# Ibu Maluku

*The story of
Jeanne Marie van Diejen-Roemen*

by Ron Heynneman

# THE AUTHOR

## W. Ronald Heynneman

Ron Heynneman was born in Surabaya (Java), and raised in Makassar (Celebes, now Sulawesi). In 1942, the Japanese invaded the Netherlands East Indies and interned the family. At the Kampili internment camp near Makassar, he met Jeanne-Marie van Diejen-Roemen, the heroine of this book.

Three and a half years later Australian troops liberated him, and the reunited family left for the Netherlands to recover.

After an engineering training in the Netherlands and Sweden, he emigrated to Canada in 1953, and moved to the United States (Chicago) in 1959.

In 1964 he returned to Canada, and made Toronto his home. In 1966 he became a registered professional engineer, and in 1968 earned an MBA from the University of Toronto.

In 1972, he married Mireille Desjarlais from Montreal, a social worker by training, now a full-time writer. They live in Toronto.

In 1974, Ron met Jeanne van Diejen again in the Netherlands and persuaded this gifted raconteur to publish her memoirs. For 25 years, Ron crossed the Atlantic almost every year to record these memoirs. He then chose to tell her story the way it was told to him – complete with Malay (Indonesian) words and expressions that the Dutch of the East Indies freely intermixed with their own language.

---

Published in Australia by
Temple House Pty Ltd,
T/A Sid Harta Publishers
ACN 092 197 192
Hartwell, Victoria

Telephone:   61 3 9560 9920
Facsimile:   61 3 9545 1742
E-mail: author@sidharta.com.au

First published in Australia 2002
Copyright © Ron Heynneman, 2002
Cover design, typesetting: Alias Design
Editing, proofreading:

The right of Ron Heynneman to be identified as the Author of the Work has been asserted by him in accordance with the Copyright, Designs and Patents Act 1988.

All rights reserved. No part of this publication may be reproduced, stored in a retrieval system, or transmitted, in any form or by any means without the prior written permission of the publisher, nor be otherwise circulated in any form of binding or cover other than that in which it is published and without a similar condition being imposed on the subsequent purchaser.

National Library of Australia Cataloguing-in-Publication entry:
Heynemann, Ron 1930 - .
Ibu Maluku: The story of Jeanne van Diejen
ISBN: 1-877059-08-0

Printed by Shannon Books
Typeset in Sabon

# REVIEWS OF IBU MALUKU

"...an emotional journey which leaves the reader inspired.."
**Kerry B. Collison (author of *The Asian Trilogy*)**

This compelling, entertaining and informative book of memoirs will provide an unforgettable reading experience for both those who have visited the Indonesian archipelago and those yet to have that pleasure. With consummate skill, Ron Heynneman has conveyed the amazing anecdotes of Jeanne Marie van Diejen-Roemen in such a way as to make the reader convinced they are listening to her tell us her fascinating story in a one-to-one conversation. The story of her life, the anecdotes, and the historical accounts of Maluku and elsewhere are invaluable not only to those interested in the history of the area but also to anyone seeking inspiration and enjoyment from the story of a remarkable human being living in a remarkable place. I found it hard to put the book down to get on with my daily tasks — Jeanne's stories kept on coming and each one was equally fascinating."

**Michael Day, Journalist (former Asia Desk Chief), The West Australian**

"*Ibu Maluku* is an amazing work — an epic. Thanks to the tenacity, patience and humanity of its author, Ron Heynneman, we, the reader, are receivers of a rare gift. It is because of Jeanne's incredible memory for detail, as if she is reliving that day and all its conversations, sights, smells and feelings, that her story is more than just an account of a great humanitarian. Her memories and her deeds, along with decades of devotion by the author, have produced a book which is enthralling, incredibly interesting, immensely readable and absolutely unforgettable. It's unforgettable because of its dimension of human emotion — joy, sadness, comedy, regret...

This lady made history and lived through so many historic events — but I have never read history in such a way that, so simply, so humanly, is so real. Thank you Jeanne and thank you Ron Heynneman."

**Wendy O'Hanlon, *APN Newspapers***

"Another masterpiece from Sid Harta ... *Ibu Maluku*. I can only hope that this book gives Jeanne the recognition she deserves for her devotion and love towards less fortunate human beings."

***John Morrow's Pick Of The Week***

# IBU MALUKU

*Jeanne Marie van Diejen-Roemen*

*Dedicated to
the people
of
Maluku*

*A selamat jalan (goodbye) from the people of Akoon village on Nusalaut, the smallest of the Lease Islands (in the Banda Sea), 100 km east of Ambon. Photo: courtesy of Mrs. Jane Wattimena-Hanser*

# IBU MALUKU

# MAPS OF REGION

*Indonesia (The former Netherlands East Indies) and its neighbours: Malaysia, the Philippines and Australia.*

# IBU MALUKU

# MALUKU ISLANDS

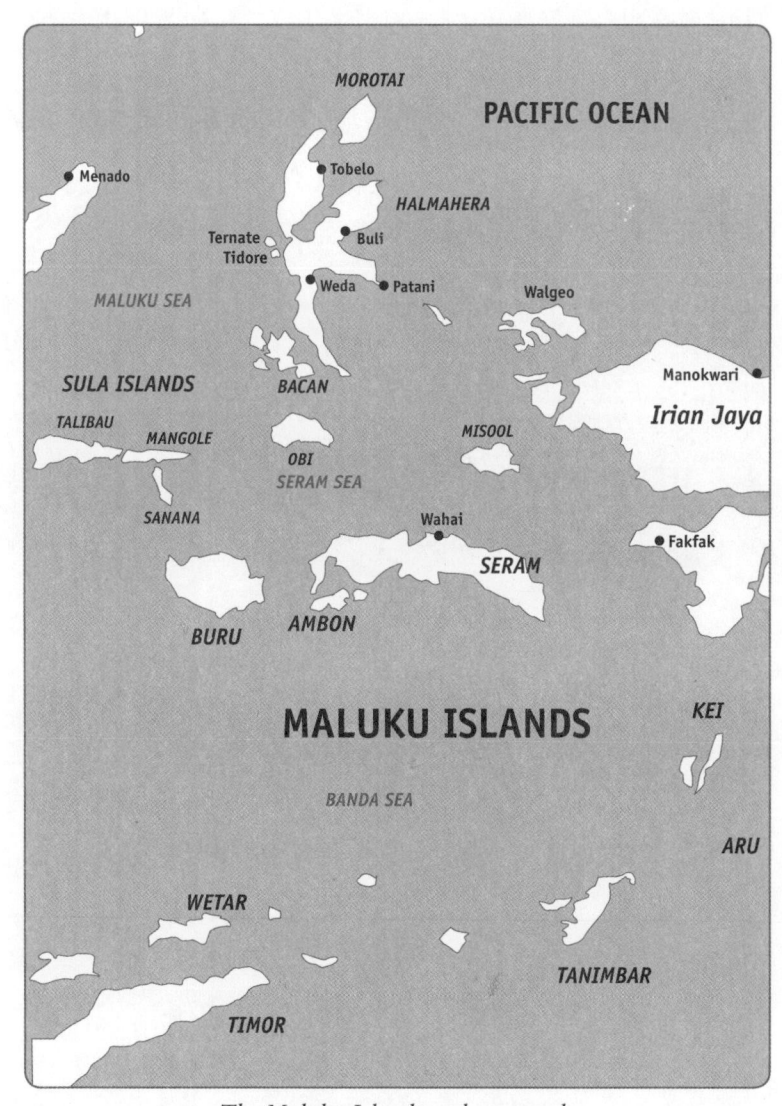

*The Maluku Islands and surrounds*

IBU MALUKU

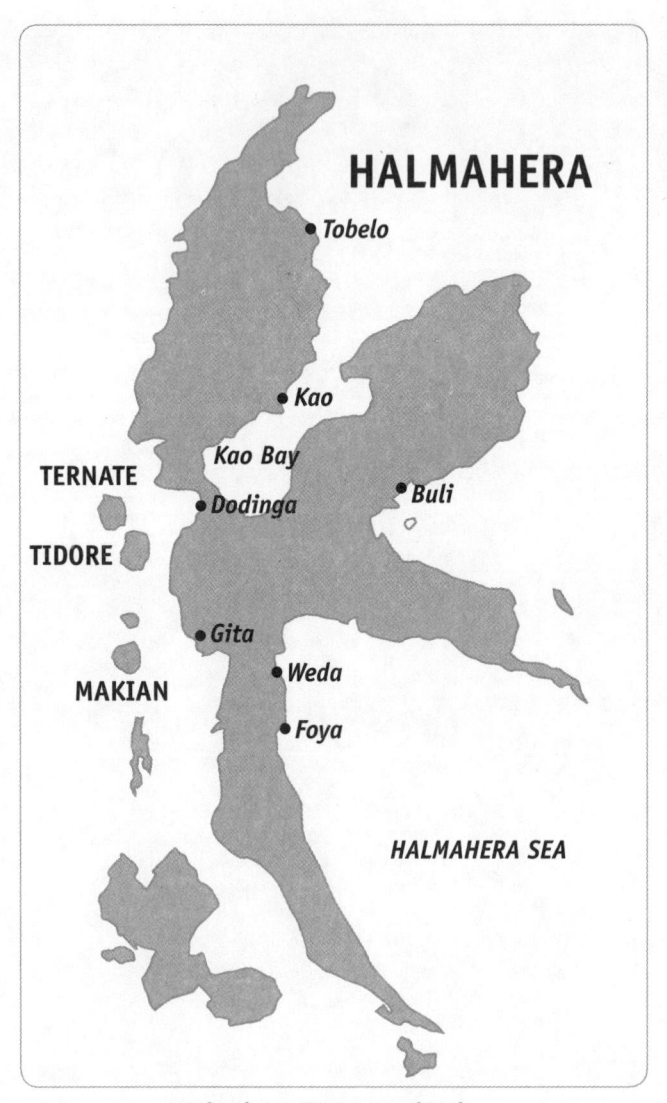

# HALMAHERA

*Halmahera, Ternate and Tidore*

# ACKNOWLEDGMENTS

I am deeply indebted to the late Nini Smits-van Dranen for typing the first drafts; to Janine Grondin for her helpful comments; to Mireille Desjarlais-Heynneman for her valuable suggestions and endless proofreading; to Jane Stuart, Robyn Walker and Natalie Silverstein for additional editing and proofreading; to Robert and Evert Heynneman, Rudy Moll, and other ex-internees who have made valuable contributions; and last but foremost, to Jeanne van Diejen-Roemen herself, for the more than 20 years of close collaboration in recalling her extraordinary, and sometimes very painful, experiences.

## EDITORIAL NOTES

When two cultures intertwine, it is natural for their languages to follow suit.

During the epoch described in this book, conversing Europeans made liberal use of Malay words and expressions in their conversations with one another. Jeanne van Diejen did likewise, and I have chosen to maintain the manner in which she told her story.

Rather than use the Dutch spelling that was in vogue before Indonesia became independent, I have used the spelling of *Bahasa Indonesia*, which thereafter became the national language. Thus, *Soekarno* is written herein as *Sukarno, and Soerabaja* as *Surabaya*.

**NOTES ABOUT THE FRONT COVER**

View of the Bay of Ternate, with Tidore in the background.
The Kedaton of the Sultan of Ternate (as it appeared at the time) is in the foreground, and Fort Orange and the City of Ternate is on the right.

Oil painting by Antoine Payen (1792-1853)
(Collection: ***Rijksmuseum voor Volkenkunde***, Leiden, Netherlands

IBU MALUKU

# CONTENTS

Preface .................................................................................................. 1

**Part One - Before World War II**

| Chapter 1 | The Wedding | Vesuvius Bay, 1920 | 3 |
| Chapter 2 | The Early Years | Europe 1896-1914 | 7 |
| Chapter 3 | The Formative Years | Europe, 1915-1920 | 21 |
| Chapter 4 | Entry into the East Indies | Sumatra, 1920 | 31 |
| Chapter 5 | A Rocky Start | Buluwaya, Mangole, 1920 | 45 |
| Chapter 6 | Getting Established | Buluwaya, Mangole, 1920 | 57 |
| Chapter 7 | Getting Acquainted | Buluwaya, Mangole, 1920 | 65 |
| Chapter 8 | Stranded | Buluwaya, Mangole, 1920 | 75 |
| Chapter 9 | The Visitors | Buluwaya, Mangole, 1920 | 87 |
| Chapter 10 | The Contract | Buluwaya, Mangole, 1920 | 99 |
| Chapter 11 | En Route to Ternate | S.S. "Pijnacker Hordijk" | 109 |
| Chapter 12 | Legal and Medical Trials | Ternate, 1921 | 115 |
| Chapter 13 | A New Posting | Tobelo, Halmahera, 1921 | 133 |
| Chapter 14 | Visions and Incisions | Tobelo, Halmahera, 1921 | 145 |
| Chapter 15 | Mon Désir | Tobelo, Halmahera, 1922-1928 | 161 |
| Chapter 16 | Our First Leave | Europe, 1928 | 175 |
| Chapter 17 | A Little Smuggling | On the high seas, 1929 | 181 |
| Chapter 18 | Home Again | Mon Désir, Halmahera, 1929 | 189 |
| Chapter 19 | Bound for New Guinea | S.S. "van Noort", 1929 | 197 |
| Chapter 20 | The Curse | Bosnik, Biak, 1928 | 211 |
| Chapter 21 | The Crash | Mon Désir, Halmahera, 1929-1933 | 221 |
| Chapter 22 | Recovery | Mon Désir, Halmahera, 1933-1934 | 235 |
| Chapter 23 | New Technology | Mon Désir, Halmahera, 1934 | 247 |
| Chapter 24 | The Medicine Woman | Mon Désir, Halmahera, 1934 | 263 |
| Chapter 25 | Dukeno's Wiles | Mon Désir, Halmahera, 1936-1937 | 275 |

**Part Two - World War II**

| Chapter 26 | The Threat of War | Mon Désir, Halmahera, 1938-1939 | 285 |
| Chapter 27 | World War Erupts | Mon Désir, Halmahera, 1940 | 295 |
| Chapter 28 | Drafted | Mon Désir, Halmahera, 1941 | 311 |
| Chapter 29 | Preparing for War | Ternate, 1941 | 335 |
| Chapter 30 | The Enemy Attacks | Ternate, 1941-1942 | 347 |

# CONTENTS
(continued)

| | | | |
|---|---|---|---|
| Chapter 31 | Surrender | Ternate, 1942 | 359 |
| Chapter 32 | Occupation | Ternate, 1942 | 377 |
| Chapter 33 | Evacuation | Ternate, 1942 | 389 |
| Chapter 34 | Internment on Ambon | Ambon, 1942 | 400 |
| Chapter 35 | Bombardment | Ambon, 1942 | 417 |
| Chapter 36 | Internment near Makassar | Kampili, Celebes, 1943 | 429 |
| Chapter 37 | The Cassava Gardens | Kampili, Celebes, 1943 | 447 |
| Chapter 38 | Life in the Camp | Kampili, Celebes, 1944 | 459 |
| Chapter 39 | The End in Sight | Kampili, Celebes, 1945 | 469 |
| Chapter 40 | Liberation | Kampili, Celebes, 1945 | 483 |

**Part Three - After World War II**

| | | | |
|---|---|---|---|
| Chapter 41 | Home Again | Mon Désir, Halmahera, 1946 | 497 |
| Chapter 42 | A New Career | Ternate, 1949-1951 | 511 |
| Chapter 43 | Aboard the "Bintang Laut" | Ternate, 1951-1954 | 525 |
| Chapter 44 | A New Challenge | Ternate, 1954 | 539 |
| Chapter 45 | Sukarno's First Visit | Ternate, 1956 | 555 |
| Chapter 46 | Sukarno's Second Visit | Buli, Halmahera, 1957 | 567 |
| Chapter 47 | The Warrant | Ternate, 1957 | 579 |
| Chapter 48 | Leaving Indonesia | Jakarta, Java, 1957 | 589 |
| Chapter 49 | Reconciliation | Tokyo, Japan, 1961 | 605 |
| Chapter 47 | Two Farewells! | Hong Kong & Ternate, 1961-1978 | 619 |

| | |
|---|---|
| Epilogue | 631 |
| Glossary | 633 |

# IBU MALUKU

# PREFACE

Jeanne van Diejen-Roemen[1] and I first met in 1943. She was forty-seven; I, barely thirteen. The Japanese had interned us with over 1,600 women and children in the south-western part of Celebes, which was then part of the Netherlands East Indies.

The name of the camp was Kampili, a former TB sanatorium. It was located some 20 kilometers from the capital, Makassar, where I had grown up. Jeanne had come from the Moluccas ("Maluku" in Indonesian), where she survived the Allied bombardment that wiped the Tantui camp on Ambon from the map.

The reason we met at all in Kampili was that she had befriended a cousin of mine, Willy Fuhrie-Broekhals. At first, both were living inside the camp boundary, which made it possible for us, my mother Madeleine Heynneman-Renaud, brother Evert, and myself, to meet often with them. We saw them less frequently after they moved outside the camp perimeter to the *kasbietuin* — the cassava garden — where, under Jeanne's leadership, a group of women grew cassava, sweet potatoes and *kangkung* (water-spinach) for the camp's central kitchen.

If it had not been for the efforts of this "garden team", I and other survivors would undoubtedly have suffered for the rest of our lives from a chronic vitamin deficiency.

The war in the Pacific ended in August of 1945. My father (Johan) and older brother Robert, who had survived the horrors of the camps at Pare-Pare, Bodjo and Bolong, joined us in Makassar. My father, who was skin over bones, needed special medical care that required us to go to the Netherlands. As for Jeanne van Diejen, she went back to her plantation "Mon Désir" on Halmahera, the largest of the Spice Islands of the Moluccas.

Later, my father, who returned to Makassar in 1947, would sell this plantation for her, and they would remain in touch.

In 1958, Jeanne went to Europe for medical studies at Lyon. She fully intended to return to the Moluccas, but circumstances prevented her from doing so.

I met Jeanne van Diejen again in Sittard (Netherlands) in 1974, and persuaded this gifted *raconteur* (with a phenomenal memory) to write her memoirs. She did (in Dutch), and — during the more than two dozen trips that I made to Sittard over the last 27 years, I fleshed out these memoirs, and complemented them with stories she told me, and with information gleaned from personal research.

I am greatly indebted to Jeanne van Diejen, whom I also call "Ibu" (Mother), for allowing me to tell the story of her life, which, for three and a half years, became intertwined with mine. The story may have been told with more frankness than she would have wanted — conscious as she was of the feelings of the living — and I accept responsibility for that.

This, then, is the result of many years of collaboration. I hope that it will give the reader as much pleasure to read it, as I have had in researching, writing and editing it.

W. Ronald Heynneman
Toronto, June 6, 2001

**Endnote**
[1] As per European custom, the last part of the hyphenated name is the maiden name.

IBU MALUKU

# CHAPTER 1

### The Wedding
*Vesuvius Bay, Sula Islands, 1920*

The chain rattled through the hawse pipe and plunged the ship's anchor into the azure waters of the Vesuvius bay, which sparkled with millions of reflections of the hot, tropical sun that stood high in a cloudless sky.

The Captain joined me at the railing, and said casually, "Your husband will be pleased that we are a full day ahead of schedule."

The look on my face startled him.

"What now, dear lady? Are you not pleased?" he asked.

"Oh Captain," I stammered, "what if John does not know that we arrived early, and cannot come in time to pick me up?"

The Captain gave me a non-plused look and in a consoling, yet somewhat teasing, tone said: "Well no, little lady. I bet that he slept on Passi Ipa last night."

I had misgivings, however, and asked him to blow the whistle now and then to signal our arrival. Laughing heartily at what he called my impatience, he instructed the First Mate to do as I had asked — and soon the ship's whistle tooted at intervals.

It made me feel much better.

All of my things were packed, except for the wedding gown that lay beside the veil in my berth. What would John's face be like when he saw me dressed in white? The salon had become off-limits for me. Two ladies of an American tour group escorted me to my cabin to help me get dressed, while the others stayed behind to decorate the salon with flowers and to set the table. The Captain and the Chief Engineer had agreed to be our witnesses.

As I got dressed, a hundred questions assailed me, and I became cold with excitement and indeterminate fear. The ladies buttoned me up, pinned a corsage on me and made final adjustments to the veil. They would escort me back to the salon as soon as the groom had arrived. But after a 15-minute wait in the unbearable heat, I asked for Father Neyens to come and bring me the latest news.

The motor sloop that ferried the ship's cargo to Passi Ipa Island had returned without John, said the pater. His *prau*[1] had not arrived there and was nowhere in sight. But the sloop was on its way again with another load, and hopefully, the groom would be there by that time.

The Captain dropped in, admired my wedding gown, and proposed that I come to the salon, where it would be cooler. I gratefully followed him and entered the beautifully adorned room amidst loud cheers.

All those present were dressed at their best. On the bedecked table stood a large wedding cake, topped by a beautiful bride and bridegroom made of sugar.

The *real* bride, upon learning the motor sloop had returned once more without her bridegroom, trembled and burst out crying.

Many willing hands dried my tears, and the ladies vied with each other to cheer me up. But the Captain said sternly, "If the groom does not show up, we'll have a party by ourselves and I'll then take the bride with me to Singapore. When the next ship comes in two months, he'd better make sure that he gets on board in time."

I took him seriously, and all life drained out of me. With a shaking voice I implored him to send another boat to find John.

The First Mate said consolingly that the motor sloop had already been dispatched. The coxswain had been instructed to bypass Passi Ipa and search for John at the mouth of the river on Mangole Island, and then return immediately — with or without the groom.

The Captain kept looking at his watch. I knew the falling tide would force him to leave soon, and I fought back my tears, not knowing what to think.

Then the Chief Engineer ran into the salon, shouting excitedly that the motor sloop was coming back with a passenger on board. Everyone rushed out, myself included. I leaned over the railing, oblivious of my beautiful gown, and forgetting the rules of etiquette that would have required me to stay behind and wait for the ladies to escort me to my bridegroom.

I did see a man standing in the sloop. As the boat got closer, I saw that he was sloppily dressed. He had a dented tropical helmet on his head, and looked shy and pitiful.

It could not be John!

The man raised his head and showed a tanned, bearded face. When he climbed the gangway, I noticed his worn shoes, and that he was covered with mud.

It could not possibly be John, and yet ...

If it was him, what had happened? What had changed him so? Was I so embarrassed by his appearance that I did not *want* to recognize him?

Father Neyens took me by the hand and led me to the top of the gangway, where this man was now standing. As if in a trance, I moved toward him and stopped several paces away. He did not speak, did not move ... he just stared. An oppressive silence hung between us as we appraised one another. It *was* John, I finally concluded, still bewildered.

"Come people," the Captain remarked dryly. "We have only fifteen minutes. Then I shall have to leave."

The spell was broken.

Side by side, John and I walked up to Father Neyens, who stood behind a table, covered for the occasion with a green cloth. Our witnesses flanked us and nodded encouragingly. Father Neyens quickly read the marriage service in abbreviated form, and asked John: "Do you take this woman to be your wedded wife?"

John looked surprised and said: "Yes ... of course ... after all I have had her already for so long."

Our witnesses hurriedly left the salon and doubled up over the railing with laughter. Father Neyens' face turned purple.

I broke down and wailed, "If you don't want me anymore, you don't have to marry me. I'll go back!"

Looking unnerved, John turned to me and stuttered: "Well, we have after all been legally married for four months. I did not mean any harm."

I kept crying.

With the witnesses back in their places, Father Neyens intoned with a choked voice: "And you, the bride, do you take this man to be your wedded husband?"

I don't know what I answered or if I answered, but everything seemed to be in order and we signed the papers placed before us. The American ladies hurriedly embraced us, and then rushed me to the cabin to help me change.

Our dinner was transferred to pots and pans and carried down the gangway to the purring motor sloop below. When I left the cabin, the wedding cake had also been brought down, and stood in all its glory in the center of the sloop's passenger bench.

As the Captain escorted me down the gangway I started to thank him, but he raised his hand in protest and said: "Bon appetit! I'll pick up the pots and pans in two months."

Demurely, I seated myself beside the imposing cake, while John said goodbye to the passengers, the crew and Father Neyens.

A moment later, he jumped into the sloop. But before he could sit down, the impatient coxswain briefly "gunned" the engine. The boat shot forward, and John landed smack in the middle of the wedding cake.

At the railing above us, everyone was doubled over in stitches.

At first I looked on bewildered as John got up with a startled look, his muddy trousers covered with squashed cake, but then I started to laugh uncontrollably.

John looked sheepishly at me, but then also burst out laughing, and so dissipated the tension that had hung over us.

Amidst much shouting and waving, we finally left for Passi Ipa. By the time we reached the quay, I had scraped most of the cake from John's trousers and had fed it to the fishes.

The roar of the sloop's engine had discouraged conversation, so I still did not know why John had come on board so shabbily dressed and covered with mud. It would have to wait.

And thus I started my married life, in the country that I had dreamt about for many years.

## Endnote

[1] *Prau* or Proa: any of various types of Malay boats, with or without outriggers.

# CHAPTER 2

## *The Early Years*
*Europe, 1896-1914*

My adventurous life started in Anderlecht, near Brussels, early in the morning of a bright day in June. The year was 1896.

Ever since sunrise, the bedroom had been filled with a golden light — definitely a good omen — but the midwife and her helpers were oblivious to the sun's overtures. A breech birth, which was what they were facing, could be dangerous.

Papa was a veterinarian, however, and knew how to handle the situation. After all, calves also arrive with the legs first. The midwife was relieved when he took over, and heaved a big sigh when I came into the world without a hitch.

Dad was proud of his first daughter, who had clearly preferred him over the midwife — or so it seemed. Right then and there, he named me after a militant saint: Jeanne (Jehanne) d'Arc. She became my patroness.

Mama's family was furious. I should have been named "Anna" after my maternal grandmother, and this break with tradition was unacceptable. So Mama's family would insist on calling me Anna, and Papa's family would call me Jehanneke (little Jehanne). It was most confusing for me.

I was barely three years old when Papa went to treat a very sick bull. Evidently, the animal had not been secured properly, for it managed to get free. Enraged by pain, it charged, thrusting its horns deep into Papa. After days of indescribable agony, he died, leaving behind a pregnant wife and two small daughters: my younger sister, Mia, and me.

Mama returned to her parental home in St. Odiliënberg in the Netherlands to await the birth of her third child. Papa's parents, who had come to Brussels for the funeral, took my sister and me into their home, which was also in St. Odiliënberg. Here we were henceforth known as "the little Brussellites". The intent was that we would eventually return with Mama to live in Brussels, but fate would decree otherwise.

Three months later the stork delivered a baby brother, Jean. Mama's health was precarious, so it was decided that she would stay with her father, and we would remain with our grandparents. Both parties were pleased with the arrangement.

Mama's father, a widower, was glad to have his daughter back — not just because he had her to look after his needs, but also because he had been given a second chance to find her a suitable husband.

He had vigorously opposed her marriage. In his eyes, Papa was just a veterinarian, who would have to live from what he earned. He himself was a farmer; he owned land. A veterinarian had no land, and was therefore a nobody. It was important that money stayed with money, he always said. Love in a marriage was fine, but wealth and accumulation of property were far more important. And so he withheld his consent and forced Mama to wait until she was legally of age, which was twenty-nine years in those days. Mama and Papa finally married, but their union was short: four years after they married, Papa was dead.

Papa's father, "Grandpapa", was grateful to Mama for the happiness she had given his son, and for letting "the little Brusselites" stay with him.

He loved children; it was a common sight to see him with a small child on his arm, telling stories to the little ones who had gathered around him.

For the next five years, we had a wonderful time. Being the only grandchildren, our unmarried aunts and one uncle spoiled us frightfully. Only Grandmama, a small spunky *Française*, was strict: she governed us, and the whole family, with an iron fist.

Grandpapa, also a veterinarian, often took us with him on his trips to the farms. Along the way he would tell us stories — each one teaching us something — and then he would test our powers of retention by asking what we had just seen or heard.

"God has given you eyes to see," he would say, "ears to hear and brains to remember, so use them."

At the farms, we children would play on the grounds and in the meadows, while he, attired in a leather apron over his naked torso, went to work inside the stable. Later, he would call us and we then had the fun of watching the farmer's wife wash Grandpapa's back and arms with soft green soap and hot water. She would tell us then that a beautiful calf or a perky foal had been born, and that we could go and see it for a moment.

Often we returned from those trips with a little lamb, a young cat or a dog; sometimes with a rabbit. This of course led to disputes between us children and Grandmama, who slowly saw her house and garden turn into a zoo.

Grandpapa would first look on with a grin; then he would step in and arrange matters so the donated animals could stay. Later, however, they would sometimes mysteriously disappear. We would grieve briefly, but then the arrival of another animal would quickly comfort us.

We received our elementary education in Odiliënberg.

In this Dutch Province of Limburg, we used German marks and Belgian francs for money, but we had to exchange them at the bank for Dutch guilders to pay for our education.

Although we were taught *Nederlands* (the Dutch language), the language we spoke outside the classroom was the *Limburger* language, or *Keuls*, which was understood and spoken in Limburg, and as far away as Cologne (Keulen) in Germany, and Liège (Luik) in Belgium.

Anything coming from the other Dutch provinces was considered "foreign" and was therefore regarded with some suspicion and, like other children, we grew up with that idea. So if, at carnival time, some relative pressed a Dutch coin in our hands, we would say a polite "thank you" and hide our disappointment; but, if it happened to be a *krentje* (a raisin, the colloquial name for a German half-mark coin), well, that was *something*!

Before Mia and I went off to school, Grandmama would always say, "Remember to stop off at Mama's and say hello, and don't forget to take Jeanne and Jean with you to school."

Jeanne was my cousin, whose mother had died when Jeanne was born. That's how it came about that Mama looked after her, as well as my little brother — and that escorting these two younger ones to school became our responsibility.

But if we could avoid it, we would not enter the house where Mama lived. We were deathly afraid of her father, who was very unpleasant whenever we did run into him. He could not stand us, for we were the offspring of the marriage that he had strenuously opposed.

*****

I was eight years old when tragedy struck again. Grandpapa was busy on a farm when two neighbors started to fight about the location of a boundary-post. Knives flashed through the air; women screamed; Grandpapa jumped in to separate the two men ... and received a knife right through his heart. He died instantly. The two men who had been fighting were horrified. They themselves did not have a scratch.

The whole village went into mourning, for he had been everybody's grandfather. We, the children, could not comprehend it: "Grandpapa gone?" It was more than we could digest. Our lives crumbled around us, and we felt abandoned.

Family arrangements followed. Grandmama did not want, or was not able, to stay in the big house. All her children were married, except the youngest one, who was studying in Brussels. So she decided to settle there for the time being and — with the general consent of the family — Mia and I were enrolled in a boarding school in Brussels.

Our glorious freedom was over, but we consoled ourselves with the prospect of spending our vacations with Grandmama. We adjusted rather easily to the new situation, and I retain pleasant memories of those years.

\*\*\*\*

As my twelfth birthday approached, preparations were made well in advance for my first communion. Both sides of the family had to be present, of course. They did not particularly like each other, but tradition had to be maintained.

To facilitate this gathering of the clans, I was taken out of boarding school for a whole year to stay in the Netherlands with Papa's youngest brother, Uncle Jean, who was also my legal guardian. He lived in Eindhoven, not far from other members of the family, which made it very convenient.

The communion took place at 10:00 am. Afterward, when we sat down for the noonday meal, I was allowed for the first time to sit with the grownups.

The Wolters (Mama's side) and the van Roemens (Papa's side) were seated at a large table, when one of Mama's brothers-in-law piped up: "We should prepare ourselves to welcome a newcomer into the family; I believe that we will soon have a new brother-in-law."

Everyone looked surprised, wondering to whom that could apply. Then, all eyes turned toward Mama — she being the only woman without a husband.

Mama was deeply disturbed by this oblique intrusion into her privacy, and the pressure it conveyed to get married again. She had no intention of doing so, but realized that her position as mistress of the parental home was shaky. Her father was getting on in years, and her younger brother, who lived there also, was planning to get married, which meant that Mama would eventually have to hand over the reigns to his bride.

There was a shoemaker in Melik, whose wife had died in child birth. The baby survived. The man was now alone with four children, two of them older than I. I had known this man from infancy, when he came to our home to take measurements for our shoes. (In those days, there were no shoe stores; the shoemaker went from door to door to ask if anyone wanted to have shoes made or repaired.)

This man had a few people working for him, while he himself was on the road taking orders or making deliveries. He got around in a carriage drawn by a small horse — it was an important possession in those days.

This shoemaker started to court Mama. To him, she must have been a good catch, for she had money, and experience in raising children, so he proposed. Mama accepted in spite of herself, but would regret this decision for the rest of her life. At her father's insistence she married with "separation of property" so she would retain control over her own money. That was the intent, but her new husband somehow got his hands on it anyway.

Initially, their union did not affect us much. During vacations we were usually with Grandmama in Brussels. Mia and I did, however, spend one vacation with Mama's new family in Melik (on the other side of the Meuse river), which is where they had settled. It was a strange experience; Mia and I felt awkward and slighted, but back at boarding school we quickly forgot about it.

\*\*\*\*

After finishing grade school, I spent two enjoyable years at the High School in Eindhoven. At the end of the second year, my stepfather invited my sister and me to spend our vacation — the whole month of August — in Melik.

When it was time to return to Eindhoven, my stepfather urged me to stay a few more weeks. I was tempted. In boarding school my only contacts were with girls of my age; here I was in the company of adults, and I also liked being with my stepfather's baby. So I yielded to the pressure, and accepted. But after those weeks had passed, my stepfather changed his tune and said that there was really no need for me to return to Eindhoven as I could continue my education with the nuns in Odiliënberg — a fifteen minute walk away. I imagine he wanted to save money — boarding school being more expensive than having me at home.

As I was underage, my protestations carried no weight.

My education progressed, but my relationship with my stepfather did not. My dislike for him grew to such proportions that I started a novena.

With my allowance I bought a statue of St. Anthony, intending to pray to him for nine consecutive days to please take my stepfather to heaven — and as soon as would be convenient.

Toward the end of this novena, the statue was accidentally knocked over, and St. Anthony lost his head. I was so disillusioned that I picked up the pieces and threw them out of the window — narrowly missing the Mayor of Melik who happened to be passing by — and I resolved never to pray to St. Anthony again.

Now, a confrontation with my stepfather seemed inevitable.

One day I was in my room, when I heard yelling. I tiptoed down the stairs and entered the living room. Mama stood cowering near the pump (every house in those days had an indoor pump) as my stepfather — his back turned to me — pummeled her with his fists. Outraged, I climbed unseen onto a chair, then onto a table, pulled up the chair, and brought it crashing down on my stepfather's head with all the force a 14-year old could muster. But it only numbed him momentarily and then, of course, he turned his anger toward me.

I narrowly escaped his clutches and ran out of the house to the home of one of Papa's sisters, *Tante* Dilia, where Grandmama happened to be visiting. I rushed into Grandmama's outstretched arms, crying my eyes out, and sobbingly told her what had happened.

"Well now," said Aunt Dilia soothingly, "perhaps it did not really happen the way you thought it did. I'm sure he did not mean any harm."

That was like pouring oil on the fire.

"I saw it with my own eyes," I wailed. "He beat her, *hard*! I don't want to go back there, ever!"

The next day, Grandmama took me to the relative safety of Brussels. She was concerned that my stepfather might employ the police to get me back, as I was still underage. But with Melik being so far away and my stepfather being practically illiterate (he could sign his name and keep track of his money, but that was all), she decided to chance it.

So I was allowed to finish my High School in Brussels.

Then the family asked what I wanted to do. What a question! I wanted to follow in Papa's and Grandpapa's footsteps and become a veterinarian, of course! Nothing else would do! But Grandmama put her foot down.

"No! Definitely not," she said emphatically. "I have lost my husband and my son because of that profession, and my granddaughter will have nothing to do with it!" And then she blamed the nuns at the boarding-school for not having squashed this "foolish notion".

The family once again discussed the threat posed by my stepfather. Now that I had finished High School, there was renewed concern that he would take steps to get me back in Melik.

A great-Aunt, a sister of Grandmama, was present during these discussions. She had lived in the southern United States, where her husband had made his fortune in tobacco. After he died, she had returned to Belgium. She now proposed, "Listen, why doesn't Jehanneke come with me for the time being. I have a house in Nice, where I live most of the time. That is far enough from Melik. Because of the distance and the language barrier, it will be highly unlikely that her stepfather will ever succeed in getting her back. And I will concern myself with her further education."

The family agreed.

This Great-Aunt had had a grandson, who had been the apple of her eye. He called her *Grootmoeder* (Grandmother) instead of *Oma*, which is what children normally call their grandmothers. Sadly, he died early from diphtheria, and from then on his grandmother insisted on being called *Grootmoeder* by everybody. So that is what I called her also.

So now I had *two* grandmothers. My real paternal grandmother, who would remain in Brussels; and *Grootmoeder*, with whom I would travel extensively over the next few years.

*Grootmoeder* and I left by train for Paris, where we arrived on a somewhat foggy September day. I immediately fell in love with the city, where I had my first ride in a taxicab. It was a high coupé on large wheels. The chauffeur was separated from us by a solid glass window. *Grootmoeder* sat on a black leather seat with our suitcases and hand luggage beside her. Behind her was a small window, covered by a curtain with little balls hanging from the bottom. I was across from her, seated on a narrow tip-up seat, watching with a mixture of amazement and fear the torrent of traffic that rushed by outside. The chauffeur dropped us off at Hotel Terminus, across from the station from where we would continue our journey to Nice two days later.

In the afternoon we walked along the Seine. The leaves were turning yellow, and there was no wind. Because of a light fog, I saw Paris as through a pearly light, and that is how I locked the city in my heart. Then and there, she became *"Paris mon amour"*. But I would never again enjoy the city as intensely as I did that first time.

We left Paris with the "Paris-Lyon-Méditerranée" train, and arrived in Nice twenty-three hours later. With the excitement of a typical teenager, I would tell anyone who would listen about this *absolutely incredible* journey. My enthusiasm amused *Grootmoeder,* but she pointed out that one should not display one's feelings so blatantly. To my dismay, many more of these discouraging commentaries on my actions would follow.

In spite of them, my sojourn in Nice was a wonderful experience.

We lived in a white, stately three-story building, called "Palais Étoile du Nord", which had two apartments on each floor.

The building belonged to the wife of a retired Russian General, Madame Vasilieff, who occupied an apartment on the third floor. Opposite her lived a Greek ship owner with an unpronounceable name; below them a Parisian family and a Polish couple; and opposite us on the ground floor lived Madame di Montebello, an Italian.

The building staff consisted of a chubby, jolly kitchen maid, who insisted on being called Madame Marie, and a tiny black-haired parlor-maid, Marina. Both spoke a dialect that I did not understand very well, but they did their best to make *"la petite Hollandaise"* feel at home.

*Grootmoeder* allowed me to take several courses in nursing, in which I had a real interest (since I was not allowed to become a veterinarian). Madame di Montebello, who was a patroness of the Red Cross, took it upon herself to fan my enthusiasm by telling me about the great accomplishments of that organization.

*Grootmoeder*'s main interest at this time was traveling.

"In times gone by," she often said, "I had a large family and was tied down. Now, I am free, and want to get to know the whole world."

She had gained a large circle of friends through her many visits to the Casino of Monte Carlo and they often invited her to visit them during her travels. Thus, in her company, I became well acquainted with Europe and Northern Africa, and began to get used to traveling by train, by ship, and even by camel.

Our first big journey took us to North Africa, one of *Grootmoeder*'s favorite places. We traveled on a German boat — a "cruise-ship" one would say today — stopping off at various harbors on the Spanish and North-African coast until we arrived at the port of Benghazi in Libya, which was then a colony of Italy.

At the invitation of a sheik, we traveled 160 km south, partly by camel, to the oasis of Agedabia (Ajdabiya) in the Libyan Desert, where I fell in love for the first time.

From a small window in the women's quarters, I spotted a young sheik, dressed in a white burnous. Flushed with ardor, I watched him mount a magnificent white horse and ride it through the inner court. Reflecting on this later, I was never sure which one I had loved more, the man or the horse!

From Agedabia, we made daily trips by camel to smaller oases nearby. They were all the property of Sheik Rida, our host. It was during these trips that I learned to appreciate goat milk and freshly picked dates.

On the way back, we visited Kairouan, the holy city of Islam in northeast Tunisia, and visited the Great Mosque, built in A.D. 705, which also served as a university. The manner of teaching seemed odd. Each professor sat on a mat facing his students, who, also seated on mats, responded to him in an almost singing manner. It did not seem to disturb other classes that were also in progress.

I had expected a university to be a more quiet and dignified sort of place.

The land journey ended in Alexandria, where we boarded the *Kaiser Wilhelm II* and headed for Athens. This ancient city with its almost 5,000-year-old Acropolis made an unforgettable impression. We continued the journey to Naples, and then back to Nice, where we arrived just before Easter.

Each evening during this trip, *Grootmoeder* had given me a lesson in geography on all the areas we had traveled through that day. She also tutored me beforehand on the customs, ethnic make-up, beliefs and economy of the people we were going to visit next. I learned a great deal and really enjoyed those trips as a result.

What I respected most in *Grootmoeder* was her stamina, equanimity, and adaptability. One of her less-endearing qualities was her unceasing criticism of my actions, which she frequently considered clumsy and childish. It made me feel like a little girl, living in a world that had no room for my age group.

In Nice, the Russian community overflowed with excitement. The Great Metropolitan — the priest next in rank to the "Patriarch" of the Russian Orthodox Church — would be coming from Moscow to inaugurate the magnificent new cathedral in Nice, and Grand Duke Paul would also attend.

Madam Vasilieff told *Grootmoeder* that we were both invited, and would be escorted by the aide-de-camp of the Grand Duke, the lively and charming Peter Petrojefski, her nephew, who was staying with her.

When we both had already shed our illusions, Peter and I would meet again under very different circumstances — as will be told later.

\* \* \* \*

In June, 1912, we returned to Belgium, where we lived in relative quiet for three months. I worked and studied at the St. Jean Hospital in Brussels, where, years later, I would graduate as *accoucheuse* or midwife.

In September, when the weather turned cooler again, I made my second visit to Paris, while en route back to Nice. *La Ville-Lumière* (the city of light) made a different impression now. This time, it was a homecoming! How beautiful were the banks of the Seine!

Months later, we left Nice to start another long journey that would take us across the Balkans and Ukraine to Russia. We traveled through Italy by train, and from Brindisi crossed the Adriatic Sea to the "white flower city" of Dubrovnik in Yugoslavia. Years later, when I visited Manokwari in New Guinea, it would remind me of this white fairy-tale city rising up from the Adriatic, decorated with thousands of flowers. It was magnificent!

The journey took us via major Balkan cities to Odessa, the main export center for Ukrainian grain on the Black Sea — which looked not black at all, but an ordinary blue! Then came the Ukraine and its capital Kiev, Peter Petrojefski's home town, from where a few years later many White Russians would flee because of the "Red Terror". They would be driven from house and home and made exiles forever.

From Kiev, we traveled through the large, lightly populated but fertile countryside toward Moscow, which was a revelation. I had never seen so many churches and golden domes in one place. We stayed there a full week.

*Grootmoeder* visited many friends, while I had to stay at the hotel to work on a travelogue. These exercises in describing my travel experiences would prove invaluable in later life. My work must have pleased her, because her critical attitude towards me was beginning to soften. Yet, I still felt awkward in her world.

From Moscow we journeyed to the northern seaport of Arkhangelsk (Archangel), and stayed with a ship-owner, who drove us around in a troika — a sleigh drawn by three horses. It was a strange, pleasant experience, but it was bitterly cold.

I was glad to be heading for the warmer climate of imposing St. Petersburg, which was then still the capital of the Russian empire. The Neva River, which runs through the city to the Gulf of Finland, has been favorably compared with the Seine in *la belle France*. It was indeed beautiful, but decidedly different.

Madame Vasilieff (our landlady from Nice) received us at her family home, where her nephew, Lieutenant Peter Petrojefsky, who was visiting also, presented his *fiancée*. After the introduction, *Grootmoeder* looked visibly relieved. Had she considered Peter dangerous for her idealistic grandniece?

After visiting the Douma, the palace-like Russian Parliament, we returned via Berlin to Brussels, where I continued to work and study at the St. Jean Hospital.

\*\*\*\*

When the leaves were changing color, we left again for the Riviera. It would be the last trip for many years to come.

Nice had changed drastically. Religious persecution had intensified.

The civil authorities had forced our parish priest out of his presbytery and made him live in the attic of his church. They had also taken away an old convent from the nuns. In the stillness of the night, they had picked up the orphans and elderly people who were living there, and pushed them across the border into Italy. Then, they had razed the convent to the ground to build a large, deluxe resort hotel, the Hotel Negresco, which still stands today at the famous *Boulevard des Anglais*.

In Nice I was thrilled to see Jules Védrines[1] and Louis Blériot[2] flying loops and corkscrews in their small biplanes. How I envied these heroes of the sky! I decided then that I, too, would fly some day — though I did not dare admit this to *Grootmoeder*. (Much later, in 1928, I did fly in a small airplane over the Maritime Alps, and would never again feel so proud and happy!)

In October, we traveled from Nice via the Egyptian pyramids and the Suez Canal to the Holy Land.

Jerusalem filled me with deep emotions. It even touched my self-assured Great-Aunt, *Grootmoeder*. Impressive as it was, what I remember most of Jerusalem, was the ever-present horde of beggars. Old women, young girls — yes, even toddlers — stammering with outstretched hands: "Bakchees, bakchees!"

Later, I would see thousands of wrecked bodies in Lourdes, but Jerusalem would always remain in my mind as the largest gathering ground for the blind and paralytic of this world. How busy Jesus must have been, healing the sick — there were so many!

Via Bethlehem, where the people were more friendly and the beggars more playful, and Crete, where the beauty of ancient Greece was conspicuous (everything seemed lighter, earthier and somewhat purer), we went to Capri, Italy, and then visited the ruins of Pompeii, and Mount Vesuvius that caused its destruction.

For the first time I stood on top of a volcano. Later, much later, the continuous presence of volcanoes in the East Indies would often remind me of that moment.

Then came Rome, that magnificent city, where we saw the Colosseum, the Forum, the Domus Aurea, and the catacombs. And at the end of our visit, we had an audience with the Pope, which dwarfed everything else.

I remember Pope Pius X as a small, white-gowned old man, with the friendly smile of a child. I curtsied and kissed his feet, and he touched the side of my face in response. Emotion overwhelmed me, and tears flowed down my cheeks.

Afterwards, *Grootmoeder* was outraged. My behavior had been disgraceful, she said. I was upset for days, thinking that older people would never understand the young.

Back in Nice, *Grootmoeder* collapsed. The trip had been too much for her.

I informed the family in Brussels. Now it was I who had to decide and act resolutely. *Grootmoeder* lay in bed with a contorted face, unable to speak or do anything for herself. Her training of me over the years had borne fruit, however, and I took care of everything. Once she was well again she even praised me — but, in keeping with her style, with certain qualifications!

Then, Love entered.

My grandmother's illness had often brought me in touch with a young druggist, who one day came to deliver medication for *Madame Grand-mère* ... and a bouquet of red roses for *la Petite Hollandaise* — me!

From her bedroom window, *Grootmoeder* had seen him coming and, wanting to order something, came to the entrance, where she met her bewildered granddaughter and the deeply blushing pill-carrier, who quickly dropped the roses and ran.

She immediately grasped the situation, but said: "It was nice of you to buy me flowers; however, I can't tolerate the smell of roses just now, so it will be better if you take them to church. They will go well with the statue of the Blessed Virgin."

Humiliated, and fuming, I picked up the roses and went to the church.

Many years later, I would meet this admirer again in the same drugstore, but by then *la Petite Hollandaise* had long since been forgotten.

※※※※

In early summer, 1914, tensions were mounting in Europe. Rumors of an impending war circulated among the foreigners living in Nice. Nobody took them seriously, except *Grootmoeder*. Prudent as ever, she decided to return to Belgium as she did not want to risk being cut off from her children if war did break out. She thought that such a war would probably only be a short one, after which we could always return to Nice.

Like many people, *Grootmoeder* had a small dog (a dachshund) that went with us wherever we traveled. In Dijon, I left the train to walk the dog, and heard over the station's loudspeakers that the Austrian heir to the throne, Archduke Francis Ferdinand, and his wife had been assassinated in Sarajevo.

It was June 28, 1914, and I was just eighteen years old.

Back in our compartment, I told *Grootmoeder* what I had heard and she said, "Oh, child, there will be war now. No doubt about it, there will be war. I shall be glad when we are safely home in Brussels."

As we pulled into the station in Paris, it was clear that the mobilization of France had already begun. Military men hurried hither and yon, trying to find the trains that would take them to their assigned posts. Even older men of 45 years had been called up. Many had outgrown their uniforms and had tied their jackets with strings, since the buttons could no longer reach their holes.

With great difficulty we managed to get a room at the Hotel Terminus in Paris, and it was there that *Grootmoeder* fell ill again. It would be a full week before we could continue our journey.

When we arrived in Brussels, we found the family in mourning. The husband of *Grootmoeder*'s daughter — the one with whom we would be staying — and the husband of another daughter had been killed when the Germans had bombed the fortress at Liège. The enemy was advancing rapidly, and travel to the Netherlands was no longer possible.

This was too much for *Grootmoeder*. Her heart gave out as the Germans tightened their grip on the capital. Convinced that she could handle any situation, she fought with all her might, but to no avail. This strong, courageous and iron-willed woman died in her 79th year in occupied Brussels.

Her death hit me hard. I now stood alone, and did not think I could carry on without her leadership. I knew the other members of the family, of course, but the people who had meant the most to me were now beyond reach. My real Grandmother in Brussels had also died, and my guardian, Uncle Jean, was far away in the Netherlands.

What was to become of me now?

**Endnotes**
[1] Jules Védrines (1881-1919) would later become famous as a World War I flying ace.
[2] Jules Blériot (1872-1936) had already made history as the first flier to cross the English Channel in July of 1909, and later became an aircraft manufacturer.

IBU MALUKU

# CHAPTER 3

## The Formative Years
*Europe, 1915-1920*

After conferring with the Brussels members of Papa's family, I decided to accelerate my studies at St. Jean Hospital and become a registered nurse and midwife. Madame di Montebello, the Red Cross patron in Nice, would have approved — particularly now, when the need for nurses was so great.

Because of the pressure and fear of those days, I got over the loss of Grootmoeder much quicker than expected. Fear (and yes, even hatred) for the enemy took hold of me, and pushed all other feelings into the background. There was so much to do, and every day presented new challenges.

The indiscriminate sinking of merchant and passenger ships[1] by German U-boats compelled the United States to enter the war on April 6, 1917.

A few weeks later, I graduated as midwife-nurse, and obtained a pass from the Germans to cross the border into the Netherlands, which had remained neutral during the war.

First, I went to Eindhoven to discuss the legalities of my coming of age with Uncle Jean, my guardian. At one point he asked: "And what are you going to do now? Are you going back to Brussels?"

"Yes *Oom* Jean, I have to go back. My permit is only good for five days."

"I wouldn't worry about that permit. Why don't you stay?" he asked. "There are many things to do here. The Germans occasionally open up the border to evacuate Belgian children out of the war zone. People are needed to receive and care for those children. You speak French, so I think you could find work immediately. It is a volunteer's job, but you would get room and board. You can also stay here, of course. If you like, I can help you make the necessary contacts."

After discussing the pros and cons, I decided to apply for the position, which would be in the city of Roermond. Uncle Jean made the arrangements for an interview, but since it would not take place until two days later, he said, "Now go and finally visit your mother. You haven't seen her in years. You can't put it off any longer."

I promised I would go right away.

On my way to Eindhoven's station, I saw soldiers everywhere, who seemed unusually busy for a Sunday. But then I remembered Uncle Jean telling me that the Dutch Army was in an almost perpetual state of readiness.

In Brussels, I had learned to keep out of the way of the military, so I automatically made a detour, choosing a quiet, narrow street where there seemed to be fewer soldiers. Suddenly the stillness was shattered by a shot! ... and another ... and a third!

People screamed and ran off in all directions, but I froze and remained rooted on the spot. For a moment I was back in Brussels, where German soldiers were hauling terrified people out of their houses with their hands up, searching house after house until they had found the sniper. Fear had immobilized me then, just as it did now.

When I came to and realized there were no Germans here, I saw a soldier running towards me. Without a word, he grabbed me, dragged me toward a shallow ditch, and pulled me down on the cold stones beside him. A split second later, a bullet whistled past his head, and ricocheted against a nearby wall.

"A soldier has gone berserk," my protector panted. "He is behind that upper window there and shoots at anything that moves."

"Why isn't anyone stopping him?" I cried out sharply, angry that he had dared lay a hand on me.

"I'm sure they are trying, but they'd better be careful. That house is full of ammunition," he replied. "Just keep your head down until they've got him!"

To distract me, he started talking. He and another conscript were the only Rotterdammers in a regiment of Limburgers, and since he did not know a soul in Eindhoven, he did not have much of a social life. But now that the Americans had entered the fray, the war would probably end soon, and when it did, he wanted to go to the East Indies.

What I knew about the East Indies had come primarily from missionary almanacs. I particularly remembered the photographs of nuns, seated on magnificent white horses, who were baptizing the Papuas. Of course, it was the horses that had impressed me most! But as this soldier talked, I recognized an old yearning in me to leave Limburg and the Netherlands some day and spread my wings.

When someone shouted "all clear", my protector helped me to my feet, and introduced himself as John van Diejen (fahn dee-yun).

I was no longer cross; indeed, I was grateful, and felt flattered by his gallantry. But I must have looked still a little shaken, for he took my valise and escorted me to the station, where I thanked him — not expecting to see him ever again.

In Melik, I had an enjoyable visit with Mama. As I did not want to run into her husband, she agreed to meet me at the home of *Tante* Dilia, where I had sought refuge after that fateful altercation with my stepfather so many years ago. Among other things, I told Mama and *Tante* Dilia of my plans to work with Belgian refugee children — and then took the train back to Eindhoven.

That evening, I wrote a "Thank You" note to John van Diejen for having saved my life earlier that day.

Contrary to expectations, a brisk correspondence followed. John wrote mostly about his plans for going to the Netherlands East Indies after the war. He was well-informed about the country and its people, and had already learned a little of the Malay language spoken there.

Eventually, I became captivated by these plans.

We started to date, fell in love, and agreed to get engaged as soon as the war had ended.

\* \* \* \*

After having been deeply involved with Belgian refugee children, who were housed in camps that were scattered all over the Netherlands, I heard that a French-speaking midwife was urgently needed by an obstetric clinic in the Hague to deal with Walloon refugees from Belgium.

This was a paying position. I applied and was accepted.

When I told John about this, he suggested that I stop off in Rotterdam on my way to the Hague and meet his family. He would ask for a one-day pass and meet me there. However, the day before the planned visit, the Allies (including British, Canadian and Australian troops) launched what would become known as the Passchendaele Offensive (the Third Battle of Ypres) in Flanders. As a result, in Holland all passes were withdrawn. Would I mind, asked John, visiting his family on my own? I did not like the idea at all, but reluctantly agreed.

Following John's detailed explanations about which trams to take, I managed to find the house on the Vijferhoutstraat, and, with some trepidation, rang the bell. The door was opened by a blind man, who had disconcertingly white, unseeing eyes. He gruffly asked, "Who do you want?"

"Mrs. van Diejen," I said, taken aback by the unfriendly tone.

"Next door," he said curtly, "ring twice." And he immediately closed the door.

I rang the same bell twice, and heard someone coming down the stairs. The door opened and I stood face to face with my mother-in-law-to-be, who was expecting to see her son.

I explained that his pass had been withdrawn, but I could see that my explanation was lost on her. She interpreted his absence as a deliberate snub. She took me upstairs, and asked if it was alright with me if she delayed the coffee until her other son and his wife came home from the 11:00 o'clock Sunday service at the St. Lawrence church.

Oh, I thought, they must be Catholics too. John and I had never talked much about religion, but he had always accompanied me to church, so I had assumed that he was also Catholic. That assumption would prove to be wrong.

"That's fine, *Mevrouw*. As long as I get to the Hague before nightfall. I have made reservations for the night," I replied, thinking about the very old couple from whom I had rented a room.

After a while, the son and his wife arrived. He, an architect, dressed in striped pants, tail coat and high hat, was an extremely tall, awe-inspiring person. She was also big and very tall. Dressed in my nurse's uniform and being less than five feet in my stocking feet, I must have looked like a child to them.

We withdrew to the "best room" that was only used on Sundays, where they started to interrogate me.

"You come from Roermond?" started the architect.

"Yes, I am from Roermond," I said, resolved to say "yes and amen" to every question they would fire at me.

"And all alone, by train?"

"Yes, *Meneer*."

"That must have been a difficult and tiring journey," he said.

"Yes, a little," I answered, but I thought: "Good God, I have already traveled a quarter of the globe!"

"Well," he said patronizingly, "I would advise you, as you continue to the Hague, to be very observant. You must always take a ladies' coupé (in those days there were separate compartments for ladies traveling alone), and if there is anything that looks a little suspicious, get out at the next station and seek the assistance of the ladies of the Girls Protection League. They carry a band around their arm, you know, and they can help you further."

"What nonsense," I thought, but I politely stuck to my self-imposed script until it was time to go.

So I left them with the impression that I was no more than a naive child from an insignificant town in a backward province, who had never been on a train before. I imagine that John had a good laugh at their expense when he told them otherwise.

# IBU MALUKU

\*\*\*\*

The end of the war came on November 11, 1918. John was discharged and we became engaged. There was no celebration, but I did receive a ring, and we started to think seriously about the future.

A lot of political tensions existed throughout Europe, including in the Netherlands. A rebel named Troelstra wanted to abolish the monarchy and change the country into a republic. The Netherlands mobilized again, this time for internal security. Soldiers from the southern provinces, known for their loyalty to the Crown, moved quickly to the west. The coup was a failure. Cheering Limburger soldiers pulled the Royal Family in a *calèche*[2] across the Malie-field in The Hague and, slowly, peace and quiet returned to the country.

Our romance, however, was starting to totter.

One time, when John came to see me in the Hague, he reproached me for never having any time for him.

"When I come, you are always busy delivering babies," he complained. "Every woman in town seems to be in labor when I arrive."

I was tired, crabby, and in a hurry to get to my next appointment, so I said, "Well, you can have your ring back. I don't want to be engaged anyway."

With that I took off the ring and threw it at him, but he failed to catch it. It fell on the pavement, and rolled until it disappeared into a sewer hole ...

\*\*\*\*

Some time later — the influx of Walloon refugees had abated for the moment — I spent several days at the home of a rich vaudeville producer, whose wife was about to give birth.

I was preparing an infusion when the housemaid came: "Nurse, there is a man for you at the door."

"What kind of man?" I replied.

"He is a postman, with a telegram for you."

"Well, please accept the telegram for me, as you can see I have my hands full at the moment," I said, displeased with her lack of initiative.

When I had finished with my patient, I opened the telegram, which said: "When and where can I see you? Cable back. Answer prepaid. Van Diejen."

I was puzzled. Which van Diejen had sent the telegram?

I thought I had broken my engagement with John. At family gatherings in Rotterdam, I had often met another brother of John, a widower, who had made overtures through his children, to which I had not responded. Could it be him?

I cabled back "come tomorrow", specifying the time and address — still wondering which van Diejen would show up.

The next morning I was busy again with my patient when the housemaid announced the arrival of a gentlemen. She could not tell me his name.

Brilliant.

"Well," I said, "let him wait in the consultation room. When I am finished here, I'll come down. Please tell him that."

When I finally came down, I found the consultation room empty.

"He's in that room," the housemaid said airily, pointing to a room where this theater family had stocked all sorts of spooky theater props, including human and animal skeletons.

She then pressed a hidden button to open the door, and there stood John van Diejen, in a high state of agitation, wondering what this grisly exhibit was all about and how he was going to open the door that did not have any knob and get out of there.

He pulled himself together as I entered, and the first thing he did was look at my legs, and say: "What strange stockings you have."

"Are you going to start by picking a fight again?" I countered, giving my white nurse's stockings a quick self-conscious glance. "What have you come for?"

"Well," he said in a more sober tone, "read this letter, will you?"

It was a letter from John's older brother, Jan, who lived in Bondowoso on Java.

He wrote that the administrator of his coconut plantation had died of Spanish influenza; that he needed a new administrator urgently and would John be interested in taking the position. "If so, and you are engaged, better get married before you come," he counseled, "because the plantation is on an isolated island."

Since he had left the Army, John had been working for the Rotterdam Drydock Company in an administrative function. He had never been trained for an agricultural role, but his desire to go to the East Indies was so strong that he was willing to give it a try.

"The whole world wants copra[3]," John explained. "The plantation has to be quickly put in order and made productive. The only problem is its location: somewhere near the Banggai Archipelago, east of Celebes. Its only connection with the outside world is a KPM-boat[4], which comes once every two months. It is not the opportunity I have been looking for, but it could be a jumping board. If I accept the position, we shall have to leave with the next available boat."

An awkward pause ensued as I examined my own feelings.

"Well," John blurted out, "what do you think?"

It was without doubt the most gauche marriage proposal ever heard, but I still had feelings for him and my desire to leave the Netherlands and spread my wings was as strong as his. So, once again, I accepted him.

A few days later we received our first disappointment. My papers had to arrive from Brussels, and this gave us unimaginable problems.

The war had left everything in chaos, and some archives had been lost. It took ages to get any sort of response, and it became clear that we could not get married on short notice.

The date of departure approached. A tropical outfit was purchased, and in February, 1919, John boarded the boat ... alone. We arranged that, as soon as my papers were in order, we would get married by proxy.

Ten months passed before I finally appeared before a magistrate to become legally married. It was a gloomy, rainy day, and the wind howled as I signed the necessary papers. It was strictly business; the lack of decorum and ceremony made the day even more dismal. What a disappointment this turned out to be!

That same day I went to book my passage, but found there was no direct passage (via the Suez Canal) available until mid-January. There was room on an earlier scheduled ship, but it was reserved for people who were urgently needed in the East Indies. "Proxies" did not count!

Not wanting to delay my departure, I dug in my pocket to pay for the longer and more expensive western route, and left for the Canadian port of Halifax.

The only excitement of the voyage occurred north of England, when we sailed past mine fields and saw the masts of scuttled German warships at Scapa Flow.

On board were several "proxies" — two Austrian, and one Dutch — and also a few Dutch missionary families with small children. All were bound for the East Indies. Obviously, they also had chosen the long route, rather than wait for direct passage to become available.

At Halifax we boarded a train, and traveled via New York across the United States to San Francisco. The magnificent trip took nine days.

Being used to traveling, I enjoyed it to the fullest. My fellow passengers, however, could not share my enthusiasm and became tired and moody. They probably thought me rather eccentric, so I withdrew a bit.

In San Francisco, I bought a wedding gown complete with veil, without having the faintest idea when or where I would be wearing it.

The journey continued with a Pacific & Orient Line ship to Hawaii. The British crew was utterly correct, but terrible reserved. They hardly mingled with the passengers. Luckily there were many children on board, so I could make myself useful as a nurse. Unlike many others, I did not suffer from seasickness. For me, the trip was a dream, and I have loved the sea ever since.

In Hawaii, we had to change to another ship. We stayed at Honolulu only a day, but it turned out to be a very enjoyable one, during which I got my first glimpse of a dark-skinned society. The natives were happy and cordial, and I can still smell the fragrance of the leis that they placed around my neck.

Our new ship set course for Japan. This time, the crew was much friendlier. They mixed freely with the passengers, and were not so formal as the British had been on the previous boat.

New passengers had joined the ship, apparently en route to the Dutch or British colonies. Both crew and veterans of the tropics soon started in on the "proxies": they wanted to know where we were going, what our husbands were doing, and especially where they were working. Then came multiple warnings about all that would be waiting for us. In the tropics, they said, an unmarried man would soon succumb to temptation and take in a *nyai*, a native "housekeeper". Once the wife appeared, this *nyai* would do anything to get rid of her — and even resort to murder. It would be better to leave this "degenerate" husband, return to Europe, and find oneself an "unsoiled" man.

The "proxies" discussed these warnings among themselves, and became apprehensive.

From Yokohama, we sailed southward. The atmosphere on board became more tense. Most passengers were suffering from boredom on this long journey, and longed for the end. When, after a stop at Hong Kong, we arrived in the large harbor of Singapore, our admirers pretended to be disappointed that the voyage was ending, but I was grateful to finally be able to escape their attentions.

At the same time, I also feared the great unknown that lay ahead.

### Endnotes

[1] Among the first passenger ships to be torpedoed was the British 31,550 ton Lusitania, one of the biggest and fastest ocean liners of the time. Its sinking in May 1915, with heavy loss of life, caused widespread indignation and mobilized anti-German feelings in the United States.

[2] *Calèche*: a barouche, i.e. a four-wheeled carriage, with or without a folding top.

[3] Copra is dried coconut meat, from which oil is extracted.
[4] KPM (*the Koninklijke Pakketvaart Maatschappij*) The Royal Packet (Ship) Line, which carried mail, passengers and goods regularly on a fixed route.

IBU MALUKU

IBU MALUKU

# CHAPTER 4

### Entry into the East Indies
*Sumatra, Java, Celebes and the Sula Islands, 1920*

I had enjoyed the journey from Europe, but had also become more anxious as I got closer to my destination. Would John in his loneliness have succumbed to the sirens of the East, as so many people had foretold? Throughout the whole journey, I had not heard from him.

In Singapore I went straight to the post office, and was relieved to find a letter waiting for me. The contents were sufficiently reassuring, but there was no evidence of a great longing for my arrival. It contained a detailed description of his work, and a list of materials that I somehow would have to purchase on Java. It was a letter written to a business partner rather than to a spouse. I had expected more, and was disappointed. Had I been influenced by the romantic courting on board?

I transferred to a KPM-ship that would take me to Padang. My heart opened up on arrival. This was truly the East Indies, the country I had hungered to see for many years! I was not disappointed. The country was beautiful, overwhelmingly beautiful, but oh, how hot it was.

I carefully looked over every Dutchman who came in sight. None of them *looked* depraved, I thought — not at all sure how depravity would manifest itself.

We sailed on to Belawan, where a young "proxy" told her devastated husband that she was through with him. She would return to Singapore, and get a divorce there. The man looked crushed, but not debased. He was an Austrian, though, and perhaps the warnings on board only pertained to Dutch men!

Upon arrival in Batavia (now Jakarta), I received a second letter:

"A warm welcome to this wonderful country! At night, close your *kelambu* (mosquito net), and watch for mosquitoes. Start looking for the material I asked you to buy."

Some romantic, this husband of mine! I was again deeply disappointed, and could not bring myself to start shopping.

In the hotel where I stayed, people expressed dismay as soon as they heard where I was heading. Most did not know where the Bangai Archipelago was, but "one boat connection every two months" defined it for them. Nobody would last there very long! I should refuse to go there, I was told, and persuade my husband to come to Java, where there were plenty of opportunities. Once again I heard the tales of degeneration, and of living together with native women. It drove me frantic!

I was glad to board the train for Bandung, where it was much cooler than in Jakarta. I registered at the elegant Hotel Homan and that evening was introduced to the famous *rijsttafel*[1].

The next morning I left the hotel for a few days to stay with John's friends, who lived high up in the Pengalengan region on a tea estate, surrounded by lush vegetation and majestic mountains. The panorama was incredibly beautiful.

The unaffected cordiality of my hosts was balm for the soul. They tried to convince me that it would not be so bad on those faraway Sula Islands. But they were friends and former classmates of John, and I wondered if loyalty to him had colored their opinions. As to the degeneration of single men in this land, the subject never came up — which pleased me. Perhaps those dire tales were exaggerations.

From Bandung I took the train to Surabaya, where I met John's older brother Jan, the patriarch of the family, who had offered John the position in this far-flung outpost of the Dutch empire. He and his wife, Koos, had lived on Java for many years. He was cordial, and talked candidly about the Indies. How one lived, worked, and especially how one could and should build a future. Throughout this talk he tried to appraise me in various ways, and it became obvious that he was very critical. Then, this exceedingly self-assured man talked at length about himself and his big successes in life. About his own younger brother, my husband, he had practically nothing to say.

Was I impressed? Disappointed? Confused? All of those, probably, because it took me many days to sort out my impressions and see life again with a degree of clarity.

Jan helped me purchase the materials on John's list. He also helped engage Chinese carpenters, Madurese brick-makers, a mason, and some thirty Madurese laborers. They would travel with me to the faraway Sula Islands to build a house for us. From this I concluded that John was still living in temporary quarters.

Jan's wife, Koos, also helped me engage a young *babu* (housemaid), Bok Punari, whom she had trained. Bok would travel with me also.

The day arrived to start the thirty-two day trip from Surabaya to the Sula islands. Our KPM ship was the S.S. *van Rees*. It created quite a stir when I boarded with my entourage, loaded down with *barang*[2] — and at that moment a spark of pride started to burn inside me.

## IBU MALUKU

I had started a new life, so business-like, so full of responsibility for people, and animals, too. I had brought a lot of poultry: chickens, geese, and ducks. Also, many tools and utensils, the names of which I had only recently learned from catalogues. Now they were familiar and had acquired an aura of indispensability.

The crew was very helpful, and the Captain, extremely fatherly. He obviously considered me far too young to handle all those responsibilities by myself.

Life on board was wonderful. Our first stop was Denpasar on Bali, where we would stay two days. While the ship was unloading and loading, I visited this paradise — the only place in the East Indies where Hinduism flourished, where the slender, graceful women did not cover their torsos, and where each task was performed as in service to the Gods.

Then, on to Makassar, an important commercial port with some 670,000 inhabitants — the "gateway to the Moluccas". As we entered the harbor, I admired the sleek sailing ships of the Buginese[3], who sail all the way to the Moluccas, to trade. "That's our biggest competition," said the Captain laughingly.

We stayed three days in Makassar. Here, too, it was very warm. The natives were different from those on Java. Men as well as women dressed in checkered, beautifully colored *sarongs*. About 3,700 Europeans (mostly Dutch) lived here, some of whom I met at the *Sociëteit* (Society) club-house, called the *"Soos"* (rhymes with "close"). All were very cordial, but they fancied themselves a lot, and I also detected some animosity between them — especially among the women.

We left Makassar and stopped at each place along the KPM route to unload goods and load mostly copra, the sweet smell of which then hung over the whole ship. On most islands, there lived only a few Europeans. The Captain always invited them on board for breakfast or dinner. Afterwards, he would give them some provisions to take home — usually raisin-bread or fresh meat. It was a very much appreciated tradition with the KPM. On some islands, we picked up a Dutch administrator, sometimes with wife and children; a representative from a trading-house; a planter's family; sometimes a doctor; and a few times even a tourist. The passengers on board were continuously changing.

Finally, we arrived at Ambon with its beautiful harbor, and its strong black men and women. Everyone was warm and outgoing. Here, I got another letter from John, which was delivered personally by a missionary, Father Neyens, who — as I would learn — had received his doctorate from the University of Louvain. His territory included the Moluccas and New Guinea. He told me that John had asked him to officiate at our church wedding, which had a much greater significance for us than the civil formality that had taken place in the Netherlands many months ago. Father Neyens would travel with me to Mangole, my destination, and then continue with the *van Rees* to Hollandia — the last harbor on West New Guinea that the KPM called on. He was accompanying a group of Americans, who wanted to tour New Guinea and Australia, before returning home.

From Ambon, we sailed past the eucalyptus island of Buru toward Sanana, the capital of the Sula Islands. This island group is made up of Sulabesi (where Sanana is located), Taliabu, and Mangole — where John was posted.

Thirty-two days had passed since I had started the journey from Surabaya, and with my final destination getting close, I became quite excited and filled with longing for my new life as a married woman.

The American ladies, who had learned about my upcoming wedding, went ashore in Sanana to get a large bouquet of flowers, while I, accompanied by *Babu* Bok, made a courtesy call on the *Gezaghebber*[4] who was the *HPB*[5] (local Magistrate) for the territory in which I would be living.

He was away on *tournée*[6], but I was received by his wife — a very kind, middle-aged woman of dark complexion, who spoke Dutch very well, but rolled her r's more than I was accustomed to. She lived in a large house, built of wooden beams. The white-washed walls consisted of interlaced stems of the sago-palm, which she called *gaba-gaba*. The roof was constructed of *atap*, made from the leaves of the coconut tree. In the front veranda stood dozens of large vases full with maidenhair fern and other beautiful tropical plants. We had tea, chatted for a while, and then, wanting to do some shopping, I asked where the *pasar* (market, usually open air) was. My hostess gave Bok directions in rapid Malay, which impressed me. The *pasar* itself, however, did not. It was a rather shabby place.

Back on board, the Second Mate helped me tell "my people" that they should get ready to go ashore. We would be arriving in a few hours. The personnel appeared relieved that the long journey was ending, and cheerfully started gathering up their belongings. Shocked at the amount of luggage they had with them, I wondered how all that could be unloaded during the short time we would be at anchor. I had already been told that everything would have to be ferried by motorboat to a small island, Passi Ipa, before the tide fell. "Don't worry," said Father Neyens, "everything will be all right." His words soothed me somewhat.

## IBU MALUKU

We sailed into the beautiful Vesuvius Bay, located between the large islands of Taliabu and Mangole. Along the coast of Mangole, I could only make out a dense jungle. John had to be there, somewhere.

\*\*\*\*

Still dazed by the rushed and definitely undignified wedding on board (as told in Chapter 1), I went ashore with John, and saw the First Mate rushing toward us with some papers.

If he noticed any incongruity in the appearance of the newlyweds — me nattily dressed and John covered with mud and remnants of our wedding cake — he certainly did not show it. He made John sign the bills of lading and wished us luck.

"See you in two months!" he said, and then made a dash for the motor sloop that would take him back to the ship.

I now had the opportunity to look around. The KPM-shed was full of shouting Chinese from nearby islands, who were loading their just-arrived purchases in their *praus* — rice, paraffin oil, soap, textiles and tobacco, which would be offered for sale in their *tokos* (shops).

John met the Chinese carpenters who had come with me, and together they inspected the goods brought from Java. John answered their questions in Malay, which I as yet did not understand. But their faces told me that they were not elated with the primitive surroundings.

John rejoined me, and explained that his Overseer, Sariowan, had already ferried the Madurese workers from Passi Ipa to the plantation with the large corporation *prau*. As soon as they had been put ashore, he continued, the *prau* would come back to pick up the Chinese carpenters, part of the goods, and the poultry. The people and animals would have to be sheltered before nightfall. The remaining goods would follow tomorrow.

"Now I have to find that *lèpa-lèpa*[8] I came with," said John.

He then told me he had been in the jungle, supervising the clearing of the plantation's border lines of trees and shrubs, when he heard the ship's whistle. The previous KPM ship had been several days late, and he had expected this one, carrying the surveyor as well as his bride, to be just as late.

The Overseer had assured him that the whistle could not possibly belong to the KPM ship. It was much too early for that. It had to be the expected government vessel that was announcing its arrival to District and *Kampung*[7] Heads.

John had originally agreed with the Overseer, but he felt uneasy and decided to go to the beach to check for himself. He cut through jungle and swamp to get to the mouth of the river, and left instructions for others to follow him with a canoe.

When he reached the beach and saw the ship in the distance, he knew there was no time to go home and change. The falling tide would force the ship to leave soon. He could not wait for his own people to catch up either, and was at his wit's end until he spotted a large *lèpa-lèpa* further along on the beach. The owners, obviously fishermen, had to be in the neighborhood. And yes, six fellows, naked except for a leaf to cover their loins, came out of the jungle, and declared themselves willing to row the *tuan* (gentleman) to the KPM ship.

Everyone got into the filthy boat. One man made a wrong move, the boat capsized, and John landed in the gooey river mud, which of course did not improve his appearance. Two men bailed out the water; everyone got in again, and the boat got under way. They were close to Passi Ipa when he saw the KPM motorboat coming toward him. He shouted and waved, and the coxswain signaled back that he had seen him. A moment later he was picked up in mid-sea. The coxswain immediately turned the boat around and set course for the *van Rees* at full throttle. John had hoped to shower on board and borrow a clean suit, but the coxswain told him there would be no time for that.

"So now you know what happened," concluded John.

I sympathized, yet found it difficult to overcome my deep disappointment. My expectations about our meeting after such a long separation had been so high. Our wedding ... well, it had been the pits!

Oh well, let the honeymoon begin!

When we arrived at the beach, the practically-naked rowers of the *lèpa-lèpa* were sitting calmly smoking a *krètèk* — a home-rolled cigarette of tobacco and dried corn leaves.

I was greeted with shouts of surprise. They looked me over from top to toe and seemed baffled when John told them, in a language I did not understand, that I was his wife, who would come with him to the Buluwaya plantation.

John took me to the *lèpa-lèpa*. It was a narrow dugout canoe with no seats in it at all. One fisherman climbed a nearby coconut tree, and sliced off a leaf with a *parang* (a chopping-knife). He came down with the agility of a monkey, cut off a piece of the stalk, and wedged it in the forecastle. Evidently, that would be my seat.

With difficulty and repugnance, I got in and promptly lost my balance as there was no flat place on which to place my feet. Luckily, John caught me, and eased me onto my seat. Four of the men jumped into the partly floating *lèpa-lèpa*, while two others pushed the vessel further off the beach.

John got in at the stern, followed by the last two fishermen. The *lèpa-lèpa* swayed momentarily but then righted itself. Then, a high wave carried the boat through the surf, and we were in open sea.

I don't remember whether I kept my eyes closed or not; I do remember I was scared and nauseated, asking myself what on earth I had got myself into.

After a while, one of the men shouted something, and when I looked up, I saw the *van Rees*, now a distant dot, sailing out of the bay. So the die was cast and there was no turning back.

In open sea, the *lèpa-lèpa* was more stable than I had expected. The six natives stood spread-eagled and rowed with unusually long oars, while John steered with a paddle.

Talking to each other was not possible. I turned around, hoping to catch an encouraging sign from John. The rowers glanced furtively at me and uttered strange sounds. No doubt they were discussing the merits of this strange creature. Looking past the fishermen would require me to lean to one side, which might tip the boat, so I was forced to look through six pairs of extended legs. It was not an elevating sight, and it made me awfully embarrassed.

The *lèpa-lèpa* stank. The edges were pasted with fresh fish scales and entrails, which in this heat gave off an unbearable smell.

I myself did not look very fresh either. My beautiful grey silken dress, which the American ladies had helped me into with so much pride, was wet and soiled. My hands, which had tenaciously clung to the boards of the *lèpa-lèpa*, were filthy; and with consternation I saw fish-polluted water swirl around my beautiful shoes. What a disaster! How long would this go on?

As we entered the mouth of the Golohaya river, John, remembering his earlier experience, warned me to sit still. "We do not want to capsize here," he said, "It is full of crocodiles." Another horror! What else would await me?

For ten minutes, we glided through a strange *vloedbos* (a mangrove forest) in which the trees stood as if on stilts in the shallow water. Then, suddenly, we were on the wide river that flowed indolently out to sea.

Along the banks were dark forests from which came the sounds of many birds. The tree tops that formed a canopy over the river allowed streaks of filtered green light to light our environment. Apart from the birds' singing, there was only the restful sound of the oars stirring the brown-colored water. Gradually, I started to discern more of my mysterious surroundings. The tall trees along the banks had strange, enormous root-systems, along which lianes were coiling upward toward the tree tops.

Suddenly there was a sound like a rifle shot. Flying strangely, almost clumsily, a flock of bright-colored lories[8] came out of one of the trees, and flew low over our *lèpa-lèpa*. A flash of green, yellow, red and purple. Gorgeous!

Enchanted, I twisted in my seat to follow them with my eyes, and in so doing caused the *lèpa-lèpa* to tilt dangerously. The rowers yelled, and with their oars quickly brought the vessel back in balance.

"Sit still!" came the angry voice from John. "That was stupid and dangerous!"

I was as much upset by the angry tone as by the event itself. Sadly, I reflected on the degeneration of single men in the East Indies about which I had heard so much. The optimism I had felt after we had both laughed at the flattened wedding cake drained out of me. Why was I sitting so far from him? Conversation was impossible. I had to cope with everything alone! Gloomily, I stared ahead, and tried to sit as still as possible in this very uncomfortable stance. I started to feel a cramp in my feet, and had great difficulty in fighting back the tears. But slowly, the surroundings claimed my attention again, and my somber spirits diminished.

The river was narrowing, so I could get a better look at the vegetation on both sides. Flights of small and large lories criss-crossed overhead, screeching loudly. Sometimes, they were followed by white cockatoos[9]. I did not dare express my excitement, but kept watching them with fascination.

The river became even more narrow and shallow. Here and there, several banks of red mud were visible above the water level. Soon, the *lèpa-lèpa* stopped, and the rowers got out. Rowing was no longer possible. The *lèpa-lèpa* was pushed now, sometimes through water, sometimes through thick mud.

John started to talk to me, but in jerky sentences, from which I understood that we were approaching the plantation. He looked inhibited, and even more withdrawn than before. How he had changed!

Finally, John also got out — the boat was now stuck in the mud — and I had no choice but to follow suit. Anxiously, I peered around for crocodiles that might be waiting to have me for dinner, but there were none that I could see.

When I saw John and the rowers scaling the river bank, I plodded through the sucking mud attempting to accomplish that *tour de force* also. John called from high up that he was sorry nobody could help me climb up, but that in the *rimbu* (wilderness) it could not be helped. This obvious discourtesy hit me hard. With clenched teeth, I tried to climb a slippery, rotting tree trunk, which was covered with moss and mud. Steps had been cut into the trunk, but they were too far apart to do me any good.

Angry and out of breath, sometimes sliding backward, I climbed laboriously — and of course much too slowly — to where John could reach out and pull me up. This was the first time we touched since he had helped me into the boat. It did not do much for me, even though I had intensely longed for some physical contact. Had he? Probably not, for he turned around immediately to say something to the rowers, who looked sheepishly and obviously had done something wrong.

They slid hastily down the slippery tree trunk to the river bank, and then I understood that our wedding dinner had been left in the *lèpa-lèpa*. They should have taken it with them, of course.

Silently, I looked sideways at John, hoping he would let go of his reserve, but he looked surly, and his face even showed dislike. I anxiously wondered if John had indeed acquired a *nyai*, and did not know how to resolve the situation, now that his wife was here. I began to wish I hadn't come. I should have listened to the advice, so freely given. Perhaps there was some truth to what had been said on board, as everything had gone wrong here from the beginning of our "honeymoon" trip.

Yet, gradually, the surroundings got hold of me again. When John instructed the naked group to bring the *barang* to the house, I relaxed somewhat and began looking at my surroundings. How still it was here, and how terribly isolated. Not a house, not a human being in sight. Nothing but green bushes, and ... mud!

We were standing on a slippery, muddy path. Here and there, sticks and bits of wood had been driven into the mire, obviously to give the ground some solidity. As I started walking, I noticed that the heel of one shoe had been lost in the river's mud. I expressed my regret to John, who looked at my shoe and said casually, "Well, those are not the kind of shoes to enter the *rimbu* with."

I looked at him in utter disbelief. How dare he say that! Had he lost all sensitivity? I shook with indignation. He did not seem to notice and added: "You'll have an unpleasant walk ahead of you, as we are still three kilometers from the house."

I angrily clenched my teeth. Not a single complaint would pass my lips!

In silence we went on, while his indifference gnawed at my insides.

Then, I remembered one of his earlier letters. In it, he told of having put all available men on the construction of a road through the swamp.

He obviously thought that to be quite an achievement. I only hoped that we would soon reach that road, for with only one heel, I tottered rather than walked.

How terribly desolate and deserted it was around us.

I hobbled along another fifteen minutes and then gave up. Desperate, I stopped in my tracks, and shouted: "And when are we going to get to that famous road of yours?"

"Dammit! You are walking on it!" John exploded. "What do you think a road through this miserable swamp is supposed to look like?"

We faced each other like fighting-cocks. John's dented tropical helmet sat askew on his head, and he had a large tear in his trousers. He looked terrible. Then, in a flash I saw myself too: dreadful! What a sight. I was now covered in mud too. There was nothing left of the fresh, elegantly dressed maiden that had so recently left the ship.

My anger dissipated; John looked perplexed.

For the first time we really looked at each other.

Then something broke up within us. At the same time we both stretched out our arms, and like two lost children laughed, cried and hugged each other in that endless mud. We disentangled, looked at each other again and, realizing the absurdity of the situation, burst out laughing again, sending a whole colony of white cockatoos screeching into the air.

Thank God! In that laughing I discovered that, although John had changed, he had remained my true friend.

As we continued our journey over this "cudgel-road" made with sticks and bits of wood, John explained how difficult it had been to construct it in this smelly, sucking swamp. There was a measure of pride in his voice.

We left the swamp, and followed a more solid road to a clearing. A strange building stood there, and I asked John if that was ours.

"Don't expect too much," said John shyly. "I'm afraid it will be another big disappointment for you." However, I felt that I could handle just about anything, now that the wall of reservedness had been broken.

The building was a cumbersome, lopsided contraption on stilts, with a shoddy roof of *atap*. An unstable stairway of tree trunks led to the main bamboo floor that swayed under my feet as we entered the house from the front veranda. The white buffet I had ordered while still in Holland was attached to a wall with thick ropes of *rotan* (rattan). Evidently, it was too heavy for the decrepit floor, which had been reinforced with boards to support an oval table and its chairs.

On the table stood the pots and pans from the *van Rees*, already being invaded by an army of black ants. In one corner stood a desk and a bookcase. That would be John's workplace. Above the table, from a strong piece of wire, hung an old-fashioned oil-lamp. There was nothing else!

The front veranda led to a long corridor. At the right was a windowless storage place. It was too dark for me to see anything in there. At the left was the bedroom. A hole in the outer wall, covered by a mat of tobacco leaves, served as a window. Against one wall stood a very large iron bed with tarnished copper knobs.

The bed was enveloped by a *kelambu* or mosquito net. Looking through the *kelambu* I could make out two pillows and two *gulings*[10], cigar-shaped pillows — the usefulness of which I still had to discover. At the foot of the bed lay two folded, striped, thin blankets and a large *sapu lidi* (a swatter made of palm-leaf ribs) with which to exterminate any pesky mosquito that might get inside.

There was, however, nothing else. I looked around in a daze. No chair, no night table, no clothes rack, and — apart from the oil lamp in John's workplace — no light. Nothing!

I was close to tears. How had John been able to live in this squalor?

John came alongside, took me in his arms and said: "It is all very disappointing, isn't it?" In a strangled voice he continued: "Oh! I had wanted everything to be different. I had so much wanted to welcome you to a decent home, but in this miserable place everything has gone wrong."

I did not answer, fearing that my voice would betray my feelings. The disappointment had bowled me over. It was almost unbearable. John tried to console me, ran out of words, and then said that my luggage was on its way.

I followed him to what he called the front veranda. My little *babu* was sitting on top of the staircase, looking wide-eyed at the strange surroundings. Her face showed neither surprise, nor disappointment.

Below, a group of people arrived, carrying coffers, chickens, ducks and quacking geese. A neatly dressed man stepped forward, and John introduced him to me as Hendrik Sariowan, the Overseer. "He has the confidence of the Board on Java, for whom he has managed the plantation for more than two years," whispered John.

I looked at the Overseer, nodded politely, and decided I did not like the man. He was too subservient, and his eyes were unpleasant. (My first impression would prove to be correct. He would always regard me as an unwelcome intruder.)

Sariowan reported that the Madurese had settled in the long-house that had been built for them. The Chinese had been sheltered in another bamboo house. He would need at least two more days to transport all the *barang* from Passi Ipa to Buluwaya.

John explained that the *emplacement*[11] and the Overseer's residence were on the other side of the river, and that Bok Punari could sleep there too. But Bok had no intention of leaving me, and asked permission to find a place for herself in our house. How grateful I was to her at that moment. Later, it became clear how much I would need this woman. She would help me through many difficult hours.

After Sariowan and the porters had left, I started to unpack. John thought it would do us good to take a bath. It was only then that I became truly aware of the suffocating heat and my longing to get out of my dirty clothes.

"Well, who will use the bathroom first?" I asked naïvely.

John chuckled. "We'll go together," he said.

I looked at him, taken aback. Imagine! What lack of propriety!

"I'll take you there." John laughed openly at me now. "It is the most ideal bathroom in the world! We shall have to walk to get there."

I was curious, and looked forward to taking a hot bath to first soak and then scrub off the hardened mud. Then, I suddenly realized there would be no bathtubs in the Indies and, embarrassed, I laughed at my mistake.

John, however, thought that I was laughing at his beard, and said: "I haven't shaved in four days, because I wanted to clear the borders before you arrived. I was up at the crack of dawn, and did not get back before dark. By that time I was so tired, all I wanted to do was sleep. But now," he continued, "the beard comes off, and you will never, never, see this monkey face again." And he disappeared somewhere in the back of the dark corridor.

*Babu* Bok was already diligently sweeping the ants off the table, grumbling they had gotten there only because there was no more water in the cans into which the once beautiful white legs had been placed.

I looked at the eroded table legs with revulsion, and firmly decided that some changes were going to be made! Good intentions, which would gradually fade away.

From the dark corridor, John heralded his impending arrival "without beard", and asked if I was ready for the trip to the bathroom. I awaited his coming with suspicion but, true, the beard was gone and now I recognized in him the man to whom I had said goodbye such a long time ago.

Smiling broadly, he took my kimono and towel from me, and helped me down the rickety stairs. We stood in the mud again, which by now had dried somewhat. I looked around, but did not see any building that might serve as bathroom.

We followed a well-trodden path and, after a few minutes came to the bank of a small river. Looking down the embankment, I could see a foot-bridge with a lean-to, from the wall of which a jet of water squirted out of a hollow piece of bamboo.

"Voilà," said John proudly. "Our bathroom!"

Flabbergasted, I looked at him: "Are you kidding me?" But John replied with enthusiasm that this was the best bathroom in the world, and he pulled me by the hand down the embankment and onto the bridge.

"Come on, now, John! If this is your idea of a joke, I can't see anything funny in it!" But John did not answer. With his back to me, he started to untie his kimono. How strange it looked on him. With a quivering voice, I asked if I had to disrobe here also.

Cheerfully, he said: "Yes, naturally. Put your clothes on the shrubs in front of you." He had obviously noticed that I had turned my back to him.

Deeply upset, I looked around. Did he really expect me to bathe here in this river that swarmed with moving things, where everyone could see us? This was too much! I climbed the embankment, dropped to the ground, and burst out in tears. The world had crashed around me, and I wished for nothing more than to perish with it.

John knelt beside me, took me in his arms, and allowed me to get it out of my system.

Drained, I finally calmed down, and felt relieved when John told me that we would leave Mangole if I could not get used to this life. I then promised to do my best. Thereafter, we bathed in the cold water. I managed to control myself, and between us there was finally a feeling of solidarity and understanding.

In the rapidly descending darkness of evening, John asked what had happened since his departure from Holland. I brought him up-to-date, and also described the life on board ship: the flirtations, the temptations, the many warnings about the degeneration of single men in the tropics, and my great fear when he did not come on board right away! In turn, John told me about his fears when, seeing the KPM ship from the beach, he realized he had no choice but to appear as he was. He did not care much about the opinions of others, but what I would think — well, that was a different matter.

Arriving on board, he had felt ill-at-ease with so many unknown people staring at him. And when he saw me, unexpectedly dressed in a beautiful wedding gown, he had become even more conscious of his own appearance. He was convinced that I would never want to share this life with him. The fall on top of the wedding cake — even if he had laughed about it himself — symbolically signaled the end, and he decided then and there to let me go back to Holland with the next available ship.

This explained why he had been so surly and stand-offish, first in the *lèpa-lèpa*, and later during the landing. He had resolutely decided not to touch me, afraid that he would lose his self-control!

Now that I knew everything, John urged me to think very carefully about whether I wanted to stay with him. But in my heart I had already decided to stay and put up with these primitive conditions.

I was determined that our marriage would survive. And so we went into the night together — my first night in the *rimbu* — to start a new life, in a new land.

**(Endnotes)**

1. Literally "rice-table", the internationally accepted Dutch word for an Indonesian culinary feast, that includes a dozen or more side dishes.
2. *Barang* – a general term for luggage and goods of all kinds. Jeanne van Diejen quickly picked up Malay words, such as this one, that the European inhabitants regularly used in conversation.
3. *Buginese (Bugis)* – a highly cultured people, living in the southwestern part of Celebes, renowned as traders and sailors and, in an earlier century, feared as pirates. The term "bogeyman" (anything that haunts one) is probably derived from "bugiman", which is what early Europeans called the Bugis.
4. *Gezaghebber* (the one in charge) – usually a part-time magistrate (often a planter by profession), who had been educated in Batavia to represent the Netherlands East Indies Government. To become a higher-ranking *Controleur* or *Resident*, one had to study in the Netherlands.
5. *HPB (Hoofd van Plaatselijk Bestuur)* – Head of Local Government, the local magistrate, who could have the rank of *Gezaghebber*, *Assistant Controleur*, *Controleur*, etc.
6. *Tournée* – a tour of duty: a business trip, or an inspection trip.
7. *Lèpa-lèpa* – a dugout canoe with one or two outriggers.
8. Lorie (pl. lorries) – a small, Australasian parrot.
9. Cockatoo – a crested (tufted on top of the head) Australasian parrot, larger than the lory.
10. *Guling* – an oblong pillow (typically 7" in diameter, by 28" long), used to separate knees and arms during sleep, thus obtaining more cooling from a freer air circulation.
11. *Emplacement* – a French word, which refers here to the hub of the plantation, where there are houses and tool-processing and storage-sheds.

IBU MALUKU

# CHAPTER 5

### A Difficult Start
*Buluwaya Plantation, Mangole, Sula Islands, 1920*

When I woke up the next morning, it was still dark. I heard John talking with Bok, and smelled the enticing aroma of coffee. But I was in no hurry, and I lay there for a while, reflecting on the events of the previous day. My marriage had been sanctified and I was firm in my resolve to make it a good one.

John was fully dressed, and welcomed me cheerfully. As we were drinking hot, sweet coffee, it was getting lighter outside. The roosters crowed to herald the sun, and under the house I could hear the animals moving about. As the darkness lifted, I had my first disappointment in this new environment.

On Java, I had always watched the sun come up with awe and intense enjoyment. At that time of day, it was still delightfully cool. The sky would be pearly, riddled with thousands of delicate hues touched with gold by the upcoming sun. I had hoped to see that splendor here too, but this early morning had brought only long veils of fog that hung between the trees and shrubs around the house. The forest stood at some distance from us, and it looked cold, dark, and threatening.

I fully expected that it was going to rain, but John thought it would be a dry, hot day. The sun would be coming through in a few hours and burn away the fog, he said. Even at this early hour, it was already as heavy and oppressive as in a hothouse.

Over a second cup of coffee, John said he had to go to the *emplacement* to discuss the work to be done by the new people. Normally, this was done by Sariowan, but the Overseer would be away supervising the transportation of our *barang* from Passi Ipa, and that might take two days.

"What is an *emplacement*, and where is it?" I asked.

"It is the hub of the plantation where the copra is processed, and where the workers live," John said. "To get there, I have to cross the *kali* — the same river we traveled on yesterday."

I walked with him to the river bank, which was surprisingly close to the house — something I had not noticed the day before.

"This is where I cross," said John, pointing to a tree trunk that connected the muddy banks, "but only if there is no *banjir* (flash flood) as a result of a downpour in the mountains. When that happens, crossing will be impossible, and then we'll have the day off."

A quick kiss, and then, with arms stretched sideways to balance himself, he stepped out onto the tree trunk, and gingerly walked to the other side. "Something I shall have to master myself, no doubt," I thought with trepidation.

John turned, waved, and shouted: "I'll be back for breakfast at eight and I'll bring some people to clean around the house and build chicken coops."

For the next hour and a half I was alone with Bok, who asked if she could have a kitchen built behind the house. She did not like my modern "Perfection" oil stove, nor the dark place in the corridor where it stood.

"Has the *nyonya muda* (the young madam) already asked the *tuan* if there is a *pasar* (market) or a *warong* (shop) on the other side of the river?" she asked.

I hadn't, and did not know the answer. However, I found out later that the closest shop was on the island of Passi Ipa!

Around eight o'clock, a boisterous group of Madurese crossed the *kali* — each one carrying either a *parang*, a shovel, or a *pacul* (hoe). They seemed eager to get down to business.

Soon after, John arrived with the Chinese *tukangs* (craftsmen), who were here for the sole purpose of building a residence for us. He said he had brought everybody — except the bricklayers, who had been dispatched to find suitable clay and to build a kiln.

We hurriedly ate breakfast, while the workers squatted outside, contentedly smoking a *krètèk* — waiting for further instructions.

I told John that Bok wanted a kitchen, and I wanted a screened window in the bedroom, and ...

"Yes," John said, "be patient. Show me first what you want done around the house."

By the time we arrived downstairs, Bok had already mobilized the Madurese, who were removing the large baskets with chickens and ducks from underneath the house, and cleaning up the dung left by a visiting wild steer.

"Nobody has been able to catch that animal," said John. "Sometimes it disappears for a long time in the *rimbu*, and then it unexpectedly comes back. The animal is considered dangerous."

"About the Chinese *tukangs*," John continued, "they have agreed to build chicken coops, and fix up the house as best they can."

"Well," I quickly said, "that rickety staircase is a good place to start."

The *tukangs* looked the house over, inside and outside, and frequently shook their heads. They said they needed to shore up the house and strengthen the wobbly floor. The floor itself could not be replaced — the roof structure rested on it — but the floor could be reinforced with a layer of freshly cut bamboo. They also recommended more internal beams to better support the upper structure. And when I asked them about putting a real window in the bedroom, they said it was no problem — and they could cover it with the fine wire-netting that I had brought.

I also asked for a door to the bedroom. John did not think it necessary, but he let me have my way.

John then instructed the Madurese, who had finished cleaning underneath the house, to clean the compound of shrubs and wild shoots; cut bamboo for the new floor; and also assist Bok in setting up her kitchen.

All morning, a tremendous amount of activity raged around us. The *rimbu* retreated before my eyes as the ducks and geese greedily picked at uprooted insects. Many times we heard a Madurese shout *"Ular!"*. Each time the workers rushed over to the one who had sounded the alarm.

"Another snake!" John would say tersely. He had explained to me that the snake would be hacked in pieces, and thrown in the river. If that were not done, then, according to popular belief, the head and the pieces would grow together into a new snake. Judging by the number of screams, this country was full of snakes, which only added to my fears.

Elsewhere, John continued, some twenty beautiful cows were running wild. Among them was also the wild bull that occasionally lodged with us. John told the Madurese about this, and promised a reward for each animal caught. They smiled from ear to ear. The Madurese *know* how to handle cattle.

At noon, John distributed rice and salted, dried fish. Soon, little fires flared up everywhere around the house.

After lunch, large bamboos were cut to measure, "de-notched", split open, and flattened. By four o'clock, the *tukangs* had furnished our front veranda with a new, green, and nice-smelling floor! Our living quarters were next.

The *tukangs* then reassembled the cupboard I had brought in knocked-down state, after which I hurriedly unpacked and placed my chinaware. When the dining table was put back in its spot — its four legs in tin cans, filled with a carbolic acid solution to protect against ants

— that part of the house looked already much friendlier.

Outside, several fires were consuming grass, wood and other rubbish. Pleased with the progress made, I showed John the shell of Bok's kitchen, and the cut-to-measure bamboo that would be used the next day to build the chicken coops.

Bok arrived with water for the chickens that were still encased in the large baskets in which they had traveled. At her side was a little boy. I had often seen him on board, sitting on his haunches in front of the baskets, silently admiring the black crested chickens. His name was Latif.

Puzzled, I asked Bok what the boy was doing on Buluwaya. Then I heard that Latif was an orphan, and that his Uncle Senen, a brickmaker, had smuggled him on board in Surabaya.

John and I looked at each other. "How can such a thing happen?" we asked.

Bok then said that she would like to have Latif as a companion. He could look after the chickens and ducks, fetch water for her, and do a thousand other things for the *nyonya muda*. And so we acquired another member of the household. John promptly instructed the *tukangs* to build a room for Bok and Latif, next to the kitchen.

Darkness had fallen. We were almost too tired and excited to eat. At eight, we were ready for bed. It had been a wonderful day, a day in which we had come closer together.

\* \* \* \*

The next day, while we were sipping our coffee, the Overseer arrived with all the workers. Everyone was assigned his task before the sun came up.

Then John and Sariowan left for Passi Ipa. Something was wrong with our *barang*, and they would not be back until noon. For the first time, I was alone on the island. Bok had gone to the *kali* to wash clothes.

Several *tukangs* disassembled the bed, moved it out of the bedroom, and covered the floor with freshly split and flattened bamboo. Soon the window was made, complete with wire-netting and shutters. It looked safe!

When John returned home around two, I immediately dragged him off to show him the new bedroom. I was pleased and proud, as if I had brought about the change myself.

At three, the Chinese had finished the chicken coops, and Latif got busy transferring the white Leghorns and the black crested chickens to their own separate pen. The reason for their separation became clear, as each rooster — after crowing its superiority — tried to assassinate its rival through, and in spite of, the chicken wire.

# IBU MALUKU

Bok's room and kitchen were ready, except for the walls. In the middle of the kitchen stood a strange contraption: a wooden table with raised edges. It was filled with a thick layer of fresh earth. On top lay several stones. With a satisfied look, Bok declared that was where she would cook. Latif had already gathered dry wood, and had arranged it neatly under the table.

I had been so busy that morning that I had forgotten to ask John about his trip to Passi Ipa. He did not speak about it either, and disappeared again after lunch. At six o'clock, he returned from across the river, where he'd had a meeting with the brick-makers. Something seemed to bother him, but he didn't talk about it. After dinner, he casually asked how long I would need the Madurese.

I looked up surprised, and said: "As I see it, it will take weeks before the *rimbu* around the house will be cleared."

John nodded, but did not comment. Only later would I understand how naive my reaction to his question had been.

The night was restless. I heard snorting and rubbing under the house. Frightened, I woke John. First, he thought that I had been hearing things, but then he said dryly: "Well, the bull must have returned. Don't worry about it. It will be gone in the morning." Then he promptly went back to sleep.

So here we were. Snakes could no longer enter through the window or by the door, thank heaven. But I did hear animals on the roof and around the house, and below me lived a wild steer. And I was expected to take all that in my stride!

\* \* \* \*

The next morning John was up just as early, and had prepared the coffee. When I entered the front veranda, the house suddenly started to shake and sway. "An earthquake!" I thought, and rushed toward the stairs to get out of the house. But John intercepted me, grabbing me by the arm.

"It's that steer," he assured me. "He's standing up now, and his hump is rubbing against the beams underneath the floor. Don't worry, he will soon leave of his own accord."

Little Latif, who had heard the animal too, ran to the river and called out to his uncle, who soon came with four sturdy fellows and long ropes. They were eager to catch "Atlas" (as I had baptized the animal), and earn the reward that John had promised. The men disappeared under the house, and I heard them rattle buckets. Latif came upstairs to ask for a handful of coarse salt. I gave it to him, and asked what the men would be doing with it, but Latif only smiled secretively. I started to follow him

49

outside, but Bok restrained me, as she thought I might get in the way.

Curious, I bent over the balustrade of the front veranda, from where I could only see the animal's snout, and the men who squatted in a semicircle around the beast. Their leader, the man in the center, had put a bucket with salted water temptingly between himself and the steer. The animal cautiously advanced, and then retreated, snorting ominously at the encircling conspirators who were waving branches.

The leader held a thick rope in one hand that he kept behind him. He lured and soothed the animal, making clucking sounds with his tongue. Now and then, he threw a handful of water toward the increasingly nervous animal.

As the animal approached cautiously, the man stayed on his haunches behind the enticing bucket, feigning total indifference. Tension mounted. The animal took another step. The man's hand shot out like lightning ... the steer snorted, pulled back, and made the whole house shake again. A cry of triumph from the men! The rope had been looped through the nose-ring of the heavy animal and was quickly let out to give the steer some leeway. The others rushed in to help their comrade pull the animal from underneath the house, and tie it with ropes to the trunk of a sturdy tree. It was only then that I noticed that Atlas had one horn missing. The men then roped one hind leg and tied it to a different tree, placed the bucket with water within reach so the animal could drink, and then behaved as if nothing had happened. Atlas pulled and snorted, rolled its eyes, and mooed like a lunatic, but gradually calmed down.

When John came home at 7:30 for breakfast, I ran out to meet him and take him to see the steer. As we watched, one steer-catcher threw some freshly cut grass within the animal's reach.

John said he would let me keep the five steer-catchers for a week, to work on the compound. Two could till the earth for a vegetable garden; the others could help clear the surrounding area.

After breakfast, John left again, and I remained outside to watch the Madurese. They hauled in the rope that was attached to the nose-ring, and Atlas fell to the ground, since one hind leg was tied. This allowed others to fashion a headstall from a strong rope. Then the nose-ring was tied up so the animal could eat. The ring had obviously been a hindrance, because — as we could now clearly see — the animal was quite thin.

Later in the day, Atlas was tied to a tree close to the river, where there was an abundance of grass, and where it could calm down. The Madurese got their reward, and returned happily to their quarters.

During dinner, John asked me to accompany him to the *emplacement* the following day. First, he wanted me to meet Mrs. Sariowan;

otherwise, she would feel slighted, and that should be avoided. Next, he wanted me to look at a few of the new arrivals who had fallen ill. And there were others who had lacerated their legs with the bamboo they had cut for our floor.

John appeared irritated, so I withdrew into silence.

How tired he looked suddenly. A stack of newspapers, already two months old, had arrived when I did. He started to read them, but fell asleep over the first one. I sat quietly, next to the softly buzzing petrol light, and it struck me that it was not still outside. There were all kinds of sounds. A large bird flew over the house with a languid wing-beat, occasionally letting out a hoarse cry. There were also some crickets nearby; and in the distance, a dog barked. I could also hear a strange chirping sound, sometimes loud, then soft; sometimes close by, then again far away. On the walls, little *cicaks*[1] (small lizards) pursued each other, stopping only to snap up a moth off the wall. Small winged creatures flew around the bright petrol lamp, became mesmerized by the light, and dropped to the floor, thus forming a ring. I noticed they had just lost their wings, and, in this naked state, looked like large ants.

Something else walked on the roof. In the dry *atap*, everything rustled.

"I should ask John to build a ceiling," I thought, feeling uncomfortable in this quiet house with the threatening darkness outside.

I woke John and asked him to come to bed. Startled, he looked around — then put out the lamp and came to the bedroom with me. How cozy it looked in the evening, so secluded and safe from the hostile darkness outside. John fell asleep right away, but I remained wide awake. A vague unrest gnawed at me.

"What is the matter?" I asked myself, feeling that John had again retreated within himself.

\* \* \* \*

The fourth day dawned. After breakfast, I would accompany John to the *emplacement*. But first I asked Latif to let out the chickens on a rotating basis, so he could clean each coop, and provide fresh water.

He committed himself eagerly to the task. "The *nyonya muda* would not have to worry," he said.

I then picked up my medical bag and apron, and walked with John toward the river. "Are there any crocodiles around? I asked. I was glad to hear they only appeared near the mouth of the river.

John helped me get down the steep bank, took my medical bag from me, and carried it across the river over the tree trunk that served as bridge. Now it was my turn. With arms outstretched to maintain my balance, I inched my way across, and breathed easier when I could step down on the other side. "Well," I thought, "with a little practice I might just get the hang of it."

We walked some two hundred meters alongside a square palm-grove. John said it contained coconut seed-beds, laid out by his predecessor. They had never been planted out; the administrator had died before it could be completed.

When I asked where this man was buried, John said he would show me later and tell me then what he knew about him. I sensed that I should not be asking any more questions, so I clammed up.

We arrived at a row of small bamboo houses. These, I learned, were the houses of the seven "old" coolies[2] — the ones who had survived the influenza epidemic and now lived here with the remaining members of their families. The houses were deserted now, the inhabitants having gone to do their daily chores.

Further on stood a large new shed, where the Madurese lived. Two of them had ugly, festering cuts on their legs, which I cleaned and bandaged. Two others had a high fever.

"Malaria," said John regretfully. "That will last a few days. They have already been given quinine pills and powders for the headaches."

"One of the Chinese coughs badly," he added, "and complains about pain in the chest." He, too, I concluded, would have to be confined to his *balé-balé* (bamboo cot), and would not be able to work for a few days.

The other Madurese had gone with Sariowan to continue clearing the plantation's borders, in preparation for the still-expected visit of the *Mantri*[3] Surveyor, who should have arrived with me on the same ship.

I would soon learn that such delays were common out here.

The Chinese lived in a bamboo house that was roomier than the ones in which the old coolies lived. But those smaller houses were at least furnished with self-made tables and chairs, whereas the Chinese had nothing in their shed, except two rows of bamboo bunks. I thought it was rather shabby, but John said they were used to it.

We walked back past the "old" coolie houses and followed the path that led to a small, pretty house, surrounded by a neatly trimmed fence of unfamiliar red shrubs.

"This is the Overseer's house," said John, "and this is where I have lived for several months."

In the front veranda stood four *rotan* chairs, and a table with a white crocheted covering.

At the entrance, John stopped and called out: *"Sepada?"*

"It means: is any body home?" said John. "That's what you are expected to say. Remember that."

Martha, the wife of the Overseer, came outside and greeted John in a glib tongue. I did not understand one word of it. She took no notice of me until John pushed me forward and said: "This is my wife."

I extended my hand, and received a weak, clammy handshake. I kept my composure, but inwardly I recoiled. Then she asked John whether he would like some coffee.

"Yes," he said, "and my wife also, please."

Martha rushed away, and returned moments later with steaming coffee and a glass jar containing home-made cookies. She talked to John only — what about I did not know. Furtively, I took stock of her, and she of me. We obviously did not care for each other.

She was a light-skinned, small woman. Her shiny, thick hair was fashioned into a *kondé* — a hair knot, on the back of the head. She wore a colorful *sarong*, and a beautiful lace *kebaya* blouse that was closed with a series of gold coins.

I realized suddenly that she had been the *nyonya besar* (the number one lady) here, and had wielded a considerable amount of influence. Now she was dethroned by me, and felt slighted. But I doubted that John had sensed this.

He kept on talking to her, and I might as well not have been there. But the situation did make it very clear that I would have to master that language soon.

After a while, I shyly remarked that I would like to go home. It looked as if John had wanted to stay a little longer, but he asked her to excuse us, and we left.

When we arrived at the *kali*, not a word had been said between us. I felt very uncomfortable, and when I asked if something was wrong, he burst out: "Could you not have made an effort, and at least talked a little to that woman? You have to realize that she is the wife of the Overseer, and that it is important to get along with these people!"

I did not reply.

Although my knowledge of Malay was still limited, I would have been quite willing to try, but John certainly had not made any attempt to draw me into the conversation. There was something strange here; first with Sariowan, and now with his wife. It made me restless, and a little fearful. In some way it seemed that John had been taken in by her, and was not aware of it. Or was it I, who did not understand these relationships? It was all very difficult.

\*\*\*\*

The next morning, John asked me if there was anything I wanted. Sariowan would be coming over soon to help sort the *barang* that the previous administrator had "temporarily" stored in the second room of the house, opposite our bedroom. Much, if not all of it, would be moved to a tool-shed that stood behind the Overseer's house.

"If that room becomes empty," I said eagerly, "I would like to make it into a storeroom, place my "Perfection" stove there, and bake my own bread. I have brought everything I need to do that." John agreed, but without much enthusiasm.

I then told John that Atlas had a broken horn and had to be treated. According to his caretaker, the wound was full of worms and maggots.

"You stay away from that steer," John replied sharply. "It's far too dangerous. I'd rather shoot the animal!"

"The thought of it!" I said. "If you do that, how are you ever going to catch the cows? After all, the steer serves as bait, and the Madurese know that."

John reluctantly agreed, but said he would instruct someone else to treat the animal. I wasn't about to give up, however, and asserted that he could not spare anyone, and reminded him that I, daughter and granddaughter of veterinarians, knew how to handle animals.

John refused to budge.

"Come now, John," I pleaded, "let me try at least. I really want to, and if I am successful in curing that animal, the people here will have more confidence in me."

John grumbled for a while, then disappeared into the dark storeroom, predicting that I would soon give it up.

At 8:30, I went to the *emplacement*, to re-dress wounds and distribute pills. Martha did not show herself.

On my way back, an hour later, I passed several men who carried tools to the new tool-shed. I was pleased. They had evidently started sorting out the contents of the storeroom. And yes, when I arrived at the house, everything had been taken outside and gathered into individual piles: rusted whipsaws, spades, hoes without handles, old rusty chains, a pump (thickly coated with grease), small containers with nails, rolled up tarpaulins (obviously intended for the plantation *prau*), crates full of old newspapers, and other possessions of the previous inhabitant.

Cockroaches — I had never seen them that large — were fleeing in all directions, and were diligently picked up by the chickens, ducks and geese.

Not wanting to be in the way, I did not enter the house, and occupied myself instead with the layout of the vegetable gardens. Senen, Latif's uncle, who served temporarily as compound caretaker, was making a fence around it. I would not be able to sow until that was finished. So I started sorting my little bags with seed, and thought about the lettuce and radishes I would be reaping soon.

When all the crates in the storeroom had been moved out and emptied, I asked John if I could use the crates to build a storage rack for our provisions. "No," said John, "the Overseer will need them for the new *gudang*[4]. But," he continued, pointing to some smaller crates, "you can have those." He then arranged to have them put aside for me.

It was wonderful to have that added space in our house — though it was still terribly dirty, and full of fungi, spiders and lizards. When Latif, who was inspecting the place with me, suggested that there were probably also some small snakes, I got out of there fast!

In the afternoon, John said a few men would be coming to clean the place. I begged immediately for the installation of a double floor and, if possible, two windows. It was so dark in there! When I said I still had enough fine wire mesh to cover the windows, John relented. The following day, he would instruct people to cut the bamboo, and ask the Chinese to work another day for me.

I felt happy and high-spirited, but my fear of snakes stopped me from entering that dark room until some windows had been installed.

The next day, John seemed more cheerful. He said that he found me a good comrade and was glad to have me with him. But ... it did not go any further. A kiss in the morning, a kiss at night, and an occasional embrace. That was it.

"Is this going to continue like that?" I asked myself anxiously. "Am I doing something wrong?

John always appeared tired. He was not often cheerful and thought only about his work, which occupied him completely. At night, he fell asleep at the drop of a hat. I worried about it, but was also very tired because of the oppressive heat and the heavy and unusual workload. Were we both responsible for this chill between us?

So ended that first week of married life.

**(Endnotes)**
[1] *Cicak* – pronounced chee-chahk.
[2] *Coolie* – probably derived from the Tamil *kuli* for "hired help", is used here to mean "unskilled laborer". By contrast, *tukang* means "skilled laborer".
[3] *Mantri* – native official or supervisor of a service.
[4] *Gudang* is a commonly used word for a warehouse, a stockroom — any place, large or small, used for storage.

# IBU MALUKU

# IBU MALUKU

# CHAPTER 6

### Getting Established
*Buluwaya Plantation, Mangole, Sula Islands, 1920*

The next day, five Chinese *tukangs* came to measure the emptied storage room for the installation of a new floor and window. I asked them to also install a door, as it would give me a feeling of security and ... home.

Would it also be possible to install a ceiling in the bedroom, I asked. They said they would try, but the superstructure did not look too sturdy.

Then they told me that John had selected a suitable spot for our new house, which would have to be built entirely of wood — without a brick foundation. The search for suitable clay to make bricks had been fruitless, and the brick-makers had already asked to be returned to Java with the next ship, as there was nothing for them to do.

Lumber was another problem, the *tukangs* said. The trees that had been cut down before they arrived were not of sufficiently good quality. They had selected better trees and had made detailed plans for sawing beams and boards. That would keep the three pairs of recently-hired lumbermen busy for a year, or longer, they said. To complete the house in a more reasonable time frame, they recommended twice as many men.

This was bad news. The *tukangs* had been hired in the belief that the lumber for the house had already been cut. It had not. So they would also have to leave. Paying and feeding them until the lumber had been sawed and dried, was unthinkable.

John had kept these problems entirely to himself. How little trust he had in me. If he had shared this, wouldn't it have been easier to bear? How could I ever convince him of this?

A few hours later, the *tukangs* were installing freshly cut, flattened bamboo over the old floor in the cleaned storage room. The next day I would make this room into a *gudang* (a storage place) and a kitchen. It would be a big step in the right direction.

When John came home, I told him how glad I was that the house was becoming more livable. He smiled shyly and said he was pleased to hear that — but he mentioned neither the setbacks, nor the impending departure of the skilled workers.

I didn't bring it up myself, in the belief that it had to come from him, but decided to drop a hint now and then. Thus ended another day of camaraderie, but without any real understanding or trust.

* * * *

After breakfast the next morning, John went back to the *emplacement*, and I joined him with my medicine bag to treat the men. I was pleased to find a woman and her sick child waiting for treatment — an indication that the families had started to trust me.

The child had infected eyes and a hard swollen tummy — symptoms that I would soon find commonplace. After treating the little one, I left John at the *emplacement* and went home to my other patient, the steer.

Atlas ignored me at first, but I now knew how to handle him. I rattled the familiar bucket with salt water and, sure enough, he came closer and stuck his head in the bucket, giving me a chance to look at the stinking wound. It would have to be treated quickly, so I asked Uncle Senen to help me. He readily agreed.

Bok supplied me with a bucket of warm water, soft soap, and a brush — to clean not just the area around the wound, but also the whole left part of the animal's head, since it was streaked with a sticky substance that had drained from the wound.

Senen pulled the steer gently toward him, making soft, reassuring sounds. Atlas yielded, and allowed us to lead him to a tree, where we firmly tied his head to the trunk. The animal struggled a bit, but then calmed down, and even allowed me to touch him.

He squirmed and wheezed a little, but did not seem to find the scouring with the stiff brush disagreeable. At least, he did not resist. Then, I smeared the soft soap on the dirty wound, and left it at that.

"We'll continue tomorrow," I said to Uncle Senen, feeling quite pleased with myself.

In the storage room, the new floor had been installed, and the Chinese were now busy constructing a cupboard from the oil crates. I was delighted! I would use it to store provisions, and make it ant-proof by sticking its legs into cans with a carbolic acid solution, as I had recently learned.

The Chinese told me they had also received orders to build a solid table there. How wonderful of John to have thought of it!

When John came home around five, the new *gudang* was in service, and my "Perfection" stove had been installed.

After a refreshing shower in the "bathroom" — which by now I had accepted as normal — I boiled water on the new stove, and drank the first cup of tea that did not have the smoky flavor that I had come to associate with Bok's kitchen.

"Delicious," I thought. "Something from the civilized world." But I was wise enough not express those sentiments, lest it be perceived as a veiled criticism.

John savored his cup too, and said how much he had enjoyed the *nasi gorèng* (fried rice) at noon, with the delicious *dadar* (omelette) from the eggs of our own chickens. He had said "our" chickens! Did I begin to mean more than just a comrade?

That evening, he didn't read his newspapers, but asked again about the long journey I had made. I only described my train trip through the United States — not wanting to belabor the romantic atmosphere on board ship, or the warnings about lonely men who were stuck in the *rimbu*.

For the first time, he laughed at a funny experience I told him about. He seemed more chummy and "normal", but was still dead-tired. After a quick kiss, he promptly fell asleep.

Oh well, patience is a virtue, they say!

****

The next day, after a cup of coffee, I again went with John to the *emplacement* to hold clinic. The people with the leg-cuts were almost ready to go back to work. Two women with children approached me on their own. I sensed that the older people had now accepted me also. I cleaned their infected eyes with boracic water, and then applied some eye-drops. One child had horrible wounds on one leg and foot. Only later would I learn that it was framboesia, or yaws, a contagious skin disease. Not knowing anything about the disease at the time, however, I cleaned the wounds as best I could, applied a wet dressing, and asked the mother to come back the next day.

Back home, Latif emerged triumphantly from a chicken coop and shouted that the black chickens had laid "painted" eggs. He ran to show me two *brown* eggs among five white ones.

Carefully I took them from him, and explained that these were going back in the nest until little chicks had hatched. From now on, we would use only four eggs per day; the remainder would be used for breeding. Was it a realizable plan ... or just another "pipe dream"?

Senen had warned me of the many snakes among the weeds that posed a real danger to the chickens. The stray duck had not returned, he said. A snake might have killed it.

I shuddered.

As soon as John had left after breakfast, Senen and I hurried with the indispensable salt-water bucket to the steer, which — did I imagine it? — had been looking out for me. The wound did not stink as much, I thought.

Senen showed me a halter he had fashioned out of a piece of discarded tarpaulin. After making sure that the animal was properly secured, Senen placed the new halter around its neck, and gently attached the nose-ring to it.

It was a pity, I said, that the heavy rope had to go through the nose-ring, thinking that it could hurt the animal. But Senen assured me that ring and rope were essential. We could not do without them.

Atlas seemed to like the new halter. As soon as the restraining ropes had been loosened, he shook his large head, snorted a bit, and then allowed me to remove the scabs and take a good look at the bleeding wound. To my horror, it was crawling with thick, white maggots, which somehow would have to be removed.

Senen advised me to apply a wad of cotton-wool drenched in tobacco juice. The maggots would then leave by themselves, he said. To keep flies away, I washed the head with Lysol and again smeared a layer of soft soap on the wound.

I would have to tell John that I was treating the steer if I wanted to get the needed tobacco from the plantation's *gudang* — and I wondered how he would react.

Returning to the house, I found Sariowan waiting for me. First, he asked me if he could bring me something from Taliabu. Then his expression changed, and he handed me a little box containing bottles of quinine tablets, castor-oil, and stomach medicine.

"This," he said, "is the plantation's medicine, which my wife had at home. She is giving it all to you. She won't need it any more now that the *Nyonya* is treating the people herself."

Startled, I looked at him. I started to protest, saying that I would like his wife to continue her charitable work, but he interrupted angrily that I would have to continue alone. Martha was coming with him to Taliabu, where she would stay a while with friends. And I could explain this to the *Tuan* myself. Then he turned around and left rapidly for the cudgel-road and the river.

"All hell will break loose when I tell John," I thought, racking my brains as to why everything seemed to go wrong here. Even seeing our improved bedroom could not cheer me up, and anxiously I waited for John to return.

## IBU MALUKU

Outside, I saw Senen and Latif sitting on their haunches near the vegetable garden, looking with fascination at each of the beds I had so lovingly planted the day before.

"I wonder if the radishes have come up already," I thought optimistically and, feeling much better, I went outdoors to see this for myself.

Then I received the second blow of the day: hundreds of ants marched back and forth over the seed-beds, carrying all my precious seeds away! My dream of fresh vegetables had just gone up in smoke.

When I returned to the house, I saw that the new ceiling in the bedroom had collapsed. The *tukangs* were feverishly trying to prop it up with a bamboo pillar, placed smack in the middle of the room. What a sight!

I sank down into the nearest chair and sobbed my heart out, and that is how John found me on his return home.

I told him about the returned medicine chest, Martha's departure, the ants on the vegetable beds and the bedroom ceiling — but stopped short of telling him about the steer.

John calmly said that it was not all that serious! It was all right that Martha had given up treating the people and would be away for a while. And the pillar, well, it was not very nice, but it served a purpose.

Consoled by the way in which he had taken everything, I suddenly found the courage to tell him about the steer.

"And you are telling me that everything has gone wrong today?" he asked incredulously. "I think it's terrific that you managed to treat that animal. You can get as much tobacco from me as you want!"

* * * *

Several days later, John asked me impulsively if I would like to accompany him to the border of the plantation, so he could explain how everything worked.

I seized the opportunity and suddenly felt very happy.

First, he told me, the Buluwaya plantation covered 700 hectares. The neighboring plantation, Tongkal, which had 1,000 hectares, was not yet cultivated. Both plots had been leased for a period of 75 years by the company of John's brother.

The borders of the Buluwaya plantation had been drawn somewhat haphazardly. An Arab who had heard about the planned Dutch concessions had quickly applied for two 20-hectare plots of timberland, located on the west bank of the Golohaya river on good, solid ground, with the beach forming the southern border. This maneuver had blocked direct access to the plantation and had forced John to build his cudgel-road through that swamp on the eastern bank.

## IBU MALUKU

The borders of the Buluwaya plantation were defined on the west by the Tongkal River; on the north by the high, densely forested mountains that contained excellent timber; on the south by the beach (partly owned by the Arab) and the mangrove forest; and on the east by a man-made boundary line running north to south, east of the mouth of the Golohaya River.

The Golohaya river ran east to west across the eastern border before it turned south, thus slicing off a parcel of plantation land where John's predecessor had built a small shed to store rice, and a large shed to house the coolies. That was the building in which we were now living.

There wasn't room for an *emplacement* there, so it had to be erected on the other side of the river, where our new house would be built also. Eventually, a good road would be constructed, west of the Arab's enclave, which would connect the plantation with the beach. Then, we would no longer have to trudge through the swamp.

Only 30 hectares of the 700-hectare Buluwaya concession had been cleared and seeded with coconut trees, which thrived there. The rest of the land was still untouched primeval forest, which was being cleared by 8 teams of 4 persons, at a cost of 75 guilders per hectare.

First, they would chop down a number of large trees in a row, such that their fall would uproot smaller trees. Then, all branches would be cut off and put together in one heap, together with small trees and brushwood, and burned when they were sufficiently dry.

John had witnessed one such burning, and had been awed by the incredible spectacle of flames reaching high into the sky. But it had rained for the last six months, and the timber was now too wet to sustain a fire. This, of course, meant a slowdown in work. Every wet day was a sore disappointment for John, who was eager to see results.

Close to the cleared area, we looked at seed-beds containing row upon row of coconut saplings. John explained that in three months, the *bibit* (seed nuts) would be transplanted to a permanent location, nine meters apart.

The *bibit* had come from Batu Gaya, he continued, a small enclave on Taliabu, the island immediately west of us. The enclave belonged to the inhabitants of a small *kampung*, who delivered 500 to 700 coconuts per month — an adequate number for the rate at which the Buluwaya land was being cleared.

We left the cleared area and entered a majestic forest, where giant trees rose up like pillars from high root skirts — eight meters or more in circumference — to form a dense canopy overhead. Several trees were marked, and I learned that these were the trees that had been selected by the Chinese *tukangs* to provide timber for our future house. Naturally, I wanted to know how they were going to be sawed, and John promised to take me some day to see the lumbermen at work.

As we went deeper into the forest, it became very quiet and mysterious. Now and then, we heard a bird take flight. Sometimes we heard the cry of a white cockatoo, seemingly a rare bird in this area. A green-yellow light filtered down through the canopy of high trees, but never reached the ground. Almost all trees were overgrown with lianas (woody vines) as thick as a human arm, and with a thorny type of *rotan*. Occasionally we would see exotic orchids that had a wonderful, but sometimes overwhelming, perfume.

The forest became more dense, hot, humid, oppressive and even a little scary as we went on, but John walked confidently and seemed to know the way. Finally, I heard people talking and chopping wood. We had reached the Tongkal River — the western border of the Buluwaya plantation.

A two-meter-wide path had been cleared along the banks of the river. It was passable, but I had to watch out for small, sharp stumps that protruded above the muddy soil.

The river was wider than the Golohaya, and it flowed strongly with a pleasant, rushing sound. When I caught up with John, who had already reached the workers, I was pleased to find among them a group of Madurese with whom I had already established a friendly relationship on board the ship. After the usual greetings, they diligently resumed their work. I soon understood why.

The work, John told me, had been contracted to the Madurese as a *borong*, equivalent to piecework in the West. They would commit themselves to a task for a certain price, and complete it at their own speed, without supervision. If they completed a three-day job in two days, they were free to work the third day on another *borong* and thus make more money.

The coolies of the plantation never accepted to do this kind of work. They worked more slowly, and required supervision to ensure that the work would be completed within the allotted time.

I learned soon that the *borong* method of working was much more efficient, and more advantageous for both worker and employer. But it was only for people who enjoyed the heavier workload in exchange for better pay.

Close to the river, we had a picnic. Someone cut a half meter long piece of a nearby liana, from which poured forth refreshingly cool, good-tasting water. How I would look for these lianas later, when I journeyed through the jungles of Halmahera!

In the forest I had been surprised by the absence of animals. Only once had we seen a snake cross our path. But here along the banks of the Tongkal River there were many types of wildlife: a beautiful *ijsvogel* (kingfisher) that perched like a blue jewel on an overhanging bush, cooing wood-pigeons, and a great many beautiful butterflies, including the exhilarating, large steel-blue hawk-moths.

I looked around for monkeys, but John said there weren't any in this area. There were wild boars and deer, but he had not seen them yet. Nor had he seen the *babi rusa* (hog-deer), an almost hairless swine, whose curled tusks in the mature male look like the beginning antlers of a young deer.

Along the water's edge were many aggressive mosquitoes. My arms and legs were already full of thick, red lumps that had started to itch badly. I realized I was not properly dressed for this outing — but I also knew that being better covered would not induce me to return willingly for another visit!

Still, I was grateful to John for this trip. I had received my first lesson in the operation of a coconut plantation, which I enjoyed — especially because John had started to open up and share with me. We had become a little closer, and I started to get a better insight into how things worked here. More importantly, I understood now what had happened on our wedding day and how it was that John had arrived on board looking like a tramp!

I had now survived for two weeks in this new world. Some of John's worries had also become mine — the major one being the lack of building materials for a new house, which would force the premature return of the Chinese *tukangs* and the Madurese brick makers.

When would our residence be built? Would it ever be built?

IBU MALUKU

# CHAPTER 7

### Getting Acquainted
*Buluwaya Plantation, Mangole, Sula Islands, 1920*

Each morning I accompanied John to the *emplacement*, where I would find my patients waiting in front of the big copra shed. The number of women and children was increasing, which I took as a sign of trust. Most of the time I was dressing wounds or dispensing quinine, drafts for the stomach, and advice.

Around eight o'clock, we would return together for breakfast. Afterwards, John would head back to the *emplacement*, and I could then start on my chores around the house.

Atlas came first. His wound was healing nicely now that the maggots were diminishing, and flies no longer had the opportunity to lay their eggs in the open wound. The animal started to know me, and no longer resisted treatment.

Next came the work in the compound: I inspected the chickens, checked the collection of brood eggs, and then drove sticks into the earth of my abandoned vegetable garden to hold the orchids that the men clearing the forest had promised me.

At home, I cleaned, sewed, repaired, cooked and did all kinds of chores specifically needed in the wilderness. Baking bread was one of them.

At the advice of Bok, I stopped using the yeast I had brought with me, because it made the bread taste bitter. Instead, I set aside a piece of the dough in a cool place. When needed, I would add some water, sugar, and flour, and the next day there would be a splendid leavening for the new batch of bread dough. I have used this method ever since, and the bread has always been excellent.

John had picked another project for the Chinese *tukangs*; namely, to build a bridge over the Golohaya River, so we could cross more easily.

The *tukangs* first built raised platforms on either side of the river, using wooden piles. Later, these bridgeheads (what a stately name!) were linked by tightly-pulled strings of *rotan*. Then, a deck of intertwined bamboo was secured on top.

After some hesitation, John decided to be the first to test this bridge. It swayed and groaned all the way, but John made it safely to the other side and gleefully raised both arms in jubilation.

"Bravo," I shouted, but my enthusiasm evaporated when he invited me to be next.

"No thanks," I said, "I'm just fine here."

But John refused to take "no" for an answer, and came back to help me across. With all the personnel watching, I felt I did not have much choice. I followed him with some trepidation, but, once across, I felt like a heroine!

\* \* \* \*

Only two ducks were still alive when Latif tearfully reported that one of the tufted chickens, his great pride, was missing. From that day on, chickens kept disappearing. Yet, the coops were well constructed from solid wire-netting. Only the doors were made from bamboo, but they were reliable and were always locked. Who could be the culprit?

We started to feel uneasy, and asked Uncle Senen to move into the room beside Bok, so he could keep watch at night. And every evening, the grounds around the chicken coops were raked, in the hope of detecting footprints.

I had asked Uncle Senen to wake me as soon as he heard something suspicious, as there was no sense in disturbing John: once he was asleep, nothing could wake him anyway!

I stayed awake much of the time, worrying. We needed the chickens and especially the eggs. What was I to do if we didn't have them anymore?

One night, Uncle Senen woke me up and asked me in a whisper to follow him. We slunk into the night, our path lit by the dim light of a stable-lantern that he was holding.

Close to the chicken coops I tripped over something that felt like a fire hose. I reached down and felt the thing moving in my hand. Uncle Senen snatched my hand away. "*Ular*," he whispered, but I did not understand him. He went on and I followed, and then saw in the light of the lantern a large python, with half its body inside the Menorca chicken coop.

Its long body hung from an opening, high in the door of split bamboo, where it somehow had managed to penetrate. Its head was raised at the height of the perch where the chickens were sleeping, and we were just in time to see it swing and strike a blow at the nearest chicken.

The stricken chicken uttered a piercing death-cry, rolled down, and was immediately caught in a coiled part of the snake's body. Both of us watched, fascinated and horrified: the chicken was crushed, and fell moments later as a long drawn-out package from the coil, while the head of the snake went up for the next chicken.

Uncle Senen charged with his razor-sharp *parang*, and cut the snake in two. The tail part outside the coop remained convulsively where it had been, but the head came with horrifying speed toward the door. Luckily it could not reach us. It then retracted itself from the hole in the door, dropped to the ground, and tried to escape. But Uncle Senen struck again, and finished it off.

Pieced together, the python measured twelve feet!

So, this was the thief — or at least one of the thieves. Just as well. It would have been agonizing for us if we had caught one of our own people in the act.

Only five chickens and two ducks remained of the livestock I had brought with me. Persuaded by John and Uncle Senen that I was outnumbered by snakes, I decided to give up. The brood-eggs were used in bread and in omelettes, and my dream of a chicken farm fizzled out: the umpteenth disappointment in two months!

Once again, I asked myself how this adventure in the wilderness was going to end. Could any good come from it, or had we, in our desire to leave Holland, made a bad choice in coming to this isolated island?

Sometimes I was close to despair and had great difficulty facing the next day. But the morning gave me renewed courage, and the awe-inspiring nature refreshed me every time. Also, people required help, and the daily chores in this most primitive environment always needed to be done.

There were little ups and downs, but being together at breakfast and doing all the things that kept us so busy, made John and me grow closer together. We began to understand each other better, and because of this, hope flourished — though it was often tough going.

\*\*\*\*

One day, John took me up the hill behind our house where there was a small plateau — the plantation's cemetery. It was here that John's predecessor, Mr. Kegenius, had been buried, together with five skeletons that had been found in various parts of the plantation. They were the remains of people who had died in 1917 of the Spanish influenza.

The administrator had not been buried in a coffin, but in a small *prau* that had probably been used to mix lime. The *prau* and its contents were not more than three feet underground. John assumed that the sick laborers who had found his body did not have the strength to make the grave any deeper.

In total, forty-seven of the inhabitants of Buluwaya had died of this virulent influenza; twenty had fled and seven had remained and were still faithfully performing their duties. It must have been a terrible scene. The sick and the dying, bereft of any medical help and far from family and loved ones. Silently, we left the cemetery, each of us occupied with our private thoughts.

* * * *

I had now been almost two months on the island. Soon, the KPM boat would be in port again. The Chinese *tukangs* were getting ready to leave. They would return when all the lumber for our residence had been sawed. The brick-makers would be leaving with the same boat and return to their villages on Java. Bringing them here had been futile — and a terrible waste of money.

For me, it was time to write my letters, including an order for Ong Kee Hong, our supplier on Ambon. It would, of course, take another two months before the deliveries would arrive.

I checked the remaining provisions, which did not take long. Two cans of milk, some sugar, several cans of vegetables, some canned meat, butter and oil. I would have to order flour, sugar, petroleum, soap, table salt, butter, milk and many cans of vegetables — since my vegetable garden had not succeeded.

I was tempted to get chickens again, but John advised not to. "They will only attract more snakes," he said. "However, I do want to get fishing gear, so we can make up our deficiency in meat and eggs with fish".

We packed the pots and pans that had contained our wedding dinner into a basket, and included a cordial thank-you note for the Captain of the *van Rees*. Then John did his administrative work, while I started on my first letter to Holland. Strange really, in two months I had not thought one moment about writing, but now, suddenly, there was so much to tell.

It was late when we both finished.

* * * *

The next afternoon the departing people came to say goodbye. The Chinese said again that, once the lumber was available, they would be happy to come back and build a beautiful house for the *Nyonya* and the *Tuan*. I was sorry to see them go. It seemed that with their departure, any hope for a real house was dissipating into thin air.

Although the ship was not expected for another two days, the Overseer would take them in the large plantation *prau* to Passi Ipa — just in case. As we had been told, in this region, the acronym KPM had been mockingly translated into *"Kom Pas Morgen"* (may arrive tomorrow) — a clear reference to the changing arrival times of their ships.

The *prau* returned the next day. Everything and everybody had safely arrived at Passi Ipa, and the people had found shelter with the few inhabitants on the small island. The Overseer further reported that the little *pasanggrahan* had been cleaned, and that we would be able to stay overnight the following day.

That would be great fun, I thought, to have this outing — even if it were only for one night. I did not yet know what a *pasanggrahan* was, but imagined it to be a small hotel. It was a small hotel alright, but exceedingly primitive!

John proposed that we leave immediately after the usually very short afternoon nap. Bok and Latif beseeched us to take them with us, apparently out of an irrational fear that they would be left behind for good.

This time, John was neatly shaved and ... dressed! I was excited at the prospect of meeting again the crew and staff of the *van Rees*, but John said it would be a different boat. There were three "Papua" ships that ran this route to New Guinea. In addition to the *van Rees*, there were the *van Neck* and the *Pijnacker Hordijk*, which all took turns on this, the longest route the KPM had.

"What about the pots and pans?" I asked, but John assured me that they would get to the *van Rees* somehow.

The water level in the *kali* was high enough for the *prau* to moor at the end of the cudgel-road. A pleasant surprise awaited me there.

John had arranged to have a stairway constructed. The slippery tree trunk that I had climbed alone with gritting teeth when I first arrived, was gone. This time, he actually gave me a helping hand. So there was some progress, and that pleased me greatly.

Unfortunately, when we arrived at Passi Ipa we discovered that the S.S. *van Neck* had arrived early in the morning, unloaded its cargo, picked up the mail and passengers, and had left the bay more than an hour ago!

I was close to tears, but John consoled me, saying that at least our mail and the all-important order for provisions had arrived. So had the long-awaited Surveyor.

But Bok was ecstatic being able to shop in the little *warong*, where she bought a piece of cloth for a *kebaya* — a blouse. Also, a small bottle of *kayu putih* (eucalyptus) oil that was difficult to get in Java and was good against a hundred ailments — so she told me. For the kitchen, she bought an enormous bunch of red onions — absolutely indispensable for the *rijsttafel*, she said.

For the plantation, we collected 30 bags of rice, five crates of paraffin (kerosene), and two crates of soap and tobacco. For ourselves, two crates of provisions, and much-needed tools that should have arrived with me on the *van Rees*.

The stay-over at the *pasanggrahan* was canceled since the high tide would enable us to transport our goods with the *prau* right up to the cudgel-road. So we got back into the boat that now rode deep in the water on account of all the provisions and heavy mailbags. One mailbag was filled with two-month-old Surabaya newspapers and magazines; the other contained business letters and private mail.

It was getting dark by the time we arrived at the plantation, and it was pitch dark before all the *barang* had been transported to our house. John immediately sent the people home. Unpacking could wait until the morning.

My mail was meager, and I was deeply disappointed. There were no letters from home. But then, everyone in Holland had probably been waiting for news from the *rimbu*, and my letters had only just been picked up by the boat that morning.

John hid himself behind the newspapers, and was unapproachable for several hours. That, too, I had to learn to accept.

\*\*\*\*

Early next morning, Senen started to open the crates. The first contained a dozen large cans of vegetables and *obat nyamuk* — indispensable against the mosquitoes that attacked at night and could infect us with the dreaded malaria. The smoke from the green spirals (which burn like incense) chased the tormentors away, but left me with a headache. There was also a large can of sugar, a barrel of nails (no wonder the crate was so heavy!), and several rolls of rope — with which to capture the roaming cows that I had yet to see.

Senen opened the second crate. On top were two bags of flour, semolina, and other foodstuffs; in the bottom, several cans of butter and one 5lb can of soft soap. In between the cans, Ong Kee Hong had stuck five steel surveying stakes that John had ordered months ago. One of the stakes had shifted during the journey and skewered the can of soft soap, draining its contents. Everything packed in bags was sticky and stank of the soft soap. The flour, the coffee, the tea, and everything else was a mess of soap and filth.

I looked with horror at all this and tears of frustration flowed. And what now? It would be two months before we could expect another shipment. This was too much!

"Luckily, there is enough rice," said John. Then he exploded, and damned Ong Kee Hong for packing in such a stupid manner.

But there was nothing we could do except put up with the situation. With a sad heart I gave instructions to get rid of all the spoiled provisions except the coffee beans. I rinsed the coffee many times, but it remained undrinkable, and finally I had to throw that away too. With barely concealed anger, I arranged for the darned stakes to be taken to the *emplacement*. Why did those things have to be packed with our provisions anyway? And what was the next shipment going to be like?

\*\*\*\*

Many weeks went by without a major catastrophe, and slowly I recovered from this disappointment.

Two more chickens had disappeared — only three were left now — and John suggested eating them, rather than leaving them to the snakes. And so we did, or rather, John did. I could not even get the tiniest morsel past my tonsils.

Afterward, John said he had not feasted like that in weeks! The beautifully made chicken coops were empty, reminding me daily of my beautiful dream that had turned to naught.

However, Atlas was doing very well. The animal was even becoming tame and somewhat spoiled! We often tied him up elsewhere as bait for the cows that had been sighted nearby. Invariably, though, he would break loose and show up at the house, mooing for salted water and treatment of the wound that had healed a long time ago!

\*\*\*\*

Apart from cultivating the Buluwaya plantation, John was also responsible for the incorporation of the Tongkal concession, which was still primeval forest. Upon my request, he explained the intricacies of leasing a concession:

"Having selected a piece of land, an applicant has to find out what, if anything, belongs to the local population or — and this makes it more difficult — to passing fishermen, who may not show up for many months. All these people have to be compensated.

"A temporary permit allows the applicant to clear a path along the boundaries. That work has now been done. The next step is to invite all interested parties to a meeting, have the land surveyed, pay out compensation, and put stakes in the ground. This will happen in a few days.

"Then it is just a matter of signing the lease, which runs for 75 years," John concluded.

A few days later, a long procession of people entered the plantation, led by the Magistrate of Sofan. Next were the Surveyor, Kampung Chiefs and *Adat*[1] Chiefs from the Mangai tribe, and woodsmen — all those who had an interest in the land that would become part of the Tongkal concession.

There was also a small group of Mangai women, who immediately caught my attention. Each was dressed only in a "sarong" of shining white tree-bark, and a *selèndang* — a continuous piece of cloth, worn as a bandoleer. In the back hung a baby; in the front, a cute black-and-brown-striped piglet. Each woman was dutifully occupied pushing the nipple of one uncovered breast in the mouth of the piglet, which sucked greedily until distracted by something else. The woman's own baby was totally ignored!

The people of this tribe were ungracefully long and thin. They had straight black hair, and eyes that looked around fearfully. The men were armed with bows and arrows. As the District Chief later explained, the Mangai had an ongoing quarrel with another tribe, the Kadai — which is why they were carrying arms.

"In the forests of Taliabu and Mangole, there are some 800 Mangai and 650 Kadai," the District Chief continued, "and there is also a smaller tribe of about 400 people[2].

"The Mangai have come from some other island. They have little contact with those living near the coast, but they do barter *rotan* and *damar* (tree resin) in exchange for salt and tobacco.

"They protect themselves against unwanted intruders by surrounding their habitat with *trous-de-loup* ("wolf-holes") — deep pits, in the bottom of which are placed fire-hardened bamboo stakes. The pits are then carefully covered with sticks, soil, leaves and twigs. They often trap pigs in these holes — a welcome booty, and a necessary food for the tribe. By the way, a pig, a live pig, is a very important possession for them, for it can be used as means of payment — or as dowry.

"The second most important possession is a dog. A litter of dogs is worth a fortune, for the dog helps the hunter in tracking down the invaluable pig.

"Another curiosity about these people," he continued, "is that when a woman goes into labor, her family takes her to a deserted spot, deep in the jungle. Here they build a little shed with a bamboo cot — a *balé-balé*. The laboring woman is placed inside, and after leaving sago and several bamboo containers of drinking water, the family carefully closes the entrance. The woman is left alone until her child is born.

"The husband goes home with other members of the family, then withdraws, moaning loudly. He imitates a woman in labor to mislead the evil spirits who might otherwise select his wife and unborn child as their next victims. After a while, a member of the family will saunter into the forest to check up on the hidden woman, and will let out a specific yell if the child has been born.

"Then, all the others arrive and open the shed. After looking the baby over, they place it back on the *balé-balé* and make a smoking fire underneath it. The baby is left there for a while, and if it survives this smoke-rite, it is considered to have been accepted by the spirits of air and fire.

"After this ordeal, the father takes the child to the nearest rapids, where he submerges the infant many times in the icy water. If the child survives that rite, it is considered acceptable to the water spirits. These spirits will protect it against the evil spirits, and the child can now take its place in the tribe.

"Arriving home, a big celebration starts, during which the mother hands the child to the father. She, in turn, is given a piglet or a puppy-dog that she will have to nurse herself until the animal is able to find its own food.

"Day and night, she will keep and caress the little animal in her *selèndang*. If she has some milk left over, which seldom happens, then her own baby will get a sip. It is the father who is now responsible for nourishing the baby. He chews the food, and then transfers it to the child, mouth-to-mouth, or by using his fingers.

"Since it is very difficult to contact these extremely shy people, the Government can do little about these barbaric practices. It will come as no surprise that the infant mortality rate is high. And, indeed, these tribes are dying out — for these reasons, and because of constant warring.

"Fighting breaks out when a tribe trespasses on the hunting grounds of another, or when it steals the barter goods left by another tribe for the inhabitants of the beach *kampungs*.

"You see, they have no personal contact at all. Communication with the other tribes is done by blowing on conch-shells. The people from the forest signal when the goods are ready. The beach people come and place their products (salt or tobacco) in the same clearing, and withdraw. Then, the foresters either signal their agreement and take "payment", or they signal their disagreement, leave the products, and wait for a better offer.

"During the bartering, the goods are left unattended, and if another tribe snatches them, war is inevitable."

I thanked the District Head, and told him I was very pleased to have learned something about the *adat* — the traditional laws — of these jungle people.

It took many hours of negotiations, but John finally signed the papers that officially incorporated the Tongkal concession with the Buluwaya plantation.

(**Endnotes**)
[1] *Adat*: customary native law.
[2] Jeanne van Diejen did not remember the name of this tribe.

# IBU MALUKU

# CHAPTER 8

### Stranded
*Buluwaya Plantation, Mangole, Sula Islands, 1920*

That night, after the incorporation of the Tongkal concession, the first baby was born on the plantation. The delivery was difficult, and I was relieved (and proud) that everything turned out so well. The parents invited me to choose the name for their new daughter, and I named her Aysah.

John invited me the next day to visit the lumberjacks, who were sawing lumber for our future home. The walk — first through the cultivated area and then deep into the jungle — took more than an hour.

A huge tree — one of those that had been marked by the now departed Chinese *tukangs* — had been cut down and had its crown removed. The heavier branches that could serve as pillars, beams or struts for future house construction, had been stripped clean and were neatly stacked to one side, covered with palm leaves to protect them against sun and rain.

The trunk had been stripped of its bark, squared in cross-section, and cut into lengths of four meters. Each piece of trunk had been placed over a hole, dug deep enough for a man to stand in. In several places, the wood cutting had begun, with one man standing on top of the block and his mate underneath it, in the hole. Both were pulling and pushing a large saw, and I was able to see, ever so slowly, the beams taking shape.

To guide them in their work, they used an ingenious little device: a small container with a crank-activated spindle that contained a thin twine. The container was filled with India ink. One lumberjack would hold the container, and his mate would pull the end of the cord out — thereby passing the cord through the ink. Standing on either side of the block, they would hold the cord taut on earlier placed markings, pull the cord up in the middle and let it snap back against the block's surface ... and voila! — a perfectly straight line. In that way, they had neatly marked the block for a total of 36 beams, each four meters in length. Simple, yet effective.

The sawing itself looked fairly easy. What I really wanted to see was how they maneuvered those heavy blocks over the holes. For that, I had to go to another part of the forest.

When we met the second group, John gave each lumberjack a cigarette. Then, for my benefit, these men — who belonged to the Bininko tribe — gave a demonstration of their skill. One of the heavy blocks of wood was lifted slightly off the ground with sturdy poles, allowing them to place long round sticks underneath. Then, the block was pushed over these rolling sticks until it was in position over the hole. It was heavy work, but it went surprisingly well.

One lumberjack gave me a bright-colored lory that he had caught with a stick coated with glue at one end. Others had gathered beautiful tiger orchids that they promised to deliver to the house that evening.

I was happy and felt that these Bininkos, who had only recently arrived from Taliabu, had also accepted me.

\* \* \* \*

One week after the departure of the KPM-ship, we finished our last batch of flour. There would be no more bread the next day; we would have to start the day with rice porridge. With forced cheerfulness, I thought we could handle that for a while. The plantation life was definitely making me more pliable.

To augment our menu of rice, and only rice, I searched the area around our house for anything that might serve as a vegetable. John, however, was dead-set against any attempt on my part to experiment with unknown plants.

Sometimes, strange scents came out of Bok's kitchen and, one day, I asked her what she ate with her rice. She first showed me a handful of small red peppers, called *ritya setan* or devil's paprika, since they were exceptionally sharp. Further, small dried fish, which stank; and a shrimp-paste, *trasi*, wrapped in a palm-leaf, which had a foul, penetrating odor.

I asked her if she would prepare something like that for us, but she said that it would not be very good without *santen*, coconut-milk, and coconut oil. Reproachfully, she added that there were enough coconuts on the plantation to spare some for the kitchen, but that the *Tuan* wanted to plant every single one. Nobody was allowed to touch them!

That afternoon, she did make us a concoction of small fishes, fern leaves and *trasi* and finely sliced *ritya setan*, in addition to the usual cooked rice.

I tried some of it, and promptly threw up. John tried some, too, but burned his mouth and then the smell made him nauseated. Thereafter, we ate the rice dry, by itself, but without much gusto. Only much later would I learn to appreciate the spices of the Far East.

\*\*\*\*

One morning, Bok sternly rebuked Latif. When I asked what had upset her, she said Latif had too many things to do in the yard and, therefore, she had forbidden him to visit his uncle. Latif looked dejected, so I cheered him up with the promise that he could come with me some other time and pick up more lories, which the lumberjacks had promised me.

When John got up early that morning, he had felt cold inside, and by the afternoon, he was trembling in spite of the heat. Thus I was introduced to the classical symptoms of *malaria tropica*.

It was a severe attack, and it took five days before he was able to go back to work. Bok helped me as best she could, and Overseer Sariowan — who seemed friendlier now — came over from time to time to remind me to give John his quinine.

On the morning of the fifth day, a sobbing Bok came to tell me that something had happened and Senen was waiting to speak with the *Tuan*. But John was finally sleeping quietly — the fever appeared to have gone — and I did not want to waken him.

A moment later, I saw three other Madurese sitting outside, whispering urgently to each other. Latif was among them. I smelled trouble, and asked what was going on — but no, they only wanted to talk to the *Tuan*. I asked them to wait until John had woken up. Then I saw Sariowan and two older coolies heading toward us. They, too, seemed greatly upset. I hastily clambered down the stairs and went out to meet them.

"They have all run away," the Overseer called out nervously.

"Who are you talking about?" I asked.

"All the other Madurese, and four Bininkos. They have taken the large plantation *prau*; only the small *lèpa-lèpa* is left."

More slowly, he told me that when the men were missing at roll-call, he had gone to the beach and concluded that they had left before midnight. I understood the implications of this further disaster. The plantation *prau* was our only good connection with the outside world!

When I went back upstairs, John had already been awakened by the excited whispering of the men near the kitchen. He asked what was going on, but, seeing the look on my face, didn't wait for an answer. He jumped out of bed and ran to the front veranda, where Sariowan reported what had happened.

John's jaws tightened, and he said angrily: "That damn malaria! If I hadn't caught it, this would not have happened." He then asked Sariowan to wait, and motioned Senen and Bok to one side to ask them what they knew about the situation.

There had been trouble between the Overseer and the workers, they said. During the distribution of the tobacco quota — which was normally done by John — Sariowan had made disparaging remarks about the Madurese.

These men had been disgruntled for some time. The situation on the plantation had not come up to expectations: there was no real village, no market, no shop, no entertainment, no *ronggèngs* (dancing girls) and no cock fights. They also missed the Chinese *tukangs* and the brick makers with whom they had made the journey from Java. Their unhappiness had been building up and they ultimately decided to leave with the next ship.

Bok got wind of the plan and advised against it. She and four other men refused to participate, and she forbade Latif to associate with the ring — afraid that the boy might be persuaded to join them. And that was the real reason for forbidding the boy to visit his uncle.

Then the previous evening, the Bininko lumberjacks — who had been hired recently from Taliabu — had formulated a new plan. As experienced sailors, they persuaded the others to steal the large *prau* and leave that very evening while the tide was favorable. Where to, Bok did not know.

John returned to Sariowan, and sent him and one rower back to the beach. They were to take the small *lèpa-lèpa* and go to Passi Ipa to register a complaint with the Village Chief. Then, they were to rent a *prau* and register a complaint with the District Head at Sofan, the capital of Taliabu, whose jurisdiction included our plantation.

In the afternoon, the rower returned alone with the *lèpa-lèpa*. On Passi Ipa, where he had left the Overseer, they had asked around but no one had seen the large *prau* from the plantation. Since the monsoons were blowing in southerly direction, it was likely that the fugitives were making for Ambon.

After five days, Sariowan returned without much success. The District Head had promised to relay the complaint to the Magistrate of Sanana and ask him to send a telegram to Ambon requesting the arrest of the deserters. But, said the Overseer, the weather was bad and it might not be possible to send a messenger to Sanana right away.

So here we were, with 16 fewer workers, and no reliable contact with the outside world. We immediately placed an order at Sofan for a large *prau*, but it would take at least two months before it could be delivered.

# IBU MALUKU

Sariowan did have one bit of good news. The *Kepala Kampung* (village chief) of Passi Ipa had promised to lend us his service *prau* when the next KPM-ship arrived. Though this event was still a few weeks away, it was encouraging news.

John remained listless after his bout with malaria. His clothes were much too large, and his face looked drawn.

One morning, I myself felt very tired and irritable. I thought it was simply exhaustion from eating nothing but rice (one did not know much about vitamin deficiencies at that time). Thinking that it might be malaria, John wanted me to start taking quinine. I did, but the pills were so nauseatingly sweet that they made me throw up.

I did not feel well for several days, but convinced myself that it would pass as soon as the new provisions had arrived — in about ten days. I tried to distract myself by working on the next provision list for Ong Kee Hong, but it did not help. On the contrary, I became more listless, could not eat, and remained dead tired.

John became worried, and reproached himself for having brought me here. But I insisted that we would pull through, once the ship had arrived. It was also possible that, at that time, I was longing for news from Holland. It had been such a long time since I had heard from home.

Then disaster struck again.

The KPM-ship was due to arrive in two days. We could not go ourselves — the *lèpa-lèpa* being too small to hold us all — but we would get our provisions and mail. Then things should be much better. The Overseer took the small *lèpa-lèpa* and left for Passi Ipa.

After several days he returned with a haggard face. The KPM-ship had entered the bay in very bad weather. During the unloading, one of the cables had broken. Our crates and mailbags had fallen in the ocean and were lost for ever. Fifteen bags of rice was all that was left of the provisions we had ordered.

John cussed loudly. How in hell was this possible! Helplessly we looked at each other. What should we do now? The next ship was two months away! And what other disasters would we be called on to face then?

A few days later, I became ill again. I could not stand another spoonful of rice or porridge. Then, a sudden suspicion entered my mind ... the throwing up ... the listlessness. For several days I lived in fear and kept my suspicions to myself. I hoped I was wrong and that it was only the start of a malarial attack. But later, I was able to confirm that I was, indeed, pregnant.

In spite of my fear, a powerful surge of happiness flooded me. A baby! I hardly dared to believe it.

Several days later, I told Bok. She calmly said that she had guessed it right away, and then asked what the *Tuan* thought about it. I sidestepped the question, since John hadn't been told, but I decided to break the news to him as soon as he came home from the sawmill. I waited apprehensively, wondering how he would take it.

After lunch I casually said I did not have malaria, but something else. But John's mind was on other things, and he absent-mindedly replied that everything would get better, once I had made up my mind to eat properly.

"John ... I am pregnant! We are going to have a baby!"

For a moment, he looked at me dumbfounded; then, with fear in his eyes he said: "But that can't be! No, not here! We have to get out of here!"

Then, he took me in his arms, and we cried from happiness and misery, and said foolish things to each other.

Later, I accompanied him to the forest, where — enveloped by the gigantic trees — we forgot we were stranded on this God-forsaken island with almost no provisions. John gathered more orchids for my collection, and promised a hundred things that were not feasible, but comforting just the same.

Life went on, with the added concern for this new life growing within me. We, the young parents-to-be, were not terribly happy about the course of events, but trusted in the Creator of this young life, and prayed for a way out of our predicament.

\* \* \* \*

I had now been more than four months on Buluwaya, and was very worried about not having received any news from home. My mother had not been well when I left. At the time, she had spoken out strongly against our marriage — the East Indies was so far away, she had said, and its future was so uncertain.

From Sariowan, John had learned about the existence of an old *dukun* on Sofan, a soothsayer with spiritual powers. Perhaps he could tell me something about home and thus reassure me.

The *dukun* let it be known that he would be willing to come when the time was favorable. But only he would know what day that might be.

That day arrived unexpectedly. The Overseer came, accompanied by a gaunt, pitifully thin old man. He was dressed in a tiny loin-apron that was kept in place by a black cord tied around his narrow waist. From the cord hung two small, beautifully woven, colorful pouches. His teeth were black, and his lips were red from betel juice — some of it was dribbling down his grubby chin. Some soothsayer! I had been expecting something quite different!

He looked at me and mumbled a few words, which the Overseer translated for me. I was to get a mat, place myself on it in front of him, and think of my mother and nothing else. That was the message.

I followed his instructions. He squatted in front of me, and took out of one pouch some dry moss and two pieces of wood — one flat, with a hole in the center; the other, round and sharpened at both ends. Placing the flat one on top of the moss, he inserted the sharpened stick into the hole, and proceeded to rotate the stick very rapidly between the palms of his hands. Some smoke soon appeared. He blew on the moss, and suddenly, there was fire.

He shoved it closer to me and heaped some wood chips on top of it. Then, out of the second pouch came some bird bones, which he placed in the flames. He blew on the fire, sprinkled something over it — I could not see what — and with one hand fanned the smoke in my direction.

Then, a very strange thing happened.

My body began to feel as light as air, and I had the sensation of flying. Suddenly I found myself walking on the old, familiar road that connects two villages in the Province of Limburg. I saw the *Kantonnier*, the district road-mender, placing branches alongside the newly graveled road — an old method to force farmers to keep their carts *on* the road and thus drive the gravel into the road surface.

I felt happy, and walked quickly along the village street that led to my mother's house. The front door was closed, so I walked around to the back. As soon as I turned the corner, I saw the familiar kennel. Our old yard-dog, Pasha, sat in front of it, wagging his tail, and looked expectantly at the back door, waiting for someone to come out.

Along the path leading to the vegetable garden, I saw the hollyhock in full bloom, with bees and drones flying to and fro. Then, the dog barked. The back door opened, and Mama came out and talked to the dog who pulled at his chain in an effort to get to her. I could not hear what she said.

Mother looked cheerful and healthy. She was dressed in a flowery dress, black with small yellow bouquets, and she had a shiny black apron on. From her left arm hung a basket; in her right hand she clasped a kitchen knife — which she put into the basket as she walked up to the dog. She stroked its head briefly, and walked on through the gate to the vegetable garden.

There she cut a few large heads of lettuce, looked around searchingly, then bent over and cut something else — I could not see what — which also disappeared in the basket. She left the garden, closed the gate, and said something to the dog who, now happy, lay down in front of the kennel to bask in the sun, and ...

Suddenly everything faded.

All around me I saw a radiant light that gradually became weaker, and then I heard the low, indistinct voice of the *dukun*, who had not moved and was still fanning smoke in my direction. Astonished, I looked around, and realized I also had not moved and was still seated on the mat.

John, Sariowan, Bok and Latif stood near me and looked at me with great curiosity. My face told them that I felt relieved and happy; but they could not know that I was, in fact, happier than I had been in a long time.

The *dukun* got up and said that Mother was fine; something had happened in the family that had kept her busy; letters were on their way, and I had nothing to worry about. All was well!

John wanted to pay the old man, but he made a declining gesture. He did not want anything, except perhaps some tobacco ... but it was I who should be giving it to him. And so I did, gratefully, and then he left as he had come: a gaunt, pitifully thin old man.

When I told John what I had seen, he remarked: "You surely have an incredible imagination, but I am pleased that the *dukun* has reassured you and made you happy."

Years later, I told the story to Mama when John and I were home on furlough. Mama said that she had, indeed, worn just such a dress as I had described. She retrieved the dress, now worn-out, from the attic. Both the dress and the vegetable basket that I had seen had been bought after my departure to the East Indies and were, therefore, unknown to me. She also showed me the basket, and then told me that her sister-in-law had been very ill at that time. She had gone over to keep house for her, and had not found the time to write to me — though she had wanted to.

Today, I can still remember vividly that experience, but I have never been able to explain it.

*****

I was absolutely certain now that I was pregnant, and I started to think seriously about what we would have to do. At times, I was filled with fear. John was also worried — and this time it wasn't the plantation he was worrying about, as that was going well.

One day, John invited me to go with him to watch the first planting of coconuts in an area of 20 hectares (50 acres).

When we had passed the seed-beds, the germinated coconuts had already been dug up. Some had leaves on them that were 40cm tall. With sharp knives, the white roots were cut off. The coconuts were then tied together in bunches of five, and two men, using long poles, carried them on their shoulders to where they would be replanted.

The replanting area was already staked out with long poles (*bellos*), nine meters apart. In front of each pole was a deep hole.

John invited me to place the first coconut in one of the holes, in such a way that one third of it would protrude above the soil. The rest of the hole under the coconut, John explained, would be filled in later by wind and rain.

We watched the proceedings for quite a while. The neat straight rows of saplings in the dark, fertile soil, were a stirring sight. In between the coconuts, corn would be planted to feed everyone on the plantation.

In two weeks, another 20 hectares would be planted. But this being the first planting, the workers would get an extra liter of rice and some tobacco to celebrate the event.

Suddenly, the future looked brighter. Once more, life enticed us, and for a brief, very brief moment, I dared forget our precarious circumstances.

\* \* \* \*

A few days later, it rained heavily. The river was swollen, which delayed John in getting to work. An unknown man approached the house. He was dressed only in a loin-apron made from tree-bark. On his head, he balanced a *tampah*, a large flat-bottomed plait basket, containing slices of smoked eel that gave off a delicious scent. He offered them for sale. John bought all of it for a little money and some tobacco, and then the banquet started — for the first time in months!

With a full mouth, I asked John if all the eel in the tropics had such coarse skin. He nodded his head, and said: "Just as well, because otherwise our eel would have been burned, rather than smoked."

We ate eel for two full days, morning, noon and night, and felt satisfied for the first time since my arrival. Later, John asked Sariowan about putting traps in the river so we could catch our own eel. But the Overseer said he had never seen any eel in the river, so that was that. John did ask him, however, to find out the whereabouts of the fisherman the next time he went to Passi Ipa, and to ask him to deliver his whole catch to us.

The theft of the plantation *prau* had set us back considerably. The boat we had ordered would not be ready by the time the next KPM-ship arrived. So, we would have to ask the Village Head if we could rent his — if it was available, which wasn't at all certain!

The *lèpa-lèpa* we had was too small to do anything with, so John started looking for something larger. After much difficulty, he managed to hire a large *prau* with a single outrigger.

Three days before the KPM-ship was due, he sent the Overseer and a rower to Passi Ipa in this rented *prau*, to deliver our mail and pick up our goods.

On the fourth day, both men returned with empty hands. The ship had not come yet, but Sariowan had come down with a severe attack of malaria, so he was taken home right away.

John immediately set off with the rower for Passi Ipa. It was getting dark when he returned, totally dejected. Arriving just beyond the mangrove forest, he had heard the last whistle of the ship, and watched helplessly as it left the bay.

On Passi Ipa, the KPM had delivered the mail and the usual bags of rice, salt, soap, paraffin oil, a batch of "Soerabaya's Handelsblad" (the commercial newspaper of Surabaya), and a box of silver coins for the payroll. There were *no* provisions for us!

John was told that a businessman on board had inquired if perhaps we had engaged a new supplier on Ternate; he apparently knew that we had *not* ordered from Ambon. Little did he know about our misfortunes, and that it had not entered Ong Kee Hong's mind that something was amiss on Buluwaya.

The disappointment hit us hard. I was despondent. John did not say a word, not knowing what to say or do. He buried himself in the newspapers. I just sat there, feeling helpless.

In the mail was a note from the Magistrate of Sanana, saying he had passed our complaint on to the Magistrate of Ambon, and had received a reply. The three Bininko deserters had indeed arrived on Ambon, but had been set free, since they were not under contract. The Madurese, who *were* under contract, had disappeared into thin air. The *prau* had been recovered and would be sent back to us on request.

We had hoped that they would have grasped the seriousness of our situation and sent back our *prau* with the KPM-ship that had just left — without waiting for an official request on our part. But we had no such luck.

John did not relish having to report our misfortunes to the Directors on Java. He expected criticism for having sent the expensive Chinese carpenters and brick-makers back to Java, without having accomplished anything.

## IBU MALUKU

I became morose, feeling that my presence had brought only unhappiness to John. That evening, the problems and difficulties we had experienced since my arrival overwhelmed me. I thought of my baby and its arrival under these difficult conditions. How would it be affected by all of this?

I was very afraid and, that night, cried myself to sleep.

# IBU MALUKU

# CHAPTER 9

### The Visitors
*Buluwaya Plantation, Mangole, Sula Islands, 1920*

The previous evening, I had not even dared ask if there had been any mail from Holland. Over breakfast, John handed me the letters that had arrived from his mother and sister. There was no mail for me, but it did not hurt so much — the visit of the *dukun* had reassured me that Mother was alright.

A few days later, toward the end of a hot, stuffy day when John had just come back from taking his bath, Sariowan showed up in the company of the eel vendor. John wanted to thank the Overseer, but before he could, the man turned to me and said in broken Dutch: "Madam, is this eel?"

"Yes," I said, pleased.

He looked at me with disdain, took a piece from the vendor's *tampah* with thumb and forefinger, and said: "This no eel ... this snake!" Dazed, I looked from him to the "fisherman", who nodded his head.

I almost fell down the stairs, pushing the "eel" vendor aside, and ran to the edge of the yard, but before I could reach it, my whole body went into continuous spasms as I threw up again and again.

Bok ran to my side. John sent the men away and then rushed over to me. He talked and talked, but the vomiting continued. Then he resolutely pulled me straight, turned me toward him and slapped me, left and right, in the face. I recoiled and ran screaming into the house, barricaded the bedroom door with the cabin-trunk and cried my heart out. Never before had I been so humiliated!

But the vomiting had stopped.

When John succeeded in opening the door, I shouted: "I want to go back to Holland, and don't want anything more to do with either you or anyone associated with you!"

John did not even try to calm me, and just retreated. How or where he slept that night I would never know. At the time, I was too miserable to care. I lay awake most of the night, looking with apprehension towards the coming day.

John met me in the morning with hot coffee. He said he fully understood why I would not want to stay, and asked if I felt comfortable about leaving on my own in the *lèpa-lèpa*, accompanied by just one rower — the boat would not carry more than two, he reminded me.

For a moment I was too choked-up to answer. Then, between sobs, I said: "How could you do such a thing? Now I cannot possibly stay!"

John got up, intending to leave and call the boatman. At that point, Bok walked in with an angry face and said that she wanted to leave with me. At that moment, I realized what would be the impact of both of us leaving — there would be no one here to make John's life even remotely bearable — and I could have died of shame. I reached out and embraced him, and we cried and talked, and I finally accepted that he had only slapped me to stop my rising hysteria.

John promised to change his priorities, and to take whatever action was necessary to improve our lot. Taking advantage of his changed mood, Bok quickly snatched several coconuts from the seed-bed and disappeared with them into the kitchen. John pretended not to notice.

Several days later, while we were planting the coconut saplings in the second 20-hectare lot, the new *prau* arrived. John and I immediately traveled with it to Passi Ipa to see if we could scrounge up something to eat. The wife of the Village Chief gave me a bunch of shallots (called *bawang mèrah*), and a small bag of green beans with which to start a second vegetable garden.

We heard that a government *prau* would be leaving for Sofan, so we dispatched a letter to Sanana with the urgent request to telegraph Ong Kee Hong on Ambon with our order for provisions. We returned to Buluwaya in a better, more cheerful mood.

\*\*\*\*

Life continued. Polyclinic every morning, as usual. The coolies increasingly trusted my medical expertise. Atlas had not been seen in several days. We assumed that the steer was on the trail of the herd, and hoped it would come back with several cows. My orchids were blooming. The lumberjacks were making progress: the pile of beams, carefully covered with palm leaves, was getting larger. I began to feel better, and I dared to dream again. But it would not be for long.

One day, John was carried home. He shivered with high fever and talked gibberish. His left leg was painfully swollen. A crippling fear took hold of me, as I realized that it was blood-poisoning. What could I do? Who could help? I was at my wit's end and my brain ceased to function.

I heard Bok saying: "*Aduh, Nyonya,* if the *Tuan* dies, what is going to happen to us and the baby?" Her remarks stung me like a whiplash and made me regain my composure. I told John not to be afraid, but that I was going to have to hurt him and would insist that he let me have my way.

I put a tourniquet on the affected leg. Extremely calm and well-centered within myself, it seemed as if another "me" had taken over and was guiding my hands.

I cleaned the area for the intended operation with pure alcohol that we were lucky to have in our medicine chest. John's razor blade — thank God that he did not use a safety razor — was held over a flaming match before I opened the artery and pressed out as much of the dark-colored blood as I could. Then, I sucked at the wound until nothing would come out any more. I then loosened the tourniquet just enough to allow fresh blood to squirt through the artery. I re-tightened the tourniquet while John hung semi-conscious in the chair, and Bok and the coolies who had carried him looked on in horror.

The fever stayed for two nights and one long fear-filled day before his temperature went down. John was on the mend again, and at that moment I felt a bit of pride stirring in me.

Thank God that I had not left Buluwaya in my foolishness. At the same time, it became abundantly clear to me that, devoid of any medical care, we were in a very precarious situation — especially with a baby on the way.

\* \* \* \*

One Sunday — it is unusual that I remember that is was a Sunday, for we worked day in, day out — the river had turned into a torrent after a whole night of thunderstorms and heavy rainfall. It would not be safe to cross, and so we had the luxury of having a free day. Bok and Latif had crossed the day before to attend some festivity, and were therefore stuck on the other side. We were alone!

The river roared.

From the front veranda, we saw the water had risen close to the edge of the banks. Trees, clusters of bamboo, banana tree trunks and palms dashed crisscross against and over one another in the brown, foaming water. It was an awesome sight.

Then we realized that our bridge, our pride and joy, was no longer there. Everything, except the bridgehead on our side, had been swept away. Just one more setback among so many!

Silently, I made a watery rice porridge with some salt and pretended that it looked appetizing. John seated himself at the table and pretended likewise. He told me he had invited a contractor from Sofan to come and discuss the possibility of building a modest bamboo house for us at the other side of the river, close to the *emplacement*.

The location he had chosen was a small hill that had been cleared recently. It was close to the Arab's concession that John still hoped to buy some day. That hill was a good place to build the house, John said, but it would not be the house we had originally envisaged. Those plans had been shelved long ago.

"The house will be like the Overseer's house, except somewhat bigger," John said, "with a room for the little one," and teasingly he added, "and a bathroom for you, since you still do not fully appreciate our present one."

"Why did you wait so long to tell me?" I asked. "Why tell me now?"

"Well," John replied, "I wanted to be fairly certain that the contractor would want to do it. I have already asked permission from the directors."

The prospect raised my spirits immensely, and I wanted to savor this happiness quietly by myself. I decided to go back to bed as it was only six o'clock and it would take many hours before the river could be crossed. But John said he would not mind stretching out himself, so we disappeared behind our *kelambu*, while the rain pelted our *atap* roof. A thin, striped blanket gave a pleasant warmth, and we talked intimately about our new house and how nice it would be for our little one. We carefully avoided any talk about our future, our worries, or our painful situation.

Sometimes I dozed off, but otherwise I savored this unusual, wonderful morning without pressure to work. Free, safe, and peaceful, thanks to a *banjir* — a flash-flood. But John could not relax, being mentally at work on the plantation. Finally, he said: "Come, let's get up and get dressed, and see who wins "the chair" today!"

This was a little game we played on rare free days. We had one comfortable deck-chair that — since we still did not trust the floor — stood safely on small boards in a corner of the front veranda. Whoever got to that chair first, could keep it for the rest of the day.

We rushed into our clothes, so the game could begin. Being alone at last, we felt like high-spirited children. Not a soul around! An unknown luxury! Then the countdown began. At "three" we took off and ran, as much as it was possible on our heaving floor. John won and plopped triumphantly down in the chair. I could not brake fast enough, stumbled, and fell on top of him. Something cracked, and before we realized what was happening, the floor caved in and we were folded double in the chair's canvas, like a child in its mother's *selèndang*[1].

## IBU MALUKU

We laughed and took great delight in the silly situation in which we found ourselves.

But when we tried to get out of this jam, we found out we couldn't! The sharp bamboo slats cut unmercifully into my bare legs whenever I tried to move. We did not, however, sink any deeper. Evidently we were wedged between two floor beams.

With his long arms, John tried to break off the bamboo on one side, but by bending over he caused the bamboo slats to cut into my leg on the other side. Finally, we lost the desire to laugh and realized we needed help — and that could only come when the *banjir* was over.

We waited silently, each one caught up in personal recriminations. How could we have been so thoughtless, I told myself. Could this have harmed my infant? A chill went down my spine at the very thought. We tried to move as little as possible. John occasionally remarked that it was raining less, or that the roar of the river was diminishing. Then, we thought we heard voices.

"See," John said, "the worst of the *banjir* must be over, and the people are crossing to come to the clinic. Boy, will they laugh their heads off when they find us like this! Listen, they are coming closer!" But the voices did not belong to plantation personnel. Timidly, we fell silent and listened.

A helmeted head appeared above the staircase. Its owner looked at us, and with a deep bass voice asked in Dutch: "Can we perhaps help the family?"

We gave him first a stunned look, then recovered, and shouted: "Yes, please! We are stuck!"

A voice called from below: "We shall give you a push! Here we go ... hop!", and John felt big hands that tried to push this sagging pouch of humanity upward. I screamed as the bamboo splinters cut viciously into my legs, and, startled, the persons below stopped.

Two more heads appeared above the staircase to survey the situation, then disappeared again. The two men now tried to carefully break off the bamboo slats from below. They succeeded, and finally, with a loud "hurrah" we were pushed out of the hole. Strong hands pulled first me, then John out of the ruined floor, and our beautiful deck-chair fell through the hole to the ground below and lay there like a discarded rag.

Terribly embarrassed, we came face to face with four hefty Dutchmen, who looked at us with pent-up laughter. How could we explain this situation? The eldest of the visitors broke the ice: "Yes, yes," he said gently, "these bamboo floors are treacherous, and will not hold two people in one deck-chair!" The subsequent laughter helped us over our shyness.

I wanted to disappear discretely into the bedroom, but the greying gentleman who had spoken first took me by the arm and made me sit in a more solid-standing chair, and said:

"Allow me to look after you for a moment. The *Mantri* is on his way to get the medicine-chest, and will treat you shortly."

The other three gentlemen were talking to John, who still had not overcome his embarrassment.

One man turned out to be the Inspector from the Department of Labor. Accompanying him was his assistant, a heavy man in a white high-buttoned-up tropical suit, who took stock of our abode with a surprised look on his face.

A shorter man in white uniform with golden buttons on his jacket and the crowned letter "W" on his cap, introduced himself as the Magistrate of Sanana, whose wife I had already met when I first arrived in this region. We were the only Europeans in his jurisdiction, he said, and he was on an official tour to collect taxes from the surrounding islands.

The fourth man, the eldest, was dressed in grey-green khaki. I did not catch his name, nor where he was from.

The gentlemen had arrived this morning in the Vesuvius Bay with the Government's steamer *Stella*. They had come to see us about the *perkara* (lawsuit) against the deserted contract workers. Because of the *banjir*, they had been delayed at the mouth of the river. Their flatboat had not been able to overcome the torrent.

"So we waited it out, and when the *banjir* subsided, we rowed upstream," said the friendly looking Labor Inspector, "... to save the family," he added with a smile.

In the meantime, the *Mantri* was painting my legs with biting iodine. It stung intensely, but I didn't dare utter a word — even after the elderly gentleman praised my courage.

*If only you knew, Sir, how tired I am of being brave!*

Finally, I was properly bandaged, and it was John's turn. While the *Mantri* bandaged his arms and legs, the gentlemen bombarded John with all sorts of strange questions. Repeatedly, I heard the phrase "Coolie Decree'. They also spoke about "impossible situations" and "necessary inspections". I didn't understand what it was all about.

In the meantime, Bok, Latif and Uncle Senen and several women had crossed the river. They struck up a conversation with the rowers of the flatboat, and repeatedly glanced in wonder at our visitors. Bok looked at the hole in the floor, then at me in bandages, but refrained from asking what had happened.

The elderly gentlemen, who smoked a short pipe, told her that the *Nyonya* was too heavy — probably because of all the good meals she had prepared — and that as a result, the *Nyonya* had fallen through the floor. Giggling, Bok disappeared in the direction of the kitchen.

*Overweight from eating too many good meals? Sir, you don't know how far from the truth you are!*

John suggested calling together the Overseer and all the workers, but the Assistant Labor Inspector would have none of it. He said the gentlemen wanted to cross the river and observe matters for themselves.

The *Mantri* had just finished treating the women who had been waiting outside, and sent them home with some medication. Then the gentlemen got ready to go over to the *emplacement*. I decided to go with them, wanting to get out of the house.

I felt bad that I had not offered any refreshments, and was afraid our visitors would find out that I had nothing to give. I sincerely hoped that, after the inspection, they would disappear as mysteriously as they had come.

Had I become people-shy?

Since our bridge was gone, we crossed the river with the flatboat. The water level was still high, but the river's force was spent. The damage it had inflicted earlier on was considerable, however. Even a part of the bank had been swept away!

The eldest gentleman — whom I thought to be the Captain of the *Stella* — had been talking to John and the Labor Inspector. He now let the others pass until I caught up with him. A little reproachfully he said:

"You are probably not very long in the Indies and are feeling a bit strange yet ... or has the isolation made you shy?" I did not know quite what to answer, so he continued:

"Well, you would want to know that here, in the Indies, we greatly appreciate a certain degree of hospitality, and staunchly uphold that tradition!"

I nodded my head in agreement and became upset, because I knew all too well that I had not been hospitable. I felt terrible.

He continued: "You are not from Holland I gather?"

"No, I am Belgian, but from Dutch stock" I answered.

"Oh," he said with an understanding tone, "Then you probably do not know that, here, we always offer our guests a cool drink or a cup of coffee."

"But we do the same thing at home!" I blurted out. He just looked at me, as if to say, "Then why did you not do it?"

I threw all caution to the wind and said bluntly: "How can one show any hospitality, if one does not have anything to offer?"

Shocked, he stopped in his tracks, looked at me aghast and said: "Excuse me, I should not have said that," and he walked on rapidly to catch up with the others.

Bewildered, I followed him. The cuts in my legs were hurting, I felt woozy and drained.

Martha — the Overseer's wife, who had evidently returned from Passi Ipa — called out to me, curious as to what had happened to me, and what this strange visit was all about. Briefly, I explained about the misery with the deck-chair. She said how sorry she was, but her eyes told me she enjoyed the humiliation that the *Nyonya* had undergone.

She herself looked like a million dollars, dressed in her best *sarong* and her most beautiful *kebaya* top, and she smelled like a *melati* (jasmine) blossom. Beside her, I felt lowly, poor and insignificant.

With swinging hips, she walked up to the group and invited the gentlemen into her exquisite home for a glass of lemonade. To my surprise, the gentlemen declined, and only the *Mantri* and the rowers accepted her invitation after having been prodded by the Labor Inspector.

After the inspection, the group returned to our house. I offered my apologies for my lack of hospitality, and said curtly and succinctly: "I have nothing in my home to offer you. We have not had any provisions for months!"

*Thank God it is now out in the open. Let them think what they will!*

The elderly gentleman grasped my hands and mumbled: "You poor thing!" and tears streamed down my cheeks as John looked at me with a chalk-white, grim face.

The gentlemen told me in unison how glad they were that they had come at this time, and said they were going to take us on board. Gently I was pushed in the direction of the bedroom as someone said: "Please put on a nice dress and dry those ugly tears." One gentleman called to Bok and Latif and invited them as well. The flatboat would come back to pick them up soon.

Everything had changed in a few minutes. The nightmare was over, and life looked rosy again. I felt uplifted and happy, and John, too, was in high spirits.

The flatboat, propelled by oarsmen, moved us downstream. The river was now almost at its normal level. I pointed out the beautiful orchids to the gentlemen, forgetting that they already knew them long before I had arrived on the scene.

The flatboat was very stable, so I could turn and twist and delight in the many-colored birds that flew all around us, without being told that we could capsize and become fodder for crocodiles.

Soon, we passed through the mangrove forest, and when I saw the beautiful white boat in the scintillating sea, I could have cheered! I was assisted on board, and everyone sat down in comfortable *rotan* chairs with beautiful cushions. A white cat jumped on my lap and immediately made me feel at home. We were offered a delicious, cool drink of unknown substance, and before long a mouth-watering smell flowed out of the cook's galley.

It was an incredibly long wait, and I felt weak from hunger, but finally someone took my arm and escorted me toward the dining salon, where all sorts of delicacies were waiting for us on the table.

The elderly gentleman said grace. It was short, and the wording unfamiliar. Then we were wisely advised to choose only from certain dishes. They were obviously concerned that, having been on a starvation diet, we might get sick if we ate food that was too rich for us.

I savored every small piece I ate. It was my first decent meal after months of rice in the morning, rice at noon and rice in the evening. I didn't know quite how to express in words my enjoyment of that meal.

It was already dark when we finished, and so we were invited to stay the night. There remained quite a bit to be discussed, and another inspection would be carried out the next day on Buluwaya and Tongkal. Gratefully, we accepted the invitation.

The shortest of the gentlemen, the Magistrate of Sanana, lent me a pair of pyjamas that was of course much too large. Toiletries had already been laid out . Exhausted from the stressful day, so full of surprises, we quickly fell asleep.

The next day, well-rested, we got up very early and went on deck to see the sun rise. The colors of the sea and sky, incredibly beautiful, were a balm for the soul after having been hemmed in by the dark, sometimes threatening, ever-present jungle. Delicious smelling coffee was waiting for us. What a luxury! Our first cup of coffee in many months!

John got into a conversation with the Magistrate, while the Labor Inspector told me a little about his work. I then asked him if the Captain was still asleep. He looked at me quizzically, and asked why that would interest me.

"I just wanted to thank him for all he has done for us yesterday, and for the splendid evening on board."

Stifling a smile, he said: "Oh, you mean the Resident[2]?"

Perplexed, I looked at him. "No, the Captain ... the tall man in the khaki suit."

The Labor Inspector burst out laughing. "Listen to this," he called out to John. "Your wife has mistaken the Resident for the Captain of the *Stella*."

The Resident, attracted by the laughter, came out of the salon to join us, and, flustered, I awkwardly offered my excuses: "I am very sorry, Sir, but I did not know who you were. I had always thought of a Resident as someone who makes his entry under a golden umbrella."

He then formally presented himself: "Resident Trips of Ternate, dear lady, at your service — but without golden umbrella. An ordinary human being, as you can see."

He said it so simply and cordially that I quickly recovered from my embarrassment. However, as a result of this mistake, the Resident was henceforth nicknamed "*Nakoda* (skipper) of the Government's Navy" — not very flattering for him.

I did see the real captain — the *juragan* — of the *Stella* a little later. He was an overweight man from Ternate, who stood on the bridge in a pair of shorts and an undershirt that looked like Swiss cheese. It was difficult to distinguish him from the sailors, but he looked stern and yelled with a commanding tone.

After an early breakfast, the Resident informed us that the whole group would return to Buluwaya. The motorboat had just returned from having towed the flatboat with the *Mantri*, the Labor Inspector, his Assistant, Bok and Latif, to the mouth of the river. Undoubtedly, they had already arrived at the plantation.

At 6:30, John and I and the other gentlemen got into the motorboat, and soon navigated the sun-drenched blue-shimmering Vesuvius Bay. We stopped at Passi Ipa to pick up the Village Chief, and then set course for the mouth of the Golohaya River. The *banjir* of the previous day was totally spent now, and the brown water flowed slowly through the mangrove forest to the sea.

The flatboat was waiting for us. We crossed over and proceeded to the beginning of the cudgel-road. I had told the gentlemen all about it, and they now wanted to see it for themselves. They also wanted to see the *gudang*, close to our house, which had drawn the keen interest of the Labor Inspector.

The stock of rice, dried fish, soap, salt and paraffin oil was checked, and John recounted the prearranged amount that was shipped every two months from Ambon. The Labor Inspector seemed satisfied, except that he did not like the quality of the dried fish. He advised to add *salted* fish and *kacang hijau* (mung beans) to the order list. He wanted to deliver personally a revised plantation order to Ong Kee Hong, together with a personal order for John and myself. I was pleased.

Finally, everything was changing for the better and I began, once again, to feel some hope.

**Endnotes**
1. *Selèndang*: a woman's shawl. With the ends knotted or sewn together, the shawl is worn in bandolier fashion to carry an infant.
2. The Resident: the governor of a residency in the Netherlands East Indies.

# IBU MALUKU

IBU MALUKU

# CHAPTER 10

### The Contract
*Buluwaya Plantation, Mangole, Sula Islands 1920*

When we arrived home, a radiant Bok was waiting. Unbeknownst to us, the Resident had given her all the provisions he could spare. She had already unpacked and stored them in the cupboard. Smiling broadly, she showed me everything. I tried to find the words to thank the Resident, but he modestly shrugged them off.

The Magistrate of Sanana promised to order emergency provisions from a reliable shop in Sanana and have the District Chief deliver them with the government's *prau*. I gave Bok permission to order whatever she felt she needed for her kitchen, and she assured me that from now on the meals would improve considerably. The *Nyonya* would be surprised!

With this done, both the Labor Inspector and Sanana's Magistrate wanted to see the books of the plantation, and the Resident asked to see John's employment contract. John handed over the books, but said self-consciously that the contract was a private matter between him and the directors. The Resident, however, insisted.

John yielded, then turned to me to suggest that, since these were business matters, it might be better if I went to the bedroom and write to the family in Holland about the events of the last two days. I gladly complied, and left the room.

Though I did start to write a letter to Mama, fragments of the sometimes heated conversation in the other room disturbed my concentration, so after a while I gave up and listened. John was clearly on the defensive. Suddenly the Resident's voice took on a commanding tone, and John entered the bedroom deeply upset to tell me the Resident had requested my presence. Apprehensive, I followed him to the front veranda, where the gentlemen were still engaged in a hot debate. The Resident stopped in mid-sentence, turned toward me, and asked:

"*Mevrouw* van Diejen, are you familiar with the contents of your husband's contract?"

"No, *Meneer*," I said. "The contract was drawn before I arrived on Java. I did not read it, because I had complete confidence that it was alright."

*It is, after all, a contract between brothers ... !*

"Well, you should have," he retorted sternly, "because it is important to both of you!"

John again brought up his promise to the directors to not discuss his contract with anyone, but the Resident and Labor Inspector insisted that I should be told.

In the contract, the Labor Inspector explained to me, John had committed himself to work as administrator of Buluwaya for seven years, starting at 200 guilders per month. After two years, his salary would increase annually by 600 guilders. He would have free use of milk from the cattle on the plantation, free lodging, servants, medical care and medicine. After seven years, he would receive a six-month furlough to the Netherlands, during which time he would receive his full salary.

Next, John had agreed to a salary deduction of 100 guilders, to pay for his passage from Rotterdam to the Vesuvius Bay, and after it was paid, the same amount would be deducted to pay for the furlough passage for him and his family.

The contract also stated that John was to commit himself fully to Buluwaya, or to any other plantation where the company might send him. He was not permitted to engage in any other activities.

Further, he agreed to name the company as beneficiary of his life insurance, as bond for the expenses that the management had underwritten on his behalf. Only after all expenses had been repaid would he be able to make his wife the beneficiary. Then followed some conditions under which the contract could be terminated — which I did not altogether understand.

Astonished, I had listened to this summary, after which the incensed Labor Inspector reviewed the matter:

"Do you know that you are entitled to habitable quarters; that in your position and in this God-forsaken dump, you should receive a starting salary of at least 550 guilders per month, and 700 after two years?"

"Further, that you are entitled to free passage to and from your posting, except if you were to leave the plantation without legitimate reason and take employment elsewhere?"

"Further, that the company can't force you to make *them* — instead of your wife — the beneficiary, and that now they can cash in if you were to leave the plantation or — and they may have had that in mind — perish here before the end of the contract?"

"Finally, that there is not one word in here about your rights and that, consequently, you can expect a big fat nothing from them?"

Trembling throughout, I had listened. Then I turned to John to ask if it was true. He nodded, and said:

"I knew soon after I arrived that I had made a mistake in accepting the contract. Since then I have often thought about asking you to stay in Holland, but I knew I could not survive by myself and I really wanted you to come. And when you arrived with people, tools and materials, I thought perhaps everything would get better. I also intended to get a new insurance policy in your name, but that hasn't happened yet, and now that you know everything, I would not be surprised if you do decide to leave me."

He was despondent and ashamed of his ineptitude, but the Resident made him understand that the company had taken unfair advantage of his inexperience, sense of duty and loyalty, probably speculating that for many years John would not get wise to them, being so completely shut off from the rest of the world.

"Well," the Resident said, "we are going to make some changes. We shall draw up a new contract in accordance with the law and currently existing norms. We shall take this contract for mailing, and I can assure you that the company will come to terms, knowing of our visit to Buluwaya."

The Labor Inspector proceeded to draw up the new contract, which contained, among other things, improved working conditions and the cancellation of the life insurance in which the company was named as the beneficiary. The last paragraph contained an urgent request to have the new contract sent as a sealed telegram with the next ship; otherwise, the Administrator would leave the plantation forthwith.

John protested against the last sentence. After all, the company depended on him and he took that seriously. He had given his word. But the Resident and the Labor Inspector persuaded him that this clause was imperative. Obviously, they were not convinced that the company could be trusted.

John signed, and the Magistrate promised to have the telegram sent as soon as he arrived at his post on Sanana. The gentlemen then impressed on us the need to transport all our belongings to Passi Ipa before the arrival of the next ship, in three weeks time.

A chill entered my heart. The gentlemen apparently did not believe that the new conditions would be accepted; in fact, it seemed they were *counting* on a refusal.

And what would happen if we missed the boat again?

The Resident assured me that, because of the special situation, he would take steps to ensure that the boat would be on time. But we would have to be on Passi Ipa the day before the scheduled arrival date. Whatever happened, he counseled us to go aboard and take a vacation in Ternate. We should also go for a medical checkup, which was urgently needed for me in view of my pregnancy. Seven days later, we could come back to Sanana with the same boat, from where — now that the monsoon was getting better — we could return to Buluwaya with the Government's *prau*.

I liked the proposal. At the same time I fervently hoped that the response from Java would be positive. I also longed for a proper medical checkup, and for a respite from our isolation. But would John do it? I doubted it. His devotion to duty could easily take priority over our personal interests.

It seemed that the gentlemen shared my concern. They urged him to be firm, and to think about himself and his family, rather than about the interests of the company.

John promised to follow their advice, and thanked them for all the effort they had made on his behalf.

*Does he really mean that?*

The gentlemen said goodbye and left. I regretted seeing them go, for now there were some matters between John and me that needed to be resolved.

For the first time, I had gained an insight into how John had been influenced by corporate dictates — of which there were many, such as:

"You have to accept a relatively small salary and primitive living conditions."

"Don't talk with third parties about your employment contract."

"Don't become too intimate with officers of the merchant marine."

"Don't talk about personal matters. It is a mark of good breeding."

"Study crop cultivation and the local languages."

"Concentrate on getting the plantation into full production."

"Treat traders and officials correctly, but keep them at a distance."

I gathered that these dictates had intimidated John, and had made him fearful of getting too close to others. John was outgoing by nature, so all this must have weighed heavily on him. But I could not make him understand the absurdity of the demands they had made on him.

"What about the life insurance policy?" I asked him. "How could you reconcile making them the beneficiary with your concern for me?"

"Of course I thought their demand very strange," John replied, " and I said as much. However, they assured me it was common practice — it was just a formality."

He had obviously trusted his superior.

"Later," John continued, "I started worrying about it, and realized something was seriously wrong when I found out the net salary of 100 guilders was insufficient to live on. Everything had to be imported, and every shipment carried an insurance cost of 25 guilders.

"The dairy products that were promised, were — as you now know — non-existent. The cattle had run wild, and our attempts to catch them failed. So milk and butter had to come from elsewhere.

"Before you came, I gave most of my money to the Overseer's wife, who washed and cooked for me. I didn't have enough left over for cigarettes, so I stopped smoking. I knew we would be in dire straits when you arrived. I was shocked by the bill for the provisions you had bought on Ambon, but didn't dare say anything."

He stumbled over his words in his haste to explain everything, but now I could at last understand his strange attitude that had caused me so much concern during the first months on Buluwaya.

John admitted to having lived under great stress. He was convinced that if I had known everything, I would have left with the next available boat, leaving him to sink back into his horrible loneliness.

"And so," he said, "I almost hated you for curing me of that blood poisoning. I would have gladly died to give you the freedom to leave this impossible place."

I spent a few bitter hours listening to his confessions and apologies, and found it difficult to console and encourage this aching man, who seemed to have lost his bearings.

*****

The days passed. We talked mostly about the hopefully soon-to-be-completed house on the other side of the river: how we would furnish it, and how we would shape the garden. Having mentioned the disaster with my first vegetable garden, our visitors had told me what to do to keep ants away from the seeds, and I was now full of new plans and intentions.

One sunny morning, while I was taking care of my orchids, I felt an internal jolt. It gave me a fright. Then I realized that my baby had shown me that it was alive and well. So great was the happiness that flooded me, that I became totally absorbed by it. My hands continued to take care of the orchids, but I was not conscious of what they were doing.

When John came home, hours later, and heard the news, he first looked at me dazedly. Then we hugged and reassured ourselves how happy we were, how promising the future was, and how everything would turn out just fine.

One week before the arrival of the ship, I reminded John that we should start packing, since he had not mentioned one word about it. He tried to convince me that the company would surely accept the conditions of the proposed contract, and that it would be insane to transport all our possessions to Passi Ipa. I just did not know how much trouble it had been to transport the furniture. And then, what was he going to tell the Overseer, when he saw that we were leaving?

I talked and talked, and only after I assured him that *he* and our possessions could go back to Buluwaya if the boat brought a positive answer, and *I* would go alone to Ternate for a medical checkup, did he agree to have our furniture packed and shipped to Passi Ipa. The bed, writing desk and a few other things would remain where they were, since they belonged to the plantation.

Of course, Babu Bok and Latif wanted to go with us to Passi Ipa. Under no conditions did they want to stay. I was somewhat bewildered, not knowing whether to say goodbye to the workers or not. We could very well be back in a few days.

John was in a somber mood. He gave his last orders to the Overseer and the workers, saying that he would return after the boat had arrived. He instructed them to take the large *prau* and pick up the usual shipment of provisions and rice.

Then, finally, we set off down the river, and I heaved a big sigh of relief.

On Passi Ipa, we moved into the *pasanggrahan*. Babu Bok and Latif sauntered in rapture through the little village.

John was very quiet. In the evening he walked along the small white beach, and talked with the Village Head and several Chinese traders. When he came in, I was already lying on a camp-cot under a *kelambu*. I was hoping that the little one would stir again, but it didn't, and slowly I sank into an uneasy sleep, full of frightening dreams.

Two days later, the ship arrived — the first one we had boarded after my arrival and marriage. Memories of those events absorbed me as we took the very first motor sloop to the S.S. *Pijnacker Hordijk*.

The Second Mate greeted us — we did not know him — and introduced us to the bulky Captain and other officers of the ship. They offered us a copious breakfast, and only then did John ask if a telegram had come for him. The Captain said he did not think so, but he was not certain, since the mailbag had already gone ashore with the first motorboat.

Hurriedly, we left and took the next motorboat back to the quay, where we found our mailbag with the First Mate. Quickly, John sifted its contents: several letters, a big bunch of newspapers, a bill from Ong Kee Hong ... otherwise, nothing! No telegram from Java; only letters from the Company, but dated well before the date on which John had sent the telegram.

John's face turned white. He had obviously counted on getting a response to his telegram.

Then he shouted rudely: "See, there is nothing, absolutely nothing! What do you want to do now?"

Astonished, I looked at him and trembled in my shoes. What should I say? What should I do? As if in answer, my infant turned. Putting my hand protectively where the movement had been, I stood squarely in front of him with a pleading face and said slowly and with great emphasis:

"John, for the sake of our child, let's leave, or we'll all die!" And before John could utter a word, I turned to the First Mate and said firmly: "We will go with you to Ternate."

John looked at me, ashen-faced, then hurried off to the *pasanggrahan*. That's where I found him later, with tears of impotence and disappointment in his eyes. But I had regained my courage now, and said that I was convinced that it would be best for us, and that we had to hurry to get our meager belongings on board.

The First Mate gave instructions to load, and we came on board ourselves with the last motorboat. Just before we left, I saw in the distance the plantation *prau* approaching Passi Ipa to pick up the shipment of rice. The people staying behind would be taken care of. I almost sobbed from relief, and went to the cabin to unpack our trunks.

"Thank God! Finally away from the daily anxieties, if only for a moment. Don't think about anything, and hope that John will accept the inevitable," I told myself.

I did admire his self-discipline. He had again withdrawn completely within himself, was coolly polite, and gazed across the railing at the disappearing island. I could not fathom what was going on inside him, except that, for the moment, I did not exist. He was again like the man I had met after my arrival eight months ago.

It was getting dark when we arrived on Sanana. The Magistrate, whom we had already met on Buluwaya, of course, came on board. John went to meet him, and I heard this Magistrate say: "A telegram for you. It arrived this morning".

John turned beet-red, took the telegram, mumbled an excuse and hurried to the cabin.

I waited a while, and then followed him. John took me in his arms, and said: "I'm going back. Everything is in order. All conditions have been met. I knew it, I knew it!" He was overjoyed!

We showed the letter to the Magistrate, who congratulated us on the good news. John promptly gave instructions to unload our furniture. This was done rapidly.

## IBU MALUKU

Was I happy? Disappointed? At that moment I did not understand myself. Had I been wanting something different, or I had come to love Buluwaya and its people, who had given us their confidence and now had been left behind?

John told the Captain that I would continue the journey alone. He wanted to return as quickly as possible, and would try to hire a government prau the next day. But the Captain, the Magistrate and his wife, who had just come on board, tried to persuade John to accompany me to Ternate. They thought we both needed some time off, and felt the father-to-be should be present during the medical check-up.

Finally, John gave in. The furniture would be sent back to Passi Ipa by the *prau*, which the District Head would take and return to Mangole the next day.

We retreated to the cabin, where John told me over and again that he knew that the Management would show good faith. When we had wound down, and realized how dead-tired we were, we went to bed. It was our first night on board. But we could not sleep: we were just too agitated. So we talked.

John told me about a passenger he had met on board: he was the administrator of a coconut plantation on Halmahera that belonged to a well-known company in Rotterdam. John wanted to talk to him again in the morning about the cultivation of coconuts and the management problems he had encountered in that area.

Had John decided to throw off his company-imposed reserve, or had the arrival of the telegram (and the resulting improvement in the standard of living) given him greater self-confidence? Perhaps it was a little of both. I prayed that the trend would continue. Finally, I fell asleep, and had an awful dream.

It was a radiant day. I was in Buluwaya and sat on the banks of a small river, in which clear water babbled quietly over a thick layer of pebbles. In the water were the tiny tots of our coolies, playing and splashing water on each other with a lot of happy laughing and high-spirited squabbling. Then the sun disappeared, and the sky turned dark and threatening. I stepped into the water to get the children out, but they were too heavy to carry up the banks. I heard a piercing scream from a mother who came running; then came the horrifying sound of an approaching *banjir*, and I saw a savage mountain of dark-colored water rushing toward us. I felt the forceful impact of the water as I fell and was swept away and tumbled and tumbled ... and a voice cried: "Dead ... dead ... dead ... and it is all your ... *your* fault!" Bathing in perspiration, I woke up.

## IBU MALUKU

I didn't know where I was and felt an oppressive agony from which I could not break free. I struggled to awaken, my mouth was bone-dry, and I gasped for air. Finally, I shook off this nightmare, and when I saw John sleeping peacefully in the bunk opposite me, I calmed down. But the fear brought on by the dream stayed with me, and I was grateful when day broke and John woke up.

\*\*\*\*

I must have looked terrible, for many people asked if I had slept badly. The Captain finally intervened, and said: "It was an abnormally hot night, and it would not surprise me if we encounter bad weather." The prospect obviously did not please him, for bad weather would slow down loading and unloading, and the KPM tried hard to adhere to a tight schedule.

I remained distressed. The Captain sensed it, and invited me to sit on the boat-deck. "It will be quiet; not a soul will pass by. And," he added with a wink, "why don't you have a little nap. You seem to need it." Considerately, he had a deck-chair brought up.

John was having a serious talk with the plantation administrator from Halmahera, and did not notice that I was going upstairs. I took some needlework with me and settled comfortably in the deck-chair. How delightful! It was indeed very quiet here, and I was so very tired.

I dozed off, and awoke when someone nudged me. It was John, who laughingly said: "Well now! Walking off without a word, and sleeping in the middle of the day!"

Then he started to talk excitedly about the conversation he'd had with the planter from Halmahera. He now knew a lot more about coconut diseases, coconut rats (a kind of flying squirrel) and about the recruitment of workers on the Talaud Islands.

John went on, at length, about his plans for the future and the expansion of Buluwaya. When I asked him to please take time to enjoy our trip, he said almost indignantly that he now had the chance to learn a thing or two, and wanted to grab the opportunity.

"Amen," said I teasingly, "for the well-being and prosperity of the directors known to us." John had the good grace to laugh. Still chuckling, we enjoyed a delicious cup of coffee that was brought by a *jongos*[1] who was exquisitely dressed in a white *tutup* (a white jacket with high buttoned up collar) and a beautifully folded head cloth on his black hair.

The Chief Engineer, drawn by our voices, left his cabin to share a cup with us. The Chief Mechanic, as this officer was called on board, paid me a compliment about my dress and asked if, on that deserted island, I had always dressed like that.

I smiled. The dress had never been unpacked, but before I could say so, John said:

"Say, I have never seen you in that. Did you have that dress in Buluwaya?" The Chief Mechanic burst out laughing, and said to John that I probably had bought the dress at one of the "exclusive" stores on Sanana, to surprise him.

"Absolutely", I said jokingly. *What exclusive store?*

We shared a good laugh, and the Chief Engineer said: "Well, I'll see you at lunch. We shall have real Dutch *hutspot*[2]." And when I looked at him unbelievingly, he assured me it would be served with spare ribs, and disappeared whistling down the stairway.

This day had not been as beautiful as the day before, and — fulfilling the Captain's prediction — it was now changing for the worse. Dark clouds were starting to accumulate in the distance. The wind started to build up, causing the boat to sway. But we were used to traveling by boat and so were not afraid of bad weather.

The gong announced lunchtime, so we went downstairs, where it was swelteringly hot. I greedily drank a glass of ice-water, and thoroughly enjoyed my first real Dutch meal in months! But storm-slats had been mounted on all tables, to prevent the china from sliding off. The First Mate had stayed on the bridge, and never did show up for lunch.

When we returned after lunch to the open deck, I asked the Captain if I could again rest on the boat-deck, since it would be cooler there. A sailor had already taken my deck-chair down below, but our cabin boy carried it up again. I followed, again with some needlework.

John joined me later, and told me about the additional things he had heard regarding the plantation business. Sometimes the swaying of the boat caused my chair to slide backward, and we made some jokes when it slid back in place.

But the sky turned progressively darker. The Captain left his chart-room for a moment to advise us to go downstairs. The swaying of the boat made it difficult for the cabin boy to carry the deck-chair downstairs by himself, and required John's assistance. I stayed behind, hanging on to the railing, to savor the fresh air for a few additional minutes.

**Endnotes**
[1] *Jongos*: a waiter or male house servant.
[2] A casserole dish of mashed potatoes, onions, meat, and carrots.

IBU MALUKU

# CHAPTER 11

### En Route to Ternate
*S.S. Pijnacker Hordijk, 1920*

Reluctantly, I left the fresh air of the upper deck to go down below. In the middle of the stairs, the ship's sudden roll knocked me against the hand rail and I lost my footing ... slid down ... and landed hard on the deserted deck below.

Before I could get back on my feet, the boat's heavy pitch threw me against the railing, and then, on the rebound, against the wall of the first cabin. I could find nothing to hang on to and yelled for help.

The *jongos* and the steward ran out of the salon, helped me onto my feet, and took me groaning to my cabin. They immediately ran out to find John, who two minutes later burst into the cabin with a scared face and asked what had happened.

I burst out in tears ... I hadn't broken anything and was unhurt except for some chafed skin and an upcoming lump on my head, but I was petrified that the fall might have hurt the baby.

The Chief Engineer, who was "doctor" on board, then turned up and asked worriedly if I were all right. One look at my face gave him the answer, and he promptly forced me to drink a glass of cognac. "So! Try to get some sleep," he said. But as he walked away, I heard him mutter to himself: "Idiot, to sit on the boat-deck in this weather. It's always those *baru's* — those new-comers ..."

Toward evening, the boat moored off Obi Island in a quiet anchorage. The storm had passed and it was cooler now, but it was raining and the transfer of cargo was therefore postponed until the morning.

I took John's suggestion to take a bath, but in the bathroom, I felt nauseous and threw up. With difficulty I dried myself and got into my kimono.

Back in the cabin, I had no sooner dropped down on the bunk bed, when a searing pain shot through my body. It scared me. Had the fall hurt me after all? The pain diminished as John comforted me with soothing words, but his eyes betrayed his fear. Then, another shooting pain. I shrank into a ball and asked if there was a doctor on Obi.

John ran out and returned with the Chief Engineer and the Captain.

Both were deeply concerned and said there was no doctor on Obi, but there was a *Mantri*, who ran a small clinic. He could, of course, be asked to come, but no one knew whether he was capable of dealing with this situation. Distressed, I asked if there was a doctor on Bachan — the next island to the north. The Chief Engineer said an Army doctor might be there on one of his periodic tours of inspection, but the chances were slim.

I asked for a sedative. The Chief Engineer gave me a bromide tablet. As I waited for it to take effect, the terrible pains returned — and suddenly I realized that they were labor pains!

*My God! Am I going to lose my baby here and now?*

I sent the men away; this was a matter for women. I would explain to John later that I was having a miscarriage; I didn't have the strength to do it just then. I realized that the malnutrition and stress I had endured on Buluwaya had now robbed me of all energy.

Bok helped me as best she could. She comforted me, cooled my hands and burning head with ice-water, and supported me when those terrible pains came. She scooted out briefly to fetch another woman, and then they both helped me through that terrible ordeal.

It was dark when it was all over. The child that John and I had longed for and already loved, was not to become a human being after all. It had moved momentarily after birth, and Bok told me later that it had been a girl.

I bled heavily, and the horrible pains kept pulling my stomach and loins together. Sometimes I did not know what was happening around me! The bleeding continued until we reached Bachan, where a doctor had not been seen for three months.

There was a small hospital, though. A native nurse arrived on board, terribly shy, to see if there was something she could do to help. But she was taken aback when she saw that I was an *orang belanda* — a Dutch person. She mumbled *"susah sekali"* — meaning this was too big a problem for her to handle — and said she would warn the *mantri*, who could give me an injection. I nodded my head in agreement ... anything at all to stop this terrible bleeding. I felt my life-force draining out of me.

The *Mantri*, a kind old hospital orderly, muttered *kassian, kassian* — you poor dear — as he gave me an injection and wrapped me in a *gurita* — a swaddling cloth.

"You must see a doctor as soon as you arrive on Ternate," he said, and then politely refused to accept payment for his services.

How typical of these people. How could I ever thank him? Just his kindly presence had done wonders for me!

Two days later, we arrived at Ternate. John asked the military doctor to come on board — but he refused after hearing when the miscarriage had taken place. I had to come to the hospital myself where he would give me a check-up ... but he let it be known right away that a miscarriage was nothing to get excited about. It happened all the time!

John was livid, but I knew that it was better so — we would have to disembark anyway. And when the boat returned in a week, I had better be fit enough to return with John to Buluwaya.

We went on foot to the military hospital. The doctor, who was more congenial now, gave me a superficial check-up and said the pains would surely go away if I were to take the pills he gave me. Only later did I find out that he had just been humoring me: the pills were quinine tablets! Their red color had fooled me, as I had only known about the white ones. It was just as well that I could not tolerate those pills; the bleeding became worse, so I stopped taking them.

We stayed at the *pasanggrahan* — a small hotel. The owner was a Eurasian lady, a caring woman who spoiled me as she nursed me ... and seemed to know everything about miscarriages. She comforted me by saying that surely I would have another baby within the year.

Aunt Caroline, as she was called, was a darling, who gave me much courage and confidence in the Almighty — being a very spiritual person herself. Yet, in spite of her loving care, I often felt so alone, so empty, so abandoned. Yet, at other times I shunned people, and longed for the stillness of Buluwaya.

\* \* \* \*

John had spent two days at the bureau of Resident Trips — the Chief Administrator of the Moluccas, whom I had earlier mistaken for the captain of the *Stella*. I knew something was wrong when he did not discuss the day's events upon his return to the hotel. Hesitatingly, I asked what was going on. John then vented his pent-up frustration and told me what had happened.

Having been shown the telegram from Java, Mr. Trips had said: "That's what I feared," and he asked John if he had noticed that something was missing from the telegram.

John had answered that everything seemed in order, and that he was very happy that all conditions had been accepted — conditions that he would not have dared propose himself.

"But," the Resident had answered, "the most important item is missing: the telegram has not been sealed and, thus, it isn't worth the paper it is written on. The company can annul the contents whenever it wants to do so."

Mr. Trips had then insisted on sending a second telegram to Java, with the urgent request to send a sealed answer. It was this answer for which John was now waiting.

He was distressed about it, feeling a second request was "undignified". He had not told me earlier, he said, not wanting to burden me with it. "You have enough to work through, and I didn't want to load you down with more problems. And I really hoped that the Resident's suspicions would turn out to be unfounded."

Another day went by, however, without a confirmation telegram.

Happily, we had a little diversion. Toward the evening we were visited by a lovely, elderly couple, who had spent 20 years in the East Indies. This in itself filled me with great respect, as they surely had experienced a lot.

While telling us a little about their past, the woman told me that she had twice lost a baby, and had then adopted a child. She herself had often been ill during the many years that she and her husband had spent in the jungle. Her life story consoled me.

Before the end of their visit, the husband, a General Agent for the MHM[1] Trading Company, invited John to come to his office for "a talk". John eagerly accepted.

The next day was a Sunday, a day of repose, which gave us the chance to meet the other guests of the *pasanggrahan*.

There was a warm, outgoing couple, whose children were in boarding school on Ternate. This couple — originally from the Dutch Province of Brabant — lived in the southern part of Halmahera, where he represented the Government as Acting Magistrate. Except for a missionary who had sent his children to Holland after his wife died, they were the only Europeans in the jungle. The village in which they lived also held a detachment of native KNIL[2] soldiers, a handful of Chinese merchants, and — "thank heaven," sighed Madame — a doctor, a Javanese.

There were as well three unmarried Dutch teachers in our *pasanggrahan*, who were also being spoiled by Aunt Caroline. They told us a little about Ternate itself, which, despite its small size, had been a major spice center for centuries.

The Portuguese — well entrenched in fortified *castellas* all over the island — were already running a thriving business in nutmeg, mace and cloves, when two small Dutch ships arrived at Ternate in 1607.

Unhappy with the misbehaving Portuguese, the powerful Sultan granted the spice concession to the Dutch, and gave them permission to build their own *castella*, Fort Orange, in the heart of the city. The

## IBU MALUKU

Portuguese were forced to withdraw from Ternate, and later, from the other Moluccan Islands.

I interrupted to tell the teachers that I had already been inside Fort Orange, and knew that besides the KNIL barracks, it also contained the Military Hospital where I had received my check-up.

They went on to say that Ternate was only 40 square miles in size, and had a 5,600 foot active volcano, the "Gamalamo", in the foothills of which lay some 30 densely populated *kampungs* and the city of Ternate.

Ternate was capital of the Residency of the Moluccas — which included Halmahera, Morotai, Bachan, the Sula Islands and the western part of New Guinea. The Dutch government, headed by Resident Trips, had to co-operate closely with the Sultan, as Ternate was a "self-rule" area.

There were a Dutch and a Dutch-Chinese grade school — both staffed with Dutch teachers. There were also many so-called *dèsa* (village) schools, spread over the surrounding *kampungs* and islands, where native teachers (*gurus*) instructed the young.

The KNIL detachment of native soldiers was under the command of a Dutch Captain, assisted by a Captain-Doctor, a Warrant Officer and a few sergeants — all Dutch or Eurasian.

Further, there were four large trading companies that imported most provisions, and exported primarily copra, *damar*, *tripang*[3], shells and fish. The island also produced *palla* (nutmeg), *cengkèh* (cloves), vanilla, *kayu manis* (cinnamon), and sago[4] — the staple food for most Ternatans.

Thus ended the teachers' description of Ternate.

It had been an interesting day, which had given my thoughts a new direction. The teachers, and the others we had met, had spoken with enthusiasm about the promising future that awaited us here in the East Indies. It had lit a spark in me, and I resolved to stop worrying. I even started to make new plans for Buluwaya, in which I myself would have a role to play.

\*\*\*\*

The days went by without the expected answer to our telegram. John became more depressed, and regretted that he had sent it. He did not think it should have been necessary: his faith in the company was apparently still unshaken.

As promised, he called on the General Agent of the MHM Trading Company who had visited us with his wife the previous Saturday. This man finally convinced John that it was useless to wait any longer. He also advised him not to return to Buluwaya under any circumstances.

## IBU MALUKU

*What did this man know about John's company that made him speak with such assurance?*

He offered John a superb job at MHM's Tobelo post in Eastern Halmahera. The conditions were favorable, with good prospects for promotion, and the work was more in line with John's experience.

The KPM ship *Pijnacker Hordijk* was expected in two days, and at John's request, I asked Bok to start packing our luggage. I awaited the arrival of the ship with much trepidation, not knowing whether we would actually be leaving with it, or not.

Still suffering from much pain and feeling quite weak, I once again visited the doctor. "The pain will go away eventually," he said. So, as far as he was concerned, I could return to our remote home on Buluwaya.

It was time for John to have one more meeting with Resident Trips, and then make a decision.

As I would learn later, Mr. Trips was very frank. The company would sue him — that was certain — but the original contract was strongly contestable, and John should not worry about the outcome.

Although he knew full well that he had been taken advantage of, John still struggled with the loyalty he felt towards his brother, but finally decided in favor of his own family[5]. When he arrived at the hotel, I heard the stupendous news that we would not be leaving after all. He had accepted the new job on Halmahera.

The Buluwaya episode was finished.

### Endnotes
[1] The "Molukse Handel Maatschappij", the Moluccan Trading Company.
[2] The KNIL (Koninklijk Nederlands Indisch Leger) is the Royal Netherlands [East] Indies Army.
[3] *Tripang* – sea cucumber, used as food by the Chinese.
[4] Sago is a starchy food, derived from the soft interior of the trunk of various palms.
[5] Jan had financed much of John's education, which may explain John's extreme loyalty toward his older brother.

IBU MALUKU

# CHAPTER 12

### *Legal and Medical Trials*
Ternate, 1921

The next day, John went to the MHM office for the first time to meet his colleagues. Apart from his boss, the General Agent, there were only two Dutch employees. The cashier and the other employees were all Chinese. The office opened at seven, and closed for lunch at noon.

When John came home for lunch that first day, he told me about his experiences that morning and said he would have to be back at two. In the afternoon, he would learn how to grade copra and *damar*, and be shown how this company operated.

*Damar* is a resin, derived mostly from dipterocarpaceous trees of south-east Asia, to make a colorless varnish. The trees are not cultivated, but grow freely in the wild in clusters of ten to fifteen. The first native who happens to pass by and understand the trees' commercial value, claims the cluster as his own. It is with this person that John would have to negotiate.

At five he returned, and we bathed in the *pasanggrahan's* large old-fashioned bathroom. In it stood a large concrete cistern, filled with clear and very cold mountain water that flowed continuously from a large bamboo conduit. With a copper *gayung* — a pan with a long handle — you had to pour the water over your soaped body. Very refreshing, that bath!

It was a little cooler outside, thank heaven, when we took our first walk through the *kota* (town). Christmas was not far off. It would be my first Christmas in the tropics, and I found it difficult to reconcile that everything around me was in full bloom and that it was so warm. To me, Christmas meant leafless trees, snow, and being cozily inside the house.

We celebrated Christmas in the *Soos* (the Society Club) with especially good food, cool beer, and dancing to music from a gramophone. There was a piano in the club, but it was sadly out of tune. I was told that a piano tuner came only once a year from Makassar to tune all the pianos along the KPM's route.

The MHM company wanted us to stay in Ternate a whole month

so John could learn the ropes. We would then be temporarily posted to Tobelo[1] on the north-east coast of Halmahera, the largest island of the Moluccas. From there, John would take several months to visit all the company's outposts, which varied in size and function.

The smaller posts served as collection points for copra and *damar*, which were sent by schooner to one of three larger posts. There these products were sorted and prepared for shipment by KPM steamer to the company's warehouses.

Once he had visited all these outposts, John could decide himself at which of the larger posts he would want to be stationed.

The new job challenged John, and soon he was completely absorbed by it. But I wondered if he had really forgotten Buluwaya.

Our first New Year's Eve was now behind us, and we entered the year 1921 full of expectations.

On January 25, we sailed with the S.S. *Sloet van der Beelen* to Tobelo, and passed many islands that spread like large bouquets in the deep-blue sea. Seen from the boat, Halmahera appeared very large. What impressed us were the many beautifully contoured volcanos — several active ones among them — that rose sharply from the coast and hid their peaks in the clouds.

We discovered that Tobelo was flanked by two such volcanoes: the Gam Gossi and the Mamuya. The hinterland to the south consisted of a long chain of shrouded volcanoes. The low-lying plain where Tobelo lay was therefore completely surrounded by these majestic mountains.

At Tobelo the boat lay at anchor in the roadstead, and the passengers and cargo were ferried ashore by a motorsloop that towed a long train of white cargo vessels.

It was a busy scene. All around our ship swarmed small *praus*, manned by dark, strikingly-tall people. Most of them were just paddling about, but some were transporting passengers who did not want to pay the separate charge for the motorsloop.

Soon, some people came on board, among them the Magistrate and his wife, and several male missionaries. Tobelo turned out to be the main post of the *Zending* (the Protestant Mission), which had a church, a training-school for native teachers, a technical school, a hospital, and a coconut plantation that was run by a Missionary-Administrator who would later become our neighbor.

All visitors stayed for lunch — as was the custom on all KPM boats sailing in these remote parts. The Dutch who lived and worked here greatly appreciated this gesture, and always looked forward to the occasion. During the meal, they covered all the news from Batavia to Ter-

# IBU MALUKU

nate. Decidedly, the KPM was the most specialized news-service in the whole East Indies!

At the quay we were welcomed by an orchestra — a group of small dark-skinned school-boys, dressed in white — playing on bamboo flutes a repertoire of Dutch national songs, among which "Piet Heyn"[2] was definitely the favorite. It was a happy, friendly welcome, — though we soon discovered it was not meant for us at all, but rather for one of the missionaries who was celebrating his birthday!

On the quay, we were met by a Euro-Chinese who introduced himself as the Overseer of the MHM Moluccan Trading Company. He said he had already made arrangements for the transportation of our possessions that were now loaded into *gerobaks* (ox-carts) and taken to our house. We followed on foot.

Tobelo looked friendly. A snow-white road, made from shimmering crushed white sea shells and coral, zigzagged its way through hedgerows full of beautiful flowers. Tidy houses stood on immaculately clean compounds. The houses were all built from wooden beams, with walls of *gaba-gaba* and roofs of *atap*. And towering above them stood the swaying coconut trees. The radiant sun beamed its light on this scene, giving it an intense beauty.

The house temporarily assigned to us wasn't much to speak of. It was a large house with a concrete floor. It had evidently served as a shop, because the wall facing the street consisted of stacked boards, which could easily be dismantled and reassembled.

Someone had attempted to clean the house, but it still looked awful. The roof looked old and not very solid. There was no ceiling. From the center of the spacious front veranda ran a wide dark corridor, with large rooms on either side, and a dining room and a provisions room at the far end.

John picked the former shop at the front for his office. The room on the left of the corridor would become our bedroom, and — since there were no separate servant quarters — Bok and Latif would use the bedroom on the right.

In the large, neglected back yard, some men were building a kitchen, adjacent to a bathroom. In one corner of this bathroom stood a water basin that had just been replastered; in the other, a little staircase that led to a high "throne" with a round hole that had no cover. That was our toilet!

We resolved to have a few things rectified as soon as possible, and the Overseer, who had just arrived with the ox-carts, promised to send six more men the following day. Finding people right away would not be possible, because it was "boat-day" — the KPM-ship had arrived — and most people did not care to work then.

We soon understood that "boat-day" here was like a national holiday in the West. What we had not learned yet was that in the East Indies nothing was cast in concrete; everything was negotiable. This time, however, we accepted the situation without a whimper.

Several days later Bok complained she wasn't feeling well. I checked her temperature and found she had a high fever. Together, we trotted off to the hospital, but the doctor was away on *tournée* and would not be back until the next day.

The *Mantri* took a blood sample, and gave Bok some quinine and something else he thought she needed. I asked him to leave a message for the doctor, asking him when we could see him. The elderly man gave me a surprised look, and then said that he would gladly tell the Doctor that we would be expecting him at our house. As a *Belanda*, one apparently did not go oneself to see the doctor.

Two days later, the doctor came. He was a *Dokter Jawa* — a doctor who had completed his medical studies on Java, as opposed to in the Netherlands.

He introduced himself as Doctor Slamat. He was Javanese, a graduate of the NIAS (*Nederlands Indische Artsenschool* — the Netherlands East Indies Medical School). The Government had paid for his tuition, which obligated him after graduation to practice three years in the Outer Possessions — that is, the regions outside Java and Madura.

He told us that he wanted to become a gynecologist, and had plans to continue his studies in the Netherlands or Germany — which eventually he did. Many years later, I would meet him as Director of Gynecology in one of the largest hospitals on Java.

He looked Bok over and diagnosed malaria. Then, I asked him to examine me. I was again very tired. The pains in my back had continued and had become more acute, and intermittent bleeding had started again.

My request made him bashful, especially after I told him about the miscarriage and the medical treatment received on Ternate. He said that the Ternate doctor, who was a *Belanda*, would surely have done everything that was necessary. But when I insisted, he did examine me.

He looked concerned, and said that the moving had perhaps been too stressful and that a rest would do me good. He then promised to return the next day for a more thorough internal examination, and he did.

After the examination, he told John and me the bad news: because of the abrupt miscarriage and the effects of undernourishment and emaciation, the womb had tilted backwards — it had become retroverted. Brief and to the point — which seemed to be against his nature — he explained what must have happened.

An operation would be necessary to correct the situation. He himself could not do such an operation, nor could this be done on Ternate or Ambon. "Thus," he advised, "you should leave with tomorrow's ship and go to Surabaya. It is the only place where they can operate, and you must have it done now if you want to have more children."

We heard him out in silence. Another set-back to digest after having just arrived at the start of a new career. I knew full well that the doctor was right and was prepared to do what he suggested, but the decision was up to John.

"How are we going to pay for all this," we asked each other after the doctor had left. We had borrowed heavily to pay for the journey from Passi Ipa to Ternate and to cover the cost of getting settled. We couldn't possibly go into more debt. The trip to Surabaya was expensive, and what about the costs of the operation and the hospital?

When I suggested to wait and see for a few months, John heaved a sigh: "If that would be possible ...!"

In the afternoon, Dr. Slamat came back with a letter addressed to a former mentor, Professor Doctor Lesk — a German, who was Medical Director of the CBZ[3] Hospital in Surabaya.

Hesitatingly I told him that we wanted to postpone the journey and the operation. He did not understand why and became self-conscious and embarrassed. Apparently, he felt that we did not consider him expert enough — few Europeans put their trust in a *"Dokter Jawa"*.

But when John explained that it was financially almost impossible for us, he relaxed and opened up. Together, we looked at the options. The doctor advised me to go now, if we really wanted to have another child. A delay could aggravate the problem to the point where it would become permanent. He offered to write the professor about our financial situation. "He is very expensive," he confided, "but he is also a human being. The hospital is inexpensive ... and even free, if necessary. So you should not worry about that."

With a fearful heart, we made our decision: the next day, I would leave for Java alone as John could not possibly accompany me.

Bok was inconsolable. I promised her I would come back with a cook from her own region, and assured her no one could take better care of the *Tuan* than she could. At that she was quickly prepared to do everything that was asked of her. Bok was not only a faithful assistant; she was and would remain almost a sister to me for as long as she was with us on Tobelo.

Fear of the unknown engulfed me. What would happen next? I might not survive the operation, in which case it would be goodbye forever. Dr. Slamat seemed to sense my anxiety, because after he had given me explicit written instructions for Surabaya, he pressed a small box of tranquilizers in my hand.

The S.S. *Sloet van der Beelen* sailed into the harbor at 6:00 a.m. as the shout "*kapal masuk*, the boat has arrived!" travelled from mouth to mouth throughout Tobelo.

The Captain and First Mate looked surprised when I boarded with my hand luggage, because only one week had passed since I had said goodbye to them. John brought the Captain up-to-date, and then accompanied me to the same cabin in which we, full of hope, had started our journey from Ternate to Tobelo.

This time, the boat did not stay long in Tobelo. The whistle blew, and I was alone. From the railing, with tears streaming down my cheeks, I watched John leave the ship.

Two days later we arrived in Ternate, and I went to the home of John's boss, the General Agent of the MHM company. He looked startled to see me, fearing something serious had happened.

In short, jerky sentences, I explained why I was there.

His wife joined us, and said consolingly that such unexpected events were part of life in these remote regions, and that even here everything would turn out all right in the end. Giving her husband a meaningful look, she continued: "Yes, my dear, now you shall have to go even deeper into debt; that, too, is the Indies, you know."

She went on talking, not giving me a chance to say anything, as I learned that this, too, would be taken care of. After all, John's potential was good, and they had faith that everything would be paid back eventually. "And so," she concluded, "Don't worry about a thing. Just do everything you can to get back your health and energy!"

Together, they took me to the boat. I did not know how to thank them. They had been so helpful, though they hardly knew us.

For many years they would be like parents to us, always concerned, doling out advice, reprimanding us occasionally when necessary, but never condescendingly. Madame, in particular, would be my support and my refuge. Their passing, many years later, would be a great sorrow and loss for John and me.

I continued my journey, reversing the route I had taken on my first trip. After 20 days, we arrived in Makassar, where I had to change and take the KPM's express service to Surabaya. Three days later, we arrived

# IBU MALUKU

at Tanjung Perak, the harbor of Surabaya. I was met by a representative of the Company, who had been alerted by a telegram from Ternate. He took me directly to the CBZ Hospital, where the doctor on duty told us that Prof. Dr. Lesk was in Malang for a consultation, and would be back in two days' time. So I was quartered in Hotel Brunett, close to the hospital, and I would stay there until the hospital could take me.

The brand-new hotel, owned by an Armenian, was almost full. Luckily, I was given a room in the rear with a small cozy veranda, where it was very peaceful and where I could have my meals by myself.

I was in no mood to visit the town. During the day, Surabaya was burning hot; also, I had become people-shy. The roaring traffic, and the swarming masses of people that I had seen from the car, scared me greatly. So I waited in my hotel room.

Finally, news arrived that Professor Lesk was back and would see me. Again, fear gripped me. I would have given a lot, at that moment, just to have had someone with me!

In the CBZ Hospital, I was registered by a young native doctor, who turned out to be an acquaintance of Dr. Slamat. She turned me over to an internist, a Belgian, who had come to the East Indies out of necessity. During the First World War, he had been a Flemish nationalist, and that had made it difficult for him to stay in his country.

With his wife — also a doctor at this hospital — he would keep watch over me. "We are after all compatriots," he remarked after having read my dossier. His words consoled me, and I returned to the hotel in a more hopeful mood. The following day I would be admitted.

The CBZ was an old hospital, made up of a cluster of massive buildings that were not laid out in any rational pattern. The rooms were very large; the ceilings, very high. The walls were whitewashed; the floor was of plain concrete. It felt like a mortuary!

My room had two high, wrought-iron beds with many curvatures. Each bed was covered by a military style blanket and a finely woven *kelambu*. There was no other piece of furniture in the room.

In the second bed lay a young Javanese woman. Her family lived close to the hospital and continuously walked in with all kinds of food for her — so the room was always full with people and filled with the pungent smell of *trasi* and garlic.

I arrived at one o'clock, and was immediately ushered into the examination room and prepared for the operation.

The two doctors and the nurses spoke Javanese to each other, which I did not understand, but I could hear that they were from Jokja, because they rolled their r's, and pronounced words in a way that made their conversation sound rigid and cut-up.

I was carried on a stretcher to the operating room, where Dr. Lesk and two assistants were waiting. Soon, I was strapped in, and all I could do then was to pray.

I forced myself to be calm, but my heart was in my mouth. I was clammy from cold sweat, and felt dreadfully alone. I was in mortal fear, once again having a strong feeling that I would not survive the operation.

Professor Lesk was aloof and short-tempered; only the assistant administering the anaesthetic said a few encouraging words to me before he covered my nose and mouth with the cap and urged me to breathe deeply.

It took a long time before I went under, which seemed to annoy the Professor. Finally, I had the feeling I was falling ... then nothing ... several times I had the sensation of being outdoors ... and then ... nothing.

When I came to and briefly opened my eyes, a native nurse was sitting next to the bed, taking my pulse. She then left to fetch the doctor on duty, who clearly wanted to talk to me, for I received two slaps on my cheeks. With difficulty, I opened my eyes again and heard him ask if everything was all right. I mumbled something in response — what, I don't remember — and went back to sleep until another doctor checked on me later that night.

The following day when I awoke, Professor Lesk stood at the foot of my bed, telling the doctors who had assisted him during the operation that I wasn't allowed to eat or drink, and had to keep quiet. Then they left.

The woman in the next bed was crying, because she would be operated on that afternoon and was frightened. She wanted to talk about it, but a conversation was not possible. She was too far away for me to understand her. Just as well, as I really felt too weak and tired. Luckily, I was not in pain.

Four days later, the doctors came back, and I felt daring enough to ask them about the outcome of the operation. Choosing their words carefully, they said it had not gone as well as expected. They had not been able to do everything, as my heart had not been strong enough to cope with a prolonged anaesthetic. Also, probably because of the brusque nature of the miscarriage, there had been more damage than expected. Scar tissue had formed, which needed to be, but wasn't, removed.

Professor Lesk concluded with brevity: "You must first stay in a cool climate to regain your strength, and in six months we shall have another go at it."

It never even entered his mind to ask if that were possible!

My world crashed around me and I sank into such an abyss of despair that nothing would have been more agreeable than to die. I felt, once again, that I was the source of all the misery that had dogged John since my arrival in the East Indies, and I fervently prayed: "Dear God, allow me to die now. I just can't take it any more."

God's answer came in the afternoon, when a vigorous male voice, asking for my whereabouts, woke me from my drugged state.

Two men entered the semi-dark room, stood beside my bed and asked, "How are you doing?" Then I recognized the Captain and the Chief Engineer, who had been the witnesses at our wedding in the Vesuvius Bay.

Confused, yet very happy to see friendly faces, I asked how they knew I was here. The answer came quick and snappy: "From the Captain of the S.S. *Meyer*, who brought you here. We are berthing in Tanjong Perak, and will be sailing for Tobelo tomorrow. We propose that you come with us."

I cried from happiness!

The Captain remained to talk a bit, while the Chief Engineer went looking for the doctor on duty. He returned with the Belgian internist, and my visitors asked if I could undertake the journey the following day.

The doctor understood the reason for wanting to leave, but said this would be impossible. Only five days had passed since the operation, and — he stressed this — it had been a major one. He was willing to talk to the Professor, but he did not hold out much hope.

My visitors then suggested that I travel express to Makassar a week later, where the S.S. *van Eck* would be waiting for me. That would allow me to stay five days longer in the hospital, and then go by ambulance to the ship. This express ship had a doctor on board. Once I was on the *van Eck*, another doctor would take over and make sure that I would arrive at Tobelo in good shape.

The Belgian doctor liked this idea better. My visitors said with assurance: "We'll see you next week in Makassar. You just get better!" And then they left.

Thank God, I had regained my equilibrium sufficiently to hope that everything would work out all right. How, I did not know, but I had the feeling that with assistance from above, a way would be found.

The following day, Dr. Lesk talked to me at length. He explained the situation, and said that a second operation was imperative if I did not want to spend the rest of my life in much pain and as a semi-invalid. The possibility of having another baby would be out of the question for the time being. There was something not quite right with my heart, which was why the first operation had to be cut short. A general anaesthetic would not be used next time, but it would be best to have the operation at the same hospital.

I listened resignedly until he was finished, and then said that I could not possibly stay on Java, and wanted to go home. He agreed to let me leave for Makassar the following week, provided — and he emphasized this — that he got confirmation that there would be a doctor on board.

I was once again in good spirits. Every day I became stronger. One last examination, followed by much advice and my promise to do as prescribed, and then I went by ambulance to Tanjong Perak. The Belgian doctors (husband and wife) accompanied me, and disembarked only after I was settled into the cabin and my care had been entrusted to the ship's doctor.

The ship left late because of bad weather, and the Radio Officer telegraphed the new expected time of arrival in Makassar. The S.S. *van Eck* signaled back they had already left the harbor but would wait for us outside. Arrangements were in progress to bring the patient on board and, they added reassuringly for my benefit, from Ambon onward, a military doctor would look after the patient.

Several hours later, the harbor of Makassar loomed on the horizon, and we could see the *van Eck* lying in wait. A steam-launch came alongside. I was strapped again to a stretcher, and a hoist lowered me to the launch, where many hands guided me to a stable place. The ship's doctor accompanied me, and ten minutes later I was hoisted on board the *van Eck* and warmly welcomed by the Captain and his staff.

The two doctors discussed their patient's case briefly. I thanked the departing doctor for his excellent care, and was then taken to my cabin, where, stressed and tired, I immediately dropped off to sleep.

The following days went reasonably well. Most of the time I lay on a bench in a quiet corner of the upper deck — alone, unless an occasional passenger stopped by for a chat. And every day, I gained in strength and spirits.

Two days before our arrival at Ambon, I learned that John's older brother, Jan, and a newly hired administrator for Buluwaya were on board. My brother-in-law had asked someone to arrange a meeting with me, but the doctor, having been informed by the Captain, withheld his permission.

The day before our arrival at Sanana where the two men would leave the ship and take a *prau* to the Vesuvius Bay, Jan forced an encounter by "accidentally" running into me while I made my way through the corridor to the upper deck. He mumbled an excuse, and said: "Oh, it is you," as if he had not recognized me in the semi-dark corridor or had not known that I was on board.

Seeing him again jolted me. When I first arrived on Java, I had stayed at his home, and he and his wife Koos had done everything to make my stay as pleasant as possible. They had agreed to all my wishes regarding the building of a house on that far away plantation, thus winning my trust. It was a pity that they'd had ulterior motives and that later everything had taken a different course.

Looking at the situation from his point of view, he probably looked on me as the chief villain in the Buluwaya drama; after all, without my coming there, John would have been like putty in his hands and would have remained as "cheap labor". That John, his own brother, would probably have deteriorated both physically and mentally, apparently had not bothered him one bit.

Jan now considered it his duty to accompany me to the bench. He pulled up a chair, and said he wanted to talk, if I could stand it. I felt uneasy, but a combative feeling awoke in me and I attacked: in a long stream of indignant words I threw out everything, and accused him of inhumanity, exploitation, manipulation, and more ...

His eyes bored angrily into mine, but he controlled himself, and merely said that business was business. Nobody had forced John to accept the proposed conditions, so no one could reproach *him* for it. Moreover, he had warned John not to get married (contradicting what he had written in the fateful letter that John had shown me in the Hague), since, during the first few years of reclamation, a wife was only a bother. If John had needed a woman, he said ruthlessly, well, he could have taken a *nyai* like any other *baru* (newcomer) — so on that point, too, I had nothing to complain about.

I seethed with anger! How terribly egoistical was this man to whom we had given our trust. As *coup de grâce* he told me that the new administrator was, luckily, unmarried and was born and raised in the Indies — and, therefore, perhaps not as difficult as newcomers from Holland.

His parting words were: "Meanwhile, your husband has been indicted, and you can bet that we shall win this case. Nobody runs out on me and gets away with it!"

So now I knew, but somehow it didn't seem to touch me much. I felt infinitely relieved that I had been able to express my grievances, and was overjoyed at having decided to return to Tobelo. Especially now, my place was with John, so we could face the difficulties together. I was convinced that we had done the right thing, and that we had friends who would support us every step of the way.

Gratefully, and with a sense of satisfaction, I saw the two men leave ship.

I would learn later that the new Administrator had been employed at a salary of 700 guilders per month (500 more than John got), with two months furlough in Java every two years. Still later, I heard that he had resigned within the year and had returned to Java.

\* \* \* \*

On Ternate I was warmly received by our boss and his amiable wife, who with deep concern asked about the outcome of the operation, and then gave me the latest news: a telegram had come from Java, addressed to John. It would be forwarded with the boat I was traveling on to Weda, where John was checking out a *damar* concession.

It probably was the telegram I had sent to tell him the operation had been a success. He certainly would be surprised to get the telegram and see me at the same time.

In turn, I told them about my experiences, in particular my meeting with the Director of Buluwaya, his lawsuit, and his assurance that he would relentlessly pursue the matter until he had won.

Our boss replied that he had not expected anything else, and that we should remain calm. "Whatever happens, don't agree to anything, respond with care, and leave everything to our lawyer. He is capable and trustworthy. At our request, he will take the case."

I stayed the night with them. Before I dropped off to sleep, I overheard a conversation, in which they praised John for the good work he was doing on Halmahera.

The following day, our boss asked me to come to the office of the Resident at 9 a.m. for a meeting. Mr. Trips told me that the Government had already had an earlier encounter with the company that owned Buluwaya; further, that a Surabayan lawyer of questionable reputation would represent the management (or, rather, its Director), and that he would pull every conceivable trick to win, since he worked on the basis of "no cure, no pay".

"But don't let this upset you," so ended the conversation, "everything will turn out all right, you'll see!" I thanked the gentlemen for their kindness and good advice, and returned to the ship — upset just the same.

Apart from these preoccupations, the journey was delightful. The weather was much better; the sea was calm. The staff spoiled me terribly, and with each passing day I became more energetic.

This time, the ship stopped at Jailolo, the second most important village of Halmahera, where I met the local military administrator, a jovial man, whose wife was English. According to the ship's officers, he could put away an incredible volume of beer without becoming loud.

The couple did not have any children, and he thought he was giving me good advice by saying: "It is better not to start; children are only a great bother here." He did not, of course, realize how insensitive this comment would seem to me.

After Jailolo, we stopped in a small harbor of the Lolodo Islands. How beautiful these islands seemed, scattered in the wide blue ocean. Their white coral beaches, fringed by hundreds of swaying coconut trees, looked like a fairy tale, seen from the sea. ( Much later, I would visit these islands often. That would be *much* later, when World War II had ended, the Dutch East Indies had become Indonesia Raya, and the situation had changed drastically.)

Next, we stopped at Galela, a small place at the foot of the Mamuya volcano near an incredibly beautiful, deep-blue lake. The village was surrounded by *kampungs*, whose very active inhabitants now gathered around the ship to load a large quantity of copra.

On the far side of the lake lived a German missionary couple, hard workers, for whom nothing was ever too much trouble. I learned that the woman made daily trips to the surrounding *kampungs*, by *prau*, to help the sick and provide them with supplies. But the population was mostly Mohammedan, and her good intentions were often seen in a bad light.

It appeared that some people even went so far as to deliberately make those persons who had been helped by her ill again. They even spread the rumor that her medicine contained pork fat — an abomination for Moslems — and that this secondary illness was punishment for having violated Moslem restrictions. In that way, the reputation of this helpful missionary was besmirched, and people turned away from her. So, even in this seeming paradise, malice sprang up — as it did elsewhere in the world.

*Something I shall have to watch out for!*

The ship continued westward along the coast of Halmahera. We would arrive the following morning in Tobelo. After dinner, the Captain dropped in for a friendly chat. I mentioned in passing that I would miss the ship's geniality, because — except for Bok and Latif — the house would be empty, with John being away at Weda.

"Yes," he said, "it would be lonely there until your husband comes back with us on the return trip." Then, his eyes took on an gleeful look, and he proposed that I *not* disembark at Tobelo, but continue to Weda.

"I would love to see your husband's face, when after opening the telegram he discovers that you are on board!" He thought that was a terrific joke, and laughed heartily when he saw the blank look on my face. He quickly added:

"The extension of your journey is a present from the staff of the *van Eck*, in recognition of your having been a good and obedient patient."

I was overwhelmed and wondered whether — after all the kindnesses I had received — I could accept this.

Other members of the staff joined us, and the Chief Engineer said that I should look upon this as a delayed wedding gift. "After all, we as witnesses should be allowed to do something special for you, *Mevrouw*." Touched by their generosity, I thanked each one of them.

At Tobelo, I did disembark briefly to go home. Bok was overjoyed at my return, but moaned when she heard I would continue my journey to fetch the *Tuan*.

Full of pride, she showed me the changes that had been made to the house — and, in truth, it looked much tidier. Everything had been whitewashed, and the ugly boards in the former office had been replaced by a proper wall with two large windows. The yard had, to a large extent, been cleaned by our first yard-boy — a happily grinning frizzy-haired Papua, who carried the fine but sorrowful name of Jeremiah.

At Bok's urging, I stayed overnight. The following morning I would get back on board, but now Bok had to tell me all the news: how the *Tuan* was, how she was, and whether she had been completely cured of the malaria.

Latif dropped in, and I hardly recognized him, so much had he grown. Bok continued, saying that the *Tuan* had ordered a horse and would make Latif the *tukang kuda* — the stable-hand. Also, that somebody had applied for the position of cook ... and on and on she went.

In turn, I told her about my adventures, and how my condition had not permitted me to look for the promised cook. I did not tell her that the operation had not been successful — afraid that I would tempt fate. As long as I did not talk about it, I would not give it any credence, I thought.

*****

The next morning, the journey continued. Two days later we arrived at Weda, where the coastline and the flora were again totally different. Coconut plantations were rare. The jungle, which reached right to the beach, contained trees with flaming red leaves, trees with strangely twisted trunks, and the *pandanus papuanus* — a kind of cactus. I heard the tough leaves were dried, dyed black, red or yellow, and then used to make special kinds of mats, hats, and little boxes — which were held together by fibers taken from wild pineapple plants.

The beaches were not white but grey — sometimes even black. According to the crew, there were many crocodiles, mostly around the mouths of coves. So, a sailor warned, it was not advisable to stroll along the beach.

It was daylight when we dropped anchor. I had not slept very much and was rather nervous: soon I would see John and have to tell him everything. How would he react to all these new problems? I prayed for courage and tact for me; strength, for him. With palpitating heart I watched the motorboat leave for shore, which was quite a distance away.

After an hour, the boat returned. From the bridge I watched with the Captain's binoculars, and saw the boat carried several Europeans. My heart told me that John was among them.

When I wanted to run down the stairs to the main deck, I felt a restraining hand, whose owner said: "Take it easy, Madame, take it easy! It will take at least ten minutes before the boat will be at the gangway."

Impatiently, I shook off his hand, but, realizing belatedly that it was the Chief Engineer, I quickly apologized for my discourteous gesture. The gentle man said understandingly: "We are a bit impatient, what? Take it easy, though. They'll be here soon," and grumbling good-naturedly, he went back into his cabin.

Once on the main deck, I forced myself to be calm. The boat was now so close that I could clearly see the people in it. But they were all strangers. John was definitely not among them, and a cold fear settled on me. Distraught, I withdrew to the other side of the deck, trying to hide my deep disappointment.

The new arrivals disappeared into the dining salon for the traditional breakfast — a sumptuous feast accorded to all visitors.

The motorboat took off again. I asked one of my fellow-passengers how often the boat would go forth and back. He told me there would be ten crossings, if not more. It all depended on the size of the cargo that had to be brought on board.

Each time the motorboat came, it towed three to four cargo-*praus* full with bags of copra or large round *keranjangs* (baskets) with *damar* — all products from the MHM company.

"Would John have something to do with this shipment," I asked myself, "or would he still be in the *damar* forests, unable to return with this boat to Tobelo?"

The thought occurred to me to ask the happily laughing people who were seated at the breakfast table, but I didn't dare, afraid of bad news. I saw the visitors leave with the next boat, and didn't know anymore what to think.

When the ship's whistle sounded the first blast, I knew that the ship would be leaving within 30 minutes.

The Captain descended from the bridge, and asked if I had found it to be a long wait. Worried, I asked if he knew what could have happened to my husband.

With a fatherly tone, he said: "He's very busy on shore. All the copra and *damar* belongs to his company, and he is responsible for its shipment. He will no doubt come with the last motorboat — as befits a good expediter."

He acted nonchalant, but his eyes beamed, and I felt differently now. With pride I looked at the long, distant train, as it came closer.

The second whistle cut through the air, and then I saw two white figures in the approaching motorboat. Moments later, I recognized one: it was John, my very own man! Surprised, I noticed how differently he carried himself — definitely more assured and confident. I had not seen him like that since Holland, and my heart swelled with pride and longing.

I ran toward my cabin, to make sure that I looked my best. The Captain met me there, and asked me to please stay in there. He had given strict orders to the Second Mate to hand John the telegram, but not to say one word about my presence!

With a pounding heart I waited in my cabin, listening intently to every sound coming from outside. Finally, I heard footsteps.

"I'll show you to your cabin myself," I heard the Captain saying. The footsteps stopped in front of my door, and I heard John's voice.

"How did you know for sure that I was returning with this boat?"

"Why do you ask?" asked the Captain.

"Because my name is already on the door."

"Oh, that is in order," came the evasive reply.

The door opened, and cheerfully the Captain called out: "Look inside! *There* is the reason your name is on the door!" and then, after casting a quick look at John's bewildered face, he smilingly walked away.

I stood rooted in my place and stared at the silhouette that filled the doorway. It took John a moment to recover. Finally he blurted out: "Are you back already?" ... and I remembered the odd reply he had given on our wedding day, when asked if he would take me as his wedded wife: "Uh, yes, of course, after all, I have had her so long already ..."

This time, I understood what he meant by that absurd remark, and I threw myself in his arms. Speechlessly we hugged, and looked at each other, and looked again, as if we could not believe that this was real!

Finally, John said: "Uh, and this telegram?" and he fished the crumpled paper out of his pocket. I tried to explain that our "fabulous" cable service did not go farther than Ternate and that, thereafter, it was up to the KPM to deliver the telegram. John didn't understand any of it. But it didn't matter. We were together.

Our mail had been dropped off at Tobelo, so John did not know about the lawsuit yet. I decided not to tell him about it, nor about the unsuccessful operation. During this short journey, I wanted to see him happy. Neither the Captain nor the staff had uttered a word, and, caught up in his own happiness, John did not ask any questions.

❧

**Endnotes**
1. Tobelo was the capital of the District of Tobelo, which included the island of Morotai. The District had 34,000 inhabitants, among which were some 80 Europeans and 400 Chinese. The Chief Civil Servant or HPB had the rank of Gezaghebber. (Source: "Geïllustreerde Encyclopaedia van Nederlandsch-Indië", Leidsche Uitgeverij, 1934)
2. Piet Heyn, a Dutchman who once served as galley-slave of the Spanish, became Vice-Admiral of the VOC (The Dutch East Indies Company) in 1623. His fame derives from having defeated the Spanish at sea three times — the last time in 1628, when he captured the Spanish Silver Flotilla, valued at 12 million guilders. The next year, he was made Admiral of Holland.
3. CBZ: *Centraal Burgelijk Ziekenhuis* — Central Civilian Hospital

# IBU MALUKU

IBU MALUKU

# CHAPTER 13

## A New Posting
### Tobelo, Halmahera, 1921

After two wonderful days at sea, we arrived at Tobelo and said goodbye to the KPM staff — the wonderful people who had done so much for us.

John took me home, and then hurried off to the shed to get the *damar* stored. Later it would be sorted, packaged, and then shipped to lacquer manufacturers in Europe and the United States. But all the copra was destined for Hamburg.

Bok was elated to have us home again, and showed it by serving us an elaborate *rijsttafel*. We quietly savored it — for the moment, all was well with the world. "But tonight," I thought, "the mail will be opened, and what will happen then?"

I had already seen the large envelope with several red seals, postmarked in Surabaya. It *had* to be the letter about the court case, so to delay matters a little, I slid it under a stack of Surabayan newspapers.

That evening, John did not go through the mail as usual, but picked out the letter from his company's Ternate office, which lay on top. At one point he interrupted his reading and said: "I'm so pleased to have you back," and then, seeing I was reading my mail, "How are things at home?"

"Everything is fine so far," I said, "but I am tired and will read the rest tomorrow."

"I'm bushed too," John said. "Let's go to bed."

*Terrific! Another delay.*

In bed, he told me about what had happened during my absence. From our talks on board it had already become clear to me that not everything was rosy in the new job.

He now filled in some of the details. Lack of supervision had resulted in shoddy work and fraudulent practices. Funds destined for *dusun* owners had disappeared into the pockets of MHM supervisors, who used the money to make loans to small plantation owners — demanding the land as collateral. At the slightest pretext, these supervisors had expropriated those lands, claiming default of payment — although the value of the land was far greater than the amount of the original loan.

This had been going on for some time, but the MHM company was blissfully unaware of it, said John. Loans had been given in the past in return for a pledge of products to be delivered later, but never before had land been used as collateral. It would be a difficult problem to solve.

I told John briefly about what I had heard in Ternate: that he would be invited to discuss his findings and plans for reorganization. This pleased him. In this job, he had at least the possibility to discuss his problems with his superiors — something he had not been able to do on Buluwaya.

Content, he fell asleep, while I worried about the inevitable court problem that would present itself the following day. I decided it would be wise to tell him about the unsuccessful operation at the same time, knowing that John could handle two blows in rapid succession far better than if they were spaced apart.

\*\*\*\*

Next morning, when John returned from the sorting shed, the time had arrived. Abruptly I said I wanted to speak about the operation. He looked up surprised. Slowly, as if it were a well-rehearsed lesson, I told him about the operation — putting the brakes on my own feelings. I saw the tension building up in him, but gave him no chance to interrupt.

Then I told him about the express service to Makassar, how they had nursed me on board, how his brother had forced a meeting in spite of the doctor's refusal to let him see me, and what had been discussed between us. John turned white with anger, but I went on to deliver the final blow.

I picked the sealed letter out of the stack of mail, shoved it toward him and said: "Read it yourself. This will be the indictment."

Slowly, John opened the large envelope, and extracted the summons. I watched uneasily as he clenched his teeth and fists in powerless anger.

"That bastard," was all he said before he ran out of the house.

I picked up the papers he had thrown on the table, and read them — though I already knew a good part of it. It did not hit me as hard as when I first heard about it, and I prayed for strength to offer John the support he would need.

Hours later he came back — his shoes sopping wet from walking on the beach. He was drenched with perspiration, and looked exhausted and beaten. I waited for him to start. Finally, he blurted out:

"So everything has been for nothing!"

"What has been for nothing?" I dared ask.

"I don't know," John said, exasperated. "My work is not earning us enough. Our debts will simply escalate, and I will probably lose the court case. And then, this unsuccessful operation ... and probably no children, ever! There is no end to it!" He threw himself across the bed and gave way to his frustration. How terrible it was to see my loved-one in such depth of despair.

When he pulled himself together, he looked at me and asked: "And now what?"

I repeated what I had discussed with Resident Trips, and said that the situation was not hopeless. A good lawyer had been proposed, and we had many friends who would lend their support.

Concerning a second operation: well, I did feel much better, we were still young and had a good doctor. "Let's wait and see. We both have our faith to hang onto, and in this instance we must leave everything to the Almighty," I concluded.

John took comfort in that, and promised to steel himself and wait for what the future might bring. I felt incredibly relieved that all the facts were now out on the table, and resolved to be undaunted, no matter what might happen.

\*\*\*\*

During the following months, life went on normally. Now and then, John let me come with him on *tournée*. Every *tournée* was a delightful experience, but I particularly remember the first one, when we went to Morotai, the largest island north of Halmahera. The company motorboat from Ternate picked us up, and took a local schooner, the *Tarim*, in tow.

To transport forest products from the islands and faraway coastal villages, the company had two large schooners, the *Tarim* and the *Angin Barat* — each with its own *juragan*, or captain, and a crew of six. All were natives of Gorontalo, Celebes, and all were excellent sailors.

The *juragan* of the *Tarim*, Captain Hassan, became an especially good friend of mine. He was well acquainted with the *adat* (customary native laws), the history and the legends of these islands, and was also a born story teller.

The crossing to Tanjong (Cape) Dehegila, the most southern point of Morotai, took five hours. Near this cape was the grave of a saint, and this had become a *keramat*, a holy place. Many childless women went there to receive the blessings from a *Haji*, who looked after the grave. If their faith was strong, Captain Hassan assured me, their desires for a child would be fulfilled. But, much later, I heard it was probably the grave of a Franciscan father, who had come with one of the Spanish ships and was murdered in 1557.

From Cape Dehegila we sailed to the next village, where we would trek into the mountains to pay the annual rent to *dusun*[1] owners and collect more *damar*. We left early in the morning, accompanied by the *Kepala Kampung*, the local MHM supervisor and a clerk from the District Chief, who, after payment had been made, would immediately collect the taxes.

A group of Alfurs[2], accompanied by their wives who carried large pointed baskets on their backs, came with us to collect the *damar*.

In the foothills, where the jungle really started, a group of fifteen *dusun* owners awaited our arrival. There were impressive specimens among them: tall and powerfully built; their heads proudly enveloped by the traditional head cloth; long dark trousers; and over it, a jacket of blue velvet with heavy silver buttons.

These clothes, dating from the Portuguese time, were kept in locked chests and only taken out for *adat* festivities and occasions such as this, when the ancestral *dusun* was to be visited. They were a proud people, descendants from pirates and slave traders who once made the sea unsafe between New Guinea and Celebes.

They greeted us gravely and with great dignity, as each one was formally presented to John and me, by name. Their leader was Masahé bin Kuabang, who would become a good friend of ours and, like Captain Hassan, would turn out to be a gifted story teller.

Slowly we went up the mountain along an ancient jungle path that was only used by hunters and *damar* carriers. The climb was sometimes steep, sometimes only moderately so. If the path was overgrown by bamboo, thorny *rotan*, or itch-causing *daun gatal*, these obstacles would be cut down quickly with a razor-sharp *parang* that every Alfur carried, pressed in the crook of his left arm with the sharp edge facing forward.

The climb continued to a height of 700 meters (2,300 feet) above sea level, where the furthest *dusuns* were located.

Sometimes we stopped to rest and drink the delicious cool water that flowed out of a one meter long, chopped-off stem of a climbing plant. It quenched one's thirst very well.

Large green wood pigeons, called *kum-kums*, cooed high up in the trees. Sometimes we heard the call of a woodcock, the *burung maleo*, whose mate lays eggs in piles of humus, which they scrape together. With each egg laying, the heap gets bigger until it sometimes measures five meters in diameter. We saw several of these *maleo* hills, but had no time to dig for the eggs.

Masahé bin Kuabang, who had taken it upon himself to be my

personal guide, mentioned the names of the plants and the trees as we went on. Some trees, he said, were several hundred years old.

Most of the time it was semi-dark in the forest, but now and then a green light filtered unexpectedly through the panoply where a giant tree, perhaps hit by lightning, had crashed, taking some neighboring trees with it.

Then, the first *damar* tree[3] loomed in front of us, towering high above the others. Its trunk was light in color and, up to a great height, free from branches. Its crown was cone-shaped and majestic. It was truly a king among trees.

The tree carried a number that identified the one person who was allowed to tap it. Attached to its trunk was a little basket, lined with banana leaves, which had collected the now-congealed golden resin that had flowed from a man-made cut in the tree's bark.

The *damar* tapper detached the basket, removed the dry banana leaves, and dropped the resin into the long, pointed basket, carried by one of the women. He then made a fresh cut in the bark, placed a new little basket under it, and moved on to the next tree.

John explained: "The resin will first be stored in a temporary hut, where the tapper lives until all the *damar* has been collected; then it will be carried downhill to the coast and delivered to the local MHM supervisor, who will weigh it, and then ship it to Tobelo for grading. This cycle repeats itself every month."

"The mature tree," he continued, "will reach a height of some 30 metres and deliver 10 kilograms of resin per month. We are not here to watch the harvesting, however, but to take inventory of the *dusuns* that we have leased, to put our mark on the trees, and to pay the owners."

This first *dusun* consisted of 37 trees — an unusually large number, they told me — and after the trees had been counted and marked, we journeyed on to the next cluster.

While the supervisor and the tapper of this lot marked the trees, our companions cleared an area, and we had a picnic: cold rice, neatly packed in bundles of plaited coconut leaves; spiced deer *dendeng* (dried meat); *achar* (pickled vegetables); and spicy *sambal* (ground hot peppers) that made me choke — much to the amusement of the others. From a bamboo container, we drank pure, good tasting water.

The journey continued to the next *dusun*, where I was surprised with a bundle of beautiful orchids that had a wonderful smell. They were olive-grey with red or rust-colored dots, and though I was very pleased to have them for my collection, my main interest, at that moment, lay with the *damar* trees.

I asked how they propagated themselves, but no one seemed to know until one *damar* tapper poked through the underbrush and found some seed cones. Animals had eaten the inner part of most of the cones, leaving an empty shell, but I found one with the seed intact, which I decided to take as a souvenir.

One of the older trees was now carefully incised, but not very deeply. After a few minutes, the first drops of gold-yellow resin started to flow. The beaming owner said it was *mata kuning* (yellow eye) resin — an especially precious kind, which is only used to produce top quality varnishes.

We were on our way to the last *dusun,* when someone ahead of me yelled a warning. Several men vaulted into action, and by the time I arrived, it was all over. A long python had dropped out of a tree onto one of the men, but a comrade had swiftly struck it with his *parang*, before the reptile could wrap itself around its intended victim.

I looked with horror at the snake's decapitated head — its jaws still opening and closing in a vain attempt to bite, its vicious eyes glaring at me. Pieced together, its still writhing, beautifully-marked body, which shimmered in the slanting rays of the sun, was three meters (10 feet) long.

It was getting dark when we came back to the *kampung*, and we therefore decided to stay the night in the house of the Supervisor. Very satisfied, filled to the brim with new plans, but also very tired and having sore feet and calves from all that climbing, I soon fell asleep.

On this first day, I had noticed how well John got along with these people. I was surprised, during payment, when he not only called out the amounts in their own tongue, but also said several complete sentences in that language. His efforts were obviously much appreciated, so I decided to learn the local languages.

Early the next morning, we departed for another post, Kampung Pitu — where, much later, the Americans would construct airfields (the "Pitu-strips") for their aerial assault on the Japanese-held Philippines.

Pitu was a small Moslem community, where a large number of foul-smelling goats was freely walking around, eating everything in sight. Its somewhat surly inhabitants were former natives of Galela, Halmahera, who had settled here years ago to earn their living as *damar* tappers or as fishermen.

In the jungle above Pitu were two *damar dusuns*, and from there we would go on foot to *dusuns* near Sangowo, the next village. As this would require an overnight stay in the jungle, John thought it would be better if I did not go. So, I stayed on board, and sailed to Sangowo — a trip of just three hours.

Sangowo was, at this time, capital of the district. There were more Chinese traders living here than in the previous villages. Most of them had their own shops and were married to Galela women. The local MHM Supervisor, Tiong Ho Seng — a *peranakan* (mixed blood) Chinese — had already left to meet John in the forest, accompanied by the District Head, several village chiefs, and the *dusun* owners.

I was received by his old, almost blind father — the first Chinese I had seen wearing pigtails. He introduced me to his son's second wife — the first one having died during child birth. The three children of the first marriage were now in Ternate with a Chinese family. The second wife had three bright boys of her own — all too young to go to school. The three of them peeked furtively at me, but did not allow themselves to be lured by the sweets that I had brought with me.

Tiong Ho Seng was well-to-do, respected, and perhaps a little feared for his business acumen. He owned a large store and a *gudang*, in which, besides MHM *damar*, he stored other products he traded in: copra, *rotan*, sea shells, and *tripang* — the much sought-after sea cucumber, which can be found abundantly in these oceans.

The old man also showed me his son's well-stocked store, which was lit at night by a buzzing kerosene-lamp. On high racks lay piles of cotton, and boxes full of colorful *sarongs*. There were also staples: rice (normally sold per *kati*[4], but here dispensed per empty milk can and not weighed); coarse, grayish salt (packed in damp, seeping gunny sacks); bars of blue marbled or light yellow laundry soap; little bottles of good-for-whatever-ails-you *kayu putih* (eucalyptus) oil from the island of Buru; the equally indispensable "Tiger Balm" ointment; tobacco and cigarettes; and, in glass jars, all kinds of colorful, wrapped candies.

From steel hooks attached to the ceiling hung all kinds of goodies, such as thick slices of deer *dendeng* (spiced, dried meat), dried salted fish, and dried *tripang*. There was also agar-agar (a gelatin-like product from certain seaweeds), rope of all kinds and sizes, fish hooks, fishing lines, oil lamps, and stable lanterns. Whatever one needed, one could get in this store.

Sangowo had a small *pasanggrahan*, the old man said, where I could stay the night. So I decided to check it out, as it would be more comfortable than sleeping on board. The bed wasn't very good, though, and I was glad I had brought my own camp cot and *kelambu*. There was a bathroom, but the *gayung* leaked badly and the water in the cistern was not too fresh. So, with permission of the old father, I bathed in Tiong Ho Seng's home, which was nearby.

The first night in the *pasanggrahan* was full of unfamiliar sounds, so I did not get much sleep. First I listened to a choir of dogs — real moon barkers; then to a lively group of men, who had fished by torch-light and were noisily unloading their catch; and finally, to buzzing mosquitos *inside* the mosquito net, whose extermination required much persistence on my part.

At five o'clock I gave up trying to sleep, and looked out. The panorama from my window was wonderful. The sea was only a stone's throw away and it glistened like grey velvet in this early morning haze. The sun had not yet come up, but the horizon already displayed a promising strip of light.

Soon after, the sun peeked above the horizon, dimly at first, then more intensely, becoming bigger and bigger, as it painted the entire sky in pastel colors of rose, green, yellow, nacre, and gold. Then it rose in all its glory from the simmering sea, setting the whole panorama aglow. It happened so fast that a painter would not have had the time to record it on his canvas. It was so beautiful, intense, and majestic, that words fail me.

Then the *kampung* sprang to life. Standing in the minuscule front gallery of the *pasanggrahan,* I saw the sleepy inhabitants getting out of their houses, one by one. No one spoke as they walked into the sea — each seemingly having a favorite spot — and lowered themselves into the cool water. The sea was soon covered with silent, unmoving, black heads. It looked like a very solemn ritual.

Just as suddenly, everyone moved. Zealous fingers "brushed" the teeth, and with a draft of sea water — which was spit out in a graceful squirt — the mouth purification ceremony came to an end. Then, the black figures rose from the gold-dusted water — the youngsters, stark naked, glistening statues of black ebony; the elders, wrapped in their body-clinging sleeping *kaïns*[5] — and all went to the wells to douse themselves with buckets full of water. Soon after, the *kampung* was alive with neatly-dressed people.

In the open kitchens the fires flamed under the cooking pots, in which they prepared bananas or *papeda* (sago porridge). From some houses came the aroma of coffee. Now and then, a woman yelled to chase away a dog that had strayed into the kitchen, or to hurry the youngsters who had to be in school at seven o'clock.

Then, peace returned: the kids had gone to school to learn a new song, and the men had left to hunt in the forest — alone, or accompanied by a pack of lean hunting dogs. All I could hear was the swishing of the *sapu lidi*, as the women swept their compounds. All was well.

# IBU MALUKU

A young girl came out of the Supervisor's dwelling with coffee and a bowl full of golden yellow bananas for me. After this exquisite breakfast, I bathed, got dressed, and went out to reconnoiter the village. I wandered along narrow paths into the *kampung* gardens, where the villagers cultivated primarily *ketella pohon* or cassava — the source of tapioca.

A cornfield drew my attention, because it was covered with white spots. A closer look revealed a multitude of white cockatoos that were devouring the young corn. I felt sorry for the owner. All his work going down the drain. Evidently I was not alone in having to learn from my mistakes. He would certainly not grow corn a second time.

In the afternoon, the men returned from the *dusuns*, and John told me that all was well. Tiong Ho Seng was running a tight ship!

Before daylight the next morning, we left by motorboat for other places along the coast, and at eleven arrived at Kampung Myra, a completely Christian community.

Many people had already gathered to be vaccinated against the black pox that had plagued them several times. The vaccinators, who had accompanied us, went to work immediately.

I watched the open air treatment with great interest. Among the patients were children of all ages with horribly ulcerated wounds on their faces, arms and legs. This was the notorious framboesia or yaws I had first seen on Buluwaya: a contagious disease resembling syphilis, and characterized by an eruption of the skin into a raspberry-like outgrowth. The children received injections of neo-salvarsan — at that time, the only available means to combat that disease.

I also saw many pregnant women. I would have liked to talk to them, but only a few understood the Malay I spoke, and the language they spoke I did not understand at all. Again, I saw the need for learning the local languages and customs of the people among whom we now lived. The *Mantri* — the supervisor of the vaccinators whom I knew from Tobelo — told me there were many cases of tuberculosis and, naturally, malaria.

The *tournée* continued day after day, until we reached the north-coast of Morotai. Here, the wide open ocean pounded the rocky coast of the island with white, frothy waves, which the natives called *air putih* (white water). A fantastic, but also a frightening spectacle.

We said goodbye to the *dusun* owners of *kampungs* Pangeo and Bido, who had received their rent for five years in resounding silver *ringgits* (2-1/2 guilder coins). I already knew that none of it would be spent. Every piece would be kept in a well-locked chest or in a bamboo tube.

Somewhere in the garden or the forest, the elder of the family would bury this treasure, and it would only be retrieved to pay for the dowry — the *mas kawin*, or wedding gold — for the sons of the family.

The weather had changed: the sea was rough with white crests. Sometimes vicious rain squalls lashed the motorboat, which sailed on imperturbably — one moment disappearing in a deep, seething trough, and the next moment riding high on top of a frothy wave. I was not afraid. I found it fascinating. Still, we were all glad when we finally entered the harbor of Wewemo. Here we could dry out and wait for better weather.

In the afternoon, the sky cleared, and the wind abated. We were, however, a day late in our schedule, so John decided to leave the schooner in port, and tow it back at a later date.

The motorboat dropped us off at Tobelo very early in the morning of the following day, and left for Ternate several hours later — taking with it the reports that had been written on the high seas.

It was good to be home again!

Doctor Slamat, who had dropped some of his reserve and had become a good friend, came over to ask with interest about our adventures in Morotai. He also wanted to know how I was. I thought the journey had done me much good, but I felt duty-bound to tell him that the pains in my back and loins were sometimes bad. It was probably due to fatigue, I suggested.

He examined me, and asked emphatically when the second operation was supposed to take place. The time was almost on us, but I told him that I had decided to wait. Despite the good income that John now had, we could not afford the cost of making a second journey so soon. The doctor gave me an understanding nod: he would contact Surabaya, he said.

Deep in my heart, however, I was afraid. I did not like the decision I had just made, knowing full well that postponing the operation could have dire consequences.

### Endnotes
[1] *Dusun* is a high-Javanese word for village, but here it refers to a "village" of *damar* trees that belongs to one person. These *dusuns* are handed down from father to son.
[2] The *Alfurs* (or *Alfuru*) is an ethnic group that can be found primarily in the Moluccas and in the Timor Sea region. They have a

darker skin color than the Malayans, and have frizzy or wavy hair.
3. The Latin name is *agathis loranthifolia*.
4. A *kati* is a unit of weight equal to .617 kilogram that is widely used in the East Indies and elsewhere.
5. A *kaïn* is a piece of cloth (usually with a pattern), 2½ by 1 meter. A *sarong* is a *kaïn*, the short sides of which have been joined.

# IBU MALUKU

# CHAPTER 14

### Visions and Incisions
*Tobelo, Halmahera, 1921*

The next KPM boat brought a letter from our lawyer with news about the pending lawsuit. The "other party" had not budged: they demanded reimbursement of John's boat fare, and payment of damages the company had suffered because of his sudden departure. If John did not comply within the time specified, they would prosecute!

In an enclosed note, the General Agent suggested that John come to Ternate to report on his last *tournée*, and also to talk about how to respond to the lawyer's letter.

John reacted with a predictable lamentation: "You'll see, I'm going to lose this case, and then what?" But I had learned not to contradict him. I knew the somber mood would go away; the problem would not. We had no choice but to come to grips with it. Some anxious days and sleepless nights followed. It took a great effort on my part to look cheerful, and the resultant stress only served to magnify the pains in my back and loins.

When the "Papua ship" came again, I accompanied John to the harbor, and watched as he busied himself with the *damar* shipping arrangements. Then it was time to go: an embrace, some endearing and admonishing words that women say to their departing husbands, and John boarded the ship.

I was grateful when the boat finally left the bay. Now I could allow my feelings to surface, and they stayed with me all night long. But then came a radiant new day and the house and garden demanded my full attention.

Two days later John returned from Ternate with the *kapal putih*[1]. It was the *"Stella"*, whose arrival at Passi Ipa (in what now seemed ages ago) had precipitated our deliverance from Buluwaya. Its appearance at this stressful time seemed like a good omen.

John brought a letter from our lawyer, who had gone on the offensive by serving a counterclaim. I did not quite understand why, but I trusted the counselor knew what he was doing. His letter gave me confidence that all would be well.

And a few months later, it was over!

The counterclaim had quashed the demand for repayment of the boat fare, but the cost of the tropical outfit[2] had to be repaid! But the really good news was that the one hundred guilders the company had been subtracting from John's monthly salary had accumulated to a tidy sum. It would pay for the tropical outfit *and* our lawyer's fee!

Thank God, the nightmare was over — but the whole affair had created much ill-feeling with John's family in Holland, who accused us of disloyalty. I myself did not mind that so much — I was just so grateful to have it over with — but John suffered from guilt for years and, I believe, never quite managed to get over it.

* * * *

A year had passed since my first operation. John and I hardly ever talked about it, but it always hung over us like a dark cloud. Only Dr. Slamat knew that the pains were getting worse, and he kept pressuring me to have that second operation. But I wanted to wait until all the debts we had accumulated had been paid off, so John would feel free again.

We had lived frugally, and I was delighted when John showed me the company's accounting books, which revealed that my journey to and from Java had been paid in full! Elated, John said: "Another year, and we shall have paid for the operation, and then, well, then ... " His voice trailed off. He just looked at me, silently, and then walked quietly to his office.

The days passed. John went on *tournée* regularly, and in the beginning I often accompanied him. For me it was an enjoyable opportunity to get to know the people of the land and to learn something about their language and culture. But eventually my presence began to bother John.

The accommodation on the ship was primitive, and having a woman on board did not make things easier. The boat was also used to transport the collected *damar*, and every bit of space was precious. So I decided to stay home, except when John went on a short trip.

There was another reason for staying home. The house we lived in belonged to John's company, and it was expected of us that we provide bed and breakfast for any MHM employee who, in the line of duty, happened to stop over in Tobelo. Somebody had to be home to receive such unexpected guests!

To fill the day, I wanted to do some gardening, but John reminded me that company rules forbade me to "lower the standing of the European woman" by doing manual work myself. We had, after all, a *kebon* to do the gardening for us. But it was not in my nature to do nothing, so I chose to ignore the company's dictates and to cultivate at least a part of the garden myself. Several hours a week, I also received instruction from a native *guru* in the local language and the *adat* (the customary law) of the various sections of the community.

John had bought a horse and a buggy, with which we sometimes toured the beautiful countryside. And on days when he was away, I found diversion in the circulating book- and-magazine box from a reading club. The Surabaya Trade Journal kept us up-to-date on world events, and I also found pleasure in reading the poems of Guido Gezelle[3] that Mama occasionally sent me from Europe.

We were getting used to life in the tropics, and were no longer bothered by earthquakes or the ongoing struggle against ants and humidity. To have some relief from the daily routine, we also spent enjoyable hours with our neighbors on a nearby coconut plantation. That's where the cows were that provided us with milk. Eventually we got to know and to like the other Europeans living nearby.

Apart from the buggy-rides and the work in my increasingly beautiful garden, I often sat in the inner gallery reading and writing, as I had a busy correspondence with Europe. One day, as I was reading at my usual spot in the inner hall, it started to get dark, so I went to light the Coleman petrol lamp in the adjacent dining room. Suddenly, I noticed somebody standing near the door leading to the dining room. My heart skipped a beat, and a chill went down my spine.

My common sense told me there could not be anyone else in the house, yet I clearly saw a person standing there who looked like a Franciscan monk. His slightly bowed head was covered by a hood that cast a dark shadow over his face.

"Who are you?" I asked in trepidation.

There was no answer.

I slid past him into the dining room and lit the lamp. When I returned to my reading, the monk had vanished.

From that time on, whenever I was reading in semi-darkness, I saw the monk standing in the same place. He never moved. I did not know any Franciscan monks, and nervously asked myself what was the meaning of his presence.

His hands were always hidden inside the large sleeves of his brown, homespun frock that was tied with a cord around his waist. His frock reached down to just above the floor, leaving his bare feet and prominent toes exposed. It was so spooky that I rearranged the furniture so I would not have to look at the door and *him* standing next to it.

When John returned from *tournée*, his first comment was: "Yech! Everything is changed here, and I can't say that I like it."

"Why not leave it that way," I answered. "It is much more comfortable for me when I am reading, and the light is better that way too."

I did not dare give the real reason, as John definitely did not believe in ghosts. Furthermore, what *could* I say except that I saw a robed, male figure that was eerily silent.

I finally stopped going through that dining room door in the evening, preferring to make a detour. Of course John noticed this.

"Why are you always walking through the veranda," he asked, leaving me no choice but to explain myself.

"I see a Franciscan monk standing there," I said lamely, giving him a full description of what I was seeing.

"What kind of nonsense is that, Jeanne?" he countered.

"Well, that's what I see."

"But there is nobody there!"

I shrugged. What could I say? A few evenings later, the same dialogue took place, and this time John got really upset.

"I'll show you there is nothing there," he said angrily. He then took his revolver out of a drawer and shot a hole in the *gaba-gaba* wall.

"See?" he shouted triumphantly. "Absolutely nothing!"

I shrugged. The bullet had passed freely through the apparition, and the monk was still standing there, undisturbed!

\* \* \* \*

During our courting days, John had always come with me to church in Eindhoven, so I naturally assumed that he was also Catholic. However, after we were married, I learned he had been brought up as a Protestant, but had never practiced his faith. At Buluwaya, there was no opportunity to worship, so the subject of religion never came up. But in Tobelo, the situation was quite different.

When we arrived in Tobelo — with the misery of Buluwaya and my miscarriage still fresh in our minds — I was deeply touched to hear the "national anthem" of the Province of Limburg: "*Waar in ons groen eikenhout, de nachtegaal zingt* — Where in our green oak woods, the nightingale sings".

It had been played by a bamboo-flute orchestra as we approached the quay in the motorboat that ferried us from our ship. I was so moved by the music that, as soon as we were on the quay, I went up to the Dutch conductor. He introduced himself as Mr. de Neef, but did not say what he did in Tobelo.

When I thanked him and said how much hearing the Limburger

anthem had meant to me, his face froze into a mask. He straightened up like a cobra that is ready to strike, and said: "Madame, you are mistaken. This is not the Limburger anthem, but the anthem of Halmahera."

"That is not possible," I said, "the words may be in Malay, but the tune is definitely from "Where in our green oak woods ... "

"Absolutely not," he insisted, "it is the national anthem of this country."

"Well, thanks anyway," I said dejectedly and left.

Shortly after, I learned that Mr. de Neef was the head of the Protestant mission, and I then realized that I had given myself away.

Knowing that I had come from the mostly Catholic Province of Limburg, the man had perceived me immediately as a threat. I was the first Catholic European to arrive at Tobelo. Horror of horrors, Rome had invaded the country! I had sensed his animosity, and it had dampened the elation I had felt upon our arrival.

I would also learn that, many years before our arrival, the Government had decreed the Moluccas beyond Ambon to be Protestant territory, strictly off limits to the Catholic Mission. However, since the law did entitle every Netherlander to spiritual guidance, a priest was permitted to enter the territory, but only once a year. (Later, it was changed to *twice* a year.) But he was *not* allowed to administer to the Catholics among the native soldiers and the Chinese; only to Dutch citizens, in accordance with the law[4].

This sharp division between Protestants and Catholics on Tobelo may have been a factor in John ultimately embracing the Catholic faith. Strangely enough, as we would find out many years later, the van Diejen family was originally Catholic. When they settled in Rotterdam, they seemingly became Protestant out of a desire to blend in with the largely Protestant population in that city.

One day we received news from Ambon that we could expect a visit from a priest, who turned out to be Father Neyens, the man who had married us. We were eagerly looking forward to his stay, as we had been on *tournée* when he had made the rounds the previous year.

John met Father Neyens at the pier, and when the priest asked about my well-being, John said brusquely: "She is going mad. She is seeing things." And he then filled in the details.

"Don't take it that way," said Father Neyens soothingly, "I'll have a talk with her."

He did, and I told him about the apparition. He could not very well tell me that I was lying; there was no reason for him to think that I would. But he did say that a vivid imagination could be playing a role here, causing the apparition to take on an increasingly clear form.

"Whatever it is," I said, "I do see it, and I don't like it. Is there anything you can do?"

Father Neyens lapsed into a pensive mood, wondering what to say next. Then, he had an idea.

"Did you have the house blessed before you moved in?"

"No. That's what we normally would have done, of course, but since you come here only once a year, it has not happened."

"Alright," he said, "that's what we are going to do! Perhaps the idea of there being a ghost will disappear." He obviously believed that the apparition was a product of my imagination.

He got a small vessel with holy water and a whisk, and asked John and me to go with him through all the rooms.

The house had an open veranda all around. Each room in the house had a door that led to the veranda, and from there to the garden. Father Neyens started on the front left of the house. From the veranda he entered the first room (with John and me following), he blessed it, then came out again. He then worked his way through all the rooms in clockwise fashion.

When he came to the last room, he asked us to stay on the veranda and say the Lord's Prayer. He entered the room alone, blessed it, and from there walked to the door leading to the inner hall. There he stopped abruptly.

We watched him from the veranda, and thought he was behaving rather strangely. His face turned red and the muscles and veins in his neck swelled.

"Keep praying, keep praying," he urged in an apprehensive voice.

After what seemed like an eternity, he took a deep breath, and said:

"Thank God. It's over!" He then entered the inner hall, and motioned us to follow him.

"Were you unwell just now?" John asked.

"I don't know," said Father Neyens, "I just could not pass over that threshold. Something prevented me from entering."

We lapsed into a silence, each one trying to find a solution to this mystery.

"Perhaps it was a lost soul," said Father Neyens finally. "Perhaps he promised to do something he had not been able to do and was, therefore, drawn to this place. I don't know."

None of us could — and never would — find a satisfying explanation for what had happened. But Father Neyens' blessing did have a lasting benefit: my fear was gone, and I never saw the Franciscan monk again.

## IBU MALUKU

Later, I heard from the Tobelorese people that a foreigner had been murdered on the premises. The story may well have been true, because when we deepened our well, we found a skull that may have belonged to a Spanish or Portuguese monk.

\*\*\*\*

With the exorcism behind us, the three of us sat down and talked for hours. I myself longed to see Father Neyens alone to talk about my own difficulties.

The biggest one: had I done right in postponing this very necessary operation for purely financial reasons? Doctor Slamat had not relented: he had pressed me harder than ever and said he wanted to speak to John to let him know that the pains were getting worse — something I had kept from him. But my conscience had started to bother me.

A few days later, our house became the gathering place for the faithful: a few Chinese girls, who had just returned from the Ursuline boarding school in Batavia; a hunter from a plantation with his wife and children — two of whom still needed to be baptized; and a few Catholic members of the constabulary of Menado. Whereas the law prohibited Father Neyens from visiting non-Dutch Catholics in their homes, he could receive them without any problem in ours!

The constant coming and going of these people who wanted to speak with Father Neyens prevented us from having a private conversation with him. It was only during his last evening in Tobelo that we finally got the chance to take a walk together. John had to mail some letters, so for the moment I was alone with Father Neyens.

We stood on the deserted pier and looked across the moonlit sea. There was not a soul around. Now was my chance. I inhaled deeply, and in one breath told him what had happened.

Calmly, he let me finish. Then, he made it quite clear that it was my obligation to act.

He affirmed for me the belief that I could not remain silent any longer. I would have to tell John about the pains, and insist on having the operation soon.

The next day, the ship that would take Father Neyens to Manokwari arrived. When it returned, Dr. Slamat would send a message to the doctors in Surabaya.

But nature decided otherwise: several days later, I had a sticky menstrual discharge that would not stop, and the pains in my back, stomach and loins became so severe that I could not hide them any longer.

Dr. Slamat arrived hurriedly, checked me over, and said resolutely that the operation could no longer be postponed. I would have to be admitted quickly! He had heard that a surgeon had been stationed on Ambon for the first time, so he immediately sent a request for assistance to Ternate, in the hope that there might be a Government ship that could take me immediately to Ambon.

Two days passed, and my condition became alarming. Toward the evening, a Government ship arrived with Resident Trips on board. It was one of the large "white boats" that just happened to be in Ternate when the call for assistance came.

At ten o'clock that night, I was brought on board, and within minutes we were *en route* to Ambon. The journey took three agonizing days. The pain was excruciating.

It was evening when the ship dropped anchor. Shortly after, an ambulance raced me to the military hospital, where, much to my surprise and reassurance, I met the Major Doctor with whom I had made the journey from Makassar to Ambon. Thank God! At least there was someone here who knew about my condition!

He introduced me to the new military surgeon, Dr. Rotter, an Austrian, just arrived, who examined me right away.

Afterwards the doctors gravely discussed my first operation, about which they had been informed by wire from Surabaya. One thing was certain: they would not be able to operate under narcosis, because of my weak heart. This did not bother me. I quickly agreed to local anesthesia and urged them to get going. The doctors went about making the necessary arrangements, and for a short time, I was left alone.

Unexpectedly, a strutting military man entered the room, who intoned that he was the Sergeant-Major Administrator. He laboriously recorded my personal particulars, and then handed me a bill for eight days in the hospital. Since I was non-military and just a civilian, I would have to pay beforehand. I would also to have to pay in advance for my funeral!

At first, I did not understand what he meant, but then he snapped that this was obligatory, and that I would get a refund if I survived the operation. When I asked him to take the money out of my suitcase, he rebuked me for having violated hospital regulations: all valuables should have been deposited at the registration desk upon arrival.

Upset, I watched as he took my purse out of the suitcase, counted its contents, and wrote out a chit for the total amount, a receipt for the eight-day stay, and one for the funeral expenses — all of which he put on the table beside my bed. Warning me that I would have to pay again if I stayed more than eight days, he departed brusquely without another word.

Still upset, I concluded that I wasn't expected to live. I did not object, really.

Unbeknownst to me, I had been given a sedative, for I was drowsy when Dr. Rotter came for me. He asked if I were afraid. I shook my head, and said: "Nor do I have any worries, Doctor, for everything has already been paid for, even my funeral!"

He looked at me dumbfounded, and — lapsing into his native tongue — he said: "*Was sagen Sie? Bestattung? Leben sollen Sie, das verbürge ich Ihnen!*" ("What are you saying? Funeral? You will live. I assure you!")

In answer, I pointed to the receipt on the table. He looked at it, asked angrily what kind of tomfoolery this was, and summoned the Doctor-Major.

This one looked at the receipt, and coolly said: "Well, this is correct, and in accordance with an old regulation. The patient is neither a military person, nor the wife of a military person, in which case the regulation applies."

The surgeon escorted the Doctor-Major out of the room, and a heated exchange followed in the corridor that petered out as they moved out of earshot.

Shortly after, two orderlies carried me on a stretcher to the primitive operating room, where three doctors were already waiting. They placed me on the operating table and strapped me in. One doctor asked if I wanted a curtain, but I refused. I was after all a nurse, and their actions would not scare me.

They gave me a series of injections around the old scar, and then stood aside, waiting for the anaesthetic to take effect.

Dr. Rotter, very calm now, asked if I could remember the particulars of the first operation. I said I did, and in a flat voice summarized what I remembered — knowing full well that it was simply a maneuver to divert my attention.

The operation started with the removal of the scar tissue. I could feel the knife cut into my flesh, but felt no pain. One doctor monitored my heart and pulse. All appeared to go well.

The curt, well-known commands were followed by the requested instrument being slapped into the surgeon's open hand. The abdominal cavity was now open, but getting to this stage had taken longer than expected.

Dr. Rotter continued, and then stopped and cursed. It sounded like "*donnerwetter*". I started to feel pain, and said so to the assisting doctor closest to me.

The doctors were now getting anxious. The local anaesthetic was beginning to wear off ... and within minutes I was begging for a general anesthetic, though it could very well affect my heart.

The doctors urgently discussed the matter. Something had to be done, but, for a general anesthetic they needed my husband's permission, and he was beyond reach.

I shouted, then screamed that I would take full responsibility for whatever they had to do to stop these horrible pains! The Austrian was livid; he was obviously not used to these primitive conditions.

A document was hastily drawn up, stating I demanded a general anesthetic and would take full responsibility for the consequences. My right arm was unstrapped. I signed with difficulty and then begged them to hurry up!

A cap of ether was put over my nose. I breathed in deeply, doing my best to slip away quickly. Then came the freeing fall and I lost consciousness.

When I came to, I was in heaven. A wonderful golden light surrounded me and I heard music. Then everything turned black again. Later, my mind became clearer. That wonderful light was still there, and I felt as if I were floating on air. I heard a voice calling me. I returned from that distant radiance, and answered sluggishly. Everything around me became quiet again, and I returned to my heavenly vision. Then I realized that the soothing golden light had been the morning sun, and I uttered a sigh of disappointment.

A nurse bent over me and asked something in a foreign tongue. Then she disappeared to fetch the doctor. He came, took my pulse, inspected the *gurita* — a long strip of wide cloth — that was tightly wrapped around my stomach, and asked if everything was all right.

I mumbled "yes" and "thirsty", and felt someone wetting my lips. That was all, and I dozed off again.

When I woke up, my head was completely clear. The nurse, an Ambonese, told me in well-articulated Malay that the operation had gone well, and that I should rest. Later, Dr. Rotter came to confirm that all was well and that I could relax. He ordered rest and then more rest. That, I got.

It wasn't until the fourth day that I had a visitor: a Dutch lady, married to a prominent Ambonese, named Kayadue. I had met her on board during my first journey from Surabaya to Ambon, and was glad to see a familiar face. It turned out she knew Dr. Rotter quite well, as he was a frequent guest at the Kayadue home. She assured me that he was a very capable surgeon — one in whom I could put my trust.

On the fifth day, Dr. Rotter dropped in for a longer chat. He said the sudden, intense pain had been caused by an inflamed appendix, which he had been able to remove before it could burst.

Then, I screwed up enough courage to ask him that most urgent question: "Doctor, can I now have children?"

Surprised, no, flustered, he looked at me as I continued: "Yes, Doctor, that was my only reason for wanting this operation, even under a general anaesthetic. Without children, life has little value for me."

From the expression on his face I could tell that he did not want to answer — or at least not right away. Perhaps he couldn't. Panic-stricken, I asked for an honest answer. I desperately wanted to know, now, and he could see I was getting more and more upset.

Brusquely, he said: "No! You will never be able to have another child. I have had to remove both ovaries."

I turned away from him, and asked why he had let me live. No matter what he said, I could not be consoled. I wanted to die. Why had he not let me slip away?

Dr. Rotter called the nurse, and a moment later I received a sedative. It helped me to endure, but inwardly, I felt dead.

\*\*\*\*

On the eighth day after the operation, the Sergeant-Major showed up again to present me with another invoice: I had to pay for the next eight consecutive days. Irritated, I told him to subtract the amount from the prepaid funeral expenses. I had not died, after all.

That was wrong, of course! The funeral money had to remain intact and would be reimbursed in full when I left the hospital. He now needed my written permission to subtract "hospital care" from the amount that I had given him in safekeeping. In a stilted, stern, yet self-conscious manner, he explained everything, and after I had signed, he saluted stylishly and marched away.

I suddenly saw the humor in this silly situation: because of a regulation that was several centuries old, the administration forced a desperately-ill person to pay for funeral expenses *before* an operation could be performed!

I burst out laughing, and although it painfully tore at my sutures, it immediately lifted me out of that horrible depression. I did not want to die anymore, and if I had to, it should definitely not be here! For the first time since I had heard the bad news, I felt liberated: I was still young, and wanted to live, live, and show that life could be beautiful — even without children. What on earth had been the matter with me? Had I momentarily lost my mind?

The nurse found me with a high temperature, and called Dr. Rotter. When he asked what had happened, I said I wanted to leave the hospital as soon as possible, and asked when this could come about. Surprised at the sudden change, he explained that my condition had been critical.

"You waited too long to have this second operation, and it is a miracle that it went as well as it did.

"You will recover completely," he assured me, "and you can lead a normal life with your husband. Only ... as I have told you ... having a child is not possible, but there are so many childless marriages that are nevertheless happy. And you could, after all, always adopt a child."

I could leave the hospital in a week, he said, but he wanted to keep me under observation for a while after that. When I protested, and tried to press for passage on the next boat, he said resolutely: "Out of the question! We will not let you go this time!" — being fully aware of what had transpired after the first operation in Surabaya.

Later, Mrs. Kayadue proposed that I stay with her after leaving the hospital. "My husband and I would be very pleased to have you," she said, "and have already prepared the guest room. We don't have any children, so it will be peaceful and quiet."

I accepted gratefully. When I left the hospital, the Sergeant-Major returned the balance of my deposited funds, and asked me to give back the receipt for funeral expenses. I refused. I looked upon it as a talisman. As someone had joked: "He who prepays his funeral and survives the operation, will surely live until a ripe old age!" I certainly hoped so![6]

Thanks to the excellent care from Mr. and Mrs. Kayadue, I healed quickly, and had an exceptionally pleasant time on Ambon. I met many people, and learned much from my Ambonese host — a teacher, who was deeply involved in politics — about the people and customs of the Moluccas.

During the month I stayed with these warm and hospitable people, I came to understand that, whereas their marriage had been harmonious while they lived on Java, there were storm clouds gathering. On Ambon, they were in the clutches of his family, and that did not augur well for their long-term relationship.

More than 25 years later, on board a ship bound for the Netherlands, I would unexpectedly meet Mrs. Kayadue again — except that she was no longer Mrs. Kayadue, but Mrs. Rotter. She had married my Austrian surgeon!

\*\*\*\*

Just before "boat day", I underwent a thorough checkup, and left the hospital with a clean bill of health. The Kayadues and a large crowd of well-wishers brought me to the ship and wished me *"Bon Voyage"*, *"Au Revoir"* and *"Amato Ambon."*

My homecoming, ten days later, was quite a celebration. John was overjoyed to have me back, safe and in good health. At my request, it was Dr. Slamat who then gave him the results of the operation.

John said nothing mattered, now that I was cured. We should be thankful for that. The rest, we would deal with later.

Inwardly, however, although he never uttered one word to me, John would always carry a deep hurt at not having any children. So did I, and it would take many years before I could be persuaded to visit a maternity ward again.

To forget the situation, I buried myself into whatever project came my way. And I insisted on the purchase of riding horses.

I rode mine in the morning and in the afternoon, and if John was absent, the *kebon* (gardener) would ride with me to exercise John's horse also.

Whenever I could, I participated in grueling *tournées*. Indefatigable, I planned and executed so many jobs that John urged me to slow down. At times he flatly refused to let me join him on his trips.

During this period, I fear, I turned into a very tough woman.

\* \* \* \*

Life went on. There was always some distraction. One day, it was oppressively hot and sultry. There was a feeling of calamity in the air, and the animals sensed it too. They were definitely getting restless, and the chickens[5] vied with each other to find a hiding place under the bushes. It became strangely silent.

I was walking on the narrow beach road, trying to cool down. An old fisherman came over and said something about the sea in an urgent tone of voice. I did not fully understand him, but noticed that the water had receded from the beach and that in the distance, above the sea, hung a strange, threatening, haze. The old man, who had walked on, turned around, and shouted a second warning. From the little houses close to the beach, as if they had heard the old man, burst forth swarms of people, who ran uphill, taking with them whatever they could carry. Although not sure why, I started to run myself, and, out of breath, reached the higher road — some seven meters above the beach.

Then the earth moved — or jumped, rather — and there followed a series of long and heavy after-shocks. From behind came a terrifying roar. I turned and saw a high tidal wave crash on the beach, dragging many collapsing houses with it as it sunk back into the ocean. Stunned by my narrow escape, I walked home.

When I arrived, I found our house like a dog sitting on its behind. The rear veranda and the provisions room had caved in; the front facade inclined steeply backward, but was undamaged. The cabinet containing our provisions struck grotesquely through the rear part of the roof. The other furniture was destroyed.

Bok and the other servants, totally disoriented, were looking at the wreckage. When she saw me, Bok started to cry. It was indeed a sorry sight. At the same time, the house looked so silly that I could not help but laugh. Then I gave instructions to cut long pieces of bamboo, to support the facade, and prevent it from collapsing any further.

John was dumbfounded when he came home from *tournée* the following night. The moon was not out yet so it was pitch dark. As he entered, he tripped over the bamboo struts that propped up the sagging house and he uttered some choice words, which woke me up.

By the light of a hastily lit stable-lantern, he inspected the mess and could see nothing funny in it. The next day, however, seeing the grotesque shape of the house, he could not help but laugh himself.

Elsewhere the quake and tidal wave had caused great damage, but, luckily, no lives had been lost. And so we chalked up another experience!

Though I was still only 26, this year I had survived a lawsuit, an operation, a tidal wave and an earthquake. What on earth could the future hold for me?

We moved temporarily to a new, very small house that Captain Hassan (the captain of the *Tarim*, the company schooner) had built for himself. We asked and received permission from the MHM Company to build a new house. The Ternate Government authorized me to design the house, gather material, and hire a construction crew. John, who had a heavy work load of his own, was pleased he could leave it all to me.

I enjoyed the work, and toiled from early morn 'til late at night. Within ten months, our new house was ready.

It was built in the classical East Indies style: a large front veranda; a wide corridor, with a large room on either side; behind, a large bedroom; and all of it encircled by a wide gallery. The adjoining buildings contained a roomy bathroom, a provisions room, two bedrooms and a bathroom for the servants, a kitchen, and a stable to shelter our riding horses.

Happy, and full of pride, we moved into our new house, and opened it to the European community with a *selamatan*[7]. It was a joyful occasion, until a mother of three, not suspecting our hidden grief, remarked that one front room ought to be quickly transformed into a nursery. It touched a raw nerve in both of us, and our delight turned to bitterness.

It would have been much better if John and I could have expressed our feelings — sharing grief is to halve grief, they say — but neither one of us would ever do so.

### Endnotes

1. *Kapal putih*, meaning "white boat", was the name given to the Government service vessels, which, contrary to the much larger KPM ships, were always painted white.
2. The typical "tropical outfit" included white cotton trousers, shirts and jackets, shoes suited for the tropics, and a tropical helmet.
3. Guido Gezelle, the Flemish priest and prolific poet from Bruges, is also known for his Flemish translation of Longfellow's "The Song of Hiawatha".
4. The Dutch population in the East Indies could be broadly divided into three groups: Protestants, Freemasons, and Catholics. To make it in this society, one had to belong to either the first or the second group. In spite of Holland's reputation for religious tolerance, there was a constant struggle between the *Zending* (the Protestant Mission, overtly aided by the Government) and the *Missie* (the Catholic Mission).
5. Chickens did thrive in Tobelo, where there wasn't the constant threat of snakes that existed on Buluwaya.
6. At the time of publication, Jeanne van Diejen was approaching the age of 106 years.
7. The Indonesian word for a consecratory banquet, preceded by a prayer, held to herald an important event or to give thanks at its conclusion.

# IBU MALUKU

# CHAPTER 15

*Mon Désir*
Tobelo, Halmahera 1922 - 1928

After having completed our new house, I became restless again. I longed for work that would give meaning and purpose to my life, and I sometimes even entertained the idea of leaving Tobelo to find a job in a hospital somewhere. (There was a small hospital of the Protestant Mission in Tobelo, but they would certainly not want a *Catholic* nurse on their staff.)

John had been on *tournée* for ten days, when a friend — the administrator of a nearby coconut plantation — stopped by for a late afternoon visit. He lived alone, so I invited him to stay for dinner. He welcomed the diversion; no one was expecting him home.

At my urging, he talked in detail about his plantation, and did it with such feeling that I was caught up in his enthusiasm.

With a touch of envy, I said: "It must be wonderful to stay in the midst of your work, rather than travel all the time like John does. His absence makes my life rather dull, as there is little for me to do here. Our servants do practically everything. But please, do go on."

"On one part of my plantation," my visitor continued, "I have three hundred so-called dwarf-coconut trees. It is a type that does not grow tall, requires only a six by six meter planting matrix, and delivers full-size nuts after only three years."

Knowing that the more common and up to thirty meters high *cocos nucifera* required a much larger matrix and took ten years to produce, I asked: "Why don't more planters switch to this dwarf tree. Wouldn't it be more economical?"

"The tall tree is productive for seventy-five years; the dwarf tree, only for about twenty years — or so it is thought. That makes quite a difference."

"Then," I pressed on, "why on earth do you have dwarf trees at all?"

"This patch is strictly for the labor force. Each person is entitled to ten nuts per month for his own use. It is not only important for their health, it also tends to stop the theft of plantation coconuts. So these dwarf trees meet a short-term need."

My visitor continued: "I have recently received an order from an American company on Sumatra. They want 100,000 dwarf-type seed-nuts for a new, large plantation, and would pay well."

My interest shot up. "But why would they order from so far away? Are there no dwarf trees closer by?"

"Yes, but not in sufficient quantity. On Halmahera and the surrounding islands, they grow in abundance," he explained.

"So?" I asked.

"Well, I cannot fill the order myself. I simply don't have the time to locate, grade and ship these coconuts. Why don't you take it on? This kind of work would keep you busy, provide variety, and cure you of boredom."

"Unfortunately, I also have my obligations here and would not be able to do all that traveling myself," I said regretfully.

That was the end of the conversation, but the beginning of a new idea: that of starting a plantation of my own, close enough to our present house so that traveling would be insignificant. The idea excited me, but I would have to discuss it with John, who, I was almost certain, would not want to have a "working wife".

As I had expected, when John returned home, he rejected the idea outright. But I longed so much for a new purpose in life that I would not it let go.

"I know your contract with MHM doesn't allow you to have any business on the side, but our marriage contract is such that I am not bound by it in any way," I said.

"Maybe not," John said, "but let me remind you that I can be transferred out of Tobelo at any time, and then what?"

"Well, we'll cross that bridge when we get to it," I countered.

A few days later I began gathering information on how to acquire land, what the conditions were, and how everything hung together. This was the start of a very exciting time.

First I made inquiries at the MHM head office. No, they would not stop me, but they repeated John's earlier warning that he could be transferred, and advised me to give that careful consideration.

I did, but decided to move ahead anyway, and every day, early in the morning, I rode out in search of free parcels of land.

Tobelo was surrounded by a number of *kampungs*. Several kilometers behind these villages were three plantations, and beyond those lay virgin forest.

I made it a point to develop good relations with the *Kampung* Chiefs.

## IBU MALUKU

They had the information I needed, and their co-operation, later, would be very important.

Jointly, these chiefs pointed out a forested parcel of land, about 100 hectares (247 acres), well placed (about 5 km from Tobelo), and ideal for starting a small plantation. About 20 hectares had been cut clear for vegetable gardens that the natives had abandoned, and were now overgrown again.[1]. Abandoned or not, the population expected compensation for having cleared the area, *and* for the existing fruit trees — mostly banana, *jambu* (guava), durian, and *langsep* (a kind of lichee) — that had been left behind. These would have to be purchased at current prices.

I consulted the Head of the District, who liked my plans. He advised me to take a 20-year lease on the *juramés* (as these abandoned gardens were called) and, later, to ask for a 75-year concession on the remaining forested land. A concession, I learned, was land on a long-term lease. The annual payment to the State for a concession was higher than for an ordinary lease, but I followed his advice.

Not surprisingly, all these new plans revived my spirits and gave meaning again to my daily life.

Soon the day arrived for clearing the boundary lines. A delegation of District Chiefs and *Kampung* Heads came with the owners of the *juramés* to stake out the property and to establish the purchase price.

Four months later I was the tenant of the *juramés*, and tenant-to-be of 80 hectares of prime forest. I was proud, and indescribably happy until John laid down the law.

He said that he did not object to my plans — provided our own life and his career would not be adversely affected. He insisted on our being together at meal times, and after 5:00 p.m. to either receive guests, visit, or play tennis at the newly formed club. What I did with the rest of my time was up to me!

I agreed to all his conditions, and assured him the housekeeping would not suffer. Our servants were excellent. Bok was in control and knew how to keep the house spick-and-span.

Of course, I had already taken into account that John would often be away on *tournée*. At those times, I could spend all day at the plantation, working along with the others. What a delightful thought. I was bubbling with enthusiasm!

I wanted to give the land a name, and settled on "Mon Désir" (meaning "My Wish" — for that's what it was). And the name stuck.

I searched for and employed five coolies: two older Papuas, Wanie and Tahir, and their much younger brother, Itunya; and two Tobelorese, Pusah and Chetèke. Their wages would come out of the household budget.

On Mon Desir, these coolies built two houses of bamboo and *gaba-gaba* for themselves, and one small house for me, which had a three-by-three meter room, a small front gallery and a primitive bathroom. It would provide shelter when it rained, and a place to sleep when John was away on business.

The European community of Tobelo was awash with gossip. In the eyes of the ladies especially, I had lost my mind. Worse, I was lowering the status of the European woman by working alongside the natives, and was also endangering John's career!

They did not shrink from warning all the Protestants in Tobelo about me. I was, after all, a Roman-Catholic and a Belgian to boot — the worst combination possible. They recalled an event from World War I, when Holland opened its doors to Belgian refugees — alleged to be mostly women from the red-light district of Antwerp — and this led them to draw the silly conclusion that all Belgian women were basically immoral!

The gossip hurt John, but did not touch me. I was only too glad and grateful that I was allowed to do something challenging, and thought the rumors would eventually stop. John, however, wanted to find the source of this gossip.

"Nonsense," I said, "why rummage through a garbage dump?"

I continued to ride my horse in the morning hours, alongside Latif, who had taken over from the *kebon*. The young lad was a good rider and John, who had little time for riding himself, trusted him with his horse.

On one such ride, we arrived in a *kampung* where I knew dwarf coconuts were growing. I negotiated with the owners to have mature nuts delivered to Mon Désir on a regular basis.

Soon, 600 of those coconuts were laid out in neatly drawn seed-beds: the beginning of my own coconut plantation. I felt so proud!

The clearing of the *juramés* was progressing well because the growth only consisted of young wild shoots, with here and there a high tree — a remnant of the dense forest that had stood there not so long ago.

After four months, the first five hectares of land were ready for planting, and the 30-50 cm tall coconut saplings from the seed-beds were transplanted in neat rows in their final location. (I had carefully studied the transplanting at Buluwaya and enjoyed turning this knowledge into practice.)

I finally persuaded John to come and see my "garden". In the past, he had stubbornly refused, saying that some day I would have to give up this "costly caprice". What he saw really surprised him. I could see from his face that he had expected something quite different.

A wide road ran from the entrance through the center of the property to the *kali*, which marked the end of the land. At the center, this road was crossed by another, thus dividing the plantation neatly into four parcels. There was also a small *emplacement*, where I wanted to build a house.

My workers and some women from the neighboring village had asked if they could plant corn and *batatas* (sweet potatoes) between the young coconuts for their own use. I gladly gave them permission to do so, for their gardening would save me the cost of weeding and thus free up manpower to clear more land.

Slowly, hectare by hectare was made ready for planting the seed coconuts. I already had eight people on the payroll, and had promoted one Tobelorese to *mandur,* or supervisor. He was in command of all the work, but also had the same daily task as the others.

One day, a man came and offered to sell me a few pigs. He wanted to return with his family to the Talaud Islands and needed money for the trip.

My first impulse was to laugh. What was I to do with pigs? But the man said very seriously that pigs would be a good source of income. The *Nyonya* had plenty of fodder, he continued, pointing to the sweet potato gardens.

Old Wanie supported the vendor's sales pitch and assured me he would take care of the pigs, if the *Nyonya* would let him earn a little extra.

I wasn't convinced and said that I wanted to think about it, but the following day I was the owner of two pigs and a pregnant sow that were delivered in a bamboo cage. Two days later they were put in an enclosure, built behind the house where Wanie lived so he could easily look after them. And that was the beginning of my pig farm.

The man from Talaud would prove to be right. The pigs would become a very good source of income.

✳ ✳ ✳ ✳

I had two riding horses now. One was ready every morning at five o'clock to take me down the five-kilometer-long road to Mon Désir. At 5:30 I held roll call, and assigned the work. If anyone had fallen sick, he received *obat* (medicine). Only rarely did I have to send someone to the doctor. Then, having checked the state of affairs, I rode back to Tobelo.

At seven o'clock, John and I had breakfast.

Afterwards, I discussed the meals with Tanta (the new cook), and gave her rice and ingredients from the *gudang*. The *jongos* received petroleum for the lamps, and I would verify later that they had indeed been filled and cleaned. I assigned the yard boy his task for the day, and gave Bok money for any purchases. I also gave her the clean laundry from the *menatu* (laundryman) to put away after doing any required mending.

The second horse would stand ready to take me to Mon Désir by nine o'clock. I made sure to be back in Tobelo between 11:30 and 12:00 so we could lunch at 12:30, after which John rested for a full hour. Fifteen minutes was enough for me, and soon after this *siesta* I was back in the saddle, and *en route* to Mon Désir.

Back in Tobelo at 5:00, we bathed, drank tea, and either received visitors, played tennis, or went out to visit someone. We dined at 7:30, and were in bed by 10:00.

I enjoyed this busy life and never knew what it was to be tired.

Sundays were strictly reserved for ourselves. We walked or picnicked, or stayed home to read or talk. Sometimes friends would drop by for a chat — there was always something to talk about — and, on occasion, John would come to see how things progressed on Mon Désir. With time, he began to enter into the spirit of things.

However, John was very susceptible to all kinds of illnesses; he often came down with a cold, a rash, or with malaria. Of course, that would force me to stay home throughout the day, and then I had to be content with brief visits to Mon Désir. Once he even came down with dysentery and was ill for several months. But with the help of so-called *yatree* injections (ordered from Java), he got better and we were both able to get back to our normal daily routine.

*\*\*\*\**

The population of Tobelo was always in a state of flux, with new people moving in and people, whom we had known and sometimes befriended, moving out. Since I had started Mon Désir, we had gone through two doctors and two magistrates.

Dr. Slamat — who had finished his three-year term and gone to Europe for further studies — had been replaced by a Menadonese, who would later become Minister of Health under President Sukarno.

He, in turn, was replaced by a Javanese, who belonged to the aristocracy and had married a *Radèn Ajeng* (a Javanese woman of noble birth), a delicate beauty, who had great difficulty adjusting to life in these "outer possessions".

## IBU MALUKU

We enjoyed their company and became good friends, so much so that their first baby was born in our house. Afterward, I nursed mother and child for a long time — which gave me great pleasure!

The first magistrate we met, a rigid disciplinarian, had a perennially unhappy wife who never became used to Tobelo. She eventually returned with their four children to Holland and sued her husband for divorce. It was not the first time I saw a marriage break up because of inability to adjust to life in the Moluccas, and it would not be the last.

The second magistrate, a widower, lived with a Eurasian housekeeper and so, perhaps for that reason, stayed away from social gatherings in the *kota* (town). After a brief period, he was also transferred.

The current magistrate, with the rank of *Controleur*, was an authoritarian person, who introduced all sorts of odd regulations that alienated everybody. His wife, a woman from Ternate, did not help matters by putting on airs.

A more delightful addition to the community was a Dutch nurse, who had joined the staff of the Protestant Mission hospital. She was happy, fresh as a daisy, and a definite bonus for the bachelors.

\*\*\*\*

Everything progressed well on Mon Désir, except that I had to look for a means to cover the ever-increasing costs, as John had balked at putting more money into my venture. I had been asked to deliver produce to the *Kweek en Ambachtschool* (an agricultural training college) and, therefore, started to plant cassava and corn to meet that demand.

Our pig family had grown to 22. They promised future cash, but they now needed space in which to roam around freely. Keeping them cooped up was becoming too expensive. So I started to look for means to set up a fenced-in area. There was ample bamboo available to build a fence, but I did not think it would be sturdy enough and would also require too much maintenance.

I regularly received a large mail-order catalogue from a U.S. company that had once sold some furnishings to John's predecessor on Buluwaya. In it, I found a type of fence that I immediately liked. It would be ideal for my purpose and last forever — but, it was very expensive.

My birthday was approaching, and when John asked me what I wanted as a present, I screwed up my courage and mentioned the fence. His answer was like a bolt out of the blue: "OK, I will give you a loan, but you shall have to pay it back with interest!"

I was flabbergasted: "My own husband dares to charge me interest? Is this a joke?" But no, he was dead serious, and I ultimately agreed to the deal. Why not! If he wanted to be businesslike, so could I — but I certainly was not very happy about it.

So I ordered the fencing material from Montgomery-Ward in Chicago, and it arrived four months later. What a joy it was! We fenced in all of the 20 hectares. No animal would be able to get either in or out. Wild animals, mostly swine and deer, could no longer damage my crops.

I now started to make plans for clearing the forested area, which, having become a concession, was now officially incorporated into Mon Désir.

I hired lumberjacks, each of whom would clear one hectare. With some helpers they would cut, burn and remove all timber within two months.

Then came the "miracle"!

A delegate from the island of Mapia arrived by boat to see me. He had heard about me and said: "We are planning to build model houses on Mapia, but there is no timber there — only coconut trees. We wonder if you could supply us with cut lumber — especially beams. Would that be possible?"

The bewilderment must have shown on my face. Had I understood him well? Was he serious? After all, I was not in the lumber business! I finally asked for time to think about the matter, doubting very much that such a venture would be possible.

But when I asked the lumberjacks the next day if there was good construction timber on my concession, they confirmed in unison that, indeed, there was. They immediately showed me a few beautiful trees that were large in circumference and straight as an arrow. They called the wood *kayu motoa* — wood from (the island of) Motoa. In addition, they were well acquainted with current prices and the rates for woodcutters.

I verified the prices with several Chinese traders, and then approached John who, pretending to be at the end of his tether, said: "Well, here we go again!".

But John did later talk to the man from Mapia, and as a result, I received a tentative order for beams. I immediately telegraphed an order for axes, saws and anything else that a sawmill would require.

I had started a new business!

A new lieutenant arrived in town to take command of the *tangsi* (the military base). He was accompanied by his wife and child. He was Eurasian, she was German — a real beauty. All the gentlemen agreed on that — much to the chagrin of their spouses. Madame enjoyed the situation, and encouraged the men. It was only a game, but a dangerous one, which created much distrust in the community.

The Lieutenant, hated pigs. The *kraal*[2] on the military base was full of them. The previous commander, a Captain, had not properly supervised the *kettingberen*[3] who had been assigned to take care of the pigsty — so the animals were badly neglected.

The Lieutenant urged me — almost begged me — to take the animals at a flat price of five guilders per animal. I went to visit the *kraal* and was shocked to see a herd of emaciated animals, covered with mud, and almost starving to death. I wondered if they would survive a change in feed. There were 70 animals, among which were 40 piglets. Knowing the risk involved, I put in a lower bid — more because I felt sorry for the animals, than out of a desire to turn a profit.

The Lieutenant gladly accepted my offer, after which a gang of *strappans*[3] (prisoners) delivered the skinny animals to Mon Désir.

Three days later, 17 animals were dead. The rest survived, and multiplied to 90 animals before the end of the year. It was time to start looking for steady buyers — which I found among the KPM ships and the local Chinese. The European community was scandalized by my business activities, but nevertheless swooped down on the Chinese butchers to buy the fresh meat.

I made good money, which enabled me to finance further land-clearing on the plantation.

\* \* \* \*

John had a new boss on Ternate. The previous General Agent — who had helped us through the critical time after my miscarriage — had gone on furlough and would settle in Menado upon his return.

John's first meeting with his new boss was disappointing. The man was quite critical on several issues, but was especially displeased with John's strict demeanor toward the forest overseers. He bluntly told John that his attitude was one of splitting hairs, and that he wanted him to become more accommodating.

We envisioned further difficulties when we heard that his wife, a Eurasian from Menado, was related to the gang of corrupt MHM supervisors who, before John's arrival, had enriched themselves at the expense of the *damar* carriers and the owners of the *dusuns*.

Very soon after the new General Agent's appointment, it became clear that the increasingly brazen overseers had returned to their shady practices. The attitude of the *juragang* (captain) of the *Angin Barat* schooner also changed drastically.

He always used to be ready to tow additional barges, or to transport passengers free of charge — like *gurus* and their families — from Morotai to Ternate. Now, he demanded payment for the trip and would only tow extra barges when he could get something out of it. He would also purchase sago, *gabba-gabba* or roof covering, stow it away on the boat, and sell these elsewhere at a profit.

All these underhanded dealings and the lack of co-operation bothered John to the extreme, and he protested against it in Ternate. This got him nowhere.

His new boss repeatedly told him that he did not understand the people and that he lacked the ability to deal with them. Over time, the remarks took on a more threatening tone, suggesting that he could be transferred out. His boss also made snide remarks about John's visits to Mon Désir — though these were few and always took place on a Sunday, when he was off duty.

As a result, John became unsure of his future with the MHM company and worried a great deal.

* * * *

At Mon Désir, the sawing of the lumber was in full swing, and required all my attention. To get an additional beam out of a block of wood, I instructed the men to saw the outer beams a little narrower. These beams, not square in cross-section and therefore not good enough to be sold, would be quite suitable for use on Mon Désir. With them, I would later build ten permanent two-family homes for the workers, close to a well that was dug for their exclusive use. The second generation of workers would be mostly born in these houses.

Driven by an inexplicable feeling of an approaching calamity, I replaced my primitive garden shed with a large, permanent house. It had a proper front gallery, inner hall, bedroom and storage room. Behind it was a kitchen, a bathroom and a servant's room. It was built in stages and was referred to as "the house that was built on the run". Later, this house would become our main residence — a safe haven during the terrifying times that were coming.

* * * *

Of course, our lives did not only consist of work. There were days when we had visitors and people who stayed over. We always put up the Catholic missionaries, who now visited Tobelo every six months instead of only once a year. Then there were new arrivals who did not yet have a place of their own, and KPM passengers who wanted to stay a few days awaiting the return of their ship.

So it happened that at one time we had a Dutch couple from Zeist (Netherlands) staying with us. He was a tireless hunter of butterflies. Accompanied by a few natives, he would leave early in the morning with his butterfly-net and equipment, and return late in the afternoon with his catch. He would then give us a dissertation on the large, beautiful butterflies he had caught, telling us about their flight patterns, what they ate and the duration of their pupation.

His enthusiasm was contagious, and in later years, catching and breeding butterflies became not only a pleasant pastime, but also a welcome source of income.

His wife was an older, calmer person, who taught me the many things one can make with thread and needle. In the little spare time I had, I even did some kilim rug-weaving and petit-point embroidery, and achieved some measure of proficiency. That too, became a creative outlet for me.

We also received the Director of *'s Lands Plantentuin*[4], Professor Leefmans, who had heard about our dwarf coconut plantation and wanted to know more about it. During the four days he stayed on Mon Désir, I learned much from him about compost fertilizer and crop-rotation for produce, and would maintain a correspondence with him for many years to come.

The livestock had grown to five milk cows, one steer and eight calves, which allowed me to breed animals for commercial use, but also allowed us to have daily milk and butter — a real advantage and luxury in this wilderness.

Every day, I learned more about all sorts of things in which I'd previously had no interest.

*****

A new overseer arrived on the scene: a Sangirese, and a descendant of the Rajah family of the Kansils. He was a quiet, competent man, who got along well with people. He was also a handy craftsman, so that much of what was previously done by expensive tradesmen, was now repaired by him.

He also knew how to build houses and train livestock. The latter was particularly important, because our young steers would soon have to be trained to pull *gerobaks* (oxcarts).

During one of my trips on horseback, I discovered a new type of coconut on the private grounds of a Kling[5] trader, who told me he had brought it with him from the island of Ceylon (Sri Lanka). This kind, called the King Nut — something between the *cocos nucifera* and the dwarf coconut — was extensively cultivated there.

"This species," he said, "has a heavier build, a rich dark green canopy and produces more fruit than any other type of coconut. The coconuts are also bigger, but have an exceptionally thin husk. These trees do not grow tall, do not get any of the known diseases, and bear fruit in abundance in four years."

Of course, I asked if I could buy all his mature nuts, which I wanted to use for seed nuts at Mon Désir. Spontaneously, the trader gave me all the nuts he had, but refused to accept any money. The *Tuan* (John) had helped him so often, he said. On top of that, he was pleased that the *Nyonya* had shown interest in his trees. Never before had any *nyonya* even looked at them — let alone noticed that they were different from other coconut trees.

This generosity was typical of these people, who trade in all kinds of fabrics (e.g., cottons and silk) and also knick-knacks, and whose shops give an exotic impression.

Two Madurese workers who had finished their contract work at Buluwaya, had followed us to Tobelo and asked to be employed at Mon Désir. Like most Madurese, they knew how to handle livestock, so one of them was put in charge of our cows and horses.

The other, Abas, who came from the same *dessa* (village) as Bok, preferred to work in the yard. One day he came to ask for an advance and permission to marry Bok. It was obvious that both were very happy. Later, they had a baby girl, Sulami, who grew up in our compound. She was a lovely, intelligent, and cheerful child, who brought much happiness to John and me and all who knew her. She would not be with us long, for Abas and Bok were already making plans to return to Java.

\* \* \* \*

Every now and then John and I would talk about taking a furlough, but each such conversation usually concluded with John saying he did not want to ask for it at this time. I was highly in favor of a furlough, for John needed it badly. Mon Désir had a good overseer, Kansil, to whom I could safely entrust the management for six months. But, would John, after the furlough, be posted again at Tobelo? That's what concerned him. Rumors were flying around that a nephew of the boss' wife needed a job, and that Tobelo would suit him just fine!

Then, fate intervened: John became seriously ill with hookworm, which had been diagnosed much too late. The doctor advised him to leave immediately for Europe, so the furlough to which he had long been entitled was granted.

John had to hand over the business and our house to his successor — who did indeed turn out to be that nephew.

All our furniture that a local Chinese had made from costly ebony and teak, I transferred to Mon Désir. Our other furnishings were auctioned off at very good prices, or sold on consignment. The total of the sale was such that it would enable us to have an enjoyable holiday.

The year was 1928. The Netherlands was in the grip of an unusually severe winter, so we decided to travel to Marseille, and stay in Nice until the summer. Bok, Abas and little Sulami would travel with us to Java, where they would then leave our employ.

Upon arrival in Ternate we found many friends waiting for us on the pier, who gave us a splendid farewell party that lasted until long into the night. Neither the boss nor his wife showed up!

The next day, we were warmly escorted on board a ship out of Menado. It brought us to Makassar, where we took the express ship for Surabaya. There was not a dry eye as we said goodbye to Abas, Bok and Sulami, who had become so much a part of the family.

From Surabaya, they would return by train to Sumber Waringin (meaning "Banyan Spring"), a little village in the eastern corner of Java. They had saved money, and could afford to buy a *sawah* (a rice-field) and build their own house. That was all they wanted.

Seduced by a strange twist of the mind — or was it the heart? — I fully expected to see them again some day. Alas, I never would.

### Endnotes
[1] When the soil's nutrients were depleted, the natives would move on, clear another part of the forest, and start a new garden. This exhaustive form of cultivation was of little concern to them, for the forest belonged to everyone, and there was plenty of it to go around.
[2] *Kraal* – the South-African word for an enclosure for animals.
[3] The term *Kettingberen* (Dutch for "chain bears"), a general name for prisoners, dates from the time when native criminals — like their counterparts in the Netherlands at an earlier time — were chained to a block of heavy material that they had to drag with them as they walked. These encumbrances were removed in 1918, and the prisoners were put to work during the period of their confinement as porters, lumberjacks, or water carriers for the military base. The equivalent Malayan name for prisoner was *strappan*.
[4] "*s Lands Plantentuin*" the National Botanical Gardens in Buitenzorg, (now Bogor) on Java.
[5] The Kling people have their roots in the Coromandel Coast and the Malabar Coast of India.

# IBU MALUKU

# CHAPTER 16

## On Leave
### Europe, 1928

We arrived in Batavia in record time: 15 days from the time we left Tobelo! What a difference from the years 1920-1921, when such a trip would have taken 32 days!

We stayed only three days to purchase some necessary clothes, and then boarded the *Tabanan*, which would sail in 28 days via Padang, Singapore, the Suez Canal, and Port Saïd, to Marseille.

On board, we found the passengers very noisy, and there was much drinking, so we stayed out of the way as much as we could. However, whenever we stopped at a harbor, we joined our fellow passengers in going ashore for sightseeing.

In Singapore, we purchased more European clothing, and from Port Saïd, we visited the pyramids and the museum of Cairo, where, in a recently opened exhibition, the incredibly beautiful treasures from the burial chamber of Tutankhamen were displayed. In Marseille, everything looked strange to us. We had undoubtedly become somewhat people-shy, and it took time for us to get used to the different pace.

In a large fashion store, John wanted to buy an overcoat and asked me to handle the negotiations since he felt his French wasn't all that good. The sales staff was exceptionally accommodating. They hauled in every conceivable type of overcoat, which was looked at, tried on, and discussed at length. To my surprise, I made out very well, although I had not spoken French in years! The sales staff reinforced my confidence in my linguistic ability with *"Mais oui, Madame"*, *"Mais non, Madame"*, or *"Certainement Madame!"*.

Then I heard John snicker. Dismayed, I suggested that he continue the negotiations himself as it was, after all, *his* coat we were shopping for and I obviously was not handling the matter to his liking.

He now laughed openly and said: "No, you go ahead! But I would like you to know that, all this time, you haven't spoken a word of French! You have been speaking Malay with a French intonation!"

I looked at him in disbelief, and then burst out laughing when I realized that he was right. This mistake would be a source of merriment for years to come.

The next day, we took the train to Nice, and installed ourselves in the Hotel Terminus. From there, we watched the entry of Maréchal Foch, who had come to unveil the monument of the unknown soldier. From our room, we threw little bouquets of mimosa, and enjoyed the impressive retinue of the famous Marshal, which included many Hussars on magnificent horses. What a colorful spectacle it was!

A week later we rented a furnished apartment on Rue Gounod, and stayed there five wonderful months. John underwent his hookworm treatment nearby and slowly regained his strength, becoming once again a cheerful companion.

\*\*\*\*

We soon made new friends. Among them were many retired veterans from the East Indies who had settled in Nice and the suburbs, as well as people who, like us, were on home leave from the Indies.

Among our close friends were two retired teachers from Ambon, who had bought an attractive apartment near the Russian Cathedral. It was because of them that I had my first flight in an airplane, which had unpleasant consequences.

More than once, I had looked longingly at the small aircraft that made short flights over and around Nice. I told John that I would love to fly, just once, before returning to the Indies. But John was strongly against it, saying that it was much too dangerous. So it looked as if I would never get my wish.

But one day, those retired teachers said they would love to go up in an airplane, but didn't have the courage to go alone. Would we come with them?

Posed with a dilemma, John did not know what to say. I broke the impasse by saying that this had also been my greatest wish, and the ladies then proposed to do it in the next few days. I was delighted, but also apprehensive about John's reaction.

I didn't have long to wait. When we reached home, he said: "I forbid it!" That was that. I answered immediately that it would then be up to *him* to tell the ladies.

At our next meeting, however, he didn't say a word when the ladies set the flight for the next day. John claimed he feared heights and so would not be joining us, but his grim face spoke volumes to me!

The flight itself was wonderful. Bundled in a leather coat, I took my seat next to the pilot. As soon as I had put on a flying cap and goggles, we thundered down the runway and were off into the sky. It was simply overpowering, and I wished it would never end. It was over all too soon, and John stood there waiting for us on the ground.

We took the ladies home. I tried to delay the parting as long as possible, knowing that thereafter the bomb would explode. But the explosion did not come. Instead, we lived together for three days without exchanging a single word! It was terrible, and I vowed never to cross him like that again.

In spite of this incident we had, on the whole, a wonderful time in Nice. Together, we visited all the (for me) familiar places, including the house where I had lived three years before World War I. I told John about my early youth and teen years, and about the enjoyable times I had spent in this part of paradise.

Toward the end of May, we left for the Netherlands, where we arrived on my birthday, June 6. The year was 1928. It had been freezing hard the previous night, and it was still bitterly cold.

It was wonderful to see Mama and the other family members again! There was so much to tell after eight years in the East Indies. Yet, it soon became obvious that they had difficulty in understanding what life was all about in those far away Moluccas. So we talked mostly about the benefits of the tropics, and omitted details of the many difficulties.

Relations with John's family were decidedly strained. His mother, in particular, was bitter about us having left Buluwaya, which she persisted in calling a "breach of contract". We quickly tired of having to explain our conduct to her, and decided not to talk about it any further. As a result, contact with them became sporadic.

John was admitted to the Hospital for Tropical Diseases in Rotterdam for further treatment of the effects of dysentery and hookworm. A neurologist who checked him out, advised him to use his furlough to get a complete rest.

I, myself, also had a complete physical examination, and a gynecologist confirmed my inability to ever have a baby. We had known this for some time, of course, but it still hit us hard! It destroyed the few strands of hope that, evidently, we had been hanging onto.

After all medical rounds were completed, we returned to the Province of Limburg to stay at a cottage in the Geul Valley, which we had rented from the well-known writer, Marie Coenen.

Scattered nearby were a few small inns, occupied mostly by tourists. In one of the inns lived an engineer and his family, with whom we developed a lasting friendship. He worked in the Maurits Mine for an English firm, Babcock and Willcox, and arranged for us to visit the mine, the largest in the province. The 500 meter descent was exciting, but I was pleased to breathe fresh air again when we returned to ground level.

From Tobelo, the news was good. The clearing of the land had progressed steadily, and all associated costs had been covered by profits from the pig farm that had grown to over 200 animals.

The news from the MHM, however, was not so good. John's successor had taken back some overseers whom John had fired. One large Chinese trader had written John to express his concern about what was happening at Tobelo. John felt uneasy about the situation, especially because this trader had heard rumors about John being transferred to another island, close to Menado.

During a follow-up visit to the Tropical Diseases Hospital in Rotterdam, John ran into an old friend, who told him about a local trading house that was expanding. The company — which already had a *damar* concession on Morotai — wanted to establish new offices in the Moluccas and in northern New Guinea. They were looking for an experienced person, who — and they emphasized the importance of this — knew the languages and customs of the different tribes.

This friend suggested that John contact the firm, and he even arranged an appointment for John.

The people he met were very business-like. They clearly outlined the firm's objectives and emphasized that the first few years would be difficult. They wanted someone who could make contacts, find good areas, and lease concessions. This would require a person who had stamina, drive, tact and courage; who had a "can-do" attitude and — most important — had experience in this kind of work.

They gave John two days to think about it, and that suited us well, since we had already planned to stay two more days in Rotterdam.

That evening, we talked extensively about the job. A big advantage was that John would be independent and accountable only to the management in Rotterdam. He would also be free from the MHM political intrigues and the underhanded shenanigans of corrupt overseers and their cronies. The disadvantage was that we would have to live somewhere along the north coast of New Guinea, instead of on Halmahera.

This meant that I would have to give up Mon Désir — or leave its management in the hands of an overseer. For me, this weighed heavily, as I had gained so much satisfaction from this undertaking. Would I be able to give it up? But I knew that John was worrying about it too, so finally I told him to exclude Mon Désir from his deliberations.

Early in the morning, John decided to leave MHM. His resignation, after some protestations, was accepted. The following day, the new contract was drawn up and signed. The conditions were extremely favorable, and signified a considerable promotion. John was walking on clouds.

Early in September, we would return to the Dutch East Indies, stay one month in Tobelo to put our affairs in order, and then sail for Manokwari, the capital of New Guinea.

In the last month of our stay in the Netherlands, with John's blessing this time, I made my second airplane flight — a short trip over Rotterdam — together with my aging mother. She thoroughly enjoyed the flight, and was greeted as a heroine when she returned home.

Finally, we set the date of departure and booked passage on the *Insulinde*, which would leave from Rotterdam. Mama would accompany us to Marseille, and then return via Lourdes and Lisieux to the Netherlands.

For Mama, it was her first sea voyage. How she enjoyed it! Together, we visited London from Southampton, and made a one-day trip along the coast, which somehow reminded me of the tropics.

In Marseille, Mama and I parted. I was never to see her again. In the Spring of 1944, on orders of the German occupation forces, she was transported under inhuman conditions from Limburg, via Germany, to Friesland, in the north of the Netherlands. Why, would never become clear to me.

The deprivations suffered during this transportation, partly on foot through the snow, partly by cattle train in a crammed wagon without food or warm cover, would have a lasting effect on her health. She died much too young, in 1946.

John and I were glad to be returning home — there was nothing to keep us here — and we longed to get back to work. Our leave had done us much good physically and we were grateful for that.

# IBU MALUKU

IBU MALUKU

# CHAPTER 17

### *A Little Smuggling*
*On the high seas, 1929*

In Port Saïd, we cut our ties with Europe by changing into tropical clothes. We did it with gusto, and laughed at our eagerness to return home.

Among the passengers were two young nurses, sisters, to whom we felt drawn. How fresh and naive they still were!

They kept pounding us with questions about the islands and the people of *Insulinde*[1]. They had big plans to set up a clinic of their own, somewhere in the interior. We gave them all the moral support we could, and wished them well!

In Colombo, Ceylon, John went ashore with these nurses to do some sightseeing. I myself was determined to visit several *kampungs* and search for King Nuts — the special type of coconut I was introduced to by the Kling trader on Halmahera.

After receiving directions from helpful Colomboans, I hailed a taxicab that drove me to a small plantation. The owner had an exclusive arrangement with a small factory, where all the nuts he produced were shelled, grated, dried, sugared and beautifully packaged for shipment to confectioners in the United States and Europe.

He freely gave me all the information I sought, and then presented me with six choice coconuts, for which he refused to accept payment. He did, however, tell me the local price for these nuts: 25 cents a piece — a pittance in my eyes, but a large amount for these people! Just before we left, the owner instructed my chauffeur, in a language that I did not understand, where to take me to buy good seed nuts.

Around noon, I was the proud owner of 30 whole, freshly picked seed nuts, and sometime during the afternoon, my chauffeur managed to find another 45.

I gladly would have bought more, but the problem was getting them into the East Indies. There wasn't enough time to get an import license from Batavia, and importing seed nuts (or other produce) without such a license was forbidden. There was no alternative but to smuggle them in. For that, I would need the co-operation of several fellow passengers.

It was late in the afternoon when I rejoined John and the two nurses on board.

When I told John about my trip on the island and the purchase of the seed nuts, he warned that I could get into serious trouble. But, I was on top of the world and succeeded in bringing him around to my point of view.

"After all, the worst that can happen is that the seed nuts will be impounded temporarily and sent to Buitenzorg (now Bogor) to be checked out ... and our friend, professor Leefmans, is there ... so?" Of course, I had made sure that the seed nuts and the source trees were free of vermin and looked healthy, as I certainly did not want to infect my own trees at Mon Désir.

A trip was planned for the next day to visit and swim at Mount Lavinia, one of the better known beaches on the Indian Ocean. John pressed me to go, too.

The following day — a brilliant one, befitting this natural paradise — we traveled 12 kilometers south from Colombo to Mount Lavinia, where we thoroughly enjoyed the panorama, the luscious vegetation, the overwhelming wealth of flowers and, of course, the exceptionally beautiful beach.

By 12:30, all passengers were back on board. Shortly after, my seed nuts were stored in several laundry bags belonging to my co-conspirators, who enjoyed taking part in this "smuggling affair", as they called it.

At 14:00 hours sharp, the *Insulinde* left the harbor and set course for Singapore, where we arrived around 9:00 the following morning.

We went ashore to shop and post our letters for the Netherlands. It was oppressively hot in the narrow shop-lined streets of the Chinese quarter, and the heavy odors coming out of the Chinese restaurants made me queasy. Most of the passengers, however, were impressed with this busy trading city, and were bowled over by the sight of the turbaned porters and the guard at the imposing Raffles Hotel — whom many mistook for Indian Maharajahs!

Toward evening, we weighed anchor and continued our journey to Sumatra, arriving the following day at Emma Harbor, a port that was black with coal-dust.

John and I were happy to be back in the East Indies. With a *sado*[2], pulled by a skinny Batak horse that partly hung in its harness, we traveled to Padang to see the city and its magnificent surroundings. Here, we introduced our fellow travelers to the milk of young coconuts.

The next day, we sailed to Belawan, where several of our fellow passengers left the ship. Among them were the two nurses, who said their goodbyes with tears streaming down their cheeks — but from whom we would never hear again.

There were also a few proxies who were met by their husbands. These brand-new husbands were clean-cut and well-dressed, and were driving well-polished cars! Discreetly, and with great interest, I watched their reactions to this, their first meeting, remembering how disheveled and muddy John had looked when I arrived as a proxy at the Vesuvius Bay. Was I envious? Amused? I am not sure what I felt, but in my mind I relived, intensely, that first meeting with *my* bridegroom.

When the whistle blew for the third time, the departing passengers and their *barang* had long since disappeared from the docks. Only a few of our fellow-passengers remained at the railings when we left the quay; the others were preparing their luggage, since they would be getting off at the next stop.

I quickly made the rounds to write down the addresses of my co-conspirators, so I would know where to contact them if I had to pick up my seed nuts there.

On the day of arrival, every passenger was on deck early to get a glimpse of Tandyong Priok — the harbor of Batavia. At breakfast — so pleasant and relaxed at other times — people ate hurriedly and said hasty good-byes before dashing to the railings, so as not to miss the docking at the as yet distant pier, where one could already discern the many white figures of expected loved ones.

Because our cabin was located in a favorable spot, our *barang* was quickly taken ashore. I had agreed with my co-conspirators that we would regroup in the customs shed.

John found an unobtrusive place, from where he could watch and see if anyone got into trouble with the laundry bags. However, everything went smoothly. Bag after bag was unsuspectingly marked with a chalked cross and carried out of the shed. Several co-conspirators winked and gave us the thumbs-up sign: we had done it! All seventy-five seed nuts made it out of Tandyong Priok.

Two days later they were placed in gunny sacks and shipped to Tobelo. How proud I was and thrilled with the results of my first and only attempt at smuggling!

We had to wait five full days in Batavia for the S.S. *van Cloon*, which would take us to Halmahera. And we took the opportunity to visit friends at a tea plantation near Bandung, where it was quite chilly — so chilly that we spent evenings in front of an open fire, and nights under woolen blankets.

We also visited the National Botanical Gardens at Buitenzorg, where we met again with Professor Leefmans, who was deeply interested in our plans. When he heard that we were going to New Guinea, he promptly introduced John to a *damar* expert.

This person informed John about the slipshod and — in his words — criminal manner in which the Papuas tapped and killed the priceless *damar* trees. John received valuable information from this man, and would keep contact by mail, even long after we had left New Guinea's north coast.

Loaded down with all sorts of things for Mon Désir and for furnishing our future house somewhere in New Guinea, we finally boarded the *van Cloon*, whose captain turned out to be an old friend.

The very first day, at the Captain's dinner table, the First Mate asked, why, in heaven's name, would anyone take seed-nuts to the coconut islands of the Moluccas. I told our dinner companions how they had been smuggled into the country — which caused much laughter — and what I intended to do with them. They wished me luck, but their faces told me that they were dubious about the outcome.

For KPMers, coconuts meant copra, and copra meant freight — and what did it matter from what type of coconut the copra came? They considered all the trouble I had taken rather eccentric, and the First Mate said teasingly: "But what can one expect from people who have come out of the *rimbu*, and, after a furlough, are oh! so happy to trek into an even greater *rimbu*!"

Life on board was pleasant and interesting. There was a constant coming and going of passengers with new stories and new destinations. It was only on board such a KPM steamer that one became aware of how much people traveled — and how frequently the Europeans working there were transferred.

Our first stop was Semarang; then, Surabaya, where we bought new harnesses and saddles for our horses. From there we made a side trip to buy a brood steer from an experimental breeding station on the Idyen plateau. The size of the herd was impressive, but the prices were out of reach. So we left this area with empty hands.

The ship then took us via the former court center of Sumenep (on Madura Island) to Bali — "the pearl in the belt of emeralds" where we made a wonderful short trip from Denpasar across the island.

The next morning at daybreak, we continued to Makassar, where we found several letters from Overseer Kansil waiting for us.

He reported that he had sold most of the pigs to cover the cost of maintaining the grounds and clearing 30 hectares of forest. Also, that he was building a new pig pen, and had placed an order for the wire fence with the Schlieper company. The wire fence had been shipped to a warehouse in Makassar. Would we bring it with us, and pay for it with the funds he had transferred to a bank in Makassar?

We did, and we were pleased to have a large sum left over, because our pocket books had become considerably lighter after the many purchases we had made. Traveling on a KPM ship was not exactly cheap either.

With growing impatience, we traveled on, counting each passing day, and greeting each harbor with a grateful heart. It was pleasant to see local acquaintances and meet new passengers, but it was always a great relief to hear the clanking of the anchor chain as it was being pulled up, accompanied by the third whistle that echoed against the volcano peaks of the Molucca islands and then died away again.

As the ship picked up steam and passed the coral islands on its northward course, our hearts beat a little faster, knowing we were getting closer to home.

We were approaching Ambon. How wonderfully did the nutmeg trees darken the flanks of the *Gunung (*Mountain) Nona, and how beautiful were the tops of the coconut trees waving against the golden evening sky. It was as if they were calling out a welcome to us: "Maluku, you are back in Tanah Maluku – the land of the Moluccas."

The ship would stay at Ambon for two days, and John used this time to discuss the plans of his new firm for northern New Guinea with the local authorities. They liked the plans and promised him full assistance in applying for concession rights.

John was relieved that all was going so well, and as the hours passed he became increasingly itchy to go to work. He would have sailed directly to Manokwari if that had been possible. But the *van Cloon* would take us only to Tobelo, and then return via Weda to Batavia. In Tobelo, there would be a long wait for the "Papua ship", and that suited me just fine, for there were many things to be done in Tobelo and Mon Désir that required John's presence.

After Ambon, the *van Cloon* took us to Buru, where we bought a large volume of *kayu putih* (eucalyptus) oil, which the island produces in abundance. Bok had introduced me to it on Passi Ipa, and I now agreed with her: it was indeed a good remedy for many ills, and could be applied externally *and* taken internally.

On Sanana — the place from where we had once traveled to Ternate under traumatic circumstances — there was a new magistrate, who asked about our first posting in Buluwaya.

From him we learned that, after John, they had gone through three different administrators. From the eager manner in which John asked about the land, I could see that he was still emotionally attached to it.

On Bachan, we were met by the administrator of the BAM[3] company and his lovely wife, with whom we spent the evening at Branka Baru, a coconut plantation in a magnificent setting.

We learned that the company had *damar* concessions deeper inland, and also on the island of Obi. The *damar* from the Bachan concession was of a very high quality — as John found out when he visited the sorting sheds the following morning. He was allowed to take a few samples with him.

While he was there, I visited the shop of local goldsmith. He displayed sparkling pearls, harvested by the local population and by professional divers who were employed by the BAM company.

The jeweler also had beautifully crafted "Bachan stones" (chalcedony quartz), which were plentiful on the island, and were polished by the natives as a kind of cottage industry. Much to my surprise and delight, I heard that the *strappans* of the local prison also polished these stones, and that the proceeds were used to pay for their keep.

The following morning we would arrive in Ternate. After that, a few more days and the journey would end. We would be home!

At Ternate, the very first thing John did was to go to the Resident's office to discuss the founding of a new company and getting new tap concessions in northern New Guinea. This was a necessary step, as that area fell under the jurisdiction of the Residency of Ternate and Dependencies.

Later he visited the MHM office to say hello to his old colleagues, who threw a party for us in the local club that evening. Once again, John's former boss did not show up. That is when we heard many tales about the current state of affairs in northeast Halmahera and Morotai, where corrupt MHM supervisors were back in the saddle. Many Europeans had been transferred, and their places had been taken by family members of the wife of the current boss — who had clearly had a hand in all of this. Some of our friends whispered that *guna-guna* (black magic) had also played a role, but we did not believe in that and simply laughed it off.

When we parted, John's ex-colleagues wished him luck in his new job, and several said: "I wish I could also escape from this bloody mess!"

It was Saturday afternoon, and the hour of departure was upon us. All of the MHM employees — except, of course, the boss — came on

## IBU MALUKU

board to see us off and to enjoy the ice-cold beer and other KPM "goodies".

Then the last whistle sounded. The visitors hurried to the gangway to go ashore, and from there waved us an exuberant goodbye.

In the distance, to the right, the mountains of Halmahera loomed up and my heart flew out to meet them. Tomorrow, we would be home!

### Endnotes

[1] Insulinde ("domain of islands") is the name for the East Indies, invented by Multatuli (Eduard Douwes Dekker, 1820-1887), author of "Max Havelaar", a bitter exposé of the abuses of the Dutch colonial system of the time.

[2] *sado*: a two-wheeled carriage for transporting people, pulled by a horse; the passengers sit back-to-back (in French: dos-à-dos, from which the name is derived) with the driver.

[3] The *Bachan Archipel Maatschappij* — the Bachan Archipelago Company.

IBU MALUKU

IBU MALUKU

# CHAPTER 18

## Home Again
### Mon Désir, Halmahera, April, 1929

When the sun started to rise from the depth of the pearly sea, the *van Cloon* dropped anchor in the bay of Galela.

The Mamuya volcano, wearing a heavy bonnet of clouds, began to light up, and the almost circular mountain range around the Lake of Galela was brushed with gold. How indescribably beautiful was this country — and how grateful I was for having been allowed to return here!

At noon, we weighed anchor, sailed around the Mamuya peninsula and past the well-known *kampungs*, and arrived an hour later at the roadstead of Tobelo.

We now turned our attention to our luggage. It had just been brought on deck, when the first motorboat returned from the pier with Overseer Kansil and six of our men. They rushed up the gangway and shook our hands as if they did not want to let go. The *"selamat datang, selamat datang"* (welcome) sounded in all keys, after which they outdid each other in getting the luggage to the motorboat as quickly as possible. There was hardly a place left in the motorboat when we took off for the shore.

On the pier we were welcomed with much arm-waving by other men, women and children of Mon Désir. We did not have enough hands to greet these good people, who escorted us with much cheering to the wide road behind the MHM shed.

Then came the big surprise: two large *gerobaks*, adorned with coconut palm leaves and flowers, pulled by four of our own steers (born on Mon Désir and trained during our absence), stood ready for us. Our buggy was also decorated. The horse recognized me and greeted me with loud neighing.

I could not speak, my throat was so choked up, and it took great effort to hold back the tears. We quickly got into the buggy, the luggage and the bags of King Nuts were placed in the *gerobaks*, and the parade got under way.

Everywhere along the road leading through the *kampungs* we were welcomed with endless shouts of *"selamat datang"*. We entered the plantation's main road, which was overgrown with grass, and drove past the first coconut trees. It seemed that the leaves were greener than usual and that they, too, whispered a *"selamat datang"*.

Then we turned into the driveway leading to our house, which was also adorned with young coconut palm leaves, and where, unexpectedly, the flag fluttered in the breeze.

In front stood the children of Mon Désir and a flute orchestra from Kampung Pitu, which promptly and joyously welcomed us with a Malay rendition of "Piet Heyn" — the Dutch Admiral, "whose name was short, but whose deeds were great". This was concluded with three shouts of *"Selamat datang"*, and only then were we allowed to enter the house.

What a wonderful welcome! We were home again!

When calm had returned to the house, Latif, who had quietly married a Madurese woman more than a year ago, came over to show us his first son, and to report on the livestock that he had supervised during our absence.

I was so glad to see him again — he was the only one left from our Buluwaya days — and then I had suddenly a terrible yearning to see my faithful Bok. How much I would have liked to have her with me at that moment!

Latif sensed my feelings, and only asked: "Is she not coming back?"

I shook my head sadly and said: "She and her husband will stay on Java, but I am, oh, so glad that you are still here. I trust that you will stay with us, I hope forever!" His face lit up. But I could not suspect that he would pay dearly for his faithfulness to us.

Overseer Kansil had stayed behind on Tobelo to take care of our *barang*. John had given him the bills of lading, and early the next day the *gerobaks* went downtown to pick up everything.

Our new *babu* Liesbeth and *jongos* Marcus, who had been engaged by the nuns of Tomohon for us, had arrived a week earlier. This morning they came to introduce themselves.

They had been married only a few years, I learned, noticing that they looked impeccable. Liesbeth appeared to be modest and dependable. Marcus was a little older and more staid, and had a fatherly mien about him. They did not have any children.

John and I were drinking our first cup of coffee at daybreak, when I noticed that the house did not look well kept. There were stains on our beautiful ebony furniture, and nicks in the chairs and even in the frames of our paintings. The floor, too, was damaged in several places.

In the dining room, a window was broken, the paint on the doors was scratched, and the lighting (provided by petrol under pressure) was defective.

The garden around the house, too, looked unkept. The beautiful rose garden in front of the house was gone. The bark of our fruit trees had been sliced deeply with a *parang* (a cleaver) and one *jeruk Bali* (grapefruit) tree had been cut down!

I continued my tour of inspection. John's horse had been properly looked after, and the saddle and the harness were beautifully polished. At least that was one thing on the plus side!

I had not noticed the damage when we arrived the day before, and now a creepy feeling went down my spine. I did not want to question the coolies about it, thinking it better to wait until Kansil was back. After all, he'd had the overall responsibility.

At breakfast, I kept my findings to myself, as John had other things on his mind. When he had finished, he left for Tobelo to pick up the mail, and to arrange various things with the local authorities concerning his new job and upcoming departure for Manokwari.

When I decided to clean the cupboards, I found they had recently been scoured and badly scratched in the process. My anxiety increased. Something was definitely wrong here!

Then I suddenly remembered the man whom we had met just before we went on board to go to the Netherlands — now 10 months ago. He had introduced himself as the new administrator of a nearby plantation, asking us if we knew of a place for him to stay. His own house was being built and was far from ready for occupancy. John had answered that he could stay at Mon Désir — although we had heard some rather disquieting stories about him.

"Could this man be responsible for the dilapidated condition of the house?" I wondered. The man, I now remembered, had looked seedy and neglected, but I hadn't paid much attention at the time. Where could he be now?

I started to become hot under the collar and was determined to seek him out and have a frank talk with him. But I soon learned that this would not be possible. Two months earlier he had been fired from his job, and had left with a native woman, leaving a mountain of debts behind.

From Overseer Kansil I received the whole unpleasant story of this man's stay at Mon Désir.

As soon as we had left for Europe, Mr. Dipso — so I will call him — arrived on Mon Désir with one beaten-up suitcase. He introduced himself to Kansil as the new administrator of Kuala Pitu, saying that he had received permission from John to stay in our house, use the servants, the *kebon* (gardener), the buggy, the horses, and the large *gerobak*, and that he would also supervise the workers.

It appeared that he had been drinking, and Kansil, afraid the man could turn violent, reluctantly gave him the key to the house. There were of course no servants, as Bok and her family had left with us.

Latif refused to work for this strange *Tuan*, and had withdrawn with the horses to a hut, far from the plantation. So when the intruder demanded a horse and buggy, Latif was nowhere to be found.

Kansil himself went to downtown Tobelo, where he heard that we had met Mr. Dipso for the first time just before our departure. He had learned all he needed to know and so returned to the plantation.

En route he met two coolies, whom Mr. Dipso had taken from their work to fetch him a case of beer and some canned food. Kansil angrily sent the men back to their work. He then assembled all personnel and gave them strict orders not to get involved with Mr. Dipso, not to run any errands for him, and to stay away from the house.

The personnel grumbled that it was not polite to act in that way, and that the *Tuan* of Kuala Pitu had promised them a liberal reward if they would cooperate with him. In response, Kansil threatened to fire anyone who disobeyed him.

Then he went to the house and made it clear to Mr. Dipso that — based on what he had heard about the conversation between him and John — he could stay in the house, but he would have nothing to say about the personnel of Mon Désir.

However, to soften the impression that the *Tuan* was not welcome, he said that if the *Tuan* needed anything, he could convey this to him, the overseer. He would do his best to be helpful, but he reiterated that he would not tolerate any meddling in the affairs of Mon Désir! The management of the plantation had been entrusted to him, Kansil, and to no one else!

Mr. Dipso first listened, then became angry and started to cuss. Then, his mood suddenly changed and with tears in his eyes he said he was a lonely man, without friends. He hungered for friendship, and all he had done was ask people to help him to get food and drink.

Following this tearful display, Kansil sent a message to the overseer of Kuala Pitu, asking him to come quickly and bring someone to look after the needs of his new *Tuan*. What was discussed between Mr. Dipso and his overseer, Kansil did not know, but it was three days before Mr. Dipso left on foot for Kuala Pitu with much sighing and groaning.

## IBU MALUKU

The plantation was only a half hour's walk away from Mon Désir! But late in the evening, he was brought back by *gerobak*, as he was too drunk to walk.

While living at Mon Désir, Mr. Dipso never paid much attention to Kuala Pitu, the plantation entrusted to his care. In the morning, he was usually sleeping it off; in the afternoon, he would walk around, and rant and cuss at whomever came near him; and in the evenings, he would get together with some buddies — Dutchmen, at first — whom he had picked up by taxicab. Then, the drinking started.

Late one night, his visitors — men and women — were too drunk to stand up. So, Mr. Dipso loaded them in two adorned *gerobaks* and had them taken home, escorted by a group of torchbearers. This caused quite a commotion in Tobelo, and the Dutch stopped coming.

They were replaced by a few Chinese, who brought their own liquor. Later, the Chinese were in turn replaced by roughnecks, who came to drink *and* gamble. It was on these occasions that much of the damage to the furniture, the house and the garden was done.

On one such a spree, Mr. Dipso and a woman from a neighboring *kampung* had fallen among the tea-roses, and had raged about the thorns in which they had landed. The next day, he had his own servant dig up and burn all of these precious rose bushes. A similar rage also caused the destruction of a *jeruk Bali* tree, and the deep machete cuts in other fruit trees.

After Mr. Dipso left, so Kansil explained, many workers came down with influenza, which explained why the yard was now in such a disorderly state.

In my heart, however, I was convinced that he had left everything the way it was, so I could see with my own eyes what had happened. Without saying it, he was telling me it was our own fault — and it was — for allowing a complete stranger to stay in our house.

To my surprise, the rest of Mon Désir had been well kept. The coconut trees looked healthy, and the workers proudly told me that more than three hundred trees were *mayang*: that they carried clusters of flowers. That was welcome news, and with pride and gratitude I went to see them. In less than a year, we could harvest the nuts!

The livestock had grown too: nine healthy calves and two magnificent colts had been born during our absence. Of the pigs, of course, only a few were left — the majority having been sold to pay the worker's wages.

The clearing of the land had progressed well: more than 40 hectares were ready for seeding. Delivery of the dwarf coconut *bibit* (seedlings) had continued, and some 150 had sprouted beautifully and were ready for transplanting. Counting the King Nuts I had brought from Ceylon, I now had a potential of 225 coconut trees — a good start.

By the afternoon, all our *barang* had been delivered, and we immediately unpacked the presents we had brought for the workers and their families, who gathered in the early evening in front of the house.

Each man received a pipe with tobacco (genuine "Van Nelle" from Holland), a real surprise. The women received a nice piece of cloth — enough to make a *kebaya* (a blouse) — and the children got large bags of *teng-teng* (candy) and ice-bonbons.

We then announced a big *selamatan* (a thanksgiving dinner), to be held the following Saturday.

When peace and quiet had returned, we went through our mail. John interrupted his reading to tell me about his meeting with the new magistrate and some of our acquaintances. I then brought him up-to-date on the state of Mon Désir. We concluded that everything had gone well, and talked little about Mr. Dipso. After all, things could have been much worse.

Later, we would meet more men like Mr. Dipso: drop-outs from society, victims of that miserable system, which often required that men — government and plantation employees alike — must be single to come to the East Indies. It also required them to remain unattached until their first furlough, six years later. This system caused the ruin of many a man. (That John and I had married before we landed, proved to be an exception.)

\*\*\*\*

In preparation for the trip to New Guinea, John had searched widely to find sturdy, knowledgeable *damar* people who could teach the local population on New Guinea how to tap *damar*.

A few butterfly catchers — led by a man named Buturu, whom we had known from the time the Zeist couple had stayed with us — begged John to take them with him. They had heard that the butterflies on New Guinea were even more beautiful than those on Halmahera. After several discussions, John agreed.

The day of John's departure arrived. He would first reconnoiter the north coast to search for a favorable location to establish a trading post. He said he would need two months — "two boats", we said — to finish the job. I would follow him then, and together we would decide what to do with Mon Désir.

After John had left, I could finally give all my attention to the plantation. In the Botanical Garden of Buitenzorg, they had advised me to plant other crops besides coconuts. They had recommended kapok, since there was a great demand for it.

I had followed up on that right away, and the ship on which John had left had brought me a shipment of kapok seed. It was a special type of kapok that withstood disease, grew quickly, and delivered a marketable product. We looked for a good place to start seed-beds, and selected the 40 hectares that had just been cleared.

I hired more lumberjacks to clear the remainder of the forest. The price per hectare had risen from 75 to 95 guilders, but it seemed reasonable to me, because the work was heavy. The price for lumber had risen also, which offset the increase in wages.

Then a major problem arose. Overseer Kansil received the unexpected news that his father had passed away. It was now his duty to return home and support his mother. As head of the family, he also had to care for the young ones, so he asked to be relieved of his duties.

I was very sorry to see him go. It would be difficult to replace such a good man. There were many who applied, but how was I to find the most dependable among them?

Upon the strong recommendation of the administrator of a nearby plantation, I hired a man who was alleged to be dependable and knowledgeable. Talakua was from the Talaud Islands (half way between Halmahera and Mindanao), and although he indulged in flattery, he otherwise made a good impression on me.

Time quickly passed. The first ship brought letters from John, full of enthusiasm. The possibilities on New Guinea seemed endless. The letters were sent with the *van Noort*, the ship that had taken him along the entire north coast. For the moment, he had settled in Manokwari, the capital, and would stay in the *pasanggrahan* until my arrival.

On Manokwari lived several Dutch families, he wrote. Also, a few Germans, who had been planters or traders in the former German New Guinea and had been "washed-up" after World War I.

They had left their homeland for this intimidating New Guinea, had put their heart and soul into their plantations, and had been proud of their achievements.

Then the war started. They had no part in it, but it destroyed them. They lost everything, and were forced to find refuge in Dutch territory. They now earned their livelihood by bartering copra, *damar*, and bird-of-paradise feathers.

Marriages were canceled, because their fiancées were not allowed to leave Germany. To substitute for this lost domestic happiness, these bereft and bitter men took native women as wives. They were partly ashamed of it and partly proud ... in a grim sort of way. With their large number of offspring, they told the world they could not care less about what was to become of them.

On Manokwari, John continued, there was also a detachment of police officers. The commanding officer was an old Navy Captain, who in a fatherly manner, had kept the peace in this difficult territory.

John had struck up a friendship with him, and had learned much about the land and its people. He had also received valuable advice on how to conduct trade and get around in that rough country.

There arose in me a desire to get to know New Guinea — although deep in my heart there was an uncomfortable feeling of an approaching disaster ...

\* \* \* \*

In preparation for my planned departure, I discussed the affairs of the plantation with the new overseer, Talakua, and in his presence explained to the lumberjacks, woodcutters and permanent workers what needed to be done. Everyone nodded they had understood me well.

The only ones that raised objections were Latif and his fellow Madurese. They did not like reporting to a foreigner, and only the promise that I would come from time to time made them curb their unwillingness to cooperate.

Talakua added that he would not concern himself much with their special task anyway. They knew how to take care of the livestock, and he would have more than enough to keep himself occupied. So, he said, he would be pleased to work together as "friends". I took him at his word.

There was, however, something I had overlooked. None of the trusted Madurese could read or write. Talakua did, of course, and he would take unfair advantage of that situation.

IBU MALUKU

# CHAPTER 19

### Bound for New Guinea
*S.S. van Noort, June, 1929*

With the second ship came the request from John to join him in Manokwari. From there, we would travel together to the island of Biak, where John wanted to establish his first post.

So with the returning KPM steamship *Swarte Hondt*, I left for Ternate, stayed there two days, and then continued the journey on the *van Noort* — the regular "Papua ship".

Captain Faber was a jolly man, who told jokes from early in the morning until late at night. From him, I learned more about New Guinea in a few days than I had in the preceding nine years. He personally knew every one of the 300 European inhabitants, and had intimate knowledge of their mutual relationships, characters and habits — even of people who had formerly lived and worked there and had long since gone.

The chronicles of these Europeans were sometimes sad, sometimes embarrassing or funny, admirable or lamentable — but always worth hearing. I began to understand why this valuable part of the East Indies had been neglected — it was so primitive and impenetrable — and that it received more attention now as a result of the economic depression in Holland.

When we approached Manokwari, Captain Faber called me to the bridge, and invited me to compare this panorama with other vistas I had seen during my young life. The *van Noort* sailed past "Missionary Island", Manzinam, into the outer bay, where the dark, almost hostile hinterland took on a more friendly face. The coast was covered with swaying coconut and screw-pine trees. In between, here and there, stood small brown houses on stilts with dark frizzy heads in front: naked black-skinned children, who waved joyfully to the ship.

When the ship turned into the inner bay, the town came into view. Built into a hill, the beautiful white houses seemed to lean against it. All of them were covered with blooming bougainvillaea, varying in color from dark purple to soft lilac, and from rose pink to dark red. Alongside the roads blazed the red and blooming *spathodea*[1], alternating with *royal poincianas* that raised their flat, brilliantly red crowns against the pale blue sky. The slopes were covered with flowering climbers that cascaded downward between green grass, like rose or white waterfalls.

"Dubrovnik!" I shouted, elated.

Yes, Manokwari did indeed look like that old imperial city on the Adriatic coast, as I had seen it one early spring morning so long ago. I saw myself again on the gleaming white deck of the German ship that maintained contact among the Mediterranean coastal cities, from Marseille to Athens.

Captain Faber enjoyed my reaction and promised there was more to come.

We dropped anchor, and John came on board to take me ashore. He wanted me to meet some people and visit Manokwari. But our visit had to be short: the *van Noort* would weigh anchor in the afternoon.

The Dutch population of Manokwari consisted primarily of missionaries. The town also had an Assistant Resident, a *Controleur*, and an Assistant *Controleur*, who made up the Dutch Government. In addition, there was a Javanese doctor; Grandpapa Klaassen (the fatherly police chief John had written about); several Dutchmen employed at a Government sawmill or engaged in an agricultural venture; and five Germans (also mentioned in John's letter) who came to the ship without their families.

Among them, I learned, was a member of the Austrian Imperial Family, who lived under an assumed name on a nearby island with a younger member of the family. He made his living by bartering with the Papua population.

This man came on board, greeted the Dutchmen and Germans with condescending affability, and then strode to the bridge to talk to Captain Faber, who later escorted him personally to the ship's gangway.

He was dressed oddly for this part of the world. He had a colored shirt, leather shorts, heavy boots, and a Tyrolean hat, complete with chamois tail.

His face looked cold and severe, and I wondered how much suffering, disappointment, hopelessness (perhaps), and disillusionment (definitely!) was hidden behind that poker face.

Human flotsam, to be sure.

The journey continued to Saonek, where the magistrate — someone with an aristocratic name — came on board. A Menadonese woman, whom everyone freely addressed as Paatje (pah-chuh), accompanied him.

We got into a lively conversation with them. He seemed to like the Papuas, but regard them as grown-up, naughty children. He assured

John that he could teach them the art of tapping *damar*, if John would give him two experienced men, whom he could train as teachers.

From the men who had come with us, two volunteered. They would stay a month on Saonek, and then catch the next ship to join us on Biak — a large island, some 200 kilometers due east from Manokwari.

In the presence of Paatje and the Ambonese District Chief who had joined us, these two volunteers were given the necessary instructions and advice. Their salaries and allowances were given to the District Chief, who would keep these funds in trust until payday. Paatje also promised them a bonus at the end of their stay.

Content, but a little unsure of themselves, our two volunteers went ashore. The first step toward training Papuas in *damar* tapping had been taken.

Next day, the *van Noort* dropped anchor in an exceptionally beautiful bay, and was soon surrounded by dozens of unsteady *praus*, filled with erect, festively-adorned Papuas, who cheerfully waved to us.

These tall black chaps, who disarmed us with their childlike laughter, were dressed with a thick bundle of leaves, colorful bird feathers and red flowers, attached with a thin string around their middle. It completely covered their *behind*. In front, they were stark naked!

They came on board with clusters of yellow-golden bananas, and a kind of *nangka* (jack fruit) — which they called *nak-nak*. They wanted to barter them for tobacco and paint, especially white and red paint, with which to adorn themselves.

They had also brought dozens of lively, colored, black-headed parrots. With a small ring around one leg, these birds were attached to a stick that joined the legs of a horse-shoe-shaped piece of bamboo — of which the ends had been carved to form a feed trough on one side, and a water trough on the other. Very clever!

This little port had a magistrate, but he was absent this day. The only Europeans here were an old German man and his young wife, Käthe, who had arrived from Berlin only a year ago. From them we learned a little about their lives in this isolated region.

At one time, he was the owner of a large coconut plantation on a Pacific island. He had a hundred thousand blooming coconut trees, a mansion, and a retinue of well-trained servants. He, his wife, a baroness, and five children lived there in great luxury.

Just before the start of the war, the three older children, all boys, went to a boarding-school in Germany; the two younger ones, girls, stayed behind with their own governess. Life was good, and he lived like a king.

## IBU MALUKU

Then came the assassination of Austrian Archduke Ferdinand that started World War I. The news arrived too late to pull his children out of Germany. The two elder sons joined the army without his permission and died in battle. The third one was wounded, and never quite recovered.

After Germany lost the war, the properties of all German citizens in the Pacific were taken over by Australia.

With his wife and daughters, he fled his island by boat, with all the money and jewels he could take. With an Australian gunboat in hot pursuit, he set course for Hollandia[2] on the north coast of New Guinea at full speed, using the furniture and every other scrap of wood on board to keep the boiler going. He managed to stay ahead, and the gunboat gave up the chase after he had entered the territorial waters of the Netherlands East Indies.

The people of Hollandia, who had been watching the race through binoculars, gave the refugees a warm welcome. He was given a piece of land, where he built a house. His wife, however, could not adjust to the primitive existence, and died within the year. He then sent his daughters to an Ursuline boarding school in Batavia, and moved from Hollandia to this region, where he first hunted, fished and bartered with the Papuas, and later purchased small, scattered coconut plantations from the native population.

He had spent much time writing petitions to the German government, whom, he thought, was duty-bound to compensate him for all he had lost. They thought otherwise. Faced with much chicanery and duplicity, he got tired of writing, and went to Germany to plead his case. He took the two girls with him, and left them with impoverished members of the family.

For two years, he battled. He spent all his money on lawyers — for whom he had no kind words — and finally did get compensation, though it was a mere pittance.

Then, Käthe came into his life. She readily came out with him to New Guinea, and, surprisingly, adjusted rapidly to her new environment. She now felt completely at home! She was a small, lively, plump blonde, who spontaneously invited everyone not needed on board to come to her house for coffee and homemade *küchen* (cakes).

We vied with each other in admiring her house and kitchen. From the primitive bamboo house, she had managed to make a cozy, attractive home.

She spent her days cooking, sewing, and ... teaching. She showed us a little shed where several Papua girls were taught how to sew. As evidence of her native ingenuity, everything produced here was used to barter with Papuas from nearby islands! A splendid idea!

We said goodbye and continued our journey, stopping at several places. On one island, we encountered a large community of pioneers: a magistrate and his family; a Eurasian doctor with wife and child; two missionary couples; and an Inspector of Police with wife and two teenage daughters, who were being tutored by correspondence.

Here, the ship took in copra, and a quantity of *damar* of exceptionally poor quality. It was a soft sticky mess, called *malengket*, which was shipped in crates. John and his tappers looked at it with disgust. They had never seen the likes of it. The shipper, who was Chinese, assured John that the *damar* from New Guinea was the worst in the world.

\* \* \* \*

Early the next day, we put into the port of Hollandia, which Captain Faber called "the most beautiful harbor in the entire East Indies".

At the crack of dawn, while dusk still hung over the ocean, I was out on deck, eager to see this harbor when it was bathed in the golden brilliance of the rising sun!

Again, I witnessed this unforgettable splendor, this orgy of colors: first the soft hues of pearly luster, which the still hidden sun daintily painted with gold. Then, the still subdued golden sun disk peeked above the misty shroud, growing steadily into a red golden arc, and then practically jumped out of the twilight. In an incredibly short time, it grew into a brilliant, blinding, fire-spitting sphere, which brought the sea to life with millions of sparkles.

Hollandia, located at Humboldt Bay (named after German naturalist and explorer Baron Alexander von Humboldt), is indeed a miracle of nature. A magnificent mountain range surrounds this bay, but there is a pass that leads to a large, fertile plain that stretches inland and touches Santania Lake.

Hollandia was the most prominent seat of government in New Guinea. It had a competent, jolly magistrate, a doctor, a detachment of police constables, two German families, several missionaries, and a few Ambonese *gurus*, who taught the Papua children.

Christianity had grown here quicker than expected, so the Papuas had built their own church, of which they were justifiably proud.

We met a German, who lived with his wife in a small house on the outskirts of the *kota*. He had also been a well-to-do plantation owner in German New Guinea, and was now a refugee, like so many of his countrymen.

He had started anew, and had built up a plantation of 30 hectares, where he now grew papaya for the production of pepsin. But this enzyme — used as a digestive and as ferment in the production of cheese — earned him barely enough to live on.

Innocently, we asked if he and his wife had ever thought about going back to Germany. The woman answered hotly:

"No, never! Our government turned its back on us. We had nothing to do with that war, but lost everything nevertheless!"

Quiet, embittered people, who now only wanted to be left alone, and live their remaining years in peace.

\* \* \* \*

The ship left for Serui (on Yapen Island), the last stop before Bosnik (on Biak), which was our final destination. We arrived in Serui toward evening, and again experienced a sunset, so beautiful, so impressive, that words cannot describe it.

It was raining the next day, so we stayed on board. John had visited the town once before, and told me a little about it.

A magistrate lived there, whose wife was on Java, recovering from an illness. He himself was on *tournée* in the interior. There were also two missionary families, two Ambonese *gurus*, a small police detachment with a cheerful Ambonese commander, a nurse, and several Chinese traders. The Papua population lived in large communal houses, built on poles over the sea — and John pointed to a few of these houses that could be seen from where we were standing. The surrounding area looked desolate, and we were pleased to leave it.

The sea had become rough when we set sail, and the ship rolled badly throughout the night.

The next day, our last one on board, we approached Biak Island. We already knew we would be the only Europeans there.

Close to the coast, Captain Faber drew our attention to the local odor of Bosnik. It was a musty smell, which made one think of a soiled, mildewed dishcloth. It was the oppressive smell of psoriasis — a chronic skin disease that was a characteristic of the population of this island.

Papuas approached in their large *praus*: tall, friendly smiling chaps with enormous frizzy heads. They surrounded the *van Noort* and shouted a welcome.

They were not allowed on board, but even from the upper deck, we could see the scaly patches on their sturdy chests and backs, and even smell the affliction from that distance. But one can get used to almost anything, and we would eventually get used to this musty odor as well.

We watched the lively, childlike Papuas with pleasure. Soon, we would be living among them. A small number had become Christian, they told us; the majority, however, were still head hunters — and to curb this practice, Bosnik had a large constabulary.

They were an exceptional jolly bunch, those head hunters. On the quay, we met many men, women and children who greeted us loudly and enthusiastically with *"Selamat malam baik"* (a very good evening to you), while endlessly scratching their arms or thighs. It almost seemed that this scraping was part of the greeting ceremony.

The women dressed nicely. They wore very tight bikinis[3] made from beads. I thought the hard beads would be quite uncomfortable — even painful — until I saw some of them skipping rope. Even pregnant women participated in this game. Would this be some special exercise for them?

The communal houses in which the Papuas lived, built on stilts over the sea, were connected by a long, narrow bridge to the mainland. At its entrance stood wooden statues with large heads, adorned with a wig made of fibers from the *arèn* (arenga) palm. Their task, obviously, was to protect the community against evil spirits.

The older inhabitants watched our arrival while standing in front of their houses and, by way of welcome, grinned from ear to ear.

"Are these people really headhunters?" I wondered.

Bosnik consisted of one long street. The roadbed was blindingly white from freshly distributed fine-grained *karang* (coral), mixed with white sand. At the end of the pier stood a solitary KPM warehouse. A little further on stood several small Chinese shops, with, off to one side, a small building for storing bartered copra.

Money was largely unknown to the Papuas. These natives bartered with the Chinese traders — copra, *damar* and *rotan* against beads, mirrors, tobacco, matches, paraffin, pots and pans, and deep red and blue fabric — and were usually victimized.

For that reason, the Government promoted the use of cash. It would put the Papuas in a better position to negotiate a price like other inhabitants of Bosnik, and finally teach them how to handle money.

The Papuas, as I had already noticed, loved brightly colored fabric. It served as the centerpiece of the bouquet of leaves, feathers and flowers with which the men covered their behinds. The red and blue, I must admit, did indeed look good. (It should be noted that the inhabitants of Bosnik were more conventionally dressed.)

The predominantly Chinese shops not only catered to the natives; they also carried wares for non-native inhabitants: the Ambonese gurus, the police, and the civil servants. For them, there was rice, salt, soap, perfumes, cigarettes; fabric for shirts, and pajamas. For the women there were colorful *sarongs*, *kebayas*, and household wares. These people did purchase with cash ... after a fierce haggle over the price, of course.

Continuing on "main street", we passed first a school, and then the government's building with the residence of the magistrate, Mr. Pastora, who appeared to have much influence with the local people, and knew how to maintain the peace. He and his wife were full-blooded Ambonese[4].

Still further on stood the *tangsi*, the barracks, where the policemen lived with their families. At the very end of this long street stood a large, desolate-looking missionary house, completely empty and neglected. This would become our residence. John had rented it when he first surveyed the area.

Someone on Manokwari had told him it had been abandoned, but did not say why. The building was large enough to also serve as a temporary home for the workers that had come with us. If necessary, part of it could also be freed to serve as *gudang* for trade products.

Opposite our house stood twelve large communal Papua houses, all built on stilts over the sea. We had a clear view of this complex, and were thus in a good position to observe them. At times, it was quite interesting. We learned quickly that these people not only had a great curiosity, but that they were also very outspoken.

With all available hands, we started to clean out this large house of ours.

It had a front veranda with an adjoining alcove, which had several times been used as latrine. It was spacious and would, after cleaning of course, be well suited to serve as dining room.

A wide corridor connected the rear veranda with the front one. Doors on the right led to three large rooms. The first one would be our bedroom. The last one would be the office, since it was closest to the rear veranda, where the Papuas could be received. Part of this veranda could also be used as *gudang*. On the left of the corridor was a cool, large hall, somewhat dark, as there were not enough windows. This would serve as temporary quarters for our workers, and a part of it could be partitioned off for our servants, Liesbeth and Marcus.

The annex was in worse shape. The bathroom had a leaky cistern, but we had picked up a few bags of cement in Manokwari and would thus be able to repair the cracks.

Fortunately, the large well in the yard yielded good water, primarily because it had been used regularly by Menadonese masons and carpenters, who were building new military barracks nearby. Their foreman was kind enough to lend us some men to make some much-needed repairs to our house. This was quite a windfall, as our own people were not qualified to handle those tasks.

That first evening, the Magistrate, Mr. Pastora, invited us to dinner. We ate a large type of crab, which feeds only on coconut meat. To that end, it climbs the tree, snips off the nuts with powerful scissors, lets them drop, and somehow opens them later to get at the coconut meat.

The crabs were delicious!

Our host invited us to stay with them the first night, but we declined because we felt we should stay with our people.

\* \* \* \*

Our first night on Bosnik was restless. We were probably too tired. It was also hot and humid — something that had not bothered us on board.

The next day, our *barang* arrived in a large *gerobak* that was pushed and pulled by a group of boisterous men. With much shouting, the cart was unloaded. If only it could have stopped there. It did not.

Our Papua friends insisted on helping us unwrap each item coming out of the crates. It then passed from hand to hand, to be admired or criticized, depending on its usefulness in their eyes.

I was especially afraid for my china and glassware. Not only did this unwrapping take forever, there was also the distinct possibility that things would disappear. We had a difficult time watching every move.

This unsolicited help was not exactly pleasant, but we did not dare to make our feelings known. After all, John had come here to win their trust, and we did not want to upset them in any way.

After a few days, the house was finally habitable. John paid courtesy calls to anyone who was even remotely connected to the local government, and in our spare time we dedicated ourselves to studying the language, since most of the Papuas did not understand the standard Malay. Our butterfly catchers learned this on the third day!

As usual, they had left very early in the morning to scout the area. In the foothills of a high mountain range that started 20 meters behind our house, they had found a well-traveled path. Soon after they had started their climb, several Papua women and children began to follow. They looked on in surprise as the men caught butterflies with nets, and gathered twigs with cocoons attached. Not understanding the explanations given in Malay, the Papuas assumed the butterfly catchers were gathering food for us, and everyone jumped in to lend a hand.

The next day we were deluged by women and children bringing live butterflies, strung together on a thin strand of *rotan* — and thus damaged. They wanted to exchange these for all the things that they had seen come out of our crates!

It was utter chaos, and in the end we had to call on the Magistrate to explain what the butterfly catchers' work was all about.

\*\*\*\*

John quickly won the trust of the local owners of *damar dusuns*, and arranged to go with them, the District Chief and several *Kepala Kampungs* to see the *damar* trees, and have our own *damar* experts also demonstrate a new way to tap.

John invited me to come along.

We brought with us a few exceptional samples of *damar* (the hard, lustrous resin, derived from the *damar* tree), to show the Papuas what the product would look like if they adopted our way of tapping. The District Chief and *Kepala Kampungs* acted as our translators, and the Papuas showed themselves to be good listeners.

After a walk of two and a half hours, we reached the *damar* trees — the same majestic trees I had admired earlier on Morotai. Sadly, the trees had been tapped in a way that ensured they would be bled dry within a few years.

The natives had built around each trunk a seven-meter-high scaffold. Standing on top of it, they had punctured the bark with sharply pointed sticks. Like a burning candle, these trees were covered with white streaks of resin, which were scraped off with much of the bark. The Papua women would gather the harvest, remove most of the impurities, and deliver the final product to Chinese traders. These, in turn, sold this mess as *malenket* to traders that traveled around on KPM ships.

Our own *damar* tappers were indignant. John advised the District Chief to stop this manner of tapping right away, if he wanted to prevent the destruction of this rich source of income for the population.

Amid admiring cries from the watching Papuas, our people carefully cut into the bark, and attached under the cut a little on-the-spot-plaited basket, in which the golden sap started to flow slowly.

We seated ourselves under this newly tapped tree, pulled out our samples, showed the Papuas what high-quality *damar* looked like, and explained what it would be worth. John offered to lease the trees at a fixed price for several years. After that, if they wanted, they could tap the trees themselves and give him the exclusive right to purchase all they would harvest.

The Papuas, who had listened attentively, then entered into a lively debate. The District Chief and the *Kepala Kampungs* agreed that the Papuas had understood the issues well, but would need time to decide.

We were pleased, though, that the first contact had been made.

# IBU MALUKU

\*\*\*\*

The forests on Biak were quite different from those on Halmahera. Excluding the tall *damar* trees, the trees on this island were shorter than those I was used to. Also, the sub-vegetation consisted mostly of brushwood and well-known fruit trees — mainly *langsep* (a cousin of the leechee), *jambu* (guava) and citrus trees. We picked several ripe fruits and took them with us.

In several places, the ground was covered with raspberry bushes, whose fruits were big, juicy and sweet. The Papuas, and even our own people, looked on in horror when I ate them. In unison, they assured me they were poisonous. They did not hurt me, however, and I later persuaded the butterfly hunters to gather them for me. I made delicious jams from them — by themselves, or mixed with *jambu* and citrus fruits.

I sometimes accompanied Buturu and his butterfly catchers on their trips, and enjoyed myself immensely. We would catch some of the most beautiful butterflies then, and I would always learn something more about the magnificent birds and orchids.

I was particularly enchanted by the *mambruk*, the blue-gray, red-eyed crown-pigeons that make their primitive nests in the bushes close to the ground, and leave their eggs for the picking. Soon, I had several of these beautiful birds parading in our yard, where I could enjoy their beauty and sonorous sounds from up close.

\*\*\*\*

We soon developed cordial relations with the traders and local population, and had also become good friends of the Pastora family. During his career in the civil service, Mr. Pastora had been posted in many places on New Guinea and had seen a great deal. But it was especially Mrs. Pastora who taught me much about the country and its people.

They did not have children. While posted at Merauke, a town on the southern coast of New Guinea, they had lost their only son to blackwater fever — a severe form of malaria that turns the patient's urine dark red, or black. I told her about myself and my miscarriage, and our mutual suffering drew us closer together.

During our conversations, she often made furtive remarks about the house that John and I lived in. Nothing specific, but I interpreted her remarks as warnings, and they made me uncomfortable.

After having lived three days in our house, Liesbeth and Marcus said they had a family member in prison, and asked permission to find quarters near the prison.

Four days later, our *damar* collectors and butterfly catchers, hardy and robust men, became uneasy. They said they did not want to sleep in the house anymore, because there were ghosts roaming around at night. Not that they had seen any, but they had heard the shuffle of bare feet and had felt the air displacements of persons walking past.

The following night, they woke us up several times to report that a stream of people had shuffled past them. Obviously they were ghosts that had been disturbed by the new occupants, they said. The house had been cursed and was haunted, and they did not want to stay.

That forced John to find other lodgings for them. This he did after some difficulty.

Early in the morning, these workers assembled in front of our house, and continued to do their assigned duties: to accompany John and a few Papuas in the search for mature *damar* trees. At night, however, after the workers had left, it became very still in this large house, and some of its strange atmosphere crept up on us. We did not know what to make of it.

A week later, I received my first visitors: the wives of two local *gurus*, who, as elsewhere, were addressed as *Nyora*.

They were demurely dressed in customary *adat* costume: the starched *rokki plooi*, a cotton skirt, pressed into hundreds of stiff, narrow pleats; the long, white *kebaya* with tight-fitting sleeves that were closed with scores of small buttons; and mules with upturned toes. In their hands, they each held a stiffly starched, ironed, white handkerchief.

They were accompanied by three other ladies, all nattily dressed: the wives of the Chief of Police, the corporal, and the Orderly from the *tangsi*.

The ladies admired the house, which, they said, had been turned into something beautiful. It was a pity that our workers had chosen to make do with a decrepit shack, rather than sleep in this beautiful house.

I tried to steer the conversation in another direction, but without success. One lady asked what these workers had seen or heard that had made them afraid to stay.

I pretended not to know, and said: "I think they were just not *senang* (happy) here."

The ladies exchanged knowing glances, pretended to shiver, and asked no further questions. They did tell me, however, about the previous owner of this house, and how it came to be built.

There had been a contractual dispute between the contractor and the owner. While the house was being erected, the owner repeatedly asked for changes, which, of course, increased the cost of construction. When he received the bill, he refused to pay for the changes. The contractor became enraged. He refused to accept a single penny, and left with his crew for Tidore after having cursed the house and all its future inhabitants.

Afterwards, among those who lived in the house, there had been a series of strange deaths in quick succession, and ultimately, the house was abandoned.

The ladies asserted that they did not see any connection between the curse and those deaths, but, one never knew. In unison, they said that we were very *berani* (courageous). They themselves would not dare to live here!

I was relieved when they dropped the subject, and told me about the small church that existed on Bosnik. Three services were given here: one for the Ambonese; one for the Menadonese; and one for the Papuas. These separate services, they felt, were necessary because of the linguistic differences, and because of the primitive state of the local population.

\* \* \* \*

As a result of our cordial relations with the traders, we received an invitation to attend the approaching Chinese New Year celebrations. We were eager to go, as it would give us some diversion and the opportunity to meet other inhabitants of Bosnik.

Once again, the *van Noort* dropped its anchor in Bosnik's harbor, bringing the two *damar* collectors whom we had left in Saonek for special training.

We had been looking forward to the ship's arrival and the mail it would bring. I longed for news from Mon Désir, as I had been worrying about it. But there weren't any letters from there.

We spent several enjoyable hours on board. Captain Faber shared his harvest of new jokes, and made me happy with the gift of a sirloin steak and a large loaf of raisin bread. When he asked us if we were ready to go back to Ternate or Manokwari, we both spontaneously answered: "Absolutely not! We are staying!" and told him about the upcoming Chinese New Year festivities.

With a heartfelt "au revoir", we then took our leave.

**Endnotes**
[1] The *spathodea campanulata,* called African tulip or fireball tree, came from West Africa early in the 20th century and was planted in Indonesia and throughout the Pacific region as a decorative shade

tree. Before it blossoms into a beautiful red tulip-like flower, the brown-green flower bud resembles a miniature banana. It is filled with water, making it a natural water pistol when squeezed.
2. Hollandia, which would feature prominently in General McArthur's drive towards the Philippines, was later renamed Kotabaru, then Jayapura.
3. The word "bikini", of course, did not exist at the time.
4. Mr. Pastora, with the rank of *Gezaghebber*, was the first native person to hold the post of Magistrate.

# CHAPTER 20

## The Curse
### Bosnik, Biak Island, July, 1928

When we arrived home from our enjoyable visit on board the *van Noort*, it was unusually hot and humid in town.

Waiting in front of the house was a group of Papuas from a faraway *kampung*, who had heard of our "unusual" habit of gathering butterflies and cocoons.

Through an interpreter, they said that, rather than gather such puny things for food, we would be better off buying from them animals with more substance — such as snakes and lizards, which they considered delicacies.

Much to the mirth of the local Papuas who had quickly gathered around us, they then showed us their wares: snakes of all sizes and colors, mostly alive and either clamped between two tied-together sticks, or kept in small plaited baskets. They also had lizards of up to one meter long, which were kept in larger baskets. Their pride and joy, however, was a four-meter long python, which they dragged up close to the house.

This undulating reptile was harnessed with *rotan* bands at the neck, the tail, and at several places in between. My old fear of snakes made me retreat inside the house, and safely watch the developments from a bay window.

I don't know what got into the heads of the animal's captors, but they dragged the python onto the front gallery and let go of all ropes, except the one attached to the band around its neck. The reptile suddenly shot forward, jerking itself free from the one restraining hand, and slithered into the corridor.

I hastily barricaded the doors leading to the bay window with chairs and a *palang pintu* (wooden cross-bar), as the doors had no locks. John ordered the captors to pursue the snake, and they finally caught it in the bathroom.

Now we had the delicate task of telling these people — without offending them — that we cared neither for snakes, nor lizards. As our words were translated, their faces registered bewilderment and disbelief. However, we continued, we would be interested in buying the skins.

John then proposed that they themselves should use the animals they had brought to prepare a festive meal according to the local custom. He would then donate — as his part in the *selamatan* — a bag of rice. The skins we would purchase from them later.

Loud cheers greeted his proposal, and the whole group took off for the beach, taking all those reptiles with them — thank God!

The inhabitants of the Papua *kampung* across from us generously donated other ingredients for the banquet: mostly fresh sago and sweet potatoes.

Some men dug a large hole, while others gathered firewood and large stones. Children came down from the mountain slopes, carrying bunches of banana leaves to line the hole with.

The snakes were skinned, chopped in pieces, and neatly packed at the bottom of the hole, with *batata* (sweet potatoes), sago, and soaked rice. This first layer was covered with heated stones. Then, the process repeated itself, until all the food had been placed. The last layer of hot stones and banana leaves was sealed with earth. Then everyone left, except a few women, who stayed to guard the pit.

Several hours later the revelers returned and arranged themselves around the pit, from where — I must admit — came a tantalizing aroma.

Curious, John and I walked over for a closer look.

They removed the upper layer of the still warm stones and stripped the scorched banana leaves to expose the food. The sago, rice, *batatas* and reptile meat had solidified into a huge cake. With large *parangs* (cleavers) they cut into this mass, and presented a piece on a banana leaf to each person present. The most important persons were served first and received the largest portions; the women and children were last in the chain.

With curiosity, we watched them consume this simple but copious meal. They presented us with a generous portion, but we politely declined, and went home, not suspecting that this day still had another surprise in store for us.

\*\*\*\*

On this coral island, it was warmer than on Halmahera. When the heat of the day had diminished, we would bathe and then take a walk to the furthest point of the harbor. A passable road led to it. At its beginning was a Chinese cemetery; at the end, a Christian one that, relative to the number of inhabitants, had many Dutch graves. This day, as usual, we made our evening walk toward the *tanjung* (the cape).

As we passed the Chinese cemetery, John remarked how strange it was that a Chinese, who seems content to live all his life in a miserably small house bursting with women, children and commercial goods, would feel the need for a huge piece of land to be buried in. The graves were indeed large and expensive, with magnificent vases, and even benches for grieving visitors.

We continued our stroll and I told John about the ladies who had come to visit me. We then visited the graves of Dutch women and children, which made us pensive. In silence, we left to walk back, and then it happened.

We were half way home, when I had a feeling that someone was following us. I repressed an impulse to look back, but the urge became so strong that, finally, I did take a quick look. In the semi-darkness I thought I saw a male figure who was fast approaching.

I took another look, and clearly saw a man, a *hadji*, dressed in the traditional garb of someone who has visited Mecca. He wore a long white caftan, and his shimmering white fez had a yellow-white cloth wound around it. One is only allowed to wear it after having finished the pilgrimage to Mecca.

My looking back irritated John, and he asked crossly why I was doing that. Then he turned around himself to see what could have drawn my attention.

Surprised, he said: "Hey! How did that *hadji* get there?" We were, after all, on a dead-end street, and had not seen him pass us. We chose to continue, but now at a faster pace.

Then, I unmistakably felt a hand on my shoulder that delivered a slight push, and I let out a scream. John whirled around to face the *hadji*, but he had already disappeared among the Chinese gravestones. John ran after him, and searched among the graves, but there was no one to be found.

Thoroughly angry, John walked faster and faster in the direction of our house, pulling me along by the hand. Instead of going home, however, he took me straight to the residence of the Magistrate.

The Pastora family was sitting on the front veranda, sipping tea, when we arrived. John did not give them any time to greet us, and urgently asked if he could see Mr. Pastora in private.

Mr. Pastora looked surprised, but immediately got up and led us to his office.

Without preliminary explanation, John lodged a complaint against this unknown *hadji* for laying a hand on his wife, in violation of customary etiquette. Then, in jerky sentences, he told him what had happened and demanded that the man be called to account.

Mr. Pastora's reaction was bizarre. He turned gray, broke out into a sweat, and with fear in his eyes stuttered: "You must ... you must not go home. You must stay here with us ... both of you!"

John exploded, and said angrily that this bloody *hadji* did not scare him one bit. We would stay in our house; no one was going to chase us out!

Mr. Pastora raised his hands in a pleading gesture and with some difficulty stammered: "No! Don't ... don't go back! There is no *hadji* on this island! Believe me ... there is not a single Mohammedan here!"

John calmed down a little and said: "But my wife and I have seen this man clearly! I chased him through the Chinese cemetery and he *does* exist. I'm *not* crazy!"

Mr. Pastora then asked us to follow him to join his wife. Much calmer now, we did as he asked.

The obviously fearful couple then told us that when the *hadji* — be he man or ghost or whatever — had made an appearance, someone always died in the old mission house that we now called our home. That is why they urged us to stay with them. There was enough room in the house, and we could stay until we could find other quarters.

However, we felt we had to decline their offer. We did not believe in these fairy tales and wanted to prove to them that it was pure superstition! So, we took our leave and went home, where our servants were waiting to serve dinner. We sent them home right away, afraid they might detect something from the way we behaved.

That evening, we did not talk much. We had recently returned from a restful European furlough, and we were in good health. Why should we worry about anything? The following evening, we would celebrate the Chinese New Year. We looked forward to this diversion, which would be doubly welcome now.

The next day, however, I suddenly felt unwell in the bathroom, and threw up violently. John pressed me to take some Norit (carbon) tablets, which usually helped in such cases. This time, though, they did not.

I became sicker with each passing hour and asked John to go to the New Year's celebration by himself. Liesbeth and Marcus would stay with me until he returned. That was the way it turned out.

John did not enjoy the party very much, not knowing what was the matter with me. He might even have thought that I had been influenced by those dire warnings and had made myself ill as a result.

However, the next day I had a high fever and did not recognize John anymore. John asked Mrs. Pastora for help. She came immediately, accompanied by her husband, the local nurse, and several women from the *tangsi* — the military police base.

They swathed me in wet bed sheets to lower my temperature, and gave me medicine. I vomited as soon as I had swallowed these pills, so they were useless. I talked gibberish, and called repeatedly for my grandfather who had passed away in 1906!

The third night, they thought I was dying. Against John's will, they put me on a field cot and carried me to the guest room of the Government's House.

For weeks on end, the *nyoras* and the *tangsi* women kept vigil at my bedside. Sometimes, I pummeled the air around me and yelled: "Don't touch me!" At other times, I begged to see Grandfather.

Four weeks had passed since the *hadji* had appeared, when the *van Noort* dropped anchor again. John, who had given up hope, begged the *état-major*[1] for help. Captain Faber and the Chief Engineer came immediately, but, in view of my condition, advised not to have me transported.

Another four weeks went by. John was absent, when — as Mrs. Pastora would tell me later — I yelled something unintelligible, sat up in bed, grabbed my throat with both hands, heaved a big sigh, and said:

"It is gone ... that big dog is gone ... through that window there!"

Then, I fell asleep, and the fever went into a decline. But I was so weak that I did not say another word; I just lay there.

The women started to feed me then, drop by drop. The food stayed down this time, which filled my caring friends with hope, and they assured John that I would live.

The crisis was over.

Later, the ladies told me I had shown all the signs of blackwater fever, but that it was definitely something else. The curse had almost claimed another victim! — so they said.

Progress came slowly. Bit by bit, I managed to get into a sitting position. Soon, they moved me outside in the shade, to regain my strength. As I got stronger, I had to learn to walk again like a little child. All my hair had fallen out. The illness had affected me profoundly, and I looked like an old woman.

Five months after our arrival at Bosnik, the *van Noort* dropped anchor again, and we decided to leave with it. I was still too weak to climb the gangway, and had to be put in a sling and hoisted aboard. With tears of joy and gratitude, we said goodbye to all those dear people, who for so many months had faithfully cared for us. We would remain friends for ever after.

John said that they had saved my life. I sincerely believe they did. At the same time, I like to think that it was Grandfather who — I don't know how — protected me with his presence. I thank him for chasing away that oppressive darkness. The experience convinced me that there are inexplicable forces between heaven and earth that can destroy us, or protect and save us.

\*\*\*\*

Six days later, we arrived on Ternate. The doctor gave me a checkup. It was the first one since our furlough in the Netherlands. He concluded that I had not had blackwater fever, which, he said, was caused by taking too much quinine. That certainly did not apply in my case: I had never had malaria and thus had never swallowed any quinine.

When I told him my *hadji* story, he shrugged. "How can a sane person believe in that nonsense!"

My greatest concern, however, was my terrible loss of hair. Would it ever grow back, or would I have to spend the rest of my life with a bald head? The doctor did not know the answer to that, but he warned that it was quite possible that I would remain bald. What a catastrophe! For a woman, even one who lives in the *rimbu*, it is a matter of life and death!

After the medical checkup, we took the next boat to Tobelo. John planned to stay one month, and then return to Manokwari, where he would take a room in the *pasanggrahan*. From there, he would make regular visits to posts on the northern coast of New Guinea. We agreed that I would stay at least one year on Mon Désir. After that, we would review the situation.

Back at Mon Désir, I was happy to be home again. For the first few weeks, John insisted that I not get involved with the plantation business. Now and then, he would tell me that, in his opinion, everything was fine and that Talakua seemed to be a capable overseer.

I knew, however, that my husband tended to readily accept everything he was told, especially if the one who did the telling was pleasant and polite. In addition, he had never concerned himself much with Mon Désir, and thus did not know much about the details of the business. So I worried, feeling instinctively that not everything was quite in order.

Soon, it was time to say goodbye again. John got a berth on a Government ship that would take him to Ternate. This would enable him to catch an earlier "Papua ship" than if he had waited for the next KPM boat.

Although I was loath to see him go, in a way his departure was a relief. Now I could take the reins of Mon Désir in my own hands.

First I found out that, during my absence, five families had left the plantation. Talakua, the overseer, offered an implausible explanation for their departure.

## IBU MALUKU

These people had been with me from the beginning. As far as I could tell, there had been no reason for them to leave so suddenly. From Latif I heard that they had been replaced by the overseer's relatives. I did not like the sound of that one bit.

Next, I found out the work on the plantation had not progressed as expected. More important, the bookkeeping listed some irresponsibly large cash advances that had been given out to the workers. There were several other matters that did not look quite right.

Talakua was much too glib and friendly. He continuously made unsolicited remarks about my state of health: that I still did not look very strong, and that he, Talakua, was concerned about me. He also said that the Tuan had given him specific instructions to look after me, and to make sure I would not become too stressed in managing the plantation. He had, after all, total responsibility, and would do his best not to get me unnecessarily involved. By nature, I am not gullible, so the flattery of this man made me cautious — and rightfully so, as it later turned out.

The coconut trees did well, however, and I was pleased to sell my very first batch of copra. It was a real success, since the trees were barely five years old. Had I planted the ordinary *cocos nucifera*, there would not have been any harvest for another five years.

The kapok seeds had sprouted well, and in several months the saplings would be replanted in an experimental area of forty hectares. The *bellos*, sticks that would provide the initial support for the saplings, were already in place, and the workers had already started to dig the holes that would receive them. If everything went well, the kapok trees would start to produce in four years — so Professor Leefmans and his co-workers had assured me.

During my first visit to the cleared land, I felt that the mood among the workers was not pleasant. It had always been so cordial before. Talakua was jovial and very friendly toward the lumberjacks, but they responded with barely restrained impudence.

They were a strange people, these wood-cutters. They came from the island of Buton, and I overlooked the matter, assuming that this surly attitude was part of their native character.

I did think it strange, however, that the earlier wood cutters, Papuas and Tobelorese, were no longer employed to clear the land. Well, I told myself, as long as the work was being done, there was nothing to be concerned about. Talakua did seem capable to direct these people. Additionally, I did not feel strong enough to get excited about anything, so, out of necessity, I let it go.

During my absence, several beautiful colts had been born. Latif was regularly busy with their training. The other Madurese took care of the horned animals, and the training of the young steers in pulling the *gerobaks*.

Four of the *gerobaks* were now used to transport harvested coconuts to the drying shed that had also been built during my absence. These same *gerobaks* would later be used to transport the dried coconut meat — the copra — to a storage shed near Tobelo's harbor. I was proud as I watched the *gerobaks* going forth and back, pulled by our "home-grown" steers. The groaning and squeaking sounds these moving *gerobaks* made were music to my ears!

Like the pig farm, the lumber business would soon be phased out. The best timber from the forest had been used up. There were still a few trunks to be sawed for some unfilled orders but, after that, the wood cutters would have to look elsewhere for work. The sawmill had been a good source of income, and the pig farm had paid for most of the reclamation and upkeep of the plantation. In the future, the proceeds from copra would have to pay for the upkeep of both the coconut and the kapok plantation.

The remaining forested land, which I hoped to have cleared within one year, would be used to plant the superior "King Nut". It would also successively replace the "dwarf coconut" trees. I had an abundance of plans, and life began to look rosy again.

\*\*\*\*

I received good news from John, but we missed each other terribly. He had shipped the first harvest of *damar* and had received a very encouraging response: the quality was as good as the best produced elsewhere. This he attributed directly to the newly introduced tapping method, and the professional manner in which the product had been sorted. For the sorting, he had to employ people from Tidore; the Papuas did not seem to have any feel for this exacting kind of work.

John described how the *damar*, collected from the forested coastal regions, was shipped to Manokwari. Here, a shed had been built to grade and store the product. The best went invariably to Hamburg and Bremen, where the demand for high-quality resins was particularly strong. The rest went to clients in the United States.

John wanted to open new concessions. Since Manokwari was part of the Regency of Ternate and Dependencies, he would have to go to Ternate and discuss the matter with the Resident.

He hoped to do this in a few months, and stop off at Tobelo on the way back. "I'll take you with me then," he wrote, which showed me — better than a long letter could have done — how lonely he felt. I, in turn, longed to see him.

## IBU MALUKU

\*\*\*\*

Buturu and his butterfly hunters, who had come back with us from New Guinea, now lived again in their own *kampungs*. Their catch had been sent to the Netherlands, Germany and France, and they were pleased with the large payment they had received. New orders started coming in that held high promise, and Buturu beseeched me to allow him to fill them. I agreed, for he and his men were competent people, and I trusted them to come up with good specimens.

Although butterfly catching had been John's hobby before, I now wanted to get involved to have something else to do. But there were problems.

We would need new nets, storage boxes, packaging materials, insecticides, and so on, and these were costly, for they would have to be imported from the Netherlands.

The high cost deterred me, initially. I did not think I could pay for them from the revenue of the plantation, and I did not want to ask John for help. That would only result in some unwanted comments and, worse, objections because of my health — which was still a sore point between us.

Eventually, I placed the order via my mother, asking her to take the funds out of an account I still had there. She probably did not understand why I was doing it this way, but she asked no questions. She also sent me many articles about catching butterflies — as a "contribution to your recovery", she wrote.

And so, I had a new task, and a new source of income. It would bring me not only much joy and satisfaction, but also help in many other ways later — when the world had caved in around us.

\*\*\*\*

My health improved gradually. One morning, my faithful Liesbeth urged me to look in the mirror, because, according to her, her efforts were bearing fruit: my head showed the growth of new hair.

On the advice of Captain Faber, she had massaged my head twice a day with a remedy he had concocted himself. She was in awe of the Captain, who had threatened to personally inspect her work from time to time. So, she had done it faithfully, even though I always protested that I could not see any good in it. Now she wanted me to see the results for myself.

Crying with joy, she guided my hands to my head. "Please, feel it, *Nyonya*, there really is new hair," she sobbed.

I did as she had asked. Looking in the mirror I thought I saw a bit of fluffy hair, but I did not trust myself. The shock of seeing my bald head made me quickly turn away, and I swore not to touch the mirror again.

I fervently hoped that, if there was any hair growth, John would postpone his announced arrival. I definitely did not want him to see me again in my present state! It was silly, and I knew it. I chafed under vehement self-incrimination, and felt very unhappy.

Liesbeth pulled me out of my depressed state. She was laughing at me! How could the *Nyonya* be so foolish. There was evidence of hair growth, wasn't there? So what was I worrying about?

She turned out to be right. A relatively short time later, I was walking around happily with a normal head of hair. Only someone who has gone through it can really understand what a traumatic experience being bald had been for me.

\*\*\*\*

Life went on. I spent full days in the newly cultivated area, and directed the planting of the young kapok saplings. Now was the most desirable time for transplanting them. A short time later, there was evidence of substantial growth.

I was now strong enough to ride my horse regularly, and several times accompanied the butterfly catchers into the forest. I became so interested that I decided to build an annex to our house, in which to raise butterflies myself.

I learned soon that cocoons were easier to find and transport than butterflies. They delivered more beautiful, undamaged specimens, which would of course fetch higher prices.

The Bosnik nightmare receded into the background as I became more involved in life on the plantation. Several children were born with my assistance. The horned animals were doing well. The employees did not complain much, and, to save aggravation, I paid less attention to the activities of my overseer.

Production had increased; the price for copra was reasonable; the sales invoices for delivered lumber were promptly paid; and, soon, all reclamation of the land would be completed. I estimated that within a year I would only have to pay for maintenance, the picking of the coconuts, and the production of copra. I could then leave the management of Mon Désir to the Overseer, and live again with John, somewhere on that still beckoning New Guinea.

We seemed destined for a golden future!

**Endnotes**
[1] *état-major*: the general staff, the officers of the ship.

IBU MALUKU

# CHAPTER 21

*The Crash*
*Mon Désir Plantation, Halmahera, 1929 - 1933*

October 24, 1929, which would become known as "Black Thursday", the day the New York Stock Exchange crashed, signaled the end of the "Roaring Twenties" and the beginning of the "Great Depression".

The first indication of what was to come was a drop in the price of copra. It had fluctuated before, so I was not particularly worried.

One day, Mr. Majoie, who had replaced the disreputable Mr. Dipso at Kuala Pitu, dropped in for a visit. He had just shipped a quantity of copra and had learned that prices for rubber, sugar, tobacco and other products had also taken a nose-dive. On Java, plantations were laying off junior employees and cutting back on production.

I asked him, of course, what the outlook was for copra. He did not think the present world slump would seriously affect it, because coconut oil would always be needed for alimentary purposes. He warned me, however, not to plant too much kapok, for which he predicted difficulties.

This, again, didn't worry me, as it would take another four years for my kapok trees to produce, and by that time, no doubt, the world market would have changed for the better. And to reduce maintenance, I could always invite our people — and even inhabitants from the surrounding islands — to plant their vegetable gardens between the kapok trees, as had already happened where the coconut trees stood. So, I remained optimistic.

Mr. Majoie promised to keep me up-to-date on the situation and the rapidly declining prices. He confirmed that the New York stock market crash was behind it all.

Nevertheless, from John I received a reassuring letter. True, the world price for *damar* had also gone down, and the head office in Rotterdam had asked him to go easy: not to stimulate production, though he had the capacity to do so. They did not seem unduly alarmed, for they had asked him to continue the search for well-placed land and concession opportunities.

## IBU MALUKU

Clearly, there was no reason to worry, wrote John. It was a pity, however, that he would not be able to earn the premium that came with increased production. I knew his salary consisted of a fixed income plus a premium of one guilder for each *pikol*[1] of copra shipped. For *damar*, the premium was higher, but it varied with the product's quality. This manner of paying was usual in these regions as it provided an incentive to ship more products. So, I could understand that John was not happy about having to curb production.

I started to get concerned, however, as the market continued its slide. Whereas the last batch of copra brought 19.75 guilders, the batch of the current month would fetch only 15.00 guilders per *pikol*. The purchaser warned that the next price could be lower still.

There were other warning signs. Nearby lay several small plantations, some of which protruded inside Mon Désir's otherwise rectangular boundary. I had tried several times to buy those enclaves so that I could straighten out the boundary lines of my concession. Each time the owners had refused my offer, being quite content with the current arrangement, whereby my people would collect all their mature coconuts, and I would buy the whole harvest from them.

Now, however, these people came to see me on their own accord, wanting to sell their properties for the price I had previously offered them.

I quickly agreed to buy the land that lay inside the boundary lines, so that I could finally fence the property. It would keep our grazing animals inside, and prevent deer and boars from damaging the young kapok plants. I did not, however, want to take the risk of buying the properties outside Mon Désir, and declined the offers made.

The disappointed owners — mostly employees of nearby plantations, who were not from this region — then tried to get rid of their land in another way. They would buy all sort of goods from local traders and then offer their properties as payment instead of cash. Often, land changed hands in this way at prices that were much below their actual value.

The news turned worse. On Java, even senior employees were now being laid off. Many plantations on Java and Sumatra had closed, and those that remained open had cut production to a trickle. The price of copra had gone down from 15 to 10 guilders per *pikol*, and buyers now demanded only top quality. Anything of lesser quality was simply refused.

This time, I became really worried. Nearby plantations had laid off *mandurs* and overseers, cut maintenance and stopped cultivation wherever possible. As a result, I received an avalanche of employment applications.

The larger plantations had either laid-off temporary workers or had kept them on at much lower wages. They were, of course, obliged to keep the contract workers for the duration of their contracts. These workers now represented an expensive, and unproductive labor force.

Driven into a corner, I sent for my overseer to discuss the changed state of affairs. When Talakua came in, he cut me to the quick. Before I could say anything about a reduction in his salary — which was high — or about the possibility of a layoff, he told me haughtily that it was John who had engaged him and that he was unwilling to discuss the matter with me. John had also decided the wages for the workers, he continued, so he did not feel compelled to discuss that subject with me either.

His last statement was definitely false. John had never involved himself with Mon Désir. To boot, the plantation was my property and I was the sole owner.

His statement about his own salary I was less certain about, however. Before leaving for New Guinea, John had spoken several times to Talakua. I was sure, however, that we had discussed and agreed on what salary the overseer would be paid.

I told Talakua that I would ask John for clarification. If John had, indeed given him the impression of being the employer, then I would ask him to give the overseer a reasonable notice of termination of employment. Predictably, from that day on, Talakua's attitude toward me changed drastically. Sometimes he even acted as if he were the owner of Mon Désir. Divisiveness spread among the workers. Some were for me; others, against.

I approached Mr. Majoie, and asked what he thought I should do to resolve the situation. His advice was brief and to the point: "Call all the people together, explain the situation and tell them what measures you will take. Then, without recourse, fire anyone who does not go along with your decisions." Luckily, all of my employees were "free workers" (none were bound by contract), so that simplified matters considerably.

After my return from the hospital, Talakua had continued to pay out the wages against my wishes, because, so he said, the task would have been too tiring for me. At the next payday, however, I took it firmly out of his hands. With everyone present, I announced that wages would have to be cut, as had already happened on other plantations. Those who could not accept it, were free to resign — immediately, if they so wished. Of course, I added, they would first have to pay back any advances that were outstanding.

Everyone fell silent. Then, most of them asked for time to think it over. That was fine, but I also warned them that if they decided to stay, there was no guarantee that the wages would remain frozen. I might be forced to lower them further at a later time. I therefore advised the bachelors to seek work elsewhere. Those with a family to support might do better to stay, as they would have greater difficulty in finding employment than those who were single.

As I talked, I was scanning their faces and also the face of the Overseer, who stood near me. He was livid and did not try to hide it. I was still talking when he walked off. Inwardly, I felt relieved, for I had expected him to oppose me more openly.

When the meeting was over, I went home to calculate how much I would still owe the lumberjacks, and what it would cost to develop and plant the remaining area. It then became clear that I could not cover these outlays if the price of copra continued to slide.

The downward spiral did continue, however: several loads of copra brought only 7.50 guilders per *pikol*. That would barely cover expenses. Soon, I would have to call on John for assistance — something I had always painstakingly tried to avoid.

In his next letter, John counseled me not to worry too much. His *damar* shipments continued, and he felt certain that the price of copra would soon go up again. Regarding the employment of the Overseer, Talakua's contention was absurd. He had never employed the man, nor talked to him about salary as an employer would to someone seeking employment. I should feel free to fire him if I considered it practical and necessary. He, himself, however thought it would be better to keep him — if necessary at a reduced salary.

After I had read the letter, I sent for Talakua. When the Overseer arrived, I told him what was in the letter. It dented his self-confidence, but he recovered quickly. A reduction in salary was unacceptable, he said, and he would resign. He would leave the plantation in two months!

Thank Heavens! This painful meeting was over, but the hatred in the man's eyes bothered me. If only I could get rid of him sooner.

Luck was with me! Several Japanese "apprentices"[2] were living and working temporarily on a sisal[3] plantation, owned by the Japanese Watanabe family. They had occasionally visited Mon Désir, and borrowed horses from us for trips into the surrounding area.

These gentlemen showed up unexpectedly one day and asked if I would sell them a young stallion, with which Mr. Watanabe wanted to start his own stable. They also wanted to buy two mares as a farewell present for the Watanabes, since they would soon leave Halmahera and return to their own country.

They looked over my stable, picked out one stallion and two mares, and offered a very good sum for them. After some haggling, which seemed to be part of doing business in their country as well, we closed the deal. They paid in cash!

Latif caught the animals and said goodbye to them in a way that tore my heart apart. He had taken care of these animals from birth, and had grown deeply attached to them. I, too, hated to part with them, but this sale would enable me to pay off the overseer and get him out of my hair.

Two days later, Talakua was gone. Only his wife came to say goodbye. She shook hands with me, and asked if I had now fully recovered from my illness. When I confirmed my complete recovery, she said she was pleased. "But" she added, "the *Nyonya Belanda* will surely not forget what has happened on Bosnik ... These things could happen again!"

Was this a threat, or just a thoughtless remark?

\* \* \* \*

The news from Holland was bad too. The whole world, it seemed, had been plunged in an unexpected crisis. With trepidation, I would wait for the next batch of mail to arrive, wishing often that John was with me, so we could face the issues together.

A letter from Rotterdam painted a vivid picture. It said the harbor warehouses were stacked to the ceiling with tropical products, such as coffee, tea, sugar, tobacco, rubber and spices. Trading had just about come to a standstill; almost no products were shipped out. Yet, every day, ships arrived with full loads. Some brokers could no longer pay for storage, and major importers had declared bankruptcy!

I knew John's company was solid, but they also imported primarily tropical products. Almost the whole nutmeg and clove trade passed through their hands. If only that would continue to go well!

Then, as a bolt from the blue came the news from Rotterdam that their manager on Morotai had stopped collecting *damar*, had taken "furlough" and had told everyone that he would not be back! In the letter, addressed to me, they asked me to transmit this news to John as soon as possible — even though he might have heard about it from another source. I wrote John the same day, and was lucky enough to catch the mail *prau* before it left for Ternate.

When this *prau* returned, it brought, among other things, a letter from Manokwari, in which John wrote that he would soon go to

Ternate. If circumstances permitted it, he would afterwards stop off at Tobelo.

"It would be better, however, if you could come down to Ternate," he wrote. "That would give you a change of pace, and it would enable us to spend a few more days together."

How I hungered to do just that! Other than saying that there was an abundance of copra along the North Coast but no buyers, the letter did not contain any sign of great concern. The suppliers were stocking the products, convinced that the prices would eventually go up again.

I also received a letter from our Priest, Father Neyens, who said he would arrive at Tobelo with the next ship. Could I put him up?

It seemed preordained! Now I would be able to talk to a trusted friend, who traveled much and knew the state of world affairs. Moreover, I would have him as company when I sailed to Ternate. I longed for the arrival of the *Swarten Hondt*.

In the days leading up to the ship's arrival, I made all necessary arrangements for my absence, and discussed them with Latif, who had taken Talakua's place and acquitted himself very well. He was the first one to hear the ship's whistle in the distance, and was in front of the house with the buggy before I had even heard it!

I was soon ready, and jumped in beside him. The horse galloped down the plantation road and ran over the big road with such speed that we were at the jetty just when the first motor-sloop arrived.

Near the top of the ship's gangway stood the familiar figure of Father Neyens in his white cassock. Captain Faber, whom I had not seen since the Bosnik days, waved from the bridge. How wonderful it was to see these familiar faces again.

It was my first visit to a ship after having regained a full head of hair — thanks to Captain Faber's concoction and Liesbeth's persistence; I had not dared to show myself before.

I quickly scaled the stairs, and found Captain Faber and Father Neyens waiting for me at the top. They greeted me warmly, and said they had an enormous surprise for me.

They stepped sufficiently aside so that I could see John standing at the entrance to the salon. We ran into each other's arms, laughing and crying simultaneously, forgetting that other people were standing around us.

Only later did it occur to me that John was unusually quiet and timid. When I asked him if something was wrong, he led me to his cabin. Here, he let out a torrent of words, from which I gathered that he had resigned from his job.

## IBU MALUKU

He had received a letter from the directors in Rotterdam with an urgent request to stop all *damar* shipments and associated activities on New Guinea. The directors explained that the warehouses in Rotterdam contained several millions of guilders worth of products for which, now, there was no demand. It was possible that these might have to be sold at bankruptcy prices to pay for overdue storage and freight charges.

"After reading about their difficulties," John went on, "I felt obliged to send them all the cash I had on hand — more than 30,000 guilders — and tell them that, after closing the business, I would voluntarily resign." Downheartedly, he added: "I can't possibly accept a salary for doing nothing."

Alarmed, I asked why he had not followed the terms of the contract. It clearly stated that its dissolution required a one-year notice, so that, had the directors asked for his resignation, he would still have been entitled to a full year's salary.

Almost angrily, he burst out: "But try to understand my position. Right now I am only a liability to them. The 30,000 guilders and my salary may save the company. Surely you can see that?"

Yes, I understood only too well. Earlier, on Buluwaya, he would rather have both of us starve to death than resign his post on his own. We were now going through a similar experience, but that was the way John was. Loyal to the extreme, but not thinking about what would become of us.

With trepidation I thought about the large sum that I still owed the lumberjacks. I also reminded myself that revenue from copra would barely cover the cost of ongoing maintenance at Mon Désir. I would gladly have gone home right then, without seeing anybody. Of course, this was not possible. I had to look after my guest, Father Neyens, be upbeat and happy, and hide the turmoil I felt. Only much later, when I was alone among my trees, would I be able to let go!

Captain Faber insisted that we stay on board for the night. Latif, who had come on board, was very pleased to learn that the *Tuan* had come home. He later took care of our luggage and said that he would be back early in the morning. He would bring the buggy for the *Nyonya* and the *Tuan Pastor* (Mr. Priest), and the white horse for the *Tuan*, he said, grinning from ear to ear.

At the dinner table, I heard all sorts of perplexing stories about the depression in which we found ourselves. Layoffs and bankruptcies everywhere; plantations being closed; and homeless Dutchmen being forced to find shelter in native villages. Everywhere it was the same.

The dinner guests were optimistic about the future of copra, however.

It was, after all, a product that would always be needed throughout the world. We could count on that — that was the consensus, and it coincided with Mr. Majoie's views.

The next morning, after a copious breakfast, we said goodbye to everyone on board, and took the motor-sloop to shore. Back at Mon Désir, where everyone showed their pleasure at John's return, I presented Liesbeth with a piece of cloth. It was a present from Captain Faber for having faithfully followed his instructions regarding the massaging of my scalp!

Father Neyens left five days later, and we were finally alone. While we had our guest, I had carefully avoided talking about John's resignation, or about the state of affairs at Mon Désir. Now, we could no longer avoid these subjects. Talking about them would not be easy.

First, we reviewed the wages; then, we covered all other particulars.

When we finished, John was quite pleased with the state of affairs. He was, as I had expected, much more optimistic than I was. As always, he was quite ready to believe that all would turn out well, and that the company would recall him to reopen the business on New Guinea. On behalf of his company, he had applied for several newly acquired concessions. By the time these applications had been processed, world trade would surely have recovered. These thoughts and hopes, he would share with countless plantation owners and many of the unemployed.

* * * *

Life went on, and we grew together again. Only now did we realize how difficult the separation had been for each of us. We became happy, as before; the depression had not changed that, thank God!

From the directors in Rotterdam, John received a thank-you note for the expedient way in which he had closed the business on New Guinea. They did not accept his resignation, however, and wrote they had no plans for laying him off. They asked him to go to Morotai to assess the state of affairs there, now that their resident manager had unexpectedly left. Of course, the cost of traveling and lodging would be repaid. The directors also wanted to pursue the possibility of John staying there temporarily as their manager.

For John, there was hope again. He quickly left for Waya Bula on Morotai, where he discovered that the business was in a sad state. Through incompetence, company personnel had accepted products of bad quality from the *damar* collectors. Also, large sums had been advanced to the workers that would be difficult to collect. Insufficient supervision in recording the exact boundaries of concessions had caused confusion, and had led to serious conflicts.

# IBU MALUKU

The *damar* sorters had left because the manager was gone. They had neither worked for nor repaid the advances they had received. New packers and sorters would have to be employed. The situation on all other *damar* posts was the same. John summarized his findings and sent off a telegram to Rotterdam.

Their response came quickly. The price of *damar* on the world market was still going down. There was still a small demand, but only for top quality. The directors asked John to collect all available *damar*, store it at Waya Bula, and leave it there unsorted until further orders.

So, after this inspection tour, and a few trips to collect and transport the *damar* from outlying posts and to sell a few houses the company had built for future expansion, the business on Morotai also came to a close.

Then, an even bigger problem appeared. Traders in nutmeg, mace, cloves and shells — mostly Chinese firms — had received large advances from the previous manager, giving their coconut plantations as collateral. Since they could not sell the copra and other products at reasonable prices, they were forced into bankruptcy. The Company took possession of these pledged plantations and asked John to supervise them.

On his advice, the company also accepted several plantations in lieu of payment from debtors that were still solvent, on the assumption that they could later be sold for a profit. John himself purchased a 250 hectare (618 acres) parcel of a coconut plantation from a trader at a very low price. He paid for this purchase with his salary of the last few months.

If the price of copra would stay at 7.50 guilders per *pikol*, this piece of land would at least bring in some revenue. I hoped with all my heart that the price had bottomed out; otherwise, it would only be another millstone around his neck.

\*\*\*\*

Early in 1933, John left for Morotai's north coast to handle additional bankruptcies. The journey was to last one week. Ten days later, there was still no sign of him, but it did not particularly worry me. Obviously, he had run into some unforeseen difficulty.

One morning in February, while John was still away, the surrounding area was covered with a layer of ultra-fine grey dust. No one knew where it had come from.

Several days later, the news made the rounds that Togutil tribesmen in the interior were responsible. They had allegedly set fire to the *alang-alang*[4] fields in the foothills of the Dukeno, a dead volcano. The Togutils did this sometimes, because the young grass sprouting up after the burning attracted many prize animals for the hunters. Presumably, the wind had been just right this time for carrying the ashes toward Tobelo.

As before, the burning infuriated the coastal people, who claimed the foothills as their own hunting grounds. They now threatened legal action unless the government put the Togutils in their place.

So the Head of the District, accompanied by a military detachment, headed into the mountains. They returned the same day with the disturbing news that the fire had not been set by man, but by the Dukeno, which had become active again. This resolved the mystery of several weeks earlier: it had obviously been a rain of ash.

The people living close to the Mamuya became afraid — and for good reason. No person alive had ever seen it erupt, but the tale had been passed down from father to son that, centuries ago, the lava from the Dukeno had flowed along the flanks of the Mamuya and had destroyed all the *kampungs*, and killed thousands of people.

In addition, tradition had it that although the volcano became active only every 200 to 300 years, when it did, it stayed active for 25 years!

John still had not returned from *tournée* and his long absence started to worry me. It was impossible to find out what might have happened, until the KPM ship — the only connection with Waya Bula on Morotai — stopped at Tobelo, eight days from now. I might not even find out then, for the ship would only stop on Morotai if there was a load to be picked up.

Several nights later, there was a series of earthquakes in quick succession. I was used to earthquakes; they happened often on this island. But these were more than mere quakes. First, the earth vibrated, then one had the feeling of being thrown up in the air, and only then the first shocks started. This was accompanied by a low rumble, which resembled distant thunder. The morning following this terror, everything was covered with a fresh layer of grey volcanic ash — a strange sight. It looked like freshly fallen grey snow, which retained every footprint.

The people closest to the Mamuya panicked and fled with all their belongings to Morotai, or to other islands off the Halmahera coast.

I now greatly longed for John's return. The KPM ship was expected to arrive the next day.

At 7 a.m., Latif thought he had heard the ship's whistle, and promptly sent a young worker to check. Sure enough, the ship had arrived and Latif dispatched the buggy to pick up the mail and possibly John's luggage, if he had arrived with this ship.

At 7:30, a local woman came running toward the house, shouting:

"*Lekas, lekas, chelaka!* — quick, quick, an accident!"

I ran toward her, and, panting, she told me she had been on her way to the *pasar* (market) when she found John lying in a ditch. He had fallen off his bicycle, so she thought, and seemed unable to get up. He had, therefore, asked her to call someone from Mon Désir.

Never in my life have I run as hard as I did on that day. Before anyone from Mon Désir had arrived, I was already at his side, holding him in my arms.

John had indeed fallen after losing control of the bicycle — his hands and legs had simply ceased to function, he said, so he had landed in the ditch.

He looked terrible, talked mostly gibberish and could not get up. When help from Mon Désir arrived, we managed to get him into the buggy and brought him home. Meanwhile, someone had gone to fetch the doctor.

I could not make much sense of what John was saying. He trembled over his whole body, and complained about a horrible pain in his legs and cramps in his hands. His legs and hands were swollen. Even the doctor was shocked to see him in this condition. He gave John a sedative and ordered complete rest.

Late in the afternoon, a man came to the house. He introduced himself as the *juragang* (captain) of the coastal schooner that had taken John to Morotai. He had returned with John on the KPM ship, had heard about the accident, and had come to inquire how he was.

From him, I then heard what had happened since John's departure.

They'd had a good wind, and arrived eleven hours later on Waya Bula. The next day, they had sailed to two northern *kampungs* to pick up a weighing scale and thirty *keranjangs* (large baskets) of unsorted *damar*. The schooner had taken this load back to Waya Bula, leaving John behind to sort out some administrative problems.

The schooner, called the *Burung Laut* (Sea Bird), had then gone back to pick up John and had taken him to a third *kampung*. They had loaded more equipment and *keranjangs* of *damar* and sailed back to Waya Bula. When they had finished unloading, the warehouse there contained 180 *keranjangs* of *damar* — an unheard-of quantity!

When it was time to return to Tobelo, the weather had turned bad. The *juragang* had planned to make a beeline for the most northern tip of the Halmahera coast, to shorten the journey through open seas. The first lap went well, but, when they sailed around the northern cape, a squall hit them ... hard. The mainsail could not be lowered in time; the mast broke in two, and the mainsail was lost. Everything on deck was destroyed and carried off, and they drifted rudderless, far from sight of any land.

When the storm abated, they thought they might be west of Halmahera, but there was neither land nor island to be seen by which they could get their bearings.

For the six men on board, there was only one bag of rice. During the first few days, they used all the wood they could break off in order to cook the rice. After that, they had soaked the rice in seawater, and ate it that way. Lack of drinking water was the worst. Twice, flying fish had landed on deck. They ate them raw, except for John, who had refused.

Finally, they were spotted by a *prau* full of Papuas, who had ventured far out from the coast. They were on their way to Serui (on Yapen Island), and told the *juragang* that he was close to it. The storm had blown them 600 nautical miles off course! A KPM ship was expected to stop there shortly, so John had given the Papuas a note for the magistrate and asked them to hand it to any KPM ship or schooner destined for Tobelo. The Papuas had left them some sago, a string of smoked fish, and some drinking water, and had continued on their way.

Two days later, John and his crew had been picked up by a regular KPM ship. They had been fed, taken care of medically and were finally able to rest.

The *Burung Laut* could not be saved. It would later land on the beach of a small island where it was broken down and used for firewood.

The following day, they arrived on Ternate just in time to catch the Halmahera ship, which had taken them to Tobelo.

John, noted the *juragang*, had said nothing about being unwell. Upon arrival, he had picked up his bicycle, which he had left with the repairman. The *juragang* noticed, however, that John had swayed a lot as he rode away. This, he attributed to stiff legs, resulting from the cramped journey on the schooner. In fact, the thought of John being sick had never crossed his mind, concluded the captain. And there lay the *Tuan*, unable to talk, let alone explain what had happened!

For a whole month John did not say much, except to complain about being terribly tired and having pain in his badly swollen legs, feet and hands.

The doctor pressed for a better diet: milk, eggs, and everything else that could help John regain his strength. Ultimately, he threw up his hands and started looking for a possible infection of the nervous system.

He pushed John to walk, and asked me to give him as much diversion as possible. He should try to bicycle now and then, or go with the buggy to the *kota* — the downtown area. Only diversion, said the doctor, would help to get him out of this lethargy.

John promised to do his best. I knew he suffered from much pain and that any exertion was difficult, but, nevertheless, I cheered him on.

One day, I persuaded him to take the buggy to the *kota* to get some provisions. With difficulty, he got in the buggy, refusing any help. When he took the reins himself, I thought that, perhaps, the doctor had been right: that all he needed was a diversion to get better. How wrong I was!

We first drove to visit a couple, friends of ours, who had repeatedly visited us over the past few weeks and had been very supportive. Their house was near the *alun-alun*[5], not far from the doctor's house.

They welcomed us warmly, and insisted that we come in to celebrate John's first outing. John and I accepted cheerfully, and I jumped out to help John in getting down. But the smile on his face faded as he grimaced in pain. He tried to get up, but could not. He could not even move his legs!

We called the doctor, who first looked him over and then tried to help John out of the buggy himself. No luck! Then he bent over, examining John's feet. He touched them with one extended finger, and exclaimed, engraving the words on my mind: "But you have beri-beri[6]! How is that possible?!"

John never did get out of the buggy. I drove him straight home, hoisted him out by myself with great difficulty, and brought him to bed.

The doctor came in shortly after, reproaching himself for not having recognized this illness earlier and having prescribed the wrong cure for so long.

He pressed me to have John hospitalized right away. The local hospital, however, did not have accommodation for Europeans, so he suggested a room in a cloister, where John could be nursed.

The next day, the doctor and two nurses arrived in an automobile. Since John could not walk himself, the nurses carried him to the car. I followed with the buggy, carrying with me everything that he might need.

The nuns would cook for him, but all the provisions would have to be brought from Mon Désir each day. We agreed on payment, after which I went home, somewhat dazed and very, very worried.

That afternoon, I received payment for the last batch of copra which I had shipped. The price had slipped again from 7.50 to 6.18 guilders per *pikol*! In the future, I was told, copra would only be purchased in batches of 100 kilograms, and only top-grade, sun-dried copra would be accepted!

❦

**Endnotes**
1. *pikol* or *pikul* = 100 kati = 61.76 kilograms = 136.16 lbs. This unit of measure is widely used in South-East Asia. It represents one "shoulder load". An adult male normally can carry two *pikols* with a yoke.
2. Much later, it would turn out that these "apprentices" were actually naval officers, scouting the area on behalf of Imperial Japan.
3. *Sisal* is a fibre from the *agave sisalana* plant, used for making ropes. It is named after Sisal, a port in the Yucatàn.
4. *Alang-alang* is a tall reedy grass that may reach to a man's chest.
5. An *alun-alun* is a large grassy square -- usually with *waringin* (banyan) trees to house powerful spirits -- located in front of the residence of a monarch or important civil authority. It is used for official and unofficial events.
6. Beri-beri is an often fatal disease of the peripheral nerves, caused by a vitamin B1 deficiency. It is marked by pain in, and paralysis of, the extremities, and severe emaciation or swelling of the body. After Dr. Eykman discovered that the polishing of rice removed that vital vitamin, rice-polishing was outlawed in the East Indies, but imported polished rice often escaped scrutiny. Vitamins and *kacang hijau* (mung beans) were used to fight the disease. By 1930, beri-beri occurred seldom, which explains why John's illness was diagnosed so late.

IBU MALUKU

# CHAPTER 22

### The Recovery
*Mon Désir Plantation, Halmahera, 1933-1934*

Early every morning, after having assigned the work at Mon Désir, I rode to Tobelo, taking with me everything needed for John's care — including chickens, eggs, butter, milk, vegetables and fruit.

John was either sleeping or staring apathetically into space, his arms extended beside his body. I particularly noticed his hands: they always seemed to be asking for something. John had beautiful, slender hands normally, but now they looked horrible. They were so swollen, it seemed that the tightly-stretched skin could burst open at any time, and from this puffed-up balloon protruded his long, intensely white and emaciated fingers. His legs were also swollen and unbearably painful, but John never complained in my presence.

We did not talk much. John either could not talk, or did not want to. After each visit, I returned to Mon Désir in an even more depressed state.

In the afternoon, I made the same trip, except I would bring clean clothes and whatever else was needed. I then sat for a while beside his bed, asking something now and then, and straining to hear the few words he did utter.

His nurse said he was an easy patient. Other than that, she had few encouraging words for me. Even the doctor was non-committal: time would show whether John would get well again; the illness had greatly affected him — psychologically and physically.

On Mon Désir, the situation worsened. I had hoped to eliminate maintenance by having the local population tend their vegetable gardens beneath the kapok trees. However, this endeavor had fallen short of expectations, and I was now forced to employ my own people to keep the ground clear of weeds. The unexpected cost would have to be paid from the copra revenue, as there would be no income from the kapok for another three or even four years. Unless the economic situation improved, we would be in for a very difficult time.

The last few hectares of forest that had been cleared would soon be planted with the remaining King Nut seedlings that still stood in the seed-beds. Just before John was taken to the cloister, I had negotiated with the lumberjacks to dig the holes and plant the seedlings — of course for an additional fee!

Now the time for getting this replanting done was quickly approaching — too quickly for my liking. Although some money had already been advanced to them, I would still have a large sum to pay these lumberjacks when the job was completed.

In addition, I needed cash to pay for John's care. How long his recovery would take, and how long I would be able to pay his bills, was anybody's guess. The situation looked hopeless, and I spent many sleepless nights searching for a solution.

In the end, I decided to ask Mama for help. She knew that John was ill, but she was unaware of the urgency of my predicament. My letter described the successively-worsening slump, and the critical situation on the plantation. I asked for understanding and help — "in rather emotional words," Mama would later write me.

My brother, sister and I jointly owned several hectares of good farming land. This land was leased to a third party, who regularly paid the rent into our bank accounts.

In my letter, I asked Mama to sell my parcel to my siblings, or to the current lessor. The rent that had accumulated over the years in my name, I asked her to send to me as soon as possible.

I knew that my request would touch a sensitive nerve in Mama. The land had belonged to her family for more than 150 years. For Mama, land was, and always would be, the safest investment. The very idea of selling it would hurt her deeply.

I anxiously waited her reply. It came quickly, and I was relieved that my proposal had not been as painful for her as I had anticipated.

The accumulated rent was promptly transferred to me, which enabled me to pay the lumberjacks in full. Since I had no further work for them, they left the plantation, except for two, who had married and wanted to stay and do other kinds of work.

And so I could breathe again, if only for a little while. During my daily visits to John, I could now talk without having this problem gnawing at my insides.

*****

One month passed after another. John's health did not improve; neither did the economic situation. On the contrary: copra dropped to 7.50 guilders per 100 kilograms. I thought that surely, by now, the market had bottomed out. How little did I know!

Having heard that John was ill, our gentle priest, Father Neyens, paid us a visit. He was well-informed about the slump and reviewed the economic situation with a discerning eye. He also had a long talk with our doctor. Both came to tell me the result of their deliberations.

John, they felt, was not going to get any better where he was. He needed a cool climate and a well-equipped hospital. His heart was weak, and he should not be subjected to any stress, as it might kill him. Shielding him from what was happening outside, the two men agreed, should be my prime objective, even though they conceded that it would be very difficult to do.

The men recognized that money was a problem. In fact, they had heard people in town asking themselves how long I — or Mon Désir — could keep on paying for John's care.

This speculation of the town's people hurt me terribly. I had faithfully paid the "hospital" bills, which often had "additional charges" added to the base amount. I had also faithfully delivered the agreed-upon provisions (though I had often asked myself who was putting away all that food). The doctor's bill, too, had always been paid promptly. It was not high, but the cash to pay for it also had to be found.

Money, money, money! Never before in my life had this word taken on such an ominous meaning. But together, we discussed what could be done.

Father Neyens suggested that John be transferred to the Tomohon Mission Hospital in the Minahasa — the northeastern part of Celebes. It was a modern hospital, and the climate was good.

I agreed, of course. I would have agreed to anything that would contribute to John's recovery, and I gratefully accepted the Pater's offer to find out about the hospital and traveling costs.

Two weeks later, everything had been arranged. There would be a doctor on board, and a male nurse would go with John to Menado, where the hospital's ambulance would pick him up. Of course, our perilous financial situation did not allow me to go with him — though John seemed unaware of this fact.

And so, again, we said our goodbyes. When John was carried on board on a stretcher, I wondered if I would ever see him again.

\*\*\*\*

A week later, the doctor on Tomohon confirmed by telegram that John had arrived safely.

The next day, something happened that was so unexpected and weird that it left me speechless.

At eight o'clock in the morning, five persons, including my former overseer Talakua, came to ask for an audience. One of these gentlemen introduced himself as a bailiff. Two were court clerks, and the fourth man was (as I would later discover) a "bamboo attorney" — a general name for a shady member of the legal profession.

When I asked them why they had come, the bailiff stated that Talakua had lodged a complaint against John for unjustified dismissal. To cover the loss of income that he had suffered, he had demanded that all assets of Mon Désir be seized before the trial. Incredibly, his demand had been granted!

I looked at them dumbfounded. Was this some kind of a joke? To my surprise, the bailiff instructed the court clerks to enter the house and list everything that was in it. Without pausing for a breath, he then turned to me and said that it would be an offense to remove any furnishings.

I realized then that this was no joke, and my blood boiled. Fuming, I yelled at the clerks to stay right where they were!

My outburst startled them, and smiling timidly, they came back to the front veranda. Talakua bellowed at them to go back and do their duty. After all, everything now belonged to him, he assured them with a sneer. The *Nyonya* would not have enough cash on hand in these difficult times to pay for what her husband owed him.

The men hesitated.

More calm now and feeling more in control, I told the bailiff that there was not one item on Mon Désir that belonged to my husband. Everything in sight was my personal property, which I could prove — and I silently blessed Mama for insisting that settlement articles be written into our marriage contract.

Howling with anger and disappointment, Talakua demanded to see the evidence, which I promptly showed him. The bailiff suddenly became very polite, and I could see that he and the clerks were secretly pleased with the outcome of this confrontation.

The "bamboo attorney", who had been silent all this time, said he would check the law and he assured Talakua that he would pursue the matter.

Thank God, they did not know that John had a coconut plantation on Morotai!

I would hear no more about this matter, but it had disturbed me deeply. I felt vulnerable, and wondered if I had the stamina to continue with this difficult existence. Just surviving seemed to be an impossible task!

\*\*\*\*

From Menado, the news was both good and bad. John's health was improving in the cooler climate, but a complete recovery would take four to six months. From where was I going to get money? The price of copra was still going down; the last batch had only fetched 5.00 guilders per 100 kilograms!

John, of course, did not know what was going on. He did not know that his own plantation earned nothing — the whole harvest being used to pay the workers who maintained the land. Nor did he know that the market for butterflies and lumber had collapsed, and that, at my request, the hospital staff at Tomohon kept him in the dark about the lingering slump in world prices and its disastrous consequences.

In Holland, the sale of my land progressed slowly, but finally — thank God — one member of the family expressed his willingness to take over my parcel. Because of the slump, the price offered was much lower than expected; however, I had no choice but to accept.

The revenue would be just enough to cover six months of hospital care and John's return trip. Any additional expenses would have to be paid by other means. So I started to sell off some of my cows. The price was less than what I had paid for them.

Times became worse still, and the whole world groaned from the effects of the slump.

Then came the *coup de grâce*. The market for copra died. A few large plantations still bought well-dried coconuts, *if* delivered along a highway, at a price of 2.50 guilders per 1000 pieces!

\*\*\*\*

After John became ill, I had maintained contact with the directors in Rotterdam, and, at their request, had wound up their affairs on Morotai.

After that, the mail diminished gradually, and the sporadic letters I did receive from them contained only more bad news. The company was in dire financial straits. The products stored in warehouses could not be sold and were rotting away. Then came the devastating news that the Director had committed suicide!

I was crushed. This man had always been a sympathetic friend, who had continuously sent us — and later, me — encouraging letters. Times would get better sometime, he would write. I had trusted his counsel, and had drawn comfort from it. Now he himself had given up.

I, too, was at the end of my tether, and for several days had to fight off the obsessive idea of following his example.

To add to my misfortunes, the eruptions became more severe. The Dukeno belched more ash and more often, which wore away the *atap* roofs of the houses well before their normal time. I had to sell five good breeding steers to pay the repair bill.

The cows could no longer be left out to graze because of the ash, and their supplementary feed had to be washed, which cut down the available drinking water, and, in turn, reduced milk production.

Even the water wells had to be deepened more often. Sometimes, new wells had to be dug, because, seemingly, the earthquakes had blocked the subterranean water arteries.

All these activities, of course, cost money.

To cut my own expenses, I sent the servants, Marcus and Liesbeth, back to the Talaud Islands. The sale of two more horses to Japanese living near the Kao Bay had made it possible to pay for their passage and to give each an extra month's salary.

I now handled both the housework and the administration of the plantation. On his own, Latif offered to resign as *mandur*, and work at the salary of an ordinary worker. His loyalty was unflinching. How grateful I was for his staunch support!

Because of John's lengthy illness, all my chickens and ducks had been consumed before he had left for the hospital. Money to buy others did not now exist. The best milk cows had been sold, and the milk of the remaining ones had to be used to feed the calves.

The cultivation of cassava for sale was a lost cause. Nobody bought these tuberous roots anymore. So we only kept a small area of it to feed the personnel and myself. The maintenance I did with the workers, who labored without pay. The harvest was, after all, for all of us.

Fortunately, the banana trees did not require any maintenance, and their fruits became an important part of my diet. Also, as a personal treat, and to remind myself of my almost forgotten origins, I feasted every Sunday on a small can of Japanese mackerel in tomato sauce. One can cost only 16 cents!

\*\*\*\*

Eventually, news arrived that John was improving and now needed a bicycle to exercise his legs. The sale of a few jewels realized enough to pay for it.

Finally, nine months later, the message came: "Your husband is virtually cured, and will return with the next ship."

"Thank God," I thought, "when we are together again, everything will improve," believing that life would soon be worthwhile again. But the letter contained a warning: "His heart is weak. Avoid stress at all cost!"

I resolved to do that — how, I did not know yet — but up to that point I had succeeded. "God, give me the strength to continue," I prayed.

## IBU MALUKU

I did hope, however, that he would at least be aware of the economic situation in the world. If not, he would certainly hear about it on board, or on Ternate, where he would have to stay over for a few days, waiting for the "Papua ship". The changes that had taken place on Mon Désir would surely be a shock to him, but that was unavoidable.

My immediate concern was the yard around the house. I would have to make certain that it looked as it had before. The rest of the plantation could wait; it was not likely that John would get around much at first.

With great longing and impatience, I counted the days. The joy I felt over John's coming gave me strength and courage; I had much more energy than before. The house and compound looked good, as if they were also pleased that "the boss" was coming home.

The big day arrived. Close to tears, I watched as some workers created a triumphal arch from young coconut palm leaves, which the women then adorned with hibiscus flowers and multicolored leaves. When Latif asked if the flag should be hoisted, I gladly retrieved it from the storage room. Soon, the tricolor was fluttering happily in the breeze. Would John be surprised!

Latif thoroughly cleaned the buggy, greased its axles, and carefully groomed the horse. Happy, I climbed aboard, letting Latif do the driving.

When we passed under the decorated arch, however, an unpleasant feeling came over me. The decor had turned out so well, and the house and compound looked so perfect, that, suddenly, everything seemed unreal.

"It looks like a fairy-tale village," I thought, "All show, and no substance!" An inexplicable fear seized me, and, searching for support, I reached out and got a firm grip on Latif's arm.

He sensed my anxiety, but let it pass. Pretending to interpret my gesture as a question, he said: "Yes, certainly, *Nyonya*. I arranged to have all the overhanging branches and coconut leaves along the road cut away. Imagine the *Tuan* being showered with ash on his arrival. The *Nyonya* can relax. Latif has thought of everything!"

After that, he just talked to the horse, urging it to do its best, as it would soon be pulling the *Tuan*. Just before the long wooden bridge, he spurred the stallion on with a Madurese yell. We virtually flew over the bridge, and its planks still rumbled after we had reached the other side.

As we turned into the road leading to the storage sheds, the nauseatingly sweet smell of copra greeted us. It came from a big pile of copra that had been put in the open air under a canvass. The pressure from its own weight was squeezing out the oil at the base, and that is where this rancid odor came from.

Full of hope, I got into the motor-sloop, which took off right away.

As we came closer to the ship, I was disappointed not to see a soul near the gangway. I had counted on John being there.

I climbed the gangway as fast as I could, and spotted a cabin boy on the otherwise deserted deck. I asked him for John's cabin, but before he could answer, the Captain came down from the bridge. Talking calmly, he led me to John's cabin, where the door stood ajar.

With trepidation, I entered the cabin and saw John sitting on his bunk, ashen-faced and looking terribly unhappy. Stunned, I stared at him. After mumbling a few words of welcome, I burst out in tears and walked over to him. He remained seated, as I clung to him. The Captain left, discretely closing the door behind him.

Dazed, I stuttered: "Is something wrong? The doctor wrote that you had recovered. Why don't you get up?"

With difficulty, John answered: "I was fine when I left the hospital, and was fine on Ternate. But now I can't walk and I feel terrible!" Then, in desperation, he cried: "I wish I were dead. Now you know it!" Sobbing loudly and writhing in agony, he lay down, turning and twisting on his bunk.

I went numb as I left the cabin to look for the Captain. I did not know him as well as his predecessor, Captain Faber, but I had to find out what had happened.

The Captain took me to his quarters and there told me briefly what he had learned from others on Ternate.

Upon arrival, a group of friends had picked John up from the ship. Instead of taking him to his hotel, they had thrown an exuberant welcoming party. The second evening, the party continued in the Chinese quarters. John's recovery had to be celebrated and they even got him out onto the dance floor. By way of farewell, they had taken him out on a boisterous picnic, somewhere along that beautiful coast. They had then brought him back on board where he had offered them a nightcap.

In the middle of the night, John had rung for the cabin boy, asking him to fetch the Chief Engineer, who functioned as "doctor". Grumbling, he had given John a sedative to reduce the severe pains in his legs.

"And this morning," the Captain continued, "I looked in on him, since he had not shown up for breakfast. I found him quite upset ... and unable to walk!"

The cabin boy had helped him to dress, and then brought him breakfast. "Later, we also brought him his lunch. And now you know everything," he concluded.

He then added consolingly: "I think he is simply overtired. I would not take it seriously, if I were you. You can imagine why these things happen when you have been in hospital for months on end. He'll be all right in a few days."

I don't know what I felt at that moment: pity, fear, anger or hatred.

Rattled, I asked the bashful-looking cabin boy and Latif to pack up John's belongings. John was placed on a stretcher, hooked up to a sling, and hoisted from board in the same fashion as he had boarded eight long months ago. I had earlier sent a message to the doctor and found him waiting on the quay with his car, ready to drive John home.

I brusquely instructed Latif to drive the buggy with the luggage home, to lower the flag, and remove the triumphal arch before John's arrival. I myself walked the long way back, brokenhearted and mired in despair and self-pity.

When I arrived, I hesitated outside the house. I had to clear my mind and come to terms with myself, before I could look John in the eye.

The doctor came outside and urged me to come in. With both of us present, he said that John's condition could only be attributed to overfatigue. Without asking, he gave me a tranquilizer shot before he left.

Later that night, I woke up and realized how cruel I had been. I admitted this to John, who was also awake, and we ended up reviewing the events of the day and comforting each other.

*  *  *  *

John stayed in bed for two full months. He was massaged regularly and fed a strengthening diet, which I managed to pay for with my few remaining jewels. Slowly he improved and started to walk a little.

I was still mindful of the doctor's orders, though: "Avoid stress at all cost! His heart is still not well!"

With great care and much effort I stuck to this injunction. However, I often had to hide in a remote corner of the plantation, where, unobserved, I could cry my eyes out and thus relieve my misery and despair.

As John regained his energy, he started asking questions. He had noticed that the plantation was not as well maintained as before. Where were the cows that used to graze around the house, and why could he not drink as much milk as he wanted? (I had, on occasion, refused to give it to him, on the pretext that it would make him fat.)

Where were the servants, and why was I doing all the housework?

It became increasingly difficult to give reasonable answers, and to prevent him from finding out what had happened during his absence.

When the doctor made the rounds again, he gave John permission to exercise his fingers on the typewriter — not realizing that this would inevitably lead to the discovery of the company's correspondence that was locked away in the safe.

Sure enough, a few days later John asked me for the key to the safe. Fortunately, his fingers were still too weak to turn the key.

With a lighthearted remark, I refused to do it for him, saying he could empty the safe when he could turn the key himself. Unseen, I put the key back in its hiding place, pleased that I had gained a few days respite.

One Sunday, however, I was less careful in replacing the key. John thus discovered its hiding place, but pretended not to have noticed.

The next day, I planned to be away for a long time: the work had to be inspected and paid for. Latif had an attack of malaria, so I installed John with a book on the front veranda from where he, instead of Latif, could inspect the cleaning of the main road.

An hour later, a worker came running with a message: "The *Nyonya* must come immediately!"

"Is the *Tuan* all right?" I asked, frightened. The man wasn't sure. The *Tuan* had come out of the house to instruct him to fetch the *Nyonya* immediately.

I ran all the way. What could have happened?

When I entered the house, John stood there, leaning lightly against the table, on which, spread out, lay all the papers and letters from Rotterdam. The safe was wide open. In his hands he held the last letter about the Director's suicide, and tears streamed down his chalk-white face.

When he saw me, he walked — yes, walked! — towards me, gripped my arms and gasped: "How horrible, how bloody awful! And I never knew anything about that!" Then came such a torrent of tears, that I thought all life would flow right out of him.

The miracle, however, had happened. His heart had withstood the shock, in spite of those dire warnings from the doctors who had treated him.

From that point onwards, recovery was swift.

John was soon brought up-to-date on all that had happened during his illness. Sometimes the news made him furious; sometimes, sad and disappointed. In the end, though, he was full of admiration for the way things had been handled and pleased that everything had come out all right in the end. We resolved then that whatever problem would crop up next, we would survive.

Two facts were in our favor. Mon Désir had remained unencumbered as there were no debts, and, most important, John was getting better every day.

As to the world crisis, there was a light at the end of the tunnel. News came that, on the world market, there was again demand for copra. But we decided to hang on to our stock and not to sell it right away.

Another month went by, and the price of copra suddenly shot up to 7.50 guilders per 100 kilograms. Early in 1934, the price went up to 10.50 guilders and kept increasing after that.

The slump was definitely over, and, slowly, the world seemed to rally.

We felt it was time to hire more workers, as the demand for them would soon increase. With a full complement, we had the plantation thoroughly cleaned. Then, the roads had to be restored, the fence repaired, and roofs — damaged at an alarming rate by the sharp-edged volcanic ash — had to be repaired again.

John now did the administration, and supervised all repairs. Three months later, he showed me that we had made a small profit. With a grateful heart, he proposed that it be used to give our people a *selamatan*.

The Feast of our Lord Jesus Christ the King, always celebrated with solemnity by our Catholic workers, was approaching. On that specific day, our kind-hearted old Priest, Father Neyens, would pay us a visit again — an ideal opportunity for the *selamatan*.

The whole plantation was festively decorated. The flag was hoisted (without the danger, this time, that it would have to be prematurely lowered). It appeared that we had embarked on a new and good life: copra now fetched 15 guilders per 100 kilograms!

Together, we went to the quay to meet our guest. But much to our regret, Pater Neyens was not there. Replacing him was a young German priest, whom we had never met. Nevertheless, the *selamatan* was a great success!

Afterwards, our guest told us what he had seen and heard during his recent European travels. Many changes were taking place in his impoverished fatherland.

There was a new government in Germany. The current chief, Adolf Hitler — who wished to be addressed as *Führer* (Leader) instead of President — had grappled with the unemployment problem and had sworn to make Germany a mighty nation again.

The present improvement in the world trade and economy, he thought, was largely due to the revived German economy with its tremendous buying power. It had an insatiable demand for tropical products such as copra, resin, rubber, oil, sugar and whatever else the tropics could produce.

However, our guest was quite concerned about Hitler having usurped all powers. He feared that it might lead to a dictatorial state, which would not augur well for the rest of the world.

How right he would turn out to be!

# CHAPTER 23

### New Technology
*Mon Désir Plantation, Halmahera, 1934*

With the economy in an upswing, we felt we could afford another furlough — the first one in six years — and decided to attend the Eucharistic Congress in Manilla. For the short time we would be away, the plantation could be entrusted to the care of Latif.

At the Congress we met a former captain of the KPM, who had stayed over a few days while *en route* to Hong Kong, from where he would continue to Japan, China and then America, where his only son lived.

Having visited Hong Kong as a proxy 21 years earlier, I expressed the desire to see that city again — this time, with John. "But that is not possible just now," I added regretfully, "not until Mon Désir is brought to full production and not until we have saved for it."

John, however, was caught by the idea, and proposed that we extend our furlough by a few weeks and visit not only Hong Kong, but also Chinese friends in Canton, who had often invited us to come and stay with them.

He talked me into it and, accompanied by the former KPM Captain, we boarded the *Tjisedane* that took us to Hong Kong.

For four days we crisscrossed this beautiful island with its magnificent harbor, and visited all the attractions. Both of us greatly enjoyed our stay — John in particular. Little did we suspect that destiny would bring him back, a short twelve years later.

Our travel companion then asked us to continue our trip with him to Japan, cross over to Shanghai and stop off at Canton (as we had wanted to) on the way back. It did not take much effort to persuade us. John, I noticed, suddenly seemed to loosen up. He, too, had been much in need of this holiday.

After visiting Yokohama (a textile center) and Tokyo, we took the train to the old imperial city of Kyoto and nearby Nara, where we admired the magnificent parks and temples, and the colorful kimonos of the industrious inhabitants, whose amiable courtesy in particular impressed us.

From Osaka we sailed to Shanghai, which reminded John of Rotterdam — it being another huge, bustling seaport. What oppressed me, however, was the sight of so many sweating, running, and panting rickshaw coolies, transporting people or cargo. Equally distressing were the many beggars.

After several days at Nanking, we traveled through the Chekiang and Fukien provinces to Canton, where our travel companion boarded his plane to the United States for the planned reunion with his son.

At Canton, we were the guests of Ang Chong Ong and family, whom we had befriended when they lived on Halmahera. They had now returned to their hometown. We spent several pleasant days with them and then it was time, finally, to return home.

With the *Tjitjalengka*, a ship of the Java-China-Japan Line, we sailed to Menado, and visited the Tomohon Mission Hospital, where John received a clean bill of health. His heart was finally in good order.

The journey had done both of us much good. We now had the energy to face the future — which at that point looked promising!

When we arrived home, John was full of plans and eager to go back to work. But when his company in Rotterdam proposed that he re-open the *damar* trade on Morotai, I persuaded him to hold off until the economy had definitely stabilized. Why not first open up his own plantation there, I suggested?

John agreed, and, since he would then spend less time on Mon Désir, my need for a new overseer became urgent. Everything on Mon Désir was going well, but it had become clear that Latif was not an ideal overseer. So I re-appointed him as *mandur*, with fewer responsibilities.

Interviewing took much time, but I finally hired a man, Sumampo, who had experience in harvesting and processing kapok.

With pride, I showed him the kapok plantation, which did look magnificent. It was so light and clean that it was a joy to walk through. In contrast, the coconut plantation, where the touching tree crowns almost shut out the sunlight, looked much more somber. The shortness of the tree trunks and the huge clusters of coconuts contributed to a closed-in feeling. With special pride, I pointed to the King Nut trees — some so heavy with fruit that they had to be shored up. The yield from these trees was fabulous, I told Sumampo.

We talked further about the need for a shed to store the kapok harvest, and another one to store the finished product. And since the old overseer's house had long since been put to other uses, a new house would have to be built for him and his family.

When I discussed this with John, he came up with another idea: since we would need to engage a construction crew anyway, why not have them also build a new house for us, and use the old one for other purposes? He talked about it with such exuberance and painted such a beautiful picture, that I finally allowed my concerns to be swept away and agreed to the building of a new house — one that would last for the rest of our lives!

But the house for the overseer was needed first, and when it was finished, Sumampo arrived with his wife, two dogs and a talking parrot. This couple had a daughter who was in boarding school in Menado, where she studied to become a teacher. She was a beautiful, spirited girl, they said, obviously expecting great things from her.

From Germany and France, I again received large orders for butterflies and insects. The London Zoo asked for assistance in finding certain rare species, and sent someone to teach my butterfly-catchers how to catch and preserve them. This person also taught my catchers how to stuff birds and snakes, and to preserve the skins of rats and other small creatures. My original cocoon nursery soon became too small and had to be expanded. In short, the work piled up.

Then, from Ternate, came three news items that were of particular interest to us.

First, the Catholic Mission was finally allowed to establish a post in the Moluccas, with a head office in Ternate. The spiritual care of the population would be entrusted to the Franciscan Friars. Two friars would be placed at Manokwari, and one, the Mission's Procurator, would become the Priest of Ternate.

The second news item was that many new companies had sprung up all over the Moluccas. The officers of the KPM ships confirmed this. There was a tremendous surge in trade, and everyone was making money!

The third news item dealt with new technology. To keep people in remote regions informed about world events, Phillips had designed a radio that worked on batteries. John knew in a flash that he "urgently" needed it, so he ordered one from a KPM Captain, who promised to bring it with him on his next trip.

His Chief Engineer readily promised to install it for us and to provide technical support. What would be needed, he said, was a large T-shaped antenna and a lightning rod. He spoke with such authority that we signed the order without further discussion and went home, eagerly awaiting the arrival of this technological wonder!

I, myself, was getting deeply involved in observing the eruptions of the Dukeno. I did this at the request of Dr. Neuman of the Institute of Volcanology at Padang, Sumatra. He had visited Tobelo earlier, and had observed the eruptions for a whole month. I had met him at that time, and had become quite interested in his work.

He was a congenial person, who spoke with a heavy German accent about the wonderful accomplishments of the *Führer*. Here was a real leader, he stated, yearned for by not only Germany, but by the whole world. We were all indebted to him for the present prosperity, he said proudly, not suspecting, of course, what was to come!

\*\*\*\*

The Dukeno became more threatening by the day. Its frequent expulsions of molten rock and hot ash had built up its cone, making the volcano higher than the Mamuya. Its normally green flanks were now scorched black; there was not one tree left.

A major eruption could happen any time, but this prospect did not particularly worry us. The lava would probably flow, as it had in 1552, along the side of the Mamuya, through the deep ravines in the Tobelo plains, and then out into the sea.

Minor eruptions now occurred regularly every three to five minutes. After persistent subterranean rumblings, it would spew out a swirling mass of black smoke that would extend hundreds of meters into the sky, form an ever-widening mushroom cloud, curl in on itself, and shower the area below with fine ash.

If the wind happened to be blowing in our direction, we would of course receive all the ash, which was like fine cement, yet felt coarse and heavy.

The ash caused many health problems for people and animals alike. It harmed the vegetation too. Growing vegetables was not worth the effort unless the beds could be shielded in some manner. The ash also affected fruit trees, resulting in lower production figures.

To keep our animals healthy, we had to cut grass, transport it to the sea and wash out the ash before we could give it to them. It was a laborious and costly process. This job had been entrusted to Latif, who fully dedicated himself to the task.

\*\*\*\*

Once the overseer's house was finished, we criss-crossed the plantation to find the best possible spot for our new house. The site had to be easily accessible and provide a good view of Mon Désir's magnificent surroundings.

In the foot hills we found a flat lot that met all the requirements, and also provided a clear view of the Dukeno.

We worked a long time on the design with an architect, who sent us magnificent drawings. They showed that the house would have a special roof and substructure to withstand the added weight of the volcanic ash, and would rest on a foundation built of stones that had already been collected from the river bed.

Construction progressed according to plan. With the foundation finished, the Chinese building contractor started on the upper structure, while John occupied himself with the layout of the grounds, which would include a rose garden that encircled the house. Beyond this rose garden would be a large lawn that included existing bamboo stools, which John wanted to preserve. It promised to become something beautiful!

Now that I had a new overseer and everything was going well on the plantation, we had more time for ourselves. We read some good books, discussed and deliberated on all things together and, once more, grew close.

Our lives were enriched by the presence of several animals: a little deer, Mieke, which we fed by bottle; a tiny striped boar — a present from a hunter — that followed me everywhere; tame birds; and our loyal dog, which was forever at war with my cats.

We made some wonderful trips on horseback or on foot, sometimes accompanied by our butterfly catchers. The long walks gave us the greatest pleasure. One, in particular, which took place on a beautiful Sunday, brought us an experience that I vividly remember to this day.

Most of the workers on the plantation were Christian and on their way to church. Everything around us was quiet and serene, and infused with a feeling of peace. We walked through the kapok plantation, which, pierced by shafts of sunlight, gave the appearance of a cathedral. The birds sang and chirped. The dog ran either after us or in front, searching for some unseen quarry. It was all so stunningly beautiful that it made us speechless. Silently, side by side, we walked on. Then, something unreal happened.

The rustling of the trees stopped, the birds fell silent, and the air ceased to move. The dog stopped in its tracks and looked puzzled. We looked at each other: what was happening here?

Then a feeling of great happiness flooded over us. We felt ourselves becoming extremely light, almost bodily detached! The silence deepened; the light intensified; and the feeling of joy became even more intense.

The silence belonged to something grand, something supernatural. We felt the urge to genuflect or kneel to that Being that enveloped us, that permeated us with this bliss and made our heads swim!

The incredible silence and indescribable feeling of happiness lingered for several minutes — and then it was over. The wind rustled through the treetops again, the light returned to normal intensity, the dog resumed its never-ending search, and birds started again to sing and to fly!

We looked at each other: tears of happiness were flowing down our cheeks. John took my hands, and whispered: "God just passed by."

\*\*\*\*

The radio arrived.

The KPM Chief Engineer made good on his promise by installing a large antenna between two nine meter-tall poles that rose from concrete pedestals. Lightning struck often in this region. Every year, we lost a few tall coconut trees because of it. So, to me, it was important that the lighting rod be made tall enough to draw lightning away from the house.

The radio drastically altered our lives: it changed our daily schedule, and also brought more visitors. Alas, it would also create jealousy.

The NIROM[1], whose signal came through crystal clear, gave us the news at 7:00 am! It was a giant step forward, compared to the newspapers that arrived every two weeks. Manilla, and even Hong Kong came through clearly as well, but European stations could only be received at night.

Apart from the radio, other changes had occurred in our environment. The Government at Ternate was no longer headed by a Resident, but by an Assistant Resident, and Resident Trips — who had rescued us from the deprivations of Buluwaya — had moved on.

More Europeans had arrived to either join the Protestant Mission — still the largest part of the European community — or to work on the plantations[2]. Among these newcomers was an Austrian doctor, who brought us the latest advances in medical science.

We also had a new broadcasting station and a customs office. New shops, owned by Chinese, Bombayers, and Arabs, were popping up like mushrooms.

The population, now that they were better paid, started to build beautiful, solid houses, most of them in a European style, with massive foundations of stone and concrete. The roofs were now made from galvanized iron — imported mostly from Belgium — that would better withstand the abrasive action of the ash rains.

With time, the Dukeno became even more violent, and earthquakes became stronger and more frequent. John once more confirmed that the ash was responsible for the decreased production. It was a major annoyance, but it did not really worry us.

Then came a pleasant surprise: Overseer Sumampo reported that the entire kapok plantation was in bloom! It came earlier than we had expected. What a spectacular sight it was! I felt I had ascended to heaven as a just reward for all the troubles the kapok had given me. (When John was ill, the kapok plantation had been the biggest millstone around my neck, for it had always *cost* money and had never brought in any revenue.)

Sumampo had now worked on trial for three full months, and John pressed me to offer him a permanent position. The Overseer had done quite well and had proved to be dependable. But I did not feel quite comfortable with him yet, and had not forgotten the misery I had suffered at the hands of the previous overseer. I therefore proposed to extend his trial period to six months.

John thought I was excessively cautious. He liked Sumampo and promised him he would talk to me. For the first time in ages, we disagreed about something and started to be awkward and stiff toward each other. I was on the point of giving in, when I saw Sumampo's wife coming to our house with homemade goodies — one of her specialties that John liked very much.

I could not stomach this gesture — not at this time. It was insincere, and it reeked of manipulation. That made me put my foot down and announce that I would review Sumampo's performance in three months time! John just shrugged and said he thought my decision was ill-advised. Luckily, he had swallowed his disappointment by the following day. It also seemed to have passed from the Overseer's mind.

Shortly after, John invited me to join him on a trip to his plantation on Morotai. I said I would be delighted to go. It would be a change, and we would again be thrown into each other's company.

We had a very pleasant trip. The weather was beautiful, and the sea calm. Best of all, on John's plantation, we were not bothered by ash rains, nor by the tiring rumble of the Dukeno.

\*\*\*\*

Back home, I started to worry about my health. For some time, I had tired quickly, and had been feeling less cheerful. Now and then, I had felt pains in my back and in the lumbar region. It was only a vague pain, but it reminded me of the one I'd had before my first operation. So I decided to ask the new doctor for a checkup. John came with me.

The Austrian first wanted to have a detailed report on the previous operations, which I gave him. He then subjected me to a painful examination, and asked me to come back the next day.

"Is it serious, Doctor?" asked John.

"How am I to know before tomorrow?" the doctor answered gruffly. How different he was from the always courteous native doctors who had preceded him.

The next day, much to our surprise, the Austrian arrived at Mon Désir in person, and now we got to know another side of this man.

The results of the checkup were inconclusive, he said. There was no X-ray equipment in Tobelo, so he could not say anything with certainty. He believed, however, that I had a tumor, and needed to go to a better-equipped hospital for further examinations.

John suggested that I go to Tomohon (the Catholic Mission hospital, where he had recovered from beri-beri) and stay there for a while, even if the results of the examination turned out to be favorable. The wonderful climate and beautiful surroundings would allow me to get recharged. To my surprise, I longed to do just that.

It would also give me the opportunity, John said, to look for workers that could be trained to process the kapok. The workers we had now would find it difficult to switch over to something so drastically different from their present occupations.

And, he continued, since I would be traveling via Menado, I could also purchase all sort of things for the house: door and window hardware; faucets and sanitary facilities; and the beautifully colored window panes that I had always wanted so badly.

John spoke so persuasively that it seemed improper to raise objections. So by telegram we booked passage on the ship that would take me to Menado two weeks hence.

Several days later, I had a visitor: a Menadonese woman, who had sewn for me and had faithfully come to church services on Mon Désir when a priest came visiting. Everyone called her *Tante* (Aunt) Donia. She had heard about my impending departure, and had come to ask if she could go with me as temporary attendant. Since her marriage, fifteen years ago, she had not been back to her native region.

I gratefully accepted her proposal. I would enjoy having someone with me whom I knew. Blissfully happy, *Tante* Donia returned home!

Till now, I had done all the cooking myself. A useful Papua boy, Lekko, kept the house clean; a girl, Nurmi, born on the plantation and now old enough to help, looked after all else. We also had a steady laundry man and a handy garden boy.

Nurmi, whom I had been training for a while, could cook for John while I was away. John did press me, however, to look in Menado for a good cook. In the new house, he joked, the *Nyonya* should not have to work in the kitchen anymore.

Preparations for the journey started. I planned the work that should be done during my absence, and advised everyone what was expected of them. And finally, with a sense of relief, I boarded the ship for Menado.

Now it was John's turn to stay behind, but under totally different circumstances. With the servants at his disposal and the radio as diversion, he would not be as lonesome and hapless as I had been when he was in Tomohon. I was grateful for that.

Two days later, *Tante* Donia and I reached Menado. Because of high waves, the ship could not anchor at the roadstead, and had to sail around the cape to Kema, where a quieter berth was found.

From Kema we had to continue our journey by bus, and this turned out to be a hilarious experience. The bus would not leave until it was full. Everyone who had bought his ticket was pressed into service to recruit additional passengers, and that was not easy, because we had to compete with chauffeurs who lured potential clients away with lower fares. It was like being pushed to play an impromptu role in a stage play at a moment's notice. No wonder we were in stitches most of the time.

Finally, the bus was filled to capacity with passengers, merchandise and livestock, and took off for the mountain region where Tomohon is located.

We arrived four hours later, and I was readily admitted to the hospital, where I was given an excellent room with a beautiful view on the Gunung Lokon (Lokon Mountain). *Tante* Diona found lodging with the auxiliary nurses. The following day, she would travel inland to visit members of her family.

There were two doctors at the Tomohon Mission Hospital. One, the Director, lived with his wife and five children in a magnificent house situated on a hill below the hospital. The other doctor appeared to be unmarried.

Both doctors examined me carefully. An X-ray photograph did show the existence of a small tumor, which could probably be surgically removed. But first, the doctors wanted to know if it was benign and, to that end, they performed a biopsy.

I went through a couple of anxious days, wishing all the time that John could have been with me. He obviously sensed my need, for he sent an encouraging telegram, followed by a detailed letter.

John wrote that Sumampo's daughter — on vacation from her studies — had arrived on Mon Désir. The girl had brought much gaiety to the plantation, was quick-witted and mature, and was a pleasant conversationalist. She had asked permission to come and listen to the radio now and then, and that permission had apparently been granted.

What caught my attention when I re-read the letter was that the girl had arrived on Mon Désir five days before I left. It was strange that I had not been told about it.

I did not give it further thought, however. After all, she would only stay a month and then return to her boarding school. Also, she would soon be bored on Mon Désir and would spend most of her time in the *kota*. And if it gave John some diversion if he received visitors now and then, well and good. Mother Sumampo would surely accompany her daughter and profit from my absence to enjoy the much-admired radio, which was for all still a miracle.

The result of the biopsy brought good news: the tumor was benign, and could be treated by means other than surgery. Treatment would start immediately, and would take not more than a month. The doctors wrote a detailed letter to John to explain the situation.

Meanwhile, *Tante* Donia had made the rounds, searching for people who might be interested in a contract position at Tobelo. I had asked her to explain clearly the circumstances under which they would have to work — including the many earthquakes and the bothersome ash rains. Knowing of her talent for expressing herself in a flowery manner, I did not think she would scare people off.

Soon, some applicants came forward, usually accompanied by wife and offspring. As a result, the veranda adjoining my room looked more like a recruitment office than the quiet gallery of a calm, modest hospital!

After many negotiations, I engaged seven married men, who wanted to come on contract for two years. They and their families would get free passage to Tobelo, and back to their place of origin after their contract had expired.

Four of the married women agreed to remove seeds from the kapok, and also do other types of work. One woman, named Leida, turned out to be an excellent cook, and was promptly hired as such. Her fourteen year-old son could be engaged as yard boy, and also look after the smaller animals. I also hired three *bujangs* (bachelors) who would do anything asked of them, but were only prepared to accept a one-year contract.

A fellow-patient gave me a tip that would save me a lot of money.

There was a small company in Menado, run by Japanese, who, with their own ship, the *Honun Maru*, would transport anybody and anything to anywhere. They would take the matériel I still had to purchase, and transport the newly employed workers as well — and it would cost a fraction of what the KPM would charge.

I proposed this means of transportation to the new recruits, and they accepted. Their departure was scheduled for two days before mine, still a month away, and we would meet in Ternate. I started to long for home.

*Tante* Donia visited me faithfully, bringing news about her friends and family, and about the ups and downs of life in the Minahasa region. From time to time, she borrowed money to buy things that were not available in Tobelo, and whose existence she had been unaware of. Her visits were always a pleasant distraction.

One day, however, she arrived at an unusual hour. At first, the nurse refused to let her in as it interfered with my treatment, but then she relented and told her to make it a brief visit.

When *Tante* Donia entered my room, she was flustered and at a loss for words — a very unusual state for her. When I pressed her to tell me what was upsetting her, she blurted out: "*Nyonya* must leave quickly! *Nyonya* must go back to Tobelo!" and she would say no more.

I laughed at her, saying that there was nothing happening in Tobelo that would force me to leave sooner than planned.

She insisted, however: "The *Nyonya* must leave!"

I felt I had to step in forcefully, and said she should not talk nonsense, and that we would soon go back together.

She started to cry, and said: "It cannot wait that long. The *Nyonya* must know!"

"What must I know?" I asked, getting a little annoyed.

Then, she opened up.

Donia had received a letter from her husband, which she had with her. In it, it said: "The Tuan has come completely under the influence of Sumampo's wife; he seems to be bewitched. The daughter is spreading the news that the *Nyonya* is finished here, and should stay away. She cannot have children, so the *Tuan* does not want her back." There was more of such foolishness and the writer then urged *Tante* Donia to make me aware of the "dangerous situation". "If the *Nyonya* does not come," so concluded the letter, "all will be lost!"

How should I take this? My first reaction was to discard it as gibberish: the rambling of a young girl who felt important, now that she had been allowed to listen to the radio. About John I did not worry. He liked to be with children, that was all. "What could such a young girl mean to him?" I asked myself, seeing an opportunity to tease him when I would tell him about the letter.

I did not want to think about this silliness any further, and tried to calm *Tante* Donia. She should forget the whole thing, and, I assured her, we would both have a good laugh about it later. But my words had no effect.

She stared at me somberly, and muttered that it would be on my own conscience.

"A *totok* (a newcomer) will never understand to what end a Menadonese will go to achieve his goal, nor what means are at his disposal!" she said. "There are many secret forces and powers, but the *orang Belanda* (the Dutch person) does not believe in them, and shall thus have to bear the consequences." With these words, *Tante* Donia left.

Later, when I had fully understood her meaning, I would remember every word of this conversation.

* * * *

John's next letter brought bad news: his radio had been destroyed by lightning! In rambling sentences, he described how it had happened.

One afternoon, while he was listening to the NIROM broadcast, he had been called away, and had forgotten to pull the plug — which he normally did, as a precaution. Suddenly, as happens often in the tropics, a storm developed. He ran home, but before he arrived, it happened: a blinding flash of lightning, immediately followed by a crackling thunder-clap, and it was all over.

When he entered the house, the smoke and stench of the smoldering radio greeted him. The room was a mess. The lightning rod and the tall T-shaped antenna had melted away, as had much of the radio itself.

"When you stop at Ternate on your way back, pick up a letter at the Post Office, in which I will give you further details," he wrote in conclusion.

I could well imagine how disappointed and lonesome John felt, now that his biggest source of recreation had been destroyed. It made me doubly glad that I would be leaving soon. I felt I had now regained my strength, and I longed to go home.

The necessary items for the house — paint, window panes, hinges and locks — had already been bought. Busy days followed, as everything had to be brought on board of the "*Honun Maru*". In the last minute rush, I also bought two robust pumps, in view of the ever changing water situation on the plantation.

The newly-employed workers had to be picked up from their *kampungs* with all their belongings, and that was no simple matter. One large bus was not sufficient to transport everything and everybody to

Menado, and it had to make a second trip.

Then it was time to say goodbye to the hospital staff and the nuns, and leave for Menado, where I would stay two days with friends, waiting for the KPM ship that would take me to Ternate.

The *Honun Maru* departed without a hitch. The workers waved cheerfully to me and called out: "See you in Ternate!" Everything had gone exceedingly well, and I was glad now to have some time for myself and catch my breath.

In conversations that took place in Menado and later on board, one could detect a recurring theme. People talked over and again about the "yellow peril", which referred to the disquieting activities of Japan. Its fleet was being enlarged, which gave credence to Japan's widely-talked-about desire for expansion.

I noted with some concern that Menado had more Japanese shops and photographers than ever before, and that these people had a steady stream of visitors.

There were also rumors that Germans, who had spent many years in the East Indies in important positions, had been recalled by their homeland. When I argued that the boom had perhaps made it easier for them to take furlough, my opinion was not accepted.

After the occupation of the Ruhr area by Hitler's troops (which was done without encountering opposition from *any* country), the speeches of the *Führer* had become more vehement, and threatening. But the few Germans I met — among them the Harbormaster — were full of praise for what this man had accomplished.

"He has the power and capability," said the Harbormaster proudly, "to remake Germany into a great nation, and that will benefit the whole world!

"There is no more unemployment in the Fatherland," he continued. "Everyone works and works well. New roads have been constructed, and business is flourishing. That is the real cause of the current boom."

Two months later, I heard that this Harbormaster had also been recalled to Germany.

When the *Bontekoe* of the KPM — replacing the regular "Papua ship" — dropped its anchor in the roadstead of Menado, I was pleased to leave.

After visiting more relatives, *Tante* Donia had made her own way to Menado, and joined me on board. At no time during the voyage did we talk again about her husband's letter. The journey went smoothly, and when we arrived on Ternate, I found two Franciscan Fathers waiting for me on the quay.

They told me that the *Honun Maru* had arrived the day before, but that measles had broken out among the children, and that they had been quarantined with their mothers near the presbytery.

The three *bujangs* (bachelors) and fathers who had not caught the disease were still on board of the *Honun Maru,* which rode at anchor some distance from shore and would leave the next day for Tobelo.

On board, everything was in order. I asked the people to continue their journey; the quarantined women and children would leave later with a KPM ship. The people agreed with the arrangement, and said they were pleased that the *Nyonya* was back with them.

Ternate had changed. The Franciscan Fathers had bought two houses. One served as presbytery; the other as church. They had also purchased a large lot on which they wanted to build a convent for nuns who would arrive soon, and a school where these nuns would teach.

In this large lot stood several small houses where, a long time ago, Papuan slaves had been kept under lock and key. This is where the stricken children and their mothers were quarantined. It was a good thing they didn't know the original purpose of these houses, otherwise they would surely *not* have accepted to stay in there.

After having satisfied myself that the children and their mothers were all right, I went to the PTT (Post, Telegraph and Telephone) Office to pick up a *poste restante* letter from John.

Outside the office, I ran unexpectedly into our friendly Käthe and her burly husband, who had aged considerably since I had first met them in New Guinea. They were on their way to Germany, from where someone had been sent to administer the plantation in their absence.

They hadn't met this person, but he seemed to be an agricultural expert. He was married to a "pure Aryan" woman, who had been trained in jungle survival. She could solder, install and service electrical equipment, repair anything, and handle tractors, trucks and inboard and outboard engines. She could also butcher animals, cut meat professionally, and preserve it as well. In short, she was a genius! — so they said.

Bewildered, I asked myself why all that expertise was needed on forty hectares of land that these people called their "estate". All they were producing there was a little copra and some pepsin from the papaya tree!

They could not tell me how long they were going to be away, and did not seem to know, or care — having full confidence in the ultimate wisdom of the Nazi party.

They would never return.

After Germany had invaded the Netherlands, our local Government unmasked this "exceptional" woman and her expert husband as notorious Nazi spies, and threw them in prison. What they were doing in New Guinea remains a puzzle. Did Hitler have dreams of getting back the former colony of Eastern New Guinea, and joining it to the western half after the conquest of the Netherlands?

The Post Office clerk silently handed me my letter. In it John described again, but in more detail, what had happened when lightning struck. He also wrote that he would be on the lookout for the *Honun Maru*, and either he or Overseer Sumampo would be on the quay to pick up the Menadonese and their belongings.

Transporting them, however, would not be as easy as before, he continued. Prolonged, heavy rains had washed away many bridges and had changed the course of the river, so that it now bypassed the bridges that were still intact. The ravines that normally carried off any overflow, were plugged by massive amounts of ash, and many areas were flooded. Moving anything from Mon Désir to the harbor had become quite difficult. As a result, copra was now transported by pram!

At the end of the letter, John had scribbled a few words: "In the *pasanggrahan* you will find another letter!"

I was mystified. What was in the second letter that he could not have said in the first one? The closing sentence of the letter surprised me even more. All it said was: "Greetings from Mon Désir."

How strange! John had never before closed a letter like that.

"He must have been quite upset," I thought. "Probably from having to shoulder all the setbacks by himself."

My heart flew out to him!

### Endnotes

[1] *Nederlands Indië Radio Omroep*: the Netherlands East Indies Radio Broadcasting Company.

[2] To give the reader an idea of how the population was made up: In the Department of Ternate -- which included Western New Guinea -- there lived 493,000 people, among which were a thousand Europeans and more than 3,700 Chinese ("Encyclopaedie van Nederlandsch-Indië", Pictures Publishers, Netherlands, 1934)

# IBU MALUKU

# CHAPTER 24

### The Medicine Woman
*Mon Désir Plantation, Halmahera, 1934*

It was time to return to the B*ontekoe* for lunch, and to arrange to have my luggage transported to Ternate's *pasanggrahan*, where I would stay and wait for the Tobelo ship.

On board of the B*ontekoe*, there was the usual flurry of visitors coming and going. It was a pleasant commotion that sprang up whenever a KPM steamer was in port, bringing the latest news from the islands between Batavia and Ternate. The atmosphere was brightened by the joy at seeing friends, but also tinged with the sadness of having to say goodbye. The visitors were loath to leave, and always waited until the third and last blast from the ship's whistle.

Having said my farewells, I went straight to the *pasanggrahan*, where the large, cool room enticed me to have a siesta. The promised letter from John was there, but I decided to read it after my bath. I had the feeling that it would contain something unpleasant. But curiosity overcame my reluctance, and I finally opened the letter.

What I read was so strange, so incredible, that I could not comprehend it right away. I had to read it several times before the message penetrated my mind.

John had written that he had done much thinking after I had left, and had come to the conclusion that it would be best for me to return to the Minahasa. Why? To obtain a complete cure, and to have the doctor conduct another thorough examination and make certain that I really could not have another child. It did not make much sense to work so hard and build a new house, without having an heir. I should ponder that!

He had also become convinced that our isolated existence on Mon Désir no longer pleased me. Not wanting to be in my way, he felt he should give me the freedom to decide if I wanted to live elsewhere. He would be willing to make that possible. "You can then," he went on, "also make that wonderful trip around the world you have so often talked about, and obviously are still longing for."

"So," he concluded, "don't hesitate to go back to Tomohon. Your arrival on Tobelo would only be a disappointment after all that has happened."

He closed with "Good wishes for a happier and less troubled future!"

I read the letter yet again, and had the horrible suspicion that the prolonged solitude and repeated setbacks had affected him mentally. Had he taken leave of his senses? He had suffered depressions before and at such moments had said and done things that he could not remember later — or, if he did, deeply regretted. But to write a letter like this one — no, that I could not understand.

With impatience I waited for the arrival of the "Halmahera ship". From the ship, I telegraphed John the date of my arrival with the request to be there to meet me.

When the ship dropped anchor at Tobelo, the first one to come on board was my faithful Latif. Anxiously, I asked him about the *Tuan*.

Latif claimed the *Tuan* had some business with the Second Mate, and had sent him to pick up the luggage. It seemed he did not want to say much else, since he only gave a short answer to every one of my questions. But perhaps this was due to the noise from the engine and our loudly-talking fellow passengers, who were getting into the motor-sloop with us.

John was still talking to the Second Mate when I stepped onto the quay. I walked over, pulled at his arm and asked if, by chance, he had not recognized me. He acted surprised, and asked politely if I'd had a pleasant trip. Then he turned to Latif, asked if all the luggage was accounted for, and — getting an affirmative answer — instructed him to transport my cases by *prau* to the plantation.

I latched onto the word *prau*, and concluded there was still widespread flooding.

Having finished his conversation with the Second Mate, he said casually: "Well, shall we go then?"

*Not one affectionate word!*

When we left the quay, it seemed that the natives who knew me looked at me with pity in their eyes.

Because of the washed-away bridges, the buggy had not made it to the harbor, and we were therefore forced to walk the five kilometers to Mon Désir.

John walked beside me without saying a word. I also held my tongue, but found it exceedingly difficult. Finally, when we had left the populated area, I could not hold back any longer, and asked what in heaven's name was going on!

Irritated, John asked gruffly if I had not received his letter.

I had, I said, but it had not made any sense.

John turned white with anger, but only said: "Well, you did come after all. Now it's up to you to decide what to do with yourself." Then he walked on with such long strides that I had difficulty keeping up with him.

When we reached the *kali*, I was surprised by how much the flooding had changed the landscape. John sat down on the embankment, and with a stick hit anything within reach — much like an angry boy who sulks because he did not get his way.

His attitude worried me deeply. I had never seen him like this before. A paralyzing fear for what was still to come seized me. How different I had imagined my homecoming when I left Tomohon.

The river's current was strong; crossing it would be difficult, and not without danger. At any other time, I would have looked upon it as an interesting, even amusing, challenge. Now it left me cold.

I had been so wrapped up in my own thoughts that I hadn't noticed that one of our workers had crossed the river with a rope. He fastened the rope to a tree, and his colleague on my side did the same. John was the first one to cross, pulling himself hand over hand along the rope to the other side.

Meanwhile, the worker who had stayed with me brought me up-to-date on the latest news. The H*onun Maru* had arrived the previous evening, he said. All the new recruits had been picked up, and were now lodged in the houses that had been prepared for them. Overseer Sumampo was now supervising the transportation of the equipment and supplies that I had bought in Menado. After that, the *Honun Maru* would take in a load of our copra. That was the first good news I had heard about Mon Désir, and it made me feel much better.

John had reached the other side, and now it was my turn. The worker told me what to do to make the crossing. A moment later, I was dangling from the swaying rope. It was unusual, to say the least, but I did succeed in getting safely across.

John had moved on; he had not bothered to wait for me. Slowly, I walked down the long road through the plantation to our house, holding back my tears with great difficulty.

When I passed the annex, I saw the Overseer's wife coming out of our house. I assumed she had brought flowers or a cake as a welcome-home gift — as was customary here.

John was nervously pacing up and down the front veranda, as I entered the house from the rear. In the corridor stood what remained of the radio. I saw also several empty painting frames, the glass of which had been blown out. That lightning bolt really had done a lot of damage!

John came inside as soon as he heard me. Again, I asked him to tell me what was happening.

No answer!

To make it easier for him, I moved to a less difficult topic: "Are you pleased with the new recruits?"

With a here-we-go-again gesture, he said loudly: "Are you sticking your nose into everything again? Don't you get it that you are not wanted here?" Then, he yelled: "I'll show you who is boss around here!"

Stunned, I just stared at him.

He looked away, and then rushed past me into the dining room, from where I heard the sounds of breaking glass and porcelain, and furniture being thrown about.

Had he gone mad?

Then I heard our dog yelp from having been kicked. Afraid, with its tail between its legs, it crept towards me. I caressed it, and it lay down beside me. Now and then it looked toward the dining room, growling softly.

I heard John go to the bathroom, and hoped that a dousing would calm him down and clear his mind. I would have to wait until a more rational conversation was possible.

It was getting dark outside. Feeling defeated, I leaned on the front veranda against a beam, and gazed across the road at the house that was being constructed for us. They seemed to have made much progress during my absence: the roof was finished. But I didn't dare go to have a look as I feared I might meet people. First, I had to get myself under control.

Then I heard some people talking softly. Two women were approaching along the hedge that enclosed the yard. I recognized the wife of the Overseer. The other person was a very slender young woman, a girl really, who was exceptionally beautiful. They pretended not to see me and disappeared down the road.

Was that the daughter of the Overseer, I wondered, and could she be responsible for John's strange attitude? I shivered.

John came out of the bathroom, and appeared to be getting dressed. Shortly after, I saw him walk down the road to the *kali*. From his vehement steps, I could see that he had not yet calmed down.

With the coast clear, I entered the bathroom. The fresh, cool water did me much good, but it could not stop the tears. I felt desolate.

I heard Lekko, the Papua boy, clean up the glass fragments in the dining room, and then set the table for dinner. Now, I did not know what to do: sit at the table at the appointed hour, or wait for John to come back? I decided not to wait.

I was still eating when John came back. He didn't enter the dining room, however, and I heard him instruct Lekko to clear the table when the *Nyonya* was finished. His voice sounded calmer. I decided to not ask any questions, and simply wait.

I was still seated, when I heard him enter the room. I didn't dare look at him. John said I could use the bedroom; he had moved his things out. Then, he disappeared and locked the guest-room door behind him.

\*\*\*\*

Early in the morning, I took a bath, dressed, walked resolutely over to John, and asked curtly if he felt capable now of giving me a reasonable explanation.

A surly stare was his only reply. Belatedly, I noticed his eyes had a weird look. And there was something so agitated and strange in his appearance, that I was shocked. Suddenly, I felt an intense pity for him.

Then I remembered the letter from *Tante* Donia's husband, which I had pooh-poohed when she showed it to me. John was under a strange influence, it had said. I had never believed in spells; to me, they were old-wives' tales! But how else should I explain John's strange state and behavior?

I left John to himself, and went searching for Latif. I wanted to find out what had happened during my absence. At first, Latif didn't want to speak. When I insisted, however, he told me enough to confirm my suspicions. Someone was indeed working on John. Then, Latif urged me to send Sumampo and his family away.

"Why?" I asked.

"Because," he said with unusual deep anger in his eyes, "Since *Nona* Ella came, everything has changed."

"First, she brought flowers for the *Tuan*. Later, she brought food and cakes. Then, she started listening to the radio with her mother."

"The mother told *Babu* Sappo, who looked after the *Tuan*, that it would be better if she went back to stay with her parents, while the *Nyonya* was away. She, *Nyonya* Sumampo, would take care of the *Tuan* meanwhile."

"Sappo did not dare to refuse and so she left. After that, the two women spent much time in *Nyonya's* house, and slowly the *Tuan* changed."

"When *Nyonya's* telegram arrived, the *Tuan* was very upset. He called for *Nona* Ella, the daughter, who stayed with him until late in the evening."

In my eyes Latif had read an obvious question, for he suddenly said: "No, *Nyonya*, she has definitely not been his *nyai*. The *Tuan* did not let it go that far."

Then, muttering to himself, he said: "As long as one is hungry, one longs for good food, but when one has eaten, one forgets how tasty it was, and tries to get rid of it."

I did not know this saying, but thought I understood its meaning. I decided to act!

I went straight home, and asked John if he were ready to talk. When I again received a surly stare, I said resolutely that in that case, I would do the talking. Something in me seemed to make him realize that he better keep quiet and listen.

"First," I said, "I want to make it clear that I am not planning to go anywhere. I will stay."

"Next, I will fire Sumampo. He and his family shall leave with the *Honun Maru — today*."

"And," I added coldly, "if you want to go too, go! I am staying!"

John turned white with anger, and was about to yell at me when I cut him off.

"Whatever you say or do makes no difference to me. My decision stands. It is now up to you to decide whether we separate or stay together and forget what has happened."

"Just remember," I added spitefully, "you will be much less of a catch for that beautiful Ella, if you don't have Mon Désir anymore!"

I then turned on my heels and disappeared, not giving him a chance to say one word. But the strange, cruel alter ego that had momentarily taken over, was gone. My hands were bathed in cold sweat and I was afraid of what might follow.

I heard John give instructions to have his horse saddled. This meant he would not be around to interfere with my plans. Good!

When I arrived at the Overseer's house, a worker told me that Mother Sumampo and her daughter had gone to Tobelo to visit friends, and that Sumampo himself was talking to the new Menadonese recruits.

I sent someone to the Overseer with a note, asking him to come to the house right away. Then I returned, dead tired, but again of steely composure, determined to follow through with what I had decided to do.

When Sumampo arrived and wanted to talk about the new workers, I cut him off abruptly and said I had decided that his services were no longer needed, and that he was fired. He would be paid two month's salary and receive free passage to Gorontalo for him and his wife. His daughter was *his* affair.

Stunned, he looked at me. Then he struck a pose of "we'll see about that". But before he could utter a single word, I told him curtly that I could not possibly keep him on after all that had happened.

His attitude quickly changed. He said he hadn't wanted things to get out of hand, but had found it impossible to control his wife and daughter. I asked him bluntly to spare me further details, and to make sure to leave *my* plantation before nightfall. Otherwise, I would take further steps.

Like a beaten dog, he slunk away. Had I just destroyed his plans for the future, or had he really been unable to control his wife and daughter? I did not know, and didn't care to know.

To calm down, I decided to walk over to the new house to see how they had progressed. It appeared that John had done nothing more about the new garden and yard. Since John was still nowhere to be seen, I went to see how the new workers were doing — but the men had gone to the *Honun Maru* and their wives had gone to the *kali* to do their laundry.

The plantation looked well-maintained. The copra makers were glad to see me, and greeted me so warmly that it brought tears to my eyes. At least there were some people here who did not want me to "get lost".

It was two o'clock in the afternoon when I left them and returned to the house. There was still no sign of John. That put my mind at ease: he would have more time to think things over.

A little later, a note arrived from Sumampo, asking permission to use the *gerobak* to transport his belongings. Lekko came timidly out of the kitchen with a teapot, several dishes and a few plates. These belonged to *Nyonya* Sumampo, he said.

Rather rudely, I ordered him to return them all and then return to the house immediately. I watched as he ran through the plantation. Moments later, he returned, out of breath, with his arms stretched in front of him to show that he was coming back empty-handed.

I then sent Latif with a letter to the KPM Agent, ordering two boat tickets for the Overseer. When Latif returned around five, John still had not come home. The *barang* of Sumampo had meanwhile been loaded in a *gerobak*, and the procession got started. When it passed the house, I summoned the smartly dressed Overseer.

I handed him the boat tickets, and thanked him for the contribution he had made to the plantation. When he stuck out his hand, however, I pretended not to see it. His wife did not come to say goodbye. She just walked on without even a glance as she passed the house. The daughter I didn't get to see at all.

John did not come home that night. I knew he was not in Tobelo, because the *kabar angin*[1] would have told me so. He had obviously gone in a different direction. I worried about him and passed a restless night.

\* \* \* \*

The next morning went by in a flash. The H*onun Maru* left with 250 sacks of our copra, and the KPM steamer returned from its trip to Weda. It was the same ship which had brought me from Ternate a few days ago, so full of hope.

I received a note from *Tante* Donia, confirming that Sumampo and his family had indeed boarded the ship and left Tobelo, and for the first time, I started to feel safe.

Late in the afternoon, I heard the hoof-beats of John's horse, and watched as he rode up the driveway. He looked disheveled, and appeared dead tired. I asked Lekko to bring clean clothes for John to the bathroom and to prepare tea in the dining room.

I remained quietly seated on the front veranda, reading, and pretended I had not noticed his arrival. But my heart pounded, and my ears strained to pick up every sound in the house. I heard the rattling of teacups, the opening and closing of the pantry and icebox. Later, I heard him walk to the guest room and lock the door behind him. I hoped it was a sign that he had decided to stay.

I knew he was engaged in a heavy battle with himself. He would undoubtedly feel terribly hurt, possibly ashamed, and would be pitying himself. If that were all, it would not be too bad — those feelings, I knew, would pass.

What I feared deeply, however, was that Mother Sumampo's "treatment" — whatever it was — might have damaged him physically and mentally. Stories I had heard about *guna-guna* (black magic) came back to haunt me now, and I was afraid! Yet, that night I slept better and I dared to hope — just a little.

\* \* \* \*

The next day, John awoke much later than usual and stayed so long in the bathroom that his coffee became cold. Meanwhile, I was sitting at the breakfast table, listening to what was happening in the house.

When John finally entered the dining room, he didn't greet me. He sat down in his usual place, and started to eat his oatmeal porridge in complete silence, except for a few words to the dog and the little deer, Mieke. For him, I did not yet exist.

I managed to be patient and started my usual activities. In my heart, hope started to sprout. Lunch was another silent meal. Then I noticed that John had no appetite and seemed to be suffering from stomach cramps after the meal. Then, he suddenly gasped for air and threw up.

I ran over to him, and he clung to me like a frightened child. Nerve spasms racked his body. Only then did I notice how thin he was, and a wave of deep compassion washed away my steely composure. I asked him to stand up, and then led him to his own bed.

He was completely unhinged. I did not ask any questions but called for the doctor, who gave *him* a sedative, and *me* a knowing look. Thanks to the *kabar angin*, this doctor, a son of the land, was well informed about what had happened here!

He could do no more, however, than prescribe sedatives, a special diet, and rest. He also advised me to be careful, and not to excite John — which, of course, I readily promised. John remained totally apathetic, and didn't talk or show interest in anything. He just stared out into space.

Without a husband or overseer, I again had to assume total responsibility for the plantation.

A few days later, *Tante* Donia came to visit. She had brought a friend, the old Mama Pina, a *dukun* (a healer or medicine woman). As John knew her well (she had once cured him from dysentery), I dared let her visit him.

John pretended to be engrossed in a book. Pina greeted him more boisterously than was usual for her, and struck up a conversation in which John participated. To my surprise, I heard her tell John that he should go outside, as she wanted to show him something. Usually, she brought with her a small plant with medicinal properties, in which John was always interested.

Lo and behold, John went outside, continuing his conversation with her. Mama Pina fetched a chair for him and placed it in the shadow of a tall *jeruk* (lemon) tree. John sat down and listened as Mama Pina kept talking. Eventually, he fell asleep! What was that old lady up to, I wondered, giving *Tante* Donia a questioning look.

Quietly, Mama Pina got up, came inside the house and asked permission to see the bedroom. "Of course," I said, in a puzzled voice.

I watched as she criss-crossed the room, sniffing like a bloodhound. She finally went to the head of the bed, still sniffing, picked up John's pillow, and brought it over to us.

What did this old woman want with that pillow?

*Tante* Donia whispered: "Let her do what she wants, *Nyonya*. She has found something harmful."

Mama Pina walked with the pillow to the copra drying shed and asked the workers to make a small fire. When it was burning well, she threw the pillow into the flames. After it had been consumed, she returned to the house. She picked up a pillow from the guest room, and put it on John's side of the bed in our bedroom.

When I wanted to know what this was all about, *Tante* Donia said curtly that the *Nyonya* had been *bodoh* — dumb! She had not even noticed that there had been a strange odor in the bedroom. But the pillow that gave out this smell was gone, and with it, the evil influence of the beautiful *nona*.

Mama Pina, who had been chewing on a fresh wad of *sirih*[2] leaves, spat out a squirt of red saliva and said: "It is all over. Everything will be all right. You can relax now." Then the two women left, leaving me anxiously waiting for what would happen next.

When John woke up, he asked me for something to drink. Those were the first words that he had spoken directly to me. Then he walked over to where the new house was being built, and returned hours later, tired out. It seemed he had done some work on the new yard.

At the lunch table, he ate little, but behaved more naturally. After the usual siesta, I saw him go back to the building site, but I didn't dare follow him.

He still wouldn't speak normally to me, but he did give brief answers when I asked him something. The atmosphere was not as tense as it had been, so perhaps the worst was over.

That evening, he closed the door to the guest bedroom, but he didn't lock it as he had before. Crying with relief, I lay down on my bed, and for the first time fell into a deep, redeeming sleep.

* * * *

A few days later, John talked for the first time about the completion of the house. The outer walls of "iron wood" were finished. The masons were busy placing the floor, he said. Would I like to go over and see it with him?

Elated, but acting as if it was quite normal, I agreed. I had longed so fervently to do that, but had always held back. John had been there every day, and not wanting to make him feel that I was interfering with the activities there, I had carefully avoided that part of the plantation. Now, we were going there together!

With immense joy, I observed that John had, indeed, been working on the layout of the gardens. It required a great deal of effort not to give him a compliment. I thought it was better to ignore the rift that had almost destroyed our marriage.

My God, how thankful I was for this change. That day we had our first normal conversation together.

But about the past, we would never utter another word.

### Endnotes

1. *kabar angin*: "news carried by the wind", i.e. rumors.
2. *Sirih:* betel, a pepper plant, the leaves of which are rolled into a wad and then chewed.

IBU MALUKU

# CHAPTER 25

### Dukeno's Wiles
*Mon Désir Plantation, Halmahera, 1936-1937*

Our kapok trees, which already bore beautiful cobs that could mature in two months, were now covered with a thick layer of the volcanic ash. Worried that the ash could destroy the harvest, I wrote the Volcanology Department in Bandung, where I regularly filed my reports on the Dukeno's activities.

By return mail, I learned that they would send an expert to advise me on the situation. It took a while, but when the volcanologist finally arrived and introduced himself with a strong Russian accent as Peter Petrojefski, I could not believe my ears.

"*Est-ce vraiment vous* — is it really you?" I said, automatically switching to French and remembering our first meeting in Nice, so many years ago, when he had been visiting his aunt, *Madame* Vasilieff.

"Ah," he responded, equally surprised, "*la petite Hollandaise. Qu'est-ce que vous faites ici* — what are you doing here?"

In the next hour, we quickly brought each other up-to-date on our adventures since we had met last in Kiev. Like so many other well-to-do Russians, he had fled his country; but unlike most, he had learned Dutch and had managed to get himself a good job in Batavia, where there was a sizeable Russian colony.

For the next seven days, I accompanied him and his staff (mostly native people) to various villages around the Dukeno. I spoke mostly in French and then translated the conversation into Malay for the members of his staff.

Peter explained that the Dukeno's performance was unique.

"This kind of ash rain happens rarely," he said. "They are difficult to predict and can be disastrous, as in Santorini in Greece. The eruptions can last more than thirty years. Then, it seems the mountain goes into hibernation, and it can take centuries before it becomes active again."

"Are you saying," I asked worriedly, "that this is no place for kapok or cotton?"

Hesitatingly he replied: "Well, I would not encourage it."

Naturally, the people from Buitenzorg who had recommended the planting of kapok could not have known that the Dukeno was of the Santorini type and would become active just at this time. I had never even considered that possibility myself!

I had read about the big eruption of 1552, and recalled an earlier report, written by the Jesuit missionary Franciscus Xaverius (St. Francis Xavier), who described it as a land of earthquakes, in which the volcano constantly spewed out stone fragments as large as the biggest houses in Madrid. He also described the heavy ash rains that blanketed forests, destroyed crops, and caused health problems among the people.

The seriousness of that report had escaped me at the time I read it, but I now wondered what the future would bring. We had invested so much in this kapok plantation, and had expected so much from it.

\*\*\*\*

The Government announced plans to set up a Copra Board, where all copra would be quality-controlled and traded at set prices. A similar board already existed for rubber. We thought it to be a good move. People often brought products of inferior quality to market, and the Government obviously wanted to put a stop to that.

Our books showed, however, that production had dropped. This could be due to theft (a common complaint on many plantations) or to the steady increase in ash rains.

We studied the flower clusters, and found the fruit crop at the bottom to be normal. At the top of the clusters and on the sides facing the volcano, however, fructification was considerably impeded — a clear sign that the ash rain was indeed the culprit.

But of greater concern was the health hazard posed by the ash.

Several people in the surrounding *kampungs* had died from throat and lung infections, so we advised our people to protect nose and mouth while at work, especially when picking the crop. Some did, and just accepted this inconvenience, but others did not — not yet being convinced of any danger.

Then a Menadonese woman on Mon Désir started to complain about shortness of breath. It was the ever-joyful Lien Sarewan, who was in an advanced stage of pregnancy. We took her to the hospital. The doctor looked somber. She had seen the same symptoms before. Two days later, Lien died and our new recruits were devastated. Ten days later, there was a second death. It was Maria's husband, the rather wooden-faced Levinus Rantani. He had been unwell for several days, but had refused to go to the hospital. He had asked his wife to pick up a bottle of *arèn* (arenga) palm wine and downed it without pausing. That night, he died in his sleep.

## IBU MALUKU

The doctor did not quite know how to list the cause of death. Levinus had complained earlier about shortness of breath and a sore throat, and his widow had said that he had weak lungs even before he left Wolowan, his home town. In our hearts, however, we were convinced that the ash rain had killed him.

The workers took time off to make the casket. We provided the necessary boards and lining material: white and black cotton. Later, they asked for more boards: the casket had to be made higher.

According to Minahasa custom, all Levinus' clothes had to be buried with him. Among his possessions was the inevitable high hat that he had worn at his wedding and at all important family gatherings. This hat also had to fit into the casket, uncrushed. So the casket-makers again asked for, and received, more boards ...

When Levinus was laid out in the oversize casket, we were invited to say goodbye and to attend the funeral. The high hat was placed between his legs, and Levinus' white-gloved hands rested on the rim. It was his face, however, that fascinated me. I had never seen him smile while alive; now, his face was beaming! Everyone looked on in wonder, but Maria, his widow, explained solemnly: "Levinus is in heaven; God has his soul."

Levinus was buried beside Lien in the new cemetery. A second grave in such a short time! After the burial, there was a funeral meal of rice, fish and all the trimmings.

Life went on as usual, but those two deaths weighed heavily on me. I gave strict instructions to protect nose and mouth during work, even though I doubted that it would really help. The ash seemed to penetrate everything.

I carefully examined each person who came to the clinic for treatment, and whenever there was any sign of a throat infection or tightness of the chest, I sent them with a note to the doctor.

We had a few days of respite, when the wind was blowing the ash clouds away, but, despite the brilliant sunshine, everything looked grey, and the slightest wind would cause the ash to fall from the trees and rooftops. How we hungered for a good downpour! But then the *sibu-sibu* (land-wind) blew the ash in our direction again ... with more grievous consequences.

Stefanus, a child from a couple recruited in the Minahasa, came home one day with a letter from the *guru* of the *dèsa* (small village) school he attended. He had fallen ill during class. I immediately sent him to the hospital, and went to see the *guru*. He told me that already five children from his school had passed away in the last few weeks!

A week later, little Stefanus returned to Mon Désir — in a casket. His parents were brokenhearted. Now there was a third grave in our cemetery!

I blamed myself for having brought these people from their beautiful country to this hellish place, and felt it was my duty to free them from their contract. But John advised me to leave the decision up to them and not make any premature move.

We had offered Levinus' widow free passage to her native town, but she had declined. She now earned her keep by cooking and washing for six bachelors who worked on Mon Désir. Three of them were from her home town; the others were from the Sangihe Islands, north of Celebes.

\*\*\*\*

One day, Paulus, one of the recently recruited Menadonese, came to report that the kapok was ripe. Together, we walked over and, indeed, saw that everywhere the large black cobs had burst open and that the white kapok protruded through the crevices.

The harvest would have to start soon, because rain could spoil this crop — our very first. The people who had come from the Minahasa had been hired specifically to harvest and process the kapok, so they could now finally be put to work. It soon became clear, however, that harvesting kapok was not as simple as picking coconuts.

The high kapok tree is covered with large tubercles, from which grow short, strong thorns. So we had to work with ladders. But our workers seemed to know how to pick, because the first day's harvest was quite impressive.

The black cobs were laid out to dry in the sun, which caused them to open up completely. The somewhat moist kapok that remained in the cob after pulling out the bulk, was manually removed by the women and laid out to dry. The many black seeds were later removed by machine. The final product was beautiful, long and fibrous, and although its color had been slightly affected by the ash, it would still bring a good price on the local market.

The harvest was in its fourth day when our worst fears materialized: there was a heavy downpour (which would have been so welcome a week earlier), coupled with strong gusts of wind, which lasted three full days. The remainder of the harvest was ruined! The work of five years had all been for nothing!

With horror I looked at the grey, filthy mass lying under the trees, and I asked myself bitterly where I should go from here.

The maintenance of the kapok plantation was too costly to continue under the present circumstances — there seemed to be no solution in sight. After due deliberation, we decided to contact the plantation that had provided us with the kapok seeds.

Their advice was devastating: "Kapok has no value on the world market unless it is of top quality and spotlessly clean. Our recommendation: Clear out the kapok trees, and switch to a less vulnerable culture!"

John now proved to be the stronger one — it was he who took the bold decision to replace all the kapok trees with King Nuts.

The men from the Minahasa were now employed to cut down the kapok trees. The wood is soft, so that felling the trees was not very heavy work. But digging out the roots was another matter. The tree-stumps had to be carefully removed and burned, since they otherwise might attract vermin that could damage the King Nut trees that were to take their place.

It was a costly affair, both emotionally and financially. The removal of this beautiful plantation, which had been my pride and joy, finally cost much more than the original clearing of the forest.

It was an awful setback. Luckily the price of copra remained high, so we could absorb this loss. Our reserves, however, were depleted.

*****

A fourth death occurred — again among the Menadonese — which plunged Mon Désir once more into mourning. It was Petrus Kegongean, a bachelor. From Paulus, we heard that Petrus had spent time in a sanatorium as a lung patient. It was now very clear that those with bronchial problems were especially vulnerable to the ash rains.

In the surrounding *kampungs*, many people and animals had also succumbed to the ash rain, which was sometimes so heavy that it had crushed clusters of bamboo cane. We hadn't seen fresh vegetables for a long time. The situation seemed so hopeless.

*****

The new house was finally finished. It looked marvelous amidst the already blooming rose beds and the lawn that John had created. He had worked hard, and the diversion had been good for him — the result had been well worth the effort.

The day of the big move arrived. To say thanks and bless the house, we organized a *selamatan* — to which everyone was invited.

We distributed an abundance of fish and meat, and soon the whole plantation became permeated with the smell of exotic dishes that were being prepared in the kitchens. Each woman would contribute something to the feast.

The Menadonese expressed the desire to cook something on their own, so we gave them permission to buy whatever they needed. Their iron cooking pots were percolating secretively on the charcoal fires, which were being fanned patiently by the women and children squatting in front.

Now and then, I made the rounds. Once, when I curiously lifted the wooden lid of a large iron pot to see what kind of brew gave out that distinct, delicious aroma, I saw to my horror the head of a big dog, whose white, dead eyes seemed to look straight into mine!

Shaken, I quickly put the lid back, while the cook cheerfully explained that her husband, Amandus, had bought this large dog from an Ambonese for only a *ringgit* — a two-and-a-half guilder coin. Later, she said, the *Nyonya* should definitely try this dish.

"The tongue is the most delicious part," she explained, "and I will specially prepare it for the *Nyonya* and *Tuan*, together with other delicacies!"

I could readily picture John's face after finding out he had been eating dog's tongue, and decided it would be wiser not to say one word about this. If told, he would not have been able to eat another morsel!

It turned out to be quite a party! The whole garden was fenced off with arches of young, yellow coconut leaves, embellished with dark-red hibiscus flowers. The children sang newly-learned songs, accompanied by a large flute orchestra — all boys who, in the course of time, had been born on Mon Désir!

There were many long speeches, during which we remembered those who lay in our new cemetery. According to the Menadonese, their spirits were undoubtedly participating in this feast, unseen, and were rejoicing with us.

It was very touching!

During the *selamatan*, I slipped away and walked to the old house. It stood there so silent, desolate and deserted. Wistfully, I walked through the empty rooms. Each one had something to tell me. We had survived a lot in this house: here, we had been deliriously happy, but I had also walked through it in terror and in untold grief. It had undoubtedly been a real home for us!

But it was time to say goodbye, and I did so with the hope and prayer that our new house would herald a safe future. At the festivities, across the way, nobody had noticed my absence. Just as well. I had wanted this to be a private farewell.

After the resplendent fireworks display, compliments of our Chinese friends, the guests left. We were finally alone to spend our first night together in our new, big home.

\*\*\*\*

# IBU MALUKU

Waking up in the new house was a different experience. Whereas the rooms in the old house were dark because of the surrounding coconut trees, here everything was light and cheerful.

The view was magnificent. Right in front was the large plateau that contained our beautiful garden. Further on, still bluish in the early morning light, stood the mountains, flanked on both sides by two gracefully-shaped volcanoes: the Mamuya on the right, and the larger Togoshi on the left. Back of them and straight in front of us stood the continually-active Dukeno. A dark ash plume hung over it, which that day, luckily, leaned away from us.

The smell of roses permeated the air. Deeply content and happy, we gratefully acknowledged: "Now, this is really the fulfillment of 'Mon Désir' — our mutual desire." Here, we hoped to spend the rest of our lives, no matter what might happen around us!"

"We've finally come home," John concluded with a sigh of contentment. But I could not help glancing at our old home across the field. For me, that old house was still "my house", for it was there that Mon Désir had its start.

\*\*\*\*

Among the guests at our housewarming party was a former Friar, who had paid his first visit to Mon Désir just before I left with *Tante* Donia for the Tomohon Mission Hospital. He was at the time accompanied by Marie, his Japanese housekeeper, who, he subtly pointed out, was his attendant, not his *nyai* (mistress).

To show that we had understood him, we treated her cordially and tried to draw her into the conversation. But this was difficult to do, because she spoke no Dutch; only bad, difficult to understand, Malay.

The story he told us during that first visit was a sad one.

He had been a Mission Friar, and had left the order because of differences of opinion with his Bishop concerning his work. He had been head of a technical school, the former Friar recounted. The Bishop had no understanding of how to run such a school, but had nevertheless imposed his views.

Then, he had met Mr. Lulofs, first Resident of Northern New Guinea, who was looking for professionals to run a modern sawmill on Manokwari. He had persuaded our visitor to take charge of this enterprise. So, the Mission lost a good friar, and the Dutch East Indies Government gained an excellent manager.

He had been on the job nine years when tragedy struck. The large sawing machine had not been working properly. While looking for the source of the trouble, he had tripped and fallen on the saw blades that were operating at full speed. Badly wounded, but by amazingly good fortune still alive, the personnel had pulled him out.

For months on end, he had been nursed night and day. Transporting him to better medical facilities had proved impossible. The lower part of his body had been and still was a mess, and for all routine functions he needed outside help.

"Then my Marie came into my life," he continued. She had come from Japan to be trained by a doctor on Manokwari. It had soon become clear that she was a born nurse. During training, she had lived with her married brother, a shopkeeper. Being the only unattached woman in the area, our Friar had offered her a good salary to become his personal aide. She had accepted.

"She has saved my life and keeps me going," so the former Friar concluded his story, which induced us to accept "his Marie" without reservation.

During the housewarming party, he told us he would soon be leaving for Holland — his first visit in forty years. He was not sure if he would return. The outward passage would be paid by the Catholic Mission.

He told us he had made suitable arrangements for Marie: the title to the house, yard and a small coconut plantation had been transferred to her name. She was also now in possession of two prize cows. But, with tears in his eyes, he asked us if we could keep an eye on her after he had left.

That we warmly promised to do, not knowing that this promise would result in a much closer relationship later on.

\*\*\*\*

Shortly after our big move, the volcanic ash claimed another victim. It was Manasse, who had been in our service since 1925. He was still young, just short of thirty years — a robust man, who had never before been ill.

A week earlier he had been hospitalized, after having complained about shortness of breath and inflammation of the eyes. He left a wife and five young children. His death was a heavy blow to us all.

Three days later, Charlotte, wife of Llelego and mother of two children, died after showing the same symptoms. Once again, the future looked black.

Fear took hold of the population outside the plantation, as they buried more and more victims of that cursed volcanic ash. Many moved to distant islands to escape it.

We told the Menadonese we would tear up the contract if they wanted to return to the Minahasa — which, in the absence of ash rains or earth quakes, started to look like paradise to me. To my surprise, only two bachelors accepted our offer; the others wanted to stay!

I suspect their decision had something to do with the arrival of Father Jan Moors, the first Catholic priest to be allowed to settle in this region after three and a half centuries of Dutch rule. He settled in our old house, which also served as church.

Especially on Sundays, the church attracted many people from the surrounding area, people whom we had not met before. Some were contract workers. Others were military persons from Central Java, Timor or Menado, who were temporarily stationed at Tobelo. Sometimes, we had civil servants of various ranks. Often, there were Chinese adherents of the faith.

Whenever the church was full, our plantation people were especially proud to enhance the service with their singing. All the members of the choir had trained voices. Another man from the Minahasa, Paulus, had appointed himself as deacon, and made sure everything went well.

Late in 1937, Father Moors moved from Mon Désir to a large Chinese-owned house in Tobelo that had been converted into a combined presbytery and church. Most of the steadily growing congregation lived, after all, in Tobelo, he reasoned, and he felt he should be closer to his flock.

Now it was we who traipsed to Tobelo for Sunday services.

\*\*\*\*

Our destroyed radio had been replaced by a new one, and it once again attracted other Europeans, who either managed plantations or were employed there. As a result, we often entertained interesting visitors, especially in the evenings.

We could then forget our personal trials and tribulations and discuss the radio news — like the *Hindenburg* airship disaster in the United States on May 6, 1937 — or our common antagonist, the volcano.

At night our guests had an exceptionally clear and magnificent view of the Dukeno, its ever-growing blackened peak sticking out from behind the mountain range. When its ash plume moved away from us and did not obscure the panorama, a rosy glow could be seen against the darkening sky, and when it turned into a fiery red, we knew a heightened activity was in the offing.

Its subterranean rumble gave the impression that, deep under our house, there was a tunnel that connected the volcano with the sea. At times, it seemed the volcano sucked in sea water and boulders through this tunnel. We would hear the rattling sound deep below our house. Moments later, we would see a glowing column of magma spill out of the crater and down its flanks into the surrounding ravines.

When this happened, we looked on in awe. It was so majestic, so impressive, that no one present could find words to express their feelings.

But, frequently, the Dukeno gave a different kind of show. It would first rumble loudly, and then every few minutes spew out red-hot fragments of stone. These spectacular fireworks would now and then be interrupted by a belching of thick clouds of black smoke. This spectacle usually occurred early in the evening or late at night and was then breathtaking to see — but, if it happened during the day, one would usually only see thick black clouds laden with ash.

The thundering of the volcano went on day and night, and sometimes it was difficult to carry on a normal conversation. The disastrous effects of its ash rains, of course, continued.

The livestock was deteriorating. We still employed a team to cut grass, transport it in oxcarts to the sea, and wash out the volcanic ash before giving it to the animals. In spite of the extra care taken, some of the animals — mostly young calves — died. Under strict supervision, they were then buried where they had died, to prevent people from eating the meat. Sometimes the people complained about this ruling, and it was difficult to make them understand the danger of consuming such tainted meat.

On a positive note, a construction crew from Java had recently constructed a long bridge over the river, with a connecting road that ran from Mon Désir to Tobelo. This made it unnecessary for us to transport our copra via waterways — a considerable saving — and also made it possible to wash grass for our livestock in the river instead of in the more distant sea.

A small victory in the endless struggle against nature.

# CHAPTER 26

### The Threat of War
### *Mon Désir Plantation, Halmahera, 1938-1939*

The press often praised the *Führer* for the continuing economic boom in the new *Reich*, and commented favorably on Mussolini, who was doing the same for Italy. Those two powerful figures seemed to dominate European politics, remaking their countries into bastions against the Russian communism that everyone feared — so we were told.

Japan also seemed destined to become a superpower, but, caught up in the excitement of their own economic expansion, Europe paid no attention to the armament build-up occurring on the other side of the world.

Every morning at 7:30, we made sure to catch the first news broadcast from the NIROM. Concerned by rapidly developing political events, we followed the radio news with great attention.

After Hitler's unopposed acquisition of the Rhineland in March of 1936, he became more brazen. He regularly held massive Nazi gatherings, and we would then hear his blustering voice, stirring up the passions of the masses. The implied threat that came through the ether tied my stomach in knots each time I heard it.

I reminded John and our guests of the events leading up to World War I, and how people had stood idly by. How the international community at the Côte d'Azur had amused itself, living it up, pushing aside all thoughts of war. And how amazed and aghast these people had been when that war appeared on their doorstep, and created so much deprivation.

But John and our guests said that I was just seeing ghosts.

I could understand their viewpoint — after all, the Netherlands had remained neutral then — but I did not agree with it.

\*\*\*\*

Early in 1938, Marie — the Japanese housekeeper of the former friar — came to live with us. Her brother, who still lived in Manokwari, had asked her for financial assistance, as his wife needed to undergo a dangerous and expensive operation in Japan. On Java it would cost too much, and nobody would be able to speak her language. Marie had rallied to her brother's aid, and had sold all her possessions, except her house. The rent of about thirty guilders per month was now her only income.

So she became the housekeeper of Mon Désir. From that time on, I did not have to concern myself with the house, and could devote myself entirely to the administration of the plantation and to my many hobbies.

After having paid for our expensive house, we decided to take a vacation. All went well on the plantation, and if anything unforeseen should happen, we felt Marie was capable enough to take corrective action.

We spent six wonderful, relaxing weeks visiting Hong Kong and Manila; two weeks in cool, ash-free Tomohon; and returned well rested to the grey lands around the Dukeno, which still spewed forth as much ash as before we left.

During this trip, we heard much about the political situation in Europe, and it dawned on us then that, in spite of our radio and newspapers, we were not as well informed as we had thought.

A recurring theme was the appeasing attitude of the "Great Democracies" — a name we did not quite understand, but which was used in contrast to the totalitarian regimes.

This appeasement had started back in 1933, when Hitler came to power and withdrew Germany from the General Disarmament Conference in Geneva and, a week later, from the League of Nations. Not one nation had registered a protest against this move.

In 1935, Hitler had re-introduced conscription to build up his air force (the *Luftwaffe*), the army and the navy. Then came the brutal occupation of the Rhineland.

Still no reaction from the "Great Democracies". Perhaps they were distracted by Mussolini's conquest of Ethiopia and the civil war in Spain; in any case, they turned a blind eye to Hitler's continuing aggression. Time and again, our news commentators lashed out against this blindness.

Our local news service also lambasted the shortsightedness and mercantile attitude of our own government. The sizeable revenue of the Netherlands East Indies should now be used to strengthen our armed forces with modern warships and airplanes, they said, for if war broke out in Europe, Japan would surely take advantage of the situation and carry out its well-publicized policy of expansion. The Netherlands East Indies would then be vulnerable to attack by the Japanese fleet, which was becoming stronger with each passing day.

# IBU MALUKU

All this we picked up while on our vacation. It made us anxious.

Upon arriving home, we again crowded around the radio. The speeches of Hitler were becoming even more vehement. He wanted unification with Austria and insisted that Kurt von Schuschnigg, the Austrian Chancellor, appoint certain Nazis to his cabinet. Among them was Arthur Seyss-Inquart, whose name we now heard for the first time[1].

Hitler gave Austria an ultimatum. Austria acquiesced, threw von Schuschnigg in jail, and accepted Seyss-Inquart as the new Austrian Chancellor. Hitler promptly sent German troops to Vienna to "maintain order" and, in March 1938, Austria became part of the German *Reich*.

Again, not one of the European powers lodged a protest. Could they not see where this Nazi *putsch* was leading? Only one man stood up to voice his concern, and that was Winston Churchill. "Oh, but that man is spooked by anything," people said. "It is not as serious as all that!"

Although troubled, we didn't feel personally threatened, as those things were happening too far away. We worried more about Japanese imperialism. Neither the pompous bellowing of Mussolini, nor the operetta-like speeches of Hitler were taken seriously. In fact, they often made us laugh. We believed that Germany would correct the problem itself. After all, there were still people in the government who were infinitely more capable than this spoiled ex-corporal!

When Hitler's next move was to demand "rights" for the Germans in Sudetenland and Czechoslovakia mobilized in response, France and England woke up and finally took notice. In September of 1938, they contacted the Nazis and hammered out an agreement in Munich, which condoned Germany's previous expansion in exchange for peace and stability.

I reminded John and our guests of the tactics employed by the Germans in 1914, but was again accused of exaggeration and unreasonable pessimism.

So, for us life went on as before.

\*\*\*\*

In the last quarter of 1938, the prices in the futures market started to go down, and with it the demand for copra. In response, the Government's Copra Board planned to build a shed for stockpiling. Several names were advanced for the board of directors — among them the name of the administrator of a large coconut plantation. Towards the end of 1938, the price for 100 kilograms of copra had dropped several guilders.

# IBU MALUKU

In the *kota*, there was renewed construction activity — perhaps in response to a growing concern about Japanese expansion policies. They were building a new *tangsi* (base) for the military, with all that went with it.

The Dukeno had finally become quieter. The subterranean rumbling, I thought, was not so deafening. The eruptions went on as usual, but the ash rains were not as heavy. We breathed easier for the moment and hoped this trend would continue.

\* \* \* \*

Between September and November 1938, many changes had occurred in Europe. The names of Daladier and General Gamelin of France, Benes of Czechoslovakia, and Chamberlain and Halifax of Great Britain had become household words. The Munich Agreement had not changed a thing, and Chamberlain's words of "peace in our time" had become a joke. Almost every evening, Hitler's threats thundered across the airwaves into our living room.

At an ever increasing pace, he and his henchmen were proclaiming the invincibility of the German *Reich*, with the slogan "No more 1918 for Germany!" — in reference to the humiliating terms of surrender the country had been forced to accept at the conclusion of "the war to end all wars".

Then came more devastating news: on March 14, 1939, Hitler had conquered Czechoslovakia and made his triumphant entry into Prague. It took *four* days for London and Paris to lodge their protest!

In August, Germany signed a peace treaty with its arch enemy, the USSR. Very confusing! Only later did we understand that Hitler had wanted to discourage Britain and France from interfering with the next part of his plan: on September 1, 1939, Germany invaded Poland.

Two days later, Britain and France declared war on Germany, and within a week, Australia, Canada and South Africa followed suit.

World War II had started.

France was convinced of its invincibility. It had, after all, the "unconquerable" Maginot Line. England had an equally unshakable faith in its fleet. Both firmly believed that Hitler had sealed his fate with this brutal attack on Poland. How soon their illusions would go up in smoke!

Hitler, of course, continued to overrun one country after another, and we now started to fear for our loved-ones in Europe. Our community was so eager to hear every scrap of news that neighboring planters offered to take their turn at manning the radio, so there would be around the clock coverage.

And so we learned that the recent economic boom was indeed

the direct result of Hitler's expansionist plans, which required the stockpiling of all kinds of supplies. Many of these supplies was still stored in neighboring countries — which, we surmised, was exactly where Hitler wanted them. By overrunning these countries, he could now simply *take* these supplies without paying for them!

Fear was spreading throughout the Dutch East Indies, and cries for more modern weapons — warships in particular — became louder. Some people considered joining the NSB[2], as many had done in the Netherlands. Already some well-known persons had appeared in public wearing the brown shirts — the trademark of the party. The authorities forbade all civil servants to join the party, but whether anyone would heed this order was the big question.

"It is the only party," people said, "which demands that the Government give top priority to armament".

So ended 1939.

* * * *

The disastrous year of 1940 started with great uncertainty for us all.

The price of copra dropped again, and the world trade started to weaken. With fear, people remembered the "Great Depression".

The Copra Board finally became a reality, and all copra producers now had to market their products through this institution. The Board demanded high quality and soon rejected "smoked copra". Only top quality "sundried" was accepted.

The price had in the meantime gone down to 7.50 guilders per 100 kilograms.

Then, on a brilliant Easter Day came the crushing news: "German troops have invaded Holland and Belgium without warning!" At the time, John was manning the radio and he shouted to me to come quickly.

When I reached him he was crying. With clenched fists he gasped: "Those bastards! Those dirty rotten bastards!" and then motioned heatedly to me to come closer to the radio and listen. The announcer was so emotional that it was difficult to understand him.

"Immediately after attacking Denmark and Norway, German troops invaded the Netherlands, Belgium and Luxembourg. Queen Wilhelmina has lodged a strong protest with the German Government.

"The Grebbe Line[3] is strongly defended. French troops are marching north to come to the aid of the Dutch Army. German paratroopers have landed in the south, west and center of the Netherlands."

We looked at each other, aghast. "War! And Holland is involved!" Distressed, we thought about our relatives in Holland and Belgium.

289

Just before the Germans invaded Holland, John had learned that his mother, aged 86, had passed away. He was grateful now that she was gone. Thank God, nothing more could happen to her!

The surviving members of his family, however, were still living in Rotterdam. John and our visitors — all Rotterdammers — were convinced their city was safe, because of its strategic importance. The Allies, who were coming to Holland's aid, surely would not allow Rotterdam or any other city in the coastal area to fall in German hands, they argued.

Most of my relatives, living in Belgium and the southern Dutch province of Limburg, would be directly in the line of attack. With trepidation I thought about Mother, who was getting on in years. All I could do now was pray for her.

On the second day of the invasion, the radio brought more bad news. The Dutch Army fought vehemently, but could not stop the advance of the German juggernaut. In Belgium, heavy bombardments were carried out on the fortresses of Liège and Antwerp. The population had fled in the direction of France.

My thoughts turned to 1914, when people fled from the German advance, and chaos reigned throughout Belgium. Now it was happening again, and my heart went out to my sister and family in Antwerp — a city as strategically important as Rotterdam — whose lives might be in danger at this very minute.

On May 12, the radio remained silent about the advance of the English and French troops that had been expected to come to Holland's aid. It seemed that they had become bogged down in Belgium. The reporter did say that Holland had been bombed here and there, and that German paratroopers were trying hard to get their hands on our aerodromes. Luxembourg had already collapsed.

The turning point came on May 13. The Dutch Government had decided to leave the Netherlands. The German troops had broken through Dutch defenses, and had crossed the Meuse. Queen Wilhelmina and the Crown Princess Juliana with her two children were leaving, with the Government, for an unknown destination.

We were speechless! We looked at each other with tearful eyes. We now realized that the situation was hopeless and that no amount of Allied assistance could change the course of events.

We couldn't think about eating and huddled around the radio so as not to miss a word. If someone started a conversation, he or she was nervously asked to please keep quiet. And when the news broadcast was interrupted with music or patriotic songs, the men just clenched their fists at this unwelcome interruption.

The news that Queen Wilhelmina had actually left her people, seemed to confound the men most.

"How could she do that?" they repeatedly asked themselves. That the Crown Princess had to be moved elsewhere they understood, but the Queen? This engendered feelings of revolt and shame in them all.

On May 14 came the devastating news that Rotterdam had been severely bombed and was now burning. Thousands had been killed and most of the city was destroyed. Words cannot describe our feelings when we learned about this dastardly act. The men cussed, and stamped their feet. There was humiliation and also fear in their eyes. For a long time, none of them spoke. Then they vowed in unison to enlist and avenge the flattening of Rotterdam. That such an action from here was impossible did not occur to them.

Later that day came more bad news: At Sedan, the Germans had broken through the French defenses.

May 15: Silently and deeply sorrowful, we heard: "The Netherlands has surrendered. Only in Zeeland are the troops still fighting. Without encountering much resistance, the Germans are moving deeper into Belgium and France."

May 16: Thank God. The first bit of good news: America, rudely awakened, asks Congress through President Roosevelt for 50,000 airplanes. "If America enters the war," our visitors said, "the Germans will soon be beaten." But ... Rotterdam was still burning.

May 17: The Germans are marching triumphantly into Brussels. In Zeeland, the fighting has stopped; all of Holland is now under German occupation. Many Dutchmen have fled to England. From Amsterdam and other Dutch harbors, ships full of refugees have escaped before a curtain fell over our home country.

May 18: "In France, the German break-through is complete, and the French Army is retreating in disorder." We listened in disbelief. Sometimes it seemed that the NIROM was broadcasting fairy tales. It simply could not be true that the German Army could overrun all those countries without being stopped at some point! The radio's continual warnings to be on the alert for falsified information made us wonder even more.

Until May 27, the Belgian Army under the command of King Leopold II and supported by an English Army unit, had maintained strong resistance in one corner of Belgium. Then the Germans issued a clear and uncompromising ultimatum: complete surrender, or else ...

The King signed the document of surrender, which started an

unpleasant argument in our living room. Some called it an act of treason! Being Belgian-born, this hurt me terribly. The small Belgian Army, aided by the British, had after all fought heroically at Dunkirk with forty thousand men of the mighty German Army in front, and nothing but the sea behind them. Young King Leopold had resisted the German advance as long as possible. Was there any other Commander-in-Chief who had done as much?

Emotionally, I pointed this out to our guests, and pointedly asked if it would have been better if the Belgian King had deserted his country and taken flight as others had done. "Oh, well! Those Belgians ..." came the muted response, and from that moment I ceased to exist.

I was furious! Could these people only think of the Netherlands? Were they blind to the suffering that was going on in neighboring countries? Thereafter, these gentlemen came less often to listen to the radio. But perhaps it was, in part, due to the strange things that were happening in our own part of the world.

First, the authorities had picked up all German nationals, even those living on remote islands. Only the men were taken; the women were told to stay put until further notice.

In rounding them up, the authorities had used some questionable practices. The Germans from small islands, for example, had been transported in small boats that lacked minimum comfort. They had been herded into small loading areas while machine guns had been trained on them. The majority of these Germans had lived in the Dutch East Indies since the end of World War I, and had become intimate friends to many Dutchmen. How could those friendships go up in smoke in such a very short time?

Next, the authorities hunted down all Dutchmen — particularly intellectuals and highly-placed persons — who were suspected of having belonged to the NSB. Among them were civil servants, KPM captains, plantation administrators, geologists, volcanologists and doctors. Effective immediately, it seemed, they had ceased to be human beings — seeing that they were now treated worse than animals.

"How is this possible?" I asked myself, perplexed.

Then, they called up the militia.

John was among those called. Early one morning he left for Ternate, where he would stay at least two weeks, to have a medical checkup and receive his uniform and weapons.

From Tobelo, only four other people accompanied him: two Dutchmen and two *peranakans* — Eurasians. One was the son of a naturalized German and an Ambonese mother. The other was the son of a naturalized Filipino and a half-Chinese mother.

All the others, even the much younger Dutchmen, had been exempted, because they worked either as missionaries, or were employed in "vital enterprises" — such as the Copra Board. From those who had vowed to revenge Rotterdam, not a single one had enlisted! They now declared sanctimoniously that it was their duty to stay at their post!

"And they are the ones who were so critical of King Leopold," I remarked bitterly to John — who was taken aback himself. He had obviously believed these men when they vied with each other in demonstrating their patriotism, and was surprised that not one had volunteered!

Even if he had not been called up, John would have volunteered right away. It would never have occurred to him to shirk his duty!

### Endnotes
[1] Mr. Seyss-Inquart later became the highest-ranking German officer in occupied Holland, where he was nicknamed "Six-and-a-quart".
[2] The NSB (Nationaal-Socialistische Beweging) or (Dutch) National Socialist Movement, was a party that -- as became abundantly clear later -- sympathized with the Nazis.
[3] This refers to the defensive line at the Grebbe River which separates the Dutch provinces of Utrecht and Gelderland.

# IBU MALUKU

# CHAPTER 27

## World War II Erupts
*Mon Désir Plantation, Halmahera, 1940*

In John's absence, everything on the plantation continued its normal course, except that Marie had started to teach me Japanese.

She herself had pushed me into it — to help pass the time, she said. But, in retrospect, I think she may have felt that a basic knowledge of the Japanese language might come in handy some day.

She was well aware of the expansionist policies of her country and I knew that she was concerned about the number of Japanese ships — especially fishing vessels — that appeared in the oceans around us.

From elderly Japanese fishermen, who had trapped tortoises at a nearby island for many years, Marie learned that the modern Japanese fishing vessels that plied our waters were equipped with large refrigerated storage chambers, which allowed them to remain at sea much longer. Even the fish they caught — mostly *ikan tongkol* (tuna fish) — was completely processed on board. There was nothing suspicious in this.

But Marie also told me something I felt I should pass on to the Magistrate: that those ships carried "passengers" who seemed to have an unusual interest in the inlets and natural harbors along the Kao Bay and around the island of Morotai.

"There is nothing peculiar about that," the Magistrate told me. "Just a bunch of curious tourists. Nothing to worry about. Japan is after all a friendly nation!"

His answer was obviously designed to pacify me, for several months later, a patrol boat was stationed at Tobelo — no reason given — and the authorities asked Marie to serve on board as a translator. Invariably, she returned from such sessions with refrigerated vegetables and fruits.

She never disclosed what she had translated, and I never thought it proper to ask. But Marie's face showed her deepening concern. At times, she would hint that something was not quite right — but that was all she would say.

Through the grapevine, however, I heard that the waters around the Moluccas were literally crawling with Japanese "fishing vessels". On several occasions, the Dutch patrol boat had to shoot a volley across their bows before the increasingly arrogant Japanese heeded the order to stop.

The radio news from Europe did not improve either.

In the Netherlands, the Germans had carried off men of all ages to labor camps in Germany. The events of 1914-1918 were repeating themselves, for this is exactly what had happened in Belgium.

In France, the English had succeeded in evacuating 330,000 men from Dunkirk, but 40,000 Britons and Belgians became prisoners of war — among them, King Leopold. During the long, lonely nights, I got up now and then to listen to the news from Europe and Hong Kong, but heard nothing encouraging. My heart was heavy and filled with worry for those who now lived under the Nazi jack-boot.

\*\*\*\*

After a month of special training in Ternate, John returned — not in the best of moods. As a private, entitled to third class passage only, he'd been forced to dig into his own pockets to upgrade to first class — the way we usually traveled.

His experiences on Ternate were not reassuring either. He had passed the medical examination alright, but the attitude of Dutch sergeants towards the Dutch citizens who were now mere soldiers was not good. John did not elaborate, but I got the picture.

The status-conscious Dutch burghers had never socialized with lowly sergeants. John had never looked down on anybody, but the sergeants still saw him as a member of the community that had shunned them, and now they had their chance to vent their hostility.

John told me that he would eventually be stationed at the new *tangsi* in Tobelo that would soon be opened with a grand celebration and a sumptuous *selamatan*. The Sultan of Ternate would come in person, and with him many other important personages.

I expressed my surprise, thinking it to be a little out of place to have a celebration while we were still mourning those who had died in the Netherlands.

\*\*\*\*

The activity of the Dukeno had increased once more. Ash and fire rained again in buckets over the already grey landscape and reduced our production by another 25 percent. But — thank God! — the ash did not affect our people as much. Perhaps the population had become immune, or the ash had become less dangerous. Whatever the reason, it was claiming fewer lives. It seemed we were finally learning to live with this major inconvenience.

On top of the significant drop in production came another setback.

## IBU MALUKU

The price of copra went down to a mere 5.00 guilders per 100 kilograms. We would soon be forced to reduce the wages again — as we had done during the "Great Depression".

Luckily, the guest pavilion and the annex to our house were now finished and fully paid for — we had also paid for a covered well and a generator that provided electricity to light the house and run the water pump. For the first time, we had running water from a tap in the house. An enormous step forward!

\* \* \* \*

On July 18, we heard that the Germans had taken Dutch hostages in reprisal for the German citizens who had been imprisoned in the Dutch East Indies. Would the Nazis also imprison the relatives of Dutch people living here? The very thought sent shivers down my spine!

At intervals of three months, John was called up for more training and then stayed two weeks at the new military base in Tobelo. There, he served with two other militiamen and was not allowed any leave.

He was now the only *Belanda totok* (full-blooded Hollander) among the draftees. The other Dutch draftee had maneuvered himself into the position of manager of the Copra Board on Tobelo and was, therefore, exempted from military service. His predecessor, who had been his boss on a plantation, had been transferred to take the same position in Ternate.

*Curious!*

Two amphibious Dornier airplanes had been stationed at Ternate to scout the waters between Ternate and the Belau Islands that are part of the Caroline Islands. The planes stopped several times a week at Tobelo, and the pilots became regular guests at Mon Désir.

Once, they took me on a short flight over the Dukeno. What a sight it was! One could see the whirling smoke billowing from the cauldron's bubbling, red-glowing witches' brew! They offered to take me over it a second time, but I declined. Once was enough. The surrounding area was completely burned, and the trees in the foothills were no longer green but charcoal black. Not a refreshing sight! From then on, I saw the volcano with different eyes.

The year 1941 rolled around. The war in Europe had increased in intensity.

In April, the BBC reported heavy air attacks on London. In turn, the RAF bombed German battleships in the harbor of Brest. Hurrah for the Brits!

In May, the British sank the *Bismarck*, Germany's largest battleship. We cheered! But then we slumped under the impact of the next announcement. In reprisal for some underground activity, the Nazis in Holland had picked up some 70 people at random and had shot them.

"Just like in Belgium during the First World War," I lamented.

But my Rotterdammer husband and friends could not accept that a cultured nation like Germany would allow its diciplined army to randomly shoot innocent civilians. There must be more to that story than was being said. And then they made the snide remark that in Belgium it might have been necessary to shoot "innocent" civilians!

*Hah!*

I did not deign to answer. The gentlemen seemed already to have forgotten the flattening of Rotterdam, where civilians were specifically targeted.

The grapevine had it that German U-boats were criss-crossing the seas around Australia and the Dutch East Indies[1]. True or not, business was bad, and *someone* certainly seemed to be interfering with the transportation of goods to the United States.

Our old house had now been converted into a copra shed, and served as living quarters for the *mandur* (Latif) as well. Almost all the roofs of the worker's houses were now covered with zinc sheeting to withstand the destructive power of the ash rains — though several roofs were still unprotected because we had run out of sheeting and it was now impossible to obtain more.

The KPM ships still dropped anchor regularly, but there was a somber mood on board. There was also much turnover in staff, so it was hard to find someone we knew. Invariably, the staff talked about the war in Europe that was still going badly. It would have been nice to talk about something else for a change.

Living in isolation, we were at times badly in need of a change — and that change came, one day, from a totally unexpected source.

John had just left for Tobelo with a shipment of copra, when I heard the familiar sound of the Dornier amphibious aircraft. It surprised me, because they had never come on a Wednesday before. As they were coming down to land, I silently hoped that the pilots would come to visit — they always had something amusing to tell.

Shortly after, I heard the sound of an approaching car. "Here are the pilots," I said to the manager of a nearby plantation who had dropped in to listen to the radio. But it turned out to be his boss, who was driving the car himself, with John sitting beside him.

"*Gezellig*[2] — How nice!" I thought, looking forward to an interesting conversation. But things did not turn out the way I had hoped.

The car tore onto our lawn, careened as it made a sharp turn, and with squealing brakes came to an abrupt halt. John and the driver jumped out and ran toward me, and — tripping over their words and talking simultaneously — they tried to tell me what was going on.

Apparently, the Japanese fleet had been spotted sailing toward the Dutch East Indies. The authorities had ordered the immediate evacuation of women and children. I, too, was to leave this instant in the car in which they had come, and leave by Dornier for Ternate.

"It has finally come to this," I thought, but I remained quite calm. That irritated the administrator who yelled that I should hurry. John nodded anxiously.

Despite the pressure from these two, I coolly tried to come to a decision. What was the sense, I asked myself, in trying to flee? No, I just could not do that. If the news was true that the Japanese were coming, I wanted to be with my workers and with John, whatever the consequences.

Briefly and pointedly, I told the gentlemen that I would not go, that I wanted to stay at Mon Désir.

The already excited administrator turned beet red and shouted that, in that case, I would not be able to count on protection from anyone. He swung on his heels and tersely instructed my guest, his subordinate, to return immediately to the plantation and prepare to receive the women and children who would soon arrive from the surrounding plantations. Then he jumped in his car and sped away.

In the meantime, John had run into the house. Still agitated, he ran back with his revolver and shouted: "When the Japs arrive, I'll shoot you, and then you can shoot me!"

I nodded my head in agreement and just looked at him until he realized what he had said — and we both burst out laughing. Then I heard what had happened.

Upon arriving in Tobelo, he had, like myself, been surprised to see the Dorniers coming in, and had gone to the "booms" where they would be mooring, to find out what was up.

One of the pilots, a newcomer who seemed to be in command, had come ashore and had asked John to take him to the Magistrate. John had obliged. During the short walk, the visibly nervous pilot had not uttered a word. He was obviously fighting to keep himself under control.

After the introductions, John had heard the pilot instruct the Magistrate to gather all women and children at the quay and have them board the planes for a speedy evacuation. The flyers had spotted a large fleet that was steaming southward to Morotai. It could not be anything but the Japanese fleet. Someone had called the Military Commander, who now dispatched messengers to all families. Our neighboring administrator, also drawn by the sound of the airplane, had driven to the *kota*. Upon hearing what was going on, he had offered to drive John home to pick me up.

That was all John could tell me. He then got dressed in his uniform. His luggage was already packed, and his carbine stood next to it. Still overwrought, he asked what we should do with the workers, and I repeated that I would stay with them.

When we told Marie what was happening, she raged against her countrymen, but the other servants shied away from her just the same, not knowing if she could be trusted.

The two planes, loaded with women and children, had hardly left when bedlam broke out right before our eyes. The road through our plantation became filled with taxis, oxcarts and bicycles laden with shop items and expensive household goods that belonged to Chinese traders, who were hoping to find a safe inland place for their wives, children and possessions. They were soon joined by the natives, who brought their livestock as well.

John waited to be called up, but nothing happened. It seemed that the militia had been forgotten. The waiting continued throughout the day and we were both getting edgy.

In the afternoon, when still no call had come, John suggested that we both go the *kota* to find out what was happening. I gratefully accepted, as the tension had become intolerable.

On the big road, we were going counter to the stream of fleeing people, who looked at us with open mouths. Strange, the *Nyonya* from Mon Désir had obviously not left with the other white women, their eyes told me, and that seemed to calm them.

We went to the house of the Magistrate, where all the Dutch men had gathered to discuss the situation. They did not budge to make room for us and obviously wanted to exclude us from the discussion. Was that because I had refused to leave?

Listening in, we learned that, secretly, two evacuation shelters had been built inland: one for the civil servants; and one for the missionaries. It was amusing to hear how each group wanted to keep the location of its shelter a secret; it was less funny to learn that no shelter had been built for the planters, the group we belonged to. We had been overlooked! It was a strange and somewhat ridiculous situation and we were glad not to be part of it.

Their discussion broke up at the sound of approaching airplanes.

Everyone fell silent to listen, and the tension mounted again.

The planes landed, but everyone remained rooted on the spot. No one felt compelled to find out what was happening, until the Military Commander saw a group of people walking to his house .. and recognized his wife among them!

With a yell, he ran towards her, closely followed by the other men. The native and Eurasian personnel of the Magistrate office looked on in disbelief. They had never seen the white *tuans* make such a wild dash!

It turned out that all the women and children had been brought back. The ladies were upset, dead-tired, humiliated and even indignant. They wanted to go home as soon as possible!

We learned later that their arrival on Ternate had been a total surprise. No one had heard the alarming news, but they were warmly received, fed, and made comfortable in the large residence of the Assistant Resident. (Though they did not realize it at the time, they had been kept there in isolation, to prevent panic among the residents of Ternate.)

Ultimately, the Assistant Resident had come himself to explain that it all been a gigantic misunderstanding. No one knew anything about an approaching fleet, Japanese or otherwise. He concluded by saying that they would be taken back to their own homes. No further explanation was given, and the pilot's lips remained sealed!

But the inhabitants of Tobelo now knew what to expect from the Dutch community if a real Japanese invasion were to occur. And this was certainly not in our favor!

Sanity returned to Tobelo, and the people who had fled inland, hesitatingly returned. Ultimately, a telegram arrived from Ternate, confirming there had been no reason for concern. Much later, we would learn on board a KPM ship that the commander of the Dorniers had mistaken floating tree trunks for enemy ships. True or not, after that incident he was quietly transferred elsewhere.

\*\*\*\*

On July 1, the Hong Kong radio station announced that the RAF had begun an offensive across the English Channel, and had bombed northern Germany, northern France and the Ruhr region. We heaved a sigh of relief. The Allies were finally fighting back!

We had started a Spitfire Fund, and collected money through rummage sales and lotteries. We also collected copper and aluminum objects for recycling, to aid the war effort. The news about the Allied initiatives did much to give this drive a welcome push.

Then, more unexpected and alarming news: Germany, Italy and

Rumania had declared war on the Soviet Union. The German SS[3] promptly picked up all communists and communist sympathizers.

Copra prices went down again to 4.50 guilders per 100 kilograms. We pulled in our belts where possible and kept the maintenance of the plantation down to a minimum.

On July 22, 1941, the Dutch East Indies introduced general conscription, and war exercises became more frequent.

The warnings from Marie took on a more serious note. The Japanese would take advantage of the worsening situation in Europe, she said, now talking openly with us about her deep concern. There were continuing news flashes from Morotai and the Kao Bay about Japanese warships, dressed up to look like fishing vessels, that were plumbing the depths and were taking photographs.

In response, the KNIL stationed scouts at several places along the Kao Bay.

In August, 1941, the BBC announced that the Germans had taken away Jewish children from the schools in the Netherlands.

On and on it went. Our conversations, thoughts and even dreams were about nothing but war ... war ... war! For us, the worst was not hearing from our relatives in Holland. The last letter from Mama had arrived in July, 1940 — more than a year ago. Nothing had come since. How were they? Would they even be alive?

Early in October, Radio Hong Kong announced the British had bombed Rotterdam by mistake! Would any member of John's family have been killed? John was seized by bouts of anger. It was incomprehensible that the Allies, our friends, would sow death and destruction on the Netherlands! How could such a thing have happened!

To add to our misery, the Dukeno ejected even more ash than ever before. We literally ate the stuff — and again lost some of our animals.

November 13, 1941: More depressing news! The Germans had sunk a British aircraft carrier near Gibraltar.

We desperately hoped something would happen that would allow us to take positive action ourselves. This uncertainty, the flood of contradicting rumors, the suppositions and ambiguous news flashes were slowly killing us.

Finally, it was announced that the United States would review their current neutral position.

"If they declare war on Germany," John said, "it will quickly turn the tables." This thought gave us all a shot in the arm.

The Magistrate of Tobelo had asked the owners of radios to buy as many batteries as they could and to use them as efficiently as possible, because soon it might be impossible to buy more. From then on, we organized ourselves into listening groups, to conserve power.

The BBC announced the Germans were marching towards Moscow, winning one battle after the other. Although the Government had forbidden us to listen to German broadcasts, some among us did it just the same. These clandestine listeners could not resist commenting on the differences between the German and Allied broadcasts, thus giving themselves away.

On December 6, Radio Manila announced the German offensive toward Moscow had bogged down, and we breathed a little easier. Would this be the turning point? We certainly hoped so!

December 7: All day there was a heavy summer storm and reception was awful. Afraid of lighting, we shut the radio off.

December 8: Thank God! The sky was clear. We hurriedly had our breakfast to be ready in time for the NIROM broadcast. As usual, John was at the radio first, nervously watching the clock.

"It's 7:30," he shouted to me.

The radio sputtered. The announcer was hard to understand, and John turned up the volume.

"He must have malaria or influenza," we agreed, but then the announcer cleared his throat and said quite clearly: "Friends, this morning, the Netherlands declared war on Japan!"

"WHAT?" We looked dumbfounded at each other. Had we heard right? Surely, this could not be true? But the voice continued, more strongly now.

"On December 7, Japan made a treacherous attack on the American base of Pearl Harbor. The American fleet that berthed there has been destroyed. The United States has declared war on Japan, and so have Great Britain, Canada and Australia."

There was more news about the landing of Japanese troops in Siam and in the north-eastern part of the Malay Peninsula, but we paid little attention. Bewildered, we stared at each other, and simultaneously said: "Well, now at least we know where we are at!"

In a way it was a relief. We were surprised at our own reaction. With a cracked voice, John said that he would get into his uniform. The call for active service would surely come at any moment.

Marie entered, deeply embarrassed, to ask forgiveness for what her government had done. Her predictions had come true. She took my hands, cried, and said: "*Nyonya*, don't let them know that you understand our language. It could benefit you to understand what they are saying without them knowing."

I put her mind at ease. "I shall be prudent," I said. Shortly after, Marie was picked up by the police. I would never see her again. She would spend the war years in an internment camp in Australia — and be much better off than those who were interned by her countrymen.

John had packed and was ready to go. All the people gathered in front of the house to say goodbye. The women cried. The men looked grim, and asked if they, too, could go to the *mèdan parang* — the "field of the machete" or battlefield. They raised their *parangs* in the air, demonstrating their willingness to *chinchang* (slice) the Japanese to ribbons.

Latif carried John's luggage, and Leida (the cook whom I had hired in Tomohon) came with a large *bunkus* (parcel) of fruit and other *makenans* — things to eat.

We did not say much as we crossed the plantation on foot. With his eyes, John said farewell to the livestock and the plantation. When we reached the bridge, he turned around for one last look, said "goodbye" and then quickly walked on.

For a moment I stood rooted to the spot, unable to speak. "Will he ever return here?" I asked myself. Then I had a horrible premonition that he had said goodbye for ever. A stifled scream escaped from my throat and I ran until I caught up with him.

Everywhere along the road the villagers lined up to say goodbye. Many asked where he was going, but John did not know what to answer. Up to now, he had served in the *tangsi* at Tobelo, but now he expected to be sent to Ternate. If so, he would likely stay at the *tangsi* for five days until the ship that was expected today had returned from Weda.

I prayed I would have at least those five intervening days to visit him in Tobelo before he left. It would mean so much.

The silence of the now deserted road was rent asunder by the sound of a ship's whistle. The KPM ship had obviously arrived sooner than expected. We walked the last two kilometers in haste and entered the *kota*, which was more crowded than on a normal "boat day". People were milling about, shouting to each other and gesturing wildly. Many walked hurriedly toward the harbor.

Among the crowd was Mansanaris, a militiaman like John. He was in KNIL uniform — plaited bamboo hat, carbine over his shoulder and cutlass dangling from his belt. As soon as he spotted John, he came running to ask anxiously what he should do.

John calmed him, and asked if he had reported to his squadron.

Yes, he had, but they had sent him away, saying militiamen could not be admitted to the *tangsi*; only career soldiers should be there now. His comrade Kriekhoff had been similarly dismissed, and, after sending Mansaris to find John, was now on his way to ask the police what should be done.

John suggested that I wait at the Presbytery until he had received his orders from Lieutenant Prins, Tobelo's Military Commander. Then he left me.

Suddenly the street became a madhouse. Military trucks, filled with equipment and provisions, were bearing down on the crowd with horns blaring. Startled, people jumped out of the way, and looked angrily back at the trucks that roared past them toward the harbor. The beat of a drum foretold the arrival of a column of soldiers, led by Lieutenant Prins. They followed the trucks, evidently intent on boarding the ship. Everything pointed to a hasty departure.

Then I spotted John and his two fellow militiamen, who were looking nonplused at the marching troops. After some hesitation, they decided to follow the military convoy to the harbor to have a word with Lieutenant Prins.

I decided to go there too. It was unthinkable to have John leave without a proper goodbye. The wives and children of John's two comrades joined me. The women cried; the nine children, all young, were jittery.

At the quay, the KNIL soldiers, standing at attention, were counted, after which the first group boarded the motor-sloop that had just come from the ship.

I saw John talking animatedly to Lieutenant Prins. Both were gesturing wildly, and the Lieutenant heatedly shook his head. John remonstrated, but seemed to have no success. He looked really upset.

The embarkation continued. The three militiamen came over to me, and John said: "We are not permitted to go with the career soldiers. They are leaving for God knows where, and no one else is allowed on board."

Thinking that all militia men would perhaps remain on Tobelo, the wives of Mansanaris and Kriekhoff breathed easier, and calmed their children. But then John said that the Lieutenant had referred him to the Magistrate, who was supposed to have the orders for the militia. So the three men trotted off to see the Magistrate.

Latif was still standing on the quay with John's luggage, and I asked him to stay put for now. The *Tuan* would surely return soon. In my heart, I was convinced that there had been a mistake that would soon be cleared up.

Father Moors joined us on the quay. He urged me, the other two women and the children to come back with him to the Presbytery. We gratefully accepted his invitation as there was no sense in waiting under the burning sun amidst the ever increasing crowd. But then Kriekhoff arrived on a borrowed bicycle to say that the women and children might as well go home. It was certain now that the militia would not be leaving with the KPM steamer.

Kriekhoff said that John and the Magistrate were trying to get passage on a Government's steamer, as they had to report to Ternate within 36 hours! Those were the orders.

"Tell John that I shall be at the Presbytery," I asked him, and left with the women and children. Kriekhoff returned to the police station, where he and his comrade would wait for John.

On the road, it was getting even busier. Many people seemed to want to leave; at least they were dragging their luggage back and forth, or had their luggage transported by oxcart. They almost fought with each other to get access to the quay. Wives and children of the departing soldiers were gathering there also, expecting to leave with their husbands. It was not to be.

A number of these women arrived at the Presbytery and told me tearfully that all the military wives were to stay behind. They would be moved to an evacuation camp that had been built somewhere inland, they said.

John found me at the Presbytery and told me that he and his fellow militiamen had been ordered to stop on their way to Ternate at the Waringin plantation and arrest the Watanabe family and any other Japanese who might be there.

John had protested. Suppose the Japanese were armed, and resisted? What could three soldiers do against that?

The Magistrate had sympathy for that point of view and telegraphed the Military Commander at Ternate to ask for clarification. The delay was welcome, because the Government's ship they needed to go to Ternate was in Morotai on business, and would not be back until the following day. No motorboats were available; the large *praus*, filled with fleeing people, had also left the harbor.

The steam whistle of the KPM ship tore through the air again, and the pandemonium in the street worsened. No traveler was allowed on board, and the arriving passengers had been forbidden to leave the ship. No freight had been unloaded, so the Chinese traders were without their bales of rice and other provisions. Only the mail had been taken ashore.

On his way to the Presbytery, John had stopped off at the post office, but had been disappointed to learn that the mail would only be distributed the following day.

A messenger arrived to fetch John. He was to report immediately to the Magistrate. A cable had arrived from Ternate!

Later, John returned alone. All three militiamen had been ordered to leave right away, and not wait for the Government's steamer. The Magistrate was trying to find a *prau* that could take the men to Pasir Putih, located deep in the pocket of the Kao Bay. They would then have to cross on foot to Dodinga on the west coast, where a motorboat from Ternate would pick them up. The Japanese planters family would not have to be picked up. It seemed the authorities had found another solution for them.

But the order to report to Ternate within 36 hours, remained in force! Since this was not possible, the Magistrate had sent another telegram to Ternate to explain the situation and so the tiring wait started anew.

Every strange sound frightened the people and set off mass hysteria. When a *prau* was sighted off a nearby island, someone screamed that the Japanese were coming. Panic was rife throughout Tobelo, but particularly around the harbor.

Father Moors' cook had prepared a *rijsttafel*, but we could not eat a thing. John drank only large quantities of iced water and became more stressed as time passed.

News arrived that a large *prau* was coming in. The three men picked up their gear and carbines and marched to the harbor, followed by their wives and children. The *prau* turned out to be too small. However, the owner mentioned that a larger *prau* from Galela was on its way, and probably had an outboard motor.

The Magistrate stationed a guard on the quay to inspect incoming vessels and hold them if found suitable. The nerve-racking waiting continued.

Now and then, the Presbytery radio gave details about the attack on Pearl Harbor. The situation was horrible. Thousands had been killed; buildings, ships, and planes were burning everywhere. In the United States, all Japanese were being picked up.

The blistering afternoon hours dragged on.

At five o'clock, a *prau* from the direction of Galela came into sight. The men once more put on their gear. They were tired and overwrought, and had trouble retaining their composure.

This *prau*, however, also turned out to be unsuitable. It did have an outboard motor, but it was defective and it would take too long to get it fixed.

Another telegram was sent to Ternate. They signaled back: "Reporting time has been moved forward by 12 hours!"

In the evening, a storm broke out with torrential rains. The stress-filled wait continued. Close to 8 o'clock, a policeman came running toward us. He had heard the engine of an approaching motorboat. He then ran off to notify the Magistrate.

This time it turned out to be a small but solid boat, which had entered our harbor to find shelter from the elements. Its destination was Galela.

The Chinese owner was ordered to unload, do an about-turn, and leave immediately with the three soldiers on board. The man protested. He was tired, and said the sea was too rough to make the journey right away. In addition, he did not have enough fuel.

Two policemen were promptly dispatched to find fuel. The tired owner could go along as a passenger as someone else had already been found to take his place at the helm.

Our men said their goodbyes. The women cried; the frightened, half-frozen children huddled together for warmth, while the heavy rain beat down loudly on the overhanging roof of the copra shed.

Momentarily lit by a flash of lightning, I saw for the last time the tense face of my husband. A final embrace, a lingering touch of our hands, and then he jumped on board.

Thunder cracked all around us, and the blinding flashes of lightning now and then allowed us to see the slowly departing boat.

I was scared. In this kind of weather, a sane person would look for shelter. But our men were being forced to brave the storm in open sea.

Mrs. Mansanaris was unnaturally calm. In a rough voice, she called her children and hastily left in the direction of her parental home. Her own house was further away, but she obviously wanted to spend the night closer by.

Mrs. Kriekhoff, on the other hand, was a despondent bundle of nerves. She kept yelling that the little motorboat would go down, and called despairingly for her husband to turn back. She tore at her clothes and her hair. Afraid that she might jump into the sea, two policemen grabbed her and led her, struggling, from the quay. I took her frightened children by the hand, and walked them home.

Father Moors had stayed with us all this time, but none of the other Dutch people had shown themselves. He offered to take me to Mon Désir, but I politely declined. At that moment, I yearned to be alone — even his company would be too much just then.

The storm was abating as I started on my journey to Mon Désir, wading ankle deep through the water that had flooded the road. The rain was still beating down. I walked automatically, as continuing flashes of lightning lit the way. I could not think anymore and felt drained and terribly lonely.

Some of the European houses were fully lit. The families were sitting happily together, probably enjoying the coolness brought on by the heavy rains. Was I envious of their security? If so, I wasn't conscious of it, but from the safety of the darkness, I looked on yearningly. How much I would have appreciated an encouraging word and a little sympathy at that moment.

Finally, I reached the bridge close to the plantation. From out of the darkness, a figure appeared and walked towards me. I recognized our faithful Latif, who had been waiting for me and now considerately held a *payong* (umbrella) over my head — drenched as I was.

I could not find anything to say, except: "The *Tuan* has left." Latif did not answer and quietly continued to walk at my side, but — my God! — how grateful I was for his company!"

When we arrived home, by way of welcome, the house was fully lit. But when I opened the door, the surrounding area was illuminated by a blinding flash of lightning, followed by an earsplitting thunderclap. A second storm had broken out this day, and John was out there in open sea, uncovered and unprotected.

I spent the night in tears and prayers.

### Endnotes

[1] The rumor was false. German U-boats did not operate in the Dutch East Indies until late in 1943. Dutch and U.S. submarines sank three U-boats in the Java Sea between 1944 and 1945. Among these was the U-183. Its commander, Captain Fritz Schneewind, born in 1917 at Padang, Sumatra, perished with his entire crew, not far from where he had been born.

[2] "*Gezellig*", the adjective of the Dutch word for companion or "buddy", refers to the pleasant, enjoyable feeling one experiences when one is in the company of good, warmhearted friends.

[3] The SS (Schutzstaffel) is the elite military unit which served as Hitler's body guard and as a special police force.

# IBU MALUKU

IBU MALUKU

# CHAPTER 28

## Drafted
*Mon Désir Plantation, Halmahera, December, 1941*

The dreadful storm passed during the early morning hours, and the day started with a brilliant sunrise.

Bleary-eyed from lack of sleep, I attacked the usual administrative problems, which I now had to resolve by myself. They kept me busy, so I didn't have much time to worry about John's safety.

I sent someone to the PTT Office to collect the mail, and then asked the plantation personnel to assemble in front of the house so we could discuss the new situation. They knew of course that John had joined the war effort, and were wondering what would happen next. Would the Japanese come soon? Should they flee inland? Understandably, the women were especially anxious.

I tried to calm their fears. "Hawaii is very far away from Halmahera, and the United States will swiftly strike back," I said, probably as much for my own benefit as for theirs. I then gave them the latest radio report:

The mobilization was in full swing throughout the Indies. All Japanese had been picked up, and — to make room for them — the interned Germans and Dutch NSB members would be moved from the Ngawi internment camp on Java to the Dutch colonies in the West Indies.

We then decided, together, that the work would continue as before, as would the picking and processing of coconuts into copra. I recommended that the women increase the size of their gardens, since the importation of produce might become more difficult. I also gave the women an advance to buy reserve clothing for their families. Elated, they went on their way to make their purchases. But the men left with somber faces, after telling me that many people along the coast — mostly Chinese traders — had moved their families and inventories inland.

In the afternoon, I finally received the mail. As usual, it contained a batch of two-week-old newspapers, some letters (alas! nothing from Holland!), and a note saying that two parcels were being held for me at the PTT Office. I decided to pick them up later that day, asking myself who on earth would surprise us with parcels at this time.

The sky had turned dark, and soon the monsoon rain beat down on the roof, and claps of thunder brought a feeling of uneasiness.

I sat tired and aimless near the radio, with my mind going around in circles. The radio came through very clear, and I tensely listened to the wheezing, agitated voice of the announcer.

The Japanese were advancing. They had landed in large numbers on Luzon and elsewhere on the Philippines.

They were getting awfully close, I felt.

"But," continued the announcer with a more upbeat tone of voice, "our fleet is ready. We shall defend ourselves and, if necessary, attack! Keep your chin up!"

So ended the broadcast.

\* \* \* \*

The rain had stopped, so I went to the Presbytery in the *kota* to see if there were any messages. Father Moors had good news: our men had arrived safely at Dodinga, and would probably be in Ternate by now. What a relief!

At the PTT Office I learned that my parcels had been taken to the Magistrate's office. All mail was now inspected there, the clerk said — until further notice.

Unsuspecting, I crossed the road to the Magistrate's office, where an *oppas* (caretaker) let me in. The chief civil servant was sitting behind his desk with a stern look on his face, and I wondered what was bothering him.

"Something has happened to John," flashed through my mind, but I kept silent.

The *oppas* was told to get the parcels for the *Nyonya* and to put them on the desk. To my surprise, they were the two neatly wrapped butterfly boxes that John had mailed five months earlier.

John had mentioned several times that he had received neither acknowledgment nor payment for that shipment. Presumably, the purchaser had moved and had neglected to send us a change-of-address notice. But I remembered neither the purchaser's name nor his address.

The *Jaksa*[1] entered and seated himself next to the Magistrate, who thrust one of the boxes toward me and asked me to read the address. The addressee was a doctor in Sukabumi on Java, a long-time collector of butterflies. In large letters, someone had stamped "RETURN TO SENDER" just above the address label.

"Do you know this person?" the Magistrate asked.

"Yes and no!" I answered. "He is an old client of ours, but I have never met him."

The second box was pushed forward. The addressee was the volcanologist from Padang, Dr. Neuman, whom everyone present had met.

"And do you know this person?" asked the *Jaksa*.

"Both you and I know this man very well," I said, "Surely you remember that he was here for a month to study the Dukeno's eruptions?"

The Magistrate nodded and then asked: "Do you know that these persons are members of the NSB?"

Surprised, I looked at him. "Of course not! I wouldn't dream of asking my clients about their political leanings!"

The *oppas* brought a screwdriver, and the Magistrate asked me to remove the screws and open the boxes.

I opened the first one, and removed the lid. On top lay the list of contents. A quick glance told me that the shipment had originally been addressed to the owner of a large construction firm in Stuttgart, Paul Kibler, and then I remembered that the box contained some very valuable and rare species.

I handed the list to the *Jaksa*, who glanced at it, shrugged, and passed it on to the Magistrate. The Magistrate also studied the list, acted shocked, and asked if I knew the code used therein.

"Code?" I asked dumbfounded, "What do you mean?" But then it dawned on me: in addition to the price, the list showed the type of butterfly, its gender (♂ for male and ♀ for female) and its name in Latin.

I tried to explain each name and symbol to these men, but they could not, or would not, understand and demanded that I unpack the entire box. The *Jaksa* wanted to help, but I pushed his hands away, saying I did not want this valuable collection to be damaged. Soon, most of the envelopes had been emptied, and the butterflies with their magnificent colors were spread out over the desk.

The last and most valuable specimen was an incredibly beautiful night butterfly with an exceptionally large wing spread. Our hunters had searched for months to find an undamaged sample of this *Sfingide*, and German and French experts had offered large sums to purchase one. Eventually, we had succeeded in breeding nine from cocoons. But the war had made it impossible to contact the original client, I explained, so my husband had sent these valuable butterflies to domestic collectors. They were better equipped to store them and he had hoped that they would either buy the specimens themselves, or store them for him until they could be sold to European customers.

The Magistrate and the *Jaksa* looked at me skeptically; obviously, neither of them believed a word of my story. They hammered away on the use of "encoded messages" and then asked me to open up the second box. When they saw that it also contained butterflies, they looked at each other, and the *Jaksa* asked me if I didn't have a more convincing explanation to offer.

I finally replied that they would have to delve into the butterfly literature at my house, in order to verify that it contained the same signs, symbols and Latin names that they had seen on the shipping lists. They then gave me permission to re-pack and close the boxes, after which they were carefully locked away in a cabinet.

The shipping lists were put into a large envelope, and the *Jaksa* and two policemen got into the Magistrate's car. Just before I also got into the car, the Magistrate ordered me "not to leave Mon Désir until further notice!"

"Would it not be better to place a guard in front of my house," I snarled.

He didn't answer, and just returned to his office without saying goodbye. By now, his behavior had made me thoroughly annoyed. I was clearly under suspicion of being a spy.

At Mon Désir, the policemen confiscated all the butterfly literature and the *Jaksa* also demanded that I hand over all correspondence. I protested that this was the private property of my husband and was very valuable, but to no avail. At least I persuaded him to place everything carefully in a suitcase.

After three days, the books, correspondence and the two parcels were safely returned to me. The shipping lists, however, were confiscated. I was also advised to send no more parcels — as if they didn't know that hunting for butterflies had stopped months earlier!

\*\*\*\*

I was very happy to receive a short letter from John which he had written upon his arrival in Ternate.

He told me that they had arrived safely, but that it had been a very difficult journey. Mansanaris was in the Military Hospital with pneumonia, but John asked me to keep the news from his wife for the moment. Kriekhoff and he had joined another group of militiamen, but he was not living with them in the barracks. He had found lodging in a private house on the Bovenweg road and was partly being fed by the nuns.

He advised me to continue with the production of copra, even though the price had sunk to 2.50 guilders per 100 kilograms.

"It's a pittance," he wrote, "but it's better than nothing!" He suggested that I pay special attention to producing a dry product of good quality. "And don't worry too much," he concluded. "It will be a short war. We have already been promised reinforcements."

But the radio didn't say anything about those promised reinforcements. It only announced that the Japanese had taken Bangkok, had landed elsewhere in Siam (Thailand) and on the Malay Peninsula, and had attacked a British flotilla near Malacca.

In quick succession, the radio also announced that on December 11, Germany and Italy had declared war on the United States; on December 13, the Japanese had occupied the American base at Guam; and on December 16, Japanese troops had landed on Borneo!

I was still standing near the radio when I heard the drone of approaching aircraft. I ran to the east side of the house, where the sound was coming from.

From behind the high coconut trees of the neighboring plantation two planes appeared, and I fervently hoped they would be our Dorniers — being too inexperienced at the time to identify aircraft by their silhouette or sound.

They flew low and aimed right at our house. Just before they passed over, I noticed the red ball on the wings, and my heart stopped.

"They are Japanese," I yelled to the workers who had come running, and dumbfounded we stared after the aircraft that were flying so calmly toward the mountain range.

"That is the direction of Ternate," I realized with a start. The war had suddenly landed right on our doorstep!

At noon, the radio announced further Japanese advances, and fifteen minutes later we saw the same two Japanese planes turning back in a north-easterly direction.

This time they didn't fly over the house, but somewhat to the left. I thought that one engine was faltering and then our workers with their eagle eyes reported that the tail of one of the airplanes had been damaged.

At 4 o'clock, Father Moors came over to tell me that the planes had, indeed, gone to Ternate and had dropped bombs which, luckily, had caused little damage. Our own airplanes had been caught on the ground, but had scrambled in time to pursue the attackers, and one of the Japanese planes had been damaged in the dog fight that followed. Our Dorniers had then taken over from the fighters and chased the Japanese deep into the northern part of Halmahera.

Would these planes come back? Had it been simply a show of force, or had it been a reconnaissance flight? We did not know.

In the late afternoon, I received a note from the Magistrate telling me that I had been called up for national service on Ternate.

I read the note with dismay. I was quite willing to go. It never occurred to me to refuse a call to duty — but what was I to do with the plantation?

As luck would have it, Father Moors was still visiting our workers, so I showed him the note. He said he didn't understand why I had been called up. It didn't seem right to him that husband *and* wife, engaged in a vital business, should both have been drafted.

"Mon Désir is, after all, a vital business that requires supervision just like the larger plantations where the employees have been granted exemptions," he said. "I think you should refuse to go," he added.

I did not agree, however, and said: "Why should I? I have been brought up to believe that one has to do one's duty, no matter how unpleasant or inconvenient it might be," and I made it clear to him that I only wanted to discuss the problem of what to do with the plantation and to have the benefit of his advice.

He then suggested that I contact a well-known Chinese, a reliable person, to ask him to manage the plantation in my absence.

"It will only be for a short time," he assured me. "You'll appreciate that this war will not last long; three months maximum. The Americans are strong and the Australians are coming to help defend the East Indies. In such a short time there is not much that can go wrong on the plantation, but a strong hand is needed in case something does."

He promised to contact the man in Tobelo right away, and if he was willing, come back with him in the evening to discuss the details.

Ang Tiong An was hired, in spite of his demand for a high salary: the price of 100 bags of copra per month, I quickly calculated. He also wanted an advance of three months. The man gave the impression of being dependable and energetic. He promised to return with Father Moors the next day.

The negotiations had left me exhausted, but I listened nevertheless for a few minutes to the radio, which announced big victories for the Russians. The German army was retreating on all fronts! Suddenly, my summons to active military duty did not seem such a big thing anymore, and even *I* started to believe in a short war!

I spent the last night in our big house reminiscing: it had been built with so much love, and with the intent that it would serve as our residence for the rest of our lives. Tomorrow, it would be deserted. I decided to offer the use of it to our Doctor and the District Chief, should they want to move their families out of the *kota* — as many persons had already done.

The next day, I discussed all operating details with Ang Tiong An and Father Moors, and, in the presence of the newly hired overseer, Benjamin, showed Ang Tiong An a storage cabinet containing rolls of textiles which — depending on need and work done — could be distributed to the workers at cost.

Then I removed personal papers, diplomas, testimonials and confidential letters from the safe to take them with me, locked the safe with our silverware in it, and handed the key to the priest.

Then came the hard part.

I distributed extra rations to the workers, thanked them for their loyalty, and asked them to remain calm and stay at Mon Désir, rather than flee. If they had any difficulties, I urged them to see Father Moors.

I also said goodbye to our house pets, horses and cattle — all of them born on Mon Désir — and to the plantation itself. So many coconuts, which I had planted with my own hands, had grown into luxuriant fruit-bearing trees. They would stay, but I had to go.

Blinded by tears I tore myself away, and hurriedly walked to the bridge — accompanied by Latif. The workers called out "good journey" and "come back soon" until their voices faded in the distance.

I didn't allow myself one last look back, but just kept going.

It was four in the afternoon when I arrived in the *kota*, where the Magistrate told me that a Government *prau* with an outboard motor would pick me up after sundown, and take me down the Kao Bay to its furthest inlet, Kampung Pasir Putih. From there I would have to cross overland to Dodinga, and find a boat to take me to Ternate. It was the same route that John had taken.

He also told me that I had been assigned the job of managing the hospital on Ternate, and would come under the command of the Army.

I had time to say goodbye to friends and acquaintances, who loaded me down with presents. Most of these people were jittery; they talked incessantly, obviously to reassure themselves. From them I learned that an urban guard and a demolition team had been formed. Also, that the military had constructed observation posts high up in the trees along the coast.

On the street I ran into the wives of Mansanaris and Kriekhoff who had come to say goodbye and ask me to take with me a parcel of clothing for their husbands. I then walked to the Presbytery to listen to our radio which I had given to Father Moors to alleviate his loneliness.

From there I saw Latif hanging about. He had not, for a moment, lost sight of me and would soon take my luggage to the quay. He was the last person from Buluwaya who was left to me, I reflected, wondering what life would now have in store for him.

The sun was setting and a fine ash rain swished down softly as I left the Presbytery for the residence of the Magistrate, where I would have to wait for the departing signal of the motorboat.

As I entered, I met several Dutch residents of the *kota*, who had come to listen to the news. Everyone was utterly polite, but nobody mentioned my impending departure.

I kept silent and sought out the Magistrate. He was busy placing a bundle of official letters in a tin container, which he asked me to deliver to the military commander on Ternate. The Magistrate's attitude toward me seemed to have returned to what it was before the butterfly affair.

Suddenly the sirens started to wail. Everyone turned pale and started to jabber. An *oppas* was sent to find out what was happening. He returned with the news that something had been sighted at sea near the islands.

Tensions rose.

The head of the destruction crew, whose name had been shrouded in secrecy up till now, asked nervously if the trucks should be started up in preparation for driving them off the quay into the sea. And when would he get the signal to put fire to the barracks and storage sheds?

The confusion intensified.

Nobody paid attention to the radio anymore. Every few minutes an *oppas* was sent out to get more information. By now the wailing sirens were resonating in the pits of our stomachs.

Then the Doctor's *jongos* came running out of the darkness, shouting for help. "*Tuan dan Nyonya Dokter sudah hampir tenggelam* — Mr. and Mrs. Doctor are drowning," he gasped.

Tripping over one another, we ran to the nearby house of our Doctor. From the backyard we heard loud cries for help. Near a covered lamp pole that swung in the breeze, we found the air-raid shelter where the family had sought refuge after the sirens started. The wretched souls were standing up to their chests in rising groundwater — each one holding a child up in the air!

Apparently, the muddy exit had become so slippery that climbing out by themselves had become impossible. Many hands eventually pulled them to safety. They profusely expressed their gratitude and were heading for the shower, when madame stopped and anxiously asked if the Japanese had arrived.

## IBU MALUKU

It then dawned on us that the sirens had been wailing all that time and no one had come to report what was going on. Not one of the gentlemen present offered to go, so the Magistrate instructed the District Chief and the Chief of Police to investigate.

When they returned, they asked to see the Magistrate in private. Everyone froze, wondering what was going on. Then we heard a heart-felt curse.

The men rejoined us, and the Magistrate told us that, whereas the coast guard knew how to turn the sirens *on*, they were waiting for the *Tuan Skepper* (the Magistrate) to tell them how to stop them!

We all had a much-needed laugh.

Relieved, I then asked permission to leave. Everybody wished me a good journey, and then returned safely to their spotless houses where, no doubt, they would watch languidly over the country's peace and their own well-being.

The *oppas* accompanied me to the motorboat with the box containing the official papers. Near the quay I found Latif, sitting alone with my luggage, hiding from the light drizzle under the protruding roof of the copra storage shed.

He told me that the crew of the boat had fled from the approaching Japanese and were now hiding somewhere outside the *kota*. I had no choice but to wait until they showed up. So I passed the night on a field cot in the Presbytery.

The next day, the radio reported the landing of many Japanese divisions north of Manila. Around eight, the crew of the motorboat returned, deeply ashamed over their flight and dereliction of duty.

It was really a relief for me when the anchor was finally raised and we set a southerly course. The *nontongers* (onlookers) called out "*Amato*" and "*Selamat jalan*".

Latif stood among them, staring at me, his face contorted with grief. I looked back with mixed feelings: sorrow, bewilderment, wistfulness ... but also with something close to a conviction that, some day, I would return.

**Endnotes**
[1] The *Jaksa* is an officer of the Justice Department.

# IBU MALUKU

IBU MALUKU

*Mia (standing) and Jeanne, with an aunt.
Brussels, circa 1905.*

*Jeanne on her 27th birthday, for the first time in sarong and kebaya.
Tobelo, June 6, 1923*

IBU MALUKU

*Jeanne, Bok and Senen (with a child on his arm)
Mon Désir, July 1923*

*A friend, Jeanne and John van Diejen.
Celebrating John's birthday.
Tobelo, September 20, 1923*

## IBU MALUKU

*Jeanne and John In front of the MHM company house,
haunted by the Franciscan Friar.
Tobelo, June, 1925*

*An oxcart with plantation children, drawn by steers born on
Mon Désir. Jeanne on horseback, John with Latif on his right.
Mon Désir, September 20, 1926*

*Jeanne and friends, ready for their first airplane flight.
Nice, March 1928*

*Jeanne and the Chief Engineer of the S.S. "van Noort",
leaving the ship in a Papua lèpa-lèpa to visit Hollandia
(now Jayapura), en route to Biak.
January, 1929*

IBU MALUKU

*Arrival on Biak Island: the van Noort's Chief Engineer,
Jeanne, and a customs official.
Bosnik, January, 1929*

*The natives of Biak Island offer one of their delicacies:
a twelve foot python!
Bosnik, Biak, February, 1929.*

# IBU MALUKU

*Father Neyens and John, who had just
resigned his post to "save his company".
Mon Désir, May 29, 1930*

*Jeanne, celebrating her birthday among the plantation workers.
Mon Désir, June 6, 1936*

*Jeanne and John amidst the sweet potatoes.
Mon Désir, 1938*

*The van Diejen's last house on Mon Désir, August, 1938
(destroyed in July 1945 by an Allied pilot, to win a case of beer)*

IBU MALUKU

*The half of the hospital that remained after the 2nd Allied bombing.
Kampili, July, 1945*

*Nuns baking bread in the devastated Central Kitchen
(author at extreme right).
Kampili, July, 1945*

IBU MALUKU

*John van Diejen's nephew Jon with fiancée, Willy Fuhrie-Broekhals.
Batavia (Jakarta), 1947*

*At the orphanage with 3-year old Djaka,
whose mother had died in childbirth.
Ternate, 1954*

# IBU MALUKU

*Former Kampili commandant Tadashi Yamaji welcomes Jeanne, who had lost her voice. Tokyo, April 26, 1961*

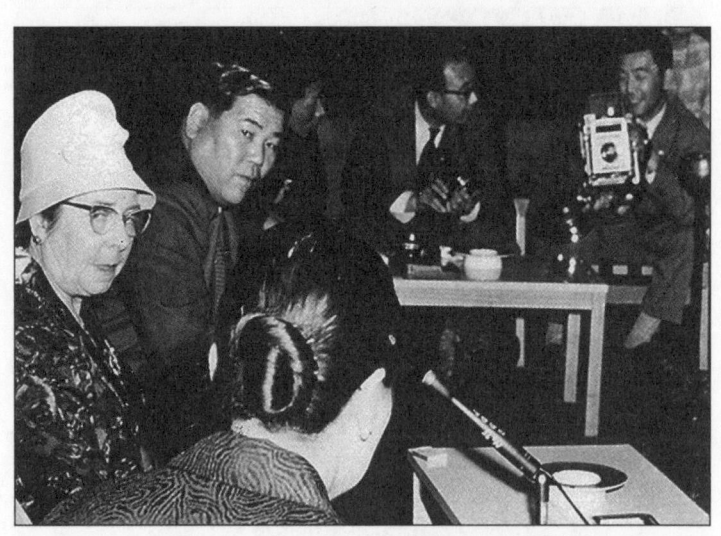

*Jeanne, Yamaji and Mrs. Oya (the translator) during the unscheduled news conference at the New Japan Hotel. Tokyo, April 27, 1961*

IBU MALUKU

*At the official Fuji-TV reception: Mrs. Hellebrekers, Jeanne, Yamaji, and former sergeant Okashima (nicknamed "Dannyboy"). New Japan Hotel, Tokyo, May 27, 1961*

*The front page of the Kampili movie brochure that was left in Jeanne's hotel room in Tokyo by an anonymous person. April 28, 1961*

*Mr Yamaji, Mrs. Oya, Jeanne, Mrs. Hellebrekers and Mr. Yamasaki of Fuji-TV in front of the Todaji Temple, Nara, April 31, 1961*

*Mrs. Hellebreakers, Jeanne, Mrs. Oya and Mr. Yamaji at a temple in Kyoto. April 31, 1961*

# IBU MALUKU

*Jeanne at her nephew's home with Yamaji's sword.
St. Job-in-'t-Goor (Antwerp),
September 14, 1975*

*Jeanne at a Chinese restaurant: with Nini Smits (standing),
Mireille Desjarlais-Heynneman.
Sittard, Netherlands, September, 1989*

# IBU MALUKU

*Nini Smits, Jeanne van Diejen, Laurette Desjarlais and her daughter Mireille, visiting St. Odiliënberg, Netherlands, where Jeanne grew up Limburg Province, June, 1991*

*Jeanne van Diejen on her 103rd birthday.
Sittard, Netherlands, June 6, 1999.
(Limburger newspaper photograph)*

IBU MALUKU

# CHAPTER 29

### Preparing for War
### Ternate, December, 1941

For 16 nautical miles we cruised along the coast and close to the foothills of the Togorih mountain, where no volcanic ash had fallen. How wonderfully green were the crowns of the coconut trees, and how pretty were the yellow-green leaves of the banana trees.

The panorama became even more beautiful as we sailed into the wide, deep Kao Bay. The large volcanos of Halmahera, which rose majestically from the land base, were sharply delineated against the sky.

We stayed close to the coast, where peaceful *kampungs* nested in their own garland of palm trees. The villages of the heathens were the most colorful, fenced off as they were with hedgerows of red hibiscus or brightly colored crotons. Another distinctive feature was that these villages were decorated with giant sea turtle shells, and had trees that projected far out over the water. The villages of the Christians were identified by their jaunty white-washed church towers. The villages of the Moslems were less colorful, for want of flowers. One could only see coconut and fruit trees on bare land, where a herd of goats provided a moving picture of black and white.

All along the coast, excited children congregated to wave a friendly welcome to us. How peaceful it was. It was hard to believe there was a war on and I was on my way to participate in it — even if my role was limited to that of managing a hospital!

Towards 2 o'clock in the afternoon we reached Kao, the seat of the District Chief. We did not stop, however, and continued on our way. One hour later we heard the drone of approaching aircraft. We nervously searched the sky, wondering if they were Japanese. We spotted two of them, and when they came closer, we were overjoyed to recognize our own Dornier aircraft!

They turned around, and went into a dive — seemingly to land on the unruffled water — and we watched, pleasantly surprised. But no, they pulled up at a low altitude and roared over our heads. Then they turned and came straight at us again, and one of them dropped something that fell into the sea some thirty meters from us.

One of our sailors dived in and returned with a cylindrical container. It contained a message from the Commander of a nearby military post, instructing us to stop off there for an urgent matter. When the fliers were certain that we had received the message, they flew on again in the direction of Ternate.

After an hour, we arrived at the military outpost and handed the container back to the Commander. I learned that six KNIL soldiers, who had patrolled the area for two months, had been recalled to Ternate and would travel with us. Within half an hour they and their possessions were loaded into the boat, and we continued on our journey.

It was now terribly cramped on board. Apart from their regular gear, the six new passengers — led by a Javanese corporal — had brought all their personal possessions, including chickens, a multi-colored lory and a noisy white cockatoo. It took much effort and many delicate negotiations to find a relatively comfortable place to sit — lying down being out of the question!

Toward the evening, it started to rain, and this turned into a short, but severe, thunderstorm that was decidedly unpleasant in this crowded situation.

Just before midnight, we entered the small harbor of Pasir Putih. Not waiting for my luggage to be unloaded, I walked with the Corporal in total darkness to the residence of the District Chief, whose assistance I needed to continue our trip overland.

It was difficult to wake him up, but he finally opened the door, holding a lantern in one hand. With a fearful look, he asked if we were being pursued by the Japanese.

I put his mind at ease, and said we needed porters immediately to help us cross overland.

With consternation he raised his hands in the air. "*Jah Allah!*" he intoned, "No one has ever walked on that road at night. You will not find anyone willing to go with you. Don't you know it is full of *setans* (devils) there?"

I showed him the Magistrate's letter, in which he was asked to give us the support we needed to complete our journey. He read it skeptically, and said he would call some people, but that he could not force anyone to make that journey in the dark. He sighed deeply and, as if to exorcize the bad spirits, he intoned several times: "*Jah Allah Ilalah!* How can anyone make such an absurd request!"

Predictably, every one of the hastily-selected porters refused — they wanted to wait until the next morning. Our boatman then stepped forward and asked us to hurry. He had received orders to turn back as soon as we had moved inland, and report this fact to the officials in Tobelo. But the porters would not budge.

Then I had an inspiration. From my luggage, I retrieved a large envelope that was closed with five red lacquer seals, and asked the District Chief if I could see him in private. With an air of secrecy, I showed him the important-looking envelope and said: "This is addressed to *Seri Paduka Tuan* (His Highness) the Sultan of Ternate; it must be in his possession by daybreak!"

Humbly and with great reference he touched the envelope. Next, he folded his hands to his heart and bowed. Then, with a strong voice he demanded — yes, demanded — that the porters carry our luggage, and then took the liberty of adding something I had not agreed to:

"The *Nyonya Belanda* (Dutch missis) will carry a large lantern and will walk in front. Then, nothing will happen to you!"

I grasped his meaning, though, and quickly added: "And armed soldiers will be walking behind you, so the *setans* cannot attack you from behind."

That broke the porters' resistance.

I had walked over this forested road once before in broad daylight, and was not pleased about having to do this in total darkness. The very thought of snakes was already making me cringe. But I had no choice in the matter.

"Well, here we go," I prompted myself, "This is no time to show fear!"

I picked up the flashlight and sharp machete provided by the District Chief, and led the way, followed by nine petrified porters and nine soldiers who did not find it much of a pleasure trip either. I was convinced that they actually feared the *setans* much more than any physical enemy.

For the first hour everything went well, except that every sound — the screech of a night bird or a suspicious rustling in the thickets — made the men stop in their tracks. An intense whispered debate about the source of the noise would follow, before they were prepared to pick up the trail again.

I was crossing a plank bridge, when it gave way under my weight. I yelped as I lost my balance and slid into the gully. The men froze, but once I had figured out what had happened and started to laugh, they came closer and pulled me out.

Luckily, the flashlight was still working. By its light I could see from the men's faces that they did not believe this had been an accident.

We continued on our journey, and it was close to four in the morning when we heard the cocks crowing in Kampung Dodinga.

At the house of the District Chief, we were served coffee and a dish of warm *papeda* (sago porridge), while a large *prau* was made ready for the last stage of our trip to Ternate.

The porters then received their payment, and started on the return trip to Pasir Putih — much relieved that it was now daylight.

At six, the large fishing *prau* was ready, and while the crew was loading our luggage, one soldier noticed that his lory was missing. It had just disappeared. Everyone was convinced it was the work of the *setans*!

Since Dodinga lies a little inland, we first cruised through a mangrove forest in which the morning fog blanketed the tangle of aerial roots. When we reached open sea, we saw the faint profile of Tidore's Kiematubu mountain and, on its right, Ternate's Gamalamo peak, shrouded in a pearly haze that slowly changed to a purple rose.

A slight breeze came up allowing the crew to put away their oars and hoist the main sail. The *Juragang* (captain) assured me that with this wind we would reach Ternate in four or five hours.

I settled into a comfortable position, and only then realized just how tired I really was. The soldiers had fallen asleep, leaning against the frame of the *prau*, and the soft gurgling of the backwater heightened my desire to sleep also. Undisturbed by the gentle snoring of the sleeping men or the occasional word that passed between the crew members, I also fell asleep.

As we approached Ternate, a sudden change in course woke me, and I asked sleepily what was happening. The *Juragang* said he wanted to approach the pier from the north, rather than head-on from the east. It would reduce the chance of being mistaken for Japanese and getting shot at.

That thought really woke me, and I stood up to have a better view. But the *Juragang* urged me to sit down again. The sight of a white woman might raise unwanted interest, and he did not want to be stopped by a patrol boat and lose time.

I collapsed back into my sleeping position, but remained wide awake. It would take only another half hour anyway to reach the harbor of Ternate, I thought. In the open boat it was now blazing hot, and I felt that my face started to get puffy, as it was already badly sunburnt.

Everyone was awake now. The soldiers stretched as well as they could, yawned, and started to collect their gear. Ten minutes later, we could see the pier, and an unexpected feeling of relief and gratitude came over me. It seemed that, deep within, I had been fearful and worried throughout this long, strange journey.

The pier was heavily guarded. When the guards noticed the KNIL soldiers in our *prau*, they dropped the muzzles of their rifles that had been trained on us. As we came closer, the guards acted tough, but they were really a bit embarrassed at having to tell me they had received strict orders not to allow civilians on the quay. But I understood their predicament and instructed the *Juragang* to row the boat to a spot further on (as indicated by the guards), where I could disembark without any problem.

When the boat landed, I looked around in surprise. The beach was unrecognizable. At every few paces, starting from the water line, sharp, pointed pieces of bamboo had been driven into the sand, followed by a rather primitive barricade. It was evidently the first line of defense for the city.

When I clambered up to the beach boulevard, I noticed that the large houses, where all the important burghers used to live, now seemed deserted. And suddenly I felt totally drained from this long, uninterrupted journey.

I was glad nobody could see me. There I stood beside my luggage, dressed in a shirt and dark riding breeches, an old tropical helmet on my head, my feet in heavy hobnailed boots, the legs tightly wrapped in grey-green puttees, a long machete in one hand, and a flashlight hanging from my belt. My face was red and swollen and I felt unwashed and uncared-for.

Finally, two soldiers showed up together with two *strappans* (prisoners) to carry my luggage. One of the soldiers I knew, as he had been posted in Tobelo for a while. Together we walked to the upper road. Then I remembered John telling me in his letter that the Army had taken possession of the beautiful homes along this road.

In one of those homes, I met the local military commander, Captain Zondag, who greeted me with a gigantic mug of *koppie tubruk* (coffee, made the native way). He pushed a dish with steaming *pisang goreng* (fried bananas) toward me, and said: "Here, eat and drink something first. We can talk afterwards."

I was very grateful, as it gave me time to collect my thoughts.

Captain Zondag busied himself with the Sergeant, who brought him up-to-date on the six men who had come with us. He then returned, welcomed me warmly once again, and said that he had only two nurses at his disposal and was glad that I had come to "lend a hand". He said he was putting me in charge of the medical center that served the needs of all KNIL wives and children, who had been lodged temporarily in a *kampung* outside the city. Later, they would be evacuated to a safer area, he explained.

Then he told me that I had in effect been drafted into the Army. I would have to wear a Red Cross arm band, and carry identification papers that would accord me the right to be treated as a prisoner-of-war if I were ever captured.

That certainly gave me something to think about!

The Captain Doctor, who had been notified of my arrival while Captain Zondag and I had been talking, arrived at noon in his beautiful new car. He was a charming man, nicknamed *"Vrolijke Kootje"* (or Jolly Joey) who proceeded to bring me up-to-date on the medical situation.

There was a military hospital inside the fortress, *Fort Oranje* (Fort Orange) — now deserted — that had a well-stocked apothecary. He would show it to me later, and he then explained my administrative duties.

Across the street from Fort Orange, closer to the sea, was the civilian hospital. It was also closed and I would have nothing to do there. He simply mentioned it, in case it should be reopened later. He then said he would take me to the field hospital — twelve kilometers inland — that would become my base camp and main area of responsibility.

The roads leaving the city had been barricaded with saw horses and other types of barricades, and soldiers had to move them, so we could zig-zag through. Once outside the city, the Doctor told me that, immediately after war had been declared, the Army had ordered the evacuation of all Dutch families living in the *kota*. They were now housed in Kampung Sangaji, close to the field hospital where we were heading. His own family was there too: his wife and children shared a small hut with six nuns. He wanted to introduce them to me, so that was where we stopped first.

We met the Mother Superior, whose face expressed shock at my appearance. I wasn't surprised. A woman in riding breeches was not exactly a daily occurrence in Ternate. Later, she would admit to me that she was particularly taken aback by the large machete that I was firmly gripping in my right hand.

The Doctor asked his wife if a place could be freed where I could sleep, but the hut was really too small to accommodate another person. I then asked him if there wasn't a cubby-hole to be found at the field hospital. We went over there to take a look, but all available space was taken by patients, some of whom were seriously ill.

There was a Chinese boy, Gerret Teng, who was burning up with high fever. He had a festering stomach wound, caused by a *dodisso* —

a deer trap, into which he had fallen while hunting. He would later become my special patient.

I also met an old orderly, an exceptionally tall Ambonese, whom everyone called *Oom Pieter* (Uncle Peter). When he heard that I had no place to sleep, he promptly offered his own shelter for as long as it was needed. He and his wife would sleep in the *gudang*. The "Sister" — which is what he called me right away — would, in any case, get their bedroom with a good bed, he stated contentedly.

Without asking for the Doctor's approval, Uncle Peter took me by the hand and pulled me along to his house. From far off he called out to his *Nyora*[1]: "Please make the bathroom ready quickly. Our new Sister needs a bath and a bed right away!"

I was greatly impressed that this unpretentious man had thought of *me*, and had quickly perceived what *I* needed. Neither Captain Zondag, nor the Doctor or his wife, and not even the Mother Superior, had given any thought to the obvious fact that — after traveling for 28 hours — I *had* to be dead tired and, most of all, was in need of a bath!

His attention touched me deeply and I gratefully accepted the help of his tiny, round, and motherly *Nyora*, who gave me a towel and soap, and gently pushed me into a small bathroom. When I came out refreshed, she gave me a cool glass of *ayer jeruk* (lemonade) and insisted that I lay down on their bed. The *kelambu* (mosquito net) was carefully tucked in, and I dropped off to sleep as soon as my head hit the pillow.

Three hours later, the Doctor came to pick me up in his car. I had put on normal clothes and now wore a nurse's uniform.

At my request, the Doctor promised to take me first to see my husband. But he could not immediately locate John and had to ask around. He finally turned into a road going inland, passing gardens of the local population, where they also grew nutmeg. How beautifully green everything was here! Not a trace of ash to be seen!

I asked the Doctor where we were going, and he said gleefully: "To the military vegetable gardens."

"Did I hear you right? What on earth is a soldier doing in a vegetable garden at a time like this?"

When we turned a corner, I saw a fenced-in parcel of land, where a few people were working. At the entrance stood a fully armed soldier. At the sound of the approaching car, he jumped to attention and saluted his superior, the Doctor. The soldier was none other than John!

Bewildered and indignant, I walked over and looked at him. Reading the question on my face, John said: "As you see, I am protecting three female weeders and a vegetable garden."

Hotly I turned to the Doctor, and burst out: "Was he called away from our plantation to do something as stupid as that?" Angry tears at this humiliation started to run down my face. John looked embarrassed, and the Doctor just stood there, not saying a word.

When we drove back, the officer said he had not known about this affair and doubted the Captain did either. Seeing I was still angry and resentful, he explained that John would have been posted there by a sergeant. He understood my feelings, however, and would talk to Captain Zondag about it. I would gladly have done this myself, but heard that, although I had been "militarized", I was still enough of a civilian to not be permitted into the *kota* after five in the evening.

The Doctor sympathetically explained the situation in which the militiamen — who were often from a higher social strata than the career soldiers — suddenly found themselves, now that the roles were reversed.

"John has already told me about this," I said, still cross, "and I can understand this to some degree. At the same time, it is highly unfair that they take it out on John. John has never talked down to anyone and has never even met any of the sergeants."

"Fair or not," the Doctor said, "I suspect that vengeance is at the back of what has happened in John's case. I will talk to Captain Zondag, I promise."

It was getting dark when the Doctor dropped me off at the field hospital. I had intended to spend the rest of the evening with Uncle Peter and his tiny wife (who wanted me to call her *Tante* or Aunty), but I had difficulty keeping my eyes open, and had to excuse myself. Soon after, I was asleep in that wonderfully large, cool bed of this elderly couple, who themselves spent the night on a not too comfortable *baleh-baleh* (a bamboo couch).

The next day, December 23, I started work early. There were many people at the out-patient's clinic whom I had to see and treat together with Uncle Peter. Around eleven, the Doctor came by to check on Gerret Teng: he still had a high fever, and the wound looked bad.

During the course of the day, Kriekhoff — the other militiaman from Tobelo — came to tell me that John had been assigned to other duties, and I made a mental note to thank the Doctor at the next opportunity.

That evening I did, after all, move into the shelter in which the Doctor's wife and her many children lived (during my first visit it had seemed like an impossibility). In a *gudang* (storage room), 2 by 2.5 meters, they had arranged a place for me to sleep. Just right for a person my size! But there was a dingy smell, and I could not sleep as my mat was always sliding — it was evidently lying on something rather slippery.

My tossing and turning finally awakened my hostess, who came to my aid. I then discovered that I had been sleeping on top of a hoarded stock of provisions. The last ship had brought the Doctor's wife two large smoked Australian hams that now — surrounded by bales of rice — formed my "bed". No wonder I was sliding around.

We laughed about that and then searched for another place to put the hams — a place where they would be relatively safe from cockroaches and ants. We finally strung them up with a rope from the ceiling and that did the trick.

On Christmas Eve something was afoot — but known only to the Army. An orderly came to tell the ladies that their husbands had orders to stay in the *kota*, so they would have to celebrate Christmas by themselves. Everyone was very disappointed.

It was getting dark when I received word that the Christmas service would take place at eight, in the nuns' quarters. I did not really want to go, because Gerret Teng was going through a critical phase, but Uncle Peter said that he and an assistant nurse would stay with Gerret.

So I left the field hospital just before eight, and tried to find my way "home" in that still strange environment. The use of a flashlight was forbidden, and the sheds were all blacked out. I stumbled around in this darkness and stubbed a toe before I found the nuns' quarters, where I was escorted to the rear.

The Mass was celebrated on the small back porch. By the light of a partially shielded pocket flashlight, the priest read the prayers, as I and many people around me knelt outdoors in the safety of the darkness. Sometimes I heard a woman cry softly, or admonish a child to be quiet. For the first time, there was a collective premonition of an approaching disaster, which was only expressed by the touch of a hesitant hand or by a fearful kiss. After Mass, I hurried back to the hospital where Gerret was fighting for his life.

Early next morning — I had to remind myself that it was Christmas Day — I took off Gerret's bandages, to clean his wound. There was a greater amount of pus than usual and Uncle Peter pointed to a dark spot in it. It turned out to be a splinter from the bamboo lance that had inflicted this terrible wound.

We removed the splinter, cleaned the wound thoroughly and then rebandaged it. Taking turns, we watched over Gerret and were relieved that, during the course of the day, his temperature slowly went down.

Late in the afternoon, the Doctor and Captain Zondag paid us a visit. Both were quite concerned about Gerret, but were pleased with his progress.

The Doctor then mentioned another serious case that would be arriving soon. "I will give you the details later," he said before leaving.

That evening, Gerret's temperature had again gone down — not much, but enough to give us hope. After I had related his progress to the nuns, they told me in confidence that all European women and children would be transported the next day to an unknown destination. How or where they got their information, I did not know and I did not ask. Before going to bed, I received a note from John. All was well with him.

The night, like the previous one, was restless. My hostess could not sleep either, and she suggested that we go outside and talk there, so as not to awaken the children. She hungered for a cigarette, but reminded herself that it was forbidden to smoke outside in the dark.

It was a beautiful tropical night. In the *kampungs* everyone was fast asleep. Above us, thousands of stars twinkled in the dark sky. It all looked so peaceful, and the war seemed so far away.

Suddenly my hostess started to cry softly. After she got a hold of herself again, she confirmed what I had heard from the nuns. Like the other women, she would have to pack all her belongings, starting early the next day. Her husband had told her, specifically, not to forget the provisions on which I had been sleeping. Clothes could be taken, but all furniture and furnishings that she had brought with her from the base in the fort had to be left behind.

I tried to console her by promising I would look after her belongings, presuming that I would be allowed to stay in her shed. Being allegedly "militarized" I would, of course, not leave with the others but have to remain at my post with my patients.

In the afternoon of the next day, the Doctor and Captain Zondag came with several soldiers to pick up the nuns, women and children. I was surprised at the amount of goods that they wanted to take with them. The gentlemen made some cuts here and there, but what was left still filled several trucks. The obviously nervous passengers would also have to be transported by truck.

The Doctor then gave me further information about the serious case he had mentioned earlier, which involved a woman who could give birth at any moment.

"It will be a difficult delivery, and it could be even life-threatening," said the Doctor. "I have been transferred to Ambon, and will be leaving with the women and children."

"Are we going to be left without any doctor then?" I asked alarmed. "What if this coming patient has complications?"

Only then did he tell me, officially, that the ship coming to pick up the women and children, would be bringing a Javanese doctor from Weda. He was no longer needed there, since the KNIL detachment he had been looking after had been moved elsewhere. There would be no time, however, for the Doctor to confer with his replacement in any detail.

Hurriedly, he showed me the apothecary in Fort Orange, and gave me the names of two blood donors, both prisoners. Their blood group he did not remember, but the orderly would know.

I did not like the situation at all! I felt like a fish out of water, and the new doctor would not know his way around either!

In the afternoon, the ship arrived and the boarding of European women and children started right away. Uncle Peter watched over Gerret, while I went to the quay to meet the new doctor.

To my surprise, I saw the ship that had brought him was the H*onun Maru* — the same ship that had brought my kapok workers from Menado to Tobelo. Concerned, I wondered if this primitive copra boat was suitable to take all the evacuees and their mountain of possessions on such a long, and possibly dangerous, journey!

The new doctor, Dr. Hassan, was a tiny, energetic Javanese, who was formally dressed in *adat* attire that was not often seen in this region. He was accompanied by his wife, a baby boy (six days old), five daughters (ranging in age from one to eight), and a Javanese *babu*, who looked after the children. His belongings were hastily unloaded, for the ship was behind schedule and had to leave as quickly as possible.

The two doctors introduced themselves, and Dr. Hassan was rapidly brought up-to-date on the major issues. When the Javanese pressed for more details, our departing Doctor — no longer resembling the "Jolly Joey" of earlier days — pointed to me and introduced us.

The evacuees lined up to embark. The children were playful and excited about the trip, but the adults looked grim. The boat was a sore disappointment to them. The H*onun Maru* had no cabins and no beds. They would all have to camp in the hold of the ship amidst their belongings. There was little room and, of course, no privacy.

The pregnant women boarded first, followed by those with small children. Then the nuns, accompanied by two Franciscan friars whom I had not seen before. It surprised me that they were leaving, believing they would have been needed here. Only one Franciscan friar, a priest who had been deported from the Communist-controlled part of China and had arrived only recently in Ternate, remained on the quay.

Finally, the H*onun Maru* weighed anchor, and pushed off. The passengers waved goodbye. I waved back. Where were they going? Would they be fortunate enough to elude Japanese submarines and airplanes, and arrive safely at their new destination?

I was deeply concerned for them all.

### Endnotes
[1] *Nyora* is normally used to address the wives of teachers (gurus).

# CHAPTER 30

### The Enemy Attacks
*Ternate, 1941 - 1942*

I suddenly realized that I was now the only European woman on Ternate, and for a moment my heart shrank and my courage faltered. Would I be able to handle the many challenges that would surely be coming my way?

My first step was to secure permission from Captain Zondag to enter the *kota* at any hour of the day or night and to have access to the apothecary inside Fort Orange. Then I moved into an empty shed closer to the field hospital.

That done, I turned to Dr. Hassan to discuss the coming childbirth case and to share with him what I knew about it.

After taking Dr. Hassan's family to their quarters in Kampung Sangaji — they would live in the shed, vacated by the previous doctor's wife — I introduced Dr. Hassan to Gerret Teng and Uncle Peter. Like the other patients, they were relieved that, once again, a doctor was present. It made up in part for the loss of the much-loved "Jolly Joey" — who was now somewhere on the open sea.

Towards seven, I received the message that the "difficult case" had gone into labor. I picked up Dr. Hassan and, in the dark, we made our way to the woman's house in a neighboring *kampung*. She turned out to be a strong, healthy woman — mother of three nice boys, who had been hastily sent to stay with friends.

A cursory examination showed that the dilation of the cervix had already progressed well. But when Dr. Hassan examined her more closely, he confirmed the prognosis of his predecessor — there was a serious complication: a *placenta preavia* (a placenta that partially or completely covers the cervix). We exchanged a worried look.

Dr. Hassan suggested that she be transported to the field hospital, but I persuaded him that in the primitive environment in which Gerret Teng and others were being treated, the chances of cross-infection were infinitely greater.

The actual delivery began and, at first, everything seemed to proceed normally. But as the baby was being born, the woman started to bleed profusely. We speeded up the delivery and then found we could not stop the bleeding by normal means. She obviously needed a speedy blood transfusion (in those days plasma did not exist), but her blood type was unknown!

We sent an urgent request to Captain Zondag to have the two *strappans* on my list brought in as quickly as possible, together with information about their blood type. But all that took up precious time.

The two donors, both healthy and strong specimens, finally arrived. However, the corporal who came with them could only confirm that they were the donors we wanted. He knew nothing about their blood type!

It was clear that the woman would bleed to death if we did not act immediately. Dr. Hassan quickly explained the situation to her husband, who had been standing by, wringing his hands. Without a blood transfusion, his wife would surely die; if he agreed to the transfusion and the blood types were mismatched, she could also die.

Anguish contorted the husband's face when he realized the life of the mother of his children was in his hands. With great effort he controlled himself, and gave permission to go ahead. He also chose the donor: the *strappan*, who was in prison for murdering a woman.

We hurriedly prepared the two people for the transfusion. The woman was almost unconscious when it began. Anxiously, we monitored her heart and watched her face for signs of revitalization. It took an eternity, but slowly the pulse became stronger, and some color returned to her waxen face.

Thank God! It appeared that the donor had been compatible. When the convicted murderer realized his blood had saved the woman, he looked blissfully happy. What was going through his mind, I wondered. Was he thinking of the woman whom he had so callously murdered?

The newborn infant was another boy. The father looked at him with great pride and delight, but his greatest joy was obviously the resurrection of his wife.

Dr. Hassan left to find a midwife who could assist me. He was successful. The midwife, a stout Menadonese woman, came in and was instructed to keep a constant eye on the patient. As a precaution, I would stay the night.

My God, how tired I was! I went into an adjoining room, laid down on a *baleh-baleh* and promptly dropped off to sleep.

A while later, something woke me up with a start — I thought it was the voice of the midwife. But no, it wasn't that. I heard a soft snoring sound and, in panic, I jumped up and hurried into the other room. The midwife was sound asleep in her chair; it was the mother of the newly born child I had heard. She was mumbling incoherently, while her hands were groping in the air.

Forgetting blackout regulations, I switched on the unshielded flashlight, turned back the covers, and was horrified to see her lying in a pool of blood. Obviously, she was having a another major bleeding.

I kicked the sleeping midwife — who yelped and fearfully looked about — and dashed out of the hut to get Dr. Hassan, who luckily lived nearby.

I literally screamed him out of his sleep: "Quick, Doctor! A second hemorrhage!" and then I ran back.

The doctor, struggling into his clothes, ran after me. The awakened husband stood near his wife, dazed and not able to utter a word.

Dr. Hassan decided to start another blood transfusion. Thank God, because of the lateness of the hour, the two donors had been put up in a nearby hut. They were hastily summoned, and arrived within a few moments.

The first donor could not give blood again so soon, so once again the husband was faced with that terrible decision. At his wits' end, he looked at us with resignation, and nodded his approval.

Again we made the preparations, greatly fearing the outcome. The law of averages was definitely not in our favor. We started the second transfusion, and watched again with bated breath, and, as the minutes passed, we once again witnessed life flowing back into this hardy woman. Once again, her life had been saved.

The midwife and I took turns watching over her for the next twelve hours and all was well. Only when all danger was past did I dare return to the hospital, which I had left three days earlier.

I was so happy to see that Gerret Teng was finally getting better! It confirmed that we had succeeded in removing all the bamboo splinters from his horrible stomach wound.

\* \* \* \*

The end of 1941 was upon us. What would the new year bring?

To my surprise and delight I received an invitation from Captain Zondag to come, with John, to the Priest's house where he and a few other military officers would join us in ringing in the New Year. Little did I know that this would be the last time we would all be together.

Quietly and somewhat ill at ease, we congregated in the darkened house where the Priest was living. Something seemed strange about him that evening, and it took a while for me to realize that he was in a military uniform. Apparently, he had been made an Army Chaplain and was, therefore, allowed to stay in the *kota*, from which all civilians were still barred.

The atmosphere was not particularly joyful. We quietly talked about the events of the war and I learned, for the first time, what had happened in the outside world during my absence from the *kota*.

On December 25, Hong Kong had fallen, and on December 28, the Japanese had landed on Sumatra. In Europe, however, everything seemed better! Rommel was retreating from the Cirenaica region of Libya; the British had re-conquered the port of Benghazi, capital of Libya; and the Russians had landed in the Crimea.

It could not be long before our American, Australian and English allies would attack Japan. Surely, in two months maximum, this nightmare would come to an end — or so we thought.

At midnight, we got up and shook hands. John bent over to kiss me, but envious eyes were watching, so I dodged his kiss although I hungered for it as never before. Deep inside me, I cried out — would John understand? He quickly controlled himself and, a moment later, we said our goodbyes.

Hesitatingly, Captain Zondag asked the new Chaplain if there was a place where I could stay the night. I understood his meaning and abruptly said that I could not accept such an offer. How could I, when such heaven was denied to the others? I caught a glimpse of John's tense face. He nodded understandingly, but the look in his eyes would stay with me for a long, long time.

When I passed the guard post at Ternate's outskirts and was by myself in the quiet, early morning hours of New Year's Day, I felt so utterly alone and deserted, that tears streamed down my cheeks. How different this evening had been compared to earlier New Year's celebrations, when everyone, the local population included, made it such a joyful occasion. Now, there was only this sad, utter stillness and desolation.

\*\*\*\*

The next day, I received new neighbors. Boki[1], the sister-in-law of our Sultan, moved into one of the sheds that was formerly occupied by the now-evacuated Dutch women. She was expecting her fourth child and, for that reason, wanted to be close to the field hospital.

I was grateful for her company, for I would have someone to talk to during the long lonely evenings. Through Boki, who spoke flawless Dutch, I got to know the other members of this friendly, hospitable and extremely distinguished family.

In the following few days, a large trench was dug in front of Boki's house. Guards from the Sultan's troops protected the house day and night and, since this protection included myself, their presence made me feel much more secure.

On January 3, I had a visitor: a young Chinese girl, named Eta, who was a Christian Red Cross worker with an *EHBO* (First Aid) diploma. Like myself, she had been permitted to celebrate the New Year in the *kota*, and had at that time offered her services as an auxiliary nurse. Her offer had been gratefully accepted, and she had come to ask if she could move in with me. I said I would be pleased to have her as a room-mate.

\* \* \* \*

On January 6, orders were issued for the evacuation of the 64 wives and more than 100 children of the KNIL soldiers. They would be moved to a safer place, inland on Halmahera, and I was to accompany them on this trip.

It took all day to get them ready, and it was already getting dark when they started to embark. Some boarded the Sultan's motorboat, others the various *praus* that had been commandeered from Tidore.

In the fast approaching darkness, it became quite a challenge to get these people and their belongings on board. I was now responsible for their health and well-being and would have to visit them regularly from my post on Ternate.

The crossing of the straits went well. Toward eleven in the evening we reached the natural harbor of Jailolo, where we were put up for the night.

Early the next morning, we started the journey inland. It soon became clear that keeping the people together and moving was to be my main problem. (How much I would have enjoyed the trip through this beautiful countryside, if the circumstances had been different!)

For the greater part of the journey, we had the use of *gerobaks* to transport the *barang* and the smaller children. The mothers and the older children had to travel the 30 kilometer road on foot. But they were all wives of the military and it would certainly not have been the first time that they'd had to make such a difficult journey.

The six KNIL soldiers who escorted the evacuees entertained the women and children throughout the trip with numerous jokes. At each *kampung* we passed, the inhabitants freely offered young coconut meat and fruits as refreshments. Some even offered eggs and live chickens!

When we arrived at the evacuation camp, we found that the Government had built reasonable accommodations from wood and bamboo in a forested area, close to a sizeable river that would provide potable water. Provisions had been stocked, and there was even a supply of medicine in a small shed. Here, I told the women, I would hold an outpatient clinic every ten days.

At high noon, the soldiers and I started the journey back, relieved that the evacuation had been carried out without a hitch. Around eight that evening, we arrived in the harbour of Jailolo and boarded the Sultan's motorboat.

I slept soundly during the entire crossing. Near midnight, we arrived at the pier in front of the *Kedaton*, the palace of the Sultan. Someone woke me up, and moments later I walked, tired and shivering — for the spray from the boat's backwash had drenched me — over the quiet road toward Kampung Sangaji.

In the hospital, everyone was fast asleep, but when I arrived home, Eta, my Chinese room-mate, was waiting for me with hot tea! Her thoughtfulness made me almost forget my tiredness. I even managed to take a quick bath before dropping onto my cot!

\*\*\*\*

The next day, rumors circulated that — under cover of night — several *praus* filled with Arabs had secretly left Ternate for an unknown destination. It made the population even more anxious. Should they also be seeking a safer haven for themselves?

On January 10, Dr. Hassan and the Magistrate decided it would be advisable to send their own families to the same camp on Halmahera where I had taken the wives of the KNIL soldiers a week earlier. The Magistrate issued an urgent order to build two additional sheds, and the wives started to prepare for their departure. The Magistrate asked my neighbor, the Sultan's daughter-in-law, if she wanted to go there too but, to my delight, Boki declined.

The radio announced that the Japanese had entered Manila a week earlier, and had also landed on Burma. The NIROM did not give us a clue as to what was happening elsewhere in the East Indies; they only broadcast soothing reports. From England came a message from Queen Wilhelmina: "She orders everyone in the Netherlands East Indies to stay at his/her post, and to support and protect the native population against the invaders."

Wryly I asked myself how we could possibly leave our posts, even if had we wanted to. After all, we were now completely cut off from the outside world!

On January 12, well before daylight, I left in the Sultan's motorboat with the two families. The youngest infants were only 10 and 15 days old; the other children varied in age from one to eleven years. Both mothers were weak, as they had not quite recovered from their last delivery. The motorboat was full, but I still found a spot for a box of medicine, which was destined for the clinic in the Halmahera forest.

The crossing again went without a hitch and the journey inland also went smoothly. At the clinic, from late in the afternoon until far into the evening, I examined pregnant women, gave out pills, operated on boils, bandaged wounds and offered advice.

Towards nine that evening, I started the 30 km trek back through the forest, *kampungs* and people's vegetable gardens. The moon was out and, because of intermittent cloud formations, gave an unsteady light. One soldier, a Javanese, accompanied me. He had been relieved from his duty to protect the women in the evacuation camp, and was pleased to be returning to Ternate.

Every five kilometers, we took a break, and then continued our trek. We didn't speak much. He was a serious and not very talkative fellow, but he answered whenever I asked him something.

At four we reached Jailolo, and a moment later we were in the motorboat and on our way back to Ternate. The boatman was ill at ease. Whenever he saw a light coursing the wide straits — which was often — he would whisper that it might belong to a Japanese boat. His muttering usually woke me, but then I quickly dropped off to sleep again.

When I stood on the Sultan's pier at seven in the morning, my legs were trembling with fatigue. I hungered for a bath and a bed. The thoughtful Sultan, who was waiting at the pier with his own car, drove me home, where I dropped utterly exhausted onto my bed.

Two hours later, Eta had to wake me for an emergency at the hospital. A seriously ill woman had been brought in. To provide her with a bed, Uncle Peter had upgraded a convalescing woman to "walking patient".

When I arrived, this upgraded patient was sitting in a rickety bamboo chair with a hurt look on her face, complaining to anyone who would listen about the injustice which had been done to her. As soon as she saw me, she lodged her protest, and then waited for my decision. But I said I would talk to her later, and went straight to see the new patient.

I had just given this emergency patient a sedative and said that the doctor would be along soon, when I heard screams coming from outside: "*Kapal udara datang*! Airplanes are coming!"

Eta said confidently that they would probably be American.

"Finally, they are coming to our aid," I agreed, feeling uplifted also.

It took a great effort to keep the patients in their beds: everyone wanted to see the landing of the Americans! Uncle Peter and Eta ran to the beach to get a better view.

I could not get away just then as I was changing the bandages of Gerret Teng. I heard the airplanes getting closer. Would they really land? What if they were Japanese? I asked myself.

Then I heard an acute whistling sound I had not heard before. It cut through the air, which, shortly after, was rent asunder by a loud explosion. It was followed by more explosions and the repeated drone of airplanes flying low over our heads.

With Gerret in my arms, I hurried outside and into my neighbor's trench. Boki, her children and servants were crying, huddled together, their hands over their ears to protect them from the deafening explosions.

Outside, people ran screaming in all directions, shouting that the *kota* was burning. I crawled out of the shelter, and saw thick, black smoke rising from the city, while the explosions continued. The sky seemed to be full of airplanes unloading their bombs on the city.

Eta and Uncle Peter came running towards me. Calm suddenly, I handed Gerret Teng over to Uncle Peter and asked him to take him back to the hospital, sure now that our Kampung Sangaji was not the target.

I pointed to the Red Cross arm-band that Eta was wearing and quietly said: "Come, Eta, we must go." Eta did not answer and looked at me with fear in her dilated eyes, but then she followed me. Together we walked to the ravaged city, where our help would surely be needed.

Along the way, we passed streams of fleeing people, carrying some of their belongings with them. They shouted that all of Kampung Tidore[2] was in flames, as were the large KPM storage sheds. Some of them yelled to us to turn back. All of them dropped flat on their bellies as several planes thundered low overhead and, as soon as the planes had passed, they picked themselves up and continued running. Where to?

From above the Sultan's palace, two airplanes dove down on the street in which Eta and I were running. For a moment it seemed they were gliding down noiselessly. Then, the pilots gunned their engines and pulled up as we dove into a ditch. Bombs whistled through the air and hit the *kampung* from where the fleeing people had just come.

We ran across the large field in front of the *Kedaton*, and found shelter in another ditch near Kampung Makassar. Running and ducking away in this manner, we reached the city of Ternate, where the road was barricaded. Close by lay two soldiers — they were beyond our help.

We worked our way through the barbed wire, and ran to the area where I knew a First Aid station had been set up. We encountered three Dutchmen who were running away from the down town area, instead of helping the wounded.

"Idiots!" they shouted at us, "Get out of here!"

"Cowards!" we shouted back outraged, and continued on our way.

Everywhere we saw the destruction of the bombardment that was continuing. From Kampung Tidore — where flames spurted high into the air — came cries of anguish and cries for help. The large storage sheds near the harbor were also engulfed in towering flames and over the city hung black clouds of smoke.

We encountered a number of Red Cross workers, who were using primitive stretchers to carry badly-wounded people to the First Aid station that we were still trying to locate. They gave us directions as to how to get there.

The First Aid station had been set up in the roomy air-raid shelter of a large school. There I found Dr. Hassan treating the wounded, aided by the orderly and a prisoner who knew something about nursing.

It was a pandemonium. Terribly wounded people were simply lying on the tiled floor, waiting their turn. They were strangely quiet — only their eyes were begging for help.

A woman was carried in. One arm had been torn off; in the other she held a baby of several weeks. A hysterical little girl clung to her blood-drenched *sarong*. The mother begged us to help her two little ones. Several minutes later, she was dead.

We bandaged the wounded, consoled the dying, advised the desperate, and sent those who had been bandaged on to the field hospital.

We had a number of volunteers when we started, but as the bombs continued to fall, they slipped away, one by one. Finally there were just five of us attending to the many, many wounded, who silently cried for help.

The dead were carried off to one corner and their places immediately taken by others who had just arrived. Our medical supplies were running out; there were no more bandages. We poured *peru balsam* over the wounds, and bound them up with clothes that had been torn into strips.

I knew there was a supply of bandages in the nunnery, and wanted to go and get them.

"There are still planes above the city. It is much too dangerous!" Dr. Hassan protested. But we had to have bandages, so I left the air-raid shelter and carefully looked around before fully emerging.

From the less-seriously wounded, who had been waiting their turn under a *canary* (Javanese almond) tree, I heard that — though planes were still in the air — the bombing had stopped and that people had gone back into the city and Kampung Tidore to look for survivors.

# IBU MALUKU

I decided I would chance it.

I took a shortcut through nearby fields, and came upon the incinerated remains of a man, shrivelled up like a roasted animal. Close to the torso, both legs had been cut off, and these stood straight up in their boots, unburned, a little further on. From the remnants of the clothes, the puttees and the hob-nailed boots, I gathered they had belonged to a soldier. Sick to my stomach, I ran on.

The nunnery and the schools had not been badly damaged and I safely reached the room where I knew the bandages could be found. The departing nuns had locked the door, so I had to go back outside and break a window to get into the store. With a priceless supply of bandages, I ran back. We would have enough — for a while.

The heat of the day was tapering off and it was getting quite late, but the treatment of the wounded continued unabated. Dr. Hassan confirmed that twenty-nine of the wounded had died, and eight were close to death. We wondered how many more dead there would be in the surrounding *kampungs* and in the storage sheds near the harbour.

Hesitatingly, several soldiers with less serious wounds entered to ask for treatment. From them we heard that, at the sound of the approaching planes, they had been ordered to leave their barracks and retreat to a nutmeg plantation located behind the *kota*. To do so, they'd had to work their way through barricades and had been wounded by barbed wire and other entanglements. We gave them a bottle of iodine and band aids, and asked them to help themselves.

While bandaging each other, they looked dazedly at the human misery around them. Then they left with a message for Captain Zondag, asking him to send soldiers who could carry some of our wounded to the field hospital, and to commandeer some *kampung* houses for their convalescence.

At seven, in the dark, the evacuation of the wounded started, which gave us more room. But soon, new victims arrived from the surrounding *kampungs*. This ultimately forced us to leave the school's air-raid shelter and move into the school itself, where we treated the wounded on benches that had been shoved together.

Outside raged an inferno. The fires, which burned particularly fiercely in the large copra sheds that were filled to capacity, threw an eery blood-red light on the surrounding area. And the roar of the crackling flames mingled with screams for help to give a vivid image of what hell could be like.

Dr. Hassan was dead-tired, the orderly could hardly stand up, the auxiliary male nurse (the prisoner) had disappeared, and Eta was close to fainting. But, somehow, we persevered! I do not remember when the last patients arrived, nor how they were treated and transported to the hospital; nor when we ourselves left the school.

People found me early next morning, sitting on the ground in the open air, fast asleep, propped up by a garden gate. Friendly hands carried me home and laid me on my cot. It was there that I awoke when John touched me and tried to wash the blood from my arms.

Dr. Hassan, overwrought and still tired from lack of sleep, started again at ten, assisted by Uncle Peter, the midwife, several nursing assistants, Eta and myself. Eta's nerves were raw, but she put up a good fight.

We were once again running short on supplies, however. With permission from the Magistrate, Police Inspector Schïauta broke open the seal of a deserted shop, where Dr. Hassan and I found the bandages, cotton-wool, towels, pillow slips, plates and mugs we so desperately needed.

In total, the bombardment had killed 59 people, wounded more than one hundred, made hundreds of people homeless, and had sowed terror into the hearts of the population.

The fire in the copra and coal sheds burned an entire week. The large KPM shed provided a bewildering and dangerous firework display for several nights — apparently, it had contained a large cache of ammunition.

When the fires were finally burned out, we found the remains of six people. Two of them were soldiers; the other four must have been civilians.

It would be the only time that the Japanese bombed Ternate.

**Endnotes**
[1] *Boki*, (which means princess), the daughter of the Sultan of Bachan, was married to the eldest brother of the Sultan of Ternate, and would eventually have 16 children. She and Jeanne van Diejen would develop a friendship that would last a lifetime.
[2] Ternate is surrounded by several villages, of which Kampung Tidore (not to be confused with the island of Tidore) was one.

## IBU MALUKU

# CHAPTER 31

## Surrender
### Ternate, January - April, 1942

In the days following the bombardment, several heavily wounded patients died, but others — even those with severe flesh wounds — were doing reasonably well, considering that they had received only rudimentary medical care.

Not wanting to risk losing our medical supplies in possible future raids, we moved some of them from the city to several spread-out locations near the Sangaji field hospital.

The panic that existed during the bombardment had decreased a little, but the news that the Japanese had taken Menado — only 156 nautical miles from Ternate — caused many natives from around the city to move inland. The Chinese followed suit and settled far into the Gamalama foothills, which made my life more difficult and dangerous. Most Chinese babies entered the world at night, when it was pitch black. Also, the mothers often had "retained placentas" that had to be removed manually and doing this in very dim light — blackout regulations were strictly enforced there too — became a perilous undertaking. But each case enhanced my reputation, and members from this community began to ask for my help even more often.

A buggy and a driver had been put at my disposal to travel to these Chinese patients. The little old horse's name was Annie, and the driver was called Pia (a strange combination, I thought, for these decidedly female names did not match the gender of either of them).

Along the roads leading into the foothills ran deep *slokkans* (ditches) to carry off rain water. Often, the wheels of the buggy would run on the rim of these ditches, which made me yell out in fear. Invariably, out of the darkness would come the soothing voice of the driver: "*Jangan takut, Pia pegang Annie, Annie sudah tahu jalanya* — Don't be afraid, Pia is firmly holding Annie, and Annie knows the way."

Small comfort!

\*\*\*\*

Two weeks after the bombing raid, I ventured a second trip to Halmahera.

At first, the Sultan's boatman refused to take me across the strait. With the Japanese being in the immediate vicinity, it was just too dangerous, he said. However, he finally agreed to take me under cover of night, when he thought it would be considerably safer.

When we arrived in the harbor of Jailolo, it was unusually quiet at the quay. The boatman called out and then waited. Silence. He called again. Then, out of the darkness, came a shaky voice asking who was there. The boatman's response seemed satisfactory, for the voice then invited us to approach the pier.

We threw out a rope and tied up to the pier. Only after we had been carefully inspected by the light of a lantern, were we allowed to disembark. We heard then that they had thought we were the enemy and that, from a nearby cove, the District Chief had sent a swift *prau* to Ternate to warn the authorities that the Japanese had landed!

It was just as well that the *prau* would not reach Ternate until many hours later. An immediate armed response to such alarming news could have embroiled us in a very sticky situation. We *hoped* that the authorities in Ternate would understand that the Sultan's *prau* had been mistaken for a Japanese vessel, but we could not be sure!

Jailolo was almost deserted, for all members of the Government of the Interior had been evacuated to the same camp where the wives of the military were housed. Only the District Chief, the *Mantri* (hospital orderly), the Kampung Head and a small civil guard were left.

Escorted by the District Chief, the *Mantri*, and several men from a neighboring *kampung* — all armed with machetes — we left immediately, and walked for the next five hours by the light of a single lantern.

Very early in the morning we arrived at the evacuation camp. All was quiet; not a soul stirred. Without waking anyone, I installed myself on the front veranda belonging to the Doctor's wife and got a few hours of much-needed sleep.

At eight I started the clinic. I examined the pregnant women and distributed medicine — also to the people from neighboring *kampungs*.

This time I was assisted by the *Mantri* from Jailolo. He had come with me to set up an emergency clinic nearby to meet the needs of civilians who had fled inland from the more vulnerable coastline. I made a mental note that, in case of emergency, the "military" women and children could get treatment there also.

An approaching delivery forced me to stay that night. The District Chief had to get back, though, and left alone. The baby was born close to midnight, and it was 1:30 by the time I went to bed.

The next day, after doing some final checkups, I walked at a relaxed pace back to Jailolo. I savored finally being alone; the 30 kilometer-long trip gave me the opportunity to reflect on what had happened since my departure from Tobelo.

A feeling of gratitude suddenly washed over me. I was quite reconciled now to having been drafted, since there was obviously important work for me to do. I did think a moment of Mon Désir, and was able, finally, to let it go!

It was dusk when I reached Jailolo. I went first to the house of the District Chief — who had made it safely back the previous day — to thank him for his assistance, and then proceeded to the harbor.

At the quay, I discovered that the Sultan's motorized *prau* was full of produce — gifts from the local population to those in Ternate who had survived the bombardment. This expression of sympathy touched me deeply, and it would greatly help the victims!

It was completely dark when we left the deserted port of Jailolo for Ternate, and five hours later we tied up at the Sultan's pier. From the palace guards I learned that the false alarm from the District Chief of Jailolo had not caused so much as a ripple. Relieved, I trotted down the road to Kampung Sangaji.

Eta had stayed up for me again, and reported that my pregnant neighbor, the Sultan's sister-in-law, Boki, was convinced that she was near her time. Sure enough, the next day she delivered a healthy baby girl.

\* \* \* \*

The days passed in nursing patients, helping midwives, or remaining glued to the radio.

The news from Europe was both good and bad: the Germans had been pushed back in Africa and Russia; but in the Netherlands, the persecution of Jews was in full swing and Dutch students were being rounded up and deported to labor camps.

In South East Asia, things were going from bad to worse. The Japanese had taken Kuala Lumpur (Malay Peninsula) and were advancing rapidly throughout the Dutch East Indies. Ambon was attacked on January 31, and surrendered several days later.

On February 4, the Allied fleet under Dutch Rear-Admiral Doorman attacked a Japanese convoy in the Strait of Makassar, but turned back after heavy attacks by Japanese bombers from Kendari (Celebes), which badly damaged the American light cruiser USS *Marblehead*[1].

Makassar was taken on February 9. Singapore and its 70,000 defenders with all their gear, artillery and vehicles, fell into Japanese hands on February 11. Banjermasin (Borneo), Bali and Timor followed within the following nine days. It was all most disheartening!

On February 18, an Allied strike force[2] under Doorman sailed from Tjilatjap (Java) in search of the Japanese fleet, and on February 27, the Battle of the Java Sea took place. The Dutch cruisers *Java* and *de Ruyter* went down with heavy loss of lives — Rear-Admiral Doorman included.

It seemed to be clear sailing for the Japanese, and on the night of February 28, they landed 60,000 men in three places on Java. We hardly dared to listen to more: It was clear that the Dutch East Indies was lost!

We also worried about the civilians who had left with the *Honun Maru* on December 27. What had happened to them? Would they now be in Japanese hands?

Thinking about them made me relive the unpleasant exchange I'd had with the high-ranking civil servant of Ternate, who had signed the order that called me up for national service. Before the *Honun Maru* left, he had ordered me to accompany his family to an unknown destination, on board of the only available Government steamer.

I refused. National service, in my view, did not oblige me to become his personal servant. The voyage of his family was a private matter, not a public one.

Of course, my refusal made him angry. In the presence of His Highness Mohammed Iskander Jahir Shah, Sultan of Ternate, he yelled that if I persisted in my refusal, I would forfeit the protection of the Kingdom of the Netherlands forever!

With a clear conscience, I replied calmly that in that case I would place myself in the hands of His Highness, the Sultan. To my relief, this protection was immediately and graciously granted. From that day on, I had little contact with this official and when, through force of circumstances we did meet, the encounter was of course severely strained.

From the very start of the war, he had spent most of his time sailing about on a *prau* that was camouflaged to look like an island, coming to the *kota* only to receive his pay check. He would then go to the hospital, where Dr. Hassan and the Magistrate regularly had their meals with me, and helped himself to our meager supplies. In recompense, he had nothing better to do than malign and cast suspicions on the three of us! War, it seems, sometimes brings out the worst in people!

\*\*\*\*

John continued to do guard duty. He also participated in training exercises — one of which had a slapstick ending, reminiscent of the bumbling Keystone Cops of the silent movie era.

On this day, the militia, consisting of 102 conscripts, was divided into two opposing groups: one to defend Fort Orange; the other to attack it. The career officers were, of course, inside the fortress to direct its defense — sure of its impregnability.

The attackers, with John in command, crept up on the *bèntèng* (fortress). Everything remained quiet inside. The men crawled into the dry moat, through the tall grass and up the high wall to the heavy gate, without meeting any resistance.

The attackers then planned on a ruse to get themselves inside. They pounded on the heavy door and commanded that it be opened in the name of Her Majesty the Queen, and sure enough, it was opened. The career officers rushed in to stop this foolishness, but were too late!

Infuriated, Captain Zondag chewed out the leader of the defending group for having opened the gate to the enemy. The leader answered wryly: "Is not enemy, Captain, is mister from Mon Désir!"

Many a time we laughed about this not too successful exercise!

\* \* \* \*

On March 1, the NIROM exultantly announced the first Allied air attack on Berlin, but the news from the Dutch East Indies, as usual, was all bad!

The Allied forces on Java, we heard, consisted of 11,000 KNIL soldiers, 10,000 English (mainly ground personnel of the RAF who had escaped from Singapore), not more than 3,000 Australians and 500 Americans. On the morning of March 1, a Japanese column had taken the Kalijati airport of Bandung by surprise, and four days later, Batavia fell.

On March 9, Java capitulated. At 11:00, the NIROM unexpectedly played the "Wilhelmus", the Dutch national anthem, and the announcer, Bert Garthoff, then said: "*Wij sluiten nu. Vaarwel! Tot betere tijden! Leve de Koningin!* We are closing now. Farewell! Till better times! Long live the Queen!"

It was over! We would now only have the BBC from Hong Kong and the Australian radio stations to listen to for news of the world situation.

From that moment on, all armed forces on Ternate wore a white band wrapped around the right arm and over Fort Orange fluttered a white flag to signal surrender. Our soldiers were still doing guard duty, but their carbines were not loaded.

The civilians in Ternate — mostly Dutch, Javanese, Timorese and Ambonese — were deeply shocked, but a few Menadonese among them seemed less sincere in expressing their regrets. The local population was unanimous in their support for the Netherlands, except the Arabian community, which became more insolent and arrogant with each passing day. This was certainly noticeable in the hospital, where they would no longer ask for medical aid, but demand it.

This demoralizing situation continued until an unexpected radio message arrived for Captain Zondag. It said, "The free troops on Ternate, Northern New Guinea, and the small group on Celebes under Lieutenant de Jong[3], must continue their resistance against the enemy!" The telegram was signed by General L. H. van Oyen, and was sent from Australia!

The euphoria of our soldiers is difficult to describe. They jubilantly ripped off the hated white arm bands and trampled them underfoot! At Fort Orange, the white flag was replaced by our tri-color. All over the island, the soldiers took up their guard posts with gusto and, this time, armed to the teeth!

\*\*\*\*

We assembled again around the radio with renewed enthusiasm.

On March 17, I heard that U.S. General MacArthur had escaped from the Philippines and had safely arrived in Australia.

On April 5, the remaining British and U.S. ships were forced to withdraw from the Indian Ocean towards Australia, with the Japanese fleet in hot pursuit. For the first time, we heard the name of Admiral Yamamoto, who would likely lead the attack on Port Moresby, Australia. If Australia fell also, who could possibly protect us then from a Japanese invasion?

Still, the mood was guardedly optimistic.

The few KNIL patrols that had been stationed at various places on Halmahera were recalled, since most of the soldiers were ill and required medical aid. The first group of six was admitted to our field hospital on March 29. Each soldier had a severe case of eczema.

Some traders — including the Chinese — returned from the interior to reopen their *tokos* (shops), seemingly assured that, even if the island was occupied, it would be "business as usual". It would be to the advantage of the Japanese, so they reasoned, to have life resume its normal course. Truly, a very optimistic view!

Dr. Hassan, in consultation with the military and civilian authorities, decided to reopen the civilian hospital in Ternate, as most of the exiled citizenry wanted to return to the immediate vicinity of the city. Before we could use it, however, the hospital needed to be thoroughly cleaned and whitewashed. The roof and the walls needed to be inspected and, where necessary, repaired, and the yard had to be cleaned of weeds. A group of laborers were put to work to do just that.

While that was in progress, I made another trip to the evacuation camp on Halmahera, where everybody turned out to be in excellent health. On the orders of Captain Zondag I had brought provisions and medical supplies, and stowed them away in several safe spots for future use. For the time being, this group would be well taken care off.

At the request of the Magistrate and Dr. Hassan, I brought their families back with me to Ternate, where their return to the city was celebrated in high spirits. Their presence made life much more enjoyable.

On Good Friday, April 3, our patients were moved from Kampung Sangaji to the revamped civilian hospital in the *kota* of Ternate. The next day we held clinic there for the first time since December, 1941. All beds were occupied: seven by soldiers; the remainder by civilians. The maternity ward held five mothers-to-be.

I was even given permission to furnish a room of my own! Finally, I could enjoy a measure of privacy that had been missing since I'd left Tobelo. I was overjoyed — and John was my first visitor!

That year, 1942, Easter fell on April 5. Amidst much cheer, I treated every patient to a colored Easter egg — for many, a first! Boiled in an infusion of onion skins, they had a pleasing brown color. It was a good opportunity to do something festive, and the patients certainly appreciated it.

There was a service in the presbytery — the first one I had been able to attend since that depressing Christmas Mass in the blacked-out shed where the Doctor's wife and the nuns lived. Our thoughts went out fondly, and also sorrowfully, to those who were absent, and we wondered if they were still alive.

That morning, Radio Australia announced that the Japanese had bombed Ceylon, and that on Sumatra the KNIL was still making a strong stand against the invaders.

"Would that do any good?" I asked myself, being somewhat puzzled by the news. Although Java had capitulated, it appeared that fighting against the enemy was still going on in isolated regions of the Dutch East Indies.

John was convinced that liberation would come in time from Australia, and all those present seemed to agree with him.

"Our area and the North East Coast of New Guinea have not been invaded so far," they argued. "The Japs seem to have no interest in occupying these remote islands, so there is every reason to be optimistic!"

Easter Sunday and Easter Monday were spent in a much more peaceful and enjoyable atmosphere than we had experienced for many months. Late in the afternoon, John and a fellow militiaman paid a short visit to the hospital while en route to a guard post at the northern point of the island. I drove them there in the car that had been put at my disposal, and we thoroughly enjoyed the beautiful surroundings.

At the so-called "Burned Corner", where several hundred years ago an enormous stream of lava had flowed into the sea from the now faintly-smoking Gamalamo mountain, we stopped momentarily to admire the weathered, but still imposing, black lava flow.

Then we drove to Kampung Sulamadahe, where John would have to stand guard, overlooking the Molucca Sea which separated us from now occupied Celebes — a mere 156 nautical miles away!

\* \* \* \*

The night of Easter Monday brought much work: two new world citizens saw the light of day. It was the early morning of April 7 when I finished the preparations for "entrusting the placentas to the waves".

Following local tradition, I carefully rinsed the placentas, wrapped them in a new white piece of cloth, and placed them in earthenware jugs that had been provided by the fathers. I intended to let these jugs slip into the sea from the hospital's small pier, adjacent to the bathrooms. The two *saudara muda* (the placentas were called "younger brothers") would then float away and thus could not harm the living, according to local belief.

Outside under the heavens it seemed to be much brighter than inside the hospital. Over the sea hung a light mist, and a faint streak of light was discernable in the distance. I walked down the pier, knelt next to the first bathroom on the damp planks, squatted on my haunches, and let the pots slide one by one into the sea.

I remained in that position for a moment to rest my back, which hurt from the long night and lack of sleep. Using my right hand to push myself up, I inadvertently looked in a northerly direction and thought I saw something far out to sea. I was not quite sure, though. The light was still so faint, and because of the haze I could be wrong — but I thought I saw the outline of ships.

I walked to the end of the pier and washed my hands. Feeling uneasy, I went back to the first bathroom, where I could scan the horizon from a higher vantage point.

Was I imagining things? I really thought I saw something in the distance, but was not sure enough to call the two young fathers, who were the only ones awake at that hour. Ten minutes later, as daylight grew, I was almost sure that, far in the distance, there were indeed ships that were sailing toward Ternate.

## IBU MALUKU

I walked back to the hospital, woke up the KNIL soldier-patients, and told them what I had seen. They were not alarmed at all! On the contrary. If there were really ships out there, they said, they just had to be the Americans who were coming to our aid! I did not believe this, but did not know why.

Thinking about the safety of the hospital, I asked them to give me their weapons and uniforms. I did not want any military gear in the hospital, I said. But they refused and I went back to the pier with empty hands.

Again, my eyes scanned the horizon. Now there was absolutely no doubt. There were ships there! I ran back inside, and, ignoring the soldiers' protests, picked up their uniforms and carbines, and rolled them into bundles. I ran back outside, down the pier, and threw the bundles near the bathrooms into the sea, knowing I was doing something for which I could be held accountable. Yet, what choice did I have? Luckily, the sea was deep here; it would not be easy to spot the bundles on the bottom.

When I returned, the other patients were awake, and I instructed the night shift to give them breakfast. Nervously, I urged the staff to quickly make the usual preparations for the day.

Having mobilized them, I had a minute to look outside. In Fort Orange there was no sign of life, of course, for all the soldiers had been dispatched to observation posts around the island after the arrival of General van Oyen's order.

I remembered I needed to get a baby weighing scale from the military hospital inside the fort. I still had the key for the apothecary in my possession — it had been given to me so I could transfer all medical supplies to the civilian hospital. If those ships were Japanese, I might not have another chance. So I snatched the key from the rack, ran to the fort, came out fifteen minutes later with the wanted scale, locking the apothecary behind me, and returned to the hospital. Mission accomplished!

It was six now, and the sun rose triumphantly. As always, a majestic event! The ships could now be clearly seen. They appeared to have come from Menado, and moved ever so slowly. But who were they — friend or foe?

Outside the hospital, people had spotted the approaching armada, and the patients who could walk tried to get closer to the pebbled beach. I sent them back inside and asked two young male nurses to keep everyone calm.

Shortly before seven, a destroyer detached itself from the others and sailed at close quarters past the hospital toward the main docks, south of the city. Its deck was deserted, and it carried no flag. It disappeared from view as it entered the harbor, reappeared a moment later, and then sailed at greater speed northward to join the other ships that were drawing near.

I looked with awe at the approaching fleet: "My God! There are so many of them," I said aloud.

They formed a single line, in what must have been a pre-arranged order, and steamed one after the other past the hospital. The clattering of anchor chains tore through the air. Right in front of the hospital, a large cruiser dropped anchor, its deck also completely deserted.

Then, slowly, all the ships hoisted flags at the stern. They did not unfurl — there was not even a whisper of wind — but we detected splotches of red and white. No one knew the Japanese ensign; everyone knew the American flag had red, white and blue. The blue was probably hidden from view, we convinced ourselves. This *had* to be the American fleet.

"But why aren't the Americans showing themselves?" asked the onlookers.

At exactly eight, we heard the drone of airplanes taking off. So there had to be an aircraft carrier there that no one had noticed before. Of course, none of us knew what an aircraft carrier looked like. As soon as the airplanes were up in the air, the decks of the ships became alive with thousands of men.

The planes flew low over the *kota*. In nervous haste I directed the patients into the trench. Apprehensive, I squatted near the new mothers, keeping their babies cradled in my arms. Thinking about the horrible bombardment we'd had earlier, I prayed for protection. But I did not hear the expected sharp whistle of falling bombs, nor any explosions.

Someone came running toward the trench, and said the airplanes had dropped something over the city — what, he did not know. But shortly after, Dr. Hassan came, accompanied by a Javanese agricultural consultant. They brought one of the pamphlets that had been dropped by the planes. It was hot of the press — the ink not quite dry.

They read the contents, which was composed in bad Malay. In blustering language it said that, after three and a half centuries of exploitation and domination of the Indonesian people by the Dutch, the hour of liberation of the chained population by Dai Nippon (Greater Japan) was at hand. There was more inflammatory language, and at the end, the Japanese called on the population to take all the Netherlanders prisoner and deliver them alive to the Japanese Marine, the representative of Dai Nippon. They were given one hour in which to do it.

# IBU MALUKU

I looked Dr. Hassan and his companion in the eye. I knew both were staunch nationalists, although neither of them had, during the months of our association, ever uttered a word about their somewhat inimical views. But times had changed and I couldn't guess what was in their hearts.

I stuck out both hands in a gesture of surrender. After all, they were supposed to arrest me and deliver me to the Japanese.

Indignantly they pushed my hands away and stated that they did not, for the time being, feel compelled to take orders from the Japanese. In this difficult time, they said, they only wanted to be friends and, where possible, to help me. The other inhabitants of the island seemed to have the same train of thought, because the hour passed without one Netherlander having been taken prisoner!

For the second time, planes took off to drop pamphlets. This time they were written in scrambled Dutch and English, and addressed directly to the civilian and military authorities.

In crude wording, they issued an ultimatum: the Military Commander, Assistant Resident, *Controleur* and all civil and military Netherlanders were to assemble at the pier within one hour. Also, white flags were to be hoisted at the fort and all public buildings, signaling surrender. If these orders were not followed, Ternate would be flattened.

They were serious alright, for the batteries of all ships swung around to face the city. The guns of the cruiser in front of us were now aimed directly at the hospital. I was almost ill with fear.

Some of the walking patients immediately left the hospital to seek shelter in the moat behind the fort. It seemed the right thing to do — Fort Orange was the only place that would afford some protection against a naval bombardment.

I kept the most serious patients and the new mothers in the trench, and looked after them as well as the circumstances permitted. All were surprisingly calm.

Every few minutes, I stuck my head out and nervously scanned the surrounding area, hoping to see a white flag going up somewhere. But nothing of that sort happened. I wondered if there was something I should be doing, and thought about the horror that would ensue if the Japanese order was ignored. Offering resistance, with less than 200 poorly-armed soldiers who were spread all over the island, would not make any sense.

I left the trench, and walked despairingly through the hospital. There were so many patients here, and they would surely die if the Japanese carried out their threat.

The time passed. Ten minutes were left; then only five. When the old clock chimed ten, the airplanes took off from the aircraft carrier and flew to the northerly point of the island — the area where John was posted, I realized with a shock. Shortly after, we heard bombs hitting their targets. The patients screamed and wanted to flee, but where to?

I saw *Controleur* Sjirk van der Goot running toward the hospital. I ran out to meet him, shouting from afar "What is being done to stop this bombardment?"

The visibly shaken civil servant, tears streaming down his cheeks, could only sputter: "The Assistant Resident is gone. The military have gone. There isn't a soul to be seen on the pier!"

We turned toward the Sultan's palace: no white flag there either!

We could now more clearly hear the impact of exploding bombs. The sky was full of airplanes. On the cruiser we could see men running to man the batteries. I could not stand it any longer and screamed: "We've got to hoist the white flag! Do you want all these people butchered?"

Drained, the man looked at me and said: "But I am not permitted to do that. I could be accused of treason!"

An icy calm settled over me, and I said I would do it and take full responsibility for it. I just had to!

I ran back into the hospital and tore a sheet from one of the beds. The *Controleur*, who had followed me inside, now sprang into action, and helped me attach the sheet to a long bamboo pole. Together, we carried this flag to the hospital's pier and attached the pole to the wall of the bathroom, praying that it would be quickly noticed.

We both wondered out aloud, if, by this act, we had committed treason and cringed at the thought of what could happen as a result. Still, we agreed it had to be done to save thousands of innocent lives.

Then a miracle occurred. From the deck of the cruiser in front of us, there was much signaling with flags. We heard one more bomb exploding, and then saw the airplanes turn back from the north.

We crouched behind a corner of the bathroom, expecting the city to be bombed next. But the planes passed over us and returned to their carrier. It looked as if Ternate had been saved!

Tears coursed down our cheeks as we shook hands and reassured the people who had gathered around us. Then I saw the *Controleur's* shoulders sag. His face became drawn.

"What is the matter?" I asked, dismayed.

Barely audible, he said: "Now I shall have to go to the Japanese ships to surrender the city," and then he slowly walked away.

I understood how difficult this was for him. I could not let him walk this agonizing road by himself, and ran after him. Also, if ever our action were to be judged as treasonable, there should be two to testify as to what had happened.

Together, we walked along the beach road looking for a boat that could take us to the fleet and came upon a beached *prau*. Inside crouched two old fishermen, who, without moving a muscle, were staring transfixed at the fleet.

The *Controleur* called out to them. Terrified, they turned around. Recognizing him, they relaxed a little and got up. When the *Controleur* asked them to row us to the cruiser, they trembled with fright, but did not dare to refuse. The *prau* was quickly pushed in the water, and we had just climbed aboard when we heard running footsteps behind us and the voice of our doctor calling for us to wait.

He had seen the white flag and said resolutely: "I shall go with you. Who knows what may happen to you on board!" We were grateful for his offer — I think ... but I still wasn't sure where he stood in this conflict.

Hurriedly, the old fishermen rowed us to the cruiser — its huge guns still pointing towards the hospital. From the cruiser's deck, the Japanese had been watching our departure. When we came alongside, someone pointed a megaphone in our direction and a rough voice asked if we understood English. We nodded and were then instructed to go, immediately, to the flagship.

Nervously, we looked up at the high, dark hull of this enormous ship, and then looked around us: "Where is the flagship?" we asked.

Hand signals from above showed in which direction we should row, and only then did we see how many ships there really were. Dr. Hassan counted nineteen; among them were two captured KPM ships.

Suddenly I noticed that my shoes and the hem of my clothes were soaking wet: the *prau* was leaking badly. Automatically, I grabbed a coconut shell, and started to bail out the water, surprised at my even having noticed it under those tense circumstances.

After fifteen minutes, we reached an enormous ship. Dr. Hassan thought it was an aircraft carrier and since it was the largest of the entire fleet, we assumed it to be the flagship. The high gangway had already been lowered for us. The *Controleur* instructed the rowers to tie up the *prau* at the bottom of the stairs and wait for our return. They nodded and then huddled together, making themselves again as small as possible.

We climbed the stairs: the two men in front, with me next. Finally we reached the enormous deck with airplanes at the far side, and just stood there looking around with boundless surprise.

Five minutes passed; then, ten. Surely, the Japanese knew we had arrived, but no one came! Then it dawned on us that we were deliberately being ignored!

Many sailors busily walked forth and back in front of us — not saying a word and pretending we were not there. Some of them almost walked into us, and others walked between us and the railing, forcing us to take a step forward or backward. It did not do much for our self confidence.

We stood stiffly beside each other, with me in the middle. I often had to wipe the cold sweat from my hands and clench my fists in a vain attempt to appear calm. Our discomfort must have clearly shown on our faces.

Finally a Japanese civilian appeared, dressed in a stylish shantung[4] suit, a smart tie, and a white tropical helmet that sat nonchalantly on his head. A cigarette dangled from one corner of his mouth. He sauntered toward us with an air of total indifference.

"Mr. Igawa!" I exclaimed in surprise, almost relieved. This man had been raised in Ternate, the son of the proprietor of a large general store whom we had known and befriended for many years!

Had he heard me? He had, for his attitude changed all of a sudden. When I wanted to greet him, he cut me to the quick and snarled: "*Dulu lain, sekarang lain. Ingat itu!* — The past is the past, things are different today. Remember that!"

Then he stood in front of the *Controleur*, whom he knew very well. His face became cruel, his eyes narrowed, and his mouth twisted to express utmost contempt. In a language which only an arrogant master might use toward a lowly servant, he hissed: "*Siapa lu?* — Who the heck are *you*?"

The *Controleur's* face stiffened and became haughty and white with anger. He pulled himself up to his full height — he was now the civil servant who had always commanded respect — and in a clear, firm voice, he gave his name, his profession, and place of residence.

The Japanese then fired numerous questions at him: "Where is Captain Zondag? Where is the Assistant Resident? Where is ...?" and in quick succession, he called the name of each Dutch citizen of Ternate.

The *Controleur's* brief answer was always same: "*Saya tidak tahu!* I don't know!" And, it was true: he did not know, not having seen anyone for a week.

"The Assistant Resident and the Captain should have been at the quay," growled Igawa. "The bombardment was their fault and your denials do not help! Speak up! Where are they?"

## IBU MALUKU

The *Controleur* shrugged, and said: "I really don't know."

Igawa was getting worked up, and, giving the *Controleur* a withering look, threatened: "Within one hour, all *Belandas* on the quay, or else ..." and his index finger moved under the chin from ear to ear.

During the course of this conversation, a second Japanese had arrived. He had stood behind Igawa, dressed in shorts, an undershirt, and a Japanese Marine kepi with flaps on the back — obviously designed to protect his neck from the sun.

He had been listening to what Igawa said, sometimes nodding his head in agreement. For a Japanese, he was a tall man. His hands were moving all the time, trying impatiently to put his undershirt that continually worked its way up, back into his pants. His gestures irritated me and I hoped he would notice it from the look on my face.

Then Igawa moved to stand in front of me with the same arrogant attitude which he had displayed in front of the *Controleur*. I looked at him questioningly. Momentarily, he lost his composure, but then said bitingly: "*Kau bikin apa di sini?* What are you doing here?"

He obviously meant: what was I doing in Ternate. So I told him, quite calm now, that I had been called up for national service to take over the administration of the civilian hospital and then pointed to my Red Cross arm band.

"Why did you come on board?" he snarled.

In a steady voice I answered: "To ask that no violent acts be committed against the patients in the hospital, nor against the population of Ternate, who are innocents in this conflict."

Igawa appeared indignant, and said: "Nippon soldiers are not animals!"

Without thought for the possible consequences, I impulsively shot back: "*Ya, minta minta*! Let's hope so!"

He jumped at me with arm raised, and I braced for a slap in the face. But he controlled himself and in measured tones ordered: "You make sure that within the hour — and he glanced at his wristwatch — all Dutch women and children are on the quay!" And he rattled off all their names, and again threatened decapitation if the order was not carried out.

I told him there were no longer any Dutch women and children in Ternate, which got him close to losing self-control again, and he snarled: "Is that so? And where are they then? After December 8, there has been no ship here!"

I said that they had all left for an unknown destination with the *Honun Maru*. He did not seem to believe me and walked with short, angry paces to where Dr. Hassan stood.

Stressed as we were, we had not noticed that other people had come on board. We saw Igawa's face change expression and when, after a hand signal from the Japanese behind him, he walked around the doctor towards the newcomers, we dared to take a look ourselves. A large group of boys from the Arabian quarter, Kampung Makassar, had noiselessly climbed the stairs and now stood with brazen faces along the railing, waving little Japanese flags.

Igawa bore down on them and thundered in Malay: "You are not wanted on the deck of a Japanese warship! Get off immediately!"

The group looked at him in utter disbelief — obviously having expected a warmer welcome. Anxiety replaced the insolence on their faces and they disappeared down the gangway as quietly as they had arrived.

Igawa came back to resume his questioning of Dr. Hassan. It did not last long. Dr. Hassan said he had come to support the request I had made. Igawa did not give him further instructions, but briefly repeated his orders to the *Controleur* and myself and then told us to leave.

In a row, with me up front this time, we walked toward the gangway. From the top, I looked down and saw that our *prau* was about to sink; only the bow was still above water. In their anxiety, the two fishermen had forgotten to bail.

I told Igawa, who had joined me, that the *prau* was now useless. He agreed and looked up toward the other Japanese who was bent over the railing, looking down at the *prau* with a grin on his face.

They exchanged a few words — sharp, raw sounds. Igawa then turned toward me and stated solemn-faced in Malay: "When I told you that Japanese soldiers are not animals, you impolitely answered *"minta minta"*. Now you will see that I was right. The *Tuan Besar* (great gentleman) has given his approval that you be taken ashore in a motor-launch.

Spontaneously, I turned toward the senior officer, bowed politely, and said: *"Terima kasih, Tuan Besar!* Thank you, *Tuan Besar!"*

Looking at it afterwards, it must have been a grotesque sight: me, in a wrinkled dress and partially wet nurse's coat with windblown hair, and the *Tuan Besar* in shorts and an undershirt.

It would turn out later that this man was Fujita Ruitaro, Commander of the 1st and 2nd Invasion Support Units that were now preparing to occupy Ternate!

# IBU MALUKU

**Endnotes**

1. In 1944, Cecil B. DeMille made a movie, "The Story of Dr. Wassell", which tells how the wounded sailors of the USS *Marblehead* escaped from Java.
2. The Allied Fleet included five cruisers — the British *Exeter*, the U.S. *Houston*, the Australian *Perth*, and the Dutch *De Ruyter* and *Java* — and nine British, Dutch and U.S. destroyers. The Japanese had four cruisers and fourteen destroyers.
3. The guerilla war on Celebes against the Japanese is described in "Guerilla in Mori", by Michiel Hegener.
4. *Shantung* textile is a heavy pongee, i.e. a silk of slightly uneven weave.

# IBU MALUKU

IBU MALUKU

# CHAPTER 32

## Occupation
### Ternate, April, 1942

While waiting for the launch, I had the opportunity to look around. What impressed me most was the size of this aircraft carrier. The planes that had carried out the raid on Sulamadahe all seemed to have returned, and nothing on this enormous deck indicated that they might take off again soon.

Flag signals from this aircraft carrier resulted in the davits of all ships being turned to outboard position. The landing barges hanging from these davits were immediately manned and lowered, practically in unison.

The invasion had started!

The motor-launch that would take us to shore arrived at the bottom of the gangway. It was full of Japanese soldiers, but none of them carried a backpack or arms — as was the case with those in the landing barges. Evidently, these soldiers had been assigned administrative duties. Igawa was already on board.

We got in and found a seat. To my surprise, the launch was towing the fishing *prau* that had brought us. Igawa ordered the fishermen, in the local dialect, to start bailing. Several hundred meters before we reached the quay, Igawa ordered us to cross over into the fishing *prau*, and, after we had complied, said, "You may no longer disembark at the quay. It can only be used by us, the conquerors!"

Our rowers did not understand this, however, and rowed as hard as they could to get to shore first. After all, they had *their Controleur* as a passenger, and he surely had precedence over those foreigners!

Slowly they shortened the lead the heavy launch had over us. The end result was a tie: we mounted the pier's stairway at the same time Igawa did! Igawa growled, but that was all, and the three of us marched smartly ahead of him down the long pier.

From the quay, we had a spectator's view of the invading forces. The long beach was crawling with running, screaming Japanese soldiers. Each one wore a grey-green kepi and canvas shoes with a separate big toe (to us they looked like monkey's feet), and carried a backpack and a rifle with a long bayonet attached. It was not a pleasant sight.

On the quay itself, everything seemed to be well organized. Japanese with "walkie talkies" (a term we would learn only much later) were walking up and down, issuing a stream of orders. Signalmen laid down telephone lines and others replaced existing street signs by plaques with Japanese names.

Then, the plundering started. From all directions, the Japanese pushed or pulled carts, laden with bicycles, sewing machines, typewriters, and even rolled-up carpets. Everything was loaded into landing barges and transported to the ships.

They destroyed the furniture in the deserted homes of the Dutch and, in front of the Resident's office, built a fire to burn all government documents. It was an unholy mess and, forlorn, we zigzagged our way through this turmoil. Nobody paid any attention to us, which enhanced the feeling that we were merely spectators on a movie set.

The *Controleur* had to go to the Police Station to check on the situation there; Dr. Hassan said he wanted to go home and see if he could find shelter for his family outside the city; and I planned to return to the hospital. So we split up, each one going a different way.

Halfway to the hospital I stopped in my tracks, for I had suddenly remembered that in Brussels, in November of 1914, one could only move about if one had the proper identity papers. Without them, one encountered innumerable problems. That could very well happen again.

So I turned around and retraced my steps towards the pier, determined at all costs to find Igawa. He certainly seemed an important enough person to give me such a certificate!

Arriving at the Resident's Office, I observed a semblance of order. Obviously, that was where the officers were getting settled in — at least, so I hoped. Unhindered by anyone, I entered the office from the gallery, and ran smack into the ever-present Igawa. Angrily he descended on me and snarled something I did not understand.

In Malay, I said I wanted to have a pass, as I was afraid the troops might take me prisoner and prevent me from carrying out his orders to care for my patients. He refused but I insisted.

A high ranking officer came out of the office. He had evidently heard *and* understood what I had said in Malay, because he handed me a scrap of paper with a small red stamp on it: apparently this was a pass for safe conduct. I thanked him, and beat a hasty retreat!

The road to the hospital seemed long. Several times, I became surrounded by screaming Japanese, who surged in waves from the beach into the *kota*. They released me when I waved my pass in their faces, but they still made mock attacks with their bayonets, which I had to dodge. Each time, I had to run to get away from those grinning tormentors.

As I passed Fort Orange, the Japanese were just launching an assault on it. Would they really think that the KNIL were waiting for them inside? I continued on my way, and finally, thank God, arrived safely at the hospital, which seemed to be deserted.

I walked through the empty women's ward to my room, intending to get out of my dirty, wet clothes. To my surprise, a soldier stood guard in front of the door: a Korean, judging by his height.

I walked up to him, and with gestures indicated I wanted to get inside, pointing to my wet clothes and my Red Cross arm band. He snarled something I did not understand but I accepted as a go ahead.

As I walked around him, I received a blow from his fist between my shoulder blades, and a second one came as I reached for the door knob. Then, he pushed the point of his bayonet against my back and forced me to walk through the hospital.

At his shouts, other soldiers came running in through the back entrance. Uttering unintelligible guttural sounds, they looked me up and down with a surprised look on their faces. They took me away from my captor and marched me to the open hall that looked out on the road.

Here, I had to stand against the wall with my hands up. I did not even get the chance to take the pass out of my pocket. Six bayonets in a semi-circle were pointing at me and, at intervals, the soldiers rushed at me with an awful yell. Each time, I thought my life would come to an end, but the bayonets always stopped — just in time.

They finally tired of this game and stopped, as four other Japanese soldiers entered the hall. The newcomers looked flabbergasted at the sight of a European woman but, luckily, had no interest in me. They had just plundered the shop of a Chinese goldsmith and dazzled their comrades with handfuls of sparkling, precious gems and wrist watches. They were obviously not used to seeing such things.

One of the new arrivals seemed to come from a better background than the others. He tried to say a few words in English, but I remained silent and avoided looking at him. That irritated him and he said, clearly this time, pointing to himself: "I help you," and he pulled my right arm down and forced me to take his rifle with the bayonet on it.

Terrified, I looked at him. What was he up to? I felt nauseous. Perhaps he noticed it for he took the rifle out of my hands and placed it against the wall, after detaching the bayonet.

Pointing the bayonet toward his stomach, he made a gesture of committing *hara kiri*[1] — the traditional Japanese atonement for disgrace, such as having been taken prisoner — and said: "You know, that means *neru neru*. Very good for you!" Then he offered me the bayonet. (*Neru neru*, so Marie had taught me, meant going to sleep). Resolutely, I pushed his hands away, and shook my head.

He looked at me, astonished. He knew that I had understood his meaning and had declined his offer. He shrugged his shoulders, picked up his rifle, and then walked out onto the hospital grounds.

The other soldiers were sprawled in front of me, playing some kind of game. Blissfully, nobody paid me any attention so I took the opportunity to listen closely to the sounds around me. It appeared that people were being brought into the hospital. How much I wanted to attend to their needs. One of the newly born babies was crying. Was it feeding time?

I was jolted back to the present, when I heard my captors grunt. They stiffened and listened intently to something that was happening outside. I now heard the rumble of wheels and the heavy footsteps of approaching troops.

My captors stopped their game and, once again, took up their threatening position around me. The troops came into view, carrying, pushing or pulling all kinds of armaments. They stopped in front of the hospital. Several soldiers with cruel, mask-like faces that spelled trouble, shouted unintelligible words to each other, left the horde and converged on my guards, screaming. To my astonishment, they started to beat them unmercifully ... and none of my guards offered any resistance!

Totally confounded, I was then taken prisoner by the newcomers and pushed roughly toward the street. Surrounded by machine guns and other armaments, I was triumphantly carried off by this sinister group through the gate and into the fort.

The *bèntèng* at first appeared totally deserted, but then I spotted a Dutchman sitting on his haunches under a large tree in the courtyard. I recognized him as the old Supply Master, a pensioned KNIL soldier.

Someone gave me a forceful shove from behind, and I tumbled at high speed in the Supply Master's direction. Whoever had pushed me bellowed something I did not understand, but I gathered that I was to squat down beside the other prisoner.

I suddenly remembered the pass in my pocket. I took it out, and held it up in the air so the red stamp could be seen. Then something unexpected happened. Talking loudly and uttering unintelligible sounds, the soldiers looked at it, gestured to me to stay where I was, and hastily left the *bèntèng*.

It became strangely quiet around us, and the old man told me how he had been taken from his house, and brought to the fort. His Chinese wife had not been permitted to join him. I then told him about my own adventures.

Outside the shade in which we were squatting, the sun shimmered on the white *karang* (coral) that covered the wide path leading from the gate into the courtyard. Only now did we become conscious of a terrible thirst, but we did not dare move.

The old gentleman started to nod. "What a blessing it is to be old," I thought. Then he woke up with a start, for from behind the fort we heard people yelling at each other in the Ternatan dialect. It did not sound reassuring.

We heard the people running outside the walls and then saw them enter the fort. They were natives, obviously intent on looting, for they were running toward the *gudang*, where the pharmacy was. They had not seen us and we counted ourselves lucky.

Moments later, I saw with dismay that priceless supplies were being thrown out of the smashed-in windows of the pharmacy. Many rolls of bandages fell apart. They stuffed everything they could find into sacks and bags they had brought with them.

The Supply Master, a resident of Ternate, recognized some of the looters. "Most of them are from Kampung Makassar," he whispered to me.

To my relief, a group of Japanese then entered through the gate and I quickly identified them as medical corpsmen! They were surprised to see us. With a sweep of the hand an officer signaled to me to get up and then pointed to my Red Cross arm band.

In reasonable German, he asked where the hospital was. I hurriedly explained that the only operating hospital was outside; then, pointing agitatedly to where the looting was still in full swing, I yelped: "Our pharmacy!"

Only then did the officer realize what was happening. A terse order sent his soldiers running towards the pharmacy. The looters, caught unawares, tried to flee, but it was too late. A few shots over their heads stopped the *jahats* (rascals) in their tracks.

One Japanese officer with a revolver lined them up against the wall with their hands up. What happened to the looters afterwards we would never know, for the old Supply Master and I were told to leave the fort and put things in order in the hospital outside. Never did I follow an order more gratefully!

In the hospital, the patients were delighted to see us. But the KNIL patients had been found out, despite all my precautions — it was the dog tags they were still wearing that had given them away. The Japanese soldiers had pulled them out of the bathrooms where they were hiding, given them a sound beating, and bound them to bamboo chairs that were placed outside in the glaring afternoon sun.

I cut the poor fellows loose, and brought them inside. Some patients I found in the trench, and a few others had hidden themselves in the *gudang* or the kitchen.

The seriously wounded patients lay terrified in their beds, ready to hide underneath at the slightest provocation. The new mothers were huddled together in a corner of the women's ward, their babies pressed tightly to their breasts. All were unharmed — thank God! My request to Igawa to protect the patients in the hospital seemed to have been respected. Or was it coincidence? I didn't know.

Not a single nurse or orderly could be found, though. All had fled and had left the patients to their own devices. This, I had definitely not expected, and a deep indignation rose up in me. There was not one Japanese in the hospital — even the guard in front of my room was now gone.

Relieved, I hurried off to the kitchen: the patients needed to eat and drink while it was still quiet. The water was quickly brought to a boil, and soon after, with the help of the old Supply Master and the walking patients, the *papeda*, or sago porridge, was distributed.

Next, I dispensed medicine and instructions, looked after babies and mothers, and helped wherever needed. And so the hours passed.

Outside, the air was heavy. I had closed the windows and doors as much as possible to keep the coolness in and yet have some air circulation, and waited for whatever would happen next.

By four in the afternoon, the heat started to lessen. There was a knock on the door, and I heard the voice of Dr. Hassan, who wanted to be let inside.

"I have come to get you," he said, "and I suggest that you put some clothes in a suitcase and take it with you. The Supply Master and the seven KNIL soldiers have to come also."

I was momentarily occupied with a baby and, therefore, did not react to his words right away. But Dr. Hassan did not lose a moment. He walked into my room and returned a moment later with a small suitcase in which he had packed some of my clothes.

"So they are in a hurry to take us away," I thought.

We walked slowly with our KNIL patients along the beach road to the downtown area. The sea was still full of landing barges traveling back and forth. The Japanese who landed at the quay never looked at us; they only paid attention to their own work.

Close to the house of the Resident, on the right side of the road, I saw several KNIL soldiers squatting together in the shade of a *johar* tree, guarded by a few Japanese soldiers. John was the only *Belanda* (Dutchman) among them. Even without a bamboo hat, he towered over his comrades. Thank God, he had not been wounded during the bombardment of Sulamadahe.

I did not dare stop, and walked on. A brief eye contact was all the moment offered and, as we passed the group, I heard John saying: "I haven't even had one cup of coffee all day!" Surreptitiously, he had made voice contact with me. But a response from me could trigger a violent response from his guards, so I marched on in complete silence.

A moment later, we encountered a group of civilian prisoners on the left side of the road. In their midst stood the *Controleur*. I was happy to see he had his wife and children with him, the youngest of which he held in his arms. But his boss, the Assistant Resident was nowhere to be seen.

Continuing on our way, we ran into a group of Japanese who were wearing Red Cross arm bands and turned out to be doctors. They wanted to know what was wrong with our KNIL patients. After I asked them to pull up the legs of their pants and take their shoes off, the doctors looked with repugnance at the weeping, crusty lesions on their legs and feet.

"Leprosy?" asked the doctors, pointing to the offending limbs.

"No!" Dr. Hassan and I answered indignantly at the same time. "Not leprosy, but eczema!"

They did not understand us, however. One doctor handed me a Malay/Japanese dictionary, which contained the word "lepra", heavily underlined, but did not list the word "eczema".

To convince them, I touched one of the afflicted legs, and slowly stated: "Eczema, not leprosy," but that only started the debate all over again.

Where was that German speaking doctor I had met earlier? As I looked around for him, I saw that the group of civilians was moving out, and that the soldiers in John's group were also on their feet, ready to move out.

Thinking that we would soon be boarding one of the ships, I picked up my suitcase to join the civilians, but a doctor stopped me and said in heavily accented English: "Stay here, you go back to hospital, and prisoners ..," pointing to John's group, "go to fort. Patients ..," pointing to the seven KNIL soldiers, " also go to fort." Tears welled up in my eyes and I let out a sigh of relief. The doctor just smiled.

In less than an hour I was back at the hospital, but stayed outside watching the fort until John's group and my KNIL patients had been taken inside. For the time being, they would be safe where they were.

Shortly after, I delivered a brand new baby into the world.

Back in my room, I had difficulty finding out what day it was, but with the help of a calendar I reckoned it was the night of April 7. I dared not switch on the radio, as it might invoke the wrath of a Japanese who might be passing by. To keep unwanted visitors from bothering me, I pasted a piece of paper on my door, which announced in large letters: "TB Dept." It was something I had learned in occupied Brussels during the First World War. It had worked then — no reason it should not work again this time!

At two in the morning, I delivered a second baby, which did not leave me much time to think about my own affairs. A third baby followed soon after that. All the deliveries had been trouble-free.

The three fathers were in the corridor between the women's ward and the delivery room, keeping each other company, while the last baby, a sturdy boy, was being washed. The door was open, and I could not help overhearing the conversation that went on outside.

The youngest father, a policeman, recounted how the Japanese had hauled Police Inspector Schiauta out of his house and beaten him to a pulp. Then, they had tied him to the car of the departed doctor and had pulled him slowly over the rough coral road, while continuing to beat and kick him.

Then they had dragged him inside the house of a native, where his long screams were finally drowned out by the raging voices of drunken Japanese. The leader and worst of the brutes was none other than Igawa, the Japanese who had grown up in Ternate!

Horrified, I listened further. When Inspector Schïauta finally died, the policeman went on, Igawa had come out of the house and yelled: "And everyone who has broken into my parents' store will receive the same treatment!"

I trembled with fear: after all, it was Dr. Hassan, myself, a few orderlies, and the now murdered Inspector, who had taken bandages and other supplies from that store in order to treat the victims of the bombardment. I was terrified for what might happen next, but the night passed without incident. Only later would I hear the details of this incident and what had really been behind it.

\*\*\*\*

In the early morning hours, the wounded survivors of the bombardment of Sulamadahe were brought in. They told me that the raid had killed more than 50 people. Some of the new arrivals were in shock; others had severe wounds. Most of them were seriously wounded in the lower part of the body and I spent hours removing deeply-embedded pieces of *karang* (coral). The patients were stoic, and hardly uttered a word.

While working on a severely-wounded woman, several Japanese doctors came in and watched. One spoke to me in difficult-to-understand English, with an *American* accent, and asked if I knew who had wounded this woman.

"Nippon!" I snapped, without thought for possible consequences.

The Japanese grinned and said: "No, the elusive Assistant Resident has done that!" and, laughing at his own wit, he walked away followed by the other doctors.

Then he stopped in front of a pregnant woman. Pointing to her swollen belly, he said in German: "*Schwangerschaft*! Pregnancy!" and, laughing shyly, he looked around the room. Then he and the others disappeared.

It was clear that the Japanese liked to show off their linguistic abilities. Yes, the gentlemen were quite vain, I was sure of that.

The next day, no one came to the outpatient clinic — and old Uncle Peter was the only staff member who showed up. A third and a fourth day passed without any major incident but, throughout the day, we had to deal with the annoying visits of armed Japanese soldiers. They were particularly curious about the women's ward and the babies, which made the patients extremely nervous. If only Dr. Hassan would show up! But he stayed away — for whatever reason.[2]

On the fifth day, a group of doctors entered the hospital. One, who spoke German, asked me to write the names of all the patients on a list, which he would collect in the afternoon. He also wanted to know how many patients there were in the fort.

When I said I did not have all the information he wanted, he commanded: "Today, the list of those in this hospital; tomorrow, the list of the sick prisoners in the fort!"

That meant I would have to enter the fort, and pass two sentries. So I fished out the scrap of paper from my coat pocket, showed the red seal to the doctor, and asked him if my pass would allow me to enter the fort.

He scratched behind his ear, sighed, and then scribbled several Japanese ideograms below the seal. My heart jumped. Would that permit me, perhaps, to see John?

In the afternoon the gentlemen returned and received the list of patients in the hospital — as requested. They made the rounds, looked at the sign on my door and .. walked on! I had been writing there when they had arrived and had left my red Parker pen on the table. When I returned, it was gone. Would one of the Nippon doctors have taken it?

Early the next day, I filled a basket with clean underwear and a pair of pajamas for John. I placed some cans of milk and vegetables on top and covered those with a layer of medicine, bandages and absorbent cotton. Then, I left for the fort.

Two sentries stood straight-backed in front of the gate. They gave me a suspicious look as I started to cross the wooden bridge and, as I came closer they picked up their rifles with the long bayonets and aimed them at me.

I approached them ever so slowly, placed the basket on the ground in front of me, and held out my magic piece of paper. It worked. One sentry said *"isha"*, which I knew meant "doctor", and allowed me to pass.

Upon entering the *bèntèng*, I noticed that all the officers' residences were now occupied by the Japanese; so where, then, were the KNIL soldiers?

To the left of the *gudang* were several buildings, and on the front veranda of one of them I saw several *Belandas* (Dutchmen). I could not recognize anyone from that distance, though, for all of them had beards! I quickly crossed the courtyard and confirmed that, thank God, they were indeed our men.

John came forward to meet me. He asked how I had managed to get in. In one breath I told him all that had happened outside and that I had permission to visit and, yes, even take care of them!

The men pressed in on me, asking questions. The militiamen asked anxiously if I knew something about their families. Alas, I could only answer that, some time ago, most families had found shelter outside the city.

I started to hand out medicine according to need, while John separated the canned food. After that, I saw my former KNIL patients with the severe cases of eczema. They complained about not being able to sleep because of the terrible itch, and I promised to bring some special medicine for them next time.

Captain Zondag told me they had been forced to sleep on the bare, cold floor tiles. He was afraid of getting rheumatism and mentioned that there was a large quantity of kapok mattresses in the *gudang*, across the courtyard.

*This required action!*

## IBU MALUKU

I straightened up and my attitude was no longer subservient when I turned and called to a few Japanese, who had been watching me from a distance. Pointing to myself, I said sternly: "*Isha*!" They nodded enthusiastically that they had understood the word. Then in rapid-gun-fire Malay and gesturing with arms and hands, I pointed to the men, yelled that they were *sakit* (ill), pretended that I was shivering, pointed to the bare floor and intoned again the magic word "*Isha.*"

"*Hai!*" panted the Japanese. They had understood. My own people first looked on in wonder and then amusement, though John was worried about possible consequences and could not appreciate my antics.

The Quartermaster Sergeant produced the key for the storage room from somewhere and handed it to me. I showed the key to the bewildered Japanese, went down the steps of the veranda, and gestured for them to follow me.

"Will they do it?" I wondered, forcing myself not to look back. But sure enough, all four of them followed me.

I opened the *gudang*, pointed to the mattresses, and then to our men. And, lo and behold, each soldier picked up a few mattresses, hoisted them on his back, ran across the yard, dropped his load on the landing, and then hurried back for the next load. Twenty mattresses and *kelambus* (mosquito nets) were thus transported to our men.

I didn't dare go further and so closed the *gudang* behind me. I should have continued while the going was good. The next day the Japanese demanded the key; the shrewd soldiers who had transported the mattresses had quickly taken stock of what else the *gudang* contained!

On the eighth day of occupation, I handed the list of sick people in the fort to the Japanese doctors, and took the opportunity to ask them to do something about the childish visits of the Japanese soldiers to the hospital.

They gave me permission to stop it myself, but I made it clear that I felt inadequate to the task because of the language barrier. In the afternoon, a sign with Japanese characters was placed at each entrance, and that put an end to those annoying visits.

A little later, the doctors asked me if I would attend to sick Japanese soldiers. In response, I pointed to my Red Cross arm band. Laughing bashfully, they accepted my silent answer. From that day on, Japanese soldiers came regularly for treatment but luckily, did not require to be hospitalized. None of them wanted to be treated by the two native orderlies who had returned to work, so I was stuck with the job.

We had recently acquired an apprentice orderly, a clever lad with a nose for business. His name was Hendrik Chiu, who was half Dutch and half Chinese. He told me that a Japanese ship had arrived that morning from Jailolo with Dutch people from Halmahera, and that they had been taken to the fort.

I had to know who they were, and thus made a second trip to the *bèntèng*. This time, I brazenly took Hendrik with me as assistant. Getting in did not pose a problem — no one seemed to object to his presence.

Once again, I had the opportunity to speak freely with our men, while attending to the sick among them. As before, the Japanese looked on with curiosity.

Meanwhile, Hendrik kept his eyes and ears open, and learned where the Halmahera civilians had been taken. With this bit of intelligence, we left Fort Orange and returned to the hospital.

Now I only needed to secure a permit from the doctors to visit them. I was sure the opportunity to do so would soon present itself.

In the afternoon, there was a great commotion outside the gate of the fort. Yelling Japanese were crowding in on something or someone. Looking out of the hospital's windows, some orderlies and patients tried to find out what was going on. Then someone yelled: "It is the Assistant Resident!"

Sure enough, the elusive Assistant Resident was walking over the wooden bridge, repeatedly bowing deeply as he approached the fort's gate. But with each bow, he received a punch or a kick from the Japanese he passed.

What a humiliation! But his behavior had undeniably provoked it. For days he had hidden himself on the island, knowing full well that the Japanese would take it out on the population if he did not give himself up. And now, he had finally been found!

"Thank goodness," I thought, "this will avert further reprisals!"

### Endnotes

[1] *Hara kiri*, meaning "stomach drill", is the common name for "*seppuku*": suicide by disembowelment.

[2] Many years later, when Jeanne van Diejen met him again and had a chance to discuss these events, Dr. Hassan confessed that he feared that his presence in the hospital would provoke the Japanese. He said he sensed, rightly so, that although the Japanese often rationalized their aggression by saying they had come to liberate their Asiatic brothers from the Dutch yoke, they looked down on these "brothers" and would not entrust themselves to the care of a native doctor.

IBU MALUKU

# CHAPTER 33

*Evacuation*
*Ternate, April, 1942*

The day after the Assistant Resident gave himself up, two ships arrived — one of them, a captured KPM steamer. Hendrik Chiu quickly found out that they had come from Sorong, New Guinea, with Dutch women and children aboard — some of them sick.

Without securing another permit from the doctors, I walked up to the sentry at Fort Orange and said that there were *kodomo* (children) inside, who needed medical attention! He let me pass, and when I met the newly arrived families, I found that many children and even adults (especially the men) had the chicken pox!

I left an adequate quantity of *Dermatol* for the adults, but the children needed a different kind of treatment, which I could only administer in the hospital.

It took time to find out who was the commanding officer of the fort, but I finally located him and got permission to bring the stricken children to the hospital. They came the next day, but ... under strict surveillance of an armed Japanese soldier!

The baths in a solution of potassium permanganate salts did wonders for the little ones, for whom being let out of the fort was a real outing. The staff and patients spoiled them, and even the police constables dropped by to treat them to all kinds of goodies.

On my next visit to the fort, the majority of internees complained that the food was inedible. They showed me a bag of cornstarch from which they somehow had to make porridge. The people from Ternate had brought provisions from home and were relatively well off, but those from Halmahera and New Guinea had nothing except this dreadful corn starch.

Hendrik Chiu immediately found a solution. It would not be difficult, he said, to deliver bread and other nourishing food to the fort, provided that it was paid for. Hendrik was definitely not a philanthropist!

But he was true to his word. Somehow, he would manage to smuggle all sorts of provisions to the internees for as long as they were detained in the fort. But, to prevent any difficulties, he was dropped from the hospital payroll.

*  *  *  *

On the twelfth day of the occupation, Hendrik learned that the Javanese KNIL soldiers would be freed; the militia would be next. Only Dutch career servicemen would remain as prisoners-of-war in the *bèntèng*.

So there was hope that John would be freed also.

When I made my daily trip to the fort, the sentries wouldn't allow me to pass. In unfriendly tones they told me to wait. One sentry trotted off and returned with ... Igawa!

He angrily told me that I would no longer be allowed to get in. When I showed him my pass with the doctor's scribbles, he snarled that the doctors had nothing to do with the fort!

My protestations did not get me anywhere, and I left. Though grateful for having been allowed into the fort this long, I was extremely worried about what Igawa might do to the internees, now that he was in command.

In the afternoon, however, something happened that sent my spirits soaring.

Once again, there was quite a commotion at the gate of the fort: many Japanese had come out of the *bèntèng* and stood on the bridge over the moat, looking at a strange procession that came from the Sultan's palace.

In front were the Sultan's soldiers in their splendid uniforms. Behind them came a procession of men in long caftans, solemnly striding along, their heads covered by large white turbans, around which were wound the thick black bolts that marked them as *Adat* chiefs — members of the supreme court of native justice[1].

As they came closer, I was surprised to recognized many District Chiefs from Halmahera. "What are they up to?" I wondered. "Is this a submission ceremony?"

However, the procession did not stop at the fort, but proceeded to the front entrance of the hospital. The Japanese from the fort drew closer, as the Sultan's soldiers broke rank and formed an honor guard, flanking the pathway leading to the hospital's entrance. Passing between them, the District Chiefs strode toward me, and stopped in front of the hospital's entrance.

In formal (high) Malay, I bid them a warm welcome, and asked why they had come.

They first gave me, with great deference, their Mohammedan *adat* salutation, touching their head and heart region with their hands, and then one of the elders spoke. He recalled that I had lived among the Tobelo people since 1920, and that they considered my husband and me as one of them.

"In Ternate, you have shown yourself to be one of us also," he said, "because when war was declared, we noticed that it was only the *Tuan* of Mon Désir who was called up to military service and that he never looked for excuses to stay safely at home.

"Later, the *Nyonya* from Mon Désir came to Ternate, and she was the only *Belanda* to attend to the needs of the badly stricken population."

He recalled the many nightly trips inland from Jailolo, and the care extended to the victims of the bombardment at Sulamadahe, and closed by expressing his admiration for my courage in going with the *Controleur* to the Japanese flagship to plead on behalf of the entire population of the island.

Deeply touched, I reached out to shake hands with each of them, expressing the hope that they, by their presence here, would not encounter any difficulties from the Japanese.

Then, the District Chief of Ternate stepped forward. He said he had confidence that for my conduct I would receive a *bintang* (a medal) from Seri Baginda Ratu Wilhelmina[2], and he expressed the hope that the war would be short, that I would soon be united with my husband and would live many years on Tobelo to receive the continuing gratitude of them all.

Then followed three cheers. While the flabbergasted Japanese looked on, we said our individual goodbyes, and the stately procession then returned to the *Kedaton*.

This royal tribute, which had moved me so deeply, would sustain me during the difficult years ahead. It also encouraged many other people to drop in for a personal visit. But ostensibly, they came as "patients", so as not to alert the invaders' curiosity.

From one female visitor, I learned more about the murder of Police Inspector Schïauta. He had been killed out of revenge, she said.

Igawa had been deeply in love with a girl from Ternate and had planned to become engaged. Before war was declared, however, the Igawa family locked their store and left — presumably for Japan. Inspector Schïauta then courted the girl and they planned to get married. On account of this impending wedding, the Inspector was alleged to have taken many items out of the locked Igawa store to give as presents to his future bride.

Igawa had learned about this through "friends", whom he had visited secretly on the first day of the occupation, and at whose place he had hoped to meet his former sweetheart. However, the girl could not be found — it turned out that the Police Inspector had evacuated her to some unknown island just before the arrival of the Japanese fleet.

Igawa then turned into a raving lunatic and went looking for the Inspector, who had gone into hiding. But he was betrayed and ultimately killed, as told earlier.

This tragic story was nevertheless a tremendous relief for me. It firmly established that neither Dr. Hassan nor I had ever been in danger, though both of us had been in the store at the same time as the murdered Inspector. I was certain, however, that Igawa did know of my actions and carried a grudge, judging by the forbidding and arrogant way in which he treated me at every turn.

Several days later, Hendrik told me that all militiamen had been set free to join their families in the evacuation camp on Halmahera, and that was where they would have to stay for the rest of the war. While waiting to be transported, the *kota* was off limits to them.

There was, however, one exception — John, the only Dutch militiaman, had not been set free. Anxiously, I wondered what they planned to do with him and, again, a great disquiet settled over me.

That evening, a heavy storm raged. All the patients were wide awake. Suddenly there was a loud pounding on the wooden shutters of the women's ward. Then harsh voices, obviously Japanese, yelled something that nobody could understand. Some of the patients wailed with fright. I tried to calm them down, and then went to the entrance to see what was going on.

In front were several Japanese standing around a car in the pouring rain. They screamed orders while two of them tried to yank something or someone out of the car. Two Japanese pulled me out into the pouring rain towards the car, where I saw the terrified face of an old Indo-European lady, Mrs. Boddendijk, the extremely obese administrator of a local hotel. How she had gotten into the car, I don't know, but it seemed virtually impossible to get her out through that small opening. She tearfully claimed she was ill, and said the Japanese wanted her to be hospitalized.

With great effort, the Japanese finally wriggled her out of the car. But then she asserted that she could neither walk nor stand. The Japanese refused to carry her, and I certainly could not do so. She did manage to stand, though, and as soon as I had grabbed her arm to steady her, the Japanese let go of her, got in the car and drove off!

There we stood in that torrential rain, lit up spookily by bright blue bolts of lightning. With the assistance of several male patients, we managed to half carry, half drag the woman inside.

The new arrival promptly demanded a private room, which did not exist in this hospital. At my wit's end and to calm the moaning woman, I gave her my room, for the time being, and received criticism about its appearance to boot! She, the richest woman in Ternate, should be entitled to more comfort, she said!

Her arrival brought unrest and trouble to our hospital. She was difficult, cantankerous, fussy, and not really sick!

Other than that, the days passed as usual. The local people came in large numbers to the hospital, grateful for whatever help we could still give them. Only among the young (particularly those of Arabian heritage) was there, at times, some noticeable insolence towards me. The Japanese walking patients were calm, even courteous, and posed no problems at all.

Early in the morning of April 20, Doctor Hassan came to tell me, on behalf of the Japanese, that all the Dutch, myself included, would be taken away in a few hours — where to, he had no idea. He advised me to pack only a small suitcase, as I would have to carry it myself over a distance of 30 kilometers. That made me think that the evacuation camp on Halmahera, which was 30 kilometers inland from the harbor of Jailolo, might very well become my place of internment.

My last and most troublesome patient, alas, would be coming too. Of course, I would continue to be responsible for her — which was something she would never allow me to forget, even for a minute.

At noon, several Japanese came to tell me to be ready for imminent departure. Upon my request, they agreed to provide assistance in transporting my overweight patient. I made the rounds to say good-bye to my people. The patients were in tears. Then, with my suitcase in hand, I went outside where everything was quiet.

The KNIL soldiers were lined up in front of the fort, guarded by armed Japanese. Moments later, they marched off in the direction of the harbor.

Then it was our turn. A truck arrived at the hospital's entrance. Several hands helped me to put Mrs. Boddendijk on a stretcher, on which I had already put a mattress, linens, blankets and pillows — all from my own bed! As soon as she had settled down, she was hoisted onto the truck's flatbed, while snickering Japanese looked on. Then the procession got under way, with me following the truck on foot.

A Japanese soldier had put my suitcase on the truck. Beside the suitcase I noticed a large kettle, with a note dangling from it. Who could have left it there? With a few quick strides I caught up with the truck to read the note. In an awkward script, it said: "*Slamat jalan dan terima kasih!* Good journey, and many thanks!" From the depth of my heart I thanked the giver, and sent him or her a prayer: "*Slamat tingal!* Farewell!"

The road to the harbor was lined, all the way, with silently-watching Japanese. None of Ternate's inhabitants dared show themselves. The civilian prisoners, visible to me only when they followed a bend in the road, walked in front of me. I recognized each man, women and child, since I had treated every one of them. They dragged suitcases, bags, a perambulator, and clothes and linens stuffed inside pillow cases. It was a pathetic sight and a dejected exit.

When we arrived at the harbor, I lifted an infant from the arms of its exhausted mother. It was one of the babies whom I had delivered in December of 1941. The little one, now four months old, seemed to recognize me and smiled.

"Poor child," I thought, "what will your future be?"

A landing craft was waiting for us. It would take us to the evacuation ship, which turned out to be an old minelayer. The soldiers — John among them — were taken on board first; then the civilian men with the luggage; and only then did the women and children get their turn.

As the last group of civilians went up the gangway, the Japanese in the landing craft placed their queer headgear on the muzzles of their rifles, raised them in the air, and shouted: "Bansai! Bansai!"

It was a strange goodbye[3] for us all, and since we did not quite know how to take it, we decided not to react to it at all.

Upon arrival at the top of the gangway, everyone was sprayed from head to foot with a disinfectant. We even had to raise our feet and have our soles sprayed! In the process, the sprayer tried to be "funny" by aiming the spray at our eyes, and I had to twist and turn to protect myself and the baby I was holding.

On deck, we were lined up and told to stand at attention, while the Japanese made a count. It seemed the sons of Nippon had difficulty counting, for they repeated the process several times!

Thank God, the abominable show and associated harassment finally came to an end. Then, spurred on by raucous shouting, the KNIL soldiers descended into the pitch-dark hold of the ship. The civilians followed. Those who did not move fast enough through the small hatch and down the narrow steel ladder, were booted inside with a kick to the back or behind. The luggage was thrown in afterward — the Japanese were seemingly too much in a hurry to allow us to carry it down.

When I landed below, I discovered that the dark hold had been divided with ropes into three parts. The right section was for the KNIL soldiers; the left one, for the civilians; and the one in the middle for the luggage. So John and I were separated and our captors made it very clear that we were not allowed to talk to each other!

There we were in the bowels of this filthy, rusty minelayer. The "civilian" section (where I was, in spite of having been drafted into the Army) contained the narrow rail tracks for transporting mines to where they were dropped into the sea. The air was stale and the cold steel floor provided no comfort. From the movement of the ship, it was clear that we were already out at sea.

Later, several Japanese soldiers distributed small square mats on which we were allowed to rest our tired limbs, but only at night — so they told us. During the day, we would have to sit up, because, for every passing Japanese, we would have to get up and bow deeply. Such deference toward our conquerors could not easily be done from a prone position! But there was one exception: Mrs. Boddendijk lay as proud as a peacock on her well-padded stretcher. Yet she never stopped complaining!

The water kettle, the precious gift from the unknown benefactor, I was able to shove across the luggage barrier toward John while our guards had momentarily turned their backs. Much later, I would learn from his fellow prisoners that it had accompanied John on all his travels.

Time had passed quickly. It was already three o'clock in the afternoon; no wonder that our throats were parched and our stomachs growled. The Japanese ordered us to stand up as they brought in large mess containers. The KNIL soldiers were the first to get their food, and when they grunted their approval, we, civilians, craned our necks to see what had been served. It smelled delicious!

It turned out to be a soup with large chunks of chicken in it: a quarter of a chicken per person! At the bottom of the container floated celery leaves and stalks. Many among us could hardly wait! Then came a tremendous disappointment. Instead of salt, the soup contained a large quantity of sugar! It was so sweet, that it almost made us throw up!

Only the children enjoyed this meal. We suspected the Japanese of pestering us, but learned later that was the way they made this soup. But nobody dared to show their disappointment. Some of us did manage to eat some of the chicken; others just kept what was left over for the children.

Later, the Japanese allowed us out on deck (this would happen twice a day) to make use of the latrine that was hanging over the side of the ship. Going there was an unpleasant and perilous experience. Sheets of canvass that were flapping in the breeze served as door and walls, but they only shielded one's lower torso. Other than that, the occupant was in clear view of the Japanese guards, who always watched the proceedings with great curiosity. It was extremely degrading!

We were also allowed to walk for a short while on deck, but the pleasure of doing that was largely negated by having to bow deeply to each Japanese we passed. We certainly were not used to this, and even found it somewhat ridiculous.

Since we were on the high seas, there was nothing to look at. Sometimes we could faintly discern land in the distance, but it would be too far away to give us a point of reference. By now, we were certain we were *not* going to Halmahera; we had already traveled too far for that. Some among us guessed that Ambon might be our destination.

Our second meal came late in the evening. It consisted of a chunk of bread and a mug of bitter tea. And that was that.

The first night was difficult for everyone, mostly on account of Mrs. Boddendijk. She was the only one who had a mattress, yet she complained every ten or fifteen minutes to me about being uncomfortable. And when, urged on by grumbling neighbors, I finally told her to keep quiet and go to sleep, she accosted every passing Japanese with complaints that I was not paying attention to her. The Japanese would only growl, and then demand silence. Finally, in the early hours of the morning, several persons had a heart-to-heart talk with Mrs. Boddendijk. Severely offended, she finally shut up and went to sleep.

****

On board, there was a Japanese whom I had seen at the hospital in Ternate. (There, it had not always been clear to me whether I was dealing with a doctor or an orderly, but I had always assumed *this* man was a doctor.) I asked for an interview because we were out of quinine and iodine. Also, I had no more sedatives for Mrs. Boddendijk!

Somewhat shyly, the doctor showed me the medicine cabinet and gestured to me to help myself. I found quinine, but no iodine or sedatives. He then gave me several large pills that looked like ordinary aspirin — oh well, perhaps they would do the trick.

In the afternoon of the second day, the doctor condescended to pay Mrs. Boddendijk a visit. It seemed her son had asked him to do so, via one of the Japanese to whom he had been able to make himself understood.

Mrs. Boddendijk cried and wailed and gestured to convince the doctor that she had been picked up by mistake. She was not a *Belanda*

# IBU MALUKU

(Dutch person), she was a native of Ternate. She repeatedly said "Ternate" and made gestures to indicate a pregnant belly and lactating breasts, to convey the number of generations that had lived there before her. There was no end to it! With a contorted face she pointed to me, and said "*Belanda*"; then, pointing to herself, she said "Indonesia".

I was profoundly embarrassed by such a performance in front of this Japanese doctor. Mother and son were practically white, but the daughter-in-law was dark-skinned, and it appeared that the doctor started to believe the mother.

Finally, several men carried her on her stretcher to a compartment where the rail track made a U-turn at the trap door for dropping the mines into the sea. The doctor allowed her son and daughter-in-law to be with her, but that did not satisfy her. She insisted that "the nurse" who had been assigned to her care in Ternate be with her at all times. She got her way; I could only follow the doctor's orders.

Then, the doctor wanted a prisoner-of-war to complement the party. Quick as a jack-rabbit, Captain Zondag pushed John out in front, pointing to his tallness and strong biceps. The doctor nodded, and said: "Quick! Quick!", anxious to have the matter settled.

And so the five of us landed in this stinking compartment. I did not know whether to be glad, or angry, at having John lie beside me on one mat, each of us embedded between the narrow rails, while the other men either made fun of us or cast envious glances. John certainly was not happy about the situation — that was quite obvious.

The night was terrible. The Japanese constantly intruded upon our little space in which *Oma* (Ol' Mama, meaning Grandma) snored, while the son and daughter-in-law lay tightly intertwined under a large *sarong* next to the stretcher. Neither John nor I dared to speak. Several Japanese came and pushed our faces toward each other, while making obscene gestures. When I got up to join the civilians in the outside section, the Japanese roughly pushed me back. And throughout the night, they continued to spy on us.

The next morning, I'd had enough! John and I each went back to our own section. *Oma* would have to make do with her own family, no matter what!

The trip lasted four full days, and with each day, the amount of speculation increased. Some had seen mountains; others thought they had recognized the peak of Sanana.

By now, we knew everyone on board. In whispers we told each other how we had been captured. Of course, each one of us had a different story to tell.

Most of those present were members of *het Binnenlands Bestuur* — the Government of the Interior: The *Controleurs* of Jailolo, Ternate, Bachan and Sanana and their families; the *Controleur* of Sorong and several missionary families with many children; several plantation people, agents of trading concerns and the KPM; and another long-time resident of Ternate, the second richest woman after Mrs. Boddendijk.

There were few Indo-Europeans among us. Most were Netherlanders, be it born in the East Indies or not. One *Controleur* was a dark-skinned native of Suriname (Dutch Guyana), married to a full-blooded Dutch woman — a red-headed, sturdy woman from Zeeland, the southwestern province of the Netherlands.

This black-and-white couple was a source of great wonder to the Japanese. They were particularly intrigued by madame's voluptuous curves; in fact, they were impressed to the point of being intimidated.

The Japanese also liked the children, and occasionally handed out bananas or candies to them all.

On the fourth day, at two in the afternoon, we were told to get ready to disembark. Agitated, we wondered where we were and what the future would hold. When we arrived on deck, we discovered that we were moored at the coal quay of the island of Ambon. We had traveled almost 270 nautical miles.

The first one to leave the ship's hold was Mrs. Boddendijk who, once again, bitterly complained when she was carried, not too carefully, through the narrow hatch onto the deck.

Our KNIL soldiers had been ordered to unload the ship. Six of them transported *Oma* and her luggage down to the quay. Another group carried her to the road, running adjacent to the dock area, and left her there with her private nurse, me, watching over her.

There was not one shaded area to be found along the road, and the sun beat down on us unmercifully. We did not see a single civilian; only the occasional Japanese patrol, that trudged along, casting curious glances at us.

I looked down at *Oma*. She was fast asleep. But the peace was soon disturbed by a series of trucks that rumbled by. One of them was full of civilian prisoners: men, women and children. They looked at us silently until they were out of view.

*Oma*, awakened by the passing trucks, complained about being thirsty. I felt deeply sorry for her, but had nothing to give her.

The waiting seemed endless, but it gave me the chance to review recent events.

On board, I had said goodbye to John. A last embrace, and a short, ardent kiss. Then John had whispered to me: "Keep your courage up, and trust in God. One day, He will reunite us, if not on earth, than certainly in heaven."

He then pushed me away, and, for a moment only, did I see a grim look on his face. "Was that goodbye forever?" I wondered, as I stood near this deserted road.

Then our men came into view: all dressed in their KNIL uniforms with wide-brimmed hats on their heads. Captain Zondag, the tallest, was in front.

The men did not dare look at us as they marched by. John was at the very end. I looked at him anxiously, longing for some sort of greeting, and hardly noticed the tiny Japanese with a huge rifle that walked right behind him.

I held my breath, as my heart went out to him.

Unexpectedly, I saw his right hand shoot up and give me a military salute.

Then it happened: The tiny Japanese lunged and attacked him with the butt of the rifle, and continued beating him until they disappeared around the bend in the road.

**Endnotes**
1. In a large area of the Dutch East Indies, the *adat*, i.e. the customary (or common) native law, was maintained and administered by these chiefs. Dutch judicial and civil servants were encouraged to study it.
2. Thirty-two years later, in 1974, Jeanne van Diejen would indeed receive a medal, not from H.R.H. Queen Wilhelmina, but from her daughter, then H.R.H. Queen Juliana. It would not be for her actions during World War II, however, but for voluntary work done in the Netherlands on behalf of destitute war victims.
3. "*Bansai*" is actually a victory cry, but the internees did not know it at the time and interpreted it as "goodbye".

# IBU MALUKU

# CHAPTER 34

### Internment on Ambon
*STOVIL Camp, Ambon, April 24, 1942*

Fifteen minutes after having witnessed the beating of John, a truck with "DOCTOR" stenciled on its door stopped near us. Japanese soldiers got off, lifted *Oma* with the stretcher onto the truck's loading platform, and then pulled me up.

One soldier gave the old woman something to drink, and then signaled the driver to get started. I found a seat on a bench, and hung on to the truck's siding as we took off for the city of Ambon.

It was strangely silent along the road. The few Ambonese we passed looked on wearily, but didn't wave as they normally would have done — they obviously feared the Japanese.

In the downtown area, we stopped at a large, shaded park. Across from it, I spotted our soldiers, but they were too far away for me to recognize anyone. I longed to see John, and wondered how he had weathered the beating.

Eventually, Mrs. Boddendijk and I were transferred to another truck, which already carried a number of civilians, some sitting, some standing. We drove through the familiar streets of Ambon, and looked benumbed at all the devastation caused by the heavy bombardments of January 31.

We stopped in front of several buildings that were enclosed by a high barbed-wire fence. At the gate was a guard-house, with several armed Japanese soldiers standing in front of it.

As we started to get off the truck, a group of excited European children appeared behind the barbed wire fence shouting: "New people! New people!" Men and women came running from all directions to join the children. Hanging carefully onto the barbed wire they looked at us and waved.

Bewildered, we waved back. So this was an internment camp! Just before I jumped off the truck, I spotted a familiar figure behind the barricade: Pater Egmond of Ternate! Thank God! So the people who had left in December on the *Honun Maru* were indeed safe, and not at the bottom of the ocean!

As we passed through the gate, I became conscious of our messy appearance. With our clothes stained with the rust and dirt of the minelayer, we looked worse than a bunch of tramps!

From all sides, the internees peppered us with questions: where had we come from, how was it "outside", was there any news from the Allies, and so on and so forth. They quieted down a little when a dignified, carefully-coiffured lady appeared, dressed in a smart batik dress.

Apparently she was the camp leader, for she bid us welcome and said we had arrived at STOVIL[1], a former training college. She explained that the buildings had been constructed for 44 students and the director's family. Now, it had to provide accommodation for several hundred internees — men, women and children.

It was not an auspicious start!

We were lodged in several halls where, understandably, the occupants did not exactly greet us with open arms, for the halls were already overcrowded and our arrival only made things worse. Also, having lived here since February, they were now used to each other, and had established themselves in groups according to social rank. Our arrival meant a change in the *status quo*.

Mrs. Boddendijk was taken immediately to a small hospital. A bed had already been prepared, but she insisted that it be made again with her mattress, her sheets, her pillow and her blankets. When I protested that all the bedding was *my* personal property, she made such a row, that I felt obliged to let her have it after all. As a favor, however, she handed me one of my own sheets — but only after a nurse had offered her one that she liked better!

There was no room for me in the hospital, so "the management" gave me a place in one of the overcrowded halls. On my left were two Captain's wives and three children; on my right was the family of *Controleur* Sjirk van der Goot, with whom I had gone to the Japanese aircraft carrier in Ternate. My personal space measured 1.8 meters long, and 4 tiles wide. This would be my home for the next year.

\* \* \* \*

I spent much of the first day getting acquainted with my fellow inmates and exploring my new surroundings. In all, there were six bathrooms and six toilets — totally insufficient for 300 people. A "water watch" had been set up, I heard, to ensure that water usage was kept to a minimum. The daily ration was one 5-lb butter can[2] of water per person — for drinking *and* washing! As little as it was, when I heard that water often came out of the faucets drop by drop and that the Japanese sometimes shut off the water to punish or annoy the internees, I concluded that I would have to resign myself to the situation.

## IBU MALUKU

Meals were provided twice a day, I was told. In the morning, it was a thin rice porridge of dubious quality, which was prepared very early in the morning in large containers made out of oil drums. The second meal consisted of cooked rice with a ladle of watery soup, in which one occasionally found some leaves and, sometimes, a piece of fish. Any extras, I found out, would have to be smuggled into the camp by enterprising merchants who were willing to risk the wrath of the Japanese.

Smuggling appeared to be a lucrative business, and I was soon approached by ladies who were in that trade. From them one could, for a hefty price, order supplementary nourishment in the form of savory *sayurans* (soups of various vegetables), buns, and sago rolls filled with *gula jawa* (palm sugar). Sometimes, one could buy *pisang goreng* (fried bananas) and, for a special occasion, it was even possible to order a roasted chicken or a cake.

Mostly, these delicacies were reserved for residents of Ambon, who had been able to preserve some of their capital and their possessions before they arrived at STOVIL. For the group to which I belonged, such luxuries were out of reach.

I later learned that not all the people who had left Ternate on the *Honun Maru* were here at STOVIL. The nuns and the wives of KNIL Sergeants had boarded another ship, and had sailed on to Java. The Doctor's family had remained in Ambon, however, because she was pregnant with her third child. She and the children were at STOVIL; "Jolly Joey" himself was locked up in Fort Victoria, within Ambon's city limits.

\* \* \* \*

In the evening, I discovered to my horror that our look-alike luggage had been switched: I had John's suitcase, and he had mine. To resolve the matter, I wrote a letter in English, which our leader, Mrs. Valderpoort, handed to a senior Japanese officer who happened to be honoring us with a visit.

Two days later, I was called to the commandant's office. Several Japanese officers grilled me for more than an hour. It was a stressful and humiliating experience.

They promised me my freedom — and suggested that my husband might be freed also — if, as a native of Belgium, I would respectfully request it. Japan was, after all, not at war with Belgium. They said we would then be returned to Ternate where we would work under the protection of Japan.

I flatly rejected their offer.

They then called in the Doctor's wife, a Hungarian, and made a similar proposal to her. Much to the disappointment and astonishment of the Japanese, she also turned it down. Being married to Netherlanders, we were, after all, according to the law Netherlanders also and, therefore, chose to be treated as such.

Chagrined, the Japanese rejected my request for an exchange of our suitcases. I was told that John would have to make do with my clothes, and I would have to be satisfied with his!

\*\*\*\*

My first night at STOVIL was troubled. Not having a *tikar* (mat), I had to sleep on the bare floor — using my clothes as pillow. The one sheet that Mrs. Boddendijk had returned to me was not enough to keep me warm during the damp and chilly night. Not being used to the hard floor, the cold, and the symphony of snoring neighbors, I often awoke with a start, and was grateful when dawn came.

I got up, and surveyed the crowded hall where men, women and children lay in all kind of positions. Stepping gingerly over the legs of the sleepers, I went outside and saw some "early birds" slinking away toward the bathrooms and the toilets. Smart. Soon, the rush would be on, and I suspected the chances of still getting some water would be slight.

Walking down the corridors that were filled with stacked crates, I looked into some of the other halls. To my surprise, I saw people sleeping in beds or on mattresses, placed on the floor. "What luxury!" I muttered.

I would learn later that those halls housed the three hundred people from Ambon itself. Shortly after the war had been declared, those people had been evacuated inland to a previously prepared camp, and had taken all their valuable possessions with them.

Interestingly, these people had convinced themselves that they would quickly return to the city. The Japanese, if they landed on Ambon, would be forced to bring back the Dutch to run the government, trade, industry and education, they argued. Without Dutch help, the Japanese would be helpless — or so they thought.

Things turned out differently. When, after fierce resistance by the KNIL, Ambon was taken in February, the soldiers became prisoners-of-war; the civilian men and their families were quickly interned — and *remained* interned.

STOVIL was the first civilian internment camp on Ambon, and everyone from the inland evacuation camp had been brought here. Awaiting better times, their possessions were in the crates that occupied much of the narrow corridors through which I was now walking. (Alas, all those crates had to be left behind, when the whole camp was transferred to a nearby coconut plantation at a later date.)

## IBU MALUKU

At the extreme left of STOVIL's entrance stood the Director's former residence with several smaller buildings as annexes to it. One annex had been converted into a hospital; the other contained a small hall that provided lodgings for the nuns of Ambon. Part of that annex had been transformed into a church.

All single men lived in the classrooms of the school building. They were still asleep when I passed, and were snoring loudly. Their rooms were separated from the main road by a covered veranda, a narrow pathway, and the high barbed-wire fence that enclosed the entire camp.

Passing along the fence to the gate, I came to the guard house, where I had to bow to every Japanese in view. I had already learned that failure to do so would result in a severe beating. If you were lucky, it meant slaps to the face that would knock you off balance; if not so lucky, it meant a thrashing with a *rotan* cane that would strip your hide.

Connected to "my" gallery were several smaller rooms, where expecting mothers and their children and young mothers with their babies were housed. Here also lived the Doctor's family from Ternate.

In the middle of the compound was a large square, where many clothes lines were strung from poles. In a few hours, I presumed, the camp's laundry would be hung up here. That turned out to be true. I also learned that the laundry had to be carefully guarded, for theft was commonplace in this diverse society.

Arriving back at my quarters, I found everybody busy rolling up their sleeping gear in order to clear their cramped space for day-time activities. But I noticed that everyone was on guard against the slightest territorial encroachment, which, when it did occur, was quickly challenged.

Only a two meter-wide path separated my building from the fence outside. Freedom was only a jump away, but the barbed wire strung diagonally across each of the hall's open windows quickly suppressed any thoughts in that direction.

Beyond the fence was an inhabited *kampung*. Smoke spiraled up from the kitchens. I smelled *pisang goreng* (fried bananas) and other delicacies, and heard people talking.

A gong sounded, and everyone in the hall began to move out with plates or bowls in their hands. It was time for breakfast. On my way to the mess hall, I learned that breakfast was distributed hall by hall on a rotating basis — with each hall having its turn at being last, to share whatever was left over.

The watery rice porridge, prepared by the missionaries, was distributed by the men. This first morning, my plate was filled by the Prior of Ternate. We looked at each other and burst out laughing.

How different was this meeting from the festive reception he had received when he visited us in Tobelo some years back. How our people had stared in awe at this dignified man in the heavy brown robe with a magnificent white beard, whose feet were shod in open sandals. Now he wore only an undershirt and a pair of shorts. He had soot on his face from the smoking fire and, generally, did not look too clean.

He greeted me warmly and muttered with a cheerful wink: "*Sic transit gloria mundi* — thus passeth world's glory."

After breakfast, the plates and bowls were quickly washed because a Japanese inspection was expected. This, I was told, invariably happened whenever a new group had arrived. Happily, the inspection came and went without incident.

\*\*\*\*

In the next few days, I learned more about the people who had arrived before me, and about camp life itself.

Shortly after the first group had arrived in the camp, dysentery had claimed many lives. The husband of our camp leader, Annie Valderpoort, and the Resident of Ambon were among the first to die.

In wooden coffins, which could still be obtained at that time, the dead were carried to the guard house and placed on a truck. Members of the family were then allowed to follow the truck to the cemetery, located outside the camp.

The places vacated by the dead were soon occupied by new arrivals from the surrounding islands, who came with few possessions — some clothes and sleeping gear, but not much more than that. A plate, a mug, or an empty butter can was a treasure for them. They had little or no money and feeding them became the responsibility of the camp executive.

A central fund was already in place then, to which everyone had contributed according to their means. Each week, a small amount from this fund was handed over to the camp executive for "expenses".

The Japanese allowed the camp executive to stock up on rice, and to buy 10 kilograms of fish and 10 kilograms of vegetables and coconuts per day. That was of course not enough to adequately feed over five hundred people, but we had to make do with that.

It had happened on several occasions that, as punishment for a minor infraction (real or imagined), the fish and vegetables had been detained outside the guard house until they were close to being spoiled. Only after intensive bowing would the inmates then be allowed to carry their purchases to the kitchen — accompanied by howls of derision from their tormentors.

I further learned that firewood for the kitchen also came from outside, which provided the Japanese with another means to punish the internees. So it was with the water, which was already in short supply. And thus it happened that there was sometimes food and firewood, but no water; or water, and no firewood.

I soon became involved in this daily battle for necessities. Through a strange twist of fate, one of our guards happened to be a member of the Watanabe family, whose plantation had been close to Mon Désir. If we were out of firewood, I would surreptitiously make contact with him and, in response, he would invariably throw some wood over the barbed wire fence.

\*\*\*\*

One side of STOVIL faced the sea. A long strip of white sand stood between us and the water. The barbed wire fence ran far beyond the high-water line into the sea, and one could walk to the very end of it when the tide was low. At high tide, however, most of the fence was submerged and posed no problem for swimmers or those traveling by canoe. It was at these times that the Ambonese smuggled many coveted goods into the camp.

We were allowed to walk on the beach, or just to sit there and think in peace and quiet. (Solitude was almost unknown inside the camp.) Often, we would stare across the water at the islands that were far beyond our reach. Or we would think about our families in occupied Holland, or about a husband or father, who, perhaps, was also on Ambon breathing the same air we did, but oh so far away. Worries and anxiety filled us all — particularly those who were alone in the camp. The members of complete families probably had a slightly easier time, but not much. Having nothing to do with one's time was bad for morale, and it made people tense and very quarrelsome, souring the atmosphere.

The executive asked me to take on the task of caring for new mothers, young mothers, babies and small children. It was no picnic, but I enjoyed it immensely.

Later, when almost no milk came into the camp anymore, I had to use all my ingenuity to keep the babies alive with other nutrients. Thank God, I succeeded.

\*\*\*\*

At the end of April, word passed rapidly that new people had arrived. I ran to the barbed wire fence as fast as others had done when I arrived — only a week earlier. Would there be anyone I knew?

The newcomers turned out to be from northern New Guinea: families of civil servants, missionaries, traders, people from plantations, and ordinary citizens, including Indo-European families of so-called "colonials". But, my God, how terrible they looked!

For seven full days they had been in the hold of a coal ship, without having been given the opportunity to wash or change clothes! Psychologically, they were a mess too. They were petrified, and kept bowing to the onlooking Japanese.

I noticed a young blond woman among them, who was shunned by the others, as if they were afraid of her. She, herself, also avoided all human contact.

"Her name is Willy Fuhrie," someone told me later. "She is the recent widow of a Captain in the Government's Marine Service, who was stationed at Manokwari.

"Following orders, he set fire to his steamer, the *Anna,* and then scuttled it at the entrance of the harbor in full view of the arriving Japanese.

"He got back on shore and fled with his pregnant wife, intending to join an escaped KNIL detachment[3] and fight with them." I was told. "But they did not make it. The Japanese captured them and took them to the presbytery where all the Dutch inhabitants of Manokwari had already been corralled.

"The people who had gathered at the presbytery already knew about the scuttled Government steamer and either praised or condemned the deed, depending on how much they feared reprisals from the Japanese.

"Two days later, the Assistant Resident, *Controleur* and Captain Fuhrie were taken away and put in prison. After two more days, the *AR* and the *Controleur* were returned as they had been found innocent of any involvement in the scuttling of the ship, as well as the flight of the KNIL soldiers.

"That afternoon, however, Captain Fuhrie was tied to a pole outside the presbytery, tortured and left there for two days. A sign pinned to his clothes read: "Anyone who inflicts damage on Nippon will be treated this way.

"At the end of the second day, the Japanese lowered their flag with great ceremony, then dragged Captain Fuhrie behind the barracks, and after a few non-lethal bayonet stabs, beheaded him. A Japanese officer delivered the notice of execution to his widow and threatened death to anyone who would "fraternize" with the wife of this criminal.

"And so," concluded my informant, "from that time onwards, that command has been slavishly followed."

"How is it possible," I asked myself indignantly, "that people can be so cruel and so cowardly!"

# IBU MALUKU

I took the pregnant widow, Willy Fuhrie, under my care — and damned the consequences. A month later she miscarried. Feeling she had nothing more to live for, she went downhill fast and was well on her way to becoming deranged. It took many, many months of constant care, but she finally did recover her health. Thus started a "mother-and-daughter" relationship that would last for several years.

\*\*\*\*

Camp life soon took on a certain regularity. Each long day passed in a continuous state of nervous tension. There was little work, too little space, too little recreation. Only the arrival of new people brought any diversion — but also renewed anxiety. For some, it brought boundless joy as they were reunited with relatives; for others, it brought endless grief when they were told — sometimes abruptly, sometimes gently — that a loved one was dead. All the Dutch people from the north, middle and south Moluccas had now been transferred to STOVIL. The only ones missing were the people from Halmahera.

A different kind of diversion was provided by a series of Allied bombing raids on the ships that were anchored in Ambon Bay, quite close to our camp.

The first raid had been a surprise, as there had been no air alarm or warning of any kind. Around eleven, six planes appeared out of the blue, skimmed the top of the *Gunung* Mona and nose-dived toward the Japanese ships.

In the absence of air-raid shelters, we dropped flat on the ground wherever we happened to be, and covered our ears as the bombs hit their targets.

There was no response from anti-aircraft guns; the Japanese had been completely taken by surprise. After inflicting heavy damage on the Japanese ships, the Allied planes retreated without a scratch, and we breathed easier when the last one had disappeared behind the mountain.

The next day, the planes came an hour earlier, and once again the Japanese were caught unprepared. A hospital ship at anchor in Ambon Bay, although clearly identified with Red Cross markings, became their primary target. The screams of the wounded could be clearly heard over the roar of the departing planes. The bombs had demolished the steam pipes of the ship and many Japanese had been critically burned by the escaping steam.

The next day, again at around eleven, the third air raid started. This time, the Japanese were ready: their Zero planes were in the air in no time at all. A fierce dog-fight ensued, and four Allied planes plunged, burning, into the sea. Only two escaped. The Japanese were overjoyed and celebrated the event by shutting off our water!

There would be other bombing raids, but only on targets further away.

\*\*\*\*

Several babies had already been born in the camp, when Jolly Joey's wife gave birth to a girl, Beatrix. She was born during the second air-raid.

In the delivery room, I had covered the window with blankets, partly out of fear for flying shrapnel, and partly to discourage Japanese guards from looking in. But three guards had somehow gotten wind of what was about to happen and wanted to see it all. They did not hesitate to hoist one comrade onto their shoulders, so he could look over the blanket and report to them on the proceedings.

When the baby uttered her first cry, nothing could stop them. With bayonets still fixed on their rifles, they shyly entered the darkened delivery room and looked around, asking: "*Komodo* — the child?"

I showed them the crying baby, and, holding their breath, they looked at it. They asked for its gender and showed their disappointment on hearing that it was a girl. They nevertheless dug in their pockets and brought out pear drops and rolls of peppermint, which, laughing shyly, they laid on the bed beside the baby's mother. I gently pushed them out the door, and then saw them dive to the ground as the Allied planes made another pass overhead.

\*\*\*\*

Every evening, we gathered in small groups outside on the grass. Gradually, the people had formed their own little cliques and clubs. Much time was spent in prayer, and in reminiscing about the past. Sometimes, fueled by rumors about Allied invasions, we talked longingly about the coming liberation.

To chase away boredom, some of us sought out those who claimed to have psychic powers. Some of these psychics explained dreams; others made predictions from cards, coffee grounds, or from the way birds flew over the camp. The so-called "cross" (a variation of the Ouija board) became standard equipment. Some even saw warning signs in the stammering of little babes. After all, those infants had a pure spirit and could "see" things — couldn't they?

Even the *tokèk*[4] (a wall lizard) was now thought to have magical powers. As soon as the animal started its sinister hawking — a prelude to its "*tokèh*" call — everyone became silent in order to count the number of calls. After seven calls, one could make a wish. So the children were taught to count with the others, and, after seven calls, to wish for the return of their dads. Too bad that the calls often stopped after the fourth or the fifth, and then terminated in a hoarse hawk.

The paranormal beliefs of the adults affected the children in a curious way. The nuns, priests and Protestant ministers all taught Sunday school. Of necessity, this had to happen in secret because, at that time, teaching was forbidden.

During one such class, a nun asked: "Children, how many gods are there?"

The hands went up in the air. A boy answered confidently: "Three, Sister".

"And who might these be?" asked the nun, surprised.

"God, the Lord, and the *tokèk*," said the boy proudly, explaining that the Catholics talked about "God"; the Protestants about "the Lord"; and everyone else talked about the *tokèk*!.

\*\*\*\*

I had been at STOVIL three weeks when I heard that the wives of the POW's were covertly exchanging letters with their husbands who had arrived on Tantui — two kilometers north-east of the City of Ambon. That camp also housed about two dozen Americans and almost 800 Australians.

In Tantui, Ambonese merchants were sometimes allowed inside the camp to sell their wares — mostly cigarettes, soap, fruit and brown sugar. One of those Ambonese had found a way to organize a fairly regular exchange of letters between Tantui and STOVIL. How he did it, no one knew.

A letter, containing only a sentence or two plus a greeting, had to be written on a small scrap of paper. Folded, it could not be larger than 2 x 3 cm. The writer would add a dime for "postage" and drop the letter at a prearranged place, which constantly changed. Who picked up the mail and the money, no one knew, and no one was allowed to know — it was a well-kept secret.

The answers arrived in a similar way. An unknown person might stop briefly to drop a letter in your lap or you might find a letter in your coat pocket, or one might be handed to you over the door of the bathroom.

Everyone was given strict orders to destroy the letter immediately after reading it. That was hard to do, because it was sometimes the only tangible evidence that one's husband was alive, and the desire was strong to reread it many times!

Not surprisingly, rumors circulated that some wives did not destroy the letters as required. The Japanese sensed that something was going on and stepped up their feared inspections.

An inspection would start with an impromptu order, demanding that all internees congregate immediately on the big lawn. One soldier would check the presence of each person on his list, and count and recount the number of people standing at attention. This was often followed by a body search, which we feared most of all.

Then came the silly part of the routine. A table and two chairs were placed in the middle of the lawn. The Japanese commander — nicknamed "Mustache" because of that big encumbrance that adorned his cruel, sly face — climbed on top of the table. Two translators mounted the chairs.

After giving us a stern look, Mustache started his blustering speech, during which he never failed to recount all of Japan's victories.

"Do you know that all of the East Indies is in our hands?" he would then ask, to which we would, in chorus, respond with "*Hai* — yes", followed by an appropriate deep sigh.

He would recount more Japanese victories, and say with great contempt:

"Do you know that your Queen has fled to England?"

"*Hai*!"

"That you are nothing now?"

"*Hai*!"

"That you are completely dependent on Dai Nippon?"

"*Hai*!"

"Do you know how many prisoners Japan has taken?"

"*Iie* — no!"

"We don't know either," he would bellow, "there are too many to count them!" and, roaring at his own wit, he would then get down from the table.

That signaled the end of his speech, but we were left to roast in the sun, while his soldiers searched through our rooms and turned everything upside down. We did not know if they were looking for something specific, but we took even greater pains to destroy the less-frequent letters from Tantui that were our very life-lines.

As unpleasant as these inspections were, the visits of high-ranking officers were worse. Panic seized us when the large black sedans drove up. The standard mounted on the right front fender indicated the officer's rank. The more stars, the quicker we sought refuge inside the buildings. Bathrooms and toilets were favorite hiding places!

As they toured the camp, these visitors traipsed behind Mustache, who would crack his feared whip left and right, looking for a possible victim: someone who had not bowed low enough or, worse, had dared look a Japanese in the eye. A mouth-to-mouth "all clear" would signal that the top brass had finally departed.

Besides bigwigs, we also received visits from sailors, whose ships were anchored in the bay. Seemingly, the camp was *the* place of attraction. In groups, they meandered alongside the barbed wire, staring, criticizing, pointing, laughing and sometimes making strange sounds. They were obviously having a good time and behaved very much like people in front of a cage full of monkeys. Accordingly, we felt like animals in a zoo. Locked up. Cut off from the outside world.

We hungered to know what was going on. The decisive Battle of Midway in June had stopped the Japanese advance in the Pacific. What a difference it would have made to our morale if we had known that!

\* \* \* \*

At intervals, more Dutch families arrived from other Moluccan and New Guinean islands as well as from coastal regions. Sometimes men were reunited with their lost families, and some women and children found their husbands and fathers in STOVIL.

One day, several nuns, brothers and a German priest arrived from the Kei Islands, 580 km south-east of Ambon. Most of them were in a state of collapse, and the elderly brothers had been badly beaten up.

The guards ordered everyone to leave the barbed wired fence and then hastily pushed the newcomers through the gate. The STOVIL nuns rushed to receive these terrorized people with their torn clothes and blue, puffed-up, lacerated faces, and led them away. The newly arrived nuns were put up by members of their own order and lovingly cared for, but they would remain silent about their experiences.

The men were sequestered in my ward, since there was no room elsewhere. We were, of course, curious about what had happened to them, but they were also too traumatized to talk. In the darkness of the long nights, I heard their muffled moans. Their lacerated backs were sore and the stone tiles made their pain unbearable. Alas, there was nothing that we could do for them.

Much later, I would read the report, written by the German priest, Father Münster, which described in detail what had happened on the Kei Islands. This is his story:

> On July 30, 1942, five Japanese warships sailed into the harbor of Tual, on Little Kei Island. The Japanese troops quickly rounded up the *Controleur*, the Police Inspector and other Europeans.
> 
> Three days later, they dug a hole. At its edge, they shot Father de

Grijs, and dumped his body in the hole. Why him?

At about the same time, a landing party crossed the strait and went ashore on Grand Kei Island at Langur. The Mission was just a half-hour's walk away. The Bishop, Monseigneur Aerts, lived there. It was also home for the missionaries (when they were not away on tour of duty), for eight friars aged between 30 and 70 (who taught in the vocational school), and myself, the only German there.

On this day, four missionaries were at home. I had just celebrated Mass, and was having breakfast in the presbytery, when a crying young boy came with a message from the Japanese landing party: I was ordered to come right away.

When I arrived at Langur, I was ordered to squat down outside the church in the rain. A soldier took away all my papers. I was then taken into the church and told to sit down on the bench closest to the entrance. In the church entrance, I passed Monseigneur Aerts, who sat on the floor amidst other squatting priests and friars.

Outside the church, the Japanese had rounded up the villagers. It seemed that they had been summoned to witness the proceedings of a mock trial.

On his knees, Monseigneur Aerts was interrogated by the Japanese commander. It was a humiliating cat-and-mouse game. The commander quickly worked himself into a frenzy, and snarled his questions and accusations at his quarry. An assistant translated his words into Malay.

Monseigneur Aerts was accused of having exploited the population, spied for the Allies and hidden firearms. Therefore, he and his colleagues would be taken to Ambon and interned there.

Toward the end of the interrogation, a Moslem boy arrived on a bicycle and handed the Japanese officer a note. His assistant translated it, without mentioning the author. It said that the members of the Mission had mistreated the local children and had turned them against Nippon. The officer shouted angrily: "If this is true," pointing to the letter, "you all deserve to die. All of you will be beheaded!"

He repeatedly shouted his verdict at the Dutch nuns who, in the meantime, had joined us. One of the nuns went berserk, and began to scream: "No! No! I don't want to die!" The Japanese then rounded up the nuns and took them back to the cloister.

For the others, there was no way out. The missionaries, with the Monseigneur in front, were led one last time past the Mission house. Then, each was escorted by a Japanese soldier to a dry part of the beach and arranged in a row, facing the sea.

A native boy was dispatched to get thirteen blindfolds and a bowl of water. The cloths were dipped in the water, and then tightly knotted around the head of each condemned man.

The officer snarled a command, and the machine guns rattled. Some fell immediately. Pater Berns and Friar van Schaik, although badly wounded, were still standing on their feet. Exploding into a blind fury, the screaming Japanese soldiers then charged their hapless victims, and finished them off with their bayonets. And so, thirteen innocent lives came to an end. The local population and I, rooted to the spot, had been forced to witness this horror.

A short time later, the boys of the Mission were ordered to drag the 13 corpses over the sharp coral to the sea. Lifting the bodies was not allowed; they had to be dragged like animals. Burying them was also forbidden, on pain of death.

"We shall be back tomorrow," shouted the Japanese officer, "to make sure you have obeyed our orders!" Then, the Japanese got into their landing boats and left for Tual.

The next day, all the corpses had been washed back onto the white sand; the sea had refused to accept them. The population, crying and praying, maintained a death watch; but still no one dared to bury the dead.

On August 1, two days after the killings, some brave souls decided to at least bury the Bishop — but it would have to be done in secret. Fearing treachery, they placed lookouts all around before getting together to plan their strategy.

The next day, however, the Raja himself gave permission secretly to bury Monseigneur in the yard of the cloister that housed the native nuns. Later that day, he decided, at his own risk, to inter the other bodies also. Terrified about reprisals, the population fled.

Then, wonder of wonders, we received support from our Protestant brethren. The *Orang Kaya* (Chief) of a Protestant village on the other side of the Strait approached the Japanese directly and asked for permission to bury the dead Missionaries.

The Japanese officer asked: "Why are you not bringing us fish any more?"

To this the *Orang Kaya* gave an Oriental answer full of Biblical clarity: "How can we go fishing, with the corpses of the European *Tuans* floating about?"

Finally, permission to bury the dead was granted after the fact! And that ends my report except to say that, aside from those missionaries, the Japanese tortured and then killed another 148 Christians.

And that ends Father Münsters Report.

\* \* \* \*

Early in August, the people from Halmahera finally arrived. Among them were men, women and children from Tobelo, and ... our priest, Father Moors, who told me that the Japanese had made Mon Désir their headquarters.

With the others, he had arrived on Ternate shortly after John and I had left, and had remained locked up in Fort Orange. Only the men had seen the outside of the fort: every day they were taken to the harbor to load or unload ships, or to maintain the roads. All of them had had a reasonably good — though stressful — crossing.

All the Europeans from New Guinea and the North and South Moluccas were now together in the STOVIL camp on Ambon.

**Endnotes**
1. STOVIL: *Stichting Tot Opleiding Van Inheemse Leeraren*: Institute for the Education of Native Teachers.
2. Butter was imported, mainly from Australia, in 5-lb cans that held about 6 cups of water. The empty cans made great containers.
3. This KNIL detachment, headed by a Captain, would for many years tramp about in the hostile interior, and wage a guerilla war against the Japanese. By means of a ruse, the Japanese would eventually capture that KNIL Captain and — though he was very ill — butcher him in a bestial manner. Some of his men did, ultimately, manage to join the Australian Army.
4. There are many house lizards in the East Indies. The *cicak* (pronounced *chee-chak*), which measures 10-15 cm long is particularly plentiful. The *Tokèk* is much larger; large enough to frighten little children.

IBU MALUKU

# CHAPTER 35

## Bombardment
*Tantui Camp, Ambon, August, 1942*

Persistent rumors circulated in the camp that our clandestine exchange of letters with Tantui had been discovered. Fear gnawed at our insides throughout the day, and sometimes at night too. In the wake of these rumors, the Japanese conducted again one of those dreaded searches. As usual, we lined up in the square under a blazing sun, awaiting the arrival of Mustache and company.

Gesturing wildly, he climbed onto his table and roared and fumed at us for what seemed like an eternity. What it was all about I didn't know — his anger made it even more difficult to understand him — but afterwards, his soldiers took away the daughter of the late Resident of Ambon (her father had died at Stovil from dysentery) together with the wife of a Lieutenant-Colonel who had been the military commander of Ambon.

We feared the worst; everybody prayed for those two women. As the hours passed, their families became increasingly despondent. Night fell and there was still no sign of them.

Two days after their abduction, the two came back. To all outward appearances, not a hair on their heads had been touched. They brought with them some buns and bananas, and appeared cheerful enough. But whatever had happened to them would remain a secret from us forever.[1]

The next day, a soldier entered our quarters and took two women — my neighbor, the young wife of a Lieutenant, and the wife of a militiaman — away to the guard house. There, they were told that their husbands had been executed. The reason given was: "*Melawan kepada Nippon* — Resistance against Nippon." Later, more deaths would be announced in this brutal manner.

The dead suffered no more, but fear for those who were still alive grew with each passing day.

\*\*\*\*

Early next morning, a palpable fear rolled like a heavy fog over the camp, eventually enveloping each one of us as we warily watched our captors.

Outside the camp walked a greater than usual number of Japanese soldiers. They acted strangely. Some soldiers cut sturdy canes from nearby bamboo bushes. Close to one end of the cane, they cut a deep groove, leaving a small cylinder at the end that was almost detached from the cane itself.

One soldier tested his weapon on a passing dog, and I was horrified to see the flexing cylinder tear off a strip of its hide. A little further on, the bleeding animal was beaten to death with a steel tube! Savagely swinging their canes, the increasingly frenzied soldiers paced forth and back along the barbed wire, searching for another victim.

Then came the order: "All Army wives must report immediately to the guard house." The children had to remain behind. Their mothers, apprehensively, left them in the care of friends.

A total of 33 women, myself included, were lined up, four abreast. The gate opened and we marched out into the midst of the waiting soldiers. They hit us with their canes where they could, screaming at us to walk faster. We gladly complied in order to get out of their reach.

They herded us into an isolated house. The women in the two outer lanes were taken one by one into a room, from where the sound of beatings and the screams of the victims sent chills down our spines. The women in the two middle lines, including myself, were pushed through the inner gallery towards a large desk.

Behind it sat a Japanese officer, with a pistol and a riding whip in front of him. He was flanked by two soldiers, their long bayonets fixed on their rifles. In the corner of the room stood another, smaller desk, complete with officer, pistol, whip, and armed soldiers.

Angrily, these officers interrogated each one of us in turn:

"Did you send letters to your husband?" they hissed.

"Who delivered the letters?"

"Who organized this exchange?"

"What did your husband write to you?"

"What did you write to him?"

If the answer did not satisfy him, the officer would pick up his whip and hit the desk, or an arm, or a face. At times, he picked up his pistol and aimed it at the person being questioned. Sometimes, the soldiers beside him would make mock bayonet attacks. Throughout our interrogation, the cacophony of trashing and screaming continued in the adjoining rooms.

The officers threatened death if we did not tell the truth and said our husbands would be killed that same night. Feeling sick, we wondered if they were in fact still alive.

In conclusion, the officer demanded that we sign a confession that he had drawn up. Most of us refused, but some mothers with children did capitulate.

The torture finally came to an end!

Only after we had been taken outside did we see how many black and blue, swollen faces and bleeding limbs there were amongst us. Huddling together, we limped back to our camp.

There we encountered the other female internees, who stood, lined up, with disgruntled looks on their faces.

In front of the gate stood several Japanese officers. They were supervising the coming and going of male internees, who were throwing provisions over the barbed wire on a heap outside. As punishment for our sins, all canned food and other smuggled goods had to be surrendered. Later, soldiers searched our quarters to ensure that the order had been complied with.

In the meantime, we, the perpetrators, were lined up near the guard house. Many of us could hardly stand. It was blazing hot, and our bloody limbs attracted swarms of flies. It was pure torture.

Then, the "throne" of Mustache was placed nearby. He climbed on top of the table and raged, screamed and denounced us in the most humiliating manner imaginable. What hurt most was being told that we had sold out our husbands and had, in fact, signed their death warrants. Had we not given him all their names and had we not confessed to having carried on an illicit correspondence?

The torment we felt was terrible.

Finally, Mustache allowed us to go to our quarters. As we entered, I heard one Dutchman growl testily: "Those damned military bitches! Thanks to them, we have lost all our canned food." What had happened to us, of course, did not concern him one little bit.

Later, I heard that we had been betrayed by the wife of a senior officer. During a search, the Japanese had found in her handbag one of those notes that she — like all the others — had sworn to destroy immediately after reading. Evidently, she had made a deal with her interrogators, because, although she was among those selected for a thrashing in one of the smaller rooms, she came out of that room without a scratch.

That a person could stoop so low was beyond me. Something close to hatred and deep contempt filled my heart and robbed me of my sleep for several days!

Then rumors abounded of the atrocities committed on Tantui. Later, I would learn that one POW, Sergeant-Major Waalwijk had been caught with letters that would have been delivered to us by Ambonese friends who were on the outside[2].

On July 12, Tantui commander Captain Ando, the terror of Hong Kong, meted out his punishment: 62 Japanese soldiers (two for each POW) beat up 31 letter writers with bats, iron bars and whatever else they could use as weapons. Three POW's were killed right away, and Lieutenant van Sandik died the next day. Many were maimed for life.

Then, irony of ironies, at the end of August the Japanese changed the rules: we were now allowed to write a short letter to our husbands — but it had to be in English, so the Japanese could read them. (Few of them spoke Dutch.) We wondered if it was a trap, but our camp leader said that it was safe to do so.

Although not fully convinced, we nevertheless did write. But it took a while before the letters were picked up. Ultimately, we received responses from Tantui. None of the letters contained much, but the signature did at least indicate that the writer was still alive. But we tempered our joy out of deference to those who had received confirmation that their husbands were now dead.

****

For some time, rumors had swept through the camp that the POWs at Tantui would be transported elsewhere, and that ships were now being readied to transport them.

Sunday, October 26, was a rainy day. The weather did not stop us, however, from going down to the beach. Sitting there, early in the morning, we looked on as several ships dropped anchor in Ambon Bay — just in front of us.

Those of us with good eyes reported seeing many whites on board. Would our husbands be among them? Anxiously we peered into the distance, hoping to recognize a loved one.

The Japanese caught on to what we were doing and wasted no time in erecting a high barrier of zinc sheets on the seaward-side of our camp. Just as quickly, we made peep holes in it but, after we found ourselves looking into the barrel of a rifle, we gave up our efforts to view the action in the bay.

Several days later, listening to the singing of Ambonese from a nearby *kampung*, we learned that many Dutch and Australian POWs had been taken away from Tantui. Where to, nobody knew, but six Dutchmen — among them "Jolly Joey", the Doctor of Ternate and father of Béatrix, had been left behind and were now living in the Australian part of the camp. Would John be among the remaining five?[3]

A month later, all 140 men of Stovil were moved to Tantui. The civilians were unhappy about it and blamed the letter writers — the military wives.

"We are and will remain the scapegoats," we, the military wives, said, shrugging our shoulders. "So be it!"

From time to time we heard bombardments in the neighborhood, seemingly in the proximity of Halong Airport. Since none of the Allied planes making the raids flew over our camp, we did not know if they were American, Australian or Dutch.

On December 28, a month after the civilian men had been moved to Tantui, the 360 women and children at Stovil were ordered to leave also. But to where?

We were loaded into large trucks together with our meager belongings, and driven in a north-easterly direction. Those who knew Ambon said that we were heading for Tantui. This immediately raised some speculation. Would we be driven past the Australian POW camp, and would some of us be lucky enough to see a husband, if only for a moment?

Eagerly we scanned both sides of the road. When we approached something that looked like a camp, Béatrix was lifted high in the air, just in case. And sure enough, her father, "Jolly Joey", stood with the other five Dutchmen behind a barbed wire fence.

A suppressed shriek escaped from the lips of his wife when she recognized him. She did not dare call out to him, but he did see the child and waved. The wives of the other Dutchmen standing around the Doctor were not in our convoy.

The trucks suddenly made a sharp turn toward the coast and drove downhill into the camp that our own military had vacated on October 26. We were indeed at Tantui.

The camp consisted of several long, low buildings distributed along the main road that encircles the island. It lay immediately downhill from a group of 50 huts where 528 Australians, 14 Americans and our 6 Dutchmen were interned.

It puzzled us that they had not been moved out like the others. Only later would we learn that they had been kept there to work as coolies on the airport, the harbor and the roads.

Our truck drove towards a large car shed, 12 by 60 meters, which stood apart from the long, low buildings. Inside the shed were long rows of bunks, made from coarsely hewn wood. There were no walls, but there was a partition of *atap* on the side facing the road. The open side faced the sea, but a manned guard-house, towering over the beach below, spoiled the view.

Our camp leader, Mrs. Valderpoort, assigned the people to their bunks. My friend, Willy Fuhrie[4], and I were given two bunk beds facing each other across the aisle.

In one corner, the nuns screened off an area for their little cloister, and set up the treadle sewing-machines they had brought with them. Thoughtfully, the camp leader had given them the street side where the partition would afford them a little more privacy.

Farther on in the shed there were several small cubicles, enclosed with boards. Evidently, those had been the quarters for truck drivers, because on the walls were drawings of trucks and girls. These cubicles were given to the women with the youngest children and some bedridden patients. Among them was Oma Boddendijk, who still insisted she could not walk and demanded attention, day and night.

Still farther, beyond a small hospital ward where Sister Josepha reigned, was a high barbed wire barricade that separated the women from the men's camp. It had a small gate, guarded by a Japanese soldier, through which, three times a day, our food was carried by an ever-changing group of men. In the morning we received a thin porridge; at noon, boiled rice with *ikan garam* (salted fish); and in the evening, again a thin gruel of some sort.

Close to the beach, in view of the guard in the watch-tower, were our bathing cubicles and primitive toilets. The water required to bathe and flush had to be carried up, every day, from the sea. The path to the beach was a set of steps carved into a coral embankment. At the bottom of the steps, before going to the sea, and again on the way back, we had to bow deeply to the Japanese guard in the tower. We would then have to wait in a bent position, face lifted up, until "his lordship" would deign to look down at us and motion us on with a sweep of his arm.

We quickly noticed that in this camp the Japanese enforced a far stricter discipline and maintained a closer surveillance. Each passing Japanese had to be bowed to, and it had to be done properly. Seemingly we had difficulty getting the hang of it for they beat us often and eagerly.

Contact with the civilian men in the adjacent camp was well-nigh impossible. The women waited eagerly for those that brought our food. Words could not be exchanged, but the eyes had a language all their own.

There were two other occasions when we might catch a glimpse of our men: when the Japanese herded them like slaves past our camp to work outside, and when, individually, they went to the latrines, which were further away on the beach, separated from ours by a barbed wired fence.

From an unobtrusive spot, the children would watch the men's latrines on the beach, and warn their mothers when they spotted Daddy. The women bristled when they saw Daddy bow low for the guard; there was not much pride left in those men, they felt. Justified or not, this griping momentarily relieved the terrible boredom, which made them ill-tempered and hard to get along with — they simply did not have enough to do to fill each day.

* * * *

News from the *kota* reached us now and then by way of songs that the passing Ambonese sang in their own language, which the Japanese didn't understand.

This time, the songs contained warnings that we could expect bombardments. The singers also informed us of a bomb depot[5] located only 50 meters from our shed that was, at all times, heavily guarded. The news scared us. Peeking through the *atap* partition that faced the road we did, indeed, see stacks of bombs in an open shed.[6]

Although our laundry was normally left out to dry throughout the day, the Japanese suddenly ordered that everything had to be removed from the clotheslines before 11:00 a.m. and that the area between our buildings and the road would be off limits to all — including the nuns, who had spent their daily period of prayer and reflection there in the shade of a few coconut and papaya trees.

Allied bombardments of the surrounding area increased steadily, until there was one raid each day. Each time we would watch the Allied airplanes flying over the bay through puffs of black smoke from exploding anti-aircraft shells.

On February 14, the singing Ambonese warned us of a singular bombardment that would occur the next day. "Stay on the beach as long as you can!" they sang.

February 15 was a brilliant day. The sea sparkled. Small waves languidly dissipated themselves on the white sand.

Heeding the warning of the previous day, we tarried as long as we could in retrieving our laundry. It was 11 o'clock, and nothing had happened. We slowly complied with the Japanese order to go back to our sheds, and wondered if it had been a false alarm.

I was still in one of the bath cubicles, when a child shouted: "Look! Airplanes!" Quickly I put on my dress and ran outside. The guard yelled at me to get off the beach, pointing at the sky. Running toward the stairs, I saw the planes coming straight toward us.

In the midst of eight shiny silver B-24 Liberator planes, I saw for the first time a large, dark B-17 Super Fortress[7], around which the Japanese fighters swarmed like angry hornets. Without breaking formation, the

Allied planes flew on unperturbed.

The leading aircraft was already over the beach when I dived into our shed. The terrifying whistle of bombs could be heard over the roar of the planes' engines, and pandemonium followed.

The first bomb hit one end of our shed; the second hit the road, close to the nun's quarters; and the third came down near the shed where the Japanese had stored their bombs.

Cries for help tore through the air; women, with children in their arms, ran outside; others walked around dazedly or tried to reach the beach. The guard tower was gone — not a trace was left.

I scooped up a terrified child into my arms and ran outside onto the beach, where I joined others who had sought cover behind some boulders. I crouched beside a pregnant woman, who clung to me in sheer terror. Her condition made me realize I had left my obstetrics case behind, so I untangled myself from her embrace, thrust the child into her arms and ran back upstairs.

I reached my sleeping place, which was still intact, recovered the obstetrics case and looked around to see if there was anything else that I should save.

Suddenly there was an ear-splitting explosion and fire engulfed me. The blast hurled me outside and I landed against the trunk of a coconut tree. I clung to it, bracing myself for whatever might happen next.

A smaller explosion followed and I looked on in amazement as the entire crown of my coconut tree came off and sailed through the air. Another explosion followed, more terrible than the first, and I saw the whole shed being picked up and blown towards the sea.

Around me, people screamed. The whole camp area was covered with small tongues of flame. Forlorn, I ran toward the steps leading down to the beach but, before I could reach it, I heard a whistling sound behind me, then a terrible explosion. Everything turned black, and I lost consciousness.

How long I was out, I don't know. When I came to, my first thoughts were: "So you are still alive." I didn't feel any pain, but I was buried under debris, and eventually succeeded in pushing enough of it away to see the sky again. I could move my arms but, when I tried to crawl away, I couldn't do so. Only then did I realize that my legs were pinned down by the badly-mutilated body of a Dutchman, who had evidently been blown over from the men's camp.

Ultimately, I managed to pull myself free. I found I was close to the stairs leading down to the beach. All around me were dead bodies, so dreadfully mangled that I just wanted to run away.

# IBU MALUKU

In front of the stairs lay a woman, whose head had partly disappeared. I crawled around her to get to the stairway, but on the first step I slipped in a pool of her blood, and rolled down the coral stairway. A nun, crouching at the bottom of the stairs, stopped my fall.

"Oh, my God!" she screamed.

"No Sister," I muttered. "It's just me, Mrs. van Diejen!"

She calmed down when she heard my name, although she probably did not recognize me. Together we ran onto the beach, which was littered with torn limbs. We then joined other survivors in running towards the men's camp, but Japanese soldiers, brandishing their rifles and bayonets, stopped us.

The explosions of the bombs in the burning storage shed continued to sow death and destruction at regular intervals. Right in front of us, the latrines in the men's camp exploded. Of the people presumed later to have been inside, there was nothing left.

Uphill along the main road stood many Japanese soldiers, who took delight in the carnage caused by the Allies. They jeered at us, and never lifted a finger to help the wounded[8].

The Allied planes had disappeared[9] and, with them, the immediate threat from the sky. But then we heard another plane coming towards us, and panic seized us again. We hit the dust as the plane roared overhead and only then saw that it was Japanese. We were so relieved there were no bombs, we almost felt like cheering.

The explosions had stopped. Several nurses ran to the beach to assist in removing the wounded. Priests from the man's camp, who had broken through the cordon of guards, were everywhere ministering to the dying. Then the Australian POW's broke through their barbed wire fence, crossed the road, and came to our aid.

An Aussie came up to me with a blanket. Without a word, he tore it in two, wrapped the two halves around me and pinned them together with safety pins. It was only then that I realized that only a few threads were left of my precious dress, and that I had been practically naked. The Aussie — bless his heart! — disappeared before I could even thank him.

Otherwise, I was alright, or so I thought. It was only later that I discovered that my ear drums had been damaged, and that my hearing would never be the same again.

Only a few people had escaped without injury. Among them, wonders of wonders, were the two old and difficult ladies from Ternate!

*****

Toward the evening, we were put on a truck and taken to Ambon

City. There was no reason to stay at Tantui. It had been wiped clean off the face of the earth.

In Ambon, we were lodged, haphazardly, in churches and other available buildings. Not until the next day did a semblance of order return, and we then had an opportunity to assess the disaster that had befallen us.

There were many casualties among the nuns. Seven had been burned alive. In total, ten Australians, six Dutchmen and twenty-two Dutch women and children had perished.

The heavily wounded were picked up and taken to a ward in the Ambon hospital. The situation was appalling: there were almost no mattresses, no sheets, or pillow cases; worse, there were no bandages nor pain killers. Several native doctors came to help examine the wounded. They gave instructions on what needed to be done but, otherwise, were helpless as they had hardly any medicine. The wounded were quiet and did not complain.

The daily bombing of the city and the immediate surrounding area continued. Transporting the wounded from the hospital to the shelters and back, during each raid, drained all our energies.

Next to the hospital was a large Japanese bordello. The shrill sounds from a raspy gramophone and the hysterical laughing and squealing of people inside sickened us. It went on at all hours of the day and night, while next door our heavily wounded patients waited for a merciful death.

The less seriously wounded were now lodged together in the churches. The continued bombing had terrified them out of their wits, and the resulting psychosis became explosive. In fact, the situation became intolerable.

Even the Japanese seemed to sense that something had to be done about the situation.

On March 17, 1943 came the news that we were to be transported elsewhere, away from this beautiful island that had now become a living hell.

### Endnotes
[1] Despite the fact that Tokyo forbade its forces to recruit women and girls from the civilian internment camps for their bars and bordellos, just the same, many attempts were made. According to Dr. D. van Velden (*De Japanse burgerkampen*), in one camp,

women attacked the Japanese officers and freed the abducted girls, but in another, the Japanese enforced their will with drawn swords. One of the Dutch girls who was abducted from the Ambarawa camp on Java, Jan Ruff-O'Herne, has written about her life in a Japanese "comfort house" in her book *50 Years of Silence*.

2 In July 1972, Jeanne van Diejen would receive a written report from Mr. J.J. Donders, one of the POW's who had witnessed those events on Tantui.

3 John and 496 other POW's, including 267 Australians, had been taken to Hainan (China's second largest island in the South China Sea). About 200 of these POW's would eventually die there, due to mistreatment by their captors.

4 Willy Fuhrie (the widow of the Captain who was beheaded in Manokwari) and Jeanne van Diejen had become inseparable companions.

5 In a report, filed by John Charles van Nooten, Lieutenant of the 2/21 Australian Infantry Battalion, who was a POW at Tantui: "About July 1942, the Japanese took over six or eight of the huts and used them as storehouses. About November 1942, they created a bomb dump of 200,000 pounds of high explosive and armor-piercing bombs within the camp area. This was within 200 feet of the camp hospital, within 15 feet of the officer's quarters and 75 feet from the compound where there were about 250 [360, actually] Dutch women and children."

6 Allied pilots had always taken pains to avoid hitting Stovil, which was located in a strategic area between the harbor and the radio station. Apparently, the Japanese wanted to take advantage of this forbearance, which is probably why the women were then moved so close to the dump.

7 These aeroplanes belonged to the 319th Squadron, 90th Bombardment Group of the U.S. 5th Air Force, based at Fenton, Northern Australia. (See *Legacy of the 90th Bombardment Group "The Jolly Rogers*, by Wiley O. Woods Jr., published by Turner Publishing Co.)

8 Although Jeanne van Diejen never saw any Japanese coming to help, a teenager, Rudy Moll, saw a Japanese medical team amputating someone's mangled leg on the beach.

9 The pilots later reported having delivered two hits on an 8000 ton ship in Ambon Bay, and having destroyed an oil dump, which sent-up a column of smoke 3000 feet into the air. They did not mention the bombs they dropped on Tantui, which destroyed the bomb dump and killed 10 Australians, 6 Dutchmen and 22 Dutch women

# IBU MALUKU

## CHAPTER 36

### Internment Near Makassar
*Kampili Camp, Celebes, March, 1943*

The harbor of Ambon was full of ships — all under steam. Our wounded were quickly taken on board the *Rio de Janeiro Maru*, a large Japanese passenger ship that used to sail between Japan and Brazil, but which now functioned as a hospital ship.

Japanese doctors assigned the serious cases to cabins, where, for the first time, they received proper medical care — excellent care.

Others were accommodated in Tourist Class. What a luxury, after so many months of camp life. We were speechless! For the first time, we ate a hearty meal. Food was so plentiful that we had to warn the patients — and ourselves — not to overeat.

The 130 civilian men from Tantui were sequestered elsewhere on the ship, and would remain separated from the women and children throughout the journey. During the air raids — there were seven in all — they were herded into the hold of the ship, with a machine gun trained on them, after which the overhead hatch was clamped shut. If the ship had been torpedoed, the men would have gone down with it!

During the raids, we — women and children — had to stay in our quarters. The portholes were closed and shuttered, but at least we were not locked in like the men were. Soon after the alarm sounded, we would hear the ack-ack from anti-aircraft guns of the escorting ships and, as long as these were blasting away, we lived in terror.

Trying to console the patients was useless. Prayer seemed the only alternative — and those who had never prayed before, quickly learned to do so.

Even during the air raids, the Japanese doctors made the rounds, and assured the patients that — since the clearly-marked hospital ship had never been hit before — it would surely take them safely to their destination. As a clincher, they reported that a baby had been born on board — a good omen, which guaranteed a safe crossing.

All nine ships in the convoy navigated a zig-zag course throughout the five-day journey that would take us to Makassar, the capital of Celebes.

We arrived on March 25, and noticed that only four ships were still in the convoy. Had the other five been torpedoed? We would never know.

As soon as the ship had docked, the men disembarked and were shipped off to Pare-Pare, a port of 400,000 inhabitants (but only a few hundred Europeans) on the west coast of Celebes, 130 kilometers north of Makassar.

Also high on the priority list for disembarkation were two pregnant women whose time for delivery was imminent, and for that reason they were carried down to the quay on stretchers. Sister Huberta and I accompanied them to the Mission hospital "Stella Maris", which I had visited several times before the war.

We were warmly welcomed by two doctors, Dr. Savary and Dr. Warouw — whom I had known from Jailolo, Halmahera — and by scores of Menadonese nuns, who asked eagerly for news about their homeland.

We told them what little we knew. None of them had heard what had happened on Ambon, but there wasn't much time to talk. We had to excuse ourselves and follow our patients, who were wheeled to the maternity ward, where they were put up in private rooms.

A Japanese doctor, apparently the Directrice of the hospital, suddenly appeared. She haughtily looked us over and, in difficult to understand English, asked for particulars about the patients. She examined them very professionally, gave one woman an injection to speed up delivery, and then dismissed us.

Dr. Warouw, one of the two doctors from Halmahera, accompanied us to a first-rate room, where a student nurse handed us clean underwear, pajamas, towels and soap. After a refreshing bath, they offered us a good meal. Then, dead tired, we stretched out on the first real bed in months.

The nuns had assured us that we would be called when the delivery started but, for some reason, their promise did not really satisfy us. I had a troubled sleep and was wide awake at 2:30. Sister Huberta was up too.

We decided to go and check on our patients, but were stopped by two Ambonese guards, who stood in front of our door and harshly told us that we were not allowed to leave the room.

One guard first looked around carefully, then bent over, placed a finger to his lips and whispered, pointing at Sister Huberta: "You have talked too much with the Menadonese nuns. There is an informant among them. Be very careful!"

Then, in a loud harsh voice, he continued: *"Tidak bolèh keluar kamar* — you may not leave your room." He straightened up, stood at attention and closed the door. I looked wide-eyed at Sister Huberta, who started to cry.

"I only told them how terrible it had been on Ambon, and that they could expect many who were badly wounded," she sniffled. The poor soul did not understand that it was better to remain silent in the situation in which we found ourselves.

After several hours, we felt the need to make use of the washroom, and asked our guards to let us out.

"*Tidak bolèh!*" one said abruptly.

The need became greater, so I approached the other guard. He called out to a passing orderly, who shook his head and walked away. But a moment later, he returned with a bedpan. What a joke!

Sister Huberta disdainfully rejected the bedpan. "As long as I am healthy, I shall not use a bedpan," she declared loftily, and started to pace forth and back.

Again I tried to reason with our guard, saying that we were not sick. We wanted a WC, not a bedpan! He chuckled, shook his head and said again: "*Tidak bolèh!*"

The situation became critical; we were ready to burst.

The door opened and a nun came in with our dinner. We rushed up to her and pleaded: "Sister, the WC, please!" With a nod of her head she told us where to go. We charged past her, ignored the shouting guards and ran down the corridor.

Sister Huberta was lucky and disappeared in the first cubicle. I ran on, found an unlocked door, opened it, jumped inside the semi-dark cubicle and almost sat down on top of a Japanese man, whom I had not immediately noticed in my haste.

The Japanese yelled angrily and struggled to get up. I flew out and ran back as I pulled down my skirt. I heard him slam the toilet door and run after me, but I had already turned the corner. I hurried into my room and quickly but noiselessly shut the door with a pounding heart.

Seconds later I heard my pursuer rant and rave outside at the guards, who — bless them — assured him they had not seen anybody pass.

The bedpan was now the only solution!

During the next two days, the Directrice allowed us three trips per day to go to the bathroom or toilet, but never alone. Each time we had to be escorted by an armed guard. What stupidity!

Seeing our patients was not allowed. However, as if to compensate for this lack of freedom, the nuns really spoiled us.

Sister Huberta received two new habits; I was given a dress and a couple of nurse's coats, which I prized more than anything. The stream of gifts did not end there. Sister Huberta asked for and was given a kitchen knife — the value of which can only be appreciated by those who have had to prepare food without one. She wanted it for the nuns in the diet kitchen, she said.

On the fourth day in "Stella Maris", we heard that both infants had been born safely and that their mothers were doing fine. We were not given permission, however, to visit them. Instead, we were told that we would be leaving the hospital that same day. Where to, nobody knew.

One nun whispered to us that the patients wounded in the Ambon air-raids had not been brought to "Stella Maris", and might have been taken to the military hospital instead. Would we be taken there also?

Our guards escorted us out of our room towards the reception hall. An angry-looking Japanese sergeant major was waiting for us. Near him stood the Japanese Directrice and the two doctors from Halmahera: Dr. Warouw and Dr. Savary. Nobody said a word.

The nuns brought our luggage. The Sergeant Major looked with surprise at the many things we had accumulated during our short stay. Dr. Warouw's eyes twinkled and Dr. Savary had difficulty in suppressing a smile. The Directrice maintained her icy composure.

Sister Huberta checked all the items that the nuns had given us, and suddenly discovered her knife missing. She could not possibly leave that behind and she pleaded with one of the Doctors to have it fetched. He was amused by this apparently silly situation, but did not respond.

The Sergeant Major became impatient. In Malay, I explained to him the reason for the delay and, without waiting for a reply, I walked back to our room.

I found the knife, which Sister Huberta had hidden under the mattress, walked back to the hall and showed it for what it was: an old, worn kitchen knife. Even the Sergeant Major could not suppress a grin now, but he quickly contained himself and growled: "*Lekas*. Hurry up!"

Outside, the sunlight was blinding. For a brief moment we looked out over the shimmering, peaceful, open sea that beckoned us. Then we climbed with all our belongings into a large luxurious automobile, and started on our journey. The Sergeant Major drove us himself. But where to?

At moderate speed, we drove through the city. Our driver grumbled something we did not understand, but we began to get his drift when he pointed to a group of white POWs who were repairing the road. They were almost naked. On bare feet, they lugged heavy loads of stones and sand, urged on by shouting Japanese guards — whose bayonets were fixed to their rifles. A horrible sight! Anxiously, I searched for a friendly face. Would John be among them?

The car turned into the familiar road that led to the radio station. Would that be our destination? But no, we passed it, and stopped a while later in front of a large building: the insane asylum!

Behind the barred windows we saw native lunatics, who pulled at the bars, made strange noises and behaved in a bizarre way. It was not a pleasant sight!

The car stopped in front of the large gate. The guard, again an Ambonese, jumped to attention. We got out, and — what irony! — our Japanese driver took out all our luggage himself. He yelled at the guard, who immediately came running to help carry the luggage inside. We did not lift a finger and just looked on in disbelief.

Inside the building was a group of Ambonese guards. They did not say a word; they just looked us in the eye. One guard helped our driver with the luggage, and then led us to a large hall which served as the hospital ward.

Here we met at last some of our companions-in-adversity who, still destitute, looked in wonder at all the things we had brought with us. In no time, a canister of cookies — a gift from the nuns at "Stella Maris" — vanished into thin air. Then they brought us up-to-date on what had happened to them

After Sister Huberta and I had left the ship, they had disembarked also: the severely wounded, on stretchers; the others, on foot. They were put onto large trucks, covered with tarpaulins, and so did not see anything of the city until they arrived at Makassar's asylum for the insane.

The hall, in which we now found ourselves, had been emptied in a hurry and only then were the patients carried in. Japanese doctors arrived to sort out the patients. Only the most severe cases were allowed to stay. The others were given a meager meal of cooked vegetables and sticky rice, and then put back onto the truck. Their destination was Kampili, a former TB sanatorium annex, some 20 kilometers outside Makassar.

Our companions, some of whom knew the area, were able to give us a detailed description of Kampili, destined to be our future home. This former sanatorium, where mentally-disturbed persons and TB patients were nursed, stood on a large plot next to an irrigation canal that ran parallel to a wide public road. There were two hospitals: one for adults and one for children. Furthermore, there was an administration building, a doctor's residence, several houses for the nursing staff and a series of small stone dwellings, where TB patients had been cared for *en famille*.

In turn, we told them about our adventures: the birth of the two babies and our experience with the Japanese in the WC — which caused much laughter. Sister Huberta showed her priceless kitchen knife and she was doubly pleased to learn that it was the only specimen in the entire community.

Sister Huberta and I then offered our services to the two female doctors amongst us, and — after learning that the only male doctor, Dr. Marseille, and a female dentist had already been transported to Kampili — agreed to be assigned to night duty.

We were glad, once again, to have something to do. When we made the rounds we found that none of the patients had experienced any setbacks from the boat trip, but it was clear that some of them still suffered from the trauma of the bombardment.

Our quarters were rather somber. Contact with the world outside was possible, however, thanks to our co-operative Ambonese guards. A rope had been lowered from one of the high-up swivel windows, by means of which we regularly received fruit. I assumed that news about what was happening outside came in the same way.

The food, allegedly prepared by insane cooks, was mediocre. In the morning it was rice porridge; at noon, rice (often burned) with *lichin* (a slimy type of gross purslane) and, sometimes, a piece of fish; in the evening, rice porridge again. Oddly enough, every once in a while, they also gave us each a large clump of cloyingly sweet *arèn* (arenga palm) sugar.

Drinking water was provided, but even that was served in unsavory copper containers, made from the same green, corroded material as our plates and spoons. Sometimes we also received kettles with hot tea. But we were never to see the people who cooked for us.

The daily routine soon became a drag.

Finally, people were selected to form the first group for evacuation to Kampili. Those chosen were mostly mothers, whose children had already moved there six weeks earlier. Of course, they were overjoyed at the prospect of being reunited with their offspring. Sister Huberta and I would also join that first group.

This time, we traveled by bus, which allowed us to see something of the surrounding area. As we passed the suburb of Sungu Minassa, the Japanese officer who accompanied us gave instructions, in poor Malay, on how we should behave in Kampili.

First, we would not be allowed to speak Dutch any more. From now on, all conversation had to be in Malay — the market language, used throughout the East Indies.

Second, we would not be allowed to talk to the guards, who, for the moment, would be native policemen.

Third, we would not be allowed to have any contact with the native population living around the camp.

Fourth, we would have to work hard: in a short time, the camp area would have to be cleared of all debris and made spick-and-span.

We listened stoically. When he had finished, I couldn't resist protesting against the order to speak Malay only — knowing that not all internees were fluent in that language.

He answered that we should be ashamed for not having mastered the *lingua franca* of the region. He had a point. But his own version of Malay was almost impossible to understand and, after he had told us he had entered the East Indies three years earlier, we furtively teased him about it — not knowing that we were talking to Colonel Ino, the highest-ranking *Kempei Tai*[1] officer, who would become one of the most feared Japanese in South Celebes![2]

Riding alongside the irrigation canal, we looked at the beautiful landscape. In the background stood a high mountain range, next to the plump shape of the Lompo Batang mountain. A magnificent sight.

Then we turned right and crossed the wide bridge that led into Kampili. We caught a glimpse of little boys swimming in the canal. So, that was evidently permitted and it reassured us somewhat.[3]

The bus stopped in front of a central building — the residence of the Japanese Commandant and thereafter referred to as the Command Post — where those who had arrived before us were waiting. Children, crying from happiness, ran into the arms of their ecstatic mothers — there was hardly a dry eye anywhere.

The Doctor's wife, who had kept only Béatrix with her, joined up with her other children, who led her to the last bungalow in a string of small houses — formerly occupied by TB patients and their families — where they had also reserved a place for Sister Huberta and myself. For the time being, this would be our home.

It was a terribly small building. One room housed five adults and three children. A second room, even smaller, was home for Captain Zondag's wife (a dentist herself), her two small children and a friend.

At the back of the house was a short landing that led to a small bathroom and a miniature toilet of the squat-down variety. In front of the house was a well, which — everyone agreed — was quickly christened "the Halmahera Well", since all of us were from that general area.

Two days later, we had to clean out this 9 meter deep well ourselves and deepen it to meet the water needs of our section of the community.

It was a challenging and dangerous task, but we did it and were proud of it.

The other "Ambon people" were lodged in the remaining six houses. The seventh, a much larger house, was divided into a nun's residence and a common room for general use.

Our enduring patients were admitted to the hospital. Among them, not surprisingly, were the indestructible two old ladies from Ternate, whose care now rested in the hands of others — thank God!

Dr. Marseille and Pater van Egmond (who had been badly wounded at Ambon) were put up in a separate building, part of which would later serve as an outpatient clinic. For a while, they would be the only men in the camp, apart from our guards.

All the buildings were made of stone and were in good condition. Spread over the camp area were four good wells, including our Halmahera Well. There was also a solid kitchen building with annexes, where our kitchen crew (those who had signed up for the job) had settled.

The ground around the buildings had once been a beautifully laid out garden; now it was one big wilderness. There were still many beautiful shrubs — such as the *alamanda* with its radiant yellow trumpet calyxes, the bright red *hibiscus* and the *lantana* with its colorful little rosettes — but they were now surrounded by stiff, tall, flammable and sharp reeds. No doubt, it was this difficult to root out *alang-alang* that Colonel Ino had in mind when he instructed us to clear the land without delay. I worried about how this could be accomplished by the very few healthy women who were left.

After we had stowed away our belongings, we gathered near the main building. Our unsurpassed, courageous, and always-dignified camp leader, Mrs. Valderpoort, welcomed the newcomers warmly, and said she would only feel at ease when all the Ambon people still in Makassar had been brought safely to Kampili. Then, the kitchen crew treated us to a mug of good, black coffee.

Until late that evening we swapped stories: the earlier arrivals talked about their experiences in the camp, and we — with Sister Huberta leading — told about our adventures at "Stella Maris", which again brought on much laughter.

The surveillance of the camp and patrol of its boundaries had been assigned to a group of native policemen. As luck would have it, their Chief, Wewenga, turned out to be the brother of one of my Menadonese workers at Mon Désir. Throughout our stay at Kampili, Wewenga would give me much help and support.

Officially we were permitted to bring in provisions from the outside, but our camp leader managed our pooled resources with great restraint, so food was sparse and all extras had to be paid for from one's own pocket.

For now, I was free from any nursing duty. There were no more babies expected, and there were a sufficient number of career nurses available to take care of the sick *and* Mrs. Boddendijk, who was as demanding as ever. So I started to look around for something else to do and, as a first step, decided with my house mates to clear the *alang-alang* and weeds from around our own house.

After the cramped quarters, fear and terror of Ambon, our stay in these much freer surroundings was soothing, and we enjoyed it. Within a week, however, the situation changed again.

A group of Japanese officers came to visit the camp. Accompanied by our camp leader and Police Chief Wewenga, they arrived at our house via a back road, which was reasonably passable.

According to regulations, we lined up in front of the house, of which Mrs. Pfeiffer was the chief. She called out the Japanese commands for the required tribute:

"*Kiotskè!* — Attention!", and then:

"*Lei!* — Bow!"

When I straightened up, I looked directly into the eyes of Colonel Ino, who was dressed in a resplendent white Naval uniform and wore high, shiny black boots with spurs.

In his mumbo-jumbo Malay, he said he wanted to explain something to us. Mrs. Pfeiffer did not understand him and asked him to repeat his words. Rather than waste time with her, he aimed a forbidding finger at me and said gruffly: "She understands Malay very well!"

As I had expected, Colonel Ino then pointed to the surrounding *alang-alang* plains, and said that they had to be cleared within one month. "Everything must be pulled out. The land must be completely cleared!"

I nodded my head, but answered that we did not have the required tools. We would have to pull the reeds out by hand. To show him the impossibility of the job, I uprooted one reed with great difficulty and without cutting my hands on the razor sharp leaves.

Ino looked on impatiently. Seeing that he was getting hot under the collar, I quickly asked for tools: spades, *paculs*[4] (hoes), *parangs* (machetes), and axes too, for all the wood would have to be taken out also. In my mind's eye, I already saw it cut up and neatly stacked near the kitchen.

In response, the Colonel yelled something I did not understand,

and the Police Chief, standing behind and to one side of Ino, gestured surreptitiously to me to remain silent. But I repeated my request: "Not to oppose you," I said. "I am just as keen as you are to remove this fire hazard, but I will need tools to do the job properly."

This time, Ino listened and agreed to provide tools, which promptly arrived the next day. The truck was full of spades, *paculs*, one axe, but not a single *parang*. So the *alang-alang* would have to be taken out with the *paculs* only.

Since every able-bodied person had already been assigned a specific task during the day, we decided to work the land from 6 to 7 each morning. Every day, we counted the number of available workers and staked out a number of equal plots. Those who had finished their plot, took off right away to do their normal chores. Some workers finished in half an hour; others — not used to this kind of work — muddled on, grumbling and complaining, but they all finished their quota before seven.

Slowly, very slowly, the grounds changed in appearance — and so did we. Apart from becoming sunburned, we learned to work together as teams — each one with a specific task to perform.

Much of the good co-operation was due to our outstanding camp leader, Mrs. Valderpoort, who worked incessantly at mediation. Sometimes, she consoled, sometimes she chided, but she always had time for each one of us, and knew how to maintain the peace.

Throughout the years, we would have many camp leaders. Some held the post for a while, most stayed briefly, according to the ever-changing moods of our Japanese Commandant. None, however, would fill this unenviable position with greater wisdom and dignity than Mrs. Valderpoort.

*****

We had been at Kampili several months, when many natives came into the camp to clear all vegetation from an open terrain west of the Command Post, moving about a lot of soil in preparation for something.

Shortly after, large amounts of building materials — mainly bamboo and *atap*, but also bricks, sand and cement — were brought in by the truck load. It looked as if they were planning to build a second camp. Curious, we tried to find out from the Police what was going on, but they would not reveal anything.

Then two cars arrived — no connection with the construction project, as we had first thought. The first car held a group of Japanese officers for whom we properly stood at attention; the second one contained large parcels of clothes for both women and children.

Since we had worked so well at clearing the *alang-alang* in the surrounding area, said the Japanese, they had organized a collection of clothes in the Malino camp. Malino, they told us, was a mountain resort where European women and children from Southern Celebes and other places had been interned.

How extremely grateful we were for these donations, for our own clothes were pretty much in tatters. After the bombardment on Ambon, the Japanese had furnished several bolts of red and black parachute fabric. There had been enough to provide scanty clothing for everyone, but the fabric was already worn to threads.

All of us received something out of the parcels from Malino. The children were blissfully happy: there were indeed many attractive clothes to choose from, and the adults were also pleased. We felt human again and Kampili took on a friendlier atmosphere.

In the meantime, the construction activities had continued. A road had been built, and on each side the native workers had put up six large barracks, each one a hundred meters long. Evidently, they were to serve as sleeping quarters.

In between those barracks, they had dug wells and around each well they erected communal bathrooms. Then, at the head of the barracks were facilities for cooking and eating, and at the other end were the latrines.

Obviously, we could expect the arrival of a very large group of people. The suspense and excitement rose with each day. Since our arrival on Kampili we had not had any contact with the outside world, and we longed for news about the progress of the war.

On May 5, a brilliant day, the feared *Kempei Tai* arrived in several black cars. High-ranking officers stepped out and went to the construction site without deigning to give us — who stood at attention and then bowed as prescribed — as much as a glance. After a while, they left.

A little later, two more deluxe cars arrived, this time with high-ranking Naval officers, who, dressed immaculately in white, did not look to us as frightening as did the khaki-clad *Kempei Tai* people.

They were followed by a series of trucks full of women and children. Amazed, we watched these new arrivals, who, in our eyes, looked so well-dressed and well-kept, and appeared even somewhat brash. Apparently, they had come from the Malino camp which had earlier donated those clothes to us.

Curious, we came a little closer, but we still did not dare to go up to them and meet the newcomers. Was it out of fear for the Japanese present? Were we intimidated by their numbers? (They outnumbered us four to one.) Or was there perhaps something in their attitude that restrained us?

Among the newcomers were many nuns. By their habits we could identify the order to which they belonged, and it did not take long before our own nuns struck up a conversation with them.

Some Malino people had come originally from the islands of Bali, Lombok, Timor, Flores, Sumba and Sumbawa; the majority, however, were from South and Central Celebes.

Malino is a charming mountain resort, a two-hour drive east from Makassar. Before the war, almost all well-off inhabitants of Makassar had a vacation home or bungalow there to escape the scorching heat of that coastal city. Trading companies had vacation resorts for their employees, as did even the nuns of Makassar. Malino was ideally placed in one of the most stunning areas of Southern Celebes and it had, of course, a wonderful climate, because of its high altitude.

After the December 7, 1941, attack on Pearl Harbor, many a man had taken his wife and children up there — just as a precaution. Makassar, with its busy harbor, was considered too vulnerable to attacks from the air.

The Japanese occupied Celebes early in February, 1942, and Malino had been under Japanese control ever since. But resistance had continued farther north, under the command of Lt. Colonel A.L. Gortmans, nicknamed *Jan Oorlog* (John War). Only after the Japanese threatened to kill all European civilians did Gortmans surrender, but on the condition that these civilians be brought together for mutual protection. The women and children were eventually interned at Malino, the men, at Pare-Pare[5].

Until their departure for Kampili, the people in Malino had been relatively free. One could not venture outside Malino itself, nor have contact with the native population, but those were really minor restrictions. What had made more of an impact was that the Japanese had burned all books, forbade the teaching of children, and made it a punishable offense to exchange letters with husbands in the Paré-Paré men's camp and the Makassar POW camp. To enforce these rules, the Japanese conducted frequent house searches — as they had done at Ambon, of course.

Other than that, it appeared that the Malino people had had it reasonably good. It followed that Kampili would be a disappointment to them. No more kapok mattresses, running water, or electricity! Now they were camp inmates just like us, and for some, this adjustment would be very painful.

# IBU MALUKU

One incident involved the wife of an Assistant Resident, a very outgoing person, whose first name was Love. Dressed smartly in white tennis shorts and a tight-fitting blouse, she walked with wagging hips up to a group of Japanese Naval officers and greeted them jovially with: "Hello boys!"

There was a moment of shocked silence. Then one officer turned and delivered a stunning blow to her face that knocked her off her feet. Contemptuous, the Japanese turned to the other officers, who had not given the incident the slightest attention. Moaning, Love got up, holding her hands to her face, and slunk away.

Later she showed up for roll-call with a raw piece of meat tied to her battered face, and from that day on, our Japanese Commandant called her *"Nyonya Bistik"* — Mrs. Beefsteak!

\* \* \* \*

The 1200 Malino people were assigned to their quarters — 100 persons per barrack; more, if there happened to be very young children.

Barrack No. 1 became the residence for 92 nuns, who lived, prayed and slept there. Their barrack was always neat and clean, and the Japanese Commandant would often mention this barrack as an example to the rest of us.

In the beginning, the Malino people (individually or in groups) prepared their meals separately. Like us, they could buy provisions from merchants who, at certain times, were allowed into the camp. Later, when their resources had dried up, our Ambon Camp leader had to step in with her funds. When finally there was no more cash, we were forced to prepare our meals together; the provisions then came from *Dai Nippon*[6]. And this brought about the formation of the Central Kitchen.

Mrs. Jo den Hond took charge of this kitchen and she was incredibly good. From practically nothing she always managed to make something.

The cooking was done in large containers (oil drums that had been cut in two) by a volunteer cooking crew who did this extremely heavy work in two shifts.

Each shift had to provide dry kindling wood. The Japanese Commandant provided firewood, but it was usually freshly cut and thus too moist for starting a fire. Once the kindling wood was alight, they shoved the soggy logs on top, hoping it would dry out sufficiently and then catch fire. It usually created a tremendous amount of smoke, which gave the food a distinctive flavor.

The morning shift, which was the hardest, started at four in the morning. The cooks then took turns standing on the blazingly-hot concrete casing around the fire, to stir the rice porridge in the high 200-liter drums and thus keep it from burning.

Rain or shine, wet or dry firewood, by six o'clock everyone was given a mug of coffee. Half an hour later, the bell rang promptly for the distribution of the watery porridge.

The midday shift started at nine. If sufficient water had been carried in, the rice could be washed, and the cleaning of the vegetables started soon after that. In later years, it occasionally happened that an underfed *kerbou* (water buffalo) was slaughtered. The meat was very welcome, but with 1,600 people sharing it, each person received only a few cubes, smaller than dice.

Our male doctor, Dr. Marseille, who also worked as butcher and general handyman, took the lot of the cooks very much to heart. Their hard work inspired him to write a "poem", in which he admired their courage, but confessed that their bedraggled appearance caused him to "desire not one among them". The cooks took his unchivalrous comments in their stride. They really didn't have much time for his botched attempts at writing poetry, nor for any other trifles.

After all, who but they could ensure that the rice would get cooked and the meals served? Certainly not the doctor! But, nevertheless, his efforts were greeted with much laughter. Without a sense of humor, we would not have survived!

\* \* \* \*

Soon after the arrival of the Malino people, I met Willy Fuhrie's cousin, Maddy Heynneman, who had come from Malino with her sons, Ron and Evert. (Her husband, Johan, and eldest son, Robert, had been sent to the men's camp at Pare-Pare.)

Several days later, Tadashi Yamaji, a heavy-set non-commissioned Naval officer, became the permanent commandant of the camp and Colonel Ino (already well known to the Malino people) now receded into the background.

Yamaji came directly from the Pare-Pare men's camp, where — in the short time he had been there — he had become feared for his brutality. Of course, we didn't know this at the time of his arrival.

His favorite form of punishment — as we would soon learn ourselves — was beating his victim black and blue with a freshly-cut tree branch. One Priest in Pare-Pare almost died from such a beating. Understandably, the men there were aghast to learn that he was to become Kampili's commandant.

Yamaji — whose most popular nickname became "de Bolle" (the round one) — had a round face, a crewcut and dark-rimmed glasses. He usually wore a light-olive cap embroidered with the distinctive anchor of the Navy, and often shuffled around in ankle high, oversized boots.

He spoke a Malay of sorts, interlaced with Japanese words — his favorite one-liner being: "*Musti pukul, dayoh?* — you must be beaten, right?" (As we would learn, in his culture, beating was not only normal; it was often considered necessary!)

Rumor had it that he turned strange at the time of the full moon. True or not, we were especially careful at that time, because — as we quickly found out — once his anger was aroused, he behaved like a madman.

During the 28 months he was our lord and master, we would learn about his never-ending fear of losing face and of not being respected. Yamaji's way to get respect was through fear. His strategy was invariably to divide and conquer. We also learned, to our dismay, that he had an infallible memory.

Yamaji had an adjutant. The first one was a menace and, thankfully, didn't stay long. The second was a young, bashful, extremely polite 20-year old, Okashima, who quickly became known as *Daantje*, or Dannyboy. The American missionaries (who had come with the Malino people) called him "Sweet Sixteen", others dubbed him *Bellefleur* (beautiful flower) on account of his apple cheeks.

Yamaji selected one woman and two boys from the camp to cook and clean his house. He was a clean person himself, and insisted on cleanliness in his house and throughout the entire camp.

Our Camp Leader — first, Mrs. Valderpoort (an Ambon person), later, Mrs. Joustra (a Malino person) — reported directly to Yamaji.

* * * *

After our funds had dried up, we had little choice but to work for the Japanese in exchange for food. Yamaji set up a sewing room, headed by a Japanese tailor, and instructed us to make uniforms for the Marines. At one time, the sewing staff consisted of 125 women.

Elderly women would knit socks and gloves and embroider cherry blossoms for badges; the younger ones would operate sewing machines. There was no problem in recruiting women to do this work. It was clean work, and it had its fringe benefits. There was always thread and yarn left over that could be bartered for other goods. The most-wanted commodity was sugar, and a Quaker Oats tin[7] of sugar (roughly a liter) became the standard unit of payment.

We also set up a Roads Service and a Water Service. The former maintained the roads and ditches; the latter was responsible for the water supply to kitchens and bathing facilities. The repair of our water pumps became the task of Dr. Marseille, assisted by one or more teenage boys.

Each adult and teenager had to deliver, every day, two buckets of water to the kitchen. It would be boiled for drinking water, coffee and tea; it would also be used to rinse the vegetables and wash out the cooking drums. One woman became the Water Chief, and her task was to make certain that everyone did indeed deliver their daily quota.

Some time after the Malino people had arrived, I remembered there had been cows on a Frisian farm near Makassar. So I persuaded Yamaji to bring six animals to Kampili and to build a shed for them. Not only did these cows give us milk for the children and the sick, but they also helped to keep short the rapidly-sprouting grass.

Yamaji put the nuns in charge of the cows — he said he couldn't trust anyone else to deliver *all* the milk that the cows produced. This posed a problem for these good souls. The Mothers Superior from the different orders got together to discuss the matter and finally decided that, yes, their nuns could milk the cows and clean the cowsheds — provided that bigger boys and girls would help cut the fodder — but that the nuns could not get involved in the propagation of the animals. They declared that this was out of bounds for their flock — and so it was entrusted to me.

Soon Yamaji looked upon me as *the* veterinarian of camp Kampili. I imagined that Papa and Grandpapa, high up in heaven, were probably very pleased and were, in fact, smiling down on me! But Grandmama was probably having a fit, knowing that — despite her strenuous objections — I had become a veterinarian after all!

### Endnotes
1. The *Kempei Tai* is the Japanese Secret Service, akin to the German *Gestapo*, but centuries older.
2. Here is another instance of infiltration of the Netherlands East Indies by Japanese advance men. Ikawa, the shopkeeper of Ternate was one; Colonel Ino was another. When they were recruited is not known, but the importance of their position suggests an early tie-in to the Japanese war machine.
3. Later, a barbed wire fence would be constructed on the camp side of the canal, which would then make swimming impossible.
4. A *pacul* is like a garden hoe, but of more solid construction, attached to a long wooden handle, and swung like an axe to till the

soil. Throughout Africa this tool is known as a *jembe*.
5   Gortmans and other KNIL soldiers were eventually interned in Makassar, where Gortmans continued to guide guerilla operations in central Celebes under the noses of the Japanese. He was eventually found out and was executed on April 6, 1944.
6   *Dai* means "great", *Nippon* is the Japanese name for Japan.
7   In the tropics, provisions quickly spoil because of the heat and humidity. Therefore, the most common form of packaging is tin cans. Quaker Oats was sold in cans. The contents had long since been eaten, but the cans were kept and used as a unit of measure.

# IBU MALUKU

IBU MALUKU

# CHAPTER 37

### *The Cassava Garden*
*Kampili, Celebes, June 1943*

The war was becoming more intense — the Allies now bombed Makassar almost every day. Sometimes they showed up at night, too, and we would then sit outside under the stars — who could sleep with all that noise anyway — and watch the searchlights criss-crossing the sky, trying to lock in on the airplanes that were unloading their lethal cargo.

For the military wives whose husbands were in Makassar it was, of course, a distressing spectacle. But the wives of the men in Pare-Pare worried too, for that city was also an important port and, therefore, a likely target.

As we watched in silence from a relatively safe distance, we were aching to know what was happening there ... and elsewhere in the world.

\*\*\*\*

Since my nursing and obstetrical expertise was no longer required (there was a sufficient number of nursing professionals in the camp) and the *alang-alang* had all been cleared, it was natural for my thoughts to turn to gardening, to keep busy and to augment our meager supply of vegetables. I was worried that the constant diet of rice would adversely affect our health and stunt the growth of the children, who needed vitamins for their proper development.

Bordering on the northern side of the camp was a fairly large area, formerly cultivated by mentally-handicapped people who had long since been moved to a psychiatric hospital at Enrekang, in Central Celebes. Yamaji turned this terrain over to us, so we could transform it into a vegetable garden, as the soil was much better than elsewhere in the camp.

The previous occupants had planted *ketella pohon* (cassava, from which tapioca is made), which was ready for harvesting. This was an unexpected bonus for us, and a welcome addition to our menu.

Some twenty women volunteered to work with me in what became known as the *Kasbietuin* (Cassava Garden). To cheer ourselves up, we often sang as we worked, until Yamaji told us to stop — no reason given. No more singing, except on Sunday during church service!

We harvested the existing *ketella*, tilled the earth with a *pacul*, fertilized the land with human and animal excrement, and planted all sorts of greens alongside the replanted cassava.

The result of our work was gratifying. Before long, the women in the central kitchen were cleaning vegetables that had all been harvested in our garden.

How proud we were!

Yamaji appointed me *Kepala Kebon*, head of the garden, and from then on, I lived with Willy Fuhrie and two other women from the "Garden Service" in a small shed in the Cassava Garden, which lay outside the camp proper. Many envied us and, over time, we were exposed to both jealousy and flattery — one being as unpleasant as the other. Although we were guarded by a policeman, it would have been easy to have contact with the natives from two nearby *kampungs*. Such contacts were tempting — they knew more of what was going on outside than we did — but it was also strictly forbidden.

Yamaji emphatically warned me that I would be held responsible for any infractions and would have to bear the consequences — his gesture of decapitation made it clear what he had in mind.

On several occasions, when he perceived that I or a member of my crew had violated his order, my life was in jeopardy and I spent many desperate hours trying to convince him that nothing had really happened. One day, Yamaji's anger boiled over and I fled. Father Beltjens kept me hidden for a whole day, which could have cost him his life. But eventually, Yamaji calmed down again.

On June 12, the day before Pentecost, Yamaji came to the Cassava Garden while I was busy protecting newly-planted eggplants against the sun with cut pieces of a banana tree trunk.

Police Chief Wewenga, with whom I'd had frequent contact since I'd found out he was the brother of my *mandur* on Mon Désir, arrived shortly afterwards to ask Yamaji's permission to go to Makassar the next day. It was Pentecost, he explained, the day for the High Mass.

"Why do you have to go to Makassar for that?" Yamaji inquired.

"Well, for a Catholic, that is the proper thing to do," said Wewenga, "and perhaps the *Kepala Kebon* will be permitted to go too?"

"You may go," said Yamaji, "but she may not leave the camp. But why do you have to go to Makassar?"

"Well," I replied in Wewenga's place, "we have no priest at Kampili, which is why I want to go too. But if that is not permitted, *apa boleh buat* — what can I do?"

Yamaji wanted to know more. What was Pentecost?

"Pentecost is a special Christian festival," said Wewenga. "It is a good time to go to confession."

"What is confession?" Yamaji asked.

Wewenga hesitated, searching for words, and again I jumped in:

"Well, that is when you tell the priest all the mistakes you have made. The priest then pardons all your sins and prescribes a means to atone for them," I said, and quickly added: "If we had a priest in Kampili, we could do it right here."

Yamaji still did not understand what a confession was all about, and asked me to give him an example. I racked my brain for an illustration that he could relate to, and said: "If you tell me and my crew to dig a ditch, and we don't do it, then we are disobedient. That is wrong, for you are the boss here and we have to obey you. In confession we would admit our wrongdoing, and could then expect some form of punishment to atone for our mistakes." (For Yamaji, punishment of course meant a good beating; he didn't know any other kind.)

Yamaji then promised quickly — a little too quickly, I thought — that he would try to get a priest from Pare-Pare. But it would have to be a versatile person who could do many things beside giving spiritual guidance.

A few weeks later, he came to tell me he had succeeded and that a priest would indeed be coming. I was elated. But when the man arrived, he turned out to be *Dominee* Spreeuwenburg, a *Protestant* Missionary who came recommended as a capable carpenter. His wife, who had been maimed by the bombardment on Ambon, was also in Kampili.

"Are you happy to have your priest now?" Yamaji asked me.

"He may be a good carpenter, *Tuan*," I said regretfully, "but he can't give us spiritual guidance. He is a *Protestant* minister." (The leader of the Pare-Pare camp, *Dominee* Bikker, may have made the switch for humanitarian reasons (to unite the minister and his wife), but I suspected that he could not pass up the opportunity to promote his own faith and thwart the "competition".)

Yamaji was clearly annoyed at having been deceived, but said that he did not dare make a second request to his superiors in Makassar.

"I am not allowed to have any men in the camp," he stated. "If I bring another man here, he will go from woman to woman and create a lot of babies. I will not tolerate such shenanigans. It is forbidden[1]."

But after I had explained to him that priests were celibate, Yamaji asked:

"Can a priest slaughter animals?"

"A priest can do anything," I answered without blinking, knowing that Yamaji had not been pleased with Dr. Marseille's performance as butcher. (Priests are not trained to slaughter animals, of course, but since most of our priests came from farms, I had a good chance of being right.)

"*Etohhh,*" sighed Yamaji, signaling that he was thinking. Then, he promised he would give it another try.

Two months passed after Yamaji made that promise and nothing had happened, so I pushed the matter out of my mind. But shortly after, he did indeed receive clearance from his superiors.

When the second request for a priest arrived in Pare-Pare, the leadership decided to send Pater Beltjens, who had never slaughtered an animal in his life, but was given a crash course by professional butchers before Yamaji came in September to fetch him.

Yamaji, still angry for having been made a fool of, drove off with the priest *and* all of Pare-Pare's three hundred pigs. He considered that proper punishment and a fitting means to regain face!

I was in the Cassava Garden when Ron Heynneman came running from the Command Post to summon me: "Mrs. van Diejen, Yamaji wants you to come to the Command Post immediately. The pigs and *Meneer Pastoor* have arrived and Yamaji is livid."

I ran back with him — my heart in my mouth — but I would never find out what Yamaji was so angry about. (He often became angry when people did not anticipate his every move, so perhaps his lordship had expected me to stand in the sun for hours, waiting for him to return from Pare-Pare.)

When I arrived, out of breath, the nuns had already lined up. They had been ordered to dress in their finest habits. What a laugh! As if they had much to choose from.

Several trucks stood in front of the Command Post, filled with snorting pigs. In the passenger seat of the first truck sat a heavy-set Dutchman, who got out and revealed himself to be naked except for a very brief pair of shorts. And what a lot of hair he had on his chest!

The nuns looked at him with open mouth, then turned to me and asked bashfully: "Is that the priest, *Mevrouw*?"

"I don't know," I answered. "I have just been told that *Meneer Pastoor* and the pigs have arrived. I have never seen that man before."

That man turned out to be Father Beltjens, making his entry from the midst of the snickering Japanese drivers who had immediately realized the acute embarrassment of the nuns.

But Father Beltjens quickly made himself at home, and took a room in the outpatient clinic. Very early in the morning, he performed his priestly duties, dressed in the few vestments that were left to him. At other times, he functioned as butcher, pump repairman, tinsmith, advisor and shepherd — dressed only in a *pèndèk* (a pair of shorts with a drawstring).

Immediately after sunrise the squat, barrel-chested Pater, carrying the necessary tools, would leave for the slaughter house in the company of a few sturdy boys. Their job would be to slaughter pigs for Japanese kitchens, and less often, a *kerbau* (water-buffalo) for our camp.

After that, he would be busy repairing pumps or other types of equipment. No matter what the problem was, he always managed to make those things work again.

He was always good-natured, and knew how to encourage or console people with a joke or a cheerful word. When necessary, however, he would not hesitate to remind one, abruptly and forcefully, of one's duties. He was averse to flattery and would indicate, clearly and quickly, if something was not to his liking.

He got along fine with Yamaji, but when necessary, the Pater was not afraid to stand up to him. His good relations with the Commandant, however, did not help him on one occasion when he received a beating for something he had not done. Pater Beltjens patiently submitted to it, but it caused such a storm of indignation in the camp that Yamaji felt obliged to apologize to him — thereby showing another side of his nature.

\*\*\*\*

Immediately upon Pater Beltjens' arrival, Yamaji had instructed me to organize a place for confessions. It was no easy task, as there were few empty spaces left in the camp. It could not be done in one of the barracks — there would be no privacy there. The Ambon nuns finally cleared a little storage room in one of the stone houses.

I found a chair with only three legs but was lucky, then, to find the fourth one. A dirty little table was cleaned with sandpaper and, after cleaning the room, I reported to Yamaji that the confessional was ready.

He came with me, and as soon he saw the place, I received a slap in the face.

"*Kurang ajar!* No respect!" he said angrily. "Don't you have any regard for the priest?" and he slapped me again.

"What on earth was that for?" I yelped. "I have done everything you have asked of me."

"You have no manners," Yamaji bellowed. "No linen on the table and no flowers! And why only one chair?"

"One chair is sufficient," I said, rubbing my cheek. "We kneel beside the priest."

"And what about me," he countered, "Where do I sit?" and then he walked out.

So that was the problem! He had wanted to hear our confessions, perhaps hoping to learn a little about our sins and what we thought of him.

How did I ever get started on this?

I found a tablecloth and an empty calabash for flowers for the confessional and, then, took my one remaining problem to Pater Beltjens: how to keep Yamaji away.

"Don't worry," he said cheerfully. "I'll fix him."

He did too. He told Yamaji that it would useless for him to attend the confessions, because he would not understand one word — they would be conducted in Latin!

"Then you can translate it for me afterwards," Yamaji insisted.

"Yes, *Tuan*, I shall do that," Pater Beltjens said obediently, but of course it never happened.

As punishment for my lack of respect, Yamaji forbade me to go to church and to confession until further notice.

\*\*\*\*

By now I had become veterinarian for the pigs as well. But the animals did not really give me much work: all I had to do was to make sure the piglets were safely brought into the world. Yamaji invariably watched from outside the pen while I helped deliver the piglets. Leaning on the railing, he would give superfluous and unwanted instructions, occasionally asking:

"*Berapa lagi* — how many more?"

The pigsty was managed and maintained by ten robust women, under the leadership of Annemarie Halewijn, and assisted by two dozen teenage boys. The pigs, at one time numbering more than 500, were kept in neat, covered sties, with wooden floors and bamboo partitions, which had to be kept spotless. The pork would, after all, be going to the Japanese in Makassar, who also provided the animals' food.

The food for the pigs consisted of tons of scraps from hotels and officers' mess-halls. This food sometimes contained desirable items, such as unpeeled potatoes that we were not able to grow ourselves. Thus, in spite of its unsavory odor, that slop was always subjected to a diligent search by members of the pig team.

\*\*\*\*

On July 23, Makassar was bombed for 22 hours, primarily in the harbor area. The air was full of black clouds from anti-aircraft gun fire, and Japanese planes — they sounded different from the Allied ones — were obviously involved in aerial combat. A few days later we learned from coolies who worked at Kampili — yes, we did communicate surreptitiously, in spite of the danger — that Makassar had been badly hit. Luckily, our men were not working at the harbor just then, but some 500 natives who were, perished.

The coolies we spoke to were obviously impressed with this display of air power, which led one man to ask if we would be prepared to take Japanese money in exchange for Dutch money. The request was, of course, turned down.

Since I spent most of my time in the Cassava Garden, I didn't get involved in the running of the camp itself, except when there were meetings with our camp leader, the barrack leaders, or Yamaji himself. I do know however, that all activities were very well organized.

During the day, every adult had an assigned task and the older children worked in the gardens several hours each day. These smaller gardens did not compete with the Cassava Garden either in size or production, but we did grow sweet potatoes there. It provided our youth with much-needed exercise and gave them something constructive to do.

The larger boys helped with all sorts of camp chores — fixing pumps, slaughtering animals, carrying water, emptying septic tanks and so on; the girls helped in weeding and watering, doing the work with a lot of zest. Slowly our camp became an organized community.

There was not much activity at night, though, for there was hardly any light. The 100-meter-long barracks, for instance, had only one measly kerosene lamp. People did make their own oil lamps, but those didn't provide enough light to do much of anything.

We learned to adjust to the hardships of camp life but, at night, loneliness took hold of us — especially for those (like myself) who had no idea where their loved ones were. We were then beset by memories, longings and fears, and struggled to cope with the hurt of the separation and the unbearable uncertainty of it all. Then we would think about Holland and all our loved ones there, and wonder if they were still alive.

Sometimes the hurt made us want to cry out and rise up in revolt — even against God, who had allowed all this to happen. But, in the end, we prayed hard for strength and courage. Sometimes, we found solace in that.

Later that month, Yamaji agreed to allow children to be taught once again. This reversed a policy, started early in 1942, which outlawed schools and resulted in the burning of most books. Both at Ambon and at Malino, however, nuns and secular teachers had secretly instructed children, in defiance of this policy.

So, from July on, we started to openly teach the 400 youngsters from grade-school to high-school level — without the use of books, of course. We covered pretty well all subjects, except the few for which we didn't have teachers. We taught them outside on the grass, in the barracks, in storage sheds — wherever.

In the following year, Yamaji gave permission to construct bamboo buildings for a kindergarten, primary school and high school alongside the irrigation canal, close to the entrance to the camp.

The teachers did a marvelous job. Many boys and girls owed their future to those dedicated teachers. Two of them, however, Sister Wilhelmina and Mrs. Logeman, would never see their pupils grow up, for they perished before the end of the war.

Another major thaw occurred in our relationship with Yamaji, when he not only allowed us to celebrate Queen Wilhelmina's birthday on August 31, but also gave us the day off *and* provided extra rations. We were flabbergasted, and uncharitably assumed that the war was not going so well for the Japanese.

The unforgettable event was celebrated with a *combined* Protestant and Catholic church service — something that would have been unthinkable before!

\*\*\*\*

Yamaji was undoubtedly a brute, and a cunning one. Invariably, he skillfully manipulated the internees' political situation to his own advantage, playing the few men against the women, and the Ambon people against the Malino people.

Yet, there was also another side to him. He was definitely concerned about the state of our health, and did much to combat the dysentery that had already killed many women and children.

Early in August 1943, we received dysentery shots and, to reduce the chance of transmission, Yamaji ordered every able-bodied person to deliver — at first only 40, later 300 or 500 — dead flies that were major carriers of the disease. Certain high-risk areas, marshes and septic areas were also dusted with quick-lime.

Dysentery patients — sometimes over a hundred — were immediately quarantined, and access to them was carefully monitored. Through strenuous effort, we managed to bring the number down to 50 in early

1945, but Yamaji was still not satisfied.

He noticed that Barrack #1 (where the nuns lived) had a higher than average share of dysentery patients and decided to track down the cause. He installed himself near my house in the Cassava Garden, watched the comings and goings to the dysentery barracks, and finally found his answer.

Unlike the other food-carriers, who left the food for the patients *near* the gate, the nuns went *through* the gate and *inside* the barracks. It was obvious, he thought, that dysentery-carrying flies settled inside the folds of the nuns' habits and were thus transported back to the barracks.

Problem solved!

Apart from dysentery and intestinal disorders, many among us also suffered from malaria. I myself would never completely get rid of it.

One day, Yamaji conceived what, at first, seemed like a foolhardy notion — to have us plant our own rice, because he foresaw that the supply of this, our staple food, might be jeopardized in the near future. So he annexed some ten hectares (25 acres) of *sawah* or rice paddy land from the native population. These lay on the other side of the irrigation canal; thus, outside the camp. I liked the idea because working there would feel like having been liberated. For a short while, we would really be "outside".

But I also had some misgivings about our own abilities. We laid out seedbeds and the *bibit* (seedlings) grew rapidly. With some apprehension I watched them grow. How were we going to transplant them and when? None of us knew anything about the cultivation of rice. This time I decided not to leave it to the Commandant and took the initiative.

Briefly and succinctly I explained to Yamaji that we would readily follow his orders concerning the planting of vegetables and *ketell*a, but that we could not plant and harvest rice. None of us had any experience in that area.

At first he listened with a surprised look on his face; then he burst out laughing. Here was, finally, something about agriculture that I did not know, he chuckled. Then his smile vanished and he reviled me for being stupid, arrogant, lazy, and more.

Resignedly I let his abuse rain down on me. When finally he ran out of breath, I admitted to being more stupid than him, more stupid even than the natives who *did* know how to cultivate rice.

He walked away angrily but, late in the evening, he summoned me to his office. Usually, this bode no good.

He received me with a long string of curses, and said we would have to manage without food if we were too stupid and too lazy to grow rice ourselves. But, he added, he felt sorry for the children and the old people about whom I did not seem to care one bit.

So, he continued, he had decided to have natives do the transplanting of the seedlings and the harvesting of the rice, under my direction. But speaking to them was and would remain forbidden; I would have to make do with gestures.

Of course I praised his wisdom and promised him my full co-operation. And so we received our own *kerbau* (water-buffalo) to pull the plow, which was quite a relief for the Garden Service that had had, up to then, only *paculs* with which to till the dry, hardened soil. Our *kerbau* now did that for us. Two sturdy women signed up: one to plow, one to take care of the animal. Both did a terrific job.

Groups of natives worked regularly with us, but they had to disappear whenever the *Kempei-Tai* came to visit. The Japanese authorities in Makassar would never have allowed such close contact[2].

The plowing with *kerbaus* and the harvesting was extremely heavy work, but the food these rice-fields produced kept us alive. Without it, hundreds of internees would surely have died.

The Cassava Garden kept expanding and became our salvation. The prediction from many fellow internees that our produce, acquired so laboriously, would only serve to feed the Japanese army, never did come true.

On several occasions, we did send Chinese cabbage (*bak choi*) to the POW camp in Makassar, but this was done at our request. The harvest had been abundant and sudden rains would have caused them to perish. And Yamaji paid our camp executive promptly for those shipments.

From October 1943 to the end of our internment, in August 1945, 31 hectares (77 acres) of land were in a constant state of cultivation for growing rice and vegetables. Of this, 2.5 hectares (6 acres) were marshlands, used for growing *kangkung* (water-spinach). The picking of this vegetable was often done by 3-8 year-old *kampung* children. Yamaji sometimes remunerated them with a piece of cloth — something that could no longer be had for either love or money.

But we also suffered from a shortage of cloth. The work on the land often had to be done in the rain. During the wet monsoons (November to April) the humidity was so high that almost nothing would dry: our clothes simply rotted away. This was also true, though to a lesser extent, for those who did not work on the land.

Later, in 1944, Mrs. Joustra, who had by then become camp leader, was able to obtain some textile. There would be enough to make work clothes for everyone. For the girls and women, a *hansop* — a "jumpsuit", sleeveless for the young, short-sleeved for those over 50. For the boys, a *pèndèk*.

Every service received its own distinct color. The Garden Crew chose lavender. However, the cloth was so thin that, after a rain shower, one might as well be wearing nothing: the thin material would stick to our wet bodies and reveal all our secrets.

The year 1943 was coming to an end. Once again, rumors circulated about an approaching liberation. The cross-stick (a variety of the ouija board) and cards predicted with increasing certainty that peace was close at hand — but really reliable information was missing. Little did we know that the tide had, indeed, turned; that the Allies were already pushing back the Japanese on New Guinea, and were preparing to take Raboul.

Expectations peaked when letters arrived from the men's camp in Pare-Pare. There was nothing in those letters about peace, however, and the mood of the camp plunged to a new low when several women learned that their husbands had died of dysentery.

For us, people from Ternate, there were of course never any letters. We still didn't know where our loved ones had been taken. Predictably, after a "letter day" with no letters we became more dejected than ever. We tried to hide it from the others, but at night, the tears would flow.

Christmas 1943: In one mess hall the Protestants held a church service, which was heavily attended. For the Catholics there was a midnight Mass in the nuns' mess hall.

It was touching to hear the little children pray for *Pappie* to come back soon. Many of them were so young that they could not know what their Daddies even looked like.

Sadly, in 1944, eleven of these little ones would also die from dysentery, intestinal disorders and unknown causes — malnutrition being the major contributing factor.

After each funeral service, when we had already left the cemetery, Yamaji always came alone to lay a wreath on the grave.

**Endnotes**

[1] To avoid such "shenanigans", the Japanese shipped the older boys — those more than thirteen — to the men's camp in Pare-Pare. One group had been sent from the Malino camp, and a second group had left Kampili on July 1, 1943. That was the last time it happened. With the war not going in their favor, one may assume that

the Japanese had more important things to do than worry about boys who were beginning to "feel their oats".

2. The rationale for this policy remains obscure. Was it part of the intimidation process? Did the Japanese fear that we might persuade the natives to hinder their war effort?

# CHAPTER 38

## Life in the Camp
### Kampili, Celebes, 1944-1945

Soon after his arrival on Kampili, Yamaji taught us basic Japanese commands, which had to be used for roll-call and when Japanese officers came to visit. They were (written phonetically): *Kiotsuké* — Attention! *Lei* — Bow! *Yasumé* — At ease! And *Mayenaré* — Dismissed! They had long since become part of our daily life.

A group of Naval officers arrived in January 1944 to inspect[1] — among other things — the Central Kitchen where the chief, Jo den Hond, had lined up her staff for the official greeting. As soon as the visitors arrived, Mrs. den Hond, who could out-shout anybody, yelled "*Kiots ... ké!*" and — lo and behold! — all officers of the Imperial Japanese Navy jumped to attention, together with the kitchen staff. The staff barely managed to keep a straight face, and of course burst out laughing as soon as it was safe to do so.

\*\*\*\*

At the end of March, we received a visit from Paul Yamaguchi, Archbishop of Nagasaki in Japan. For the Catholics in the camp, this was a great blessing.

Yamaji graciously made his bedroom available to allow Father Beltjens to confess to the Monseigneur. Afterwards they strode through Barrack #1, where the nuns were already on their knees to receive the Monseigneur's blessing. Yamaji stood at the entrance looking in, surprised that the Monseigneur's race made no difference to the nuns. When the Mother Superior came over to thank Yamaji for having arranged the visit, he looked embarrassed, and mumbled something unintelligible.

Yet, though he accepted the nuns' behavior as natural, when I also knelt in front of the Monseigneur, I got slapped afterwards for not showing him, Yamaji, the same deference! That was Yamaji. Totally unpredictable!

\*\*\*\*

The internees of Kampili consisted of several groups — the largest one containing the wives and children of Dutchmen and Eurasians who had been born, or had settled, in the East Indies.

A special and close-knit group were the nuns: ninety-two devout, hard-working, ever-cheerful women, whose own difficulties and fears never mattered, and who were always ready to help others. Without them, life in the camp would have been unbearable for most of us. Anyone could call on them for help. No one was ever turned away! If a mother fell ill and had to go to the hospital or to the dysentery barracks, the nuns would collect her children and look after them until her return. The little ones could find no better care!

There were also a number of Chinese women. Among them were the female relatives of the *Majoor-Chinees*[2] who, with his sons, had been executed by the Japanese. Just because they were Chinese? As their forays into China had abundantly demonstrated, the Japanese seemed to have a special hatred for the Chinese, which may have had its roots in antiquity.

There was also a Jewish family, called Meshmoor, which created a bit of a stir in the central kitchen. The mother refused to eat what was provided because it was not *kosher*. She ended up cooking for herself and her family, receiving the best tubers and vegetables the garden could provide.

There were also other nationalities — Americans, Armenians, British, Russians and others — most of whom were assembled in the international barracks under the leadership of Mrs. Darlene Deibler[3], an American missionary.

During June and July, the feared *Kempei Tai* took two small groups of people to Makassar for questioning about a supposed hoard of stashed-away money. The two groups were eventually returned, unharmed. But then the *Kempei Tai* took away three American missionaries — Darlene Deibler included — and when they were returned ten days later, Darlene's companions had been driven insane.[4]

The two women were cared for in a shed in the Cassava Garden, next to another hut that functioned as jail. One day, Yamaji came to visit, and one of the ladies ran up to him, embraced him and cried out: "Dear commandant, the victory of the Lord is here."

Yamaji was shocked and looked very sad. A moment later he shouted angrily at a few adult bystanders who had been giggling. That they could laugh at something so terrible, he could not understand. I couldn't either, though it was probably only a nervous reaction — people were under a lot of strain.

****

During the course of 1944, tension mounted as more and more

# IBU MALUKU

Allied planes appeared in our immediate area — especially at night.

Searchlights in Makassar would then slash through the black sky, and we would hear bombs exploding. But there were also new targets: Mandai, Makassar's airport; and Limbung, just south of us, where the Japanese had built an air-strip.

In response to this close-proximity bombing, Yamaji brought in natives to dig a number of open trenches throughout the camp, and a few covered shelters — one for him and his staff, just beside the Command Post, and also beside the hospital. Aware of the military installations that existed close to our camp, he sensed danger from the air, and ordered us to camouflage our white-washed houses and barracks with mud.[5]

All this activity made us hunger even more for news from the outside. Not one plane had dropped pamphlets; no one knew anything!

Once in a while we did have a clandestine "conversation" with our Police Chief Wewenga, who would only tell us which party had been the "winner" in a recent action. If the Japs had scored well, he would say: "The mosquitoes were bothersome last night."; otherwise, "My pension flew over last night[6]." Fear of Yamaji's cane prevented him from saying more.

\*\*\*\*

For me, the operation and control of the irrigation system for the *sawahs* had serious consequences. For months on end I had pains in my feet and knees, which became so swollen that for a while I had to enter the hospital. Our doctors diagnosed it as rheumatism. Yamaji was livid. That was his response when things did not go the way he wanted.

I was not the only one who was incapacitated. Several of our loyal co-workers were laid up in the dysentery barracks and were not expected to return. Their job — to transport manure from the pigsty and the cowshed to the Cassava Garden — was taken on by a few sturdy young women, who did this unpleasant job with zeal and even cheerfulness.

The harvest from our *sawahs* was often so abundant that we had to set up an extra shift to transport the vegetables over the wide, outside road into the camp. To draw the necessary extra part-time help we had to promise special rewards. Our boys were keen on doing this work, especially when it involved hundreds of cucumbers or eggplants. As a reward, they could pick out the largest item for themselves. It was usually eaten on the spot as our children were always hungry and were very much underweight for their age. The smaller children hardly grew at all.

Often, there was no room in our hospital for those youngsters, many of whom suffered from dysentery or malaria. So sometime during 1944, we set up a separate area for dysentery patients, with one ward for the adults and another one for the children.

****

Strange as it may seem, we did have parties in our camp — with Yamaji's permission, of course. In fact, he encouraged it to relieve the palpable tension which he sensed in us. Heaven knows who started the idea of parties, but when the Central Kitchen's anniversary approached, it was decided to celebrate that event.

The other work groups followed suit, and soon a competitive spirit developed, one group trying to outdo the other. People composed verses, practiced singing, and rehearsed theatrical performances. Also, the work group that was celebrating would receive the necessary ingredients to prepare a "banquet" — always a popular event.

For the Cassava Garden, the celebration occurred on October 1. The ladies went all out. Yamaji provided an abundance of rice and a butchered goat — heaven knows where he got it! — and enough extra sugar to make several *tapeh* (fermented cassava) pies. The Camp Executive provided extra coffee. Prolonged beating of coffee extract with sugar produced the famous imitation whipped cream, popularly known as "spit". It was delicious; more importantly it *looked* and *felt* festive, just like real whipped cream. It made you feel, well, ... different!

It was just as well that Yamaji did not join the party. His unpredictability would have made people ill at ease. But he did watch with great interest from a hiding place in the garden, and I wondered what he felt at that moment.

Throughout 1944 and beyond, there was also a type of celebration held in a community center, inside the camp. The only people who were invited, initially, were the camp executive and heads of the various departments — the so-called *honchos* (Japanese for "heads"). Yamaji would then be our host and would even wait on us. It was really an executive meeting, a formal and stiff affair — a far cry from the spontaneity that made the Cassava Garden celebration such an enjoyable occasion.

During one of these executive get-togethers, the camp executive asked Yamaji for permission to now and then import eggs for the sick and for the steadily-weakening children.

Yamaji's response was to build large coops, and stock them with chickens that, regrettably, had been purchased from the local population with little forethought. A hundred of them had to be killed soon after their arrival because they were sick. But they were still edible and provided an unexpected boon for the diet kitchen — the kitchen that catered to the sick.

Thereafter, the new chickens were selected with more care. We also purchased ducks, which were carefully tended by two, later four, women. Among them was one of the two American missionaries whose mind had become so unhinged by the treatment meted out by the *Kempei Tai*. She fulfilled her task with an extreme and often compulsive fervor.

The women tending the chickens obviously enjoyed their work. One, Mrs. Hofker[7], complemented her work by making funny drawings. Yamaji caught her at it and quickly found something else for her and her companions to do. He instructed them to scoop up all chicken droppings and lay them out to dry in the sun. Then, they had to be mashed with a wooden rice mortar into a kind of guano, which was to be used to fertilize the garden. It was dirty work, and also very tiring. Even the garden crew hated this chicken manure, for it had to be distributed by hand.

Later, we used the contents of septic tanks to fertilize the smaller vegetable gardens inside the camp. Boys were recruited to do that stinking job and the smell that hung over the camp at such times was revolting.

\*\*\*\*

At the end of October, we were devastated to hear that the men's camp at Pare-Pare had been bombed by the Allies on October 20 and 21. Seven women were told that their husbands had perished. Most of them were from the northern part of the Moluccas.

Fear crept over us. "How long is this horror going to continue? Will it now be our turn to be bombed again?" Those questions were never uttered out loud, but were always on our minds — at least on the minds of the Ambon people. The Malino people had not yet lived through a bombardment and so had difficulty understanding the fear we felt, and showed, whenever we heard the roar of approaching airplanes.

Yamaji told us that the survivors of the Pare-Pare bombardment had been transferred to abandoned pigsties, seven kilometers from Pare-Pare near the Bodjo river. Even Yamaji, himself, was livid at that indignity.

For seven months those men would be forced to live in filth and manure; they suffered terribly from hunger, dampness and the cold (it was high in the mountains). About twenty-five men would perish before the remaining 625 were moved to Bolong, in the mountains of the Toraja-lands.

Those dirty, but still living, skeletons would eventually survive the war. Many would be broken for life; the others would find that, although they were eager and capable to go back to work, society no longer wanted them.

\*\*\*\*

On November 14, the natives from the surrounding villages brought in forty incendiary bombs that had been dropped within a two kilometer radius of our camp.

This, in addition to the bombardment of Pare-Pare, made Yamaji increasingly nervous, and he ordered everyone to be in the trenches within minutes after the alarm bell had sounded.

During an alarm, late in December, two women were assisting an elderly lady towards the shelter. They were not moving fast enough for Yamaji, and he shouted: "*Lekas* — hurry up! When they answered they could not, he immediately slapped all three of them and ordered them to report to the Command Post.

There, he beat the elderly lady, Oma Zimmerman, with a bamboo cane and sent her packing. Then he grabbed a wooden bat, told the younger women to raise their hands and beat them until their behinds were raw. For weeks, they would not be able to sit or lie on their backs.

"Next time," he thundered, "you run!"[8]

His anger gone, Yamaji then ordered 500 pairs of pants to be made for the Pare-Pare men who were still in Bodjo. Apparently, they didn't have much to wear anymore.

\*\*\*\*

The year 1944 was coming to an end. Cross-woods and cards once again predicted that liberty was near. We did not know it, of course, but General MacArthur was already firmly entrenched on Morotai, which he would use as a springboard for driving the Japanese out of the Philippines.

There was now a more upbeat mood in the camp, because we enjoyed more freedom. Things that would never have been permitted before, were possible now — a clear indication that the tide had turned in our favor.

Christmas was celebrated in the large *Kerkloods* (Church Barrack), where a stage had been built. On either side — oh wonders of wonders! — hung larger-than-life-size portraits of Queen Wilhelmina and her late husband, Prince Willem, *with full permission of Yamaji*!

They were drawn in charcoal and colored with dyes made from home-grown vegetables and roots. And, of course, there were also orange banners in honor of the Royal House of Orange.

Yamaji somehow managed to have a piano brought in[9]. Mrs. Olga Duyvenée-de Wit, a Russian concert pianist who had married a Dutchman, started a Russian folk song choir that would perform regularly in the Church Barrack.

# IBU MALUKU

Thereafter, the Church Barrack was sometimes jokingly referred to as the "Opera House". However, those who attended the Sunday Protestant or Catholic services there would always refer to it, more respectfully, by its former name.

Even in the little room where the *honchos* sometimes dined together with Yamaji, the walls were now painted with early scenes from the life of the Royal family — enlarged from clippings that someone had managed to hide away.

There was also a large portrait of Queen Wilhelmina. When Yamaji entered the room for the first time, we, the guests, looked on wide-eyed, as Yamaji bowed deeply in front of this portrait!

These were just a few of many things that signaled a change in the war situation. But many among us started to doubt that we would live long enough to see freedom. The optimists insisted that liberty was just around the corner; the pessimists could not see the light at the end of the tunnel any more and thereby soured the general mood. This pessimism also affected Yamaji. Once again he became capricious; he would often burst into an uncontrollable rage for seemingly no reason at all.

One day, he rode his brown-and-white-spotted horse like a madman through the camp, howling and screaming at anything that moved. I was walking cautiously on a muddy, slippery path when I met him. From afar he yelled that I should walk faster. Fearing his whip, I ran! Suddenly I slipped, fell hard, scrambled to my feet — and discovered that my left arm and wrist were broken!

Yamaji, who had caught up with me, became even more enraged and lashed out with his whip. Ducking, I was able to avoid the lash. I ran away fearing that he might pursue me, but he didn't. I then walked the long road to the hospital, where my arm and wrist were splinted — without anaesthetic or sedative of course.

A week after the accident, a wobbly *rotan* chair was delivered to my little house, intended, presumably, for me to rest in after work. Was it Yamaji who had sent it? Was it a peace offering? An apology? I don't know.

However, most of the time I found the chair outside in the shadow of a mango tree, and Yamaji himself would be in it, sleeping like a log or simply enjoying the quietness which he could not find in the busy camp.

This chair became a object of mockery but was, nevertheless, enjoyed by all who could use it now and then. It was the only easy chair to be found in the entire camp.

\*\*\*\*

Allied bombardments around our camp increased in frequency and intensity. Suddenly rumors bolted from barrack to barrack: "The Allies have landed in France, and are now in the Netherlands also!" From then on, we eagerly followed the course taken by the Allied planes that flew around — but never over — the camp.

Then, a great silence fell over Kampili. We heard *nothing* anymore; not a single snippet of news penetrated the barbed wire boundaries of the camp. But the activity in the air increased; planes passed over in ever increasing numbers. As a precautionary measure, more shelters were dug throughout the camp. Some were open; others were covered with tree trunks, interwoven strips of bamboo and earth — in that order.

In addition to occasional day-time raids, we now had a raid every night. The drone of planes kept us awake and in the shelters throughout much of the night. After one bomb had dropped close by, Yamaji ordered us to vacate the barracks in the early evening, and spend all night in the shelters. This would be particularly hard on mothers with small children.

Early each evening, we would spread our thin sleeping *tikars* (mats) on the damp earthen floor of the dark musty shelters or trenches. To save space, the children would be placed alternatingly head-to-toe, wherever that was possible.

The lack of sleep, dampness and constant tension brought on more illness. The number of dysentery and malaria patients grew steadily.

The air raids on Makassar and other important targets invariably started around eleven each night. Since they were far off, we were not overly concerned. But there was one lone plane that flew near us, which we got to recognize by the manner in which the pilot flew it. It rattled and clattered through the darkness, occasionally dropping a small bomb in our immediate vicinity. Seemingly, the pilot's task was to keep the Japanese awake. One of his bombs landed on a native cemetery, creating fear and outrage in the *kampungs*.

Though we were not supposed to have any contact with the natives, we knew that they suffered — possibly even more than we did.

The Imperial Army seized eighty percent of their rice and vegetable crop, grabbed almost all their fruit, and exercised strict control over the natives' dairy production. Each hen had to produce a specified number of eggs for the sons of Dai Nippon, and if the quota was not met, the Japanese meted out swift and inhuman punishment.

As a consequence, many chickens developed an imaginary illness, or disappeared from the *kampungs* with their owners, who sought refuge in the forests and the mountains, where the Japanese would not find them.

\*\*\*\*

In December of 1944, a new enemy appeared on our doorstep. A rabid dog attacked three children. One, Jaapje Wesseling, was bitten in the arm; the other two, in the legs and buttocks.

Since there was no anti-rabies serum nearby, Yamaji immediately requested that it be flown in from Bandung (Java), although he doubted that it would come, and knew it would be too late even if it did.

Dr. Marseille burned out the bite wounds as well as he could, but it was too late for 7-year old Jaapje. Three weeks later, on January 4, he died a horrible death. His mother, in the hospital herself at the time, was inconsolable.

There was little we could do to defend ourselves, since the dogs had easy access to the camp. Yamaji instructed the local population and the policemen to kill all roaming dogs, and even had his own dog put away. But fear would remain with us.

Five months later, a pack of rabid dogs appeared in the evening. Our own night guard was doubled and armed with clubs.

During one of the nightly air raids, a dog attacked Mrs. Vreeden in an open trench and bit her in one ear. A quick-thinking person cut off that earlobe and saved her life. Then the dog attacked Nelly Filet who was on her way to the toilet and bit her severely in her arms and face.

Another dog (or was it the same one?) attacked a mother with a child on her arm in an open trench. Luckily she had wrapped herself and her infant in a heavy blanket just before the attack occurred. (It did get chilly at night.) The dog's teeth did not penetrate the blanket, so she got off with just a scare.

Still another attack occurred near the pigsty, where Mrs. Toos Hoogeveen — the daughter of former Governor de Haze-Winkelman — stood on guard, armed with a club. In the darkness, Toos did not see the animal fast enough, and the club clattered to the floor as she tried to defend herself with her bare arms.

She managed to get her hands around the animal's throat, and yelled for help. Mrs. Dahler, who lived near the pigsty, came running and stabbed the animal to death. But by then it had bitten Toos in the hands and arms, and she was covered with deadly slime. Dannyboy was sent to Makassar to fetch the serum that had arrived there, and in the afternoon all the bitten ladies received injections. But is was too late for some.

Nelly Filet died first.

In the Toraja-lands, Toos' husband, Roel Hoogeveen celebrated his wife's birthday on July 24 with a large cup of coffee, not knowing that she was on her death bed.

Toos was fully conscious and aware of what was happening. She accepted her lot patiently, and without protest, and passed away six days after her birthday.

### Endnotes
[1] With the war going badly for them, one wonders in retrospect why high-ranking officers would take the time to make these inspections. Was it concern for retribution when the war was over, or was it simply to find relief from their military duties?

[2] Literally, the Chinese Mayor, i.e. the head of the Chinese community in the capital, Makassar.

[3] Darlene Deibler, would later describe her experiences in her book, *Evidence Not Seen*, published in 1988 by Harper Collins.

[4] It is alleged that the Japanese questioned the American ladies in an unsuccessful attempt to learn the whereabouts of a transmitter that had belonged to Lieutenant de Jong, who had waged a guerilla war against the Japanese until he and his men were caught and beheaded on August 25, 1942. One of his soldiers, however, eluded the Japanese until the end of the war and may have kept on using the transmitter the Japanese were looking for.

[5] In doing so, however, he unwittingly succeeded in making the camp look more like a military installation.

[6] This curious saying was his way of expressing his belief that his pension would only be assured if the Allies pushed the Japanese out of the East Indies.

[7] Mrs. Hofker and her husband, both well-known artists, lived on Bali until the Japanese moved them to Celebes.

[8] Yamaji's orders were not as unreasonable as the manner in which he reinforced them. We learned later that there was an ammunition dump close to our camp.

[9] My mother, Madeleine Heynneman, and I recognized it as the one we had left behind in our home in Makassar.

IBU MALUKU

# CHAPTER 39

### *The End in Sight*
*Kampili, Celebes, 1945*

On January 1st, 1945, at 6:30 a.m., the *honchos* gathered in front of the Command Post to wish Yamaji a Happy New Year. Yamaji in turn conveyed his best wishes to all the internees, and expressed the wish that the Emperor of Japan *and* the Queen of the Netherlands (!) would start the New Year in good health. He then handed out cigarettes to the few women who smoked and also to Father Beltjens and *Dominee* Spreeuwenburg, giving the men permission to get drunk — as if there was anything to get drunk on!

The natives from the surrounding villages and the police detachment also came with gifts to wish the Commandant a Happy New Year. Yamaji again handed out cigarettes.

Two days later, Yamaji again switched camp leaders. He had had enough of Mrs. Joustra because in any dispute, he said, she always chose the side of the internee — right or wrong. Yamaji seemed to favor Mrs. Deibler, the American Missionary, whose impartial views he respected. But the mostly-Dutch inmates were not happy with that choice, so Mrs. Valderpoort, who was loved and deeply respected, became leader again after a lapse of only six months.

Both leaders were capable, but their motivation differed widely — Mrs. Valderpoort was a born leader who loved to help her fellow men; Mrs. Joustra was a consummate politician who loved power. Both did yeoman service — for the job of camp leader was an exceedingly difficult one.

Over time, the adversarial mood that had existed at the outset between the Japanese commandant and ourselves had become less acute. We had to admit, grudgingly, that — in spite of his unpredictable behavior — Yamaji did have our best interests at heart.

Early in January, he brought two Japanese doctors from Makassar to look at four children who were seriously ill. All had the same symptoms: stomach cramps and an inability to hold down food. There was not much the doctors could do. In their presence, one girl even slipped away and died.

He also arranged for inoculations against typhus and cholera, and built more trenches so we would have shelters during an aerial attack, which he felt was a distinct possibility. He took that threat so seriously that he began building a backup camp in a nearby forest — unbeknownst to all but a few of the *honchos*.

Yet, we were still fearful of Yamaji and felt relieved when he was away in Makassar. Animals were also afraid of him, and that really bothered Yamaji. One day, he was sitting in the easy chair that had so mysteriously appeared at my doorstep, when a cat jumped, uninvited, onto his lap. At first, Yamaji was too moved to speak, then he looked around proudly, and said: "Look at this puss, it came without being called."

It made his day.

Once, uncharacteristically, he talked about himself, and said that his family was poor, and that he had been forced to forego an education in order to help his younger brothers through school.

He never talked about his own family, but I assumed that he was married and had children. He also said that he would like to be seen as a caretaker, rather than the enemy, and confided that his life was no bed of roses either. True, he ate better and lived better and could get out of the camp once in a while, but the rest of the time he was also behind barbed wire, bereft of friends and leisure time.

With time, Yamaji began to show more interest in our ways and our culture. He asked about our traditions and ceremonies and took lessons in Dutch and English from Father Beltjens. Soon he started to practice Dutch, always with a delighted grin on his face. "Oh lah lah" — though it originates from French — became his filler, and he once gleefully addressed Mrs. Emmy Korteman — the alarm-bell ringer, nicknamed "Bellemie" — as *Tante* (Aunt) Emmy. He had heard children call her that.

Once, he called the teachers together and gave them a lecture on moral fortitude, commenting that they had to be an example to the children and could not allow themselves to get downhearted.

"If people complain," he said, "you must not complain with them, but be strong internally. The Almighty gives us this time as punishment — I mean as a test, to try us."

"I also think that you should talk more with the children's parents — the mamas and the papas," he continued, and then, realizing his mistake, he stroked his chin shyly, and said laughingly: "Of course, there are no papas here."

"I cannot talk so well," he concluded, " but all the *nonyas* here are so smart, that they will understand my meaning." He was of course suggesting that we hold parent-teacher meetings. Then he bowed politely as the teachers filed out of the room.

It is not surprising then that we began to see Yamaji less as an enemy, and more as a human being, trapped like ourselves in a situation beyond individual control.

Later in January, Yamaji left unexpectedly for Makassar, saying he would be back for lunch. But he returned instead at 8:00 that evening and was in a deeply depressed state of mind that would stay with him for weeks. Perhaps the war was not going so well for the Japanese, we concluded, but then there was also talk about Yamaji leaving us. Later, I was able to piece together the whole story:

He was, indeed, supposed to leave us. Rumor had it that he would go back to Japan, but that does not seem plausible, given the war situation at that time. Perhaps he had received a promotion with the option to transfer out. Two ladies had even given him gifts for his wife.

The man who applied for Yamaji's job turned out to be an unsavory person, widely known as "the beast of Menado".

When this man came to Kampili to get acquainted, Yamaji decided to make the visit as unpleasant as possible, hoping to discourage the man from taking the assignment. One trick he arranged was a visit to the slaughterhouse. A pig had been bound — but not too tightly — and when Father Beltjens stuck a knife into the animal, it wrestled free, ran away from the pater and his carefully-placed helpers in the only direction it could, charging directly at Yamaji and his visitor — blood spurting everywhere. Yamaji, yelled at his visitor to climb the tree next to him, which he knew was full of red ants, and climbed himself into one that was not!

It took the pater's helpers an unusually long time to wrestle the bleeding animal to the ground, and when the howling visitor finally came down, he danced in pain as he beat the ants off his arms and legs and from inside his pants and shirt.

Yamaji chuckled when he told me the story. Then, becoming serious, he said he had saved Kampili from a real swine. I concluded, from this story, that he had given up his furlough or transfer for the sake of the camp.

Yamaji had been trained to mete out physical punishment, and to take it without flinching when he was on the receiving end.

Once, two not-too-sober Japanese soldiers from a nearby garrison entered the camp, presumably looking for a willing woman. Yamaji, just returned from Makassar, intercepted the two men and took them to the Command Post, where he proceeded to beat them to a pulp — yelling all the time at the top of his lungs. The two soldiers, knocked off balance with every slap, immediately jumped back to attention, and literally took it on the chin. It was a frightening spectacle, and everyone who was close, slunk away.

Dannyboy was also frequently beaten up. Often, we didn't know what for; perhaps he did not know either, except when he had left a Malay-language newspaper lying around for everyone to read. It had happened once before and it was thus that Mrs. Valderpoort found out that Paris was in the hands of the Allies.

Yamaji also beat up the natives. He would cut a fresh branch from a tree, and swing until he was satisfied or until his victim had collapsed. Once he beat up a policeman — reason unknown; another time, he beat a man who had diluted the milk he delivered for the children.

The food situation was still bad. We had rice and vegetables, but hardly any protein, fruits or fats. We received one banana every two weeks and one egg *per year*. We were always hungry. To augment our diet or at least have some variety, we started eating *bungkil* — what is left of copra after the oil has been pressed out of it. It still contained B-vitamins — or so we thought. Mashed and roasted, it gave a enjoyable flavor to our rice porridge. Alas, we didn't get it for very long — it seems that the pigs needed it more than we did.

\*\*\*\*

Throughout May, without ceasing, Makassar to the north and Limbung to the south were subject to nightly bombardments. Each evening at ten o'clock we would once again pick-up our mats, blankets and clubs (to ward off roaming rabid dogs) and head for the nearest trench, where we could expect to spend a good part of the night.

At 10:30 the airplanes appeared. They could have been American, Australian or Dutch. In the darkness, there was no way to tell. As during the previous bombardments, those damp trenches did not do much for our health and, once again, many people fell ill. Some people were so tired from lack of sleep that they stayed in their barracks, willing to risk a beating from Yamaji.

On May 14, Yamaji had been with us two years. "Yes," he reminisced in an uncharacteristically humble way, "I made some mistakes, but I had a great responsibility for my young age. When I started at Kampili, I was only twenty-nine."

After May, we had a brief respite, but on June 5, the nightly bombardments resumed and continued unabated for three more weeks. On several occasions we heard strange whistling sounds, and found that our Allied friends were throwing beer bottles out of their planes. One narrowly missed people sitting in a open trench and drove itself deep into the soil. (The bottle carried the name of the Richmond Brewing Company of the United States.)

"They really don't have any manners!" said Yamaji angrily.

On June 22, two Allied planes bombed Limbung airport during the day and were attacked by a Japanese Zero fighter that dived down "out of the sun" and kept shooting until we thought it would ram its quarry. But it dived off to one side, and was caught in a stream of bullets that came from the B-24's bottom turret. The Zero burst into flames and started its plunge to earth.

We cheered. The pilot jumped out and we saw his parachute — a little cloud in the sky — drift down. We anxiously watched the B-24 that had been the main target. Had it also been hit? It circled a few times, but then flew off, seemingly unperturbed.

Yamaji later rebuked us, saying we should not cheer when an airplane was shot down. "It involves human life," he said. "I know that the pilot was badly burned and may not live."

On June 25, three American P-38 Lockheed Lightning fighters flew so low over the camp that we could see the pilots and wave to them. (We dared do this, because Yamaji was in Makassar.) One plane jettisoned a 165 gallon fuel tank. Luckily it landed in an uninhabited area.

Almost every day, from then on, we saw more of those graceful fighters close to the camp. This convinced us that the Allies knew there was a camp here with women and children, and it made us feel much safer.

With the war going so badly for Japan, Yamaji said that, as a military man, he would have to commit *harakiri* before the Allies arrived. He admitted that the Japanese people had been led astray by the men at the top. "We did not want the war, and would not have minded remaining as farmers," he concluded.

At our cemetery, which he often visited with Sister Corine, whom he liked very much, he counted the many crosses, and said he was sorry there were so many. But it was a nice place, and, if he could not go back to his homeland, then this is where he would want to be buried, pointing to a place under a tree.

One June 27 we were surprised to find pieces of pamphlets strewn about. They probably had been dropped during the night. Yamaji immediately clamped down: it was forbidden to read these pamphlets, and they should be handed in at the Command Post right away.

Of course, the pamphlet fragments were first pieced together and read anyway. It showed a gorilla-like caricature of a Japanese, with the caption — in several languages, including Japanese — saying that the power of the beast had been broken.

On the night of June 30, the Allies resumed their bombing of the usual targets and, for the first time, used bombs that lit up the sky before they exploded just above ground level. A little later, they threw out *orange*-colored pamphlets that we were again supposed to deliver — unread! — to the Command Post.

Ha!

Strict blackout regulations had to be observed, of course, if one did not want to incur Yamaji's wrath. So Father Beltjens and Mrs. Joustra hid inside the "confessional" with one of the pamphlets. Father Beltjens crouched half under the table and, while Mrs. Joustra spread her skirt over him and the table, the Pater read the pamphlet out loud with the help of a pocket light. Then Mrs. Joustra kneeled down, pulled her skirt over her head — this was no time for modesty! — and looked at the picture of Prince Bernhard and an aid who waited at the bottom of the ramp from which Her Majesty was descending.

In Malay, it said that Queen Wilhelmina was back on the throne in the Netherlands, and would do everything possible to free the people of Indonesia from the Japanese.

Father Beltjens and Mrs. Joustra decided to spread the news as quickly as possible, but to warn everyone to remain calm, so Yamaji would not notice that something special had transpired. Dr. Marseille and *Dominee* Spreeuwenburg were pressed into service and, within the hour, the whole camp had heard the stupendous news.

A tremendous joy surged through us: "Liberty is close at hand!" we cried. Hope flared in our hearts and we prayed with renewed fervor.

What a boost it gave us!

\* \* \* \*

July 17, 1945, was an exceptionally beautiful day. I marched with a large group of cheerful women into the *sawahs*, where many small native children had already picked baskets full of *kankung*.

At 9:30 those kids went home, each one carrying several tubers of cassava, and — as a bonus — a large *tèrong belanda* (egg-plant).

Around 10:00 we heard the drone of planes and shortly thereafter the tumult of bombs striking targets in the vicinity of Makassar. When the explosions became disturbingly close, a co-worker suggested we return to the Cassava Garden, where we would feel less exposed. The others agreed, so we picked up our tools and crossed the irrigation canal to sit it out.

About 11:00 we heard the roar of approaching airplanes, and yes, there they were, and this time they were coming straight at us! We counted 23 silver birds. When they crossed the camp's perimeter, one plane expelled a white trail, which we took for pamphlets.

We jumped up and cheered: "Those are Allied planes!" and with moist eyes we saw them pass overhead. These had to be our liberators and, with hope, we looked up into the blue sky, searching for pamphlets. But there were none and, sorely disappointed, we watched the airplanes disappear into the distance, leaving that white trail hanging in the sky behind them.[1]

It was too late now to do any significant amount of work on the *sawah*, so I let my co-workers return to the camp. Three women stayed with me in the garden. Among them was Mrs. van Sandik who had lost her husband on Ambon in so tragic a manner[2], and who was now caring for four small Chinese children whose mother was in the hospital.

The four of us decided to make a dugout beside our house, sensing that the war was getting much closer. We had only just begun when we heard again the drone of approaching aircraft. Our hopes revived: certainly this time the expected pamphlets would come!

The same squadron of B-24 Liberators that we had seen earlier, flew at low level straight towards us and dropped a string of canisters that came apart in mid-air.

"Bombs!", we thought. With our heads down, we braced ourselves for explosions. But all we heard were soft thuds.

"Those must be pamphlets after all!" we hoped, sitting on our haunches in the partly dug shelter. As the airplanes passed over, one woman looked up and screamed: "They are dropping fire bombs! Look! The cassava field is in flames!"

Aghast, we looked around and saw that the pigsty was also in flames. Within seconds the air was torn by the piercing squeals of 500 terrified pigs trapped inside.

Close to us lay a burning cylinder that threatened to set fire to a hedge and the dysentery wards next to it. Willy Fuhrie ran towards it and extinguished the flames with handfuls of scooped-up earth.

Flames shooting up nearby caught our attention: the chicken coops were also burning. Shortly after we heard the roar of flames and blasts of bursting bamboo: more than half the camp was on fire.

Mrs. van Sandik hurriedly got up and ran toward the burning buildings to be with the children who had been left in her charge.

The flames shot up three to four stories high and spread an intense heat, while a massive, churning, black column of smoke darkened the sky. The Liberators returned in wave after wave to unload their deadly cargo over the houses and barracks, and over the running women and children, driven mad with fear. It was an inferno!

Everything around us was now in flames, yet the planes returned to drop still more incendiaries. Some that remained bundled like stacked bottles, fell in the midst of the screaming people. In most cases, the heavy bands holding these incendiaries together came apart in mid-air — as they were probably supposed to — and the bombs, some burning already, would spread out and make their own way down to earth[3].

Upon hitting the ground, a soft plop would eject the burning jelly, which would tumble through the air like a flaming baton before returning to earth to find its mark. From the containers that had launched them and were now deeply embedded in the earth, long streams of light-blue gauze fluttered in the breeze like so many umbilical cords.

The bomb downpour was so dense that almost every square meter of the camp was covered with four to seven individual bombs. Some burned, some didn't, but they still scared us. Not knowing whether they were spent, we feared they might still explode.

Feeling unsafe in the half-finished trench beside our house, the three of us ran towards the *sawahs*. The planes, now coming toward us, continued to strafe anything that moved. We jumped into an irrigation ditch and crept along, on all fours, to put distance between us and the camp. Several scorched pigs and a loudly-squealing one that was still burning moved in among us. It was as if they were seeking our help.

We were pressing ourselves as deeply as possible into the slithery mud, when a gunner spotted us and opened fire. Bullets bored all around us in the stinking mud and one landed where only a moment before I had pressed my head into the moist earth. The realization of my narrow escape almost paralyzed me, but, determined to survive, I crept along with the others.

The aircraft returned in formation with the others, and its gunner continued his deadly game with three defenseless women. How long this ordeal lasted, I don't know. Some said it was an hour; others said it was more. I had the feeling that several hours had passed before the strafing stopped, and the horrible drone of those aircraft faded away into the distance.

We clambered out of the mud and returned to our home in the Cassava Garden. The chicken coops were one smoldering pile; the surrounding area was strewn with incinerated chickens that had shriveled into little balls. The dysentery barracks were untouched, and our house was also undamaged. In our partially completed trench lay five un-detonated incendiaries!

## IBU MALUKU

We hurriedly rinsed the stinking mud from our bodies and rushed toward the camp, where our help might be needed. The roofs of the stone-walled houses where the Ambon people had been living were in flames.

The two hospitals and the Commandant's house were undamaged, but two-thirds of the bamboo barracks of the Malino people had already been reduced to ashes. The remaining cluster of barracks presented one sea of flames, and the sharp explosive booms of the thick bamboo uprights that burst open from the heat terrified us.

The roof of the central kitchen was also aflame, and the wood that had been carefully stacked beside it to dry was reduced to charcoal. In front of the kitchen stood several Japanese soldiers from a nearby garrison. We watched a grim-faced Yamaji, pistol in hand, as he forced a handful of Japanese soldiers to enter the burning building and rescue large drums of boiling hot food from the fireplace. Thanks to him, we would still have a midday meal.

The people we met were shattered. Scared and trembling, they banded together. They had escaped by the skin of their teeth; what few possessions they'd had before were now lost in the fire. How many had perished, we did not yet know. We searched for the wounded and the dead inside the camp and outside on the *sawahs*. Predictably, those who had stayed behind in open trenches were hit hardest.

We found a seven-year old girl from Tobelo, Berthe Ploeger, who had lost her mother and sister during the Allied bombing of Tantui on Ambon. A single bomb had nailed her to the ground. We hoped that she had died quickly.

Mrs. Dahler, who had killed the rabid dog near the pigsty, had received a canister through her right thigh. Freddie Paul, an Armenian boy who had been lying face down, received a bomb in the right buttock and it had almost detached his right leg. A Belgian teacher of French, Mrs. Coumans, had been injured below the knee. All were rushed to Makassar. Only the teacher would come back alive — minus one foot.

Mrs. van Sandik, who had left us before the strafing started, did find the children who had been left in her care. They were in an open trench. When another hail of incendiaries came down, she had covered the little ones with her own body, exposing her back to the flaming jelly that rained down from the sky. Like a burning torch she had run out of the trench into the fields, possibly in search of water — which would not have helped. Badly burned, she would die two days later.

We learned that immediately after the first drop of incendiaries, Yamaji had rushed through the barracks on foot, and later on horseback, shouting to everyone in sight to leave the camp by the bridge over the irrigation canal. They did, just in time, for the area that they had just left was hit with the next wave of incendiary bombs.

Japanese soldiers from the Limbung garrison rushed into the camp. Some, standing amidst the fleeing women and children, shot with automatic weapons at the Liberators, who immediately shot back. It was a miracle that none of us were hit.

With the aircraft finally gone and parts of the camp still in flames, Yamaji summoned the *honchos* and said he had foreseen the possibility of such a bombardment and had ordered the construction of emergency quarters in a nearby forest — as a few of our leaders already knew.

These not-as-yet-completed emergency quarters turned out to be a series of primitive bamboo barracks in a small, dense forest, which made the camp invisible from the air. We soon referred to it as the *boskamp* — the jungle camp. Our people would have to snuggle up tightly, because under normal circumstances these barracks would only be able to accommodate a fraction of the camp's population of 1,670.

In the meantime, the still smoldering camp crawled with fully-armed Japanese soldiers — bayonets mounted — which stirred up new fears among the already frightened women and children. Were they here to maintain law and order or, like earlier in Ambon, to revel in our misery? We didn't know, but we interpreted their distressing presence as a possible foreboding of an even greater calamity.

Night brought an unusual coolness and many people in the *boskamp* were too cold to sleep, not having anything with which to cover their bodies. For us in the Cassava Garden, sleep did not come any easier. The night was full of frightening blasts from overheated bamboos bursting open.

The forest camp had no toilets, nor water, and the people were forced to go into the bushes, or wait till the darkness of night enabled them to use the wall-less latrines in the old camp with some measure of privacy. Most of them could not wait that long, and it was comical — if that's the right word — to see a long string of squatting figures being silhouetted against the red background of the darkening horizon.

It was the ultimate humiliation.

Later that night our house was lit up by leaping flames: the *trunku* (jail) had caught fire. The night wind had rekindled some smoldering embers and had ignited the door and roof.

Yamaji, who could not sleep either, arrived and ordered us to quickly put out the fire, fearing that it might attract unwanted attention from Allied pilots.

All night long we drew water from the well to quench the flames and also threw water onto burning sacks of chicken manure that were spreading an awful stink.

To cap it all, that little rattling and clattering plane arrived again to make the rounds and drop a bomb here and there. We did not dare go back to our house now. My God, how rattled we were!

The next day, many despondent people sifted through the ashes hoping to find remnants of their meager belongings. An Austrian Countess, reputed to have kept some jewels, poked with a twig through the ashes, as tears streamed down her cheeks. The jewels, her only hope for a bit of security, were gone.

The Garden Crew quickly picked some vegetables and tubers from the gardens, and then left. Fearing another air raid, we did not want to linger in the open for longer than necessary.

In the partially-ruined kitchen, a meal was being prepared just as hurriedly. The food was carried in large washtubs to the *boskamp*, and drinking water was transported in a similar fashion. Around eleven, the bombardment of Makassar resumed in all its intensity, and we wondered if it would ever stop.

We hastily dug graves for our dead in the little cemetery, and were on our way with one casket, when the alarm sounded. We dropped the casket on the road, and fled into the *sawahs*. Here we hid again in the muddy irrigation duct, engulfed by the putrid smell of 500 decaying pigs that had drowned or had burned to death the previous day.

Father Beltjens dove in beside us just as we heard the drone of an approaching aircraft. He gave us all general absolution and, remembering yesterday's strafing, we waited tensely for what would happen next.

Much to our relief it was only a single Allied plane — probably a scout, for it flew low over the burned barracks, perhaps to take pictures of the devastation. We breathed more freely when it disappeared in the distance. Then we returned to the abandoned casket and continued with the burial of our dead.

*\*\*\*\**

July 19 was also a brilliant day. The sun shone and shimmered on the charred ruins of the camp. Two people, who had been wounded in the bombardment, died.

Around eleven, the kitchen crew had finished cooking. The food was hastily transported to the *boskamp*, where Mrs. Valderpoort had been appointed leader. Mrs. Joustra, who was back in favor, would be leader of the old camp — what little remained of it. Teams of boys were still carrying the last tubs with water, when the bombardment of Makassar started again.

Except for a group of boys who were burying the rotting carcasses of the pigs in an open trench near the pigsty, the camp behind us was deserted. Even the sick had been moved from the hospital wards to the dysentery barracks outside the camp proper.

Four of us were in the *sawahs*, covering over some saplings to protect them against the scorching sun, when we heard airplanes coming closer.

We had just ducked under a little bridge when we saw the planes coming right at us, and we had the uncomfortable feeling of having been spotted. They flew close overhead and dropped one bomb that landed nearby and splashed us with mud. We tensed for the explosion, but there was none. Relieved, we saw the planes disappear. They were probably the ones that had just completed their mission over Makassar.

Then we suddenly became aware of two Liberators that were circling the camp at some 20,000 feet. All hell broke loose when the first one dropped its load of heavy explosives amidst the remaining stone buildings and the half-burned Ambon houses.

A minute later the second plane had its turn. The bombs seemed to come out of the tail of the aircraft like little round beads on a string, right over our heads. Then the round dots became pear-shaped, eventually emitting a piercing whistle that ended in a thunderous series of explosions, with shrapnel flying everywhere.

The biggest bomb — perhaps a 1,000-pounder, judging by the crater it produced — landed next to the hospital and sheared the building at a 45 degree angle. Other bombs destroyed most of the remaining stone buildings, including the Commandant's house.

In the *boskamp* the terrified people crowded together on the damp forest floor, seeking protection between the high surface roots of the tall trees that formed a solid canopy over their heads. They found some comfort in knowing they could not be seen, but the fear persisted that the Allies might find out about this camp and bomb it just the same.

The bombing finally stopped. Thoroughly shaken, we left our hiding place under the bridge and went home. We did not dare return to the *sawah*.

That afternoon, Willy van Sandik was buried. She had suffered horribly from her burns before a merciful death finally claimed her.

We were on the verge of despair, but refused to give in. Life had to go on; people had to be fed. So, early next morning, we went out again to pick vegetables and cassava from the fields. Whatever was left of the kitchen after the first bombardment had been obliterated by the second one, so we would have to cook under open skies. With general approval we decided to make only a thick soup, and as usual, Mrs. den Hond managed to make something savory from what little ingredients were at her disposal.

The next day, several planes flew over the camp. They were probably on a reconnaissance mission, for they didn't drop any bombs. Yet, the people were panic-stricken as long as they were around. The total destruction of the women's camp was apparently to their liking, for the planes then disappeared without further ado.

There is little doubt that the Allies knew that this camp housed women and children. Four weeks earlier, the pilots of low-flying P-38 airplanes had seen large groups of schoolchildren that could not possibly have been mistaken for Japanese soldiers.

Why then, this fire-bomb attack? Why the second bombardment? One assumes that these questions were asked after the war. Were the answers ever made public?

We, the victims, would never be told.[4]

### Endnotes

[1] That white smoke trail was probably a navigational marker.
[2] Lieutenant van Sandik was beaten to death at Tantui in the letter exchange affair.
[3] The M-69 Incendiary Bomb Cluster contained 32 individual bombs that broke apart in mid-air. Each bomb was a 2-foot long metal cylinder with a 3½-inch octagonal cross section. It was filled with a gauze-wrapped, highly inflammable jelly-like substance that would later be known as napalm (NAphtha PALMitate).
[4] Forty-five years later, my younger brother, Evert Heynneman, a young teenager at the time of the raid, would meet many U.S. airmen of the 13th Air Force, who carried out these raids from their base on Morotai. Some members of the 307th Bombing Group, who had dropped the incendiaries, knew that they had hit a civilian internment camp. Whether this intelligence was derived from direct observation or from studying photographs taken during the raid, is not known. What is known is that this intelligence did not get passed on to the 868th Bombing Group before it took off to drop conventional bombs on us. A similar lack of communication may explain why the earlier observations of the low-flying P-38 pilots did not get disseminated either.

# IBU MALUKU

# CHAPTER 40

## *Liberation!*
*Kampili, Celebes, July 1945*

On July 22nd, a lone P-38 Lockheed Lightning attacked Limbung airport, and spread panic among the women and children in the forest camp, where the sound-filtering effect of the trees made the airplane seem closer than it really was.

The people were still so traumatized by the earlier bombings that the mere sound of trucks passing in the distance would set off a mass frenzy ... and a mad dash for the nearest tree with high root skirts that might provide some protection against shrapnel.

Many of us therefore preferred to be out in the open and *see* what was happening and risk *being seen*, rather than be cooped up in this claustrophobic forest.

Hygiene — or rather, the lack thereof — was fast becoming a critical issue, so natives were brought in to dig latrines and erect walls of dried coconut leaves that gave some privacy, but not much. These latrines did not improve the quality of the air of course, but a dusting with quick lime did help somewhat.

The Meshmoors, the Jewish family, had lost everything also. The mother refused the food from the central kitchen and prayed unceasingly for a miracle to happen. It didn't — so concerned neighbors furtively persuaded the children, one by one, to eat with them. The children thanked God every time and then, presumably, carried some of the food away with them, because Mama did survive.

The bombardment of the surrounding area continued until the end of July, though nothing more fell on the old camp itself. We did, however, receive more pamphlets — some carried by the wind, others brought in by the native police. After having read them secretly, we faithfully delivered them to the Commandant.

In one pamphlet, written in Malay, it said that all women and children had to be cleared from a 30 kilometer radius around Makassar because the area would be targeted for total destruction. We were well within that radius.

The Camp Executive petitioned Yamaji to transport us elsewhere, but he answered that it was not possible and that we should not press the point. "You do not know what may still happen to you!" he warned.

After the war, we learned that the Japanese Command had actually formulated a plan to transport us to Borneo and have us perish there in the desolate jungles of the interior. Yamaji obviously knew about this plan.

To alert other Allied pilots as to our whereabouts, he marked an open grass field with "DUTCH WOMEN" in large letters, and pinned red, white and blue banners in the grass beside it.

At the end of July, Yamaji informed the *honchos* that, in two months time, the barracks would be rebuilt. He also gave a pep talk, saying that the war was still on; we should not complain about little things; we should obey without questioning; and we did not have to think, since he would do the thinking for us!

Once again, he proposed to make the American missionary, Darlene Deibler, head of the forest camp. In his opinion, Mrs. Valderpoort was too tired and placed too much emphasis on unimportant things. He then studiously ignored her.

When Mrs. Valderpoort confronted him about this, the "unimportant things" turned out to be the absence of proper latrines, wells with potable water, and blankets! Since she considered those things extremely important, Mrs. Valderpoort tendered her resignation, and asked him — referring to his recent behavior of ignoring her — why he had not accorded her the same courtesy that she had always shown him. Then she left him, without asking permission to do so.

This event was the precursor of a more serious incident. Various versions of what happened would be floating through the camp. This is what I was able to piece together, after hearing Yamaji's version.

Just outside the boundary of the forest camp ran a little brook — the only nearby source of water. Although it did not meet all our water requirements — supplementary water still had to be carried from the old (burned down) camp — it was an important source just the same. Yamaji had assigned two women to guard the brook and to chase away would-be trespassers.

One day he came by on horseback and found Mrs. Valderpoort and another woman chatting, unaware that children were playing in the brook and muddying our drinking water. Yamaji flew into a rage, and instructed Mrs. Valderpoort and her companion to report immediately to the Command Post.

As it happened, I had to see Yamaji about something, and, after hearing where he was, I walked from the old camp to the forest camp over the dirt road that had become slippery from spilled water and soup that was carried there daily.

Halfway there I ran into Yamaji — riding his horse. I had, of course, no inkling of what had transpired in the forest camp. He was wearing a white sailor's cap with the sides pulled down. That cap always signaled to us that he was in a black mood, so I automatically tensed up.

Forty yards from me, the horse lost its footing on the slick road, and Yamaji flew over the animal's head and landed on his buttocks, legs up in the air — a burned-out cigar still in his mouth.

His posture was so comical that I burst out laughing — I'm sure my taught nerves desperately needed this release — but, what was worse, I could not stop.

Yamaji was fit to be tied, of course, and thundered at me to report immediately to the Command Post.

When I arrived, he told me to have a grave dug in the cemetery (the order was later again given to Police Chief Wewenga). Only later would I understand that it was not meant for me.

Mrs. Valderpoort and her companion arrived. The companion was sent away and Yamaji beat Mrs. Valderpoort on her behind with a bamboo stick, and then instructed her to stand at attention outside the building.

"She has a bad influence on the camp," he told Mrs. Joustra, "and I am going to put an end to it and don't you try to interfere. Go and tell her."

Mrs. Joustra, scared out of her wits and not knowing if Yamaji was serious or not, did as she was told.

"What did she say?" asked Yamaji when Mrs. Joustra returned.

"Nothing."

"Good," said Yamaji, "I shall ask the *Dominee* to make a coffin and write her will. You go and ask her if she has a last message for her husband and children."

In the Central Kitchen, Yamaji unsheathed his sword, and started to sharpen it on a whetstone, mumbling to himself: "This sword wants to taste blood" again and again.

Mrs. Jo den Hond overheard him as she entered, and said: "Pater Beltjens is late in slaughtering a *kerbou*, so why don't you do it, if your sword wants to taste blood?"

Yamaji, looked up as if he'd just come out of a trance and asked what she had said. Mrs. Den Hond repeated her words, but the spell had already been broken.

The execution of Mrs. Valderpoort was canceled.

The dignified camp leader went home, but was too traumatized to talk.

Yamaji later said that he had planned a spiritual death — to bury the old (bad) person, so that a new (better) person would arise. He'd wanted to teach her a lesson, but believed she had learned nothing from the experience.

\*\*\*\*

To repair the valves of our pumps, we needed leather. Yamaji had, with great difficulty, obtained some strips of cowhide from Makassar and had given them to Father Beltjens. However, when the Commandant visited the repair shop sometime later, the strips could not be found. They had probably been stolen.

Yamaji flew into his usual rage, and beat up the innocent Pater. The whole camp was in uproar — Catholics and Protestants alike.

Around midnight, Yamaji came to our house in the Cassava Garden and knocked on the window. "*Buka pintu* — open the door," he said.

"I won't open the door," I said through an open window. "It is midnight."

"*Musti* — you must!" he answered. "I know you are angry with me."

"Of course I am angry with you," I said. "You have no business beating up our Priest. He hasn't done anything wrong." I opened the window further and leaned out to get a better look at him. (The house was built on stilts.)

There he stood, his head newly-shaven bald, dressed in a white kimono (for the Japanese, the color of mourning), with his sword in his hand. Was he contemplating suicide?

"If I were in your place," I said, "I would be careful with that sword. One of these days you will behead one of us, and when the war is finished and Japan has lost, you will be condemned as a murderer. So, I would not carry it around anymore."

There was a long silence, and then he said: "Come with me, and I will give it to you so you can keep it for me."

"Don't go," warned Willy.

"If I don't, he'll get angry and may drag you out of here as well," I countered.

So I did go, trembling — not only because I feared his unpredictability, but also because I didn't want to run into any of the big apes that roamed the Cassava Garden at night looking for corn to eat.

At his office, he took a strip of white cloth and wrapped it around the sword until it was completely covered, like a mummy. Then, with tears in his eyes, he bowed ceremoniously and presented me with the sword

— holding it horizontally in one hand.

I took it and ran all the way home, having the irrational fear that he would change his mind and shoot me in the back. Somewhere along the way, I threw the sword into the tall *alang-alang*. I surely did not want it in my house, where he could demand it back at any time.

Many years later, I would ask him what had ailed him that night. "*Sudah lupa* — I've forgotten," he said, obviously not wanting to talk about it.

\* \* \* \*

Once again, speculations and predictions about the end of the war made the rounds. Some people started making plans for this elusive peace-time, but several women just could not cope anymore. They pined away before our eyes, died, and were buried.

In the primitive forest camp, the situation had become untenable: too many people, cramped in too little space, with too few facilities. The promised new barracks would alleviate the situation, but their construction would also signal a prolongation of our primitive existence. It was more than we could bear, and our courage withered and almost died.

Several weeks passed, and then it was August 15 — a day like all the other days, full of work and worry. Early in the morning, the Garden Crew had gone out to harvest vegetables and cassava. The mood was dark.

Suddenly one woman dropped face down to the ground, crying her eyes out. Between sobs, she stuttered: "You have said that we would be free on August 15, and that's today and we are still in this horrible camp!"

Taken aback, I remembered having said something like that when she went through a similar crisis a few months earlier.

"Why did I say a dumb thing like that?" I berated myself silently. I waited until she had composed herself, and then sent her back to the forest camp.

Around noon, a black car arrived from Makassar. "No doubt it is the *Kempei Tai* again," we feared. Shortly after, Commandant Yamaji left in that car. Beset by a vague trepidation, we anxiously waited for his return. He did come back that night and went to bed. It seemed that nothing special had happened!

Thursday, August 16, was a brilliant day. Everything was quiet until 10:00 a.m., when Mrs. Joustra, our camp leader, left with Yamaji for Makassar. Two hours later, they returned and called the *honchos* together. Mrs. Joustra looked serious — but serene. For a long time she remained silent, as did Yamaji.

"We are surely going to be taken elsewhere!" we whispered to each other. "Where will they take us now?"

Then Mrs. Joustra announced: "Everybody — including the sick who can walk without help — are urgently requested to assemble on the cow meadow at 2:30 sharp."

The wildest rumors buzzed throughout the camp. Everyone, tall and small, was present on the meadow at the appointed time, their faces tight with expectation.

We didn't have to wait long. Yamaji arrived, accompanied by Mrs. Joustra, Father Beltjens and *Dominee* Spreeuwenburg. The faces of the three Netherlanders beamed. Behind this party came Yamaji's orderly, Dannyboy, with a chair.

Yamaji mounted the chair, and announced quietly:

"*Perang abis* — the war is over!"

His voice was so subdued that only those in the front rows had heard him. He stopped, and bowed his head momentarily as emotion overpowered him. He then stepped down and silently motioned to Mrs. Joustra to take over.

"Commandant Yamaji has asked me to tell you," she started, speaking in Dutch, "that the war is over! You will have to remain in this camp for the time being. Since we don't know what the situation is outside, we have asked Mr. Yamaji to remain here as our protector, and maintain order and peace in the camp."

Yamaji nodded, turned around, and silently left the meadow.

No, we did not burst out cheering. Most of us were too moved. Many cried, remembering a husband or a son who had been swallowed up by the war. Now we, their wives and mothers, would have to go on alone! And those of us who still knew nothing, would we see our loved ones again? The Ambon people still didn't know where their husbands had been taken.

Thousands of memories crowded in on us — things we had almost forgotten because of the day-to-day worries, illness, fear, rabid dogs and bombardments. Now we were free — and yet not free: we were still prisoners of the camp, but above all, we were also prisoners of our own fears and anguish.

On August 17, the inhabitants of Kampili gathered in one of the new barracks, to plan for the future. Some demanded that the Dutch flag be hoisted over the camp. Father Beltjens and Yamaji advised against it. The Japanese flag had never been flown there either. The Japanese had spared us that humiliation!

Others wanted to leave the camp right away and be taken to Makassar. That did not appear to be possible because of the uncertain situation there. The Allies had not landed yet, and the Japanese were still in control there. It was finally decided to move only our very sick to the hospital in Makassar.

The food did improve, and the people from the forest camp were moved into the newly built barracks. Impatiently, we waited for our liberators, whoever they might be!

An overwrought Yamaji came to ask me for his sword, which he would have to hand over when the Allies arrived.

"I'm sorry *Tuan*," I said, "I have thrown it in a grass field, and don't know exactly where it is."

Yamaji was very unhappy, and feared the Allies would not believe that he didn't have a sword. But I really couldn't help him. And he never asked me for it again. But after much searching, I finally retrieved the sword and, years later, gave it to my nephew in Belgium, who still has it today. Yamaji would never know.

\* \* \* \*

On August 31, we joyfully celebrated the birthday of Queen Wilhelmina. A depressed Yamaji went to live outside the camp but remained in charge of the native police, who would still be responsible for our safety. But when native gangs made repeated attempts to plunder our camp, we decided to reinforce the police with our own guards.

The first call from outside arrived: at the request of her husband, Mrs. Ehlhart and her children would be flown with the first available plane to Morotai.

"So Morotai is already in Allied hands," I thought, "So close to home. Halmahera may be liberated also," and my thoughts went back to Mon Désir.

Agitated and expecting to be called at any minute, I started making plans to leave Kampili. Alas, nothing happened. When Mrs. Ehlhart and her children left a few days later, I remained behind.

I wondered if John would already be home. We had agreed that, wherever we might find ourselves at the end of the war, we would go back to Mon Désir and wait for each other there.

Every day, groups of people left for Makassar, where the Japanese military still held sway. But there was no call for me.

Then a small group of men arrived in Kampili from the Pare-Pare camp to look for their families. My God! How awful they looked! Walking skeletons, with horribly swollen bellies, large sunken eyes, and literally dressed in rags! They left with their loved ones in open trucks, driven by Japanese soldiers.

## IBU MALUKU

Later, I would see many of those couples in the divorce courts. Not surprising, really. The camp experience had drastically changed people. Many of the women had become more assertive and wanted out; and those who wanted to stay in the relationship often had their marriage broken up by young, healthy-looking females, freshly imported from Holland.

An Allied aircraft came over and dropped instructions: we were to clearly mark the camp as a Prisoners-of-War camp, and with strips of cloth indicate how many we were — one strip for every 100 persons. They did not provide enough strips, however, and a hospital bed sheet had to be torn to pieces so we could signal that there were almost 1,700 of us. In large white letters, we painted "POW" on a large grassy area, marking it also as a drop zone.

More aircraft came over to drop goods, packed in cylindrical containers — many hitting the ground before the parachute had opened to slow their decent. What a disappointment: they had obviously not understood that this camp was full of women and children — there were only things for men. The three men in the camp — Father Beltjens, Dr. Marseille and *Dominee* Spreewenburg — were therefore well taken care of!

Two B-25 Mitchell bombers with Dutch markings flew over a few times, dipping their wings in greeting. As they flew off, another aircraft appeared, a Dutch Catalina, which flew very low and sowed panic amongst the children.

From the cockpit and the plexiglass blisters we could see people waving at us. Then they dropped long-since-forgotten delicacies, this time without parachutes. It rained little drums of dried fruit and cans of sweet condensed milk, and bars of chocolate that soon melted in this tropical heat!

Unfortunately, many drums and cans broke open on impact and their precious contents flew all over the place. The chocolate and sweet condensed milk literally dripped from the *kasbie* leaves and stems.

Everyone was out in the field to pick up the raisins, dried apricots, pears and apple slices, and to scrape up whatever chocolate could be saved. That evening, the whole camp enjoyed hot chocolate milk. What luxury! Except for the kitchen staff, nobody noticed the layer of sand on the bottom of the cooking drum after all the chocolate milk had been consumed.

We made daily shipments of vegetables and cassava to a central kitchen in Makassar that had been set up for the people who had moved there. Every time a house became available in that city, more people left Kampili.

# IBU MALUKU

Then we received word: "The Dutch are coming!"

Commandant Yamaji was beside himself: he would now have to surrender officially — and without a sword!

A black car arrived with a Dutch flag fluttering on it. Breathless, we watched as a Dutch woman, dressed in uniform, got out. That we had never seen! She looked terrific: beautifully-curled hair, immaculate make-up. Gracefully swinging a large shoulder purse, she walked toward us.

The disdainful expression that appeared on her face as she eyed us made us suddenly conscious of how awful we looked: barefoot; shabbily dressed; unkempt hair bound together with strips of cloth; faces burned brown by the sun.

She looked around casually, showed no interest in wide-eyed Yamaji and said she was a member of NICA[1] — the interim government of the Dutch East Indies. She didn't inquire about the situation in the camp, but just distributed a few pear drops among the children — making sure she did not get too close — and then left, without saying another word. So that was the first representative of the new regime! And that was our liberation!

Yamaji said: "*Kasihan* — I pity you. You thought you had troubles in Kampili. If that was your liberator, your troubles are just starting."

These would turn out to be prophetic words.

\* \* \* \*

The camp became emptier as time wore on. All our sick had already been transported to Makassar, where many families were now united in temporary lodgings.

Two more graves had been added to our cemetery. For the last time we, the remaining internees, passed by the thirty-seven graves, and we planted a local type of yellow and purple bell-flower by way of saying goodbye.

Then our last day dawned.

On October 16, 1945, the last internees — myself included — left Kampili. Yamaji came with us.

Makassar was in a state of chaos. At the center of major intersections stood surly Japanese soldiers, each armed with only a 12-inch thick *rotan* club. Natives, still remembering the solid beating they received for not paying proper respect, bowed deeply to these traffic cops (if that is what they were), before they passed on. Japanese officers drove around in large cars while the casual and relaxed Australians — the first of the Allies to land — raced around in the popular American Jeep.

Willy Fuhrie and I were lodged in a large house, next to the hospital

"Stella Maris", where Sister Huberta and I had been so long ago.

The Australians took Yamaji into custody, and would eventually hand him over to a Dutch military court. On July 5, 1947, almost two years later, he was sentenced to a prison term of seven years for mistreatment of interned civilians.

The Australians thought this was too severe, particularly in view of a petition signed by former Kampili interns, which asked for Yamaji to be set free. During the trial, however, another charge was read — something that happened in Makassar, before Yamaji was assigned to Pare-Pare and, later, to Kampili.

The son-in-law of the *Majoor-Chinees* (the Mayor of the Chinese Population of Makassar) had escaped, and the prison's warden — who was Yamaji's brother-in-law — *had* to capture the escaped man or forfeit his life. (Whether this is according to Japanese military law, is uncertain.)

Yamaji volunteered to help his brother-in-law. The two split up to cover different areas. Yamaji found the man first, and beheaded him on the spot. The problem was: he did not have orders to support this action; only his brother-in-law did.

Yamaji, who had been visited frequently by *Dominee* Bikker (Pare-Pare's former camp leader) and became a Christian during his prison term, pleaded guilty despite the protestations of his lawyer, and incurred, as a result, a longer jail sentence. Afterward, Yamaji was firm in not wanting to appeal.

"I have become a Christian[2]," he said, "and Christianity says: if the hand does wrong, then it must be punished, and this hand has wielded the samurai sword."

I don't know if he served his full term, but he was eventually returned to Japan.

*\*\*\*\**

After a restless night, Willy and I reported to the NICA building, where Officer Wagner received us rather coldly, and did not bother to offer us a chair!

Next we were thoroughly checked out by internists, dentists, and ophthalmologists. Then they offered the widows with children two alternatives: a permanent stay in the Netherlands, or a temporary stay in Australia to recuperate. A stay in Australia was also offered to single women whose health was precarious. The healthy ones among us were pressed to stay and help in the reconstruction of the East Indies.

I put myself in the latter category and expressed the wish to be flown to Moratai, where a large reception camp had been built to serve as a stopping-over-point for those, destined for Australia. I felt that, once there, I would have no trouble getting a native boat to take me across to Tobelo.

A few days later I was told that for me, a "stayer", there would — "until further notice" — be no opportunity to go to Morotai. Passage would only be granted to those going to Australia for their convalescence.

"So those wanting to rebuild vital enterprises will, for now, not get the chance to do so," I thought. "What a strange outlook!"

One day, Willy and I were asked to come to the Australian headquarters, in connection with some jewelry — a medallion and a gold-plated case — that Yamaji was supposed to have stolen. I was able to tell them that two Kampili women had *given* those items to him for his wife, when he was scheduled to leave Kampili. The ladies now obviously regretted their earlier actions!

While I was there, I took the opportunity to ask an Australian Colonel about my returning to Tobelo. He was more receptive than NICA officer Wagner and immediately pulled from a file an aerial photograph that showed our house at Mon Désir. My heart leaped!

"I believe there is a later photograph of that region," he continued, and after some searching found the one he was looking for.

To my horror, it showed that our house was completely destroyed and tears welled up in my eyes. "Why?" I asked him. "This was not a military target, was it?"

Before the Colonel could answer, a young pilot, who sauntered past our table, supplied the answer:

"Oh, I remember that one," he said airily, looking over my shoulders at the photograph. He then related how his squadron had been returning from a mission with bombs to spare. They had been authorized to hit any target that might be of military importance. There weren't any around, yet they had to get rid of their bombs before they could land at their base on Morotai. Then he had spotted an isolated house and had challenged his fellow pilots:

"The first one who makes a direct hit wins a case of beer."

"Well, I was the one who won it!" he told us proudly. Oblivious to my tears, he then walked away.

The Colonel started to say something, but I just got up and with Willy left the building, hardly being able to see where I was going.

The house that John and I had built with so much love, the house where we said we would meet again after the war and where we had planned to stay for the rest of our lives, was no more. It had been flattened for a case of beer!

## IBU MALUKU

\*\*\*\*

December arrived. Life in Makassar was as boring as could be, because there was nothing to do.

The native population, friendly at first, became untrustworthy and turned decidedly anti-Dutch in the wake of Sukarno's declaration of independence. In the local shops we were unwanted visitors. Merchants did come to our houses in secret, but only wanted to be paid in clothes. Looting was rampant, and the Australian forces were powerless to stop it. Soon after their arrival, the Red Cross shipments somehow disappeared without a trace.

An exception to this dissident behavior were the several hundred Javanese laborers who had been brought here by the Japanese and had now been abandoned. They sat along the streets, waiting for some good Samaritan to feed them and bind their smelly, ulcerated leg and arm wounds. They were not wanted by the local natives, and therefore looked toward us for support.

They usually waited in small groups of two or three in front of the houses that we now occupied, waiting silently for us to come with whatever food we had left over. They were infinitely worse off than anyone else in the city.

We, the Ambon people, still had not received any news about our men. Would they still be alive and, if so, where in the world would they be? Finally we received unofficial word that the Japanese had taken them to the island of Hainan, off the Chinese coast.

Then ... Mrs. Valderpoort came, in person, to tell me that John was dead.

He had died on April 20, 1945, she said, just four months before the end of the war! So now there would be no reunion on Mon Désir, or anywhere else for that matter!

My thoughts immediately went back to Ambon and the last time I had seen him: when, after giving me that stirring salute, the little Japanese had jumped him from behind and had pummeled him with the butt of his rifle until both had disappeared around the bend in the road.

Since the news Mrs. Valderpoort had brought came from a semi-official source, I clung to the possibility that there might have been a mistake in the records. But much later, after having waited many long and sorrowful months for his return, I did receive official confirmation that John had, indeed, died. How, or from what cause, I wasn't told.

\*\*\*\*

On December 24, Willy Fuhrie and I left with an Australian airplane for Balikpapan on Borneo. There I met many ex-Kampili inmates who were stranded, waiting for transportation to Morotai.

Early in January, the first KPM ship after the war arrived in Balikpapan. It was the S.S. *Tegelberg*, which had been used extensively as a troop transport ship during the war, and was now sailing under an English captain.

With this ship, Willy Fuhrie and I finally left for Morotai.

The boat stopped at Ternate, where I met Sultan Jahir Sha again. He was now the CONICA (Commanding Officer, NICA) for the Moluccas. He entreated me to return to Tobelo as soon as possible to assist the population that had sought refuge in the forests.

I also paid a visit to Mr. Sjirk van der Goot, the *Controleur* with whom Dr. Hassan and I had gone to the Japanese aircraft carrier to surrender, more than three years ago. From him I learned that the Japanese had moved all my furniture from Mon Désir to Fort Orange, and that he had used part of it to furnish his own house.

Since I had nothing at all, I asked if he could give me some of the stored furniture that, after all, had belonged to me — but he coldly told me that this was not possible: "Nothing belongs to anyone anymore, everything in the fort is now NICA property!"

Frustrated and embittered by such hardness, I left Ternate.

When we arrived at Morotai, several people on board had come down with measles. It seemed that the *Tegelberg* was contaminated with it. Because of this acute infectious disease we were, of course, not allowed to enter the reception camp and were quarantined in cardboard houses on the outskirts of the town. Unfortunately, Willy Fuhrie also came down with the disease.

For a long time we were left to ourselves. Only once in a while did an English doctor come to see if the disease had run its course. That was all the attention we received. Eventually, we were let out and were allowed to mingle with the other inhabitants.

Morotai was full of white and black Americans, and rugged Australians. They were later joined by a KNIL detachment, commanded by Colonel van Rooyen. The island was under NICA administration.

To get permission to go to Halmahera, I went to the NICA office, which was staffed with shapely young ladies, freshly imported from the Netherlands. The ladies turned down my request because Halmahera was "not safe". They also forbade me to visit John's plantation, Sangowo, on Morotai itself. That also was "too dangerous".

The Overseer of John's plantation, having heard of my arrival, came to visit with several of the workers. Ignoring NICA's refusal, I went with them to the plantation by *prau*, a distance of 27 kilometers.

News traveled fast, because a short time later, a *prau* arrived from Tobelo with my *mandur*, Benjamin, who had come to ask me to return home.

With the help of a former magistrate, I secured permission to go to Halmahera, but "at my own risk". He also helped in getting me some provisions: 10 kilograms of rice, six cans of jam, and six cans of milk. It was pitifully little, seeing that the Dutch on Morotai were given three full meals a day! But that was all that I was given to enter the jungle with!

A compassionate sergeant did provide us with a tent and two field cots. An Australian gave us some military clothing, much too large of course, but we were nevertheless grateful to have it.

On February 2 — Mama's birthday, I remembered — Willy and I finally arrived at Tobelo. There were still many Japanese soldiers about the town.

The place was unrecognizable. The Japanese had plowed and planted the roads that had led to Mon Désir; the bridges and the surrounding *kampungs* had either been burned down or demolished, and many areas were full of land mines.

With Benjamin's help, we finally came to Mon Désir itself. It, too, was unrecognizable, except for the "King Nut" coconut trees that were still there. Everything was completely overgrown and neglected.

Only the bougainvilleas that now covered the foundation like a large purple shroud showed where our house had stood. Now I knew with certainty:

"John, it is over!

"What remains for me now is the promise you made during our goodbye at Ambon, on April 23, 1942:

"Trust in God," you said. "Some day we shall see each other again ... if not on earth, then surely in heaven!"

**Endnotes**
[1] NICA stands for Netherlands Indies Civil Administration. It consisted of young Netherlanders and Indonesians from all over the world (including the liberated Netherlands), who received their training first in Melbourne, and later in Brisbane at Camp Columbia.
[2] Jeanne van Diejen doubts that Yamaji really understood the difference between Catholicism and Protestantism.

# CHAPTER 41

## *Home Again*
### *Mon Désir, Halmahera, February, 1946*

*Mandur* Benjamin brought me up-to-date on what had happened on Mon Désir during my three and a half years absence.

At the end of April, 1942, shortly after having occupied Ternate, the Japanese had landed at Tobelo and taken up residence at the *rumah mèrah* (the red house), which is what they called our abode on Mon Désir. They stayed until August, 1944, and up to that time, the garden around the house had been meticulously maintained.

When the Japanese arrived, the plantation was deserted; the workers had fled into the forest. Latif had taken the horses and had hidden them farther into the foothills. The horses meant everything to him, and once they were safe, he returned regularly to look after the other animals.

The Japanese he met on those occasions had ordered him, several times, to bring back the horses — they obviously knew they existed[1]. Latif probably pretended not to understand them, and did not comply.

To make an example out of him, the Japanese took him to the beach, trussed him up, buried him up to his neck in the sand, and left him there to die.

So my devoted Latif, who had been with me since the Buluwaya days, was dead. I recalled the last time I had seen him, his face contorted with grief, as he watch me leave Tobelo for my assigned post on Ternate — an eternity ago.

Tears welled up in my eyes. Benjamin pretended not to notice.

"In July, 1945, a bomb reduced *Nonya's* house to rubble," he continued.

"*Mengapa* — Why?", I asked bitterly, wiping my eyes.

Benjamin did not know what to say, and I did not tell him what I knew. How could I explain that it had been destroyed by an Allied pilot, one of *ours*, on a mere whim ... ?

Benjamin then pointed to our safe that lay further on in the yard. It had been opened with dynamite and blown a good distance from the house. It was empty of course. It had only contained some papers, because, so I learned from Benjamin, Father Moors — to whom I had entrusted the keys before I left — had taken out the silverware and had given it to Benjamin for safekeeping. He had buried the pieces in glass jars underneath a pigsty and now gave them to me — somewhat tarnished, but still serviceable. It would be the only memento left from our former existence.

As I made the rounds with Benjamin, it became clear that it would require much work to rebuild the plantation. How to do it I did not know, for I had neither funds nor workers.

Benjamin told me that most of the local natives — including my former workers — were hiding in the forest. They were weak from malnutrition and still afraid of the Japanese — 65,000 of whom were now being rounded up and transported to the Kao Bay, where they would wait until ships were available to take them back to their homeland.

I also learned from Benjamin that on the whole of Halmahera there was only one Dutchman present: Lieutenant Brunning, who, aided by twelve Japanese soldiers, had the unenviable task of guarding several thousands of so-called *Hei-Ho*'s in Galela, 39 kilometers from Mon Désir. These *Hei-Ho*'s were native militia men, who had been in the service of the Japanese. They were hated by the local population and, in turn, they hated everything that had to do with the Allies.

Since Lieutenant Brunning was our only neighbor, I thought it prudent to make contact and let him know of our whereabouts. So I wrote him a letter and asked Benjamin to deliver it right away.

Willy and I cleared an area for our base camp. Having been well trained at Kampili, we did not waste time and before nightfall our tent was pitched.

The next day, I received help from Benjamin and a few returning locals to deepen the well and to clean up the annexes, which were only lightly damaged by the bomb that had leveled our house. Several rooms, the kitchen, the servant's room and the bathroom could be made livable — as soon as materials and workmen could be found.

One morning, we had a surprise visit from several Australian officers, accompanied by a native civil servant who had just returned to Tobelo. With him as guide, the Aussies had managed to find their way through the dense forest. Somewhat embarrassed by my scanty attire, I went out to meet them.

They explained that the Allied Forces now had the obligation to feed the Japanese soldiers who had been interned at Wasilé. Among other things, they required fat, which meant ... coconuts. The question was, could I deliver them? Against payment, of course.

I did not have to think twice. This was my chance to get going again.

But, I had no workers!

The Aussies offered to supply the necessary manpower — the Japanese themselves — who, using their own means, would transport the coconuts to their base.

I quickly laid out the conditions. The Japanese would be divided into two groups of equal size. One would start clearing the plantation; the other would pick the coconuts, transport them and also provide food for those who worked on the plantation. Also, the Japanese would have to build their own quarters, which would then be turned over to me when the time for their repatriation arrived.

The gentlemen agreed, and also accepted that the work would be done under my supervision and according to my instructions.

Two days later, a Japanese construction crew arrived. In one day, they built several temporary shacks of bamboo and *alang-alang* grass. To me they were exceedingly polite! After they had settled into those temporary quarters, the real work began.

Each morning I held roll call in Japanese fashion, as we had learned in the camps. *Kiotsuké* – Attention! *Lei* – Bow! *Yasumé* – At ease! Then I assigned the work, with the help of an interpreter, Lieutenant Nogami, and in the evening, I again held roll call.

We started off with one group building permanent barracks and kitchens from good quality lumber, while the other group, commanded by a Captain, cleared the existing premises and removed the rubble from the ruins of the main house.

The foundations emerged undamaged; the bricks looked as if they had just recently been cemented in place. The annex buildings were made livable, so that Willy and I were then able to fold our tent and move into what used to be the servants' quarters.

We started a vegetable garden, much to the surprise of the Japanese, who offered to do that for us in their spare time. Of course, we spurned their offer: this was *our* thing!

Later, they built a hospital ward and clinic on the grounds of Mon Désir. It also provided accommodation for a Japanese doctor, who arrived with a large supply of excellent medicines — which also benefitted the local people who were slowly returning.

One day, I received another unexpected visitor: it was Jon, the nephew of my husband, whom I had met as a ten-year-old at his parents' house in Ambarawa on Java, when I first entered the East Indies.

The van Diejen family was obviously enamored with the name John in all its variations. There was John (my husband), his older brother Jan (who had given us so much trouble) and Jan's son, Jon — pronounced with the "J" as in the French name Jean.)

Jon was flabbergasted to find me lording it over 200 Japanese soldiers. "How is this possible?" he asked repeatedly.

Like his uncle, Jon had been drafted into the KNIL. He was captured by the Japanese and put to work on the infamous Burma railroad. When Japan surrendered, Jon was shipped to Singapore and then prevented by the British from entering the areas of the East Indies that were under their control. (Only later did it become clear that the English feared getting embroiled in the struggle for independence , if they allowed the Dutch military to enter Java.)

From the Dutch authorities he learned that his father, Jan, had died in the POW camp at Surabaya, and that my husband — whom he barely knew — had died in a labor camp on Hainan. So this confirmed as much as I knew. But the actual details were still missing.

Why the Dutch authorities did not know that I was alive in Makassar at that time remains a mystery, but they gave John's meager belongings to Jon instead of to me.

When the English command finally permitted him to enter Java, Jon learned somehow that I had survived, though he had no idea where I was. He finally tracked me down to Mon Désir and came to bring me John's belongings: his wedding ring, two letters I had written in Ambon, his rosary and an envelope with a banknote of 25 guilders.

That was that. It felt very strange to touch these objects, the only legacy from the man with whom I had shared so many years of joys, heartaches and tears. My feelings of the moment were suppressed, however, as I had a much more pressing problem on my hands[2].

The problem was that I had berri-berri and pellagra (a protein deficiency disease). It was so bad that the doctor advised me to leave for a cure in the Netherlands as quickly as possible. It was at exactly this time that news came from the Government that Willy and I — as ex-prisoners of war — were eligible to travel, as evacuees, to the Netherlands, where I had not been in 20 years. I would gladly have left right then and there, but my presence was still needed on Mon Désir to supervise the cultivation of the plantation and the production of the copra.

Willy and I discussed the problem, and Willy, who, in the few weeks that Jon had been with us, had fallen deeply in love with him, suggested that Jon, a trained planter, might be persuaded to manage the plantation in our absence. But Jon didn't want to have anything to do with the Japanese and returned to Java at the end of his furlough.

Then seven months after their arrival, we received a sudden notice that all the Japanese had to leave; they would be picked up at Tobelo by an American ship with a Korean crew. The news hit us like a bolt out of the blue. Only a third of Mon Désir had been brought into a state of readiness. Where would I get the manpower to complete the job?

Luckily, some of the returning natives applied for employment. Their own *kampungs* were still in ruins. Their fear of the Japanese was still so strong that they had not yet dared to start rebuilding them. Thus, they needed the shelter that Mon Désir — thanks to my Japanese crew — could now provide.

I assigned the newcomers to the task of building a proper drying shed for the copra. Production had better increase if we wanted to get some income; up to now, we had barely covered the costs.

It became clear that the new laborers were no longer used to working with any regularity. I also perceived a political change in them. The former distance between manager and the native worker had now changed. They now saw the relationship as more of a partnership, which sometimes caused problems, but the differences were always amicably resolved.

The other very time-consuming problem was how to remunerate them. The copra (which was now, in part, sold again through the Copra Fund) was partly paid for in cash and partly in goods, such as textile, rice, sugar, crockery and pans. But since everyone wanted something different, there were endless discussions. Not that they wanted to be difficult; the problem was that some of the bartered goods were just of no use to them, and invariably it was I who got stuck with them. This created many cash flow problems for me.

It was encouraging, however, that the work on the plantation progressed very well. The roads were repaired, and the revenue from the copra increased with each passing month. But the supervision became increasingly complex and, because of my illness, I reached a point where I could no longer continue.

I started to make plans for a year-long recovery in the Netherlands together, of course, with Willy. Neither of us had had any respite since our departure from Kampili, and Willy also needed time to recover.

Again, she suggested that Jon, who was back on Java, could take over in our absence. She thought that now that the Japanese had left, he might be interested. Jon wrote that he was indeed interested, and proposed that Willy become his partner. The problem, however, was that he was still in the Army and it would take time to get him discharged. But I could not wait, so an interim manager had to be found.

I arranged with a Chinese manager of the Copra Fund in Tobelo, to temporarily take over the reins, just until Jon was free. I also instructed a Chinese carpenter to build, while we were away, a new, more austere house on the foundations of the old one. I also re-appointed Benjamin as *Mandur*, and saw to all the hundreds of things that needed to be done before one could leave on furlough.

The Sultan of Ternate eventually heard about our planned departure and asked me in a letter, if, during my furlough, I would contact "Holland Helpt Indië" — a private philanthropic organization started by a business group.

"They have given 250,000 guilders to the City of Ambon to build a technical school. Would you try to get a grant to build a school for girls in Tobelo," the Sultan asked.

"For five years," he wrote, "the population has lived in the jungle and the girls who have grown up there do not have the foggiest notion about keeping house and what it entails. They have never even seen a needle and thread!" That I already knew, for when I had mentioned those items to them earlier on, they didn't know what I was talking about.

The Sultan then wrote:

"Would you try to get the necessary funds? We could begin with the daughters of the *Kepala Kampungs* (village heads) and teach them some of the basics of housekeeping."

By return mail, I promised I would. The one problem that concerned me was: who would teach the girls? I knew many things, but I was no teacher. But that too, I was sure, would resolve itself. I eventually concluded that, in spite of any misgivings about myself, I could certainly teach by example. But would that leave me enough energy to manage Mon Désir?

The day of departure arrived. An old KPM ship lay at anchor in the roadstead, and when Willy and I stepped into the sloop that would take us there, that familiar, uncomfortable feeling took hold of me again. Would I ever return here and, if so, in what state would I find Mon Désir? I felt most despondent.

Used as I was, before the war, to traveling first class, it was a disappointment to be assigned to a 2nd class cabin. The Government of the Netherlands apparently did not consider us evacuees worth more than that — and we were not permitted to pay for the difference ourselves. Along the way, the ship picked up additional ex-camp-inmates, who were also having their first furlough since the outbreak of the war — they, too, were assigned 2nd class accommodation.

In Batavia we disembarked and were put up in the dormitories of the educational Wilhelmina Institute, which had been converted into a reception center.

# IBU MALUKU

I immediately started pulling all available strings to get Jon out of the Army, on the grounds that he was urgently needed in the reconstruction of the country. I succeeded and felt comforted knowing that Jon would soon be sailing for Tobelo.

In total, we stayed in Batavia about four weeks under rather trying circumstances, and were then put on board of the *M.S. Nieuw Holland*. No cabins, this time. We were taken to the cargo hold of the ship, where we would have to sleep in uncomfortable hammocks, or else on the floor. There was no privacy, of course, nor any way in which to protect our belongings from theft — except to guard them at all times.

The journey itself went smoothly enough, and grateful that this ordeal was behind us, we eventually arrived in the harbor of IJmuiden.

As the ship continued slowly through the waterway towards Amsterdam, I took in the scenery. How strange looked the green meadows. The land was flat; the horizon, wide. There was not a single mountain in sight. Obviously, I would have to get used to this landscape again.

Finding lodgings in the Netherlands was very difficult, and we had to rely on the help of relatives. Willy was offered a room with an aunt in the Hague, where Willy's mother and younger sister also lived. There was no room for me, but I was offered a place with Willy's grandmother, whose house was within walking distance.

Like other repatriated Netherlanders who had arrived for their first furlough after the war, we received for twelve months 200 guilders per month per person on which to live. After those twelve months, we were expected either to have found a job or to have left the country. (In those days, pensions did not exist.)

From the 200 guilders, one first had to pay 20 guilders tax, and from the remainder, one had to pay for lodging, food, clothes and all other necessities. We had to start from scratch, because we had nothing; all our possessions had, literally, gone up in smoke.

The medical care in Holland was excellent, but our encounters with the civil servants — on whom we depended for identity papers, allowances and food coupons — were often unpleasant. They were openly jealous of the things we, the evacuees, received and made us feel unwanted and very unwelcome.

Our encounters with other citizens were equally disappointing. They were full of how much they had suffered under the German occupation — I *knew* they had — and it seemed that these experiences had anaesthetized them to what anyone else might have suffered. They were totally indifferent to what had happened to us under the Japanese.

On several occasions, I visited my family in Antwerp, where I was relatively free from the lack of empathy and downright antipathy I had experienced in the Netherlands. Nevertheless, these visits did not give me much satisfaction either. Many members of the family had died; many surviving members had been bombed out of their homes, and were preoccupied with their own problems. Much of the time I was made to visit graves, which didn't do much for my state of mind either.

Other evacuees must have had similar experiences, because there was a run on the ticket offices of shipping lines. Everyone wanted to return home to the Far East as soon as possible. As a precaution, Willy and I also placed ourselves on the waiting list even though our furlough still had quite a while to go.

These experiences made Willy and me draw closer together, and we maintained almost daily contact. Of course we talked much about Jon — who should be on Mon Désir by now — and about the marriage that would take place when he and Willy were reunited.

As I had promised the Sultan of Ternate, I contacted the *Holland Helpt Indië* Foundation, and succeeded in getting a grant of 2,500 Dutch guilders to build the planned housekeeping school at Tobelo. From the *Pelita* foundation I also received textiles: some for the school, some for the poor in our district. These gifts I would personally take with me when I returned.

\* \* \* \*

One day, Willy's grandmother asked me to do her a favor: would I visit a well-known clairvoyant for her, and inquire about the future of two of her grandchildren: a boy of thirteen and a girl of fifteen, who lived in her house with their newly-separated mother. Grandmother wasn't feeling well enough to go herself.

I was not overjoyed with the idea. Clairvoyants were not exactly my cup of tea; I did not put much faith in their counsel. But Grandmother didn't give up. She thought that the children were not doing well in school. The separation from their father had obviously scarred them psychologically and Grandmother thought that to be the reason why they paid so little attention to their studies. So she asked me again:

"I would really like you to go see this woman. I want to know if they will pass their exams. I am afraid they won't, because they always want to see their father." It was obvious that she did not approve of these visits.

"It is very simple," Grandma continued, "all you have to do is to show her these personal effects of the children," and she handed me two sheets of paper that the children had written on.

"Oh yes, and here is a *rijksdaalder*," she added, handing me a 2-1/2 guilder coin. "That's what you'll have to pay her."

It was hard to refuse the lady who had taken me in, so I went to Rotterdam to see this clairvoyant, Allagonda Damasue, feeling a little embarrassed just the same.

Upon arrival I found that the kitchen served as waiting room. I was not impressed. I sat among many people who were eager to go back to the East Indies and talked about the difficulty in getting passage. Presumably they were here to find out what was in store for them. I overheard someone saying:

"Everything she says has come true."

"Full of expectations beats my heart," I thought sarcastically, picking up the words from a song that children sing on December 5, when they celebrate St. Nicholas Day.

When my turn came, I first handed Mrs. Damasue the writing of the boy. She took it without looking at it, and rubbed the paper between her fingers.

"Yes," she said, this concerns someone in uniform ..."

"Good grief," I thought, "a boy of thirteen in uniform? That's pure nonsense." I did not comment, however, and handed her the second piece of paper.

"Yes," she said, "this concerns a man who is in great difficulties, but it will not last long. The wife will die in a few months and then he will marry her sister, the one who keeps house for him now."

"Well," I thought, "that takes the cake!". The gender was wrong, and the girl, Thea, was only 15 years old. She was not ill and had neither a husband, nor a sister. So this was nonsense, as I had suspected from the start.

"No," she continued, "Just a minute. It concerns two people here. Please tell the grandmother who has sent you [*I had not told her that*] that she must see a doctor right away, because she is ill. If she does not, she will end up in hospital in a much worse condition. And she does not have to worry. These two are studying diligently, and will pass their exams. But she should allow them to see their father as much as they want and not interfere. That is the message you can give her."

"Well, put *that* in your head!" I told myself, surprised at the sudden turn of events.

As I got up to leave, Mrs. Damasue asked:

"Don't you want to ask something for yourself? You don't have to pay for it. Don't you have a letter from someone about whom you would like to have some news?"

I just happened to have a letter from Jon in my bag, which I hesitatingly handed to her.

"This is about a man in uniform," she started, "and he is on board of a ship."

"Thank God," I said impulsively, straight from the heart. Jon was obviously on board of a KPM ship, on his way to Tobelo. The relief I felt showed how worried I had been about the timing, hoping that Jon would get there before the man from the Copra Fund had to report back for duty.

"No," said Mrs. Damasue, "you are mistaken. He is not sailing to the place you are thinking of. He is on his way to the Netherlands."

"But that's impossible," I said, convinced that *had* to be nonsense. I had been meeting Willy practically every day, and if that had been true, she would have told me.

"It is true." insisted Mrs. Damasue. "In four days, he will be standing in front of you."

I thanked her and left, a little upset, but firm in the belief that she had made a mistake.

Back home, I relayed the message about the children to Grandmother. Then it turned out that Grandmama had torn a leaf out of her granddaughter's notebook, where Thea's teacher had made a sketch and written some remarks. It was the teacher's hand-writing that Mrs. Damasue had picked up initially. As to why she was wrong about the boy, I never found out.

Then I told Grandmother about what Mrs. Damasue had said about Jon being on his way to the Netherlands. Grandmother could not believe it and said:

"Let's call Willy and ask her to come over."

Ten minutes later, Willy arrived, and Grandmother said:

"Willy, I want you to give me an honest answer. Jeanne has just visited Mrs. Damasue, who has said that Jon is on his way to Holland. Is that true?"

Without a moment's hesitation, Willy answered:

"That is not possible. You have misunderstood what she said. If he is on his way to Holland, I would be the first one to send him back right away, because our future is at stake here."

Those words put my mind at ease, and convinced me that Mrs. Damasue had indeed "missed the boat" here.

However, four days later I happened to go to the house where Willy lived and rang the bell. The door opened, and there stood Jon in the vestibule.

In utter amazement I looked at him and asked:

"What are you doing here? I thought you were on your way to Tobelo!"

Suddenly Willy appeared beside him. The deep disappointment I felt must have been clear to them both.

"And what now?" I asked.

"Listen, Jeanne," Willy answered. "The first time, I married by proxy. For my second wedding I want my family to be present. Jon has been imprisoned for a long time and also needs a rest."

"If that is so," I countered, becoming more emotional with each passing minute, "why have you not told me so before this, then I could have made the necessary arrangements for Mon Désir? What kind of underhanded business is this?"

"Well," Willy said, "we thought that if you could return home now, that would give us an opportunity to get back our strength. In a year, we could join you, take over the plantation and you could then devote yourself to the building of that school for girls."

"I see," I said, "you have it all figured out, and have made all the decisions without even asking me. I don't accept that from *anybody*, not even you, Willy. Goodbye!"

I did not wait for an answer, turned around, and left, afraid that if I stayed I might say things I would later regret. With tears of anger and disappointment I told Grandmother what had happened. She also had difficulty in accepting it.

It is often impossible to make sense of affairs of the heart, but Willy's breach of trust hurt me deeply and would drastically change the course of my life. More through circumstances than through intent, I would have no further contact with the woman whom I had loved, and still love, as my own daughter.

I had been in Holland only five months of the twelve-month furlough, but Jon's change of heart forced me to shorten my stay and to return immediately to the East Indies. Mon Désir could not be left alone much longer.

Passages were very difficult to get, as I already knew. So I was extremely pleased to hear from the Rotterdamsche Lloyd that they had a cancellation on the MS *Oranje*, and offered me this one place.

A week later, I was on board with the gifts from *Pelita* and the money for the school on Tobelo. This time, I paid for my own passage from the amount that I had been permitted to withdraw from my bank account in Batavia before I left.

I intended to enjoy this trip, first class, and to rest-up from my furlough. My health was much better and I felt I would be fit enough to return to work again — in fact, I longed for it with all my heart.

In Batavia, I found there was money in the bank for my continued journey to the Moluccas, and I departed in high spirits. In Ternate, I informed the Sultan of the gift from the *Holland Helpt Indië* foundation. His Highness was greatly pleased and, together, we discussed the building plans for the school.

Finally the long journey came to an end in Tobelo, where I was so warmly welcomed that I had trouble keeping my composure. How different were these wonderfully warm people from the indifferent folks I had met in Europe. I was truly home again!

The new house, built with Willy and Jon in mind, was ready for occupancy; only the annex buildings needed to be properly fixed-up. The plantation, however, was a disappointment. Practically no maintenance had been done during my absence. The roads were overgrown with vegetation and the area around the houses had also been neglected. And the remaining part of the plantation was still in the state in which I had found it immediately after the war.

With great sadness, Benjamin explained that, in my absence, the workers had been frequently in conflict with the temporary manager and had finally left Mon Désir. It had been very difficult to find new workers, as they always demanded higher wages and often refused to take payment in the form of goods. On top of that, they seemed to have formed a Communist-leaning union. In short, Benjamin was not hopeful for the future.

As a result, I started to lose courage and this also affected me physically. As time went by, the management of the plantation slowly became a millstone around my neck.

The negotiations for the construction of the school, however, went well, and gave me consolation.

Slowly, ever so slowly, my attention started to shift to the school, and I began to hate Mon Désir with its never-ending problems. It turned into an obsession, and I did not know what to do. I realized that the rebuilding of the plantation would take more energy than I had and, therefore, started to look for another solution.

I didn't want to work with a new administrator — in fact, the thought scared me. And so I finally reached the point I thought I would never reach: I decided to sell Mon Désir.

Through a friend in Makassar, Johan Heynneman[3], I found a buyer: someone from Java. I arranged for easy terms, and the deal was closed.

Part of the sale agreement was that I could stay in the house until the school had been built. Every morning I walked with an eager heart the

## IBU MALUKU

5 kilometer-long road to the school's construction site and then walked back again in the evening, longing for a good night's sleep.

Finally, the construction of the school was completed, and it was time for me to move out of Mon Désir. It was as if I was saying goodbye to a loved one who had passed away. Yet, that evening, when darkness provided me with the privacy I craved, I could not resist walking through the familiar places, saying goodbye to the houses, and the coconut trees that I had seen grow up from tiny seedlings.

When I came to the last tree, I hugged it with all my might and let the tears flow until there were none left to be shed.

Then I looked up into the vastness of the star-studded, cloudless sky and suddenly felt liberated. The die was cast. Mon Désir was now behind me, and I was free to start a new existence.

### Endnotes

[1] They must have heard this from one of the many high-ranking Japanese officers (disguised as business people or apprentices) who had visited the Watanabe family on their plantation before the start of the war. Those officers had often hired horses from Jeanne van Diejen. They were skilled riders, she said, well-educated, and always very polite and helpful towards her.

[2] During the writing of this book, when I telephoned Jeanne van Diejen for details about John's meager belongings, she told me later that after the call she was seized by such an intense anger, that she wanted to smash something, a window, a mirror, a glass, anything! It was an anger directed against the Dutch Government — safely exiled in London then — that had committed the people in the East Indies to this ill-prepared, unsolicited war that cost John his life; a Government that had promised full restitution for damages suffered, but instead confiscated what little of her furniture was recovered after the war. This anger was further fuelled by later bureaucratic bungling that robbed her of a good part of her war widow's pension and *all* of the restitution money — little as it was — to which she was entitled. A neighbor calmed her down before she could smash anything, but this explosion made clear how deep these feelings had been buried over the years!

[3] My father.

IBU MALUKU

# CHAPTER 42

## A New Career
*Ternate, 1949-1951*

On August 1,1949, the first rural housekeeping school of Halmahera was officially opened. An elderly District Chief christened it *"Lina Ma Maratana* — Hope for the Country of Lina", the cradle of the Tobelorese people.

The first class held twenty charming interns, all daughters of District Chiefs or Kampung Heads — as decreed by Sultan Jahir Shah of Ternate.

The girls ranged in age from twelve to seventeen years. All had mastered reading and writing, but none had received any schooling during or since the war, having lived almost 5 years hidden in the forests. They had no idea of how a normal family was supposed to function, and it was precisely this lack in their upbringing that the school would address.

The question of tuition fees never came up. The parents contributed all the necessary food, and the students — as part of their curriculum — learned how to transform it into delicious and nutritious meals. The terrain around the school was plowed into a garden, which would eventually provide all sorts of vegetables and fruits. Thus, feeding the girls would never be a problem.

The girls took turns doing the laundry, cleaning the living quarters and maintaining the buildings and gardens. They learned to grow flowers and fruit, to sew, to darn and even how to embroider — all according to a strict schedule. Every day, a team of eight girls prepared the meals — a task that everyone enjoyed.

Once the school started to operate like a cohesive family, the girls were taught the rudiments of nursing. Periodically, we sent them out to various homes to take charge of a mother and her new-born child. They received practical experience in providing community care and social assistance and, thus, gained in self-assurance and spontaneity.

Without much effort, they learned geography and physics. Their evenings were filled with games, dance, gymnastics and story-telling. Many of them recalled old folk stories and traditions, which they presented beautifully.

Soon, non-resident students applied and two months after the school opened, the number of students had doubled to forty. We were now thankful for the gardens, for they provided the additional food needed to feed them all adequately. The girls were eager to learn and felt safe and privileged to be at the school.

Lina Ma Maratana was not, however, an accredited school. The students did not have the necessary prerequisites, nor did the teachers have the required diplomas. Nevertheless, it achieved its intended objective and was greatly appreciated by the population.

Then on December 29, 1949, three years after the draft agreement on a Netherlands-Indonesian Union had been signed, the transfer of power took place in Amsterdam.

The daily chores left me with little time to brood about the past, or the present political turmoil around me. I kept up-to-date on current events, but did not allow them to disrupt my life.

The Dutch Government was still in the hands of a very young *Controleur*, a rather straight-laced man who had come directly from the Netherlands. Parallel to the civilian government, there was also a military one, headed by a Captain. He had spent some time in Australia, and had recently enlarged the Dutch community with his wife and children. The schools, hospital and post office all functioned as they did before the war, and some of the Protestant mission families had returned. Tobelo had become alive again. Yet, one could sense that the political winds would soon change that situation.

On August 17, 1950, the civil administration was officially handed over to an Indonesian civil servant, who became *Kepala Pemerintah Setempat* — the local magistrate.

A short time later, all Dutch civil servants and the KNIL Captain and his troops left Tobelo; those who remained became subjects of the State of *Indonesia Raya* — Great Indonesia — which had Sukarno as its first President[1].

For a while, everything continued as before. We still used the same money of the Dutch East Indies, and the new government functioned as did the one before it. A squad of Indonesian policemen arrived under the command of an ambitious Ambonese Inspector. Other than that, everything remained pretty much the same.

But this would turn out to be the calm before the storm.

\*\*\*\*

One day, late in 1950, the new Government ordered everyone to come to the Post Office and hand over all paper money — except the bills of 2-1/2 guilders. We looked on in shock and disbelief as our bills were cut in two. The halves bearing the head of the Queen was confiscated. We were told they would eventually be replaced by stocks or bonds from the new State[2]. The other half was returned to us: it was to be temporarily used as legal tender, but at half of its original value!

For me, it was a major catastrophe. Only a few days earlier, I had received the final instalment on the sale of Mon Désir. By its action, the new Government had reduced this large sum — and my savings and securities as well — to half of its original value!

I was deeply troubled. The money received from the *Holland Helpt Indië* Foundation had not been enough to pay for the construction of the school, and I had used my own funds to complete the job. On top of that, I had administered the school without salary, and had also paid the salaries of the teachers out of my own pocket!

I decided to discuss the matter with Sultan Jahir Shah on Ternate and propose to him that the buildings and the operation of the school be turned over to the State, as had always been the intent.

I took the next available boat and arrived the following day at Ternate. The audience took place, and His Highness said that he would personally take care of the matter and expedite the transfer as quickly as possible.

With that promise, I returned to Tobelo. But, again, events would take a different course from what I had planned.

Upon arrival, I sensed that the mood had changed. All inhabitants were now required to carry an identity card that had to be produced on demand. A new civil guard had been organized, made up of noisy, lanky youngsters, who checked ID-cards, questioned shoppers, and patrolled the streets until late into the night. Their actions slowed down traffic considerably, and their menacing attitude made life decidedly unpleasant.

Rumor had it that American and Dutch troops had landed from New Guinea and were regrouping in the forests, in preparation for an all out attack — supposedly, to recapture Halmahera and rejoin it to New Guinea. This rumor made it very uncomfortable for the Dutch. Of course, we were now suspected of being collaborators!

The next night, a noisy gang came to my house. Fists rained down on the door and high-pitched voices demanded that the door be opened. The students were instantly awakened. A teacher ran to my side as I walked to the entrance. I opened the door and looked nonplused at several hate-contorted young faces that were eerily lit by the light of flickering, smoking torches.

"Surrender all your weapons immediately!" they cried.

I froze momentarily as a boy of not more than fifteen years leveled a large pistol at me. Shouting wildly, he waved his weapon around recklessly. I prayed to God that it was not loaded.

Several youngsters, obviously the ring leaders, tried to push their way into the house, but I did not budge and firmly refused to let them search the dormitory. But in order to placate them, I quickly instructed the teacher to go to the kitchen and fetch our ax, *parang*, large chopping knives and anything else that might be considered a weapon.

"That's not what we came for. We want your rifles and pistols!" someone shouted.

From their prattling I understood they were absolutely convinced that — since I was a *Belanda* and lived outside the city and near the forest — that the rumored American and Dutch "military units" had hidden a cache of arms in our school.

Perhaps it was due to my firm, uncompromising attitude, or to my stern schoolmistress' voice, but I succeeded in driving that silly notion from their minds, after which they noisily demanded some beer.

I patiently explained that our building was a school and not a clubhouse, and proposed to have some coffee made instead. The leaders accepted my offer, albeit in a haughty tone of voice. All that yelling had made them thirsty and the coolness of the night was making them shiver. My uninvited guests then installed themselves around a table, enviously watched by their less fortunate comrades who were still outside, in the cold.

After the coffee, feelings calmed down somewhat, but they ordered me not to let anyone leave the building. In front of all the doors leading outside, and even in front of my bedroom, they placed guards, armed with *bambu runching* — sharply pointed bamboo sticks. Then the rest of the gang left to terrorize some other hapless citizen.

This unpleasant situation continued until the afternoon of the next day, when a growing uproar in the distance once more made us ill at ease. People converged from all directions on the market and we heard them shout: *"Tentara ada"* — the Army is here." And yes, a company of Javanese soldiers slowly marched towards us, and stopped in front of the school building.

A sergeant stepped forward and informed me, very politely, that the school had been requisitioned to house his soldiers. I started to protest, but soldiers had already entered the school building and were busy installing themselves in the classrooms. So I asked to see his commanding officer. The Sergeant obliged, and came back with a Javanese captain.

I explained the situation, but the Captain said there was nothing he could do. The school was the only suitable building and, within a week, he would also have to house the soldiers' families there. But the teachers, students and myself were allowed to stay in the dormitory!

The future looked gloomy indeed. Lacking classrooms in which to teach, we had to drop the non-resident students. This left twenty-two pretty girls in the dormitory, with only one person as their protector: me! I'd had no experience in getting along with Javanese people and foresaw that misunderstandings could easily occur. I found this too great a responsibility to handle, and decided to send the girls home on vacation.

Within three days, most of the girls had left. Five stayed because the monsoon rains had made their villages inaccessible. So we continued teaching them, and maintained our normal schedule as best we could.

The soldiers were quiet and well-behaved, and did not present any problems. But the situation changed drastically when their women and children arrived with a company of Engineers. The women took over the kitchen and all it contained. The toilets and the wells became public property, and our vegetable gardens were quickly plundered.

Concern about my wards drove me to have the remaining five girls sheltered with friendly neighbors. The teachers and I would try to stay in the dormitory as long as it was possible.

After several more weeks, the Corps of Engineers started to stack their provisions in front of our windows, including a large amount of *ikan garam* (salted, dried fish) which gave off a pungent smell. This was more than we could take. I approached the usually considerate Captain, who flatly turned me down. He could not help me in this matter, he said. The fish would have to stay where it was!

The smell was intolerable, so I decided to close the dormitory. The two teachers were sent home to Menado on vacation, and I planned to go to Ternate for consultations. I informed the Captain of my plans and he promised that the dormitory would be left untouched during my absence.

Ternate was full of Javanese soldiers. Some of the senior civil servants had been transferred to Java and had been replaced by Javanese. This was the start of a migration that would continue in the years ahead.

My consultation with the Sultan brought no results. He advised me to relax and wait it out. The school would be reopened when the soldiers in Tobelo had their own barracks. That would soon happen, he predicted. The present Police barracks were already being enlarged for that purpose.

Dispirited, I returned to Tobelo.

The Corps of Engineers had disappeared, but the other soldiers and their families were still there. The school buildings now had the unmistakably bedraggled appearance of army barracks. The local mood was gloomy.

Then came another bolt out of the blue. One somber evening, an official came to say that all Dutch people would have to leave the next day with a specially chartered ship of the KPM. The reason, he said, was that the Government could no longer guarantee their safety. I told him that I had nowhere to go, and would stay and take my chances. And so, the next day, I became the only Dutch resident of Halmahera[3].

Rumors, however, about American troops in the foothills increased in intensity. The mood of the people was becoming ugly because the Netherlands had refused to cede New Guinea. I then received orders to come immediately to Ternate.

So, once more, I left Tobelo, wondering if I would ever return.

I found temporary quarters in Ternate, and tensely waited for the first day of 1951, when the transfer of New Guinea was supposed to take place. That fateful day came and passed, but nothing happened.[4]

The threatening attitude of some instigators was still there, but the steam had gone out of it. So in mid-January I returned to Tobelo with the two teachers who had returned from their vacation in Menado.

We found the dormitory ransacked. Everything in the large kitchen had disappeared. The school furniture and my own furniture was also gone. My request for a police investigation was refused.

Being at the end of my tether, I transferred title of the buildings to the Head of Government, sent the teachers back home, and left Tobelo, my beloved city, for good.

\*\*\*\*

Back in Ternate, I found lodgings at *Sekolah Gadis,* a housekeeping school for girls, and started to look for work. I soon received some offers, and after due deliberation chose a job as journeyman in the Department of Social Affairs where I was, in fact, on probation.

The new job excited me and I felt a new person. Instead of the young woman whose aspirations had often been inhibited by circumstances, I had now become a mature person who wilfully and consciously had given a new direction to her life. I felt free to do as I wanted. There was now nothing left that tied me to the past and I decided to dedicate myself to the welfare of the people of the North Moluccas.

I realized that Social Assistance was in its infancy, and that a massive education job lay ahead. The people had never even heard the term

## IBU MALUKU

"social assistance", and did not understand what it meant.

The first few weeks of my new existence were hard — especially psychologically. After the *pesuruh*, the errand boy, I was the lowest paid civil servant in the Department.

The staff consisted of three young men who worked — or were supposed to work — in Accounting, and three young girls who honed their typing skills, leafed through manuals, listened to Social Work lectures, or took courses in the new *Behasa Indonesia*[5] in which I also eagerly participated. My colleagues accepted me without animosity, but there was a certain timidness in treating me as a fellow worker.

Our boss was an elderly Menadonese. He had once followed a course in Social Work, and had then put his knowledge into practice. He did not quite know what to do with me, however. He would not, or could not, give me any guidance in my work. For several weeks — during which I simply listened and reflected on every word he uttered — I had no idea what I was supposed to do.

Whenever I approached him, he would say: "Find out for yourself. You know the people. Take your time thinking about what you can do best." In retrospect it may have been Oriental wisdom — allowing me to find my own way — but at the time I found it very frustrating.

Fed-up with all this inactivity, I visited my trusted advisor, the Sultan, and told him about my problem. He advised me to be patient but he also gave me some valuable insight into the make-up and the needs of the population on Ternate.

Slowly, a picture emerged of what I might be able to do and I hatched a plan that I felt I could present to the Sultan, his advisors and my indecisive boss. With the latter I had to be particularly careful because he was ambitious and proud. But I'd had a glimpse into his character and thought I would, with care, be able to get him around to my point of view.

I planned my approach carefully, making sure he would not feel upstaged. He not only listened receptively to my plans, but also gave me unqualified approval to start implementing them immediately.

My first task was to do an extensive survey of the many *kampungs* around the capital. The survey would not start until several weeks later, so I used the available time to visit all the District Chiefs, Kampung Heads and old civil servants, whom I remembered so well from the time of the Japanese invasion — seemingly a century ago.

From them I received an even better understanding of the lives and traditions of the natives, which would prove later on to be invaluable. They all pledged full co-operation, and promised to inform their people about my planned survey and its place in the framework of the Government's Social Services.

For the time being, I remained as guest of the teachers at *Skola Gadis*. The evenings I spent with them not only provided a welcome relief from my daily excursions, but also taught me much about the many unsuspected traps that I would still encounter.

At the end of the month, I received my first salary of 140 rupiahs — 40 rupiahs more than the errand boy — which amounted to 11 American dollars!

\*\*\*\*

One day, I was unexpectedly interrupted in my work.

"*Tabeh, Ibu* — good day, Mother," said a soft, melodious voice.

I looked up from my papers and saw, in front of my desk, a small, delicate woman. Her feet were sheathed in high-heeled, brown velveteen sandals. Her sarong, tightly wrapped around her tiny waist, fanned out into numerous, neatly pressed pleats, and the *kebaya* was modestly closed around her slender neck with a dainty cambia broach.

Thick, black hair was combed high around her small head, and two big brown-black eyes looked at me from a delicate face. At the corners of the cherry-red mouth fluttered a half-expectant, happy smile. A graceful hand was extended to me, western style.

Surprised, I got up, took her hand and looked this *mademoiselle* in the eye. She introduced herself as Habiba Jafar and, hesitatingly, sat down on the corner of a for her rather high chair.

"And," I asked cordially, "what is the purpose of your visit?"

Her smile widened expectantly as she handed me a neatly filled out employment application form.

I read that Habiba was 18 years old. She had passed the elementary school exam, taken a course in typing, and had completed one year of high school. She now wanted to become a *pegawai sosial* — a social worker.

I urgently needed a good assistant for my planned surveys, but the position required a high school diploma — at least on paper.

We did have one person on staff, the corpulent, indolent and much too jolly Safura, who did have the required diploma. However, her work was good only when she wanted it to be, which was not often. If it had been up to me, I would have sacked her a long time ago, but she was the daughter of an influential *Haji* (a Muslim who has gone on a pilgrimage to Mecca) and, therefore, had to be kept on the payroll for political reasons. And there were others like her.

The clerk, Abdul Rachman, was chairman of an important political party, and though he spent more time on political matters than on his work, he was also untouchable. The junior typist, Miriam, was a vain creature who flirted non-stop with Mohammed, the son of a Javanese Department Head. So these two were also declared irreplaceable.

The two remaining employees were: Salim, an Indo-Arabian bookkeeper who was my right hand, and the lethargic, morose Papua girl, Imram, who was often away on sick leave.

All these personages flashed through my mind as I looked at this fresh, neatly dressed figure in front of me who stirred in me a desire to give her a chance. I then asked her the usual questions about her family, health and faith.

She was the eldest of a family of seven children. The father had had an accident that had forced Habiba to quit school and look for work. She had her heart set on social work, and was eager to improve herself and — she added sweetly — be of service to the *Ibu*.

I laughed and said that would be fine presuming that she really wanted to do this wonderful but heavy work, and had the energy required to sustain her. Habiba countered boldly that she was not discouraged easily; that she was diligent, and would succeed.

I decided to take a chance and took her on, feeling gratified that here was, finally, a person who was employed for what she was, not because she had an influential father or was politically important.

The first week, Habiba navigated with grace around the tables and cabinets still nattily dressed in *sarong* and *kebaya*. Then she came in a flowery dress, self-conscious at first, but perking up when I gave her an appreciative nod.

Her work was neat, and she learned with astonishing rapidity. Soon she became an indispensable assistant and I found her attentive in ways that the other girls were not. Occasionally I would find a modest bouquet in a small can on my desk. At other times I would notice that everything had been carefully dusted. When a sunbeam shone in my face, she would unobtrusively close the curtain.

Once she asked, with genuine concern, how the orphans were getting on. We discussed it at length, and Habiba then demonstrated to me that she had a social conscience and was deeply interested in the work I was doing.

One time, she asked discreetly if she could come along and assist me in doing the planned surveys of the *kampungs*, which really should have been the job of the slow-moving Imram.

Pleasantly surprised, I agreed, because I knew that my work was not important enough to interest the others. They would reluctantly accompany me only if I gave them a *perintah keras* — a firm order. So the spontaneous interest of Habiba did me much good.

\* \* \* \*

Early in the morning of the next day, Habiba and I left Ternate on foot as the city was starting to emerge from its slumber.

The sun had just risen above the horizon, and we watched with delight as it increasingly brushed this ever-beautiful panorama with its golden rays. Dewdrops sparkled on the blossoming hibiscus flowers. The creamy-white and lily-like flowers of the *sedap malam* (the commercially important tuberose, originally imported from Central America) smelled wonderful. Everything looked and smelled fresh and new.

We walked at a good clip, for there was much ground to be covered, and we had no means of transportation except our legs.

We arrived at the first *kampung*, a fairly large one. There were 500 inhabitants, both young and old. The *Kepala Kampung*, whom I knew, had someone signal our arrival on the *tong-tong*, and soon the curious population assembled in front of his house.

Right away, we faced a serious problem. Since this was a Moslem village, there was no registry of births and deaths. This made registration far more difficult than in a Christian village, where a baptismal register would at least provide some insight.

We explained the nature of the survey we were conducting, and then inquired if there were any widows or orphans.

The widows came forward spontaneously, but often could not explain how or when their husbands had died. The younger ones had usually remarried; the elderly ones invariably lived alone under very trying circumstances.

The registration of the orphans also caused much confusion. Whoever had lost both parents stepped forward — young *and* old. We encountered this misunderstanding in all villages, and quickly learned to address it beforehand. The word "orphan", we would explain, applied only to children under fourteen years.

Of course, we then ran into the problem of kids being passed off as being younger than they really were, but, in the absence of birth certificates, it was difficult to argue about the claims made. Eventually I would develop rules of thumb to overcome those obstacles.

When we turned to the elderly, another problem cropped up. None of them knew how old they were. So we had to gauge their age by some major event that they might recall: the name of an old Sultan, a natural disaster, or some other important happening.

To my surprise, I found that old men were respected and reasonably well cared for in the homes of their children, whereas old women were not. They would only be welcome so long as they were useful in keeping house or in looking after their grandchildren. If they could not do that any more, they were usually banned to a kitchen outside the house, where they spent their last days in abject misery. This group was clearly in great need of social assistance.

After this admittedly crude census, we surveyed the villagers' state of health. The blind, deaf, handicapped and those suffering from eye diseases, malaria, dysentery and other tropical illnesses had to be prodded and persuaded to come forward. Then came the mothers with their infants, framboesia-marked children (those with strawberry-like birth marks, often a sign of yaws, a contagious tropical ulceration), and those with lesser ailments. I treated them as best I could, but had to refer some cases to the outpatient clinic in the capital, where there was a doctor. Later, when I visited people living outside Ternate, I frequently would have to function as a doctor, insofar as it was within my capabilities.

Then, I checked into the state of their drinking water, their eating habits, way of life, the way in which they earned their living, and the products which they imported and exported. In short, I checked into anything that could affect the villagers' well-being, and made notes on all conversations with the *Kampung* Head, the *Mufti* (Islamic jurist), the *Hajis* (Mecca pilgrims) and with the people themselves.

The eagerness with which the population participated impressed me. They clearly expected something from this survey — particularly in terms of material aid — even though they were not used to getting assistance from outside their village and were, by nature, a little skeptical in this regard.

For centuries, the people of the North Moluccas had followed their strict *Adat* rules, the so-called *gotong royong*, voluntary aid or self-help in case of natural disasters.

For example, if a house had burned down, the villagers would erect a new dwelling; if a *prau* was lost at sea, they would build a new one; if a widow was not able to weed her garden or fix her leaky roof, they would give immediate and spontaneous assistance. The *Adat* prescribed this, and no one needed to be prompted. It was second nature to them, and this provided me with a good foundation on which to build.

When the survey of this — our first — *kampung* was finally completed, the *Kepala Kampung* spontaneously invited us for a meal, which we gratefully accepted. It had been a long session, and it had been very hot on the veranda where we had interviewed hundreds of people. With most of them gone, it was a welcome respite to enjoy our food in relative peace and quiet.

We then said good-bye to the few people who were still around, and left for the next *kampung*, which was only 4 kilometers away. The news of our coming had apparently traveled ahead, because, when we arrived, the villagers were already gathering in front of the house of their *Kepala Kampung*. These people spoke the Ternate version of Malay, which I knew, so there would be no language problems.

When I learned that this village had a school, I decided to visit it right away, because it was getting close to 1:00 pm — the time when schools close in this tropical country.

I figured that the school could well reflect the social health of the community. If the children looked neat and healthy, well and good; if, on the other hand, they looked unkempt and sickly, we would have to check into the community's lifestyle and eating habits. An interview with the *guru* and pupils would also provide clues as to the community's level of development and social standing. All these subjective criteria would assuredly provide an important framework for the survey itself.

As expected, this first school visit taught me plenty and it broke the ice. The villagers appreciated my immediate interest in their children, and that smoothed the way for the interviews that were to follow. I decided then to start all future surveys by asking if there was a school, and, if so, if I might visit that first.

After the school visit, during which I had made many notes, the teacher and students escorted us to the house of the *Kepala Kampung*, where we interviewed and registered everyone and encountered the same problems as before. One important difference, however, was that the villagers expressed a greater interest in the medical part of our program. The women even asked quite freely about pregnancy checkups — something I had not dared hope for, having expected these country people to be less open to modern medicine than the city dwellers.

After completing this second survey, we started on the 9 kilometer long trek back to Ternate. Habiba was exhausted, but the coolness of the afternoon revived her somewhat.

It was getting dark when we entered the *kota*, tired yet excited about our plans for the next day, when we would have to start on the report for our chief. We intended to draft and type it with care, since the continuation of the project depended on it.

This day had been a decisive one for me. I had learned much and concluded that this work held a promising future for me. I was determined to pursue it.

The next day, we started to draft our report. It would have to be written in "Church Malay" — also known as *Bahasa Tinggi*, or

## IBU MALUKU

High Malay — because none of us had yet mastered the new *Bahasa Indonesia*, even though, like all civil servants, we had been enrolled in speed-courses as a condition for keeping our jobs.

Two days later, we submitted the report to our chief and waited anxiously for his answer. We should not have worried. He approved it in its entirety and gave us the green light to continue along the same lines!

I was delighted, of course, and started to see our work in a different light.

What we were doing had never been done before. The former Dutch Government had restricted itself to giving subsidies to the Protestant and Catholic Missions, the Salvation Army, other Christian organizations, and to private initiatives. But the new Government was the first one to pay attention to the well-being of the population on a broad basis.

### Endnotes

[1] In *Indonesia Handbook*, Bill Dalton has written the following epitaph for the 210,000 Dutch settlers and Civil Servants of the Netherlands East Indies: "By governing through local leaders, this tiny nation on the other side of the world in the cold Atlantic came to dominate this sprawling archipelago in the Java Sea for over 350 years. The Dutch established the first estate crops and, thus, the first economic wealth of Indonesia. They used the considerable wealth generated from the Indonesian land to increase agricultural export and trade, and also to support the manufacturing development in Holland. They upset the ecological balance by introducing new health schemes so Indonesians lived longer. Population growth in Indonesia for 100 years after 1830 was stupendous (growing to 60 million). By bringing to bear their organizational skills, technologies, European education, egalitarian ideas, and ideologies, the Dutch finally made themselves superfluous and brought about their own extinction in the area."

[2] Many years later, those half-bills with the Queen's picture were exchanged for Government bonds that were of little value. Since she was not allowed to transfer the cash out of the country, Jeanne eventually gave it to the Catholic Mission where it might do some good.

[3] The indigenous population never showed any animosity towards Jeanne van Diejen. The problems that occurred were always the

work of a few instigators from elsewhere, she said.
4   After much diplomatic wrangling which, at one point, involved Bobby Kennedy and other envoys of the United States, the Netherlands agreed to relinquish New Guinea in May of 1963 — more than 12 years later.
5   During the war, the Nationalist movement decided to establish the Sumatran variant of Malay as the national language for a new and independent Indonesia. This made sense as, for centuries, *pasar Malay* — or "market Malay" — had been the trading language throughout the East Indies.

# CHAPTER 43

### Aboard the Bintang Laut
### Ternate, 1951-1954

Eventually, it became normal for Habiba to come with me on *tournée*, and even though this made it more difficult for her to do her other work, she never asked for anyone to replace her. We made long trips over Ternate Island, visiting all the *kampungs* along the coast and in the mountains and Habiba proved that she had, indeed, a lot of persistence.

On these trips, the lovely traits in her character came to the fore. She always had something for the children, be it a fruit, a peppermint, or now and then some beads or shells that she had picked up from a beach along the way. Sometimes she cleverly used these gifts as bait to persuade a scared child to submit to an examination or a painful treatment of a wound.

Calmly, she would make notes as an examination progressed. She encouraged the sick, cracked a joke now and then, and in some fashion or other managed to turn the examination into a more pleasant experience.

Physically, Habiba also progressed. Her figure blossomed out, her skin color became more healthy, and her cheerfulness and joy in her work also increased.

Three years later, Habiba had progressed to where she could sometimes fill in for me, and when she did, she came through without fail. But the days of our association might be numbered. I heard unofficially that I might be transferred to the Social Services' Inspection Branch, and since this involved much more traveling, it meant that I would have to be replaced. If that came about, I fervently hoped that my successor would understand and appreciate her. If not, then I would fear greatly for this sensitive girl.

In time, I did indeed get transferred to the Inspection Branch, and immediately embarked on a four-month long tour. My replacement would arrive after I had left.

When I returned, I saw my devoted foursome — Sofura, Mirjam, Imram and Habiba — standing on the pier, waving a large bouquet of flowers.

As soon as the gangway had been lowered, the four ran up to greet me. Three of them excitedly told me the latest news: how much fun it was at the office now; how the new chief had made many changes; and that more people had been hired — not forgetting to mention, of course, the important families these new employees had come from.

Habiba, however, was distant and didn't say much, but just stayed devotedly close to me. She looked pale, and had lost weight. I gave her an extra nod and asked if all was well with her. Shyly, she nodded, but then her beautiful eyes suddenly filled with tears. It was neither the time nor the place to ask for an explanation, so I decided I would find out what this was all about later on.

Arriving at the office, I found that all the furnishings had been moved about; the walls were plastered with loudly colored posters; all desks had been pushed against one wall; and my replacement had created a private office, walled off with filing cabinets. There he sat with an unknown girl, also Javanese, who had usurped Habiba's position.

To my dismay I learned that Habiba had been classified as unqualified for the job, because she did not have a high school diploma. The girl who had replaced her, did. A protest from me would not help. The man had been hired as my replacement and could do as he pleased.

Before I left for a different office, I tried to arrange for Habiba to be transferred, but her mother, pregnant with her ninth child, needed her at home to help cook and launder for the family. A transfer to another place was out of the question.

A year later, I returned to my previous post for an inspection. My faithful foursome stood on the quay again to welcome me.

Mirjam introduced her first-born, and Sofura giggled non-stop as she showed me a photograph of her fiancé, a heavy-set Arab. Imram was still the melancholy girl I remembered, and Habiba, well, she was a shock. She was a shadow of her former self.

Deeply concerned, I asked:

"Dear child, what has happened to you?"

She smiled wanly, and said:

"Oh *Ibu*, I am so happy to see you again. May I come tonight and talk to you?"

She did come that evening, but did not say much. The next day, I took her to the hospital for a check-up. The doctor diagnosed TB, and urged that she enter a sanatorium immediately.

Two weeks later I left Ternate to make an inspection tour of the Minahassa on North Celebes (now Sulawesi). I took Habiba with me and left her in the well-known hospital of Tomohon, where the wonderful mountain climate should do her much good.

Throughout later travels I kept in contact by mail, and eventually learned that she had regained her strength and would soon be going back to her family and her work.

Then, at the beginning of 1957, I unexpectedly arrived in Ternate. Of course, there was no one there to greet me this time; no one knew I was coming. I spent the morning at my old office, discussing business matters. Habiba was not there and nobody mentioned her to me.

After the meeting, I was told, in answer to my questions, that Habiba had indeed returned to work three months earlier, but had been absent from the office for a week now. I decided to visit the family in the coming days.

Then, that afternoon, I was driving down a narrow road and stopped at the side to pay my respects and make room for a Mohammedan funeral procession that was coming towards me.

Imram, who was with me, said:

"Look *Ibu*, it's a young girl."

As the procession went by, I noticed that most mourners were from Habiba's village.

As I got out of the Jeep, an old man came up to me, gripped both my hands, and cried out:

"Thank you, *Ibu*! Thank you for coming to see Habiba on her last journey."

Thunderstruck, I looked at him, and asked:

"Habiba? Habiba Jafar?"

"Yes," he nodded, "She passed away this morning. She never stopped asking for you."

My mind went numb, and I don't remember what I said. Moments later I found myself in the procession, tripping over stones and potholes I couldn't see because of the tears that wouldn't stop.

By the time we entered the Mohammedan cemetery, I had gotten hold of myself. The grave had been dug. Two people stood in it, ready to receive what had once been Habiba, but which was now just a shapeless pack, dismally white and stiff, lying on a stretcher. Was this the affectionate and courageous girl, the cheerful comrade of so many work-days, whom I had come to love as my own daughter? I could not accept this.

The stretcher-bearers arrived at the grave and stopped momentarily to allow the mourners to gather around. The old man, who had spoken to me earlier, suddenly stood beside me and touched me — a rare gesture.

"*Ibu*," he said, "your child ... *how wonderful that sounded* ... your child is being laid to rest without having seen you. Can we let her go that way?"

Tears filled my eyes again, and what had never happened in a Mohammedan cemetery before, happened then. The old man went up to the stretcher, loosened the wrapping around Habiba's neck and pulled the shroud away from her face.

"Look," he said, "the *Ibu Belanda* — the Dutch mother — may say goodbye to her child before she is laid to rest!"

I knelt and desperately wanted to touch her, but Mohammedan custom forbade that. So I could only stare at that still-lovely face and mumble a prayer. And then I said goodbye to her.

"You may cover her up again," whispered the old man with a trembling voice, "and then you may, together with me, her father, pick her up and carry her to her grave."

This also breached the ethics and traditions of these people, so I was deeply touched by the beautiful gesture of this man, who knew exactly what his daughter would have wanted.

Habiba was put in her grave on her side. Her face was uncovered once again and pressed into the cool earth, facing Mecca. A mat was placed over her and then the grave was filled half-way with earth.

The men — the women were absent as custom dictated — kneeled around the grave and in supplication raised their hands with palms up to the Almighty, while the Imam recited a chapter from the Koran. Seven times, they pleaded with Allah to be merciful to Habiba. Bowing repeatedly, they lamented that the girl was still so young, and prayed that she would find favor in His eyes.

Then the diggers closed the grave and inserted a head-board and foot-marker. After a few minutes of contemplative silence, the mourners slowly turned and went home.

Back at the office, the staff feigned not to have known about Habiba's death. Perhaps the relentless pursuit of their own happiness did not permit any feelings to surface, but it appeared to me that they had already forgotten their fellow-worker.

Of all her co-workers, her "white mother" was the only one who had accompanied Habiba to her last resting place.

\* \* \* \*

Now I will backtrack a few years. Habiba was still alive then, and we were pleased to see what was happening as a result of all our surveys. The District Chiefs and *Kepala Kampungs* had started to implement our recommendations, with the full support of the population who had started to believe in the program.

My original ideas on the future of social work in the Moluccas became more and more accepted — and appreciated. A year after I had started, I was promoted to the better-paying rank of *Pendidik, Penjuluh Sosial* — Instructing and Investigating Social Civil Servant. Soon after, the people, large and small, started calling me *Nyonya Sosial* — Mrs. Social.

Then a big change occurred in the territorial makeup of the Moluccas, which would change the focus of my work forever.

The Sultan of Ternate, His Highness Mohammed Iskander Jahir Shah had been transferred to Jakarta to become Special Advisor to President Sukarno[1], and Ternate itself had been absorbed by its historical rival, Tidore. The Sultan of Tidore, H. H. Zainal Abidin Shah, had been named *Kepala Daèrah* (Regional Head) of this enlarged region.

I knew him well, and my relations with this former Dutch civil servant had always been extremely cordial. So, although I deeply mourned the loss of a friend and advisor, it was with a positive frame of mind that I met with His Highness in his office on Ternate.

We mutually agreed to start surveying the islands of Tidore and Makian — using the same approach as I had used on Ternate — and to later include the islands of Morotai, Bachan and the hundreds of smaller islands that make up the Moluccas.

We knew that the latter group would require careful planning, because whereas some islands were inhabited all year around, others were only populated during the fishing season.

I soon realized that I could not count on commercial ships or boats to get me where I wanted to go, and decided to obtain a boat of my own.

I bought a schooner, which I had rebuilt to accept a 25hp outboard motor. Inside, there was room for a spare motor, four fuel drums of 200 liters each, and sleeping quarters for a crew of five. There was also a cargo space to store a supply of rice, sugar, soap, clothes and, of course, medicine.

For crew, I engaged an experienced *juragang* (skipper) named Om Erest (a variation of *Oom Ernest* — Uncle Ernest), a helmsman named Senen (Nen for short), and a cook called Mahmud. All of them were descendants of slaves from New Guinea who had eventually settled as free men on the Moluccan islands.

Now I was able to leave whenever I wanted, to reach any island, however far and in any kind of weather. This boat, which the natives called the *Bintang Laut* (Sea Star), would serve me well until the end of 1957.

By means of this boat, and assisted by the experienced crew, I would eventually visit and survey all the islands of the Moluccas. Bad weather often plagued us, but I never feared for my life except once — and that was not because of bad weather. In fact, at the time, the sea was quite calm.

We were on our way to the island of Sanana when our skipper, miscalculating the impact of low tide, ran aground on a coral reef. The crew immediately jumped overboard to try to cut away the coral under the boat and get us adrift again — but all to no avail.

Spotting a fishing boat in the distance, we managed to attract their attention and asked for help in pulling us off the reef with a brand-new Manila hemp rope that I had recently purchased. The fishermen agreed.

My crew jumped overboard again, to lighten the load, and the fishermen pulled with all their might, but with no success. After a few more tries, they gave up, cuts us loose and left — taking most of my Manilla rope with them as payment for their services.

My men climbed back into the boat, angrily shouting at the disappearing fishermen; but their anger was soon replaced by despair. With the tide going out, it was clear that the bottom of the boat would soon be crushed by the coral, and we were too far from land to swim or hope for a timely rescue.

The men, all born sailors, were, for the first time in their lives, at a loss as to what to do and asked me — for they were all Christian — to lead them in prayer in preparation for certain death.

The men squatted in front of me. I stood up, closed my eyes and addressed Judas Thaddeus (St. Jude), the Saint to whom one appeals when one is in dire straits:

"Judas Thaddeus," I prayed fervently, "if you really exist, help us now as we are in mortal danger." I don't know how long I kept on praying, but a sudden movement of the board made me adjust my footing and open my eyes.

The awestruck men then told me excitedly that it seemed as though two invisible hands had lifted the boat off the coral reef and had placed it into deeper water.

We were saved.

Was it a miracle? I like to think so.

\* \* \* \*

My first trip outside Ternate in the *Bintang Laut* took me to Tidore.

Tidore, slightly larger than Ternate and only one kilometer from its closest shore, is a beautiful island. Its gracefully-contoured volcano, the 1,730 meter (5,676 foot) Kiematubu, dominates the southern half of the island. The lush forests that fill the deep ravines are full of *chèlengs* (wild swine) that often ravage neighboring gardens. For that reason, the farmers always welcomed hunters with open arms — the more so because the largely Islamic population loathed those animals.

# IBU MALUKU

Visitors to Tidore may be forgiven for thinking that they are in Portugal[2]. The white-washed houses with their neat little shutters are of Portuguese style, both inside and out, and the language is full of Portuguese words. Festivals and dances also date from the Portuguese era, and even family names and school children's dresses reinforce the impression of being in that country.

Whenever I entered a school, the children would get up without prompting, stand beside their desks, and sing a song to welcome me. I found the *kampungs* on Tidore well maintained and prosperous. The population was intelligent, courteous and co-operative; and the survey, which had been well planned in advance from Ternate, went smoothly.

However, I encountered more sick people than I had expected, and also discovered a small number of *bona-fide* war orphans who, having no one to stand up for them, had fallen victim to exploitation. Something *had* to be done for them!

After surveying a few small neighboring islands without difficulty, we sailed south toward Makian. The crossing was rough. A violent rain storm whipped up the waves, and the *Bintang Laut* was heavily knocked about. We were pleased that the storm passed over as we approached the harbor of Ngotakiaha, the capital of the island.

Makian, dominated by a volcano with a split cone, made a different impression than Tidore — as did the Makianese people. They appeared surly and rather suspicious. As a result, the survey took much longer than planned.

In the capital was an outdoor clinic, filled to capacity with patients who had all sorts of skin disorders and eye diseases. The *kampungs* outside the capital were not well maintained — yes, even unkempt. I duly noted everything in my report.

From Makian, we continued the *tournée* along the west coast of Halmahera, where there were several *kampungs* that were included in the Region of Tidore. Dealing with the inhabitants was difficult at first, but thereafter everything else went according to plan.

In all, the survey took us three weeks, and netted unexpected information about orphans, war widows, blind people and many others who were not able to fend for themselves.

Upon my return to Ternate, I learned that my boss, the Head of Social Service, had been replaced by a Javanese — a man of courtly manners who had, nonetheless, a captivating personality. His name was Pak Latif (which, of course, made me think about my faithful Latif).

I would need time to get used to him, but our first meeting was pleasant.

He showed great interest in my work, and we discussed it objectively for several days. I learned that on Java one did not make *tournées* like I did; there, tours of duty were made either by car or train. My *Bintang Laut* was, in Pak Latif's, eyes an uncomfortable and dangerous means of transportation. I assured him that it was quite safe, and invited him to join me on the next *tournée*, and then on the one after that. He declined politely at every turn, and so never learned to love the sea as I did.

\*\*\*\*

The next *tournée*, which would last six weeks (twice as long as the first one), would take us to the heavily-populated western and northern coast of Halmahera.

Dr. Tan, the Chinese doctor on Ternate, provided us with as much medicine as the boat could carry. The Department of Education supplied educational materials for new village schools, where young men and women were enrolled in a 3-4 year elementary Adult Education program. Here, interested people of all ages could learn how to read and write. The Social Service Department also wanted me to distribute free food, clothing, and other items, as I deemed necessary.

The boat was so full that I had to slide over boxes and bags to reach my quarters — a board of just two meters by 55 cm — where I would live, work and sleep.

Life on board was very primitive, of course. We cooked on the roof of the cabin. The stove was a petrol can with a layer of sand covering the bottom. Steel pins that diagonally pierced the wall near the top formed the grill. The stove was fired with wood, which was inserted through a hole near the bottom. It was part of the cook's duties to gather firewood in each village we visited. He also had ample time to do other chores while we were doing the survey.

The necessity of a daily bath was not always met, because not every *kampung* had a good water well or other bathing facilities. Bathing in a nearby river was not always possible either, because of crocodiles or because the river was a so-called rain-river that dried up during the dry season.

When we did find a river to suit our purpose, we took our time and bathed and laundered at length. After a tiring survey, or after not having been able to bathe for several days, it did us much good to relax in this way.

Although I always traveled with men, there never was any problem about getting the privacy I needed — be it on the boat or in the river. A sign or a look from Om Erest to the other men was all that was needed.

One of the Captain's duties was to make sure that we had an adequate supply of water on board. It was a constant worry for him, because, strangely, on many islands it was difficult to find potable water. Even if they did have wells, the water was often brackish or polluted. It took much of my time, tact, and persuasiveness to get the villagers to clean the wells. Sometimes, I had to twist their arms by refusing to distribute rice, clothes, or medicine, until the well had been made usable again.

Some islands had water reservoirs constructed by the former Dutch Government, but the war had damaged many of them, rendering them useless. Some islands had to import water by canoe, which was mostly done by women and children, some of whom lost their lives in stormy seas.

The villagers sought my advice in these matters, and thus I became involved in all sorts of affairs that were really outside the scope of social work, yet were vitally important and had to be reported.

We often had to leave the *Bintang Laut* at anchor, and take a small *prau* through mangrove forests to reach the villages to be surveyed. Those forests were sometimes exceptionally beautiful; sometimes they were oppressive and heavy with the unpleasant smell of crocodiles. The rivers beyond those mangrove forests were usually wide and clear, with villages spread along their banks.

Once, we arrived at a village early in the evening with the intent of getting a good night's rest there. The next morning brought an interesting spectacle, which reminded me of the early-morning "sea-dunking" procession I had seen in Sangowo, on the island of Morotai. The entire population, dressed in blue sleeping sarongs, left the *kampung* with solemn expressions on their faces and descended the steep river bank. One by one, they disappeared silently in the water, each one finding a private spot. Only their heads showed. Nobody moved; nobody uttered a word. After a little while, the masses stirred: they "brushed" their teeth with their fingers, rubbed their limbs, and bobbed up and down a bit. Then, one by one, the silent figures hurried back to the village to rinse themselves at the well and put on fresh clothes. Only after that was done did they start to talk.

Under the houses on stilts or in the little kitchens, fires were lit, and soon the aroma of coffee, fried or cooked bananas, *papeda* (sago porridge) and small fish spread over the *kampung* and the river.

Normally, the church bell would have rung at this time to summon the children to the Christian village-school; the women, to their gardens; and the men with their dogs, to the forests to hunt swine. That would have been the usual course of events. However, since the *prau* of the Social Service had arrived, everything else was pushed aside, and the entire population assembled in front of the house of the District or Village Chief.

Whenever we stayed overnight at other villages, we invariably witnessed the same early morning proceedings that we had seen in the first village. Most of the time, the people were friendly and co-operative. They particularly appreciated receiving the medicines and so the medical checkups became, increasingly, the focal point of the visit.

Our next destination was the many groups of islands along the Northwestern coast of Halmahera, which are little more than tiny blips on this vast stretch of ocean. Among them are the Northern and Southern Loloda Groups.

The Southern Group is located just north of the beautiful 1,635 meter (5,364 foot) high Gamkonora volcano on the mainland, where one can look straight into the fiery crater. At night, its radiant glow was a truly magnificent and awesome sight.

The inhabitants of the Loloda Islands are fishermen, very peaceful in nature, whose houses of bamboo and *atap* sit on the hillside. In the evenings, their little harbors are calm and peaceful. One feels good. Through slits in the bamboo walls of the houses shine warm lantern lights that make the houses look very cozy and inviting — enough to make any sailor nostalgic.

Above the islands sparkle millions of stars in a cloudless sky. They look like a gigantic king's cloak on which Orion and his entourage shine as twinkling jewels; the Pleiades functions as a broach; and a string of stars embellish the cloak's fringe. Moonless nights there, in particular, are like fairy tales.

There was no one to help me with the survey of those islands. My colleagues didn't like the long rough *tournées,* nor the hard work associated with them. Thus, all the administrative work fell on my shoulders.

After each visit, I had to write a complete report, give names and aliases of all the people I had talked to, outline the general situation, and comment on how Social Assistance might play a role in the future of the village.

This report-writing took much time and energy, and usually had to be done while en route from one island to the next. Sometimes it was done in the evening, while we were at anchor close to, but never in front of, a *kampung* — so as not to give offense to them. Then, my diary was updated by the light of a stable lantern, while the *Bintang Laut* tugged at her anchors, or rocked back and forth from a swell. By then the crew was asleep, and their soft snoring made me hanker for a long, undisturbed — and often badly needed — sleep.

It would be late at night before I could put away my diary. Perhaps it was just as well, for it allowed little time to think about the past. As it was, I barely managed to remember my loved ones in my prayers before I put my head down to sleep.

At one of the islands, we had to drop anchor far from the beach since a coral reef prevented us from getting closer. The population gathered on the beach and Om Erest — using a megaphone — asked them to send a *prau* to fetch us. They ignored our request. Then Om Erest explained the reason for our visit. Nobody moved. Finally Om Erest told the beach crowd that if they did not send a *prau* in one hour, we would leave and never return. Still no response, so, after one hour of waiting, we packed it in.

On all my *tournées*, it only happened three times that the population refused to receive us. Yet every time, it struck me like a whiplash; I had great difficulty in accepting it.

Sailing north from the Loloda Islands, as I wrote my report, we soon approached *Pulau* Doi[3], where an Arab worked a manganese mine. He received us royally and invited us to an Arabian wedding. The very young bride, seated on an elaborately-decorated bed, received her guests with great dignity, and appeared impressed by our presence. It was a pleasant diversion for us.

From Doi Island, we sailed around the northern tip of Halmahera and headed for several large coastal *kampungs* that were also part of the Tidore Region.

In each, the reception was different. The inhabitants usually co-operated, but sometimes worked against us, depending on their nature and their religious views.

In the Moslem villages, the people were usually more surly than in the Christian ones. Moslem villages could be recognized from afar: they were usually unkempt and smelled of the many goats that were kept there. By contrast, the Christian *kampungs* were more inviting, for they were clean and well-kept, and the people were also more genteel.

The least-inviting *kampungs* were the so-called heathen ones. From afar, we could recognize them by the large shells of turtles that hung as trophies from the trees along the beach, but also by the lush, brilliantly red hibiscus that bloomed in every garden. Evidently, this plant, which has medicinal properties, was the one most prized by the natives, who also used them to decorate their hair.

Whatever the cultural stripe or size of a village, the inhabitants always expressed great surprise about the existence of an organization in the as-yet-little-known Republic of Indonesia that would concern itself with the well-being of the entire population. That was unheard of! And that this work was being done by a Dutch woman, who either spoke their language or was learning it, and who did not seem to make any distinction between rich and poor, old or young, well or sick ... that was even more unusual!

People talked among themselves about this *Ibu Sosial* (Social Mother), for whom no one lived too far, and for whom no village was inaccessible. This created admiration and trust, which was a great boon for the kind of work I was trying to do.

\*\*\*\*

The weather had changed for the worse when we left Doi Island and took to sea again. I instructed the Captain to follow the Halmahera coast for a while before crossing the open sea to Morotai. Every crew member was against it because of the worsening weather. But, knowing that their fears were partly fed by the belief that Morotai's coast was bewitched, I persisted.

At Laumadore, we brought the boat about, leaving the relative safety of the Halmahera coast behind us and headed for the large, silent ocean that contained not a single island. The unbridled power of nature was awesome. For a long time, we saw nothing but black water, whipped into high waves by a ferocious gale.

Finally, the rocks of Morotai emerged from the undulating sea. It was a breathtaking view: wave after wave crashing onto the high rocks, exploding into geysers with a thunderous roar, and returning to the ocean in white streams of foam. It was terrifying and magnificent, but also dangerous. That we understood very well. But our boat performed beautifully, and its motor did not quit on us. If it had, it would have meant certain death. One moment we straddled a high wave; the next, we were thrown into a deep valley between two high, dangerously curving mountains of water. But every time, the boat courageously climbed to the crest of the next wave.

The faces of the crew, which had been drawn with fatigue and tension as we fought our way past these dangerous rocks, broke into smiles as we left that watery violence behind us and approached the more protected cape of the island. On shore, we were received by an excited District Chief, who repeatedly expressed his admiration for our piece of bravado, and then served us a meal fit for a king.

Morotai is inhabited by a totally different mix of people: Butonese, Malaysians, Ambonese, Galelarese and Tobelorese. Compared to the other islanders, we found these people, as a result of the war, very politicized. From the Japanese they had inherited an anti-Dutch complex; from some very red Australians, communism; and from that motley crowd of Americans, rowdyism. Later they had been exposed to the under-trained Dutch NICA government that — in spite of its inexperience — had succeeded to put an end to the piracy of American stockpiles, and had also stopped the barter of weapons and clothes for strong native liquor.

Now the islanders were dealing with the growing presence of Javanese soldiers who considered themselves vastly superior. On orders of their political bosses, these soldiers had whipped up the citizens — especially the young — against any Dutch person who had stayed behind in this young Republic.

This made it necessary for me to approach these islanders with great caution, every step of the way. Each word had to be weighed carefully — especially because the Javanese and their supporters saw me as a spy for the hated Dutch, who were still holding on to New Guinea and hindered communication with family members still living there. Interestingly, their scornful remarks showed that they were quite jealous of these far-away family members, who were still paid for their labors in Dutch silver *ringgits* (two-and-a-half guilder coins), whereas they, inhabitants of Morotai, had to be content with scrappy and worthless paper *rupiahs*.

The people often did not understand my mission — partly because it had not been properly explained to them by their own leaders. Sometimes I was heckled. This hurt me, and brought about stresses that were difficult to overcome. Yet, in spite of these and other difficulties, I did make some progress, and it became increasingly clear that this island was also badly in need of some form of social assistance.

Along the southern coast of Morotai were many *kampungs* to be surveyed. In one, I found out that the black-pox had killed many people. Now the three members of my crew were able to appreciate the importance of the vaccination that they received before leaving Ternate. I knew that, at the time, they had submitted to it only to please me!

I knew this coastal area well — having visited here many times when John was still alive — and I was pleased to run into many old friends who greatly helped in getting the surveys done. At night, when we had some time to ourselves, we met again to relive old memories.

During the Japanese occupation, the population had suffered much. In my survey, I documented the plight of an exceptionally large number of war victims: widows, orphans and abandoned seniors.

Having finished with the other coastal areas, we sailed south to survey the Tobelo Islands, and then stopped at the mainland city of Tobelo to obtain fuel. I was very close to Mon Désir then, but did not have the time to find out what had happened to it. Probably just as well!

We had used up more than 900 liters, and could only refuel in harbors — like Tobelo — where there was a military post, because it was the military who controlled all gasoline supplies. The negotiations were often painful, and it usually required much diplomacy and demonstrated humbleness on my part to get the required fuel.

This time, I had to bargain with a young lieutenant of the TNI (*Tentara Nasional Indonesia*, the National Indonesian Army), who was very courteous, but also *very* curious about my activities, especially on Morotai. However, I received 200 liters of gasoline from him, enough to get us home.

Three days later, we entered the safety of the Ternate harbor during a heavy storm. We had been away 40 days and had surveyed 77 *kampungs*.

The report was typed directly from my diary in the prescribed eight copies. Om Erest, Mahmud and Nen received a few days' paid leave, and then extra time to fix up the boat and prepare it for the next trip.

For them, as for me, it was good to be home.

### Endnotes

[1] He had been "promoted away", as part of Sukarno's policy to replace influential leaders with his own people in order to strengthen his grip on the former Dutch empire. The Dutch government was in fact being replaced by a deeper entrenched Javanese government. Bloody resistance to this policy would erupt in many areas, especially in Ambon, Celebes, and, much later, in Timor, Aceh (north Sumatra) and Borneo.

[2] The Portuguese were the first Europeans to reach the Moluccas. They arrived in 1512 and started the lucrative spice trade. However, the Dutch dislodged them in 1605.

[3] *pulau*: island

IBU MALUKU

# CHAPTER 44

### A New Challenge
### Ternate, 1954

After two days off from work, I had a long meeting with Pak Latif, who had changed much during my absence. Evidently, he and his family were homesick and had difficulty adjusting to life in Ternate. He would never be *senang* (happy) either in his work or in his private life, and would soon return to Java.

We discussed the bulky report of my journey. As a result, he asked me to go to Java for meetings in Jakarta and Jokja. It was clear to him, he said, that two major initiatives would have to be launched: an orphanage for at least 40 children, and a care center for the elderly. My task would be to convince my superiors on Java to provide the necessary funds.

Within a week, I boarded a KPM boat to Menado, Celebes (now Sulawesi). Then I climbed aboard a Dornier aircraft that would take me to Java. It was my first flight as a civil servant of the Republic of Indonesia.

Most of the time, the aircraft followed the coastline. Flying overland was considered too risky, because guerrillas were battling Government troops. Close to Makassar the aircraft was indeed fired upon with small arms, but we were not hit, and at 19:00 hours landed safely at Anchol Airport near Jakarta.

A car from the Ministry picked me up and drove me to the mess hall of Social Affairs at Tanah Abang (a district in central Jakarta), where I met a few colleagues — one of them, a Dutchman, who helped me get settled in the dormitory part of the building.

These colleagues advised me to take great care to speak proper *Bahasa Indonesia*. The Ministry promoted, relentlessly, the *Satu Nusa, Satu Bangsa, Satu Behasa* (One Country, One People, One Language) concept, as one could easily read from the banners that were plastered everywhere, including on the walls in the mess hall. I resolved to do my very best.

The next morning at 6:45, I went with my colleagues to a large new building that housed the ministry of Social Affairs. My superiors received me with unexpected friendliness, yet with utmost propriety.

My reports were pulled from their files. It appeared that they had already been carefully studied. The gentlemen even praised my correct usage of Malay — the language in which the reports had been written — and then expressed surprise at my having mastered the new *Bahasa Indonesia* fairly well.

The need for an orphanage — as recommended in the conclusion of the report — was discussed, and before the offices closed for recess at 14:00 hours, I had their approval in black and white. The details would have to be discussed with heads of other departments. I also received an advance of 200,000 rupiahs to care for the aged, but the funds needed to buy, lease or build a seniors' home, I would have to find elsewhere.

Two days later, Secretary General Sekjen informed me that I had been promoted. It was a substantial promotion. I no longer belonged to the rank and file, so it appeared that I had finally been accepted.

More discussions followed that, from their point of view, were only exploratory in nature. However, I was pleased to perceive a genuine concern for the Moluccas and its inhabitants. After a week of conferences, during which I met several more colleagues, I received permission to return home.

A plane took me to Makassar, where I boarded a ship heading for Ambon. Here, I visited the ISORI organization — the inspection arm of the Ministry of Social Services — whose region, besides Ambon, included the North and South Moluccas.

I discussed the details of the orphanage plans with the highest ISORI official, an imposing Sumatran, who warmly received me. We got along very well, and over the years would maintain an excellent relationship. Fourteen days later I landed on Ternate, and, with my colleagues, celebrated the success of what had been achieved with the Government on Java.

*****

A week later, my crew and I readied ourselves for the next *tournée*, which would cover the southern region of Halmahera and all the islands — except the Gébé Group that, because of limited fuel supplies, lay for the moment outside the range of the *Bintang Laut*.

This *tournée*, which would last six weeks, would once again give a new direction to my life — and start me on a project that would soon absorb all my time and energy.

It was Monday, very early in the morning. The *Bintang Laut* was loaded to capacity with rice, clothes, medicine, soap, four reserve drums of fuel and a spare outboard motor. All was ready for departure. It was still foggy, but a dim light on the horizon told us where the sun would rise.

## IBU MALUKU

With the helping hand of the *juragang* I slid over the cargo into my accustomed seat, and we raised anchor. When the sun made its triumphant entry, we were already half-way to the Halmahera coast, where the first survey of a village was scheduled to start at 7:30.

Having finished there, we worked our way southward, coming upon some fairly large *kampungs*. The drinking water in most villages was contaminated and brackish, and had made many people sick.

Five days later we had surveyed all the west-coast villages, and arrived at Cape Libobang, the most southern tip of Halmahera, known to all navigators as a dangerous area. There was a considerable swell and a heavy rain. The sky was black with storm clouds.

As we rounded the Cape, incessant squalls hit us from ever-changing directions. The small dinghy, that we had brought with us for the first time, was torn from its deck moorings, and smashed to bits on the rocks. Cape Libobang had exacted its toll.

Following the local tradition, we threw a few handfuls of rice into the churning sea — which calmed all of us — and then, unexpectedly, we entered more tranquil waters where steering the boat became much easier.

The *kampungs* along this desolate coast were few and far between. The people were poor and bashful, not having seen many visitors, but the surveys went reasonably well. The villagers were especially grateful for the medicine.

On our way to Weda, we passed the Widi-Widi Islands — the so-called "bad" islands — which had no potable water and were only now and then inhabited by a few fishermen. Sometime in the past, the captains of passing ships had given these islands joyless names, such as Difficult Island, Lost Island and Sad Island.

Because of treacherous coral reefs, we navigated with great care through the straits that separated these islands from the high, forested coast-line. One crew member remained at the stern of the boat at all times, watching the shifting colors of the waters below and searching for a small passage to a lagoon where we could find a quiet, safe berth close to the village to be surveyed.

The weather again became awful. A strong headwind slowed us down considerably, and the rain pelted us unmercifully. We struggled continuously with tarpaulins to keep our cargo dry.

As we traveled farther north, the weather improved, which made our job easier. Finally we reached the capital of Weda, which I knew well from the days when both John and I had traveled with the KPM line.

There was a governmental post here and, as usual, I first reported our arrival to the police, with whom I also had to negotiate for a new supply of fuel. They were not at all co-operative, but when I discovered that they were short on medicines, I was able to close a deal for 200 liters of fuel — more than I had expected. I was pleased, because we still had a long journey ahead of us.

At the small hospital, the *mantri* (orderly) warned me that the pox had broken out farther up the coast and that each area had been marked with banners attached to long poles. He regretted that he could not give us any shots, for the *mantri* in charge of inoculations was on *tournée* and had taken all available vaccines with him. I put his mind at ease, saying that we had already been vaccinated.

We left Weda and called on several Islamic villages that were similar to the ones we had visited earlier. We also surveyed a few Alfur villages, where we were received warmly and, in the evenings, treated to their *chakalélé* war dances.

We stopped at Patani and rounded the eastern leg of Halmahera at Tanjung Ngolopopo. From there on we encountered more and more Christian *kampungs* and, finally, we reached Buli, the capital of the district.

From the District Chief I learned about the existence of a native group who lived in the rugged mountains, cut off from the rest of the world.

"They call themselves the Biri-Biri," he told me. "They are Alfurs of the Tobelo tribe, who are so afraid of outside contact that they will kill anyone who crosses their path."

Intrigued, I asked him to tell me more, and then learned that, farther east, there was a more peaceful tribe, the Linos. They were hunters and foragers who lived in the foothills and were more accessible. Near the Telaga Lina Lakes, the original hunting grounds of these people, there were even a few settlements where Protestant missionaries were setting up schools. This information would prove useful in my later travels.

Leaving Buli, we sailed along the northeastern arm of K-shaped Halmahera, admiring the extraordinarily beautiful coast that would, someday, make an attractive tourist area. After surveying Lilai and Jiriway near Cape Gamchaka (now Cape Lelai) we changed tack and headed for the deep, magnificent Kao Bay.

During the war, this bay had been the largest Japanese naval base, from where the entire East Indies' war effort drew its supplies. In 1945, more than 60,000 Japanese servicemen were stationed here. At that time, the bay was usually full of ships, providing the Allied's Air Force with a "fish-in-a-barrel" shooting opportunity. Once this base had been destroyed, General MacArthur could relax, bypass the East Indies and concentrate on the Philippines.

Thousands of Halmaherians died from the bombardments — or from hunger, when the Japanese, cut off from food imports, seized local supplies. All the villages were destroyed during the fighting. The survivors, who had fled inland but had since returned, now lived in shacks made from asbestos paper and rusted corrugated steel sheets. Their health was poor and there were many widows and orphans.

The journey through this magnificent bay took many days. To our left was a chain of high volcanoes that — particularly in the early morning — made an unforgettable impression as their peaks, protruding above a hazy shroud, were touched by the golden rays of the rising sun. Closer to shore lay the ruins of large coconut plantations. They had been destroyed, in part by Japanese axes, in part by MacArthur's bombs. The District Head of Wasilé gave us a vivid description of what had happened there.

Finally we reached the bottom of the sack-shaped Kao Bay, and followed its western shore line. Here, the *kampungs* were almost entirely hidden from view by banana plantations. The people spoke a different language and we had quite a struggle making ourselves understood.

Halfway up the bay was the former base of the Japanese fleet, which had been protected by fighter aircraft from aerodromes further inland. The harbor was still full of partly, or completely, submerged ships that had become havens for large schools of fish. From the locals, we heard about the many atrocities committed during the war.

In the very first *kampung* that we visited after leaving the entrance to the bay, something unusual happened. The Village Chief readily answered all my questions about the villagers' state of health, but often in a hesitating, faltering voice. I felt he was hiding something.

My suspicions were confirmed when I later interviewed a couple of invalids. They told me that the Chief had some relatives living high-up on the slope of the Togosi mountain. For some reason they had been banned from the village, they said. Why, they would not tell me. That was *rahasia* — secret. Asking others later on, I discovered that these relatives were the Chief's brother, with his wife and children.

Thinking that this was, perhaps, a family matter, I didn't question the Chief further, but decided to ask around in the next village. There, I still didn't get any straight answers, but I did understand that the separation was *not* the result of a family feud.

I felt an inexplicable urge to go and visit this exiled family. After much prodding, the villagers hesitatingly explained to me how to get there. It meant a good two-hour climb into the mountain.

## IBU MALUKU

As a precautionary measure, I packed an ample supply of medicine, rice and warm clothing into my rucksack and took off, leaving my crew behind.

Initially, the trip took me through gardens and banana orchards, but soon there was nothing but jungle. The path I followed narrowed down to a swine trail, and the climb became steeper. After clambering for a long time with my *parang* (machete) firmly held in one hand, I heard a dog barking in the distance. Probably some hunters, I thought, expecting to run into them at any moment. The smell of a wood fire told me I was getting close.

Coming to a slight clearing, I discovered a shed. Under the roof's overhang sat a woman, who gazed attentively into a pot that sat on stones placed around a crackling fire. Around the fire sat four children, dressed in rags, whose bodies — I could see from afar — were ravaged by framboesia (yaws).

The dog noticed me first and started to growl. I approached hesitantly and called out a greeting. The woman jumped up and raised a wooden spoon, ready to strike.

She became embarrassed when she saw that I was alone, and shyly invited me to come closer. Pointing to the fire, I softly asked if I could have some warm water. She gave me an astonished look and then shoved a wobbly bamboo stool in my direction.

Luckily, I understood her language. I told her what I had come to do, and emptied the contents of my rucksack while the wide-eyed children looked on. Hesitantly they accepted some cookies. I took the last one by the hand and said that I wanted to apply some medicine and bind his wounds. The child did not pull back. The mother let me treat this child, and didn't object when I then treated the others.

By the time I was finished, the mother had boiled some water. She dropped a few slivers of bark in the steaming water, and offered it to me.

As I drank the tea, I recounted my experiences in her village of origin: what I had done, and what I had heard. Her face suddenly hardened and, with bitterness in her voice, she said that she would rather not hear about that.

Carefully searching for the right words, I asked her about her life, so high up in the mountain: too far for the children to go to school and too far to receive medical aid from the traveling *mantri*. She muttered that, like her husband, she had attended school, but that she did not consider it necessary to have her boys educated.

The conversation switched to her livelihood. How did she sustain herself? Did *batatas* (sweet potatoes) and corn grow well this high up?

And was her husband perhaps attending the gardens, or was he out hunting?

The children had listened quietly, but attentively. When I talked about the father, the eyebrows of the eldest boy shot up and his eyes darted furtively toward the shed's door that was slightly ajar.

Catching his glance, I asked: "Is your husband ill?" and, before she could reply, I quickly moved to the door and threw it open. A suffocating smell hit me as I approached a *balé-balé* — a bamboo sleeping cot — where a human form lay, covered from head to toe with a sleeping *kain*. I pulled the cloth away and saw a man, covered with the same lesions as the children had.

"How strange," flashed through my mind, "that an adult would have framboesia."

With difficulty, the man sat up. I reached out to help him get up and lead him outside where, in daylight, I could get a better look at his condition. But I didn't get that far.

The wife, who had run into the room with the children, now tried to pull me back as she took turns cussing her husband and shouting at me: "Don't touch! *Kusta-kusta!*"

I did not understand what "*kusta-kusta*" meant, and told her, calmly, that I wanted to inspect his wounds. At my request, one of the children, his face contorted with anguish and tears streaming down his cheeks, brought me a bowl of water. Seething, the wife ran outside, leaving the children as if rooted in place.

I asked the man, who was almost blind, what "*kusta-kusta*" meant, and somehow he made me understand that he had leprosy[1].

All the blood drained from my face. Had I understood him properly? Was I now washing a leper? I broke out in a cold sweat and it took a great effort not to show the terror that had gripped me.

I left all my medicines and provisions with those wretched souls and left — forcing myself not to run. Like an automaton, I followed the path down the mountain slope, holding my offending arms in front of me.

"Am I now contaminated?" I raged. "Am I now also a leper?" Fear overwhelmed me and made my imagination run wild. I hurried down the path until I came to a brook, where I washed my hands, arms, face and legs for a long time in the cool, flowing water. Inside, I felt cold and paralyzed. My mind was numb; I could not think anymore. All I knew was that it would take a full ten days before I would see Dr. Tan in Ternate, the only one who could help me.

The remainder of the journey was pure hell. I did not dare confide my fears to anyone — my crew would surely have abandoned me in the middle of nowhere if they had known.

Finally we left the last of the 61 villages that we had surveyed and, on a brilliant Sunday morning, we sighted Ternate. As soon as I set foot on the wharf, I abandoned the boat and its cargo to the care of the crew, and — as soon as I knew they could no longer see me — I ran as fast as my legs would carry me to the home of my trusted Doctor, Karel Tan.

As soon as I entered his house, I held out my hands and shrieked: "Doctor, I have caught leprosy!"

Dr. Tan looked at me for a split second, then made me sit and gulp down a sedative, before sitting down himself to listen. Haltingly, and stumbling over my words, I told him what had happened.

Calmly, he asked: "Did you have any open wounds or cuts from *alang-alang* on your hands when you washed your hands after making contact with those people?"

Surprised, I looked at him, then shook my head. Not being sure, however, I carefully looked at my hands, but could not detect anything.

Calmly, he continued: "Don't you know anything about leprosy? Did you not know the local name for it?"

Sheepishly, I admitted to believing that all lepers were immediately rounded up and placed in a leprosarium.

Dr. Tan explained that this affliction was widespread among the native population, and that those who had it were invariably ejected from their communities and condemned to live in hiding under indescribable conditions. As he continued to tell me what he knew, his calm voice drove my fears away and I started to relax and become interested in what he had to say.

It dawned on me that I had never encountered this malady during all my surveys and none of the natives had mentioned it. I then realized my error in not having questioned the villagers about it, and wondered how, as a member of Social Service, I could help those unfortunate creatures without getting infected myself.

Dr. Tan seemed to have read my thoughts, for he gingerly asked: "Would you like to know more about leprosy? If you do, you would have to take a special course in Jakarta. I could help you get a leave of absence and a traveling authorization from the Governor of Ambon, who will be here tomorrow."

Somewhat more at ease now, I thanked him and said I would discuss it with my boss, and then went home.

In the afternoon, I visited Pak Latif at his residence. Surprised and somewhat alarmed, he listened to my story. When I had finished, he stated flatly that the fight against leprosy had nothing to do with Social

Service. It was clearly the domain of the Ministry of Health. He very much doubted that ISORI (the inspection arm of the Ministry of Social Services) on Ambon, let alone the Ministry itself in Jakarta, would give me permission to take that leprosy course.

Undaunted, I persisted in my request, and tried to persuade him that I had to know where I was at — I had to know how to prevent infection if I should meet lepers again. Whether he felt my resurgent fear, I did not know, but after Governor Latuhahary provided me with a travel authorization to Jakarta, Pak Latif also relented in his opposition to this plan.

Three days later I reached Menado, and in the early morning of the next day I landed at Jakarta. This time, nobody met me at the airport. With fear in my heart, but resolute nevertheless, I took a cab to the Ministry.

Quite unexpectedly, I had an opportunity to speak directly with our new Minister. He listened to me and then firmly declared that he would never grant my request — repeating Pak Latif's words that this work lay outside the scope of the Ministry. Then, in a more soothing voice, he told me that, anyway, there was no room for me in the dormitory of the mess hall as it was booked solid.

"But I can stay with friends in Jakarta," I countered. "He is a doctor, who happens to be the Secretary General at the Ministry of Health and also a member of the Cabinet."

Taken aback and misunderstanding my meaning, he said disappointedly: "So you want to be transferred to *Kesehatan* (Health)?"

I quickly put his mind at ease: "No, I want to stay in Social Services, but to do my job I must take this leprosy course. Our greatest challenge lies in helping those banished lepers, and I can't help them if I don't know how to."

Finally, though still uncertain, the Minister gave in.

"Three months to take the course, then I shall return to Ternate," I promised, and added: "*Sungguh mati*, I give you my word!"

Still unsure, he got up and shook my hand.

"See you in three months!" I said gratefully, and jubilantly left the Ministry. The die was cast.

The next day I met the Director and medical staff of the Leprosy Institute, participated in discussions, toured the wards and the laboratory, and met many of the patients. For the first time I got a good look at the incredible devastation that this illness can wreak on the human body, and I was pleased to learn that a new medicine, Promin, had arrived from the U.S. that promised to arrest or even cure this disease.

When I told the doctors of the fear I had felt when I met the lepers high up in the mountain, they nodded understandingly. They also had felt that paralyzing fear, especially the older ones, who remembered the time when there was no cure and all they had was the difficult-to-administer chaulmoogra oil[2]. At that time, it was the only known medicine.

"Luckily," they reminisced, "that is a thing of the past. You will be taught how to use the latest drugs."

Having enrolled in the course, I was exempted from having to do nursing duties. However, I felt that dealing with the patients in person would teach me things that the classroom could not, and I wanted to cram as much into those three months as was humanly possible. So I asked the supervising doctor to put me to work, preferably that very first day. And so it happened. The incumbent nursing staff readily accepted me and liberally shared their knowledge with me.

Among the patients were a few Dutch and Eurasians, who were seriously affected and badly disfigured. All were eager to try the new drug that promised them a better life. These pour souls had no idea how the cards were stacked against them on the outside. How could they earn their livelihood without having usable hands and feet? But in spite of their malformation, the patients were full of hope. They liked being nursed by me, and I learned much from them.

The course was difficult. I had to learn many new procedures that, when I had been trained in Belgium so long ago, either did not exist or could only be done by doctors. But I quickly learned, eager as I was to uncover the secrets of this horrible disease: its origin, how it was transmitted, and everything else that was even remotely connected to it. All my time was given to study and practice, and I learned how to treat, and deal with, leper patients and to win their confidence.

Some patients died during the new treatment. Why, we did not know, but we later learned that the doses had to be adjusted to the needs of each individual patient. We learned also that a special diet was the best means to assure the success of this new drug.

Some patients reacted quickly to the drug, improving visibly day by day. In spite of their rapid progress, however, it would take a long time before they could be pronounced clinically cured. Regular check-ups over an extended period would be a must.

I was also put to work in the outpatient clinics that had been established throughout the metropolis. Many people, including lepers, came for treatment every day, and I learned that leprosy could take

# IBU MALUKU

many different forms. Most of the lepers who arrived at the clinics had already passed through the Leprosy Institute, and had come for the usual follow-up treatment. It happened, however, that some cases required more than just that.

One day, I saw in front of one clinic a very beautiful woman, who was furtively looking around. I went up to her and started a conversation. Suddenly she gripped my hand, started to cry, and asked to be examined. I asked her to come in, but she wouldn't enter. So I invited her to meet me in the mess hall of the Institute. After bowing gratefully, she left.

She came in the afternoon and, after some casual talk, took off her beautiful *kebaya*. On her left arm, she had the by-now familiar white spots that were numb to the touch. There were no other telltale signs. She was in the early stages of leprosy and I gently told her that.

With dazed eyes she looked at me, and sobbed that no one in her family had ever had the disease. How and where could she have caught it? With desperation in her voice, she told me that she had already been at the Leprosy Institute and had seen the horrible destruction that this disease could cause.

How young and beautiful she was. I talked with her at length, and she promised to let herself be treated by Dr. Benjamin, the Director of the Leprosy Institute. However, to my knowledge, she never did go and I don't know what happened to her afterward. But I will never forget her eyes, so full of despair, fear and horror.

Another case involved the father of a large family, who came with his three young children. He'd had a good job, and had lived in the house of the company he worked for. When rumor had it that his children had contracted leprosy, he was fired. He sold all his belongings to pay for the trip to Jakarta, but he had already given up hope of ever finding another job. Who would employ him now?

The children were checked out. No trace of leprosy was found. They did, however, have a minor skin disease that required a short treatment.

Upon hearing the diagnosis, the eyes of the man and his wife, dulled by despair, became radiant. But then, just as suddenly, they showed unspeakable anger at the injustice they had suffered at the hands of the husband's employer. At that moment, there was murder in those eyes.

From this and other cases I learned how much misery could be caused by fear alone: it would often cause the patient to delay seeking medical help, or not to seek it at all, and it could cause relatives and friends to prematurely shun a suspected sufferer.

# IBU MALUKU

Giving each person with a skin disorder a thorough examination, as early as possible, seemed to be the answer. So I took an oath to train people back home in early detection procedures: to get into the habit, for instance, of checking each other during bath times. Later, this resolution did, indeed, become part of a practical program.

The day of the exam arrived — and I passed.

It is difficult to describe my happiness. It doubled when Dr. Benjamin, the Director, gave me enough Promin to completely cure four people in Ternate.

The Minister of Social Services was also pleased with the exam results, and greatly relieved that — in spite of strong pressures from the Minister of Health to join his department — I would keep my promise and stay with Social Services.

A few days later, I booked passage on the *Kalabali*, a KPM ship. I was overjoyed to be able to take with me all the necessary furnishings for the Ternate orphanage that was being built for 40 children. By personally supervising the loading, and pledging several cartons of cigarettes to the *bayos* (harbor workers) if nothing was lost, I was able to deliver all the furnishings to Ternate in good condition.

\*\*\*\*

Back home, discussions with Pak Latif led to leprosy research becoming an integral part of the *kampung* surveys.

Dr. Tan asked me to start in the Sorofo Leprosarium in Ternate, and select four of the 172 patients for the initial Promin treatment.

The selection process required, among other things, checking the patient's hemoglobin level. The blood had to be taken by scratching or puncturing the nasal septum, which was a very painful procedure. Nevertheless, everyone submitted to it.

The result was an unpleasant surprise. None of the 172 patients had a sufficiently high level to start the cure. Three men and a woman were close because they had received supplemental nourishment from outside the leprosarium, so I selected them, feeling that with liver shots, milk and eggs, their hemoglobin level could be quickly raised. Luckily, all four were educated and could easily understand the reason for delaying this remedial cure.

The nourishment of other patients was also augmented to qualify them for treatment with either Promin, Diasone, or DDS, the least-expensive of the drugs known at that time.

The joy of the selected four mounted, as each blood test showed that their hemoglobin level was indeed going up.

Then, the trouble started.

I had my weekly meeting with all of the patients, during which I gave them the latest information on the treatment, and also urged them to eat better and to work outside to strengthen their weakened bodies.

Somehow they had got it into their heads that Promin was a miracle drug, and that just one injection would cure them. So all of them now demanded to be given this one miraculous shot. The mood rapidly grew ugly, and the favored foursome had to be taken out of the room for their own safety.

I tried to reason with the rest of them, but they would not budge, demanding one shot for each and every patient — no exception! It sent a chill down my spine to see this threatening, hideous, pitiful mob moving about with clenched fists, yelling and cursing — devoid of any reason.

At the end of the third day, I was desperate and threatened to destroy all existing Promin ampules and withdraw from the work for good. Only then did reason finally return. The patients calmed down, and treatment was allowed to begin.

It was a real victory when, three years later, the first four patients could be declared clinically cured. Four people, whose lives had once been written off and who had withered in the leprosarium for so many years, were now cured. It was truly a miracle!

Accompanied by an official from Social Services, this foursome traveled to Jakarta. One man became a bookkeeper at the Leprosy Institute at Jakarta, where he would marry and have five healthy children. The woman and the two other men were trained for nursing, and then returned to Ternate. One man became head of the Leprosarium; the other, a traveling leprosy pamphleteer. The woman became a nurse. All received a good salary and could now look forward to a Government pension.

They had become a symbol for the community, which enabled me, eventually, to make all of the people in the Moluccas conscious of the dangers of leprosy. It required ongoing research and extensive counseling in word and deed to accomplish this. In spite of many disappointments, misunderstandings and, yes, even downright obstinacy, this area became a shining example of the fight against leprosy for the hundreds of islands in the "Ring of Emeralds" that make up the Indonesian Archipelago.

\* \* \* \*

I soon discovered that fighting the disease in Ternate's leprosarium was child's play compared to fighting it on the outside. The patients at the leprosarium had lived with their fellow-sufferers for some time and had come to accept their own condition in keeping with their faith: it was the Almighty's will, so one could not revolt against it. Acceptance of their lot was also aided by the knowledge that the hospital would care for them until they died.

Finding and treating the outcasts who were hiding on small islands or in remote inland places, well, that proved to be quite a task. For their fellow-villagers these pariahs were already dead, so bringing up the subject was often exceedingly difficult.

Then I found a way — previously discarded as impossible — that did work.

During a regular survey, I separated the patients with skin disorders from the others. Whenever I saw suspicious-looking patches, I told the patient that leprosy often started with such spots. Casually I would add that I thought it was quite normal to talk about the disease; that this supposedly incurable illness was just another skin problem, and that it *could* be cured; and that on behalf of the Government I would give the necessary drugs free of charge (which was important to them). I emphasized that I was not at all afraid to touch these patients, to give them a check-up and, if necessary, to treat them.

The response surprised me. The *Kepala Kampung* bent forward and whispered to me that in *his* village no one had this feared illness, but in the next village some people had disappeared. Supposedly they had moved to other islands, or had been sent to visit hitherto-unknown distant relatives. Well, *Ibu Sosial* (Mother Social) could draw her own conclusions from this, and find out for herself what had become of those people.

Finally, I had a lead, but I knew that it would require great diplomacy and tact to uncover the true facts. How and in what manner I succeeded would take too long to describe here. Suffice to say that I had to do a lot of detective work.

Soon, I came across villages where I was asked, spontaneously, to visit this or that island or remote bay, or to trek into the interior where — sometimes alone, often in small groups — the lepers lived in abject misery, waiting for a merciful death.

Thus I found a mother and six stricken children living in a shabby hut on a small atoll with the healthy father, who had stuck by them. They were in a weakened condition, living from whatever the sea would provide, plus a little sago that passing fishermen would sometimes leave for them on a nearby island. The husband fetched drinking water from a well on a large island, but only dared to go there at night, afraid that he might be spotted and prevented from coming again.

High up on the Gamelamo volcano I found a child, barely six years old: a small deformed boy with a ballooning stomach and a disfigured face, who wobbled on mutilated feet and spindly legs, covered with wounds. My assistants and I were able to creep up and surround the child, because his attention was fixed on opening a nut with a stone. As soon as the boy saw the men converging on him, he dropped everything and ran, as it happened, right into my outstretched arms. I will never forget the animalistic fear in the boy's eyes as he struggled to free himself and get away from those humans who had banished him from their communities.

His father, so I later learned, had died. To attract a new husband, his mother had kept the infant hidden, feeding him at night when everyone was asleep. But the new husband discovered them and threw her little son out, threatening bodily harm if he ever showed his disfigured face again. It was a miracle that he had survived alone in that jungle!

Resisting continuously with all his might, the child was taken to the leprosarium, where he calmed down amidst his fellow-sufferers. Slowly, very slowly, he would learn again to trust his fellow man. Eventually he was cured, but his scarred face and misshapen hands and feet of course remained. Twenty-five years after I had found him, I met him again, and he told me proudly that he was now married:

"*Ibu*," he said, "I have a healthy son, Kadir, who is happy to have a family and a home!" And his eyes sparkled as he recounted his story to whomever would listen.

Another case involved the only child of a respected couple, little Soradiah, who had probably been infected by an old aunt. The child had lived with her desperate parents in exile for several years, when I found them quite by accident.

On a remote cape, I had seen a man walking, who suddenly disappeared as the *Bintang Laut* came closer. I dropped anchor, tracked him down, and listened to his sad story. I then persuaded the parents to return with me and allow me to treat their daughter. The child, however, was mad with fear. She bit, hit, and kicked, but we managed to get her on board. Eventually, she was cured. She married in the leprosarium and gave birth to a son, who became a lawyer.

Little Korsiah was found sitting on top of a garbage dump, where she was scraping pus off her afflicted legs with a sea shell. She lived in a remote place with her aged grandmother, who had infected her. She was also taken to the leprosarium and would eventually be cured. I could not persuade the grandmother to come also, and when I looked for her during my next trip, I heard that she was dead. She had been burned alive in her hut that had been set ablaze. Was it an accident? Arson? Suicide?

These are just some of the many cases that I encountered during my surveys in the jungles and on the smaller islands. During the six years that I was privileged to do this work, I found more than a thousand lepers. Of course, their families and close associates also had to be checked out. In total, some 6,000 people were examined.

When I left, I had the satisfaction of knowing that the people of the Moluccas had indeed become leprosy-conscious, and had accepted this disease as a normal illness. As a result, the community allowed a leper's healthy children to go to school, as well as cured patients to live in their midst, where they could earn a living and, once more, be happy.

The horrible, paralyzing fear of this illness had been conquered!

❦

**Endnotes**

[1] In India, as far back as 1400 B.C., leprosy was referred to as "kushtha" in the sacred Vedic scriptures. (source: www.webspawner.com)

[2] This fatty oil, extracted from the nuts of the Kalaw tree and known officially as Gynocardia oil in Britain and as Oleum Chaulmoograe in the U.S.A., may have provided some relief, but tended to nauseate most people. (source: www.botanical.com)

IBU MALUKU

# CHAPTER 45

### Sukarno's First Visit
*Ternate, 1956*

Shortly after having returned from the leprosy course, I learned that President Sukarno would pay us his first visit.

Ternate was buzzing with excitement. Various groups in the community came together with the President's advance men to organize the reception and make sure that nothing would go wrong. But there was a huge problem. These groups didn't trust one another.

The people of the Moluccas have a reputation for being expert "poison brewers". Without doubt, the President's high-level representatives in Ternate knew this. So it was imperative that the meals be prepared by trustworthy people.

After endless deliberations, the committee decided that, since the President's visit was of a social nature, the Ministry of Social Affairs should have the responsibility for lodging, hosting and feeding the President and his entourage. Logical or not, that is the way it turned out, and much of the responsibility landed in my lap!

Luckily, there were still a few nuns in Ternate. I knew them well and had no difficulty in persuading them to accept responsibility for the meals. That solved one big problem.

We also tracked down and hired people who had before the war been employed by company presidents or other upper-class Europeans. Those former servants would be housed in the *Kedaton* — the Sultan's Palace — and be responsible for transporting, storing and serving the meals. We carefully checked out their manners and gave them strict instructions on how to proceed inside the palace. Security inside and outside was the responsibility of the military.

The schools soon competed with one another in learning songs of welcome, while the Socials Affairs staff went from house to house to borrow chinaware, bed sheets and furnishings to make the *Kedaton* fit for the important guests.

The Islamic population — the main supporters of the Sultan when he resided here — grappled with two serious problems: the large chandelier in the *Kedaton* would not light up; worse still, the snake that had inhabited the *Kedaton*'s attic since time immemorial, had disappeared. This signaled doom for anyone who entered, and double doom for anyone who stayed overnight, because the snake was the *Kedaton*'s guard — its protecting spirit.

The faithful fasted and prayed in their mosque and, for good measure, the *Kedaton* was once again cleaned inside and outside, and special flowers and other offerings were placed at strategic places within.

Then, yet another catastrophe occurred. Some heavy beams in the *Kedaton*'s roof structure needed to be replaced. The old ones had already been removed, but, try as they would, the Chinese carpenters could not get the new beams into their assigned places. So they burned incense, and waited.

Then, suddenly, the snake reappeared. It slithered over the new beams, and — lo! — the beams miraculously dropped into place. So I was told.

Now, everyone focused on the remaining problem: the chandelier. The electricians checked and rechecked the circuitry, and finally discovered a wiring defect. It was quickly repaired and, the evening before the President's arrival, the chandelier lit up in all its glory.

All of Ternate breathed a sigh of relief. We were ready to receive the President.

The next day, everyone was up bright and early, doing whatever small chores still remained to be done. The military men put on important faces and swaggered back and forth. The civil authorities were running themselves ragged doing last-minute checks and then nervously gathered at the quay when the President's ship came into view.

The disembarkment went smoothly and without incident. Standing in a festive army jeep, flashing his winning smile, President Sukarno then made his triumphant entry into the city.

The route to the *Kedaton* was lined with cheering children — their parents standing protectively nearby — who waved their flags and flowers. Other schoolchildren had gathered in the *Kedaton*'s large front courtyard and, at the right moment, started to sing their well-practiced song of welcome.

At the bottom of the stairs leading into the *Kedaton*, stood, in order of rank, the District Heads, Kampung Chiefs, the Mosque's staff, and the Sultan's guard, all dressed resplendently in their traditional *adat* attire. But everyone looked rather solemn and I wondered what was going through their minds at that moment. Did they miss their own Sultan, Iskander Mohamed Shah, who had been "promoted away" to serve as the President's advisor in Jakarta?

# IBU MALUKU

The President stepped out of the jeep, followed by the Sultan of Tidore, Zainal Abidin Shah, who, as Resident, was now the official host. When, with a sweep of the arm, he invited the President to ascend the stairs with him, a discontented murmur arose among those present.

The Sultan stopped in his tracks, hesitated, then took one step back and, deeply embarrassed, beseeched the President to go up the stairs by himself. He would meet him upstairs in the great hall. Then, he dashed off toward the Palace's side entrance, leaving the President standing by himself.

The crowd uttered a sigh of relief. The President looked momentarily surprised, but then, smiling warmly and shaking his head slightly in disbelief, he climbed the grand staircase. However, he didn't immediately enter the Palace's main hall as expected — was it a slight rap on the knuckles of his host? — but strode to the balustrade of the spacious front gallery to wave to the crowd, while the children's choir once again belted out their welcome. Only after his own entourage had joined him did the President proceed into the main hall where the Sultan could finally bid him a warm welcome.

A flock of journalists and photographers followed the President inside. They were openly critical of the Sultan's behavior — some even called it offensive. Since few of them understood what had happened, I volunteered to tell them about the curse.

"Some 300 years ago," I told them, "the Sultan of Ternate had brokered a marriage between one of his sons and a *Boki* (Princess) of Tidore. The two Sultans agreed on the dowry, and Ternate prepared to give the young bride and her entourage a royal welcome.

"On the wedding night, when the bridegroom removed the veil of his young and beautiful bride, he discovered, to his dismay, that the House of Tidore had replaced her with a much older and more-homely woman of lower rank.

"Pandemonium broke out! The Sultan of Ternate angrily sent back the substitute bride, had her mother thrown out of a Palace window, and put a curse on the House of Tidore: none of them were ever to enter the *Kedaton* by the front door again; if anyone did, the members of the House of Tidore would die!

"It is perhaps hard for you to believe," I continued, "that the fear for a 300-year-old curse would still be so strong. But you have seen what happened. The Sultan obviously didn't dare enter through the front entrance. Whether he explained his puzzling behavior to the President, I don't know."

The journalists chuckled, and wondered aloud whether or not they should print the story. Shaking their heads in disbelief, they then wandered off.

The President's visit lasted three days and passed without further incident, and everyone breathed easier when his ship left Ternate harbor and disappeared into the distance.

As a postscript to the 300-year old curse: In 1956, Zainal Abidin Shah, Sultan of Tidore, became the first Governor of the new Province of Greater Irian. This Province included the territory of Ternate, the former Sultanate of Jailolo on Halmahera, and the Sultanate of Tidore — including the contested territories on New Guinea that were still in the hands of the Netherlands.

In establishing the new Province, the Indonesian Government clearly expressed its contention that the Netherlands should cede the last part of its former colony. The transfer finally did take place in May of 1963, but the Sultan was never to be the Governor of that region. Just before the transfer, he died under very strange circumstances.

It is believed that, after the Ternate *Kedaton* was transformed into a museum, he thought it safe to enter the former palace through the front door. After all, the status of the *Kedaton* had changed and the curse would no longer apply — or so he thought. It is a fact, however, that not only his spouse, but also every one of his sons disappeared from the area in an inexplicable manner.

To all outward appearances, the curse had indeed come true!

\*\*\*\*

After the strain of the Presidential visit, life resumed its normal course. As before, I traveled a lot, but my *tournées* were often cut short by orders to appear in person on Ambon and in Makassar, Jakarta or Solo.

In Solo, a new ministry had been set up for the development of the primitive tribes living in the jungles of Halmahera, Ceram, and some areas of Sumatra.

The work had been started in response to my urgent reports about the original inhabitants of Northeastern Halmahera, who were grouped under the name of *Orang Tugutil* — the people of Tugutil.

More than 300 years earlier, these people lived in Tobelo and the surrounding area. Their tribal land lay around a large lake, which they called Talagalina. They grew nutmeg, cloves and other spices on the largest plain of this huge island. For centuries they had traded, first with the Chinese, then with the Arabs, and finally with the Portuguese and Spanish. This trade was the source of prosperity for them, and for the Sultans, who collected taxes paid in gold, pearls, Chinese porcelain, manual labor, and slaves.

Eventually, Dutch traders found their way to the Moluccas. Their company, the VOC (East Indies Company) became firmly entrenched on Ambon and Banda, where they cultivated nutmeg for the European market. To force out the competition, they destroyed the Halmahera plantations — with the blessing of the Sultans, who had grown tired of the Spanish and Portuguese. The Tugutils who resisted were either killed or forced off their land. Many escaped, either to the rugged interior, or to other islands.

It is with those who had settled in the interior that the new Ministry at Solo, Java, now concerned itself. They wanted to bring these tribes — spread over a wide area of north-eastern Halmahera — into the 20th century by enticing them to leave the jungles and settle in villages along the coast.

Under my supervision, five new villages were built for that purpose — of which two were immediately inhabited by the Tugutils on a trial basis.

Although interesting, this project consumed much of my time. Finding and coaxing these people-shy jungle inhabitants to leave their accustomed habitat required an enormous amount of energy and patience, and my other work suffered as a result.

\*\*\*\*

Improvements were made to the leprosarium, and the general examination program became part of my regular work. For lepers who could not be accommodated in the hospital because of lack of space, we had to build a few out-patient villages that would be run and supervised by Social Affairs.

For their construction, we needed the help of a distant village. I left them the plans and returned a few weeks later with my boat crew to see how they were progressing. Alas, nothing had been done. I told the *Kepala Kampung* that I would be back in one month and, if nothing had happened by then, the Army would have to get involved.

On my way back, I stopped for a rest at one of the villages about which the Sultan had warned me never to accept anything — no drinks, no food — because its inhabitants were expert poison brewers who used visitors as guinea pigs for their newest concoctions. They would not specifically target me because I was a *Belanda*, the Sultan told me, but because I was a *outsider* — not one of their village.

I had earlier passed the warnings on to my crew members, asking them to be extra alert. But a new helmsman, temporarily filling in for Nen, was so thirsty that he asked for a young coconut in spite of the warning.

The *Kepala kampung* fetched a few coconuts, sliced off the top of one, and with the tip of a knife made a hole in the top. It being the first one to be opened, it would normally have been offered to me. But the thirsty helmsman made a grab for it and started to drink right away.

The *Kepala Kampung* proceeded to open the second one, presumably to offer it to me, and as I watched him cut the hole, I noticed that the coconut meat touched by the knife started to change color.

With my fist, I knocked the coconut out of the hands of the helmsman and said: "Don't drink any more. There is poison in there."

Sure enough, the helmsman soon fell ill and, on the way back to Ternate, he died. So the warnings the Sultan had given me really were true. From then on, I was doubly careful about where to accept something to drink or eat.

\* \* \* \*

Apart from the out-patient villages for the lepers, Social Affairs built a large and well-furnished orphanage for the orphans from the surrounding islands, and started a hospital for the infirm elderly. Land was also cleared for the construction of a reception and treatment center for handicapped children. This land, full of nutmeg trees, was next to my residence. It had been given to me by the KPM, but I had no plans to use it for myself.

All these activities kept me so busy that there was no time for relaxation. Perhaps it was just as well, for it prevented me from becoming involved with the city dwellers, who occupied themselves with politics and mutual squabbles.

There were only a few Dutch citizens left in Ternate: the odd trading house manager, many Indo-Europeans who owned nutmeg plantations that sustained them; seven Dutch nuns with their Mother Superior; and several *Paters* from Tilburg (the Netherlands) — the so-called MSC's[1] — who had replaced the Franciscan friars.

The nuns and their Mother Superior, the female teachers, and the head of the school all had opted for Indonesian citizenship. So had one of the priests, the head of the Catholic Mission and I, myself.

For me there was no other choice. I had to earn my bread in Indonesia and felt I should continue with this important work I had been given to do. So I applied with the others.

The Sultan of Tidore, the Resident at the time, gave us a small yellow card with his seal and signature as proof of application, but none of us would ever receive confirmation that we had, indeed, become citizens of Indonesia. Fearing that something like that could happen in this young

## IBU MALUKU

State, we kept our Dutch passports!

At the advice of a trusted friend, a KPM Captain, I applied to have my passport extended. The Captain took it with him to Makassar, intending to speak personally to the Dutch Consul, whom he knew well.

At the Consulate, however, the Captain learned that the Consul was away on furlough. Before he realized what was happening, the Chargé d'Affaires had destroyed my passport, stating that, since I had applied for Indonesian citizenship, I had lost my Dutch one.

The destruction of my passport — which, to this day, I think of as a great injustice — made me, in effect, a stateless person, and would cause all sorts of problems later on.

In Ternate, many changes were happening in the political arena. Little by little, influential people — municipal authorities, teachers, and federal civil servants — were "promoted" elsewhere and replaced by hard-line Javanese who, together with the Army, shamelessly exploited the indigenous population.

Two instances come to mind.

There were no *sawahs* in the Moluccas, so rice had to be imported from Java. Since high demand had made rice too expensive for the local people, it was ruled that every family — regardless of size — could buy 10 kilograms per month through Government outlets at a controlled price. But, by the time the people arrived at Tidore from the surrounding islands to make their purchase, the civil servants had sold all the rice on the black market for a much higher price — with the difference going into their own pockets.

For some people, a return trip by boat took ten days — during which time they could not fish, harvest sago or attend to their gardens. So it was a double calamity for them.

Another product that channeled profits into the wrong pockets involved salt, which was also sold in stores at exorbitant prices. To secure the market, anyone who tried to make salt from seawater was thrown in jail.

Apart from exploiting the locals, these Javanese hard-liners also incited them to prepare for war with the Netherlands, which was still hanging on to New Guinea, the last remnant of the former Dutch East Indies. They introduced the abusive term *"Belanda Busuk"* (Rotten Dutch), precipitated misunderstandings and enacted provocative regulations, which eventually undermined the trust and goodwill that were so important in my work.

But, thank God, their hate campaign only affected the urban population. The native people in the outlying villages remained devoted and co-operated with me, no matter how much abuse was heaped on my head.

In preparation for the eventual unification of New Guinea with the Republic of Indonesia, a complete provincial government would be set up in Tidore. Construction crews were brought in that at a feverish pace built new schools, a modern hospital, a town hall, a palace for the Governor, roads, bridges and military barracks.

All this activity brought large-scale corruption and raised the price of land. Many civil servants bought land from the local population at rock-bottom prices, then turned around to sell it at astronomical profits to the Indonesian Government.

Tidore soon became deluged with ministers and delegations from Java. These visitors had to be picked up from the airport of Menado (North Celebes). My own boat, the *Bintang Laut* had to be used initially to ferry them between Menado and Tidore.

Soon, however, my boat was judged as not comfortable enough for these very important people. So the authorities decided that I should get a *real* boat, and — to my surprise — they asked *me* for advice about what to get.

As it happened, during my last visit to Jakarta I had met the owner of a shipyard on Sumatra, who took me across the straights to see a splendid yacht, powered by a Rolls Royce inboard motor. It had been built as part of a covert plan to free a former KPM agent, Mr. Jungsläger, who was at the time a political prisoner in Indonesia. However, by the time the yacht was finished, the prisoner had died.

I mentioned to the Ministry of Social Affairs that the yacht was probably for sale, and they quickly decided that this boat was the right vessel for criss-crossing the new province *and* enhancing their public image.

I was asked to go to Jakarta to negotiate its purchase. That done, I hired a crew, sailed the beautiful boat to Ternate, and handed it over to the Government. But I would never use it myself.

The boat affair, though not of great importance in itself, led to a chance meeting in Jakarta with Dr. Leblanc, a leprosy expert, who had served in one of the French colonies in Africa. He told me about the work that was being done at the Leprosy Institute of Lyon, and urged me to apply for a one-year furlough to take a course there and learn the latest in leprosy immunization.

I did take his advice and, sometime during 1957, applied via the Ministry of Health to the Ministry of Social Affairs. Attached to the application was a petition, signed by Dr. Leblanc, Professor Benjamin of the Jakarta Leprosy Institute, the Governor, the Resident, various medical authorities, and more than 1,000 leprosy patients and former patients.

The Ministry approved my application on the condition that I would first pay all expenses out of my own pocket. Upon my return, the expenses would then be refunded jointly by the Ministries of Health and Social Affairs. The leave of absence was to start on December 31, 1957.

\*\*\*\*

I soon learned that, during my absence in Jakarta, the war propaganda machine in Ternate had continued at an ever increasing pitch. A heavy-duty radio transmitter had been installed, which beamed its inflammatory messages non-stop to a large part of Northern New Guinea. The tension mounted with each passing day and, eventually, precipitated an incident on a distant island, west of Halmahera.

When the greater part of the Dutch East Indies had been transferred to the young Republic, this island, Gag, which was part of the Gébé Group, had remained within the territorial waters of the Netherlands, with little thought for the consequences.

For centuries, Gag had been the breadbasket for Gébé Island, whose inhabitants had grown coconuts, cassava, corn, *batatas* (sweet potatoes) and various vegetables there, because their own soil contained too much nickel to grow anything. So now the people of Gébé were completely cut off from their food source.

The matter was discussed with the Dutch Government, which solemnly pledged to allow the islanders access to Gag four times a year to plant and harvest and make their copra. However, the copra would have to be sold to traders on New Guinea.

Nobody objected to that. The islanders knew full well they would be paid in *rijksdaalders* (silver coins) that could be exchanged for a large number of Indonesian *rupiahs*. Well and good.

From time to time, a Dutch patrol boat would stop at Gag to ensure that no one would be on the island during the off-season and, for a while, all went well. But one day the patrol boat arrived during harvest time. In violation of the agreement, the armed crew arrested all fifty-two men and took them to the nearest Government post on Northern New Guinea. But two young boys escaped the dragnet. Being experienced sailors in spite of their young age, they sailed home and gave their families the sad news.

Each of the captured islanders eventually received a prison sentence of several years. The Indonesian media learned about this and made the most of it. Particularly on Java, the propaganda machine urged military action.

A few months later, I unexpectedly received orders to take a shipload of food, medicine and clothes to the fifty-two families on Gébé, and report on the general situation there.

The *Bintang Laut*, festively adorned, would also take on board the Assistant Resident of Tidore and a Javanese Agronomist whose job it was to find out if produce could be cultivated on Gébé in some way not previously considered.

To complicate matters, I was also asked to take a Dutch nun, Sister Dionysia, back to Tobelo. She had been in Ternate for medical treatment and was now cured. The fact that taking her home meant a huge detour that would keep us many more days at sea, did not seem to matter — orders were orders.

Three days later, we arrived at Gébé, where the population had gathered on the beach. Using a megaphone, I asked them to send boats and people to help unload the cargo. Nobody moved. After all, why should they listen to a *Belanda Busuk* — a rotten Dutch person.

They shouted back that they wanted to hear from the Assistant Resident, Salim Fabanje, who was standing beside me. But Salim refused to get involved, saying that the boat and its cargo belonged to Social Affairs. He had nothing to do with it. The Agronomist did not volunteer his services either and remained hidden inside the cabin.

Then Sister Dionysia decided to make an untimely appearance. As she emerged from the cabin and strode to the railing, the crowd began to yell and shake their fists.

I gave them some time to vent their feelings, and then, with as much of a commanding voice as I could muster, I yelled that the Indonesian Government had sent me with food, clothes and medicine to help them, and that I would stay one hour, and not one minute longer. If the cargo had not been unloaded by that time, I would leave and never come back. This was their last chance!

Stupefied, they let me finish. For a moment there was an anxious silence, but then it became clear that my threat had had its desired effect. Suddenly there were candidates galore. They came with their *praus* alongside and quickly went to work, anxious to get the cargo ashore within the given time limit.

When everything had been unloaded, I decided to have someone row me to shore. Sister Dionysia, afraid to stay on board alone with men, begged me to take her with me. Rather than risk a fate worse than death, she preferred martyrdom at my side, convinced as she was that we would be murdered. I quickly put her mind at ease, saying I knew the people too well to have any fear for that.

As I had expected, everything went smoothly, and in co-operation with the District Head and Village Chiefs — the only men on the island — I did my usual survey routine. Since every step required careful consideration, I divided the workload. Sister Dionysia, who had suddenly been accepted, looked after the distribution of food; the distribution of clothes — always a precarious task — was my job, as was the medical check-up and the registration.

It took three tiring days to get everything done, and then all the island's women and children accompanied us as we returned to the boat.

"Most women do not really mind the absence of their husbands," someone whispered to me. "In prison they are put to work, for which they get paid *real* money, which we can save for dowries. Also, they get all the *obat* (medicine) they need, so they will come back in good health. And in the meantime, we can do what we want. *Ibu* will understand what that means."

"And what about the food question," I asked, barely able to suppress a smile.

"Oh! We have resolved that pretty well now. The first four months were really hard, but we have found some fertile soil here and there, where we have grown *batatas*. *Ibu* will see for herself when she arrives on board."

I did. Much to my surprise, I found not one, but six gunnysacks full of freshly-harvested *batatas* on board, destined for the Governor of Tidore.

I understood the message right away. In a nice way, they were telling the Governor that the Government certainly had waited an awfully long time before coming to their rescue. Just the same, they had survived on what the sea could provide, until their *batatas* were ready to be harvested.

For Sister Dionysia, there was a gunnysack full of precious sea shells as thanks for her assistance and as a token of the population's respect. Perhaps it was also intended as an apology for their initial mistrust. As I had explained to her, they had never seen a nun before. Sister Dionysia was elated, as much with the shells as with the fact that she would soon be home.

Three days later, we arrived at Tobelo, much to the relief of her sisters in the religious community, who had worried about their "lost" sister — she had been expected back much earlier. We said goodbye to

Sister Dionysia and her fellow nuns, and left.

A few days later we were back in Ternate, and, before the day was done, the *batatas* had been deposited on the doorsteps of the Governor's palace.

The Gébé message had been delivered!

### Endnotes
[1] MSC: *Missionarii Sacratissimi Cordis* — Missionaries of the Sacred Heart

IBU MALUKU

## CHAPTER 46

### Sukarno's Second Visit
*Buli, Halmahera, October 1957*

With the passage of time, the confrontation[1] between Indonesia and the Netherlands became more heated, which made my life increasingly difficult.

One outcome of this dissension was a series of covert operations which illustrate that history does, indeed, repeat itself. Prior to invading the East Indies, the Japanese recruited Indonesians to infiltrate the country and sow unrest; now Indonesia was sending its own agents into Netherlands New Guinea for the same purpose.

Presumably on orders from Java, these agents had been recruited from small islands close to New Guinea and promised a large sum of money and a life-long pension in return for their efforts. Apart from sowing unrest among the natives, they were also supposed to report on military installations and troop movements.

Soon after having landed, however, these untrained agents were quickly picked up and thrown into jail. The Dutch kept them locked up for a while and then returned them to the Indonesian authorities, who brought them to the provincial capital, Tidore.

The Government's Office there quickly passed them on to Social Affairs, and that is how I became involved. We had to house and feed these would-be agents until they could be returned home to the islands from where they had come.

Each group of agents arrived on our doorstep with a crowd of shouting sympathizers, who secretly hoped to be repaid for their troubles with a share of the bounty — cigarettes, tobacco, rice, or money — that their heroic compatriots would surely receive as a reward for their "exceptional bravery".

Loudly supported by this choir of sympathizers, those hapless agents first touted their heroic deeds outside our offices, and then brazenly forced their way inside to noisily demand what had been promised at the time of their recruitment. But their self-confidence quickly evaporated when I calmly explained that Social Affairs could do little except offer them primitive accommodation and food, until they could be repatriated to their own islands.

When it dawned on them that they had been duped, they aimed their anger first at the Government, then at the Governor, and finally at me — who had refused to hand over the promised bonuses. They felt they had been robbed, of course, and this frequently made for an ugly and very tense situation.

Often, however, such a situation would just as suddenly change into a comical farce. Abandoning their self-professed patriotism, the infiltrators would then, *en bloc,* proclaim their love for the Dutch who had treated them so well in prison. There had always been an abundance of cigarettes and tobacco; they had eaten three solid meals of rice and fish; and they had always received good medical care. They would not have minded staying there longer, really. No, in contrast to what they had been told, it was much better across the border. Then, with arms raised in unison they swore that, upon arriving home, they would "get even" with those miserable agitators who had swindled them!

\*\*\*\*

Radio Station Tidore continued to hurl the most absurd threats at Netherlands New Guinea. As before, the agitators were agents who had come from other parts of Indonesia.

By contrast, the indigenous population continued to hope that the Netherlands would hang on to *Tanah Papua,* as they called New Guinea. After all, many had family members there who worked on plantations and were paid in silver *ringgits*. The silver, of course, kept its value, while the *rupiah* continued its downward spiral. Under cover of darkness, there was frequent contact with those distant relatives. Many profited from the bartering that took place and, therefore, wanted to maintain the status quo.

For me, however, the continuous agitation caused nothing but problems.

During my *tournées* I depended heavily on the goodwill of the military, particularly with respect to obtaining fuel. I had to avoid confrontations at all cost, even though it became increasingly difficult to remain calm and ignore the sneering *Belanda Busuk* remarks. These remarks seriously influenced the members of my crew and the local population, and made my surveys sometimes very disagreeable.

I started to ache for the planned leave of absence that would allow me to study in France. Approval finally arrived while I was on the Bebseli Coast overseeing the building of more homes for the Tugutils. The leave of absence would not start until the end of the year, which gave me just enough time to train someone to manage these villages.

## IBU MALUKU

I was lucky to find a native of Ternate, and succeeded in having his appointment approved. That in itself was a victory; I would have been most unhappy if Social Affairs had forced me to appoint a Javanese. He would not have been close enough to the Tugutils to understand them; in addition, he would have had great difficulty in adjusting to a very different life style.

After having finished the training of the new manager, I returned to Tidore, where I was introduced to my new boss, Mr. Darmono, a Javanese who would make the remaining months before my planned leave of absence extremely unpleasant. He hated the Dutch in general, and me in particular, and had a knack for undermining my authority.

He encouraged the staff to ignore my orders, or made them believe that the orders had really come from him. The *esprit de corps* that had always been so good before, now soured so quickly that it frightened me. Little did I know that my salvation would be closer at hand than I had anticipated.

\* \* \* \*

On October 19, 1957, it was announced that President Sukarno would pay us a second visit, arriving on board a warship that the Dutch had given Sukarno. On board were the representatives of seven Communist countries.

His original destination had been Gébé Island. Sukarno had wanted his Communist friends to learn first-hand from the island's women how the Dutch were mistreating their imprisoned husbands on New Guinea. He obviously wanted to persuade these friends that *Tanah Papua* had to be liberated from the Dutch yoke as quickly as possible and at any cost, and hoped to receive their support.

However, Sukarno must have had second thoughts about the islanders' allegiance. The inhabitants of Gébé belonged to a strict Islamic sect that had severely criticized the President for having married a divorced woman. Did he fear a demonstration that might damage his public image and, thus, popularity with his Communist friends? In any case, giving a small change in the weather as the reason, Sukarno decided to cancel his trip to Gébé.

Instead, his warship would take him to northeastern Halmahera, to the biggest and most important city of Buli, once the bulwark of the Dutch Protestant Mission. This itinerary contrasted sharply with the original one, which specified that only Islamic villages were to be visited.

I happened to be in that general area, not too far from Buli, helping the victims of a flu epidemic, when a dispatcher from Tidore arrived aboard the fastest available motorboat — with orders to take me immediately to Buli.

Reluctantly, I left my patients. On board, I learned that my job was to persuade the mostly Christian inhabitants of Buli to rebuild the decrepit jetty so that the *Gajahmada* — the new name of the warship — could moor there. If that was not possible, the jetty should at least be fixed up to allow passengers to go ashore from a smaller vessel. The inhabitants of Buli, so I learned, had refused to undertake this work and had scrapped with a dozen Javanese soldiers who had been sent there to oversee the job.

Had Sukarno known the whole story, he would undoubtedly have changed his plans yet again. As it was, he must at least have known something, for he had his ship sail up and down the Halmahera Sea so as to give the people of Buli more time to fix the jetty.

Upon arrival, I talked at length with the Bulinese who knew me well, and was able to persuade them to undertake the task, thus avoiding a nasty confrontation with the military. Within 24 hours they had built a fairly sturdy wharf that was long enough to hold a large motorboat, but certainly no warship.

I also organized a welcoming reception for the 200 guests who were on board the *Gajahmada*. This was not easy. This erstwhile prosperous village had fallen upon hard times, and it was difficult to scrape together enough dishes, cutlery and cookery for the occasion.

Hurriedly, we assembled a group of Papua girls to sing a welcoming song in *Behasa Indonesia* — the new official language that none of them had as yet mastered. A few Islamic women set about to make a garland that, in accordance with the new mores, would be placed around the neck of the President. The solid rattan ring that would serve as frame turned out rather large — too large, I thought — but, not wanting to interfere, I said nothing. I did, however, make a floral contribution of my own by gathering a few exquisite orchids for the traditional bouquet that would have to be presented in addition to the garland.

The District Heads from the surrounding area gathered to form a welcoming committee and decided that I, being the most senior civil servant present, should personally receive the President and his guests. The three-year old son of one District Head, who was to be seated on my arm, would offer Sukarno the bouquet of orchids.

All available *praus* were cleaned and festively decked out to take the visitors to shore, while the onlookers periodically scanned the horizon. Excitement mounted when someone thought he had seen a dot in the distance, but it turned out to be a false alarm.

The sun was high in the sky when the public call was finally heard:

# IBU MALUKU

"*Kapal perang ada!* The warship is here!" — and everyone scurried to take his place or make last-minute adjustments.

The choir hastily rehearsed the welcoming song once again; and the toddler on my arm was rushed one more time to the toilet while I brushed off the ants that had crawled out of the orchids onto my moist arms.

Shouts announced the arrival of guests in a motorboat. I fervently prayed that the jetty would be strong enough to hold everyone. Luckily the sea was calm and, although the jetty swung ominously to and fro, all 200 guests came safely ashore.

At some distance from the landing place stood the welcoming committee, with me and the infant in the front.

Preceded by President Sukarno, the delegates walked toward us. I was pleased to find among them the two Governors from Ambon: The Resident (civil governor), a regal Sumatran; and Major Pieters (military governor), an Ambonese born on Tobelo, whom, when he was a child, I had often chased out of my mango trees.

Haltingly I stepped forward, encouraging the three-year old to say "*Selamat datang* — Welcome", and helping him to extend his tiny arm with the bouquet of orchids.

The President, who had been beaming at the people to his left and right, presently caught sight of me. He recognized me and I saw a cloud pass over his face. For a moment, anger flashed in those eyes and I quickly realized why: the first person to welcome him on this trip to win support for his anti-Dutch campaign was ... a Dutch woman. What impression would this make on his Communist friends? This was a major loss of face for him — and he made me feel it right down to my bones.

A split-second later, however, he had regained self-control. Beaming royally for the cameras, he accepted the flowers without greeting me and then took the child in his arms. For him I did not exist.

The Islamic women stepped forward with the garland. He took it from them and placed it around his neck himself — and, in a flash, I pictured Napoleon, placing the Emperor's crown on his own head.

As I had feared, the rather large garland quickly slipped off one shoulder. When the President made another sudden movement, it slipped off the other shoulder too and slid down to his plump hips, from where it spiraled around his legs, hula-hoop fashion, to the ground.

Nonchalantly he stepped out of that colorful obstacle and then stood still to listen to the Papua girls singing — alas, out of tune. His entourage stood erect and listened politely. The entire population looked on breathlessly. The journalists, jockeying for the most advantageous position, flashed their cameras and scribbled furiously in their notebooks.

I had, somehow, become separated from the welcoming committee and soon found myself at the rear of the assembly that was moving slowly toward the rickety school building, where the District Head would officially welcome the visitors, using the pulpit that had been borrowed from the church. Then, there would be *pidatus* (speeches) from the President and other important guests. At least ... that was the plan.

People were still milling about looking for a seat, when suddenly, there was Sukarno standing in the pulpit. As the outmaneuvered District Head looked on with a perplexed face, Sukarno greeted the industrious people of Buli and praised them for their affection, devotion and obvious refinement — as clearly demonstrated by the many floral decorations, and of course, the newly constructed jetty. He also praised them for the large school complex in which he found himself, from the existence of which he could only conclude that they were also well educated.

Since the school had been built and run by the Dutch Protestant Mission, he continued, he assumed that they could sing Dutch songs. He confided that, as a youngster, it was through these songs that he had begun to learn Dutch. He then asked the audience to join him in singing *"Piet Heyn"* — the rousing ode to the Dutch naval hero who had captured the Spanish silver fleet.

Sukarno sang in Dutch; the people knew only the Malay translation.

Then followed *"Zie de maan schijnt door de bomen"* (see the moon shining through the trees), a song for children, normally reserved for St. Nicholas Day in early December. The President sang again in Dutch, and the aroused audience — who had never expected such a display of camaraderie — followed again in Malay.

At the end, a brief silence ensued. The Presidential face then took on a cunning expression. His eyes contracted — a familiar sign to those who knew him that an unpleasant surprise was coming. In a flat voice he addressed the crowd, first praising them for their good voices, then, in a cold tone, he asked them to join him in singing *"Indonesia Raya"* — the national anthem of the young Republic.

Silence followed. None of the local inhabitants knew this song.

Unconcerned, the President started the first stanza. Only a few among the important visitors joined in. In the middle of the second stanza, the President stopped and, with glittering eyes, thundered that he would teach them how their national anthem should be sung!

Two hours later he was finally satisfied that everyone knew the melody and the words. Throughout the music lesson, the ignored and utterly bored guests managed to stand respectfully at attention, while unobtrusively sipping the lukewarm drinks that had been quietly pressed into their hands.

After the singing, there were no more speeches. No one was permitted to step into the pulpit; or more likely, no one dared. Everyone uttered a sigh of relief; the show had finally come to an end, and the crowd could disperse.

Some of the out-of-towners went to see the village, but there was really not much to see. The President and his guests left for the District Head's residence, where the wives of the *gurus* — also called *nyoras* here — had prepared a festive meal.

The principal ingredient, rice, had been taken from my stock on board of the "Bintang Laut". Parting with it had been difficult for me. The rice had been intended for the victims of the 'flu epidemic, whose need, I knew only too well, was infinitely more urgent than the need of those well-fed visitors.

Everyone sat down at tables that were covered with multi-colored table cloths. The dinnerware was a mish-mash of stone and chipped porcelain plates and dented enamel dishes. The cutlery was a motley collection of hastily-scoured copper forks and spoons, as well as some brand-new, shiny knives supplied by the Chinese shops.

Not having been at the meal myself, I don't know whether the exotic dishes were a success or not. I do know, however, that the attention of the guests was not so much on the food as it was on the President himself, who well knew how to keep his guests occupied and entertained.

The President ate sparingly: a little rice, some half-raw vegetables and a soft-boiled egg was all he consumed. When he was finished, he clapped his hands to signal the meal had come to an end. Most of his guests had not yet finished, but they took the hint, hastily got up, and walked out to find some coolness under the trees. Here, they waited for the customary folk dances that would take place in the early part of the evening.

The male dancers dispersed to pick-up their gear for a war dance; some guests left to take a quick shower; and the journalists departed for a photographic expedition through the village, much to the delight of the inhabitants — young and old alike.

I used the time to wash my hair, take a shower and don fresh clothing, hoping to then escape to the *Bintang Laut* for a rest. When I tried to slip away, however, I found my way barred by a crowd that was flocking in to see the dances. All I could do, at this time, was to retreat to the annex of the District Office.

The folk dances were announced, and then started by the elite women and girls from Buli. Twirling finely-embroidered handkerchiefs, they chose their dancing partners from among the onlookers who, according to tradition, could not refuse the invitation. After the President came the two Governors, and then the delegates. This would go on until every guest had had his turn. Thereafter would come the war dance, performed by the men of the village.

I sat in the darkening shadows of the annex when I spotted two men who were obviously searching for someone or something. Thinking that I could perhaps help them, I stepped forward and recognized the two Governors from Ambon: the Resident, and the Military Commander, Major Pieters.

Seeing me, the gentlemen rushed over to warn me that the audience was getting restless because of my absence. After all, the planning committee had chosen me as their official hostess and my non-participation in the festivities could lead to trouble. So the gentlemen pressed me to make an appearance, if only a short one. I should at least participate in one dance, they insisted.

I promised I would on one condition — that I would not have to be in the company of Sukarno. I didn't explain to them why but, although I had regained my composure after the President's slight near the jetty, I wanted to avoid further unpleasantness, especially one that I might unintentionally trigger myself.

The gentlemen promised solemnly they would make certain that I would not even get close to Sukarno and, thus assured, I accompanied them onto the dance floor.

A snake-dance was in progress, in which dancers follow one another with their hands placed on the shoulders of the person in front. I had the honor of placing my hands on the soaking wet shoulders of the panting, obese Egyptian Ambassador and was, in turn, followed by a Czech envoy, a tall, severe-looking, haughty blond man who deigned to touch me, but only with his finger tips — as if he were touching a reptile, I thought.

The music stopped abruptly and the dancers stood still. The performance was over and I stood right in front of Sukarno, who — seated on a small bamboo stool and leaning forward with a Marshall's baton shoring up his chin — had been looking at the dancers with a serious expression on his face.

Then, what I had dreaded most, happened. Both Governors got up, came over, and, in spite of their solemn promises to me, escorted me to the President who looked up as if surprised.

Major Pieters mumbled something and, addressing the President with a bashful smile on his face, said:

"Our *Ibu* is a little annoyed with *Bapak* President, because in all the commotion, *Bapak* President has forgotten to shake her hand."

*The Governors should know how annoyed I was for having been made such a fool of!*

Sukarno immediately extended his hands to me and said:

"I am sorry for that! Here, take both my hands!" and he then invited me to sit beside him.

The villagers, who had been watching the proceedings closely, applauded. Their *Ibu* had been shown proper respect. The unrest amongst them that had so worried both Governors was gone and, with it, the danger of an ugly incident.

Everyone relaxed; it was safe now to start the war dance.

To those who were seeing it for the first time, the dance was fascinating and intimidating in its display of coiled-up violence that seemingly stood on the edge of becoming unleashed. It totally absorbed the foreign envoys and excited the journalists whose cameras were clicking away at a frenzied pace.

At the end of the dance, the President and I struck up a conversation and discussed, among other things, the methods I was using to bring the Tugutil jungle inhabitants of Halmahera into the modern world. He was astonishingly well informed about my work, to which he pledged again his full support — as he had done during previous encounters.

Yet I had the impression that his mind was not totally focused on the subject at hand. Sometimes he looked around as if in doubt about what to say. Then suddenly, his voice became more resolute, as he finally spoke his mind:

"I hear that you are going to America," he started in a roundabout way.

"Then you have been misinformed, Mr. President," I replied. "I am going to France. I have received approval to go to Lyon to learn more about leprosy. We know now how to cure it, but not how to prevent it. That's what I hope to learn."

"No," Sukarno answered, "I think it is better that you go to America, because you know the situation here and there — pointing toward New Guinea — and you can tell them that we have solid plans to develop New Guinea. Also, that we have a group of capable civil servants — all trained by the Dutch. So it is better that you go there."

I then understood that he was referring to a post at the United Nations. I should have been honored by his offer, but the tone in which it was made kept me on my guard.

His proposal, he went on, meant an enormous advancement. I would be traveling through many parts of the world, doing useful work in the political and social arenas. I quickly perceived that he wanted my assistance in getting New Guinea away from the Netherlands, by convincing the UN that a capable government for that region was already in place.

I felt a great repugnance growing inside of me. If I accepted his proposal, I would be betraying my own roots *and* the trust of many people: the jungle inhabitants, who had finally given me their confidence; the many lepers who had signed the petition in the hope that their family members would be protected against this dreaded disease; and the Ministry of Social Affairs, whose hard-to-get support had finally been obtained.

Sukarno kept pressing, and — though I became vaguely aware that unknown people were crowding in on us — I finally blurted out: "And what should I tell them in America, Mr. President? Should I tell them the truth — that we lack doctors, hospitals, roads, and houses? Should I tell them that our people go hungry because rice is disappearing into the black market, and that your soldiers are throwing my people in jail for making salt from seawater, whereas before we were *exporting* salt?"

To soften my harsh remarks and to buy time, I added: "Give me a year to complete the work I have started, and then ask me again."

But Sukarno's eyes narrowed, and his face turned into a mask. Only then did I realize that we were surrounded by journalists, who had diligently noted every word we had said. Shocked, I realized I had gone too far. I, a *Belanda,* had offended the President of Indonesia and made him lose face! I immediately asked his forgiveness for my bad behavior, but he haughtily refused, got up abruptly, clapped his hands, and announced curtly that the festivities had ended and that all guests should return immediately to the ship. Then he brusquely turned around and left.

I stood rooted to the spot, numbed, confused, and not fully comprehending the seriousness of the situation. I felt drained. I had blown it, and there was nothing I could do to repair the damage.

Everyone left for the harbor, and I followed in a daze. As I watched the guests get into the boats, I once again prayed fervently that the pathetic jetty would hold until all of them were on board of the *Gajahmada,* convinced as I was, that an accident would surely occur, which would seal my fate.

# IBU MALUKU

Everything went well, however, and I was blissfully grateful when I finally could stretch out my exhausted body on the hard couch of the *Bintang Laut* and let my tears flow under cover of darkness.

The events of the day pressed in on me. Sukarno had told me many times, in the past, that I had *carte blanche* with him: "Ibu Maluku (he was the one who started calling me that) can tell me anything and ask me anything, because I know it is for the people of Maluku." What, then, had gone so terribly wrong?

I went over the disastrous conversation sentence by sentence — and then I realized, with a sinking feeling, which words had offended him. "*Your* soldiers are throwing *my* people in jail for making salt from seawater, whereas before *we* [the Dutch] were exporting salt."

Why, oh why, had I said that? And then I realized it had been said out of annoyance with the Sultan of Tidore, who *should* have brought up these matters with Sukarno, but had not.

What had happened could not now be undone, but I was at peace with myself. I had remained true to myself, and true to the people of the Moluccas whose care had been entrusted to me.

So be it. Whatever would happen next, would just have to happen!

**Endnotes**

[1] Indonesia wanted *all* of the former Netherlands East Indies; The Netherlands wanted to keep New Guinea as a penal colony for members of the NSB, a group of Nazi collaborators.

# IBU MALUKU

IBU MALUKU

# CHAPTER 47

## The Warrant
*Ternate, 1957*

The next day at the crack of dawn, we sailed out of Buli harbor and set course for the influenza epidemic area, where my treatment of the sick had been cut short by the President's visit.

The events of the previous day still weighed heavily on me, but I felt good about having given Sukarno a frank and honest answer. The task that lay ahead soon occupied my mind and the presidential visit and all the rigmarole that had been part of it, receded into the background.

After fourteen days of tending the sick, we set sail for home. Near Jailolo, we encountered a severe storm and were very pleased to get through it and to see the peak of Ternate, painted in gold by the bright Sunday morning sun.

It was low ebb when we arrived, so we dropped anchor in the roadstead. We would have to wait there for the tide to rise before we could moor at the quay, which was deserted at this early hour.

As the sun rose, the beach boulevard slowly came to life. A few soldiers appeared who seemed to take an unusual interest in us. One soldier took a bicycle away from a fisher boy, and pedaled hastily into town. I wondered if that had anything to do with me. A short time later, a former KPM agent appeared, accompanied by two *strappans* (prisoners) — easily identified by their rust-red clothes. He called out that the Governor wanted to see me as soon as possible, and that the two *strappans* were there to carry me ashore, so I would not have to wade through the mud myself.

His commanding tone irritated me. It was, after all, Sunday; I was dead-tired, and was neither dressed nor in the mood for an audience with the Governor[1].

Although the *strappans* were not exactly steady on their feet, I did get to shore without taking a mud bath.

Still annoyed, I walked to the Governor's residence, which was one house removed from mine, where I found him in a highly agitated state, still dressed in his pajamas.

He apologized for possibly having scared me, but it was urgent that he let me know that I should leave Ternate by 6 o'clock that evening. A ship of the PELNI[2] was waiting for me at the quay. He said it was my only chance to make a connection in Jakarta for my intended journey to Europe.

"But what is the reason for this sudden switch?" I asked, confounded. "I've already booked my passage on a KPM ship that will arrive in ten days, and I couldn't possibly leave earlier. I still have to find someone to take my place. I also have to hand over the funds. It is Sunday today, most of the office staff is in church, so this is definitely not possible!"

The kind-hearted Governor let me finish, and then he explained:

"Mrs. van Diejen, *no* KPM ship will come to Ternate anymore. All ships bound for Jakarta have on arrival been seized by the military on arrival and the KPM has recalled all its remaining ships back to Amsterdam."

I just looked at him, speechless.

"Your staff has been notified," he continued. "They will be in your office at noon. You can hand over the funds and the books to a temporary replacement — the bookkeeper strikes me as a suitable person. Dr. Tan has been told also, and he will come to discuss the leprosy cases with you. But I urge you, strongly, to leave with this PELNI ship."

I brought up all sort of difficulties, and suggested that I could always sail with the *Bintang Laut* to Menado and fly from there to Jakarta.

The Governor shook his head. Deeply embarrassed, he took a letter out of his breast pocket and handed it to me. It was an order for my arrest! I was accused of what one could call *lèse majesté*. It seemed that I had, indeed, offended the President of Indonesia.

Drained, I looked at him. "Is this serious?" I muttered.

He nodded and begged me to leave before he would be obliged to carry out the order, which could sweep along many others in its wake.

"I don't want to run the risk of a revolt among my people — especially the lepers — when this becomes known. So please ... "

I acquiesced. There was no time to say goodbye to close friends. At noon, I transferred the Departmental books and funds, as well as my house and belongings to the First Bookkeeper, Mr. Paät, a man from Wolowan, who was dependable. I handed the care of the Tugutils to an assistant, Baut Hadi, who had received elementary training in this work, and then I went to pack a suitcase.

Dr. Tan arrived at five, helped me to lock up the house, and then took me to the harbor. Dazed, and dressed in the same clothes in which I had spent a stormy night on board of my ship, I followed him up the gangway to my cabin. A quick hand clasp, *"selamat jalan"* (good journey) and I was alone.

Night fell quickly. Standing at the railing, I could barely make out the lights of the houses in Ternate. After having worked here for more than 39 years, this, then, was the last that I would see of my beloved Spice Islands. I could not accept it, and tears flooded my eyes. My still uncomprehending mind searched for words that could express the anguish in my heart, words that would not be spoken aloud:

"Goodbye Ternate, goodbye orphans, farewell residents of leprosarium Sarofo. *Ibu* has to leave you now. May God protect you and guide you through all the difficulties that await you!"

\* \* \* \*

The *Batang Hari* — that was the name of the PELNI ship — sailed via Bachan, Sanana and Buru to Ambon. The boat carried all the passengers it could. Among them were students returning to their schools in Makassar or somewhere on Java.

The ship was new. It was even more beautiful than the KPM ships that one usually took to traverse Indonesian waters. I was lucky to be given a first-class cabin.

The Captain and Chief Engineer were Dutch. Most of the staff were Menadonese or Makassarese, with the lower ranks consisting of people from all over the archipelago.

Five days later we arrived at the roadstead of Ambon, where many memories overwhelmed me. All places at the quay were occupied by large KPM ships, so our ship would have to wait at anchor until a berth became available.

A motor-sloop arrived from shore. A uniformed figure, standing up, shouted through a megaphone that no one was allowed to leave the ship. The man then turned his attention to the many *praus* that were floating around our ship and sent them away. Our ship's gangway remained in hoisted position.

Early next morning, a few military men came on board to see the Captain. A little later, the Captain's voice boomed over the intercom instructing all passengers — without exception — to pack their bags and prepare for disembarkation.

All passengers crowded around him, protesting that none of them had Ambon as their final destination. The Captain expressed his regrets, but said he was merely following orders from the military, who had commandeered the ship to transport a detachment of soldiers with their families and possessions — including livestock.

This news was particularly unpleasant for the students. They didn't know anyone in Ambon and had no money to pay for lodgings or alternate means of transportation. This delay would also cause them to miss classes. It was sad and depressing to see them meander about without being able to help them. The military authorities obviously didn't care about their problems.

I went ashore and managed to see the Military Governor, Major Pieters, to whom I complained loudly about his broken promise that had precipitated the incident at Buli. If I couldn't continue my voyage on the *Batang Hari*, I said, it would only be a matter of days before the order for my arrest would reach Ambon. And then what?

The unrepentant Major thought the matter over and, in view of the priority normally assigned to my tours of duty, gave orders — assuming that I wouldn't object to traveling with soldiers — that I could continue my journey with the *Batang Hari*.

After two days of pointless waiting, it became clear that the need for transporting the military had somehow evaporated. So the *Batang Hari* left Ambon — empty, except for a load of lumber — with Makassar as its destination. None of the dumped passengers were permitted to continue the journey — except myself!

Five days later we arrived in Makassar, where we would stay for at least one day. The sea journey had done me good, and I felt completely rested.

A few hours after the ship had moored, I went ashore to discuss various matters concerning the Province of Irian Barat with the head of Social Affairs, Mr. Lego. Of course, for him this was simply a courtesy visit, a stop-over on my way to Europe for a legitimate leave-of-absence. He had no inkling that an order had been issued for my arrest.

In the afternoon, I visited the nuns at the Stella Maris hospital, where we exchanged news of our latest adventures amidst much laughter. This went on until well after dinner.

At ten o'clock I was back on board. No new passengers had arrived. The crew had gone on shore leave, and the Captain wondered out loud how much longer this fruitless waiting would last.

The next morning, since no sailing orders had arrived, I stopped again at the Social Affairs Office, and visited the Maternity Clinic "Maria Fatima", which was run by the same missionary nuns who ran the Stella Maris hospital. I was back on board for lunch and spent the rest of the day reading — an unheard-of luxury.

In the afternoon, a few military men came on board to talk to the Captain. At dinner time, I heard we were to sail for Pare-Pare, north of Makassar, where the European civilian men had been interned during World War II.

"We probably shall be taking on a detachment of soldiers there, but even that is not certain," remarked the irritated Captain, who wouldn't comment on it any further.

We left very early in the morning and moored at the quay of Pare-Pare four hours later. All was calm. No military men came on board, so I visited the local hospital, run by missionary nuns whom I knew well. I was talking to a doctor, also a nun, when a messenger arrived and asked her to come to the Government Office as soon as possible. Still having some time on my hands, I then decided to accompany another nun who had to visit a few young mothers in a nearby village.

When I returned to the harbor, all sorts of vehicles were driving back and forth with livestock, luggage and household goods. The embarkation had obviously begun.

Near the top of the gangway I spotted the doctor, who had been called away earlier in the day. Surprised, I asked what had brought her here.

An hour before, so she told me, she had been drafted for military duty! Her task was to check all the military and their families, and weed out those requiring medical attention. She then gratefully accepted the help I offered. She would check all the soldiers; I would take care of the women and children.

As the first group climbed the gangway, I noticed the Captain and Chief Engineer gleefully watching us. With grimaces and gestures, they signaled their amusement at the irony of the situation: here were two Dutch women ostensibly helping the Indonesian Army prepare for a possible war with the Dutch over New Guinea. It didn't seem to occur to them, however, that they themselves were also caught up in circumstances beyond their control.

The medical inspection went smoothly, and we finished around seven that evening. Dead-tired, I went to my cabin and found, to my surprise and slight amusement, that it had been taken over by two women, five children, four beer-drinking officers, a number of chickens and a lory (a Malayan parrot).

The people looked at me, just as surprised. The women, speaking at the same time, indicated that I should feel free to also make use of this cabin. My bed had, in the meantime, been remade on the upper berth — without my permission, of course.

I thanked them amicably for having thought of my needs — what else could I do? — and politely took my leave to ask the Captain if the officers also had to stay overnight in the same cabin.

The Captain put my mind partially at ease: the men would be

assigned to another cabin; the women and the children ... alas, he could not place them elsewhere. However, the chickens and the lory would be taken outside for the night. And I could take a shower in the ship's officers' quarters, since all the water in the passenger section of the ship had already been used up — something I had not known before.

The crossing to Surabaya took three days and three long nights. All the military disembarked there and boarded a train that was waiting for them. In the afternoon, with more breathing-space on board, the *Batang Hari* raised anchor and finally set course for Jakarta.

Thirty-eight hours later we moored in Jakarta's harbor of Tanjung Priok and, that same evening, I was hosted at a dinner reception given in the mess hall of Social Affairs at Tanah Abang. It was November 30, 1957.

The next day I went straight to the Indonesian Immigration Office in downtown Jakarta to apply for a passport. They refused to give it to me since I could not prove that I was an Indonesian citizen, and referred me to the High Commissioner of the Netherlands.

Here I was received by a dark-skinned man from Suriname who quickly labeled me as *spijtoptant*, pidgin Dutch for "sorry optant": one who had opted for Indonesian citizenship, was sorry about it, and now wanted the Dutch citizenship back. Beating his dark chest, he proudly declared himself to be a Netherlander, adding that he would never give it up.

According to him, I was a *Warga Negara* — an Indonesian citizen. That no paper had ever been issued to prove that, didn't matter. He would only consider giving me a visa for the Netherlands if I showed up with an Indonesian passport.

I stopped next at the Ministry of Social Affairs to let them know I had arrived, to discuss the transfer of my duties, and to get letters of introduction for the Embassies in Belgium and France.

The matter of funding was dealt with at a high level. I would, initially, have to pay for the voyage myself — as I already knew. Upon my return, they hoped to have enough funds to refund my travel expenses. The voyage in Europe would be arranged by the Indonesian embassies in Brussels and Paris. My salary would continue to be paid during my absence and deposited into my account. Regarding funds to pay for the course, for that I would have to approach the aforementioned embassies.

To my dismay, I was asked to go to Jogjakarta before my departure, to discuss the Tugutil project. This could not be done in Jakarta, they said. The gentlemen impressed on me, once again, the necessity of speaking good *Bahasa Indonesia*, pointing to the many banners inside and outside the building that proclaimed "One Country, One People, One Language". I promised to adhere to that policy to the best of my ability.

To make the trip as quickly as possible, they put a new Jeep stationwagon at my disposal. The vehicle was slated for inspection work at Tidore, and "would I please give my comments on the suitability of this type of vehicle for its intended purpose."

There were other matters the Departmental Heads wanted to discuss, but I managed to persuade them that these were really not that urgent. By this time, I had become anxious. My time was already extremely limited, and here they kept giving me more work to do.

My anxiety was also due to the roadblocks I had run into — the passport situation being the worst one. In addition, I didn't know how long the Governor of Tidore could sit on my arrest warrant. Eventually, my absence would surely spark a general alert.

The political situation in Jakarta was perilous. The New Guinea conflict was being used to whip up anti-Dutch sentiment, and it was becoming increasingly dangerous for any white person suspected of being Dutch to be seen in the city.

Money-wise, I was also tied up in knots. I could use my savings in the Escompto Bank as long as I was in Jakarta, but I couldn't transfer money abroad nor purchase foreign currency with it. After much wrangling, I succeeded in getting special permission to buy a measly 2,700 *rupiahs*-worth of Belgian francs for my three-month stay in Belgium. Transfer of additional funds to the Netherlands was flatly refused. How I was supposed to live in France was none of their concern, and that was that!

With the question of New Guinea not yet settled, Sukarno had begun reprisals against the Netherlands, and on December 1, seized $1.5 billion in Dutch holdings.

The next day I left for Jogja at 4 o'clock in the morning with a chauffeur assigned to me by Social Affairs. Taking turns at the wheel of the Jeep, the chauffeur and I drove along the hot coastal road, stopping now and then to eat something purchased by the chauffeur from street vendors. I, myself, didn't dare get out of the car.

We didn't stop in inhabited places, as I was frightened for my life. Banners and posters with horrible, inflammatory obscenities against the Dutch could be seen everywhere, and it was scary.

Without difficulty we reached Ungaran, but by then we were just about out of fuel. Under cover of darkness, I managed to purchase enough fuel from a Chinese merchant to reach Jogja, where I spent a short night at a reception center for handicapped girls.

At seven in the morning, I was at the office complex of the Social Affairs' Department of Civilization. The civil servants were courteous and helpful and we immediately got down to business.

During the meeting, which was conducted in the new *Bahasa Indonesia* that not everyone had completely mastered, I described the Tugutil situation and used a few sociological terms. One gentleman finally interjected:

"*Ibu*," he said, somewhat embarrassed, "we don't know these terms in *Bahasa Indonesia* yet; we do know them in Dutch, so why don't you speak in Dutch to us."

I could not resist looking pointedly at the sign on the wall that proclaimed "One Country, One People, One Language", but remained silent when I saw the look in his eyes.

The rest of the meeting continued in Dutch.

All the remaining points on the agenda were quickly dispensed with and, before noon, I was on my way to Solo (Surakarta), to discuss the construction of a reception center for handicapped children in Ternate. It was getting dark when we finally left for Jakarta. We drove straight through the night, stopping only to take turns at driving and cat-napping, and arrived in the early afternoon of the following day.

My first stop was the large KPM building, where I wanted to see the KPM's legal advisor, Mr. Voorthuizen, and pick up the deed for the parcel of land that the KPM had given to me, which I intended to use for a handicapped children's reception center.

To my surprise, the office was in a complete state of turmoil. Shouting and laughing Indonesians were walking back and forth. I sought out the old *mandur*, the superintendent, whom I had known for many years, who told me that the new Indonesian bosses had fired all white employees, including Mr. Voorthuizen and the Director. However, since Ibu's business concerned the well-being of Indonesian children, he was certain he could find someone to fetch Mr. Voorthuizen.

"But what is going on?" I asked, puzzled.

"*Ibu Sosial* has obviously not seen the flags on top of the building when she arrived." Taking me outside, he pointed upwards. Beside the red-and-white flag of the Republic of Indonesia fluttered a red flag with yellow hammer and sickle.

Still bewildered, I looked at the old man, who then explained that the entire KPM had been taken over by the PKI — the Indonesian Communist Party! It then dawned on me that some kind of a coup was in process.

Little did I then know that hundreds of thousands would die and that Sukarno would be replaced by General Suharto before the struggle for power was over.

## IBU MALUKU

In the meantime, Mr. Voorthuizen had been picked up, and moments later I had the valuable document in my hands. Mr. Voorthuizen then gave me the well-meaning advice to escape from "this hornet's nest" as quickly as possible.

I took the streetcar to Immigration in central Jakarta to make another pitch for an Indonesian passport. Again, I was referred to the High Commissioner of the Netherlands. This scenario repeated itself the following day.

In the harbor, one KPM ship after the next was put under embargo, and tension mounted. My ship, the *Karimoen* of the Maatschappij Nederland — which was not subject to seizure — would be leaving on December 8, so I would somehow have to obtain my passport and visas before that date.

On December 6, I went again to the increasingly dangerous downtown area for a final attempt at getting an Indonesian passport. Once again I failed, and I left the Immigration Office with the staff's jeering remarks still ringing in my ears.

Thoroughly dispirited, I walked past a guard post that was manned by Ambonese soldiers whom I had always greeted cheerfully when I had passed on previous occasions.

One soldier walked over to me and said:

"Hai, *Ibu Maluku*." This was how they had addressed me from the beginning.

"We have seen you pass here almost every day. The first day, you laughed; then you stopped smiling and started to look angry; and today, your face looks *kaya anjing punya pintu belakang* — like the rear end of a dog!"

Normally I might have burst out laughing at this descriptive, if unflattering, phrase. Instead, all my frustrations suddenly erupted and, in one breath, I told him that on behalf of the lepers in the Moluccas I had to go to Europe for further study and that Immigration did not want to give me a passport.

The soldier asked me to wait a minute, and then called over his armed comrades.

"Come with us, *Ibu*," is all they said, and in a Jeep we raced off to the Immigration Office.

With fierce expressions on their taciturn faces, their fingers on the trigger of their stenguns, they marched with me into the office.

The people standing in front of the counter quickly dispersed and ran out the front door. But the officials behind the counter had nowhere to hide, and their faces turned ashen as they stared apprehensively into the barrels of the machine guns.

An Ambonese voice snapped:

"Hai! Why have you refused to give our *Ibu Maluku* a passport?"

A sputtering answer was cut short with a brief order:

"Make out her passport! Now!"

Stunned, I surveyed the situation. Would this really work? Two men moved and seemed to obey. Except for the rustling of papers and the wall-clock ticking away, there was a deadly silence. Not a word was said.

Fifteen minutes later, my passport was ready and, trembling from both happiness and trepidation, I left the Immigration office with my escort.

Triumphantly, the Ambonese soldiers helped me again into their Jeep, and we drove at breakneck speed to the Belgian Embassy where my benefactors left me.

While waiting for my visa, I told my story, which evoked much laughter. The amiable Ambassador took me in person to his French colleague, who saw to it that I received my visa right away. The French Embassy staff car then took me to the Dutch High Commissioner, where I finally received a visa for a one-time entry into the Netherlands.

Blissfully happy, I arrived in time for dinner at the Ministry's mess hall at Tanah Abang, where an urgent message had been left for me: the departure of the *Karimoen* had been moved up one day. I would have to be on board the next day before twelve noon.

I skipped dinner and started packing. In trying to use up all the Indonesian money in my possession, I had bought many things that now posed a real problem. It took time, but finally everything was packed.

I then wrote a few letters of farewell to people in Ternate and called some friends to say goodbye. Sleep now seemed impossible.

The still very real threat of arrest, as well as the uncertain future in Europe were on my mind until the sun rose on a new day — December 7, 1957.

### Endnotes

[1] This post was still held by the Sultan of Tidore.
[2] PELNI, a division of the KPM, which was 55% owned by the Indonesian Government.

IBU MALUKU

# CHAPTER 48

### Leaving Indonesia
### *Jakarta, Java, December 7, 1957*

At 8 o'clock sharp, I left Tanah Abang by cab for a last ride through Jakarta. Although glad to be on my way, I could not as yet relax knowing that anything could still happen before I boarded the ship. My heart was in my mouth each time we were stopped at one of many military roadblocks, but finally we arrived at the harbor without incident.

At Tanjung Priok, Jakarta's harbor, I negotiated with belligerent porters and then endured an aggravating inspection at the hands of sardonic custom officials. They slowly and deliberately pulled all my carefully-packed possessions out onto the counter, before telling me I could go. The *Karimoen* had already sounded the first whistle ... but it would take me at least 20 minutes to re-pack all my precious things.

Suddenly, my Ambonese soldier-benefactors of the previous day appeared out of nowhere, quickly put all my scattered belongings into a wicker basket, and rushed with me up the gangway. It was just five minutes before the appointed hour when they deposited me on the deck with my empty luggage case and that magic wicker basket.

Out of breath, I thanked them profusely. They each gave me a broad grin in response ... and then left my life as suddenly as they had entered it.

On board, the tension was so thick that one could cut it with a knife. Eleven high-strung passengers welcomed me — I was the last one to come aboard — and after perfunctory introductions, I left them and entered my cabin, almost crying from relief.

The *Karimoen* was a freighter with limited passenger accommodation, under the command of a Dutchman, Captain Meyer. At 12:30 we left the quay and sailed slowly past the many KPM ships that were no longer allowed to leave the harbor.

We could see Indonesian soldiers on the almost deserted decks of these commandeered ships. The white crew members, whose future was anything but certain, waved to us furtively. I wondered what was going on in their hearts and minds as they watched us leave.

After all the anxiety of Jakarta, I savored the relative safety of this Dutch ship. By amazing good fortune, the order for my arrest had not surfaced. Yet, I only felt really safe when it was announced that we had left Indonesian waters and were heading for British Borneo.

Our first stop was the harbor of Miri, where, almost 16 years earlier, the Japanese Navy's Second Fleet had landed the Emperor's first invasion force onto the shores of the East Indies. The *Karimoen* would stay there a week in order to take on a load of precious lumber. So the other passengers and I decided to go ashore to explore.

Everything was very different from the East Indies. The architecture, road construction and even the many golf courses were decidedly British. In contrast to the unruly masses in Jakarta, the Islamic inhabitants were extremely friendly toward us.

A week later, as we were sailing towards Singapore, I made a pleasant discovery: quite by accident, I found, in the outer pocket of my old *tournée* handbag, an envelope containing a sizeable amount of Indonesian *rupiahs*. I probably had put it there when I hurriedly left to prepare for Sukarno's fateful visit, and had completely forgotten about it.

It was a miracle that it hadn't been found during the very thorough customs inspection at Jakarta. Otherwise, it certainly would have been impounded. It was equally surprising that it hadn't been stolen at my lodgings in Tanah Abang, where the handbag had been left lying around.

All in all, this was an enormous windfall as, otherwise, I would have had hardly a cent to my name. This stroke of good luck would resolve many problems for me.

At Singapore, the first one to come aboard was a money changer. I received so many Singapore dollars for my newly-found treasure-trove that I was able to buy shoes, warm clothes and many other necessities — and still have some money left over, which I changed on board into Dutch guilders..

During the voyage from Jakarta to Miri as well as during the subsequent trips ashore, the passengers had come to know each other and learn why each of us had left Indonesia[1]. Inevitably, there were many similarities to the stories.

Most of the Netherlanders were men who had worked on contract for the Indonesian Government. A major part of their monthly salary had been deposited in a bank in the Netherlands; only a small portion — but still enough to live on — had been paid in Indonesian money, making any further savings on their part unnecessary.

A few had been plantation administrators; some, technical experts of one kind or another. Invariably — and perhaps inevitably in this new Republic — they'd had to work under Javanese, who knew little or nothing about the management of the plantation or enterprise. The Government's hate-campaign had soured relations with the personnel. Some of the men had been threatened, others had been subjected to humiliating house arrest. All had eventually been fired. Most of them were glad to be leaving Indonesia.

The only tourist, an American, turned out to be of Dutch descent. His heritage alone made him decide that it would be prudent to cut short his trip and leave the country.

I listened with great interest, but didn't participate much in the conversations. Once again, I observed in myself a shyness and a certain difficulty in understanding the life-styles of these people. How would it be once I had arrived in Europe, I wondered?

After two days in Singapore, we left for Ceylon (today once again "Sri Lanka").

We were already well on our way when the Captain received a telegram from Holland, ordering him to turn back and pick up some women and children from Medan on Sumatra. Apparently, the political situation there had deteriorated so much that the shipping company considered it unsafe for the families of their employees to remain there.

My heart sank when the Captain announced the turn-about, for we would be entering Indonesian waters once again!

The *Karimoen* was quickly reorganized to take on twenty new passengers. Most, though not all, of the single cabins were changed to accommodate two people. Some of the passengers had complained so much about the threatened "invasion" that in order to keep the peace, the Captain had also freed up some room in the ship's officers' quarters. The decks also had to be partitioned off so children could safely play there.

The small, cozy salons would, no doubt, become crammed with people, and we would have to abandon any further notion of a pleasant, quiet journey to Europe. The passengers were not exactly overjoyed at this, but had little choice in the matter. They would just have to adjust to the coming inconveniences.

It was New Year's Eve when the *Karimoen* docked at Medan on Sumatra. The harbor, normally very busy, was unusually quiet. Three unsightly Russian ships lay moored at the quay. They were probably there as part of Russia's foreign aid plan; it was highly unlikely that Indonesia would have paid hard cash for those rusting hulks.

There were no other ships, except for a KPM-steamer that was making ready to leave port. The Dutch flag fluttered at the stern beside the red-and-white flag of the Indonesian Republic. At the far end of the quay we spotted many schooners and fishing vessels.

The quay itself was deserted except for a few soldiers, who peered at the *Karimoen* with lingering suspicion. In view of the tense political situation, the passengers thought it prudent to avoid a staring contest and so returned to their cabins.

The harbor officials came on board and sent the Second Officer to collect all the passengers' passports. They would be returned as soon as the *Karimoen* was ready to leave, he said. He also passed on the officials' instructions: we were not permitted to leave the ship, nor to have contact with anyone on shore. His eyebrows shot up when I gave him my passport, which of course differed in color from the Dutch ones, but he left without a word.

Moments later he returned and asked me to follow him. He then led me to a group of Indonesian soldiers who had come aboard unseen. Their commander, a very young Captain, was studying my passport. He introduced himself very politely and then asked, quite pleasantly, if I was pleased to be celebrating New Year's Eve in Indonesia again.

In response, I mumbled something incoherent. What could I say? My heart was in my mouth. I was convinced that my freedom had come to an end and that I would soon be escorted off this ship, which — more than ever before — felt like a safe haven.

The Captain, however, was in no hurry to put manacles on me, for he quietly talked about some of the details in my passport that had drawn his attention. Suddenly he asked:

"Are you perhaps from the Province of Irian Barat?"

"Yes," I answered, " I live in Ternate."

"What did you do there?" he asked.

In a controlled tone of voice, I answered this and other questions he posed, but finally blurted out:

"Captain, why did you send for me?"

He suddenly became shy and said that my passport had made him curious for personal reasons. He then mentioned somebody's name and asked if I knew that person.

"Yes, of course, Captain," I said surprised. It was the name of an employee who handled the correspondence in my office — the only Sumatran among my staff.

The Captain smiled and then inquired about the man's health, which I was able to tell him about in detail. The young man had become terribly homesick shortly after his arrival at the solidly-booked *pasanggrahan*, where he had contracted malaria. I had taken him home and had looked after him, until he had regained his health and I had found him more congenial quarters.

"Was he a good worker, and is he used to Ternate now?" asked the Captain.

Still wondering where this conversation was heading, I answered:

"Yes, Captain. I am pleased to say he is doing fine on both counts."

Much to my surprise, the Captain then said:

"Then you must be *Ibu Maluku*! What a coincidence! This man is my only brother. He has written about you, but I had difficulty in believing that a Dutch woman would be head of Social Affairs out there in the *udik* — the backwoods. So he really told us the truth!"

Relieved, and pleased with the direction the conversation had taken, I nevertheless had to ask him:

"Captain, I hope that my answers have satisfied you but I wonder if, perhaps, you had another reason for wanting to see me."

"Well, yes," he answered, turning somewhat shy again, "there is another reason." He then pulled a piece of paper from his breast pocket, and proceeded to read it to me:

"It is the duty of every person stationed at airports, harbors, or stations, to track down Mrs. Jean Marie van Diejen-Roemen and return her, under guard, to her post because of indispensability."

Instead of *"lèse majesté"*, the reason for my arrest had now changed to "indispensability" — a curious choice of words, I reflected.

I gazed at him intently, and, controlling my voice with difficulty, said:

"With your permission, I will now leave to pack my bags. Thereafter, I will follow you wherever you want to take me" — already picturing myself behind bars.

Spontaneously he grabbed both of my hands, shook his head and said, emphatically:

"No, *Ibu*, that won't be necessary. Let me explain. After reading the order for your arrest, it occurred to me that Mrs. van Diejen and the *Ibu Maluku* my brother had written about were one and the same person, and that your ship just might stop in Medan. I then asked to be assigned to harbor duty, so I could keep an eye on the situation. I can promise you that you will be safe, as long as you stay on board. Unlike the other passengers you may, of course, go ashore. But if you do, I will not be able to protect you should you run into trouble with other patrols."

I heaved a big sigh of relief, and thanked him profusely.

The Captain and I then continued talking about my trip to Europe and its intended purpose. At one point, I abruptly stopped in mid-sentence and looked on in wonder as two KPM ships — with the Dutch flag hoisted high — sailed past us in opposite directions: one, coming into the harbor; the other, leaving it. How was that possible under the present circumstances?

I looked quizzically at the Captain, who laughed, and explained:

"In Medan, we would not dream of impounding the KPM ships. We are faithful patriots, but we are not about to ruin our economy like they are doing on Java. Here there are two KPM ships: one is docked and supposedly kept under embargo, while the second one is out picking up cargo at other Sumatran ports. When it returns, the first one goes out again. It's as simple as that!"

With a twinkle in his eyes, he then gave me an impeccable salute, wished me *selamat jalan*, and left the ship with his men.

I watched him go ashore, reflecting on my good fortune of having run into him, rather than into some hard-line colleague of his. Certainly, somebody up there was looking out for me. Needless to say, I didn't tempt fate and remained quietly on board that New Year's Eve.

Soon, a lot of activity drew my attention: the new passengers were coming aboard and the voices of children and their mothers filled the air. That effectively signaled the end of any peace on board. The *Karimoen* had now become an evacuation vessel, with all the attendant difficulties of such.

Three days later, we continued our journey and all went well until we reached Port Saïd, where I, once again, ran into difficulties on account of my questionable Indonesian citizenship.

The Second Officer had passed out forms to all passengers in order to apply for free housing assistance in the Netherlands. The Government would receive us in Amsterdam and provide free transportation to wherever in the Netherlands they had arranged accommodation for us.

On orders from the Captain, the Second Officer returned a short time later to retrieve the form that he had given me to fill out. Somewhat embarrassed, he explained that, because I had given up my Dutch citizenship, I was not eligible for free housing and transportation. But he was not embarrassed enough to add that, if they had been aware of my status in Sumatra, they would most likely have put me ashore at Medan!

The passengers rallied around me and protested to the Captain — but to no avail. Unbeknownst to me, however, they also sent a protest telegram to HRH Prince Bernhard. Apart from this unpleasant incident, the trip from Port Saïd to Amsterdam was extremely interesting.

The *Karimoen* had not been able to take on a full load because of the political situation in Indonesia. The Captain had therefore been ordered by his head office to pick up other cargo on the way. This afforded the passengers several unexpected opportunities to explore other ports of call. One such opportunity came when we docked at Pôrto, in Portugal, which I had never before visited.

It had a beautiful, but very small harbor — too tight, really, for the 10,000 ton *Karimoen*. The Captain, however, proved to be an expert helmsman. He executed an extremely tight turn and brought the ship to within 25 cm of the dock. The passengers gave him loud applause for this remarkable performance.

The ship planned to stay there a few days, so a few other passengers and I took the opportunity to explore this part of Portugal that I had not visited before.

Apart from the very attractive university town of Coimbra, we visited other towns and small villages — all of which reminded me very much of Tidore. In the yards, older women — the younger generation probably being away at work — were cooking with wood on a few assembled stones. The air smelled of forests. Family names sounded so familiar, the language was so similar to the dialect spoken in Tidore, and I felt so comfortable with the people that — if I would have to stay in Europe for good — I felt I could be quite happy in this lovely place.

When the ship reached IJmuiden — the last stop before Amsterdam — a certain Mrs. Wickers, who was head of the Pelita Institute, came on board to see me. She brought me warm clothes and showed me a letter from Prince Bernhard, asking Pelita to provide me with whatever assistance I needed. It was only then that I learned about the telegram that my fellow passengers had sent to the Prince on my behalf.

Deeply touched by their unselfish act, I warmly thanked each one of them. However, I was still deeply hurt by the persnickety attitude of the ship's senior officers and, thereafter, declined further offers of help. I would also decline future offers from Pelita that were presumably made on behalf of the Government of the Netherlands.

The ship arrived in Amsterdam on the evening of January 28, 1958. My sister, who had arrived from Antwerp, was waiting for me. I hadn't seen Mia in many years, so we had a lot of catching up to do. Fortunately, because of the late hour, the custom officials were very easygoing. We slept in Amsterdam and left the next day by train for Antwerp.

In Roosendaal, a Royal *Maréchaussée*[2] boarded the train to check the passports. He expressed surprise at my short stay in the Netherlands, noting that my visa was for only a single entry. If I wanted to return to the Netherlands — which I had to do in order to obtain my war widow's pension — the Constable politely advised me to see the Dutch Consulate in Antwerp and apply for a multiple-entry visa of longer duration.

This I did the next morning, accompanied by Mia. My Indonesian passport caused great hilarity among the staff, who joked about it — at my expense. My sister angrily demanded to see the Consul himself, to whom she expressed her indignation at such unprofessional behavior. He did make the guilty ones apologize, but I knew this was simply a prelude to what was to come, and it made me apprehensive.

I then filled out a visa application form, and was told it would take a couple of weeks. In Jakarta I had received my European visas within 15-20 minutes, but it seemed that this Consulate was not able to match that. I would be advised when to come back for it.

A few days later, Mia and I visited the Indonesian Embassy in Brussels. The Ambassador, himself, received us with great courtesy. He spoke in *Bahasa Indonesia*, inserting a Dutch word now and then to clarify a concept, from which I concluded that His Excellency spoke Dutch fluently.

We talked about my long stay in Indonesia and he asked some pointed questions about the developments in the as yet provisional Province of Irian Barat — provisional, because the largest part of the province, New Guinea, was still in Dutch hands. He also showed a keen interest in the reasons for my visit to Europe, and the purpose of the study in Lyon.

As to obtaining any financial assistance, he had to disappoint me, he said. The Embassies in Brussels and Paris simply did not have the money — there was hardly enough to pay the staff. "But," he said, pointing to my bag of alligator skin, "that bag will fetch a tidy price here, which may be enough to cover most of your expenses."

My sister bristled, and started to express her outrage at the suggestion that I should have to sell my own personal belongings to fund a study underwritten by the Republic of Indonesia. But I quickly shushed her as I didn't want any trouble. We were, after all, on Indonesian soil and, if the Ambassador knew about the warrant, he could arrest me then and there.

The Ambassador let the moment pass, and said he would be pleased to help me in other ways, such as providing letters of introduction or introducing me personally to influential people.

With that pledge in my pocket, I returned to Antwerp. Although disappointed, I had half-expected such an answer. My sister, however, was outraged — which I could understand, but then she lived in a very different world from the one I had just left.

In any case, since the course in Lyon was now beyond my reach, and since returning to Indonesia seemed impossible in the immediate future, I decided to focus my energies on the present: how to make ends meet and, in particular, how to get my war widow's pension reinstated. I had not received a cent since September 1952. Neither had any of the Indonesian war widows and orphans in the Moluccas. The ones on Java, however, had continued to receive theirs — but I would never find out why this had happened.

Two weeks after my unpleasant visit to the Dutch Consulate, I received a one-week visa for the Netherlands. The next day I took the train to the Hague and called on Mrs. Wickers — the head of Pelita, who had visited me in IJmuiden — to ask for her advice. She advised me to contact SAIP — the Society for the Administration of Indonesian Pensions — but warned me that I would be entering a lion's den.

It certainly didn't sound hopeful!

She further advised me that I had just missed the deadline for receiving a rehabilitation remittance of 3,000 guilders, paid out to repatriates from Indonesia. If the *Karimoen* had not returned to Medan to pick up the endangered civilians, had not stopped at so many unscheduled ports and *had* arrived in Amsterdam on the scheduled date of December 28, I would have received this much-needed amount — which was really a small compensation for the possessions I had lost during the war with Japan. When I made further enquiries later on, I found that Mrs. Wickers had, indeed, been right. I had missed the deadline, and would never receive this compensation!

Then, accompanied by a friend, Mrs. Malgo, I went to the SAIP office at the Neyhuyskade in the Hague, to have an interview with its Chief, Mr. Bargsma.

He acknowledged that my war widow's pension had been unjustly withheld from 1952 to 1957 — the year when I had opted for Indonesian citizenship — but since I did not have a bank declaration to that effect, he couldn't help me. I would have to engage a lawyer, and he pleasantly recommended one to me.

On the other matter, to get my pension reinstated, he said, I should reapply for Dutch citizenship. When I said I had never received the Indonesian citizenship, I heard once again the old cliche: that since I had *opted* for it, I had thereby forfeited my Dutch nationality.

"Well," I shot back, "if it is that easy to change nationality, then I hereby opt for the Dutch nationality." But that did not wash, of course. Getting out was one thing; getting back in was something else — or so it seemed.

"If you had taken the Belgian, French, or even Russian nationality," he continued, "you would not have forfeited your rights. But you chose the Indonesian one and, well, that was just too insulting!"

It was "too insulting" because of the ongoing fight over New Guinea, no doubt! Mrs. Malgo was getting hot under the collar, and so was I.

"Mr. Bargsma," I replied, "I would like to remind you that Minister Lieftink, speaking for the Dutch Government, made a radio broadcast urging all Netherlanders who wished to remain in the former Dutch East Indies to ask for Indonesian citizenship, and thus be in a better position to foster good relations between the Netherlands and Indonesia."

"Do you have that in black and white?" asked Mr. Bargsma.

"I don't know of anyone who has ever seen a radio broadcast in black and white." snapped Mrs. Malgo angrily.

Mr. Bargsma just shrugged. He seemed happy to interpret the political mood of the Dutch people, but did not feel called upon to interpret the policies of the Dutch Government.

I tried one more time:

"Mr. Bargsma, I would like to remind you of another broadcast, made by Queen Wilhelmina from London, immediately after her government declared war on Japan — and even before the United States and Britain did. In that speech, she *ordered* everyone in the Dutch East Indies to remain at their station; no one was allowed to leave; and she assured her subjects that all damages resulting from this declaration of war would be fully compensated.

"I would like you to know," I continued, "that the Dutch Government has never honored that promise!"

I might as well have been talking to the wall.

"It has nothing to do with me, Mrs. van Diejen," he concluded, "but if you can regain your Dutch citizenship, I will try to get your war widow's pension reinstated from the date of your arrival in the Netherlands." And so ended this hopeless, frustrating and humiliating conversation.

The pedestrians a block away must have heard Mrs. Malgo and myself giving vent to our feelings as we wended our way to the office of the recommended lawyer, to see if I could file a claim against the Government for the pension that had been wrongly withheld.

The lawyer quickly made it clear that putting in the claim would be a very complicated procedure. He would have to send someone to interview the pension administrators in Bandung and the banking and government officials in Ternate, and this would be quite costly. Thus he felt obliged to ask for a retainer of 5,000 guilders!

Since I had neither income nor savings and was entirely dependent on the generous help of my sister — something that Mr. Bargsma of the

SIAP Institute knew full well — I had to abandon the pursuit of this claim. The pension that had illegally been withheld from me over five years would never be recovered.

I went back to Pelita to review my options. Mrs. Wickers urged me to apply, as soon as possible, to regain my Dutch citizenship, offering me all the support I needed until it had been achieved.

I was ready and willing to do that, but new difficulties arose. To apply for Dutch citizenship, I would have to *live* in the Netherlands; it could not be done from Antwerp. In addition, finding accommodation in the Netherlands was well-nigh impossible, due to the influx of repatriates from Indonesia. Dutch citizens had the right to temporary shelter in hostels which had been contracted by the Government, but, once again, I was not eligible for such assistance.

As chance would have it, however, on the train taking me back to Antwerp I overheard one elderly lady telling another one that she was living in the Caritas home for the elderly in Sittard (Limburg Province) that was run by Roman Catholic nuns. She even mentioned the address of this home which I, unobtrusively, jotted-down.

After consulting with my sister, I wrote to this home and received the promising reply that a small room would become vacant in June, some five months hence. I immediately registered as a resident with the Registration Office in Sittard, so I could start applying for my Dutch citizenship.

There were many bureaucratic difficulties to be faced, but I managed to overcome them because, luckily, I had all the necessary personal documents in my possession. After depositing 200 borrowed guilders, my application was finally accepted.

For five months I depended on the hospitality of relatives and friends in Sittard and elsewhere. The most onerous task I had during that time was having to report to the Aliens Police on a weekly basis, come rain or shine. Many a time, when I had serious attacks of malaria, I had to drag myself out of bed and report to the police of whichever town I happened to be in at the time.

In the smaller towns, the police often didn't have a clue as to why I had come. The result was endless waiting while they called the office of the Aliens Police in the Hague who had dreamed up this dreadful ruling.

One fine day in June, I finally took possession of this, indeed, very small room at the Caritas Home in Sittard. The rent was 175 guilders per month, and my sister — who had come over for the occasion — had to pay twelve months in advance!

However, I was pleased to have a permanent place of my own —

even though I did have great difficulty getting used to the smallness of the room and to the strict house rules that were in force there.

On the third day, I went out to buy a small carpet in a shop that was located on the second floor of a downtown building. I was on my way up when a stair rod holding the runner in place came undone. I lost my footing, fell down the stairs, and broke my left leg in two places.

It was not an auspicious beginning, but it turned out to be a blessing in a way. Now I was forced to stay in my room with my splinted and plastered leg, and reflect on what I was going to do with myself once the leg had healed. One thing was certain. I was too young to be in a home for the elderly, and too active to do nothing. Then, quite unexpectedly, a solution presented itself.

On a particularly nasty, cold and rainy day, I received my first visit from the Mother Superior. She asked if I spoke Malay — which of course I did. She then asked me if I would be willing to become a translator at the Carita Center, where the staff had great difficulty dealing with non-Dutch speaking repatriates from Indonesia.

I gratefully seized the opportunity offered. Firstly, because I desperately longed for contact with people from Indonesia, and secondly, because I wanted again to earn my own living.

Since I could neither stand nor walk, the director of the center had to come over to discuss the job offer. However, it soon became clear that it was a non-paying job; I would have to work as a volunteer. He could look into the matter — he himself favored paying me a good salary — but then, he warned, I might not get the war widow's pension that I had applied for.

I reflected on this briefly. I would soon be 65 and, as a salaried person, would probably be forced to retire in favor of a younger person. It was not worth jeopardizing my pension for. I wanted the job as the work matched well with what I had been doing in the Moluccas — so I accepted to be a volunteer.

Arrangements were made to wheel me from my room to the center on a daily basis. I was soon deeply involved with mostly middle-aged Indo-European and Indonesian women, widows of former KNIL soldiers, who had never spoken a word of Dutch and who just couldn't cope with this strange society.

Now, all of a sudden, there was someone to whom they could open up in their own language; someone who didn't need many words to understand their problems; someone who consoled and encouraged them; someone who, just like that, had become a "grandma" to them all.

Needless to say, the work and the contact with these people made me happy again, and it helped, immensely, to ease the long wait for the arrival of better times.

After my leg had healed, I was approached by the local Child Welfare Council and later appointed guardian for several children. Some lived with their family; others in foster homes.

This brought some diversity to my life. I now met regularly with the Juvenile Bureau, and since it shared quarters with the Aliens Police — where I still had to report every week — I quickly became one of the family!

After staying nineteen months in my small cubicle at the Caritas Home, my deliverance arrived — in three rapid steps.

First, the Aliens Police told me that my weekly visits had come to an end: I was once again a Dutch citizen, as officially announced in the Legal Gazette No. 247-248 of 1959.

Next came a call from the City Hall, asking me to drop in and fill out an application form for my Old Age Pension.

And then, wonder of wonders, came a call from the Housing Department: would I please stop by and pick up the keys to a brand new apartment! This last one was largely due to the intercession of my friends at the Sittard Police Station.

Incredibly, these three calls came on the same day!

My mind reeled; I couldn't believe my luck. I was finally free again: free from the stringent house-rules at the Caritas Home; free from the weekly visits to the Aliens Police, and, most importantly, free from having to depend on the kind financial assistance of others. Now I could look after myself again!

I then thought about contacting the Leprosy Institute in Lyon about the course I had planned to take, but my doctor stopped me in my tracks. In view of my recurring attacks of malaria, he strongly advised me *not* to return to the tropics. The clincher, he said, was that the undernourishment in the Japanese internment camp had permanently affected my health.

After a long internal struggle, I gave up. In my heart I had always kept the hope of eventually returning to Ternate, but the dice were loaded against me.

I wrote to the Ministry of Social Affairs in Jakarta to tender my resignation. By return mail, I was told that they would consider the matter upon my return. The letter also said I would be eligible for a pension — in fact, far better than I had expected, because included in the calculation were the many years which, as a private citizen, I had devoted to the care of the sick, even in the remote *kampungs* of the Moluccas.

However, I decided not to go. My health was one consideration; but the outstanding order for my arrest was the other. That had not been resolved yet.

A third consideration was an invitation I received from the Pelita Institute to become their volunteer representative throughout the Province of Limburg. As traveling expenses would be reimbursed, I eagerly accepted. It was an opportunity to once again do useful work.

By this time, most of the repatriates had already left the contract-hostels in the large cities and had settled in homes that were scattered over a wide area. Traveling by bus, by train, and on foot, I thus got to know many of beautiful Limburg's smaller villages..

For the repatriates, "Pelita" soon became a household word. I loved this work and it filled my days in a unique way.

Some time later, as I was casually chatting with my priest about my experiences in Kampili, he asked:

"Did you have spiritual guidance there?"

"Yes, Father, we had Father Beltjens."

"Well, we should give him a call and say hello," he suggested.

"That would be an expensive phone call, Father, because he is on the island of Flores in Indonesia."

"Not at all! He is half an hour away in Heerlen, where he is rector of the school for midwives."

And so, once again, I got in touch with that warm and humorous Pater P. Beltjens, who, after Kampili, had continued teaching physics and mathematics on Flores. Trained in Hollywood in the art of making films, he had just returned from a seven-month stay in Japan, where he had made a number of films on the missionary work there.

It was wonderful to hear his voice.

As we chatted, he said, "Do you know that there is another Kampili inmate living close to you? It is Mrs. Nini Smits-van Dranen."

He spoke a little more about her difficult personal circumstances, saying that she badly needed to move and make a fresh start. And so it happened that Nini later moved to Sittard into an apartment close to mine, and became my faithful companion and co-worker in the work of Pelita.

\*\*\*\*

While in Sittard, I ran into a Mr. Pinkster, a former KNIL sergeant, who was now employed by the Municipal Traffic and Water Department. From him I finally learned the details of how John had died.

The senior officer in the camp had received orders to provide 50 POWs for a certain project. He couldn't find enough able-bodied men and so, not wanting to get into trouble with the Japanese, he had taken some people from the sick bay. Among them was John, whose body was badly swollen from beri-beri.

On the site, John worked a while before collapsing. The Japanese guard then walked over and beat him with a club until he was dead.

Mr. Pinkster was one of two people assigned to carry John's bloated body back to camp, and said: "I certainly was not pleased having to do that. Your husband was unbelievably heavy with all that fluid which had accumulated in his body."

I was overwrought for many days — as much by the news as by the callous way in which it was told to me.

### Endnotes
[1] Unbeknownst to them, a massive exodus from all parts of Indonesia had started around this time. By the end of December, some 10,000 Netherlanders had left Indonesia, on orders of Sukarno.
[2] *Maréchaussée* — a French word adopted by the Dutch for their national (originally mounted) police force.

# IBU MALUKU

## CHAPTER 49

*Reconciliation*
*Japan, May, 1961*

In mid-March, Pater Beltjens, Nini Smits and I went to Antwerp to see a Japanese movie about Kampili, *Shiroi Hada to Kiiroi Taicho* (*White Skin and Yellow Commandant*), which had its Belgian debut at the Ciné Paris, a small theater on the Keizerlei. The movie was dubbed in French, and had Flemish/Dutch subtitles.

I learned later that it was based on the book by that name written by Masao Kikuchi, who had been attached to the Administration Section of the Japanese Navy, presumably in Makassar. As I also learned later, the author's intent had been to show that humanity can and does flourish in the midst of the hatred and bitterness wrought by war.

As to the movie, well, that was another story. The lurid publicity of the theater should have warned us of what was to come. When we came out, we were thoroughly disgusted. Perhaps five percent of the movie had some truth in it; the rest was pure fabrication.

It portrayed the camp commandant as a knight in shining armor who had saved thousands of disorganized, disoriented, sex-crazed women from themselves and from being dishonored by Japanese soldiers!

Perhaps the movie had been made to fill a Japanese craving for nobility, for something that would show their military in a more favorable light — but for us, the prisoners, it was highly unflattering, to put it mildly.

Back in Heerlen, Pater Beltjens contacted a Flemish journalist and gave him his opinion about the movie, in the hope that he would bring the real story to the public. One thing led to another, and the end result was that the movie was banned in the Netherlands.

Six weeks later, I received a letter from Mrs. Joustra, one of the former leaders of Kampili. It came as a total surprise, since we had never been close during our internment. Much later I was to find out that her letter was directly linked to the movie we had just seen.

She had received a letter from Kampili's former commandant, Tadashi Yamaji, in which he invited her and two friends, on behalf of the Fuji Telecasting Company, to come to Tokyo — all expenses paid — and appear with him on a TV show called *Higashi wa Higashi* (East is East), a program that may be likened to the U.S. series "This is your Life".

"... I eagerly wish to realize my dream of you visiting Japan," wrote Yamaji in English. "As you recall, this has been my long-cherished desire. I have often talked in Campiri [Kampili] about how wonderful it would be to show you my country.

"If you can be with us in April," he continued, "it will be the prettiest season. Japan will be full of cherry blossoms." And in a postscript, he added:

"Among those three who are invited, please include either Mrs. van Diejen or Mrs. Fuhrie, if possible, thank you. Enclosed please find a copy of the letter from Fuji-TV addressed to me ..."

The attached letter, signed by Publicity Director Goshu Nishimura, explained that Fuji-TV wanted to bring out Yamaji's exemplary leadership and promote understanding and co-operation between nations.

In her letter, Mrs. Joustra explained that she could not accept the invitation. She had a broken wrist that was not mending well; it would make traveling difficult. Would I go in her place? (I concluded later that the real reason was not physical, but political: since she was a civil servant working on a World War II documentary, she preferred not to appear in a foreign television program where that war would be discussed.)

My first impulse was to decline, but the letter from Fuji-TV made me reconsider.

One reason was that a TV interview would provide a unique opportunity to tell the Japanese people about Kampili *and* about other camps, where the behavior of the Japanese had been anything but exemplary. I recognized that my views might cause some embarrassment to the Japanese, but they were obviously willing to risk it.

Another reason for going was that this trip would enable me to visit the grave of my husband in Hong Kong. After the war, John's remains had been transferred from Mashio Lang on Hainan to the English Military Cemetery in Hong Kong. I had never before had the opportunity to visit his grave; now the possibility existed to stop there on my return from Tokyo.

After discussing it with Father Beltjens, I decided to accept the invitation. I wrote Mrs. Joustra about my decision and asked if she knew the whereabouts of Willy Fuhrie, now surely married to my late husband's nephew.

I also fired off a letter to Mr. Goshu Nishimura in which I accepted the invitation, and asked him if he could arrange for the participation of former Lieutenant Nogami, who had, from February till July 1946, been interpreter for the Japanese soldiers who had worked on Mon Désir.

# IBU MALUKU

By return mail, Mrs. Joustra wrote that she had checked with an official at the Ministry of External Affairs, who said he could not forbid our participation in a TV program, but considered it undesirable! Mrs. Joustra also wrote that Willy Fuhrie was just about to open a *pension* — a boarding house — and would, therefore, not be able to go.

It was too late to back out now. I had already accepted and I would go alone, if I had to. At the last minute, however, I found someone who had never been in an internment camp and, thus, had no axe to grind. Her name was Mrs. Hellebrekers, a supervisor in a fashion store in Sittard.

On April 24, Mrs. Joustra came to see us off at Amsterdam's Schiphol Airport. She gave me a series of photographs of Kampili that I had never seen before, and asked us also to take with us a present for Yamaji: a thick treatise on the war in the former Dutch East Indies that was hot off the press.

At the ticket counter I learned that KLM had changed our route. Instead of flying over Rome, we would be flying over Iceland and Alaska, and would, therefore, arrive in Tokyo much earlier than expected. I tried to warn Fuji-TV about the change in arrival time, but couldn't get hold of anyone there.

We took off at 7:30 p.m. in an airplane that was full of Dutch military personnel destined for New Guinea. The crew was Australian.

During the stop-over in Iceland, I caught a cold, and by the time we reached Tokyo, I had lost my voice and could only communicate with note-pad and pencil.

After we left the plane at Tokyo's Haneda airport, I looked back with a heavy heart at the airplane that would soon leave for New Guinea. How I wished I could be on it.

There was no one to meet us at the terminal, of course, since we were not expected until several hours later. A KLM attendant called Yamaji for us and contacted him at the trucking company he owned. But Yamaji thought there was some mix-up, and refused to come to the airport unless he could hear my voice on the telephone!

I didn't have any voice, of course, but I did manage to mutter a few barely-audible Malayan words into the horn that had the desired affect. Yamaji said he would arrive in about an hour.

Mrs. Hellebrekers and I installed ourselves comfortably in a corner from where we had a good view of people coming into the terminal, and I wondered if I would recognize Yamaji. Sixteen years had passed since I had seen him being taken away by Australian MP's.

When 45 minutes had passed, I carefully looked over every man who entered the hall and finally spotted someone who looked like Yamaji. He threw a quick glance in our direction but didn't see us, so he turned and walked away. I hurriedly got up, ran after him and grabbed his arm before the crowd could swallow him up.

Sure enough, it was he: neatly dressed in a civilian suit in which, of course, I had never seen him. He was forty-seven or forty-eight now, and somewhat heavier than I remembered. However, he recognized me right away, and blurted out:

"*Bigi mana di sini* — what are you doing here?"

I pointed to my throat to signal my inability to speak; then pulled out the map to show him that we had flown a different route and, consequently, arrived earlier than expected.

"*Tida bisa*! That's not possible." he said obstinately.

"Well, it is! I'm no ghost!" I wrote.

"*Ah, so des!* — so it is!" he muttered. Then taking charge of the situation, he excused himself to call the Fuji-TV people. A moment later he told us that they would arrive in a few hours — Haneda airport being quite a distance from Tokyo. With them would be a few people from the association "East is East", who were the sponsors of the show by the same name.

Three hours later, Mrs. Hellebrekers and I were introduced to the gentlemen, and I was pleased to find my former translator, Lieutenant Nogami, among them.

On the way to the hotel, we stopped off at a doctor to have my throat checked. He cleaned my throat with something similar to a brush that one uses to clean the glass bell of an oil lamp! I was neither impressed nor amused. It was distasteful and it hurt. But I just hoped it would do some good!

Our hosts then took us to one of the biggest and most modern hotels in Japan, called "New Japan". A silent elevator whisked us up to the ninth floor, where we entered a large air-conditioned room, which had all the modern conveniences, and more. It quite overwhelmed us.

The gentlemen suggested that we take a hot bath and rest for a while. At 9:00 that evening they would pick us up for an intimate reception that would take place in a small room of the hotel. There, we would also meet our official translator, Mrs. Oya, the wife of a professor at the University of Tokyo.

A luxurious bath did wonders for us. We then dropped into bed and slept two short hours before having to get ready for the reception.

At 9:00 p.m. Mrs. Oya came up to introduce herself. She spoke fluent Dutch and made a pleasant impression on us both.

She explained that nothing was scheduled for the next morning, and asked what our plans were. I asked her if she would take us, first thing in the morning, to the Dutch Embassy.

"Why?" she asked, perhaps feeling that her qualifications as translator were being questioned. "That won't be necessary."

"Yes," I assured her, "it is necessary." I wanted to consult the Ambassador on what I intended to say at the upcoming TV-interview, but did not feel obliged to explain this to her. With a nonplused look on her face, she agreed and then took us downstairs where the reception committee was waiting.

Besides the directors of Fuji-TV and the "East is East" Association, there were two dozen press-photographers. As flash bulbs popped, we received large bouquets of flowers and then listened to a welcome speech, duly translated by Mrs. Oya.

During the evening, it slowly became clear that our invitation to come to Tokyo to appear on the TV program was directly linked to the movie about Kampili that we had seen in Antwerp.

When the formalities were over, our hosts took us to a small but exquisite dining room where we enjoyed our first Japanese meal. The lobster dish, in particular, was delicious.

At 11:30, our hosts escorted us back to our room, where we presented them with our gifts: mostly books about the Netherlands, famous Dutch bonbons and eau de Cologne. It was almost one o'clock in the morning when we finally stretched out to enjoy our first night on Japanese soil.

\* \* \* \*

At 9:30 the next morning, Mrs. Hellebrekers, Mrs. Oya, Mr. Yamasaki of Fuji-TV and I were at the Netherlands Embassy, where Ambassador N. A. J. de Voogd received us politely, but with little warmth.

The reason for his reservedness became clear when he said: "I have been requested to ask you not to go ahead with the television interview."

He did not specify who had made the request; nor did he mention (as I later discovered) that he had received an ominous telegram from NIBEG (an association of ex-internees in Amsterdam) which had been addressed to me.

"No problem," I wrote on my note pad, "I shall cancel the interview, but must ask you then to refund Fuji-TV for my travel expenses. I have no money and I do not wish them to be duped."

"What exactly is the purpose of your visit," he asked, changing his approach.

"To make clear what did happen in those camps, and to correct the negative image created by a Japanese movie about our particular camp. I have drafted two speeches, and have discussed them with our former camp priest. He thought that one draft was too sharp, but gave his blessing to the second one."

"Do you have those drafts with you?" asked Mr. de Voogd.

I nodded, pulled the typed speeches out of my bag, and handed them over.

He read the two drafts pensively, and then picked the *sharper* one as being the *better* one of the two.

"Is it your intention to read this in front of the press?" he inquired.

I nodded, and wrote: "What else would they expect of me, except to talk about the camps?"

"And your companion?" he asked, looking at Mrs. Hellebrekers.

"Never been in a camp," I jotted down, "She's my impartial witness."

His face relaxed a little.

"Would you be amenable to making a few changes to the text?"

"I am open to suggestions," I wrote, "but would then want them retyped. I don't want to risk getting confused in front of the cameras."

"I will have a typewriter and some Embassy stationary delivered to your hotel," he said, and then started to make notes on the draft he favored. When he finished, he looked relieved. He handed me back the papers, cordially escorted us to the exit, and wished me good luck. It was 11 o'clock.

We made a small detour to see some of the city sights, passing the white walls of the Imperial Palace with its many entrances, and arrived half an hour later at our hotel.

Someone from Fuji-TV met us in the princely lobby, and asked us to hurry and get dressed for the official reception that would start at 13:00 hours.

As we changed hurriedly, another messenger arrived: there would be an unscheduled press conference before the reception. I was not exactly thrilled about that.

When we arrived downstairs, we came face to face with a horde of 50 journalists, who — as became clear later — had assembled in response to a telegram from the NIBEG which had been leaked to the world press.

It may have been embarrassing for my hosts, but this press conference gave me the chance to speak openly about the dozens of other camps in the former Dutch East Indies, which — in contrast to the under-the-circumstances reasonably good Kampili — had been places of abject misery, incredible brutality, hunger and death.

At first I wrote down my answers, but slowly — perhaps prompted by my eagerness to communicate — my voice started to function again, hoarsely at first but more smoothly toward the end.

This press conference was attended by my former translator, Lieutenant Nogami, the former Japanese priest of Makassar, Mr. Nakamura, Mrs. Oya of course — who handled the translation — and Mr. Yamaji, who sat squirming beside me and elbowed me a few times in an attempt to dampen my frankness. By contrast, the journalists cheered me on with an unequivocal "yes" when I asked them if they really wanted to know what had happened. And so I let them have it.

I concluded with the plea, "If, God forbid, there is another conflict in the future, please leave women and children out of it!"

There were many questions. When one tough one came up, Yamaji said: "*Jangan menjawab* — don't answer," and extended his arm to restrain me. But I was riding high and slapped his hand. The journalists roared their approval, and I answered the question without holding back.

I was drained of energy when the press conference ended.

An American journalist from Associated Press sauntered over, and said:

"You probably think that there has been a leak at your Embassy."

"I think nothing of the sort," I answered defensively.

"Well, I can tell you that we did *not* get our story from that source. It is the NIBEG people who released the contents of the telegram to the press themselves."

"I have yet to see the telegram you are talking about," I said.

"You will," he answered, "but I don't have a copy to show you."

He then pulled a piece of paper out of his jacket, and handed it to me.

"I know that after the TV interview, you will be making a trip to Kyoto, Osaka and Nara. If, on the way, you see anything that looks suspicious, give one of our people on this list a call. They will know what to do and will be able to help you."

I thanked him with a mixture of surprise and concern — he knew more about the upcoming schedule than I did — and watched him join the other departing journalists.

I then turned toward my hosts, somewhat worried about their reaction to what had just happened. It was clear that they were bewildered. This press conference had not been on their agenda. However, in unison they said they were glad it was finished, and now they could proceed with their own program!

But the reception was somewhat of an anticlimax. After the usual welcoming speech, we were introduced to other members of "East is East". Then they played the "Wilhelmus", the national anthem of the Netherlands, followed by the Japanese anthem. Everyone stood at attention and listened respectfully.

A charming children's choir sang and danced, and was followed by a little girl who performed a classical dance that dates back to 1720. Afterwards, our hosts presented us with two dolls, dressed also in the costume of that period.

Two little dancers then stepped forward to offer us magnificent bouquets of white lilies and red carnations. There was a coming and going of VIP's. We shook hands, bowed, and accepted the business cards that were offered. Meanwhile, the music played, the little girls danced and the guests partook of the cold buffet that had been spread over many tables. There was no hard liquor: only sherry, port, coca-cola, lemonade, and a green, somewhat bitter tea.

Then Mr. Yamaji's entire family arrived: his wife, dressed in a magnificent kimono; his daughter of eight, and son of six; his father-in-law, aunt, uncle, brother and two sisters-in-law.

Mrs. Yamaji, especially, was very emotional, thanking me profusely for having forgiven her husband for his misdeeds of the past and for having accepted him again as a *bona fide* member of the human race!

I also met former Sergeant Okashima, aide to Commandant Yamaji in Kampili, whose bashfulness had earned him the nickname of "Daantje" (Danny Boy) by the Dutch, and "Sweet 16" by the Americans and English. He now earned his living as a tailor.

At one point, Father Nakamura and Father Kobayashi came over to congratulate me for my spirited performance at the press conference, saying that I had spoken the truth.

By this time I was extremely tired and longed for the reception to end, which it finally did around 7:00 pm.

Our room resembled a flower garden. The chamber maids had placed the flowers everywhere, even in the bathroom. We had barely had the time to freshen up when there was a knock on the door.

It was Mr. Yamasaki of Fuji-TV, who invited us to go to the largest theater in Tokyo, the Kukasai Theater, also called the Tokyo Odori, after which we would have dinner at a very special Chinese restaurant.

My head was spinning, my throat was sore, and a nasty headache was developing. I would have much preferred to go straight to bed, but after the embarrassment created by my fiery words at the press conference, I didn't have the heart to refuse. So I assured Mr. Yamasaki that we were, indeed, looking forward to an enjoyable evening.

We had half an hour to rest and get ready, and then at 8:00 we left the hotel with Mrs. Oya, Messrs. Nogami, Yamasaki, Okashima and Yamaji, and were driven to the Asakusa district.

The Kukasai theater is immense. It is lit by more than 10,000 lamps, holds 3,300 spectators, and has a 36-meter high stage measuring 48 by 90 meters. Every year it presents four different shows which involve more than 500 actors — all women.

Places had been reserved for us in the front row. Many seats behind us were already occupied by uniformed school children, who, so I learned, would have to submit a written report on what they had seen and heard, *and* write a poem about it.

The play had already started when we arrived. It dealt with princess Akemi and her loved one, the sculptor Harokiko, who was in strict seclusion, having been given the task of sculpting a statue of Buddha. In his quiet isolation, the sculptor forgets his beloved Akemi, which drives her insane. She seeks to destroy him, setting fire to the temple that houses the statue, and both perish in the flames. Only the statue survives.

Other performances followed, including some Western-inspired dances like the can-can, and a shortened version of Japan's famous flower festival dance, the Hanamatsuri, that was danced in the traditional costumes. (The unabridged version takes a full 20 hours.) Spectacle 15, during which all the artists appeared on the stage, concluded this superb show.

At 11:00 we emerged from the theater and admired the imposing and very beautiful neon signs of Tokyo. In two cars we drove to the famous Dai Hanten restaurant, where we sampled the very best that Chinese cuisine can offer.

It was past 1 o'clock when we returned to our luxurious hotel room, where we found that the Embassy had indeed delivered the promised typewriter and stationary. There was also a letter from the Ambassador, which read:

"I have the honor to inform you that this afternoon a telegram was delivered to the Embassy, sent from Amsterdam by the Secretary of the NIBEG, Mr. van Ketel, with the following contents:

PLEASE TRANSMIT TO MRS. VAN DIEJEN ROEMEN THE FOLLOWING CABLE:

NIBEG, WITH ITS THOUSANDS OF FEMALE EX-INTERNEES FROM THE JAPANESE CAMPS, DEMANDS THAT WHEN YOU ARE INTERVIEWED BEFORE THE JAPANESE TV, YOU RECALL EMPATHICALLY THE MISERABLE CONDITIONS FROM WHICH

THE DUTCH INTERNEES SUFFERED IN GENERAL. STOP. THE BAD TREATMENT OF THE INTERNEES WAS ACKNOWLEDGED BY THE JAPANESE GOVERNMENT THROUGH THE PAYMENT OF THE JAPANESE SMART MONEY. WE THINK IT APPROPRIATE TO WARN YOU OF UNPLEASANT REACTIONS FROM THE INTERNEES ON YOUR RETURN TO THE NETHERLANDS.

CENTRAL COMMITTEE NIBEG, VAN KETEL, GENERAL SECRETARY.

The letter, signed by his Excellency N. A. J. de Voogd, was dated April 27, although, judging from what the journalist had told me, it had probably arrived when we were still waiting at Haneda airport for Yamaji to pick us up.

Why the Ambassador didn't mention it when we met in his office has remained a mystery. Perhaps I would never have seen that telegram, if the NIBEG had not released it to the press, thereby forcing the Ambassador's hand.

How the NIBEG got to know about my trip to Japan was another unsolved mystery, but I suspected that Mrs. Joustra, or her contacts at the Ministry, had been indiscreet. They were the only ones who knew about this trip, except Pater Beltjens who was, of course, above suspicion.

I was too exhausted to think straight, and decided that this thoughtless telegram and the threat it contained would just have to wait till the morning.

\*\*\*\*

The next day, April 28, we slept until 9:00. After a hearty breakfast, I sat down at the typewriter and used the Embassy stationary to redraft my speech for the upcoming TV interview.

At 12:30, we had a sumptuous lunch, and were driven to the Fuji studio, where we met His Eminence, Paul Yamaguchi, Archbishop of Nagasaki. Mrs. Hellebrekers and I knelt in front of him and received his blessing.

This brought back the memory of his visit to Kampili on March 31, 1944, when the war was still in full swing. Enemy or not, he was a Bishop, and his position held a special significance for us Catholics. I had also knelt in front of him then to receive his blessing, and had been slapped in the face afterwards by Yamaji, who angrily asked why I had never shown him similar deference. I reminded Yamaji of this event in front of the Bishop, who broke out into laughter as Yamaji's face became flushed.

After another short session with Associated Press about the NIBEG telegram, we hurried to the studio and at 2:30 sharp started the TV interview, during which Mrs. Oya translated the contents of my rewritten speech.

At 7:30, we were back in the hotel. Our room was still full of flowers.

We dined with our hosts on the terrace near a beautiful water fountain, during which Mr. Yamasaki told us that we would leave the next day by train for the old imperial city of Kyoto — which I already knew from the American Associated Press journalist.

It was past midnight when we returned to our room. Although exhausted, I did notice something I hadn't seen before. Half hidden amidst the flowers stood an attaché case. Where had it come from? Who had left it there, and when? And ... why?

A chilling thought entered my mind, but I quickly rejected it. The NIBEG would not ... surely ... or would they? I drew up close and listened. Not a sound. With my heart beating wildly, I carefully opened the latches, not allowing them to spring back by themselves. Then, slowly, ever so slowly, I opened the case a crack, and peered inside. I couldn't see anything suspicious and so opened it up a little more. I could only see a large, thick envelope which I gingerly fished out of the still almost-closed case. I opened the loose flap and took out the contents. It was a stack of publicity photos and fliers about the Kampili film which I had seen in Antwerp. No note. No explanation. Nothing!

The mystery of who left it, when, and why would never be solved.

Relieved, however, I dropped into bed and slept like a rock.

\* \* \* \*

At 9:30 the following morning, we joined Mrs. Oya, Mr. Yamasaki and Mr. Yamaji, and, on the way to the station, became trapped in a gigantic traffic jam.

Small wonder. It was April 29, the 60th birthday of Emperor Hirohito, and hundreds of thousands of people, dressed in traditional clothes, were in the streets on their way to the palace to wish their Emperor a happy birthday.

Our car progressed very slowly but, luckily, we made it to the station in time. To our surprise, a special salon car had been coupled to the locomotive for our exclusive use. It contained every imaginable luxury.

Tokyo being a massive city, it took quite a while before we entered the countryside, which was resplendent with cherry blossoms. The sun was out, the air was clear, so we had a splendid view of magnificent Mount Fuji, while we enjoyed an excellent Western style lunch.

After spending two days visiting Kyoto and Nara, meeting swarms of journalists at every turn, we stayed overnight at the Osaka Grand Hotel. The next day, May 1, we encountered a fiery anti-American labor demonstration on the way to the station. A similar demonstration was simultaneously taking place in Tokyo, but by the time we arrived there in the afternoon, everything had quieted down.

And so we returned to the New Japan hotel, this time to be given rooms on the seventh floor. The decor was now in mauve, in contrast to our previous rooms which had been entirely in gold and silver.

There was only time to freshen up a little and get dressed for the next event. Yamaji had invited us to spend our last evening at his home. We were driven through narrow winding roads, past small wooden dream houses and flower gardens, and arrived at his residence that was located in a modest district.

The whole family — Yamaji, his wife and their two young children — were dressed in kimono and stood at the entrance, bowing deeply. We took off our shoes and were escorted to the dining room, which was enlarged by pushing aside the sliding walls.

In the middle of the room stood a low, lacquered table, with pillows all around it for us to sit on. We took our seats with as much grace as our Western legs would allow.

On the table stood a hibachi, and a large flat dish with all the ingredients, freshly cut, to make the famous sukiyaki, which Yamaji himself prepared for us and for his son — the female members of the family did not join us. We managed exceedingly well with the chop-sticks, and really enjoyed the meal.

After dinner we toured the house, and I recognized many artifacts that could only have come from Holland. Yamaji pointed to each one of them, saying: *"Dari Nyonya Joustra"* — from Mrs. Joustra. They had obviously been much in contact with each other. I also learned that Father Beltjens had been a guest here, while he was filming in Japan.

After being shown the unique communal bathroom, we were taught the secrets of how to wear a kimono. Mrs. Hellebrekers and I each received a kimono with a beautiful obi, and then we bid the family an emotional farewell.

The night would be short, because it was 2:00 am when we finally went to bed.

\*\*\*\*

May 2 was our last day in Tokyo. First we revisited the Ambassador of the Netherlands, who was extremely amiable this time. I handed him a copy of my response to the NIBEG telegram, which I had written in the Osaka Grand Hotel. I told him that I had also sent a copy to the Ministry of External Affairs in the Hague.

His Excellency was pleased with the reaction of the press, and expressed the hope that the TV interview to be broadcast on May 6 would be equally favorable.

He was especially pleased to have received an invitation from Fuji-TV to attend the first screening, with their assurance that if there was anything disagreeable in the presentation, Fuji-TV would alter the video in accordance with his wishes.

He then thanked us for our co-operation, and wished us a good journey and a safe return to the Netherlands.

We left the Embassy and drove to the Fuji-TV building, where we would lunch with the managers and then, officially, take our leave.

On the way, Yamaji gave us the first eight photographs of the TV interview. Several hundreds had been taken, and Mr. Yamasaki promised he would put them in an album and send them to me.

The reception at Fuji-TV was heartwarming. We had a chance to speak with all those who had participated in the TV interview, and then sat down for lunch with members of the executive. The president of "East is East" joined us later, as did Mr. Takaho Ito, president of Shiseido, well-known for its perfumes and soaps, who presented us with a priceless box of cosmetics.

The beautiful dolls that we had received during the Fuji-TV reception were carefully packaged for us, and then we left with a warm *"sayonara"* — until we meet again.

We still had three hours to shop and to see something of the city on our own. Up to this time, we always had been in the spot light. Everything we had said had been translated word for word. Every trip, every visit had been pre-planned and was recorded by camera. Now we were alone with Mrs. Oya, who spoke Dutch very well indeed. No further translation was required which gave us a wonderful feeling of being free again.

Mrs. Oya took us to the well-known pearl cultivators, Miki Moto, owned by her father-in-law. The factory made a disorderly impression, but the necklaces, rings, earrings and bracelets that came out of there were exquisite.

Time passed quickly, and we soon took off for Haneda airport. Our flight to Hong Kong would leave at 4:00. It was a good thing that we had allowed ourselves extra time, because once again, we got caught in a horrendous traffic jam. It took us a long time before we were out of the city that has the dubious distinction of having the greatest number of traffic accidents in the world.

At Haneda Airport, a surprise awaited us. Several Fuji-TV managers, Messrs. Nishmura, Yamaji, Okashima (alias "Dannyboy"), Kamasaki, several beautifully dressed ladies, and members from the children's choir of "East is East" were standing there with magnificent floral bouquets, to bid us goodbye.

Yukari Uehara, the little girl who had presented us with large bouquets during the TV interview, stepped forward to give me some photographs that she had taken herself. Mr. Nogami's daughter, Yukiko, then came forward to give us some embroidery that she had made.

After more pictures and another emotional farewell, we walked, loaded down with flowers and packages, to our departure gate, accompanied only by a sobbing Mrs. Oya.

A last handshake, and then we boarded our Pan American Airways plane bound for Hong Kong.

IBU MALUKU

# CHAPTER 50

### Two Farewells
*Hong Kong ... and Ternate, 1961 - 1978*

We took off at 4:00 p.m. and soon reached an altitude of 21,000 feet. More than an hour later we flew over Okinawa, where hundreds of thousands of soldiers had died during the last stages of World War II.

Then we passed over Taiwan — also called Formosa — where General Chiang Kaischek still ruled over some twelve million Chinese. At 7:30, the lights and huge neon signs of Hong Kong peered at us out of the darkness below, and half an hour later we were on the ground at Kowloon airport. The first stage of the journey home had been completed.

After custom formalities, we discovered that the excellent care of Fuji-TV had been extended to this city as well. A limousine of the Park Hotel was waiting for us, and after a 20-minute ride through the wide, neon-sign-lit streets of Kowloon, we arrived at this palatial hotel and, thankfully, went straight to bed.

The next day, we took a taxi to the harbor, boarded the ferry for Hong Kong, and then found another taxi for the one-hour ride to the Military Cemetery at Saiwan Bay, where John had been re-buried 15 years earlier. They had brought him here from Hainan, where he died on April 20, 1945 — only five short months before the end of the war.

The cemetery is beautifully sculpted into a hill, terrace by terrace. It is surrounded by other hills and looks out on the sparkling blue bay. In the distance are the dark green-blue mountains of the Chinese mainland.

I found the Dutch section, located on the lowest terrace of this field of honor. John's grave stood close to a high granite cross with an unsheathed sword chiseled on it.

I stood there, alone, for a long time recalling the many years of separation. At this moment, for the first time, the irrevocable finality of his death hit home.

The upright gravestone with his name carved under the national emblem of the Netherlands — the standing lion with the sword in its paw — told me what words never could. It was over: John would never come back. My mind had accepted it before; my heart, never — not until now. Here he rested amidst other Netherlanders, many of whose wives and children had been interned with me, first at Ambon, later at Kampili.

On all the graves blossomed beautiful red and yellow roses, gerberas and daisies. The different sections were delineated by blossoming *kembang sepatu* (hibiscus) and gardenia hedges.

We distributed the flowers we had received at Haneida airport over John's grave and the neighboring ones also — graves that would probably never be visited by a wife or a child.

Time had passed quickly; it was time to go.

I picked a few twigs from the hibiscus, in the hope that it would become a living memento of my visit here. Then I said a final goodbye, with total acceptance of the inevitable and full trust that we would be reunited. A brief prayer, and then I mounted the stairs to leave.

At the entrance stood a beautiful gate. In one of its pillars was an opening that contained a guest-book. I leafed through it and noticed how few Netherlanders had visited this field of honor. It motivated us to write our names in it, together with a few appreciative words. I did so with a deep gratitude in my heart for having been given the opportunity to come here.

We flew to Rome, stayed three days, and then returned to Amsterdam. As we went through customs, the customs officer asked if we were the ladies who had been on TV in Japan.

"Well, yes," I said, frowning.

"There is a rowdy crowd waiting for you outside," he said. "Follow me, please" and he took us down a deserted corridor leading away from the main exit, and brought us to a cab that was waiting for us. I thanked the customs officer, and after loading all our luggage and packages in the trunk, we left.

Throughout the trip home, I was deeply upset. First, because someone's indiscretion had caused our trip to become a public matter, and second, because the time of our arrival had been leaked to people who evidently acted first and thought later — if at all.

None of these people had bothered to find out what my motives were, or what had been said in Tokyo. My letter to NIBEG, in response to their rude and threatening telegram, was never answered.

Back in Sittard, it took a long time before I recovered from the often vicious attacks on me in the newspapers[1]. My conscience, however, was clear. In Tokyo, I had said nothing that would in any way damage the image of the Netherlands or diminish the suffering that had taken place during World War II.

\*\*\*\*

## IBU MALUKU

In Limburg Province, the repatriates were glad I was back and ready to continue with the Pelita Institute's work. Nini Smits moved from Heerlen to Sittard to join me in this work, and we became known as the "the Pelita Ladies".

We got along famously, became inseparable, and made many unforgettable trips throughout Europe and South Africa which gave our lives a new dimension.

In 1969, twenty-four years after the end of the hostilities in the Far East, a new law was enacted that granted benefits to victims of the war. Nini and I were recruited to find and to register the many civilians who had become destitute or in some way disadvantaged as a result of the war in the former Dutch East Indies.

Later, at our urging, several thousands of nuns, priests, and missionaries — whose needs had heretofore been left up to their Church — were included in the benefit program. They were spread all over the Netherlands. Finding and interviewing them required much research and travel, so we arranged for someone else to take over our work with the civilians in Limburg Province.

On March 20, 1974, my Pelita work was recognized: I was honored with a golden medal of the Order of Orange-Nassau. Two years later, when I turned 80, I felt the time had come to end my part in this important work.

Making this decision was extremely difficult, but the extensive traveling and the emotional pain from continually having to relive the war years had started to sap my energies, and so I reluctantly resigned.

On February 20, 1978, Pelita honored me with a golden medal of its own. I was pleased, of course, but the real reward for my work was the many friends I had made along the way. It is this continued friendship that has given substance and meaning to my later years. It is something for which I am extremely grateful.

* * * *

Throughout the years that I spent in the Netherlands, the Moluccas were never far from my mind. With the leprosarium and the orphanage on Ternate, I maintained a regular and impassioned correspondence, which often made me feel that I was still very much part of their lives.

Many times I had been asked to come and visit Ternate, but uncertainty about the status of the warrant for my arrest made me hesitate. I didn't want to expose myself to unnecessary risks at this stage in my life.

But as my correspondents in Ternate pointed out, the situation had changed in Indonesia. Sukarno had passed away, and his successor, General Suharto had different ideas. In fact, if I were to come, they would push for official exoneration from the charge of *lèse majesté* that I was supposed to have committed in Buli, when I refused Sukarno's request to go to New York and plead for the peaceful transfer of Dutch New Guinea to the Republic of Indonesia.

Everything was different now, my friends insisted. They pressed me to return, and celebrate one of my birthdays in the Sorofo Leprosarium in Ternate.

Dr. Tan, with whom I had worked harmoniously for so many years, offered me accommodation, and when word spread, many Mother Superiors whom I had known and who were now living in the Netherlands, offered me accommodation in Indonesia wherever they had a convent.

And so Nini and I decided to celebrate my 82nd birthday in Ternate, as a worthy conclusion to our co-operation.

On May 23, 1978, we left Schiphol Airport on a Boeing 747 of Singapore Airlines destined for Jakarta, full of expectations and a longing to visit again our beloved Indonesia!

It was a profoundly emotional trip. This is what Nini had to say about it:

\*\*\*\*

> Via Rome and Bahrein we arrived in Singapore, transferred to a plane from Garuda Airlines, and arrived late in the evening at Jakarta's Halim Airport.
>
> Two Ursuline nuns picked us up and drove us to their convent on Jalan Pos, where we were warmly received. We immediately felt at home, and were pleased we could stay here a week to get used again to the heat, and also to recover from the jet lag — after all, neither of us was getting any younger!
>
> At the invitation of the Mother Superior, on May 26 we visited the leper half-way house "Maria Fatima" at Tangerang. There were quite a number of *Ibu*'s ex-patients there, who were greatly surprised and delighted to see again the person who had been responsible for their recovery.
>
> One of them had become director of the center; another, the most mutilated one amongst them, had become head of the carpentry shop and furniture factory. Not having any legs, he was strapped to a dolly to get around, his head barely reaching the top of the workbenches. Neatly dressed and holding an attaché case under one arm, he recounted how *Ibu* had saved him and had taught him how to use his stiff and warped hands again, by exercising them in a bowl of warm water. He, the most rebellious among all the patients,

thereby became a human being again, and went on to become the community's architect and the boss of this factory. Proudly, he presented us with his printed business card as a memento of this success.

Sister Francisca showed us the other buildings. There was a cardboard factory, a poultry farm, a clothing factory and a hospital — in addition to the furniture shop we had just visited. All the work was done by former patients. Here, also, we encountered some ex-patients of *Ibu*, whose reunion with her was deeply touching.

It profoundly impressed me that the center allowed former lepers to regain a sense of self-worth and to earn their own bread, after having been cast out by the villages in which they lived.

On May 27 we visited the military cemetery, Menteng Pulo, at Jakarta, where, for the first time, I saw the grave of my father who had died in a Japanese internment camp in 1945.

At four o'clock on June 1, we left for Halim Airport (formerly Kemayoran Airport), and boarded an airplane of the *Merpati Nusantara* (Dove Indonesian) Airline that would take us to Makassar.

There we had a very long wait for the 9:15 am plane that would take us to Ambon. As the departure time got closer, we watched the clock with mounting alarm, wondering when the boarding announcement would be made. When it dawned on us that the automatic display unit was probably defective, we ran with an Indonesian fellow-traveler across the tarmac to the aged Fokker D29 that was already in motion for take-off.

Luckily the pilot saw us and stopped. Helping hands pulled us inside, and the door was barely closed when the aircraft roared on toward the end of the landing strip. We were already up in the air and looking down on the airport before we had found our seats!

After flying two hours, the aircraft developed engine trouble. Luckily, we were close to Ambon, and the pilot radioed Halong Airport — just in case. We slowly lost altitude and practically skimmed the water of Ambon Bay, but we landed safely amidst fire trucks and ambulances that had been put on alert. Phew! Were we glad to set foot on solid ground!

The Mother Superior of the Otto Luyck Center, accompanied by several nuns and a brother named Piet, was waiting for us at the gate. In a minibus, they took us to the medical center where we would stay for two nights.

We were warmly received by Father Rutgers, master builder,

artist, and assistant to the Bishop, Monseigneur Sol, who was on furlough in the Netherlands.

The next day, Father Rutgers drove us around in the Bishop's car over well-paved roads to various places of interest, and I wondered what went through *Ibu*'s mind as we did our sightseeing. It was here in Ambon that she had seen her husband John for the last time, and it was here, also, that Allied bombs had caused so many lives to be lost in the Tantui camp where she had been interned.

Very early the next day, Brother Piet drove us and two nuns to Halong Airport for a 7:15 a.m. flight of Merpati Airlines to Ternate. The plane was rather small as it could carry only fifteen passengers.

Waved at by the three missionaries, we took off, and soon delighted in seeing the paradise-like splendor of these islands of the Moluccas — the Spice Islands — that lay beneath us in the crystal-clear, light-blue sea with its famous aquatic gardens. How incredibly beautiful!

Around 9:00 am we landed on Ake Huda, the military airport of Ternate. Since we were supposed to arrive on the second daily flight two hours later, we didn't expect anyone to meet us there. So we were very surprised to see a crowd of ex-lepers standing at the gate. Longing to see their *Ibu*, they had been convinced that she would arrive on the very first flight; not for a moment had they expected otherwise. With arms outstretched, each one eager to be the first, they rushed towards us.

Tears flowed freely as *Ibu* and I shared their embraces. Their *Ibu*, their Mother was home again! Words cannot possibly describe the emotion of that moment. *Ibu* was pulled hither and yon, and everyone wanted to capture her attention.

"*Ibu*, listen to this ..."

"We can go everywhere now!"

"We don't have to stay in the hospital any more!"

"We do like normal people!"

"*Ibu*, this is my wife, you remember her!"

"*Ibu*, this is my son ... my daughter ... and they are healthy!"

"Listen to this ... you must know, *Ibu* ..."

Poor *Ibu* was short on eyes and ears. All the news had to be told; all questions for advice had to be asked. Who better than *Ibu* would know what should be done!

She had been away 20 years, but it felt as if she had just returned from a mere week-long *tournée*.

More people squeezed into the reception hall that had become too small to hold them all. They were the orphans, now grown up and married. All told how they now had good jobs, and how they had followed *Ibu*'s counsel given so many years ago, or in later years by correspondence. It was the most moving reception I have ever witnessed, the most beautiful reception that *Ibu* Maluku could have been given!

For a healthy person like myself, who had never experienced their misery, it was difficult to imagine what these people had gone through. I looked at the faces of these, *Ibu*'s most beloved children who, banished from their communities and facing death in agonizing isolation, had been saved and brought back as happy, productive and self-reliant members of their society. To me, it seemed close to being a miracle.

*Ibu* herself seemed to take it all in her stride. Quietly, she sat among her children, listening with undivided attention, or giving advice, or praising them for their accomplishments. The joy, courage, enthusiasm and trust that radiated from their faces made a deep and lasting impression on me.

At eleven, the official welcoming committee arrived at the airport: it included *Ibu* Boki (daughter of the Sultan of Bachan and daughter-in-law of the former Sultan of Ternate); Dr. Tan and his wife, the Mother Superior, Sister Aldegonda, and Sister Iviolata, who arrived out of breath on a bicycle.

All were surprised, and disappointed, that we had arrived earlier, and decided there was no sense now in going through with the carefully planned reception. The ex-lepers and the orphans had clearly stolen the show and their shining faces showed they knew it.

We were taken to Dr. Tan's residence and shown to a separate bungalow, close to the main house, where we would be staying.

For the next two days we received old friends and the people that streamed into Ternate from the surrounding islands. We also met all the newcomers to the leprosarium and the orphanage: each came up to admire *Ibu*, to be admired in turn, and to receive a hug from this *Oma* (Grandmother) from Holland.

And so the sixth of June arrived: the day for which the people of Ternate had prepared so long — the day of *Ibu*'s 82nd birthday.

Very early in the morning a group of adults and children came to escort us past an honor guard of Scouts into the church, where they offered us a seat on the front bench.

The priest, a native of the Kei Islands, celebrated a solemn High Mass, and brought us to tears with a long, touching tribute to *Ibu*

*Maluku*, in which he summarized all that she had done for her suffering fellow men in the Moluccas.

After the service, the Scouts stood again at attention, as members of the organizing committee led us to a decorated car that would take us to the Leprosarium, where the festivities of the day would be held.

In front of the richly embellished gate, two poles held up a huge banner, proclaiming: "Welcome honored guests from the Netherlands, *Ibu* van Diejen-Roemen and *Ibu* Smits-van Dranen".

When our luxurious car arrived, a loud cheer arose from the assembled officials, lepers and children, all waving little flags and colorful balloons high in the air. Helpful hands reached out to help us get out, and no sooner had we straightened up than the Director of the Leprosarium solemnly hung a garland of beautiful orchids around our necks and bid us a warm welcome.

We entered through the gate into the large yard of the Leprosarium. To the left and right were numerous bungalows where the patients lived. Each one was festively decorated for the occasion.

We entered the big, exquisitely decorated hall where once again we were given a place of honor under another welcome banner. The officials sat down beside us; the other guests found seats at the many tables placed along one side of the spacious hall.

An orchestra made up entirely of patients fervently played a series of well-known melodies, and then the Director of the Leprosarium, Mr. Habib Assagaf, gave the welcoming speech. A former patient himself, he had been among the first to be cured. His face was still scarred, his hands were still mutilated, but he could write beautifully, and still spoke Dutch flawlessly.

Mr. Assagaf spoke passionately about the Leprosarium and its founder. She gave us hope, he said; she told us not to feel sorry for ourselves, and to get back to work, in spite of our handicap; she made us believe that we were worthwhile human beings and owed it to ourselves to do everything possible to get better.

The next speaker was Saadia Syaffi, now a married woman with two healthy, beautiful children. I had heard her story many times. When *Ibu* had found her, she was a little girl already badly maimed. Her parents had kept her hidden in a little shack away from where they themselves lived, fearful of contamination, fearful also of being exiled from their community. The child screamed, kicked, and resisted with all her might, when *Ibu* and her helpers took her to the Leprosarium. Here, an older female patient, Malie Kneefel, who was badly mutilated herself, would care for her as lovingly as if she had been her own child.

Saadia recounted her own experience with bitterness, hitting hard at the hostile attitude of the people in Ternate. Her tone softened when she narrated how she began feeling human again, largely because of the regular visits of *Ibu*, who was never afraid to hug her.

"She treated me as a healthy person, empathized with me, encouraged me, and praised me when I made progress."

*Applause.*

Then her tone changed again:

"You, Mr. Governor," she said, looking directly at the senior civil servant, "you are, today, the first Government official who has dared to set foot in this Leprosarium! Our *Ibu* already did that way back in 1950, when there was still no known cure for this illness!"

*Another applause.*

*Ibu* got up; she had obviously lost her composure. With tears streaming down her cheeks she crossed the crowded hall to thank Saadia, which sparked another loud round of applause.

The Governor, the *Kepala Daèrah* (Head of the District), then spoke briefly, followed by Father Bosse, who had never before met *Ibu*.

He recalled that during the many *tournées* he had made, the first question he had always been asked was:

"Where is *Ibu Sosial*?"

Not knowing who this referred to, he inquired back in Ternate, and became quite impressed by stories of the exploits of this woman: how she had traveled alone on foot or by boat to the most remote villages, and how much she had accomplished in her time. So, he concluded, he was very pleased to finally meet her in person.

After the speeches, *Ibu* was loaded down with gifts, and then, while the band played again, she was escorted outside. Mr. Assagaf showed her the many improvements that had been made in the brick factory (which made good money) and in the hospital (which housed the critically-ill patients).

No matter how ill they were, each patient had a smile for *Ibu*, who responded with a hand shake and some encouraging words. Before leaving, *Ibu* discussed those cases with Dr. Tan, and it seemed as if no time had passed since her last visit.

Back in the large hall, we and 200 other guests were then each offered a cheerfully-colored cardboard box that contained a substantial *rijsttafel*. And those for whom there was no room inside, were handed their boxes through the open window. *Ibu* had installed herself amidst the untiring musicians, who appreciated this gesture and played again, as soon as they had finished eating.

After dinner, it was *Ibu*'s turn to walk up to the microphone and express her thanks. The words stuck in her throat, but she managed to utter a few sentences. However, it didn't matter; everyone understood, and knew that these words came straight from the heart.

After much hugging and crying and shouts of "*Selamat Jalan*" (Good Journey), we walked, surrounded by the crowd and the playing musicians, to the car that took us home for a much-needed siesta — before going to another festivity that same evening, hosted by the nuns.

Once again we were loaded down with gifts and flowers. There was also a stack of letters and telegrams that had arrived from the Netherlands, Canada and other corners of the world. Oddly enough, all of them had arrived on *Ibu*'s birthday!

The following day we spent visiting the homes of many of *Ibu*'s friends and the now grown-up orphans, and the last day we traveled all over the island.

Everywhere we met people who remembered *Ibu*. Many brought up memories from the war. The inhabitants of Kampung Sulamedaha, especially, remembered how *Ibu*'s actions had stopped the bombardment of their village by Japanese planes.

Later that day, the inhabitants of Ternate, with the patients of the Sorofo Leprosarium in the lead, escorted us to the airport. Here, we were literally pushed inside the small plane; it was so full of flowers and presents that there was hardly any place for us to sit.

****

As a foot note to Nini's account, the people in Ternate who had known about Sukarno's order for my arrest, went out of their way to make amends during this unforgettable visit.

When the festivities were over, Nini and I went to visit the house where I had lived until my hasty departure in December 1957. At that time, I had simply locked up and taken the keys with me. Those keys were now in the pocket of my coat.

We found the house and I asked a passerby: "Who lives in this house?"

"*Tidah tau* — I don't know."

I asked other people the same question and always received the same answer. Eventually I found out that the military were living there. They had simply taken possession, some time after I had left.

Saying farewell to Ternate and my many wonderful friends was extremely difficult. I knew this would be my last visit. If I were ever to come back, I surely would not have the strength to leave again.

My resolve to leave now was only due to having promised Nini that we would complete our present tour (a visit to the Minahassa in Northern Celebes and Makassar in Southern Celebes was on our itinerary) and return together to the Netherlands.

Had it not been for that promise, I would have stayed in Ternate, for this is where I belonged, this was my home, and this is where my life and work has had meaning for me and for my beloved Moluccans.

### Endnotes

[1] Some of these 'Letters to the Editor" attacks were motivated by racism; some, by bitterness over the hardships endured. Evidently, some of these former internees had not been able to put their suffering behind them and get on with their lives. For them, sadly, the war was *not* over.

ICU MALUKU

# EPILOGUE

Few would have expected, including Jeanne van Diejen herself, that she would become a centenarian and outlive most of the people who played a significant part in her often very difficult life.

On June 6, 1996, she celebrated her 100th birthday at the Kollenberg Home in Sittard amidst friends and relatives. She received many congratulatory letters, including a letter from Her Majesty Queen Beatrix and the Governor of the Province of Limburg. The Mayor of Sittard and his wife arrived with a huge cake, and the Kollenberg Home staff pulled out all the stops to make the event a warm, happy celebration.

Alas, her dear friend, Nini Smits, could not be there. Two years earlier, in 1994, she unexpectedly collapsed in Ibu's arms and died. It was a great loss. To Jeanne, she had been like a daughter; the two had been doing everything together since they had met again in the early '60s.

Another "daughter" was my cousin Willy Fuhrie-Broekhals, with whom Jeanne spent the war years at the Ambon and Kampili internment camps, as well as some time at the plantation, Mon Désir. A separation occurred, as disclosed in this book, but Jeanne would dearly have liked to see her at this, her 100th birthday. Willy and her husband, Jon van Diejen (the nephew of Jeanne's husband) started a pension in the Hague in the early '60s. Some twenty years later, a stroke incapacitated Willy. It is not known if she is still alive.

Tadashi Yamaji, the Japanese commandant of Kampili, died in a car crash in the mid-80's. Pater Beltjens has also passed away. Mrs. Oya, the translator from Tokyo, is alive and well and roaming the world, stopping every so often in Sittard to say "hello" to Ibu.

Ibu's knees are giving her much discomfort now, which is probably due to having stood for hours on end in the flooded *sawahs* of Kampili. Her heart has never been strong. Her hearing and sight have deteriorated, but her mind is as sharp as ever, and she is still deeply interested in world events and people's lives — especially those with whom she has shared so many joys and sorrows.

She still carries on a busy correspondence with her people in Maluku — especially with Boki, the daughter-in-law of the Sultan of Ternate — but also with others on Ternate, Ambon and Bachan, giving counsel and material aid where needed. Their letters — always neatly written in perfect Dutch or Bahasa Indonesia, and displaying the greatest possible deference to their Ibu Maluku — have been a lifeline for her and may hold a clue as to why she has attained such a venerable age.

The economic turmoil in Indonesia (1998), however, has forced many of her Indonesian friends to curtail their correspondence, as they cannot afford to pay 17,800 Rupiah to mail a letter to the Netherlands. But that, too, shall pass.

As long as there is a breath left in their Ibu, they will find a way to communicate with her, knowing they can count on her unwavering support and love.

Contrary to Rudyard Kipling's frequently quoted words that "East is East and West is West, and never the twain shall meet", this story shows that the twain can meet, and work together to make the world a better place.

# GLOSSARY OF TERMS

*(Indonesian words, except as noted.)*
*[D] – Dutch, [E] – English, [F] – French, [J] – Japanese*

| | | |
|---|---|---|
| *adat* | | traditional native law |
| *aduh* | | an exclamation expressing pain or surprise |
| Alfur | [E] | member of a Papuan-Melanesian ethnic group |
| *arèn (palm)* | | arenga palm, the sap of which is used to make sugar and wine |
| *atap* | | roof covering, made of palm leaves |
| *babi rusah* | | hog-deer |
| *babu* | | a female house maid |
| *balé-balé* | | a bamboo sleeping cot |
| *banjir* | | a river flash flood, caused by heavy rains |
| *barang* | | a general term for goods, luggage, cargo |
| *baru* | | new |
| Belanda | | Dutch |
| *bello* | | stake, to support a plant |
| *bèntèng* | | fortress |
| *bibit* | | seed, seedling |
| *bungkusan* | | parcel |
| *cicak* | | a small wall lizard (formerly *tjitjak*) |
| *cingcang* | | to mince (formerly *tjingtjang*) |
| cockatoo | [E] | a large crested parrot |
| copra | [E] | dried coconut meat, from which oil is extracted |
| coolie | [E] | an unskilled laborer |
| *damar* | | dammar, copal-like resin |
| *dèsa* | | a village (formerly *dessa*) |
| *dukun* | | a healer, or medicine man/woman |
| *dusun* | | an orchard |
| emplacement | [F] | central place of work on a plantation |
| état-major | [F] | staff officers as a group; herein the, the officers of the ship. |
| *gaba-gaba* | | interlaced stems of the sago-palm, used to construct walls |

633

| | | |
|---|---|---|
| *gayung* | | a water scoop (also *gayong*) |
| *Gezaghebber* | [D] | the rank of a local magistrate (see *HPB*) |
| *gerobak* | | (ox) cart, for transporting goods |
| *gudang* | | storage place, warehouse |
| *gunung* | | mountain |
| *guru* | | teacher |
| *Haji* | | Mecca pilgrim |
| *hansop* | [D] | jump suit |
| *honcho* | [J] | leader |
| HPB | [D] | *Hoofd van Plaatselijk Bestuur* — Local magistrate of various ranks: e.g. *Gezaghebber, Controleur*, etc. |
| *Ibu* | | mother, Mrs. |
| *jongos* | | male (house) servant, waiter |
| *juragan* | | skipper (also *juragang*) |
| *kali* | | river, stream |
| *kampung* | | village (formerly spelled *kampong*) |
| *kati* | | catty, a weight of about 1-1/3 lb. |
| *kayu putih* (oil) | | eucalyptus (oil) |
| *kebaya* | | a lady's blouse or jacket |
| *kebon* | | garden (often used for *tukang kebon* - gardener) |
| *Kedaton* | | Sultan's palace (in the Moluccas) |
| *kelambu* | | mosquito net (around a bed) |
| *Kepala Kampung* | | head of a village |
| *Kepala Daèrah* | | head of a region, district |
| KNIL | [D] | *Koninklijk Nederlands-Indisch Leger* Royal Netherlands-Indies Army |
| *kota* | | city |
| KPM | [D] | *Koninklijke Pakketvaart Maatschappij* - Royal Packet (Boat) Service Its ships carried mail, passengers and goods on a fixed route. |
| *krètèk* | | a cigarette rolled in corn leaves, rather than paper |
| *lèpa-lèpa* | | a dugout canoe with one or two outriggers |
| *lory* | [E] | a small multi-colored parrot [*luri* in *Bahasa Indonesia*] |
| *Maluku* | | the Moluccas |
| *mandur* | | supervisor |
| *mantri* | | counsellor, superintendent, ordely, civil |

## IBU MALUKU

|   |   |   |
|---|---|---|
|  |  | servant [from Sanskrit] |
| MHM | [D] | *Molukse Handel Maatschappij* - Moluccan Trading Company |
| *Meneer* | [D] | Mister, Sir |
| *Mevrouw* | [D] | Missis, Madam |
| NSB | [D] | *Nationale Socialistische Bond* — a pro-German organization in the Netherlands and the Netherlands East Indies |
| *nyai* |  | a housekeeper, in the employ of Europeans at that time |
| *Nyonya* |  | Missis |
| *nyonya besar* |  | great missis (indicating importance) |
| *nyonya muda* |  | young missus |
| *Nyora* |  | the name used to address the wife of a teacher (*guru*) |
| *obat* |  | medicine |
| *pacul* |  | hoe (formerly *patjol*) |
| *parang* |  | heavy (1/8 to 3/16" thick) steel hack-knife |
| *pasanggrahan* |  | guest house, small hotel |
| *pasar* |  | a generally open market place |
| *pèndèk* |  | a pair of shorts with a drawstring |
| *peranakan* |  | person of mixed blood |
| *pikol* |  | a weight equal to 100 *kati*, or about 133lbs |
| *prau* |  | a proa, any of various types of South Pacific boats (*perahu* in Behasa Indonesia) |
| PTT |  | Post, Telegraph and Telephone Office |
| Resident |  | the (civil) governor of a residency, e.g. the Residency of the Moluccas |
| *rijsttafel* | [D] | a multi-course Indonesian dinner (literally *rice-table*) |
| *rimbu* |  | jungle, forest (*rimba* in *Behasa Indonesia*) |
| *rotan* |  | rattan |
| *rupiah* |  | monetary unit of Indonesia |
| *sapu lidi* |  | a broom made from palm-leaf ribs |
| *sarong* |  | a tubular garment, worn by both sexes |
| *sawah* |  | rice field |
| *selamat datang* |  | welcome |
| *selamat jalan* |  | good journey |
| *selamatan* |  | a benedictory (thanksgiving) meal |
| *selèndang* |  | a continuous piece of cloth, worn as a bandolier |

| | | |
|---|---|---|
| Sultan | | hereditary ruler, king |
| *tangsi* | | military/police barracks or base |
| *tanjung* | | cape |
| *toko* | | a medium to large shop |
| *tournée* | [F] | a tour of duty, an inspection tour |
| *trunku* | | jail |
| *Tuan* | | Mister |
| *tukang* | | a craftsman, a trained worker |
| *ular* | | snake |
| *warong* | | small shop (*warung* in *Bahasa Indonesia*) |

**Another great title from Kerry B. Collison**

# INDONESIAN GOLD

## KERRY B. COLLISON

*Based on events surrounding the infamous BRE-X gold fraud and the determined few who destroyed so many lives in their all-consuming quest for gold in Kalimantan (Indonesian Borneo).*

SID HARTA PUBLISHERS

## *Best-selling titles by Kerry B. Collison*

**Readers are invited to visit our publishing websites at:**

http://www.sidharta.com.au

http://www.publisher-guidelines.com/

http://temple-house.com/

**Kerry B. Collison's home pages:**

http://www.authorsden.com/visit/author.asp?AuthorID=2239

http://www.expat.or.id/sponsors/collison.html

http://clubs.yahoo.com/clubs/asianintelligencesresources

email: author@sidharta.com.au

# *Also from Sid Harta Publishers*

OTHER BEST SELLING SID HARTA TITLES CAN BE FOUND AT
http://www.sidharta.com.au
http://Anzac.sidharta.com

***

HAVE YOU WRITTEN A STORY?
http://www.publisher-guidelines.com
for manuscript guideline submissions

***

LOOKING FOR A PUBLISHER?
http://www.temple-house.com

*New Releases...*

*Cold War Cornhuskers*

307th Bombardment Wing (Medium)
Strategic Air Command

Lincoln AFB, Nebraska
1954-1965

370th Bomb Squadron
371st Bomb Squadron
372nd Bomb Squadron
424th Bomb Squadron
307th Field Maintenance Squadron
307th Operational Maintenance Squadron
307th Armament & Electronics Squadron
307th Air Refueling Squadron

# Cold War Cornhuskers

## The 307th Bomb Wing

## Lincoln Air Force Base Nebraska

## 1955-1965

Mike Hill

Schiffer Military History
Atglen, PA

Book Design by Ian Robertson.

Copyright © 2011 by Mike Hill.
Library of Congress Control Number: 2011923417

All rights reserved. No part of this work may be reproduced or used in any forms or by any means – graphic, electronic or mechanical, including photocopying or information storage and retrieval systems – without written permission from the copyright holder.

Printed in China.
ISBN: 978-0-7643-3751-2

We are interested in hearing from authors with book ideas on related topics.

Published by Schiffer Publishing Ltd.
4880 Lower Valley Road
Atglen, PA 19310
Phone: (610) 593-1777
FAX: (610) 593-2002
E-mail: Info@schifferbooks.com.
Visit our web site at: www.schifferbooks.com
Please write for a free catalog.
This book may be purchased from the publisher.
Please include $5.00 postage.
Try your bookstore first.

In Europe, Schiffer books are distributed by:
Bushwood Books
6 Marksbury Avenue
Kew Gardens
Surrey TW9 4JF, England
Phone: 44 (0) 20 8392-8585
FAX: 44 (0) 20 8392-9876
E-mail: Info@bushwoodbooks.co.uk.
Visit our website at: www.bushwoodbooks.co.uk
Try your bookstore first.

# Contents

Acknowledgments ............................................................................................................................. 6
Foreword ............................................................................................................................................ 7
Introduction ....................................................................................................................................... 8

Chapter 1: 307th Bomb Wing: The Early Years ....................................................................... 10
Chapter 2: 1955 .............................................................................................................................. 18
Chapter 3: 1956 .............................................................................................................................. 32
Chapter 4: 1957 .............................................................................................................................. 58
Chapter 5: 1958 .............................................................................................................................. 82
Chapter 6: 1959 ............................................................................................................................ 110
Chapter 7: 1960 ............................................................................................................................ 138
Chapter 8: 1961 ............................................................................................................................ 163
Chapter 9: 1962 ............................................................................................................................ 186
Chapter 10: 1963 .......................................................................................................................... 211
Chapter 11: 1964 .......................................................................................................................... 241
Chapter 12: 1965 .......................................................................................................................... 268

Memorials ...................................................................................................................................... 277
307th Bomb Wing Aircraft Assignments .................................................................................. 279
Flight Crews .................................................................................................................................. 290
B-47 KC-97 Walkaround ............................................................................................................. 294
Lincoln Air Force Base Then and Now ..................................................................................... 303
Glossary ......................................................................................................................................... 308
References ..................................................................................................................................... 311
Notes .............................................................................................................................................. 312

# Acknowledgments

I would like to express my profound THANKS to the following for their help in this project.

Gene Aenchbacher, Sigmund Alexander, Louie Alley, Neal Amtmann, Graham C. Andoe, Dick Arens, Mary (Bowling) Ashton, David Avery, Gerry Bachner, Charles Baker, William Barnicoat, William Bathurst, Roger Beamer, Gerald Berger, Richard Berggren, Harold Beucus, Charles Bird, Larry Boggess, Dave Bowersock, R.T. Boykin, Jan Campbell, Dale Christians, Neil Cosentino, Robert Cox, Bobby Cox, Lee Cullimore, Rolland England, Bill Erickson, Rene Erickson, William Filpula, Roger Flanik, and H.A. Frost.

Donald Fudge, Ed Godec, Darwin Godemann, Morgen Goodroe, Dick Grammes, Charles Grant, Hank Grogan, Patricia Hall, Mark Hamilton, John Herder, Glen Hesler, Don Hickman, Earl Hill, Don Ivie, Harry Jones, Don Kellum, Jim Kendall, Jeff King, Mike Koczorowski, John Koudsi, Jarvis Latham, Robert Loffredo, Billy Lyons, Bob Matich, Tony Minnick, Donald Mowery, George Nigh III, and Bobby Odum.

Al Ottaviano, John Parks, Tom Pauza, Ernie Pence, Shirley Pudwill, Robert Purcell, Gerald Putnam, Clayton Robson, James Rusher, Orin Shellhammer, John Sinclair, Merrill Sinclair, James Sutton, Everett Sutherland, Larry Talovich, T.R. Taylor, Paul Trudeau, Doug Valen, James Villa, Bert Vorchheimer, James "Wally" Whitehurst, Ken Wikle, and Billy Williams.

I must say a SPECIAL THANK YOU to the following:

Mike Gingrich and Pete Todd for their support and guidance. Also for reading the manuscript and checking for accuracy.

Ken Tarwater for his work and help in contacting members of the 307th ARES.

Paul Koski was like a big brother to me at Lincoln. He answered my call for help with over a hundred pages of 307th memories. THANKS PAUL, REQUIESCANT IN PACE.

Sedgefield D. and Wilda Hill, my parents for years of support in my book projects.

Pastor Jason Hill and family. Our father-son trip to the 2010 307th Reunion at Dayton, Ohio, will always be remembered.

My daughter and her husband, SSgt Christopher Rast (USAF), for their computer skills and downloading photos.

Finally, a Special THANKS to my wife Linda. Her support and understanding has always carried me through "another book project." She is one in a million.

# Foreword

I joined the 307th Bomb Wing in the summer of 1961, about two thirds of the way through its eleven year residence in Lincoln, Nebraska. This was my first operational duty assignment after completing pilot training and nearly a year TDY (temporary duty) at various training courses. As a very green first lieutenant, I recognized I had a lot to learn.

Much of what I learned about the history and traditions of the wing was delivered by the "old heads" through innumerable bull sessions on alert and various social occasions. Much of what I learned about flying, teamwork, professionalism and leadership came from the day-to-day associations with the commanders, combat crews, maintenance professionals and staff members throughout the succeeding fours years. However, it was to be over thirty years later before I fully grasped the depths of the camaraderie that had formed between 1954 and 1965 within the 307th Bomb Wing.

Early in 1996, Mike Gingrich called and invited me to be the guest speaker at the opening reunion of the 307th Bomb Wing B-47/KC-97 Association that he was coordinating in Dayton, Ohio. While attending that reunion, I was amazed to learn that almost a quarter century after the wing had closed at Lincoln, a small group of former members had conceived the idea of reuniting with old friends and comrades in arms, and thus was the Association born. Some years later I was honored to be elected president of that Association, and in June 2010, the *thirteenth* biennial reunion was held again in Dayton.

What enabled the 307th Bomb Wing B-47/KC-97 Association to form and thrive? Was it the shared values, shared experiences, shared purpose and all the triumphs and heartbreaks that marked life in a Strategic Air Command Bomb Wing? I think it was all of that and more. There were dozens of bomb wings, but few produced associations with a sense of identity and mutual support that 307th has. What was the " X-Factor" that made the 307th Bomb Wing such a success and gave "legs" to the Association?

Mike Hill's exhaustively researched and expertly written history of the 307th Bomb Wing answers that question through the thoughts and recollections of the men who lived it. His brilliant narrative literally brings the wing back to life, giving the reader an insight not only into *what* was accomplished during those eleven years at Lincoln (and elsewhere), but also into the hearts and souls of those who made it happen. This remarkable author has a rare ability to turn back the pages of time and make you smell the jet fuel and feel the roar of engines as the B-47 and KC-97 flight crews and maintainers preformed their mission of deterrence day after day.

This is his tenth book, may it be his finest.

Harold W. ("Pete") Todd
Maj Gen, USAF (Ret)
President
307th Bomb Wing B-47/KC-97 Association

# Introduction

A gentle breeze drifted down the flightline at the "patch," and shimmering waves of heat danced upward from the concrete. Looking around, I could see row after row of parked B-47s on the ramp. To the south sat KC-97s with their ever-present puddles of dripping oil. The flightline was a beehive of activity that day. Young troops working to get the birds ready for the day's flying schedule, Reflex or Alert.

At the north end of the patch sat the alert birds. The tires bulged under the weight of JP-4, their bomb bays full of Mark-28 weapons and horse collar ATO racks strapped to their bellies for added thrust in case of a EWO launch. A short distance away sat the Alert facility, or "mole hole." Inside, alert crews were whiling away their time with games of poker, reading, watching the boob tube, or trying to catch up on some sack time.

There was a tense calm within the walls of the mole hole. Those on alert knew the calm could be shattered by the blare of the Alert Klaxon. When the horn went off, there would be instant pandemonium as they rushed to their aircraft. Heaven help anyone who got in their way as they charged through the halls like NFL running backs.

Would the Klaxon signal another Green Dot practice alert, or would they get the message to launch? Would they get back to the poker game, or would they find themselves headed for their target in the Soviet Union? Within moments of strapping into their seats and starting engines, they would know if the day would finish with poker or nuclear Armageddon!

A KC-135 was on short final for Runway 17. Could it be General "Sundown" Wells, the SAC IG, arriving for a no notice ORI? Or was it just a tanker shooting touch and go landings? If the 135 carried the SAC IG, the ramp would be in turmoil moments after the start of the ORI.

"Dad, did you get him?" I pressed the shutter on my camera and looked away from the eyepiece. The rows of B-47s began fading to phantom shapes, then disappeared in the shimmering waves of heat. Shaken back to reality; it wasn't 1959, it was 2005. The KC-135 was a Nebraska Air Guard tanker shooting touch and go landings. Looking about, the flightline was devoid of any other living soul except for Dad, Jason and I. But, for just a few fleeting moments, I had crossed the boundary of time and saw the flightline as it was forty-some years ago during those hectic days when SAC was SAC.

If you are hoping to read about aircrews flying through flak filled skies, locked in mortal combat in war torn skies, close the cover and put the book on the shelf. You will find nothing like that within these pages.

This is the history of a different kind of war. It is the day-to-day story of combat during the Cold War.

Back then, it was the American Eagle against the Soviet Bear in a no holds barred duel of ideology. Freedom, as we knew it, or Communist domination of the world! It was a time before spy satellites and instant world communication. There was no CNN or Fox News. We got our world news once a day, on the evening news with Walter Cronkite. There were no home computers or cell phones, and letters were delivered by the mailman, not through the Internet.

Members of today's generations will say we were paranoid about the capabilities of our Cold War advisory. Perhaps we were. Revisionist historians would have us believe that it was all a government lie, as they have tainted the Cold War with the benefit of looking back with twenty-twenty hindsight. Yes, perhaps we were paranoid, but back then we actually trusted our elected officials.

Those who filled the ranks of the 307th came from all walks of life and every corner of the nation. The core personnel were veterans of World War II and Korea who stayed in the military. Serving alongside was the second generation who heard the call of duty, to serve the nation in another time of need. Regardless of their background, they shared the same devotion and dedication to duty that is the hallmark of the American service man.

Their pay was low, hours long. They endured tours of TDY and Reflex away from home and family. The tension of knowing the next Klaxon could signal nuclear war was almost unbearable at times, yet they served with professional calmness, in freezing cold and torrid heat. No matter what their particular job, aircrew, crew chief, mechanic, cook or commander, they were all an important part of keeping the wing combat ready at a moments notice.

For this history, missions and special operations were reconstructed using information obtained from the microfilm history of the wing and are as accurate as they can be after nearly fifty years of time. They are included to provide a general idea of where the wing flew on the various operations.

At this point I would like to interject a word on the format. You will find the use of military rank absent most of the time. I have used military rank when it was known at the time of the incident. If I have offended anyone for the lack of military courtesy, I ask your forgiveness.

This has been a personal trip down memory lane. For almost eight years, our family called Ring Trailer Park on West "O" Street home. I

# Introduction

wasn't officially assigned to the 307th; I served as a SAC BRAT, a military dependent in official jargon. My boyhood memories of those years at Lincoln are filled with fondness. Long summer days fishing at Oak Lake, swimming at the base pool and Capital Beach. There were school days at Garfield Elementary, Everett Junior High and Lincoln High School. Memories of sitting off the end of Runway 35 watching the planes land or take off and "spying" on the base. There are memories of those who were with us as friends. T.R. Taylor and his cheek bulging with the ever present chaw of tobacco. Paul Koski's smile and chuckle. Bob Conway's steely-eyed glance.

There are other flashbacks to those days in Lincoln. Waiting in line for a table at Valentino's Pizza, chicken dinners at Lee's and, yes, a hamburger and those fabulous onion rings at King's. Ah yes, those were the days.

Then, there are memories of the alerts at the base, ORIs, and how dad and the rest of the men sweated it out over how the wing would do. The pride in the unbroken record of on-time takeoffs. The euphoria when the wing won the Fairchild Trophy. The sadness when we lost an airplane and crew.

I hope as you read these pages that you will pause for a moment and think about the dedication and sacrifice of the men of the 307th Bomb Wing. They, along with thousands of other SAC warriors, gave themselves to maintain the peace of the world. They fought a different kind of war from the plains of Nebraska. They were the *COLD WAR CORNHUSKERS*.

This history of the 307th Bomb Wing is dedicated to all of the men and families who served with the 307th Bomb Wing at Lincoln Air Force Base. Your service helped win the Cold War. God Bless all of you for serving your country.

*Cold War Cornhuskers: The 307th Bomb Wing Lincoln Air Force Base Nebraska 1955-1965*

# 307th Bomb Wing - The Early Years

The guns of World War II fell silent with the signing of the formal surrender of the Japanese aboard the USS *Missouri*. The greatest armed conflict in the history of the world was over. With peace finally at hand, the 307th Bomb Group returned to the United States.

With the euphoria of peace, there was no longer a need to have such a large military force. The 307th Bomb Group was deactivated and the personnel released to return to their families and start their lives all over again. They had served their country in a time of war and had distinguished themselves in the Pacific.

The ink had hardly dried on the deactivation orders when the 307th was reactivated on August 4, 1946. The Group was to be stationed at MacDill Field, Florida. With the new activation the Group would be equipped with the Boeing B-29 Superfortress and designated as a "very heavy" bomb group.

Shortly after arrival of the first personnel and aircraft at MacDill, word was received that the 307th would be under the control of the Strategic Air Command (SAC). Strategic Air Command had been established on March 21, 1946, with the mission of providing global bombing capabilities. The 307th was part of the second activation of groups to fulfill SAC's mission.

After a period of fitting out with B-29s and transfer of personnel to man the group, the 307th began training for their new mission. That mission was to become specialists in anti-submarine warfare along with other bombing capabilities. Another mission assigned the 307th was to do research on high altitude maneuvers. To help accomplish that mission, the 307th had six F-80 fighters assigned. The fighters helped train gunners on how to track fast moving jet targets.

Shortly after the end of the war in Europe a new specter arose in the East. The Soviet Union had taken over most of the Eastern countries of Europe and made them satellite countries under the control of Moscow. The Soviet leader, Joseph Stalin, wanted to bring Russia up to the same status as other world powers and to dominate Europe.

Although Russia had been part of the Allied forces during the war, the other Allied governments realized the Soviet Union could not be trusted when it came to holding the peace. For the first few years after the war there was an uneasy peace in Europe.

The 307th honed their skills in anti-submarine warfare to a razor's edge. They practiced by hunting down Navy subs and tracking them along the coastal waters of the United States. Now granted, there may have been a few whales that were followed, but after all it was just training.

When, in 1948, the Soviet Union set up a blockade around Berlin, the United States and England decided to supply the city by air. Since Berlin was well within the area controlled by the USSR, the flights into Berlin would be interesting to say the least.

During a reorganization of Air Force units, the 307th was changed from a Heavy Bombardment unit to a Medium Bombardment unit on July 12, 1948. Later, on December 16th, the unit was placed under control of the 15th Air Force.

Since the Soviet Union was rattling their saber, the Western Allies would need to respond. In a show of force the 307th, along with several other groups, were deployed to England. Here, they flew training missions and projected their presence so that the Soviet Union would know there were American bombers close at hand in case they were needed. With the end of what has been called the first Berlin Crisis, most of the 307th returned to the U.S.A. and resumed routine training. The last contingent of the 307th didn't get back to MacDill until May 2, 1949.

In 1949, the 307th led one of the waves during the flyover in honor of President Truman's inaugural ceremonies. To say the least it was an impressive demonstration of American air power, as wave after wave of aircraft flew over Washington, D.C.

The 307th was subjected to an Organizational Readiness Inspection (ORI) on August 15, 1949.[1] This was a SAC Headquarters directed test to see if the 307th was ready to perform their mission. ORIs would become a mainstay in the life of SAC. There always seemed to be a vulnerability for SAC to throw an ORI at a unit to keep 'em on their toes.

North Korean forces attacked South Korea on June 25, 1950. The invaders moved across the 38th Parallel and pushed the defender further and further south towards the southern most tip of Korea.

The 307th was alerted for deployment on July 30, 1950, and began packing for action. The deployment started with the movement of men and equipment from MacDill AFB in stages. The first stop was Fairchild AFB, Washington. From there the group moved on to Hawaii. After a brief stop there they flew on to Kwajalein, then Guam. The flight across the Pacific could be classified as hours and hours of constant boredom. There was nothing out there to see except a lot of water. Most of the men flying in the B-29 hoped that the navigator was doing a good job. After all, miss the next island stopover and there was nothing else to do but ditch in the vast Pacific Ocean and hope that they would be found.

The group arrived at their new base, Kadena, on the Island of Okinawa. They didn't even have time to settle in when they were alerted

## 307th Bomb Wing - The Early Years

to prepare for a mission. That first mission came on August 8, 1950, just ten days after getting the alert for deployment for overseas action. By all standards, it was an incredible accomplishment.

After the first mission the 307th continued to fly missions against bridges, troop concentrations and other targets as deemed important, to push the North Koreans back. On November 15, 1950, the 307th attacked the Sinuiju Bridge with poor results. The bridge ran north to south along the Manchurian border. The B-29s could not cross the border, so they had to bomb on an East to West axis. Hitting a 40 to 60 foot wide target from 20,000 feet with a crosswind and under attack from fighters was an almost impossible task.

November 26, 1950, saw the 307th going after the Chongsongjin Bridge. This time the 307th didn't have a crosswind to contend with and clobbered the target. Post-strike photos showed that two of the spans on the bridge had been hit and dropped into the valley below. The 307th finished the year with almost daily missions to targets in both North and South Korea.

On October 23, 1951, the 307th attacked the Namsi Airfield. The group was escorted by F-84s from the 40th and 136th Fighter Wings. Near the target the formation was jumped by over 50 MiG-15s. Although the fighter escort went after the MiGs, they were no match for the nimble swept wing fighter.

The MiGs broke through the escort and attacked the 307th. The lead B-29, flown by Capt Thomas Shields, was raked by gunfire from the attacking MiGs. The B-29 was hit hard by cannon fire and, after the second pass, fire erupted in the B-29. Capt Shields maintained his position in formation and led the B-29s to the target in spite of the fire. After the post target turn the burning B-29 finally headed down towards the Ocean. Capt Shields stayed at the controls until everyone was able to bail out. By that time the blazing B-29 was too low and Capt Shields went in with his ship.

The MiGs were finally beaten off by the escorting F-84s. A young Navy exchange pilot in one of the F-84s had managed to shoot down one of the MiGs. The young Lt Wally Schirra would go on to get a couple of more MiGs, and later become one of the original Mercury Astronauts.

By December 1951, losses over North Korean targets had mounted to the point where it became necessary to change tactics. The B-29s were no match for the attacking MiGs during the day. With that, the 307th began flying the "night shift." They also began to use "Guardian Angel" ECM tactics. The tactic was simple. An ECM designated B-29 flew a figure eight over the target area jamming enemy radar while the formation attacked the target.

The 307th continued to fly missions throughout the Korean Conflict. One of the more notable missions was a double attack on August 14 and 15, 1952, against a supply center at Anak. The results were reported as excellent. A lot of rice and ammo wouldn't be used against United Nations troops after that visit by the 307th.

By July 1953, the missions flown had become tactical in support of the ground troops in South Korea.

On July 3, 1953, the 307th at Kadena was alerted to the approach of Typhoon "Kit." Plans were made to deploy the aircraft to a safer location in case "Kit" actually came calling. The storm was expected to make landfall at about 1600 hrs with winds of about 170 knots. Without any further warning "Kit" changed course and missed Okinawa.

On July 14, 1953, the 307th attacked front-line troop positions of several Chinese Divisions. Twelve B-29s dropped over 120 tons of bombs along a 50-mile front.

Rumors that a peace agreement was about to be reached ran rampant across the flight line at Kadena on July 26, 1953. Rumors didn't stop the planned mission. The mission that night would be the 573rd mission that the 307th had flown since deployment to the Pacific. The B-29s took off at 6 PM local time and headed for the northwest corner of North Korea to bomb two airfields. Radio Operators in the B-29s had their radios tuned to Armed Forces Radio for the usual evening news.

The mission was led by Col Austin Monett. The flight ran into thunderstorms near the Yalu River. The flight crews were also treated to a full eclipse of the moon, which spawned comments that, with the darkness, the MiGs would not be able to find the formation. Due to the thunderstorms and the eclipse, the MiGs never got off the ground. The B-29s hit their target and returned to Kadena to hear the news that the conflict in Korea was over.

During their deployment to Kadena, the 307th had flown 6,052 combat sorties and amassed 55,473 combat hours. They had dropped 51,757 tons of bombs on targets in support of United Nations Forces. The 307th had played a key role during the "Police Action" in Korea. It may have been called a "Police Action," but the men of the 307th knew better. Those 51,757 tons of bombs couldn't really be classified as "traffic tickets."

Most of the men of the 307th believed that with the end of the conflict would come the redeployment of the group back to the good old USA. Not to happen in the near future, they were told. The "powers that be" weren't about to cut orders to send the 307th home until they were sure that the Korean pot wouldn't boil over again. Gene Aenchbacher recalled:

"I was first assigned to the 307th as Commander of the 372nd Bomb Squadron in December 1953, then located at Kadena AFB, Okinawa. The mission then was to maintain combat readiness in case the peace failed. From an operational viewpoint, our most critical decision was whether to deploy or ride out the typhoons. In one case we deployed to Clark in the Philippines. On another, the decision was to ride it out. Our aircraft were parked on small revetments that were hardly large enough to turn around on and were very slippery when wet. As the typhoon approached and the wind began to rise, a pilot, copilot and flight engineer would man the aircraft. The ops staff would go to the tower and would advise us when to start engines and, as necessary, what direction to head the aircraft to keep it into the wind and using whatever power needed. It was an eerie experience to say the least, and most crews agreed the trip to Clark was preferred."

For the moment the 307th would be assigned to the Far East Air Force for training and maintaining a strategic bomber force. That training continued during the next several months. In October, the 307th flew practice missions to Tori-Shima Island.

On December 4, 1953, the group flew Operation Watch Dog II. This was a penetration mission to test the defenses in the Far East. Six B-29s flew a round robin type mission to Formosa, then to the Philippine Islands, and then back to Okinawa. There were several fighter intercepts over the Philippines, but none was observed over Formosa.

During December 1953, 101 airmen were sent back to the United States. Rumors spread that since they had sent that many people home, the rest of the group would follow shortly. Again the know-it-all clerk in supply, who always got the straight dope from his buddy at Headquarters, got it wrong. They may have sent 101 airmen home, but the group got 130 airmen to replace them.

By May 1954, the 307th had pretty well settled into the fact that they were going to be at Kadena for some time to come. This was compounded by the fact that the 307th had just absorbed most of the personnel from the 19th Bomb Group, which was due to rotate out of Kadena.

Col Louis Thorup assumed command of the 307th on June 7, 1954. Shortly after that it was learned that the 307th would come under the control of the 20th Air Force, which had control of the Pacific area at that time.

*11*

# Cold War Cornhuskers: The 307th Bomb Wing Lincoln Air Force Base Nebraska 1955-1965

With the change in command, the 20th Air Force directed a mission to be flown against defenses on Formosa, Luzon and Okinawa. This was another mission to test the defenses in those areas. This time there were two fighter intercepts as the 307th approached Okinawa.

Again the rumor mill started working. This time the word was that the 307th was going to leave Okinawa and head back to the States. The word was, the 307th was going to get a new mission aircraft called the B-47. They were also going to Lincoln, Nebraska, somewhere in the middle of the country, they believed. Ah yes, the rumor mill was full of juicy information about Lincoln, Nebraska.

For once, the rumor mill was correct; the 307th *was* moving back stateside. They were going to change their B-29s for B-47s, and yes, they would be stationed at Lincoln, Nebraska.

Meanwhile, back in the states, SAC Headquarters cut General Order #64, dated September 19, 1954. This order activated the 818th Air Division at Lincoln Air Force Base, about seven miles northwest of downtown Lincoln, Nebraska. With that activation, the 307th was "officially" notified they had been invited to rejoin the Strategic Air Command and take up residence on the plains of Nebraska.

The 307th flew their last Unit Simulated Combat Mission from Kadena on September 29, 1954. As always, the 307th passed the test and showed the 20th Air Force that they were still a crack outfit.

The 307th was "officially" relieved of duties at Kadena and transferred to the 15th Air Force on October 15, 1954. Kadena was alive with activity as the men of the 307th packed their equipment and got ready to return to the land of "round eyed women, big cars, and drive ins."

The movement back to the states began shortly after the Wing came under control of the 15th AF. Personnel began boarding military transport aircraft for the flight back to the states. A lot of these were personnel going back to attend school on how to manage and repair the B-47. Other personnel served their enlistment and were getting out of the Air Force, especially in view of the fact that the next base was in Nebraska.

The 370th Bomb Squadron aircraft left Kadena on October 22, 1954, under command of LtCol Robert Christy. They were followed by the 371st on October 25th and the 372nd on the 28th. The movement back to the states, as usual, was a drawn out affair with stopovers at Guam, Wake Island and Hawaii. The last B-29, 42-94032, arrived at the boneyard at Davis-Monthan AFB on November 4, 1954. This was the last B-29 bomber version that had served in SAC. The Wing remained attached to the Far East Command until 2400 hours on November 19, 1954. At that time the 307th "officially" closed down APO 239, San Francisco.

When LtCol Christy arrived at Davis-Monthan, he was greeted by none other then Nebraska Lt. Govenor Charles Warner and a group of Lincoln businessmen who had traveled all the way to Arizona to say "hello" and welcome them to their new home at Lincoln.

307th Bomb Wing Headquarters was ordered to open at Lincoln AFB at 0100 hours on November 20, 1954. The Wing may have been ordered to open the Headquarters at Lincoln on November 20th, but there wasn't very much there to open with. Besides, where the heck is this place called Lincoln Air Force Base, Nebraska?

Lincoln Air Force Base began as a grass landing field for barnstormers in the 1920s. One of the more famous barnstormers was Charles Lindbergh, who took flying lessons in the Lincoln area. It is almost certain that he landed on the grass strip that would become Lincoln Air Force Base. In later years, the city officials at Lincoln actually proposed naming the field after Lindbergh when he became famous for crossing the Atlantic in 1927.

The field was situated about seven miles northwest of downtown Lincoln, on a large open plain. The grass strip became a full-fledged airport with the arrival of airline passenger service by United Airlines in 1927. In 1928, the field became an airmail stop. For years, the field was used as a stopover for the airline and provided a convenient field for the occasional flying circus that would appear as if by magic.

After Pearl Harbor, the Army began looking for airfields in the Midwest to serve as training bases for the growing war effort. Lincoln seemed to be a perfect location. The city had a railway and major highways running into it. Since it was in the middle of the country, it was safe from any enemy air attacks. The Army announced that they would have a training base in Lincoln on February 27, 1942.

Under wartime priorities, Lincoln Army Air Field sprouted from the plains of Nebraska like a cornstalk. The main runway was lengthened and hangars were built, along with workshops, barracks, and mess halls to feed the troops. A hospital and support buildings were built on the northwest side of the base. Nearby a chapel was built for worship.

The base served proudly during the war years. It was the Phase 3 training base for several bomb groups before they went overseas. It also served as a modification center for aircraft getting last minute upgrades before heading off to war. The citizens of Lincoln soon got used to the sight and sounds of B-17s, B-24s and the huge B-29 Superfortress. For the duration of the war there were planes coming and going on a daily basis.

After the war, the base was used as a personnel center for those who were mustering out of the service. It was also used as a depot for returning aircraft before they were sent to the boneyard. Shortly after the war, the Nebraska Air National Guard took over the field as their home base. At first they were assigned the nimble P-51 Mustang that had become a legend during the war. Later they upgraded to the jet age with the F-80 Shooting Star.

For the most part, the buildings from the wartime base stood empty. In 1949, the hospital and the nearby buildings became housing for the University of Nebraska. Known as Huskerville, it was a small city with a grocery store, barber shop and the nearby chapel.

During the Korean War the Navy moved a contingent of the Reserves to Lincoln and set up shop in the old hangars on the West side of the runway. The Reserve contingent flew training missions from the field for the next several years.

The city fathers of Lincoln heard the Strategic Air Command was in the market to station their bombers in the Midwest. They figured that Lincoln was an ideal candidate; after all, they already had a runway and buildings at the old Army base. The city of Lincoln sent their proposal to Senator Kenneth Wherry, who in turn placed the activation proposal on a bill in the Senate. The city officials lobbied in favor of the bill, which finally passed. With the passage of the Bill and pending arrival of the Strategic Air Command, work began on bringing the old World War II base up to modern Air Force standards.

Two large hangars were built at a cost of over a million dollars each. New barracks were constructed to house the incoming airmen. At the time there was no housing for the married personnel, but plans were underway to take care of that problem. The course of the small Oak Creek was diverted so it ran through the base around the south end of the runway.

It would take a few years to transform Lincoln Army Air Field into a mighty SAC base. Those that would arrive in the first months after activation of the base would have to put up with the constant construction and changes that were underway at Lincoln Airplane Patch.

The 307th AREFS (Air Refueling Squadron) had been activated at MacDill AFB, Florida, on June 16, 1950, and attached to the 307th Bomb Wing. At first, the squadron flew the KB-29M. This was a hose type refueling tanker. Before they could learn very much about refueling, the squadron was transferred to Davis-Monthan AFB, Arizona, and attached to the 43rd Bomb Wing in September 1951.

*12*

## 307th Bomb Wing - The Early Years

Later that year, the unit was sent to Walker AFB, New Mexico, and given the KB-29P, which had the new "flying boom" installed. The Squadron moved again in July 1953. This time, their new home was Bergstrom AFB, Texas. This was a short stay, as the Squadron was deactivated on November 18, 1953. The men and aircraft were dispersed to other refueling squadrons in SAC.

The 307th AREFS was again activated by General Order 7, dated February 26, 1954. The squadron would be stationed at Maxwell AFB, Alabama, until being transferred to Lincoln. Under General Order 71, dated October 18, 1954, the 307th Air Refueling Squadron was transferred to Lincoln Air Force Base from Maxwell AFB. The Squadron had been attached to the 321st BW stationed at Pinecastle, Florida. The actual date of arrival of the first KC-97 at Lincoln was November 8, 1954, with personnel arriving during the next few weeks.

On arrival at Lincoln, the tanker squadron didn't have a parent Bomb Wing in place to be assigned to. The 307th Bomb Wing was on the way, but at the moment the tankers were on their own. SAC couldn't have that, so the Squadron was placed under administrative control of the 98th Bomb Wing at Lincoln.

That may have seemed like a good idea at the time. However, the assignment of the tankers to the 98th would cause all kinds of problems. The 98th had just arrived at Lincoln and was in the process of training to become combat ready. As such they really didn't have time or facilities to be saddled with an orphaned squadron of tankers.

Everett Caudel of the 307th AREFS recalled:

"I arrived at LAFB on Labor Day 1954. There wasn't a single B-47 on the ramp. The conditions were sparse. Our crewmen worked for months on the warped hardwood floors in the barracks to get them habitable. Our 'orderly room' was first in one of the barracks, then an office in a hangar, and I believe finally a large room at the end of the engine test stand stalls. That engine test stand building was a hazard. The snow would blow in under the entrance door, make a drift, melt slightly and then freeze, making a six to eight foot long ice slide just inside the door. More than one tailbone was hurt there. I believe Lt 'Frosty' Frost and I built the briefing platform. As the Squadron didn't have any lockers for flying suits, parachutes, etc, we also built 'outhouse size' lockers for each crew out of liberated CE lumber. We *were* resourceful out of necessity."

The KC-97s that arrived at Lincoln for the 307th came from Hunter AFB, and were well-worn "F" models. Because of this there were subtle differences between these and the newer "G" models in the 98th. Small differences, but enough to cause all kinds of problems in maintenance. John Sinclair recalled some of the early days:

"Our crew was sent to Lincoln as one of two instructor crew to help form the 307th AREFS. Capt Smoltz headed up our crew, and I believe the other instructor crew commander was Capt Fletcher. We came from the 310th AREFS out of Salina, Kansas, and were quite new to air refueling ourselves, but someone said we were instructors and instruct we did. I can still remember teaching a grizzled old B-29 gunner who was attempting to make his first contact with a B-47. He was lying on the ironing board in the boom pod and I was right on top of him so that I could keep my left hand on the extension handle and my right hand on the stick. You could get thrown out of the service for doing that these days! Many of our students were fresh from the Korean War, where they had flown the B-29. Most weren't too impressed with the likes of this 20 year old 'boomer' instructing them on anything, much less playing hunky-bunky on an ironing board in the rear of a tanker!"

The oncoming Nebraska winter caused more problems. There was limited hangar space to house the big tankers, so most of the routine work had to be done on the flightline in snow and freezing temperatures. Engines had to be preheated to perform within safety limits. The cold weather also caused fuel leaks and radio problems, and turned the pliable rubber tires into rock hard donuts.

Before any of the planes arrived, several members of the new 307th had arrived from Tech School. Young Marv Nystrom had arrived in early summer of 1954. There wasn't anyone in place for him to report to. Kenny Smith arrived on July 21, 1954, and found a Navy Reserve Clerk to sign in with. He recalled, "We were pretty much left alone to do whatever we wanted to do, just show up for morning report."

Paul Koski recalled arriving at the Trailways Bus Depot about 7 PM on November 11, 1954, after a two-day bus trip from Amarillo Texas:

"I asked the clerk about a bus going to the base. He had no idea what I was talking about, but said, 'There is a pick up point on 'O' Street where people sometimes get a ride to the base. Just west on 'O,' you can't miss it.'

"I found the pick up point; the temperature was about twenty degrees with blowing snow. My first impression of Lincoln was that no one lives there. I stood there for over an hour, and during that time I could have shot a cannon down 'O' Street and not hit a single car. I did get a ride to the base from a lieutenant and checked in. I was the seventh person to sign into the Squadron. I pulled CQ for a couple of weeks, and then they farmed us out to the 98th to get some hands-on experience on the B-47."

On November 24, 1954, 66 officers began transition training to the B-47 at McConnell AFB, near Wichita, Kansas. The next contingent from the 307th began training on December 14, 1954. Most of the men who retrained at McConnell believed that the base had been named for Joseph McConnell, the top scoring fighter ace of the Korean War. Actually, it had been named after the McConnell brothers, who had served with the 307th Bomb Group in World War II.

The advance party had arrived at Lincoln in November and began taking care of some of the problems faced by the incoming 307th. The advance party was led by Maj William Minor. Other members of the party were Maj Dale Samuelson and Sgt Paul Tasler.

There may have been a few members of the 307th who noticed a lot of activity brewing on the north end of the ramp on 7 December. Near the large north hangar a group of airmen were standing in formation; they appeared to be waiting for something. That something was the arrival of the first B-47. That afternoon a shiny B-47 made a pass over the runway and then peeled off for landing. As she taxied in, a couple of the guys from the 98th noted her tail number as 51-2207. She would be the first of many B-47s to be assigned to Lincoln.

Slowly, other newly assigned members of the 307th began arriving at Lincoln. Jerry Kilgore arrived on 12 December and signed into the 372nd Squadron. He recalled that it snowed on 27 December and didn't melt till spring. Quite a shock for a Texas boy.

It had taken awhile, but the 307th had officially arrived at Lincoln.

# Cold War Cornhuskers: The 307th Bomb Wing Lincoln Air Force Base Nebraska 1955-1965

Activation Ceremony, August 4, 1946 MacDill Field, Florida (307th BW)

The 307th flew it's first combat mission just ten days after being alerted for deployment to Kadena, Okinawa. (USAF)

## 307th Bomb Wing - The Early Years

A B-29 from the 307th drops it's payload on a Communist Target. (USAF)

Col. Louis Thorup assumed command of the 307th BW on June 7, 1954. (USAF)

# Cold War Cornhuskers: The 307th Bomb Wing Lincoln Air Force Base Nebraska 1955-1965

370th Bomb Squadron (USAF)

372nd Bomb Squadron (Aenchbacher)

B-29 42-94032 receives a Farewell from Hickam Field Hawaii on her way to the United States and retirement. She was the last true B-29 bomber in service with SAC. (307th BWAssoc)

The World War II Chapel still stands at Lincoln Air Park. (M.Hill)

## 307th Bomb Wing - The Early Years

KB-29s taxi out for another mission at Davis Monthan, AFB. (Stolt)

KB-29 on short final at Davis Monthan. (Stolt)

Downtown Lincoln Nebraska as viewed from the observation area of the Capital Building. Lincoln Air Force Base can be seen in the distance.

# 1955

The year 1955 began clear and cold at Lincoln Air Force Base. Day by day, more arrivals reported for duty with the 307th. Most of the wing activity centered on trying to get organized. Each new arrival had to sign in, find quarters and unpack his gear. Since there was no base housing, married officers and airmen had to find housing off base in the city of Lincoln. Unmarried airmen would be assigned rooms in the barracks.

On Tuesday, 11 January, Col Louis Thorup left Lincoln for McConnell AFB, Kansas, to attend B-47 pilot update training. After all, if you are going to command a SAC Wing, you had better be able to lead your crews into the air. In his absence, Col Ernest Hardin Jr. assumed command of the 307th.

While things were getting organized at Lincoln, the new aircraft commanders and copilots were learning how to fly the B-47. Most of them had flown B-29s or the giant B-36. At the time, the B-47 was the only all-jet bomber in existence to carry out SAC's global deterrent mission.

Now you just don't don your brain bucket, strap in and blast off into the wild blue in a B-47. First, the flight crews had to pass the academic portion of the training program. In order to pass, they not only had to read the book, but commit much of it to memory. That piece of required reading was the T.O.-1B-47E-1, or "Dash-1." Almost everything in the world you wanted, or needed to know about how to fly the B-47 was contained on the printed pages of that manual!

Along with the Dash-1, crews attended classes on the how, what, and why of all the different systems within that aluminum package known as the B-47. Electrical, hydraulic, fuel and flight control systems were studied, memorized and tested on. Only after passing the final test in the academic training did the crews even get near a real B-47.

There she was! Sitting on the ramp at McConnell, she was big, sleek and beautiful. Even if she was just a TB-47, she was still a B-47, and the crews could hardly wait to get their hands on her. From wing tip to wing tip she measured 116 feet. She was over 109 feet long, and stood over 27 feet on her landing gear. Hanging from each wing were three big J-47 engines that would get her into the air. She was sure a beautiful sight sitting there on the ramp.

The first flight in a TB-47 was an orientation flight. Usually a take off, a couple of trips around the pattern, then head for the designated training area. If you had sweet talked the instructor enough, maybe he would actually let you take the controls and fly her straight and level for a few minutes, just to get the feel of her. And what a feeling, all that power and speed rolled into one package.

The days passed by in a blur. Each time they went up, there was something new to master. Everything from formation flying to letdown and approach had to be mastered by the fledgling B-47 pilots. Each step was done under the watchful eye of the instructor. One mistake could lead to a setback or, worse yet, washing out of the program.

Without a doubt, the trickiest part of flying the B-47 was getting her off the ground and back down in one piece. Her J-47 engines took time to spool up to full power. It seemed to take hours to gain full speed, so everything had to be done by the book.

The unique bicycle landing gear presented special quirks on landing that only a fellow B-47 pilot could appreciate. If you touched down on the forward gear she could bounce and porpoise on you. The idea was to touch down on both front and rear landing gear at the same time; that's a greaser. A lot of pilots figured if you got her up and then got her down without pranging it was a successful mission.

There was another aspect of flying a B-47, as Gene Aenchbacher related:

"It may seem strange to some single-engine pilots, but bomber and other multi-engine pilots prefer to have a side by side cockpit seating arrangement when flying two-, four-, or six-engine aircraft, and some of us admit the adjustment to the tandem cockpit of the B-47 was disconcerting, at least in the beginning [Some say they never liked it]."

After all the book work, testing, flying and check flights, it was graduation day. Pilots were now qualified to fly the B-47. Qualified yes, but most pilots will tell you that the real learning process to become a SAC Combat Crew was just about to begin.

Joseph Anthony describes how the new navigators fit into the upgrade program. He recalled:

"Shortly after Christmas of 1954, I, along with William 'Bill' Bathurst, Frank Goetz, Dick Gromberg, Earl Johnson and several others reported in to the 307th at Lincoln, Nebraska, after completing our navigator B-47 electronic computer (bombing/navigation) training at Mather AFB, California. Upon my arrival at the 372nd Bomb Squadron orderly room, I was informed that I was the first combat crew navigator to report for duty since the squadron had returned from overseas.

## 1955

"Because the 307th did not possess any B-47 aircraft and to justify my base pay, etc., I had to perform some tasks until I could be assigned to a crew and start training for what I was selected to do. I was assigned to the 307th Air Refueling Squadron Field Maintenance office to 'shuffle papers' until the 372nd was ready to use my services.

"After what seemed like an eternity, I finally met my other crew members: Maj Bill Holden, aircraft commander, and Capt Carl Germundson, copilot. We were designated as Crew N-61.

"Shortly after I joined my crew, the 307th started receiving its first 'worn out' early model B-47Es (the ones that still had the window in the nose and just forward of the navigator's left foot). They were equipped with the 'K' bombing/navigation system and a six-inch APQ-23 radar scope.

"Our next move was to McConnell AFB, where the pilots received flight training in TB-47s. The navigators were exposed to ground school only—understandably so, since the TBs weren't equipped with bombing/navigation systems and, more importantly, they didn't have an ejection seat in the nose compartment.

"Our combat crew flight training began when we returned to Lincoln. Our first flights were on a volunteer basis, since they were 'local area' sorties for the benefit of copilot training. I believe at this time the 307th had acquired three or four 'instructor crews' from Castle AFB, California, who took us under their wings and taught us all they had acquired as 'combat-ready' B-47 navigators. The one instructor-navigator, whom I shall long remember, was Capt Frank Leslie. He certainly knew how to instruct.

"Wouldn't you know it—as soon as my crew and Bill Bathurst's crew accumulated 200 flying hours in the B-47, we were assigned to standboard! And if ever there was an impetus to learn your trade, it's being thrust into an evaluator role."

While the officer crew members were learning to fly, navigate and bomb with the B-47, there were a lot of enlisted men learning how to keep those birds in the air. There were several technical schools for ground crews. The one they attended depended on what they were going to have as a specialty.

Crew chiefs had to know every system, backwards and forwards, blindfolded. From nose to tail, every rivet down to the last zerk had to be mastered. The mission and the lives of the flight crew would depend on how well the crew chief kept his bird.

To help the crew chief keep the planes ready there were specialists for every system on the B-47. There were Bomb/Nav, Engine, Hydraulics, and Armament and Electronics specialists who had to be ready to tear off a panel and dig into the guts of any problem bomber. Nobody flew until the plane was as mechanically perfect as possible.

The only flying being done by the 307th during January and February was being done by the 307th AREFS. After all, they had the only planes, but they weren't getting off the ground very often. There were several reasons the tankers weren't getting much flight time. First, they had been attached to the 98th Bomb Wing for administrative purposes. Since the 98th was trying to get combat ready, they didn't have time or facilities to operate two tanker squadrons. In view of this, the 307th AREFS was released from their attachment to the 98th on February 1st.

Nebraska winter weather didn't help either. The 307th AREFS lost 122 flying hours in February due to freezing rain, snow, and below-minimum weather conditions. They did manage to spend 405 hours in the air and make 572 hook ups. They transferred over 540,000 pounds of JP-4 during those hookups; not too shabby for a new outfit.

Then there were the planes themselves. The original tankers were well-worn KC-97Fs the squadron inherited at Maxwell and brought to Lincoln. These tankers were well traveled. They had been stationed at Hunter AFB near Savannah, Georgia. Coming from the south, they hadn't been winterized and weren't used to sitting on a cold, snowy flight line. The onset of cold weather had brought on a rash of problems, everything from cracked prop blades to fuel leaks.

The squadron had also received some new KC-97Gs. These were new from the factory, and once they were checked out and got the factory bugs out them, they were great.

There wasn't enough hangar space available at Lincoln at the time. Since the 307th AREFS had been detached from the 98th BW, the 98th had been authorized by SAC to take over almost all of the hangar space on the base. The 98th had arrived on Base first. Well, you know the old saying, "First come...!"

No hangar space meant almost everything that had to be fixed had to be done outside on the ramp. Major work that did require hangar space had to be scheduled through the 98th. Pushing paperwork and getting the space was about as fast as... well... molasses in January.

The 307th spent the first two months of 1955 getting organized and settling in at Lincoln. Manpower grew day-by-day as more officers and airmen reported for duty in Cornhusker Land. The 307th still didn't have any B-47s to work on or fly. Everyone was more than ready for the first real B-47 to arrive so they could get going.

Early in March, the rumor mill started cranking out almost daily ditto sheets of the latest "straight poop," on the arrival date of the wing's first B-47. A couple of the wheeler-dealers even had a pool going. A buck a square was all you needed for a chance to win the pot. There were even some side bets going on over who would win the pot.

Whoever picked Monday, March 14th, won the pool. Members of the 307th were told to report to the flight line in Class A Blues for the arrival ceremonies. There was the usual shuffling around trying to get organized on the south side of the big south hangar. A flat bed trailer and sound system were ready for the anticipated arrival. So, there they were, all lined up in squadron formation, decked out in their fine blue suits waiting for the scheduled arrival time, which came and went.

Anyone who has served in the military is all too familiar of the adage, "Hurry up and wait." That day was no exception to the rule. At least they were on the south side of the hangar where the sun could shine on them. Wasn't long before the troops were stamping their feet and blowing into their cupped hands trying to fend off the cool of the day. After about thirty minutes of doing the "cupped hands shuffle" they heard the unmistakable sound of approaching jet engines. Expectant eyes scanned the sky in anticipation of the sight of the first B-47 to arrive at the 307th BW.

There she was, 52-054, flown by none other than Col Louis Thorup, the Wing Commander, Maj Edwin Jenkins, was copilot and Maj Frank Remmele was up front in the nose navigating. Col Thorup made a low pass so his boys could see what they had been waiting for. He followed up with a nice landing and then taxied toward the formation. The Base Commander began his speech, "This is a proud day for the 307th Bomb Wing." His words were lost in the whine of the six jet engines as 054 taxied in, then stopped on the ramp. All eyes turned, expecting to see a bright new B-47 from the factory. Paul Koski remembers that day:

"The aircraft taxied in and instead of cheers, there was dead silence. We had been working on the 98th aircraft, which were 'E' models, brand new, right from the factory. They were like a new car with that new car smell and no major maintenance problems. This thing that taxied in was like a bad dream. It had red doors on the forward landing gear and the wings were splashed with green chromate paint. The whole aircraft looked dirty."

## Cold War Cornhuskers: The 307th Bomb Wing Lincoln Air Force Base Nebraska 1955-1965

Col Thorup climbed down the ladder and moved to the flatbed to address his troops. Even he seemed a little disappointed with what he brought to Lincoln that day.

"Needless to say the commander's speech wasn't well received," Paul Koski recalled. "When someone asked why the 98th got new aircraft and we got hand-me-downs, his answer, I thought, was very good, even if we weren't too happy with it. 'We are in a training mode, and when we can show what we can do to make these planes combat ready, then we will get new aircraft. Until that time comes, we *will* bring these aircraft up to 307th and SAC standards.'"

That same day eight more B-47s arrived at Lincoln. They didn't look much better than the first one. They were all well-worn "E" models that hadn't been sent to the depot for update to the 731 standard. Like the tankers, these B-47s had come from Hunter AFB, Georgia. Seemed like everything the 307th was getting was from Georgia. Maybe so, but they sure weren't peaches.

Not only did the 307th get their first B-47s that day, the first large contingent of maintenance personnel arrived. They were mostly system specialists who had been training at various locations around the country. Judging from the looks of the nine B-47s sitting on the flight line as the sun went down, those specialists were going to be needed in the next few weeks.

Each squadron was assigned three of the newly arrived B-47s. Each plane was assigned to a crew chief, whose job was to check the old gal out and see just what shape she was really in. During the next week, the crew chiefs went over the aircraft with a fine-toothed wrench. The results were about as expected; each plane had an average of 83 discrepancies. The fewest were found on 52-066, while the first "Dog Award" went to 52-120.

During March, the 307th AREFS was alerted for a TDY deployment to Goose Bay, Labrador. John Herder recalled:

"When I heard it was going to happen, I mustered up my courage and went to Lt Col Thurlow, our squadron commander. I suggested to him that since I had spent a year in Iceland in an Air Rescue Squadron, I really didn't want to go where it was cold. If we were going to the Bahamas, I would be more than happy to go. Maybe he could leave me at Lincoln and I'd watch over his office for him. He missed the humor of it all and made me a lead navigator—'and don't get us lost!!'"

A lot of the crews reflected John's thoughts. It was cold at Lincoln; going to Goose Bay would be like going from the fridge and into the freezer.

With the impending trip to the North Country there was a flurry of activity on the south end of the flight line. Crew chiefs worked long hours to get their tanker ready for the trip north to DA GOOSE. The tankers had to be winterized. Every hose connection had to be checked and tightened. Flexible lines had to be checked and retightened. Spark plugs had to be changed over to a special type that was supposed to be better in cold latitudes.

A large contingent of new flight crews arrived from McConnell on Monday, 28 March. With their arrival, the 307th was ready to begin training to become a Combat Ready SAC wing. Ready, yes, but these crews had just completed their basic flight training in the B-47. Again, there would have to be a period of organization before the real flying could begin.

By the end of March, the 307th was manned by 1,368 airmen and 280 officers. They had nine B-47s and 33 crews to man them. There were three crews that would serve as instructor crews for the wing.

The B-47 conversion program began early on Monday, April 25th. The flight crews had completed flight training at McConnell and were ready, willing and eager to get going. The conversion program was divided into three Phases. In Phase One the crews had to fly four basic missions and complete a special Field Check Ride. As soon as they passed the check ride they would begin Phase Two.

Phase Two began with another check ride just to make sure they knew what they were doing. The check ride was followed by five missions with instructors on board. These flights were to include mission planning, navigation, gunnery, and air refueling. Then, the crew would fly a solo mission followed by a night mission. Finally, they would fly a heavyweight mission with refueling. Every aspect of flying would be done over and over, checked, rechecked, and then for good measure rechecked by a Senior Instructor. So, until the crews were Combat Ready, it would be a constant routine of plan, then fly, plan and fly, then do it all over again. Day by day, night by night, the crews flew and got better and better at it.

Every time a crew returned from a mission, the Crew Chief and ground specialists would check the Form 781 for write ups, then start getting the bird ready for the next mission. The B-47 was serviced with JP-4, oxygen, engine oil, and any other fluid that needed topping off. Any problems were trouble-shot and repaired. It was a never ending cycle of fly, fix and fly again.

Anytime a bird left the roost on a mission, the Grim Reaper could be flying as an additional crew member. On May 24th, 52-054 took off at about 1700 hours for a night navigation mission up to Montana and Idaho. The crew that night was John Koudsi (AC), Dean Knight in the back seat and James Evans up in the nose to navigate. Ed Seagraves was the Crew Chief on 52-064, which was down for maintenance. He was aboard 054 to get his time in for flight pay. The crew had no idea the Reaper was along as the fifth crewman.

The flight was routine until 054 returned to Lincoln at about 0100 hours that next morning. On approach, they were advised there were rain showers in the area along with gusty crosswinds at Lincoln. They checked their gross weight and the charts for the correct cross wind and gust component for a best flare speed and landing. Airspeed was added to compensate for the gusts. Final approach was a bit bumpy, but nothing serious at the moment.

In typical Nebraska fashion, the weather changed within a matter of moments. The crosswind died as the B-47 crossed the threshold. With the extra airspeed, the plane kept flying beyond the touchdown point. 054 just kept floating through the air, eating up runway with each second of flight.

054 finally touched down with a spray of water from the wet runway and John Koudsi called for the drag chute. Dean Knight reached for the handle with his right hand and pulled it. There should have been a tug of deceleration as the chute billowed; there wasn't. Dean Knight shot a glance over his shoulder. The chute had failed to deploy.

The B-47 charged down the runway like a runaway freight train. Koudsi was tramping the brakes, trying to slow the big silver locomotive. On a puddled runway it seemed futile. The reaper smiled from his fifth seat; he had them in his icy grip. In a move born out of desperation they tried to ground loop the careening B-47. Ed Seagraves remembered:

"The runway was being extended and there was an excavation at the end of it. There was a concrete slab with lights on it marking the end of the runway. We hit the slab and the forward main gear linkage broke. The forward main retracted backwards into the bomb bay. When the plane came to a stop the forward part of the fuselage was in the dirt. The inboard engine pods had rotated and the exhaust cones stuck up into the flap wells. The outboard engines were lying flat on the ground."

# 1955

In the last frantic moments, John Koudsi pulled the fire shutoff switches to cut off fuel to the engines, hoping to prevent a fire and explosion. The emergency canopy release was pulled to unlock the canopy. Seagraves recalled the next few moments, "The aircraft commander, copilot, and I pushed the canopy off and we exited the plane, down the fuselage and down the right wing. We were clear of the plane before the crash trucks arrived." The navigator wasn't far behind.

John Koudsi and crew cheated the Grim Reaper that morning aboard 054, but they wouldn't get off scot-free. An accident investigation board would be convened to find out what had caused the mishap.

The 307th AREFS left Lincoln in early April for their tour at Goose Bay. They were going to be gone about 45 days. The winter in Lincoln seemed to last forever. When the tankers left, the snow was almost gone and some of the trees were starting to get buds on them. Flying to the northeast towards DA GOOSE, the KC's flew from spring back into winter as they got closer to their destination. Frank Harvey remembered:

"Lt Pavlas was the AC and I was the copilot. The initial approach and landing is the most vivid memory I have of the entire time there. We landed in a canyon of white. So much snow had fallen over the winter that it was piled above the level of the cockpit of the KC-97. The tower was out of sight as we rolled out on landing. There were these little passageways cut for us to taxi into the ramp. Snow was so high in front of the base operations building that a tunnel was cut through the snow to the doors."

Goose Bay was built during WWII to help defend Canada against a possible attack by Nazi forces. It is situated at the far end of Hamilton Bay. Because of the cold weather, isolation and Spartan living conditions it had quite a reputation in SAC. It was an old saying that if you screwed up, you'd end up at "Goose." The 307th hadn't had time to really screw anything up, yet here they were at Goose Bay.

On arrival the crews wanted to get to their quarters and get some chow and then maybe some sack time. The meal wasn't good and the quarters weren't much better. The 307th was assigned to an area near the main runway. The barracks were open bay leftovers from the war, with maybe one or two oil burning stoves to heat the building. If you were close to a stove you roasted and froze if you happened to have an end bunk.

Back to the mess hall, hoping the chow would be better; no such luck. For the rest of their tour it would be the same basic chow: lots of hamburger, powdered eggs, creamed corn, beans, dry bread and the old military standby Spam. The cooks tried to come up with different ways of using the stores they had on hand to please the troops. Let's face it, there may be a hundred ways of cooking it, but Spam always was and ever will be Spam.

If flying from the plains of Nebraska in the winter was hard, it could be classified as almost impossible from Goose. The cold weather and snow posed all kinds of problems. Some of the worst problems were caused by bad carburetors and fuel valve malfunctions. At the time of the TDY, the squadron was hampered by the lack of qualified ground personnel. Anything that could go wrong in normal conditions was compounded by the weather. Just getting the four big R-4360 engines started was considered a major victory. They had to be preheated for several hours just to get them to turn over.

Shortly after arriving the tankers began flying in the harsh weather conditions, which would test just how well the 307th AREFS could perform their mission. The primary mission was to provide tanker support for the 55th SRW during Operation Meadowlark II. During that operation, the tanker crews flew over 43 hours and offloaded enough JP-4 for the 55th to complete their mission. H. A. "Jack" Frost wrote:

"I only flew one mission from Goose. It was an orientation flight to Thule and BW-1. BW-1 was an abbreviation for Bluie West 1 in Greenland, a combined military and civilian airport located at the end of a fjord. It was a sticky visual approach type airport that you committed yourself to land if you passed a certain landmark in the fjord that was the point of no return. You landed straight ahead and took off in the opposite direction. As we got near, an engine started backfiring over the water so we returned to Goose. A day or so later I fell on the ice, breaking my foot, and became a ground pounder."

"Frosty" was fitted out with a cast from his toes to his knee. Can't just have a troop sitting around, so he was assigned to SAC Operations for the duration.

Another day, another mission to fly. This time it was to refuel a flight of F-84 fighters on the way to England. Everything went well, except that they got a mixture of JP-4 and AVGAS. This isn't usually a problem for the J-47 engines on the B-47. However, the F-84 had J-65 engines and the AVGAS just didn't burn well in that engine. A couple of days later a message came into Goose saying that there were 25 engine changes when the fighters arrived in England.

Flying out of Goose was anything but routine. John Herder recalled:

"We took off one morning. As usual, the AC and copilot were handling the flight controls and the flight engineer was standing behind the throttle quadrant with both hands on the throttles, moving them as the AC told him to. We were climbing out, when suddenly we hit the prop wash of the plane in front of us. Our plane bounced and the flight engineer fell backwards, still holding the throttles, which caused loss of power on all four engines!

"Out of the front windows, I could see the **base** of the mountains ahead of us, and the lake or river. I yelled to the AC—the AC, copilot and engineer were yelling at each other, 'MORE POWER! MORE POWER!'—'I'M TRYING!!' I yelled at the AC to aim for the water—maybe it would put the fire out after we crashed.

"As we continued downward, it dawned on me that we were not dumping fuel. I yelled at the engineer to dump it. He yelled back that he couldn't because the AC hadn't given him the word. I told him to dump it or I'd shoot him. I don't know with what, a rubber band? Anyway he started dumping. That combined with more engine power and I could now see the middle of the mountain. We were getting closer to it, but climbing. With one last grunt we made it over the top of the mountain. I figured there might be a pine tree stuck in the boom, but there wasn't. A week or so after the flight, the A/C and copilot were sent home and we got new ones.

"Both seemed like nice guys, so if they could fly, things would be fine. Our first flight with them was at night. We took off and were climbing out nicely. Suddenly, one of the scanners in the back called and said it looked like #3 was one fire. The new copilot looked out the window, said 'Yep,' and the #3 was shut down.

"The A/C told the engineer to dump the fuel, then asked me for a heading back to the base. Rather than telling him just to turn around, I figured it sounded more professional to give him a new heading, even though it was just a 180. We got back and landed safely."

Every tanker squadron in SAC was always proud when they could chalk up a "save." A save was just that, a tanker being able to get enough fuel into a receiver to get safely back to a base instead of crashing due to lack of fuel. The 307th was credited with a save while at Goose Bay.

The crews were briefed for a night Mass Gas mission. Mass Gas refuelings were always interesting. They usually had six tankers flying in

# Cold War Cornhuskers: The 307th Bomb Wing Lincoln Air Force Base Nebraska 1955-1965

a loose formation in the rendezvous area. The receivers would arrive and try to find their assigned tanker. Then it was move into position, hook up, and wait for the lead receiver to give the word to begin transferring fuel. Doing this at night increased the pucker factor by 100%.

Everything went as briefed except for one of the bombers. They were running low on fuel. They found their tanker and flew into the observation position, then moved in for contact. They radioed their leader and asked permission to take on fuel since they were just about dry. The leader told them to hold off till the other B-47s were ready. This left the low fuel bomber hanging on the boom waiting for the rest of his flight while burning fuel that he didn't have to spare.

The boomer apparently heard the plea for fuel and started pumping fuel without the "official" go ahead. They had taken on about a thousand pounds of fuel when they got the word "Commence Transfer." Without warning, the rear engine mount on the "early bird" gave way, causing the #6 engine to rotate upwards into the leading edge of the wing. The drag and asymmetrical thrust caused a momentary uncontrolled yaw and then an out of limits disconnect. The boomer could only watch as the B-47 headed down towards the Atlantic.

Lady Luck was the fourth person aboard the B-47 that evening. The first bit of luck was that the refueling track was on about the same heading as Harmon AB, Newfoundland, so they didn't have to make any major heading changes. The damaged B-47 was able to make an emergency landing after some tense time in the air for the crew. H. A. Frost recalled:

"A few days later, we got a message from the AC gratefully thanking the tanker crew for the unauthorized early transfer of the fuel. The thousand pounds of fuel they got was about all they had left when they landed at Harmon. If the boomer hadn't started pumping fuel when he did they would never have made it."

Days grew longer, the temperature was warmer, and the high banks of snow seemed to dwindle lower and lower with each passing day. Several recall that, with the melting snow, there appeared a rather large melt pond, which they named Lake Thurlow in honor of the Squadron Commander.

All flying and no fun makes for bad morale. There were the daily poker games that went on into the night. Several were introduced to the pleasure and rigors of trying to catch a fish through the ice. As always, skill and luck governed who would have a fresh fish supper to supplement the regular chow.

Since they were in the land of snow and cold, there were plenty of spur-of-the-moment snowball fights. There was always someone waiting in ambush to fire a firmly packed snowball at the unwary. Favorite targets included anyone who happened to be in the danger zone. Rank was never considered a safety factor, as everyone from the CO down to airman was fair game for the white missiles.

The night before departing Goose for the long trip back to Lincoln, some of the men thought a farewell departure party was in order. One last time to get the antifreeze level up in the old bloodstream. They pooled their money and sent a committee to get the good stuff. That night the booze flowed like a melting glacier. Clay Robson remembered, "Needless to say, there was a lot of throwing up at the barracks later. You had to stand in line to get outside between the snow banks."

The following day, with light hearts and heavy heads the 307th AREFS bid farewell to DA GOOSE and headed back to the Beef State. It is safe to say that the throbbing of the big R-4360 engines didn't do a lot of good for those who were suffering from the previous night's self-inflicted wound. Even oxygen didn't do a lot to help those wounds.

It was a long flight back to Lincoln. There were a lot of hello hugs and kisses when they arrived back home. The base had changed a little, the kids had gotten a little bigger and, most important, their wives were a lot better looking.

While the tanker squadron was at DA GOOSE, the bomber crews were busy at Lincoln. Training was the name of the game. They were cramming as many flying hours into the 24-hour day as possible. That meant flying during the day and night, around the clock, only pausing long enough to service the aircraft, fix what was needed, plan and get back into the air. The crews were seeing a lot of the United States. That is, what could be seen from 35,000 feet in the air. By the end of June the Wing had 15 crews that were combat ready.

Then, there was the "great fuel boom mystery." One day, in the spring, Nebraska Farmer Brown showed up at the main gate with a bent up refueling boom sticking out of the back of his pickup. "I dug this up while I was plowing the other day, here Sunday, a week. Looks kinda like one of them there pipes you fellas have on some of those planes you have there."

The item in question was indeed a refueling boom. A quick check showed it was a boom from a KB-29P, not a KC-97. A message was sent to SAC Hq, who in turn replied, "Not one of ours, could be from sister TAC." Who knew!!! There hadn't been a KB-29P over that part of the Cornhusker State in a coon's age. "By the way, Farmer Brown, we can't pay you for your trouble, but thanks anyway." To this day the how, when, and why the boom ended up in that Nebraska field is a mystery.

On the afternoon of 30 June, Capt Joe Pavlas and tanker Crew T-04 departed Lincoln for a routine training flight. Fly out to somewhere, refuel someone, navigate to Point B, and then return to Lincoln. Just another flight. Frank Harvey flew copilot and wrote:

"We had been on a mission that brought us back to the base at around 0200 hours (July 1). It was a black night without any moon and maybe an overcast. We were directed to park over a refueling pit at the north end of the ramp opposite the 98th AREFS.

"There were no lights around any of the airplanes, no vehicles either. We called the Command Post to ask them to get some maintenance people out to our pit and direct us over it. We waited awhile, but no one showed up. We were tired and wanted to go home. So we decided to have A1C Willie Ezell (Asst. Boom Operator) go outside and direct us over the pit.

"Only the inboard engines (#2 & #3) were running. All exterior lights were on. The wheel well lights were on so that there would be light in the area around the pit when we were over it. The Boom Operator (TSgt. Norman Doland) briefed Willie to go outside the #1 engine and go around the front where Pavlas could see him and give hand signals to direct us over the pit. It was practice never to go near the running engines. However, we always went between #2 and the fuselage when the engines were NOT running.

"Willie goes out the back entrance door. Now, he is out of sight of everyone in the airplane. The next sound we hear is a heavy dull thump and the #2 engine RPM drops a few hundred revs, but immediately returned to 800 RPM for idle. Pavlas looked out the window and could see Willie lying on the ground in front of the #1 engine.

"I called the tower and told them we have an injured man that was hit by a propeller and please send an ambulance immediately. We shut down the engine and the Flight Engineer James O'Conner went out the front hatch to see if he could do anything. By the time I got out, I could see Willie was dead. We all suspected that he tried to duck between the #2 prop and the fuselage."

The investigation could not determine exactly what had caused A1C Willie Ezell Jr. to accidentally walk into the running #2 propeller. Joe Pavlas and his crew were devastated. Their fellow crewman and friend would fly with them no more. In a cruel twist of irony, the crew recalled that Willie was going on leave shortly to get married.

News of the accident spread like wildfire through the ranks of the 307th that day. Morning report was subdued by the news. Few, if any, really cared that Lincoln AFB was now under control of the 8th Air Force. They had lost a member of the wing, but more important, they had lost a brother in arms.

8th Air Force headquarters at Westover AFB sent a directive for the refueling squadron to fly Operation Picket Fence. The mission was to support the 9th Bomb Wing during their Unit Simulated Combat Mission (USCM) on 6 and 8 July. The 307th AREFS put 15 tankers into the air for the two-day exercise. During that time they offloaded 580,000 pounds of JP-4 to the thirsty bombers. Most of the mission went according to the profile. The most notable problem was weather along the refueling track.

Capt Don Chambers and crew were flying 52-2795, call sign Purdue 19 during the mass gas refueling on the night of the 6th. Darwin 30 from the 9th BW had made contact and was taking on fuel. There were thunderstorms in the area and the turbulence was giving both aircraft a roller coaster ride. Both aircraft went up and down like a couple of yo-yos with Darwin 30 trying to stay on the boom.

There were several disconnects as the airspeed fluctuated and both tanker and receiver bounced around the track. The tanker banked 10 degrees to the right to avoid some fast building cumulus cells. Then they banked 10 degrees to the left to miss another cell. Darwin 30 stalled out and fell away from the boom completely inverted. The pilot was able to recover, gain the altitude back, and rendezvous with Purdue 19 about 50 miles down the track and complete the offload.

Reports of the incident were written and sent to Offutt. There were also several letters of "What the Hell Happened" exchanged between the commanders at Lincoln and Mountain Home AFB. Everyone agreed that it was a miracle that no one had been injured in the incident.

Doing a mass gas was always an interesting exercise. Tony Minnick recalled:

"We formed our cell of six B-47s over north central Kansas at an altitude of around 30,000 feet. Number 2 was 500 feet above number 1 and one mile to the right and a mile back. Number 3 was 1,000 ft above Number 1 and two miles to the right. Four, Five and Six were positioned in a like manner.

"Weather had briefed us the refueling area would be problematic, with clouds or bad weather in the area. As we approached the descent point, the lead tanker said he thought we'd be OK, as he could see all his tankers. It was nighttime, and we could see the lights of our tankers in the distance. The decision was to descend to our refueling altitudes. The lead was at 17,000 and plus 500 feet for the rest of us. Our altitude was 16,500 as we started moving towards the tanker. At this time, we started in and out of clouds. At first not much, but quickly we were in almost solid clouds. The navigator had a good clear contact on his radar and kept reporting our position: 5 miles, 4 miles, 3, 2, 1 mile, still no visual. The copilot said he could not see any other aircraft.

"We continued to move forward. The radar/nav said we were right behind the tanker, so we continued very slowly. We were now at a half-mile or closer. We decided to continue, but ever so slowly. I had slid up a bit, so I was only 200 feet below refueling altitude. I was about to call it quits, but I saw a glow in the gloom, and it had to be our tanker. We reported a not so clear visual, and shortly thereafter the boomer said he had us. The lights on the tanker were like in a fog. We made contact and took on our fuel with no disconnects. While we were refueling, we did have another tanker move above us (we think) as we heard the engine sounds as it went by. Don't know how close they were, but certainly close enough to be heard."

The 307th AREFS flew Operation Front Point, supporting the 340th Bomb Wing on 15 and 16 July. Then they turned around and flew support for the 90th Strategic Recon Wing in Operation Deep Rock on Saturday, 23 July. The tankers were busy and kept flying even with the problems of maintenance and inherent problems with the aircraft.

SAC headquarters sent a detailed operations order to the 307th in early July. The code name was Operation First Out. It was designed to prepare the Wing for combat readiness. It would be a profile mission flying from Lincoln back to Lincoln, with all kinds of interesting things to do along the way. There would be navigation legs, air refueling and bomb runs on two separate targets.

Operation First Out began on 26 July with a briefing for the nine crews that would fly the mission. Every moment of the flight was gone over in great detail. After all, this was their First Time Out.

Wednesday morning, 27 July, the nine flight crews reported for the final briefing. The nine crews that would fly the mission were commanded by:

Cell 1: James Sullivan, Fred Ouderkirk, Thomas Peebles.
Cell 2: Robert Hoover, Anthony Minnick, Louis Webber.
Cell 3: William Holden, Joseph Hull, James Mann.

The bomber cells would depart at one hour intervals, with one minute between aircraft launch. For the first time the 307th AREFS would provide support for their parent wing in the operation, with three tankers for each cell. Takeoff for the tankers would be at one-minute intervals. They would fly to the refueling rendezvous area, Green Airway 3, and be ready when the bomber cells arrived.

The first cell left Lincoln and took up the briefed heading towards Des Moines, Iowa. At the correct time the other cells departed and headed out for the mission. Shortly after each cell departed, the supporting tankers for the cell struggled into the air with their heavy loads of JP-4 and headed for the refueling point.

Passing over Des Moines, the cells turned and headed towards Worthington, Minnesota, then turned and flew to Sioux Falls, South Dakota. They made a slight heading correction and headed for the refueling rendezvous point near Grand Island, Nebraska. After closing the gap between each of the bombers the cell formation flew towards the waiting tankers.

The briefed route then took them on a heading back to the southeast. That heading would take them just south of Lincoln. From the refueling altitude the crews had a panoramic view of Lincoln and their home base as it slid below the formation. Rendezvous with the waiting KC-97s was about 14 miles southeast of Beatrice, Nebraska.

Weather was excellent, and the thirsty bombers had no trouble finding the tankers in the clear Nebraska sky. On command of the cell leader, the B-47s moved into position, hooked up, and began taking on fuel. By the time they reached Dodge City, Kansas, they had taken on the required fuel load.

**"Transfer complete. Disconnect when ready!"**

Near Alamosa, New Mexico, the cells crossed over into "enemy territory"; from here on, they could expect "Red" fighter attacks until they finished their penetration runs. The enemy must have been caught napping, as there were no fighter attacks on the run to Las Vegas, Nevada, or the return run back out to Hobbs, New Mexico.

With the penetration runs and fighters behind them, the cells began a grid navigation leg from Austin, Texas, to Greenwood, Mississippi, then on to Montgomery, Alabama. Reporting in over Montgomery, they turned for the first briefed target run. They were still over enemy territory, but no fighter attacks were scheduled for this part of the mission.

## Cold War Cornhuskers: The 307th Bomb Wing Lincoln Air Force Base Nebraska 1955-1965

The bomb run began over Eufala, Alabama, at about 35,000 feet. The navigators in the nose of each B-47 were busy setting up the "K" System for the run. At Paducah, Kentucky, they made the call, **"Departing IP. Second station has the aircraft."**

The time to release indicator began to wind down as they approached the target. **"30 Seconds to release, Tone ON!"** The high-pitched squeal stabs into the ears of the crew. **"Ten Seconds... Five seconds..... Bomb Away, Tone Break and Turn!"** Below, the city of St. Louis had been "destroyed" by a radar bomb.

After the breakaway it was off to the next target. This time they were to drop on a radar scoring target at Kansas City, Missouri. The process was repeated again until the tone cut off, indicating the release of another simulated bomb. They made a breakaway from the target to simulate escaping from the blast of a nuclear detonation, and then it was back on course for the return trip to Lincoln.

Operation First Out was in the bag. As the crews returned they assembled for debriefing, where they reported how the mission had gone and filled out the necessary paperwork. Everything had gone pretty well, considering it was the first simulated combat mission the wing had flown. The scores from the targets showed eight of the nine drops were close enough to be scored as effective. The nine bombers had flown a total of over 8,200 nautical miles. The KC-97s had off loaded over 361,000 pounds of JP-4 during the mission. For the "First Time Out" the 307th had scored better than expected.

Becoming combat ready meant you had to learn new methods and techniques to accomplish the mission. SAC began using what were called "heavyweight" takeoffs for the tankers. Simply put, the KC-97s would take off with a maximum combat load of fuel. This would bring the total takeoff weight of the tankers to about 175,000 pounds, give or take an ounce or two.

The dubious honor of making one of the first heavyweight takeoffs seems to have fallen on Capt Leroy Kutcher's crew in 793, known to her crew as "Baby Doll." Gerald Putnam remembered that they had to use the shorter runway and took off towards the Southeast:

"It was the only time the AC required the entire crew to be in crash landing positions on departure. There was a very tall brick building off the end of the runway and we would have been a lot more comfortable if we had cleared it by more than we did."

Anyone who ever took off or landed at Lincoln will recall there was a low hill or ridge just off the end of Runway 17 and "O" Street was just beyond the hill. This area was farmland, and a cornfield was nestled on the north side of the ridge. It wasn't a high ridge, just enough to be classified as a "vertical obstruction," which had to be cleared on takeoff. H. A. Frost recalled a heavyweight departure on Runway 17:

"All the engines ran fine. Acceleration seemed slower than normal, but then we expected that, didn't we? When we broke ground it was at a higher speed than computed lift off and rising terrain with a cornfield loomed ahead. We cleared it, but just barely. As we climbed out through 13,000 feet still at METO (Maximum Except Take Off) power to meet the B-47 waiting for fuel, #3 engine belched and blew its oil out the breather, so we feathered it. The aircraft immediately began to descend and we starting dumping fuel. We landed without further incident."

The Flight Engineer calculated how much fuel they had sprayed over the countryside and found out they had been 10,300 pounds over the War Emergency maximum gross weight. The air refueling tank gauges had been miscalibrated. The overweight condition was verified when over 10,000 pounds of fuel was drained from the tanks.

While the crew was checking the weight and draining fuel, the crew chief was looking at the feathered prop on #3 engine. Something just didn't seem right to his well-seasoned eyes. He glanced at all four props, then shook his head. He could have sworn the props tips had been painted yellow when they left the base. Now they were chlorophyll green! The only logical explanation was that they had done a little "corn husking" when they went over the top of the ridge.

We can only imagine the thrill West "O" motorists had when the huge tanker roared over from behind the ridge without warning and crossed the street a couple of hundred feet overhead. If there had been a Highway Patrolman there he may have tried to give them a speeding ticket.

In mid-August, the 307th was directed to fly another combat readiness preparation mission. This one would be a little more involved than the first one. Col Louis Thorup left Lincoln for Loring AFB on 17 August for a meeting of 8th Air Force Wing Commanders. At that meeting he was supposed to submit the mission plan and brief the 8th Air Force command staff on the progress of the 307th.

The 307th AREFS flew two major missions during the first weeks of August. Operation Knee Length was flown on the 10th and 11th supporting the 98th Bomb Wing. Then, they flew another tanker support mission for the 320th Bomb Wing's Operation Billy Club on August 19th through the 21st.

As always there was a problem with supply. Base Supply always appeared to be out of parts needed to keep the planes in the air. Now there was another problem. On 16 August the Wing sent a simple supply request, stating the wing needed 50 new flight suits. Supply came back with a note that there were no flights suits available. They mentioned flight suits were a SAC-controlled item and, as a result, the request would have to be forwarded to SAC.

X-Day for Operation Second Out was set for Tuesday, August 23rd. With that date fast approaching, the flight line was a beehive of activity to make sure the aircraft were as ready as possible for the mission. The operations plans called for the tankers to be loaded to the max for a heavyweight takeoff. That meant the crew chiefs had to double-check the engines and make sure that they were in tiptop shape.

Operation Second Out would be flown in two parts. Alpha would be flown on Tuesday; Bravo would be flown a week later on the 30th. The plan called for nine B-47s to fly on each part of the mission. The crews would have to complete cell tactics, heavyweight refueling, and strike two targets.

Alpha was flown as scheduled by the nine selected crews with very few problems. They hit the tankers, took on fuel and finished all the navigation legs without being very far off the money. From 37,000 feet the navigators put the cross hairs on the southwest corner of the Charleston Hotel, in Salt Lake City, Utah. As they broke away, it disappeared in a make-believe nuclear flash.

Second Out Bravo, flown on 30 August, was a horse of a different color. The mission appeared to be FUBAR from the get go. During engine start, one of the B-47s had a hot start on the #1 engine. Capt Bill Holden's plane had oil pressure fluctuations after engine startup. Then, during engine run-up on the end of the runway the oil pressure fell to zero. It would take twenty minutes to find and correct the problem. This was kind of embarrassing, since Col Thorup was aboard as mission commander.

Shortly after taking off, Capt Hal Brooks' aircraft lost the entire radar system. They managed to join up with their cell visually and more or less tag along. At Marysville, Kansas, the cells took up a heading for Strutter, Illinois, and continued to climb to altitude. At Strutter they turned for a short leg to Beloit, Wisconsin, where they turned towards Marshalltown, Iowa, and began descending for refueling.

Problems with the rendezvous radar in both the tankers and bombers made refueling an interesting game. It could be compared to the blind

24

## 1955

trying to find the blind in a dark room. On top of the radar problems, they were also having problems with the radio equipment.

In spite of the problems everyone met near the Refueling Rendezvous Point, found their tanker and took on the briefed load of JP-4 before they flew over the end refuel point near Harlan, Iowa. After dropping off the tankers, the bombers turned and started climbing as they headed for Sioux Falls, South Dakota.

At 37,000 feet they changed heading for Mitchell, South Dakota, to begin a grid navigation leg that would take them to Rawlins, Wyoming, then north to Yellowstone Lake. Following the mountains, they flew to Missoula, Montana, then turned towards the Pre IP at Boise, Idaho.

Over Boise, they corrected to a heading of 121 degrees for a 123 nautical mile flight to the IP at Burly, Idaho. The bomb run was on a heading of 141 degrees towards Salt Lake City. The radar picked up the north end of the Great Salt Lake as they crossed into the Beehive State. Off to their left lay the Wasatch Range. Far below, in the small town of Willard, a group of children were playing baseball. For a few moments they called time-out and watched the contrails cut a white ribbon in the sky.

At 37,000 feet there was no time for looking at the mountains or the Great Salt Lake. In the cramped nose of the planes the navigators were busy making final adjustments to the bombing system and checking the radar returns on Salt Lake City. At the precise moment the navigators called, "Bomb Away, Tone Cut off, Break Left!" Since Hal Brooks' B-47 had the sick radar system they could not bomb by radar. They gave it the old college try and made a visual run on the Charleston Hotel. Their run was scored as having hit somewhere in the state of Utah.

After the run on Salt Lake City, the cells headed across the mountains to hit the Denver bomb plot. Hal Brooks tagged along and gave it the old college try once again over Denver. The results were about the same. The bomb landed in Colorado. The old saying that close counted in horseshoes, hand grenades and atom bombs just didn't cut it in SAC. They wanted the bomb to hit within 2,500 feet of the target.

Post-mission debriefing was rather quiet and subdued. Of the nine planes flying the mission, only four were scored as effective. Brooks' crew was given "E" for effort. The only high point was Col Thorup's comment about the fact that this was a training mission, and as such a lot had been learned.

During August, the 307th AREFS was hampered by all kinds of problems. It was a wonder that they got planes in the air at all during the month. First, SAC sent a directive concerning propeller defects on the KC-97s. This grounded three tankers for the entire month. Six others were down for six to ten days while the tech orders were complied with. Then there were problems with worn throttle brackets causing slipping of power settings during flight. There were problems with spare parts available from supply. The biggest problem was manpower; the squadron was authorized 107 trained mechanics, but they had 91 on the squadron roster.

On 3 September Tech Reps from Boeing declared 52-054 as non-repairable. Her crash landing back in May had caused enough damage that she would be stricken from the rolls. The wings were removed and loaded aboard a C-124, and returned to Wichita to be used on other B-47s. The rest of the hulk was towed to the north end of the base and placed behind an old warehouse that had been designated as the Auto Hobby Shop.

Mission directives kept rolling down from SAC Headquarters at Offutt. Some felt since Omaha was only a stone's throw away, the wings at Lincoln were under the watchful eye of SAC more than any other wings. Not so, as SAC kept a watchful eye on *all* of its Wings.

The operations order for Melon Rind arrived in early September. Like before, the complexity had increased to hone the 307th's edge closer to razor sharp and combat ready. Operation Melon Rind would be flown over a four-night period beginning Thursday, the 16th. Each Squadron would prepare and fly eight B-47s for the ten-hour mission. Air refueling support would be 12 tankers from the 307th AREFS and 12 from the 98th. The force would take off at one-minute intervals to fly the profile mission, Lincoln to the target and back to Lincoln, with all kinds of challenges in between.

The mission plan called for the B-47s to leave Lincoln and climb towards the south, leveling off near Beatrice, Nebraska. They would then proceed on course to Las Vegas, New Mexico, then on to Tucumcari, New Mexico, and descend to the refueling rendezvous point over the Dodge City, Kansas, VOR. After refueling, the bombers would climb back to 37,000 feet and level off near Nebraska City, Nebraska. At that point the cells would separate and fly their own profiles. These profiles were basically the same route, with only a few degrees difference in heading and timing.

Minneapolis was the next navigation checkpoint, then a slight turn towards Alexandria, Minnesota, then a turn towards Sioux Falls, South Dakota. Over Sioux Falls they began a celestial navigation leg to Lake McConaughy, Nebraska. Passing over the lake they turned for the IP at Sterling, Colorado. Each of the B-47s made a bomb run on the Denver bomb plot, then turned back towards Lincoln.

The overall results for the four nights of flying were listed as good. Sunday showed the best results of all the missions. The CEA (circular error average) was listed as 1,557.5 feet from the target. During the nav legs, the navigators were within 15 miles of their planned positions, scoring 80% for the mission. These results were considered very good in view of the fact that two planes were scored as aborts due to radar malfunction.

The rest of October found the 307th flying a toned down flight schedule. This was designed to allow ground crews a chance to catch up with a backlog of maintenance. The missions that were flown were routine training flights to try and get more crews listed as combat ready.

In his summary report for October, Col Thorup noted the biggest problems centered around fuel leaks and the unreliable "K-System" for bombing and navigation. He mentioned there were several special technicians at Lincoln that were working on the fuel leak problems, but so far they had had very little success in finding any of the Gremlins. His report went on to point out the 307th AREFS was still short of mechanics, parts and other personnel. He underscored this with the fact that at the present time there were only eight repairable propellers on the base and it had been that way for the last three months.

November was spent trying to figure out the reason for the constant fuel leaks in the B-47s. New sealers, ranting, raving and a lot of "dirty rotten blankity, blank blank" were tried. No matter what, those "damn" fuel cells just kept dripping JP-4 on the ramp.

If the onset of winter weather caused problems for SAC operations, it also brought on the hardest part of the year for the local wildlife. One of the great game birds in Nebraska was the Ringneck Pheasant. Don Person Sr. recalled, "I remember working on the engine test cell at Lincoln. It was a flat bed trailer down on the south end of the flightline. During engine runup in the winter, the pheasants would come and sit in the exhaust to warm themselves."

The 307th AREFS spent the month trying to fulfill the operations orders contained in Winter Wind. This started on November 11th and continued until the 25th. The SAC directed mission was to test how well the squadron could transport personnel to overseas locations. To accomplish the mission the tankers had to do a lot of flying. Problems plagued the tankers from the start, and it took them almost the entire month to accomplish the mission. Since they finished the operation on the day after Thanksgiving, everyone was more than thankful it was over.

The Wing started December, wishing it was summer again. Winter had arrived with subfreezing cold and piles of snow covering the flight

## Cold War Cornhuskers: The 307th Bomb Wing Lincoln Air Force Base Nebraska 1955-1965

line. If you didn't like the weather, wait five minutes. Sure enough it got worse!!

On Saturday, the 10th of December, the 307th BW flew an 8th Air Force-directed mission called Pacesetter. The powers that be at Westover thought it would be interesting to have each wing fly a mission against the same targets. The primary difference would be the route each of the wings flew to the targets.

The 307th managed to get 13 B-47s into the air before old man winter stepped in, causing the remaining four birds to abort. In view of the 307th being the new kids on the block, the results for Pacesetter I were considered Excellent.

Sunday, December 18th, was the last day of the monthly Navy Reserve duty for the "Weekend Warriors" at Lincoln. Another day of Flying for Freedom in the Midwestern Navy. Get it over with, and then go home for Christmas with the family.

The weather was typical for that time of year at Lincoln. Cold, maybe 20 degrees at the most. Snow on the ground, ice on the ramp causing lots of slipping and sliding. Just another winter day in Nebraska land.

The Navy Reserve Squadron at Lincoln had about 20 aircraft assigned to maintain flying proficiency. It was a mixture of F-9F Panthers, P2V Neptune patrol bombers, and a couple of TV-2s (the Navy version of the T-33 trainer), along with a couple of twin engine Beechcraft.

One of the old World War II hangars served as the headquarters and maintenance facility for the Reserves. They had a pretty good canteen, and a lot of the 307th would go in and get a greasy gut bomb hamburger. The 307th AREFS used part of the building for mission briefings before moving to a different area.

Lt (jg) Vernon Chapman had flown combat during the Korean War off the U.S.S. *Philippine Sea*. The Grand Island native had been flying with the Reserve Unit for about a year. Today he would fly a routine flight to qualify for his monthly flight pay. Like he had done hundreds of times, he climbed into his assigned F-9F Panther and began to start the engine. His cockpit checks complete, he waited for his wingman to taxi towards the runway.

Without warning, the jet engine went from a gentle whine to a full power roar. The Panther lurched forward; the special metal chocks used on icy ramps were no match for the thrust coming from the tailpipe of the Panther.

The Panther now became an unleashed tiger, lurching forward over the chocks, and knocked a Navy Crew Chief to the icy concrete. He scrambled out of the way, clawing at the ice as fast as his hands and knees could move. The runaway Panther barely missed the scrambling chief as it roared forward.

Chapman's wingman, Lt Harry Nelson, had just taxied past the runaway jet, missing it by a matter of about three feet. Nelson glanced over his shoulder and watched helplessly as the jet careened towards a parked P2V Neptune.

Roy Lewis of the 307th recalled, "I was coming back from the south end of the flight line. I heard a loud noise. Realizing it was an airplane, I turned my attention to the Navy jet that was running full power."

The Panther was on a collision course for the Neptune. Lewis and several others saw Chapman trying to stand up in the cockpit, flailing his arms trying to warn anyone away from the jet. With the engine running at full throttle the Panther slammed into the patrol bomber just behind the wing. Pieces of both aircraft flew in all directions. The impact turned the remains of the Panther towards another Neptune. That collision produced another shower of jagged aluminum.

The hulk of the once proud Panther was now headed for the wooden hangar. A twin engine Beechcraft SNB was parked in front of the hangar doors. Without a pause, the jet slammed into the tail of the SNB and disappeared into the hangar.

Lt Roy Highberg was inside the hangar working as Liaison Officer for the Reserves that day. During a news interview he recalled, "I heard this whining noise and thought someone was buzzing us. I looked out and saw this plane coming and wondered why he was headed for the hangar. There was a crash and the plane broke into flames almost immediately."

Punctured fuel tanks sprayed JP-4, which became a boiling mass of flames engulfing the inside of the wooden hangar. Reservists scrambled like "rats leaving a sinking ship". Only this wasn't a ship, it was a burning hangar! Within moments the hangar was a blazing inferno.

Every fire truck on base responded to the alarm. Within minutes they were spraying the inferno with foam, trying to contain the blaze that had once been a hangar. Other units were fighting to contain the fires that dotted the wreckage lying on the flight line. Tom Parsons of the 307th recalled:

"I was in the barracks when it happened and went out there and helped get the Coleman Tractors from between the two hangars. One of them wouldn't start, so we hooked a cable or chain to it, and I steered it while it was being pulled. That thing was kind of hard to steer without the engine running for the power steering. I kept thinking and hoping that the wall on the burning hangar would not fall towards us while we were trying to get the Coleman moved."

Other 307th and Navy personnel worked frantically to move planes and equipment out of harm's way as the fire on the flight line and hangar spread. With Herculean effort they managed to get six aircraft out of the hangar before the inferno closed down their efforts. Several fire trucks from the Lincoln Fire Department raced from town to help battle the firestorm.

By late afternoon the flames had been beaten down to a smoldering pile of embers. The Navy began to take a roll call to see who had managed to escape from the hangar. Kenneth Newman and Hubert Tracey were missing. The Lincoln Reservists were later found in the rubble of the hangar. They never had a chance to escape.

Monday morning the men of the 307th reported for duty as usual. The area between the 307th and 98th was a scene from a war movie. Shattered hulks that had been proud planes of the Navy Reserve last Friday lay broken and twisted on the frozen concrete. Paul Koski remembered, "The hangar was gone, the damaged aircraft, but most of all were the water pipes that had broken; they had frozen into fountains."

The accident that terrible Sunday had cost the Navy Reserve Squadron dearly. Lt Chapman, Kenneth Newman and Hubert Tracy had perished. Several other Navy personnel were burned or injured. A total of six aircraft had been destroyed and several others had been damaged.

## 1955

It was an ironic twist of fate for the Navy at Lincoln. It was well known that Gen. LeMay wanted his SAC bases to be occupied by SAC, and only SAC. The Navy was scheduled to turn the hangar over to the Air Force and move to their new big hangar across the runway in January.

Col Thorup finished the year by getting the year-end paperwork out of the way and sent off to SAC, 8th Air Force and the 818th Air Division. His reports brought out the fact that flying and training time had been lost during the year to weather, maintenance and lack of trained people. Problems with fuel leaks and the unreliable "K" system on the B-47 headed the wing's problems. Propeller problems on the tankers and lack of parts caused the primary loss of flying hours in the refueling squadron.

He pointed out an example of how things compounded themselves. The K-4 Bomb Nav System on the wing's B-47s caused as many problems as any other item on the B-47. This system had given SAC fits ever since the B-47 rolled off the production line. The system had about 370 vacuum tubes and some 20,000 other parts, most of which were buried in the guts of the aircraft. If something went wrong during a mission the navigator could only change a few fuses and hope for the best.

It didn't take a college professor to figure out that a specialist was needed to trouble shoot and repair such a monster system. Now, the bottom line was the wing only had 20% of the authorized personnel to work on the gremlin-infested Bomb/Nav System. Throw in the fact that those specialists had to share shop space and test equipment with the 98th, and it was easy to see it would take a while to iron things out.

Along with his reports to the higher commands, Col Thorup and a lot of other men in the 307th may have sent a Christmas wish list to the man in the red suit at the North Pole. Topping the list were newer updated B-47s to fly, more trained crews and mechanics, more propellers for the KCs, and a lot of nice warm winter parkas and pants.

Sitting on the ramp, the B-47 is an impressive sight the first time you got up close and personal. (USAF)

One off the first navigator classes assigned to the 307th. Back row 4th from left, Cecil Davis, Extreme R. Bill Palmquist. Center 3rd from L, Don Hesse, Extreme R, Dick Gronberg. Front Extreme L, Joe Anthony. (Anthony)

Approach chute out, another training mission almost over as a B-47 lands at McConnell AFB, Kansas. (USAF)

# Cold War Cornhuskers: The 307th Bomb Wing Lincoln Air Force Base Nebraska 1955-1965

Equipment and personnel required for the KC-97 to fulfill it's refueling mission. (Boeing)

KC-97s in the hanger for maintenance. (USAF)

A factory fresh KC-97G leaves the Boeing plant for a SAC assignment. (Boeing)

A B-47 about to touch down at McConnell. Graduates of B-47 pilot training would soon begin formal training to become a combat ready SAC crew. (USAF)

## 1955

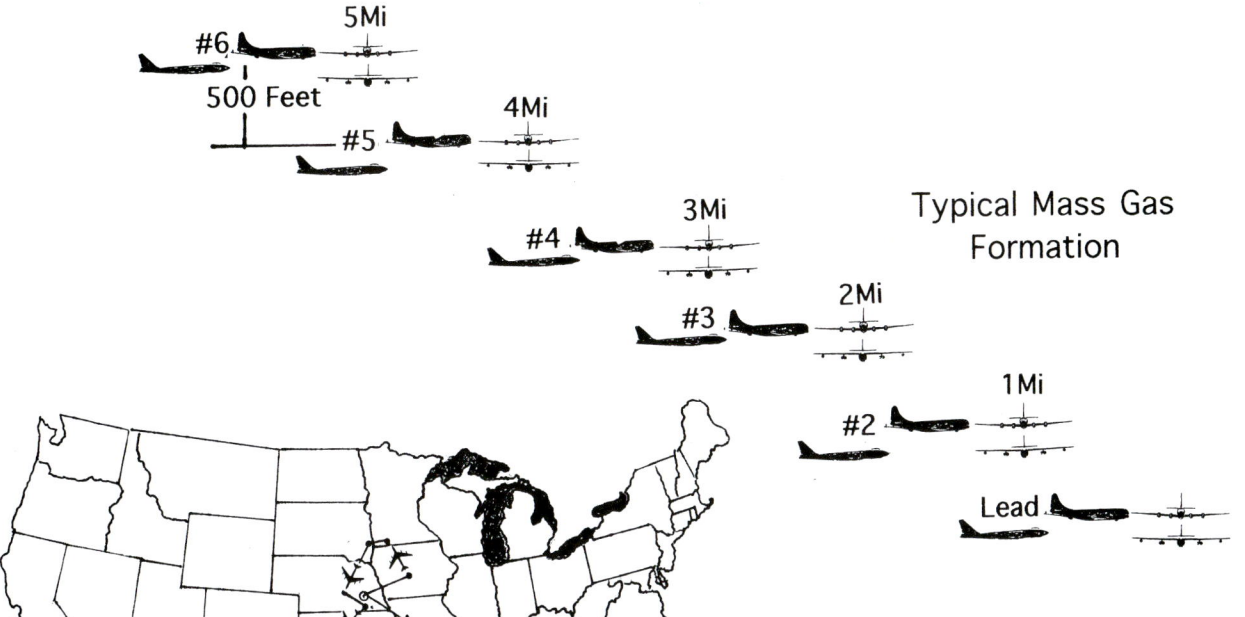

**Typical Mass Gas Formation**

#6 — 5Mi
500 Feet
#5 — 4Mi
#4 — 3Mi
#3 — 2Mi
#2 — 1Mi
Lead

Operation FIRST OUT: July 27, 1955

Touring the country at 40,000 feet. (307th BW Assoc.)

A KC-97 on short final was quite a site for motorists on West "O" Street. (Campbell)

# Cold War Cornhuskers: The 307th Bomb Wing Lincoln Air Force Base Nebraska 1955-1965

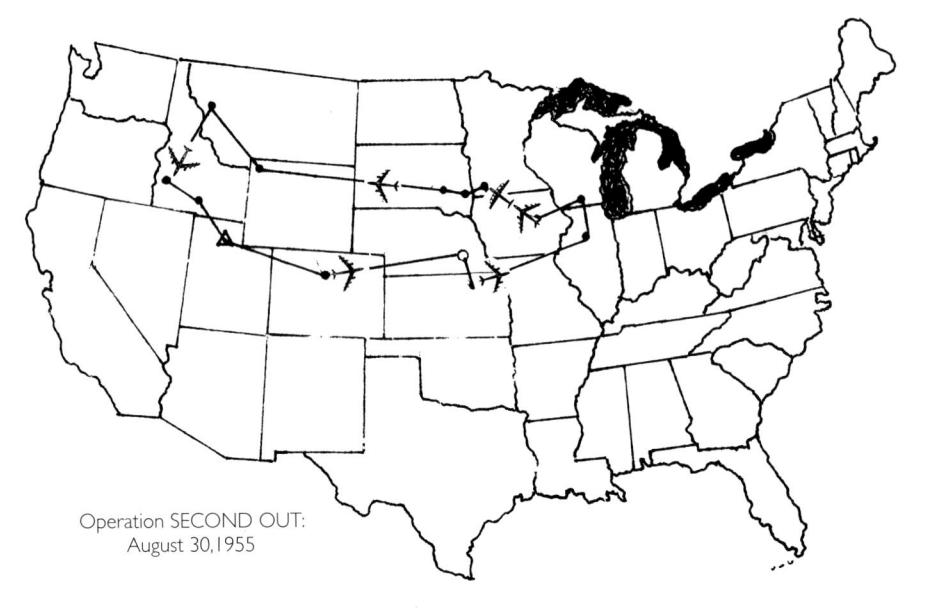

Operation SECOND OUT:
August 30, 1955

Cecil Davis and crew getting ready for another training mission. (Bundy)

The original control tower at the base. It would become Job Control for the 307th after the new tower was built. (USAF)

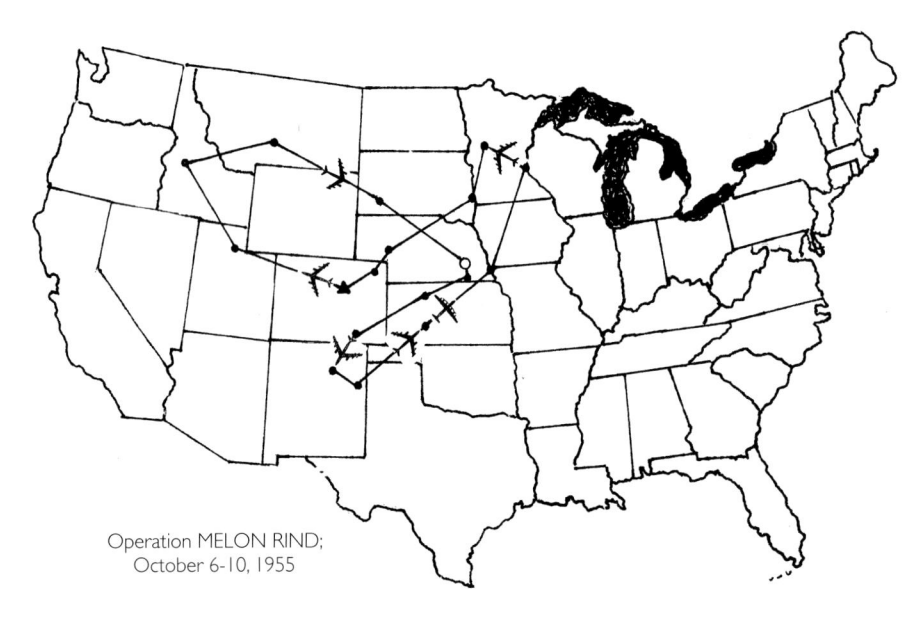

Operation MELON RIND;
October 6-10, 1955

# 1955

B-47 on short final for Runway 17. (Dunlap)

PACESETTER crews. (307th BW Assoc.)

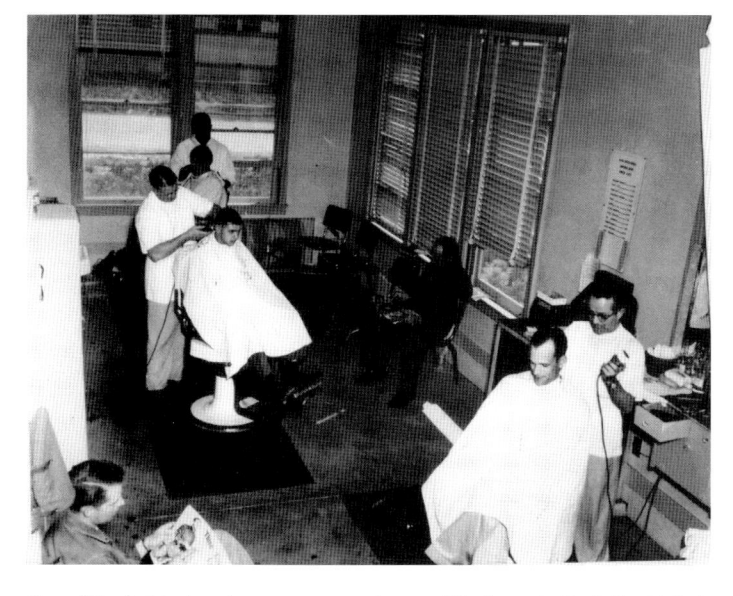

One of the first barber shops was a room in one of the barracks. That's Fred Lally in the chair on the left. (Lally)

The hanger on fire after the F9F Cougar jumped the chocks and plunged through the Hanger wall. (Lally)

Another photo showing the devastation on the ramp. (Sinclair)

# 1956

Nebraska farmers called it "old man winter"; men of the 307th referred to it as "the Hawk". Whether it blew in from the Rockies or came charging down from the north as an Alberta Clipper, there was nothing to slow the cold and snow from reaching Lincoln, except for a few fences and fewer trees.

January 1956 found old man winter taking up what seemed permanent residence at Lincoln. So far, it looked like it would be another record-breaking winter. It was nice for the farmers who needed the moisture, but it was bad for air operations at the base.

On January 3rd, a snowstorm blew in from the west. Snow and blowing snow made air operations impossible and 56 flying hours were lost to the blizzard. Well, if you can't fly, let's have a practice alert. Those on base responded to the 818th Air Division Alert. Anyone off base was required to fulfill the telephone pyramid alert.

Apparently, Santa found his way to Lincoln and made a stop at Base Supply during his Christmas Eve rounds. Paul Koski recalled, "They found some used parkas and winter flight pants. They were clean, but well worn. We didn't care as long as we could be comfortable when working outside."

That's all well and good; however, to get deep into the innards of a B-47, they had to take off most of the warmer clothes. The parkas were just too bulky and could get caught on any one of the thousand and one fittings or metal edges that reached out from all over the insides of the aircraft.

With each snowfall came the process of clearing out the snow. Paul Koski wrote:

"I had to sweep snow off the aircraft and shovel it out. Once, I was sweeping the snow off the left wing root, and I slipped. I dropped the broom and grabbed the leading edge of the wing so I wouldn't slide off the back of the wing. I was hanging on so tightly that I know my fingers were embedded in the wing skin. Just then a gust of wind hit and the aircraft rocked; a little bit, but just enough to start me sliding down the wing, still clutching the leading edge for dear life. My speed was picking up. All I could think about were the vortex generators (little airfoils on top of the wing to guide air over the ailerons during flight). I went through them so fast I didn't have time to think. I heard a ripping sound, slid off the wing and landed in a snow pile. I looked at my stomach, expecting to see blood, but the only thing I saw was my shredded parka."

The 8th Air Force liked competition among the wings under their control. On January 11th, the squadron commanders were at Westover for a special competition held just for squadron commanders. They flew missions against targets at Kansas City and Little Rock. The crews from the 307th did pretty well considering they were still pretty green. LtCol Delos Richards (371st) placed 3rd, LtCol Arthur "Gene" Aenchbacher (372nd) was 4th, and LtCol Roy Showalter from the 370th came in 8th overall.

Col Thorup was at Westover on Thursday, January 19th, for an 8th Air Force commanders' conference. During those three days he was briefed on an upcoming SAC-wide operation called Swan Dive. He was also told April 1st was the projected date for the 307th to be combat-ready.

After the three-day commanders' conference, Col Thorup left for a routine flight back to Lincoln. Col Thorup and crew would fly 52-0288 and use the flight to fill in some training requirements. By 0900, 0288 was in the air and headed for Huskerland.

The crew finished a nav leg and a bomb run on a radar target. Passing near Akron, Ohio, they discovered they were using fuel at an alarming rate. Quick calculations showed at the present fuel consumption rate they would not have enough fuel to reach Lincoln with adequate reserves. Col Thorup contacted Lincoln and declared a low fuel emergency.

Within minutes of the emergency call, Capt Vernon Cole had been notified of the situation and directed to report to Base Operations for an emergency refueling mission. Vern said a quick goodbye to his family, grabbed his flight bag and headed for Base Operations. By the time Cole and the rest of his crew arrived, the ground crew had 52-2796 ready for the mission.

MSgt. Melvin Patterson's hands danced across his engineer's panel like a concert pianist as he got the four big radial engines turning in record time. Capt Cole and his copilot, Lt Paul Nystrom, taxied the tanker to the end of the runway and made a rolling take off.

Climbing out, the navigator, Lt Gordon Newhouse, gave instructions for a turn that would put 796 on a heading for Lamoni, Iowa, the refueling orbit point. By air, in a KC-97, Lamoni is about an hour away from Lincoln. The tension-filled hour passed quickly as the tanker crew stayed busy rechecking everything for the rendezvous.

Over Lamoni, the tanker orbited until radar contact was made with Col Thorup's thirsty B-47 about seventy miles away. The tanker banked to a heading for Columbia, Missouri, the refueling area. With the B-47 closing at jet speed the distance between the two aircraft closed rapidly.

32

In the back of the tanker, TSgt Bert "Clancy" Skinner moved to his cramped pod and laid down on his "ironing board". From here, he watched to the rear through his small windows in the pod. Over the radio, he could hear position reports until finally he made visual contact with 288 coming up from below the tanker.

Now began an aerial ballet, as the B-47 slowed to match the tanker's airspeed. Slowly, Skinner coached the bomber into the observation position. His skillful hands grasped the pistol grip boom controls and began flying the refueling boom into position.

**"Up six feet, right three, up three, Contact!"**

Within seconds of the contact fuel was flowing through the boom and into the bomber. Without warning the tanker hit a small pocket of turbulence and there was a disconnect. Again, the B-47 moved back into place and Clancy flew the boom in for another hookup.

After hanging on the boom for about eight minutes, there was enough fuel in the tanks to complete the flight to Lincoln. With a hearty "Thanks" and friendly wave, Col Thorup dropped off the boom and slid away from 2796.

Back at Lincoln, the crews met for mission debriefing. They agreed it had been a good mission. There were several comments about how the mission would make a great newspaper story to show how SAC bombers are refueled in the air and how emergencies are avoided.

Well, that's exactly what happened. The entire mission had been planned and staged for the benefit of the local news media. Reporters and photographers had followed the entire mission. They not only took photos aboard the tanker, they even took some of Capt Cole saying goodbye to his family. The article appeared in the Lincoln Evening Journal on January 26th.

The 8th Air Force sent a directive to all wings to fly another Pacesetter mission. This one was a little longer and more complex then the first one. This time, there were three radar targets to hit along with navigation legs.

The initial mission briefing was held on January 24th in the 307th AREFS briefing room. The wing would use 28 aircraft for the mission. The operation would be flown at night and was to include a night celestial navigation leg over Canada. The wing would be divided into two waves. One would fly on January 25th; the second would execute the mission on January 26th.

Station time was an hour and a half before takeoff. Each crew went through their preflight walk around. Last-minute checks on the weather en route didn't bring any major surprises. Local weather called for cold and a slight chance of snow.

One by one, the B-47s lumbered into the air Wednesday evening at 10-minute intervals. They climbed out and headed towards Trenton, Missouri, then turned to a heading for Centerville, Iowa. By the time they reached Centerville, they had reached 37,000 feet. At this checkpoint they turned for Quincy, Illinois. Over Quincy they began the first bomb run towards the Pre-IP at Springfield, Illinois. They called the bomb plot as they departed the IP at Effingham and identified themselves for the bomb run. The target at Mt. Carmel, Illinois, would be scored as a practice run, then the real mission would get underway.

After the practice run the bomber stream headed for Ashland, Kentucky, and then over the Alleghenies to Frederick, Maryland, for the next target. Asbury Park, New Jersey, was their Pre-IP. As they departed the IP at Darby, Connecticut, the navigators fine-tuned the bombing system for the target at Springfield, Massachusetts. As they pulled away from the target, the navigators set their sights on the next target.

Montreal, Quebec, was the third and final target. The bomb run was made from 35,000 feet. When the tone cut off, the B-47s turned and beat a hasty retreat out of Canada. All they had to do now was finish the mission and go home. For good measure they completed a celestial navigation leg with a final checkpoint and turn over Lake Michigan near Traverse City. One last checkpoint near Chariton, Iowa, then it was a quick flight back to Lincoln.

The results were scored as good, not outstanding, but good enough to please the 8th Air Force.

January went into the wing history as another month of fighting Nebraska weather, aircraft problems, supply delays and lack of equipment. Weather accounted for the loss of 63 flying hours. Fuel leaks on the worn B-47s added another 126 hours to the loss column.

When Col Thorup returned from Westover after the commanders' briefing for Operation Swan Dive, he carried the plans for the mission in his briefcase. This operation was from SAC Headquarters via the 8th Air Force. It was bigger and more complex than any of the previous operations the 307th had been handed. Now all they had to do was figure out how to carry it out with the equipment that was on hand.

Special training for Swan Dive began on Friday, January 30th. Each crew that would fly the mission was required to attend at least three hours of arctic survival refresher training. Special areas covered were keeping warm, how to build a shelter and signal for rescue. Hmm! That meant the mission would take the boys up north.

Swan Dive would be the first time the 307th would fly with "special weapons" hanging from the shackles in the bomb bay. The directive called for each B-47 to carry a Mark-6 weapon for the entire mission. That meant some special training and security briefings. The Mark-6 weapon was a lightweight version of the earlier Mark-4. It could be configured to deliver yields from 8 to 160 kilotons. It was big, fat and ugly, just like the *Fat Man* weapon that was dropped on Nagasaki. Depending on the yield, the weapon weighed 7,500 to 8,500 pounds as she hung from the shackles.

The briefing for the crews was held on Saturday, February 4th, in the 307th briefing room. Every part of the mission was presented in great detail. The 307th would launch 28 planes in three waves. The waves would consist of two cells launching two hours apart. Each wave would launch at twelve-hour intervals. The mission would include two air refuelings, two celestial navigation legs, cell tactics, fighter attacks and camera attacks on four different targets. The final briefing would be at Base Operations one and a half hours before take off. X-Day for the mission was scheduled for February 7, 1956.

Crews listed to fly Swan Dive
First Wave Feb. 7 (Tue):
Cell 1.  Wayne Herman, William Darden, Joseph Hall, Harold Morrison, William Boudreaux.
Cell 2.  Paul Nordstrom, William Holden, William Bifford, Harold Brooks, Chester Shaver.

Second Wave Feb. 8 (Wed):
Cell 1.  Louis Webber, Joe Hull, James Mann, Tom Peebles, John Crook.
Cell 2.  Anthony Minnick, Russell Bowling, John Gieker, George Biggs.

Third Wave Feb. 8
Cell 1.  Marvin Pope, Leon McCrary, John Koudsi, Herbert Wheeler, Carl Phillips.
Cell 2.  William Sullivan, Lee Kohlscheen, Robert Hoover, Clarence Guy.

Crew chiefs worked through the day and into the night on the first wave aircraft. When their plane was ready for the weapon, the command post was notified. Convoys of slow moving transporters moved the weapons from the storage area northwest of the base to the northwest gate, then across the base to the flight line. When the weapon arrived it would

## Cold War Cornhuskers: The 307th Bomb Wing Lincoln Air Force Base Nebraska 1955-1965

be loaded. During the whole process the crew chief had to be present at his aircraft.

Each Mark-6 was configured as it would be during a real EWO mission. The only difference was the absence of the arming package, or "pill," to make the weapon "hot". Even with these safeguards, loading was done by the checklist. Dropping one of these three-ton uglies on someone's foot would really ruin his day. After final safety checks, the bomb bay doors were closed and security guards placed at each B-47. Their job was simple: don't let anyone get near the aircraft without the proper clearance and password.

8th Air Force sent the execution order to the 818th Air Division, which in turn gave the "go" order to the 307th. Crews flying in the first wave reported to Base Operations for the final briefing and weather updates. Then, it was out to the aircraft for preflight.

The first cell aircraft started their engines, taxied out, and held short of the runway for the final take off clearance from the tower. One by one the aircraft commanders pushed the throttles forward to 100% power, then hit the water-alcohol and started down the runway. Cell #1 managed to get into the air without a problem.

An hour later, the second cell was ready to take to the air for Swan Dive. Like before, the engines were fired up and the B-47s taxied to the end of the active runway. This cell would have problems getting everyone into the air. Ed Seagraves, crew chief on 52-064, recalled:

"We were parked near the end of the runway and the aft main gear was on the seam of the concrete and black top apron. We were all set to go, engines idling when we got a call that a plane had a ground abort. We were assigned as standby in case someone aborted. The aircraft commander asked the tower if he could run his engine checks in place there, then take the runway. He was cleared and proceeded to spool up to full power.

"I was on the interphone and out in front of the aircraft when a six to eight square foot section of asphalt blew up on the right side. It broke over the leading edge of the horizontal stabilizer and broke into small pieces. One piece penetrated the skin of the vertical stabilizer just in front of the rudder. Another chunk broke into the aft fuselage just forward of the tail turret. I signaled to cut the engines and got back on the interphone. The pilot wanted to know what was wrong; he was all set to go and hadn't felt anything. We may have been the first B-47 knocked out by flying asphalt. 064 was out of commission for about 90 days while repairs were being done."

The two cells headed for Grand Island, Nebraska, after takeoff and rendezvoused with their tankers in the "One Step" refueling area. Refueling went off without a hitch as they headed north over Sioux City, Iowa. They dropped off the tankers near Fargo, North Dakota, and crossed into Canadian airspace a few minutes later. Near Trout Lake, Manitoba, the B-47s turned and flew to the northern tip of Maine, then north towards Gaspé, Quebec.

Near Harmon AB, Newfoundland, the B-47s came down from cruising altitude for their second refueling in the "Willie" refueling area. This refueling was at night, which was always fraught with excitement and danger. To make matters worse, there was a brilliant display of the Northern Lights that night. Trying to hang on the boom was hard enough at night. Throw in the strange glow of the Northern Lights dancing across the night sky and, bingo, the possibility of vertigo. Several pilots were hit with such a bad case of vertigo that the copilots had to get on the controls and help keep the B-47s steady under the boom.

After getting their fuel and getting over the effects of the Northern Lights, the B-47s climbed back to altitude and coasted out over the Labrador Sea for the celestial navigation leg. This far north, all the crews could see was white being reflected into the night sky. If there was a problem and they were forced to eject, they would need every bit of the survival training they had received.

Coast-in was at the northern tip of Newfoundland. Several of the navigators had trouble identifying the coast from the ice pack on their radar screens. A quick heading correction got them back on course. This would be the longest straight-line navigation leg on the mission. As they approached the CONUS border, everyone gave a sigh of relief. They were glad to be near the states since they were carrying nuclear weapons. No one wanted to have an accident and cause an international incident.

When they reached the control point near Saginaw, Michigan, the cells broke up and changed headings for bomb runs on their briefed targets at Chicago, Indianapolis, Dayton, or Louisville, Kentucky. Each plane would then fly a short nav leg back to home plate at Lincoln.

As each of the birds landed and taxied back to the ramp they radioed the tower, "We request to be parked in the designated area for radiation monitoring and decontamination. Request you notify the Decontamination Team."

Wave 2 was scheduled to takeoff 12 hours after the first wave. The winds had picked up and turned to the north. An Alberta Clipper had arrived shortly after the first wave had gotten into the air. Now, it was the 307th against the clipper. The runway had to be kept clear along with the taxiways. Snowplows charged up and down the concrete like raging bulls. Crew chiefs and ground crews grabbed brooms and shovels and attacked the piles of white to keep the snow and ice off the B-47s. Takeoff time slipped backwards about as often as the intrepid souls working on the flight line.

Takeoff was delayed two hours, then four. Finally, the snow dwindled to flurries and the wind changed from a cross wind to a gentle breeze right down Runway 35. Wave 2 launched five hours late. The delay meant they would have to do some last minute shuffling in the celestial and nav leg schedules.

Since the second wave was late taking off, that set the third wave back five hours. Changes were made to the control points to compensate for the new launch time for the last wave. These delays were not good for the scoring of the mission; SAC Hq in Omaha was having the same weather, so they knew what the 307th was up against.

When each aircraft returned from the mission, the "special weapon" was removed and returned to the storage bunker. The B-47 was checked for any radiation that may have leaked from the weapon. When everything was checked and rechecked, the plane was returned to the flight line.

As with all SAC missions, the final results and scores arrived at the 307th Headquarters. The crews were assembled for the "who did and who didn't" part of the mission. It was like waiting for the teacher to give you your report card. Did you get an "A" or did you flunk, was the feeling going through the room.

Most of the unsatisfactory bomb scores were the result of problems with the "K" Bomb/Nav System. Lou Webber's crew (R-33) had a bombsight malfunction. John Koudsi and Crew R-03 aborted the bomb run when they lost the radar system. His navigator changed a fuse three times and it blew every time. Jim Mann aborted in 52-071 prior to the IP when the whole "K" System went on the fritz.

There were other problems, too. Rocky 30's tanker had a boom malfunction and he was unable to take on the first fuel load. Rocky 23 lost the #3 engine thirty-one minutes after taking off and returned to Lincoln to be scored as an abort.

Navigation was scored as very good. Overall, the mission average showed the planes were less than 20 miles off the route at any one given moment. Bomb scores were rated as satisfactory. The average circular error for the entire mission was 6,732 feet.

## 1956

The best results of the mission were turned in by Joe Hull's Crew R-35. When the score arrived from the radar scoring unit, it showed an error of zero. They were awarded a "shack", or direct hit. Right in the old "pickle barrel" as they said in World War II.

SAC Hq liked to throw things at the wings to keep 'em on their toes. While the 307th was flying, "enemy saboteurs" (actually OSI agents) slipped in during off-duty hours. They infiltrated the flight line and "destroyed" nine B-47s. How'd they do it? They posed as snowplow drivers, inspectors or just plain Airman "Snerd". They all had flight line badges, so they looked legitimate. The problem was, the pictures on the badges were photos of characters like Donald Duck, Mickey Mouse or a chimpanzee, instead of actual mug shots. So, the score at the end of regulation play was OSI 9, Security ZIP!

In March, the 307th began seeing a few changes for the better. A small, yet important, change was the opening of a Base Commissary in one of the old WWII warehouses. At least now families wouldn't have to go downtown and pay higher prices for their groceries.

Santa was about two months late, but another item on the 307th Christmas wish list began arriving in March. These were several newer B-47s that had gone through the depot and been updated to the "731" standards. They had the newer MA-7 Bomb/Nav system, which was supposed to be more reliable than the old "K" System. They also carried an external fuel tank on each wing to give them longer range.

Everyone who stepped onto the flight line knew it could be a dangerous place for the unwary. This was brought out in spades on Monday, March 19th. An A&E specialist was in the cockpit of a B-47 doing a routine check on the A-5 fire control system. He depressed the 20 mm guns and swung the turret. Anyone on the flightline can attest to the speed that the turret moved. At that moment, a mechanic happened to walk past the moving turret. Luck was with the airman; he spotted movement out of the corner of his eye and ducked as the turret and guns came at him. Quick reflexes and lady luck prevailed. The incident was written up and sent to the Ground Safety Officer.

Six tankers from the 307th AREFS took off on March 20th to fly Operation Home Run. The 55th Strategic Recon Wing from Kansas was headed north for Thule for another round of photographing the northern borders of the Soviet Union. The four RB-47s would also test their photo equipment in the arctic conditions while at Thule.

The KC-97s, Call Sign "Runner Ann", would meet "Pigtail" over Green Bay, Wisconsin, for a mass gas refueling. This was a hush-hush operation, so everything was done under strict radio silence. Before leaving, the boom operators had to review the procedures for radio silence in the Dash-1 so they knew how to signal the bombers with the boom.

Two tankers launched early to fly to the Green Bay area and scout the weather at the refueling altitude. They reported that everything looked pretty good. They began flying an oval racetrack pattern waiting for the other KC-97s to arrive and join up.

At the appointed time, heading and altitude, four RB-47s arrived and moved into a pre-contact position beneath their assigned tanker. The boomer wagged the boom up and down, then extended eight feet of the tube to let the bomber know they could move in for contact. They made contact and began to transfer fuel at about 3,500 pounds per minute. At that rate, the bomber would be on the boom for about twelve minutes to get the required 40,000 pounds of fuel. The KCs of the 307th AREFS chalked up about 40 flying hours during the mission. The tankers transferred over 150,000 pounds of fuel to the RB-47s.

In March, an Operations Order called Red Cap came down from Offutt. The order was the initial notification to the 307th that they would be heading overseas on Temporary Duty (TDY) within the next six months. Six months would give plenty of time to figure out just how the wing was going to accomplish the move.

307th personnel noticed there were a lot of high-ranking officers milling around the 307th area during the month. They were interested in just about everything the wing was doing. They were checking records, flight schedules and personnel files. Turned out these "big wigs" were from Offutt, and were at Lincoln to see how the wing was coming along towards becoming combat ready.

During the month the wing managed to fly a total of 480 hours of training. By the end of March there were 53 crews listed as combat ready. Everyone figured that wasn't too bad in view of the continued problems encountered. Weather was still causing delays, aborts and the ever-present fuel leaks. Tankers were having the same propeller problems, along with not enough specialists to fix them.

On 1 April, CINCSAC endorsed a readiness report on the 307th Bomb Wing. The message sent to Lincoln was, "Effective April 1, 1956, the 307th Bomb Wing, Lincoln Air Force Base, is Combat Ready." Another message proclaimed April would be a "free training" month. The wing didn't have to worry about SAC Reg. 50-8 Requirements. They just had to fly and train as much as possible.

If SAC wanted the wing to fly and train, then that is exactly what they would do. The wing began on April 2nd with a bomber stream mission. They would follow up with another bomber stream mission on the 11th and 12th just for good measure. In between, crews would fly regular profile missions to hone their skills.

Friday morning, April 6th, Capt James Sullivan and his crew, 2Lt Lawrence Schmidt (CP) and Lt Anthony Marcanti (Nav) reported for a routine profile flight. The flight plan called for a nav leg, air refueling and a bomb run. A1C James Berry, crew chief on 53-4209, was going along that morning to get his time in for flight pay.

Preflight was routine that morning. The crew climbed aboard and went through the checklist for engine start as they had done so many times before. Engine start, taxi, and runup were normal. The weather was cool and overcast with a 4,000-foot ceiling.

At 1123 hours, 4209 lifted off Runway 35 and began climbing to the North. Those who watched the takeoff saw a routine departure of the newly arrived B-47. Several on the ground watched the B-47 until it faded from the sight of the naked eye.

At 1130 hours, Ceresco, Nebraska, was rocked by an explosive concussion. Three miles south and a mile east, near Highway 77, Oscar Spader was in his farmyard doing some morning chores. He had watched a lot of the B-47s fly over near his farm. Like many times before, he glanced skyward to see his tax dollars at work. He later recalled, "The plane was about 1,500 to 2,000 feet in the air, just below a layer of clouds. I saw the plane explode and it came apart in the air."

Pieces of the B-47 rained down on several farms. Wreckage was strewn along a mile and a quarter path. Most of the wreckage impacted just south of the Martin Johnson farm at the base of a small hill. Flaming debris caused several fires to erupt.

The concussion of the exploding B-47 was also felt at the base. On the flight line, several airmen saw the fireball as it fell to earth. Word spread across the flight line, then spilled out onto the base. It was evident that "we had lost one."

Crash and fire trucks from the base raced towards Ceresco and joined the local fire department to contain the fuel-fed fires. Several units from the City of Lincoln also responded to help fight the growing conflagration. There was some difficulty in getting close to several of the fires due to the terrain and the country roads surrounding the crash site.

It didn't take long for sightseers to show up and clog Highway 77 and surrounding country roads. A Lancaster Country Sheriff's Officer believed there might have been as many as 2,000 cars turned away from the crash site area. Before the site could be secured, some of the more ghoulish sightseers had picked up pieces of the B-47 to take home as souvenirs.

The investigation team began sifting through the wreckage almost before it was cool. Back at the base, all of the records dealing with 4209 were being brought together for the investigation. Interviews were conducted with anyone who had actually witnessed the explosion and crash. When the onsite investigation was completed, clean-up of the site began with the wreckage being transported back to the base.

Several of the witnesses stated that 4209 had turned back towards the base. This was confirmed at the crash site. There had been no radio contact from 4209 giving any indication they were having any problems or that they were returning to the base.

The #6 engine was found some distance from the main impact area. It appeared the rear engine mount might have failed. The investigation board was not able to discover the exact cause of the accident. The board believed the engine might have had problems, causing the crew to turn back towards the base. They theorized the engine mount failed, causing the engine to rotate upward, depart the aircraft, and strike the horizontal stabilizer. Fuel from the broken lines may have ignited, causing the explosion.

This was the first fatal flying accident at Lincoln since the base reopened. Memorial services were held for the crew at the Base Chapel. April may have been designated as a "free training" month, but it had cost the 307th dearly.

Training continued despite the loss of an airplane and crew. On Monday, April 9th, there were classes on Special Weapons for the crews who were non-combat ready. Then, on the 18th, an altitude chamber refresher was held. Since there was no chamber at Lincoln, the students were transported to Offutt for the actual chamber qualification.

Crews were also spending a lot of time in the simulator making special landing approaches for Goose Bay, Harmon, Lakenheath and Upper Heyford, in the United Kingdom. This was part of the preparation for the upcoming TDY. After all, you don't want to wait till the last minute to learn any of the quirks of landing at a faraway base.

In mid-April, the second 307th Maintenance Bulletin hit the flight line. The newsletter was full of timely tidbits for the crew chiefs and ground personnel. They were introduced to Airman Loose Screw, a comical sad sack type character. He seemed to live up to his name and couldn't do anything right. A little corny, yes, but there were a lot of good tips and information within the pages of the little paper.

The return of warmer weather brought back a distinctive sound to the flightline. It was mentioned in the Maintenance Newsletter and called "Engine choo-choo". It usually happened during start up and runup when the power setting was below 85%. The cause of the distinctive sound was fluctuating fuel flow to the combustion chambers. It sounded similar to the choo-choo sound of the old steam locomotive, hence the name "engine choo-choo".

The condition was more annoying than dangerous. The engine would usually work itself out of the condition once fuel flow stabilized. Sometimes it could be corrected by short fast throttle changes. If that didn't work, the Dash-1 suggested turning the fuel selector switch to ME on the offending engine.

Operation Date Roll began on Thursday, April 26th. This was another bomber stream mission. It was to be flown in two parts, Alpha and Bravo, with six B-47s in each flight. The plan called for a mass gas refueling, nav legs and radar bomb runs on selected targets.

While the crews were flying Date Roll, other crews were attending training classes on Special Weapons starting at 0900. The outline included the process for loading the Mark-6 into the bomb bay, safety procedures, and how to arm, and then disarm the nuclear device. For safety, a training unit was used instead of a real weapon.

The 307th traded in thirteen of their older well-worn B-47s during April. On the 26th, 52-245 from the 371st Bomb Squadron left for the depot at Marietta, Georgia, to be updated to the 731 configuration.

As more of the older B-47s were traded in for newer updated B-47s, the 307th began a new policy. Crews would now be assigned a specific aircraft. The names of the crew and the crew chief were stenciled on the side just above the entry door. The planes were assigned to the older, more experienced crews as kind of a "well done" for these crews and incentive for others. By the end of April, there were 15 of the newer 731-updated B-47s gracing the flight line.

May was the first month in the SAC 50-8 training period. The wing had its free month, so now everything they did counted. It was time to start filling in the training squares for real again.

Out on the flight line, two crews were preparing for a night launch to fill some 50-8 squares on Wednesday, May 2nd. Preflight, engine start and taxi to Runway 17 were routine. Arriving at the end of the runway, they were advised to hold short for an inbound B-47 on short final for a GCA approach.

Holding short of the runway, they watched the landing lights of 52-450 approach and then begin to climb back into the sky as they finished their low approach. Within a few minutes, the two B-47s pulled onto the runway and launched into the night sky for their mission.

Meanwhile, Adams 60 from the 98th Bomb Wing had continued its pattern work and was setting up for their seventh and final approach. This one would be flown by the copilot. The GCA controller noted the approach began at 2234 and had 450 fly a wider pattern than normal so the co pilot could take over. The aircraft flew the pattern and turned onto final five and a half miles out.

At 2238, when Adams 60 was about three and a half miles from the end of Runway 17, it disappeared from the GCA scope. At almost the same instant, the sky to the north lit up with a brilliant flash, followed by what was likened to a distant thunderclap.

Fire and rescue equipment charged out of the fire stations and headed towards the crash site. For the next several hours, they fought the conflagration until there was just a swath of smoldering wreckage. That morning, when the two 307th aircraft returned to the base they flew over the wreckage of Adams 60.

The loss of Adams 60 and her crew was the result of the wider than normal pattern flown on the last approach. The extra distance was not compensated for by the GCA controller and the crew. The aircraft was flown into the ground before reaching the end of the runway.

Going TDY to England meant the wing would have to cross the Atlantic Ocean also referred to as "the pond". That meant a lot of flying over a lot of water. So, bright and early on Monday, May 7th, aquatic survival training began at the base pool. Training began with lectures on equipment, how to land after bailing out and the proper way of boarding the life raft.

Lecture over, time to get wet! Only one way to simulate bailing out and a water landing. That's right, off the diving board with flight suit, harness, boots and helmet. It may have been May, but those who went into the drink wondered how long the ice had been out of the pool. After a couple of hours of climbing into rubber rafts and showing off their skills on the diving board, the cold-soaked trainees were more than happy this particular square on the training board was filled in.

While some of the guys were having the "pool party", six crews were getting ready to fly Date Roll Bravo, the second part of the operation. Pre-mission briefing was at 1530. Any last minute changes were gone over, along with problem areas that had surfaced during the first part of the mission. Enroute weather was presented by the weather section. Then, it was out to the aircraft for preflight and engine start.

## 1956

At 1700 hours Rocky Lead, flown by William Boudreaux, took off to begin the mission. At five-minute intervals, the remaining five B-47s launched for the mission. From Lincoln, they would climb to their first turn point over Beatrice, and then head for Russell, Kansas, about 120 nautical miles away. Over the Russell VOR, the navigator called for a heading change for North Platte, Nebraska, for the next 155 nautical miles. The mission profile called for the B-47s to join up and fly formation for the leg to the refueling area. To link up would require precise timing and flying to get everyone back together and into a formation.

At North Platte, the lead aircraft turned to a heading of 348 degrees and began a timed flight for 12.5 minutes on that heading. The second aircraft would fly the same heading for 10 minutes. At the end of their timed run, they would begin a timed four-minute, 180-degree turn to the left. The last B-47 over North Platte began their four-minute turn over the VOR. If everyone was on time they would all be tucked in nice and tight with each other. Rocky Lead gave everyone another three minutes to adjust, then banked into a final four-minute turn back towards North Platte.

The formation left on a heading that would take them to Sioux Falls, South Dakota, the refueling IP. The tankers were waiting between 15,000 and 17,000 feet. The formation rendezvoused and began the intricate aerial dance behind the KC-97s. Fuel tanks were full by the end-refueling point near Pontiac, Illinois. From here, the formation would fly to Indianapolis, where they broke up to fly their individual briefed routes.

Rocky 3, flown by Anthony Minnick's Crew R-31, would fly about 30 miles south of the break up point, then turn and fly to Charleston, West Virginia, where they would circle for six minutes to establish separation from the bomber stream. On their last turn, they took up a heading towards Pittsburgh for the next leg of about 145 nautical miles. Over Pittsburgh, they made a radio call at the checkpoint, then turned towards their IP at Johnstown. A camera-attack run was made on Harrisburg, Pennsylvania, then on to the turn point at Lakehurst, New York, for a bomb run on Springfield, Massachusetts.

Rocky 3 then flew north for another bomb run; this time, the target was Montreal, Quebec. After "destroying" the target with a radar bomb, they beat a quick retreat out of Canada for another camera attack on Rochester, New York. Rocky 3 flew south to Altoona, Pennsylvania, and the next turn point. They began a celestial navigation leg passing over Akron, Ohio, and ending at Chicago.

The final leg was from Chicago back to home plate at Lincoln. After landing, the crews turned in the camera film and reported for mission debriefing. The flight was gone over in fine detail, noting any problems that they had encountered along the way. When the final results for both Date Roll Alpha and Bravo were sorted out, scored, then written up, the 307th had chalked up mission accomplished, "Results, Very Good."

Bomber stream missions were flown on May 11th, 22nd, and again on the 24th. These were designed to fill training squares required on the SAC Reg.50-8 Board and to update crews. Each mission was flown as briefed with only a few problems.

Lincoln Air Force Base opened the gates to the public on Armed Forces Day, May 19th. It was a beautiful Saturday and the base played host to nearly 30,000 visitors. The 307th provided two B-47s and two KC-97s for the event. There were also several flyovers for the crowd. All agreed the simulated air refueling was the hit of the day.

During the month there were all kinds of training activities going across the base for the 307th. Classes in Special Weapons were conducted for aircrews and crew chefs. More water survival classes were given at the base pool. Crews spent hours in the simulator practicing approaches to various bases in Canada, England and Morocco. There were even classes on the proper way to fill out the Form 781 for crew chiefs.

During the month the Wing continued the "out with the old" and "in with the newer" B-47s. May saw fourteen of the original B-47s leaving for update and modification to 731 standards. Competition for the shiny, newly arrived B-47s was fierce. Every crew chief wanted his name stenciled on one of the "new birds".

At this time, it was an established policy of SAC to send units that had just become Combat Ready on Temporary Duty (TDY) to a selected forward base around the world. The purpose was twofold. First, it placed the unit closer to prospective Soviet targets. Second, it provided a test to see how well the new unit could undertake and accomplish the movement of the entire wing in case of a national emergency.

For the last several months, the 307th had been preparing for just such a movement. Crews had been flying approaches to several overseas bases in the simulator and arctic and water survival classes were being held. The men of the 307th figured, with all that kind of training going on, it was just a matter of time before SAC would give them a chance to try it out.

On June 15th, the 307th published Operations Order 74-56, which had arrived several months ago. The code name on the order was Red Cap, and the 178-page document outlined in detail just where and when the wing would be going. The orders were broken down, printed and distributed to each section so they could begin getting ready.

The first wave of the advance party was scheduled to leave Lincoln on June 20th. They would travel to Goose Bay on C-124 transports and be in place to provide any support needed for the wing. The advance party would carry several engines for both B-47s and KC-97s, along with a supply of parts that may be needed.

After June 19th, there was a general halt to flying routine missions. In view of the impending long flight across the Atlantic, aircraft maintenance became the number one priority for the flight line crews. The last of the original B-47s, 52-270, left for the depot on the same day. Now, the 307th had newer B-47s to take across the pond.

The orders for the deployment included a Special Weapons exercise to be conducted on Monday, June 25th. This would test the ability of the wing to load and unload special weapons. It would be scored by the 3908th Strategic Evaluation Squadron. The mission was to prepare, load, then download thirty-two B-47s with a Mark-6 weapon. Each aircraft would be assigned a flight crew whose job was to assure the aircraft and weapon were loaded to the exact condition it would be in at the time of release over a target. The crew chief of the aircraft would remain with his aircraft during the entire exercise.

Aircraft Assignments for Special Weapon Exercise:
**First Wave: June 25**

| Aircraft Commander | Crew Chief | Aircraft |
|---|---|---|
| Herman, Wayne | Owensby, William | 53-4224 |
| Bifford, William | Harding, Calvin | 53-1902 |
| Webber, Louis | Otten, Gerald | 53-4220 |
| Pebbles, Thomas | Lauk, Richard | 53-2139 |
| Hall, Robert | White, William | 53-1912 |
| Morrison | Mosser, Homer | 53-2141 |
| Brooks, Harold | Lechot, W | 53-4235 |
| Hull, Joe | Vensky, Steve | 53-2134 |
| Gieker, John | Wright, Beotis | 53-2413 |
| Biggs, George | Holmes, Frank | 53-4232 |
| Bowling, Russell | DeWitt, James | 53-1911 |

## Second Wave: June 25

| | | |
|---|---|---|
| Mattick, Steve | Lovett, Richard | 53-4227 |
| Sullivan, William | Filpula, William | 53-1909 |
| Mills, Bruce | Wilson, Robert | 53-2143 |
| Wheeler, Herbert | Rosario, Joseph | 53-1917 |
| Nordstrom, Paul | Pepper, James | 53-4223 |
| Hoover, Robert | Issacson, Richard | 53-4228 |
| Guy, Clarence | Truckness, David | 53-1918 |
| Kohlscheen, Lee | Nieman, Rudolph | 53-2416 |
| Hoffman, William | Alexander, Allen | 53-4226 |
| Mann, James | Mowry, Donald | 53-2144 |
| Koudsi, John | Lancaster, James | 53-4222 |

## Third Wave: June 26

| | | |
|---|---|---|
| Boudreaux, William | Martin, William | 53-2417 |
| Shaver, Chester | St. Louis, Richard | 53-1916 |
| McCrary, Leon | D'Eustachio, Ed | 53-4241 |
| Holden, William | Finfinger, Leo | 53-2128 PHASE V |
| Hibden, Floyd | Johnston, Garth | 53-4219 |
| Echelbarger, Paul | Nigh, George | 53-2140 |
| Darden, William | Stanton, Donald | 53-4230 |
| Crook, John | Koski, Paul | 53-4214 |
| Phillips, Carl | Arsenault, Norman | 53-1900 |
| Bath, Frank | Noland, Lawrence | 53-1915 |

The Armament and Electronics Squadron was given the task of transporting the weapons from the storage bunkers to the flight line and making sure the weapons were ready for uploading by 2400 on June 24th. With a lot of Mark-6 weapons sitting around waiting to be loaded, the Security Force was assigned to guard the entire flight line.

SAC always rose early in the morning. June 25th was no exception to the rule. After all, there was a lot of work to be done. At daybreak the first wave of loading began. According to the orders, the crews had six hours to load, be scored, and then download the weapon from the aircraft. Now, this may not seem difficult on the surface, but the flight line was crowded with B-47s, and KC-97s from the 307th. There were also several C-124s waiting to load the advance party.

Across the flight line, the men stood ready by their assigned B-47s. At the pre-arranged time, the signal was given for the first wave to begin the upload. The crew chiefs had already completed the preflight up to the point of engine start. To prepare the B-47s for their cargo, the bomb bay door actuators had been disconnected so the doors could be opened as wide as possible.

The weapons dollies were manhandled into position under the bomb bay and the task of loading the Mark-6 began. This process would be accomplished in three separate waves of eleven aircraft, until each B-47 had been loaded, scored and unloaded. It was a slow methodical process, each step done according to the loading checklist.

While most of the flight line was busy with the weapons exercise, there was a lot of activity going on down on the south end of the ramp too. Several C-124s were being loaded with engines and other equipment. By mid-morning they were loaded, and then 102 officers and airmen marched up the ramps into the cavernous cargo compartment. They settled into their "first class" MATS accommodations and waited for takeoff. They left on the first leg of the journey to England. After what seemed an eternity aboard "Old Shaky" they landed at Harmon, Newfoundland, for refueling and rest. The next day, several of the C-124s departed for the flight across the Atlantic to England. The ones that remained behind would stay at Harmon until the wing had arrived in England in case any of the deployment aircraft had trouble and needed maintenance.

The weapons exercise continued on Tuesday, the 26th, for the third and final wave. Like the day before, the aircraft would be loaded, scored, and downloaded. The weapons would then be returned to the storage area. Another long day on the flight line. It wasn't a routine day, but it was long and hectic under the watchful eyes of the umpires.

On the 26th, KC-97 51-377, flown by Joe Pavlas' crew, departed Lincoln with the advance party for the tanker squadron. As they lifted off the runway, Flight Engineer John Lynch called out, "Wheels up, flaps up, balls up too; old 377 is in the blue." It was his usual statement after takeoff on every flight. They would land at Harmon, Newfoundland, refuel and continue to their TDY base at Greenham Common the next day. At least that was the mission plan. Lee Cullimore recalled what happened:

"377 was the lead aircraft for the 307th deployment to RAF Greenham Common in England the summer of '56. We left Lincoln the last week of June with 39 people aboard. The #1 engine started acting up about an hour after we left Lincoln. The oscilloscope had quit working so there was no way to determine what was going on. When we got somewhere over northern New York or Maine, the turbo in #1 engine blew up, threw pieces of a blade into the carburetor, and set the engine on fire. Pavlas called for it to be feathered and fire bottles, pulled back the throttle on #1 to under a thousand RPM, and watched with horror, when within a few seconds, the other three engines lost power, also. John Lynch (flight engineer) had forgotten to flip the abort switch off automatic after takeoff, so when #1 came off power, the others did what they were supposed to do under that scenario, and did we fall!!

"I was sleeping on the deck behind the cockpit when it happened and I recall being lifted some inches off the floor as the dive began. We were at 29,000 feet altitude when the show started and didn't recover until under 10,000. After recovering we continued to Harmon Field in Newfoundland. Lincoln was contacted and after some discussion they decided to send a fresh engine from there, and that took three days. In the meantime, I pulled off the damaged engine and stripped it of the parts needed for the new one.

"I was laboring under some difficulty in doing this because, in spite of my having an MOS for reciprocating engine mechanic, and having been previously assigned to an engine build up unit (for B-29s) at Kadena AFB, Okinawa, I had very little hands-on experience with the beasts. Fortunately, there were a couple of more experienced hands around who pitched in and helped me get it all running right. We left Harmon, after being there five days and made it to England without any problem."

For the next several days, the flight line at Lincoln mirrored the deployment scene from the movie *Strategic Air Command*. The south end of the ramp was crammed with C-124s from the Air Force and R6D-1s (C-118s) from the Navy. The gaping doors of the Globemasters swallowed pallets of equipment, J-47 engines, fuel trucks and people just like in the movie. When the C-124s taxied the brakes squealed like trumpeting elephants. The only thing missing was the musical soundtrack from the movie and, of course, Jimmy Stewart.

Practically everything the 307th would need for the next three months had to be transported, lock, stock, bag, bunk and junk aboard the Military Air Transport Service (MATS) cargo planes. By the time they arrived in England, it would amount to over 366,840 pounds of equipment transported by MATS alone.

Everything seemed to be progressing according to the OPSORD. Well, almost everything, except for down in the 307th AREFS area. Problems with the solid steel props on the KC-97s had plagued the fleet before and had reared its ugly head again. Several props were found to have cracks in them during a routine inspection. There weren't enough props on base

# 1956

to change all of the bad props that were found. There was only one thing to do. Each KC-97 would have to have the props inspected and repaired or replaced as needed. On a long flight across the Atlantic you sure didn't need a blade to break or come loose. In view of the problem, the departure date for the tankers was placed on hold.

A general briefing for the first-wave crews was held on Monday, July 2nd. The briefing, as usual, outlined the general route to be flown, who would fly where in the formation and what would be accomplished during the flight across the pond.

As with the weapons exercise, the operation orders called for a rather ungodly hour for the first wave to take off. Takeoff time for the first wave was 2100 on July 3rd. True, a strange time to be launching into the wild dark yonder, but SAC had a method in their madness. Taking off at that hour would make the arrival time at the destination during daylight hours.

Most of the crews used the time for last minute packing, making arrangements for their families, then trying to get a little rest before they had to leave. They all knew that no matter how well they planned, there would be something they forgot to do or take care of. Mary (Bowling) Aston wrote:

"Before Russ left for England, he said three things to me that haunt me to this day. The first was, 'I don't want to wish my life away, but I wish this TDY was over!' Second, there had been two B-47s crashes at the base that spring and Russ said. 'I wonder who the third is going to be.' Then he said to me. 'If you have any premonitions about me when I'm flying, don't tell me.' I was filled with them when he was preparing for that TDY and I didn't have any reason to be."

Aircraft deployment schedule for the TDY flight
**First Wave: X-Day**

| Aircraft Commander | | Tail # | Call Sign "ROCKY" |
|---|---|---|---|
| Hoover, Robert | 53-4240 | 39 | (Col Louis Thorup: Red Cell Lead) |
| Bifford, William | 53-1911 | 36 | |
| Webber, Louis | 53-4234 | 42 | |
| Hoffman, William | 53-4220 | 34 | |
| Williams, William | 53-4218 | 43 | |
| | | | |
| Sullivan, William | 53-2143 | 24 | White Cell |
| Biggs, George | 53-4232 | 19 | |
| Crook, Jack | 53-1916 | 23 | |
| Ouderkirk, Fred | 53-4210 | 15 | |
| Clark, Roy | 53-1919 | 12 | |
| | | | |
| Nordstrom, Paul | 53-2128 | 63 | Blue Cell |
| Gieker, John | 53-2417 | 59 | |
| Boudreaux, William | 53-2413 | 60 | |
| Heller Jr., Russell | 53-2144 | 50 | |
| Terry, Everett | 53-4225 | 54 | |

**Second Wave: X-day + 1**

| McCary, Leon | 53-4241 | 18 | Col Robert Christy: Green Cell Lead, |
|---|---|---|---|
| Peebles, Thomas | 53-1901 | 13 | |
| Brooks, Harold | 53-4236 | 10 | |
| Ecelbarger, Paul | 53-4235 | 22 | |
| Mills, Bruce | 53-2140 | 14 | |
| | | | |
| Kohlscheen, Lee | 53-2416 | 61 | Brown Cell |
| Hull, Joseph | 53-4223 | 55 | |
| Wheeler, Herbert | 53-1900 | 64 | |
| Dodge, Hale | 53-1906 | 58 | |
| Reilly, Stanley | 53-2141 | 51 | |
| | | | |
| Darden, William | 53-4226 | 31 | Amber Cell |
| Guy, Clarence | 53-1915 | 37 | |
| Ames, Melvin | 53-4227 | 40 | |
| Bath, Frank | 53-2138 | 38 | |
| Hibdon, Floyd | 53-4219 | 44 | |

**Third Wave: X-Day + 2**

| Holden, William | 53-1910 | 57 | Col. Ernest Hardin: Pink Cell Lead |
|---|---|---|---|
| Mann, James | 53-4217 | 52 | |
| Burford, William | 53-2144 | 50 | |
| Phillips, Carl | 53-2134 | 53 | |
| Morrison, Harold | 53-1917 | 62 | |
| | | | |
| Mattick, Steve | 53-1902 | 33 | Orange Cell |
| Hall, Robert | 53-1912 | 30 | |
| Bowling, Russell | 53-4228 | 41 | |
| Peterson, Pete | 53-4230 | 32 | |
| Behan, Joseph | 53-1918 | 35 | |
| | | | |
| Herman, Wayne | 53-4224 | 20 | Black Cell |
| Shaver, Chester | 53-4208 | 11 | |
| Koudsi, John | 53-4222 | 17 | |
| Dandrich | 53-2139 | 21 | |
| Trudeau, Paul | 53-4214 | 16 | |

Final briefings were held at Base Operations. The latest en route weather conditions were double-checked. A hundred and one last-second details were ironed out. Parachutes, helmets, Mae Wests and flight lunches were gathered. Some of the guys went to the snack bar and got a last minute burger to fortify them for the flight. Others said a last-minute goodbye to their families.

Across the ramp, fifteen crews packed their gear on their B-47s, then began the preflight walk around. When everything was checked, checked, and rechecked, they climbed the ladder and settled into their cramped home for the next ten to twelve hours. Now, it was just a matter of time before the engines would whine as they started up to idle power.

It was an impressive sight, even in the dark, as the first wave taxied towards the runway. Each B-47 was loaded with enough JP-4 to get them to the refueling point over Eastern Canada. One by one, they moved down the taxiway and took their place in the long silver stream.

At 2130, Robert Hoover in the lead B-47 called the tower,

**"Rocky 39, Ready for take off."**

Power came up on the engines, brakes released.

**"Rocky 39... Rolling."**

Along with the rest of his crew was Col Louis Thorup, 307th Bomb Wing Commander, serving as mission commander. As usual, most of the men on the ground watched the takeoff. 53-4240 lifted into the air and disappeared into the dark sky. At one-minute intervals, the remaining B-47s rolled down the runway. Anyone who may have been taking in the flick at the West "O" Drive Inn that night would find it impossible to hear the movie over roar of the B-47s. Ah yes, but what an impressive show of their tax money in action. The 307th was on the way!

Mother Nature waved her weather wand to mess things up for the departure of the second wave on the 4th. She provided natural fireworks in the form of thunder, lightning, gusty winds, and a good old Nebraska

## Cold War Cornhuskers: The 307th Bomb Wing Lincoln Air Force Base Nebraska 1955-1965

frog-strangling rain. For safety, takeoff for wave two was reset for 1800 on the 5th. The second wave would be followed by the last wave later that night. It meant changing refueling times for the second wave, but at least the entire wing would get to England as outlined in the orders. That is, if everything went according to plan during the flight.

Crews for the last wave reported for the final briefing. Robert Hall's crew would fly in the last wave as Rocky 30 aboard 53-1912. His copilot was Robert Frank, from the small town of Tyler, North Dakota. Robert Hill would navigate for their trip across the pond. They were known as "The Three Bob Crew; Bob, Bob, and ReBob". Going along with them would be Richard Jones Jr., a reporter from *The Tulsa Tribune*. He was going to write a newspaper story about SAC crews and flying across the Atlantic.

Waiting for takeoff, Bob Frank went to the snack bar at Operations and had a banana split. Bob Hall spent a few extra minutes saying goodbye to his wife, Patricia. Bob Hill spent a little extra time looking over the charts and route that they would soon be flying.

Rocky 30 started engines at 2209. The crew went through the usual checks after engine start and proclaimed everything was ready. Now all they had to do was wait their turn for take off and they would be on their way to Jolly Old England.

Orange Cell lead launched at 2237; the mission was underway. Rocky 30 rolled down the runway at 2239. Takeoff was normal, and the aircraft climbed to altitude and took up a heading for Des Moines, Iowa. Over Des Moines the cell leader reported in, then turned to a heading of 030 degrees and began another climb to 30,000 feet about 28 miles northeast of Ames, Iowa.

Orange Cell lead made a radio check with Green Bay, Wisconsin, at the appointed time. With that, the navigators began a celestial navigation leg. Using the sextant, they looked for the stars Altair and Arcturus to pinpoint their position. The cell was cruising at 31,000 feet; the stars were like little diamonds in the dark sky. The flight leader checked in and cleared with Sudbury Radio in Ontario. The time hack was 1245; everything was on time.

The flight plan took the cell deeper into Canada. During the flight, the crews were busy with radio checkpoints. The navigators plotted their course and checked their position with star shots. Flying towards the East at jet speeds, the black night turned to aqua blue, then orange as the sun peeked over the horizon. It was one of the fastest changes from dark to light they had ever witnessed.

The cell leader called to report they had the tankers on radar. They would refuel in the "Pepper Box" refueling area just north of Goose Bay. It was time to move into close cell formation, rendezvous with the tankers and get a SAC gulp of JP-4. This was critical, so the bombers would have enough fuel to make it to England. Miss a tanker and it was a night at Goose Bay.

"ReBob" Hill spotted the tankers on the radar scope and gave a course correction to his pilot. Up in the front seat, Bob Hall approached the boom of the lumbering KC-97. Gentle adjustments in speed and the B-47 slid into the observation position.

**"Up five, left two Standby.....Contact!"**

Hanging on the boom, the fuel gushed through the pipes and into the fuel tanks on the B-47, while copilot Bob Frank monitored the fuel panel during the hookup. Bob Hall pulled off a textbook refueling. About twenty minutes after contact the transfer was complete. The total refueling was done in what they called "one gulp" (without a disconnect).

The cell was still together as they departed the refueling area and headed further out over the Atlantic. They would maintain this close formation for the next two hours. The cell leader called his "chicks" to move into formation for the required gunnery portion of the mission.

Bob Frank turned his copilot seat around and warmed up his gun-laying radar and guns. With the barrels of the 20 mm cannons pointed towards the water he waited for the word to commence firing. This could get hairy if Rocky 30 had a problem. With the seat facing the tail, it would be next to impossible for Frank to eject if he had to. After the "clear to fire" was received, Frank started firing short bursts, then a cool off period. Every time the 20 mm guns fired, a faint vibration was felt along the airframe of the B-47. After about 250 rounds the guns failed. A link had jammed and the next round wouldn't feed. Nothing could be done to clear the jam in the air. Frank recorded the number of rounds fired and turned his seat back around.

After the fireout, Orange Cell separated into a looser formation and continued the flight across the pond. During this part of the flight, the navigators were using time to practice pressure pattern navigation along with dead reckoning.

Bruce Mills and crew were flying 53-2140, call sign "ROCKY 14". He recalled:

"We were to refuel on coast-out of Canada and, of course, my tanker aborted and didn't show up. I started back to Goose Bay. Koudsi said, 'Call Goose Command and get another tanker.' So I did. Goose said they had a tanker whose bomber didn't show up, and I turned around and made a head on rendezvous.

"We hooked up with the copilot's help and the tanker pilot said, 'Open all your tanks-I'm going to emergency override and pump gas fast. The weather at Goose was getting really bad; it's closing in, and I've got to get back.' The son of a gun got me so heavy, I swear he had to tow me through the air. When the boomer said, 'Breakaway,' he disconnected and I dropped like a rock 5,000 feet. He said goodbye and when I finally got flying speed, I got all the way up to 26,000 feet. When I got to England, I was still so heavy I had to fly around another hour just to burn gas. So we made bomb runs, one radar and one visual with radar over a solid undercast. Good old Kuko got one with less than 150 feet CEP!"

George Nigh was flying on 2140 as crew chief for the trip over the pond. He recalled the trip was long, and the fourth man seat got hard as a rock after awhile. "At least I could get up and move around the aisle between my seat and the navigator's area."

Hours passed and miles of ocean drifted below them. By now the crews really began to feel the parachute straps cutting into their bodies. Helmets felt like a twenty pound piece of concrete on their heads. And talk about pressure points and hot spots on the backside. Bob, Bob, and ReBob were getting anxious to get down on the ground and stretch their legs.

Over the Command Radio, the Cell Leader called to advise they had the Irish Coast on radar about 150 miles ahead. The call was confirmed by ReBob as the coast slid into view on the next sweep of his radar. "Hot Ziggity!" Cell leader called for a gentle turn to a heading of 123 degrees for approach to the English Coast and the coast-in point.

Orange Cell was cleared by traffic control to land at Lakenheath. One by one the bombers made their jet penetration for landing. The Three Bob Crew went through the checklist and put 912 on the runway with a "no sweat" landing. After taxiing in and engine shut down the 3 Bobs and their reporter passenger were happy to put their feet on English terra firma after over ten hours in the air in the cramped confines of Rocky 30.

They collected their gear and baggage and waited for the truck to arrive to take them to Operations. While they waited, they watched the rest of the cell approach and land at Lakenheath. The 307th had arrived!

There wasn't much time to stand around and watch other planes land. They were dog-tired and needed to check in for debriefing, get something substantial to eat, find quarters, then get some well-deserved sack time.

While the newly arrived crews got a nap, the ground crews got busy turning the planes around. Any baggage or equipment brought over in the bombers was removed and sent to the appropriate area. After that, it was panels open so the maintenance crews could get inside and fix anything that had gone wrong during the flight. Within twenty-four hours, most of the B-47s were ready for whatever was planned.

Meanwhile, back across the pond at Lincoln, the tankers were trying to get things rolling and get headed for Jolly Old England. KC-97s had had problems with the solid Hamilton Standard propellers almost from the beginning of their service with SAC. H.A. Frost recalled:

"SAC's answer to the problem was: 1. Restrict the maximum crew aboard to only essential. 2. Max takeoff weight reduced to 155,000 lbs, except in case of a War Emergency. 3. All propeller blades were to be inspected and magnafluxed prior to the next flight and at intervals thereafter. 4. All crews were issued a 4-5 inch magnifying glass to inspect the blades for cracks and/or scratches on their pre-flight inspections.

"Post-accident analysis of recovered blades and inspections disclosed that many of the failures started under the rubber deicer cuffs at the base of the blade, so the magnifying glasses were only useful to look closer at scratches. Later, a requirement came out that each aircraft commander, copilot and flight engineer were to have a simulator session within one year demonstrating this engine/prop loss and how to fly it with the control problems in order to be rated "Combat Ready". When someone figured the only C-97 simulator was at West Palm Beach and belonged to MATS, more action had to be taken or all the tankers would be grounded after a year. Another directive came down that a standboard crew would check each crew on a check flight using differential power, cowl flaps and adverse flight control trim inputs. This was logged for training requirements, not as pilot proficiency flights, but as (get this) a Simulated-Simulator flight!"

By the 10th of July, most of the tankers had been inspected and any defective props magnafluxed. There were still weight restrictions, which meant some of the extra equipment wouldn't be going overseas on a KC-97. Departure was set for Thursday, the 12th, so any last minute details could be ironed out.

At the briefing, the crews were assigned their take off times. There would be two waves of ten KC-97s, taking off at one-minute intervals. Since the tankers would be carrying passengers the boom operators were given the extra duty of acting as stewards. According to the orders, it was their responsibility to make sure there were enough flight lunches to feed everyone. They were also told to have extra "barf cups" in case of rough weather.

**KC-97s deployed to UK**
**First Wave:**

| Aircraft Commander | Call Sign "Purdue" | Tail # |
|---|---|---|
| Fletcher, George | 10 | 51-375 |
| Veiluva, Edward | 15 | 52-2798 |
| Nutty, Jean | 13 | 51-378 |
| O'Brien | 27 | 52-2800 |
| Franklin, Denny | 17 | 51-382 |
| Cole, Vernon | 23 | 52-2796 |
| Maxwell, Phillip | 11 | 51-376 |
| Cragun, Calvin | 24 | 52-2797 |
| Caudel, Everett | 14 | 51-379 |
| Grammes, Richard | 30 | 52-2803 |

**Second Wave:**

| | | |
|---|---|---|
| Thornton, Jack | 16 | 51-381 |
| Chambers, Don | 22 | 52-2795 |
| Dodds, Richard | 19 | 51-384 |
| Sheffer, Leonard | 29 | 52-2802 |
| Tiede, Norman | 28 | 52-2801 |
| Westerman, "Bud" | 21 | 52-2794 |
| Armstrong, Jim | 18 | 51-383 |
| McLennan, "Mac" | 26 | 52-2799 |
| Watt, James | 15 | 51-380 |
| Kutscher, Leroy | 20 | 52-2793 |

The first wave of KC-97s, led by George Fletcher in 51-375 (Purdue 10), departed Lincoln and headed for their first layover at Harmon AB, Newfoundland. Crew chief Russ Geisler remembered, "When we left for England, we lost an engine over Iowa. We had to turn around and go back to Lincoln. We changed the engine and did our test flight. We ended up going to England all by our lonesome."

The last plane in the first wave was 52-2803 (Purdue 30), flown by Richard Grammes. Also aboard the plane was LtCol Everett Thurlow, the squadron commander. He was flying "tail-end Charlie" to make sure everyone in the first wave got off the ground. Grammes had other passengers on 2803 for the flight. He recalled the Flight Surgeon was aboard, "just in case." Protestant Chaplain Copeland was also aboard as a passenger. "I guess they figured I needed all the help I could get."

The second wave, led by Richard "Bud" Westerman in 52-2794 (Purdue 21), climbed into the Nebraska sky. Sitting in the right seat was H.A. Frost, who recalled the flight:

"The flight over was interesting. We flew to Harmon AFB, Newfoundland, the first day and left for Greenham Common before dawn the next morning in horrible weather, heavy rain and high winds with lots of turbulence at low altitudes right after takeoff. We took off at five-minute intervals and maintained 500 feet altitude between aircraft. Once underway, the weather was clear and smooth. We had the most experienced navigator on our crew since we were standboard. 'Blink' Blinkinsop was one busy guy taking drift readings, sun shots, etc., and scribbling madly. A few hours into our eleven and a half hour flight, Blink asked to use the VHF radio and began comparing data with the other navigators coming along behind. We got occasional small course correction as we bored along.

"Landfall within three miles of the flight plan and five minutes of the ETA was essential to avoid intercept by the RAF, so the navs worked hard at it. A couple of hours out, I tuned in the BBC broadcast located roughly in the center of England at a known Lat-Long coordinates. I turned on the weather radar for land mapping to paint the coastline picture when we got within range. Bud Westerman, the AC, and I were noticing the ADF needle was pointing more and more to the left of the nose position and pretty soon the radar was painting the coastline.

"I got out my WAC charts and started trying to find the shoreline we were painting. The needle was now pointing thirty degrees off the nose, so I got the WAC chart showing the southern coast of England and the northern coast of France. The radar image was a very distinct one and, Eureka!, it matched a section of the French coastline exactly. Since this was a graded navigation leg for 'Blink', the pilots weren't allowed to give him any help, but this was getting ridiculous. We told him the location the ADF was pointing to and told him to come and look at our radarscope. He was leery of accepting that he might be in error, but shortly afterwards, he gave a left course change of about forty-five degrees and we gave a revised ETA to Oceanic Control. The rest of the flight was uneventful and we did our best not to rag 'Blink' too much!"

Back in the tanker stream, radio operator Richard Roberts was busy at his station:

"My position as radio operator was very insignificant, but occasionally we found a few duties to perform. In 1956, I was one year shy of being old enough to buy beer, legally. Needless to say, as a newly checked-out RO, this hop across the pond was very interesting for me. It was also my first over-water flight where the RO was responsible for all communications once outside of UHF/VHF range.

"I shared this experience with six or eight other new operators who were experiencing the same adrenaline rushes that I was. Everyone followed the same route at about ten-minute intervals. Our HF radio equipment saw very little use in the States (as did radio operators) so, as a result, several of the ROs had trouble contacting the ground stations on the flight across to England. Someone came up with the brilliant idea of relaying their messages to our copilot then having me send them on to the appropriate ground station. Well, when we arrived at Greenham Common, I had about four pages of radio logs."

After the last KC-97 had taken off from Harmon, the support party began to repack their equipment and tools. They had been there at Harmon in case anything had gone wrong on the incoming tankers and needed to be repaired. Bob Matich wrote:

"LAFB to Newfoundland was non eventful. After the KCs and 47s went by, we got ready to leave and I noticed this oil leak on #3 engine. I told the flight engineer about it, and he said, 'No problem, normal seepage.' Well, that normal seepage went from the aft wing root to the empennage and also covered the right side cabin windows.

"We took off and, at about 500 feet in the air, we lost #3 engine. Luckily, due to a valley we got enough air speed for a go around and we landed. Then we waited two weeks for a backup C-124. We had about 50 souls onboard, 2 complete R-4360s, our own tools and luggage and two complete flyaway boxes. The trip after that was uneventful."

While the tankers were trying to get off the ground at Lincoln, the bomber crews were settling in to their temporary lifestyle in the English countryside. Dale Christians recalled:

"While we were there we were all housed in a big barracks across from the Officers' Club. I was copilot on Crew R-21 with Capt. Paul Trudeau as AC. As you entered the barracks, we had the first three single rooms on the ground floor to the left across from the latrines."

Dale recalled that some of the parties at the "O" Club would spill over into the barracks. Some of the single crewmen would bring British Flowers over for "a nightcap." News of this activity filtered back to Lincoln and the squadron commander had to go back and assure the wives all was fine in England. Now, legend has it, some of the wives got together and had a party of their own back at Lincoln. After all, what's sauce for the gander is sauce for those who held down the home front.

Starting on Monday, July 9th, the 307th began flying a four-day operation called Bee Sting. It was an orientation mission to familiarize the new arrivals with flying in the British Isles and surrounding parts of Europe. The mission included celestial navigation, one hour of depressurized flying, and radar bomb runs on Paris and London. There was also an attempt at shooting the tail guns for a fireout score. Results were listed as "good"; the 307th placed third among the wings participating in Bee Sting.

"We had just completed our mission," Paul Koski wrote. "Most of the mission went smoothly, except we were to have a fireout of the 20 mm cannons. After about 100 rounds, the guns jammed and wouldn't move from the down position. We aborted the fireout and returned to the base.

"The AC notified Lakenheath we would be landing with hot guns. Control wanted to know if we wanted to have someone meet us to put the gun turret switch to the safe position. The AC said, 'We have a crew chief on board and he could do it.' The tower said, 'to expedite your egress of the runway since other aircraft were on approach.'

"I opened the cockpit door and stood on the entrance ladder. I was waiting for the aircraft to stop before extending the ladder. This is where the fun began. We were off the runway and taxing when we hit a bump, the ladder jumped out of the latches and there I went, ladder and all, landing on my back. Luckily I had my chute and helmet on, so no harm done except some bruised fingers.

"I went to the tail and set the turret switch to safe. Since the entrance to the aircraft was too high for me to get back in, I notified the AC through hand signals that the switch was set and motioned for him to taxi in without me.

"I had about a mile to walk carrying the ladder, parachute and helmet. It seemed like it took me an hour to walk to the parked aircraft, but it was only about ten minutes. When I got there they were still trying to get the crew and equipment off the plane. They had a B-4 stand and a stepladder in the entranceway. They were having a time of it. They hadn't seen me walk up so I stood there a moment watching this three-ring circus and then asked them if the ladder would help. The next morning at roll call we were briefed that you don't open the hatch until the aircraft stops, citing me as an example. Did I have a red face?"

Friday, July 20th, most of the 307th Wing Staff journeyed to South Ruislip to attend a 7th Air Division briefing on upcoming operations that would affect the 307th Bomb Wing. While the staff was at the briefing, the simmering pot in the Middle East came to the boiling point. Egypt's leader Gamal Abdel Nasser's forces seized the Suez Canal. Military forces across Europe went on increased readiness in case the Suez pot boiled over.

Crew R-38, Capt Russell Bowling (AC), 2Lt Carroll Kalberg (CP) and Lt Michael Selmo (Nav), were on the flying schedule for Saturday, July 27th. They had planned a routine mission over the British countryside, staying within 200 miles of Lakenheath. They were also to test the radar system on the aircraft. They made two bomb runs on the London RBS, then an air refueling with a KC-97 from the 307th AREFS about 120 miles south of London and finished the mission with practice approaches and touch and go landings. Since there had been some problems with the Bomb/Nav System on the aircraft, TSgt. John Ulrich from the A & E section went along to make sure the problems had been fixed. After three touch and go approaches, 53-4230 started for the fourth and final approach; from the ground it looked like a textbook approach.

All of the pilots who had landed at Lakenheath soon found out about the "hump" about a third of the way down Runway 07/25. If you didn't watch out for it, it could really give you a big surprise. Several crews had already had an unexpected thrill because of the hump.

4230 touched down and passed over the hump, which launched the B-47 back into the air, causing it to porpoise. The B-47 became a runaway, the right wing dropped, and the outboard engine hit the runway. That caused a hard roll back to the left until the left wing came down and smashed into the ground. Shedding parts, the aircraft traveled over 3,000 feet down the runway. Out of control, yawing and rolling, the B-47 headed for a bomb storage bunker.

William Bathurst was watching from the window of the BOQ. "The B-47's left wing tip was above the hangar, then it disappeared and the right wing tip came up. I yelled at Sully and Wayne Herman, 'The plane is going to crash!'"

Smashing into the bunker, the plane disappeared in a boiling cloud of fire and smoke. The fire spread and covered several of the bunkers, causing a new danger. These were storage bunkers that contained Mark-6 nuclear weapons. Lakenheath had a Broken Arrow in the making if the fire was not contained.

Fire crews responded to the conflagration and fought the blaze to a standstill. Parts of the base were evacuated in case of more explosions. Several rows of transient F-84 fighters were latched onto and towed to the far end of the ramp. Charles Bird recalled:

"I was a new SSgt in charge of the Radio Field Shop and was in a maintenance meeting when the plane was trying to land. I saw the whole event, as there was a large plate glass window that faced the runway. The entire A & E building was evacuated to the perimeter fence as far away from the site as we could go. Fortunately, no bombs detonated and few were damaged. A TSgt from the A & E Squadron was on board doing a Quality Control in-flight check on some of the equipment."

Lakenheath was closed to air operations for two days following the accident. Time was needed to assess the damage to the bunkers and assure there was no danger of further explosions or radiation leaks.

The investigation was unable to determine the exact cause of the accident or who was actually at the controls of the B-47 on the fatal approach. It was believed 2Lt Carroll Kalberg might have been flying from the copilot seat. From the back seat it would have been impossible to judge exactly where the runway hump was. It was believed Russ Bowling might have taken over the controls as the plane began to porpoise, but was unable to regain control in time to prevent the accident. The board listed the hump in the runway as a "significant contributing factor" to the accident.

A Memorial Service was held at the small chapel at Lakenheath for the crew several days after the accident. Col Louis Thorup attended and led the service along with Chaplain Copeland. Everyone who knew Russ and his crew were shocked and saddened by their loss. After that dreadful Saturday, England wasn't quite as "Jolly".

The 307th AREFS would spend their TDY deployment at Greenham Common and fly operations from there. Like the bomber crews, they had to fly orientation flights after their arrival. They found flying over England was a lot different than back in the States. First, there was the weather, and then there was the air traffic control, or seeming lack of it.

Like the others, "Bud" Westerman's crew took their turn at getting to know the English countryside. Copilot H.A. Frost recalled:

"Our orientation flight was a big circle up to Scotland, down the East Coast and back over London then home, all in solid overcast conditions. In an hour period, we just missed a B-29 going in the opposite direction over us and a few minutes later missed a Convair C-131, which went from right to left at our altitude. We were pretty shook up until after we got safely back to base. We were under radar control, but when we were off-airways, ATC didn't provide separation. They would only tell you about traffic if they had time. If they said you had head-on traffic, you had best make a turn one way or the other quickly. The RAF owned all the airspace below 200 feet AGL in those days. It wasn't unusual to see a flight of two or so jet fighters cooking along in the mist just above the obstructions."

Not all of the flying in England was for orientation. Paul Koski remembers:

"We were at Lakenheath and my aircraft 4214 was scheduled for a four hour pilot proficiency check ride. Our call sign was ROCKY 42. Some colonel from RAF Brize Norton needed to get a check ride to maintain his rating. Since this was to be a short flight, it was an ideal time for me to get four hours for flight pay. Preflight was completed and the engines started. The colonel had the front seat and the major had the back seat. I was lucky to ride in the navigator's position, since we didn't need one for local missions.

"Takeoff was uneventful. We bored holes in the sky for about two hours. Since I was in the nav position, I could look out the little window on the right side of the nose of the aircraft. This was great, since the crew chief usually didn't see out in the 4th man position, but after a while it got boring.

"Part of the proficiency check was takeoffs and landings. We were making GCA touch and go landings. The colonel was a very good pilot. He greased all the landings without so much as a bump. I wasn't even sure when we touched down most of the time. He was nailing it on glide slope with little if any deviation. After about six touch and gos, the major told the colonel his check ride was over and complimented him on his skills.

"This is where the fun begins. The major said we still had some time left and he hadn't made any back seat landings for awhile and would the colonel monitor him.

"The first attempt, GCA said he was high on the glide slope and too far to the left and gave him corrections, but he was still too high as we came over the end of the runway, so we missed approached and went around.

"The second attempt wasn't much better; GCA told him he was too low on the glide slope. 10 feet, 25 feet and back to 15 feet. Another missed approach and go around executed. It should be noted that landing from the back seat is like flying blind. You can't see straight ahead through the back of the aircraft commander's seat, so you have to lean one way or the other to see where you are going.

"On the third attempt, the major said, 'I'm going to make it or else.' Well, we were low, then high. Dumb me; I was standing up looking out the window to see how he was doing. When I saw the hangars go by, I knew we were halfway down the runway and about fifty feet in the air. I jumped back in the seat and buckled up in record time.

"Power came up and I thought we were doing another go around, but the aircraft started shaking and it seemed the bottom fell out. We hit the runway so hard that amplifiers on the wall popped out. We bounced back into the air with all engines screaming. The aircraft was still shaking, as well as my knees. The colonel said, 'I have the aircraft.' I know we weren't gaining any altitude, but air speed was picking up and the shaking stopped. I think what saved us was that the ground sloped down at the end of the runway and we just followed the terrain.

"There was a little town in the valley, which had a church steeple that people said we just missed. I don't know how close it was because I was really strapped in and had the straps been any tighter, I wouldn't have been able to breathe. I did hear the tower on the radio ask, 'ROCKY 43, are you in trouble.' They kept repeating it over and over. It seems we had dropped from radar and couldn't be seen from the flight line.

"As cool as can be, the colonel answered as we pulled out of the valley, 'Lakenheath Tower, this is ROCKY 42, were you trying to reach us?' He notified the tower that we would be making a full stop landing this time.

"The colonel made another perfect landing and then we had to debrief. They wrote up the aircraft for a hard landing. This meant we would have

## Cold War Cornhuskers: The 307th Bomb Wing Lincoln Air Force Base Nebraska 1955-1965

a lot of X-rays to do and inspection of the landing gear and engines. The colonel logged in the time as 3 hours and 55 minutes. I asked him if he could make it 4 hours. He said we only flew the amount of time that he entered and he wasn't going to change it. I had to fly another mission to get my flight pay for the month. I didn't really mind, since I owed the colonel a lot."

With the situation in the Middle East at a near-boiling point, the 307th had to be ready for a real mission if the balloon went up. The training drill was to load one B-47 with a "weapon," then have each crew fly a short mission and perform In-flight Insertion and Extraction of the arming device. These training flights went on until one mission when the "pill" fell out of the aircraft as it taxied back to the ramp. The device was surrounded by Security Forces until it could be removed to the proper storage area.

Operation Pink Lady began on Tuesday, August 14, 1956. This would be another scored bomber stream mission. The B-47s would take off at fifteen minute "hacks". There would be three waves of aircraft. British weather had to cooperate for the mission. Minimums for takeoff had to be at least five hundred-foot ceiling and a mile visibility. For landing, they had to have a thousand foot ceiling and two miles visibility. The targets for the mission were Paris and London.

Capt John Koudsi flew the lead position in ROCKY 17. They flew the navigation legs and made their runs on Paris. According to the briefing, his navigator placed the Polar Mode Switch to Polar Position for an "Eskimo" run. Then it was coast-out near Normandy, turn and make a run on London. Their target was the center of the bridge at Windsor Castle. The second offset aiming point was the sewage disposal area on the west side of the London Airport. They hoped the offset point wouldn't cause a "crappy" bomb run.

By the end of the third day, everyone had flown the mission. Good old British weather caused several problems on the bomb runs on London. At least two of the runs did, in fact, go right down the old sewer pipe. Overall results were listed as very good, proving once again that the 307th could bomb the crap out of a target.

All work and no R & R made the men of the 307th, well, not happy while away from home. Some of the guys did manage to get to London to see the sights and visit Piccadilly Circus. Robert Richards was one of those lucky enough to get to London. "Our crew got a weekend pass into London which was a great experience for this old Kentucky boy. In London, we had to check in (by phone) with our aircraft commander periodically. As for me, the trip was an experience of a lifetime." Now, the reason the boys had to check in was because of the ongoing situation in the Middle East. After all, we couldn't have the boys having fun if an alert was called and nobody knew where they were.

Richard Grammes recalled "We had a golf course only a stone's throw away from our quarters. So some of us took up the game. Calvin Cragun was an average golfer. He liked to challenge all of us. Frank Strom and I played him a number of times. I don't recall us winning."

Then there was the Peddling While Intoxicated Caper. Seems that several of the hard-working crew chiefs went to the Enlisted Club to have a couple of brewskis. Close to closing time the boys thought a couple more cool ones at the barracks would be a great way to call it a night. There was a strict rule against taking beer outside of the club. To make sure the rule was enforced, the bartender would open the cans in the club. Now, if these guys could delve into the innards of a B-47 and figure out what makes it tick, they could certainly figure out a way of getting a beer or two (or three or four) out of the club. The solution was simple: pass the cans out the bathroom window when no one was looking. So be it! The leader secured the cans inside his shirt, being careful not to spill a single amber drop. Our intrepid crew chiefs were off on their bikes towards the barracks. The rider of the beer laden bike happened to hit a bump and made a three point landing on the concrete. There happened to be a Security vehicle nearby and the APs saw the bad landing.

The biker was a bit bruised and, needless to say, covered with suds and reeked with the aroma of booze. The APs issued a ticket for Peddling While Intoxicated. No cold brewskis in the barracks that night! On top of that, the biker had to report to his CO on Monday and try to explain his way out of that one. The CO let the scraped up crew chief off with a verbal, "I hope you learned your lesson!"

Robert Rose recalled:

"A2C Mauer and I were sent to Ben Guerir Air Base, French Morocco, to support four of the 307th's B-47s. We flew down on a C-119 with a spare engine on board. About three quarters of the way down, we lost an engine on the C-119 and a crusty old captain ordered us to prepare to bail out if he gave the order. We made it to the base and right at touchdown the other engine quit.

"The temperature there was around 120° and we spent about three weeks there trying to get the 47s off the ground and back to Lakenheath. Our quarters were next to an all-girl band from England and, needless to say, we had a great time there."

Operation Side Car found the 307th flying missions on September 4th, 11th and 18th. Another bomber stream mission with celestial navigation, possible fighter attacks and three bomb runs. After the nav legs, the first target would be London. Then over the countryside and coast-out over the White Cliffs of Dover and head for Paris. After the run on Paris, it was back for another try on London. The results were scored as "very good". This would be the last major operation for the 307th while on TDY.

It may have been the last major operation, but there were always local missions to fly to keep in practice for the big one. As always, flying any mission could go from routine to "hell in a hand basket" in a matter of moments. Take for example the crew flying KC-97 51-375. Russ Geisler remembered:

"We lost three engines coming back from a mission. We just about put 375 into a hill on our approach. We managed to get one engine back before we landed. We barely missed a church steeple. When we got back on the ground, we got out of the plane and our AC said, 'Well, fellas, about another thirty seconds and we would have augured into that hill.' Then he said. 'Now, we're all gonna go and get a drink.' A couple of days later we heard that some people had complained about us flying so low. When the situation was explained to them, they were glad we had made it to the base."

Because of the situation in the Middle East, there were rumors the 307th would have their TDY extended for an indefinite period. It was just that, the good old rumor mongers stirring up the rumor pot. With the end of the TDY in sight, the 307th began packing their bags for the return flight back to good old Lincoln, Nebraska.

Beginning the first week of October, it was Operation Red Cap in reverse. Equipment was inventoried, packed and loaded for the trip home. There was a lot of last minute work on the planes to get them ready for the flight. Everyone was anxious to get the show on the road and get back to their families. After all, three months was a long time to be away from loved ones.

Military Air Transport Service (MATS) had to help get everybody back to Lincoln. Huge C-124 Globemasters would land, open the big nose doors and gulp down equipment and people. Then they would taxi out and use almost every bit of the runway to claw their way into the air.

## 1956

"Our crew didn't have an aircraft to fly back because we ferried a KC-97 back to Tinker AFB, OK at the end of July for IRAN maintenance," Wrote H. A. Frost. "Since we didn't have an aircraft to bring back, Bud Westerman and I were assigned as OIC and Asst OIC of a thirty-five man crew, tool boxes and two Quick Change engine assemblies on a MATS C-124 for the return maintenance support at Goose Bay. That was a long, noisy and alternating hot and cold ride in the cargo compartment with a crew rest stop at Lajes enroute. When all our aircraft were off and headed home from Goose, it was back on "Ole Shaky" so we could go home too. But #2 engine failed right after takeoff so we got to spend another night at Goose while the MATS crew changed an engine."

Like the trip over, the Navy was there to help bring the 307th home. On Wednesday, October 10th, they brought in several R6D-1 (C-118) transports from Air Transport Squadron 6 (VR-6). They were to load personnel, baggage and leave. Everyone checked the manifest to see which plane he was scheduled for. Dave Avery was supposed to fly back on the Navy R6D-1, #131588, scheduled for a later take off. His wife Betty was expecting a baby. A2C Dale Brockman told Dave he could have his seat on an earlier flight. So, Dave packed his bag and headed home. There were several other last minute changes as men traded places or were bumped.

Robert Rose was one of those bumped at the last minute. He recalled, "I was waiting in line to board a C-118 to go back to Lincoln at Lakenheath. The man ahead of me was A1C Herbert Banks. He looked back at me and said, 'Rose, I've got a feeling that we are going to have to swim before we get home.' We both boarded the C-118 and I sat in a seat near the entrance. Someone came on and pointed to me and said, 'Get off'."

Marv Nystrom was one of those who boarded 588. "We sat there in the aircraft, seemed like hours. After a long wait we were told to go back to the barracks, that the airplane had some problems. After a few hours we were told another aircraft had come in and they were moving us up to take that one, which we did. The next group was changed to take the one we were originally scheduled for."

Fifty members of the 307th boarded 588 that day. They were full of smiles of anticipation; after all, they were headed home to their loved ones. The flight crew fired up the four big engines and taxied to the runway. Last minute run up and mag checks were completed. The navigator had his charts laid out and ready for the first leg to the Azores.

Takeoff was textbook. The big transport lifted into the air, sucked up the gear, then disappeared in the distance. About an hour later, another Navy transport lifted off with another load of homeward-bound members of the 307th. They landed at Lajes Field, Azores, on schedule. On arrival there was a strange buzz in the air: Navy 588 was overdue and there had been no contact with them since a routine radio report placed them near Lands End, England, on a course for the Azores.

Several other planes left England that day. They were asked to keep an eye out for the missing Navy plane. It became painfully evident the aircraft was down somewhere when the maximum fuel endurance hour came and went with no word from 588.

Bob Matich recalled, "After we left RAF Greenham Common, we heard about the C-118. When we got to the reported area, we orbited for a brief time, fuel allowing. Then we headed for Lajes AFB, where the runway has an uphill run. We were there overnight. There was a "one-armed bandit" in the church lobby and I left my total $3.00 there. When we got back to Lincoln, I was broke."

Search and rescue planes were launched from England, the Azores and Spain looking for any sign of the lost transport. It would become the largest search mission mounted in history up to that time. Every aircraft that even came near the area was told to look for the downed aircraft. Ships were dispatched to the area to comb the sea in hope of finding some clue, yet there was no sign of the aircraft.

Friday's *Lincoln Evening Journal* ran a headline of hope:

### S.O.S. SPURS HOPE FOR LOST AIRMEN

Several airliners had picked up what was believed to have been a distress signal about 150 miles north of the Azores. Another search of the area revealed nothing.

The men of the 307th were devastated by the loss of fifty of their fellow airmen. These were their friends, men with whom they had worked, eaten and shared a can of beer. They were fellow brothers-in-arms. Now, they were gone. Sorrow and, in some cases, a feeling of guilt soaked the ranks of the 307th. The chapel at Lincoln Air Force Base overflowed on Monday, October 29th, for the Memorial Service.

The wing was home at Lincoln and faced the chore of putting grief aside and getting on with the job at hand. No better way than to keep flying and working on the planes, to keep 'em ready for anything that SAC could come up with.

On Friday, November 16th, the men of the 307th couldn't help but notice a lot of activity up north on the 98th's home turf. The activity culminated with the arrival of a KC-97, tail number 53-3816. It was the last KC-97 to come off the production line at Boeing. She was clean and shiny; wouldn't the 307th AREFS crew chiefs like to get their hands on her!

Another day on the flight line at Lincoln. For mid-November the weather was beautiful. Sunny skies and mild temperatures in the low fifties. There was a forecast of light snow in the panhandle, but that wouldn't be anywhere near Lincoln till Monday or Tuesday.

The situation in the Suez Canal area had cooled down to a slow simmer. SAC had a lot of B-47s on alert just in case the situation would begin to boil again. As a precaution, SAC Headquarters had placed a lot of the tanker force in strategic spots in case they were needed. The 98th had sent tankers to Harmon AB, and had the tankers of the 307th standing by as a follow on force if needed.

Lee Cullimore recalled, "377 was put on overseas standby because of the situation in the Suez Canal area. Orders were cut sending us to RAF Mildenhall in England, but we never went. However, for two weeks we lived on the flight line, hat in hand and ready to go. Not much fun."

On Friday, a flight of Nebraska Air National Guard F-80s left Lincoln for Casper, Wyoming, for weekend gunnery practice. The weather in Wyoming was bad and the "weekend warriors" wouldn't get much trigger time due to low clouds and light snow.

While the situation on base was tense, it wasn't the real hectic pace usually found during a world crisis. There were a lot of aircraft sitting on the ramp in various stages of readiness, just in case. All in all, it was a good day to finish any write-ups on the Form 781, clean up the birds and get ready for the upcoming flying schedule.

A1C John Delancy found a fuel leak on a fuel pump in the bomb bay of 53-4235. That meant changing the faulty pump. The B-47 was towed to Refueling Pit 14 and the process of defueling to safe limits was started. 52-369 from the 98th was sitting at Pit 13, just to the north of Pit 14. Her ground crew was in the process of fueling the bird for the mission. They had taken all of the safety procedures as outlined in the checklist.

Lt Robert Cox had recently arrived at Lincoln and was waiting to be assigned to a crew. He had the duty of supervising some of the refueling and topping off tanks on several other B-47s on the ramp. Simple duty, kind of boring, yet a vital link in the chain mail of SAC.

SSgt Paul Koski had spent the afternoon working on his bird (53-4214). He was putting the nose cowling on the #2 and #3 engines when

45

## Cold War Cornhuskers: The 307th Bomb Wing Lincoln Air Force Base Nebraska 1955-1965

John Delancy drove up. John pitched in as usual and helped secure the cowling. John had been to supply to get a new fuel pump and was on his way back to his aircraft. His assistant, A2C Don Price, was busy removing the old pump from the bomb bay.

John and Paul chewed the fat for a few minutes. They agreed it was about time to call it a day, button things up and go to town. John's assistant could change the pump. Sounded like a plan; it would be good to get off base and relax a little. Neither of the airmen noticed Nebraska Air Guard F-80 #44-85284 taxiing towards the end of Runway 17.

Lt Robert Young had not been able to make the trip to Casper with the rest of the flight. He had spent the day going over training material and making flight plans for an early evening local training flight. He would spend about an hour in the air making night instrument approaches and touch and go landings. Just routine training, get some stick time for flight pay to help pay his tuition at the University of Nebraska.

The sun slid below the horizon at about 1700 that day. A combination of humidity and 44 degree temperature caused a low haze to descend as twilight fell on the flight line. Lt Young lifted Sombrero 15 off the runway at about 1745 and barreled to the south climbing into the Nebraska twilight.

A1C Roger Smith and A2C Melvin Werschky of the 98th were busy refueling their B-47 at Pit 13. Smith was in the cockpit monitoring the fuel panel, while Werschky was standing near the rear of the right wing at the refueling point. They wanted to finish for the day and maybe get a "cold one" after supper.

Sombrero 15 had requested to make a practice jet penetration and was advised by the tower to report over Sprague for an approach to the north. Three miles south of the runway Sombrero 15 requested a low instrument approach to the field. The tower told Lt Young to maintain at least 500 feet over the runway due to a B-47 preparing to take off. Lt. Young acknowledged that he would maintain 3500 over the field.

Young then requested a low frequency approach from the north. Sombrero 15 crossed the field at about 3500 feet and continued north. After clearing the field Lt Young crossed the outer cone and turned inbound and was cleared for the approach. At the inner cone he requested permission for a touch and go landing on Runway 17. He was cleared for the touch and go and advised to touch down on the east side of the runway due to a repair patch on the west side of the runway. Young acknowledged, "Sombrero 15 on the go."

So far it was another routine approach, just like he had done many times before. Easing back on the throttle, he lined up on Runway 17 and let his F-80 settle towards touchdown. As he flared out, a B-47 suddenly emerged from the twilight haze directly in front of him. Frantically Young pushed the throttle forward and pulled back on the stick trying to get back into the air. There wasn't enough time for the jet engine to spool up to full power.

In the cockpit of 52-369, Roger Smith was looking down at the refueling panel. "I saw a flash and looked up, everything was orange. I sat there petrified, fearing I was trapped. I managed to climb out. There were flames all around. I looked for 'dark spots' where there were no flames. I ran, beating out flames on my left arm as I ran for safety."

The F-80 slammed into 369 at nearly takeoff speed. It sliced through the bomber and careened into John Delancy's bird a few yards away. In the bomb bay Don Price never knew what had happened. John Delancy was under the left wing and turned to run, but there wasn't enough time to outrun the boiling conflagration.

Across the flight line there was instant pandemonium. For those dangerously close to the erupting flames, the first reaction was to run "like hell" towards safety as the heat built to an intolerable level. Then their training started to kick in.

Lt Bob Cox was about a hundred yards from the explosion. "I yelled at my crew, 'Let's Go!'. As I was running toward the burning equipment I glanced back to see my crew running the other way, a very lonesome feeling. However, they saw that the best action was to move all of the aircraft away from the fire. As I arrived near the aircraft, I saw men on fire so I used my parka and jacket to put out the flames on their clothing."

Within minutes of the accident, base fire crews responded to fight the growing inferno. A call went out to the Lincoln Fire Department for trucks to head to the base and stand by in case they were needed. The firefighters hosed the area with streams of foam, trying to beat back the boiling river of flames. The heat kept the crews on the outer edge of the boiling inferno. They had to contain the spreading river of flaming JP-4 from reaching other aircraft on the flight line. At one time, the flames had spread over a hundred yards from the crash site.

Across the ramp, men grabbed tow bars and jumped into Colemans to move aircraft away from the fire. H.A. Frost and Ozzie Parrish scrambled aboard their tanker and fired up the engines, then taxied it toward the runway, away from the inferno.

Everett Sutherland recalled, "We were in the mess hall getting ready to eat supper when we heard the explosion. We were called out and had to go to our planes in case we had to move them. Seeing all of that fire out there on the flight line scared the hell out of me."

Paul Koski recalled, "The heat was so intense that static electricity was building up. The radio truck, Alpha 1, showed up and said for everyone to get off the flight line, now! With all the static electricity, they thought the whole area could go up in flames."

Slowly, the firefighters beat back the flames, then moved towards the mangled wreckage of the two B-47s. Several of the firemen were injured and taken to the base dispensary. By about 7 PM, the fire was under control thanks to the Herculean efforts of the firemen. In the darkness of night there was little more to do except spray foam on the hot spots of the smoldering wreckage.

The scene on the flight line the next morning was one of complete devastation. Two B-47s were just a pile of mangled and charred junk. Parts of the F-80 were mingled with the other wreckage. The grim task of searching the crash site for victims began. No one really knew how many men had been working on the B-47s. Paul Koski had hoped his buddy, John Delancy, had made it to safety. Paul was devastated when he learned John had not made it.

When Lt Bob Cox reported for duty the next morning, his friends gazed at him like they were seeing a ghost. His parka and dog tags had been found near the crash site. They figured he had perished in the flames. Not so, he was very much alive and kicking.

The accident claimed three lives. Lt Robert Young died in the cockpit of his F-80. Airmen Don Price died in the bomb bay of his aircraft. John Delancy was overcome by flames as he ran towards the left wing of the B-47. A total of seven other men were injured, including three firefighters. Paul Koski remembered that it was very hard to attend the memorial service for his buddies who perished in the accident.

The investigation that followed was never able to come to a conclusion as to why Lt Young had mistaken the taxiway for the active runway. He was an experienced pilot and had used Runway 17 many times during his service with the Air Guard. Could it have been the twilight haze caused by the sunset conditions? There was also rumor that someone in the control tower had accidentally turned off the runway lights while reaching across the panel for something. Ultimately, the board was only able to conclude that pilot error had caused the horrific accident on Saturday, November 17.

From November 27th to December 11th, SAC conducted Operations Power House and Road Block. During the two-week period, B-47s and

KC-97s flew over one thousand simulated combat missions over the arctic and Continental United States. The entire operation was SAC shaking its mailed fist in a show of power in case the Soviet Union had any idea of intervening in the Middle East.

One of the last missions flown during Operation Road Block was flown on December 11th. The 307th AREFS would provide refueling support. Lt Earl Bullock's crew was assigned to act as weather scout; that is, fly to the designated refueling area, scout out the weather conditions and report back to Lincoln. LtCol Everett Thurlow, 307th AREFS Commander, would fly along with Earl's crew that day.

Preflight was normal: all the rivets, props and tires in the right place. No major leaks spotted, so everything was ready to go. What could go wrong, good old 375 had just gotten back from updates and IRAN. Crew briefing out of the way. Nothing to do now but climb aboard, check everything inside and start the engines.

**"Ground ready on #3, Prop Clear! Fire Guard standing by."**

The thirteen-foot diameter Hamilton Standard propeller turned through twenty blades, then the engine coughed to life, sending blue gray smoke billowing in the propwash. One by one the other three R-4360s came alive with the deep throaty rumble and groan that only a big piston engine has.

Earl taxied 375 to the end of runway and called the tower for takeoff clearance. Cleared for takeoff, last minute checks, cowl flaps, mags checked, mixture Auto Rich, flaps set, windows and hatches closed. The crew may have given a little tug on their seat belts just to make sure they were secure.

At full throttle, the KC-97 vibrated under the power surging through it from the four big turning fans. At the release of the brakes, the heavy tanker inched forward, then rolled faster as she trundled down Runway 35. Earl kept her headed down the runway with his left hand using the nosewheel steering wheel.

**"Coming up on 70 knots.... Hack!"**

At S2, take off speed, Earl nudged the wheel back. The nose wheel lifted ever so slightly, and seconds later the main gear left Runway 35, and the KC-97 was airborne. Once again, fear and superstition was overcome by science and technology.

**"GEAR UP!"**

The altimeter slowly wound upward as the tanker gained altitude. Slowly the crew milked the flaps up. Everything was going according to the checklist. Another routine take off from Lincoln Air Force Base.

Passing through five hundred feet, the crew was getting ready for the climb-out checklist. Without warning, #3 engine coughed and started to backfire. On take off that's a real attention getter. MSgt Melvin Paterson pulled the power back a little and the engine quit its coughing spasm. With a sick engine they couldn't climb at their take off weight. They were too low to bail out, and a crash landing? Well, that was out of the question, since they were loaded with a lot of JP-4.

The "engine-out-on-takeoff" procedures raced through Earl's mind. In nanoseconds he had his plan. They had to try and stay in the air long enough to dump fuel, fly the pattern and make an emergency landing. After all, the book said it could be done. Besides, at this point, they were running out of options and time.

Radio operator A2C Rosario Deals got on the radio and contacted the tower to let them know what was going on, then declared an emergency. The tower acknowledged and hit the emergency button to alert the fire trucks. Flight engineer Paterson hit the Air Refueling Master Switch and turned the Dump Switch, and JP-4 began spewing from the boom, raining down on the snow covered fields north of the base.

Just after the left hand turn in the pattern, the #4 engine backfired once, then started coughing uncontrollably. Pulling the power back didn't help. No time to mess with it, so they pulled the throttle back to Idle Cutoff and hit the feathering button for #4. Then #3 engine started to backfire again. MSgt. Paterson played the throttle like a concert violinist, but to no avail; #3 was sick and nothing could be done to save the partial power. His only option was shut that engine down and feather the prop.

Earl made a slow careful left turn into the sun and onto the downwind leg. Airspeed was about 190—should be able to stay in the air if nothing else went wrong. They were pulling 42 inches of manifold pressure at 2700 RPM. They kept dumping fuel, trying to get the weight down for landing. All they had to do was fly the downwind leg, then base, turn onto final approach and get the sick plane back on the ground.

Since the whole squadron was getting ready to fly, there were a lot of people on the flight line when 375 took off. When the fire trucks came busting out of the barn, everybody knew in an instant there was trouble somewhere. Hundreds of eyes scanned the sky till they spotted the KC-97.

**"There he is, over there to the northwest. JEEZ! He's on fire!"**

It wasn't fire streaming from the tanker. The late afternoon sun gave the illusion of flames licking back from the troubled KC-97 as they dumped fuel on the Nebraska farmland.

375 made a long gentle turn to the base leg, still showering the countryside with JP-4 until they had dumped over 20,000 pounds. They dropped the landing gear and pulled in some flaps on the downwind leg. A five-degree bank and a lot of opposite rudder to keep her straight and the KC rolled onto final approach at about 250 feet.

Anyone who may have been trying to do any cross-country skiing at Pioneers Park would have been treated to a common, yet rare sight. It was common for tankers to fly near the park on final for the base. But to see one with two engines shut down on the same side? Well now, that was a rare sight!

Looking out front, Earl could see the runway in the distance. Between the KC and the runway threshold was the railroad switching yards or "hump". North of that was the West "O" Drive-In, "O" Street, and then the runway. They had to stay in the air for about another thirty seconds.

Crossing "O" Street, they had to make it over the hill between the highway and the threshold. Airspeed was about 160, Copilot Nystrom kept calling out airspeed and altitude. The KC-97 thundered over the hill; no matter what happened now, they would make the end of the runway one way or another.

The tanker crossed the end of the concrete. Throttles back a bit, more rudder, let her float a little. The tires touched the concrete and squealed in protest of going from zero to over a hundred miles an hour in a split second. As the speed bled off, the nose wheel touched down and they were safe. The grim reaper had been foiled again.

A lot of folks were there on the ramp to greet the crew when they shut down the two-engine tanker. Standing there on the ramp was the crew chief, looking at his KC-97 and shaking his head. "Well, you brought her back with two turning and two at attention, but at least you brought her back, and in one piece."

The crew chief told Earl he thought he might know what happened. The KC-97 had just returned from the Depot for updates and IRAN. The crew chief was right. The investigation found the spark plugs had come loose during the heavyweight take off. They had not been torqued to the specifications while at the Depot. Somebody down there was certainly going to get chewed out royally.

By mid-December, the first units of the new base housing were opened to those who were on the waiting list. There was no grass planted and the streets were not paved. They were the usual military type duplex units. Nonetheless, it was an early Christmas present for the families who were able to move in.

47

# Cold War Cornhuskers: The 307th Bomb Wing Lincoln Air Force Base Nebraska 1955-1965

The base newspaper, *Jet Scoop*, came out on Friday, like it always did. The issue for December 21st was full of Christmas messages, and last-minute sales for those who needed last-minute ideas. It also mentioned that two crews from the 307th had been selected to attend B-52 upgrade training. Capt Paul Nordstrom, Capt Robert Dinah and Capt Francis Leslie were listed as one crew. The other crew was the 3-Bob Crew of Capt Robert Hall, Capt Robert Frank and Capt Robert Hill.

The paper also announced that Crew R-39 from the 371st Bomb Squadron had been selected as the crew of the month for the 307th. That crew was commanded by Capt William Hoffman, with Capt Franklin Pease as copilot and Capt Edward Burden as navigator.

The year ended with the usual Holiday festivities. Those who attended Candlelight Services took a moment to reflect on the past year. The 307th had come a long way. They had flown a lot of miles, participated in SAC Operations, became combat ready and gone TDY to England. The 307th had lost a lot of friends in accidents but, day-by-day, the 307th was getting better and better at helping preserve "Peace On Earth".

Sybil Webber had written a take off of *'Twas The Night Before Christmas*. It appeared in the Officers' wives *Jet Skirts*. It was later read by Arthur Godfrey on national TV.

*The Flight Before Christmas*

'Twas the night before Christmas and all through the base,
Not an aircraft was flying in outer space.
The planes were parked on the ramp with care,
In hope that he would leave them there.
The Airmen were nestled all snug in their sacks,
While visions of Pacesetter kept coming back.
And Mom in her robe and I in my cap
Had just settled down for a much needed nap.
When all of a sudden there arose such a clatter,
I grabbed the phone to see what was the matter.
"Oh no!" I cried and reached for my shirt.
"Merry Christmas my love, they've called an alert!"
I left the house in somewhat of a hurry,
And started the car with the usual flurry.
I rushed to the flightline, and out to my plane,
With all those important things crammed in my brain.
The word had been given, not by St. Nick,
That voice on the phone said "Better be quick!"
More rapid than eagles, his aircrews they came,
With orderly shouting and checking of names,
Now bombers, now tankers, now air crew and ground,
The ramp is alive with the power cart's sound.
To radar, to cannon, to gear and munitions,
The specialists check for the proper conditions.
The air crews arriving all laden with gear,
And fastened the straps that hold them there.
My Observer and pilot are strapping in too,
The interphone muffles the voice of my crew.
Checklist complete! Ready on four!
A whine, then a rumble, an ear splitting roar.
Now five, now six, now three, two and one,
The thing's ready for the race to be run.
I can't help but think, that there so far,
He's watching the sky as he puffs his cigar.
And waiting out here for my takeoff time,
I wonder if families-- yours and mine,
Will see SAC's Christmas trees up in the sky
With hundreds of contrails blazing high,
Weaving a network of silvery gray,
Our gift of Security--on this Blessed Day.

## 1956

Nice photo showing the sleek B-47 at her best. (USAF)

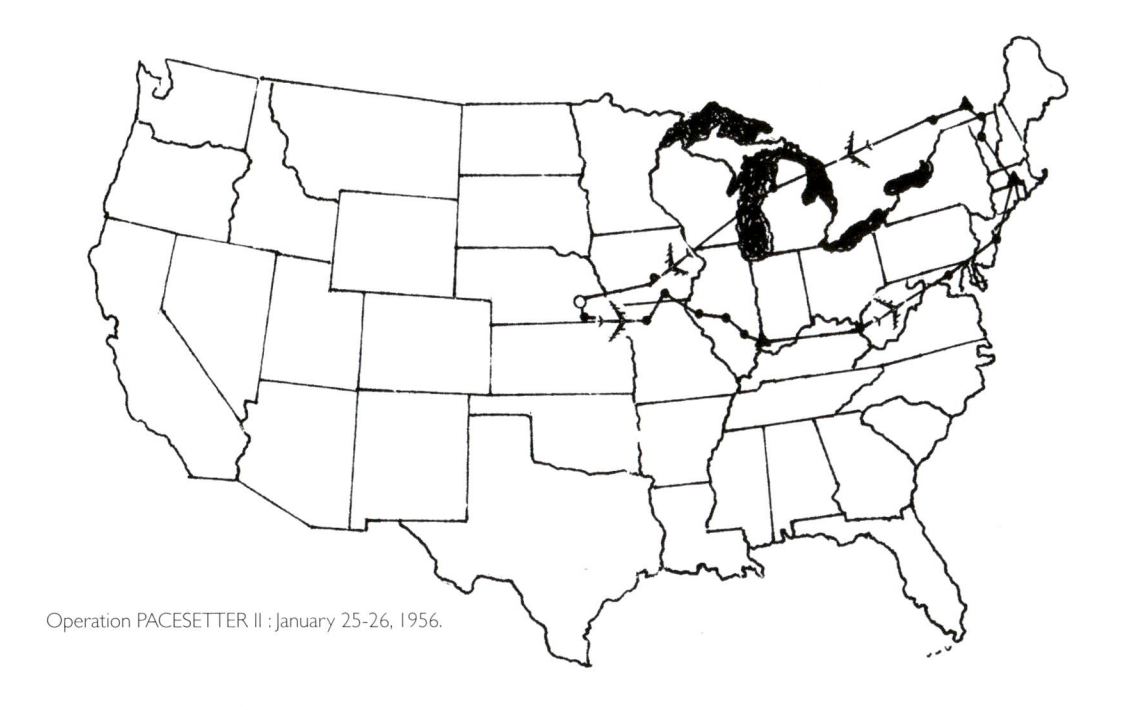

Operation PACESETTER II : January 25-26, 1956.

A Mark 6 nuclear weapon. (M Hill)

This warehouse from World War II served as the first Commissary. (M.Hill)

# Cold War Cornhuskers: The 307th Bomb Wing Lincoln Air Force Base Nebraska 1955-1965

Interesting view of a KC-97 refueling a RB-47. Note the flap position on the RB-47. (USAF via Consentino)

Crash site near Ceresco showing one of the main landing gears. (Avery)

Main crash site of 4209 (Avery)

The #6 was found over a mile from the main impact area. (Avery)

Leo Beers examines the remains of two of 4209's J-47 engines. (USAF)

# 1956

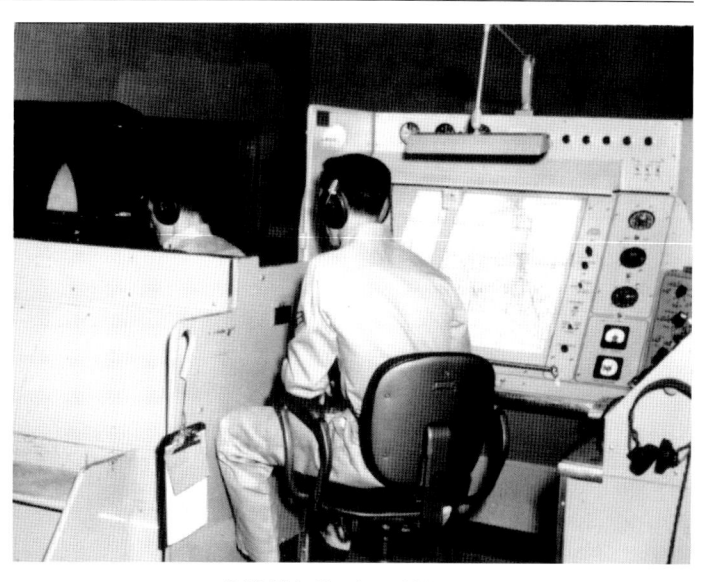

The Adventures of Airman Loose Screw (USAF)

C-11 Flight Simulator. (Gillstrap)

KC 97 tankers in formation waiting for the thirsty bombers (309th ARES)

Open House at LAFB. Naval Reserve Neptune and Cougar (RT). Note the KC-97s parked at the edge of the flight line. (Dunlap)

*Cold War Cornhuskers: The 307th Bomb Wing Lincoln Air Force Base Nebraska 1955-1965*

"OLD SHAKEY" (C-125) would transport most of the 307th to England during the summer of 1956.

53-4232, Call-sign ROCKY 19 was flown overseas by George Biggs and crew. (307th BWA)

53-2128, Call-sign ROCKY 63 would lead Blue Cell. Paul Nordstrom and crew would take her to England. (307th BWA)

Three Bob Crew. L-R Bob Hall, Bob Frank, Bob Hill, Richard Jones Jr. from the Tulsa Tribune would fly with them and write the story for his paper. (Tulsa Tribune)

52

## 1956

Refueling complete, the B-47s would be able to make England with their full tanks. (USAF)

53-2144 (ROCKY 50) at Lakenheath, England, during the deployment. (Mowry)

Ground crews worked overtime to get the tankers ready for the long flight across the pond to England. (USAF)

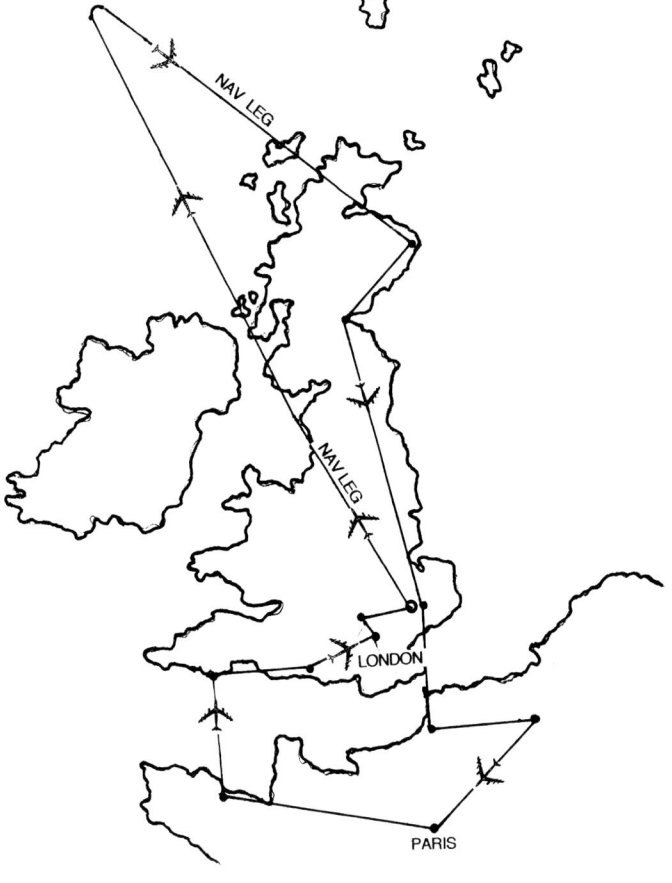

Operation BEE STING July 9-12, 1956

# Cold War Cornhuskers: The 307th Bomb Wing Lincoln Air Force Base Nebraska 1955-1965

Paul Koski (Rt) and crew check out the #6 engine of 53-4214. (307th BWA)

L-R Msgt Atwood, Col Thorup, Msgt Baugher. (307 BWA)

L-R 2Lt Carrol Kalberg (CP), 1Lt Michael Selmo (NAV), Capt Russell Bowling (AC), July 22, 1956. (Mary Ashton Bowling)

Memorial Service for Russell Bowling and his crew. (Dobbs)

## 1956

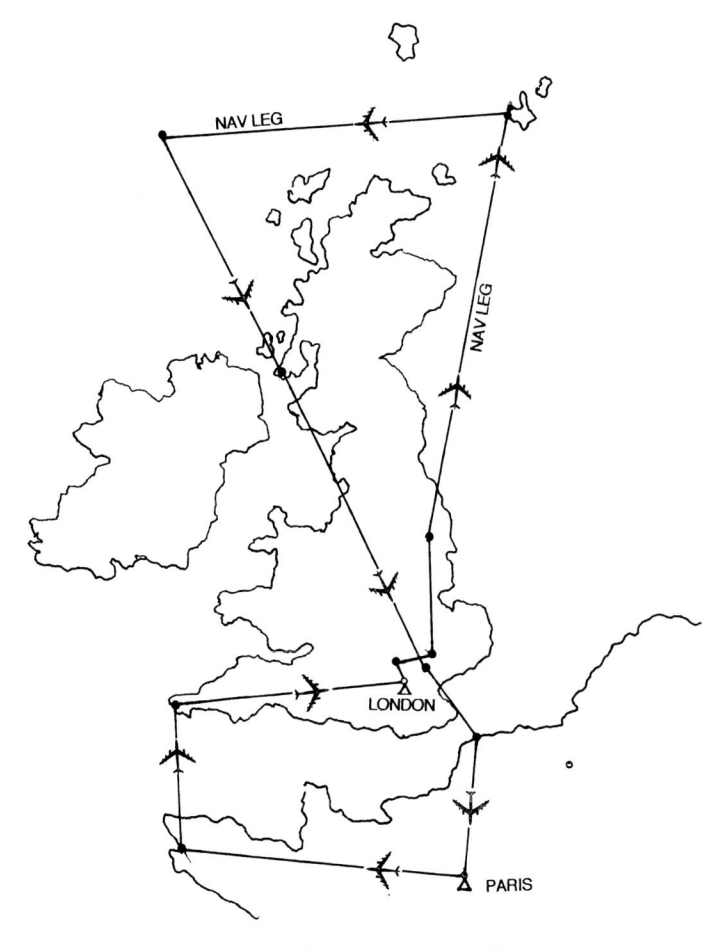

Operation PINK LADY August 14, 1956

Crew L-61. L-R Capt. Leo Beers (CP), Lt. Joe Anthony (NAV), Maj. Bill Holden (AC), and unknown RAF Officer. (Anthony)

T.R. Taylor and his bird 53-1901 at Lakenheath 1957. (Taylor)

307th FMS at Lakenheath (307th BWA).

# Cold War Cornhuskers: The 307th Bomb Wing Lincoln Air Force Base Nebraska 1955-1965

307th FMS take in a ball game during deployment to England. (307th BWA)

307th Engine Shop. L-R Galloway, Mikoloski, Conner, Howard. (Rose)

Rear L to Front Reese, Swanson, Nichols, Curel. Right Rear to Front: Swinson, Shaetley, Oliver. (Rose)

Left side: Lovelace, Seay, Raynor. (Rose)

L-R: Murray, Zanetti, Lehr, Person, Raynor, Rhinehardt, Nystrom, Askew. (Rose)

L-R: Heller, Gilstrap, Short, Unknown. (Gilstrap)

## 1956

Welcome home after a long TDY deployment.

53-6244, the last B-47 of the line was assigned to the 307th on October 23, 1957. (NDAF Collection)

53-3816, the last KC-97 built, was assigned to the 98th BW on November 16, 1956. (NDAF Collection)

Fire crews battle the conflagration after the Nebraska Air Guard F-80 crashed into two B-47s near Refueling Pit 14. (Lincoln Journal-Star)

Above right: The scene of devastation the next morning. Remains of 52-369 in foreground. The wing of 53-4235 can be seen in the background. (USAF)

Right: Earl Bullock's crew. L-R Earl Bullock, Paul Nystrom, Gorgon Newhouse, Melvin Patterson, Rosario Delash, Leroy Hollbrook Jr. (Bullock)

# 1957

Just like last year, "old man winter" held Lincoln Air Force Base in his icy grip on New Year's Day. Snow and ice covered the flight line. Snowplows worked overtime to clear the piles of white snow from the runway and taxiways. After all, in theory, no SAC base is ever closed to operations.

The wing was alerted by 8th Air Force that there would be another Pacesetter mission, scheduled for the last part of the month. To get a jump on the bomber stream, the 307th flew a practice Pacesetter on Wednesday, the 16th. Thirteen crews flew the exact route as the real operation. The practice mission posed all kinds of problems. Of the thirteen planes flying, only seven made bomb runs on all three target cities. The target at Binghamton, New York, presented the most problems. The radar return on the target was marginal, causing poor results. At least they would have a better idea of where the target was during the real operation. The practice mission for Pacesetter VI set the stage for the real one scheduled for January 28th and 29th. Sixteen B-47s would fly each day. 8th Air Force required twelve hours of target study. Most of this was accomplished on the practice run. It would be the most intense Pacesetter mission so far: three targets, navigation legs and possible fighter attacks.

Getting a B-47 started for Pacesetter, or any mission, required one very important piece of equipment, the MD-3 Generator. Last April, the 307th had received forty-five of them. 8th Air Force Headquarters sent a message to send seven of them to another base in October. Two of the units were destroyed in the flight line accident in November. So, the supply of MD-3s was getting low.

The 307th sent four requests for replacement units. The requests were denied because, according to the depot, the 307th still had forty-five units on hand. On January 15th, the wing sent a priority message to Warner Robins AFB to straighten out the paperwork and get the generators moving. The next day a reply came back saying control of that supply item had been transferred to Gadsen AFB and the MD-3s wouldn't be available until the latter part of June.

Monday, January 28th, the 307th was ready to fly the first wave for Pacesetter VI. Low clouds hung over Lincoln; wind was from the north and gusty. The weather didn't look good for the home team. Snow was in the forecast by takeoff time. The weather continued to go downhill as the takeoff time drew closer. Going downhill may not have been exactly accurate. It soon became impossible to see beyond a couple of hundred feet as the snow was whipped around and across the flight line. It became apparent that there was no way the 307th could launch aircraft safely, so the first wave was postponed.

The storm was a fast mover and blew out of the area by late that evening. When the snow slowed to flurries, the snowplows attacked the runway and taxiways with a vengeance. The ground crews hit the flight line armed with shovels to dig the birds out of the drifts. When they were finished, there were a lot of airmen reaching for the liniment to soothe their aching backs.

Wave 2 lined up for takeoff on schedule on January 29th. At ten-minute intervals they took to the sky and headed for Yankton, South Dakota, the first checkpoint. Abredeen, South Dakota, was the next checkpoint, then on to Alexandria, Minnesota. By now, they were topping out at 35,000 feet as they changed heading for Redwood Falls. The H-Hour Control Point (HHCP) was reached at Lyndon, Minnesota, and they turned for the IP at Storm Lake, Iowa.

From their altitude of 35,000 feet, the bomber stream began their bomb run on Omaha, Nebraska. The target city was well defined on the radar scopes as they approached. When the Time To Go Indicator reached zero the tone cut off, signaling "Bomb Away". That is, in all of the planes except one. The tone continued wailing after the target. The navigator was so busy trying to figure out the problem he didn't hit the manual tone cutoff. They were scored as a gross error on the target.

The bomber stream turned on a heading for Ottumwa, Iowa, then to the IP at Quincy, Illinois, for the run on St. Louis, the second target for the mission. Below them, St. Louis spread out in a beautiful vista. In the distance, the Mississippi River rambled on its course to the south. But there was no time to sightsee; they had to complete the run and release their radar bomb. Again, the tone failed to cutoff on the same B-47 as it had over Omaha. This time the navigator reached up and hit the cut off. Even with his effort, they scored a big goose egg for St. Louis.

At the release point, the B-47s were to execute a "Hi Jinks" tactical breakaway. This had been added to SAC training requirements in January 1956. This was a maximum turn at 50-degree bank to the left at .74 Mach for thirty seconds. After that the B-47 was rolled back to level flight.

Pulling away after their "Hi Jinks", the mission continued to Johnstown, Pennsylvania, and the beginning of a navigation leg. From there it was towards navigation check points at Hardin and Lancaster, Pennsylvania, then towards the IP at Wilkes-Barre for the target at Binghamton, New York.

# 1957

The "tone deaf" B-47 elected to abort the target. By this time they had developed major problems with the Bomb/Nav System. They left the bomber stream to the left about 60 miles from the target. Since they had aborted the final target and had missed the other two with their malfunctioning tone, they were scored as an abort for all three targets. There was nothing for them to do but return to Lincoln.

The final portion of the mission was a long celestial navigation leg from Geneva, New York, to a Ground Control Intercept (GCI) site near Galesburg, Illinois, codenamed "Postcard". After checking in with "Postcard" the B-47s turned for home.

Wave 1, which had been grounded by the weather, got off the ground to fly the mission on February 1st. One B-47 aborted with fuel system problems between Omaha and St. Louis. They were having trouble transferring fuel from one tank to another. They had fuel on board, they just couldn't use it. They managed to get back to Lincoln, where they declared a fuel shortage emergency. The crew spent the last few minutes watching the gauges like a hawk and praying they didn't see "red" lights on the fuel panel followed by silence when the engines flamed out. They were one happy crew once they got on the ground.

Five gross errors were charged to the wing. Three of them from the "tone deaf" B-47. Navigation was scored as "very good" for the entire mission. The radar scores were listed as "good" overall. When the final results were tabulated the 307th placed fifth in the 8th Air Force for Pacesetter VI.

During the first month of the year, the wing lost forty-one sorties to weather. It appeared every time the 307th was scheduled to fly; the snowflakes would just beat them to it. Then there were problems with the KC-97s. Again, cold weather caused fifty-three hours of flying to be lost. Pilot upgrade training time was lost because of 8th Air Force Headquarters directed missions. Topping off the problem was the shortage of qualified flight engineers in the squadron.

The 307th Wing Planning Staff started February trying to come up with a program to fulfill SAC Programming Plan "Stand Down". This was a directive from Omaha for the wing to conduct a special upgrading program. According to the directive, "No score will be completed in the Operations section of the SAC Management System." The wing would be scored on items contained in a pamphlet. Items that would be scored included AWOL rate, personnel and flying safety. The Stand Down program was to begin on March 1st and run for about four months, or one "SAC Quarter" according to the SAC standard calendar.

Five members of the 307th left Lincoln on Saturday, February 5th, for Stead AFB, Nevada. These intrepid souls were headed there for the survival course. The TDY orders listed Capt. Guy, Capt. Beers, Capt. Phillips, Lt. Whitehurst and Lt. Wilson as the lucky travelers. "Wally" Whitehurst remembered:

"It was the worst time of the year to go there....very cold and lots of snow. We were issued snowshoes, and walked a lot of miles in them. There were three men assigned to each group...had a tough time getting enough to eat. We were issued three pounds of beef, three cabbages and three potatoes to sustain the three of us for nine days... walked somewhere near fifty miles, or so they said. I lost seventeen pounds in those nine days. I had to lug the HF radio generator for the group and had it attached to my backpack; after the first hill climb it became VERY heavy. This generator was hand-cranked and was used to give daily position reports back to Stead. I remember one of our group climbing a tree and pushing a porcupine off a limb to the ground, where he was viciously attacked by several of us with our survival knives. We did cook it and eat it and it wasn't all that bad... we were really hungry!"

The 8th Air Force decided to try and get as much out of the 307th as possible before the standown. They sent another operations order for the wing to fly something called Lone Dozen. The wing would fly on February 13th and again on the 27th. That is, if "old man winter" would permit such a thing.

The plan called for the usual mission profile: a night celestial nav leg, night mass gas refueling and high-level formation flying. A new twist was thrown into the profile. Seven crews were selected to make a real bomb run on a target off the coast of Florida, dropping a special training weapon. The 307th AREFS would provide tanker support for the mission.

X-Day for Lone Dozen arrived with the usual pre-mission frantic activity underway on the flight line. Planes were fueled and last minute checks were made to make sure that the mission birds were ready. With all the activity going on, few were aware of a special honor being awarded at 307th Headquarters. Under Special Order #18, A1C Paul Orem from the 307th A&E Squadron was named 8th Air Force Outstanding Maintenance Man for January.

Later that day, the wing was ready for the main event. At 1700 hours, Robert Hoover's crew led the first cell into the air. Nestled in the bomb bay of 53-4240 was a training weapon. At one-minute intervals, the rest of Blue Cell made the takeoff run and climbed into the air. By 1733, the last of the first wave was off the ground and heading for the first checkpoint at Redwood Falls, Minnesota.

The tanker force began taking off as soon as the last bomber was in the air. They climbed out and took a heading for the refueling rendezvous point near Grand Island. They would orbit there in a racetrack pattern and wait for the B-47s to appear on the radar scope.

The bombers made the first checkpoint, then turned towards Huron, South Dakota, then turned towards the waiting tankers. The tricky task of finding the tankers in the dark began over the Nebraska plains. The lead bomber made radio, then radar contact with "Iceman Lead".

**"Iceman Lead, Rocky 39, I have you 5 degrees left at 50 miles."**

The bombers descended, to place them behind and below the tankers, then slowly crept closer to the flying gas stations. Everyone in the cell found their assigned tanker and moved into position. Staying in the envelope for refueling during a daylight hookup is hard enough. Doing it at night was another story: try driving within about 38 feet of a big 18-wheeler on a dark interstate without your headlights. On second thought, *don't try it!* Except for the lights on the tanker, there was very little visual reference to work with. Depth perception is next to nothing in the dark sky.

By the time they reached Dalhart, Texas, the bombers had taken on the required 33,000 pounds of fuel and were ready to drop off the boom. On signal, the B-47s dropped away and made a slow turn to the right. When everyone was clear of the tankers, they started climbing towards Childress, Texas.

Over Childress, everyone checked to make sure the oxygen system was working and their oxygen masks were tight against their face. The next leg from Childless to Waco would be flown with the aircraft depressurized. At 35,000 feet a malfunction in the oxygen system would be deadly in a matter of minutes.

Passing over Waco, the planes were repressurized and the crews could literally breathe a little easier. By now, their helmets felt like twenty pounds of lead and wearing the oxygen masks had given them a rosy pair of "mask hickeys".

From Waco, the stream headed for Lake Charles, Louisiana. The crews scheduled to make the live drop ran the checklist and made sure it was complete before arriving over the checkpoint. With the checklist complete they headed for the IP at New Orleans, then coasted out over the Gulf of Mexico for the bomb run. For the mission, the target wasn't a radar bombing site. It was just a set of coordinates, 25 degrees N, 88 degrees W. Just a point in the Gulf of Mexico, about a hundred and sixty miles south of Mobile, Alabama.

# Cold War Cornhuskers: The 307th Bomb Wing Lincoln Air Force Base Nebraska 1955-1965

In the nose of the B-47s, the navigators were busy in their cramped little office. The coordinates for bomb release had been entered into the Bomb/Nav System. Through the maze of vacuum tubes, control boxes, radar units and stabilizers the system had computed the bomb drop solution.

**"AC, NAV, One minute to release."**

The navigator peered into the radar scope. Not much of a return to look at out there over the water.

**"AC, NAV, 30 seconds to go. Stand by for Tone. Bomb Bay doors open."**

Glancing up at the Time To Go Indicator, the navigator watched it unwind towards the bottom of the dial.

**"Bomb Away!!, Tone Break, Break Right!"**

Electrical impulses opened the shackles and the bomb fell from the B-47. With the weight gone, the plane gave a slight upward lurch. The AC took control and rolled the plane into the practiced breakaway turn.

Each aircraft in the stream would hit the same target. Those that carried weapons released, while the others would use a radar bomb to accomplish the run. The impact of the large training weapon sent huge geysers of water skyward as they hit the surface of the Gulf and then sank to the bottom.

The cells rendezvoused over the Gulf and reformed their formation, then turned towards Tampa Bay. The next part of the mission was to fire the tail guns. Copilots turned their seats on the tracks and faced towards the tail. They switched on their gun laying system and checked the system to make sure it was operating. Sweeping the rear of the aircraft, they could see there was no traffic in the danger zone of the depressed 20 mm guns. When the Cell Leader gave the word, they were clear to "fire out".

Passing over Tampa, the flight turned north for Cross City, then on to Brunswick, Georgia. At Brunswick, the formation began a nav leg that would take them over checkpoints at Greenville, South Carolina; Lexington, Kentucky; Indianapolis, Indiana; Peoria, Illinois; and Des Moines, Iowa. From Des Moines it was contact home plate at Lincoln, let down and land.

The second wave repeated Lone Dozen on Saturday, the 27th. They flew the same route as the first wave. This time only two B-47s carried training weapons. One of them dropped on the target as briefed. The other had a radar malfunction and brought the big "egg" back home to Lincoln.

Bad weather caused problems with the mass gas refueling during the second wave. Each receiver had to take on at least 3,000 pounds of fuel for a score. Because of the weather, there wasn't enough gas passed in the entire cell to achieve a score. Regardless of the problems on wave two, the overall results of the mission were listed as "very good".

During the monthly meeting at 818th Air Division headquarters, the newly arrived Commander, Col. Perry M. Hoisington, chaired the meeting. He announced plans to create a recreational lake near the northwest corner of the base. He felt a lake on base would provide a place to spend off duty time, thereby helping to reduce traffic violations and off-base accidents. It would become just one of "Perry's Pet Projects".

On February 26th, the wing staff boarded a KC-97 and flew down to Whiteman AFB, Missouri. The purpose of the visit was to observe the 340th Bomb Wing. That wing had been testing ground alert procedures for a fast reaction launch. This was the first gentle breeze in the winds of change heading for SAC wings across the nation.

March started the four-month stand down for intensive crew upgrade training. After looking over the program outline, most thought it looked like the flight training program they had at McConnell. In fact, it was basically just that. The 307th was going to go back to basics and start over again.

Although the wing was standing down, 8th Air Force handed the 307th a special project to undertake. The Ordnance Test Center at Eglin needed to test and evaluate the Mark-36 nuclear weapon.

The Mark-36 was a large weapon, weighing over 17,000 pounds. It was over twelve feet long and four and a half feet in diameter. Someone said it looked like an overgrown oil barrel with little stubby fins. Eglin wanted to know if the big oil barrel would fall on a straight and true trajectory. The only way to find out was to take one up in a B-47, drop it, and see what happens.

The Operation, called Black Duck, was scheduled for March 7th and 14th. Four B-47s would be loaded with the Mark-36 shape at least three hours before takeoff. A typical Emergency War Plan (EWP) profile mission would be flown. To add realism, a minimum of seven hours would be flown prior to the target, along with one air refueling. The strike aircraft would be under security guard protection at all times after loading.

The wing was assigned two targets, designated B-1 and B-52. B-52 was a land target on the Eglin range. B-1 consisted of a radar reflector on a sled about four miles offshore between Destin and Ft. Walton Beach, Florida.

Flying Operation Black Duck almost became Operation Black Eye. The mission was scheduled, canceled and rescheduled a total of nine times. Several cancellations were because Eglin sent a no go message at the last minute. Then, there was the typical Nebraska weather that moved in to cause more problems.

The wing received a letter from Col. Hoisington on March 9th. He called for "shakedown" inspections of vehicles and quarters due to the increase of airmen found in possession of concealed weapons, narcotics and other "contraband". The letter went on to say that everyone below the rank of SSgt should be carefully screened, take driving classes and receive written permission to drive on or off the base.

He also implemented what would become a weekly feature in the JET SCOOP. It was the infamous "Roads Gallery". Anyone who had a accident or traffic ticket would not only have to explain it to his commander, but would have his name appear in "Roads Gallery" for the entire base to see. There was also the Saturday morning "Traffic Court". Anyone who had a violation during the week would have to appear before Col. Hoisington and explain why he had received the violation. Legend has it that during the first session of the Saturday event a young airman fainted at the prospect of appearing before the Division Commander. From then on, there was a Medical Officer present during the court sessions.

The "Traffic Court" and "Roads Gallery" put the "fear of Hoisington" into the troops. No one wanted to appear in the JET SCOOP for the entire base to see. Sometimes the person was downright lucky, as Billy Cox recalled. "I remember that Gen Hoisington was really tough on you if you got a driving ticket. When I was reporting into the base after three years in Germany, I made an illegal left turn at, I believe, 14th and O St. The policeman took pity on me and gave me a warning. He didn't want me to get in trouble. Ha!"

High gusty winds on the 11th and 12th of March necessitated the use of the shorter secondary runway. Using it meant take off weights had to be reduced. This always made the take off just a little more interesting.

The refueling squadron was still having problems. Again, as for the past several months, there was a severe shortage of built-up R-4360 engines for the tankers. The results were obvious: several tankers were listed as out of commission for parts and engines changes.

There was still the problem of a lack of trained flight engineers. The squadron had three replacements arrive during the month. One had completed basic training in the position, but had not passed any qualification flights. The third hadn't even been in a KC-97, let alone sat at the engineer's station. A harsh letter was sent to 8th Air Force about the situation.

Black Duck was on again for March 24th. The planes were loaded and the security guards were in place. A fast moving Alberta Clipper came roaring in from the north and started dumping snow on the base. It didn't take very long for the ramp to become covered in a blanket of white. The mission was called off, again.

Wing officials realized you couldn't have loaded B-47s sitting outside in the snow being guarded by intrepid security forces even if they weren't real nukes on board. Planes were shuffled around and the four strike aircraft were towed to the big hangar or the nose docks area to be out of the weather.

This turned out to be a real "polar bear" of a storm. Roads to the base became clogged with snow and closed down for the next two days as the white stuff swirled and drifted in the high winds. Snow crews fought a losing battle to keep the runway clear. They were finally called in when one of them got lost and plowed a new taxi strip on the east side of the runway.

Snowplows hit the taxiways when the snow slowed to flurries on the 26th. They formed long conga lines and attacked the snow like troops storming a beach during an invasion. By the time they were finished, snow piles over twenty feet high lined the taxiways.

Saturday, March 27th, Black Duck was finally underway. The planes were out of their cozy hangars and on the ramp for the mission. Briefing was at 0800 in the briefing room. The first SAFEWAY aircraft was in the air by 1000 followed at one-minute intervals by the other three.

Climbing out of Lincoln, they headed towards North Platte, then into Wyoming. From their altitude they could see Cheyenne off to their right as they passed. Just to the west of Bear Lake, Utah, the B-47s turned and flew over the mountains to Yellowstone Park, then to a turn point at Livingston, Montana, then to Miles City. From there, they crossed snow-covered North Dakota without changing course until the checkpoint over Alexandria, Minnesota. Here, they began coming down from altitude to meet their tankers at the refueling point near Grantsburg, Wisconsin.

Tankers from the 307th and 340th AREFS were waiting for the B-47s. Rendezvous and hook up went as briefed, with 30,000 pounds transferred to the thirsty bombers before ending the refueling just south of Madison, Wisconsin.

Near Rolla, Missouri, the bombers split according to which target range they would release on. Those that would hit the land target flew to Texarkana, Texas, then to Lake Charles and Lafayette, Louisiana, then on to Mobile, Alabama, and the bomb run. The others turned for Campbell, Kentucky, then Royston, Georgia. From there they crossed the IP at Blountstown, Florida, and on to the release point.

Each aircraft had to make a practice run to identify the target. When they received the OK from Eglin AFB, Florida, they were cleared to make the live run at least ten minutes before the release. The Bomb/Nav System was set up in each of the aircraft. Approaching release point, the tone came on 15 seconds before release. Over the target the big Mark-36 fell from the bomb bay towards the target, and the B-47s were racked into the usual tight turn. The post strike message was sent.

**"Ramey..This is Safeway 33. Relay to Ringleader Bravo and Fellow.. Zippo..0812 Zulu--G Golf. Over."**

After hitting their targets the cells turned for home. Those who had hit the land target turned and flew north through Alabama, while the other cells flew towards Texas before turning north towards home plate at Lincoln.

The JET SCOOP came out on Friday, March 29th, as usual. It was filled with news from around the base and across the flight line. A lot of people checked the "Roads Gallery" to see who had scheduled themselves for a session with the traffic court. The Hinky Dinky stores in Lincoln were running a special sale. Their ad included:

46-ounce can of Tomato Juice, 2 cans for 35 cents.
Beef Roast at 29 cents a pound
Jumbo Shrimp 69 cents a pound or 5 pound box for $3.39.
A large box of Tide detergent 25 cents.

The wing had been alerted that they were to participate in Pacesetter VII, scheduled for April 16th and 18th. There was an immediate exchange of messages between Lincoln and Westover. According to SAC Headquarters, the 307th was under the guidelines of Operation Stand Down. Under these guidelines, the wing was supposed to be exempt from all other higher headquarters operations unless directed specifically from Offutt.

Westover contacted Omaha and pleaded their case. After all, the 307th was going to fly Black Duck and other special training missions during the stand down. Pacesetter was considered as "special training", so the special training and competition would do the wing good. Westover won; the 307th would fly a practice for Pacesetter on April 10th.

April 5th began like any other day at the patch. During the morning, the 307th launched five aircraft for routine training missions to fill some SAC Reg 50-8 squares on the board. Five more were scheduled for later in the afternoon and evening.

The weather that morning was typical for April in Nebraska. There was a 2500-foot overcast with about ten miles visibility. The temperature hovered around 33 degrees. What made the weather interesting was the wind. It was from the northwest at 18 knots, gusting to 25 knots. The slight crosswind combined with gusty conditions made take off a little more interesting than normal.

Around 1500, several B-47s returned from their morning missions. By this time, the winds had picked up and were howling with gusts to 30 knots from the northwest. The returning crews refigured their landing weight and computed the gust component for landing.

Flight line troops paused for a moment and watched the birds trying to get safely back to the nest. Several of the B-47s got caught in a gust and bounced a couple of times before being able to keep the plane firmly planted on terra firma. After taxiing in and climbing down the ladder, several pilots commented about their "hairy landing with those gusts out there".

At 1600, another B-47 pulled into the pattern. It was 52-456 from the 98th Bomb Wing. They had taken off in the morning and were returning for some pattern work, including several touch and go landings. About this time, the crew got the latest weather update. The tower reported several gusts to 35-40 knots.

Several troops glanced to the south as 456 crossed the threshold. She was crabbing into the wind a little, but everything seemed to be going according to procedures. The B-47 started to flare for landing when she was rocked with a gust of wind, which caused the right wing to drop rapidly. The pilot corrected with left aileron, rudder and power to the right engines. The right wing continued to drop until the wingtip hit the ground about 2675 feet from the end of the runway and about 12 feet off to the side of the concrete.

From the 307th area it looked like the runaway bomber was headed for the Air Guard area on the east side of the runway. Several of the onlookers made a plaintive yell, "Hold on to her Newt!"

The wing scraped along the ground until the main gear settled on the ground, at which time the B-47 started skidding to the right. The plane continued to skid to the right, leaving the runway in a cloud of smoke and churned up turf. When the B-47 came to a stop, it had traveled over 800 feet to the east of the runway centerline. She was sitting on the taxiway on the east side of the base.

The pilot pulled the throttles back and hit the cutoff switches. The copilot pulled the canopy release. The canopy didn't separate completely due to the warping of the fuselage. Inside the aircraft, there was a mad scramble to get out before the B-47 caught fire and exploded.

Through the combined efforts of the crew they were able to get the canopy far enough back and scramble out of the opening. About a minute and a half after the plane came to a stop, a small fire broke out under the left wing and spread to the fuselage. Fire crews arrived about five minutes after the plane came to a halt. By then, the aircraft was engulfed in flames.

Everyone who saw the accident knew the crew had been very lucky. During the next few days, the flight crews dug out the trusty Dash One and reviewed the proper procedures for landing a B-47 under severe crosswind conditions.

The wing flew the real Pacesetter VII on April 16th and 18th. The mission included nav legs, air refueling and hitting targets at Atlanta and Little Rock. When the final results were tabulated and sent in from 8th Air Force, the 307th had placed 4th overall. Several crews placed higher in individual areas like bombing and navigation.

8th Air Force believed in rewarding crews that placed high in the Pacesetter Competitions. William Bathurst flew several of the Pacesetter missions, "If you met the qualifications the crew was awarded an inscribed Zippo lighter. Our crew won one in January 1956 and another in January 1957. I didn't get two lighters; they inscribed the first one with the second date. I guess they were out of money."

Up on the northwest corner of the base a small army of heavy equipment had arrived. Now that the weather was improving, the initial excavation for the lake could begin. Bulldozers and other equipment attacked the fifty-acre site. The plans called for a circular doughnut shaped lake, about eight to fifteen feet deep. A picnic area was planned for the area on the south side of the lake.

April ended with a general briefing on the upcoming Pacesetter VIII mission on Thursday the 30th. As before, the mission would place the 307th in competition with other wings within the 8th Air Force. Since the first Pacesetter, these operations continued to be more and more complex with each directive that came down the pipe from Westover.

The wing would fly a practice mission on May 2nd, 8th, and again on the 17th. They would fly the exact route as the real mission so they had an idea of what they would do when it came time for the real one.

An advanced survey party from the 307th AREFS left Lincoln on May 6th for Thule AB, Greenland. The purpose was to look the place over and check out the facilities along the way for the upcoming TDY deployment to Thule. On the way they stopped at Westover, then dear old Goose Bay for refueling and crew rest.

Monday the 13th may have been the start of the week, but events of the day show, it should have been Friday the 13th. Paul Koski recalled the events of that day:

"My aircraft had a forward aux tank leak. They changed the bladder tank and had a 24-hour leak check. The next mission, we started the engines and, on my walkaround before flight, I found the area just in front of the wheel well wet with fuel. The flight was canceled and the fuel cell personnel changed the cell again, 24 hour leak check and no leaks. The aircraft had been down for two weeks for leaks and people were getting unhappy; they had lost two missions and training time.

"This time they put a packet of dye in the cell after they changed it. 24-hour leak check, no leaks. We were ready to start engines and the area in front of the wheel well was wet again. The flight crew wanted to know how bad a leak it was and I told them it was dripping. They said they would take the aircraft anyway. They said it was their decision. I said no! I was putting it on a Red X and the maintenance officer would have to release the aircraft. We canceled the mission.

"The fuel leak didn't have any dye package or color so it had to be coming from somewhere else. Since the fuel people had come out to try and find the leak, my flight chief told me to help launch another aircraft. Jokingly, I said that aircraft had a bomb bay leak and wouldn't go either. The flight chief and I went over to the aircraft and I ran my hand under the belly of the aircraft. Sure enough there was a fuel leak. I couldn't believe it; that aircraft was also scratched.

"The flight chief told me to help in the next launch and I said, with my luck, an engine would fall off. They started engines and went to the end of the runway, went to full throttle, then the #6 engine rotated and launched off the aircraft. The aft engine mount had broken. The flight chief told me to get off the flight line and don't come back until tomorrow. I think they thought I was bad luck. I left the flight line and didn't come back until the next day."

While Paul was having a bad day, the Thule survey crew returned from their trip to the far north. In their bags were the results of the survey trip. Their report was full of vital information the squadron would need for the TDY to the top of the world.

They found the quarters were adequate. There was a shortage of bedding, so extra sheets and pillows would need be taken along. Office materials would have to be brought in from Lincoln.

Two hangars were set up for KC-97 maintenance. Each hangar could hold two tankers. The parking area was about two miles from the hangars and shops. There was a radio dead zone that covered about twenty-five percent of the parking area. There was an incline on the parking area between there and the hangars. This had caused a lot of slipping and sliding when the ramp was covered with snow and was a huge safety concern.

Sweeping compound for cleaning and drying the hangar floor was an essential item. When the 91st AREFS was at Thule, they used over 3,000 pounds of Speedy Dry. The compound had to be brought in with the unit since it was not available through supply at Thule.

The party found the maintenance facilities at Thule left a lot to be desired. There were no Magnaflux units, and repairs had to be done outside, unless hangar space was required. Props were hung with a manually operated A-Frame. Some of the older Sarges would say, "Just like we did it back in WW II."

Late in the afternoon of Wednesday, May 15th, the 307th acquired a "new" B-47. Well, at least it was new to the 307th. Those on the ramp watched as 51-2087 taxied in and shut down. They wondered what in the world they were going to do with a TB-47. Obviously, if you have a training B-47, you are going to use it to fly training missions and upgrade crews.

Friday night, May 17th, there was a special Armed Forces Day program at Pershing Auditorium. One of the featured performers was Andy Devine. Andy was a well-known actor, appearing in a lot of movies. The author knew him as "Jingles" from Saturday mornings' Wild Bill Hickock TV program. Andy visited the base that day, and included on his tour was lunch at the O-Club and a tour of the base. He was particularly interested in the work being done on the lake. He liked the idea and promised to make himself available for the dedication of the lake if the base would like to have him.

On Saturday, May 18th, the 307th Bomb Wing held a Change of Command Ceremony at Wing Headquarters. Col. Louis Thorup was leaving the wing for his new duty assignment at Westover with the 8th Air Force. Taking over command of the 307th was Col. Elkins Read, Jr. Col. Read had served as Deputy Commander of the 98th Bomb Wing. Since he was just moving down the ramp from north to south, he had a unique understanding of the situation at Lincoln Air Force Base.

# 1957

Col. Read hardly had time to place his name tag on his desk when he got a letter from Col. Hoisington at Air Division Headquarters. The letter said in no uncertain terms that the squadron commanders would take any steps necessary to reduce the number of traffic accidents and violations. He further wrote that because of the low standing of the 818th Air Division in this area, he "was personally embarrassed at the 8th Air Force commanders' conference."

From the day the base reopened there had been a tense relationship between the people of Lincoln and the "prop heads" at the base. City officials always maintained everything was hunky dory, but that wasn't always the case. It was well known several of the frat houses at the university would "black ball" any coed caught dating military personnel. Several of the local nightspots refused to serve base personnel. Having a base sticker on your car was an open invitation at times to be pulled over for almost any minor traffic violation. To help combat the situation, base personnel had to sign a pledge not to have an accident while driving off base. Then there was the infamous traffic monitor program.

At one period the Base Commander toyed with the idea of placing the entire city "OFF LIMITS" during non-duty hours. This obviously wouldn't work, since a lot of personnel lived off base and had to do their shopping off base.

In an effort to show Lincoln just how important the base was to the community, the base came up with a dramatic and novel idea. When over 2,000 military personnel lined up for payday, they signed for and received their pay in two-dollar bills. With all of the two-dollar "Frogs" hopping around Lincoln, it didn't take an accountant to see the base was pouring a lot of money into the city. Relations improved somewhat, but there were always those locals who didn't appreciate the long hours in freezing cold or summer heat the "prop heads" were putting in to keep the Cold War from becoming a nuclear shooting war.

During the last weeks of May, the wing's flight time was restricted to ferry flights and test flying. Seems SAC was feeling a budget crunch during the last part of the fiscal year. At this time, JP-4 cost about eight cents a gallon. This doesn't sound like a lot of money. If, during a mission, a tanker off loaded 30,000 pounds of JP-4, the cost of the fuel alone was about $400. Take that times six for a mass gas refueling, then multiply that across the entire command, and it is easy to see that just refueling could be a real budget buster. The budget crunch was bad enough to cause 8th Air Force to postpone the Pacesetter mission indefinitely.

On top of budget problems, there was the ever-present shortage of spare parts. Cannibalization became a way of life. There was always someone trying to take parts off one airplane to go on another. This wasn't always on the up and up. In several cases, parts were obtained by "midnight requisition," much to the dismay of the victim crew chief when he found the entry ladder missing.

May would go into the wing history as just one of those months. The wing was hampered by the slowdown in flying due to the budget cutbacks. In spite of the cutbacks, the wing was able to accomplish 48 of the scheduled bomb runs against Radar Bomb Scoring sites. The tankers made a total of seven mass gas refuelings. Not bad considering the shortage of flight time.

Budget problems from May spilled over into June, bringing the wing to almost a complete standstill. The wing managed only 417 hours in the air. There were a total of ten refueling sorties with nine scored as effective. The wing was forced to implement a schedule of short, four hour missions, which did very little to maintain proficiency. About all that could be accomplished was a quick run to the Hastings Bomb Plot, a short nav leg and get back to Lincoln.

Despite the slowdown in total flying hours, the wing posted some of the best bombing scores since becoming combat ready. Overall the wing achieved a one hundred per cent effective rating in visual bombing and night celestial navigation.

Since the wing couldn't spend a lot of time in the air, it was a good time for getting any backlog of maintenance done. Six B-47s were towed down to the new nose docks for periodic inspection and repairs. Each of the aircraft would take about forty-eight hours to complete. Three other aircraft were sent to Marietta, Georgia, for ECM updates. Paul Koski recalled an incident:

"My aircraft had just come out of post docks and had been refueled to 110,000 pounds of fuel. It was scheduled for an eight-hour mission. Preflight went as usual with no problems. The aircraft taxied out on time and started its take off. Just about half way down the runway, all of the backbone panels opened up. The aircraft made a normal take off but had to bore holes in the sky to burn off fuel. The post dock inspection included checking all the flight control cables, which meant opening all the panels on the backbone of the aircraft. They had closed the panels, but failed or forgot to fasten the panels. It's not part of the preflight to climb on top of the aircraft and check these panels. From there on, I always checked the top of the aircraft. The aircraft made a normal landing with the fire department standing by, but they lost a training mission. There was no damage to the panels, but there was an incident report written up. The flight crew said they didn't know how the plane would have flown if the panels were torn off the aircraft."

The flights to Marietta were usually routine. Paul Trudeau recalled a return flight that was not routine:

"My crew and I had flown to Lockheed Marietta, Georgia, to pick up and deliver back to base, either a new bird or one that had gone through modifications. Those of you who had the experience will verify the royal treatment received upon arrival at Marietta. A delightful and pretty Georgia gal met us at the airport and chauffeured us to a hotel. She and the Limo would be our wheels for the length of our stay. I believe this was to jolly us so we would waltz through the release forms we had to sign off on the aircraft to be picked up. At any rate, it was late Friday evening when all the details were taken care of, the aircraft was ours.

"We filed our flight plan to arrive at Lincoln sometime after midnight. The flight back was normal although I did note that the landing gear came up immediately after liftoff and before I called for it. We arrived over Lincoln, made a normal downwind, lowered the gear which extended normally, but as soon as the gear lights showed four in the green, up they came again. The copilot made the remark that they had come up on takeoff before he raised the gear handle.

"After several attempts with the same results, it was decided to lower the gear, pull the proper circuit breakers, then crank them into the green. The maintenance job control officer was in the tower and an emergency had been declared. A normal landing was made and we stopped at the end of the runway to wait for maintenance to insert the down locks. We wrote the problem up and retired for the night.

"A few days later, while playing golf on a day off, a staff car came racing down the fairway, out jumped the Director of Maintenance. Seems as though the aircraft had ground checked O.K. and was cleared to fly. After completing a mission the crew had encountered the same problem. A tanker had been alerted for refueling while the situation was researched. After repeating the procedure we had used, the bird landed O.K. I don't remember getting any merits or demerits for this incident, but my tours on alert and Reflex seemed to come one on top of another."

63

# Cold War Cornhuskers: The 307th Bomb Wing Lincoln Air Force Base Nebraska 1955-1965

On June 11th, 307th AREFS ground personnel were busy as usual working on the tankers. They paused momentarily to watch as a Coleman towed a tanker towards the south end of the ramp. 52-2804 was being transferred from the 98th to the 307th to augment the squadron.

On the 16th, high winds hit the Lincoln area, along with several very strong thunderstorms. The winds caused a maintenance stand to crash into the left inboard engine pylon of a B-47. There was damage to the sheet metal to the tune of about $155.00. In view of the wind and storms there could have been a lot more serious damage to the aircraft on the flight line.

During June, the 307th AREFS spent a lot of time preparing for their trip to Thule. The crew chiefs spent extra time going over the Form 781, making sure their bird was up to snuff. Engines that were near maximum flight hours were changed out so they wouldn't have to worry about doing it in the cool air of Thule. Several of the tankers were sent to the depot for IRAN.

There was concern about some of these aircraft coming back from the depot. They still had the same N-1 compass they had departed with. This update to the new compass should have been accomplished at the depot. The N-1 compass was virtually useless up north since the magnetic pole was actually south of Thule. There wasn't enough time to return the tankers to the depot, so the squadron would just have to make do with the old style compass.

Several messages were fired off to 8th Air Force Headquarters regarding the ever-present shortage of flight engineers. The reply from 8th Air Force was not encouraging. Their reply was to the effect that there was a SAC-wide shortage of engineers, so the squadron would have to take it on the chin until more engineers were available.

At the end of the month, Col. Read sent his monthly report to Westover. In the report were the usual statistics showing manpower, flying hours, aircraft availability and who did what, when and where. The report recommended that any wing undergoing upgrade training under stand down status be exempt from competitive bomber stream missions such as Pacesetter. The wing used the most experienced crews for the competition. This drew resources away from the upgrade training and focused on competition.

On Monday, July 1st, there was a Change of Command Ceremony. This time it was at Offutt AFB. Gen. Curtis E. LeMay was turning control of the mailed fist of SAC over to Gen. Thomas S. Power. Gen. LeMay had been CINCSAC since October 19, 1948, when he had taken over from Gen. Kenny. It was an impressive ceremony with all the pomp and circumstance a major command change required. LeMay would leave Offutt and travel to Washington to assume the duties of Air Force Chief of Staff.

Good or bad, LeMay made SAC what it was. He had taken a ragtag outfit and turned it into the most potent strike force in the world. He did it by imposing his iron will on those who served under his command. He may have had the hard-boiled, cigar-chomping image, but underneath, he was genuinely concerned for the men under his command. Thanks to his efforts, there were better housing, quarters for airmen, commissaries, spot promotions and hobby shops.

There were those in SAC who hated LeMay and those that liked him. No matter which side of the fence they were on, they all had respect for him and for what he had accomplished. To all, he would always be "Father SAC".

Gen. Thomas Power had served as the Deputy Commander in Chief of SAC. Like LeMay, he had a tough-as-nails reputation. LeMay himself referred to Power as "a mean, almost sadistic SOB." Like LeMay, Power would continue to work for better conditions for the warriors of SAC. It was the only way to try and take care of his own.

Early on the morning of July 2nd, the south end of the ramp was again a beehive of activity. The 307th AREFS was getting ready for another trip. This time they were headed for the top of the world, Thule, Greenland.

The advance party had departed on June 30th. That party had taken a couple of C-124s along with their KC-97s. They loaded eight built up R-4360 engines in case anyone needed a quick engine change along the way. The party would wait at Goose Bay until everyone was at Thule.

Last minute details were checked and rechecked. Preflight walkaround was completed. Flight crews reviewed all the forms and checked the weight and balance sheets. Everything was loaded, including the 7,790 gallons of fuel they needed to get to Goose Bay.

**"Ground, Fireguard standing by. Clear on #3."**
Engine Start Select Switch to #3. Start switch pressed.
**"Turning #3."**
Ground and fireguard watch as the big Hamilton Standard prop turns through 20 blades.
**"Ignition On, Boost and Prime."**
The big engine coughs to life in a cloud of bluish smoke, blasted backwards by the spinning prop.
**"Oil Pressure at 50, 1000 RPM. Ready on #4."**
One by one, the four engines on each tanker came to life under the skillful hands of the flight engineers. Engine runup completed, everyone strapped in, hatches and windows closed; the first KC-97 was ready to roll.
**"Lincoln Tower, Prescott 25. Ready to taxi."**
With a slight nudge of the throttles Prescott 25 moved forward. The pilot grasped the nose wheel steering and turned the big tanker to the right towards the taxi strip. At the end of the runway, the crew went through the checklist.
**"Lincoln Tower, Prescott 25, ready for takeoff."**
At 0900, Prescott 25 began the take off roll. At the calculated airspeed the big tanker left the runway and began to climb into the Nebraska sky. At 15-minute intervals the KC-97s rolled down the ribbon of concrete and headed towards the north.

The KCs leveled off near Shenandoah, Iowa. Prescott 25 was at 11,000 feet. Prescott 13 would hold and maintain 13,000 feet to keep the briefed 2,000-foot vertical separation. In each of the aircraft the navigators fine tuned the APN12-76 radar units to help keep the separation correct.

There was a mandatory radio check over Ft. Wayne, Indiana, then the tankers headed for Elmira, New York, for another position check. Over Elmira, there was a heading change towards Canada. By the time they were over Quebec City everyone was tired of the throbbing drone of the engines. They still had to check in at Seven Islands and then on to "Da Goose".

Arriving at Goose Bay, those who had been there before noticed a big change. It was GREEN! Gone were the piles of snow along the runway and taxi strip. You could actually see the tower! The hills were covered by green trees and the bay was a crystal clear blue.

The next morning it was back to the task at hand. The flight crews had rested, the planes had been serviced. Everything was ready to get going again. The first tanker left Goose Bay at 0900 and headed north. Like before, they would maintain the same separation for the final leg.

Heading out over the Labrador Sea, the KCs droned farther and farther north towards the Arctic Circle. That far north, the magnetic N-1 compass was about as useful as a screen door in a submarine. They had to navigate by polar grid, sun shots and a little dead reckoning thrown in for good measure.

For Ken Tarwater, this was his second trip to the north. He made the trip to Goose, now he was going a lot farther north:

64

# 1957

"About twenty of us were in the front lower section of the old KC-97F. We had K-ration type meals on the way up. We were trading fruit for cookies and such when somebody decided to open a can of Spam and eat it out of the can. We were all a little airsick anyway, but this airman lost his lunch (Spam) and all of us were sick and losing our lunches. We were so glad to get to Thule. We were probably the happiest guys ever to set foot at Thule. We were glad to get out of the airplane and get some fresh air and boy was it fresh."

The 307th AREFS was lucky; they arrived at Thule during the balmy days of midsummer. Balmy for that far north, yes, but don't put your parka and long johns away. It is still far north of the Arctic Circle and, even during summer, it could get pretty nippy. One of the first things the new arrivals did was look for the pretty girls behind every tree they had heard about. Well, this far north there were no trees and obviously no pretty girls.

Back at Lincoln, there was a lot of open space on the south end of the flight line with the tankers gone. So, for the time being, the bombers spread out a little. The extra space also provided a convenient place to park transient aircraft that happened to drop in from other bases.

There were several more trips to Whiteman AFB to observe the new alert program. There had been alerts called in the past. Under the new program, there would be B-47s and crews loaded and ready to respond at a moment's notice, twenty-four hours a day, seven days a week. Everyone who had heard of the new alert program couldn't help but wonder just how it would affect daily life at the patch.

Monday, July 22nd, commander's call was held at the base theater. Col. Read presided over the event. After going over the "how we're doing, and how we can do better," the meeting turned to the "attaboy" part. Col. Read announced that twelve crews had been cited by M/Gen. Sweeney, Commander of the 8th Air Force, as "outstanding" for their performance during Pacesetter VII, last April. The stars indicate the number of times the crews had been cited by 8th Air Force. The crews were listed as:

| | | | |
|---|---|---|---|
| R-09 | Erling Chapelle | Thomas Pauza | Jack Jones |
| L-71 | Hale Dodge | Frank Wanek | Leslie Walrath |
| N-76 | Alfred Horner | Charles Ohrvall | James Wilson |
| R-16 | Paul Ecelbarger | Robert Goodrich | Noble Timmons ** |
| R-08 | Harold Brooks | Harold Struemple | John Mattioli *** |
| R-74 | Stanley Reilly | John Parks | Robert Meyer ** |
| R-79 | Samuel Myers | Perry Esping | Maurice Welch |
| S-05 | Leon McCrary | John Bible | Richard Gronburg |
| R-11 | George Biggs | Dean Knight | James Evans |
| R-65 | William Boudreaux | Richard Mckenzie | Carter Hart Jr. ** |
| R-41 | Dale Peterson | Roland Behnke | Archibald Sams |
| R-33 | Anthony Minnick | John Philips | Ward Allen ** |

These crews couldn't have scored as high as they did without the hard work of the crew chiefs to get the aircraft ready for the mission. Col. Read handed out letters of appreciation to twelve crew chiefs who had "kept em flying." One of the crew chiefs receiving the letter was George Nigh. Finally, SSgt. Billy Hill was named Outstanding NCO for the month for keeping his bird, 53-0353, mission-ready and not missing a takeoff.

Although he was at Thule, Capt. Everett Caudal was named Pilot of the Month by the 8th Air Force for landing his KC-97 with a nose wheel problem. He wrote:

"The KC-97 nose wheel incident was dramatized and over-inflated. When we tried to retract the gear after take off, the nose gear did not retract. The wheels were cocked some 45 to 60 degrees to the right. Attempts to recycle were ineffective. We were sent to Wichita, where they foamed the runway. Upon landing, we let the nose gear settle very gently to the runway a time or two. The nose wheel straightened out, and the landing was uneventful. We made a right turn off the runway, and then found the nose wheel <u>steering</u> would not turn back. We got onto the taxi way using brakes and throttles. Once we were clear of the runway, they hooked a tug on us."

While commander's call was underway, several flight crews were busy flying practice missions for the upcoming Pacesetter VIII. The practice would follow the route that was scheduled for August 6th and 8th. Another Pacesetter meant a lot of work for everyone. Most members of the 307th were of the opinion that all of these Pacesetter missions were a waste of time. They were all bomber stream missions, which meant they were easier to plan, but not very realistic in a real world crisis. Did anyone really think that SAC would fly a bomber stream towards targets in the Soviet Union? Maybe not to the Soviet Union, but years later, SAC would do exactly that during the Linebacker II campaign against North Vietnam.

While the bomber crews sweated it out in the August Nebraska sun, the tanker crews were basking in twenty-four hour daylight at Thule. Their mission at Thule was to provide tanker support for aircraft deploying to and from Europe. They also provided strip alert for any aircraft that was running low on fuel. One important aspect of the mission at Thule centered on supporting RB-47 recon flights. RB-47s from the 55th Strategic Recon Wing were conducting both photo and electronic intelligence flights along the northern border of the Soviet Union. These flights were highly classified. If an RB were lost to hostile action, they would be listed as having been lost during a "routine training" or "weather" flight.

Thule, Greenland, had become one of the most important outpost bases during the Cold War. It sat 921 miles south of the North Pole. By the great circle route, Seattle was 2,457 miles away, while New York City was 2,477 miles, and Moscow was 2,760 miles. The base was 725 miles northeast of Prince of Wales Island, the magnetic north pole. Any compass at Thule would point towards Prince of Wales Island, making navigation out of Thule a real nightmare.

The TDYers settled into their quarters on arrival. These were specially built to meet the unique problems of living in the North. Unique problems, you betcha! During the winter, there are twenty-four hours of darkness; the sun never rises above the horizon. Temperatures hover at -35 to -45 degrees Fahrenheit, and that's on a warm day or night. The winds come right off the North Pole, adding chill factor to the frigid weather.

Quarters were built using Clements Panels. These were large panels that had been used in the states to build large walk-in coolers. At Thule, the principle was reversed: to keep the warm air in and the cold out. To prevent melting of the permafrost, the buildings were placed on piles above the ground. Entry into the buildings was through an entryway with two doors.

Water had to be trucked in from the water plant and stored in each building. There were three storage tanks: one was for drinking water. The second was for bathing and washing, which was stored after use and recycled to flush the toilets. The third tank held, you guessed it, sewage.

Toilets bore a close resemblance to the "head" on a submarine. A valve was used to charge the toilet bowl, then you had to turn off the water valve to avoid a wet surprise. When finished, a foot lever pump was used to flush the bowl and water into the third tank. When full, the third tank was pumped into a "honey truck". There was the inevitable spillage, which resulted in large, multi-colored ice towers in the winter and pungent ponds when they melted in the summer.

# Cold War Cornhuskers: The 307th Bomb Wing Lincoln Air Force Base Nebraska 1955-1965

Weather at Thule was unpredictable at best. There were no weather satellites circling the earth to beam down the latest weather photos from space. Nope! These were the days of weather observation, charting, and predicting which way the weather pattern was going to move. Some weather forecasts were issued using the SWAG (Super Wild Ass Guess) method.

The most severe, life-threatening weather event at Thule was a foehn wind. This occurred when two low-pressure systems were close enough to generate high winds across the base from the ice cap. A foehn was divided into three parts. Phase I was with rising winds and snow. Phase II, strong wind, blowing snow with restricted visibility. Outdoor activity restricted, with mess halls and other facilities closed. Phase III, very high wind, visibility zero. "Take cover," remain in the building where you are located. These storms could last for two or three days. Each building was equipped with a pantry filled with "C" and "K" rations in case a foehn blew in. There were also survival huts strategically placed around the base in case people got caught out in the open.

Snowstorms weren't the only weather problem that made operations at Thule interesting. Ken Tarwater recalled:

"One very foggy night at Thule, three or four of us in a weapons carrier, were headed for the KC-97 parking ramp. Normally, when you got to the end of the runaway you flashed a light at the tower and they gave you a green light to cross the active runway. This night, we couldn't see the tower and they couldn't see us. We shut the engine off and listened for any aircraft noise. All we could hear was the wind blowing so we decided to go ahead and cross the runway. Talk about bad timing. Just as we started across, a B-47 came over the top of us. I don't know how close the B-47 was to us, but it rocked that weapons carrier and scared the Hell out of us and I can still remember the noise as he went over the top of us. We couldn't believe he was landing in that fog, we could barely find our way to the KC-97 parking ramp. I guess we were lucky that night in Thule, Greenland."

On August 30th, the 307th AREFS provided tanker support for Operation Sun Dog. The tankers offloaded fuel for RB-47s gathering electronic intelligence on the "Red Bear". Before all of the tankers could get back, the weather at Thule fell below GCA minimums, causing several of the KC-97s to divert towards other bases and sweat out their fuel reserves.

August 31st found several crews on strip alert in case any of the RBs got into trouble. Word came in there were a couple of RB-47s that were short of fuel, so the tankers would have to launch. Weather at the time was not the best, with almost zero visibility because of the ice fog. William Schmuck was the Navigator on Crew T-24, commanded by Maj. Jean Nutty. There was a bird in trouble up there somewhere, so they scrambled to 51-378 and fired up the engines. After all, there was a bird in trouble out there somewhere:

"We were launched and made a rendezvous with a RB-47 who was returning from a "USSR" mission and was extremely low on fuel. We made contact off of northern Greenland and escorted and refueled this aircraft until we could no longer hang in and still hit a base in Greenland. We were on final approach and the engineer (Sgt. Worm) said we had no fuel for a go-around, my radio operator (A1C Harold Beucus) said, 'I'll be p....d if we crash,' and Maj. Nutty brought us in with 600 pounds of fuel." Harold Beucus remembered the flight as "an interesting experience for a nineteen year old kid."

The mission is perhaps best recalled by the letter of commendation the crew received from Maj. Cletus Kressge from the 55th SRW. He wrote:

"On August 31st, 1957, I was the Aircraft Commander of Ascot 33 returning from a classified flight to this station (Thule). Arriving in the area, I was informed of the local weather being zero/zero and directed to an alternate some fourteen hundred miles away. Since my fuel (after ten hours of flying) was depleted, it was necessary to have an immediate refueling sufficient to allow for another four hours of flight.

"One of your tankers had already taken off in zero/zero conditions, was well established on the strip alert track, and properly prepared to effect a rendezvous and refueling. After several thousand pounds had been transferred, the tanker called for a "Breakaway" denoting emergency conditions. As I disconnected, a flow of hydraulic fluid was noted from the left wing root of the tanker. Apparently with minimum hesitation, the malfunction was isolated, hydraulic servicing made and another hook up effected.

"During the fuel transfer, which was now at half-rate due to the loss of one engine driven hydraulic pump, your aircraft commander (Maj. Nutty) requested to know my "minimum fuel in tanks requirement at end of air refueling." Since the refueling was unusually lengthened by the above conditions, it was necessary for him to transfer up his reserve of aviation fuel and this was accomplished without complaint. At the conclusion of refueling, all necessary information was received to allow an orderly departure to our alternate including weather and filing of our clearance by this tanker.

"Needless to say, this Detachment is certainly appreciative of the outstanding performance of this crew and their professional approach in saving an 'H' model RB-47. We are indeed indebted to your organization."

The other KC-97 was flown by Herman Tiedes' Crew T-23. Enid Samuelson recalled the trip back after the refueling:

"We had to head for Sondrestrom after completing refueling. The RB-47s headed for either Goose Bay or Fairbanks. When we hit the coast, we were informed that Sondrestrom was below minimums. We had about three hours of fuel left and it was 2.5 hours to Frobisher, the next closest airfield, so we headed there. About fifteen minutes later Sondrestrom called and informed us they were above minimums and expected to remain that way so we changed direction and headed there and landed after dark. While on final, the tower asked us how we wanted our steaks cooked. After landing and parking the aircraft, we had our steak dinner waiting for us. The next morning we saw the mountain right next to the runway, glad we did not know it was that close when landing that previous evening. The runway was only 5500 feet long. We spent a very nice holiday weekend, and even enjoyed the flush toilets in the BOQ before returning to Thule." Enid's crew also received a letter of commendation for their mission.

Lincoln Air Force Base started September by playing war games on the first of the month. The 818th Air Division called for a practice run of Operations Plan 10-58 (Base Evacuation). Under the code Red Coat, base aircraft would disperse to preselected civilian airfields. The bombers were to take off and orbit near Redwood Falls, Minnesota. When everyone was tucked in, they would head for Des Moines, Iowa, land, and wait for the all clear. Tankers were to assemble over Mason City, Iowa, and land at Sioux Falls, South Dakota.

# 1957

Paul Koski related the experience for the rest of the personnel on base:

"We formed a convoy of Military and civilian cars and went to Seward, Nebraska, a small town west of the base. The convoy was several miles long and had gas trucks as well as wreckers in case anyone had any trouble. There was a small park in the town and that's where we all parked. We were there about six hours; the townspeople were out in force and cheered us on. They thought it was a parade.

"They passed out C-rations. I got a can of pasta and meatballs. Some people had enough sense to put them on the engine blocks to warm up. I got to scrape the grease off the top of the can and eat it that way. The pound cake weighed about that and the chocolate was bitter. Heaven help us if we had to weigh in after eating all of this."

The wing operations plan for September called for the wing to fly 290 training sorties. Each of the missions would last about seven hours. Since September was the first month of the SAC training quarter, survival refresher classes were being held at the Ashland National Guard Camp. Two crews would be scheduled to journey to Ashland, near the Platte River, and spend three days living off the land. Their orders reminded them to bring a set of fatigues or flight suit, boots, jacket, gloves, extra socks and a sheath knife.

A Devil Fish mission was flown on September 17th and 20th. These ECM missions were yielding more and more information about the capabilities, or lack thereof, the B-47 fleet had in case they launched for an actual EWO mission. In view of the results, SAC was beginning to change some of the tactics that would be used in the event the fleet was launched.

Back in February, 53-2128 and 53-2138 had been sent to the depot for some special modifications and updates. At first glance, they appeared different than when they had been sent out. There was a distinctive bulge where the bomb bay doors should have been. No, there weren't going to be any baby B-47s running around the flight line in the near future. These B-47s had been fitted with the Phase V ECM capsule and related equipment. The Phase V B-47s were supposed to be part of the answer to the increase in Soviet Air Defense capabilities. The purpose was to have the pod equipped B-47s fly with the strike force and provide special electronic jamming for the strike force. It was like a lineman laying down a block for the running back in football.

Now, for its day, the bomb bay of the B-47 was fairly large. But putting a two-man pod inside took up every square inch of the bay. As a matter of fact, the pod hung down about eight inches from the bottom of the aircraft, giving a somewhat pregnant look. The pod was crammed with all kinds of electronic jamming equipment to complete the mission. There were two ejection seats facing towards the tail. These were downward firing and had a special cutter to blast through the fiberglass bottom if the crew had to bail out.

Earlier in the month, the wing had been alerted for a no-notice exercise code name Blue Light. When the execution order arrived, the wing was to generate a force of seven B-47s and three Phase V-equipped jammers. The wing would fly a decoy mission while the jammers provided jamming for the 42nd Bomb Wing as they approached the primary targets.

The execution message for Blue Light arrived on the afternoon of September 17th, and the race was on to generate the aircraft for the mission. Takeoff would be on Wednesday, if the 307th was ready. Planes were towed to the refueling pits and serviced for the mission. The three jammers were also prepared for the mission. When they returned to their parking spots on the line, the two "pod people" made sure there was a parachute in the pod and one in the regular crew area. Everything was ready for the mission; now all they had to do was wait for the "go" from "Dropkick".

The word arrived from "Dropkick" in a three-part message. After decoding the message, the command post gave the launch order and the mission was on. The strike force had already been preflighted by the crews. A quick walkaround was all that was needed to make sure there were no leaks that may have sprung up and it was time to "turn em, juice em and give em spark."

One by one the B-47s taxied towards the end of the active runway. After making their final checks they turned onto the concrete ribbon and pushed the throttles forward. When the power was stable at a hundred percent, the spring loaded water-alcohol injection switch was pushed and held at the START position.

**"Six Reds Out, WAI on!"**

Clouds of dense, choking, black exhaust billowed from the engines as the water augmentation kicked in to provide extra thrust. Within fifteen minutes all of the aircraft were airborne, trails of black smoke marking their climb into the sky.

Climbing through five thousand feet the pod people began the hazardous journey to their pod in the bomb bay. They had to open the inner pressure door and climb down to the crawl way. Not an easy chore considering they had to put their full weight on the entry ladder and hope it would not give way and slam them against the main entry door and perhaps into space. Then there was the tunnel itself. It was just big enough for a man to crawl through, scraping his knees on the protruding ribs.

During the climbout the B-47s formed into two cells before the first turn point near Grand Island. There they turned towards the north and flew to a mandatory checkpoint at Pierre, South Dakota. At Pierre the navigators called for a fifteen-degree heading change, to the right, for a radar nav leg into North Dakota. Within a few minutes the radar was painting the outline of Bismarck, North Dakota, along the Missouri River. At this point they checked in with Bismarck Radio.

Passing just to the east of Devils Lake, North Dakota, the formation started picking up a crosswind that was stronger than the weather people had forecast. It was soon evident that the jet stream had shifted. By the time they had crossed into Canadian airspace they had to make several heading adjustments to compensate for the crosswind.

The cells were now listening on their radios for a message from "Drop Kick". As usual, it would be a standard message to "Sky King". The message they were listening for would be directed to "Safeway", and would read "*Casket, Kilo, Oscar.*" The message would be decoded and when authenticated would give the 307th the go-ahead to proceed on the mission.

On over to Winnipeg, then to the turn point on the west shore of Lake Winnipeg. The formation turned and flew towards Trout Lake. Now, the crosswind became almost a tail wind as the strike force headed towards the east. Trout Lake was the point where the formation was to break up into two groups. The ECM aircraft continued on their easterly heading. The rest of the force turned south for a decoy run toward Minneapolis. The decoy was designed to draw off enemy fighters that may have been scrambled. When the three jammers reached 59 degrees-N, 89 degrees-W, they turned south and took up a heading for their individual target corridors.

Down in the ECM pods, the "Ravens," as they would be called, had checked all of their equipment and were ready to "start their music." One jammer would head for Des Moines, Iowa; one would go to Ft. Wayne, Indiana. The middle jammer would sweep a corridor towards Springfield, Missouri. If they did their job, the bombers from the 42nd Bomb Wing would have a fairly clear path to the target.

Over Lake Michigan, one of the planes picked up a possible "Little River," or fighter lock-on. Immediately they started kicking out RR-39

## Cold War Cornhuskers: The 307th Bomb Wing Lincoln Air Force Base Nebraska 1955-1965

chaff from the left hopper to break the lock. The lock was broken, then reappeared. More chaff fluttered into the slipstream. Looked like the bogey had a solid lock. More chaff and heavy music, bordering on "acid rock," then the lock signal disappeared, this time for good.

The 42nd Bomb Wing strike force pulled in behind the blockers, right on time. The three attack units would use the path being cleared by the jammers to get to their target. So far, everything was going exactly as planned and briefed.

Near Traverse City, Michigan, a fighter picked up the jammer headed for Ft. Wayne. Chaff was kicked out and the Ravens turned the volume on their music up. The fighter attack broke, but then came back for another look. There was enough foil fluttering down to cover a hundred Christmas trees, yet the fighter hung on. The copilot turned his seat around to his gunnery station and was trying to track the incoming bandit. It was a cat and mouse game. Lock, break lock, lock, chaff, then lock again. This time the Ravens couldn't break it. It was up to the gunner, that is, the copilot, to defend the B-47. Without warning his gun radar went "haybags". They were meat on the table for the fighter. Then, the fighter just broke lock and pulled away. The crew on the B-47 couldn't believe it, they were off the hook.

The jammers kept the music playing until they were fifty miles past their target city. Then they shut everything down and turned towards Lincoln. Their part of the mission was done. All they had to do was wait for the scores to be posted.

8th Air Force scored the mission and sent the results to SAC. The final results were typed and sent to Gen. Power's office. At the next meeting of the Headquarters staff, the results of Blue Light were discussed. Those present thought they detected a hint of a smile on "Big Tommy's" face. When the final score was sent to Lincoln, the jammers had accomplished their mission with "excellent" results. It was brought out one fighter claimed a kill on one of the bombers, but it was denied when it was determined the fighter had broken lock before he fired.

Since its debut, SAC had enjoyed the luxury of having bombers ready to respond to a national emergency in about eight to twelve hours. That was about the flight time for a Soviet bomber to get close to the USA and a potential target. With the advent of long-range missiles, that luxury was becoming a thing of the past. SAC could see the writing on the hangar wall. They knew they had to come up with a way of getting the mailed fist of SAC into the air a lot sooner than ever before. Offutt knew the Soviet Union was improving their long-range strike capabilities with missiles. They had been trying out various methods of getting the aircraft generated and in the air as quickly as possible. It had started in February 1955 with Operation Open Mind. This was followed by Operation Watch Tower.

Plans for putting the 307th on continuous alert arrived on September 1st. Col. Read and members of the wing staff had visited Whiteman AFB and had a good idea of what the program was like. Since their visits, they had worked on a plan to implement the ground alert program at Lincoln. SAC Headquarters had placed the target date for the first alert aircraft to be ready as October 1st. With this date in mind, five aircraft were selected based on their reliability and current flying schedule. The alert operations plan set forth in great detail the how, when and what things would be accomplished for placing the wing on alert.

Each of the selected B-47s would be loaded with a Mark-6 unit. The weapon would be loaded using the checklist to insure it was done according to the book. During the upload, a designated flight crew would be present along with the aircraft's crew chief. When the aircraft was loaded security guards would be placed at each aircraft to prevent sabotage.

The "cocked" B-47s were to be placed in the designated alert area on the south end of the flight line. B-47s would be parked on Uniform Row while the tankers would be parked on Tango Row. The alert crews were to make sure their personal equipment, such as parachute, helmet and other flight gear was aboard their assigned aircraft. The aircraft was also checked and loaded with at least two flight lunches per crewman, personal weapons and preflight checklist. Most important, they must have the current and next effective KAC-1 code books for checking any messages that may arrive.

Beginning at 0900 each morning, the alert crew assigned to the aircraft was to complete the preflight according to the Dash-1, up to the start engines portion of the checklist. The MD-3 power cart would be positioned with the power cords plugged into the aircraft. When the daily preflight was finished, the alert bird would be considered as "cocked".

Crew changeover was to begin at morning preflight at 0900 on the designated changeover day. There would be a three-hour overlap in duty hours to insure the aircraft had been preflighted and accepted by the new crew. If an alert were called during this time period and the new crew had not signed for the aircraft and weapon, the old crew would launch.

After completing the preflight, the new crew would report to Building 1758 for the formal changeover. The crew would sign for the weapon, inventory and sign for the Combat Mission Folder, obtain the combination for the safe, and review and replace all material in the CMF. Then the crew was to notify the Wing Control Room they were now on alert. As soon as that word was received, the old crew would be free to leave.

At first, the Alert Crews were pretty well tied down while on Alert. There were only three specific locations they could be during the first days of Alert: they could stay at the Alert barracks, which was Building 1758 (BOQ); the Alert Aircraft; or the designated alert dining area at Dining Hall 2.

By the end of September, the days were getting even shorter at Thule. Perpetual day had given way to longer, cold nights. The Air Refueling Squadron was getting restless to get out of the deep freeze and back to Lincoln before the long cold night of winter arrived. They had supplied tanker support for a lot of transient aircraft. Overall, they had chalked up ten mass gas refuelings, offloading over 170,000 gallons of JP-4. The squadron had also been credited with at least five "saves" during their time at the top of the world.

The Strategic Air Command officially began continuous ground alert on October 1st. By 1000 hrs, the 307th was ready with five cocked B-47s sitting on Uniform Row along with five birds from the 98th Bomb Wing. Tankers from the 98th AREFS were ready to provide strip alert. Dave Fehnel recalled the first days of ground alert:

"The alert crews were housed in the BOQ away from the flightline. The crew folders were kept in a safe at the BOQ. We got to the flightline and our bird by bus from the motor pool or private cars. You can see why things had to change.

"When the horn went off, the navs and copilots went to the bus and the ACs went to the safe (they were the only ones with the combo to the safe). I recall one event when after about 5 to 10 minutes waiting, a nav went in to see what was going on with the safe opening, and found none of the ACs could open the safe. Things had to change. Then, it was the ride to the flight line and drop off the crews. The 307th had some of the best crew chiefs going, because they would have the dust covers removed and the power unit going by the time the crews got to the bird.

"I don't recall the order of changes, but a rental car was assigned to each crew, the crew folders were kept in the plane, and things began to improve. Each crew was on its own, no more waiting for the crew kit or the slow bus ride to the birds. The crews could now travel the base in their rental car. Things were getting better.

"Some other things I recall. Drag racing the rental cars. Passing the card that hung around the neck of the AC to the next crew coming on, sitting on the flight line for hours during some problem overseas with power carts running and standing by the radio waiting to go. I recall being told that there would not be any more alerts one day except for the real thing, and then going to the movie theater, and watching the RED light go on. We did not move as fast that night, as we should have, with the thought that this was it! YES.., THOSE WERE THE DAYS TO RECALL!"

From now on, standing Alert would be a daily part of life for the men of the 307th. From time to time there would be changes in alert procedures and duration of standing alert. If the klaxon went off, you never knew whether it was another practice alert or for real. There was always the chance that someone on either side had pulled the nuclear trigger. All would agree, tension in SAC had risen to a higher degree.

On October 3rd, the 307th AREFS packed their bags and bid a not-so-fond farewell to Thule, Greenland, and the land of no trees or pretty girls. Like the trip up, they would make it in two hops. The first would end at Goose Bay for refueling and crew rest, then on to Lincoln the next day. Several had hoped they would be able to make the trip without stopping. After all, they were more than ready to see their families.

Mid-afternoon on Friday the 4th, a large party assembled to welcome the 307th AREFS back to Lincoln. The Lincoln Lions Club was on the flight line; they were the adopted sponsors of the refueling squadron. Wing and Base command staff were also waiting, along with Miss Nebraska. Now, this was all well and good for the returning hunters from the frozen hill. However, the people they really wanted to see were their families and sweethearts. After all, three months in the frozen north was a hell of a long time.

The first tanker arrived and taxied to the ramp. Excitement grew as the engines were shut down and the plane just sat there. How long does it take for them to get the darn doors open so the boys can come out? Finally, when the forward door opened all eyes strained to catch a glimpse of who would be the first off the plane. After a brief welcome home speech, the men were able to finally get a well-deserved "welcome home honey" kiss and hug. About every fifteen minutes, another tanker would land and the tired northern explorers would at last be home. The returning members of the squadron were given three days off to make up for lost time with the family.

That posed the question as to just how do you make up for the lost time? The tankers had been gone for three months. There had been a lot of water passed under the bridge during that time. Some of the kids had taken their first step, or said their first word while dad was gone. Maybe the car had broken down or the washer or dryer had gone on the fritz. Oh sure, you could give the guys a few extra days off, but they would never make up for the memories lost, or what could have been if dad hadn't been off with the squadron defending the nation at the top of the world.

While the tankers were celebrating their return to Lincoln, the nation was reeling in shock over the news that the Soviet Union had launched a man-made 184-pound satellite into orbit around the earth. The effect in Washington was dramatic, with almost everyone wondering how the Russians had beaten the United States into space. If they could launch a satellite into orbit, they may have nuclear tipped missiles aimed at the United States. Senator Lyndon Johnson summed up the near hysteria in Washington. "Soon they will be dropping bombs on us from space like kids dropping rocks onto cars from freeway overpasses!"

The United States had been experimenting with ways of launching a satellite into space for several years. When Sputnik started "beeping" from space, a whole new sense of urgency was placed on the space program. Sputnik not only changed the priorities for the space program, it changed the way SAC would conduct operations from that day on.

Even though the concept of Alert had been proven under several of the test programs, SAC Headquarters wanted to have a final proof of concept test. A special Operations Order arrived from Omaha outlining Operation Romeo Alert Stake Out at several bases that would fly the test mission. The 307th was one of the wings elected to carry it out. Under the Alert concept there were four types of Alerts:

<u>Alfa</u>: The crews would report to their aircraft and, when ready to start engines, contact the control room and report.
<u>Bravo</u>: Crews report to aircraft, start engines and report to the control room, "Ready to Taxi."
<u>Coco</u>: Start engines, contact control room when ready to taxi. Then taxi to the runway, hold brakes, go to full power, then reduce to idle and return to alert area.
<u>Romeo</u>: This was a launch order alert.

For the operational test, six "cocked" B-47s were selected. The alert crews assigned to them were given a special briefing on the mission profile. This was going to be a full-scale test to validate the alert concept. The aircraft would carry real weapons, a full fuel load, ATO for takeoff and hot guns. The selected crews spent extra hours reviewing the special mission folders so they knew exactly what was going to be expected of them.

Three aircraft would fly a non-refueling route while the other three would fly the same route, except they would rendezvous with tankers and take on fuel. ATO would be used during the take off. For safety, the ATO rack would not be jettisoned unless there was an in-flight emergency. All safety wires would remain in place on the Mark-6 weapon and no detonators or "pills" would be carried. Everything was ready; now, all they had to do was sit around and wait for the horn to go off.

Thursday, October 10th started off like any other day on the flight line. Everyone was going about the usual activity, working on the planes, pumping JP-4, or fine tuning the electronics in the Bomb/Nav System. The Alert birds had been given the required morning preflight and the alert crews had returned to the alert quarters. Nothing to do now, maybe watch some TV or get a card game going. Later, go to lunch and see what "Cookie" had prepared for the noonday bill of fare.

Routine is shattered by the ear-splitting wail of the alert horn. Instant pandemonium, as the alert crews respond on a dead run for the doors of the alert quarters. God help anyone in their way. Air Force officers and gentlemen were instantly transformed into NFL running backs, ready to stiff-arm their way to the alert vehicles.

Alert vehicles were fired up and hit the driveway to 9th Street, then highballed across Oak Creek. Break right on "H" Ave and down to Cheney, and a two-wheel turn to the east and onto the flight line gate near Base Operations.

Within minutes, the crews were scrambling up the ladders to their planes. Ground power units rumbled to life, putting power on the aircraft for engine start. Contact was made with the Control Room to find out if this was it or another practice alert.

**"Execute Romeo Alert Stake Out. Break Break**
**Authentication is PAPA, OSCAR, ECHO. Repeat.."**
Down the line, there was a low whine as engines began spooling up. In moments the whine was replaced by the roar of thirty-six J-47 engines coming up to taxi power. Inside, the crews ran the checklist.
**"Adams 35, Ready to taxi."**
The B-47s moved out of the alert parking ramp and turned onto the taxiway. At the active runway there was a momentary pause for final checks and contacting the tower to see if the alert was go or no go. Throttles were pushed up to 100%, water on.

# Cold War Cornhuskers: The 307th Bomb Wing Lincoln Air Force Base Nebraska 1955-1965

**"Adams 35, Rolling!"**

Clouds of black water-alcohol smoke billowed backwards from the engines. Slowly at first, then gaining speed, the B-47s rolled down the runway.

**"Fire ATO!"**

The planes literally jumped into the air with the extra thrust of blazing rocket motors. Heavy plumes of smoke boiled backwards, hanging on the runway and in the air like a building cloud. Motorists along Cornhusker Highway were treated to a spectacular show, better then any air show they had ever seen. One by one, the six B-47s literally blasted into the air and disappeared in the distance.

The Combat Mission Folder called for three planes to fly the refueling route, while the other three flew a standard route. The alert tankers were right behind the bombers so they could be waiting at the rendezvous point at Big Boy.

Once in the air, the aircraft turned to the heading for their assigned part of the mission. Crews flying the mission without refueling took a heading for Sioux Falls, South Dakota. Passing over Sioux Falls at 35,000 feet they continued north to Fargo, North Dakota.

At Fargo, the cell turned and began the first navigation leg to their checkpoint over the Minot VOR. Just north of Minot, the B-47s turned to the west and headed for the next checkpoint at Lewiston, Montana. Within minutes of their turn, the cell passed near the small farm town of Powers Lake, North Dakota. On the ground, a few residents may have looked skyward as the white ribbons in the sky approached. No one in the sleepy town could imagine that there were planes loaded with nuclear weapons flying overhead.

Over Flathead Lake, Montana, the three B-47s turned southwest and flew to the last checkpoint on the nav leg near Klamath Falls, Idaho. There they turned back towards the east and made a radio check at Boise and Burley, Idaho.

Near Riverton, Wyoming, the cell broke and headed for their specific targets. The lead aircraft would make a run on the Belle Fouche Reservoir near Belle Fouche, South Dakota. The second would hit the Angostura Reservoir in South Dakota, while the third B-47 would head for Lake McConaughy in western Nebraska. As outlined in the orders, the bomb run was aborted fifteen miles from the target. After the run the aircraft headed back to Lincoln.

The cell that was to complete the heavyweight refueling had taken a heading for Akron, Colorado, after leaving Lincoln. Passing Akron at 25,000 feet, they did an about face and flew back to Grand Island. At Grand Island the cell turned towards Pierre, South Dakota, and the air refueling rendezvous point.

The three B-47s moved into the pre-contact stable position behind Seaman flight. With small throttle adjustments they moved into position so the "boomer" could fly the boom and hook up. JP-4 surged through the nozzle and into the B-47s. For a change the weather was halfway decent, so there were very few disconnects.

Over Minot, the bombers dropped off the booms 30,000 pounds heavier and slid below and to the left of the tankers. Climbing back towards 25,000 feet, they took a heading for Livingston, Montana. From this point they flew the same mission profile as the first cell had flown.

When the planes landed, they were refueled and recocked for alert status. The crews went to debriefing and went back over the mission step by step. There had been no aborts, refueling rendezvous was on time, and everyone got the briefed off load.

When the final results of the mission were tabulated and sent to Offutt, the staff at the head shed was extremely pleased with the way the mission had gone. This was the first time alert aircraft loaded for "Bear" had been launched from Lincoln. It was clear SAC could flush the birds from the nest and fly a mission. The big question was, could SAC sustain an alert posture indefinitely?

SAC's goal was to have at least one third of the bomber force on alert. It looked good on paper, but accomplishing the goal would take time. There were all kinds of details to be considered. You can't have a force of B-47s sitting on the ramp cocked and not have them guarded twenty-four hours a day. So you have to get more security guards. Putting one third of the force on alert meant fewer planes available for daily training operations. Fewer training flights meant loss of the razor edge for the crews.

Then there were other details to consider: quarters for the alert crews, transportation, scheduling for planes and crews, etc. It all added up to more of almost everything, including money. It didn't take an accountant to see it would be some time before the mailed fist of SAC would meet the goal. In the meantime, they would have to make do with the resources on hand.

Sharp on the heels of one operation came another. This time, it was yet another Pacesetter mission sent down from 8th Air Force Headquarters. This one was scheduled for October 16th and 17th. Yep, another Pacesetter; this time it would be number nine in the series. It seemed they just kept coming, bigger and tougher with each mission.

Plans for Pacesetter IX called for fourteen aircraft to fly on Wednesday, followed by thirteen on Thursday. Each aircraft would fly the same mission profile. The profile included a grid and celestial navigation problem, ECM jamming, maximum fire out and bomb runs on three targets. Bombing on two of the targets would be using offset aiming points. At bombs away, they were to perform the "Hi Jinks" breakaway. The Phase V-equipped B-47s would make ECM runs with the strike force to cut a path in the "enemy" defenses.

As per operations instruction, the crews spent eight hours devoted to target study and planning. When they knew the route and timing they filled out the Form 1a, or Mission Flight Plan. They went back over the form several times to make sure all of the altitudes, headings, distances and fuel estimates squares were filled in and double checked.

Bright and early Wednesday morning the crews arrived for the last minute briefing to see what the weather was going to be along the route. No major changes from the original forecast and briefing; good, that makes the mission a little bit easier. All in all, it looked like a good morning to go flying.

At 0901, Capt. Paul Ecelbarger began starting engines on his assigned aircraft, 53-1909. This would be the lead aircraft for the mission, call sign Adams 12. Ten minutes later he moved out towards the runway. Behind him the other fourteen B-47s were starting engines and getting ready to taxi.

At the end of the taxi strip the crew made their final checks. Take off gross weight 196,000 pounds, looks like about 9,500 feet to get airborne. That is, if everything went according to plan. At 0936 Paul pushed the throttles to one hundred percent and let the power stabilize. Water-alcohol injection activated, brakes released. Adams 12 lurched forward with the speed of a turtle until the thrust of the engines overcame the gross weight. Clouds of black exhaust billowed from each of the engines.

**"Coming up on 70 knots......Now!"**
**"Hack"**
**"Coming up on S1.....Now!"**
**"Hack! Speed looks good, We are committed!"**

No matter what happens now, they were committed to take the B-47 into the air. There wasn't enough runway to stop the hurtling B-47.

**"S2....Now!"**

A slight pull on the yoke and Adams 12 left the concrete just after passing the nine thousand foot marker.

# 1957

**"Gear up.....Four Green!"**

The B-47 continued to climb out over the countryside, leaving a long dark smudge of smoke drifting across the sky. If everything went according to the profile, they would be back in about eight hours.

At ten-minute intervals the B-47s took off, climbed, and then turned towards Beatrice, Nebraska. Over the small town they checked in with the base and turned to a heading that would take them to Grand Island, the level off point at 25,000 feet.

By the time they reached a turn point near Mankato, Kansas, they had finished the climb to mission altitude at 35,000 feet. The first major event of the mission began with a grid navigation leg between Mankato and Lawrenceville, Illinois.

The ECM blockers started their music as they passed just south of Springfield, Illinois, and kept playing their tunes beyond the Lewisville turn point. They wouldn't stop playing their music until they were well south of Nashville, Tennessee. The jammers weren't playing any music that you would hear at the Grand Ole Opry. They were trying to jam "S," "L" and "X" band radar.

The navigation leg ended as they coasted out near Panama City, Florida. One crew reported completing the leg two minutes before actually passing the GCI station at Eglin and were given a big goose egg.

Over the blue waters of the Gulf, the copilots rotated their seats and took up their gunnery station. As they approached Warning Area W-15, they checked the radar for anything within the lethal range of the twin 20 mm guns in the tail.

Aboard 53-1901, Adams 13, the copilot hit the fire button. Nothing happened; a fuse had blown. Trying to replace it, he dropped the fuse. The fallen fuse could not be found and they were scored zero on the fire out.

After the fire out, the crews turned the bombers towards the coast-in point near Cross City, Florida. There they began setting up for the first bomb run on Charlotte, North Carolina. This would be the first target using the offset aiming point (OAP) technique. This meant having one or more points on the ground, readily identifiable on radar. Knowing the distance and bearing from the OAP to the planned target, the Bomb/Nav system computer guided the aircraft to the bomb release point for the actual target.

Adams 12 reached Charlotte four hours and thirty-eight minutes after leaving Lincoln. The Bomb/Nav System was set up using the offset points and they made the run. At tone cut off, Aircraft Commander Ecelbarger racked Adams 12 into the breakaway "Hi Jinks" turn.

From Charlotte, it was a short run to the second target at Richmond, Virginia. Then over the Appalachian Mountains to the third target at Columbus, Ohio. This target gave the 307th the most problems of the three assigned targets. Four gross errors were scored over this target.

Crew R-13 flying Adams 13 was scored a gross error when they started their "Hi Jinks" break five seconds before bomb release. Judging from the problem during their fire out and what happened over Columbus, Crew R-13 flying in Adams 13, was just plain unlucky 13.

Heading west from Columbus, the bomber stream made their last checkpoint over Peoria, Illinois, then on home to Lincoln. Adams 12 popped the drag chute seven hours and fifty-six minutes after takeoff.

Beginning at noon the next day, thirteen bombers began climbing into the sky for the second wave of the Pacesetter mission. 53-2140 led the way into the air. Col. Read was aboard as mission commander. They would fly the same route as the day before. By the time Pacesetter IX was over, the 307th had flown a combined distance of about 86,000 nautical miles in the two-day mission. All they had to do now was wait for the results to be tabulated and posted.

Lt Gen Walter Sweeney Jr., 8th Air Force Commander, paid Lincoln a visit on Thursday, October 21st. His two-day visit was a general inspection of the base facilities. He and his staff poked into almost every nook and cranny of the base. He was impressed with the construction in progress on the lake, but he hit the ceiling over the condition of the floors in the new operations area. It seems the wax being used didn't have enough shine.

Col. Read held a wing staff meeting on Wednesday the 30th. During the meeting he discussed the last Pacesetter mission, and the fact that the 307th could look forward to another one in December. He also mentioned he was going to set aside time from 1600 to 1700 to do his paperwork. He would appreciate no interruptions unless it was important. The meeting ended with mention of the upcoming production of *No Time For Sergeants* at Pershing Auditorium beginning on October 31st, with encore presentations during the weekend.

On Saturday morning, November 1st, the Pacesetter crews gathered in the wing briefing room to get the word on how they had done. Overall, the 307th placed 8th with 808.14 points, while the 98th had placed 9th. The wing had the best fire out ever achieved. Fourteen of the twenty-six planes had scored one hundred percent fire out. The overall fire out average was 75%, which gave the wing an excellent rating. ECM results were excellent, along with navigation. Bombing was the area that caused the wing to place in the lower half. There were a total of seven gross errors, four coming from the target at Columbus. The one bright spot was Crew R-31 in Adams 40. They scored a "shack" at Charlotte while flying in the second wave.

The November 1st JET SCOOP was dedicated to traffic safety and how to prevent accidents. Col. Hoisington declared all-out war on violations and accidents. Under his plan, all personnel under twenty-five *must* take drivers' education before they were allowed to drive off base. This put a lot of stress on the personnel living off base. The whole program was labeled as another of "Perry's Pet Projects".

On the 6th, two crews returned from the 1957 Bomb/Comp held at Pinecastle AFB. During the last week Crew L-08, commanded by Harold Brooks, and Crew L-39 lead by William Hoffman had represented the 307th in the World Series of Bombing. They managed to place 33rd overall.

The 307th AREFS flew tanker support for the 340th Bomb Wing during Operation Iron Bar. The tankers flew on two consecutive days starting on November 8th. On the first day they refueled the receivers in the "Fat Cat" area, which ran northwesterly near Green Bay, Wisconsin. During the second day they used the "Rainy Day" area in western Minnesota.

The Nebraska winter arrived with a vengeance on November 18th. Twelve missions scheduled for that Monday were canceled. Heavy blowing snow began early that morning and continued the entire day. Going along with the snow, the colder weather brought back the old familiar problem of fuel leaks.

In September, the 307th had placed an order for forty-five of the special covers for the noses of the B-47s. By November the wing had received four of them. The lack of these covers caused late take offs due to radio and radar malfunctions.

The concept of placing aircraft on alert had been proven. That didn't mean everything was going along smoothly. There weren't enough crews and supplies to maintain the alert posture and carry out the daily routine. SAC planners had some ideas floating around the hallowed halls of the big hangar up in Omaha. It would take a while, but the wind of change was becoming a gentle breeze.

A new item was introduced to the training schedule. It was called "Pop Up". Basically, it was a tactic to go from low level to a higher altitude during the bomb run. It would become a required square to fill on the big board.

1Lt Robert Cox was awarded the Soldier's Medal for heroism displayed during last November's tragic crash of the F-80 on the taxiway that destroyed two B-47s. The citation commended Lt Cox for smothering the flames on a burning victim and, despite personal danger, searching for other victims until he was sure none remained in the danger area. (In April 1958, A2C Melvyn O. Werschky, 98th OMS, was also awarded the Soldier's Medal for his actions in responding to the same emergency.)

November ended with a letter from Col. Hoisington arriving on the 29th. He was not happy with the results of Pacesetter IX. He gave instructions for the wing staff to form a committee to monitor crew results. Crews that hadn't performed well during the last Pacesetter were to be given special training. He believed that, by knowing how they placed and what was done well, they would be able to do better in future operations.

The wing started December by getting one practice mission for Pacesetter X in on the 1st. Like always, they flew the route that would be flown on the real one. Weather raised its ugly head during the flight, causing all kinds of problems. The crews were hopeful the real one would be better than the practice mission.

Judging from the weather that greeted those reporting for duty on the 2nd, everyone was glad they had flown the day before. Cold and snow brought Lincoln below minimums for flying. Another training day lost, so time was spent going over the details for the real mission.

Any snowfall meant extra work. Snowplows hit the concrete to clear the snow off the ramps. It also meant extra work for the ground crews. The snow had to be removed from the entire aircraft. Then they had to shovel the drifts away from the bird.

There had been several incidents in the first couple of winters of people falling off the aircraft while removing snow. Falling off the wing of a B-47 or KC-97 would ruin anybody's day. To prevent serious injury, a directive came in stating a safety harness would be worn. Wearing a harness didn't always mean you were safe. It depended on what or where you anchored it. Paul Koski wrote:

"We had a crew chief servicing water-alcohol and was short of help, so he tied the rope to the water truck. He serviced the aircraft and passed the hose back down to the truck driver. He then went back on the wing to secure the service caps. You guessed it, the driver drove off! The crew chief played Superman for a few seconds as he was yanked off the wing. He was about fifty yards down the ramp before he got the truck stopped. What was amazing, the crew chief only had some minor bruises!

"I was sweeping off the backbone of my aircraft, removing snow and frost. I slipped and fell over the side, but, luckily, I had my harness on and landed gently. Everything seemed OK until I heard a scream from the other side of the aircraft. It seems, my assistant had tied the rope around his waist and since I weighed 200 pounds and he only weighed 160, I went down and he went up. That rope almost cut him in two. He was sore for several weeks."

Flight crews reported at O-Dark Thirty on the morning of December 7th to fly Pacesetter X. What a time to fly, on a Saturday. Who cared if it was the sixteenth anniversary of the attack on Pearl Harbor? It was dark and cold as they shuffled into the briefing room. Well, at least the coffee was hot.

The 307th put the most experienced crews in the first wave. Harold Brooks' Crew S-08 would lead off. He would be followed by Jack Crook (L-06), Paul Ecelbarger (L-16), John Koudsi (L-03), George Biggs (L-11), Bruce Mills (L-14), Paul Trudeau (R-15), William Hoffman (L-39) and Clarence Guy (L-40).

The briefing was over before it began. Word was received from 8th Air Force that en route weather and weather at several of the alternates was below limits. The mission was postponed twenty-four hours. The crews were told to go home and get some rest.

Twenty-four hours later, again O-Dark Thirty, the crews shuffled into the briefing room. The coffee was hot and someone was passing out donuts. Coffee and sugar to wake the men up! The briefing went smoothly, no major weather problems to report except for the weather near Montreal. There was one major change, however. Instead of two waves, the 307th was to fly one long bomber stream. Twenty-one B-47s would take off and fly the mission. There would be five standby crews in case of an abort.

Hal Brooks' crew took off at 0636 that Sunday morning and climbed into the dark sky. He would be followed every ten minutes by another B-47. For the next three hours, the roar of one take off was replaced by another.

Climbout was to the northwest, turning near Columbus to a heading for Hastings. Ten miles west of there was the next turn towards Falls City, Nebraska, for the beginning of the navigation leg. At this point they had been in the air about forty-four minutes.

The next two hours would be jammed with sextant shots to check position, figuring lines of position and checking time and distance. Looking down from 35,000 feet, small towns drifted by, visible in the dark only by the outlines and glow of their street lights. The route would take them up through Iowa and to the east of Minneapolis.

Approaching the turn point near Duluth, Minnesota, the crews took another sextant shot, perhaps looking for the star Betelgeuse in the constellation Orion. Then they took a heading towards Houghton, Michigan. They flew out over Lake Michigan, ending the navigation leg near New Liskeard, Ontario.

It was time to set up for the first bomb run on Montreal, Quebec. Heading east, the sun seemed to jump up over the horizon, bright rays of piercing light, right in the kisser. By now, the bomber stream had caught up with the weather system that had delayed the mission the previous day. Solid undercast, no sign of the ground, just clouds. Montreal was reporting heavy snow and gusty winds. No problem, bombing would be by radar, just compensate for the wind.

By the time the lead bomber reached the IP at Mont-Laurier, Quebec, the navigator was ready for the bomb run. His aiming point was the southeast corner of the Verdan Industrial Building. Using the tracking handle, the cross hairs were moved to the aiming point. Countdown to release, then tone cut off as the radar bomb headed towards the target.

As the bomber stream continued to arrive over the target the navigators were finding they were in the jaws of a tremendous change in the forecast winds. They had picked up a jet stream moving at 170 knots from right behind them. That increased their ground speed to almost 700 miles an hour. That would make hitting the target almost impossible. Wally Whitehurst recalled the run:

"I remember the Pacesetter X mission. The bomb run at Montreal and the final aiming point used was the bridge abutment that was not well defined on radar. I did a bit of radar interpretation to locate what I thought was the point in the 'blob' that we thought would be well defined and made the run on that point. Those of us that did that early on the run did well. I believe I had the lowest circular error of all on that target. There was a tremendous wind change on the run. If I remember correctly, I noticed that I couldn't keep up with the changing wind and I did a final wind run quite close to the target which allowed me to kill the wind as it was changing rapidly near release. I also remember that others reported there was a jet stream in close proximity to the release point and the sudden wind shear, caught a few with their pants down. Walt Hudkins was flying with us in the "fourth hole" and was watching me over my shoulder on the runs. He wasn't real sure of the aiming point either. I stuck to my guns and made the run."

After the run on Montreal, the bomber stream coasted out near Bangor, Maine. When the gunnery area was reached, they called Dow, Maine, for clearance to commence fire. A quick check of the area to make sure it was clear and 20 mm rounds began arching out and falling into the ocean below.

Coasting in near the IP at Portland, Maine, the navigators set up for the run on Springfield, Massachusetts. They had run away from the jet stream they had encountered over Montreal. Compared to that run, this one would be a piece of cake. The aiming point was the tower on the east side of the U.S. Armory Building at Springfield. The planes made contact with the Radar Bomb Scoring unit on Channel 8, gave them set-up information and confirmed their identification for scoring.

The next target was Columbus, Ohio. The lead bomber had tone cut off six hours and seventeen minutes after leaving Lincoln. They were right on time for the flight plan. So far they had covered about 2,700 miles since take off.

They flew a short leg to Peoria, Illinois, then on to Ottumwa, Iowa. Within a few minutes, the crew would run the checklist for descent. They made a call to Lincoln requesting a jet penetration and the latest weather, wind and altimeter. They crosschecked fuel remaining and figured their gross weight for landing.

Engine Stall Prevention Switch--ON
Windshield Anti-Ice--ON
Bombsight Cover--CLOSED
Landing Gear-- FOUR DOWN-FOUR GREEN!

Throttles back to idle, nose down. Adjust and maintain 4,000 feet per minute decent. Make the penetration turn about halfway down to minimum penetration altitude. Run the landing checklist.

Double check, gear down-FOUR GREEN
Zero Second Lanyard Attached-CHECK
Flaps- DOWN
Cabin Pressure-DUMPED
Approach Chute-DEPLOYED

After the checklist was completed they lined up on the runway. Power adjusted to the best flare speed, across the fence... hold her straight for touchdown, easy does it, easy...easy!

A puff of smoke and squeal from the rear main tires as they kiss the concrete and spin up to match the forward speed. The brake chute pops from the tail and the B-47 starts to slow down. Once again they have tamed the tiger.

All they had to do now was taxi in, shut down and go to debriefing. Only a couple of items to write up on the Form 781. The mission had taken eight hours and twenty-seven minutes. All they could do now was wait for 8th Air Force to send in the scores.

The results came in and the crews reacted to the good—or bad—news. The calm was shattered by dead silence: the 307th placed tenth out of the eleven wings flying the mission. It was the worst showing the wing had made in the entire Pacesetter series. If Gen Hoisington was upset about the results of the previous Pacesetter mission, he would really hit the roof after this one.

Navigation had been scored as "Outstanding". No crew was more than fifteen miles off the route at the end of the navigation leg. Gunnery was "Excellent", with an overall score of 72%. The problem was in the bombing scores. It doesn't count if you can navigate to the target and not hit it. The old saying that close counts in horseshoes and atom bombs didn't cut the mustard in SAC.

The wind shear over Montreal caused most of the bomb scores to be poor. There were ten synchronization errors on that target alone. The target at Springfield was second with five gross errors, while Columbus had three. One aircraft aborted before the first target when the Bomb/Nav System went "haybags". The overall score for the wing was 74% effective in bombing. NOT GOOD!

There was some good news: five crews were given an "outstanding" rating by 8th Air Force. The best score for the wing and the entire 8th Air Force went to Crew R-51, commanded by James Houghtly with Thomas Sutton copilot and Alfred Merrell, Navigator. They had a three-target circular error average of 656 feet, with one bomb scored at 200 feet from the target. The other crews were listed as:

R-50: Ray Coley AC
Sidney Goyer CP
Niles Peak Nav
Circular Error = 1123 feet

L-11: George Biggs AC
Leroy Potter CP
James Evans Nav
Circular Error = 1230 feet

L-75: Hale Dodge AC
William Lawson CP
Oleah Short Nav
Circular Error = 1326 feet

R-80: Richard McKenzie AC
Samuel Martin CP
James "Wally" Whitehurst Nav
Circular Error = 1340 feet

Wally Whitehurst mentioned he thought he had the lowest circular error on the target at Montreal. The bombing results showed he was correct with a circular error of just 155 feet from the target.

Crew L-06 (Capt Crook, Capt Biaett, and 1Lt Brumbaugh) were acknowledged by 8th Air Force for their "outstanding performance" during the mission while flying 53-2140. Crew chief George Nigh received a letter of appreciation. Col. Read added a personal note at the bottom of the letter. "Thanks for the hard work and long hours you put in to get me off in 140 on Thursday night."

The only other bright spot was a commendation for the Phase V ECM crews. They provided ECM jamming on three targets. 8th Air Force Headquarters mentioned the jamming was rated as "Outstanding". So Pacesetter X was over.

In order to get strike aircraft closer to potential Soviet targets, SAC came up with a novel idea. Move closer to the targets by placing aircraft at bases overseas for short periods of time. In other words, surround the Russian Bear. It was like flexing a muscle to show the "Reds" that SAC was strong and ready for anything. Since it was a flexing of muscle then coming back to the States, it would be called Reflex.

On Friday, December 13th, the 307th published Operations Order 96-57, Reflex Action. Under the plan the wing would maintain five aircraft and crews on Alert at RAF Greenham Common, UK. The B-47s would rotate about every fifteen days. Supervisory and support personnel would rotate every ninety days.

The plan outlined routes that would be used to fly across the Atlantic and outlined the responsibility of each of the squadrons. The flight over would be used to fill as many training squares as possible. During redeployment, the crews would make bomb runs on Montreal or Omaha.

On the afternoon of December 13th, Lincoln Air Force Base was rocked with news of a 98th Bomb Wing B-47 crashing near Duluth, Minnesota. The B-47 (52-186) was attempting an emergency landing

## Cold War Cornhuskers: The 307th Bomb Wing Lincoln Air Force Base Nebraska 1955-1965

at Duluth after reporting they had an engine and wing fire. The aircraft crashed about a mile and a half from the Duluth runway, killing the three crewmen.

Dover 23 had departed Lincoln at 0922 and began a routine training flight that was supposed to last about five and a half hours. The flight was a normal training flight until approximately 1151, when Dover 23 contacted Duluth Tower. They reported they had shut down three engines on the left side. A fire warning light on number one engine had come on and they had a "fire in the left wing". The pilot advised the tower there were three crew on board and they had 49,000 pounds of fuel remaining. He requested an emergency GCA landing. The tower cleared them for landing on Runway 27.

During the next ten minutes there was constant communications to try and get the troubled aircraft down. At 1207 the tower asked Dover 23 if they were landing on that pass. The pilot answered, "I am having trouble turning. I don't think I can make it." At 1208 the left wing was observed dropping, followed by the aircraft hitting the ground.

The accident board found an ironic set of factors causing the loss of Dover 23. First, there was a malfunction in the fire warning system, causing the fire warning light to come on when there was no fire. Second was the phenomenon of aerodynamic condensation over the wing, giving the impression of smoke and fire in the left wing. The crew had shut down three perfectly good engines, then tried to land at an unfamiliar airport in an aircraft that exceeded the 125,000 recommended maximum gross weight for landing.

The wing was scheduled to launch the first Reflex flight of five B-47s on January 8th. That would be followed by flights on January 15th and 22nd. On paper it looked good. However, it left the wing staff scratching their heads as to exactly how many people and planes it would take to cover the Reflex commitment.

On the tenth of December, two special technicians from Tinker AFB, Oklahoma, arrived to help troubleshoot the fuel leak problems. They looked at the dripping JP-4, shrugged their shoulders and said, "Well, here's your problem." They tried new sealers, dyes and may have even tried chewing gum. Nothing they tried got the leak gremlins to go away. They left to go back to Tinker on the 19th without accomplishing anything to prevent the fuel leaks.

'Twas the Night before Christmas, and all across the patch, everyone was checking his wish list for Santa. Col. Read had a long list and made sure it was filled out correctly, in triplicate, as per SAC Regs. Topping his list was more personnel for Alert and Reflex, along with more personnel in almost all areas.

The scheduling section wanted B-47s that didn't cover the ramp with pools of JP-4. Crew chiefs wanted the nose covers to protect their birds. The Alert crews wanted to be home with their families. Most of all, everyone wanted PEACE ON EARTH!

Winter on the flight line and the ever present MD-3 power cart. (USAF)

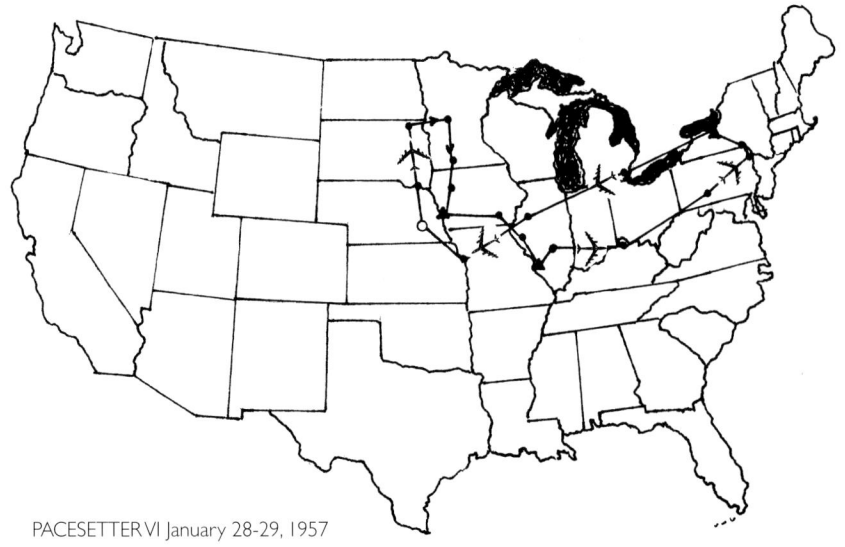

PACESETTER VI January 28-29, 1957

74

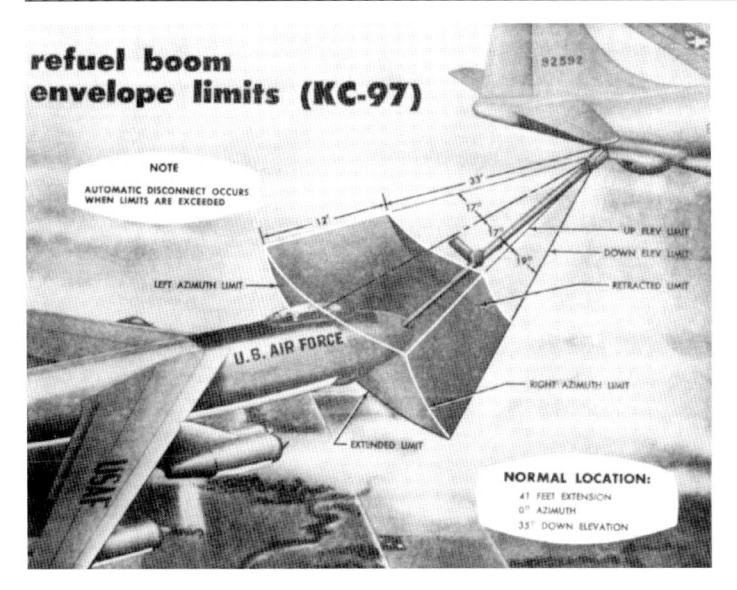

# 1957

Diagram of refueling limits from the B-47 Dash-1. (T.O.1B-47E-1)

Mark 36 nuclear weapon. (USAF)

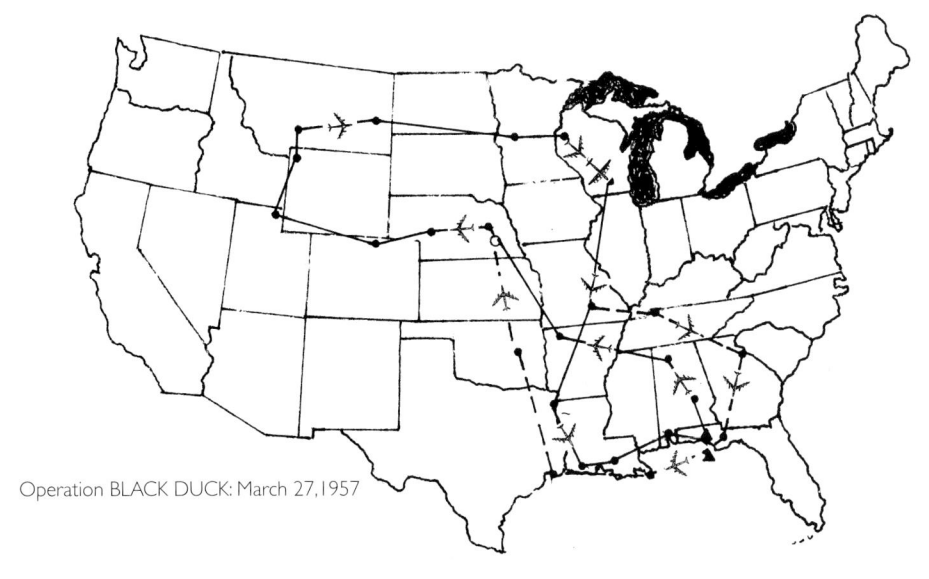

Operation BLACK DUCK: March 27, 1957

PACESETTER crews. Back Row 3rd from L Tony Minnick, Standing Extreme Left Bill Holden. Front Extreme Left Joe Anthony, Marv Pelletier. (Anthony)

# Cold War Cornhuskers: The 307th Bomb Wing Lincoln Air Force Base Nebraska 1955-1965

Heavy equipment working on what will become Bowling Lake. (Mary Aston Bowling)

Pershing Auditorium.

Col. Elkins "Pete" Reed Jr. assumed command of the 307th on May 18, 1957. (USAF)

KC-97s fill the north end of the ramp as they prepare for deployment to Thule, Greenland. (Tarwater)

## 1957

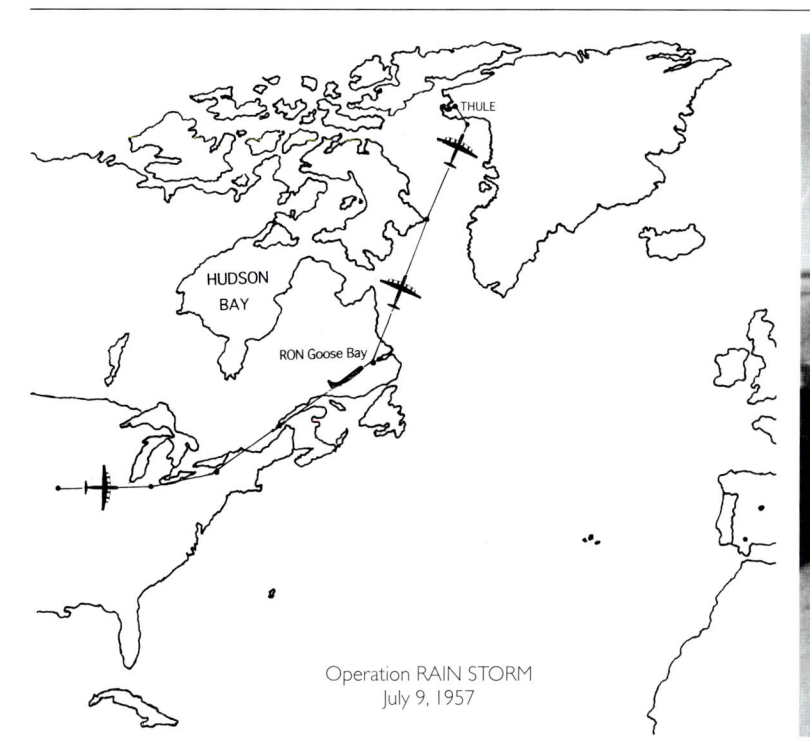

Operation RAIN STORM
July 9, 1957

Thule Greenland- What Trees! What Beautiful Women? (Tarwater)

As soon as the 307th arrived, this KC-97 would be relieved to return to its home base.

Mt. Dundas and Thule Air Base in the distance. (Erickson)

# Cold War Cornhuskers: The 307th Bomb Wing Lincoln Air Force Base Nebraska 1955-1965

Thule quarters, Mt Dundas in the background. (Tarwater)

KC-97 on the flight line at Thule. (USAF)

A welcome frostbite check for this lonely guard. (USAF)

Even in the spring, the area around Thule is not very hospitable. (Erickson)

*1957*

Front L-R. Alfred Brooks, Vincent Locey, Paul Smith. Rear L-R. Jerome Hart, Calvin Cragun, Roger Hammerli. (Kaya Cragun Staehlin)

307th KC-97 refuels a RB-47 returning from a "hush, hush" mission to gather intelligence on Soviet defense along the northern target routes. (Brannon)

Flight crews sprint for their B-47s during a practice alert. (USAF)

Maj. Nutty and crew after their mission that saved a 55th SRW RB-47. L-R. Maj. Nutty, Lt. Berry, Lt. Schuck, Sgt Worm, A1C Beucus, Sgt McLain. (Beucus)

# Cold War Cornhuskers: The 307th Bomb Wing Lincoln Air Force Base Nebraska 1955-1965

First Class seats in the Lincoln bound KC-97. (Tarwater)

It was always nice to get home to those who had stayed behind and tended the home front. (USAF)

Moments after the Klaxon went off, crews hit the ladders to start Operation: ROMEO ALERT STAKE OUT. (USAF)

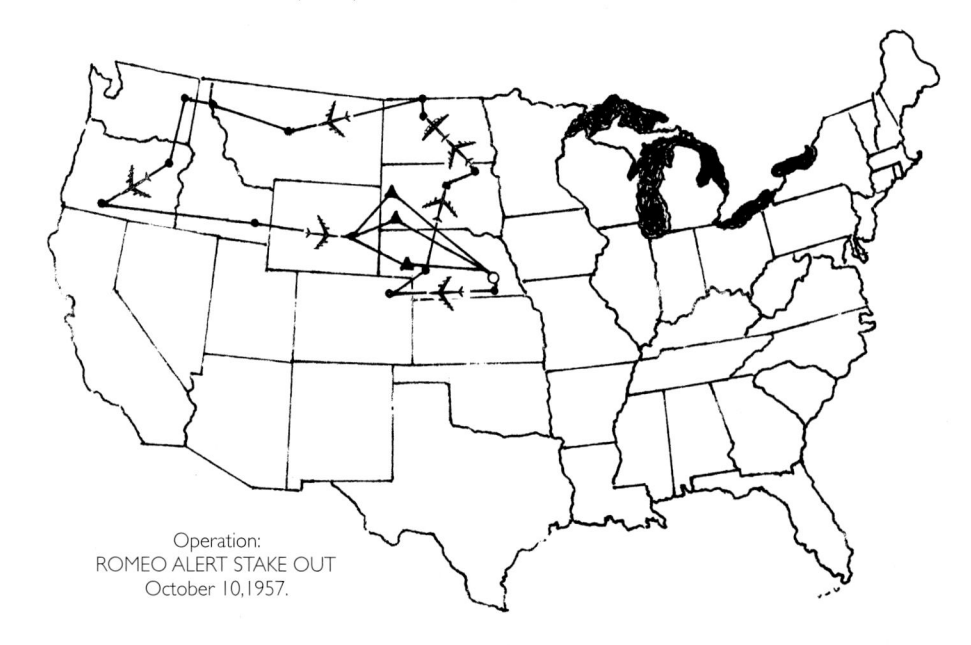

Operation: ROMEO ALERT STAKE OUT October 10, 1957.

80

## 1957

Alert Taxi Plan November 1957.

Lt. Robert Cox was awarded THE SOLDIERS MEDAL for his action during the November 1957 F-80 crash that destroyed two B-47s on the flight line. (Cox)

Operation PACESETTER X
December 7-8, 1957

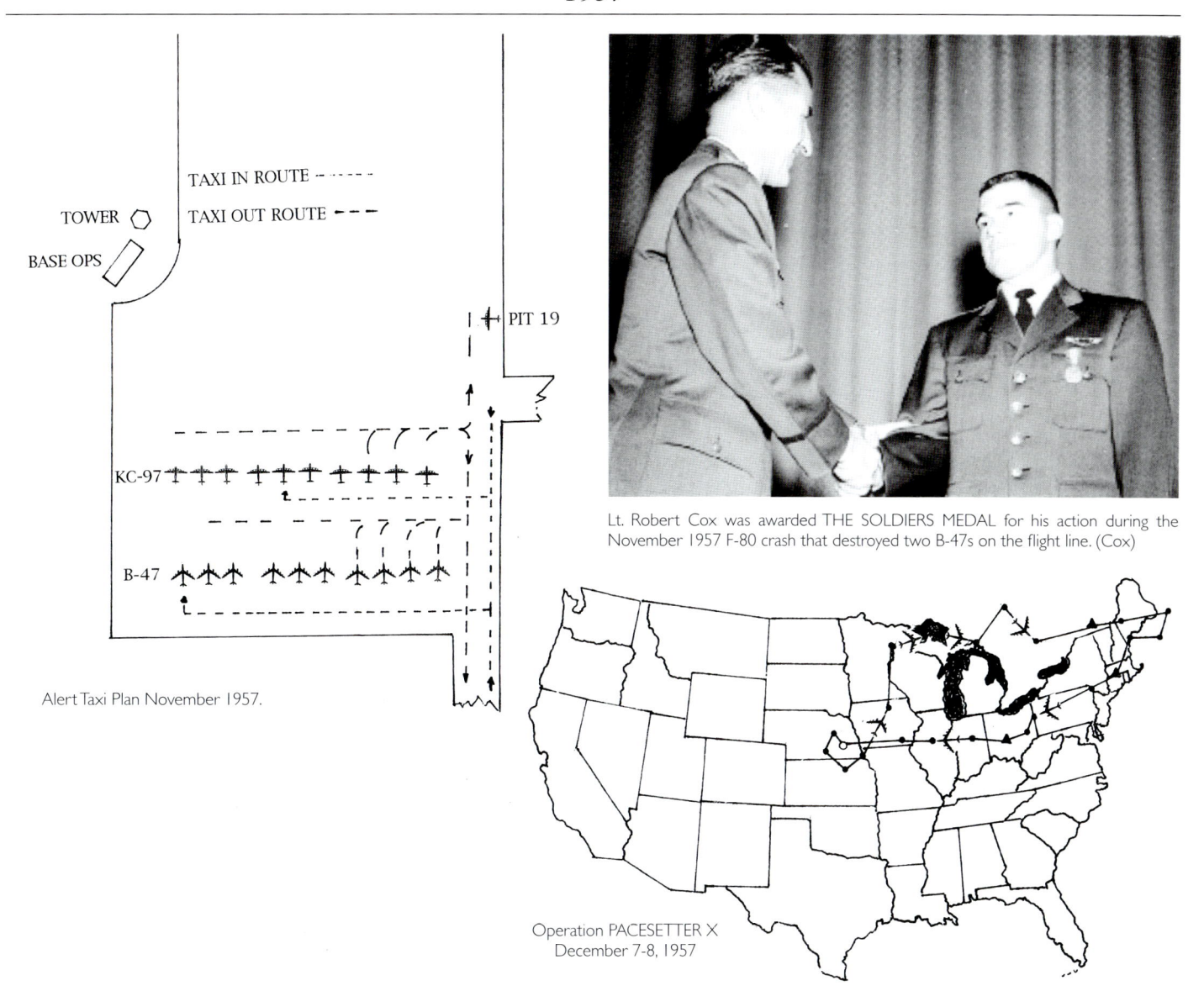

Streaming black smoke, a B-47 lifts from the runway on another training mission. (USAF)

# 1958

1958 would be a year of dramatic changes for Strategic Air Command and the 307th Bomb Wing. More and more giant B-52s were rolling off the production line at Boeing to equip new wings. Long-range missiles were no longer a fantasy, but reality. Soviet air defense capability had grown, making high level attacks almost suicidal. SAC had to change to remain a viable deterrent force. If SAC changed, the 307th would have to follow suit and change with it.

The 307th began the year with over nineteen hundred officers and airmen. There were forty-eight combat ready bomber crews and nineteen combat ready tanker crews. There were forty-seven B-47s and twenty KC-97s sitting on the south end of the flight line.

Winter weather closed in on Lincoln on January 4th. High winds piled up the heavy snow into drifts in town and on the base. Duty personnel had a difficult time getting to the base from town. For safety, there was a general slowdown till the storm moved on and the plows had time to clear the roads.

By the 6th, operations were approaching normal for winter. The flight line and taxiways were clear and the planes dug out. Crews assigned to fly the first Reflex deployment met in the briefing room and went over the last-minute details. At the briefing, the weather wizards mentioned they were watching a low-pressure area moving out of the Rockies. Depending on how it moved, another round of old man winter could be arriving at the patch by the afternoon of the 7th.

Out on the flight line the crew chiefs were getting the five Reflex birds ready. The first five B-47s to make the Reflex flight were 53-2141, 53-6244, 53-2413, 53-1906 and 53-2134. They had been selected for the first Reflex because of their proven reliability record.

Sure enough, about 1200 on the 7th light flurries began to drift down on the flight line. By 1500, the flurries had turned to heavy snow. At 1800 it was downright nasty with heavy snow, gusty winds and almost zero visibility. It was soon evident the Reflex flight would be rescheduled.

The snow abated around midnight, then the snow removal crews hit the concrete like Marines hitting the beach. Working through the night, they had everything fairly well cleared by O-Light hundred. It was up to the ground crews to man the shovels and dig the planes out, then get them ready for the flight.

The Reflex operation was able to launch that evening. It would be a long night for the crews. From Lincoln they flew to the northeast over Green Bay, Wisconsin, and on towards Maine. Off the coast, they met their tanker support and took on their "SAC Snack" of JP-4 to get them across the Atlantic.

It was a welcome moment when the lead navigator spotted the English coast on a sweep of his radar scope. Not too bad a job; they were only about ten miles off the route centerline. Now, all they had to do was contact the traffic center and clear into British airspace, then find Greenham Common. When the planes arrived, the ground crews were waiting with wrenches in hand to get the birds turned around. They had to completely service, repair and cock the birds that had arrived. After a sleepless night, the aircraft were declared "cocked" by 1313 Zulu on January 10th.

Fuel leaks continued to cause problems for air operations. 53-1901 would be listed as Out of Commission (OOC)) from January 11th to the 26th due to leaks. 53-6243 went OOC on the 16th due to leaks. She wouldn't be back on the flying schedule until the last day of the month. January would see a total of twenty-one sorties canceled because of leaks in the fuel system.

8th Air Force postponed the Reflex launch on January 14th due to bad weather along the route and at the forward base. The launch on January 21st was also held back twenty-four hours due to bad weather and lack of tanker support. Old man winter was standing in the way all across the USA and the tankers were grounded. Maybe, the name should be changed from Reflex to Noflex.

None of the Reflex crews leaving on the 22nd, or the residents of Lincoln, had any idea of a brutal event that had taken place during the day in the Belmont area of Lincoln. When the news of three residents found murdered in a run-down frame house hit the papers several days later, it would be just the prelude to fear and panic that would grip not only Lincoln, but also the entire state of Nebraska.

Even with the bad winter weather, the 307th managed to fly 198 sorties for just over 1200 hours in the air. These sorties included 34 "pop up" training bomb runs. The B-47s of the 307th made 68 refueling attempts with 38 scored as effective.

The 307th AREFS flew a Texaco Tanker mission on the 25th. The lone KC-97 left Lincoln and flew to Grand Island. For the next five hours they flew a racetrack orbit from Grand Island to Sioux Falls. Four receivers arrived and practiced dry hook ups, transfer and disconnects, then did it all over again. The last item on the profile was to practice emergency disconnect and breakaway.

# 1958

The tankers were busy in January. They supported not only local sorties, but also other wings stationed in the Midwest. They flew tanker support for Operation Gallant Stride. The squadron transferred a total of over a million pounds of JP-4 during the month.

On January 27th, Lincoln police were summoned to the Belmont area of Lincoln to investigate a strange situation at the home of Marion Bartlett. Members of the family had tried to contact the family of the run-down frame house for over a week. The police found the house empty, and there was a note on the door saying everyone was sick and to stay away. During a search of the property the police made a horrible discovery. The bodies of Marion Bartlett, his wife Velda, and their two-and-a-half-year old daughter Betty Jean were found in several of the buildings on the property. Missing was young Caril Ann Fugate, Marion Bartlett's stepdaughter.

What the police didn't know was that Caril's boyfriend, Charles Starkweather, had committed the crimes. Caril and Charlie had stayed in the house for several days after the killings. He and Caril were now headed for Bennett, Nebraska, about fifteen miles southeast of Lincoln.

On the way to Bennett they got stuck in the snow. Bennett High School students Robert Jensen and his date Carol King stopped and offered their help. Charlie responded by murdering them and hiding their bodies in a storm cellar at a nearby abandoned farm. At Bennett Charlie killed an old friend of the family, seventy year old August Meyers. Later that day Charlie and Caril returned to Lincoln.

On the evening of the 28th, Lincoln police were dispatched to the home of Lauer Ward, President of Capital Steel. In the opulent home on the southeast side of Lincoln they found the bodies of Lauer, his wife Clara, and their housekeeper Lillian Fend.

Five B-47s were scheduled to launch on a Reflex deployment on January 28th. The ground crews seemed antsy, in a hurry to get the birds launched so they could button things up and get home. As soon as the Reflex aircraft were England-bound, the ground crews went home as soon as they could. They had heard about the local murder spree and wanted to make sure their families were all right. The aircraft launched on time, but had to divert to Goose Bay when the tankers didn't show up.

So, who was this Charles Starkweather? He was born on November 24, 1938. Growing up, he was always being picked on by other boys in his school because of his thick glasses. He spoke with a noticeable speech impediment. His only real interests were guns, guitars, and his prized 1949 Ford hot-rod. He liked to talk about girls, especially his girlfriend Caril Ann Fugate. He wore his blondish hair in the popular combed forward ducktail and bore a striking resemblance to the actor James Dean.

T.R. Taylor moonlighted at a gas station on "O" Street. T.R. recalled that Charlie would stop in once in a while during his route on the garbage truck. He was usually quiet and liked to talk about fast cars and girls. What T.R. didn't know was that Charlie's first victim was Robert Colvert, a gas station attendant, on December 1, 1957.

Robert and Genelle Cox lived on 42nd St., just off "O". Genelle recalled:

"One time, Bob was on the roof adjusting the TV antenna. Bob saw our garbage man (Starkweather) trying to persuade a little neighbor girl who lived across the street to go with him. He was walking thru the alley behind our place. The mother saw this and called her child into the house and phoned the Lincoln Police. A motorcycle policeman immediately came by, but Starkweather was nowhere to be found."

Lincoln, Nebraska, was gripped by terror when the news of the latest murders broke. The Sheriff called for a posse of a hundred men; he got more then two hundred, armed with everything from sidearms to shotguns. The National Guard was called out to guard banks in the Lincoln area. Several businesses reserved whole blocks of hotel rooms for their employees so they didn't have to go home.

Lincoln was transformed into Dodge City, Kansas, on a Saturday night. It was very common to see people walking down "O" Street near Gold's Department store armed with loaded Winchesters, shotguns or packing a Colt. Sales of firearms skyrocketed as citizens armed themselves for personal protection.

On-base security was increased. Air Police patrolled the housing area around the clock. Children were kept inside and not allowed to play with friends on the playground. Wives of deployed crews kept tabs on each other just to play it safe. Tom Pauza recalled:

"I was on Alert at the base during the height of Starkweather's rampage. I called home to see how Anita and the kids were doing. She said, 'We're doing fine. Mary (Watt) and Gail (Mulkey), our neighbors, are here and we're having coffee. We've locked the doors of the house, parked the car outside, unlocked and left the keys in it.' I asked her, why? She replied, 'If Starkweather is in the neighborhood and he is looking for a car, we don't want him coming in the house to look for the keys.'"

Since Charlie worked on a garbage truck, he knew the streets of Lincoln like the back of his hand. Even so, he realized that things were getting too hot for him in Lincoln. Charlie and Caril drove out Cornhusker Highway past the base and headed west on Highway 34. Charlie and Caril were captured near Douglas, Wyoming, on January 29th, but not before they added one last victim to their rampage. Their killing spree may have been finished, but for months Lincoln remained an armed camp.

The wing received Operations Order 215-58, code name Noon Day, on 3 February. This was a Joint Chiefs of Staff directed mission to test the 37th Air Division. The 307th was to provide maximum support for the operation. The 307th would fly the Bravo and Romeo portion of the mission. The mission would include three RBS runs, navigation, fighter attacks and maximum use of ECM-equipped B-47s. There was no execution date; the wing would be vulnerable for this operation until 3 June.

On the 5th, a directive came in from SAC Headquarters. The directive prohibited practice fighter attacks during all future missions. The directive was a direct result of a mid-air collision between a 19th Bomb Wing B-47 and a F-86D during a training mission. The pilot of the F-86D was able to eject safely. The crew of the B-47 managed to drop the Mark-15 bomb in the ocean off the mouth of the Savannah River and make a safe landing.

For several weeks, the military mounted a massive offshore search for the missing Mark-15. The news media stirred the rumor pot with claims that the Air Force was searching for a "highly classified, armed, atomic bomb". Classified, yes; however, it had never been armed while aboard the B-47. The weapon was never found, and as far as can be determined still lies somewhere off the mouth of the Savannah River.

A special order was received by the 307th on Tuesday, 11 February. The wing was to generate the force and be ready to fly Operation Noon Day upon getting the launch order. The wing would fly on two consecutive days. The first wave would fly Bravo route; the next day the second wave would fly Romeo route. Maximum use of ECM aircraft was directed on both days.

When the launch order arrived on the 12th, the 307th was ready to go. Twelve B-47s launched at one-minute intervals. Two Phase V ECM-equipped B-47s launched to provide jamming for the strike force. Leaving the base, the force would climb and head for the first turn point over Beatrice.

Passing through 3,000 feet, the Ravens began the move to their pod in the bomb bay of the B-47. This wasn't the easiest trip in the world to make. During take off, the Ravens had to be in the forward section of the

## Cold War Cornhuskers: The 307th Bomb Wing Lincoln Air Force Base Nebraska 1955-1965

aircraft. To get to the pod they had to open the pressure door and carefully climb down the stowed entry ladder, then move sideways while hanging onto the ladder into the narrow crawlway, referred to as the "hell hole".

Now, it was about a fifteen-foot crawl to the pod. Fifteen feet wasn't very far to crawl on your hands and knees, right? Well, they didn't call it the hell hole for nothing. First, it was dark, narrow and claustrophobic. Once inside, there was no turning around. If you had to go back you had to crawl backwards. Then, there were the aluminum ribs, spaced just right so a knee would end up on one of them with almost every move forward or back.

At the far end of the tunnel, the first Raven would have to open the pressure door to the pod and squeeze through the opening, climb over the chemical toilet and wiggle into his seat. The other one would have to close the pressure door and make his way around the equipment and into his seat.

The two pod dwellers would strap in, pressurize the pod, make sure the heaters were on and the oxygen system working. They would report when they were ready so the climb could continue.

Sitting in the pod facing to the rear, the two occupants would warm up their equipment and check the frequencies so when it was time to start playing their "music," everything would be ready for the outgoing "mail".

After turning at Beatrice, the flight headed for a turn point near Des Moines, Iowa. At Des Moines they made a radio check and turned for the first target at St. Louis, Missouri. By the time they reached the IP at Hannibal, the Bomb/Nav systems were warmed up and the bombing parameters set. Radar returns on the target were beaming brightly in the scopes. Contact was made with the scoring station to record the run. When the tone cut off signaling "bombs away", the bombers were pulled around into the breakaway turn. One target down, two to go.

The navigation leg began at Decatur, Illinois. The leg would take the flight north to Green Bay, Wisconsin, then out over Lake Michigan for gunnery in the R-502 range. After fireout, the planes headed for Sault St. Marie, Michigan, and then turned to the northwest, continuing the nav leg with a checkpoint at Paqua River, Ontario. Crossing back into the United States near Thunder Bay, Ontario, the bombers continued to Ashland, Wisconsin, the IP for the RBS at Minneapolis. After hitting the target, the mission continued to the next IP at Fort Dodge, Iowa, then back to the target at Omaha. The aiming point at Omaha was the highest grain elevator at the Updike Grain Co.

After Omaha, the force flew down the Missouri River to Nebraska City and began letting down for approach to Lincoln. Once below 10,000 feet the Ravens had to move back through the crawlway and squeeze through the entryway. The pressurization had been dumped so they could get the pressure door between the crawlway and the cockpit open. After flying the tear drop approach, the B-47s came back for landing at the patch. All that was left was debriefing, finish up the paperwork and go home.

The next day the 307th flew the Romeo portion of the operation. It was the same route, with the same targets. The only major difference was there was no fireout over Lake Michigan. At the last minute a new twist was added. 8th Air Force added a page to the operation order called Noon Day Sierra. This aspect of the operation had not been assigned to the 307th in the original operations order. Now, it became a test to see if the 307th could pull off the last minute change.

The plan called for three Phase V B-47s to fly a special route, timing their flight to arrive at the control point in time to provide jamming for the 340th Bomb Wing during their target runs.

Takeoff for the three-ship cell was spread out at one-minute intervals. Their initial climb-out heading was towards Norfolk, Nebraska. Passing through 3,000 feet, the Ravens headed for their nest in the pod. Until they were needed they would just sit back and monitor their equipment.

With the Ravens snug in their nest, the cell turned towards Alliance, Nebraska, to begin a navigation leg towards the north, checking in over the Minot, North Dakota, VOR. At Minot, the navigator gave a correction to heading 040 for the next leg into Canada. The next checkpoint was Winnipeg, Manitoba, then northeast to Lake Winnipeg and the H-Hour Control Point (HHCP) about fifty miles north of Thunder Bay, Ontario.

The cell was right on the time hack to pick up the incoming 340th Bomb Wing. The ravens were ready to start their music and send out the mail. To add to the confusion on the ground, the jammers turned off their Identification Friend or Foe (IFF) transmitters and separated for their assigned ECM target corridors.

All along the three corridors the Ravens sent their mail and dispensed chaff into the stream. Over Lake Superior, they picked up indications that fighters were heading out from Duluth, Minnesota. The Ravens picked up the incoming "Little Photo" and sent some special "Chatter" their way.

Post-mission results showed the 307th had performed very well on the Bravo and Romeo missions, as there were only three unreliable bomb runs. Navigation was rated as excellent, with everyone making the end navigation checkpoint within fifteen miles of the route centerline. One B-47 aborted the mission due to fuel leaks but was replaced by a spare. The last-minute addition of Sierra caused some problems in generating the Phase V aircraft. Thanks to some dedicated ground crews, the aircraft were turned around and ready for launch on time. The 307th was scored as "outstanding" in their ability to provide jamming support for the mission.

While the crews were busy with Noon Day, the wing staff received another directive from Omaha. This one was code named Team Play. SAC would initiate a series of no-notice practice alerts. This would be a ground response exercise. Alert aircraft would perform a Coco alert. A follow-on force would then be generated. Execution for Team Play would be by standard SAC voice execution message.

Just a routine start to another Reflex day at Greenham Common. Alert crews had finished the morning preflight by 1000 on 18 February. Now, just sit around and wait for the horn to go off for another practice alert, or maybe the real thing. By now, the crews had turned alert response into an unofficial competition called "Who's Gonna Be First". Some took the competition to the extreme. One navigator at Greenham Common sat in a jeep for seven and a half hours so his aircraft would be "first" in the next alert.

Later that Tuesday afternoon, Granville 20 from the 340th BW departed Greenham Common for a return flight to Whiteman AFB, Missouri. Shortly after take off they called the tower declaring an emergency. The aircraft commander had fire indications in the left inboard engines. With two engines out, they had to get the heavyweight B-47 lighter for an emergency landing. The tower told them to jettison their wing tanks over the designated on base drop area, which ran parallel to the runway. Caught up in the emergency and trying to maintain control, the pilot lost visual contact with the runway and called the tower for help.

During the conversation between the tower and Granville 20, the base commander arrived, responding to the emergency. He interrupted the transmissions, distracting the tower personnel. At one point he countermanded the instructions that were being given to the flight crew. Within moments, the situation on the ground and in the air was going to hell in a hand basket in a hurry.

Those on the flight line watched as the small drogue chutes appeared from the tail cones of the two 1,700-gallon wing tanks. Departing the B-47, they started failing towards the ground. Near Hangar 2 (Building 301) people watched for a moment, then started running like hell. One of the tanks was hurtling towards the hangar. The other was headed for a B-47 that was being preflighted. Like the people at the hangar, those around 53-6204 began to scatter. Others watched transfixed as the two tanks fell towards the flight line.

One of the tanks smashed into the hangar; the other made a direct hit on 6204. On impact, over 20,000 pounds of flammable jet fuel sprayed across the flight line and through the hangar. In the blink of an eye the fuel ignited, causing red-orange flames to roll and billow into a growing column of boiling black smoke. Tom Pauza was on Alert that day:

"It was mid-afternoon at RAF Greenham Common when the klaxon was sounded. Jeff Finch, Joe Cameron and I responded. On our way to the ramp we realized this was more than a practice Alert. We saw billowing smoke and fire in the hangar and near the refueling pit. We were able to drive between the two and get to our Alert aircraft, which was on the opposite side of the entrance to the ramp.

"Boarding the airplane, it was obvious what we had to do; we were parked about 150 to 200 yards from the pit and an aircraft on the pit was burning. We had no idea what configuration the airplane was in and we were close enough to feel the heat. It seemed forever before we got the engines started. I can't remember if we had any contact with the tower or if we started all six engines. Anyway, between a lot of 'hurry ups,' checklist responses, and 'watch outs' we did manage a brief moment of levity. Jeff and I exchanged a few comments that amounted to 'where would you rather be than where you are.' Jeff was a laid-back sort who handled 'pucker time' well. We taxied the airplane out of immediate danger. We were quite relieved that there was no explosion."

Within minutes base fire crews responded to the scene of the accident. Fire crews from RAF Welford were brought in to help contain the fire. 6204 had been serviced and was fully loaded with fuel when the accident happened, adding more fuel for the growing conflagration. The fire was contained, but it took over twelve hours to completely douse it.

The next day, the investigation team began the grim task of sifting through the accident scene. The crew chief of 6204 and an A & E technician perished in the accident. A2C Clive Wilson of the 307th was injured. Several personnel inside the hangar were also injured. Then there was the rumor that, at the height of the emergency, the base commander left the base and went to Bournemouth.

The final accident report found almost everyone involved in the emergency to be at fault. The investigation ruled pilot error for the pilot of Granville 20, even though he was able to make a safe landing. Tower personnel were cited for failure to maintain control of the situation. The base commander was criticized for having caused confusion in the tower by interrupting tower personnel and countermanding instructions, and he was subsequently relieved of duty.

Along with the loss of life and the destruction of a B-47, the accident caused the complete loss of Hangar 2. This meant Base Operations, Maintenance Control, Weather and several other offices had to be moved to other locations on base.

The 307th finished the month with over 1,300 flying hours. They made a total of 102 effective refuelings. "Pop up" training suffered due to the weather, alert and Reflex. By the end of the month the 307th had made 40 Reflex deployments.

On 6 March 6 the Command Post received a voice message.

**"THIS IS COTTER PIN. PREPARE TO COPY.**
**BREAK..BREAK**
**THIS IS A PRACTICE, REPEAT PRACTICE, SAC ALERT.**
**TEAM PLAY GROUND RULES APPLY. NOTIFY THE SENIOR COMMANDER PRESENT AND INITIATE ALERTING PROCEDURES.**
**BREAK..BREAK**
**AUTHENTICATION IS, YANKEE, MIKE, KILO, ALFA"**

When the message had been authenticated the Klaxon began its ear-piercing wail. Crews dropped everything and began the sprint for the birds. Alert vehicles jockeyed for position as they sped to the alert area. When they arrived the cars skidded to a stop. Crews piled out and hit the ramp on a dead run towards the hanging entry ladders. Within minutes the first B-47 reported.

**"Adams 32, Ready to Taxi."**

One by one the alert birds reported, then taxied to the end of the runway. The first B-47 moved into takeoff position. Clouds of exhaust blasted back as throttles were pushed forward to one hundred percent. Brakes released, the heavy bomber crawled forward to begin the takeoff roll. Then the roar of the six jet engines fell off to a high-pitched whine as the throttles were pulled back. One by one each of the alert birds took the active runway, went to full power, released brakes, then pulled the power off and taxied down the runway.

As they arrived back at the alert area, each was met by the crew chief, ready to guide the plane back into the parking slot. When the crew came down the ladder, they let the crew chief know if there were any problems to be fixed. During the Coco alert, the planes had burned several thousand pounds of fuel. The fuel and other fluids had to be checked, topped off, and the gross weight of the aircraft refigured. Then the crew had to go back through the process of "cocking" the aircraft all over again.

According to the orders, the follow-on force would now be brought up and made ready for launch. There was a constant stream of aircraft being towed to the refueling pits for servicing. The aircraft were towed back to their slots, reparked, and loaded with everything needed for launching on the mission. Under the outline for Team Play-Ground Rules, everything would be accomplished up to the point of launch. The entire exercise was a ground response with no launch of the aircraft. Just another exercise to keep the troops on their toes, or dying feet.

Overall the alert went well. All alert aircraft made the runway and returned to the alert area. The follow-on force was generated according to the operations orders. The 307th was given a score of "Excellent" for the first Team Play exercise.

Anytime there was a major accident in SAC, word of the accident spread across the command like the plague. There would always be speculation as to what had gone wrong to cause the accident. Was it something mechanical, weather or crew error? On Tuesday, 13 March, a B-47 assigned to the 379th Bomb Wing at Homestead AFB, Florida, crashed on takeoff, killing the crew. On the same day, a TB-47 crashed near McConnell AFB, Kansas, when the left wing failed near Butt Line 35. Two major accidents in one day!

SAC Headquarters sent a triple flash message to all wings on 18 March. Starting immediately, nuclear weapons would no longer be carried during training flights. This was a direct result of an accidental dropping of an unarmed nuclear weapon near Mars Bluff, South Carolina.

A B-47 from the 308th Bomb Wing was flying a routine flight. The navigator was in the bomb bay practicing the in-flight insertion of the detonator when the aircraft hit some turbulence. In the confined space, he grabbed for something to hold on to. He happened to grab the bomb salvo cables, releasing the unarmed nuke.

The weapon landed in a backwoods farmyard. The explosives in the bomb detonated, blowing out windows and causing injuries to the farm family. Since the weapon was not armed there was no nuclear reaction, just one very large explosion. The result was a huge hole in the South Carolina countryside and a lot of medical bills to be paid by SAC.

On Friday, 21 March, B-47 52-244, from the 306th Bomb Wing, left MacDill on a training mission. They made a series of low-level bomb runs

## Cold War Cornhuskers: The 307th Bomb Wing Lincoln Air Force Base Nebraska 1955-1965

near Avon Park, Florida. Then, they made a low pass by the control tower to check the landing gear. After the low pass, they began a climbing turn to the left. Without warning the right wing folded over the top of the aircraft, sending it into a spiral dive towards the ground. The original members of the 307th may recall that 52-244 was one of the original B-47s assigned to the wing back in 1955.

Returning from a mission on 29 March, the crew of KC-97 #52-2803 noticed a vibration and unusual sound coming from the left side as the tanker landed and taxied to the ramp. An examination of the left main gear found a crack in the wheel extending all the way to the rim. It was not noticed during preflight due to it being on the inside of the dual wheel assembly. Needless to say, the crew chiefs grabbed their flashlights and double-checked the wheels for cracks on their own tankers.

By the first week in April, construction on the base lake was underway again. At an 818th Air Division Staff meeting earlier in the year the lake had been given a name. It was to be named after Capt Russell Bowling, who had perished in the crash of his B-47 in England during the TDY in 1956.

Another item came out during the meeting: Col Hoisington thought it would be a good idea if everyone on base would "volunteer" eight hours of his spare time to help build the lake. So began a long line of "volunteers" clamoring to be first in line for the project. Yeah, Right!

On 3 April, in response to the B-47 accidents in March, the Oklahoma City Air Material Area (OCAMA) at Tinker AFB issued a flight supplemental warning. The warning limited the maximum airspeed on the B-47 to 360 knots. It also placed a 1.5G limit on any maneuver. They also required that a field inspection of the wing root area be conducted.

April 8th turned out to be a very interesting day. By the end of the day, paperwork on three potentially dangerous flying incidents would be filled out (in triplicate of course) and forwarded to SAC Headquarters.

That Tuesday, 52-4218 was deploying back to the U.S. from a Reflex commitment. They had to divert to Goose Bay when their tanker didn't show up for refueling. As they taxied in, what appeared to be fuel was streaming from the bomb bay, all the way back to the brake chute doors. The bomb bay doors were opened and fluid poured out onto the ramp. The aircraft was carrying a "pickled" J-47 engine during the flight back to Lincoln. This was quite common; just hoist an engine pickle barrel into the bomb bay and attach it to the shackles. Somehow, along the way the container had been ruptured and the "pickle juice" leaked out, covering the bottom of 4218. The safety report brought out the fact that an incident of this kind could have been a disaster due to the fire hazard presented by the leaking fluid.

During a refueling mission, 52-2804 had been assigned an altitude of 18,000 feet by air traffic control (ATC) at Omaha. Entering the sixty-mile radius of the Omaha bomb plot, they ran into some clouds. The KC-97 was advised to climb immediately to 20,000 feet, as there was a B-47 somewhere between 18 and 18,600 feet. A quick check with Omaha found no other authorization for that altitude had been given. The B-47 had been ordered to climb or let down as necessary. Radar indicated the two aircraft passed each other after almost merging on the screen.

Later that night 53-1906 was returning from a flight. After landing, the crew stopped to jettison the brake chute. The copilot watched the chute drift away, and then he noticed sparks following along with the chute in the darkness. The crew was unaware of a serious fuel leak until it was spotted as they parked the aircraft. The combination of flying sparks and leaking fuel was enough to cause the fire trucks to be called out of their stations, just in case.

To preclude the possibility of SAC bombers being caught on the ground, the concept of Positive Control was initiated on April 15, 1958. Under this system, the Commander-in-Chief of SAC could launch the Alert bombers and get them in the air and headed toward their targets. A geographical point was assigned to each sortie. After launch, the crews would fly to the designated Positive Control Turn-Around Point (PCTAP). Upon reaching it, the strike force would hold in an orbiting pattern if they had not received the "go" code. If the "go" code was received, it had to be authenticated by the crew. If the message were an authentic strike message, the bombers would continue to their targets. If the code could not be verified, the bombers would return to their bases. Pete Todd recalled:

"In those days, because of the expectation of intentional as well as collateral jamming, SAC had elaborate, redundant, overlapping means to push the go-code out to the crews. Primary source was the three numbered air force (NAF) HQs via High Frequency radio. Alternate means included SAC's airborne command post, UHF radios aboard launched rockets, crew to crew, UHF-- literally **any** available channel was to be employed to disseminate the go code. All crewmembers would normally be monitoring all available channels and the copilot on the B-47 would copy the message, crosscheck authentication with the AC and, if the message were valid, the AC and Nav would break open their plastic authentication documents ('crack open the cookies' in crewmember jargon) and compare the strike codes with those in the message. If everything was valid, they were authorized to depart the PCTAP and strike their target."

Pete continued:

"That reminds me of one of my long-forgotten giggles. On every training mission, the crew was required to copy and authenticate one or more so-called 'Foxtrot' messages, which were transmitted on HF at designated times. These were 'canned' messages that had no meaning in and of themselves, but were designed to simulate positive control message traffic. Any SAC Command Post and control tower was supposed to maintain the latest Foxtrot message and transmit it to flight crews on request. On a night mission early in my crew training, my AC told me to get 'Foxtrot traffic' from the Little Rock AFB tower. I dutifully called the tower and asked, 'Do you have traffic?' to which they dutifully replied, 'Traffic is one B-47 in the pattern and one KC-97 on short final.'"

"Pop Up" training continued during the month when weather was favorable. These missions were flown in specific areas where low-level flying would not cause problems with population centers. As always, this kind of flying could be dicey at times.

On 16 April a crew departed Lincoln in 53-2278 for a routine pop up training mission. There was an instructor pilot on board that day. They made the first run over western North Dakota, then flew towards Fargo and turned to the southwest into South Dakota. The instructor had flown the same route several days earlier. He mentioned to the pilot that he had spotted a radio tower that was higher than 500 feet above ground level and the approach to the tower was deceptive. It could only be spotted at the last minute. He also mentioned they were going to be approaching that area in a few minutes.

Approaching Wessington Springs, South Dakota, the IP mentioned they should be approaching the area where the tower had been spotted. Within seconds the aircraft commander spotted the tower dead ahead, 12 o'clock high and pulled 2278 into a steep, gut-wrenching bank to avoid the tower. The B-47 hurtled past the tower, missing it by about one hundred feet. There were actually two towers near Wessington Springs. Both towers were over six hundred feet tall and neither of them was on any of the flight charts. A note of interest: those towers are still there, just south of Wessington Springs. There is a low level training route in the area. Both towers are now clearly marked on the Sectional Chart. Oops!

That same day a crew was flying pop up training in 53-2139, heading south from the IP near Storm Lake, Iowa. They were flying at 19,630 feet. Without warning, another B-47 crossed in front of them, dangerously close. The other aircraft had not cleared through the bombing range and the bomb plot had no knowledge of the stray B-47. Oops again!

News arrived that a B-47 had exploded and crashed during a refueling flight on 8 April. The crash site was near North Collins, New York. Then, on the 15th, two B-47s crashed. One was from the 306th Bomb Wing at MacDill AFB, Florida; the other was from the 509th Bomb Wing at Pease AFB, New Hampshire.

The MacDill B-47 took off with thunderstorms in the area and crashed about five minutes after takeoff. Initial report was there was a stress crack in the wing that failed in the turbulence of the thunderstorm.

SAC had lost six B-47s in less than a month. Three of the accidents were a direct result of wing failure. SAC's initial response was a Command-wide directive to inspect for stress cracks in the wing area. The initial inspection found cracks in more aircraft than originally expected. Then a real bombshell hit the fleet. The investigation of the North Collins, New York, crash showed one of the main wing-to-fuselage fasteners had failed, causing the entire wing to buckle and fail.

SAC's fleet of B-47s was in deep trouble and so was the nation. At the time, the B-47 was the only jet bomber in the SAC inventory with sufficient numbers to maintain a strong nuclear attack posture. Without the B-47 on alert, the Soviet Union had an open road to try something if they wanted. At this point, the B-47 was a danger to her flight crews and the nation was in danger of losing its main deterrent force.

Boeing and OCAMA started burning the midnight oil trying to figure out the problem and how to fix it. During construction, the left and right wing assemblies had been bolted to the wing center section with twelve bolts. The wing was mated to the fuselage and secured in place by two large milk bottle shaped pins and two smaller pop bottle shaped pins. The solution was complex. Every B-47 in the fleet would have to be sent to a depot and have the milk bottle pins inspected and replaced if needed.

On 24 April the B-47 was placed under special flight restrictions. Takeoff weight, cruising speed and climbing speed were all reduced. Jet penetration descent was limited to 300 feet per minute. The restrictions were intended to reduce stress on the B-47 wings until they could be returned to the depot and be repaired.

On 25 April, Lincoln AFB was devastated by the crash of a B-47 assigned to the 98th Bomb Wing. The aircraft had taken off from Goose Bay and crashed on the ice a few moments later, killing 2 of the crew. That made seven Class A accidents involving the B-47 in less than a month. The crash at Goose Bay was ruled pilot error. The wings had not failed, and the accident was not attributed to the ongoing crisis in the fleet.

The Reflex crews at Greenham Common were tested with fourteen Alfa and sixteen Bravo Alerts in April. The average response time had improved. It may have improved, but waking to the blare of the horn at 0200 was a real pain in the butt. Not only was it a pain, it robbed the crews of sleep. Try going back to sleep after the adrenaline level had been blasted to pucker level ten, with the thought you may be headed into the wild blue yonder to incinerate targets in a nuclear doomsday.

May began with increased effort to complete Bowling Lake. It was scheduled to be finished by the end of the month. More "volunteers" were needed for the final push to completion. A group of Civil Air Patrol cadets had a week encampment at the base in early May. They "volunteered" to help for several days on the lake.

Every morning "volunteers" would line up for their shovels, then head for their assigned works areas. There are a lot of memories of working on the lake, most of them not happy. One volunteer recalled marching to the work area with a group whistling the tune from the movie *Bridge On the River Kwai*.

Another volunteer recalled helping place rocks along the shoreline to prevent erosion. During his riprap tour of duty, he happened to look down the line of rock pickers. There in the mud and grudge was none other than his wing commander, Col Elkins Read, Jr., covered with mud just like the rest of the rock pickers. He was impressed with his boss, as there were no other "full birds" down in the mud and muck.

The schedule for Reflex was changed again in an attempt to make it easier to find enough crews and aircraft to fulfill the commitment. Reflex would now be fourteen days overseas.

Because of the recent rash of accidents with B-47s, SAC decreed the entire B-47 fleet would be scheduled for inspection and repair of the wing center section. Aircraft would be sent to several depots to insure the fleet could be turned around as quickly as possible.

About the same time, the Phase V ECM-equipped B-47s were to be either transferred or reconfigured back to Phase IV-equipped aircraft. SAC believed the pod-equipped aircraft should be placed in wings dedicated to maintaining ECM capabilities.

Another message from Omaha curtailed all "Pop Up" training missions until further notice. Again, this was the result of the impending "Milk Bottle" program. No sense putting undue stress on already stressed aircraft. The flight crews were glad about the news. They wouldn't have to fly missions in aircraft that might have a wing fall off during the mission just to fill in a square on the board.

On 14 May, Andy Devine was back in town for another show at Pershing Auditorium. Like last year he visited the base. He wanted to see how well the lake was coming along. Members of the 370th Bomb Squadron were requested to assemble at the lake wearing their red squadron blazers. Nobody really knew why. Well, one thing was for sure; if they were to wear their red blazers, they wouldn't be expected to work in the mud.

Arriving at the lake, they found Col Hoisington and several other staff officers giving "Jingles" a tour of the lake. There was also a photographer following the entourage. After a lot of the usual shuffling and moving around, the group was in the right pose and the shutter snapped.

Andy Devine had served as a gunner in World War II, and he always felt a special kinship with the Air Force. While on tour, he liked to visit any air base that might be near the city where he was performing. Before he left the base, he donated money to build a small lighthouse on the point at the lake marina. He also promised to be back for the formal dedication of the lake in June.

By 19 May almost all of the work on the lake had been completed. Water was being pumped from nearby Oak Creek to fill the donut shaped lake. There was some last-minute concrete work to be done at the boat ramp and construction of Andy's lighthouse. Several members of the 307th commemorated the event by inscribing the date and "307th BW" in the wet concrete.

The men of the 307th could look out across the lake and smile with a certain amount of pride. The lake had been the brainchild of now B/Gen Perry M Hoisington. He had started the project as a way of providing on-base recreation for off-duty hours. He made sure there were enough "volunteers" to complete the project. The lake was just one of his pet projects. Members of the 307th could look at it, boat on it, and maybe even catch a fish or two. They would give a little grin and say, "Yep, I helped build 'Perry's Puddle!'"

In 1992 Jim Frise happened to run across Gen. Hoisington in Washington, D.C. Jim was able to spend a little time with him at a chance meeting at Duke's restaurant, which was a popular place to eat. During their conversation, Hoisington gave Jim some insight about the command structure and problems at Lincoln. One interesting bit of conversation centered on the lake. Gen. Hoisington revealed to Jim that while working at the lake, Hoisington lost his father's West Point ring somewhere in the muck and mire. He never told his dad the ring had been lost. So for any

# Cold War Cornhuskers: The 307th Bomb Wing Lincoln Air Force Base Nebraska 1955-1965

treasure hunters in Lincoln, somewhere around Bowling Lake there is a West Point ring waiting to be discovered.

The flight restrictions on the B-47s due to Project Milk Bottle were having an adverse effect on the 307th. Over 200 hours were lost during May due to the Milk Bottle restrictions.

If you can't fly enough to complete the 50-8 requirements, then the time should be used to get the birds in the best possible shape. The nose docks were busy all through May. 53-1916 spent time in the docks undergoing five engine changes. 53-1906 had five engines changes and sheet metal work on the ailerons. There were a total of 17 engine changes on B-47s during May.

The 47s may have had flight restrictions, but the KCs had no such problem. The 307th AREFS provided five tankers every week for "Texaco Tanker" and "Taxi Cab" refueling missions. They also flew regular missions outlined on the flying schedule. Boomers transferred over 205,000 gallons of JP-4 during the month.

On 27 May, the first two B-47s assigned to the 307th left for Milk Bottle updates. These were followed on the 29th by two more. This started a constant back and forth stream of B-47s for the updates.

In his monthly report to Omaha, Col Read had the usual statistics showing how the wing had done during the month. There were bright spots and dull spots to report. His overwhelming concern was the effect Project Milk Bottle would have on the wing. He believed, with the restrictions on flying and movement of aircraft to and from the depots, the 307th Bomb Wing would not be Emergency War Order (EWO) capable.

A ground safety incident crossed Col Read's desk. It had him and everyone involved shaking their heads over how lucky everyone had been. The incident brought out a well-known fact; the flight line was a dangerous place to be. The unlucky would be claimed by the grim reaper; the unwary could only believe that dumb luck had prevailed.

Crew chief Merrill Sinclair was working on his bird, 53-4210, parked facing south at Papa 5 on the flight line. During the gunnery portion of the previous day's mission there had been a problem with the 20 mm guns. A crew from the Munitions Maintenance Squadron (MMS) had removed the ammo cans and cleared the feed belts after 4210 had landed. A crew from the A & E Squadron was troubleshooting the problem. What happened next is best told by Merrill:

"Capt Jack Crook was visiting with me at the front of the aircraft. We were out in front near the power cart. Ernie Pence was cleaning the bomb bay doors. Capt Crook had started walking north towards the next row of B-47s. All of a sudden, there was a loud BANG, BANG!! I immediately looked to the rear of the aircraft and saw one of the fire control airmen do a complete 360-degree spin, just like in the old westerns. I set out for the rear of the aircraft at a dead run. The airman was lying on the ground, not hurt, except for a hearing problem.

"We were joined by Capt Crook, who was white as a ghost. Ernie joined us at the rear of the plane. He was also white as a ghost. By this time, the other fire control airman, who was in the cockpit, joined us along with half the personnel on the flight line. The airman was O.K., but lost his hearing for a few days, a very lucky airman.

"Capt Crook had just left and walked towards the next row, when the guns went off. The two rounds bounced off the concrete and flew over his head. No wonder he was white as a ghost.

"When the fire control technicians check out the system, they put a wand up the barrel of the gun to check out the electrical firing circuits. The other technician would dry fire the guns from the cockpit. In this case they had removed the ammo cans, but had forgotten to check and clear the chambers. One round was left in each of the cannons."

Ernie Pence wrote:

"Cadillac Crook was working his way to Base Operations, when there was this very loud BANG! The two rounds dug into the concrete about four inches and ricocheted over Crook's head. I never heard a noise like that; it literally scared the hell out of me, for a short time, anyway. The gunnery tech was laying on the ramp, face down. Nubby (Merrill Sinclair) turned him over, his eyes rolled back in his head, out cold. The MMS crew had pulled the ammo cans, cleared the feed chutes, but had failed to remove the rounds from the chambers. Fortunately, no one was killed."

June kicked off with a constant stream of B-47s coming and going to be updated under the Milk Bottle project. June 2nd found crews flying 53-1916, 53-1853 and 53-1910 to Tinker AFB, Oklahoma, for the project. 307th Field Maintenance checked the records of all the B-47s to make sure the aircraft with the highest flight hours were sent to the program first.

Since the B-47s were going to Tinker on a regular basis, standing Alert and going across the pond on Reflex, there weren't many B-47s left to fly training missions. There was the lone TB-47 assigned to the wing. It didn't have a Bomb/Nav System, so it could only be used for maintaining proficiency of the pilots. Also, since it didn't have the pesky bombing system it required fewer man hours to keep it flying. Paul Koski shared crew chief duties on the old TB:

"It didn't break and all we had to do was service it, preflight and launch. Since it only flew about four hours each time, we were turning it around, or as they say, 'double and triple banging it.'

I used to win lots of bets on it when I would ask if anyone knew where the vortex generator timer switch was located. Naturally, they would say the vortex generators didn't give off electricity. It was like asking for a left hand monkey wrench, or sending a new troop for a bucket of prop wash. I would show them, the right side of the forward bulkhead in the bomb bay, the vortex generator timer switch, clearly labeled. It was originally designed to supply current to the generators for deicing, but was deactivated."

June 5th saw the usual activity going on out on the flight line. 53-4224 launched on a routine profile mission. The flight was to include a nav leg, bomb run and air refueling. Tanker support for the flight would be from the 6th AREFS. After completing the bomb run the B-47 began descending for the refueling rendezvous near Columbus, Ohio. The navigator picked up the tanker on radar and gave the AC a slight correction to the left.

As they closed the distance on the tanker, they started running into more and more building cumulus clouds. The closer they flew, the higher the clouds billowed and boiled. Visual contact was made, then lost when the tanker was swallowed by the clouds. It now became a combination of hide and seek on a roller coaster as they went in and out of the clouds.

Over the static filled radio came the call. "**Breakaway, Breakaway, Breakaway!**" Breakaway? They weren't even hooked up yet! 4224 stayed in position until they broke out of the clouds. The KC-97 was nowhere in sight, not even a blip on the search radar. The crew of 4224 finished the rest of the mission and turned towards home.

At debriefing, the crew was wondering what had happened to their tanker. Well, it turned out the tanker called for the breakaway and aborted the mission, just like that, no hello, goodbye or God bless! So, the crew of 4224 was scored as non-effective on the refueling portion of the mission. It was no practice, no points, and a hot under the collar crew.

This was only the first fouled up refueling for June. The 307th had forty-two sorties scheduled with refueling support provided by the 6th AREFS from Walker AFB, New Mexico, and 96th AREFS from Dyess

# 1958

AFB, Texas. Fifteen of these were scored as ineffective, thirteen from the 6th AREFS alone.

The 307th AREFS was also having a less-than-stellar month. Several KC-97s were out for major repair or parts. Then, there was the adverse weather in both the primary and secondary refueling areas that kept causing problems. There were other refueling areas that had clear weather, but couldn't be used under current operational directives. So again, it was no practice, no points, and a lot more hot under the collar.

By Tuesday, June 10th, preparations for the dedication of Bowling Lake were in full swing. The huge aqua-air show had been in the planning for several months. Everyone in the area was invited and the show was billed as the largest special event in the history of the base.

The donut shaped lake covered over twenty-seven acres near the northwest corner of the base. As we know, a lot of the last minute finishing touches were completed by the "volunteers" from various units at the base. By now, over eighty-five million gallons of water had been pumped from Oak Creek to fill the lake. Andy Devine's lighthouse had been built on the point at the marina. Construction of the sportsman's lodge on the north side of the lake was almost complete. All that was left were the signs in the parking lots, traffic control, and a thousand and one last-minute details.

Several months ago BGen Hoisington had held a planning session for the dedication. He suggested that a memorial plaque with Capt Russell Bowling's name and story on it be unveiled at the dedication. Lou Webber wrote:

"I told Gen. Hoisington that I felt strongly that we needed more than a plaque that said Bowling Lake. I said it needed something like a statue. He replied, 'Well, make a statue then.' So, I got a book by a sculptor named Zorack, and set out to make a statue. By the way, my statue of Russ was my first.

"The statue was made of plastalene, which is a clay-like material that never hardens. It will get softer when warm and harder when cool. After making the original plastalene figure, I had to create a mold of liquid rubber, reinforced by metal rods imbedded in the plaster. Then I removed the mold from the original, cleaned it and put it back together, and filled it with hydocal, which is a plaster-like material, but much harder and stronger. Then came the bronze paint to give it a patina that looks like bronze. I don't remember how long it took. I would guess several months."

Thursday, June 19, 1958, would be the culmination of over a year and a half of planning, excavation, rock hauling, and mud- and muck-slinging. Before the day was finished, Bowling Lake would be dedicated and the big celebration would be underway. Over 25,000 people were on hand around the lake to witness the dedication and show.

Around noon participants started arriving at the Lodge for the dedication. The list of dignitaries was impressive. The Strategic Air Command Band came down from Omaha to provide music. Lincoln Mayor Bennett Martin arrived, followed by Victor Anderson, Governor of the State of Nebraska. Staff cars brought in BGen Perry Hoisington, Col Felix Hardison (Base Commander), Col Elkins Read Jr. (307th Bomb Wing Commander), and the Commander of the 98th Bomb Wing. For this special occasion, Lt Gen. Walter Sweeney, 8th Air Force Commander, and Lt Gen. Joseph P. McConnell, 2nd Air Force Commander, had flown in from their respective Headquarters. Robert Johnson from KOLN-TV would perform the duties of Master of Ceremonies. Everything was ready. Lou Webber's statue was in place, covered by a parachute. The SAC Band began playing a musical prelude concert at 1245, and at about 1252 the dignitaries were seated.

The Base Chaplain delivered the Invocation to begin the dedication ceremonies. Everyone near the podium stood as the SAC Band began playing the Star Spangled Banner. Hand Salute or hand over the heart, honor guard present arms with the Stars and Stripes fluttering in the Nebraska breeze.

As the last bars of the National Anthem echoed across the lake, a flight of Nebraska Air National Guard F-86s approached from the East. Just before they arrived, one F-86 pulled up away from the formation. The other three passed over the lake with an open slot, in the traditional Missing Man Formation in tribute to Capt Russ Bowling and his crew.

Robert Johnson introduced the local and state officials attending. He followed with the introduction of the Division and Wing Commanders. Each stood and was recognized by the crowd. Johnson then introduced Andy Devine to the assemblage. Andy moved to the podium and began speaking in his trademark raspy, two-tone voice. Andy introduced Lt Gen. McConnell and then Lt Gen. Sweeney, who addressed the crowd.

General Sweeney's remarks are lost to history. It was almost sure he explained Capt Bowling's service and sacrifice for his country. He then introduced Mrs. Mary Bowling, Capt Bowling's widow, Sarah Bowling, mother of Capt Bowling, and his brother Preston.

With the speeches and introductions finished, the party of dignitaries moved to the doorway of the lodge. Andy Devine escorted Robert and Rebecca Bowling to the parachute draped statue of their father, while members of the family and dignitaries gathered around. "Jingles," along with Robert and Rebecca, moved forward and pulled the rope, releasing the parachute cover, revealing the statue of Capt Russell Bowling. It was a solemn moment, and the two children's eyes welled with tears. Very few noticed that "Jingles" wiped a tear from his eye with the sleeve of his suit coat.

The dedication ceremony of Bowling Lake was officially over. It was a dignified tribute to an airman and crew who had given their lives defending the country they loved. Now was the time for the traditional photos and special chitchat. Andy Devine spent a moment to autograph Mary Bowling's program. Just to the side of the letterhead for the 818th Air Division he signed *Andy Devine "Jingles"*, a small memento Mary still cherishes to this day.

The dedication on Thursday was just the beginning. For the next three days there would be all kinds of activities. Every day there were morning boat rides and ski lessons. The crowds were thrilled by demonstrations in the air performed by the Air National Guard Minute Men demonstration team. Helicopters "rescued" downed flyers from the lake and island. There were other flying demonstrations, highlighted by a near supersonic pass by an F-102 and F-106 that really got the attention of the crowds. The big event of each day was the water ski show. The show was put on by Tommy Bartlett's Water Ski Show. It featured just about everything that could be done on water skis.

The festivities ended each night with a huge fireworks show. Base families lined up around the lake, while others jammed nearby roads to watch. Hundreds of rockets, aerial bombs and star shells erupted skyward from the island and covered the Nebraska evening sky in magnificent bursting colors and noise. Those attending would always remember it as one of the greatest celebrations they had ever seen at Lincoln Air Force Base.

By the end of June, eleven of the 307th's B-47s had returned from Project Milk Bottle. The wing had forty-five B-47s and one TB-47 assigned, along with nineteen KC-97s.

Col Read's monthly report highlighted problems maintaining EWO capabilities under the constraints of Alert, Reflex and Milk Bottle. He also outlined problems caused by aircraft going in for Periodic Inspections.

# Cold War Cornhuskers: The 307th Bomb Wing Lincoln Air Force Base Nebraska 1955-1965

One major sore spot for the Colonel was personnel arriving from upgrade training at McConnell who were not adequately trained, requiring another two to three months before they were able to be placed on a combat ready crew.

Midsummer at Lincoln, and the 307th would turn in a busy month for July. There was the constant movement of B-47s for Milk Bottle. With each return the wing had one more B-47 with stronger wings. These would be placed on Alert and Reflex schedules as soon as possible.

Nebraska is well known for its long, hot, humid summers. Farmers would drive along the country roads and watch the corn and milo grow. Youngsters spent lazy afternoons at their favorite fishing hole, hoping a big old catfish would bite. If you were stationed at Lincoln, there were two things that were well remembered during the summer: thunderstorms and "skeeters"!

Sitting on the Eastern end of the state, Lincoln was in the heart of "twister" country. Weather systems would develop, then move across the plains drinking up moisture and then boiling upward. By the time the thunderheads reached Lincoln they contained millions of gallons of water vapor. The water vapor was so heavy that the clouds couldn't hold another drop. They would produce what Ernie Pence called, "a frog-strangling chock washer."

A young airman, just out of tech school, remarked about the size of the skeeters making his life miserable on the flight line. Not only were there a lot of 'em, they were huge. An old cigar-chomping crew chief looked at the airman and smiled. "Big! Son, you ain't seen a real big skeeter yet. Last year they were, I mean, *really* huge! Hell, we latched onto one with a Coleman and towed him down to the pits. We pumped 35,000 pounds of JP-4 into him before we realized it wasn't a B-47!"

Roland England remembered the "mosies":

"One night, while working on the south end of the parking ramp, the mosquitoes got to be such a great number that my crew could hardly work for fighting them off. The windshield of my Metro became so 'messed up' from smashed mosquitoes that I had difficulty seeing through it. Right across the fence south of us was a fair-sized swamp. I called for a smoke truck. Finally, after pleading and finally threatening to pull my crew off the flight line, a captain came out from somewhere. He looked around awhile, then made a smoke truck available."

July began with some of the most severe summer weather Lincoln had ever seen. On the first of the month the area was hit by thunderstorms that dumped over two inches of rain on the eastern part of the state. That was followed on the second and third by another three inches of rain. Then, on the 4th, Mother Nature provided a spectacular aerial display by pummeling Lincoln with severe thunderstorms, hail and a total of four inches of moisture. Along with the storms high winds hit the area, making air operations difficult.

Everett Sutherland recalled coming back to Lincoln in a KC-97 on a night with high winds:

"The wind was blowing just like a hurricane, it seemed. We tried to land a couple of times but the wind kept blowing us off the side of the runway. So we headed for Ellsworth AFB near Rapid City, South Dakota. The pilot and navigator almost got into an argument about our ETA and fuel reserve because we were already running low on fuel. Anyway we headed for South Dakota. We lost an engine on approach and another one as we touched down when they ran out of fuel. I'll tell you, my heart was up in my throat. We got it on the ground and taxied in on two engines. When they dipped the tanks they could hardly get anything. That's how low on fuel we were that night. We tied the plane down because we had just beaten the storm front in.

"We had a mag go out, so we sat there a day or so until they found another mag. Anyway, I'm out there by myself working on the engine. I put the mag on and had it 180 degrees off timing. Well, you know what happened when I fired the engine up. I had flames shooting out the back of the engine till it appeared past the wing. By the time I could really do anything, I had fire trucks sitting out in front of me and everything else."

On 11 July there was a mass gas refueling scheduled for five KC-97s. During the weather briefing it was reported there would be the possibility of thunderstorms in the refueling area. It was also noted there might be thunderstorms in the Lincoln area by the time the flight returned. Capt Thomas Morgan would be flying the lead tanker, taking off at 1820 that evening.

The route to the refueling area was changed several times due to weather along the planned route. Reaching the refueling area, the flight found the refueling track smothered in thunderstorms. The refueling track was changed to avoid the weather and rendezvous with the receiver aircraft was accomplished. With the mass gas accomplished the tankers turned and headed back towards Lincoln.

Between Sioux Falls, South Dakota, and Sioux City, Iowa, the flight received word from Lincoln that weather in the area was bad, with severe thunderstorms. The flight was directed to turn for their alternate at Minneapolis. At almost the same time, 8th Air Force sent a message for the flight to divert to Bunker Hill AFB, Indiana, instead of Minneapolis. Capt Morgan got on the radio and stated rather harshly that was the wrong alternate. His protest fell on deaf 8th Air Force ears. At this point Morgan contacted the other four tankers for a status report on their fuel reserves for the new alternate. All reported they had enough fuel to make Bunker Hill. The tankers headed towards Des Moines and on to Bunker Hill.

The flight was routine, with the exception that the diverted aircraft had received no reports on the weather at their new destination until they were about fifteen minutes from Bunker Hill. At that time they received a report from Indianapolis Center, and it didn't look too good. Bunker Hill was reporting scattered clouds at 2,000 feet, with four miles visibility due to fog. It was also reported the conditions were starting to go downhill rapidly.

Gary McGill was navigator on the fourth KC-97 in the flight. He recalled:

"I wasn't with my regular crew, I was flying with Vic Pelter. We were in number four position and were the last aircraft to land successfully that night. We were coming in on instrument approach. When we broke out, I stood up from my navigator's position, looked out, and saw we were to the left of the runway. Vic made a beautiful S-turn and came right in and kissed it on and we got down."

Flying in the number five position was Richard Grammes' crew in ol' 793, call sign "Handcuff 20". He recalled:

"We were a flight of five tankers departing Lincoln to refuel B-47s. On return to Lincoln, thunderstorms prevented our landing there. We were directed to Bunker Hill AFB, later known as Grissom AFB, at Kokomo, Indiana. Upon arrival, the weather was deteriorating. The first four planes were able to land. I was then told the field was below minimums. I told them we were getting low on fuel and needed an alternate location. After about five minutes, we were told we were cleared to make a GCA approach at Bunker Hill, with weather conditions reported obscured one mile with fog.

"All went well until we hit the nose wheel on the overrun. The nose gear strut came into the cockpit with a loud bang and jolt. Immediately a go around was made with severe vibration, due to the two inboard propellers striking the runway. The airplane filled with smoke and we prepared to bail out. However, as throttles were reduced at fifteen hundred feet, the vibration lessened. The smoke also dissipated and we learned later that it was from the auxiliary power unit being jarred during impact.

"We were very low on fuel and were directed to Weir Cook Memorial Airport, Indianapolis. A successful crash landing was accomplished with no foam on the runway. The reason they didn't foam the runway was because they only had one truck of foam and they were preparing to use it after the big bang and fire. The airplane was repaired at Weir Cook by the Tinker AFB depot team.

"Subsequent accident investigation concluded that there were thirteen contributing factors given such as; erroneous weather forecast (not a mile visibility, but zero visibility), diverted to an unsuitable alternate, no high intensity approach lights, etc. However, I was given the primary cause of the accident by allowing the aircraft to descend below two hundred feet and not making an immediate go-around.

"The 8th Air Force Commander, Lt Gen. Walter C. Sweeney, Jr., instructed my wing commander, Col Elkins Read, to court martial me prior to the board's convening. Col Read took a stand and said he could not do this as Lt Grammes did not willfully disobey an order, but made an error in judgment by not making an immediate go-around. Col Read gave me an Article 15, which was subsequently removed from my file within two years. I have Col Read to thank for his great effort to keep me on flying status and in the Air Force. Col Read didn't make BG, but was an outstanding officer, commander and friend."

At one time or another, almost everyone who served in SAC saw the movie *Strategic Air Command*, staring Jimmy Stewart. Take out the Hollywood melodrama and the movie gave the public a fairly accurate account of SAC in the mid-fifties. Hollywood aside, it featured some of the most beautiful in-flight B-36 and B-47 sequences ever filmed.

The central character is "Dutch" Holland, third baseman for the St Louis Cardinals and Air Force Reserve officer. "Dutch" (Jimmy Stewart) is called back to active duty in SAC at the height of his baseball career. The movie follows his tour of duty in the B-36 and the fledgling B-47.

In real life, Jimmy was a full Colonel in the Air Force Reserve and ultimately attained the rank of Brigadier General. Now, Jimmy Stewart was no Hollywood Colonel. He made a lot of public relations films for the Air Force and was always ready to promote the Air Force. The fact that he was a mega movie star always helped to get his message across to the public.

Stewart was a rated pilot in both the B-36 and B-47. He maintained his rating by flying the aircraft as part of his Reserve M-Day service. He was also working on becoming rated in the new KC-135 tanker. We have set the stage for what I have come to call "The Jimmy Stewart Caper".

Late one afternoon a KC-135 appeared on approach for the patch. Coming in from the south, it cleared the hill and settled onto Runway 35. As she taxied onto the flight line, wary eyes watched her taxi towards Base Operations. An unannounced visit like this usually signaled the start of an ORI.

Bill Cox from the 307th AREFS went over to get a better look at the big jet tanker. After all, it was the first time he had seen a KC-135. Talking with one of the crew, he found out none other than Jimmy Stewart was aboard, flying in from March AFB, California. Good time to get an autograph, but alas, Colonel Stewart had already disappeared into Base Ops.

Col Stewart's visit to the patch was no accident. It was actually a pre-planned arrival so Jimmy could fly a B-47 back to California and maintain his rating in the Stratojet. So, it was a simple task of meeting with the crew he would fly with, plan the mission and get ready for the early morning flight.

Several days before Jimmy arrived, William Sullivan, Joe Hangar and Bill Bathurst had been alerted they would fly with Jimmy for the flight to California. Checking the flight schedule, Bill Bathurst found he was scheduled for a Standboard evaluation mission on the day of the special flight. A quick check of the flight schedule showed Bill Burford, Gene Hickman and Walt Hudkins were scheduled for an early morning flight. A quick shuffle of the schedule and the team of Burford, Hickman and Hudkins would fly with Jimmy Stewart.

Bright and early the next morning the troops on the flight line were getting started for another day. 53-4208 had been serviced and was ready for her special flight. Her crew arrived and was ready to begin the preflight walk around.

The exact preflight conversation was never "officially" recorded. It most likely went something like this from Ernie Pence, in the way only his rapier wit could recall:

"Jimmy Stewart arrives at our playpen. He will fly 4208 back to the land of strange people. He shows up at the plane, says, 'Well ah, well ah Chief, ah is she ready to go?' The crew chief, proud as punch, replies, 'Yes Sir, she's ready to go!' Stewart replies, 'Well ah, well ah, butt ah, button her up, ah let's ah, let's ah get a cup of coffee.' Doesn't get any better than this: a movie star you like trusts your judgment and integrity enough to forego the preflight and wants to get a cup of coffee."

Sitting next to 4208, William Filipula was working on his bird, 53-1909, getting her ready for the next mission. Looking over at 4208, he recalled seeing Jimmy:

"What I remember about Jimmy Stewart was that he was very tall, thin and had gray hair. He was standing by himself and I was about twenty feet away from him working on my aircraft. I wanted to go over and get his autograph on my 781 form and take a picture with him, but he was a Colonel and a famous movie star and I was too shy to approach him. How I wish I would have conquered my fears and followed through with my thinking. What a wonderful keepsake that would have been. However, it is still a great memory for me."

It was time to head for California. The crew climbed the ladder, settled into their seats, went through the checklist, and then started the engines. Of course, with such a famous person sitting in the front seat, everything was done according to the checklist.

4208 moved out of her slot and taxied to the end of Runway 17 for a south take off. With everything ready, the final items on the checklist were completed. "Ah, canopy coming closed. Ah, Lincoln tower ah, 4208 requesting, ah, takeoff instructions." The tower gave 4208 clearance to take off and final departure frequencies. In the front seat, Col Jimmy Stewart pushed the six throttles forward and waited for the power to come up and stabilize. As soon as the power was available they would hit the water-alcohol injection and start the takeoff roll.

As the power reached one hundred percent something went wrong in the number four engine, causing it to seize and begin tearing itself apart. Parts of the engine punched through the cowling and flew off into the air. Other parts hit the runway and bounced in all directions. In the cockpit, Stewart and Burford pulled the throttles back and hit the cut off switches on four and five.

The tower was advised of the problem and in turn hit the button for the fire trucks to respond. Within minutes, the fire crews were headed towards 4208. Lady luck was aboard 4208 that morning. There was no fire after the engine blew.

# Cold War Cornhuskers: The 307th Bomb Wing Lincoln Air Force Base Nebraska 1955-1965

As soon as it was safe, with no other threat of fire, 4208 taxied back to her spot on the ramp. Merrill Sinclair recalled:

"When 4208 came back from the end of the runway that morning, I was working on 4236 and I remember looking toward the north east where 4208 was parked. Jimmy Stewart and the crew were looking at what was left of the engine."

Of course there were photos taken for the investigation. Then the crew went to Base Ops and began filling out the paperwork on the incident. They were debriefed on exactly what had happened at the end of Runway 17 that morning.

When the paperwork was finished the California bound crew headed back to the flight line. This time they headed for 51-15808, one of the oldest operational B-47s still in service. T.R. Taylor recalls, " I remember Jimmy flying 5808. I was the crew chief."

The exact date Jimmy Stewart was at Lincoln is lost to history. We know he was at Lincoln and flew a 307th B-47 back to California. Research, based on collected memories of those who were there and aircraft records, indicate Jimmy was most likely at Lincoln during the first two weeks of July 1958.

The Middle East had come to a boiling point over the Suez Canal in 1956 while the 307th was in England. The uneasy peace in the Middle East started simmering again in 1958. This time it wasn't the Suez Canal, but the city of Beirut, Lebanon.

By 15 July the situation was serious enough for President Eisenhower to authorize U.S. Marines to be sent in to secure and occupy the Beirut Airport under Operation Blue Bat. The operation called for over 8,000 Army and 5,000 Marines to secure not only the airport, but also approaches to the city and the seaport.

At the 307th Command Post, the alert came in.

**"Break, Break... This is Moonbeam...**
**Stand By for a triple flash message.**
**This is an execution order, Repeat.."**
**This is an execution order, for**
**Operation BLUE BAT SIERRA BRAVO.**
**Authentication is**
**Oscar..Bravo..India..Lima."**

This was a no-launch, real-world, authentic alert message. The Command Post set the alert notification in motion. All leaves were canceled; flight crews not on alert were called in for briefing. Possible targets were selected in case there was a launch.

As with all alerts, the ground crews began generating the force. This time the follow on force would be generated and cocked. That meant real bullets, chaff and nukes. By the end of the week, SAC had over a thousand B-47s sitting on ramps across the nation and Reflex bases worldwide, "cocked" and ready.

Since this was a real-world alert, all practice alerts were canceled until further notice under SAC guidelines. If the horn blew it would be for real, or would it? On Thursday, July 24th, someone at Offutt forgot about the guidelines and initiated an Alfa alert to test communications.

Within seconds there was pandemonium at command posts around SAC. Was this a comm check, or the real thing? How do we respond? Should we hit the horn? At several bases the horn blared, sending the alert crews scrambling to their birds. Offutt realized what had happened within moments and issued a standown recall, putting an end to the accidental alert.

With a real-world alert going on and the ramp full of armed B-47s, there wasn't a lot of training going on. The TB-47 was getting into the air almost every day. It amounted to short proficiency flights, not real crew training. For the rest of July, the 307th spent long days and dark nights sitting on pins and needles.

The 307th started August by saying farewell to BGen. Perry Hoisington on 1 August. He had been the 818th Air Division Commander since 1956. He would be remembered for his list of "Perry's Pet Peeves". Number one on his list was his constant battle to reduce traffic violations and accidents. His legacy would always be the beautiful Bowling Lake, or as the troops called it, "Perry's Puddle". Col Thomas Corbin took command of the 818th Air Division at Lincoln Air Force Base.

By 7 August, the situation in the Middle East had cooled down and Omaha sent word to stand down the follow-on force. The tension was released. The 307th lost very little time uncocking the force and trying to get back to normal operations.

Normal operations meant getting back in the air and filling those SAC Reg 50-8 squares. So, it was back to routine mission planning, preflight, and hit the local RBS plots. Then, back to Lincoln, get the bird turned around and ready for the next crew and mission.

Enough B-47s had been run through Milk Bottle to resume "Pop Up" training flights on a limited scale. These flights were a pilot's dream come true and, at the same time, his worst nightmare. Flying the profile allowed the pilot to legally fly low, say 500 feet above the terrain. However, flying that low meant everything was rushing by in a blur, leaving little room for error.

Back in July, before the Beirut problem, the 307th AREFS had been alerted for Operation Sand Tiger. The orders outlined a TDY deployment to Harmon AB, Newfoundland. The tanker crews could only shake their heads in disbelief. Just got over a TDY and another looms in the not-so-distant future. The date for the deployment was set for 22 September.

Men of the 307th didn't know it, but there was another real-world pot starting to boil. It wasn't in the Middle East, or Europe. This simmering pot was just off the coast of Communist China. Few men of the 307th had any idea of where or what Quemoy or Matsu was. Well, they were two small islands just off the coast of Red China. At the present time they were under the control of the Nationalist Chinese on Taiwan. The islands had been a sore spot for the Eisenhower Administration since the spring of 1955. Since the islands were just a few miles offshore they were under constant harassment by the Chinese Communists. The U.S. had supplied large howitzers to defend the islands. These guns were more than a sore spot to the Reds; they were a real thorn in their backside.

Early on 23 August, the nervous calm on the islands was shattered by incoming artillery rounds from Mainland China. This time it wasn't harassment fire by the Chinese Communists; it was a massive barrage, lasting all day and into the night. Red Chinese patrol boats lurked offshore to block any aid that might be sent to the beleaguered islands.

President Eisenhower responded by sending a Naval Task Force into the area as a show of force to prevent any invasion of the islands or Taiwan. Soviet Premier Nikita Khrushchev countered by saying any attack on Red China would be viewed as an attack on the USSR. The situation in the Taiwan Strait was going from simmer to a rolling boil in a hurry.

The Joint Chiefs of Staff called for an increase in U.S. military readiness. So, once again, for the second time in less than two months, SAC would be called on to shake its mailed fist. Ernie Pence wrote:

"Before anyone can blink an eye, we are deep in aircraft returning from training flights, water alcohol trucks, combat chaff, H.E.I. 20 mike-mike and nuclear weapons. We maintenance types do our standard thing: nobody goes home until all aircraft are ready to load. That means no sleep, damn little to eat, nothing but behinds and elbows.

"'Cadillac' Crook was a godsend. We are all out there getting after it for who knows how long, and who shows up in the 370th section of the ramp, but Jack. The trunk pops open and—presto!—what to our bloodshot eyes should appear but a cornucopia of sandwiches and coffee from the O-club! At times like that it, comes over as good as a sit-down dinner in an excellent restaurant.

"All birds are loaded and cocked, the crews are using the BOQ for alert quarters, and the crew chiefs are living in the bomb squadron buildings. No practice alerts; if the horn blows, it is a real launch. This low-pressure cauldron boiled for about two weeks. You could physically feel the tension, but no one let on it was tight. We were professionals. Time passed with endless card games, sleep, preflight, Russian roulette, stories and freshening the crew water bottles in the planes."

The alert continued day after day with no relief in sight. The requirement for Air Police to guard each cocked B-47 ate into the available manpower for the base security staff. The solution seemed easy: cross-train office personnel and supply clerks. After all, all they had to do was stand there in front of the aircraft with an M-1 Carbine and challenge anyone who came near. Easy, right? Ernie continued:

"About a week into this thing–it seemed an eternity–Howard Berry's crew decided to have fresh water put in the bottles that day at preflight. They brought them down and told Berry to put in fresh water and leave them in between the front main tires. They would put them up in the morning.

"Bored, absent-minded, stupid or a combination of the three, about 1400 hours, the make-believe policeman decided the bottles had been transformed into a deadly bomb. He calls in a bomb threat. We all hear the Klaxon. A lot of money was lost that day, cards, money, chairs, everything went straight up in the air. For those of you who have not had the privilege of thinking you are about to incinerate the world, you cannot imagine the plethora of thoughts that go through your mind in a millisecond. In that short span of time, the world stands still, no audible sound is uttered, then the whole area erupts as everyone accelerates to the max, instantaneously.

"The crew chiefs of the 307th went through the Base Ops building as one would think a tornado would. The door flew against the wall and we rounded the second corner jockeying for position; no words, just the noise of a normal stampede, labored breathing and a hell of a lot of fast moving feet.

"I can still see the guard at the door, eyes big a saucers, reaching for the leading airman's flight line badge. Fifteen of us ran the poor man down without hesitation. We literally ran over the man. A witness told me the fellow had just managed to get up to his feet when Col Thompson rounded the corner and hit him like a linebacker.

Fire trucks, bayonet nozzles at the ready, were poised in front of the endangered bomber. An NCO from the Air Police was standing in front of the nose of his pickup, red lights flashing, mobile strike team at the ready. When Berry's crew arrived, he walked over, picked up the two 'bombs' and sheepishly handed them to his crew, who then mounted the ladder and stored the offending units.

"To bring a short story to fruition, suffice to say that the command post saw fit to inform all crews the alert was over a week later by initiating *another* alert. Everyone scrambled to the birds as before, only to have the copilots informed by radio that the alert was terminated. When the hell did telephones become redundant?"

With the end of the crisis and alert, the task at hand was to download all of the cocked, follow-on force aircraft. That meant taking all of the nukes out and trucking them back to the storage area. After the nukes had been removed the planes had to be taken back to the pits and defueled, if they were not going to fly in the very near future.

Word came down on Monday, September 1st, there would be a major change in the way things would be done out on the flight line. Some of the changes would be for the better, while some were not well accepted. The primary reasons for the changes were the constant changes in alert and Reflex procedures.

Up till now there were three tactical maintenance areas. Field Maintenance performed everything on the flight line. Periodic maintenance did the scheduled inspections and maintenance that would require the aircraft to be out of commission for a long period of time. Armament and Electronics was responsible for the Bombing and Navigation and fire control systems. This had been known as the directorate system.

Under the old system aircraft were assigned to a specific bomb squadron. Each squadron had a great deal of pride in their aircraft and the ability to keep them flying. Each squadron also had a distinctive colored strip emblazoned near the top of the tail in the appropriate squadron color.

Under the new system, the wing would be organized under a Deputy Commander for Maintenance and a Deputy Commander for Operations. Under this concept, everything on the ground fell under the responsibility of the DCM. Every aspect of flying fell under the control of the DCO. The aircraft now belonged to the DCM and were "loaned out" to the bomb squadrons for flying.

The initial program of reorganization had started at Loring AFB, Maine, under Project Head Start. There would be a gradual changeover to the new system within SAC. The program also called for the activation of a fourth bomb squadron in the wing. This would add more aircraft and personnel. Lincoln AFB was scheduled to be one of the first bases to make the changeover.

With the year filled with alerts, Reflex, Milk Bottle and changes, 8th Air Force hadn't had time to call for any more Pacesetter missions. So Westover came up with a new wrinkle called Golden Hour Tango. These were designed to test the wing's ability to carry out a USCM. It all started with a Coco Alert. After the planes were back at the alert pad the crews would recock the aircraft, and they would then be tested on Emergency War Order procedures.

While the alert crews were busy taking the test, a pyramid alert was started to call flight crews and maintenance personnel to report for duty and generate the force. After about four hours of playing war games, the stand down order would arrive from Westover and almost everyone could go home.

Now, these alerts weren't called "Golden Hour" for nothing. Most of them would be called during off duty hours, with a very strong tendency for the phone to ring after the golden hour of 2400. So everyone got jolted out of bed, taxied the birds and recocked, tested, briefed, and were then told, "Thanks for coming, have a nice night, what's left of it". 8th Air Force loved the idea and let everyone know they could expect at least one Golden Hour Tango a month.

On 1 October the 307th Headquarters published OPSORD 22-58, code name Grand Slam. This was a mission to test the wing's ability to conduct air and ground operations during a no-notice USCM. The wing would be vulnerable for the ORI until 25 February of the next year.

The 307th AREFS began the month with preparations for their trip to Harmon. The squadron was scheduled to leave Lincoln on or about 7 October for ninety days in the North Country. They had lucked out in going to Thule during the summer; the trip to Harmon would be another story.

On the 4th, word came down from Omaha that visual release bomb runs would no longer be part of the training requirements. Apparently, there was a shortage of the MB-4 "Blue Beetle" practice bombs. Shucks, if there was a shortage of the little blue bombs, they could just stop down

# Cold War Cornhuskers: The 307th Bomb Wing Lincoln Air Force Base Nebraska 1955-1965

at Surplus Center on West "O". They had plenty of them stacked up in crates. The going price was about 25 bucks a bomb.

By now, most of the B-47s had cycled through Milk Bottle. As of 4 October forty of the assigned aircraft had the beefed up wings. "Pop Up" training and qualification were added back to the schedule on almost a daily basis.

All training flights with navigation legs towards the north of Lincoln now included a fireout requirement over Lake Michigan. On 7 October 53-6244 flew a mission and achieved a 75% fireout score. It would be the best fireout for the entire month.

Ken Tarwater was on the KC-97 scheduled to be the advance party for Harmon. He wrote:

"The 97 that I was on was selected to go a couple of days before the rest of the squadron to take over alert duties at Harmon. At the time I think it was called 'strip alert'. We landed at Ernest Harmon AFB, refueled and were put on alert. The flight crew and ground crew were assigned two station wagons and put together in alert quarters that were more or less in the center of the base. We had just been in the barracks a short time when they sounded an alert. We all got in the wagons with officers driving both and sped to the flight line with red lights flashing. We cocked the 97 and were ready for anything. It was soon called off and we returned to the barracks. The aircraft commander of our crew was called to task for running stop signs and breaking speed limits on our way to the flight line. They told him maybe in the US he could get by with this, but not here in Newfoundland. What a crock! What we did that day was set a speed record getting to our alert aircraft, a record that probably was never broken because alert vehicles were to obey all of Newfoundland's traffic laws."

On 7 October the south end of the LAFB ramp was a beehive of activity. Along with the usual KC-97s, there were several huge C-124s. Tons of equipment were being onloaded through the gaping nose doors. It seemed that the Globemasters had an insatiable appetite as they gobbled barrels, engines and palettes of equipment. After they had been filled and fueled, the cargo planes took off and headed for Harmon, Newfoundland.

Early on the 8th, the KC-97s' engines began coughing to life in clouds of blue gray smoke. Every ten minutes a KC-97 would taxi out and make the long take off run. Climbing out, they took up a heading for Green Bay, Wisconsin, their first mandatory checkpoint. After the checkpoint, the tankers continued northeast and made another checkpoint near Montréal, Québec. Then it was over to Gaspé, Quebec, up the Gulf of St. Lawrence and on to Harmon.

Omaha was always coming up with great ideas on how to test the troops and keep them on their toes. One of the ideas was called Operation Battle Cry. The Operations Order called for the launch of alert aircraft to fly a simulated attack authentication mission under positive control. When the execution order was received, the alert birds would perform a Coco alert. The aircraft would then be downloaded and stand by for a Romeo launch message from Omaha.

At 0132 hours on the morning of the 8th, the command post received a message from 8th Air Force to initiate a Golden Hour Tango. After the message was authenticated they hit the Klaxon. Alert crews were jolted from dreamland by the blare of the horn and scrambled to their aircraft. While they were scrambling the alert pyramid was initiated.

Phones in base housing and Lincoln rang off the hook until they were answered. Drowsy voices responded to the call, then called the next two phone numbers on the list. Within a few minutes there was a steady stream of cars heading out "O" Street and from the housing area, all headed for the main gate.

Alert crews hit the ladder and started engines, then checked in when they were ready to taxi. Then it was down the taxiway, take the runway and push the throttles briefly to 100% for the Coco alert. Down the runway, pull the power back, return to the alert area and shut down the engines.

After the alert birds were recocked, the crews shuffled into the room to take their test on EWO procedures. Everyone else who had reported for duty was briefed and preparing to generate the follow-on force. Then, there was a session to see if there were any problems during the pyramid telephone alert. One big one was always voiced; it was too damn early in the morning for this kind of fun and games!

About 0530 the stand down message arrived from Westover. By now, the alert birds were about recocked and back on alert. The crews were back in their bunks and the ground crews were thinking of getting a little sack time before the routine day started. All in all, it was another night shot to Hell.

Dawn at Lincoln, with the sun poking up over Cornhusker Highway, looked like any other morning. Everyone reported for duty and started the usual morning ritual of alert preflight. As 20 October progressed, the routine training flights were getting ready to launch.

As usual, without warning, the command post got a message from Offutt, and the tension rose by six levels. After acknowledging the message it was authenticated. The message was a valid Green Dot execution order for Battle Cry. So, here we go again: Klaxon blaring, crews scrambling for the ladders.

**"Fire guard standing by on 4."**
**"Voltage" "Rotation" 5,6,3,2,1.**
**"Ready to taxi"**

Down the ramp, full power, back to the alert area. As the aircraft arrived back at the alert area, the bomb bay doors swung open and the downloading of the weapons began. The download checklist is followed down to each comma and period until the weapons are secured to the transport dollies and headed back to the igloos.

The crew chiefs were busy topping off fuel and checking their aircraft for anything that may have popped up during the Coco alert. Hopefully, everything ran fine so there wouldn't be anything to fix. Within a few hours all the alert birds were ready to go in a "sorta cocked" status.

Now, everyone was sitting around on pins and needles waiting for the launch order to arrive so they can get the show on the road. Even though this was going to be a practice launch, every move would be scored under the watchful eyes of SAC.

Headquarters 8th Air Force called an Alfa alert seven hours after the initial Coco had been called by Omaha. This caused not only confusion, but also tempers to reach near boiling point in the command post. As soon as tempers cooled a little, a message was fired off to Westover regarding the fact the wing was already standing by for a SAC launch execution order.

The order to execute Battle Cry arrived on the 21st. As per the OPSORD, the message was an authentic launch order within the guidelines set up for the operation. The alert crews responded as they would for any alert. Engines were spooled up and they taxied to the end of Runway 35. A final check with the tower and the lead aircraft rolled. At the predetermined speed the ATO was fired. With the added thrust of the ATO, the heavy B-47s sprang into the air trailing thick, boiling clouds of acrid smoke. Every minute or so, another B-47 left the ground and began climbing into the sky.

While climbing out there was a slight turn towards Omaha, then to the level off point just northeast of Des Moines, Iowa. Passing over Des Moines at 35,000 feet, the B-47s made a heading correction towards the gunnery area at Lake Michigan. So far everything was on time according to the profile.

# 1958

They crossed the coastline of Lake Michigan near Sturgeon Bay, Wisconsin, and approached the restricted gunnery area. When they were well inside the area, the copilots reached down and pulled the ATO rack release handle. Most of the racks released cleanly and fell towards the water, or a couple of quick wing wags and any sticky racks came loose and fell into the lake.

The stream of bombers crossed into Canadian airspace just south of Sault Ste. Marie, Michigan, and flew on towards the next radio checkpoint near Sudbury, Ontario. Straight on course, they continued northeast across the St. Lawrence River.

Within the bomber stream, the navigators kept busy checking and rechecking their position. The positive control point was coming up fast! So far there had been no recall, and no "go code". At 49 degrees N, 67 degrees W, they reached positive control point. This was as far as they could go without a valid "go code" message.

With no message to proceed beyond the positive control point, the B-47s turned away and the crews opened the special folder they had been given before takeoff. It contained information as to how the mission was to proceed. The profile was now a grid navigation leg to 52 degrees N, 75 degrees W. This was a turn point for the next leg to the southwest. Looking down from their altitude, there wasn't very much to see. Below were frozen lakes and snow-covered tundra. Not a very nice place to get out and walk if anything went wrong and they had to eject.

The nav leg ended when they crossed Lake Superior and passed over Marquette, Michigan, the final checkpoint. All they had to do now was set up for the bomb run at the Minneapolis bomb plot, then head home.

The results of Battle Cry were listed as excellent. All of the aircraft had left the roost within the time guidelines. Navigation to the positive control point was considered dead on the money. Nav legs into the Canadian tundra were within limits. Bomb scores were very good. Only one aircraft was given an ineffective score when their radar went on the fritz after passing the IP. SAC Headquarters was very pleased with the entire 307th performance during the operation. If SAC was pleased, then the men who flew the mission were overjoyed.

While Battle Cry was being flown, ground crews were busy uploading six B-47s to alert "cocked" status. After all, there can't be any gaps in alert coverage just to fulfill a higher headquarters mission. By the time the mission aircraft returned, the newly cocked aircraft were squatting on the ramp, ready for the blare of the Klaxon.

Up at Harmon, the 307th AREFS had settled into a daily routine. Their primary missions were to provide alert tankers and refuel returning Reflex aircraft. There wasn't a lot to do during off-duty time. You could play cards or go outside and watch the clouds go by, or maybe take a hike.

Ken Tarwater and Russ Geisler decided to do some exploring:

"We decided to take a walk up in the hills north of the base. While we were up in the timber overlooking some small lakes, they sounded the alert horn and all we could do was watch the KC-97s roll down the runway and then return to the ramp without taking off," Ken remember. "We walked a little further and walked right into an MP holding a gun on us. We had blundered right into a very restricted missile site. The Air Policeman was not impressed with our 307th flight line badges, but we convinced him that we were just a couple of dummies out for a stroll in the woods and were not Russian spies. About that time, we heard a jeep coming up the hill. He informed us it was his NCO in charge and he would probably throw the book at us. The AP, I wish I could remember his name, told us to high tail it back to the base and be quiet. Boy, did we get down that hill. So much for sightseeing at Harmon."

By the end of October, the 307th had flown over 2,000 hours without a serious accident. There were the occasional interesting moments, but nothing that would warrant an incident write-up. October also found ten more crews becoming "pop up" qualified. That gave the wing a total of twenty-eight crews qualified for "pop ups". You could be assured that as more and more became qualified, it would soon become a standard requirement for all profile missions.

From its beginning, SAC had almost complete use of the ocean of air above 25,000 feet. If you saw another contrail while flying a mission, it was almost assured a SAC aircraft was making it. That all came to an end in October. The Boeing 707 was entering the commercial airline fleet. Now, SAC aircraft would have to share more and more airspace with the civilian jet fleet.

The 307th started the month of November with a three-ship Reflex launch on the 1st. One of the B-47s had to abort enroute because its tanker didn't show up, so they diverted to Goose Bay. After refueling and crew rest, they departed for England the next day.

Reflex deployment, or any flight for that matter, may not always go according to the planned profile. Glen "Pappy" Hesler wrote in his book, *The Heart of the Tiger*:

"One time we were on our way on a Reflex deployment when we were radioed that our refueling tanker was disabled and we would need to land at Goose Bay, Labrador, to be ground refueled. As I prepared for the descent to land at Goose Bay, I went through the "prior to descent" checklist. One item on the list was to place the windshield heat on max high several minutes before starting the descent. This was accomplished well in advance by my copilot, Tom Crocker. He was always on the ball and expected me to respond to each item on the checklist. If I did not do so, he was right there until I did respond. The procedure is still used today by professional pilots.

"We were established on our descent, still in the 30,000 feet range, in solid weather and on instruments. One cross check around the cockpit including checking out the windshield for traffic in case we became visual. I was absolutely shocked when my windshield suddenly became a crossword puzzle of cracks that made it impossible to see anything out of it, even for landing. There was no emergency procedure for this mess.

"The windshield was nearly two inches thick with electrical wires throughout. It was called Nesa glass. The wires were heated electrically which kept the ice from accumulating on the windshield. There was no way for the pilot to know if the system did not operate. Even if he knew, there was nothing he could do about it. Now was the time I had to test Larry (Boggess) on that equipment he had up front. The only way I could safely find the runway at Goose Bay was for Larry to guide me down to the final approach. Then when we were close to the runway, I would crack the canopy open and use peripheral vision. With Tom's help, just <u>maybe</u> we could get her down safely.

"It was a situation few pilots have experienced. There was no training for such a mess. I notified Goose Bay tower of my predicament. They quickly radioed back that they had no traffic, and wished me luck. The fire truck was on its way. There was some light snow on the runway, but I could make out the runway lights. I opened the canopy about halfway to ensure that we would stay on the runway even after slowing down. With the drogue chute out, I could slow down to 140 knots with a light aircraft. It seemed like we were going like a bat out of hell. Any pilot will tell you that with some moisture from that snow, it seems a better landing can be made when one is not sure of the asphalt beneath the plane. We made it with no damage.

# Cold War Cornhuskers: The 307th Bomb Wing Lincoln Air Force Base Nebraska 1955-1965

"The next day I learned a great deal about replacing a new Nesa glass windshield in a B-47. After it was installed, there had to be a three-day soaking period before the plane could fly again. This meant hours and hours of nothing to do in Goose Bay. We checked out every item in the BX and bought nothing. It is times like this that cemented crew members together."

As part of the changeover to the Deputy Commander system, the 424th Bomb Squadron was assigned to the 307th Bomb Wing on 1 September. Although it was assigned, the squadron would take several months to get organized and be officially activated. The assignment of the fourth bomb squadron was designed to help alleviate problems with aircraft and manpower for alert and Reflex.

Wednesday, 12 November, the 307th Command Post got an advanced condition of readiness message from "Jumbo" (SAC HQ). It was the notification to generate the force for Grand Slam. Unlike most SAC exercises, this one did not start with a Coco alert.

The operation order for Grand Slam required the 307th to generate thirty B-47s for the mission. This simulated mission would be the closest to a real combat mission the 307th had flown to date. Each B-47 was to be brought up to combat mission status. The only difference would be that no "special weapons" or ATO would be carried. They were to have a full fuel load and 20 mm ammo loaded. Escape and Evasion belts would be issued along with morphine syrettes and personal effects envelopes fifteen minutes before the mission briefing.

"Jumbo" was always trying to figure out new things to throw at the crews during these special operations. Grand Slam was no exception. While the birds were being generated, the planners and command post staff were busy preparing the Combat Mission Folders (CMF). The contents of the folder outlined important details, such as route to the target, alternate targets, and weapons and target defenses. For this exercise there were three special envelopes containing the "go code".

As each B-47 reported ready, a wing staff member would load the CMF into the aircraft safe box. The 307th was required to launch thirty aircraft. Half of the force would get a valid "go code" while the other half would carry the recall code. The wing planning staff and Col Read were the only members of the 307th who had access to the "who gets which" list.

At the briefing, the mission plan and route up to the positive control point were reviewed. Air refueling areas and offloads were discussed. There would be a total of ten three-ship cells. There were three separate primary targets and one alternate. Nobody in the briefing room knew their specific target or if they would get the "go code". They would only know the target after receiving a correct message from "Jumbo" to fly the profile. The whole purpose of the mission was to test the ability of the wing to plan and execute an EWO mission. Receiving and authenticating a "go" message was the most important aspect of the mission.

Late on the afternoon of 13 November, the 307th received a "151 Delta Sierra" message from Jumbo. It was the launch execution message for the first fifteen aircraft. This was not a wild scramble to the boarding ladder like a regular alert. It was a routine launch for the crews, only under USCM guidelines.

Scarlet cell launched at 0113 hours local time. Lemon cell would go at 0213, followed by Ivory at 0513, then Tan at 0713. Peach would be the last cell of the day, leaving Lincoln at 1013 hours that morning. Take off would be at one-minute intervals. According to the message, they were to stand by for a "Noah's Ark" message before they reached the H-Hour Control Point, which would also serve as the positive control point for the first cell.

After takeoff the B-47s climbed out and turned over Schuyler, Nebraska, taking up a heading for Sioux City, Iowa. Minneapolis was the first radio checkpoint.

" Minneapolis radio, Squad Car 22 at 35,000 feet with a three ship cell.
Grand Slam Mission"

The next checkpoint would be as they passed over Grand Marais, Michigan. The next leg was a straight flight to a point just northeast of Quebec City for another radio check. After the radio check, there was a heading change that would take them almost due north.

By 0500, the first cell was dropping down from their perch to meet the tankers orbiting in the Silver Fox refueling track. Right on time, they saw the tanker blips on radar and started closing the range. One by one they found their assigned tanker, moved into the slot and ran the refueling checklist. As they closed in for refueling, there was quite a sight to behold. All across the horizon there seemed to be thousands of red, green and white stars, twinkling in the sky. They all seemed to be at about the same altitude. They weren't stars; they were blinking nav lights from other aircraft. The men of the 307th didn't know it, but almost the entire 8th Air Force was flying that morning.

Moving into position under the tankers, they heard some familiar voices over the radio. Some of the tankers were from the 307th AREFS. They had flown out of Harmon to provide support not only for their fellow Three Ought Seveners, but also for the other wings flying the mission.

After hanging in position long enough to gulp down 38,000 pounds of JP-4, the B-47s dropped off the boom, cleared the tankers and climbed back up into the frigid Canadian stratosphere. The next leg would take them farther north, almost to the Labrador coast. Turning back towards the southwest, they flew a straight navigation leg with timing checkpoints. Ever since they had refueled, they had been above solid clouds. That far north, there wasn't much to see on the ground anyway.

The navigator's radar picked up St. John's Bay on the southern tip of Hudson Bay. Anyway, it looked like it should be St. John's Bay; hard to tell water from land with everything frozen over. Finally they were able to pick up the outline of Amrimiski Island, then a faint signal from Wapisk weather station; they were right on course for Nippigon, the end point for the navigation leg on the north shore of Lake Superior. Over Lake Superior, the lead cell picked up a message coming in on the high frequency AN/ARC-66 radio.

"SKYKING...SKYKING...
This is Jumbo with a message for all SKYKING aircraft.
Stand by. Message to follow. Break ..Break."

After copying the message, it was decoded by the crews. Checking the mission folder for the results, some of the aircraft received the coded message "Beer Can", the recall order. These aircraft would finish the navigation leg and return to Lincoln. The other aircraft decoded the message "Scarlett O'Hara", the "go code". They would make a bomb run on their assigned target outlined in the folder.

The strike aircraft crews made a short study of their target. The 307th had been assigned three primary targets: Estherville, Iowa; Fort Dodge, Iowa; and Newton, Iowa. The aiming point would be the center of each city. The profile called for the bomb run to be made at .810 mach from 36,000 feet. Radar scope photos were to be taken on each target at release. After hitting their targets, the strike aircraft did a "Hi Jinks" breakaway and took up a heading for home. Since the last cell didn't leave Lincoln until 1013 hours, there would be aircraft coming and going for most of the day.

# 1958

While the bombers were flying Grand Slam, the 307th AREFS was providing support from Harmon. Their part of the huge joint SAC and 8th Air Force operation was called Full Force. Not only was the 307th AREFS flying, but almost every air-refueling asset in the 8th Air Force was in the air. Bad weather in the lower forty-eight caused most of the tanker force to recover at Harmon. This caused a hell of a traffic jam. Earl Bullock remembered:

"There were so many tankers on base we couldn't taxi to the refueling area. We had to sit on the ground waiting in line to refuel with our engines running. One of the pilots got tired of sitting and waiting. He radioed the tower and told them that if the line didn't move pretty soon he was going to divert to his alternate."

Ken Tarwater wrote:

"KC-97s were coming into Harmon from all over. They were flying long refueling missions and the ground crews were thinking maybe we were at war. Our aircraft would come back, we would refuel, check the logs and, if it was flyable, another crew got aboard and off they went. Sgt Jack Wilkins and I had gotten the plane back to our parking area and had it ready to go. We hadn't eaten for some time, so we decided to go get some chow. When we came back twenty minutes later, our plane was missing and no one knew, or would tell us, where it was or who took it. Sgt Wilkins didn't know what else to do, so he went by the book, of course. He reported it as stolen, I guess so we wouldn't have to pay the Air Force for a KC-97. About four hours later, old 377 showed up. The flight crew's assigned 97 had to have some maintenance, so they checked our log and had one of the crew chiefs kick them out."

Everyone who lived at Lincoln knew it was in the heart of the Central Flyway for ducks and geese flying south for the winter. Every fall, a lot of members of the 307th would dust off the old shotgun, grab the waders and head for the duck blind. It was nice to get away from the grind at the base, go hunting and bag a couple of ducks or geese for the table. However, ducks and geese could be bad news for a low-flying B-47.

On 18 November, 53-4222 returned from a mission. They had done well on navigation, bombing and the other items on the mission profile. They also managed to bag a duck. Crew chief Paul Koski remembered:

"My plane landed in the early evening and the recovery team had parked it and done the post-flight. I reported for roll call the next morning and the flight chief was briefing us on what the day's activities would be. When he got to my aircraft, he said it had a bird strike and I would need a B-5 stand at the aircraft for the investigation and pictures.

"My plane had indeed taken a bird (duck) strike on the leading edge of the left wing, between #1 and #2 engines. The hole was about the size of a football. It not only damaged the wing, but also blew up the hot air duct that ran inside the wing.

"We moved the aircraft into the hangar, assessed the damage and ordered parts. The leading edge was attached with about 25 Allen-head screws and could be reached by removing the lower wing access panels. These were located just aft of the bottom leading edge of the wing and were six inches by six inches, just big enough to put your hand into. You were basically working by feel since you couldn't put your hand and a mirror in at the same time. We couldn't loosen the screws, so we had to call the factory and ask for help.

"They said when the wing was assembled, it was flat and not drooping down like it is when attached to the aircraft. They said that we would have to jack the aircraft up to relieve the pressure on the screws and, since we were working with two skins that had to line up, that we shouldn't take the aircraft off the jacks until the job was done.

"Well, we jacked the aircraft for several hours until we could remove the leading edge and remove the pieces of the hot air duct. We ordered all the parts on a priority AOG and were promised overnight delivery. We placarded the aircraft to not remove the jacks and went home.

"The next day, we went to the hangar and found they had moved the aircraft outside. They said they had a higher priority for a retraction test on another aircraft. When we finally got the aircraft back inside, we spent the next three days jacking it up and down, trying to get all the holes to line up. Finally we got everything to line up and completed the work. That's why I hate ducks."

In November, the 307th was one of three wings to begin a test program of field repair of jet engines. Instead of sending engines to the depot, the engine shop would repair the J-47s locally. The program was designed to save time and money for engine changes and repair. It appeared to be a good idea and, with the increase in workload, maybe the shop would have a few extra bodies to help turn the wrenches.

The wing started December on a high note. Word came in from 8th Air Force that because of their efficiency and ability to accomplish their mission, the 307th AREFS had tied for the coveted Golden Boom award in November. It was some great news for the guys working in the freezing temperatures and snow at Harmon.

The December *Nuts and Jolts* hit the flight line on the 6th of December. This issue was devoted to the arrival of winter and the impending yearly duel with the "Hawk". Most of the flight line troops had already dug out their long johns and parkas so they would be ready for Old Man Winter's arrival.

There was a timely section on how to dress in layers to help ward off cold temperatures. Then, there was a section on the importance of the buddy system while working out in the cold. It stressed the importance of keeping an eye out for frostbite and checking your partner for signs of exposure. It mentioned that gloves should be worn at all times when working with cold soaked tools. That's great advice, but have you ever tried to thread a nut to a bolt with gloves on? Have fun! See you in the spring!

Finally, crew chiefs were told how to properly care for power cords and ground communication cables. It mentioned they should always be coiled and hung up out of the snow. Never leave them on the ground when not in use. Why, you ask? You only had to chop fifty feet of communication cord out of the ice with a screwdriver one time to learn that lesson.

A night mass gas refueling was scheduled for 10 December. Mass gas refuelings always increased the "pucker factor". Visualize six B-47s coming down from their cruising altitude to find the orbiting tankers. The real fun started when everybody started trying to find their assigned tanker. Doing it at night or in bad weather? Well, that would increase the pucker factor to plus ten. Dale Christians recalled:

"Sometimes refueling was real hairy. I remember once when George Biggs was leading a flight of three B-47s and we were letting down through the clouds to get behind the tankers. The navigator had a signal on his radar to tell how far we were from the tankers, but in the clouds, he had to go into a different mode on the radar to keep track of the other B-47s. I remember I had to make a pull up pretty hard to keep from hitting Biggs. I couldn't turn to the side as I had another aircraft over there."

The mass gas refueling mission on the 10th went well. Everyone got their offloads and returned to the roost at Lincoln. During the postflight, the crew chief on 53-2111 gave his bird the usual look-over to make sure the flight crew had brought her back with the wings still attached. The wings may have been fine, but there was something strange about the #1 engine. The ring cowling was blown inward while the islands looked bent outward. The internal skin of the cowling was forced inward into the airflow intake. Obviously, there had been some kind of internal problem.

After pulling the cowling and digging into the innards of the engine, it was the usual "Well, here's your problem!" The relief valves around the aft ring of the nose cone had failed to release the excessive pressure. This resulted in a mini explosion, causing the damage. The flight crew had had no indication of any problem. No vibration, no change in EGT, no nothing. The engine just kept turning like a fine tuned watch. The first indication of the problem was during the recovery post flight. Snatched another one from the gods!

Unexpected danger lurked not only in the air, but also on the ground. Paul Koski remembered:

"My aircraft was due for a periodic inspection. This was just about the only time we got to wash the aircraft since the inspection team wanted a clean working environment. As it was the middle of winter, the wash rack was closed for ice. They were using the jumbo hangar to perform the periodic and elected to wash the aircraft in the hangar the day before the inspection.

"Work stands were positioned and the aircraft opened up, cowling removed. The pre-inspection meeting had taken place the day before. The 781 was checked for open write-ups and parts ordered. We were ready for the inspection crew. They arrived around eight o'clock and wheeled the rectifier (power for the aircraft) in place, laying out the ground power cables to get ready to connect to the aircraft. They had to plug the rectifier's power cable into the hangar floor to power up the rectifier. When they did, all hell broke loose.

"It seems that when they washed the aircraft, water had gotten into the receptacle and when they plugged it in, everything shorted out. The power cable that was going from the rectifier to the aircraft began flopping around and everything it touched, sparks would fly. It was like a snake; you didn't know where it would strike next. It was also like a cutting torch and when it hit the wheel well door, it cut right through the skin, leaving a big gash across the door.

"The only thing I could think of was to save myself, because if it hit the work stand I was on, I would be fried and, even worse, if it hit a fuel line or fuel cell, the whole hangar would go up in flames as well as the people and aircraft.

"I ran, jumped or flew off the stand and it had to be twenty feet before I touched down. I was all the way across the hangar and starting to open the door, when someone yelled it was under control. Someone had had enough sense to grab the cable so it wouldn't cause any more damage. That person had to be very brave, or didn't have any choice. I came back to the aircraft and there was Airman Gary Browns, holding on to the cable, hollering at the top of his lungs to get someone to turn off the power. No one knew where the power switch was and it took about ten minutes to locate it. Gary had to hold that cable all that time.

"Even though we could have lost a lot of people, hangar and the aircraft, there were no medals or recognition of what he did. I think it was because no one wanted to admit the mistakes that were made. The landing gear door was repaired and the inspection completed on time. One thing did come of this mess: No more washing aircraft in the hangar. All washing would take place on the wash rack, weather permitting."

Up at Harmon, the tankers were up to their booms in snow. It may have been balmy when they arrived, but now it was December, which meant cold weather and snow, lots of it. It didn't take long for everyone to start disliking the weather man. It seemed the only word in his vocabulary was "snow".

Every time it snowed the KC-97s had to be swept clear of the white stuff. The boys developed a unique way of removing it from the top of the fuselage. They would sling a rope across the top and then walk it back and forth till most of the snow was gone. Crude, but effective.

Often the tankers had to be dug out. Bill Novetzke wrote, "Sometimes we helped the ground crews literally shovel out a path in front of the main and nose gear to allow us to taxi off the blocks."

Just getting the engines started was a special chore in the cold. Sitting on the ramp, the tanker looked like an octopus with the engine preheat ducting hanging down like tentacles. It took over four hours to preflight and preheat engines using the ground unit or onboard APU.

Starting engines wasn't the only problem. The almost daily Bravo alerts at Harmon were causing an overabundance of spark plug fouling on the R-4360 engines. The crews dug into the Dash-1 and went through the procedures for defouling the plugs on the ground. That involved running the engines at 800 to 1,000 rpm for about two minutes, then gradually reducing the mixture until there was a drop in the rpm. Then, run the engines for at least another two to four minutes. Cowl flaps had to be adjusted to maintain proper cylinder head temperature. It all meant a lot of extra work out there in the cold.

Anyone who ever worked on a R-4360 engine would remember changing spark plugs. Ken Tarwater was assistant crew chief on several KC-97s:

"One of the last things the flight engineer did was scan the engines with the engine analyzer and make write-ups on the plugs, coils and leads. All could be identified with a cylinder location and which problem we had. This was very important because on a KC-97 and its four 'corncobs', there were 224 spark plugs, 224 sparkplug coils and 224 sparkplug leads for a total of 672 possible problems.

"Lucky for us, the earlier engines had more problems with plugs than our models. So, lots of times we had only to take off the lower cowl ring, but not always. Seems like the lower plugs had more oil fouling than the upper ones. The spark plug coil was mounted very close to the cylinder that it went to and it had a low voltage lead coming from the magneto coming in one end and a high voltage lead going to the plug coming out the other end. As I remember, some of the plugs were very hard to get to and others were out in the open.

"The part you have to take into consideration is that all of this was done on the flight line at Lincoln, Nebraska, or wherever we were at the moment. You could be in anything from a dust storm to rain or blizzard conditions with snow and cold, cold wind blowing up your you-know-what. I can still remember my fingers being so cold I couldn't feel them and you couldn't tell if you had a plug in your hand or not, or so hot during the summer you burnt your fingers. If you dropped a plug you had to send it back for reconditioning. The spark plug leads always wanted to cross thread and you had to make sure they weren't before you put a wrench on and tightened them, or else you had another lead and plug change.

"Everett Sutherland told me about a spark plug event that happened to him on 52-2800. He had been working on a plug change on the upper front cylinder when they sounded an alert. He quickly installed the cowling forgetting to put the spark plug wire on the plug. When the flight crew started the engines, Sutherland noticed sparks coming from the front of the #2 engine. Knowing what he had done, he entered the aircraft, opened the left overwing door and crawled out onto the wing. The flight crew had shut down the #2 engine and Sutherland crawled out to the front of the engine and sat on the nose dome of the prop, reaching in and hooked up the spark plug lead. If you don't think this wasn't quite a feat, think about

## 1958

crawling out there on that round slick cowling with the #1 engine running and a big Hamilton Standard prop spinning at about 1,000 rpm just a few feet away from you."

Everett Sutherland recalled the incident:

"As soon as they started up the engine, I knew what I had forgotten to do. So I climbed out there and hooked up the lead. I remember it was hot as hell in my hand as I was trying to hook it up. Some officer in a truck spotted me out there and came over and was yelling at me to get off the prop dome, I said, 'Not till I get it hooked up.' Of course, with the engines running he couldn't hear a word I said. The aircraft taxied on time and I caught hell for getting out there with the #1 engine running. Well, you know how it was when you were young and foolish."

At the last staff meeting before Christmas, Col Read went over the yearly recap. The 307th had put in a busy year. Reflex had caused problems all year. Hopefully the increased manning of the 424th in January would help with scheduling. The alert force had achieved an 89% effectiveness rating for the entire year. He also mentioned that the 307th, along with the 818th Air Division, would be transferred to the 2nd Air Force effective January 1st.

Christmas was on final approach. Everyone in the 307th was busy as little elves. They were trying to get as many 50-8 squares filled as possible before the holiday break. After all, when "Santa SAC" checked his list, they wanted to be in the "nice" column.

Depending on the flight schedule, the men of the 307th AREFS deployed to Harmon spent Christmas Eve in various ways. Some exchanged small gifts with each other. Bill Novetzke recalled:

"I remember sitting at the Club bar listening to Christmas Carols, looking at whiskey labels behind the bar, and feeling lonesome for home and family. Also, I recall the heating unit in the BOQ going out and having to keep warm by burning some of the furniture in the dayroom fireplace. Some of the guys (Fraker and Store as I recall) put blankets over their heads and did a takeoff on the three wise men."

Earl Bullock's crew was scheduled to fly on Christmas Eve. The actual reason for the mission is lost to history. It was most likely a routine refueling mission. Legend has it that they were supposed to head up to the "Silver Fox" refueling area and stand by to refuel a special flight coming down from the North Pole. Earl's crew was ready with preflight almost done when bad weather moved in and their flight was called off at the last minute. The special flight from the North Pole would have to find an alternate area and tanker to refuel the eight tiny reindeer.

Men of the 307th ARES man the shovels after a visit from "The Hawk" (Zester)

Reflex B-47 on the boom off the coast of Maine. (303rd ARS)

# Cold War Cornhuskers: The 307th Bomb Wing Lincoln Air Force Base Nebraska 1955-1965

Fuel transfer complete the B-47 droops away from the tanker and continues towards England. (303rd ARS)

Crawlway looking towards Bombay (Bright)

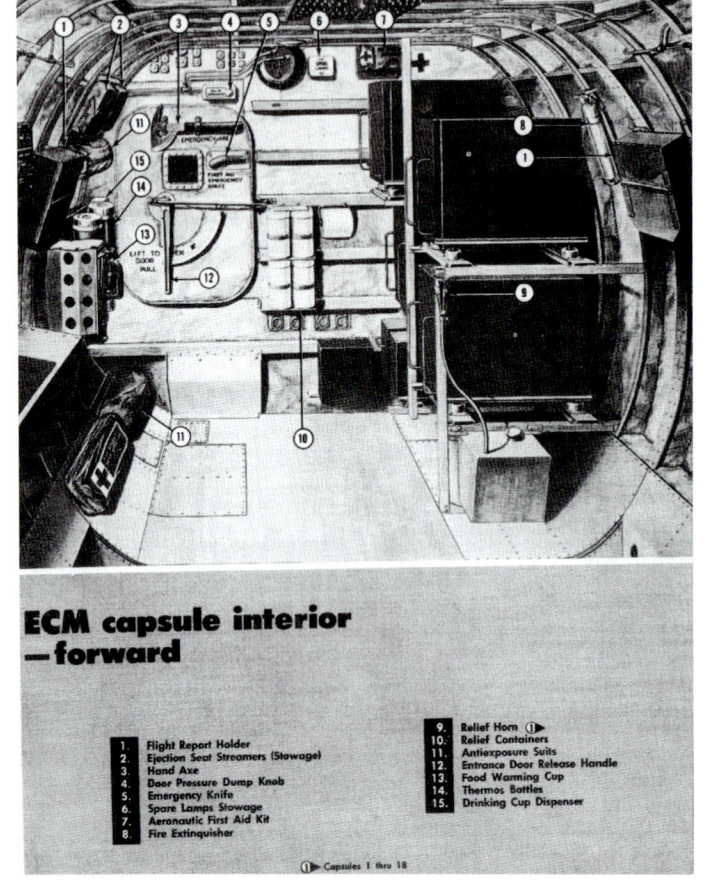

ECM Capsule diagram from the B-47 Dash-1.

Bombay interior looking forward. Capsule entry door would connect with crawlway at left. (M.Hill)

# 1958

B-47s taxi towards the north during a COCO Alert. (Tarwater)

With the Klaxon still blaring, crews hit the Alert Ramp at Greenham Common. (USAF).

Leaving a long trail of water alcohol augmentation and JP-4 smoke, a B-47 leaves Lincoln for a training mission. (USAF)

An airman stands guard by a cocked B-47 waiting for the crew to arrive. (USAD)

*Cold War Cornhuskers: The 307th Bomb Wing Lincoln Air Force Base Nebraska 1955-1965*

Andy Devine and members of the 370th Bomb Squadron. (307th BWA)

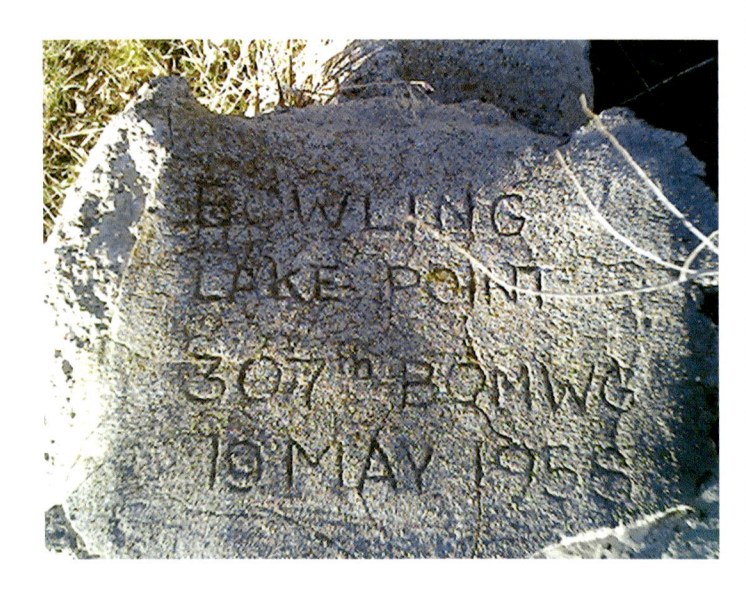

A Alert Vehicle arrive in a blur. The Crew Chief is busy pulling engine intake plugs. (USAF)

Bowling Lake Point. The date was commemorated in concrete. (307th BWA)

A&E technician bore sighting the 20mm tail guns. Dangerous at any time, as Merrill Sinclair and his ground crew found out. (USAF)

# 1958

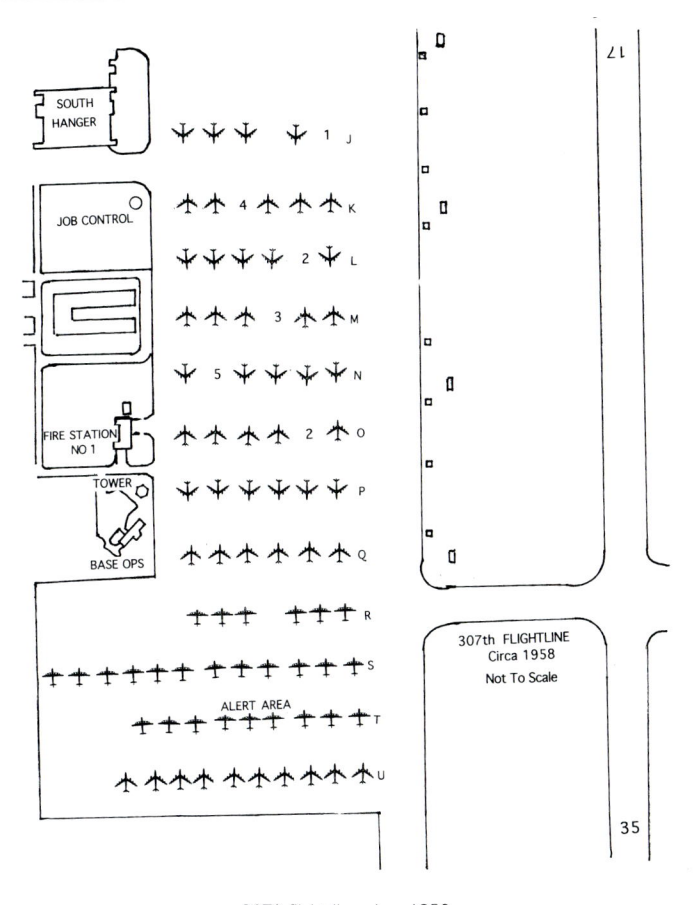

307th flight line circa 1958.

Lou Weber's statue of Russell Bowling. (Mary Aston Bowling)

LAFB Flight line, Row Q. Front to Back: 52-0214, 53-6236, 53-1910, 52-0075, 51-5248, 52-0323. (USAF via King)

103

# Cold War Cornhuskers: The 307th Bomb Wing Lincoln Air Force Base Nebraska 1955-1965

Bowling Lake Dedication. L-R Becky Bowling, General Walter Sweeney, Mary Bowling, Preston Bowling (brother), Sarah Bowling (mother). (Mary Aston Bowling)

Nebraska Air National Guard F-86s approach the crowd moments before changing into the missing man formation. (Mary Aston Bowling)

Governor Victor Anderson addressed the crowd. (Mary Aston Bowling)

Gen. Sweeney addressed the crowd. (Marty Aston Bowling)

Andy "Jingles" Devine, Becky, Robert and Lou Weber, moments after the statue was unveiled. (Mary Aston Bowling)

L-R. B/Gen Hoisington, Mary Bowling, Preston Bowling, Robert Bowling, Sarah Bowling, Becky Bowling, and Andy Devine. (Mary Aston Bowling)

# 1958

The Bowling family and Andy Devine. (Mary Aston Bowling)

The family surveys the lake. (Mary Aston Bowling)

The crowd was treated to a water ski show. (307th BWA)

An Air Force helicopter demonstrates rescue capabilities. (307th BWA)

Andy Devine's Lighthouse. (Mary Aston Bowling)

53-4227 off the right wing of the tanker before climbing back to mission altitude. (Vorchheimer)

# Cold War Cornhuskers: The 307th Bomb Wing Lincoln Air Force Base Nebraska 1955-1965

#793 starting engines. That's Vern Cole leaning out of the cockpit window during an earlier mission. (Bullock)

Jimmy Stewart played Col. "Dutch" Holland in the movie *Strategic Air Command*. He flew a real B-47 from the 307th to maintain flight proficiency. (Paramount Studios)

KC-97 794 on the flight line preparing for the trip to Harmon AB, Newfoundland. (307th BWA)

An interesting and rare view of a KC-97. (303rd ARS)

## 1958

A B-47 departs the base in a cloud of smoke. (Joe Bruch Collection)

Pilot's view of the tanker. (307th BWA)

Air operations at Harmon, AB, Newfoundland. (USAF)

During refueling for Operation GRAND SLAM the boom operators met up with B-47s from back home at Lincoln. (307th BWA)

# Cold War Cornhuskers: The 307th Bomb Wing Lincoln Air Force Base Nebraska 1955-1965

Msgt Jack Wilkins and Ken Tarwater work on an engine on their tanker. (Tarwater)

Four triple deuce on the LAFB ramp. She suffered a bird strike on November 18th. (307th BWA)

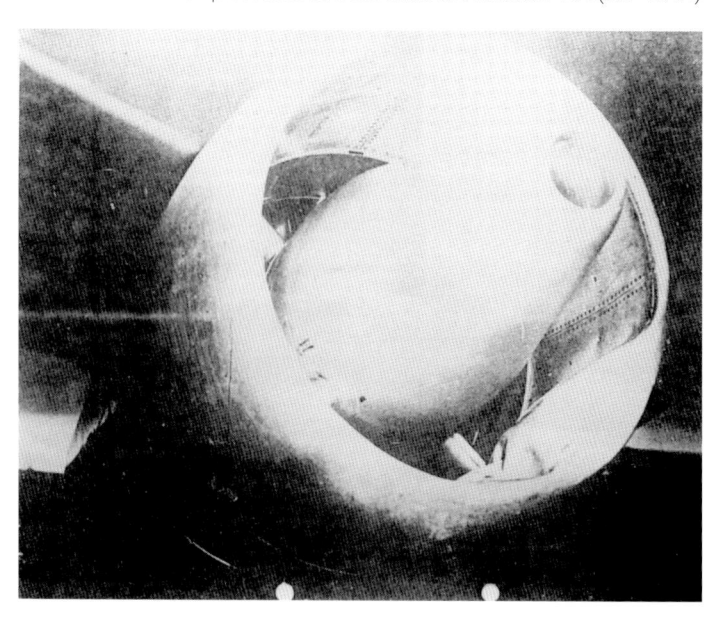

Bent inlet on the #1 engine. (USAF)

Bent inlet on #2111. (USAF)

Weather briefing for the 307th ARES at Harmon, December 11th. According to the board the forecasted high for the day would be 16 degrees. (USAF).

## 1958

Cleaning snow of the wing using the Mark-1 broom. (307th BWA)

Another day at Harmon AB, Newfoundland. (USAF)

2804 getting ready for another refueling mission at Harmon. (USAF)

Crews working on the #3 engine on the cold snow covered ramp. (USAF)

Above left: Diagram from the KC-97 Dash-1 showing the engine pre-heat ducting. (USAF)

Left: Earl Bullock's crew preparing for their Christmas Eve "special" mission. (Bullock)

# 1959

The 818th Air Division and both wings at Lincoln Air Force Base were officially transferred to the 2nd Air Force, effective January 1, 1959. The real bright spot for the 307th was there would be no more Pacesetter missions. However, it was soon learned the 2nd Air Force had its own version called Heads Up. Along with the change, Major Charles Fries assumed command of the 307th Headquarters Squadron effective on the first.

At roll call on the morning of 3 January, the flight line troops had some special instructions. They were to make sure the area around their aircraft was clean and spiffed up. They were also reminded to make sure they had sewn the reflective tape to their parkas or field jackets and to wear clean fatigues to work on 5 January. The reason for all of this special cleanup and tape sewing was that Lt Gen Joseph P. McConnell, Commander of the 2nd Air Force, would be on base that day to meet the new members of his command. So, it was a special "look sharp" for the 2nd Air Force boss and make a good first impression.

On Wednesday, the 7th, the lead wave of the 307th AREFS returned from the North Country. The ramp was covered with snow, the wind was blowing and it was cold, but the returning tanker troops were sure happy to see their families.

The second wave of tankers was scheduled to arrive on Thursday, but bad weather moved into Lincoln and the tankers had to divert to other bases. Reunions were placed on hold till Old Man Winter would cooperate. Ken Tarwater was in the second wave and recalls:

"We got to go to Whiteman AFB, Missouri, for the night and went to Lincoln the next day. While at Whiteman, the Captain told us we had a really bad oil leak on one of the engines and had used a lot of reserve oil. We were all ready to get to Lincoln so we just serviced the oil, took off, got to altitude and then feathered the engine and flew on to Lincoln on three engines.

"I remember my Dad, brother and brother-in-law had come up from Harrisonville, Missouri, to pick me up. They were waiting an extra day and night. Because of the storm, the only lodging they could find was an old hotel downtown. The next morning, they were back out to the base waiting with several other folks when the Air Force informed them they would feed and house them until we got in. So, after all, they had a good time seeing where I worked and lived and the Air Force fed them all."

On Friday, the 9th, Capt Donald Love left Kearney, Nebraska, in his little Aerocoupe for Lincoln. He was coming to Lincoln for a weekend with the Nebraska Air National Guard. By the time he got near Lincoln, the weather had turned from fairly nice to almost zero-zero visibility because of fog. He called the tower and declared an emergency. The tower managed to get him turned over to the GCA folks, who in turn got him into an orbit around the KOLN-TV tower.

Capt James Campbell from the 818th AD and Maj Jack Crook of the 307th scrambled in a Base Flight C-47. They were able to pick their way through the soup, found the little Aerocoupe and managed to find a couple of holes in the fog. With the help of GCA and a healthy portion of skill and luck, they were able to get the little plane down safely. Their exploits were written up in the 16 January edition of the *Jet Scoop*.

The 424th Bomb Squadron was officially activated on 9 January. Lt Col Walter F Duch was the first squadron commander. It was hoped that the activation of the fourth squadron would make scheduling of alert crews and crews for Reflex commitment a lot easier for the planning staff. With the extra aircraft coming in, there would be an influx of additional personnel to fix and fly. That is, if everything worked out as planned.

Because of Old Man Winter at Harmon, Lincoln, and points in between, it took several days for Military Air Transport Service to get the entire 307th AREFS home to Lincoln. Families waited at the Service Club for the planes to dribble in. While they waited, Family Services and the Lincoln Lions Club played movies for the children and served lunches. It was a long wait, but by the 10th, all of the hunters were home from Harmon.

The 307th put four B-47s in the air to fly a Devil Fish mission on Wednesday, the 14th. These missions were in support of the Air Research and Development Command. Leaving Lincoln, the flight took the crews almost due east. Near Cleveland, Ohio, they met tankers from Dow AFB, Maine, in the Tea Shop refueling area and took on 30,000 pounds of JP-4. After refueling, the planes turned north for Quebec City. There, the B-47s turned and made a bomb run on Boston using as much ECM jamming as they could pump out. These missions were used to help calibrate SAGE system radar stations along the East coast and a research facility at Massachusetts Institute of Technology.

Friday, January 16th, Col Read held his weekly staff meeting. He spent most of the agenda going over the goals for the wing during the coming year. He brought out that during his visit to the base, Lt Gen Francis Griswold, Vice Commander-in-Chief of SAC, had been pleased by what he had seen in the 307th area.

He also mentioned several comments from the 818th Air Division. The commander wanted all of the doors in the barracks repainted. Name tags were to be placed on the doors and lockers. Finally, flight suits should be dry cleaned to prevent them from shrinking.

Word came down from SAC that visual bomb release using the MB-4 blue training bomb would again be a training requirement. The crews would remember it wasn't long ago that the visual release was taken out of the training program. Apparently SAC found a source for the "Blue Devils", so now it was back on the schedule. Squadron wits speculated that they had gone to the Surplus Center on "O" Street and bought out the store's supply of the little blue bombs.

The *Jet Scoop* hit the ramp on 16 January like it did every Friday. There was a lot of news about the 307th AREFS returning from their TDY. There was also the infamous "Roads Gallery". A high point was the advertisement from the Surplus Center on West "O". They had a special on the famous black Korean Boots. You could get a pair for $10.95. Some of the flight line boys took advantage of the sale and bought a pair. At least they would have warm feet the next time the north wind blew in.

On the 21st the wing launched a Big Blast mission, similar to the Devil Fish missions. They would use maximum ECM capabilities against the Air Defense Command. These missions would become a routine part of the SAC flying schedule. A lot of information was gained by flying these missions.

Maj William Minor left the wing for a new assignment at SAC Headquarters. He had been a member of the 307th advance party that arrived in November 1955. He helped get the wing set up at Lincoln and had watched the wing grow during his five-year tour. He was the last member of the original cadre to leave the 307th.

The 307th AREFS tied for the "Golden Boom" award in November with TDY at Harmon. Lt Col Oliver Fowler, Squadron Commander, received word the squadron had won the "Golden Boom" award for December. 8th Air Force awarded the trophy to the squadron, even though they were now part of 2nd Air Force. It was a nice way to give recognition for a lot of hard work in the frozen north.

January went into the wing history as a routine month. The 307th chalked up 39 late takeoffs during the month. Weather conditions cost the wing 161 flying hours. As for the Management Control System (MCS), the wing scored 100 % effective. As usual during the winter, weather caused most of the problems. It caused fuel leaks, lost flying hours and lost manpower hours when people couldn't get to the base and report for duty.

February kicked off with a message from SAC Headquarters on the 1st. It directed the 307th AREFS to provide refueling support for the 340th Bomb Wing during their ORI. The liability period for the operation was from February to April 15th. The squadron would be required to provide twenty-one tankers for the mission.

February was filled with routine training flights, Alert, Reflex, and the daily grind on the flight line. Aircraft were coming and going with redeployments and profile flights on a daily basis. That is, when the weather was suitable for safe flying.

During the last several months of 1958, the wing transferred out twenty-five of the 1953 model B-47s. Eight of the Phase V ECM aircraft were sent to Lockbourne AFB, Ohio. The wing received replacements; however, seventeen of them were 1951 and 1952 models. This caused problems in maintenance due to the subtle differences in parts and fittings. It also caused problems for the flight crews due to the different switch positions, equipment, seats and systems.

The difference between the aircraft was brought out in February when a navigator grabbed a handle that was in a different place than he was accustomed to and released the escape hatch. This small difference could have spelled disaster if the aircraft had been in the air. Luckily, it happened during engine start and the mission was aborted. Since the mission was aborted, the wing lost MCS points due to a situation they had little control over.

On the 15th, Lincoln was hit with a good old-fashioned Nebraska snowstorm. So what's new? The storm caused two Big Blast sorties to be canceled. Snow piled up hour after hour, causing seven routine missions to be called off. Not a good situation for the squares on the 50-8 requirement board. At least the kids in the housing area enjoyed an extra day off from school.

Friday, February 17th, dawned clear and bright. The snow had stopped falling late that night. Snow removal crews were on the job, hitting the roads like a "duck after a June bug". By late afternoon they had the runway cleared and as much of the flight line as possible. Ground crews would have to finish the job of digging the planes out so air operations could get back underway.

At the Lockheed plant at Marietta, Georgia, a test crew took off in 53-4208 for a test flight. The aircraft had been through IRAN, and the test flight was needed to make sure the updates were working. Something went dreadfully wrong during the flight and the aircraft crashed, killing the crew. The aircraft was still officially assigned to the 307th. However, since it was at the depot at the time of the accident and not flown by a crew from the 307th, the accident was not counted against the wing as a Class A accident.

On 27 February Col Read held Commander's Call. During the get-together, he awarded B-47 1,000 hour pins to crewmen who had accumulated at least a thousand hours of flying in the Stratojet. He also pointed out license plates on cars would expire on the 28th. He hoped everyone had their new plates on their cars so there wouldn't be any violations in the wing.

March got off to a start with six Big Blast sorties on the 5th. This was followed on the 8th with four Devil Fish missions. Two of the Devil Fish sorties had to divert to Bunker Hill AFB, Indiana, when bad weather moved into Lincoln. The same bad weather caused six training sorties to be called off.

The execution order for Operation Daisy Fox, the 340th Bomb Wing ORI, was received on 10 March. The 307th AREFS generated their tankers and launched the first nine tankers within the time window for the operation. With all of the loose snow, the tankers churned up a mini blizzard as they fired up and taxied out. From Lincoln they flew over Omaha to the orbit point near Storm Lake, Iowa. Then they set up the racetrack pattern and prepared for the arrival of the 340th BW, coming up from Missouri.

About forty minutes before the 340th arrived, the navigators in the tankers warmed up their APN-69 radar sets. Until contact with the incoming B-47s was made, the tankers would orbit and paint the sky with their radar. It was like trolling on a lake, waiting for a big Northern Pike to home in on your lure and let you know you had a strike.

**"Handcuff... Ranger 10, ETA ARCP is 15 minutes. Over."**
**"This is Handcuff Flight.**
**Roger, ETA is 15 minutes."**

When the B-47s were within fifty miles of the rendezvous point, the lead navigator in the tankers started calling off the range every 10 miles. The B-47s were descending from their cruising altitude of 35,000 feet. When they were about 500 feet below the refueling altitude they leveled off and kept closing the distance.

# Cold War Cornhuskers: The 307th Bomb Wing Lincoln Air Force Base Nebraska 1955-1965

Within twelve miles of each other, there were constant one-mile calls from the navigator in the lead tanker, until they were within five miles of each other.

**"Ranger 10... Handcuff 15.
You are four miles out. Heading 270.
Take over when you have visual."**

By now, the B-47 pilots should see the tankers at 12 o'clock high. If not, the navigators in the B-47s had them on radar. The receiver pilot pulled the power back a little to bring the closing speed down a little. Within a few moments they were within three miles of each other, closing slowly. The B-47s had to be careful not to overrun the oncoming tankers.

He was known by several handles: the boom operator, boomer or "Clancy". Lying on his ironing board in a small pod beneath the tail of the tanker, he was the next player in the aerial ballet. Looking down from his windowed pod, he could see his receiver approaching. The bomber had to be within the refueling envelope, which is very small considering the size of the two aircraft and the speed they were flying.

Skillful flying put the B-47 about twenty-five feet below and one hundred feet behind the KC-97 in what was known as the Observation Position. Now the real fun was about to begin. The tanker pilot had to fly straight and level and maintain a stable platform. When the receiver was in the correct observation position, "Clancy lowered the boom.

**"Ranger 10. Handcuff 15. You are in the slot. Stand by.
Up five. Left two. Up three."**

Clancy extended the refueling boom and, grasping the ruddervator control grip, he flew the boom into position.

**"Slipway door open. Up two.
Stand by for contact. Up one!
Contact."**

In a heartbeat latches closed, securing the aircraft together; hydraulic pressure pushed the boom valve open and JP-4 flowed down the boom at about 5,000 pounds per minute. The mission profile called for 35,000 pounds of fuel to be transferred. There were several disconnects when the receiver slipped beyond the boom limits. In spite of the disconnects, the receivers hung in there and got their fuel.

**"35,000 pounds complete, disconnect when ready."**

**"Roger, can you get the windows, and don't forget the Green Stamps this time."**

By the end of the refueling the formation was approaching St. Cloud, Minnesota. The bombers dropped off the booms and continued their ORI mission. The tankers turned and began a nav leg near Fargo, North Dakota, running to Rapid City, South Dakota, then back home to Lincoln.

The results of Daisy Fox were rated as "excellent" for the 307th AREFS. There was one tanker ground abort, which was replaced by a spare. The 307th AREFS tankers arrived on time at the Air Refueling Control Point (ARCP). Only one tanker failed to complete the 35,000 pounds of fuel offload when there was a problem with the boom.

Sunday, March 15th, was a special day at the Base Chapel. It was the celebration of the first SAC Memorial Sunday. The special service was to honor all of the men and women who were serving in SAC. Special honor was paid to those who had given their lives in the line of duty. The names of those who had made the ultimate sacrifice while serving at Lincoln were read, accompanied by a special lighting of memorial candles.

Weather forced a virtual halt to activity on Monday the 16th, as a major winter storm arrived from the west. Fifteen inches of snow blanketed not only the flight line, but also all of eastern Nebraska. Travel on base was restricted; only essential personnel were asked to report for duty—that is, if they could make it. With all of the snow on the ground, it would be a few days before operations would return to normal.

A B-47 from the 307th launched late on the afternoon of 27 March. It was a routine mission: climb out, refuel, nav leg, and a couple of bomb runs. In actuality, it was more than a normal mission. When that B-47 left Lincoln, it was the first in a never-before-or-since-matched record string of on-time takeoffs.

March had come in like a lion and roared through the first three weeks of the month. Then, all of a sudden, Old Man Winter returned to his snow cave and fell asleep until it was time to blow his icy breath again. With him gone, March went out like the proverbial lamb.

March may have gone out like a lamb, but there was still one major winter holdover: SNOW! Lincoln had recorded a near record snowfall for the winter. With moderating weather and spring-like temperatures, the mountains of snow dwindled on a daily basis.

The by-product of a near-record snowfall is, of course, near-record runoff. Before long, Oak Creek was flowing almost to the banks. Low areas on base were transformed from sparkling fields of white to shimmering mini-lakes. Speaking of lakes, Bowling Lake was brimful, which meant a great boating season.

They say April showers bring May flowers; well, not in Nebraska. Heavy April showers on top of the melting snow means farmers can't get into the fields and get the crop in. Getting the crop in wasn't the main concern of the flight crews; they had those 50-8 squares to fill.

On 3 April Col Read held a wing staff meeting. The wing was scheduled to begin an intense crew upgrade training period. This was designed to raise crew status to the highest possible level. It was also announced the new base housing would be ready to occupy in August.

Other topics brought out included that the 307th would begin a Reflex commitment at Morón Air Base, Spain, starting in July. Advance personnel would have to be in place by 1 July. So instead of Reflex in England, it would now be in Sunny Spain.

The staff was updated on the construction of the new alert facility on the north end of the ramp. The alert parking ramp is almost finished and construction on the building is set to begin in late June. When the facility was complete, alert aircraft would be moved to the north end of the flight line.

April 9th, and another nice day to fly and fill 50-8 squares. Crew R-17 commanded by Lt Howard Solomon, with Lt Mike Gingrich in the copilot seat and Lt Joseph Miller III plotting their course, took off in 6244 for a training flight. Mike Gingrich wrote:

"It was a normal mission with a celestial nav leg and one GCA approach. It was a crystal clear night and there may have been some aurora to the north. We over flew Chicago westbound, and I remember looking down at the city lights and the lake and that it was very clear. I had been daydreaming somewhat, but the vista got my attention. There was a lot of hoopla at the time about the opening and dedication of the St. Lawrence Seaway, with the Queen's visit and Chicago rolling out the red carpet. As we flew over, it was either in progress or imminent. Of course our guys who Reflexed to the UK over flew the Queen all the time."

Coming back towards Lincoln, the crew contacted the base for a practice GCA. Everything went according to plan until the final approach. Mike recalled:

"We were a couple of miles out on final for Runway 35 when number 6 engine flamed out. We shut it down and continued the landing."

April was the first month in 1959 that the flying schedule wasn't hampered by snow, freezing rain or cold temperatures. Fuel leaks caused by cold weather sealed up with warmer temperatures. N3-B parkas, Korean boots and heavy gloves were put away for the fast-approaching summer.

On the 15th, the wing flew six B-47 sorties to fulfill the monthly Devil Fish requirement, only now it was known as High Wind. The launch of these six sorties was in conjunction with an 818th Air Division test alert called Big Sickle. It was bad enough for SAC or 2nd Air Force to call practice alerts, but add the local Air Division calling one, well, it meant a lot of extra work and pressure for everyone.

The operation was fairly simple. First generate the force, then the wing staff was to select fifteen aircraft and crews to fly the mission. When the aircraft and crews were ready they would launch at fifteen-minute intervals and fly the profile.

After takeoff the bombers were to fly to Sioux Falls, South Dakota, and hook up with their tankers. Fuel transfer would be a minimum of 8,000 pounds to score as effective. Then, the B-47s were to head for the Bismarck RBS for a bomb run. From Bismarck, the strike force would change heading and fly towards Kenora, Ontario.

Flying northeast, the route took the bombers over the Red River Valley of North Dakota. From over 30,000 feet, the fliers looked down on the snow-covered countryside. They passed over the small town of Hoople, the potato capital of North Dakota. The flyers didn't know it at the time, but a lot of the potato chips they ate came from the potatoes grown in those fields below.

At Kenora, Ontario, the stream turned and headed for the checkpoint at Thunder Bay, then over Lake Superior for another checkpoint over Sault St. Marie, Michigan. At this checkpoint they turned to the southwest. Over the Lake Superior gunnery range, the copilots turned their seats to the gunnery station, depressed the 20 mm tail guns, and checked the radar to be sure the area was clear. When they were clear, they depressed the fire button and commenced firing.

Over Green Bay they changed heading again for the IP at Eau Claire, Wisconsin. At the IP they contacted the RBS at Minneapolis and verified their position. The run on Minneapolis was made from 35,000 feet at Mach .80. When the tone cut off signaling bomb release, the pen lifted from the plotting paper and the bombers pulled into a breakaway turn, then headed for Lincoln.

When the results of the missions were posted, the 307th had "beat the pants off the 98th". The 307th scored a whopping 98% effective in navigation and refueling. Better yet, the wing was scored 99% effective on the bomb runs. It was the best mission the 307th had flown on a competitive basis.

That mission helped the wing in the quarterly MCS standings. For the first quarter of the year, the 307th had scored 96.8% in the MCS, placing the wing in first place in 2nd Air Force and third overall in SAC. Lt Gen Joseph McConnell, 2nd Air Force Commander, sent a message to the 307th congratulating them on the outstanding performance during Big Sickle and on the MCS standings. He stated, "The achievement was the result of outstanding individual performance to ensure the completion of the wing's mission."

The city of Lincoln had been planning their Centennial Celebration for over a year. It was going to be a huge celebration, with special entertainment, parades, concerts and school competitions. For the summer, "O" Street downtown had been turned into a giant outside park.

The entire Centennial Celebration kicked off on 1 May with an Open House at Lincoln Air Force Base. The gates opened to the public at 1000. The 307th provided a B-47 on static display. There were flyovers by a B-47 and KC-97 in a simulated refueling. The Nebraska Air National Guard made a formation flyover in their F-86L Sabre Jets. One of the main attractions was an RAF Victor bomber. It had arrived earlier that morning after a short flight from Offutt. This was the first time an RAF bomber had landed at Lincoln Air Force Base. Despite a record-breaking temperature of ninety-three degrees, over 30,000 people passed through the gates and sweated on the sun-baked ramp just to see their tax money at work.

The Centennial Parade formed up on Saturday morning. It was the largest parade Lincoln had ever seen. Starting at noon, it took over two and a half hours to make its way down "O" Street to the Mall Area, then to the south and on to Pershing Auditorium. "Lonesome George" Gobel was the Grand Master of the parade. Later that night, "Lonesome George" kicked off the evening show and the Centennial Ball at the auditorium.

While the party was going on downtown, Capt William Barnicoat, Lt Neil Cosentino and Lt James McElvin were preflighting 53-2349 for a routine flight. SSgt Harold Morillo was on hand during the preflight to make sure the wings were still glued on and there wasn't anything dripping from the wrong places. After everything checked out the crew climbed aboard, spooled up the engines and taxied to the active runway. At 0105, Sunday, May 3rd, Capt Barnicoat lifted 2349 into the air to become the 500th sortie to fly without deviating from the flying schedule.

Col Read held the weekly staff meeting on Friday, the 8th of May. On his agenda was the training program for the next four months. Again, visual release of the "Blue Devil" training bomb was back on the training program. One item that took considerable time was a recent security test that the sister wing at Lincoln had failed. Col Read stated if any altimeter was found to be set at 10,000 feet plus or minus incorrectly, a "Seven-High" sabotage alert was to be called immediately.

On the 11th, four B-47s flew a Tan Glove mission. This was the new designation for the old Big Blast mission. This was to be a daylight mission. Leaving Lincoln, the route would take the B-47s to Green Bay, and then they would do a fireout over Lake Michigan. After the fireout, there were several nav legs taking them up to Hudson Bay before turning back and commencing their ECM runs on selected targets along the East coast.

The 307th flew a High Wind mission on 13 May. The six B-47s flew the scheduled mission without any major problems either during launch or during the mission. Along with the standard High Wind profile, the B-47s packed as many training items as possible into the eight-hour mission to fill a few of the 50-8 squares.

On 17 May the new altitude chamber was opened on base. This was a welcome addition to Lincoln Air Force Base. Flight crews wouldn't have to go to Omaha or Shilling for the yearly training and qualification. Now they could be scheduled for the chamber locally. The qualification included going up to altitude and learning the signs of hypoxia after taking off the oxygen mask. Flight crews also learned what to expect during rapid decompression.

Under the training schedule for the month, a mass gas refueling was to be flown every Tuesday during the night missions. The mass gas on the 19th was noteworthy for an in-flight incident. During the refueling turbulence caused several disconnects. One of the B-47s had a problem with the disconnect latches which caused a brute force disconnect. The only damage was to the refueling door, which was torn off. The crew brought the bird home without the door covering the receptacle in the nose and perhaps some wounded pride over the incident.

The month ended with the wing completing almost all of the 50-8 requirements for the month. There were four mass gas refuelings, which filled in squares on both tanker and bomber slots. As of the 31st, the 307th had chalked up 798 sorties without a deviation from the flight schedule.

Visitors to Bowling Lake noticed some new arrivals on the island in the middle of the lake. A small herd of sheep had been ferried across the lake and placed on the island. The sheep were going to live on the island, acting as resident lawn mowers. A small shelter was built for them in case of inclement weather. The sheep seemed to be happy on the island. After

## Cold War Cornhuskers: The 307th Bomb Wing Lincoln Air Force Base Nebraska 1955-1965

all there was plenty to eat, and all they had to do was put up with the noise from the boats.

June would be another busy month for the 307th. The primary activity would be the constant training flights to fill in the squares on the big board. The wing would launch sorties around the clock in an effort to get the 50-8 squares filled in. Some of the squares were taken care of on 3 June. SAC was always coming up with new ways of evaluating not only the crews, but also the system. Sometimes, Offutt would combine different types of missions into one. That was the case with the High Wind missions in June. SAC decided to combine High Wind with something called Spring Tonic.

The first combined mission was scheduled to be flown on 3 June. Six B-47s would fly High Wind, and six would fly Spring Tonic. The crews flying High Wind would take a route into Canada as far north as Hudson Bay, then back into the USA, sending out as much ECM music as possible for a standard Phase IV equipped B-47.

Spring Tonic would be flown at low altitude to evaluate the ability of the crews to fly, navigate and bomb from an altitude of about 500 feet or less. The route for the low-level part of the mission would take the six B-47s northwest from Lincoln across the Sandhills region of Nebraska to a checkpoint at Murdo, South Dakota. From there they would continue to Miles City, Montana, another checkpoint. At Miles City they ended the navigation leg for that part of the mission.

Anyone who has traveled in that area of Nebraska and South Dakota knows it is sparsely populated: no major cities, just a lot of wide open space, so flying low wasn't going to bother anyone. A great place to fly while hugging the deck. You never knew what was just over the next rise.

One crew popped over a ridge and down the other side at about 200 feet. There, in front of them was a large heard of cattle and some cowboys who had apparently just rounded up the dogies. It was hard to say who was more surprised, the cattle or their keepers. The bovines scattered in all directions as the big silver bird hurtled over them and continued like a bat out of hell down the valley and over the next ridge.

After turning southwest at Miles City, the route took the bombers to a turn point to fly down the Big Horn Valley. Hugging the Eastern edge of the valley, they followed the Little Big Horn River towards the south. This wasn't a sightseeing tour, but perhaps they managed to glance off to the left and catch a glimpse of the Custer Battlefield as they hurtled towards the south. Looming ahead were the Big Horn Mountains. A slight heading change and the B-47s were hugging the foothills, masking the planes from any radar that might be searching for them.

Flying down the East side of the Big Horns was a history buff's dream come true, if they could only stop and look around. No time for that, so again, just a fleeting look as they roared over the sights of the Wagon Box Fight, Fetterman's Fight and old Fort Phil Kearney. Then it was on to Laramie, Wyoming, then to the turn point near Greeley, Colorado.

At Greeley, the strike force flew towards eastern Colorado and into their home state of Nebraska. The last part of the mission was to complete a pop up bomb run on the Hastings bomb plot, then home to Lincoln. Spring Tonic had covered a lot of ground. During their run down the east side of the Big Horn Mountains, the flight crews had covered more miles in a few minutes than early settlers could cover in days.

Thursday, June 4th, 53-4217 was scheduled for a training flight. During preflight the crew found a problem with the N-1 compass. A quick check found a fuse had blown, so it was replaced. During engine start the fuse blew again. After some trouble-shooting, the problem was found to be in the directional gyro. The string of non-deviation from the flight schedule was in serious jeopardy. Two specialists tore into the guts of 4217 and changed the gyro unit in record time. 4217 departed for the mission within the established guidelines.

Every time a B-47 from the 307th launched without deviating from the flying schedule the string that began back in March continued to grow. By now, SAC Headquarters was keeping a close eye on the 307th. They even sent several teams to Lincoln to check the records and make sure there wasn't any cheating or shuffling of the schedule going on. At this point, no one wanted to be the crew responsible for breaking the string. In some cases, a bird may have been accepted by a crew that may not have been a hundred percent ready to fly. As long as the crew believed the aircraft was safe to fly within the safety guidelines, they went ahead and flew it.

On June 15th, six B-47s flew another Spring Tonic operation. They flew the same route down history lane as the first mission had followed. There was one addition to the flight. At the last minute, Offutt added a requirement for a bomb run on Denver, before the turn towards Hastings. So the crews flying the mission would get credit for two "pop up" training squares.

In the early evening of the 16th, Crew T-36 from the 307th AREFS was busy preflighting 52-2804 for a refueling mission. The crew for the mission consisted of Capt Joseph Lloyd in command; Capt Richard Stonckiny, copilot; Lt Robert Voight, Nav; TSgt Edward McNeil, Engineer; A1C Otis Owen, RO; SSgt Charles Stroud, BO; and SSgt Sam Sloan, Crew Chief.

Sam Sloan and his assistant, Ken Tarwater, had completed the preflight, and the crew made the required walkaround to make sure everything was copacetic. The wings were still attached and the R-4360's were not dripping any more oil than usual. Everyone climbed aboard and checked the interior, then buckled up and prepared for engine start.

Sgt Sloan was on the ground headset and Airman Tarwater stood by the #3 engine as fireguard. The big Hamilton Standard turned 20 blades, then the engine coughed to life, sending copious clouds of bluish smoke billowing across the flight line. Within a few minutes, all the engines were purring like big kittens and oil pressure looked good on all four. The KC-97 moved forward, and Sam and Ken flashed a sharp salute or thumbs up.

At the end of the runway, 2804 paused for a moment while the crew made their final checks and ran up the engines. At the prescribed moment, the brakes were released and the tanker inched forward down the runway. At 1940, 2804's tires left the runway to become the 1,000th sortie to launch without a schedule deviation.

Keeping 2804 ready for a mission wasn't always easy. Ken Tarwater wrote:

"I remember lighting up the sky one night. On KC-97 804 we had a carburetor change (you jet mechanics probably thought these came only on cars) on number 3 engine. I can't remember who changed it, but it was my job to run, trim check for leaks and do the full power check, all per the maintenance manual, of course. Everything was going good until it was time for the full power check. As I was slowly taking it to T.O. power, the engine backfired. This was not a normal backfire; this was more like an explosion. It blew the turtle back cowling (this piece of cowling covered the aft accessory section including the carburetor) right off and down the ramp behind the aircraft. Luckily no one was in the way of it.

"The engine was still running at part power and burning like crazy. The guy on the headset was telling me what was going on. While this was happening, someone notified the fire department, or they may have seen the flames; I don't know which. I slowly pulled the power back to idle, it backfired again and I cut the mixture. The flames went out when the fuel was shut off, thank goodness. I could just see the airplane burning up.

"That same night, the guys put another carburetor on and it checked out fine. The next day we took the aircraft to the south hangar and the sheet metal people repaired the damage done when the cowl was blown off. Ol' 804 was once again ready for whatever needed to be done. It was determined later the carburetor was faulty and we were not at fault. In fact, we were praised for handling the situation and staying the night to get the new carburetor installed then checked out."

During a routine mission, Lt William Berry from the 371st got permission to remove his oxygen mask for a moment. Within seconds he felt strange. He started getting a headache and his vision blurred. He recognized the signs of hypoxia he had experienced during training in the altitude chamber. He was able to get his mask back on and the problem went away. A crew check showed a malfunction in the pressurization equipment. The aircraft commander took the B-47 to a lower altitude and continued the mission. Lt Berry stated, "I owe my life to that simple little test and that high altitude training."

Another Tan Glove mission was flown by six aircraft on the 17th. These monthly ECM missions not only helped calibrate the defenses along the East coast, they also opened SAC's eyes to just how inadequate the jamming capabilities of the B-47 force were. Changes would have to be made to update the ECM systems in order to give the force better capabilities to jam Soviet radar.

The maintenance section of the 307th published the first official edition of "*Nuts and Jolts*". It was a new version of the newsletter for ground crews. As before, the publication was full of timely tidbits for the boys who kept the birds ready to fly. One of the editors was MSgt William Atwood. The publication had more and more statistics and how to gain MCS points out on the line. KC-97 52-279 and 52-2802 were still listed as the "best birds" for the 307th AREFS for the month.

"*Nuts and Jolts*" wasn't just full of tidbits on maintenance. No, indeed; this issue contained a fishing report:

"Word had been received through the grapevine that trout fishing is at its PEAK now in Nebraska. TSgt Robert Conway of Red Section hooked into a few (nine by number) of the beauties, but does not care to divulge the location."

June ended with the 307th still near the top of the MCS totem pole. The wing flew 262 B-47 sorties and 102 sorties for the tankers. There were sixty-two crews rated as combat ready. Plans were underway for the Reflex commitment at Morón, Spain, which was to begin on 15 July.

There were several changes in the command staff effective on the first of July. Capt Earlen Seawards replaced Maj Charles Fries as Commander of Headquarters Squadron. Maj William Burford relieved LtCol William Miller as the 372nd Squadron Commander.

Also effective on the first, the names of the streets in Base Housing would be changed to honor Air Force Medal of Honor recipients. Within a few weeks the new street signs were in place with names like Zeamer, Metzger and Bong.

Operation Short Punt got off the ground on 3 July. A single KC-97 departed that Friday for Harmon AB with the advance party. Landing at Harmon in July was a lot better than touching down on a snow-choked runway like the last time they were there. Instead of snow, they were greeted by green trees and blue water on final approach.

The next day, after the KC-97 had been refueled and the crew had a good night's sleep, they departed on the next leg of their journey. Their destination was Lajes Field, on the Island of Terceira, Azores. The flight would be just over 1,900 miles, or about eight hours. Except for the first part of the flight after leaving Harmon, it would be all over water. Needless to say, there was a last minute briefing on emergency ditching procedures for everyone aboard.

Takeoff was at 1300 hours. After climbout, the KC-97 headed out over the blue waters of the Atlantic. It didn't take long for everyone to settle down into the flight routine. The flight crew was busy flying the plane and checking the route. The flight engineer sat at his panel and kept an eagle eye on the gauges and a well-tuned ear on the sound of the engines.

First-class seating on the KC-97 was nothing more than canvas roll-up seats along the right side of the fuselage. With extra equipment and cargo aboard, there wasn't a lot of room to move around and stretch the legs. Add to that the continuous throbbing drone of the four big radial engines and it didn't take long for the passengers to get a case of tired butt and ringing ears.

After the sun sank out of sight behind them, the passengers hoped the navigator would be able to find the Azores. After all, they were just a group of small islands out there in the Atlantic. Miss them and there was nothing solid to land on till the coast of Africa. The navigator was on the ball; at about the correct time according to his dead reckoning, the islands showed up on the radar, right where they were supposed to be. Everyone was happy to get back on the ground, stretch their legs, collect their gear and get some shuteye.

Operation Shotgun Delta was the code name for the Reflex deployment of the 307th to Morón, Spain. The first crews departed Lincoln on 7 July. Their departure was different than the usual Reflex departure. The three crews left in style (well, sort of) aboard a KC-135. All they had to do was sit back in the web seats and relax and let the flight crew do the driving, so to speak.

Eight KC-97s left for the Azores on Wednesday, July 8th. They were loaded with passengers and crammed with cargo that would be needed during the three months on the islands. They would fly to Harmon that day, refuel, and continue to the Azores the following day. While the KC-97s were headed towards the Azores, six B-47s flew one of the monthly Tan Glove missions.

The deployment of the KC-97s to the Azores didn't go exactly as planned. During the flight to Harmon, Earl Bullock's KC-97 lost the #2 engine due to a G-rotor pump, causing a loss of oil pressure, and had to divert to Plattsburg AFB, New York. They were there for two or three days for repairs, then went on to Harmon. Since the rest of the tankers had already passed though, Earl's crew had to make the trip to the Azores as a single ship. Earl recalled:

"After a couple of days at Plattsburg, we finally got the engine changed, flew a test hop and got all the passengers on board for the trip to Harmon. I think the tail number was '380'. It was an F model KC-97 because all the passengers had to be seated in the lower compartments. The crew included Hans Logerloef (CP), Jerry Henderson (Nav), Jim O'Conner (RO), and Rosario Delash (Boom Op). We accepted the engine change knowing there was a problem with the magnetos on #2 engine and it performed OK enroute to Harmon.

"On the way to the Azores, we shut down #3 engine just past the point of no return for "no oil pressure". The Radio Operator was unable to determine if he was reaching the Azores with his messages regarding our situation. I began going through cigarettes when the engine that was changed at Plattsburg began giving us indications that it was not delivering the power that the other engines were delivering. I don't remember descending to a lower altitude, but we continued on and did land at the Azores. I must have OD'd on cigarettes during the final hours of the flight, because I felt terrible and quit smoking cold turkey!"

The first three B-47s for Shotgun Delta Reflex deployment to Spain left at 0430 hours on 9 July. The B-47s would fly the *Gold Route* (Lincoln to Nashville, Tennessee), then take a heading for a point just north of Charleston, South Carolina, where they would coast out over the ocean.

## Cold War Cornhuskers: The 307th Bomb Wing Lincoln Air Force Base Nebraska 1955-1965

The three B-47s met their tankers in the Salt Spray refueling area near Bermuda and took on 45,000 pounds of fuel.

After refueling and climbing back to cruising altitude, all the crews could see was a lot of sky above and water below. The three Stratojets had about 3,000 miles of water to cross. In the cramped nose quarters, the navigator was the busiest member of the crew. Navigating across the Atlantic was a combination of dead reckoning, pressure pattern, and celestial, with maybe a little SWAG method thrown in for good measure.

To break up the hours of boredom, the crews could dig into the lunch bag and see what was there to chow down on. Let's see: tuna fish, ham and cheese, or maybe peanut butter sandwiches that were made sometime yesterday. Or maybe they had those nice little steak cubes they could warm up on an amplifier. Another cup of coffee or sip of water and they were good to go for a while.

A flight lunch may have taken care of the growling stomach, but it wouldn't do anything for the acute case of tired butt. Ejection seats were not designed for comfort on long hauls. By now, they felt like a block of concrete. The parachute harness was cutting into all kinds of places and helmets weighed a ton. They were making pressure points and hot spots all over their skulls. And the oxygen mask, well, it would take hours for the pressure marks to go away. And how about that dry oxygen throat? An ice-cold beer about now would sure taste great!

The coast of Spain appeared on the radar at about 250 miles out. Too far to swim in case of an emergency, yet they were almost there. A few minutes later the coast emerged through the haze on the horizon. They coasted in near Ourense. You just can't fly nearly five thousand miles and not make a bomb run. So, before heading to their home away from home, they made a run on a bridge in northern Spain.

After landing at Morón there was the downloading of equipment and personal baggage. Then off to debriefing and get assigned to their quarters. The B-47s were checked out and serviced, then quickly cocked for alert. Within hours the newly arrived B-47s took their place in the alert force.

On Sunday, the 12th of July, the Lincoln flight line was again full of hustle and bustle. Eleven KC-97s were being serviced for the final stage of departure for the Azores. By early evening the planes were loaded with fuel, equipment, and any last minute items that needed to go to the Azores. All that was needed were the passengers and crews.

Personnel going to the Azores as passengers were to report by 2300. One of those reporting was TSgt Sedge "Red" Hill. Right on time he reported for departure, only to find his assigned tanker was not scheduled to leave until 0200. Since he was going to be gone for three months the family decided to stay and see him off.

The waiting area isn't anything like a regular airport terminal. Nope, it's a series of several rooms in one of the hangars, reeking of fuel and hydraulic fluid. No comfortable chairs either, just a couple of old well-worn couches, real comfy! Not a lot for a young SAC BRAT to do during the wait. Mom and dad were busy going over last minute details and things that may pop up during the next three months. Then, SAC BRAT would spot a stack of "official" looking magazines sitting on a corner table. Ah, his salvation was at hand! For most of the next three hours, young SAC BRAT read every issue of *Combat Crew* magazine on the table. Finally it was time. "Goodbye Dad, see you in three months. Bring me something real neat from the Azores."

Three crews from the 424th Bomb Squadron departed Lincoln for a Reflex deployment to Morón on 13 July. One of the crewmen who flew that night recalled:

"We were a flight of three; the leader was Maj Bill Howard and his copilot was Joe Rogers. The #2 aircraft was flown by Capt Bob Byrom, Pete McKay CP, and Ken Wikle, Nav. The 372nd Bomb Squadron had sent three crews over a week earlier. Capt N.V. Meeks was one of the ACs. Lt Col Walter Duch, CO of the 424th also went over with the 372nd to become Reflex Commander. The 307th was relieving a Reflex force from Little Rock AFB.

"Before departure, we sat in the cockpit at Lincoln for two hours because of weather in the refueling area that was in the general area of Bermuda. This was the southern route to Spain, 1000 miles longer than the North Atlantic route, all of the additional distance over water. Finally, after a two-hour sit, we got the GO order.

"Everything went according to the plan until we arrived at the refueling area. There was a problem with the tanker and we didn't get the complete offload of fuel. After checking the fuel log we were about 20,000 pounds short of fuel. The flight leader was getting impatient and wanted to get going. After checking the log again, we figured we had enough fuel to make it to Spain.

"The weather was beautiful and dawn came up shortly after we crossed the Azores. In the meantime, I had been checking and rechecking the fuel log, we were about 20,000 pounds short. I was forecasting something like 8,000 pounds remaining over Morón, well below the 20,000 pound planned reserve.

"We coasted in about Lisbon, and the flight was scheduled to swing north and do a camera attack against a target in Valladolid, before heading south to Morón. I rechecked the log and we were burning fuel faster than normal. We would have about 5.000 pounds over Morón.

"The bomb run was completed and we swung south. In the meantime, I was getting more "nervous in the service" as I saw fuel being burned faster than expected. I was really squirming with an estimate of 3,000 pounds remaining. Then the flight lead elected to do a three-ship close formation overhead approach with a fighter-style tactical pitchout to impress the folks on the ground at Morón. My overactive imagination pictured the lead or number 2 blowing a tire on the runway in front of us and the runway closing down and us ejecting due to fuel starvation.

"Anyway, we landed uneventfully as I am here to testify. As we shut down, the fuel totalizer was bouncing around 1,000 pounds. After fourteen and a half hours strapped in, it took awhile for the legs to get working and the butt to stop aching, but the fact that we arrived OK made up for that.

"We were met on the Morón ramp by the Little Rock crews we were replacing and they were a particularly slovenly bunch. The guy who greeted me at the bottom of the ladder had a sweat soaked flight suit, no T-shirt, and unzipped down to his navel. Well, Col Duch was determined that we, the 307th, would rectify the lousy image of the Reflex force. He laid down a set of rules. One was that each morning we would have an open ranks inspection on the ramp before we entered the flight line ops building for the morning briefing.

"We all made sure that we had a clean flight suit, haircuts, shaved and polished in general. We assembled and did the little dance step in response to 'Open ranks, march'. Duch walked slowly up and down the three ranks formed by the eighteen men, looking closely at each individual and then moving to the next. He paused in front of 'Soldier' Meeks (who had started his military career as a teenager in the Texas National Guard cavalry). He looked Meeks up and down, and spoke. 'Meeks, your boots need shining.' Meeks slowly turned red in the face, his jaw quivered twice and said, 'Gawd dammit, Colonel. I haven't been chewed out about my boots since I had horseshit on my heels in the cavalry.' All decorum was immediately lost."

Ken Wikle recalled the first Reflex to Morón:

"Col Duch wanted the 424th to make an 'entrance'. Orchestrated by former USAFE Acrojets team leader Bob Byrom, our arrival was a tight

*116*

three aircraft buzz of the runway followed by the best imitation of a bomb-burst you can do in a B-47. Not that I could see any of this from the navigator's seat, even looking through the optics. But, what I could see, after we landed, was Colonel Duch making a beeline for our crew. Not headed for Bob to give him an 'attaboy' for the buzz job; he was looking for me.

"The base commander at Morón (pronounced 'more-OWN' by the Spanish; I reverted to the anglicized pronunciation after the Great Godman glider gig) was one Colonel Godman. He had taken it into his head he wanted to fly gliders in Spain. He had acquired two such machines and wanted to start glider pilot upgrade. Col Duch had informed him that I was the ace of glider aces, a famed sail plane competition performer and, last but not least, a certified instructor. Just what Godman needed.

"My protestations that I was a 200-hour private pilot with the ink on my glider rating barely dry and not legally entitled to instruct anyone, especially a fifty year old colonel, were deftly handled by the infallible logic that was the hallmark of Col Duch. He reasoned that: 1. We were in Spain so US licenses didn't make any difference. 2. The gliders were owned by the Spanish Air Force so civilian licenses didn't count. 3. I was going to be Godman's instructor because he (Duch) was telling me to. 4. If I ever told Godman I was not a licensed instructor, he (Duch) would personally break my neck. I weighed the persuasiveness of his argument and gave a reasoned response. 'Yes Sir', I said. But, there was a limit. NO WAY was I not going to be on the Gooney Bird for Mallorca at the end of the first week of alert. 'Fair enough,' said Col Godman, 'We'll fly gliders while you are on alert.' Caramba!

"Not having a glider winch, I told him that if he got me 1500 feet of tow-target cable with a safety link and hook up rings, we could auto-tow, like we did at Wichita. Presto, out of the shops of Godman's Little Acre the hardware appeared and we were ready.

"We used a mowed field on the 'Spanish side' of the base. The entire Reflex Alert force was there, alert vehicles parked at the side. The only way to move the glider was to pick it up and carry it, which nine B-47 pilots and navigators could do easily, the trainer having an empty weight of maybe 400 pounds. Thus, we carried the glider to the launch pad. The launch vehicle was, as I recall, an Air Police jeep. I was given a parachute, also on loan from the Spanish, which was of British origin, with the center point strap hookup. Duch had flown with the RAF, got me into the chute and briefed me on how it worked. Then, off we went in to the very wild blue yonder. I made a quick circuit of the patch, pausing only for a stall entry so I would have some clue as to what airspeed to fly on final. I learned that the craft was light on the rudder, heavy on the ailerons, and had the glide ratio of a greased safe. It had little utility in making Godman a soaring master."

Before Ken could get Col Godman up in the air enough times to make him a glider pilot, their Reflex tour was over and they had to return to Lincoln. Before they left, Col Godman promised he would have all the details on launching the other glider worked out before the next Reflex tour in November. Thus ended part one of the Great Godman Glider Gig.

Operations Plan 31-60A for the 1959 SAC Bomb/Comp was released on 15 July. The plan outlined the procedure to select four crews to compete for two berths to represent the 307th at the upcoming World Series of Bombing to be held in October. According to the plan, the crews "will be divorced of all duties not pertinent to the competition training as of August 1."

The four crews selected to represent the 307th in Operation High Sand were:

S-06
Capt John Koudsi AC
Lt William Bailey Jr. CP
Maj Vernon Biaett NAV

S-16
Capt Dale Christians AC
Lt Donivan Jordan CP
Capt Noble Timmons NAV

Crew L-55
Capt Richard Mitchell AC
Lt Darrel Norris CP
Lt Keith Kinyon NAV

Crew L-86
Capt John Parker AC
Lt Ralph Utech CP
Lt Donald Kellum NAV

The first return Reflex flight from Morón left on Thursday, July 23rd. The return route was the northern, or *Silver* route. The returning B-47s made a heavyweight take off; they were loaded with enough fuel to fly all the way across the Atlantic. The returning aircraft would meet their tankers in the Tow Bar refueling area near the coast of Labrador and take on at least 20,000 pounds of fuel. If they missed the tanker or didn't get their offload, they would have to divert to either Goose Bay or Pease AFB. Once they got their fuel, the homeward bound "Squad Car" B-47s would continue to the USA, flying along the St. Lawrence Seaway. The last thing to accomplish before arriving home was to make a bomb run on either Minneapolis or Omaha. Then, it was home and a happy reunion with their families.

Maj Ray Coley's crew was scheduled to fly on Thursday, July 30th. Lt Robert Corti, CP, and Lt Leroy Kerchner, Nav, had planned a routine mission. That afternoon they preflighted their assigned B-47. Crew Chief SSgt Don Mowery stood by 53-1872 while the crew fired up the engines and taxied to the active runway. They got clearance from the tower and rolled down the runway. As she lifted off in a cloud of black smoke there was a cheer heard along the flight line. The 307th had just launched the 1,500th sortie without deviating from the schedule.

In Spain, the Reflex crews had an interesting experience one morning. Mike Gingrich wrote:

"Back in July 1959, those of us on the Alert Force, while lined up on the Morón ramp awaiting Col Duch's open ranks inspection, were amazed to watch an apparition from Wild West Days appear at the south end of the runway. It took the form of a railroad train... of sorts. It seems that a narrow gauge track ran through the end of the overrun before entering the supply area. At the head of the train was an ancient locomotive followed by a couple of decrepit freight cars, all of which looked like they had been last used in our Civil War to haul union troops to battle. The train leisurely chugged through the overrun, occasionally emitting a feeble high-pitched shrill "toot-toot" from its whistle. It was totally fascinating and we soon christened it 'The Toonerville Trolley'.

"Maybe I saw it, or perhaps it's an invention of my aging but overactive imagination, but I still have a vivid mental picture of an incident involving the Toonerville. One fine day, we were launching a Reflex redeploying bird when, for some reason, its water alcohol was late coming on and, as a result, it was using up much more runway than normal. Simultaneously, Toonerville appeared around the bend, chug-chug-chugging, toot-toot-tooting along at its usual warp speed of about five miles per hour. The engineer must have looked out his cab window to reestablish his situational awareness and observed a great aluminum beast snorting clouds of intense black smoke behind itself bearing down rapidly on his future position of well being. What went through the engineer's mind one can only speculate, but since the aluminum beast did not yield to the plaintive appeal of his whistle, one must assume he did not forecast a favorable outcome. With that conclusion in mind, he frantically applied the brakes accompanied by a great squealing of metal on metal and then, deciding he wanted to live to engineer another day, he leapt out of the cab over the side.

"The outcome was favorable to all: Toonerville stopped short of the overrun, preserving its cargo of goodies for the base, the B-47 became airborne well before the overrun and conveyed its crew home to LAFB and, after he stopped shaking, Casey remounted to the cab."

Mike's memory has a postscript. While visiting Spain in 1993, the family he was visiting took him on a tour of Madrid. There in a park, preserved for eternity was none other than The Toonerville Trolley, "in all its glory."

July ended with the usual monthly reports being typed up and sent off to Omaha. It had been a busy month for the 307th. The wing had deployed the refueling squadron to the Azores and began the Reflex commitment to Spain. On top of that, the flying schedule had been jam-packed with sorties to make up crew training. The wing had a total of 5,016 Alert hours with 7 uncocked hours for the B-47s. The tankers pulled 2,892 Alert hours with only one and a half uncocked hours. On top of everything, the wing had recorded 1,500 sorties without a deviation from the flying schedule. Not too shabby, considering Reflex and sending the tankers to the Azores.

The first of the month saw an operations order come down from 818th Air Division called Red Mike. The plan outlined a USCM for a no-notice ORI. The wing would be vulnerable for the mission from September 1 to June 30, 1960.

August was the last month of the SAC training quarter. There would be a lot of flying to finish any 50-8 requirements. To accomplish the training, there would have to be some last-minute shuffling of the flying schedule for flight crews.

On the heels of the 818th operation order Red Mike, the 307th got an order from SAC for another special mission. The order was to provide receiver support for the Griffiss AFB tanker force. The mission would be flown in October. The 307th would generate the force on receipt of an execution order from SAC Headquarters.

Two crews competing for a Bomb/Comp slot flew a practice mission on 5 August. The other two crews flew on the 6th. The crews would fly three B-47s selected for the practice. The three aircraft selected were 53-2134, 53-2416, and 53-2392. The B-47s were selected because of their high performance and reliability records for the last several months. Before the competition there would be the final selection for the competition bird.

There was a mass gas training flight flown on 4 August. Six B-47s were scheduled for the flight. Since the 307th AREFS was in the Azores, the 98th AREFS would pitch in, providing tanker support. Except for a couple of thunderstorms in the refueling area, the mission went according to the profile.

While the B-47 crews were flying training missions over the USA, the tanker crews were leading the Life of Lajes. According to Ken Tarwater:

"Our living quarters at Lajes left a lot to be desired. They were old, open-bay Quonset huts that I'm sure had been there since World War II. The first day, getting settled in the huts, two locals got in a knife fight right there in our Quonset hut. Seems one of them had invaded the others laundry and boot care area. I think it was just a show for us and no one was actually hurt. I let the so-called winner do my laundry. Little did I know they starched and pressed everything including your shorts. You could actually stand them up in the corner. We had to make him understand: 'no starch in the underwear'."

The KC's didn't just sit on the ramp gathering dust. There was a job to do. After all, that's why SAC had sent them halfway around the world. The tankers were there to provide refueling support for B-47s flying Reflex. They would also travel up to RAF Upper Heyford, UK, and Morón, Spain, to pull strip alert.

Flying out of the Azores was always interesting. The islands were just a speck of land in the ocean. Navigation had to be on the button. Miss them and there was a good chance you were going to go for a very long swim. Bill Novetzke wrote:

"The flying was dicey. Gusty winds on landing were always present. The Atlantic winds blew over the island like a small hurricane. Since only the rudder controls were boosted on the '97', it would sometimes take both pilots on the controls with the engineer handling the throttle setting during landing."

Charles Grant, an engine specialist with the 307th AREFS, recalls:

"We were taking off one day from the Azores and the #2 engine started pumping oil out somewhere. The crew thought they had lost an engine. We didn't have much time because we were losing altitude pretty quick. I told them to put the turbos on which gave extra power to the other three engines. They brought her back around and we made an emergency landing. When we got back and parked, the three engines were smoking and what was left of the engine oil was dripping out.

"They had to change the three engines and this one officer wasn't to happy about it. Changing three engines was better than putting a KC-97 in the water at the base of the cliff. Especially with me on it!

"What happened was, when they serviced the aircraft, they left the oil filler cap off. The oil drained out. In the air, we couldn't know what happened. We thought the #2 engine was going out.

"Now, there was a guy in the squadron and he just hated to fly. They almost had to carry him on the plane to go TDY. He wanted to see a refueling mission. He said he would go along since nothing ever happened when I flew on a mission. It scared him half to death when the alarm bells started going off. When we got back, he said he'd never ride on a plane again; he'd walk back to Lincoln if he had to."

Ken Tarwater recalled going to Morón for a two-week Reflex:

"On the way over, we lost an engine and the KC-97 that was on alert had to stay until we got an engine and tools to change it. You had to have hangar space to work in the daytime at Morón, it was just that hot. We couldn't get the hangar, so we worked at night.

"The main off-duty attraction in the Azores, other than going to town, was going to the beach for a dip in the Atlantic. Ah yes, the beautiful clear blue water of the ocean. But, alas, there was a certain element of danger lurking just offshore. The base dumped a lot of garbage off the cliffs into the water. Garbage in the water attracts all kinds of marine life for a free meal. It's well known sharks are scavengers. Hence, lots of opportunity for free meals means lots of sharks. The beach had lifeguards and a siren that blew whenever a menacing fin was spotted."

Sedge Hill recalled about the only thing he had time for was helping service the KC-97s and keeping them ready. He only got to town twice during the ninety days at Lajes. During one of the trips he found a shop and was able to pick up a couple of Dinky Toys to take home to his SAC BRAT.

Meanwhile, back at the patch, the Bomb/Comp candidates were busy flying practice missions. On August 19th, the crews journeyed to Barksdale AFB for preliminary briefings and practice for the upcoming competition. Now, you can't have a tanker from the 98th refueling a B-47 from the 307th during the competition. It just wouldn't work out. There was always the chance of the sister wing sabotaging the 307th's chances at winning by not cheating fair. A message was sent to the Azores to send a KC-97, two crews, and support personnel back to Lincoln, posthaste.

The *Jet Scoop* issue of 28 August found the 307th AREFS dominating the Crew Chief Totem Pole in front of Base Headquarters. At the top was Ozzie Peterson with 44 on time takeoffs. Next was P.R. English with 34 and Sam Sloan with 33.

The bombers had been scheduled to fly 217 sorties during August. By the end of the month they had chalked up 217 to keep the string of not deviating from the schedule alive. As of August 31st, the 307th had 1,931 sorties without a miss. This was an incredible record in view of twenty-four Reflex sorties and the tankers on TDY.

September began by deploying three B-47s to Morón AB, Spain, for Reflex. The three bombers launched on time at 1400 hours for the twelve-hour flight. As before, they would fly the southern route to Sunny Spain and refuel near Bermuda. During the month there would be a Reflex launch every Tuesday in order to keep the Alert force manned and ready.

There was a mass gas refueling mission on the first of the month. Nothing like getting off to a fast start. The mass gas was marred when two tankers aborted before rendezvous. The receivers came up short on their fuel offload and had to divert to Pease AFB to refuel before returning to Lincoln the following day.

On Tuesday the 4th, 52-060 departed Lincoln for a profile mission. She was scheduled to be transferred to the 98th along with eleven other B-47s from the 307th. She may have been scheduled to leave the 307th, but not before she was credited with the 2,000th sortie, without a deviation.

The 307th needed tanker support for the upcoming Bomb/Comp. The solution was already in the works by recalling a tanker from the Azores. The tanker selected was 52-2804. The tanker had just returned to the Azores from pulling strip alert at Morón. Ken Tarwater wrote:

"My crew chief, SSgt Sam Sloan, and I had no more than gotten back to the Azores when we were told to pack our bags. Our KC-97, 52-2804, and ground crew had been selected to go to the Bomb/Comp in early October. Sgt Sloan got to handpick the support people to go, so my stay in the Azores came to a quick stop and we were headed back to Lincoln with two flight crews that would have a big part in the Bomb/Comp."

Out on the flight line, the 307th was in danger of breaking the streak of takeoffs. 51-5234 was on the schedule to fly a mission. There was a problem with one of the wing fuel tanks. The problem was found, but the only solution was to change the big tank. MSgt Jim Rutherford, TSgt Earl Higgins, TSgt John Burke and A1C Calvin Brennan grabbed their toolboxes, stands and dollies and tackled the big tank. In less than forty-five minutes they had downloaded the tank and replaced it with another. 234 launched on time to keep the string alive.

September was the beginning of the final quarter in the SAC training cycle. It was also the beginning of the next Management Control System statistics. The MCS as first conceived by SAC was a useful tool to find problem areas in wing management. As time passed, the MCS became littered with new things to manage; points were added or subtracted for almost anything. So many points for duty schedule, overtime, reporting for duty on time and physical fitness to mention a few. As time wore on, a lot of guys thought how you used the latrine would show up soon. Starting this quarter, Technical Order Compliance was added to the MCS.

Routine missions could be just that, but it only took a split second to go from routine to pucker factor plus ten. Ed Godec recalled one of those moments while flying a mission in 53-2139:

"We–AC Thomas Dance, copilot Ed Godec, navigator Robert Kretschmer–were on a routine training mission which included RBS runs on the Denver Bomb Plot.

"Having finished the last run we were headed back towards our cruising altitude, probably around 35-38000 feet. I was engaged in going through some routine checklist duties involving the fuel panel at my position, when I looked up for a quick check of the sky. I noticed a heavy contrail approaching from about 2 o'clock position. It seemed at some distance, yet I brought it to the attention of Capt Dance saying, 'Hey Tom, you got that contrail at 2 o'clock?' He acknowledged seeing it, so I returned to my fuel panel and associated paperwork. After less than thirty seconds at this, I again looked up to see another B-47 pass immediately in front of us from right to left and, as well as I could tell remembering how fast it all happened, at our exact altitude. Our aircraft gave a tremendous lurch as we passed through the wake of the other B-47, which inspired Bob Kretschmer, who couldn't have seen the other airplane, to sharply remark, 'What the hell's going on up there'."

Six B-47s flew the monthly Tan Glove mission on 9 September. Again, these missions were part of the schedule each month and were flown to gain experience with ECM procedures and how well the Eastern coast defenses could detect incoming intruders.

The lead aircraft in the Reflex flight that left on the 9th carried a special folder to be given to the Reflex Commander on arrival at Morón. Carrying special communications from Lincoln to the Reflex Commander was a common practice. The folder contained a special operations order for Operation Sky Hawk. This was a no-notice exercise directed by the Pentagon to test NORAD units. The purpose was to test NORAD's ability to detect, identify and intercept an aerial attack on the North American continent.

The B-47s returning from Reflex would act as an incoming enemy bomber strike force. The bombers would depart Morón as normal. If they were to implement their attack profile, they would get the "go code" via a "Noah's Ark" message. If it was authentic, they would attack three cities as outlined in the orders. The operation would be executed sometime between September 15th and October 2nd.

On September 11th, the 307th was named to the Strategic Air Command Hall of Fame. The wing was awarded this honor based on the fact that the wing had gone for at least a full year without a flying safety accident. There had been a couple of close calls, but no major accidents. The Wing Staff expressed their thanks to all members of the 307th for a job well done.

The 307th was alerted for yet another "no-notice" operation liability. This one was called Operation Fast Move. The 307th and the 98th would provide a total of fifty-eight B-47s to act as receivers for the Griffiss AFB tanker unit. They would also act as enemy bombers for a NORAD training exercise. The operation would be flown sometime during October. Reflex deployment would be postponed if the operation was called on a Reflex launch day.

The September *Nuts and Jolts* hit the flight line with more tips on how to fine-tune a B-47. One article mentioned that Maj William Lindsey was now the 307th Job Control Officer. Ernie Pence remembered Maj Lindsey:

# Cold War Cornhuskers: The 307th Bomb Wing Lincoln Air Force Base Nebraska 1955-1965

"Major William Lindsey was, to say the least, different from most officers envisioned while working your way through basic and tech school. He was a short man, heavy of beard, uniform shirt always finding its way out of his pants. His cap had most of the silver trim worn off and it was a little black on the topside, from nosing under and around B-47s. Quiet most of the time, but dark eyes that would give away a laugh before he would. He was a man that totally understood enlisted humor and flat enjoyed it. He also had that sense that enabled him to judge a man's capabilities to do his job, and how long he would endure something before blowing his cool. His little brown Plymouth seemed to fit his demeanor as he made his rounds. It, too, was a little faded. But when the chips were down, he was hell on wheels and knew the book inside out or quoted it in such a fashion that others never questioned his knowledge."

Then there was the question about nuclear safety. "What's the difference between 'radiation' and 'contamination'?," asked the instructor in the Atomic Training Center. The young airman from Nebraska thought a moment, then gave a definitive example that rated 100%: "Radiation", he drawled, "is when you smell manure; contamination is when you step in it."

Col Read held Commander's Call at the Base Theater on the 21st. As usual, his agenda was full of how the wing was doing and where improvements could be made. Under the "attaboy" category, SSgt Robert Ketchum of the 307th OMS was named the Outstanding NCO for the month of August. SSgt Donald Mowery was given the title of Crew Chief of the Month. The 372nd was the Outstanding Squadron for the month.

Three B-47s departed Morón on 24 September for their trip back to Lincoln. After coast out, they headed for the Modest Lady refueling area just north of the Azores. The tankers were right where they were supposed to be. The voices on the radio were familiar. Sure enough, when they got close enough, there was the green tail stripe of the 307th AREFS.

The B-47s slid into position beneath the tankers and the boomers plugged the booms into the snouts of the B-47s. JP-4 flowed like wine through the boom and into the tanks on the 47s. With full loads they could make it across the Atlantic or at least to an alternate. "Thanks for the juice. See you guys in a couple of weeks when you get home."

Climbing back to cruising altitude, the HF radio came alive with more than dull static.

> "Sky King, Sky King, This is Blackjack Oscar
> with a Noah's Ark Message for all Sky King Aircraft.
> Prepare to copy a four-part message.
> Break, Break. Part One
> TANGO, ZULU, INDIA, FOXTROT, HOTEL, HOTEL
> Part Two
> UNIFORM, MIKE, BRAVO, PAPA
> Part Three
> INDIA, SIERRA, JULIET, WHISKEY, HOTEL
> Part Four
> UNIFORM, ECHO, GOLF, KILO. Break, Break
> Authentication
> YANKEE, YANKEE, FOXTROT."

As with all messages to Sky King aircraft, the navigator or copilot copied the message, then got the latest KAC decoder and figured out what the message was all about. The decoded message was just two words, "SCARLET SEA". A quick check with the Aircraft Commander verified the message. It was the "go code" to execute Operation Sky Hawk.

They pulled the Combat Mission Folders and reviewed the mission profile. The B-47s were to act as enemy bombers and attack the USA to test NORAD and see just how good they were. It wasn't just the 307th participating in this mission. All across the Atlantic, other SAC aircraft had received the same message. Those that decoded Scarlet Sea were now classified as enemy bombers.

As per the profile, the B-47s continued their routine radio communications under Shotgun Delta Reflex return. As they crossed the H-Hour Control Line (HHCL) at 44 degrees W, they ended all radio communications and went to radio silence.

Just off the coast of Newfoundland, southeast of St. John's, the three B-47s broke up their cell and began a bomb run on their respective target cities. The lead ship would fly to Pease AFB and make a camera attack. The second would make a run on Logan International Airport near Boston, while the third would go to Worcester, Massachusetts. After the turn for target run, maximum ECM tactics would be used. After each camera attack, the B-47s would contact the nearest GCI site and report "Mission Complete". All three would then land at Plattsburg AFB, New York, and refuel, reform the cell and return to Lincoln.

NORAD had been caught with their pants down. None of the B-47s reported any radar or fighter lock-ons! All three B-47s had been able to penetrate U.S. airspace and take some very nice camera attack photos of their targets. So the final score for Shotgun Delta was 307th-3, NORAD-zip.

On the 29th, the four Bomb/Comp crews headed back to Barksdale for the final cut with the two top teams going to the big event in October. Since this was the final round, competition was sharp among the crews. It was no-holds-barred as the four crews flew each mission with a very competitive spirit.

Each crew would fly one mission. The profile included air refueling, a night celestial navigation leg and three bomb runs. The targets were located in St. Louis, Missouri; Dallas, Texas; and Joplin, Missouri. To make sure there was no stretching of the rules, an umpire would fly in the 4th man position.

After a week of furious competition the final scores were posted. The scores placed Capt Richard Mitchell's crew in first place in the B-47 category. With the win, his crew would represent the 307th. Of the three remaining crews, Capt Dale Christians' crew was the next highest scoring crew. His crew would also go to the World Series of Bombing.

At 1847 hrs, on October 1, 1959, Crew E-53, commanded by Capt Albert Masserini, departed Lincoln on yet another training mission. Flying as copilot was Lt Vincent Kovacich and Maj Alan Simkins was in the front to navigate on the mission. Their sortie was the 2,327th to be flown without a deviation from the flying schedule.

The record string was broken later that night when a B-47 aborted takeoff due to a mechanical problem. During the last 188 days the 307th had not deviated from the flying schedule. The B-47s had 1,553 sorties, the KC-97s chalked up 774 sorties. Col Read commented, "This could only be accomplished by the concerted and continual efforts on the part of maintenance and the flight crews. This is truly a fine effort by everyone in the 307th."

When the 307th had posted the 1,000th sortie, SAC Headquarters had checked the records of every wing in the command. They also checked the records of the 307th to make sure there was no fudging going on. Everything had checked out five square. So, at the 1,000th sortie, the 307th had set a new record. With this string of 2,327 sorties, the 307th had set a record that was never topped by any other wing in the Strategic Air Command.

The 307th AREFS bid farewell to Lajes, Azores, on 2 October. The first wave departed and took up a heading for Kindley AB, Bermuda. The flight from the Azores to Bermuda was about 2,500 miles, and every bit of it was over water. Needless to say, the small island was a welcome sight when it appeared on the horizon.

After refueling and overnight rest, the travelers boarded the tankers for the final leg to good Ol' Lincoln Airplane Patch. As with all returns, there were tearful reunions as the hunters came home from the hill, or island in this case. A lot of SAC BRATS got a new supply of Dinky Toys when dad finally unpacked the old B-4 bag.

The squadron was given a few days off to take care of home matters and relax a little. Col Read sent a message to Omaha regarding the scuttlebutt he had heard from members of the squadron:

"There is a potential morale problem with the 307th AREFS. From October 1958 to October 1959, the unit has spent over six months overseas on TDY. During 24 weeks at home, the unit was on Alert on average of six weeks per crew. This left approximately 120 days out of the year for crew members to consider 'normal at-home' duty. In addition, while on TDY, each crew spent almost one third of the time on alert. There is also a difference in 'per diem' for tanker crews."

Thursday, October 8th, another day of fixing and flying is on the schedule. The crew chiefs were busy making sure their birds were in the best possible shape. B-47 51-5248 had returned from the refueling pits after having her tanks topped off. She was scheduled to fly a training profile at 1140 that morning.

The mission was to check pilot proficiency and upgrade training. Lt Joseph Morrissey would be the aircraft commander. Maj Paul Ecelbarger, 372nd Bomb Squadron Commander, would fly as copilot and instructor on the flight, Capt Theodore Tallmadge was the navigator, and Capt Lucian Nowlin would fly as instructor navigator.

The mission was to start with an ATO takeoff, then north into the Dakotas for a bomb run on the Bismarck bomb plot. Then there were several navigation legs so Capt Tallmadge could be scored on his navigation. Finally, a couple of hooks-ups in the refueling area and then back to Lincoln.

The crew went through the usual preflight inspection of 5248. Everything was in the right place, including the ATO rack. Everything on the Form 781 had been signed off, and 5248 was ready to go. The four flyers climbed the ladder and buttoned the B-47 up for the mission. With routine precision, the six engines were started and the B-47 taxied towards the end of Runway 35.

Power on the six engines was brought up to 100%, then the water alcohol kicked in as the B-47 began the take off roll. Airspeed acceleration check was good. At the correct indicated airspeed the ATO was fired. Smoke and flames blasted from the ATO bottles, giving the bomber extra thrust.

Paul Koski had just relieved the Senior Controller in Job Control so he could go to lunch. Sitting in the old control tower, Job Control had a bird's-eye view of the flight line. "The aircraft was due for an ATO take off and had an instructor pilot riding in the back seat." Paul recalled:

"The aircraft started its takeoff roll with black smoke trailing as he kicked in the water alcohol. The B-47 was about a quarter of the way down the runway when he fired his ATO.

"Instead of flying normally, the nose pitched up about forty-five degrees. I said to everyone in the room that he was in trouble. I got on the radio and told all Alpha vehicles to stay off the air, that we had an emergency on take off. The B-47 went about 500 feet in the air, then the water and ATO quit. The pilot got the nose over but the wings were wobbling, he continued descending until the aircraft hit the ground, which was about three quarters of the way down the runway and to the right. The aircraft exploded and was engulfed in flames. Alpha 5 (tow team supervisor, TSgt Sedgefield Hill) radioed that an aircraft had crashed and where did I want his tow team? I told 'Red' to stand by, we didn't have notification and were checking.

"We called the fire department, but someone had alerted them since I could see the fire trucks already responding. It was too late to do anything; the plane just went up in flames too fast. All of us were silent for a few minutes; then there was disbelief and a sick feeling in our stomachs."

The B-47 impacted the ground near the intersection of the main runway and the shorter diagonal runway. Flaming wreckage covered both runways, as well as an open field to the east of Runway 35. Fire crews were on the scene within minutes of the accident and began fighting the flames with flame-suppressing foam. By 1300 the fire was under control.

The runway was closed to all military and civilian traffic. Several Frontier and United Airlines flights were diverted to Omaha. The crews worked all afternoon to clear the runway of wreckage and restore operations. By late afternoon, two National Guard F-86s were able to take off, flying over the smoldering crash site.

The investigation found that, when the aircraft went to the fuel pits for servicing, it had been listed as scheduled to fly a local mission for pilot upgrading. There was no indication there had been any change in the mission profile requiring more fuel to be pumped into the tanks. The forward main and wing tanks were only partially filled. The board concluded that, when the ATO was fired, the added thrust caused fuel to shift towards the rear, causing the center of gravity to shift, ultimately causing the B-47 to pitch up and stall.

Members of the 307th were shocked and saddened by the loss of the crew and Maj Ecelbarger. When the memorial service was held at the Base Chapel, the service was packed by fellow crews and ground personnel who sat in silence in memory of their friends who had given their lives in the line of duty.

On Monday, 12 October, the wing received a standby execution order for Operation Fast Move. The wing was to provide 30 aircraft to act as receiver support for the 41st AREFS stationed at Griffiss AFB. As outlined in the operation order, the wing would begin generating aircraft and stand by for the launch order.

The strike force would consist of three aircraft per cell, launching at one-minute intervals. There was to be one hour between cells. Each cell would fly the mission profile and monitor radio traffic for a specific "Noah's Ark" message giving the "go code" to continue the Fast Move mission. If the cell did not receive an authentic "go code" message, they were to revert to a standard training mission outlined in the "Bravo" mission folder.

Crews slated to fly the mission spent the day reviewing and planning the mission profile. Later that afternoon they attended the formal briefing, where everything was gone over in detail. So far, the weather at Lincoln and along the route didn't appear to be a factor in conducting the mission.

While the flight crews were busy reviewing their part of the mission, the ground crews were busy generating the force to fly the mission. Out on the flight line, fifteen B-47s were being prepared for the first day's launch. The birds had been serviced with JP-4, oxygen, and any other fluids needed for the mission. The post-flight records were checked to make sure all maintenance had been accomplished.

Final briefing began at 0600 on 13 October. The mission profile was gone over a final time. Weather still looked good. Each crew was given their combat mission folder to be placed in the "lock box" during preflight. For added realism, the folders had been placed in a random order. No one would know who would get the "go code" and who would fly a standard profile training mission.

Flight crews reported to their aircraft and went through a routine preflight. They loaded their personal gear and brought the aircraft to

# Cold War Cornhuskers: The 307th Bomb Wing Lincoln Air Force Base Nebraska 1955-1965

a simulated "cocked" status. With everything as ready as possible, the fifteen crews went back to their "alert" area to wait for the Klaxon.

The Klaxon went off at 1122, sending the real alert crews to their aircraft for a Bravo alert. Crews flying the Fast Move responded by reporting to their aircraft. The first cell crews boarded their aircraft and started engines. They were given the green light to taxi and launch. One by one, they taxied to the end of Runway 35 and rolled down the runway at one-minute intervals. For the next five hours the 307th would be busy launching aircraft for the mission.

Climbing out from Lincoln, the first cell turned and headed for Grand Island, Nebraska, then turned south towards Mankato, Kansas, to begin the navigation leg. After checking in over the entry point they flew to Kansas City, Kansas, the first navigation checkpoint.

A slight heading change was made to place them on a course for Quincy, Illinois, and another checkpoint. From there they headed for Rochester, Indiana, and another mandatory checkpoint. At this checkpoint the cell turned northeast and flew to Sandusky, Michigan, then out over Lake Huron.

The navigation leg ended when the cell checked in over Sudbury, Ontario. After checking in the cell began descending to refueling altitude. There was a slight heading change to get the bombers on course for the Chess Set refueling area. By now, the navigators had the tankers spotted on radar.

Entering Chess Set, the cell split apart with each bomber heading for its assigned tanker. It was a three ship mass gas refueling. Each tanker and receiver was at the same altitude with a five-mile horizontal separation. Rendezvous, hook up and fuel offload went according to the mission profile.

Leaving the refueling area, the cell headed for the positive control point at 51 Degrees N, 66 Degrees W. So far, they had heard nothing on the radio giving them the "go code" for the rest of the Fast Move portion of the mission. Without the proper message, the aircraft would abort the exercise and fly the routine training sortie.

Just before arriving at the positive control point, the cell received the "Noah's Ark" message they had been waiting for. The message was copied and decoded. The next part of the flight would depend on what was contained in the message. If they decoded a valid "go code" they would continue to fly the Fast Move exercise as outlined in the combat mission folder.

Strike aircraft flew south along the western border of Maine. Along the route, they used maximum ECM music and chaff to confuse ground radar. They also kept a keen eye peeled for any indication they were being intercepted by fighters.

The Pre IP for the first target was Wilkes-Barre, Pennsylvania. At the IP, they contacted the bomb plot at Youngstown, Ohio, and transmitted identification for the bomb run. When the tone cut off, the pen lifted from the plotting paper in the bomb plot scoring station. One target down, two to go.

The flight path took the strike aircraft to Columbus, Ohio, and on to a turn point over Cincinnati. Here they turned northwest towards Wisconsin and began setting up for the next bomb run. Passing near the "Windy City" of Chicago, the crews stole a quick glance at the panorama below.

Winona, Minnesota, was the designated IP for the target at Minneapolis. Again, they identified themselves for the bomb run on Target Y and began the bomb run from 30,000 feet. At tone cut off, the aircraft commander pulled the B-47 into a steep left combat break and headed for their final target at Omaha.

On Wednesday, the 14th, the second wave of fifteen aircraft repeated the entire mission. When the final B-47 recovered, the crews felt they had flown a good exercise. All they had to do was wait for the final results to be posted on the nav legs and bomb runs.

The final results gave the wing an overall rating of "Outstanding". Navigation was right down the center of the nav legs. The best news was the bombing scores. There was only one unreliable bomb run. Even better news were the eight shacks that were scored. Fast Move had been one of the best missions the 307th had flown.

The following Tuesday, the Reflex deployment left as usual; well, almost as usual. Billy Lyons recalled:

"On our first Reflex trip, we had a maintenance delay and couldn't launch with the other two aircraft in our cell. It was a twenty-four hour delay and you normally lost your tanker with a full day delay, but we were able to get a KC-97 refueling in spite of the twenty-four hour delay. We launched as a single ship and, approaching the refueling area over the Gulf of St. Lawrence, made contact with our tanker. The tanker pilot advised that they had one sick engine and would have to use higher power settings on the other engines to try and give us the airspeed we needed for refueling with them. We rendezvoused with the tanker and were attempting to hook up at about ten knots below our requested airspeed.

"The AC got an initial contact, but it was tough going at ten knots below. We got about fifteen hundred pounds of fuel and had a disconnect. As we were getting back to pre-contact position, the supercharger on one of the tanker's good engines blew up. Big ball of blue flame and it sounded like a shotgun blast in the cockpit. The tanker started down on top of us. We couldn't get out from underneath him. We finally fell off on a wing, lost about five thousand feet and, by the time we recovered and were flying straight and level, the tanker was right down beside us. We got the flaps up, cleaned up the checklist, and headed for Goose Bay. We spent the night at Goose because we didn't have enough crew duty day left to refuel at Goose, do some replanning, launch and get to Morón. We learned that the tanker recovered safely. What an introduction to Reflex! But, the fun was just beginning.

"We launched from Goose Bay the next evening and headed across the North Atlantic. The primary means of navigation was celestial (shooting stars and planets with the sextant) with some assistance from pressure pattern, ships stationed out in the Atlantic, and dead reckoning. After level off, I put the sextant in the port in the canopy at my station and hooked it up. Something was wrong-- no light in the sextant. Seems the circuit breaker for the sextant light kept blowing, so, I had to use my flashlight to shoot the sextant. Not the best way to get accurate observations, but somehow we made it across the ocean and found the Iberian Peninsula. We coasted in at Averi, Portugal, tuning in to a low frequency radio beacon located there, and headed for Morón AB, located in south central Spain about 35 miles southeast of the city of Seville. We considered ourselves lucky for not coasting in over France or North Africa."

The crews headed for the Bomb/Comp flew a couple of last minute practice missions to keep a razor sharp edge. By now, the crews were flying the aircraft selected for the competition. The B-47 was 53-2134, now known as *City of Lincoln*. 52-2804 would represent the 307th AREFS as the tanker. The two aircraft had been selected after reviewing the individual aircraft records and finding they had one of the highest reliability rates in the wing.

During the last few days before leaving for Florida, the crew chiefs and selected ground crews went over each aircraft with a fine-tooth comb. Everything was checked and rechecked. They even took a little time and touched up some of the paint job. Couldn't have a shabby looking bird at the World Series of SAC.

Capt Richard Mitchell's Crew E-55 climbed aboard *City of Lincoln* and headed for Florida. Capt Dale Christians' Crew S-16 would fly to Florida as passengers on 2804 with the ground crews and the other tanker crew. After arriving at McCoy AFB near Orlando, the equipment and passengers were taken off the tanker. Then she departed and flew to Homestead AFB outside of Miami. Homestead was the base that tankers would stage from during the competition.

The official competition didn't begin until the 24th. The crews had some time on their hands. Using the convertibles provided, some went sightseeing. The ground crews used the extra time to go over the birds one more time to make sure everything was shipshape.

At 1000 hours, the competition crews gathered for the welcoming ceremony. On hand was Gen. Thomas S Power, Commander-in-Chief of SAC. He welcomed the crews and stressed the importance of the activities for the upcoming week. The commanders of the 2nd, 8th and 15th Air Forces were also on hand to welcome the participants.

It was quite an assembly. There were 188 crews representing 47 wings from SAC. They were the cream of the command, having gotten their seat in the competition the old fashioned way: they earned it. Sitting there, some of them looked around at the faces in the crowd and wondered, "Who is the best?"

Crews attended a general briefing at 1400. The rules of the competition were gone over in minute detail. Everyone had to know exactly what they were going to do and when. The mission routes were outlined for the crews. All flying would be done at night. There would be an air refueling, nav leg and bomb runs on three different targets. Bomb scores would be relayed back to McCoy in code, then decoded and placed on the big score board.

The schedule of who flew and when was determined by a drawing conducted by the wing commanders. It may have been a stroke of luck or the head sheep herder's skill, as Col Read drew two of the best capsules for his two bomber crews. Capt Mitchell's crew would fly on the first night. Capt Christians would be the last B-47 to fly on the last night of the B-47 phase of competition. The 307th would know how well they stood at the beginning and how well they would have to do at the end.

After the briefing, the crews spent the rest of the day planning their flights. Fuel loads were computed, navigation checkpoints reviewed and times for each leg were figured. Aiming points and radar films were studied to get the picture of how the target would be identified and bombed.

At Homestead, the process was the same for the tanker crews. They would take off, refuel their receiver, then fly a navigation leg before returning to Homestead. Everything that was going to be done from now on, whether flying or working on the ground, would be under the watchful eyes of the umpire.

The B-52s threw out the first pitch, flying the first wave on the first night of the competition. The crews from the 307th used the time for last minute review of the mission profile. Ground crews were tweaking *City of Lincoln* until she was as mechanically as perfect as possible. They didn't want any last minute surprises.

Capt Mitchell's crew reported for their mission on time. Last minute weather reports were gone over, then it was out to their bird for preflight. The umpire and his ever present scoring sheets on his clipboard stood by, watching like a hawk.

*City of Lincoln* lifted off the runway at McCoy at 2300, right on time. Climbing out, they headed for Lakeland, Florida, climbing to 35,000 feet. At Lakeland, they turned and headed for Gainesville, Florida, then to Lake City and on to Jessup, Georgia. At Jessup, they made a heading change to Vidalia, Georgia, then a westerly heading change toward Cordele, Georgia, the refueling rendezvous point.

As they approached the refueling area they scanned the area with the radar. Ahead, right where they were supposed to be, was Maj Normandin's crew in 2804. *City of Lincoln* slid beneath the tail of 2804, and A2C Larry Kessler lowered the boom and gently grasped the ruddervator control stick. Looking down from his dust bin pod, he eased the boom into the receptacle and started transferring fuel. Between Coffeeville, Alabama, and Laurel, Mississippi, the aerial refueling continued until the full fuel load was in the tanks. One of the major aspects of the mission was over.

Dropping off the boom, the crews wished each other luck on the next portion of the mission. The B-47 climbed back to 35,000 feet, while the tanker turned for their navigation leg. The tanker would head southwest for a turn point just southwest of New Orleans. Then, it was out over the Gulf before turning back and coasting in near Tampa. After ending the nav leg, the tanker headed home and recovered at Homestead, AFB.

When *City of Lincoln* reached cruising altitude they were over Natchez, Mississippi. Here they changed direction to the northeast and headed towards Bastrop, Louisiana, the beginning of the night celestial nav leg. From Bastrop, the bomber headed towards the northeast for the next turn point between St. Louis, Missouri, and Evansville, Illinois. Then it was a straight run to Richmond, Virginia.

At Richmond they turned for the first bomb run. Their target was the main building of the Parks-Cramer Company. Seventy miles out at the IP, they contacted the mobile scoring unit for positive identification. As they had done hundreds of times, the tone came on fifteen seconds before bomb release. Below, in the plotting room, a pen traced their bomb run on paper. At tone cut off, the pen lifted from the paper indicating bomb release. In the scoring shed, ballistic tables were used to compute the trajectory of the simulated bomb and determine where it would have detonated.

Their next target was the center smokestack of the Alpha Portland Cement Company at Birmingham, Alabama. After release they maintained their heading for several minutes, then turned south to Montgomery, Alabama. Passing over Montgomery, they turned for the last target at Macon, Georgia. Lt Keith Kinyon put the cross hairs on the intersection of the two runways at the Macon Airport. When the tone cut off over Macon, *City of Lincoln* flew the breakaway and turned for the coast. Near the coast, they turned south and followed the coast back to Daytona Beach and home to McCoy.

Tired after their seven hours-plus in the air under the watchful eyes of the umpire, they figured they'd scored pretty well. When the scores were decoded and posted on the standings board, it was better than pretty good! They had scored 390.5 points out of a possible 500. That put the 307th at the top of the heap at the end of the first inning.

B-47s from other wings continued flying the same profile. Every time the scores were posted the 307th stayed on top. The sheep herders from Lincoln got a major scare on Wednesday night. A B-47 crew from the 100th Bomb Wing scored a "shack" on the target at Macon. That mission moved the 100th into second place with only a few points separating the two wings.

Since there were several days between missions, the crews and support personnel had a little free time. Ken Tarwater recalled:

"When we got to Homestead, each six guys got a car to get around in. The great part was, this was Sgt Sloan's stomping ground. His parents lived in Hollywood, Florida, and we went to visit one night while we were there. I was the designated driver, since I didn't drink. The other five guys said everything was on them while we were there. We went to a fancy nightclub that had different acts that would come out and do their thing. It was a great place and I was enjoying it, drinking my cokes and watching the show on stage. I heard one of the guys arguing with the waiters and, before I could whistle Dixie, we were thrown out of the club. Found out later, the Sarge had refused to pay the cover charge on every coke I ordered, each coke was costing five dollars, a lot of money back then and more than they were paying for the booze."

# Cold War Cornhuskers: The 307th Bomb Wing Lincoln Air Force Base Nebraska 1955-1965

October 28th was the final night of the competition for the B-47 wings. At this point the 307th was still leading the pack by 14.5 points. A narrow lead in view of the fact, the last wave of the B-47s and B-52s still had to fly. Capt Dale Christians' Crew, S-16, would be the last B-47 to leave McCoy that night.

The Bomb/Comp has been called "The World Series Of SAC". Well, here we are, the ninth inning, the 307th is holding onto a slim lead. It's going to be up to Dale and his crew in *City of Lincoln* and Murray Jett flying 2804 to team up and hit a couple of home runs to cushion their lead. Dale Christians recalled his mission:

"My crew was the 27th and last crew to take off on the third night of the competition. Our takeoff time was around midnight for a seven and a half hour mission. Normally the hardest parts of the mission for the aircraft commander are the takeoff, the air refueling and landing. The rest of the time, you put the bird on autopilot and follow the instructions from the navigator. However, this night was different as we had a lot of pressure on us to come through in the clutch. Our tanker was commanded by Capt Murray V. Jett. Air refueling with a KC-97 was a lot harder than with a KC-135, as it was a lot slower. The tanker would be going as fast as it could at around 12,000 feet and the B-47 had to slow down to match the tankers speed. During the actual refueling, the tanker would be able to speed up as it transferred its load of fuel and became easier for both aircraft. The competition was to transfer around 40,000 pounds of JP-4 without a disconnect in the shortest time possible. We did that without a disconnect.

"We then climbed back to the designated altitude and started the navigation competition. My crew was fortunate in that the copilot, Lt Jordan, had been a navigator before going to pilot training. He could find the stars that we needed and take sextant shots very accurately. Meanwhile, Capt Timmons would plot the fixes and determine any course changes that we needed to make. We had an umpire riding with us to see that everything was done legitimately. I can't remember our score, but it was very good.

"Following the nav leg, we headed for the bomb runs at the three selected RBS sites. They would pick us up at about seventy miles from the target, make sure they had the right airplane, then track us as we approached the target. At about thirty seconds before bombs away, we would turn on a tone, which would stop when the radar showed bombs away. We did not get our scores until we landed. They were forwarded to McCoy and posted on a giant wallboard. When we landed around eight a.m. the following morning, we found that we had scored 381.5 points and the 307th Bomb Wing was still in the lead for the Fairchild Trophy."

Final night, or the bottom of the ninth. All eyes were on the B-52s as they lumbered into the sky for the final round of competition. Col Read's "sheep herders" were hanging in there. At this point, only a three-shack mission by a B-52 crew could knock them off the top of the scoreboard.

"On the final night of the competition," Dale wrote", about everyone in the 307th Bomb Wing was in the hangar, watching the scores of the B-52s." When the scores started coming in, the men of the 307th began a quiet computation of the standings. With the posting of each score the quiet grew to a murmur, louder and louder with each posting. When the final B-52 score was posted, the men of the 307th went wild with cheers, back slapping, hoots and hollers. The 307th was still at the top of the board with a total of 772 points! The coveted Fairchild Trophy belonged to the 307th Bomb Wing!

On Friday, October 30th, the award ceremonies were held at McCoy AFB. Gen. Thomas Power was on hand to pass out the hardware. The Bombing Trophy went to the 100th Bomb Wing. The Best Crew award went to the 100th Bomb Wing. The 55th SRW took the Navigation Award in both bomber and tanker categories. The 55th also took the Best Refueling trophy.

Finally, Gen. Power presented the Fairchild Trophy to Col Elkins Read, Jr., and the crowd from the 307th went wild. Col Read held the trophy up so his "fellow sheep herders" could get a look at their prize. Several of the 307th noticed they had never seen Col Read smiling like he was at that moment. They also noted a special gleam in his eyes, or was it a tear? Perhaps it was the same gleam a dad has when his son hits a home run to win the Little League game. These were his boys; they not only hit a home run, they had won the World Series of Bombing.

Word of the win arrived at the 307th Headquarters at Lincoln. The news spread across the wing and spilled out onto the flight line. Even though they weren't at McCoy, every member of the wing knew they were part of the winning team.

Gary McGill remembered the flight back to Lincoln in the KC-97:

"We flew up to McCoy to pick up the support crews and extra crew for the B-47 section and the Deputy Wing Commander, Col Raleigh Smith. We had to stay overnight there at McCoy, so the next day we took off for Lincoln. It was the most casual flight I ever had in Strategic Air Command. At the navigator's station we started tuning in the local radio stations, listening to music. I put it on the speaker so it went out all over the flight deck. The popular song at the time was Bobby Darrin singing "Mack the Knife". We must have heard "Mack the Knife" a dozen times going across country. There were no flight requirements so we were just sitting up there laughing and hollering. All of the extra pilots on board were hopping in and out of the right seat. I don't think Bill Novetzke got much flying time that day. It was a flight like you had never seen in SAC before."

When the victorious 307th arrived back at Lincoln, the base literally rolled out the Red Carpet. Ken Tarwater remembered trying to hide in the back of the tanker; no such luck. He had to face the crowd just like everyone else. It seemed no matter which way they turned, there was someone poking a camera in their face taking pictures for posterity.

October 1959 would be remembered as one of the best and worst months in the history of the 307th. The wing had chalked up an unbeatable string of not deviating from the flying schedule. They brought back the Fairchild Trophy from the Bomb/Comp and were proclaimed World Champions. This would be the last time a B-47 wing would win the Fairchild Trophy. The high points were dulled by the tragic loss of a crew in a flying accident.

November started with a directive from SAC Headquarters. With increased capabilities of the Soviet air defenses and the growing number of commercial airline flights in the United States, training flights were officially brought to low-level altitude. SAC and the FAA established seven low-level navigation "Oil Burner" routes across the country. These routes were about twenty miles wide and five hundred miles long. Aircraft were restricted to 1,000 feet above the local terrain. The routes were located over sparsely populated areas. SAC would start flying the "OB" routes on the 23rd.

On the first of the month, three B-47s (53-1932, 53-2364, 53-4219) departed Lincoln for Reflex in Spain. When they arrived at Morón, the crews that were to be relieved were glad to see the new arrivals. *More* than glad; you see, the normal Reflex had been delayed and the Reflex crews had been extended another week. Billy Lyons wrote:

"This Reflex tour was supposed to be the normal 23-day tour, but our replacement crew had been delayed several days and we were extended a week. We finally got off, flew across the North Atlantic, refueled with our tankers east of Boston and headed for Lincoln. However, we were advised the weather at Lincoln was below landing minimums in a blizzard! Nobody has a blizzard in early November! But, it was true, and so we headed for our alternate, Plattsburg AFB, New York, to RON (remain overnight). Got home the next day. Not too many kind words from wife. Left her there with two small boys, no snow tires on the car, and no money for the rent, food, gas, etc. I had counted on being home in time to get my check at finance on the first of the month and deposit it in the bank, the old way. That got changed quickly. Luckily, she was able to borrow some bucks from the AC's wife. We were learning lessons fast about SAC aircrew duty, Reflex Operations, the 307th Bomb Wing and how bad weather can get in Lincoln in a short period of time"

The storm Billy mentioned didn't just mess up his return from Reflex. It caused all kinds of problems for Lincoln and the entire Midwest. It all began with freezing rain and drizzle. That turned to snow, and lots of it. When the winds picked up, the snow swirled around and drifted on the roads, buildings and planes.

The B-47s on the ramp were coated with ice and snow. It took a while to shovel out the planes and sweep the snow off the wings. But, what about the ice build-up? Just call for the MB-3 deicer vehicles, right? That's all well and good, but there were only two units for the entire base. It takes between fifteen and twenty minutes to deice a B-47. Figuring all of the B-47s and KC-97s sitting on the flight line covered with ice, it might have been spring before all of the planes would be free of ice.

This prompted 818th Air Division Commander Col Thomas Corbin to fire off a message to SAC about the lack of deicing equipment at Lincoln. He said at least six units were needed. He brought out the point that two units wouldn't even be enough to deice the alert aircraft to maintain EWO status, let alone the entire fleet.

SAC liked to test you whether you were up or down. The 307th was at the top of the heap with the recent win at the Bomb/Comp and were literally down because of the recent blizzard that had clobbered the base. Wouldn't it be a great time to throw an ORI at the wing? On Monday, 9 November, SAC did just that. The SAC Inspector General arrived at the Command Post and initiated a no-notice ORI code named Red Mike.

The ORI began with the harsh blare of the Klaxon. Alert crews scrambled to the cocked B-47s and started engines. Checking in with the Command Post, they were directed to execute a Coco Alert. They taxied to the end of the runway, accelerated briefly down the runway, then returned to their parking spots. Back at the alert pad, the planes were downloaded and serviced. These would be the first aircraft to launch during the ORI.

Out on the flight line, the ground crews shifted from normal hustle and bustle to overdrive to generate the force for the follow-on flights. Overdrive yes, but not the kind you would expect during an ORI. No one knows, or cares to admit, exactly how or when, but the 307th knew the ORI was coming. Someone had leaked the execution day to the 307th, so most of the force was almost generated when the SAC IG arrived.

The Alert crews were briefed on the ORI mission. The ORI would test every aspect of how the wing conducted not only flying, but also the daily business of the wing. That meant personnel records, aircraft records, manpower hours and physical fitness records. The wing had to be ready to produce documents on anything the IG Team wanted to see. Not only that, the IG Team would be snooping around the buildings looking for chipped or peeling paint, unlocked lockers, and anything else that may suit their fancy. Some believed the IG even checked the erasers on pencils. Erasers that have been worn down meant mistakes have been made. Everyone knows you can't make mistakes in SAC!

According to the operation order, the 307th would launch four B-47s per cell with one spare aircraft available. The first four cells would be made up of the aircraft that had been on Alert. There would be no maintenance done on these birds unless a problem violated flight safety. That way, SAC would know how well the alert birds would have performed on a real EWO mission launch.

The first cell launched at the prescribed time and climbed out towards Beatrice, where they changed course and headed for Hastings, Nebraska. As they approached Hastings, they began searching for the tankers waiting in the Donald Duck refueling area.

The tankers were waiting, and the rendezvous and refueling control time were on the money. On a heading of 023 degrees, the B-47s eased into the slot behind the tankers, hooked up and started transferring fuel. After taking on the 35,000 pounds of JP-4, the bombers dropped off the boom and started climbing out of Donald Duck near Sioux Falls, South Dakota.

Flying to the northeast, the cell passed overhead near Brainerd, Minnesota, and then on to Hibbing. At Hibbing, they turned to a heading of 264 degrees and headed towards Grand Forks, North Dakota. Shortly after turning, the cell tuned up their ECM and started playing their music all the way to Grand Forks and on to Minot.

Near Williston, North Dakota, the B-47s completed the ECM run and turned the music off. Turning to a heading of 235 degrees, the cell began the nav leg towards Yellowstone Lake, Wyoming. Over the lake they turned and flew south making a radio checkpoint with Denver. At Denver they turned towards Oklahoma City, where the cell would separate and space themselves for the bomb run. There was a slight dogleg turn to McAllister, Oklahoma, the Pre IP. The lead bomber called the bomb plot at the IP over Ft Gibson, Oklahoma. Positive identification was established for the bomb run at Joplin, Missouri.

When the tone cut off over Joplin, the B-47s made their tactical breakaway, then began the set-up for the next target. The route would take them along the northern border of Arkansas, then to the Pre IP at Paducah, Kentucky. Over Paducah they turned northwest for the IP at Sparta, Illinois. The aiming point was the Highway Bridge across the Missouri River at St. Louis. After release the bombers headed towards Iowa, where the next wave of tankers were waiting in the Rainy Day refueling area for a short refueling before heading home to Lincoln.

According to the Red Mike plan, the 307th was to launch the ten alert birds and a follow-on force of twenty more. That would mean a lot of aircraft launching over a twelve-hour period. The ten alert birds launched within the ORI guidelines without an abort. When they returned to Lincoln they were recocked and put back on Alert as quickly as possible.

For a while, the outcome of the ORI was a little shaky. 53-2140 was late getting off the ground because of problems with the water-alcohol system. Capt Erling Chapelle's crew also lost their UHF radio after takeoff. Even with their problems, they managed to make the HHCL on time and were not scored as an abort. Three aircraft were originally scored as ineffective on the St. Louis target. 53-2416 had a circular error of 5,700 feet when the score came in. Later the radar film showed it was a good run, so the ineffective score was changed.

Sometimes an ineffective bomb run score was the result of what could be labeled "the best laid plans of mice and men". Gene Aenchbacher recalled:

"Another incident that was humorous–up to a point. We were authorized to make a run over the planned target cities, so on one occasion we picked a very bright offset aiming point at St. Louis. Then on the night of the mission we could not find it anywhere. When we investigated we

## Cold War Cornhuskers: The 307th Bomb Wing Lincoln Air Force Base Nebraska 1955-1965

found that the bright spot had been selected on a night when the St. Louis Cardinals were playing baseball, but, alas, they were away on the mission night and the parking lot was empty of autos with their highly reflective roofs."

By the time the last B-47 launched, the command post was getting disturbing news from the Donald Duck refueling area. Weather at the refueling altitude was getting rough. 53-4224 poured on the coal and headed for Donald Duck. When they arrived they found solid clouds, but were able to rendezvous with their tanker. They managed to hook up and tried to hang on to the roller coaster-like boom. Turbulence tossed both planes up and down, side to side, back and forth. They disconnected, then hooked back up again, only to lose the boom at the next pothole in the sky. After half an hour of bumping and grinding across the Nebraska and South Dakota sky, they had managed to take on only 4,000 pounds of fuel. They called it quits when it was no longer within the safe limits of flying to try it again.

When Red Mike was over and the final scores posted, the wing scored 97% for generation of the force. Mission effectiveness was rated at 90% and the bombing was scored as 96.2%. The average circular error for the entire mission was 1,120 feet. The 307th was rated "Outstanding" for Red Mike.

During the ORI, the fire department had trouble dispatching equipment to a simulated fire on the flight line. The problem was, they couldn't find the location of the aircraft parked on the flight line. Not a good situation, especially when the prying eyes of an ORI team are looking at you.

TSgt Sedge Hill had a simple solution: get the fire department a big board, like the one they had in Job Control. OK, sounds like a simple solution, "Red," how about volunteering to build the board. "No Sweat," said Sedge. So, it was off to the sheet metal shop to get the needed material for the board and get the project underway.

The board was a simple piece of sheet metal. Then, the aircraft parking rows on the flightline were painted on the board along with other essential information like the fuel pits, hangars and taxiway. Small aircraft representing B-47s and KC-97s were cut from sheet metal and had a small magnet riveted to the bottom so they would stick to the board.

Painting the aircraft was an "off duty" project, so "Red" brought the small sheet metal planes home. The kitchen table became a mini-flight line as he labored over a hot paintbrush. Now SAC BRAT, being plane-crazy, thought this was kind of neat and wanted to help. During the next few nights, Great White Father and SAC BRAT painted the planes in the red, blue and yellow squadron colors. After painting what seemed the entire production run of B-47s and KC-97s they were done. Well, not really. The next step was to paint the tail numbers on the metal planes. With fine point paintbrushes from SAC BRAT's model plane junk box, the two spent several more nights getting the tail numbers on the small planes. It wasn't a professional job, but it was good enough for their purposes.

The board finally went up at Fire Station #1. Everyone seemed pleased with the project. Now it was a simple matter to put the metal planes in the appropriate rows and move them around the ramp as they went to the refueling pits or to the hangar. Just pull the plane off the parking spot and move it to the new location. It was now possible to see at a glance where the aircraft were in case of an emergency. Another ORI problem taken care off.

"Sarge" Hill was awarded a check for $25.00 for his Yankee ingenuity. Helping paint the planes was not only a great father-son project; it was SAC BRAT'S small contribution to help win the Cold War.

Ever since the 307th AREFS had returned from the Azores, there were rumors floating around on the south end of the flight line. The rumor was the Squadron was going to be deactivated. Then, there was the rumor they were going to upgrade to the KC-135 jet tanker. Another had the squadron moving to Texas, Florida, Ohio, or, God forbid, Minot, North Dakota.

At this time, SAC was placing more and more tanker units farther north in the States. Moving the tankers north would make it easier to refuel outbound EWO bombers. So that threw Texas and Florida out the window. Most of the more well-informed rumor mongers believed the squadron was going to change over to the KC-135 and go north. Since the 906th AREFS had just taken up residence at Minot, well... they wouldn't be going there, Thank God!

All of the rumors were thrown out the window when the official word arrived from Omaha. The 307th AREFS would transfer PCS from Lincoln to Selfridge AFB, Michigan, in June 1960.

The *Jet Scoop* came out as usual on Friday the 13th. As always, it was full of news from around the base and the command. And, as usual, Miller and Paine had the last full page devoted to advertisements. Their Toy Land was opening for the big Christmas season just ahead. There it was! The "official" Steve Canyon jet helmet for young aviators. They wanted $2.95 for the little beauty. Now, I don't know about other SAC BRATS, but I had to have one!

After checking my pop bottle deposit slush fund, I had more than enough pennies, nickels and dimes to get one. After doing some sweet-talking and downright begging mom and dad for a ride downtown, I had my prize. I was a little disappointed with "STEVE CANYON" plastered across the front of it under the visor.

Later that night, A1C Hugh "Duane" Wells stopped by to say "Howdy". His family lived two trailers down from us. He was my "big brother friend", so I had to show him my new prize. I told him it would be better if it didn't have that "official" Steve Canyon stuff on it. Well, he secretly left that night with my helmet. A couple of days later he brought it back. WOW! "STEVE CANYON" was replaced with my name in fancy script. The 370th Bomb Squadron insignia was emblazoned on each side of the helmet. It was beautiful; I could hardly wait to climb aboard my Bike-47 and fly a mission.

Reflex sorties continued on November 16th, when the next three B-47s left Lincoln for Spain. On arrival, the crews they were going to replace were more than happy to see that familiar green stripe on the tail as the B-47s landed at Morón.

Ken Wikle was back in Spain on Reflex. It was time for his second go-around with flying gliders in Spain. He wrote:

"I told Godman that the Kranich was the preferred vehicle for glider instruction. The best way to maximize training was to air-tow. 'Fine,' says Godman, 'use one of the base Aero Club Cessna 150s.' 'Okay,' says I, 'we need to contact Cessna engineering for tow hook installation data, not to mention the answer to the question, could a 150 tow a monster like the Kranich.' Then, the President of the Aero Club rendered the whole issue moot. He was a captain who had been around awhile and worked in base weather. He found me in the BOQ and delivered a short but understandable message: 'You guys are not touching any Aero Club aircraft,' Oh well, back to the tow-target cable.

"The Kranich was huge. It was the biggest sailplane I have ever seen before or since. It must have weighed 1500 pounds. Made in the thirties, it had a large, two-place tandem cockpit with a canopy that looked to be an exact duplicate of the famed Stuka dive-bomber.

"This time, the launch would be from the taxiway and an alert vehicle–one of those Ford station wagons with the red roof lights–would tow. My instructions from Col Godman were that I should probably land after a hour or so and that if I saw red lights flashing, I was to land near the alert ramp and proceed to my aircraft and not to worry about the tower, he'd given those folks the word. I told him that 900 feet (some 300 meters on the Kranich's altimeter) would be about maximum on the auto tow, my chances of snagging a thermal big enough to make the monster climb were less than nil, but he seemed interested.

"Shortly before launch, a USAF staff sergeant appeared on the scene. He was an Aero Club member, spoke Spanish, and had flown with the Spanish club and had actually taken instruction in the Kranich. He was willing to go with me. I refrained from kissing him and invited him into the rear seat. His first words of advice were never to deploy the spoiler-air brakes while airborne because they tend to bring the aircraft to a stop unless you had the nose pointed pretty much straight down. Maybe it was made for training Stuka pilots.

"We made an uneventful launch, flew a downwind leg that took us over the alert ramp and landed back on the taxiway. Colonel Godman seemed disappointed that was all I could make it do. That was our last flight of the day and forever more at Morón. When Crew E-10 next returned to Morón, Godman was gone and so were the gliders. From all of this foolishness, I claim a record. I was the only one on Reflex Alert ever to make an actual launch."

Ken's glider flight was an interesting way of breaking up the humdrum of alert duty. Most of the time there wasn't anything as fascinating as flying a glider. Paul Koski recalled alert duty:

"There are many stories of things that happened while on alert. When you are on alert, you have hours of boredom and rushes of adrenaline. We were trained like Pavlov's dogs: when the Klaxon sounded, your blood pressure went up and you raced to the aircraft, you had fifteen minutes to launch the bird; after that you were late and you could kiss your rear end goodbye.

"When we were on alert at Morón, Spain, our normal routine was forty-eight hours on and forty-eight off duty. You knew you were going to have a couple of alerts, if not more, during your shift.

"Our first shift, we went the whole shift without having an alert; everyone was on edge, but we were glad the shift was over. The next shift we didn't have any alerts either. Now, everyone was on edge, we began snapping at each other, card games and conversations were curt, any remarks were taken wrong. We felt sorry for the next shift, since we knew they were going to catch it.

"We went six days without an alert. You talk about trying us; our friendship with other crew chiefs from other wings was very thin, as well as between ourselves. The seventh day, all hell broke loose. We had so many alerts we lost count. We even had an unexpected incident, when the power station that supplied lights to the base blew a transformer and the whole base went black. Our first reaction was that we were under attack because of the loud explosion we heard when the transformer let go.

"We ran to the aircraft, using flashlights to guide us. The guards were hollering for us to stop and be identified. We didn't know if they would shoot us or not since there was so much confusion. We finally got the power units going so we could have lights and the flight crews were showing up. We spent the better part of the night at the aircraft. They finally got the power back by morning and we were glad the shift was over."

The November *Nuts and Jolts* was published late in the month. There was just one major problem. It was now called "Monthly Maintenance Order". Gone were the cartoons and timely news or tidbits. Reflecting the growing influence of the SAC MCS, it was almost entirely graphs and pie charts showing this and that figure. An interesting and helpful newsletter had become an instrument for helping crunch the MCS numbers.

Speaking of number crunching, the wing flew a total of 216 sorties accumulating 1,629 hours. The KC-97s flew 99 sorties for 559 hours. The wing lost 161 flying hours to the early arrival of old man winter. One major problem was the wide fluctuations in temperature, causing frost build up which had to be eliminated before takeoff.

On November 25th, the Bomb/Comp participants were summoned to the State Capitol. Nebraska Governor Ralph Brooks had a special evening planned in honor of the 307th Bomb Wing. First they were fed a great meal. Then, each of the Bomb/Comp participants was given a proclamation making them Admirals in the Great Navy of the State of Nebraska. Later, the winning flight crews were presented with a special Bomb/Comp ring with a beautiful blue stone. Emblazoned on the sides were special engravings of a B-47 and KC-97 refueling on one side and 1959 Bombing Competition on the other side. All in all it was a great evening, with members of the 307th getting special recognition and being able to rub shoulders with the State officials and otherwise do some serious, well-deserved hobnobbing.

December started just like November. The base was hit with snowfall on the 5th. It wasn't enough to halt flying, just slow it down. The lack of deicing equipment made getting the frost and ice off the aircraft a time consuming job.

On the 7th, three B-47s launched to fly a Tan Glove sortie. Like always, these missions would not only help SAC and NORAD get information on ECM, they would also cram as many training items as possible into the flight to meet 50-8 requirements.

Flying on the new low-level "Oil Burner" routes started in December. There were seven routes in the United States. The closest OB route for the 307th was a route terminating near Hastings bomb plot. The other six were scattered across the country.

A message arrived from Offutt with new orders for the Reflex commitment starting in January. The 307th would continue its Reflex to Morón, Spain. The orders outlined the checklists for equipment and what the procedures would be on arrival in Spain.

One major change in the order was a change in the route. The wing would fly over using the "Blue Route" or northern flyway to get to Spain. The Reflex bombers would refuel in the Farm Boy refueling area. Refueling would begin near Albany, New York, and end at Presque Isle, Maine. In case of bad weather, the Tow Bar refueling area would be the alternate refueling area.

For the last couple of months there had been a lot of construction going on up on the north end of the flightline. Near the end of the secondary runway they were pouring a lot of concrete and creating a rather strange looking building. It had funny-looking metal culvert-like tubes running from below ground to the surface. This would turn out to be the new Alert facility, scheduled to be completed in March.

SAC had been working on a way of getting the alert force in the air as quickly as possible. The new method was tried out under Project Open Mind beginning in late November. The 307th had their opportunity to try it out on December 12th.

It was called Minimum Interval Take Off, or MITO. The concept was simple in theory. If the alert force must be scrambled a Delta alert would be sounded. As usual, the pre-takeoff checklist would be completed as they taxied to the active runway. The launch would be a rolling takeoff, not stopping at the end of the runway. The bombers would roll down the runway at fifteen-second intervals until the force was airborne.

The approaching Christmas season found the flight crews checking the Alert and Reflex schedule to see which crews would be stuck with the "Holiday Duty". Actually they knew who was on the list, but there was always hope and the outside chance that there had been a last minute reprieve.

## Cold War Cornhuskers: The 307th Bomb Wing Lincoln Air Force Base Nebraska 1955-1965

The 307th Headquarters and 424th Bomb Squadron held their Christmas Party at the O-Club on December 18th. The A & E Squadron had their party at the NCO Club on the 21st. Over 450 attended the bash. Santa made a rush trip from the north to be on hand to give out presents to the children. The A & E Squadron took first place in the wing Christmas decorating contest. They were proud of the sleigh and reindeer that 1st Sgt "Bones" Minard had spent a lot of time building and painting.

Just in time for Christmas, Bruhn's Freezer Meats on Cornhusker Highway ran a special in the *Jet Scoop*. If you bought a half a beef, they'd give it to you at twenty-five cents a pound. Or, you could get T-Bone Steaks for thirty-six cents a pound. Pork chops were nineteen cents a pound.

The month ended with the usual reports to SAC being compiled, typed and reviewed to make sure all the i's were dotted and the t's crossed. There was also a review of the quarterly MCS points sent down from Division. There were several areas that may have raised Col Read's eyebrows.

The main area of concern was the loss of points because of aborts on the low level Oil Burner routes. At this point, the 307th didn't have the navigation charts for the routes. Without the charts the crews couldn't fly the routes accurately or safely. So, the 307th lost points for something over which they had no control. So much for the accuracy of the MCS.

It had been quite a year for the 307th. They had established an unbeatable record of sorties without deviating from the schedule. The wing maintained a high efficiency rating for Alert and Reflex. The 307th AREFS had a successful TDY deployment to the Azores. On top of everything, the 307th went to the World Series of SAC and came back to Lincoln as the World Champions.

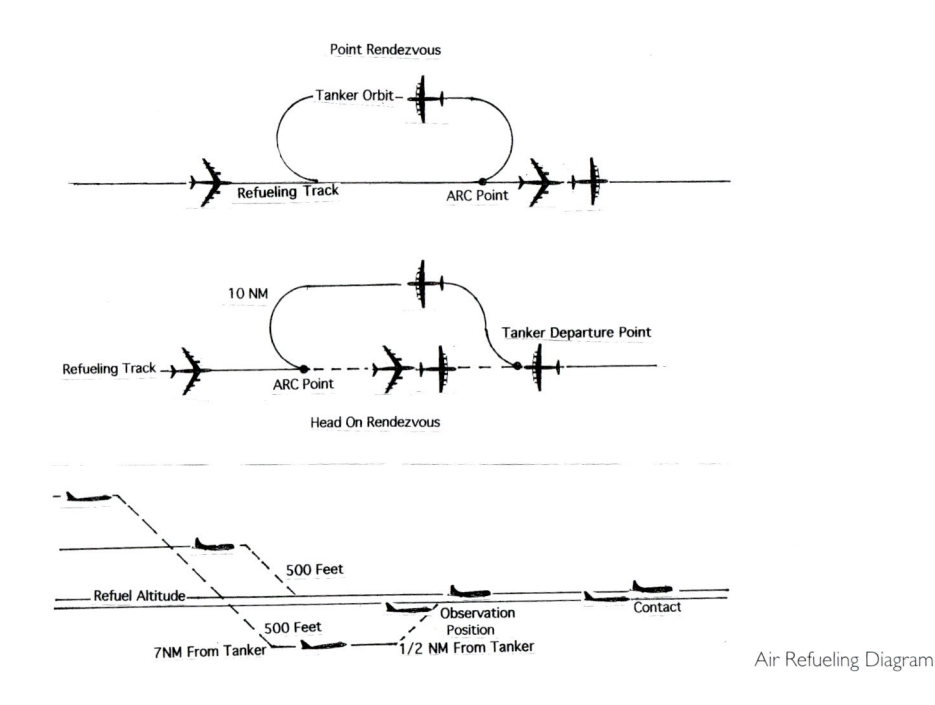

Air Refueling Diagram

After each visit from "The Hawk", snowplows would hit the ramp to clear the snow. (JET SCOOP)

Refueling over the snow covered Dakotas. Willie Martens was the boom operator. (Vorchheimer)

128

# 1959

SAC Memorial Sunday. (JET SCOOP)

Crew Chief Totem Pole. April 3, 1959 issue of the JET SCOOP. H.D. Mosser and Leo Finfinger from the 307th are on the right. (JET SCOOP)

Old reliable 6244 on the flight line at LAFB. (Villa)

2142 near one of the old hangars. (307th BWA)

# Cold War Cornhuskers: The 307th Bomb Wing Lincoln Air Force Base Nebraska 1955-1965

Operation: SPRING TONIC June 3, 1959.

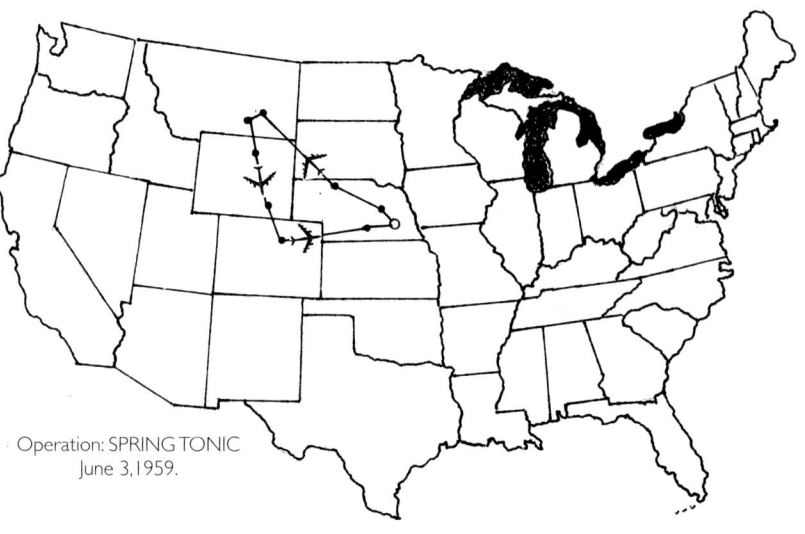

Hopefully, when the Sergeant finishes computing the bomb drop, it will be a SHACK. (USAF)

1000 sorties without a deviation from the flying schedule. L-R Rear: Col. Raleigh Smith, Capt. Joseph Lloyd, Capt. Richard Stoneking, Lt. Robert Vogel, TSgt. Edward McNeil, A1C Otis Owen, SSgt. Charles Stroud, L-R Front. MSgt. Robert Gould, SMSgt. George Rothenbach, SMSgt. Thomas Roch, MSgt. Eugene Stachen, SSgt. Samuel Sloan, Col. Elkins Reed, SMSgt. George Henry, SMSgt. Houston Page, SMSgt. Richard Carson. (Jet Scoop)

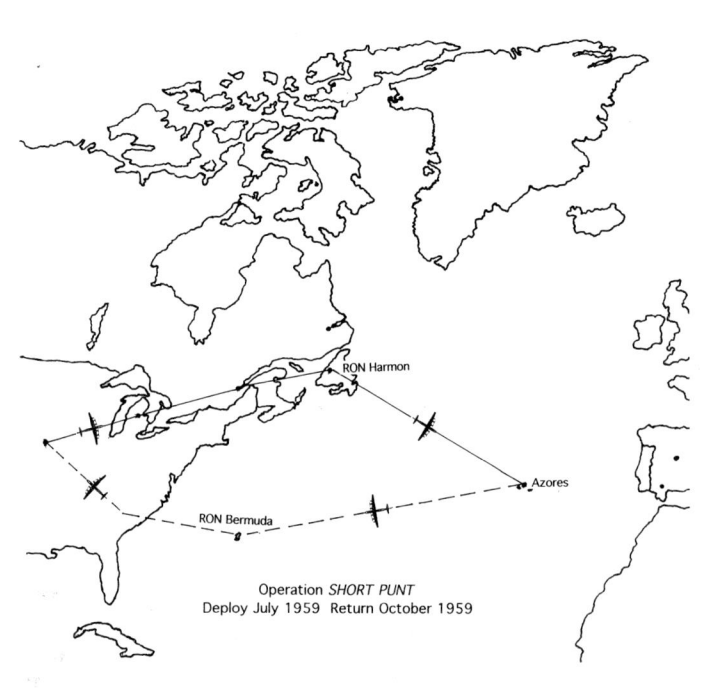

Operation: SHORT PUNT Deploy July 1959-Return October 1959

# 1959

Losing an engine over the Atlantic increased the "pucker factor" by several notches. (303rd ARS)

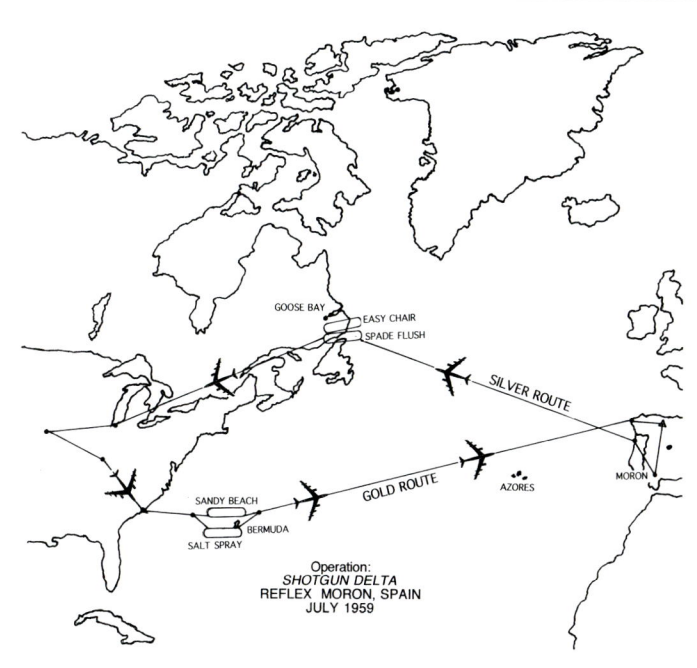

Operation: SHOTGUN DELTA REFLEX MORON, SPAIN JULY 1959

KC-97 landing at Lajes AB, Azores. (303rd ARS)

Lajes AB, Azores (307th BWA)

307th KC-97s on the flight line at Lajes, AB, Azores. (307th BWA)

Ken Wilke contemplates his fate before launching the glider. (Gingrich)

131

# Cold War Cornhuskers: The 307th Bomb Wing Lincoln Air Force Base Nebraska 1955-1965

A successful launch of the glider. (Gingrich)

Crew J-58 at Lajes Field. L-R Ray Normadin, Nick Nikkell, Bill Novetzke, Gary McGill, Larry Kessler. Departing for alert duty at Moron, Spain then R&R at Palma de Majorca. (307th BWA)

1500th Sortie without deviation from the flying schedule. Back Row L-R: SMSgt Thomas Roach, LtCol. John Thompson, Maj. Ray Coley, Lt. Robert Cort, Lt. Leroy Kerchner, Capt. George Biggs, LtCol. Lyle Cochran. Front L-R: Msgt Samuel Coffia, Col. James Britt, SSgt Donald Mowery, A3C. Elmo Thompson, LtCol. Lyle Cochran. (Mowery)

2000th sortie without deviating from the flying schedule. (307th BWA)

Col. James Brit congratulates Frank Kisner, Don Daley, Earl Buys and Thomas Sterling after the 2000th sortie. (307th BWA)

132

## 1959

Ken Tarwater rides in the "1st Class" area of the KC-97 on the way home from the Azores. (Tarwater)

L-R Tom Dance, Ed Godec, Bob Kretchmer. (Lally)

53-1872 flew the 2,327th Sortie. L-R Unknown, Capt. Albert Masserini, Lt. Vincent Kovacich, Col. Elkins Reed, Maj. Alan Simpkins, SSgt Donald Mowery, Unknown. (Mowery)

Celebrating the milestone. (307th BWA)

Crash site of 5248. (USAF)

Aerial view of the crash site. (USAF)

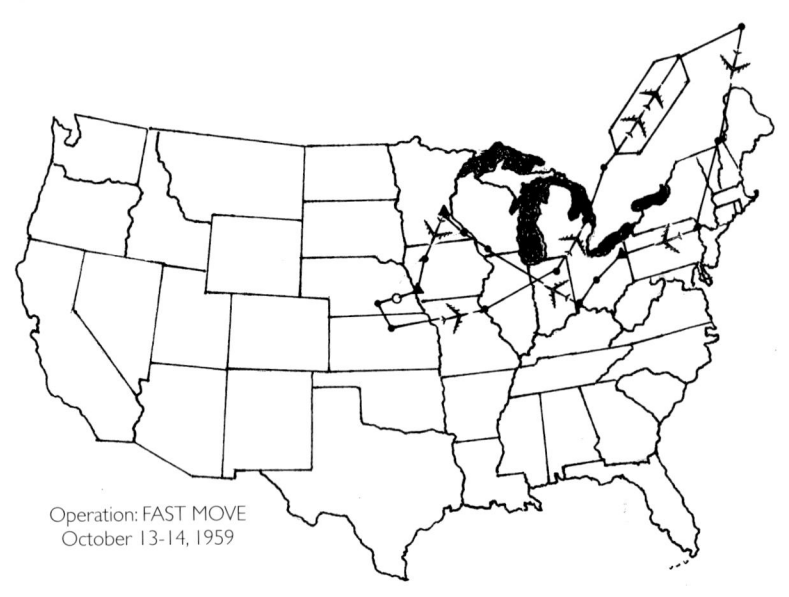

# Cold War Cornhuskers: The 307th Bomb Wing Lincoln Air Force Base Nebraska 1955-1965

Operation: FAST MOVE
October 13-14, 1959

53-2134 *City of Lincoln*. Competition aircraft for the 1959 Bomb Comp. (JET SCOOP)

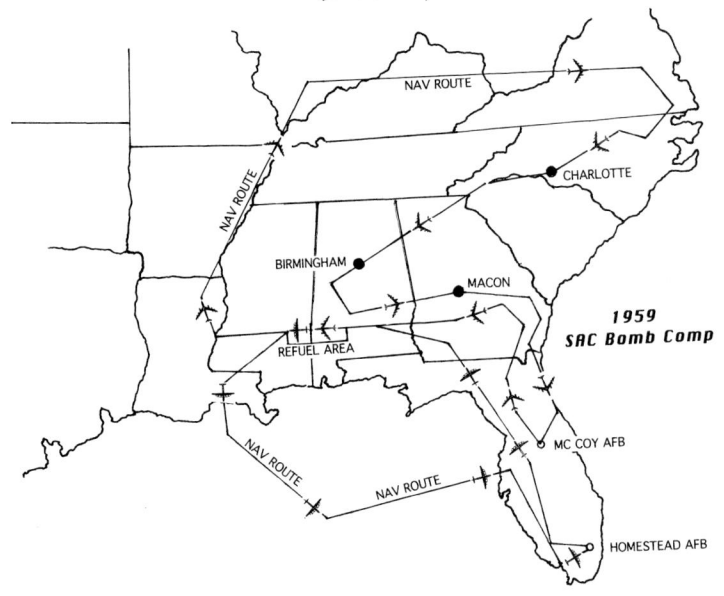

1959 SAC Bomb Comp

L-R: Capt. Richard Mitchell (AC), Lt Darrell Norris (CP), Lt Keith Kinyon. (NAV)

134

## 1959

L-R. Capt. Noble Timmons (NAV), Lt. Don Jordan (CP), Capt. Dale Christians (AC). (Christians)

1959 BOMB COMP Patch (Christians)

To the victors goes the Fairchild Trophy. L-R Keith Kinyon, Col. Reed, Darrell Norris, Richard Mitchell. (307th BWA)

The Fairchild Trophy. (USAF)

135

# Cold War Cornhuskers: The 307th Bomb Wing Lincoln Air Force Base Nebraska 1955-1965

JET SCOOP photo of the victorious 307th.

Bomber ground crew for the 1959 Bomb Comp. (JET SCOOP)

307TH ARES ground crew for the Bomb Comp. (Tarwater)

Col. Corbin congratulates Capt. Jetts' crew and ground crew from the 307th ARES after returning to Lincoln. (Tarwater)

## 1959

Paul Trudeau, Al Leet and Mike Gingrich on Reflex to Moron, Spain. (Gingrich)

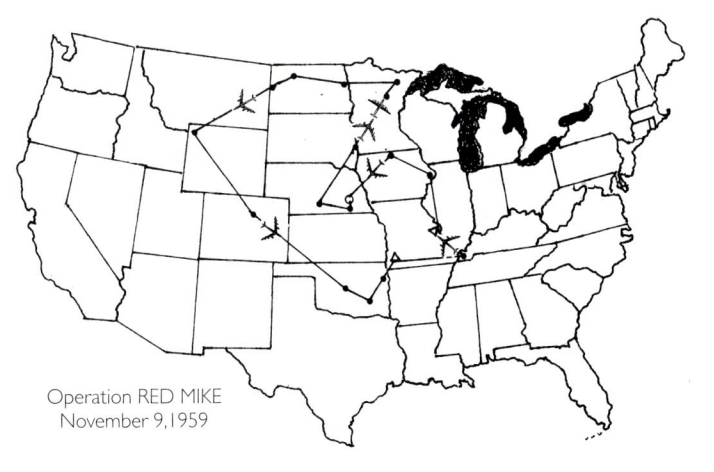

Alert Vehicles at Moron, Spain. (Gingrich)

Operation RED MIKE
November 9, 1959

The flight line board at the fire station. (S.D. Hill)

Reflex bound Hank Grogan took this beautiful photo off the coast of near Cape Cod. The crew of 1844 consisted of Jim Pumford in the front seat, Jim Forgas in the back and Bob King hiding in the nose. (Grogan)

Left: With the new board, it just took a quick glance to find out where a certain aircraft was. (S.D. Hill)

# 1960

Bouncing Baby New Year arrived at the stroke of Midnight on Friday. Since New Year's Eve was Thursday, there weren't as many heavy throbbing heads as there might have been if the holiday had fallen on the weekend. The real workweek would start on Monday, so there were a couple of extra days to recover if one was inclined to party a little bit.

The first Reflex deployment of the year left Lincoln on Monday, January 4th. As per the operations order, they would fly to Spain using the Blue Northern route. The route was about a thousand miles shorter than the southern route; still over water, but a thousand miles shorter to swim if you had to eject.

Leaving Lincoln, the three-ship cell flew east towards Chicago, then on to Detroit. From Detroit they headed for the Farmer Boy refueling area to meet the tankers. The end of the refueling area was near Presque Isle, Maine. Coasting out over Nova Scotia, the cell began the long overwater flight to Spain.

On the 11th, another three-ship cell departed for Spain. They followed the same route as the first cell. They ran into trouble during refueling. Air traffic control in that area had restricted altitudes for refueling. These were above the altitudes published for high gross weights of the B-47. That put the planes closer to the deadly "coffin corner". The cell was able to get their fuel, but it was getting kind of hairy towards the end of the refueling track.

Returning Reflex aircraft had a hard time getting back on the 12th. Using the return corridor for the Blue route, they ran into strong headwinds. The copilots had to keep a keen eye on the fuel gauges. At one point they were almost below fuel reserves if they missed the tanker. Thankfully, everyone was able to hook up and get the badly needed fuel.

On the 12th, KC-97 52-2804 was scheduled to fly a routine mission. The crew had planned for a refueling with a B-47 over western Nebraska, then a navigation leg and on home to Lincoln, no sweat. Sgt Sam Sloan met the crew and helped with the preflight walk around. Like always everything was in the right place, so the crew climbed aboard and fired up the engines.

During runup and mag check at the end of the runway, they ran into a problem when the #1 propeller stuck in reverse pitch. The Engineer pulled the power off the engine and tried to feather the prop. No luck; the prop wouldn't budge from reverse. There was nothing the crew could do but shut the engine down and taxi back to the ramp on the other three engines. Sgt Sloan could only shake his head in dismay. He and his assistant, Ken Tarwater, would have their work cut out for them trying to figure out why old reliable 2804 had aborted.

A Reflex flight returning from Spain on the 13th achieved something that had never happened on a Reflex flight. To the surprise and joy of the flight crews, all of the aircraft achieved a 100% fire out over the Atlantic. At least they'd get some extra MCS points for the flight.

Wing Headquarters received a directive via 2nd Air Force. The 307th AREFS was to send two tankers to Lockbourne AFB, Ohio, to maintain strip alert. The aircraft would remain at Lockbourne for two weeks and then return. This rotation would continue through July. Crews for the alert aircraft would rotate on a weekly schedule.

The first two tankers were scheduled to deploy on 14 January. That Thursday, the best laid plans of mice and tanker toads were spoiled by the local weather. Up to then, winter had been fairly mild by Nebraska standards. There was snow on the ground, but not enough to hamper regular flight operations.

That morning started with low clouds hanging over the flight line. By 1000 a light freezing drizzle was falling. At 1200, the aircraft on the ramp were covered by a thin glaze of ice. Everything, literally, slid to a halt on the flight line. All air operations were canceled for the rest of the day.

The 307th AREFS was supposed to begin sending their KC-97s to the depot for updates and propeller modifications. Cracking and blade separation had been constant problems with the KC-97 props since it came into service. With the change to the 34G60 solid aluminum propeller the problems declined. The bad weather on the 14th canceled the first departure for the KC-97s' update.

Saturday dawned bright and sunny. With the sun shining, the ice started melting off the planes. On the 16th two tankers departed for the Alert assignment at Lockbourne. On the same day, two tankers left for the modification depot. It all boiled down to the fact that, in Nebraska, you had to fly when the weather was good.

On the 25th, the tankers were getting ready to take off on a mass gas refueling mission. The fireguard was posted at 52-2804 for engine start. The #3 engine coughed to life after the usual twenty blades. Then the crew began to turn the prop on #4. After twenty blades the huge engine coughed to life, then backfired. A huge ball of flame came out of the exhaust pipe followed by black smoke. Within seconds fire was streaming from under the cowl flaps. The ground crew yelled "Fire in #4!" The engineer pulled the power off and hit the cutoff switch. The fireguard moved into position

138

## 1960

and started shooting his fire bottle up at the engine cowling. Within a few seconds the fire went out. The base fire trucks responded to stand guard against further flare-up.

Col "Pete" Read, representing the 307th Bomb Wing, and Col Thomas Corbin, 818th Air Division Commander, began a campaign to higher headquarters about the MB-3 deicing units which were supposed to have arrived, but hadn't. Their letters of consternation yielded the fact that the delivery date for the units had slipped another sixty days. By the time the equipment arrived it wouldn't be needed.

Ugly weather continued to hamper air operations. On Wednesday the 27th, there was a combination of drizzle and freezing rain. Weather was making life miserable on the flight line again. Anything out in the open was being coated with layers of ice. No better time than now to see how the men would react to the old SAC curve ball.

What began as a simple fire drill that day turned into a proverbial Chinese Fire Drill. It all started up in the 98th area. The crew chief of B-47 #178 was informed, "This is a simulated fire. You have a big fire in the cockpit of your plane." The umpire looked at his watch and noted the time as 1115.

The crew chief pulled the power unit away from #178 and started moving other equipment away from the "burning" aircraft. Interesting that he made no effort to report the fire until prompted by the umpire, "You have a fire; don't you think you should report it?"

At that time the crew chief announced, "We have a 'Broken Arrow'". The umpire was taken off guard; there had been no reference to the aircraft having a weapon aboard. The north end of the flight line was transformed into an anthill of activity within a matter of moments.

The Broken Arrow standby signal was given at 1119. Coleman tow vehicles slid into the area to tow a couple of tankers away from the fuel pits. Two of the Colemans didn't have the right tow bar to latch onto the nose wheel of the tankers. One latched onto #759 and moved it away from the pit.

By 1123, the Explosive Ordnance Disposal (EOD) team was on the scene, followed by the fire department. By the time they arrived, the "fire" was deemed out of control at 1125. Two minutes later, the "fire" reached the bomb bay and the signal to withdraw was given. Almost everyone in the area scrambled to get away from the impending disaster.

At 1136, the flight line was rocked by an "explosion" as #178 blew apart, showering the area with debris and flaming JP-4. People stood around and watched as the "fire" spread across the ramp. The umpire finally had enough and called the exercise to a halt at 1140. Activity on the flight line would resume normal operations. The drill would continue for the medical, disaster and other personnel until almost 1300.

After it was all over, the umpires got together to write up the report. Their report and comments brought out a comedy of errors. The largest was in the reporting of the incident. The drill was supposed to be a routine fire drill. They recommended personnel should be cautioned not to call a Broken Arrow unless a weapon was involved.

They also pointed out that the wrong tow bars were brought to tow aircraft. Security and disaster teams must be briefed on their respective duties. During this type of drill, all personnel in the area should be encouraged to participate. It was brought out that over fifty percent of the personnel within the 1,500 foot danger zone continued their normal duties and did not withdraw from the danger zone. If it had been a real emergency, the umpires scored eight KC-97s and six B-47s that would have been destroyed or damaged. Several power units, heaters and a Lorain crane also would have been lost, not to mention death and injuries to personnel standing around with their hands in their pockets.

The Broken Arrow was bad enough, but the weather was worse. The freezing drizzle continued on and off all afternoon, causing ten aircraft to launch late and two sorties to be canceled altogether.

When the reports of the Broken Arrow hit Gen Power's desk, he hit the roof. Some observers at Lincoln swore they saw a mushroom shaped cloud in the distance towards Omaha. He immediately sent out orders to the effect that, due to the results of the Broken Arrow exercises around the command, it would be mandatory to hold a practice Broken Arrow at every base on a monthly basis.

During a Tan Glove mission on 29 January a refueling sortie was lost. As 52-2804 pulled into the refueling track the Engineer reported the oil pressure on #4 engine was falling. They were close to the rendezvous with their receiver, so the pilot told the engineer to watch it. Watch it he did, as the oil pressure continued to fall. The engineer told the pilot it was still falling, and they had better shut the engine down or risk a major problem, like throwing a prop. The engine was shut down and the tanker had to abort the mission.

January ended with more freezing drizzle, causing a slowdown of just about everything on base. The 307th had been scheduled to fly 201 sorties, but they managed to get only 155 off the ground. January may have started with mild weather, but the last half of the month was a typical Nebraska winter.

February started where January left off, with bad weather holding Lincoln in an icy grip. Freezing drizzle coated everything in a cold glaze of ice. With limited deicing equipment available, the men on the flight line had to revert to the age-old method of removing the built-up layers of ice from the planes. The sound of rubber banging against aluminum reverberated across the ramp as personnel tried to beat the ice into submission with rubber hoses.

The first Reflex deployment for February left for Spain on the 3rd. The three B-47s flew the northern route, refueling in the Farmer Boy refueling area, and then heading out over the Atlantic and on to Spain. Reflex deployments would continue every week during the month.

As soon as the B-47s arrived at Morón they were unloaded, serviced and cocked for alert. The flight crews got some chow and then tried to get some sack time before relieving the alert crews the next day.

When the ground crews finished getting the aircraft serviced and cocked, they would go back to their alert quarters. There wasn't a lot to do while waiting for the klaxon to interrupt the tense routine of just waiting.

Every now and then the routine would be broken by a different kind of tense moment. Paul Koski wrote about just such a moment:

"We were at Morón AB, Spain. We had finished preflighting all the aircraft and were back at the alert shack, relaxing, playing cards and just waiting for the klaxon to blow. (The alert shack was a cinder block storage building that was converted to our alert facility). This was also our sleeping quarters while we were on alert.

"One of the crew chiefs said he saw a mouse, so we thought we would try to catch it. There were six of us and only one little mouse, or so we thought. We moved the bunks out of the way and cornered that sucker. The only problem was, it wasn't a mouse; instead, it looked like an overgrown Wolf spider. It was crouched against the wall, cornered.

"As we approached the spider, with thoughts of killing it, we were shocked, dismayed and scared when that spider jumped at us from six feet away. I didn't know they could jump that far. All the big, strong crew chiefs stumbled over each other, as well as bunks, trying to get out of its way.

"We didn't see where it went, so we started tearing the beds apart and moving anything that wasn't fastened down. Would you believe it? We couldn't find the darn thing. Needless to say, none of us got any sleep that night. I think the spider won that battle."

When the resident Alert crews were relieved by the new arrivals, it was time to plan for the return trip to Lincoln. The flight would cover the northern route across the Atlantic. They would also refuel in the Farmer Boy area and coast in over the good old USA. To fill a couple of training requirements they would make a bomb run on Omaha before landing at the patch.

There was an accepted tradition of bringing back all kinds of things during the Reflex flights. If it could fit in the bomb bay of a B-47, it was fair game to bring back at one time or another. Items included special yard goods, stereos, cuckoo clocks and pieces of fine granite. The most popular category was booze, and lots of it. Doug Valen recalled:

"On one particular trip with Crew E-03, made up of Maj Lloyd Timmons, Capt Doug Valen, and Capt Norm Menke, we landed at Lincoln and waited for the Customs guys to show up. On that particular trip, Sgt Rivers, a crew chief, was riding the jump seat and had a B-4 bag tucked under his feet containing no small amount of booze. Needless to say, he was very concerned about getting caught with too much in the bag. The customs guy came up the ladder, looked around and asked about our booze. We said we each had about a gallon and he went back down the ladder and departed. Sgt Rivers was smiling from ear to ear and laughing about how clever he was, packing his booze in a B-4 bag that looked like the Pubs bag of charts and maps.

"We called the motor pool for a baggage truck and started unloading everything on the ramp, waiting for the truck. As we were all talking and having a great time, we suddenly heard a very distinct sound of breaking glass. We turned around and the baggage truck had backed over Sgt Rivers' bag of booze and broken every single bottle. His stash of booze was slowly spreading in a large circle around his bag. I thought he was going to cry. He was totally destroyed and couldn't believe the unfortunate occurrence."

Bringing booze back in a B-47 is not always the best way to transport the golden liquid, as Paul Koski relates a tale of a Champagne Flight:

"The bomb bay had a cargo rack installed and it was completely filled, as well as the crawlway and the cockpit. The copilot had bought a case of pink champagne for his wedding and wanted to take it on the aircraft. I told him we didn't have any more room and he would have to send it on another aircraft. He wasn't very happy and was telling one of the ground crew his problem. This person, trying to be helpful, said he knew where there was room.

"They put the champagne in the aft ECM antenna pod, which was behind the aft main gear. We landed at Lincoln and off loaded the boxes. The only problem I had was that there was this pink stuff dripping from the ECM pod all the way back to the 20 mm cannons. I knew it couldn't be hydraulic fluid since there wasn't any hydraulic equipment in the ECM pod. You guessed it! The pod wasn't pressurized and all of the bottles had popped. We washed the plane down and changed the champagne-soaked cannons. For the next few months, we had this pink stuff leaking out of the seams every time the aircraft flew."

On February 15th, the 307th AREFS got word that, instead of maintaining their strip alert at Lockbourne, they would maintain alert at Selfridge AFB, Michigan. To the crews who had to sit on alert it made sense, since the squadron was going to be moving to Selfridge in the summer.

Word came in from 2nd Air Force for Operation Red Mike. This would be another no-notice ORI mission. The Command Post thought perhaps 2nd Air Force was running out of special names for special missions. They recalled they had already flown an Operation Red Mike. It turns out it was the same operational name, just a different route and mission details. The wing would be vulnerable for this one until 30 June. Since the wing hadn't had an ORI in several months, everyone figured they would get the call for Red Mike a lot sooner than June.

Typical winter weather continued to plague the 307th's efforts to get off the ground during February. It was a constant cycle: snowstorm moves in, dumps snow, plow, snow dumped again, then clean it all up again. Piles of snow fifteen to thirty feet high lined the taxiways. In all, the wing lost over 206 flying hours to winter weather during the month.

March roared in like a lion. High, gusty winds lashed the ramp, sending anything not tied down flying off to who-knew-where. The cold wind introduced the troops to something called "chill factor", a combination of temperature and wind, which lowered the danger point for exposed flesh. With the snow blowing around the flight line the troops were glad to have their nice, warm N3-B parkas. They were great; you could zip the front up all the way to the hood, pull the hood over your head and form a snorkel to protect your face. It was great protection, but you couldn't see a heck of a lot. More snow fell on the flight line and, again, the snow crews battled old man winter with their well-worn snowplows. Everyone was hoping spring would arrive pretty soon.

Coming back from a mission and getting the aircraft safely on the ground could sometimes be a problem. Dave Bowersock recalled:

"We had completed all phases of our B-47 training mission and were descending for a night landing a Lincoln. In the descent, we lost the defrost system for the windscreen (glass in front of the cockpit). The situation was serious. The Command Post discussed a plan to launch an emergency tanker for us, but my copilot calculated that we didn't have enough fuel to rendezvous with it. The Command Post cleared us to land.

"It was a dark night and, even though the sides of the canopy were clear, I had no forward visibility. It was black as the inside of an ink bottle, but Thank God for strobe lights (a row of intense flashing lights extending out from and indicating the center of the runway). They were just visible thru the frost and helped keep us lined up until over the runway. From that point on, I could see the runway lights only from the side and that was all the reference I had as to how high we were from the ground. The copilot and nav both remarked, that on a clear, no-wind day, I could land hard enough to break concrete, but that night my landing was as smooth as glass."

Word was received from SAC Headquarters that the 307th AREFS alert commitment would change from Selfridge back to Lockbourne. The squadron had just gotten squared away in Michigan and now it was back to Ohio. In typical military fashion, this whole alert thing was becoming SNAFU. The tanker boys were hoping the people in the "head shed" at Omaha would make up their cotton pickin' minds.

Monday, the 7th, started another freezing week at the frozen patch. Low-hanging gray clouds covered the base. Ernie Pence reported for duty and cast his keen weather eye skyward. He could almost sense a change in the weather and the approaching "Hawk". Sure enough, by 0930 the wind had shifted; the clouds were dipping even lower. A fine drizzle started to drift down from above. Yep, Ernie was right: the Hawk approacheth.

The blare of the klaxon wailed across the base at 0940. Crews scrambled or, in some cases, skated to the alert birds, hit the switches and spooled up the engines. Contacting the command post, they got the word to execute a Coco Alert. The first B-47 reporting ready moved forward towards the taxiway. Turning on to the strip was dicey due to the thin layer of ice deposited by the drizzle. The planes taxied as fast as possible under the prevailing conditions, which was about as fast as a turtle. At the runway, several planes had trouble making the turn onto the active runway.

# 1960

The flight line crews found out this was not just a simple Coco Alert. Word came around; the Coco alert signaled the beginning of OPSODR 312-60 code name Red Mike. The 307th had been tagged with a no-notice ORI. Regardless of the weather, if the wing was hit with an ORI, it's DAMN THE WEATHER, GENERATE THE FORCE!

The Alert birds were downloaded, serviced, and made ready to launch on the first ORI sortie. The follow-on force would be readied for launch within the guidelines of the ORI and launch after the first wave.

Col Read had been out on the flight line when the alert aircraft taxied during the scramble. He didn't like what he saw. The aircraft were having all kinds of problems moving safely under the conditions. Ground crews were slipping and falling on the frozen concrete. Watching his boys slipping and sliding on the ice-covered ramp, he was getting more worried with each frozen pellet that fell.

The wing was able to get ten B-47s and eight tankers into the air in spite of the ice and drizzle. The last tanker off reported they had trouble getting into the air because ice on the runway and ice building up on the wings, even with the anti-ice equipment going full blast on the plane.

Freezing drizzle continued to fall while the planes were being readied for the ORI flight. With only two MB-3 deicer units available on base, it was a losing battle against old man winter. Col Read made another trip around the flight line, then headed back to the Command Post. It wasn't safe for man or sheep herder out there on the flight line. He wasn't going to put his "boys" in further jeopardy, ORI or not!

Col Read fired off a message to 2nd Air Force, telling them in no uncertain terms that the 307th Bomb Wing would continue the ORI as directed. However, due to the weather, operations would continue at a slower, safer pace until the weather improved. He also contacted SAC Headquarters with the same message. Col Read had made a command decision that could curtail his chances of ever pinning a star on his collar. It may have been an ORI, but under peacetime conditions, he wasn't going to put the safety of his men above his career.

2nd Air Force replied by canceling further generation of the force for the time being. Later that night, 2nd Air Force came back with a message to continue the exercise by launching the remaining aircraft as soon as weather permitted. The aircraft already in the air flew a scaled-down profile and recovered at McConnell AFB, Kansas, due to the bad weather at Lincoln.

The rotten weather stuck around for another couple of days. On Friday, March 11th, the clouds moved out and the sun beat down on the flight line. With the ice melting from the aircraft and ramp, the wing was able to launch and fly Red Mike. The ORI was over, or was it?

The jet engine shop had been suffering from understaffing for the last several months. They performed thirty-two inspections, shipped two engines to Reflex bases, and completed eight unscheduled engine changes. On the 14th, they went to twelve-hour shifts to accomplish the workload. The hydraulics shop was also short four people. Col Read started his never-ending stream of letters and messages to higher headquarters requesting more trained people to keep the wing in the air.

The new Alert Facility opened on 16 March. The building was a self-contained building on the north end of the flight line. It looked like a building that had culverts coming out of the sides instead of doors. It had sleeping quarters for the officers and airmen that would pull Alert. There was a mess area, day room, communications center and briefing room. Alert crews could pull their entire tour of Alert without going outside of the building—except for daily preflights and the occasional Alert—if they wished.

By mid-afternoon, Alert birds were parked on the "Christmas Tree" and the crews had been assigned their quarters. To christen the new Alert pad, 2nd Air Force called a Bravo Alert at 1720 that afternoon. After everyone was back inside, most agreed that it was a lot easier getting to the planes from the new building than driving helter-skelter across the base. The only complaints were the lack of telephones and the smell of freshly painted green walls.

For the last several months, several low-level bomb runs had been lost in the Clearview Oil Burner route. Control of the airspace was shared by Kansas City and Denver Centers. Col Read wrote:

"Numerous low-level bomb runs have been lost at Hastings Bomb Plot due to no clearance from Denver (ATC) for bomb-run-only aircraft, if another aircraft has been cleared on the navigation portion of the Clearview route by Kansas City Center. Unless coordination between the two centers can be affirmed, it is recommended that the Oil Burner route Clearview be relocated to place it entirely in the controlled area of one Center since no such problems exist on the Oil Burner Flat Rock. Until such time as this can be done, it is recommended that the SAC REG 50-8 requirement for RBS scored low-level runs be reduced a commensurate amount to the Oil Burner time utilization without a 'Bomb Run-only' capability."

Monday morning, March 28th, started another new workweek at the patch. Alert crews did the morning preflight on the alert aircraft, just like every morning. Ground personnel reported for duty and got their work assignments. The weather wasn't the best. A lot of people had to slow down driving to the base because of the patchy fog in the area. By the time the Alert crews reported back from preflight, the fog was getting thick enough to cut with a knife.

The Command Post got a message to execute Operation Red Mike. What, again? Alert crews raced to the aircraft, which was a lot of fun on the fog-covered ramp, and hit the ladders. Within moments, the sound of ground power units was matched with the growing whine of jet engines spooling up to power. Checking in with Alert Control, the crews reported when they were ready to roll. With the heavy fog covering the base like a blanket, the alert was downgraded to a Bravo response.

Both Col Corbin and Col Read were on the horn to 2nd Air Force. They expressed their strong concern about conducting another ORI under the current weather conditions. Barksdale replied that the force would be generated according to the outline for Red Mike. Flying would proceed as soon as the fog lifted and it was safe to fly.

While Col Read and the wing staff sweated out the weather, the ground crews were busy generating the B-47s for Red Mike. There may have been fog thick enough to cut with a knife, but within eight hours, most of the force was ready to fly.

Tuesday the 29th, everything was ready to fly the mission. The low clouds, fog and flurries had moved on to the east. It wasn't CAVU skies, but the weather at Lincoln was good enough to get off the ground. Crews reported for the mission briefing. The weather boys gazed into their crystal ball and pointed out that the frontal system was moving slowly to the east and the weather over the route to the targets was questionable.

Later that morning, the relative quiet on the ramp gave way to the low whine of jet engines spooling up again. The south end of the ramp was awash in blue smoke as the tankers fired up for the mission.

One by one the lumbering aircraft taxied towards the runway, looking like a silver wagon train, brakes squealing like trumpeting elephants. It was an impressive sight; twenty-seven B-47s and sixteen KC-97s were strung out from the ramp to the end of Runway 35. They would take off at one-minute intervals and climb towards the north.

As 53-4219 taxied towards the runway, the crew noticed a strange vibration coming from the left side of the aircraft. A quick check by one of the Metro truck crews provided the reason for the vibration. The left outrigger wheel was wobbling like a bad grocery cart wheel. When 4219 stopped, the boys in the Metro would pile out and try to fix the wobbler.

*141*

A certain amount of intestinal fortitude was required for this. Even though the engines were powered back to idle, there was still considerable danger being that close to the intakes and tail pipes of two jet engines. Try as they might, they couldn't fix the problem. It wasn't safe to try to take off; the outrigger could fail completely. When 4219 reached the end of the taxiway, the crew pulled off and moved down to the compass rose to get out of the way. 4219 was scored as a ground abort.

The tankers headed for Grand Island after launch to get in position to refuel the bombers. Approaching the area, 52-2667 was having problems with the boom. A quick radio call to home plate was made to launch a spare tanker to replace the troubled KC-97. Within minutes of the call, another tanker was launched and heading towards the refueling area.

The bombers had flown north to Sioux Falls, South Dakota, then turned for Alexandria, Minnesota. Over Alexandria they turned towards Fargo, North Dakota, then southwest towards Pierre, South Dakota, to meet the tankers. About the time the bombers began descending from altitude there was another problem developing in the tanker force.

52-2804 was losing oil pressure on one of the engines. The engineer pulled the power back, hoping to keep the engine running long enough to make the fuel transfer. No such luck; the oil pressure kept falling. They had no choice but to shut it down, feather the prop and return to Lincoln. The rest of the tankers stayed in the refueling area and managed to make the rendezvous and offload the fuel. Sadly, as there wasn't enough time to launch another spare tanker, 2804 was scored as an air abort.

After refueling, the bombers headed back upstairs to the mission altitude of 30,000 feet to begin the first nav leg towards Denver. After checking in over Denver, the B-47s turned towards the next checkpoint at La Junta, Colorado. From there they headed for the end of the nav leg at Oklahoma City. They turned north and flew to Wichita, then turned for the first bomb run on Kansas City, Missouri.

The bad weather hadn't moved away from either of the target cities, just as the weather people had predicted. ATC gave a special IFR clearance in that area for the mission. The bombers made their bomb runs from the newly approved altitude of 35,000 feet. After radar bomb runs on the targets they turned and flew to Des Moines, Iowa, then back to home plate at Lincoln.

The ORI was over; everyone could only wait for the scores to come in, be posted, and the final results gone over. The final results: bottom line, the 307th passed with no recommendations. Preparation and generation were scored as "Outstanding". The execution phase was "Satisfactory". Navigation was rated as "Excellent" in spite of the bombers running into high cirrus clouds over two thirds of the nav leg. There was one ground abort and one air abort. The wing was glad to see that twenty-four of the twenty-seven B-47s were scored as reliable on the bomb runs.

Even though the wing passed the ORI with no recommendations, Red Mike would go into the books as one fouled up ORI. First, there was the weather that had caused the first attempt to be slowed down, called off, and then flown. Weather caused problems when the klaxon sounded the start of the second shot at Red Mike. The ORI was also notable for the fact that Col Read had stuck his neck out a mile for his fellow sheep herders by slowing things down in view of the weather. The men of the 307th knew the boss' neck was on the line and they went all-out to pass this one for their head sheep herder. He may never wear a star, but he had the respect and admiration of the men in his command.

April arrived with the typical showers to bring the summer flowers. Most of the snow had melted and, in a lot of places, the grass was turning green. At least the weather was warming up and, with that, air operations would be a lot easier in the upcoming months.

During Project Open Road, SAC had validated the concept of using the Minimum Interval Takeoff, or MITO, as a method of getting the alert force into the air in the shortest time possible. With the advent of long-range missiles, it was obvious that the old method of launching the fleet was no longer a viable option. Pete Todd recalled:

"The Minimum Interval Takeoff (MITO) was an emergency launch of the SAC Alert force, designed to get the maximum number of aircraft off the ground and a safe distance away from their base in the minimum amount of time before a presumed nuclear attack from ICBMs could obliterate the force.

"The MITO procedure was simple in concept. Each aircraft was to cross the painted 'hold line' from the taxiway onto the active runway fifteen seconds behind the one ahead, making a rolling takeoff with throttles set at about 80 % power in the turn, controlling speed with brakes, then applying full takeoff thrust when aligned with the runway. At a precomputed speed, the aircraft commander would fire the ATO bottles. If everything went well, all aircraft would have safe separation from each other throughout the takeoff and liftoff.

"Nevertheless, the tremendous jet wash and smoke from the engines and ATO plus the wake turbulence of the aircraft, themselves, would create real control challenges, especially at night. It's one of the few times you would hope for a brisk crosswind at takeoff, which would carry the turbulence and smoke off to the side of the runway and provide the crew a more stable air mass for the flight controls and better visibility during the takeoff roll and liftoff.

"To further ease the control problems, the lead aircraft was expected to turn about 30 degrees to the right of the runway heading as soon as possible after liftoff. Number two would turn 25 degrees, number three 20 degrees and so on, avoiding flying through the jet wash of the plane ahead and creating a fan of safe airspace during critical moments immediately after lifting off. Everyone would drop their ATO racks after burnout and proceed individually on their designated route of flight.

"As I recall, each crew had to qualify annually on the MITO procedure. As a peacetime training exercise, it was very carefully controlled, for obvious safety reasons. Before I arrived at Lincoln, there may have been some "mass gaggle" takeoffs, but I can't remember performing a MITO at Lincoln with more than two or three airplanes. I never saw one that included ATO.

"In addition to the annual takeoff requirements, the first part of the MITO procedure was practiced on each Coco exercise (in which the alert force would be scrambled, taxi to the runway, perform the MITO protocol up to applying takeoff power, then reduce to taxi power about 1,000 feet down the runway and then return to their parking place.) Each ORI for a SAC bomb wing was initiated with a Coco exercise and the MITO simulation was a pass-fail item. If I recall correctly, the criterion was that the alert aircraft had to cross the hold line within fifteen minutes of the sounding of the klaxon.

"There was one critical aspect of the wartime MITO that was rarely discussed openly, namely, what happens if an aircraft in the takeoff stream experiences a major malfunction. Under peacetime rules, of course, there was a clear-cut course of action: if there's a safety of flight problem before decision speed, the aircraft will abort takeoff and all following aircraft will also abort.

"In wartime, however, when the survival of a significant fraction of the retaliatory force might be compromised, it was pretty much understood by everyone that, once you started takeoff roll, you were committed not to impede those behind. Whether that meant risking death by continuing takeoff or veering off the side of the runway, we all understood that aborting takeoff on the runway wasn't an option. I don't recall ever seeing anything in writing about it; it was just that invisible '800-pound gorilla' that everyone knew was there."

## 1960

Three B-47s departed for Reflex on Thursday, April 14th. As before they would fly the northern route to Spain. There were several reasons for SAC changing the route for Reflex. The primary reason for the change was that it was a thousand miles shorter. Fewer miles meant less fuel used to get the Reflex force moved to the forward bases. That meant less time in the air and money saved. It also meant crews would spend a couple of hours less in the air, which should help reduce fatigue.

There may have been another underlying reason for the change. Mike Gingrich recalled that, in August, his Reflex return was delayed for almost a week due to their replacement crew being stuck in Bermuda with mechanical problems with their aircraft.

While SAC never published a survey on mechanical problems encountered along the southern route, there seemed to be more breakdowns and missed tankers along this route. It may have been just the fact they were flying more miles. Then, maybe it was because they had to fly through the Bermuda Triangle.

Friday, April 15th, almost everyone was thinking of the upcoming Easter weekend. Some of the men were looking forward to some time off and catching a space available flight to sunny California aboard an outbound KC-97 that morning.

52-0919 was the newest KC-97 in the squadron. She had arrived a couple of months earlier and she was still bright and shiny. Her crew chief, MSgt Robert Chapin, kept her looking like the day she left the factory and ready to fly at all times.

The crew for the morning flight was commanded by Capt Thomas Hedge, and Lt William Novetzke was the man in the right seat. Then there was Lt Thomas Artman, Nav, Lt Berthold Mueke, Nav, Lt Robert Munn, Nav, TSgt Robert Watson, Flight Engineer, and A2C Wilbert Heath, Boomer. Sgt Chapin and his assistant crew chiefs, A2C Eugene Shelton and A1C Melvin Ferguson, were also going along on the flight.

The extra navigators were flying to gain experience and training for upgrade to a combat ready crew. Along with the extra crewmen, there were fourteen passengers headed for California. The mission was scheduled to include several navigation legs for training. There was not going to be any in-flight refueling, so it was safe for the passengers to go along. After completing the training portion of the mission, the KC-97 would land at March AFB, California.

The crew went through the usual preflight walkaround. Everything looked good; no major drips or danger signs, just the usual oil stains always present under the big radial engines. Inside, the passengers settled into their "first class" web seats and buckled in. They listened to the safety briefing and perhaps made a mental note about the nearest emergency exit hatch.

The flight crew fired up the four big engines and went through the checklist. After contacting the tower, the KC-97 moved away from its spot on the ramp and taxied to the north end of the runway. After going through the takeoff checklist the throttles were pushed forward, brakes released, and Milan 11 began the takeoff roll at about 0951. "California, here we come!"

Rolling down the ribbon of concrete, Milan 11 gained speed with every turn of the tires. Everything was normal, just as it should be during a routine takeoff. A little more rudder pedal to counter the torque of the four spinning props, engine instruments and oil pressure all normal for takeoff. A little bouncing and vibration as the tanker continued to roll towards takeoff speed.

In a heartbeat routine became a pilot's worst nightmare. The KC-97 began veering away from the centerline of the runway. Both Tom Hedge and Bill Novetzke fought to get 919 centered again. Nose wheel steering wasn't helping; neither was opposite rudder pressure. The KC veered left, then right; the side of the runway was close, too close for comfort. Then, the big tanker left the runway and the nose gear was sheared away by either a runway light or the rough terrain.

Props spinning at over 2,000 RPM dug into the runway and ground, sending showers of sparks and dirt cascading into the air. Prop tips bent back as they continued to grind away at takeoff power from the four engines. In the back of the plane the passengers were bouncing around in what many thought was the roughest takeoff they ever had. Those near a window could see that they weren't taking off, but sliding off into the grass.

Sliding to a stop in a veil of dust with her tail in the air, Milan 11 stopped just off the right side of the runway near one of the fuel pits. Smoke billowed and began to boil skyward as fuel from ruptured tanks caught fire. Everyone aboard knew they had mere seconds before the fire would reach the main tanks, exploding the tanker into small pieces.

In the cockpit, Tom Hedge and Bill Novetzke pulled the emergency release handles on the two sliding cockpit windows so they could get out of the airplane. Hedge went out the left side and dropped to the ground. Novetzke recalled that, as he tried to get through his window, one of the navigators stepped on his hand and wiggled through the window. Bill followed through the window and down to the ground. He recalled, "Since there was no nose gear, it was a short distance to the ground."

It wasn't so easy for the men in the back of the plane. With the tail jutting into the air, they not only had to fight smoke, but also gravity. The emergency releases on the hatches were pulled upwards and the hatch yanked out. Someone grabbed the emergency rope and threw it overboard. Passengers grabbed the rope and slid to the ground like in a Tarzan movie. Others managed to get out through the over-wing exits and drop off the trailing edge of the wing. Ken Tarwater wrote:

"I watched the troops exit off the right wing. No one was hurt too much, maybe a sprained ankle or two from jumping from the wing, which was a pretty good drop. Also the assistant crew chief (Ferguson) couldn't locate his crew chief (Chapin), so before he jumped, he went back into the burning aircraft looking for him upstairs and downstairs. When he was satisfied that his crew chief wasn't on board, he got out by the skin of his teeth. I talked with him after the crew chief was found unharmed. In the confusion, they were both looking for one another and the smoke was unbelievable. The plane was burning and his face and hands were as black as if someone had painted them black, a picture in my mind that I never forgot."

Fire trucks from the base raced to the scene and began fighting the growing fire. Luck was with the souls on board that day; the tanker didn't erase itself in a massive explosion. It just sat there and burned until the shiny KC-97 was consumed by fire. By the time the fire had been beaten down and was under control, only the wings and tail could be recognized as having been a shiny KC-97.

There were twenty-four souls on board that morning. Only SSgt Annas Thompson and A1C Edward Sennett had to be hospitalized. Both had suffered a broken ankle when they jumped from the flaming hulk. Five others were treated for minor burns, cuts, scratches and bruises. The only regular member of the crew that was injured was TSgt Robert Watson, the flight engineer, who suffered minor burns.

Everyone aboard knew they had been very lucky that morning. The Grim Reaper could have claimed everyone in a blinding flash. They were lucky to have cheated death or serious injury. Was it luck? Or was a higher authority riding in the jump seat on Milan 11 that Good Friday morning?

Reflex deployments continued during the month. A flight of three B-47s would leave Lincoln every week and three would return from Spain, usually within a day or two of the relief crews arriving in Spain.

# Cold War Cornhuskers: The 307th Bomb Wing Lincoln Air Force Base Nebraska 1955-1965

Along with Reflex, there was the constant chore of maintaining the ground Alert. Pulling Alert was about as much fun as going to the dentist. At times it was painful, being away from family and friends just to sit around and wait for the klaxon to blow, the word to launch, then maybe destroy the world as it was known. Crews passed the time on Alert in a lot of different ways. Doug Valen recalled:

"On one of my first Alert tours at Lincoln, I walked out of the Alert facility one summer evening and found several crew members sitting around in lawn chairs. As you recall, the Alert facility was just off the north end of the runway. I asked what was going on and someone said, 'We're WATOLing!' I wasn't familiar with that phrase so I asked what it meant. They said, 'We're WATCHING AIRCRAFT TAKE OFF and LAND!' That turned out to be a favorite pastime, both while on Alert and off."

"How about Dave Roebuck's mongoose?," Larry Boggess recalled. "Dave had a large wooden box that he said contained a live mongoose. There was a partition in the box that had a little hole cut in it to allow the mongoose to come out in the half that had a screened top for viewing. The story was that 'he goes for your throat'. While wearing his flight jacket backwards to protect his neck and wearing gloves, he would tap the box to get the mongoose to come out in the viewing area. While tapping the box, he aims it for the middle of the crowd, or intended victim. Dave would then release the catch on the box and the spring-loaded top would fly open (with a loud bang) and propel a furry coon tail toward the victim hitting them about the throat. It was great fun and once taken in on the joke, people would seek out others they wanted to get. Dave would say it had to be kept a secret because it was illegal to have a mongoose in the States. People would beg to see it."

A Tan Glove mission was flown on April 20th. The profile for this one was a lot different. The usual profile would take the crews north to Hudson Bay, then turn south for an ECM run on Boston and the East coast. For this TAN Tan Glove, the B-47s flew towards Charleston, South Carolina, on what appeared to be a routine Reflex deployment along the southern route.

The flight coasted out near Charleston and flew on towards Bermuda. North of Bermuda, they picked up the tankers and took on over 35,000 pounds of fuel. At this point they climbed to 35,000 feet and turned north. When they reached a point about five hundred miles east of New York City, they began descending to 15,000 feet. Due east of Boston the flight turned towards "Beantown" and set up for their ECM run.

Ever since refueling the flight had maintained radio silence. There were no routine calls for ATC. The flight was flying under the concept of Military Assumes Responsibility for Separation of Aircraft (MARSA). This Tan Glove wasn't just going to help calibrate ECM equipment. This mission would also test NORAD to the hilt.

By the time the flight roared over the beach they were between five hundred and a thousand feet above the sand. They were playing their ECM music at full blast. There wasn't any flying up and down the coast on this mission. They flew directly to their target cities, pulled up to about five thousand feet, and made camera attacks on Boston Logan Airport. As soon as they had completed their mission they climbed higher and reported to ATC by saying, "Tan Glove, Mission Accomplished." ATC and NORAD replied, "Huh! What Mission?"

SAC Headquarters was very happy with the results of the Tan Glove. The stations along the coast had been aware that Tan Glove was in progress, and everyone was waiting for the bombers to come in from the usual direction. Nobody was looking out towards the water. After all Soviet bombers would be coming in from the north, right? Yeah Right!

Few men of the 307th ever heard of Project Overflight. It was a sure-fire cinch no one had any idea of what a U-2 was. That all changed shortly after 1 May 1. A U-2 flown by Francis Gary Powers was shot down by a Soviet missile. Powers was flying over the Soviet Union taking high altitude photos as part of Operation Overflight.

The flights had been going on for some time. Up till now everything had gone fairly well. Soviet radar had tracked the U-2s on every flight. They had fired missiles trying to bring one down, but so far they hadn't been able to hit one of the high-flying spy planes. On this flight Powers had a problem with his engine and had to come down from his mission altitude. He was just low enough that the missile was able to bring his U-2 down.

At first, the Eisenhower Administration denied the United States was conducting spy flights over the Soviet Union. They tried to explain the incident away by claiming it was a weather flight that had gone off course. After the wreckage of the U-2 was placed on display in Moscow, President Eisenhower could no longer deny the true nature of Project Overflight.

With a real-world situation bubbling towards a crisis, SAC increased readiness throughout the command in case it was called upon. Across the command extra alert aircraft were generated. Lincoln Air Force Base was placed on "Standby Alert". Everyone on base was ready to respond at the ring of the phone.

The loss of the high flying U-2 had not only created a tense world situation, it also brought out the fact that, if the Soviets could shoot down a U-2, B-47s attacking at high altitude would be sitting ducks for the SAMs. This was to have a profound effect on SAC tactics. Suddenly low-level attack wouldn't just be a training requirement; it was now a matter of survival in order to penetrate the air defenses of the Soviet Union.

On almost every mission the crews would now have to include a low level flight on one of the "Oil Burner" routes. Mike Gingrich recalled flying an oil burner route:

"Once, with Solomon, we flew a daytime route starting at Camp Atterbury in Indiana, south to the Ohio River at Evansville and downstream along the river. I was flying from the back seat and I won't say we were low, but several times Solly told me of a tall tree ahead. On the north side of Evansville, he told me to add another fifty feet; seconds later, we passed over a high school. That must have excited them! Then Solly took over, and descended down into the river valley, executing a 70-degree turn to the right. He leveled off over the water and we passed a large riverboat. I remember looking UP at the boat's bridge! Man, those days were fun."

During May, the south end of the flight line was buzzing with all kinds of activity. The 307th AREFS had been sending tankers to Lockbourne to stand strip alert since January. Along with strip alert, KC-97s were now flying training flights with a landing at Selfridge AFB, Michigan. After landing there they off loaded all kinds of cargo. It was all part of the move from Lincoln to Selfridge.

Everything that belonged to the squadron had to be inventoried, marked, packed and loaded for the trip to Michigan. When SAC transferred a unit, they had to have a complete record, from aircraft down to the last pencil and paperclip. It also included personnel records, which were checked, then rechecked.

There were those who were "getting short," that is, their enlistment was almost over. Ken Tarwater was one of the "short timers". He could either re-up (reenlist) or say goodbye to the Air Force. He recalled:

"I had decided to get out of the Air Force and my discharge was coming up in July. So I had to either reenlist or extend to go to Selfridge. It was the toughest decision in my life. Then, Col Vieluva gave me his re-up speech and I was really close to reenlisting. I had time in grade for staff sergeant and he promised me staff stripes and that I would be crewing my own KC-97 in the near future. But, I had a job waiting for me on the outside and was ready for another adventure. I only spent four years in the Air Force, but it had a lasting impact on how I did my job in General Aviation and for TWA. I was among some of the greatest men that I have met in my lifetime. I am very proud of my time with the 307th AREFS at Lincoln Air Force Base."

As the date of departure for the 307th AREFS drew closer, there were more and more farewell get-togethers for those leaving and those that were staying at Lincoln. One of the young airmen who would transfer to Selfridge with the 307th AREFS was George Kenton Sisler.

Friends in the squadron knew him as "Ken". "I got to know Ken soon after he arrived at Lincoln", remembered Ken Tarwater. "Probably because he was from Missouri. And talking with someone from your home state was a little bit of home. That's just the way it was. I can remember going to his room and watching some of Ken's home movies of him before he joined the Air Force, as a smoke jumper in southern Missouri, parachuting into forest fires that he had taken from a helmet-mounted movie camera. I remember him having that camera and taking movies of us. He loved to talk about parachute jumping."

George Sisler went to Selfridge with the squadron and finished his tour of duty in the Air Force. After discharge he went to college and earned a degree. "Ken" heard his country's call to duty again and enlisted in the Army this time. With his college degree he earned a commission.

With his experience and love of parachuting, it was natural for him to go to jump school at Fort Benning, Georgia. After jump school, Ken won the coveted Green Beret and served with Army Intelligence. Serving with the 5th Special Forces, he was sent to the Republic of South Vietnam.

Lt George "Ken" Sisler was leading a patrol deep in "Indian Country" on February 7, 1967. While on this patrol, his platoon was ambushed by a company-sized enemy force. Ken deployed his men for defense and called for air strikes. Being the leader, Ken rallied his men and shouted not only orders, but also encouragement to them. Two members of his patrol were wounded by enemy gunfire. Without hesitating, Ken left his platoon and ran back to his wounded men while under enemy fire. He grabbed one of them and started carrying him back to the perimeter when he again came under increased enemy gunfire. Ken laid the wounded man down, grabbed his rifle, and killed three of the charging enemy soldiers. He then threw a grenade, knocking out a machine gun nest that was firing at his men. Ken ran back to the wounded man and dragged him into the perimeter. By this time the enemy was attacking the left side of the position and several more men had been wounded.

Without hesitation, Ken grabbed several grenades and charged the advancing enemy force. He kept throwing grenades and firing his rifle at the oncoming enemy. His action caused the enemy assault to falter and they began to break off the attack and withdraw. He continued to move around the area, directing his men in the defense of the perimeter and calling in more air strikes on the enemy as they left the area. During the final phase of the battle Ken was hit by enemy gunfire and mortally wounded.

For his heroic action that day 1/Lt George Kenton Sisler was awarded the Bronze Star medal with V for Valor device attached and the Purple Heart. But the story of Ken's valor was not over. Members of his platoon who were there with Ken, along with fellow Green Berets, would not let his story of bravery and self-sacrifice fade. They filed after-action reports documenting Ken's actions and his heroism.

On June 27, 1968, Secretary of the Army Stanley Resor presided over a presentation ceremony at the Pentagon. The citation read:

"For conspicuous gallantry and intrepidity at the risk of his life above and beyond the call of duty...His extraordinary leadership, infinite courage and selfless concern for his men saved the lives of a number of his comrades. His actions reflect great credit upon himself and uphold the highest tradition of the military service."

1/Lt George Kenton Sisler was posthumously awarded the Medal of Honor. Our nation's highest award for heroism was presented to George's wife, Jane, and two sons by Secretary Resor on behalf of the President of the United States.

By the end of May most of the 307th AREFS had made the trip to Michigan. There were still a few last-minute items to be taken care of, mostly paperwork in the form of double checking the inventory to make sure everything that belonged to the squadron had either been shipped or was about to be shipped.

By the end of May SAC had reached the goal of one third of the total bomber force standing fifteen-minute ground Alert. Around the country and across the ocean there were now more aircraft loaded with nuclear weapons standing Alert than at any time in our history.

Effective June 1, 1960, under the provisions of SAC General Order 43, dated 25 May 60, the 307th AREFS was officially relieved from assignment to the 307th Bomb Wing and transferred to the 4045th Air Refueling Wing. With that order the 307th Bomb Wing no longer had a dedicated refueling unit.

By the end of the first week in June the south end of the ramp was bare. The tankers were gone, and along with them the deep throaty throb of the R-4360s, clouds of bluish oil smoke, and the squeal of the brakes as they taxied. All that remained to mark their passing were numerous oil stains on the concrete.

Harold Beucus wrote a fitting requiem for round engines:

"The round engines put heart in the plane and made the plane throb. They leaked oil, hydraulic fluid and fuel. They burned tons of engine oil, smoked like a steam engine, they caught fire, had runaway props that often flew clean off the propeller shaft. They backfired, snorted and farted when they are started BUT--there is nothing like the sound of the round engine on the ground and in the air. Those were the days of REAL flying and those who never experienced it, well, they just would not understand the romance of flying the big bird with four roaring radial engines that vibrated and shook the coffee cups right off the tables in the control cabin. WOW, what a feeling! And we were young kids doing it too; that made the thrill even better."

June brought warm temperatures to the Nebraska plains. Along with warm temperatures came the possibility of thunderstorms and rain. This had been a wet year so far. Lincoln had gotten a lot of snow during the winter. So far, spring showers had kept the plains green with new grass and plants. That was all well and good, provided you landed on the runway. Paul Koski recalled:

"It was late in the evening, my B-47 airplane had just landed and, as I was installing the down locks, I stared in disbelief as the whole aft wheel well was caked in mud and old cornstalks, about 2-3 inches thick.

"The flight crew had just gotten off the aircraft and I asked the pilot if he had any problem on landing. We started the post-flight walkaround and he said, 'There might have been a problem, since he felt a bump on approach and may have touched down a little short of the runway, but if it did, it was just for a second.' (The south end of the runway has a little hill and this is where the cornfield is.)

"As we walked around the aircraft, everything seemed OK until we got to the aft wheel well. He was shocked to see so much mud. He was sure there wasn't any damage since the bump was so soft. I told him that until we cleaned up the mess we couldn't determine what damage there might be and only an inspection would determine that. He said they would be back out first thing in the morning to help clean up the area.

"The next morning I talked it over with my flight chief. Since we hadn't written anything in the forms, we would wait until the area was cleaned up and then determine what was to be done. If nothing was found broken or bent, we probably would be OK. We didn't want to jump the gun and get the flight crew in trouble if this was a minor incident.

"We got the fire department to use their high pressure hoses to wash off most of the mud, but the rest of the cleaning had to be done by hand with brushes, putty knives, rags and a lot of water. The flight crew pitched in and helped clean up.

"No damage was found, but we did change the tires and brakes since we couldn't get them clean enough. The feeling was that this wasn't a hard landing and no incident reports were made, but I wonder what the farmer thought when he saw the tracks. UFO or USAF?"

Reflex deployments continued on a weekly schedule. B-47s left on Tuesday and returned after being relieved by the arriving aircraft and crew, usually on Thursday. Returning from Spain the crews would be going against the prevailing westerly winds. At times the headwind caused all kinds of excess fuel use. By the time the aircraft arrived in the refueling area they were often down to minimum fuel to recover at an alternate. A tanker sitting up there in front, right where she was supposed to be, was always a beautiful sight.

Since the 307th AREFS was now at Selfridge the wing didn't have a dedicated tanker force. For the time being, the 98th AREFS would supply the needed tanker assets. Other refueling units from around the command would also pitch in to fill the need for refueling.

In his monthly report to SAC, Col Read outlined the usual areas where the 307th was having problems. His biggest concern, as usual, was the shortage of people. The 307th A & E squadron was one of the areas that were working with low manpower. The photo maintenance area was also short of trained personnel. Col Read brought out that, in the last two months, the wing had lost sixty-nine sorties due to problems in the Bomb/Nav and camera systems. There was also a shortage of personnel in the jet engine shop. This area had been short of people for over nine months. Col Read finished his report with an emphatic, "You can't fly 'em, if you can't fix 'em!"

July 1st found the wing getting off to a shaky start for the month. 53-2111 taxied to the end of the runway to begin the mission. The crew called the tower for takeoff clearance. There was no response to any of their repeated calls! The radio seemed to be dead. The aircraft returned to their parking spot and the launch crew started figuring out the problem. After they tightened all the UHF antenna connections the radios worked and 2111 launched.

That day, high over the Barents Sea, a lone RB-47H, 53-4281, assigned to the 55th Strategic Recon Wing, was flying another ELINT mission. These missions were to gather electronic intelligence along the northern border of the Soviet Union and were long, sometimes over twelve hours. They were usually routine, although every now and then Soviet fighters would come out and intercept the aircraft and fly alongside just to let the crews know they were being watched.

The crew on this mission was made up of six officers. The aircraft commander was Maj William Palm, Capt Freeman Olmstead, copilot, and Capt John McCone, navigator. There were three electronic warfare officers, or Ravens, aboard: Capt Eugene Posa, Lt Dean Phillips and Lt Oscar Goforth.

About six hours into their mission the Ravens picked up signals that they were being tracked by Soviet airborne radar. That meant only one thing; fighters were in the area. Within moments there was a MiG-19 sitting on the right wing. Then he disappeared. The next thing the crew knew they were being fired at by the MiG.

Cannon shells hit the left inboard engine pod, which caught fire. The crew could hear more cannon shells hitting the aircraft in the fuselage. Within seconds Maj Palm gave the order to eject. Capt Olmstead blew the canopy and ejected. Olmstead observed that everyone ejected, but one crewman's chute did not open. Olmstead landed in the near-freezing water and was able to climb into his one-man life raft. After over six hours in the raft he was picked up by a Russian fishing vessel. There was another American already on board, Capt John McCone. There was no sign of any of the other members of the crew.

SAC went to a higher level of readiness, just in case the Soviet Union wanted to make something more about the shoot down. The Soviets claimed the RB-47H had violated their airspace, which of course the United States denied. It would be over seven months before the two officers would be freed from the Soviet Union. They would be questioned over and over by the KGB about their mission. The Soviets were eager to expose another "American act of aggression." During their captivity the two officers were not allowed to see each other. They were finally released on January 23, 1961.

Wednesday, 6 July, started with the daily reporting for duty, briefing, and the morning FOD walk for the flight line troops. The coffee and donuts would turn out to be the highlight of the day. A lot of the troops thought they should have stayed in the sack, when they saw how the day was going.

It all started at the refueling pits. A valve stuck during the fueling of a B-47. Flammable JP-4 flooded across the ramp, causing a potentially explosive situation. Fire trucks responded and sprayed the area with retardant. Obviously everyone in the area forgot about taking a smoke break until the mess was cleaned up.

A B-47 appeared from the south on short final. Those that could take a minute paused to watch the landing. It was picture perfect; the aft main tires kissed the concrete with a puff of smoke. Within a nanosecond the front mains were on the ground. The brake chute came out, just like it was supposed to. The bird watchers waited for the chute to billow and slow the charging B-47 down. 53-1956 hurtled down the runway; no chute could be seen, just a streamer of fluttering nylon where the billowing chute should be. The crew pulled the throttles back to idle and let the beast roll. It took a lot of runway and the brakes may have been a little hotter than normal, but 1956 finally slowed and taxied back to her slot on the ramp. During postflight the ground crew would have to check the brakes, tires, and steering. They would also be looking at the drag chute to see why it didn't deploy.

Just after chow the klaxon went off. Crews scrambled to the Alert birds. It was a Bravo, so all they had to do was start engines and report. Two aircraft couldn't get the ground power unit to fire up. The others started engines and reported when they were ready to taxi. Another uncocked incident for the ground crews to work on.

Later that afternoon, SSgt T. R. Taylor and his crew were doing preflight on 51-15808 for a late afternoon takeoff. They found several nicked rotor blades on the number five engine. No flight today; nicked blades meant an engine change. So it was call Job Control and get the engine shop boys to set up the change for the next day.

About the only thing that could top the day's events was if the warm sticky weather would produce a twister. Well, that evening there wasn't a twister, but there was a good old fashioned "trash mover" of a thunderstorm.

# 1960

After the engine change, T.R. and his crew were going to try and get 5808 back in the air on 8 July. During engine start one of the alternators would not come on line. The circuit breaker kept popping. In spite of the problem the crew flew the mission. Later, a short was found in the control panel. On the 15th old 5808 was going to fly again. As the crew began to taxi the nose gear would not steer. While the ground crew was troubleshooting the problem, the steering engaged and the crew flew the mission.

It wasn't that 5808 was a "dog" of a "bird". As a matter of fact, T.R. recalled she was actually a pretty good airplane despite all her hours in the air. She was just starting to show her age. At the time she was one of the oldest B-47s still in front-line service with an active wing. Nonetheless, every time she had a problem T.R. could only grit his teeth, leaving deep marks in his trademark cigar.

On the 16th, construction crews moved out to repair the main north-south runway. They were going to put an eighty-foot wide overlay down the center. Hopefully this would take care of some of the humps and bumps that had developed. They began working at 0700 and worked until 1700 every day until the job was finished.

This construction meant a change in the flying schedule. Flying would have to be done at night, or at least take off and landing either before or after the daily runway work was finished. So for about the next two weeks, take offs would be between 1700 and 0700 daily.

During the construction, there was a lot of concern that loose oil might cause problems with aircraft components. There was also concern that loose gravel could be sucked into the engines. There were only three engines that were damaged by FOD during the construction.

Since the wing couldn't fly during the day, it was a perfect time for SAC to pull a special "war game" in the form of a Broken Arrow. This time it was the 307th's turn to play war games. Unlike the Chinese fire drill in January, this Broken Arrow was played out according to the procedures. The men stopped what they were doing and played along with the umpires until the area was declared safe. The wing was rated as Outstanding for the way they responded during the initial phase of the exercise.

With the warm days of summer there was no better way to cool off than at the pool. All during the month, aquatic survival refresher classes were held. Crews that hadn't gone through the survival training during the last year grabbed their flight suits and headed for the pool. By the end of their dip they had reacquainted themselves with the one man and five man life rafts and how to get aboard the tricky little devils.

The swimming pool could be used by Alert crews on the weekends so the families could spend some time together. Dave Bowersock recalled:

"One Sunday afternoon, my family, Gene's (Van Meter) family, Neal (Amtmann) and his girl friend were together at the base swimming pool. In response to someone's question about an exercise, Gene said that we never had an exercise on Sunday and that if the klaxon blew it would probably be for the real thing. I think that it was within the hour the klaxon sounded.

"There were other crews there and we all instinctively grabbed our flight suits, yelled goodbye and ran for our trucks while the wives and girl friend sat stunned and a little frightened. Just before reaching the truck, I looked back and there was my wild-eyed, six year old daughter, Terri, running right along with us. I scooped her up, ran back to where Loretta was standing and practically tossed Terri to her. Of course it was just an exercise and of course it spoiled the whole afternoon, not to mention scaring the daylights out of our families. Lorreta didn't come out to visit very often. She said it felt like visiting a prison. I sometimes suspected that her attitude toward visitations began that Sunday."

During the first half of the month, air refueling support for the 307th was provided by the 928th AREFS out of Ellsworth AFB, South Dakota. They were flying KC-135s, which meant the refueling could be done at higher altitude and faster airspeed. No matter what tanker was used, refueling in the air still took a lot of skill and always increased the pucker factor. Starting on the 16th, refueling support would change to the 906th AREFS out of Minot, North Dakota. Like Ellsworth, they flew KC-135s.

On Tuesday the 19th, three B-47s left Lincoln for Spain. They flew the northern route and met the tankers according to the Reflex profile. One of the tankers was having a boom problem. The boom was stuck in the intermediate position and would not lower to the correct refueling position. The receiver had to divert to Pease AFB and spend the night before heading across the pond as a single ship.

On the 22nd, 53-4222 was scheduled for a training flight. During the ground preflight, the launch crew noticed something dripping from the #6 engine. Using the old "rag wrench" they wiped the fluid away, only to see it reappear. They applied the "rag wrench" again, and again, the fluid kept dripping. Pulling the cowling, they found the oil pump was leaking. Job Control got another unit out to the aircraft in record time. After changing the pump the team found it was defective. Another pump arrived and it was also defective. Finally, in this case the third pump was the charm, but 4222 launched fifteen minutes late.

July 27th would turn out to be a busy day for the 307th. The runway construction had been finished in record time, so the flying schedule was back to normal. That morning, three B-47s launched to fly a Big Blast mission to the East coast. On their return trip, they were to make a low-level nav leg and bomb run on the Iron Man Oil Burner route.

Later that morning, four B-47s launched for a mass gas refueling mission. From Lincoln, the bombers headed northwest to meet the tankers near Rapid City, South Dakota. Radio contact with the tankers from Minot was made about three hundred miles from the rendezvous point. This was going to be a head-on rendezvous. As they approached each other the closure distance was called out at about one hundred mile intervals, then at fifty miles. The receivers were offset to the refueling track by about ten miles. The tankers closed the distance until they were at the turn point for the refueling heading. An easy one hundred eighty degree turn and they were on the correct heading. As they rolled out, the receivers were about twenty miles behind and closing. Exxon flight maintained the heading and the B-47s kept closing the distance.

Visual contact was made and the receivers moved into position behind the big KC-135s. With higher jet speeds the bombers were soon in the observation position, slowly moving closer to the hanging booms. About a mile behind the tankers, the receiver crews ran through the Pre-Contact Checklist.

**"Bombsight Cover-CLOSED"**
**"Auto Pilot-OFF"**
**"Anti collision Lights and Nav Lights-ON"**
**"ESP Switch-ON"**
**"Slipway Door-Open and Deicing-ON"**
**"Fuel Panels-CHECKED AND READY"**
**"Ready for Contact."**

In the front seat the Aircraft Commander moved into the slot using small, smooth adjustments in power and controls. From his seat the boom loomed ahead; it looked like a huge telephone pole heading right for his head. The boom extended and bounced in the slipstream, making slight movements back and forth as the boomer flew the boom towards the bomber's nose.

As soon as they made contact latches closed, holding the boom in the receptacle. JP-4 flowed through the boom at 4,000 pounds a minute. While the fuel flowed the copilot watched the fuel panel, making sure the fuel was sent to the right tank to keep the center of gravity correct. Watching the aerial ballet on film it looks so easy and beautiful. Inside the bomber, the aircraft commander and copilot were working about as hard as they would during any part of the mission. Keeping a B-47 in the refueling slot took a lot of constant adjustments. Over-control and you could get a boom in the beak real quickly.

With fuel tanks full the receivers called for the disconnect. A little residual JP-4 spray on the windshield got whisked away by a combination of the airstream and the wiper. The bombers dropped away and slid to the side as the KC-135 climbed a little to get safe separation.

After refueling the bomber cell separated apart, each crew getting ready for the next part of the profile. It may have been on to Hurley, Wisconsin, for entry into the Iron Man Oil Burner route. Maybe it was on up to the Dakotas and a bomb run on Bismarck. After completing their profile the bomber crews headed back home to Lincoln.

Whether it was cold and snowy in the winter or hot and humid in the summer, weather was always a factor on air operations at Lincoln. Anyone stationed at Lincoln will remember those long hot summers. Air conditioners ran full blast to try and cool down quarters and offices. That is, if there were air conditioners. There was always a big crowd at the two base pools. Or you could always head for Capital Beach or Muni for a cooling daily dip.

Those warm days made getting a B-47 off the ground very interesting at times. Put together the combination of temperature, humidity, and field elevation and you came up with something known to pilots as density altitude. The higher the density altitude, the longer it took to get the old gal into the air. Combine this with a heavyweight takeoff and watch the pucker factor go to plus ten in a hurry.

Nothing like rolling down the runway on a hot, muggy day, watching the runway markers flash by and the old gal not even thinking about clawing her way into the air until the overrun appears to be just a few feet away. Then, at the last apparent second, the aircraft lifts off the concrete and struggles into the air. Ah yes, once again science and technology overcome fear and superstition.

The heat and humidity also combined to produce another afternoon Nebraska thrill. It would start with cumulus clouds rolling across the sky like puffs of cotton. With the warm air rising, they would begin to billow and boil upward, punching towards the heavens. If the clouds were to the east of you, the sun shining on the boiling mass would make them so white it almost hurt your eyes if you looked at them. If they were to the west with the sun behind them, they would appear dark and menacing as they moved in.

If they were building to the west, that meant they were heading towards you. The low rumble of thunder across the plains would signal the approach of the storm. On arrival, the wind would suddenly die, then change as the gust front arrived. Heavy rain, wind and possible hail signaled the "trash mover" had arrived.

Returning to Lincoln after a long mission was always welcomed by the tired crews. Flying the approach and getting the bird down in one piece was always a challenge. Doing it with bad weather in the area made the challenge border on difficult, if not downright impossible. Bruce Mills wrote about one of his experiences with the local weather:

"Another practice mission was to fly up into Canada, refuel over Hudson Bay, radar bomb some forgotten site in Minnesota and return to Lincoln. Piece of cake. However, two things happened. First, the forward aux fuel tank refused to work and my CG (center of gravity), of course, went to hell. Next, I called the control tower and found out that a big bad Nebraska thunderstorm was moving in from the south. I split for home. When I crossed the homer at 20,000 feet, I could see the air base. But, the storm was only about ten miles south. The tower gave me permission to land. I made the descent teardrop pattern and crossed the low key. The tower closed the runway. Seems the wind had changed 180 degrees. By that time I was 200 feet high, gear and flaps down. I didn't think I could get back up to altitude and get a tanker off Lincoln or Offutt, rendezvous, hook up, and get refueled before my CG went nose down. Well, thank God for Kudo, my nav's, magic fingers. He started giving me distance and course to the runway. I made a 45-degree turn, flew out four minutes, turned back, (by that time we were in the clouds) and began computing time, airspeed, distance and altitude. I crossed the fence at 40 feet high, saw the runway and yelled at the crew, 'gear down, full flaps, run the checklist yourself—deploy the chute'."

During a storm, it was also dangerous for those working on the flight line. Roland England wrote:

"It was storming so bad that my troops were working with several inches of water on the ramp. There was lightning flashing all around. It nipped at my guys several times. It was extremely hazardous to be out there doing any maintenance. There were several tornadoes reported within fifteen miles of the base. I took my crew to a shelter for about forty-five minutes. Job Control knew where I was and had contact via a land line."

Paul Koski had his share of memories about storms on the ramp:

"It was one of those dark, rainy nights with winds 20-30 knots. Water was standing on the ramp around two to three inches deep. The thunder and lightning were banging away all around. The lightning made it look like daylight outside, it was so bad. The flight line was no place to be in a storm.

"This A3C one striper, just out of tech school, was assigned to guard three aircraft that were on Alert. I knew he was scared, since I have been working in these kinds of storms and have been knocked down just by static electricity. A bolt of lightning had a direct hit on one of the aircraft he was guarding. The bolt of lightning hit the JATO rack and fired off some of the bottles. The fire department, flight crew and ground crew reported to the aircraft. After determining what had happened and finding no damage, they replaced the JATO rack and recocked the aircraft.

"It was then they discovered the guard was nowhere to be found. The poor guy took off for the tall timber. When they did find him, he refused to work the flight line. He went through a medical evaluation, I was told, and he was reassigned to administrative duties. He also got an Article 15 for deserting his post."

The wing flew another mass gas mission on 29 July. Six aircraft launched and started for the refueling area over western Minnesota. Climbing out, they could see a line of thunderstorms building ahead of them. Luck stayed with them and the storms were further away, not in the refueling area. The six B-47s rendezvoused with the tankers, took on their fuel and flew the rest of the mission.

Once again, Col Read sent his reports to Offutt. Once again, it included his plea for adequate manpower to complete the wing's mission. He noted the A & E Squadron was only 71% of authorized strength. More missions and MCS points had been lost to equipment failure. Some of the equipment failures were directly attributable to maintenance, or lack of it, which in turn was due to lack of manpower.

# 1960

It is interesting to note that every commander of the 307th had waged a constant battle with higher headquarters to obtain adequate personnel to fill the ranks of the maintenance squadrons. From the beginning, almost every section had suffered from shortages of properly trained personnel. The fact that the 307th not only fulfilled their mission, but excelled at it, stands as a tribute to all of the men who worked long hours, with little rest or chow, and kept the fleet in the air fulfilling the wing's mission.

The wing had flown a total of 1,586 hours during July. Each of the missions averaged about seven hours flying time. In view of the two weeks of runway repair, which shifted the flight schedule to an almost night-only flying schedule, the wing had done pretty well.

Then, there was the monthly look at the wing MCS point standings. There were more areas that had been added to the list of MCS points. Under the revised MCS, the old On The Job Training (OJT) was now listed as Individual Proficiency Training (IPT). Sounds professional, but it was still OJT with a different name and point standing. After crunching the MCS numbers the 371st Bomb Squadron was on top, followed by the 424th, 370th and 372nd. As always, someone had to be on top and somebody had to be at the bottom.

Speaking of the top, the best bird standings for the month of July were posted.

Top Crew Chiefs as of 2400 July 31:
R. E. Bergene  53-1906  113 sorties
S. L. Vensky   53-6244  92 sorties
J. R. Yandle   53-2392  91 sorties
K. W. McGee    53-2143  81 sorties
H. D. Knight   53-2417  76 sorties

For July the Top performing aircraft in sections:
"A" Section      "B" Section        "C" Section
53-2140 = 81%    51-7065= 80%       53-6244= 76.9%
53-4224 = 87%    53-4217= 80%       53-1958= 75 %
53-2111 = 76%    53-2266= 77%       53-1906= 75.2%

Along with the best aircraft standings came the announcement that Merrill Sinclair (307th OMS) had been honored as Crew Chief of the Month for July.

August started with changes in the Reflex operations orders (296-61). The changes reflected the increased transatlantic commercial air traffic. Reflex deployments would follow the same "Blue Route" and basic schedule. The primary changes were increased radio checkpoints. The changes also related to which ATC channels had to be monitored and used for reporting. There were also a lot of ATC procedures for hand-off locations and control times. It all boiled down to the fact that SAC no longer owned the skies on the Atlantic crossing routes. Contrails in the sky could be anything from a Boeing 707 to a B-52. If you spotted three contrails fairly close together, chances were it was a Reflex flight.

The first Reflex flight to use the new changes departed for Spain on Tuesday, 2 August. The cell leader had to make constant radio checks with Kansas City, Chicago, Indianapolis, Detroit, Pittsburgh, Boston and New York. It was due to the increase in civilian air traffic, especially at high altitudes and around the East coast.

The return flight on the 4th was a reverse of the deployment flight. The lead aircraft had to contact New York Center as they were ready to coast in.

**"New York Center, Sanka Flight with a cell of three. Reflex Action. Lucky Guy. Over"**

After transmitting "Lucky Guy" the cell would be given priority for bomb run-only clearance for a bomb run at Watertown, New York.

On the 4th, the wing launched six aircraft to fly the monthly Big Blast mission. It would be combined with a mass gas refueling over western Minnesota. The bombers met the tankers near St. Cloud and took on their fuel. There was some bad weather in the area. Turbulence caused some hairy moments and a bumpy ride for both tankers and receivers. Fuel transfer was completed according to the profile, and the rest of the mission was flown according to Big Blast profiles.

2nd Air Force Strategic Evaluation Group arrived at Lincoln on Monday, 8 August 8. The purpose of the visit was to conduct Standboard Evaluations of the crews in the 98th and 307th. Their evaluation flights would be flown under the guidelines called Top Ring. At the end of the visit, a total of sixteen crews at Lincoln were placed on probation for failure in critical areas of EWO procedures and flying proficiency. Four of the crews were from the 307th Bomb Wing.

On 11 August, another Big Blast/mass gas combo mission was on the schedule. This one would have a new twist to it. The briefing called for a special training square to be filled. The takeoff would be a MITO launch. The last three aircraft would be flown by crews who needed the MITO to be qualified for an actual EWO launch.

That morning, the six aircraft spooled up and prepared to taxi. They moved out of the parking area and lined up on the taxiway. When they were cleared from the tower, the lead ship began moving down the taxiway, followed by the others at about fifteen second intervals.

When the lead aircraft turned onto the runway, everything had been checked before the final turn. All six engines were pushed to a hundred percent, water on, lead was rolling. For those who hadn't seen a MITO, it was impressive to watch six B-47s rolling down the runway with only fifteen-second separation. At one time, there were three B-47s rolling down the runway at full power. The black smoke billowing would have been an environmental nightmare in today's world. The noise was almost beyond a painful decibel level.

Within a minute or two it was over. All six aircraft were in the air and climbing towards the north, leaving black strings of smoke in the air as they fanned out. The smell of burned JP-4 wafted across the flight line. Ah yes, I love the smell of JP-4 in the morning. It smells like freedom!

After the MITO, the aircraft climbed to refueling altitude and headed for the refueling area near Green Bay, Wisconsin. After the mass gas refueling they continued to fly the Big Blast profile. Coming home, the B-47s did a low level run through the Iron Man oil burner route, climbing out near Hurley, Wisconsin. The total time in the air was about seven hours.

On the 12th, the wing received OPSORD 11-60, code name Sky Shield. The orders outline had a certain air of cloak-and-dagger attached to it. The 307th, along with other wings, were to act as an enemy strike force and attack the United States, testing NORAD. The cloak-and-dagger was to keep as much about the mission as possible away from NORAD. E-Day for the mission was set for 10 September.

Monday, 15 August, a triple flash message arrived at the Command Post. The authenticated message was an execution order for Hurry Home Bravo. This was a "Team Scrimmage" operation, so both the 98th and 307th would be busy for the next several days. "Team Scrimmage" meant the force had to be generated and a mission flown, in contrast to a "Ground Rules" exercise, which was a total ground response with no launch of the aircraft.

The first phase started with the klaxon going off, followed by the scramble to the Alert aircraft. Runway 17 was the active runway so the taxi distance was short. The 47s hit the runway simulating a MITO, then taxied back to the north end of the ramp and back to the Alert area.

*149*

The Alert aircraft were met by ground crews, who started downloading the nukes from the aircraft. When they were uncocked, they would be serviced for the initial wave of aircraft for the mission. Only items that presented flight safety problems could be repaired before the flight.

While the Alert birds were getting ready to fly, the follow-on force was being generated to fly phase two of the mission. The orders called for the 307th to have a total of 24 strike aircraft and one weather scout aircraft to fly during the three day ORI.

When launch time arrived, the first eight aircraft started engines and taxied into position. They would launch in a modified MITO. Each aircraft was to roll within a minimum of thirty seconds after the preceding aircraft. Aircraft would hold short of the active runway until it was clear before turning onto the runway and rolling.

After launch, the aircraft climbed out and headed for the refueling area over western Kansas. The tankers were waiting right where they were supposed to be. The bombers made the rendezvous and moved in for the hookup. Thunderheads were building in the area, and there was considerable turbulence to deal with. They had been through this kind of refueling before, so they had some experience refueling on a roller coaster.

After refueling, the strike force headed for a low level run at La Junta, Colorado. After the run, the bombers began a low-level nav leg towards Wichita, Kansas. At low level, with the thermals rising from the plains, it could turn out to be a teeth-chattering ride due to the turbulence. The second target was at St. Louis, Missouri, then up to Des Moines, and the final leg back to Lincoln.

August 16th was the second day for Hurry Home Bravo. The next eight aircraft were loaded and ready to go. Everything looked good except for the weather in the St. Louis area. Possible thunderstorms were forecast about the time the force would arrive. Crews were briefed to monitor several radio channels for possible weather updates.

The flight crew assigned to 53-4217 arrived and began their preflight walkaround. Crew chief Frank Logan was standing by in case they spotted anything that didn't look right. No problems were found, so the crew climbed the ladder and buckled in.

The ground crew stood by as fire guard as the engines were started. Engine start went according to book until the fireguard moved to engine #1. The engine spooled up to idle, then the copilot noticed the oil pressure fall back to zero on the gauge. The pilot gave the throttle a little boost, but the oil pressure stayed at zero. Throttle back to idle, then boosted a little, still no pressure on #1 engine. The crew signaled they were shutting the engine down.

The launch crew moved in and pulled the cowling off to get at the engine. They found the shaft on the oil pump had sheared during start up. They called for another pump to replace the broken unit. They tried desperately to change the pump and get the bird in the air, but there wasn't enough time; 4217 was scored as a ground abort.

Everything else went like clockwork until the bombers were heading for the target at St. Louis. The weatherman hit the forecast on the nose. Nearing the area to enter the low level run to the target, the planes were blocked by a line of thunderstorms. They called the command post for advice. Kansas City Center gave new clearance for getting around the storms and the B-47s picked their way around the front.

By the time they got around the thunderstorms, the H-Hour control point was canceled and changed to a new one. With bomb run-only clearance from ATC the bombers made their attack, then got the hell out of Dodge or, in this case, St. Louis. All of the strike force was able to get to the target and make their runs.

Heading towards Des Moines, the bombers were again facing the line of thunderstorms, which were now between them and Lincoln. They had to fly north, almost to Minneapolis, Minnesota, before they could get around the building storms and head back to Lincoln. By the time they got back bad weather had already visited Lincoln. The runway was wet, but the winds were almost calm as the birds came home to roost.

The third and final day of the exercise started with the same weather forecast as the day before. The strike aircraft flew the exact route and ran into thunderstorms at about the same area as the previous day. Like before, the route had to be changed at the last second. This also meant changes in ATC clearance. The changes were made, new clearances were granted, and the B-47s plowed through the low level route and hit the target.

This time the planes had to return to Lincoln by heading back through Kansas, then jogging back to the north. They ran into a couple of small "thunderbumpers" along the way, but nothing like those building over Missouri.

The final results of Hurry Home Bravo were some of the best that the wing had ever posted. The wing was given an "Outstanding" rating.

Generation= 100 %
Bombing= 95.8 %
Equipment Reliability = 91.2 % (due to the one ground abort)

Although the wing had scored very well during the exercise, there were several things that came up for recommendation and were sent back to higher headquarters.

First, it was felt "TEAM SCRIMMAGE" rules should be adjusted when takeoff times were affected by Air Traffic Control delays. It was also felt there should be an alternate mission profile already in place in case of bad weather over the target area or route. These are peacetime exercises and flight safety should be the paramount concern.

August 24th: 53-4266 was on the flying schedule for that Wednesday. It was a typical flight to fill some 50-8 squares. Preflight, engine start and taxi were done according to the mission plan. Sitting on the end of Runway 17, throttles were pushed to a hundred percent, then the water alcohol was applied for extra takeoff oomph.

Rolling down the runway, the crew made their timing check and acceleration was on the money. Then the crew felt a vibration on the right side of the aircraft. A quick scan of the engine instruments showed the oil pressure on #6 had fallen to zero.

### "ABORT, ABORT, ABORT!"

Throttles were yanked back to idle and the copilot deployed both chutes to help slow the beast down. The #6 engine was pulled to idle cutoff. The aircraft commander pushed the brakes and held them, cycling the antiskid system. The crew could feel a momentary lurch and shudder each time the antiskid system kicked in.

For several heart-stopping moments it didn't appear that 4266 was slowing down. Then a combination of lack of thrust, brake chutes and braking brought her speed down so she could turn off the runway. A little power from the remaining engines and she taxied back to her slot on the ramp. A sheared oil pump shaft had starved the engine long enough to cause another unscheduled engine change for the boys in the engine shop.

The crew on 4266 was lucky that day. The emergency happened before they had reached decision speed, or S1, so they were not committed to take off. If the engine had failed after being committed, the crew would have had to take the aircraft off the ground one way or another. Failure of an outboard engine was one of the worst case scenarios a B-47 crew could face during takeoff. The asymmetrical thrust could cause uncontrollable yaw unless the crew reacted immediately. The problem was so critical that

## 1960

SAC and Boeing issued a special supplement to the emergency procedures section of the Dash-1 devoted to the problem.

The supplement outlined how to detect the possible problem by monitoring the engine tachometers and EGT (Exhaust Gas Temperature) gages. This would help identify the failure of an engine before the yaw was actually felt. Loss of an outboard engine on takeoff was practiced during simulator missions.

Col Read wrote the month-end report and sent it on up through 2nd Air Force and SAC Headquarters. Like numerous times before, he wrote about the manpower shortages that continued to plague the wing. There were shortages of manpower in every section of the 307th. It was also noted the wing had continued to transfer flight crew personnel to the B-52 and B-58 programs.

At the end of August the wing had 69 combat ready crews. The wing flew fifteen Reflex deployments to Spain. The last Reflex aircraft departed Lincoln on 30 August using the "Blue Route". The wing had accomplished sixty-six air refuelings during the month. They also flew forty-three high altitude synchronous RBS bomb runs with a 99 % effective rating. The average circular error for the bomb runs was 1,490 feet from the target.

Throughout the history of SAC there were changes that had to be made with changing technology, as well as the temperature of the cold war. During the last several years SAC had made changes in several areas, including refinement of Positive Control procedures and the scramble MITO launch concept to prevent the force from being caught on the ground.

The tactics for weapons delivery also had to change. The old "pop up" was now called "Long Look". Then there was a drop tactic called "Short Look". An aircraft approached at tree top level, climbed to about 6,000 feet, made the bomb run and dropped back down. SAC also devised variations of the two. There was "Long Look Large Charge", where the bomber would have more than one release on a single bomb run against different targets in the same area. Add to this a "Side Step" zigzag to try and confuse enemy air defenses and it is plain to see that trying to stay current was a never-ending chore for the flight crews. Along with the changes came new procedures and methods to make sure that everyone knew what the changes were and how to use them.

September began with a TWX arriving from SAC Headquarters with some long-awaited news. Lincoln Air Force Base was awarded priority for delivery of the MC-1 sweeper. The unit was designed to sweep concrete and vacuum at the same time. Arrival was scheduled for November. The unit would help eliminate all the pesky little items that had a nasty habit of being sucked into the jet engines. The MC-1 could help spell an end to the morning ritual FOD WALK by the flight line troops.

Word was also received the Jet Engine Field Maintenance program would be discontinued. Since November 1958, the 307th has done all major work required on the J-47 engines at the engine shop. They were the only jet engine shop doing major repair at the local level. With the phase-out of the program, engines would be sent to the depot for major inspection and repair.

At 0600, Wednesday, 7 September, three B-47s launched for a seven-hour mission called Sword Fish. This was a modified Big Blast/Tan Glove type mission. Instead of heading towards the East Coast, the three-ship cell flew to Green Bay, Wisconsin, then up to Hurley, Wisconsin, for a low-level run on the Iron Man route. After the low-level run they made a high-altitude run on the Minneapolis RBS.

After visiting Minneapolis the cell headed for Grand Forks, North Dakota, and then over to Minot using maximum ECM to help calibrate radar stations at both bases and at a large radar base thirteen miles south of Minot. Two F-106s from the 5th Fighter Interceptor Squadron were scrambled to test the ground intercept radar procedures. The two "Spittin' Kittens" made the intercept using the ground based radar for initial positioning of the fighters. Since this was a mission to help the Spittin' Kittens get their radar procedures up and running, the B-47s just flew straight and level like sitting ducks.

After playing targets, the B-47s dropped back down to low level for a nav run, then headed back to Lincoln. At postflight debriefing, the crews mentioned the sleek F-106 was a beautiful airplane. If only they had a camera, they could have gotten some great shots of the "Six Pac" sitting off their wing.

The first Reflex of the month departed for Morón, Spain, on 7 September while Sword Fish was underway. When the B-47s arrived in Spain, they were to make a bomb run on San Pablo and San Jarlo airfields. Then it was on to Morón, land, debrief and get ready to stand Alert just like they had done for months.

Thursday, the 8th, another day on Alert. Morning preflight accomplished without any aircraft having problems. So all of the planes stayed "cocked". The Alert crews went back to their quarters and continued with their tense routine.

The normal calm was shattered by the ninety-decibel wail of the klaxon. Now began the mad dash for the Alert birds. Was this the real thing or just another practice Alert to keep everyone on their toes? Doesn't matter. A klaxon is a klaxon; respond as if it were the signal to launch on a real EWO mission.

Everything went like clockwork. The crews buckled in while the ground crews got the power carts fired up and power on the aircraft. The klaxon's wail was replaced by the low whine of J-47 engines starting to spool up to idle. Each crew reported to alert command center when they were ready to taxi. They were told it was a Coco Exercise.

Runway 35 was the active runway that day, which meant a fast taxi of about two and a quarter miles to reach the end of 35. As 53-2139 reached the south run up pad, the aircraft commander felt a sharp thud. They turned onto the active and gave a fast check of the outriggers on both sides of the aircraft. They saw nothing out of the ordinary.

Turning onto the runway, the pilot pushed the power up and began the simulated takeoff. Speed came up, then the power was pulled back; all they had to do was taxi down the rest of the runway, then back to the alert pad.

However, another B-47 still on the way to the end of the runway spotted something wrong with 2139 as they taxied past on the taxiway. The right outrigger was on fire! They called the tower and reported the problem. The tower, in turn, made a quick call to 2139 to let them know what was happening. Then the tower called the fire department.

The crew followed the emergency procedures for aborting takeoff and brought 2139 to a stop about 3,000 feet down the runway. With the emergency in progress, the other B-47s throttled back and held their position. Since they didn't have any idea just how bad the fire was, the crew left their wounded bird posthaste. After a short sprint from the aircraft they turned and watched the firefighters arrive and spray foam on the outrigger. Within a few moments the fire was out. 2139 was towed off the runway and downloaded pending the investigation of the incident. Another B-47 was cocked and placed on alert to take its place.

It was determined that the "thud" the aircraft commander heard was most likely the tire blowing. The tire actually left the rim about 500 feet down the runway. The wheel continued to roll, creating enough friction to freeze the bearing and start a fire in the bearing grease. By the time the aircraft stopped, the wheel had been worn down to the axle. One can only imagine what might have happened if this had been a real launch.

So far, it had been a busy week at Lincoln. On top of everything, the flight line troops were working overtime to get the force ready for Sky Shield, which was scheduled to be flown on Saturday. Then a major monkey wrench dropped into the gears.

# Cold War Cornhuskers: The 307th Bomb Wing Lincoln Air Force Base Nebraska 1955-1965

At the direction of the Joint Chiefs of Staff (JCS), Sky Shield was moved forward by twenty-four hours. The 307th was almost ready to fly when the change came in. There were several reasons for the change, the major reason being the weather forecast for the scheduled E-Day.

Sky Shield was a JCS-directed mission to evaluate NORAD. It was designed to test the ability of NORAD to detect, identify and intercept an aerial attack on the United States. All civilian and military aircraft not participating in the exercise were grounded. This tipped off NORAD as to the day; however, they had no idea of the route the attacking bombers would use.

The 307th was scheduled to launch eight B-47s for the mission. The first B-47 left the runway at 2130 local, followed by the other seven aircraft at one-minute intervals. Sanka 15 climbed to 10,000 feet and leveled off over Sioux Falls, South Dakota.

Sanka 15 crossed into Canadian airspace at 49 degrees North, 95 degrees and 52 minutes West, and stayed on course to the north. Looking out the windscreen, they could see the Northern Lights dancing across the horizon. Good thing there was no air refueling scheduled on this mission. The shimmering Aurora always posed problems during air refueling. First, there was the interference with the radios and radar. The biggest problem after finding the tanker was trying to hook up and stay on the boom with the distraction of the dancing glow which, in many cases, caused extreme spatial disorientation for the pilots.

Shortly after crossing into Canada the flight began climbing to 31,000 feet. Sanka 18 had been having trouble with their radar since crossing the border. Changing fuses didn't help. Flying deep into the Canadian north without radar posed a flight safety concern, so Sanka 18 aborted and turned for home.

North of Churchill, Sanka 15 began to fly a large orbit so the other aircraft of Sanka flight could catch up and get into formation. Sanka flight formed up, and then entered a spacing triangle for the turn and run back to the United States. The B-47s were now spread out over a one hundred and forty mile front, using twenty-mile lateral separation and five hundred feet vertical separation until they reached the H-Hour Control Line at 56-46N by 93-21W.

With spacing accomplished Sanka started back towards the States, descending until they were only about two thousand feet above the ground. At 0115 local time they started blaring their ECM music. Four aircraft would make camera runs on targets at Crystal Falls, Freda Falls, Ontonagon and Tula, Michigan. The strike aircraft continued their ECM music until they crossed the end-ECM line running through St. Joseph, Missouri, at 0305 local. From there, the aircraft turned towards Lincoln and final approach. By 0430, the last of Sanka flight had popped the brake chute and taxied back to the ramp.

The overall results for the 307th were listed as "Excellent". It was believed the mission would have been more effective if chaff had been used. This may have defeated six Nike missile lock-ons that were encountered. It was suggested visual fighter attacks on low-level runs be eliminated due to the safety hazard at night. The X-Band ECM jammers caused problems with the Bomb/Nav system. This was not considered a major problem since the X-Band was only used for a short time to break lock-ons. One pilot remarked he did not see a single interceptor until over the Lincoln TVOR prior to landing.

In conjunction with Sky Shield, the rest of the wing played a war game called April Fool II. It was designed to test the wing's ability to operate after a nuclear attack. After the attack, all personnel except for the umpires went to preselected shelters. This was supposed to help gain knowledge in generating aircraft under nuclear conditions.

April Fool was an appropriate name for the exercise. It was a case of SAC conning SAC into believing the force could be generated after a nuclear attack. Everyone knew a ten-megaton air burst over the Capitol building would have been close enough to insure there wouldn't be much left at the patch to generate except for smoldering junk.

Starting engines for a mission didn't always go according to the Normal Procedures section of the Dash-1. On Thursday, 15 September, the flight crew had gone through a routine preflight on 53-1901. Engine start went according to the manual until they started turning #3. The EGT (Exhaust Gas Temperature) went to over a thousand degrees for several seconds. It was long enough to shut her down and call the engine shop. There would have to be a complete inspection and engine change before 1901 would be in the air again.

Speaking of engine starts, here's a memory from Paul Koski:

"The flight crew had finished their before-start checklist and said, 'Ground ready to start #4.' I replied, 'Ground clear on #4.' The AC said, 'Starting 4.' I replied. 'Rotation' when the engine started turning. This was a night launch and engine start always gets exciting. We had fuel fumes going past the flaps and fuel leaking out the tail pipe. I told the AC that we had no start and asked, 'Do you have the ignition switches on?' I wish I hadn't said that because he turned them on and a ball of fire rolled out the tail pipe and all the fuel vapors behind and around the flaps also ignited.

"My assistant hit the flaps with the CO2 and I took my shirt off and beat the flames out around the tire and on the ground. The AC kept the engine running and blew out the fire coming out of the tail pipe. I can remember the AC shouting, 'Ground, put the flames out,' over and over. He wanted to know if there was any damage on the ground. I said, 'No' and we continued engine start on all engines. I did ask if he had a hot start. No hot start, EGT was normal. Flight went on as scheduled."

The 307th may have had high priority from SAC for the MC-1 FOD sweeper to keep the ramp clear, but not all of the FOD was on the ramp. On Thursday the 29th, three B-47s were homebound from Reflex. As they were letting down one of the crews felt a faint thump, followed by an increase in EGT on the #1 engine. They shut the engine down and finished the approach on five engines. During post flight, bird feathers and remains were found around the intake section of the engine.

Bird strikes were not an everyday occurrence, but they did happen from time to time. Dale Christians recalled an encounter with a bird:

"We were coming back from a pilot upgrade flight when we hit this bird right in front of the windshield. We immediately declared an emergency and got clearance to descend and land. I was in the back seat instructing. The pilot wasn't hurt but he couldn't see a thing because of the windblast in his face. We all went to a hundred percent oxygen, slowed the plane down and I landed it from the back seat."

Col Read authored the monthly report and got it ready to send out to Headquarters. As he had done since May 1957, he pointed out that the wing was short of people. The 307th A&E Squadron was short fifty-two airmen. Other areas in the maintenance sections were also short of manpower. Eleven late takeoffs were attributed to maintenance. "There are not enough people to complete system checks and repairs", he wrote.

In his conclusion, Col Read stated emphatically that, without proper manpower to complete needed repairs, system checks and regular maintenance, it was only a matter of time before there would be a major flying accident. In one of his previous reports he had said, "You can't fly 'em if you can't fix 'em!" He took it one step further in his final sentence. "If you can't fix 'em, it isn't safe to fly 'em!"

When Col Read signed the report for September, it would be the last time he would endorse a monthly report from the 307th Bomb Wing. Col

## 1960

Read would be leaving Lincoln next month. It was time for him to leave his fellow sheep herders and move on to another assignment.

The 307th was scheduled to fly a Big Blast on 6 October. The only change from the regular profile for that kind of mission was in the takeoff. It would be a three-ship MITO for the first three aircraft to launch. The other three would make the regular one-minute separation for their departure.

During 51-7065's engine start for the mission, the oil pressure on #4 dropped to zero shortly after power was pushed to 65%. The engine was shut down and the launch crew moved in to investigate the problem. A spare aircraft was launched in 51-7065's place.

Afternoon routine on Friday, the 7th, was shattered by the klaxon. The Alert was a Bravo Exercise. All aircraft started engines and reported to Alert Control when ready to taxi. Within minutes of the end of the Alert, there was the customary rush to recock the Alert aircraft.

Anytime the klaxon blared, there was the mad scramble by everyone standing Alert. Across the base, everyone knew an Alert of some kind was underway. Buildings either had a klaxon or rotating red lights that would start flashing when an alert was called. Outside, there were rotating red lights at almost every street corner. Everyone knew when the lights started rotating, Alert crews were on their way and, above all, they had priority over everything. Heaven help anyone who happened to be in the way.

As a SAC BRAT, I remember being on base several times when the klaxon went off. Once, we were in the BX doing some shopping. There were several flight suit clad SAC warriors at the counter near the door when the horn went off. They hit the door like NFL running backs, just as a young lady was reaching for the handle. She went flying backwards as the door flew open in her face. One of the rushing crewmen yelled "Sorry!" as they passed the prostrate figure. Then, there was a Sunday morning at chapel service. As the chaplain was delivering his message, the two red lights at the front of the chapel began to turn. A reverent rustle came from the back as the Alert crews left their pews and headed for their vehicles. The service went on as if nothing had happened.

There was a farewell get together for Col Read on Saturday, the 8th. That night at the O. Club there was a large crowd to wish their commander well on his next assignment. This was the last time he would be able to spend quality off-duty time with his officers. His farewell remarks that night were filled with emotion as he related some of his memories of commanding the 307th for the last three and a half years.

Monday, 10 October: nothing like starting the week with another test from Omaha. This one was called Great Effort Bravo. It was a maximum effort designed to test and improve the EWO capability of the wing. Since it was listed as a "Team Scrimmage", both wings at Lincoln would fly the mission.

The exercise didn't start with the klaxon blaring and a rush for the Alert aircraft. It started with a quiet briefing to lay out the activities, rules and time lines for the next three days. As always, from now until the last plane landed, everyone would be under the watchful eyes of 2nd Air Force and SAC umpires.

Phase one consisted of preparing twenty-four B-47s for an EWO mission. Each aircraft would be loaded with a single Mark-28 nuclear weapon. The aircraft would carry a full EWO fuel load and ATO units for takeoff. The first twelve aircraft were to be generated to EWO configuration on the first day.

With the start of the exercise, twelve weapons were brought out of storage in the weapons igloos and transported to the flight line. The loading was done by the upload checklist. No one wanted anything to go wrong and get a bad score or, worse yet, have a real "Broken Arrow".

ATO racks were carted to the aircraft, then jacked and jockeyed into position and secured. The tail guns were loaded with "20 mike-mike" (20 millimeter) ammunition and the turret safetied. When all the safety checks were double-checked and the safety plugs in or out according to the checklist, the aircraft was declared ready for EWO.

According to SAC regulations, B-47s couldn't sit on the flight line loaded with nuclear weapons unless they were on alert. The umpires made their final scoring checks and finished filling out their score sheets. As soon as the scoring for the upload was finished, the umpires gave the word to begin downloading the weapons. So the ordnance people moved in and started the download checklist. It was late that night when the final nuke was put back to bed in its storage igloo and secured until the next exercise.

Day two, Great Effort Bravo started with the first twelve crews attending a briefing for the mission. The first wave of twelve would take off in four three-ship cells. Each cell would take off using MITO tactics. The cells would then climb out and make a run on the first target from high altitude.

After the high altitude run, there was descent to low altitude and a low-level nav leg, culminating in a low level "Short Look" bomb run on the second target. The crews were informed they could expect fighter attacks during the high altitude run and missile attacks during the run at low-level. They were to use maximum ECM and chaff to break any lock-on. Leaving the second target, the cells would return to Lincoln.

It was time to kick the tires, climb aboard, and spool up for the first three-ship cell. As they taxied, the next three aircraft were spooling up. There was to be a five-minute separation window between the cells. All four cells launched and climbed out heading for Sioux Falls, South Dakota. From Sioux Falls, they made a slight heading change towards Alexandria, then turned for the IP at St. Cloud, Minnesota. Approaching Minneapolis, the navigator set up for release on the target, the west end of the Mendota Bridge over the Mississippi River. After tone cut-off, the B-47s headed into Wisconsin before turning south for the next part of the mission. Over La Crosse, the bombers turned south and began coming down from 30,000 feet. They flew across Iowa and into Missouri.

The strike force contacted Kansas City ATC Center for clearance into the Rough Road Oil Burner route. The route was clear of traffic and the B-47s started a low-level nav leg. After the nav leg, they finished Rough Road with a "Short Look" bomb run on the Joplin RBS. After the run on Joplin, the B-47s turned and headed for home.

While the crews were flying the first wave, the second wave was going through the EWO upload, servicing, scoring and then, like before, unloading everything and waiting for the scores to be posted. During this phase, the troops noticed some unusual activity to the north in the 98th area. There were a lot of flashing red lights. Later, they found out a couple of 98th A & E technicians showed up to work on one of the uploaded birds. All was well except for one little thing: the crew chief noticed the gizmo guys didn't have their flight line badges on and called a "Seven High" sabotage alert.

Wednesday, the 12th, found the 307th preparing to fly the second wave of Great Effort Bravo. The twelve aircraft were serviced and ready for the crews to arrive. Takeoff would be in three-ship MITOs, then fly the same route and make runs on the same targets as the first wave.

The first three B-47s started up and taxied towards the runway. 53-4223 was listed as Sortie 15, so she would be the third ship in the first cell. The first two aircraft rolled down the runway. Forty-five seconds after the first ship began rolling, 4223 started to roll. Monitoring the instruments, the copilot noticed the oil pressure on the #4 engine fluctuated, then fell to zero.

**"ABORT.ABORT.ABORT!
No oil pressure on #4!"**

## Cold War Cornhuskers: The 307th Bomb Wing Lincoln Air Force Base Nebraska 1955-1965

The AC pulled the power off and pulled the drag chute handle. 4223 slowed and finally turned off the runway. She taxied back to the ramp on five engines. The other B-47s in the next cells pulled onto the runway and blasted off without any further problems. It was fortunate the abort happened when it did. If it had been one of the other planes in the cells, the abort would have thrown the timing off for the rest of the mission.

The mission went according to the profile until the last cell approached the low-level nav leg. Low-hanging clouds had moved into the area, and thunderheads were building all around. The crews made a quick call to the Command Post for advice, which in turn contacted ATC to try and get things changed and cleared up. The last cell had to make a "bomb run-only" entry into the oil burner route. Rough Road lived up to its name as the B-47s flew through cross winds, turbulence and rain squalls all the way to the target.

Back home at Lincoln, the weather was also going downhill. Another system was moving in from the west with low clouds, wind and rain. By a stroke of luck, the weather held off arriving until the last bird was on final approach. The wind was starting to shift, which meant a probable change in the active runway. The last plane's tires kissed the runway and the chutes blossomed just as the north end of the runway disappeared in a rain squall.

The final results of the mission scored the wing "Outstanding" in all phases of the operation. There were several areas that caused problems. Four of the low-level "Short Look" runs were unreliable. This may have been because the RBS site was unable to maintain lock due to ground return interference.

The largest problem was the weather on the final day. Thunderstorms in the area caused last-minute changes in the profile. The change to bomb run-only caused the loss of four low-level nav legs. Of the nav legs that were flown, all were rated as reliable. Bombing was rated as "Outstanding". Twenty-three aircraft were scored as reliable on both targets.

While the 307th was flying the mission a notable incident occurred in New York City. Soviet leader Nikita Khrushchev was present to make a speech to the United Nations on relations between the major powers of the world. At the height of his diatribe he took off his shoe and beat the desk with it. Uttering his famous proclamation "We will bury you!," he pounded the desk to the amusement of the delegates, then walked out of the Assembly.

The formal change of command ceremony took place on 14 October. Col Elkins Read, Jr., handed the wing over to Col Walter Berg at Wing headquarters. Col Berg had served as Vice Commander of the 305th Bomb Wing at Bunker Hill, AFB. Col Read may have been leaving Lincoln, but he wouldn't be very far away; he was being assigned to SAC Headquarters at Omaha.

The rest of October was taken up with the regular flying schedule. The wing flew 241 sorties, not counting the higher headquarters exercises. There were 73 effective refuelings during the month. During training, the wing scored 99% effective on 53 RBS bomb runs.

It was noted that, during the last several months, the wing had been having problems at the RBS site at Minneapolis. This was due to Nike missile lock-ons in the area. The Nike lock-on was indistinguishable from the RBS lock-on signal. This had resulted in jamming of the Nike site, yielding an early jamming score from the RBS site.

November started with a three-ship Reflex launch on Tuesday, the 1st. The crews used the Blue Route for the deployment. They reported some difficulty refueling due to clouds and turbulence in the refueling track. They managed to get the fuel load and made the long flight to Spain without any further major problems.

That same morning, the wing received a standby message from Omaha for Operation Top Team. The wing staff pulled the folder out and looked to see what the mission included. The plan was for a SAC-wide test of the tanker force. It was to see how well the tankers could react to a simulated EWO mission. The tanker wings' planning and battle staffs would also be tested on their performance.

The 307th was to generate and launch twenty B-47s in exercise configuration. No weapons or ammo would be carried. The generation of the force would begin eighteen hours before H-Hour. Crews flying the mission had to be available either at base housing or on base at the BOQ.

Generation of the force began that afternoon. Selected aircraft were double-checked to make sure all 781 discrepancies had been taken care of before the mission. The planes were towed to the fuel pits and serviced for the mission. After the fuel pits, they were towed back to their slot on the ramp and serviced with oxygen and any other fluids that were needed.

That Tuesday morning would turn out to be a lot busier than normal. SAC had been looking at different ways to improve the survivability of the strike force in case of a national crisis. They came up with an idea called Clutch Pedal. The idea was to disperse aircraft to selected civilian airports large enough to accommodate a B-47. The concept looked good on paper, but like every plan on paper, it had to be tried out in real life. The 307th was one of the wings that would test it and help iron out the wrinkles.

Two B-47s would deploy to Mitchell Field, Milwaukee, Wisconsin, and two would fly to O'Hare Airport at Chicago. Glenn "Pappy" Hesler's crew was one of the crews selected for the trip to Chicago. Earl Freeman and his crew would fly the other B-47 to O'Hare.

The idea of sending B-47s to civilian airports wasn't just any fly-by-night idea cooked up in a staff meeting at Omaha. The whole plan wouldn't be worth the paper it was written on if the airports couldn't support the military aircraft. Cities across the nation had submitted required paperwork to show SAC they were up to the job of supporting SAC any time of the day or night.

Glen wrote about the first Clutch Pedal flight in his book *The Heart of the Tiger*:

"A rainy, cloudy day was selected for the surprise. Flight plans were always filed. This rule was never broken, especially during bad weather and when landing at a field as large and as busy as O'Hare. I filed no flight plan for this flight. The Kansas City center made all of the arrangements for the procedures and implemented the cover-up. As our flight approached Chicago, I called the O'Hare tower for landing instructions using the ILS for the designated runway of which Kansas City center was aware. The senior tower operator knew of the cover-up so he came on my frequency as soon as I called. Very quietly he cleared us to land on a certain runway via the ILS system. There were no further transmissions until I touched down and deployed my brake chute. The drogue chute was already out.

"I was told later the tower people thought it was an invasion from Mars. They had never seen an airplane deploy a large chute like this one. The senior tower advisor assured them all was well. As I was clearing the runway, I saw Earl touching down also so I jettisoned both chutes while I was still on the taxiway. The wind helped the chutes to clear all hard surfaces. The tower told me that a "Follow Me" truck was on the way out and would park us.

"Television cameras were at the landing end of the runway and were in on the 'invasion'. Those cameras were also in my face as I deplaned, another surprise. General LeMay had explained just what I was to say as I stepped out of the entrance door. This is what I demanded: 'I want 70,000 pounds of JP-4 fuel and fill the oxygen bays to the top. I have very little time as I am on my way at the direction of SAC.' The ground crew just looked at me, dazed at such a request. They finally confessed that they had only 5,000-gallon fuel trucks available and no single point refueling for our military type receptacles. They never responded to my request for oxygen."

"Pappy's" navigator, Larry Boggess, recalled:

"We were told that we would be on the evening news broadcast with Huntley & Brinkley. As it turned out, Lyndon Johnson was there on the 1960 campaign and we got bumped. The next morning there was a picture of one of us landing there and the caption was, 'JET MAKES PARACHUTE LANDING' as it was new to them to see a plane use a brake chute and an approach chute."

Execution notification for Top Team arrived on 2 November with the blare of the klaxon. Alert crews scrambled for the aircraft and started spooling engines. They were informed that it was a Bravo Exercise. They shut the engines down and climbed back down the ladders. Fuel trucks were already arriving to top off the tanks and get the fleet recocked.

Aircraft that were to fly the mission were ready for the crews to arrive from the final briefing. One by one they started engines, taxied and launched at one-minute intervals. Within thirty minutes the force was in the air, heading for their first checkpoint at Des Moines. After the first checkpoint they headed for a nav leg to Chicago, Detroit, Toronto, and on to Montreal, Quebec.

After Montreal the bombers headed for Goose Bay, then turned for the Elm Tree refueling area. Approaching the refueling track, the strike force began running into bad weather. There were high clouds in the area. Turbulence was getting worse by the minute. Tankers that made it to Elm Tree were also starting to report they were picking up ice. Several of the tankers turned away, aborting the mission.

Bob Byrom, Mike Gingrich and Bill Heald were flying 53-2416 on the mission. Due to the combination of weather and aborting tankers, they had to abort when they weren't able to get fuel for the rest of the mission. They headed back towards Pease Air Force Base. They were not alone; a total of twelve 307th aircraft had to divert to the missed-refueling alternates.

The eight aircraft that were able to refuel then continued the mission by flying back towards the States and heading for the assigned target. The surviving mission aircraft set up a timing triangle over Lake Superior between Houghton, Michigan, and Duluth, Minnesota, to get ten-minute spacing for the bomb run. At the proper spacing, the aircraft would leave the triangle and head for Ashland, Wisconsin, their Pre IP. From there, they flew to the IP at Spooner, Wisconsin, and made contact with the RBS at Minneapolis. After the bomb run, the B-47s continued south to Omaha and then turned for the short leg to Lincoln.

The eight aircraft that were able to complete the mission were rated as "Outstanding". The bomb runs on Minneapolis were each scored as effective. With twelve aircraft aborting due to missed refueling, the profound effect of weather on operations was made very clear.

The SAC training and MCS quarter was almost over. The wing posted a busy flying schedule to fill in the rest of the squares before time ran out. There were training flights leaving on a daily schedule along with Reflex deployments every Tuesday. The schedule for the TA-2 trainer was jammed and crews found it hard to get in for some "sim time".

Our nation had gone to the polls to elect a new President during the month. Voters had chosen the young Senator from Massachusetts, John F. Kennedy. The campaign was historic. There was the usual mud slinging and rallies across the nation. For the first time in our nation's history, the two candidates squared off in debate, which was televised across the nation. The young Kennedy seemed relaxed, while Richard Nixon looked tired and nervous. Kennedy won the election by one of the narrowest margins in the history of the United States up to that time.

With a new Administration about to take the reins of leadership in January, a lot of military men couldn't help but wonder how things would change with the new President and his Administration. During the campaign, Kennedy had made a lot of comments about the fact that the Soviets had more long-range missiles than we did. To meet these threats and others there would have to be changes in the nation's deterrent posture.

On the 17th, 53-1918 aborted a mission before she even had a chance to start. She was still in the big south hangar. Several days previously, 1918 had a mid-air encounter with a UFB (Unidentified Flying Bird). The bird hit the windshield, causing it to crack. After the investigation and filling out the paperwork, she was taken into the hangar and the windshield was replaced. The sealant used hadn't had enough time to cure before the next scheduled flight.

Thanksgiving Day arrived with all the trimmings. The cooks in the 307th mess halls went all-out to provide the troops with a good meal. There was a full menu of all the goodies that one would find in a home-cooked meal. Roasted turkey, cornbread stuffing, mashed spuds and gravy, along with sweet 'taters and just a hint of cranberries were on the bill of fare. There were also all kinds of desserts, especially the holiday favorite, pumpkin pie.

Airmen and families lined up with hearty appetites to chow down and give thanks for the bounty. The meal was great! The cornbread dressing was different for those accustomed to sage and bread dressing. About the only thing negative about the meal at the mess hall—you guessed it: no leftovers for a late afternoon turkey sandwich.

Winter arrived on the 28th. It wasn't a major storm, just a lot of rain that shortly changed to freezing rain. Later that afternoon the freezing rain turned to snow; just enough to cancel four sorties that were scheduled for the day.

Col Berg wrote his month-end report for November. His report was similar to the reports that Col Read had written. Like his predecessor, his major plea was for more qualified personnel to keep the aircraft fixed and ready to fly.

December got off to a shaky start. A Reflex return deployment arrived home on Thursday, 1 December. Everything seemed fine except for 51-15808. The flight crew wrote her up for using excessive oil in the #2 engine during the flight back. After checking the write ups on the Form 781, the crew chief pulled the cowling in search of what should have been an obvious oil leak. No leak was found, so they fired the engine up to try and figure out why she was using so much oil. They ran the J-47 for an hour at various power settings; no leak. Then one of the ground crew thought the engine seemed to be wobbling around in the mounts. Power was pulled back, then shut down, and the crew moved in for a closer look.

What they found scared the daylights out of them. One of the engine mount bolt pins was missing! With the pin missing, the entire engine could have torn loose during the flight from Spain. The fact that the engine stayed in place was a miracle. They chalked it up to Lady Luck beating the Grim Reaper to the draw.

Since December was the last month of the SAC training quarter and with Christmas coming, the flight schedule was crammed. There were a lot of last-minute flights to try to take care of last-minute squares that had to be filled by the crews.

On the 6th, three crews prepared to deploy for Reflex. The aircraft scheduled were 53-4217, 53-1911 and 53-2143. During preflight, a problem was found in the radar on 2143. 53-4227 was substituted and everything appeared copacetic for the launch. About three and a half hours before launch, the ground crew found a problem in the oxygen system on 4227. They tore into the innards trying to locate the gremlin. The other

## Cold War Cornhuskers: The 307th Bomb Wing Lincoln Air Force Base Nebraska 1955-1965

two aircraft launched on time. The $O_2$ gremlins were found and 4227 was in the air nineteen minutes after her cell mates launched.

By the time they reached the refueling area they were back together in a three-ship cell for the Atlantic crossing. The crossing was long and filled with tension, since they had received word the weather in Spain was not the best. As they approached the coast, they were advised that weather was getting worse and they were to divert to Ben Guerir, Morocco.

On the 7th, Crew R-89 was up flying a mission. Capt Charles Watt (AC), Lt Orin Shellhammer (CP) and Lt Robert Bauer (nav) called Minneapolis RBS and identified themselves for the bomb run. It was a textbook run to the target. When they got the score, it had indeed been a very good run. As a matter of fact, they scored a shack. Orin Shellhammer recalled:

"I've got several 'shack plaques' as we called them. Of course, the nav is really the one who earned it, but the whole crew got the award. If it was way off, only the nav got the flak. It was quite a thrill to receive the bomb scoring site's radio message (which we always received after a bomb run) and it was the 'secret additive', same as we were using for the day, which meant when you subtracted it from the report, it gave the distance and bearing from the target. If the additive was the same as the radio message, that meant the distance and bearing were 0-0, or a shack."

The arrival of cold weather brought on the age-old problem of JP-4 finding ways of leaking from the tanks and puddling the flight line. On the 5th, the bottom had fallen out of the thermometer. The next day, 53-4235 was listed out of commission with a leak in the forward auxiliary tank.

During the last several months, the reenlistment rate had been the lowest it had been in several years. During this period of time the reenlistment officer had been conducting interviews and taking notes on what was said. The notes were typed up and sent to SAC Headquarters.

The report brought out there was a prevailing sense of insecurity about being able to pursue a military career. Then there was the MCS point system. Lose points in certain areas and you could be booted out of the Air Force. Old Timers, close to retirement, were "running scared" they might "stumble" and not be able to make it all the way to their retirement.

It was pointed out that the only thing promised on reenlistment was the re-up bonus and thirty days' leave. Previously, an airman could re-up for the base of choice. Now, it was for base of preference with no guarantee of getting it. On top of that, the airman had to reup *before* stating his base of preference. It was also brought out that the present system for promotion left much to be desired.

Several other suggestions were listed. The main one was to get rid of "Roads Gallery" in the *Jet Scoop*. It was felt there should be the old management axiom of "Praise in Public, Punish in Private". Also, the military should go back to the old rank of "Buck Sergeant" for the three stripers and let them join the NCO Club. Some of the suggested changes would be implemented. However, some of them would take years before they would be seen by the flight line troops.

The klaxon blared on the 16th and the crews responded to a Coco Alert. During engine start, an alternator on 53-1912 would not come online. As 53-2392 started to move, they noticed the steering disconnect was inoperative. Since they couldn't steer they couldn't taxi, so 2392 was stuck on the pad. That meant two 307th birds aborted the Alert and were uncocked. The steering disconnect was repaired and the alternator drive unit was replaced. Since they were uncocked, it meant MCS points down the drain.

The last Reflex flight before Christmas left on 20 December. The three crews were not the happiest campers in view of the date. They could either have a late or early Christmas. Either way, it meant they would be far away from family during the holiday. Maybe their personal sacrifice of family life would help assure "Peace on Earth".

Regular duty ended on Thursday the 22nd. Except for Alert and emergencies, all routine work was put aside until 27 December. That is, if everyone around the world would just observe the true meaning of the season and not cause a world crisis demanding an increase in readiness.

Christmas arrived on the crest of the new-fallen snow. Not much of it, just enough to make for a White Nebraska Christmas. That Sunday, families packed up the car and made the trip to the "mole hole" to visit dad while he was on Alert. They were glad to spend some time with him even if it was at the "mole hole". Most of all, they were glad the klaxon stayed quiet.

Work and flying started again on Tuesday the 27th. Weather was pretty good for this time of the year. You could almost actually see the end of the runway. Crew E-74 launched to fly one more mission before the end of the year. Capt Pete Hershey and Capt Jerry Dove did some refueling from the front and back seats while Lt Laurie Bunten kept track of where they were and how to get there. With refueling and the nav leg over, they headed for a bomb run of the Minneapolis RBS. Lt Bunten adjusted the bomb nav system and double-checked his offset points. It looked like a good run all the way to tone cut off. When the results were sent back, it was a shack!

Getting a shack was like hitting a fly with a BB Gun from a block away. On every bomb run the crew wanted to be scored as reliable. If you scored a shack it was icing on the cake, maybe a couple of extra MCS points thrown in for an exceptional job, or a "well done".

Another year had come and gone in the history of the 307th Bomb Wing. As always, there were high points and low spots during the last 366 days. The wing said farewell to their tanker friends and had a change in commanding officers. Reflex and Alert procedures had been revised for the umpteenth time. The 307th has passed every test Omaha and Barksdale had thrown at them. The men of the 307th looked back with pride at what they had accomplished. They looked forward with hope that SAC would continue to maintain a strong deterrent and that peace would prevail for another year in the Cold War.

53-1867 Reflex bound. (Hood)

*1960*

In the cold air at high altitude, vapor trails stream back marking the B-47's flight path. (307th BWA)

Reflex sunset, a companion B-47 can be seen in the distance. (307th BWA)

Light snow covers "the patch". Looking towards the south end of the flight line and alert area. (307th BWA)

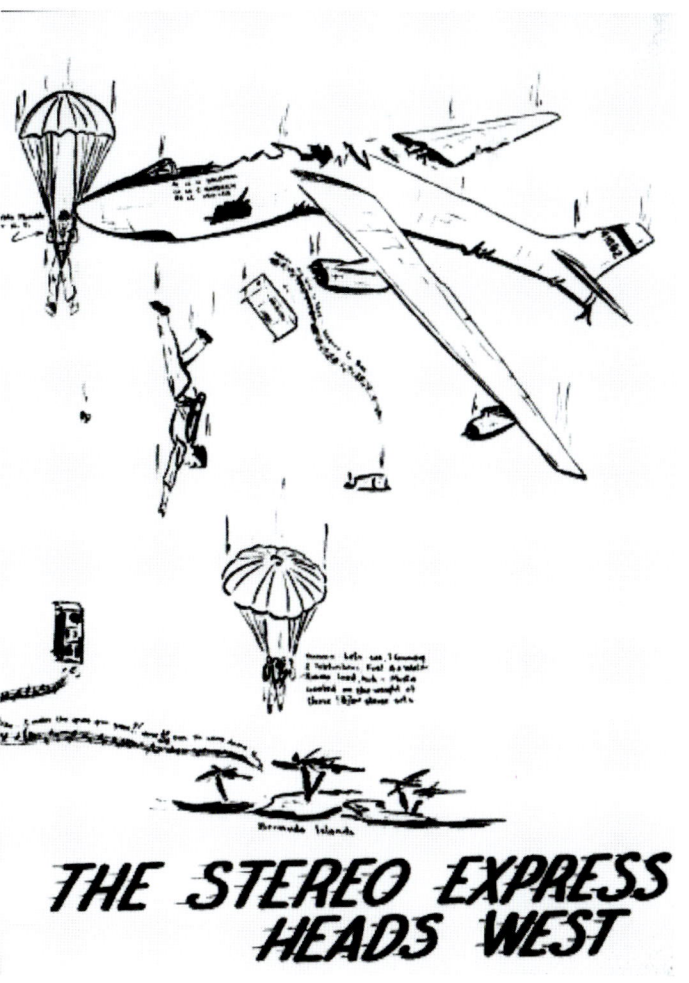

STEREO EXPRESS (307th BWA)

THE STEREO EXPRESS HEADS WEST

# Cold War Cornhuskers: The 307th Bomb Wing Lincoln Air Force Base Nebraska 1955-1965

The snow plows would hit the roads before "THE HAWK" was finished. (JET SCOOP)

Air Force Commendation Medal presented to the top four Crew Chiefs for the period of December 22, 1958 to November 1959. L-R SSgt. Bergan (98th), SSgt Lawrence Powers (307th), SSgt. Merrill Sinclair (307th), SSgt. James Yandle (307th). (Sinclair)

Alert facility with "cocked" B-47s in the background. (JET SCOOP)

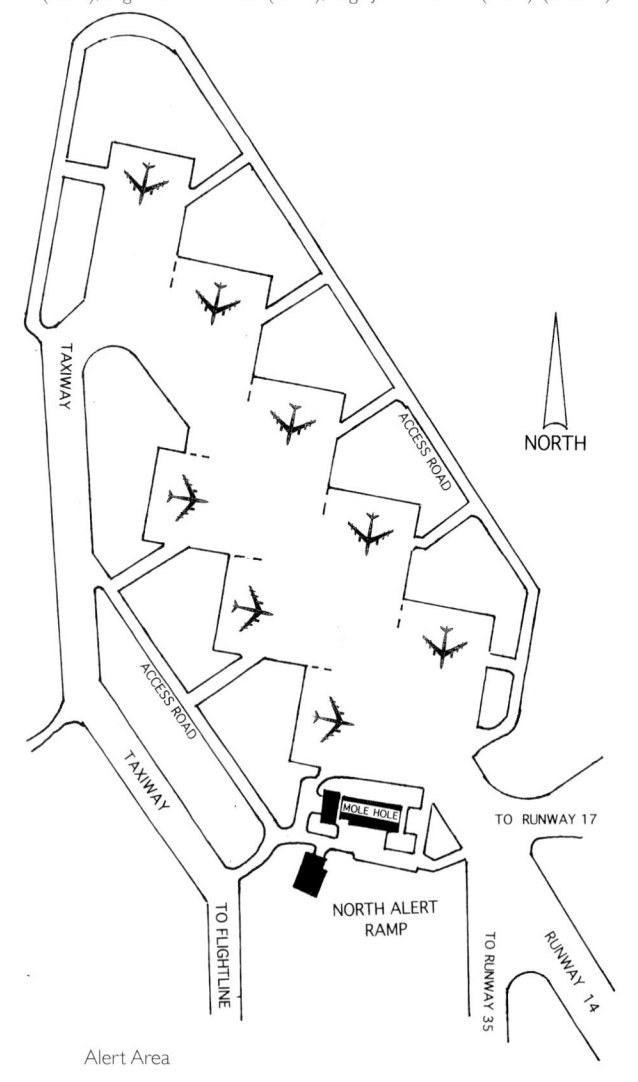

Alert Area

*1960*

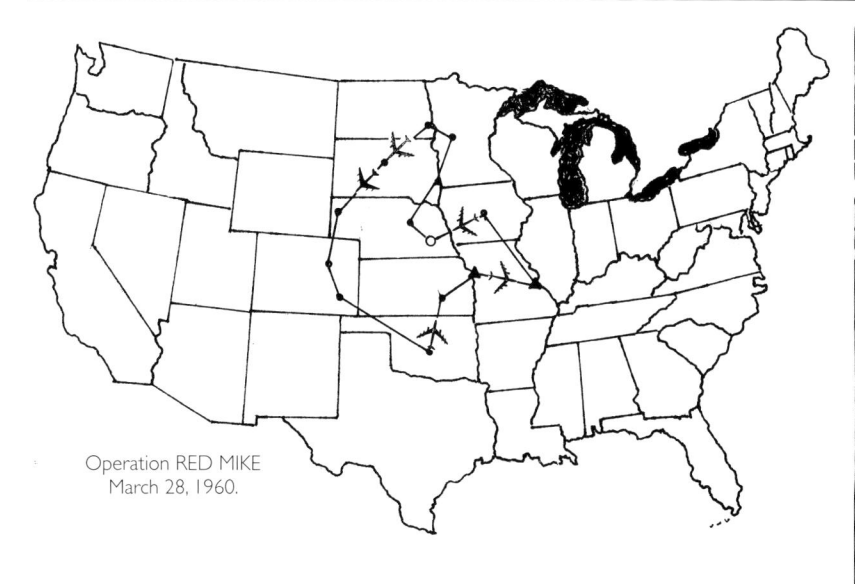

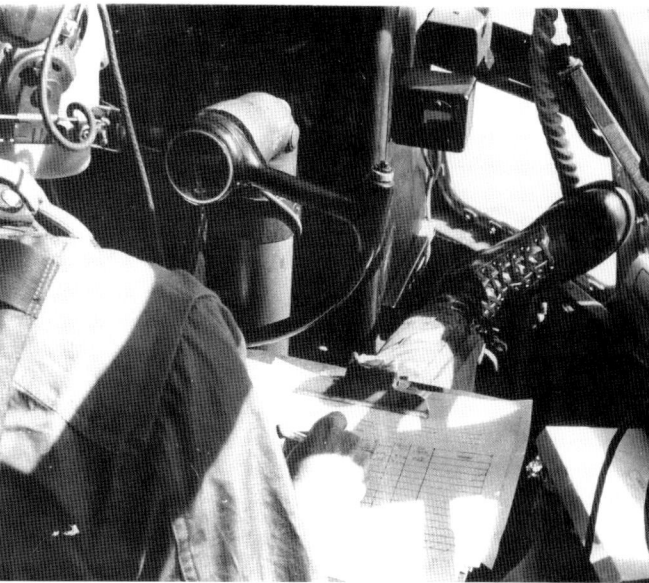

Operation RED MIKE
March 28, 1960.

A tanker copilot relaxes while filing out report form during a long mission. (Zester)

Members of the 307th OMS, March 31, 1960. (Lally)

2804 on the snow covered flight line. (Tarwater)

Smoke billows from the burning KC-97. (USAF)

Ground view of 0919. The two officers are looking at a propeller. (USAF)

# Cold War Cornhuskers: The 307th Bomb Wing Lincoln Air Force Base Nebraska 1955-1965

Firefighters move in close to spray more foam on the wreckage. (USAF)

A once proud KC-97, now a pile of burnt aluminum. (USAF)

George Kenton Sisler, Medal Of Honor. (Tarwater)

By mid-June, the south end of the ramp was absent of the familiar KC-97s of the 307th ARES. (USAF)

*1960*

Tactical Squadron Award. (307th BWA)

Refueling Boom Envelope Diagram from the B-47 Dash-1.

A 906th ARES KC-135 launches from Minot AFB, North Dakota, to provide refueling support for the 307th. (M. Hill)

Summer on the flight line. (307th BWA)

# Cold War Cornhuskers: The 307th Bomb Wing Lincoln Air Force Base Nebraska 1955-1965

307th B-47 on the LAFB flight line. (307th BWA)

Col. Walter Berg assumed command of the 307th BW on October 14, 1960. (USAF)

53-4216 prepares for a night mission. (USAF)

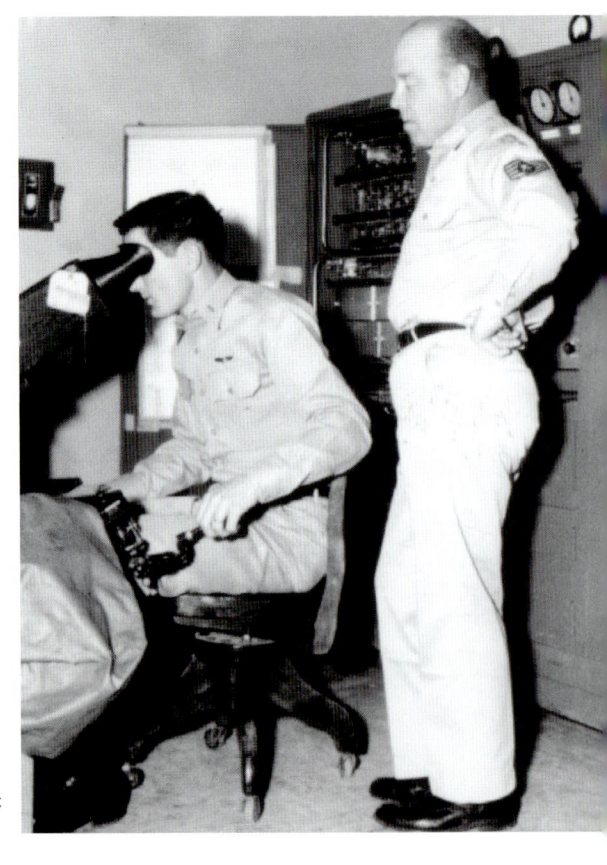

Filling in some 50-8 training squares on the T-1A tail gun trainer. (Gilstrap)

# 1961

Gentle falling snow greeted the stroke of midnight and the New Year. It wasn't heavy, just a nice gentle snow to cover any old snow that had been soiled by human encroachment. Within the first hour of the New Year, a blanket of fresh white had covered the flight line again.

On the Alert ramp, silent sentinels stood their lonely posts, guarding the Alert birds. Their only defense against the snow and cold were their heavy N3-B parkas and winter flight pants. They had the hoods drawn up over their heads and the snorkel cinched up to ward off the falling snow and freezing cold. Every now and then, if they were lucky, a Metro would pull up; climbing inside, they stole a few minutes of warmth and maybe a quick smoke and a cup of java to warm their innards. Then it was back out into the cold, to walk their post and leave fresh footprints in the fallen snow.

During the early morning hours, the snow stopped and the clouds broke up. The long first night of the New Year ended with a growing glow on the eastern horizon. When the first rays of the rising sun came over Cornhusker Highway, they almost blinded the lonely alert ramp guards as the rays reflected off the fresh snow. The guards stood their post in the snow and cold that night without any fanfare or special recognition just because it was a New Year. They would stand many more nights, those nameless men who silently stood ready to challenge anyone who came near their charges. This was *their* "Cold War".

It was back to regular duty on 3 January. What better way to start the duty week than with the klaxon jarring everyone from their holiday lethargy? The first crew reported ready to roll, six and a half minutes after the horn. It was a Coco Exercise, so the B-47s taxied, went to full power, then taxied back to the alert area to be recocked. The Alert crews went back to their tense routine of waiting for the next klaxon.

Pulling Alert was never considered "fun". It was about as much "fun" as a visit to the proctologist. Consider, for a moment, the alert experience. As soon as the crew became combat ready and EWO-certified, they knew it was just a matter of time before their crew number would appear on the alert schedule. That was a SAC FACT! When their crew number came up, there was a certain amount of preparation on the home front. This was before the days when most families had more than one vehicle sitting in the driveway. Wives had to pack dad off to the Alert pad so they could have the car. If payday was at hand, arrangements had to be made to get paid and get it into the bank. Remember, these were the "good old days" BP (Before Plastic). About the only credit cards were for the major oil companies. There was no Internet, so online banking and bill paying was a thing of the future.

After crew changeover, the new crew would settle in for a routine that would last for the next seven days. There were the briefing and target study, then morning and afternoon aircraft checks. They could look forward to three trips through the chow line. When that was done, what lay ahead for the rest of the duty day?

When SAC first started pulling ground alert, things were not very structured for the crews after the daily aircraft checks and briefings. As time passed, Alert became more and more structured for the crews. There was target study, classes on Alert procedures, EWO procedures, and Positive Control procedures, along with written tests on their knowledge of any and all procedures.

Free time was whiled away in a thousand and one different ways. First, there were endless cards games. You name it, it was played, somewhere, sometime on a SAC Alert pad. Marathon games of Canasta, Whist, Bridge, Pinochle and, of course, the favorite Poker. Of course, there were at least a hundred and two variations of poker, everything from Five Card Stud and Texas Hold 'em, all the way to Seven-Toed Pete.

Those not inclined to try their luck at cards used time on alert for other things. Some built models of—what else?—airplanes, either balsa or plastic. There were endless bull sessions covering every topic from politics to sports and any subject in between. A lot of people furthered their education by taking extension courses. Many post-Air Force careers were prepared for while standing Alert.

After chow, crews would amble into the day room for the Evening News with Walter Cronkite or Huntley and Brinkley. After the news, there began a constant "Channel Check" for favorites like *Have Gun Will Travel*, *Ed Sullivan*, *The Untouchables* and *Gunsmoke*.

No matter what the world situation was at the time, being on Alert was filled with tension. No matter the time of day or day of the week, the blare of the klaxon hung over the heads of the alert crews like a hangman's noose. The wail of the klaxon could be just another test to keep the crews on their toes, or it could be the signal to pull the nuclear trigger and Armageddon. Dave Bowersock relates an alert memory:

"We were on alert at Lincoln AFB. One night, Gene Van Meter and Neal Amtmann wanted to see a movie, but I was taking college classes and needed to study. The crew in the room next to ours said they would be in all night and I could ride in their truck if we had an exercise.

# Cold War Cornhuskers: The 307th Bomb Wing Lincoln Air Force Base Nebraska 1955-1965

"About the only time we didn't wear our flight suits and boots when on Alert was when we were in bed, at the pool, or working out in the gym. Even then, everything was within reach at all times. That night, I was wearing my flight suit, but it was cool in the room so I had my white terry cloth bathrobe over it. My boots were off, sitting by the doorway.

"When the klaxon sounded, I grabbed my jacket and, for some stupid reason, I sat down and put my boots on. When I got outside, the last two trucks were just pulling away. The one I was supposed to ride with was already gone so I jumped into the truck bed of the nearest one to me. While we were on the way I took off my white robe, put on my flight jacket and then tied the arms of my bathrobe around my neck. I soon discovered that their airplane was in the first row, whereas ours was next to last.

"When the truck stopped, I jumped out and started running between the planes. I had perhaps 70 or 80 yards to go. We had a good moon that night so the tail numbers were easy to read. Gene and Neal were ahead of me and the power cart was already going. I scrambled up the ladder, threw my bathrobe in the crawlway and climbed up into the front cockpit. When I got my helmet on I expected some smart remark from Gene about me being late, but there was a lot of chatter going on between the aircraft and questions coming from the Command Post. Gene explained that several pilots had seen a white something or someone going between and even under the wings of some of the planes. The security force was sweeping the area.

"As Gene and I started the checklist, something in the bright moonlight caught my eye. It was my white terry cloth bathrobe lying in the crawlway. I was the intruder, the ghost in the night. I think I told Gene and Neal, but I'm sure I didn't tell anyone else."

Even after the tour of duty, Alert Crews remained "nervous in the service" for several days after leaving the "mole hole". It was hard to change your mind set after pulling a week under the constant threat of the klaxon. There are a lot of memories of coming off alert and trying to relax. Then the klaxon blares and the troops were headed for the door on a dead run, then it hit them. "Hold it, I just got off Alert this morning." They may have felt a little sheepish, but it was a normal Pavlovian reaction.

After several tours on alert, an individual's response to the growl of the klaxon could definitely become Pavlovian, which under certain circumstances could be downright humorous. Mike Gingrich relates the following:

"In our bachelor days, Bob Boulware and I shared a basement apartment where it so happened the doorbell had a very throaty growl reminiscent of the klaxon. It happened also that one Saturday morning at 0700 the doorbell/pseudo-klaxon sounded. Boulware bounded out of the bunk and into his flight suit, which he had just taken off several hours earlier upon returning from a mission. Meanwhile, I was there watching, laughing my ass off at Boulie's unconscious reaction to the external stimulus. It turned out that the doorbell was the postman with a special delivery letter from my parents…according to post office procedure, it must be delivered whenever it arrives at the local post office, which happened to be 0700. I next made the mistake of telling my parents about the time of arrival and Boulware's reaction, which tickled their wicked sense of humor.

"Well, the next Saturday morning at 0700 the doorbell rang again, and again Boulware jumped about a foot in the air before gaining consciousness. Once more, it was a special delivery letter from my parents. It consisted of a note 'Good Morning, time to rise and shine!' Boulware's comment after he calmed down: 'Mike, ya gotta get yourself some new parents'."

On 4 January, Capt James Jacobs was flying as a replacement navigator with Maj Robert Hanson and Capt Roger Beamer on a routine round robin mission. After refueling, they headed for a practice run on the Ironwood RBS. When the score came in, they had scored a shack.

Then, on the 7th Capt Jacobs was back in the nose of a B-47 with his regular crew. Capt Garland Gee was his AC and Lt Theodore Childress was flying in the backseat. Their mission included a Short Look run on the Rough Road oil burner route. When the score came back from Joplin bomb plot it was a shack. That made two shacks for Jacobs on two consecutive missions! His two shacks were the third and fourth for the 424th Bomb Squadron since 7 December.

January 17th saw the arrival of the long overdue MC-1 sweeper. It may have been winter, but they put it to work right away sweeping the flight line. In the first eight days it picked up over thirty-five bushels of junk that could have played havoc with the engines.

There was, however, one type of material that was acceptable to be sucked into a running engine. Older crew chiefs know the answer to this one; why, of course, walnut shells! That's right, ground up walnut shells were used to clean compressor blades. The procedure was simple, with a certain element of risk. Strap someone, usually a one striper, into a safety harness and hook him up to the bumper on a Metro. Start the jet engine and run it at about fifty percent. Then, with the one striper attached to the safety harness, approach the front of the engine and throw a bag of walnut shells into the intake. Poof, a little black smoke out the exhaust and, bingo, nice shiny compressor blades! It may have been crude, but it was effective.

John F. Kennedy was sworn in as President on January 20, 1961. His speech to the nation was impressive. He mentioned that the torch had been passed to a new generation. Perhaps the most remembered thing he said was, "Ask not what your country can do for you; ask what you can do for our country." A lot of SAC troops were already doing a lot for their country. Under the new Presidential Administration they would be called upon to do a lot more.

If there is one word to describe life on the flight line in January, it would be "miserable". It was always bitterly cold out there, even on sunny days. Add something called "chill factor" and at times it was life-threatening. Troops working on the ramp had to attend briefings on cold weather and its effects on human flesh.

There were a lot of ways to try to stay warm out there. Marv Nystrom recalled:

"The damn cold nights changing engines, so cold you put the ground heater tubes up your parka; sleeping on the ramp so damn tired; trying to align the throttles when it was so cold you couldn't stop shaking."

"We all remember what it was like trying to stay warm for 14 to 16 hours or so while fixing up the Old Girl for the next mission," Ernie Pence recalled. "Sam, in his infinite wisdom, had issued us all Arctic clothing that was marvelous and snuggy-pooh. One major problem, though, was that you had to take it off to get at anything on the bird. We all know what warm skin does when it contacts 20° below metal. But everyone had their particular way to get around that issue. Some wore fat man's clothes with many layers of whatever they could find under it. Others tried to use ground heaters whenever possible. Downside was, that only worked if you were in the cockpit or crawlway. Not too many boost pumps or EGT probes there.

"My garb was a mix of military clothes, civilian clothes and my long underwear. Let's start at the top. Russian pile hat with flaps. Upper torso: t-shirt, navy knit longwear top, fatigue shirt, OD brown army sweater, civilian suede zip-up jacket covered by a black and yellow diamond flight line taxi jacket. Lower torso: jockey shorts, navy knit long underwear

164

bottoms (no trap door), Levis covered by fatigue pants. Feet: one pair black socks, one pair knee length heavy wool socks (2 if below 20 degrees) and mukluks. Hands: a real show stopper; elbow-length buffalo mittens with curly buffalo hair everywhere except the palms and bottom side of thumbs. (Present from my wife's grandmother, who had immigrated to Nebraska when there were still hostile Indians in this part of the country. They were the real McCoy!) There were many who would have stolen them, but how the heck would you have hidden the fact that they were one of a kind. They obviously weren't mil-spec, but due to the weather conditions, a lot of considerate people let it slide."

Sadly, Ernie's prized buffalo mittens met a sad end when they became soaked with JP-4:

"Working at about 0100 hours, I entered the radio truck to order parts. I had been working on the fuel system and some JP had gotten on my gloves. 'Some JP' turned out to be a lot more than I thought! Someone on the radio truck lit a cigarette about 4 feet from me and my gloves blew up. FIRE, SMOKE and the most God Awful smell you ever put your nose to. There was no saving them; I suppose age, old hair and leather had a lot to do with it. This 'SAC Trained Killer' lost a good friend that night."

Not all methods used to stay warm on the ramp were exactly according to SAC Regs:

"We had a late launch and had been working all day to get the aircraft ready," Paul Koski remembered. "The temperature hadn't gotten above 20 degrees. We had to keep checking each other for frostbite. The radio truck would come by now and then and we would get out of the wind and try to warm up a little. We tried to get a ground heater to warm the cockpit and ourselves, but they were either in use or broken.

"The maintenance officer (Maj Crook) came by to check on us and sign the release on some forms. He had a white Cadillac convertible and always had a case of booze in the trunk. He had brought us a 12 oz. foam cup that we thought it might be coffee, but it was Coke. He said, 'Drink a little bit of it and you will warm up.' He had sweetened it with a little bourbon. It tasted pretty good and we did feel a little warmer.

"The flight crew showed up and smelled our breaths and the AC asked if we had been drinking. We didn't lie to the Major, but said we had only one to keep warm. Did he have a fit! He wasn't going to take the aircraft and was going to take action against us. We were really worried until Maj Crook intervened and explained to him we had been out there in the cold and he had given us the drink to warm up. The AC didn't like it, but he took the aircraft, although not until he thoroughly inspected it himself. I think we were very lucky."

February started with the notification from SAC that the Ballistic Missile Early Warning System (BEMEWS) was operational. The system was a series of special radar sites in the far North between Thule and Nome, Alaska. The sites were designed to watch for anything coming over the North Pole from the Soviet Union. They were designed to provide fifteen minutes warning of any missile launch, so the Alert aircraft could be launched and out of nuclear harm's way.

The wing launched six aircraft on Wednesday the 1st to fly a Big Blast ECM mission. The mission was flown according to the usual guidelines except for the recovery at Lincoln. Low clouds and freezing drizzle forced five of the aircraft to divert to Whiteman AFB, Missouri, and then return to Lincoln on the third.

For the last nine months, SAC had been working on the concept of an Airborne Command Post to ensure the "go code" could be transmitted to the strike force in case the main SAC Command Post had been destroyed. Specially modified KC-135s had been taking off from Offutt and flying to a designated area. Then for the next eight hours they would fly a racetrack pattern. They had special equipment on board to be able to transmit the orders to any aircraft that had been launched. Each of these aircraft had a battle staff on board commanded by a general officer. The "Looking Glass" Airborne Command Post became operational on 3 February. From then on there would be one Looking Glass in the air 24 hours a day, seven days a week.

Since February was a short month, with only nineteen days on the flying schedule, it was packed to the limit. There were at least seven aircraft launching each day during the week. The T2A trainer was also packed with crews trying to fill in the squares on the quarterly training board.

Launch crews were getting 53-4217 ready for a training profile mission on 6 February. During their preflight a problem with the bomb bay doors was discovered. They would not close completely. Troubleshooting found one of the motors was not working. A replacement arrived and the troops started changing the unit. While they were working light snow started falling. Before they could finish the snow was really starting to pile up. Just after getting the work completed, the crew was informed the flight had been canceled because of the weather.

Three B-47s left for Spain on 7 February. Billy Lyons recalled a Reflex flight:

"Our first Reflex tour of 1961 was in the January- February time frame. As typical this time of the year, the headwinds were so strong on our departure date from Spain that we couldn't make our missed refueling alternate on the East Coast of Canada. So we sat for a few days waiting for the winds to decrease enough so we could at least get to Goose Bay, Labrador. We launched single ship late in the afternoon. Not much to navigate on except sun shots and that didn't help much. (You don't know where you're going, but you know how fast you're getting there). About an hour after we coasted out and headed across the North Atlantic, I noticed the sun was off our left side when it should have been more or less off the nose, as we were supposed to be headed in a westerly direction. I took a quick true heading shot with the sextant. We were on an almost northerly heading. Headed for Iceland. Didn't want to go there. I advised the crew and the nav quickly computed a three-body fix using the Sun, Moon and Venus. We were lucky we could see the Moon and Venus. We got a good fix and altered course. Made it to Goose Bay with enough fuel, but it could have been a disaster if we hadn't caught the precessing N-1 compass problem."

Freezing rain and drizzle arrived again on 8 February, causing all kinds of problems with flight operations. By mid-afternoon the flight line was covered with a thin glaze of ice and further flight operations were called off. Up in the Alert area, the maintenance troops were trying to get the MB-3 deicer off the shelf and deice the alert birds in case the klaxon went off. It was a losing battle since there were only two units on base.

There was another problem on the Alert ramp. Seems a "Light" Colonel had decried the MB-3 unit would not be used because of the cost of operating the unit and the deicing fluids. Good thing there was a budget-minded officer in charge. After all, it's better to save some money than have the Alert birds deiced in case the flag goes up. Well, since the troops couldn't use the MB-3 unit to deice the birds, get out the rubber hoses and beat the ice off the aircraft.

A Reflex deployment on 21 February was marred by problems. First, there was a four-hour delay in the launch time due to weather at Lincoln. The next problem was in the refueling area. The tankers were nowhere in sight or on the radar screen. The three B-47s had to divert to Goose Bay, where the weather was going downhill in a hurry. Thanks to some good work by GCA, the B-47s made it to DA GOOSE.

They were able to refuel, get some crew rest and ground stage on to Spain the next day. As they approached the coast, they were informed that weather at Morón wasn't the best. In spite of the weather they were able to land; they were a day late, but they had arrived.

The crews that were relieved from Alert departed Morón a day late. They ran into the same rotten weather flying towards the United States. Another added problem was the headwinds, which meant the fuel gauges were decreasing at an alarming rate. Two of the B-47s managed to refuel and get home, while the third had to divert to Pease AFB, New Hampshire, when its tanker missed the refueling area.

Whether going or coming back, Reflex flights were long, tiring and filled with anxious moments. Doug Valen recalled some Reflex memories:

"These flights generally departed Lincoln around 6 pm and arrived in Spain during the early morning hours the next day. It seems like it was normally a two- or three-ship loose formation, but each aircraft was kind of independently navigating.

"The most popular flight lunch for the long flight was bite-size steak, individually wrapped in tin foil. These could be heated up on the amplifier rack along the left side of the cockpit. We carried two large thermos jugs and filled them both with coffee on our first trip. We then learned that we became dehydrated and later carried coffee in one and water in the other.

"We used celestial navigation so, as copilot, I spent a good bit of time hanging on the periscopic sextant above my seat. Incidentally, as a smoker at that time, the open periscopic sextant port was a very efficient ashtray cleaner. It was like a high-power vacuum cleaner and sucked the ashes out very effectively.

"Since most of the flight time was during the hours of darkness, there was not much sightseeing on these trips. At one point, someone in the upper levels of SAC decided that, if we ever went to war, we would be doing the bomb run at the end of a long flight. So they began a program whereby, coming home to Lincoln, we would overfly the base and do a bomb run at the RBS site at Hastings, Nebraska. This would turn a 16-hour flight into an 18-hour flight. This was not well accepted by the flight crews, but we did it.

"We did not normally have a nuclear weapon on board during these flights and there was usually a cargo platform in the bomb bay. Occasionally, a weapon needed to be ferried to Spain and then we carried an unarmed, inert weapon in the bomb bay.

"There was never much conversation between crew members on these flights. We did a 'station check' every hour and the normal checklists that required response, but not much small talk. Everyone was fairly busy and we all just did our thing.

"As I look back on this experience, I usually had mixed feelings about it. Leaving home and family for a month was hard, but flying to Spain, going on Alert, and going R&R—it really was kind of exciting for a small town kid from Butterfield, Minnesota."

Sgt Vern Dixon and his ground crew were getting his bird 53-1902 ready for a flight on 24 February. One of them spotted a crack in the right forward gear door. Now, if the crack wasn't too big, the usual procedure would have been to get out the old drill and drill a small hole at the end of the crack. However, this crack was near the actuator rods, so simple stop drilling wouldn't be a safe fix. The door was replaced.

During February SAC revised the MSC point system. What, again?! There would now be incentive points awarded in certain areas. Thirty incentive points would be awarded per crew for each additional fifty refueling hook ups. Under the MCS points were the name of the game. So if SAC wanted to play the numbers game, so be it. To be a good SAC combat crew, you had to rack up the points on every mission and beat SAC at its own numbers game. It was easy: just drive up to the tanker, hook up, disconnect, then practice a couple of dry hooks ups, then disconnect, back off, move back in and take on the fuel load required. Beaucoup points, but not much practical training other than hooking up with the tanker. Pete Todd recalls how the MCS led to abuses:

"From a crew standpoint, the system assigned point values to certain training activities, bomb runs, celestial navigation, fighter attacks, etc. Crews were 'graded' on the efficiency of their training missions in terms of points per hour of flying time, which tended to corrupt the system and induce the crews to do the dumbest things to stay 'competitive' with their peers. The worst example I know of involved fighter attack training.

"This training was designed to give Air Defense Command fighter crews practice in attacking bombers and bomber crews practice in evading and defeating fighter attacks, potentially valuable training for crews who would have to penetrate enemy air defense nets at high altitude. The training was scheduled in advance with fighter units and was usually conducted under ground-based radar control.

"The MCS assigned something like five points per fighter attack. Some sharp 307th operator figured out that the definition of a fighter attack was flexible so, after rendezvous, he'd have the fighter sit in a high perch to the left rear of the bomber and swing across to a high perch on the right rear. Then reverse, then do it again. Back and forth, five points per pass. Zero useful training for either crew, but thirty MCS points per minute. When the bomber crew came back and 'truthfully' reported hundreds of points for their mission, they looked good on paper, but sacrificed both training time and a slice of their integrity in the process."

News of a major aircraft accident travelled through SAC like wildfire, especially when it involved one of your own. On 28 February the 307th AREFS was undergoing an ORI at Selfridge. Late that afternoon, the flight crew was preparing for a mission as part of a thirteen-tanker stream to refuel bombers. The takeoff appeared to be normal until those on the ground noticed the #1 propeller was being feathered, then the #2 prop seemed to slow down. The aircraft started to descend and clipped several power lines several miles off the end of the runway. The KC-97, 53-331, crashed about two miles from the end of the runway. The five crewmen were fatally injured in the crash. The crew had been stationed at Lincoln before the tankers had moved to Selfridge. Lost in the crash were Capt Lindell Hagood (AC), Lt John Dibble (CP), Lt Robert Lewis (Nav), TSgt Robert Derby (FE), and SSgt Ernest Lemoine (BO).

At the end of February the 307th was still short of manpower, just as they had been from the very start at Lincoln. There were 1,067 airmen and 340 officers assigned to the wing. The A&E Squadron was still 43 officers and airmen below authorized strength. So, once again, Col Berg crunched the numbers and filled out his monthly report for Headquarters.

March arrived in typical Nebraska fashion. Cold weather that gripped the base in February was still hanging over the Midwest. Almost every day during weather briefings there was a chance of freezing drizzle or snow in the forecast. So it was fight the weather to get the aircraft ready, then fight it to get airborne and fight it again to get back on the ground.

Word came in from Omaha outlining Operation Big Switch. The orders stated that the 307th would conduct a special operation involving "seeking out and bombing an RBS attached to a train." The prototype train was being built at the Army Depot at Ogden, Utah. The 307th would be one of the first wings to try it out when it was completed.

## 1961

Low clouds and freezing drizzle greeted the troops reporting for duty on Monday, 6 March. Those who watched KOLN-TV weather the night before knew that yet another weather front was moving towards the patch. There was a slight chance it would go further to the north, but with the base's luck so far this year, it didn't seem likely.

Sure enough, about the time they headed to the mess hall for lunch the wind was starting to pick up and the drizzle had turned to snow. Nice heavy wet stuff that stuck like glue to any surface it touched. They all figured the rest of the day would be interesting trying to get the aircraft free of snow and into the air.

One of the birds on the flying schedule was 53-1853. Her crew chief, Roy Long, had called for the deicer truck and had her ready when the flight crew arrived for preflight. Everything looked good, so they packed the brake chute and closed the compartment doors. The crew climbed aboard and buttoned up for engine start.

At the end of Runway 17, the crew went through the checklist and prepared to launch into the wild gray yonder. Throttles were pushed to a hundred percent and stabilized. Water alcohol switch was pushed and held until they had "Six Reds Out". Brakes were released and they were rolling. After traveling about fifteen hundred feet, the RPM on #1 engine dropped like a rock as the engine went into compressor stall. They hadn't come close to decision speed, so it was a relatively easy aborted takeoff.

The sixth seemed to be a bad day all around. Later, 53-4227 aborted takeoff when an alternator drive shaft sheared during engine run up. Two other launches were canceled late that afternoon when the heavy snow had piled up enough to preclude safe operations.

Snow continued to fall all night and into the morning of the 7th. It was the heavy wet stuff, just right for making nice, fat, round balls to pelt anyone who wasn't looking. Boys will be boys; any time there was enough snow there would be the obligatory snowball sailing through the air, which of course had to be countered by another one flying in the opposite direction, until it escalated to all-out snowball warfare for a few minutes. After the foe had been vanquished it was back to the more serious work of defending the country. By afternoon the snow had piled up to about six inches on the ramp. Two more sorties were canceled that afternoon.

March saw the wing flying the usual schedule of special missions. Six B-47s flew a scheduled Big Blast mission on Friday, 10 March. This was the standard ECM mission to the East coast and back. On the 11th, two sorties were flown to O'Hare under the Clutch Pedal program.

Reflex to Spain continued with some more changes in ATC procedures reflecting more and more civilian usage of the transatlantic airways. There was also to be a maximum attempt to accomplish as many of the 50-8 requirements as possible during the Reflex flights.

March was not the best month for dropping radar bombs on far-away bomb plots. The wing had thirteen unreliable runs during the month. Nine of them were chalked up against one bomb plot alone. Two bad runs were made on the Minneapolis site. Anyone who flew in the nose of a B-47 and peered into the radar bombsight will tell you that the secret to hitting the target is to have good, accurate information entered into the bomb system.

Larry Boggess relates some of the fine points of hitting the target:

"In a bomb run, you are solving the wind problem by taking wind runs on the radar scope. If the system knows the wind, the system will track what the cross hairs are on, but if the wind is wrong, they will drift off the target. This is most of the problem. To start off, you need to know your altitude above the ground, so you need to measure the altitude at some known point near the target at which you know the ground elevation. You will be flying a pressure altitude during the run, but there should be little variation between the measuring point and the target.

"The altitude above the target, or burst altitude, is used to determine the ballistics. You need to know two things: first is the actual time of fall (ATF). This is in seconds and is looked up in a chart. Second is the Trail. Trail is the distance in feet that you are beyond the target when the bomb explodes. On an RBS-scored run, this is determined by the scoring site by actual measured altitude and is used to score where the bomb hits.

"Since most targets are something you can't see (e.g., the aiming point may be a geographic point between multiple targets that you intend to destroy by a single bomb), offsets are used as aiming points. The system is given the distance in feet North or South, and East or West from the actual target to the aiming point. This is computed and put into the system so you can 'aim' at a point easily seen on the radar and be able to hit the target as desired. Aiming points are many times a point of land-water contrast, such as the corner of a dam, end of a bridge, center of a bridge, a large building or whatever is available. If there was enough time and a second offset was available, an offset could be changed during the Large Charge run and still have time to make the second drop.

"During the bomb run you are solving the wind problem by making wind runs, as many as possible. Once you are close enough (less than 60 miles) to set the counters on the target and switch in the offset, you begin the actual bomb run.

"Once you are on target, you have the pilot center the PDI, then the bomb/nav system can steer the plane to the release point. At ten seconds to go, the nav turns on the 'tone'. When the tone breaks, it signals 'bomb away' to the RBS site. When they score the drop, they measure the ground speed and use ballistics to determine ATF from your measured altitude and back up the trail distance along your heading. It is rumored that if you 'kick' the heading a few degrees, you can impact your score to the right or left if you were not really on the target at release.

"There were also optical bomb sights and a 'B' scope for bombing. The 'B' scope was a magnified radar picture that you saw with your left eye and the right eye viewed the optical sight. Optics were rarely used as most targets or aiming points were usually obscured by clouds. These two systems were line-of-sight and not north-oriented as was the regular radar scope."

All too often, the bomb run didn't go exactly as it had been planned during mission planning. Doug Valen recalled one that missed:

"Norm Menke was a first rate bomb/nav guy and earned a reputation for excellence. But, he wasn't perfect and we pitched a few bombs out there that haven't hit yet. One night, we had some problems and got a bad bomb. As we departed the RBS site, Norm admitted he screwed things up by setting the 'offsets' in backwards. Many crewmembers at this point would start thinking up ways to explain this simple mistake. We ended up in front of some kind of board, and when Norm was called on to explain his error, he simply said, 'I set the offsets in backwards!' I think the board was prepared to hear a litany of feeble excuses and was completely taken aback by the simple truth! I'll never forget the looks on their faces. It was kind of like Jack Nicholson's line-'You can't handle the truth!'"

On 28 March President Kennedy gave a speech on the National Defense Budget. In his speech he mentioned the accelerated phase out of the B-47. He also mentioned SAC would have to increase its alert posture. This was the first hint that SAC would begin to put fifty percent of their bombers on fifteen-minute ground response alert.

March had been a month filled with fighting the weather during the first weeks of the month. It appeared it would go out like a lamb when spring-like weather dominated the latter part of the month.

The 307th chalked up a pretty good month. One hundred percent of the 50-8 training requirements were filled. The wing flew twenty-six high-

# Cold War Cornhuskers: The 307th Bomb Wing Lincoln Air Force Base Nebraska 1955-1965

altitude RBS runs and scored 96% effective. It was noted in the month-end report that crew error was responsible for forty-two unreliable bomb runs. To find the problem and help correct the situation, the Deputy Commander for Operations interviewed the crews.

April got off to a rather bad start on Monday the 3rd. The wing suffered two late takeoffs. During takeoff the water injection on 52-0353 failed to kick in. After taxiing back, everything checked out fine during troubleshooting and 053 launched an hour late. The right wing tank fuel valve on 53-1918 stuck, causing a fuel leak. Repair of the problem caused a two-hour delay in the launch.

Three B-47s launched for Reflex on Tuesday, 4 April. It was a routine Reflex deployment if you consider spending over twelve hours in the air as being routine. By this time SAC had been sending aircraft across the pond for several years so, yes, considering the basic operation, Reflex had become a matter of routine. If you consider how it disrupted families, stress of flying those hours and then going on Alert after arriving, Reflex was anything but routine.

Putting aircraft on Alert and keeping them there was a work-intensive process. One of the most tedious and dangerous procedures was loading the nuclear weapons. First-generation nuclear weapons were large, bulky and hard to handle. Every time an aircraft was scheduled for Alert, a weapon had to be taken out of storage, checked, then transported to the flight line. Then it had to be literally manhandled into position and hoisted into the bomb bay. Depending on the type of weapon, it could take four to six hours to load a weapon into a B-47.

Second-generation weapons helped simplify the upload process, but they still had to be loaded one at a time by the checklist. This was about to change. On 11 April a conference was held with the wing staff and project officers for Project Clip In. The conference outlined modifications that would be made to the 307th aircraft to reconfigure them to carry up to four Mark-28 weapons.

The bomb bay would be modified to accept the MHU-20C Clip In assembly. To accomplish this, the bomb bay would be reconfigured with the MAU-5A rack assembly. When all of the subassemblies were in place, each B-47 would be able to carry four weapons and hit four different targets. Maj John Mealka was the project officer; Capt Arnold Hollenber would be his assistant. TSgt A. G. Oredson was the NCOIC for the project.

The conference brought out a tight schedule for the project. Four B-47s at a time would be pulled off the line for the modification. It was estimated it would take a least four days to complete the modifications on each aircraft. Teams from Tinker AFB and Boeing would be on hand to do the work.

Wednesday, April 12th, was just another day at Lincoln Air Force Base. People reported for duty and crews manned the Alert pad. Several B-47s launched for routine missions to hone their SAC skills. Later that afternoon, six birds launched for a mass gas refueling over the Dakotas. Just routine, but this would prove to be a historic day on planet Earth. That night on the evening news, it was reported the Soviet Union had beaten the USA into space again. Soviet Cosmonaut Yuri Gagarin was launched into space and made one orbit of the Earth. His flight lasted one hour and forty-eight minutes from launch to landing. Reaction to the first man in space ran from A to Z. Scientifically, it was a great step forward. As with Sputnik several years previously, the U.S. was going to take a back seat to the "Great" Soviet Union in space.

SAC's reaction was to increase readiness to counter anything the Soviets might try. With BMEWS on line, SAC was certain they could spot any missile launch from behind the Iron Curtain. SAC Looking Glass aircraft were in the air to relay the "Go Code" if needed. At Lincoln, each wing put two more birds on ground alert just in case.

Six B-47s launched out of Lincoln on Thursday the 14th for a mass gas refueling. Their flight took them up into South Dakota, where they rendezvoused with their tankers and refueled. After they completed the mass gas refueling, the bombers slipped away from the tankers and flew their individual profiles.

The 818th Air Division sent the 307th the Operations Order for Quick Kick Bravo. This plan would be used for a no-notice ORI by either SAC or the 2nd Air Force. The operation called for heavyweight take off, celestial nav, rendezvous with tankers and refueling, low-level nav leg, Short Look RBS runs and runs on Nike sites. The 307th would launch two aircraft per cell in four waves with half an hour between waves. The exercise would take three days to complete. It was noted that the 307th would be vulnerable for the next nine months.

Some of the Alert crews had finished chow early and plunked themselves in front of the television for the nightly news on April 17th. The big news of the night centered on the island of Cuba. That day, Cuban exiles had landed in an ill-fated attempt to wrest their country from the grasp of Fidel Castro's pro-Communist regime. When the Kennedy Administration opted not to give further U.S. military support the invasion crumbled. The Bay of Pigs fiasco would go down as Kennedy's first major foreign policy blunder. Again, SAC increased readiness in case the situation in the world started heating up any more than it was.

A Clutch Pedal practice dispersal flight to O'Hare was flown on the 19th of the month. 53-4222 flew a standard profile training flight, landing at Chicago. After refueling and crew rest, the B-47 returned to Lincoln on the 20th.

Project Clip In was scheduled to get underway on the 24th. The work hit a big roadblock right off the bat. The adaptors needed to configure the Mark-28 weapons had not arrived. 53-1909 had been towed to the docks for the project. Since the parts hadn't arrived, the technicians spent the day moving templates around and marking the position for the adaptors to be placed in the bomb bay. Again, it was a case of the best-laid plans of mice and men going astray.

The *Jet Scoop* appeared at the usual spots on base on Friday, the 28th. The 307th Crew Chiefs dominated the Honor Totem Pole for on-time take offs.

Robert Bergene: 53-1906 = 151
Kenneth McGee: 53-2143 = 119
James Yandle: 53-2392 = 108
James Booth: 53-1911 = 87

The month-end report to 2nd Air Force and SAC showed the 307th had turned in a good month. There had been 159 air refuelings scheduled and 159 accomplished. In the bombing category, the wing was scored with a 93% effective rating. The Short Look Large Charge bombing was the lowest score with a 91% effective rating.

Project Clip In finally got started on May 1st. With almost a half a month lost in delays for parts, it was decided to have some of the work done at the modification centers at Tulsa, Oklahoma, and Marietta, Georgia. Aircraft would be ferried to the two locations, then return to Lincoln after the modification was completed. With work going on in three different places, the project was expected to be completed in record time.

May's first Reflex deployment left on the 1st of the month. Capt Leroy McMath led the flight in 52-0353. There had been no changes in the basic operation plan for the month. The three aircraft flew the northern route, refueling near Newfoundland, then heading on to Spain.

With the 307th listed as vulnerable for an ORI at any time, 10 aircraft and crews were launched for a practice ORI mission on the second of the month. For the next five days, the wing would launch aircraft each day to fly the ORI profile. Although it was practice, everyone played it out like it was the real thing. After all, the outcome of the real ORI could depend on how well they flew during the practice.

During the practice mission on Friday, May 5th, the nine B-47s hooked up with the tankers for a mass gas refueling. The tankers were KC-135s from Ellsworth Air Force Base near Rapid City, South Dakota. The six tankers were waiting in the refueling track over western Minnesota. Everyone in the flight got their briefed offload.

While the wing practiced for the ORI, our nation took a step towards closing the gap in the space race. At Cape Canaveral, Alan Sheppard sat in his Mercury spacecraft waiting for the countdown to reach zero. There were delays after delays until, finally, the countdown resumed and the launch clock reached zero. The Redstone rocket didn't have enough power to get Sheppard into orbit. His suborbital flight lasted about fifteen minutes. It wasn't a spectacular orbital flight like the Russians, but at least the United States was on the space race scoreboard.

During the afternoon of May 9th huge cumulus clouds billowed skyward, bringing on the threat of thunderstorms. That afternoon three crews were getting ready for Reflex to Spain. About 1530 the clouds were close enough to Lincoln for the rumble of thunder to be heard across the base. Within the hour the flight line was pelted by rain and wind. The Reflex deployment schedule for launch at 1750 was delayed an hour so the storms could move on to the east.

Capt Paul Pudwill and his crew lifted off the runway in 53-1887 at 1850 and climbed towards Beatrice. They were followed at one-minute intervals by 53-1932 and 53-2139. Over Beatrice, the B-47s turned to the northeast and continued climbing to altitude.

Ahead, they could see the building thunderheads that caused the delay in their launch. Using radar and the good old Mark-1 eyeball, they managed to snake their way between the clouds. It was a little bumpy going through a couple of valleys between the storms, but the flight got through without any major problems.

There was another line of "thunderbumpers" building in front of the Spain-bound birds. They got clearance from ATC to deviate from their flight plan and skirt the clouds by flying to the north, then zigging back to their original route. All of the cloud skirting was using fuel. The tankers would be a welcome sight so they could refuel. After refueling the rest of the flight was a piece of cake, so to speak.

Project Clip In was not progressing as it had been planned. Parts were not arriving within the scheduled time frame. There were also problems scheduling time in the nose docks to complete the work. In view of that, SAC sent word to increase the movement of B-47s to the depots for modification. At the same time, priority was to be given to scheduling of aircraft locally to expedite the program.

The monthly Big Blast mission was scheduled for Wednesday, the 17th. Five aircraft launched and headed north over the Canadian wilderness. After flying the route north they turned back towards the States. They spread out to maintain a ten-mile lateral separation and were stacked up from 29,000 to 31,000 feet.

Approaching the H-Hour Control Line, they started tuning up to play their music with a "parrot check". For ECM scoring, the lead aircraft reported to a GCI site and let them know Tan Glove was in the area. For the next hour and a half the 307th's Tan Glove aircraft would fly straight and level, play their music, take no evasive action and record each lock on they detected.

After playing targets, the Tan Glove leader again identified the flight. After finishing the rest of the flight checked in with the lead aircraft, then turned their navigation and anti-collision lights on. The flight headed for Detroit, Michigan, to meet the tankers for a mass gas refueling. Although it was dark and they couldn't see the markings on the tails, the voices on the radio sounded familiar. Yep, the tankers were from the 307th AREFS. They had flown out of Selfridge to meet their old friends and make sure they had enough fuel to get home. When the B-47s had their fuel in the tanks they headed back towards Lincoln.

There was a Reflex deployment back to the states on May 18th. The flight back was uneventful until the aircraft coasted in. There was a problem with the tankers. For a few hair-raising minutes there was no sight of them. No radio, no radar, no visual. Then, all of a sudden, they were on the radio and radar. The B-47s moved in and got a drink of JP-4. There never was an explanation about where the tankers had been.

Another Clutch Pedal deployment was flown on May 29th. 53-1843 and her crew landed at O'Hare after a regular planned mission. The crew found there was still no single point refueling so they had to be refueled by trucks. There were also no facilities for liquid oxygen. The taxiways were just wide enough to accommodate the B-47. Security guards were flown in from Bunker Hill Air Force Base, Indiana.

The last Reflex deployment of May departed Lincoln on May 30th. That afternoon 53-1917, 53-2143 and 53-4219 launched at 1750 to begin the long flight to Spain. Arriving in Spain, they relieved the crews scheduled to return to Lincoln or go on R&R.

During the three-week Reflex tour the crews would be on Alert for a week. The second week was usually spent on R&R, with the last week on Alert again before cycling back to the states. A lot of the crews could hardly wait for the week of R&R. It gave them a chance to hop on the R&R Gooney Bird and see some of the sights Europe had to offer. Dale Christians had this R&R memory:

"One time while pulling alert at Morón AB, Spain, the night before going on a C-47 down to Palma de Majorca, Spain, we had gone to Seville and drunk too much of that good Spanish wine. The next day on the plane, I was stretched out on the seat with my parachute on when Matyas yelled, 'Bail Out'. I jumped up and was almost to the door when they reeled me in. They all thought it was funny. HA HA! I didn't."

Billy Lyons offered a couple of R&R memories:

"I had heard about the city of Palma de Majorca in the Balearic Islands off the East Coast of Spain. We blasted off in the Base Flight C-47 and, after arrival on Majorca, went to the Bahia Palace Hotel, supposedly the best hotel on the island. Our first day there, I went down to the dining room for "supper" about 5:30 PM. and found the dining room locked up tight. After pulling and knocking on the door, one of the waiters came to the door and advised me that the dining room did not open till half past eight! I told him I would probably be starved to death by that time, but somehow I survived. I met some of the other guys on R&R and we went to the hotel bar to wait out the opening of the dining room. We finally got seated about 9 PM. I didn't know if I liked the idea of not having dinner until 9 PM, but got used to it and later found out it was best to adjust to the customs of the country we were in.

"On our next Reflex, we went to Rome on R&R. Good experience. Lots of culture. Next R&R went to Palma again- getting springtime- good time to rent scooters, go to the beach, get some sun and drink some beer. One of the copilots had a mishap on his scooter, hitting the median of a divided street and sliding across the brick street on his face. Didn't look too good, but he could still pull Alert.

"Then, there was the guy that went over a cliff on his scooter on the way out to the beach. Seems he was looking back at his fellow R&R guys on their scooters as they raced out to the beach. He broke his arm and couldn't pull Alert. No more scooters for a while.

# Cold War Cornhuskers: The 307th Bomb Wing Lincoln Air Force Base Nebraska 1955-1965

"In the fall of 1960, three of us 'bullet proof and invincible' copilots put together an R&R trip to spend time in Madrid, Paris, Copenhagen and back to Madrid. We made it, had a great time in all these cities that were new to us, but got back to the base broke and worn out. I had money from several countries and went to the money exchange window at the airport at Copenhagen and pulled out my coin currency from these different countries and had a grand total of $1.85 US money. But, we got back to Madrid where we could cash a check at the club and made it back to Morón to pull the last week of Alert."

May went into the books as a very good month for the 307th. The wing scored almost 100% in all areas. The flight crews chalked up 100% reliability in night celestial navigation, high altitude bombing and low-level bombing. There were 153 air refuelings scheduled and the wing made every one of them. The wing flew 212 sorties and spent 1,619 hours in the air.

Clip In continued to fall behind. Parts arrived late due to supply problems at Tinker AFB. By the end of May, the wing had twenty B-47s modified for the Clip In system. Several B-47s were transferred to the 307th from the 321st Bomb Wing at Grand Forks AFB, South Dakota, that were already upgraded with the Clip In system. When Clip In was completed, loading the aircraft with weapons for Alert would be easier and take a lot less time.

June started with events across the world that would have a profound effect on SAC and the 307th. President Kennedy had flown to Vienna to meet with Soviet leader Nikita Khrushchev. All hoped that the meeting between the two leaders would ease world tensions. The Soviet leader believed the younger U.S. President was weak in his foreign policy commitments and could be pushed around. Therefore, he maintained a hard line during the meetings. He went so far as to suggest the Allies should pull out of Berlin altogether. Kennedy was stunned by the boldness of the Russian leader. The trip to Vienna was another complete foreign policy disaster for the new Kennedy Administration.

When Kennedy returned to Washington, he called several high level meetings with his military advisors to plan how they would meet the growing Soviet threat in Europe. The advisors were part of the Defense Department under Secretary of Defense Robert S. McNamara.

McNamara had been the president of the Ford Motor Company before being chosen by President Kennedy to head the Pentagon. McNamara came to Washington without much respect for or understanding of the military. He packed the offices of his department with a group of young, number-crunching advisors who would become known as the "Whiz Kids".

One of his first acts as the new Secretary of Defense was to order the rapid phase-out of the B-47. Everyone knew the B-47 force was aging; however, at the time it was still the only bomber in sufficient numbers to maintain a strong deterrent posture. He believed the money saved could be better used for the *development* of other weapons systems. The key here is these future weapons systems were still in the development phase and not operational.

He cut the budget in some areas so there would be more money for his pet projects, like the TFX fighter to be used by both the Air Force and Navy. The TFX would later become the F-111, and would experience so many problems in development that the Navy finally lost all interest in it. It would later perform to expectations in Southeast Asia, but that employment was almost ten years away.

His "rob Peter to pay Paul" style would become a trademark of his administration. His budget realignment reduced the per diem compensation that Reflex crews would be paid. After all, they were getting "three hots and a cot" just being in the military; what more did they need? His scrooge-like attitude towards the military caused financial and mental hardships for those who served in the military. While the Joint Chiefs of Staff fought for higher pay scales, McNamara cut the military budget while increasing the pay scales for government employees in the Pentagon.

His centralized micro-management of the department became another hallmark of his tenure. It took most of the control away from field commanders and placed it in the Pentagon. This number-crunching, central control style would have profound effects in the mismanagement of the military years later in the jungles of Vietnam and the skies over Hanoi.

His disdain and contempt for the military was evident by the way he would completely disregard the advice given to him from the Joint Chiefs of Staff. If it didn't come from his "Whiz Kids", it wasn't considered good information. After all, they had the statistics to prove what they were saying. It didn't take very long for the military to start feeling the same way towards their chief in the Pentagon. Col Sigmund Alexander served as a navigator in the 100th Bomb Wing at Pease AFB. He recalled McNamara was referred to as "Sweet Old Bob". SOB, for short.

After President Kennedy met with his advisors, plans were formulated to meet the possible crisis that was beginning to brew over Berlin. There would be a gradual build up of military readiness. For SAC, that meant putting more bombers on alert and sending more aircraft to forward bases. All of this with the manpower available at the time.

The first Reflex deployment for June left Lincoln on the 5th. That Tuesday, the three B-47s departed at 1830 due to a weather delay. A line of thunderstorms hit Lincoln about 1700 with gusty winds and heavy rain. The Reflex aircraft had to have their refueling schedule modified due to the delay.

Training flights to fill the 50-8 squares were being launched on a daily basis. When the flights returned, the crews would go through debriefing, then head for the personal equipment area to put their equipment away. Doug Valen recalled:

"Sometime in 1961, Crew R-03 (Capt Timmons, Lt Valen, Lt Menke) had flown a training mission and returned to Lincoln AFB sometime after midnight. After the maintenance debrief and normal paperwork requirements, we were in the 370th Bomb Squadron locker/equipment room putting away our gear and getting ready to go home to our families for the night. For some reason, I started humming the old gospel hymn titled *I'll Walk in the Garden Alone*. It really surprised me when Bud Timmons kind of joined in and it was clear he was familiar with the words. So the humming turned into singing, and we even harmonized a bit.

"When we came to the end of the song, we looked up and LtCol Steve Mattick, the 370th Squadron Commander, was standing in the doorway listening. He explained his presence at that late hour by saying he couldn't get to sleep and had some work to do, so came over to the Squadron and was working in his office down the hall. He heard a song that he remembered from his distant past and came down the hall to see who was singing. He knew my father was a Lutheran minister, but was not aware that Bud may have been versed in gospel hymnology. He said he enjoyed our rendition and went back to his office.

"About 30 years later, I ran into Col Mattick at a 307th Bomb Wing reunion--at Lincoln, Nebraska, I believe. I was sure he would not remember me, so I introduced myself. He looked at me and said, 'Your Daddy was a preacher wasn't he?' I said, 'Yes he was,' and then he said, 'I still remember that night when you and Bud Timmons were singing *I'll Walk in the Garden Alone* about 2 AM in the Squadron Building'. He said he had always liked that song and enjoyed hearing it that night."

Project Clip In continued during June. Aircraft modified locally were requiring an average of four days to be brought up to TOC (Tech Order Compliance). Aircraft returning from the Modification Depots were

*170*

coming back with discrepancies in the Tech Order that required more work locally. The situation was causing a general slowdown of the project.

An example of the problem was found when 53-2278 returned from the depot. Inspection of the work found it did not meet the project Tech Order. She was sent to the docks on June 13th and required another 160 man-hours to complete the work. 53-1843 came back from Tulsa with seven defects. She went to the docks on June 15th and wasn't released until June 30th.

Capt Russell Holst's Crew S-64 was pulling Alert duty on June 14th. They were scheduled to fly a training mission on the 18th after they got off alert. He and his crew spent part of the day planning for the round robin mission. They would complete both high- and low-level bomb runs and a celestial navigation leg. Lt Thomas "Wally" Wesner, copilot, figured the weight and balance and filled out the forms for the mission. With the planning completed, all they had to do was wait to be relieved from Alert.

About 1730 on Sunday, June 18th, Capt Holst and his crew arrived at Base Operations for final flight briefing. Along with copilot Wesner, the crew was made up of Capt Albert Marinich, Navigator, and Capt Allen Matson would fly in the fourth man position.

The crew was informed their aircraft for the flight, 53-2111, had been serviced with more fuel than their mission plan had called for. No problem; they made some quick calculations on the load adjuster and refigured the new weight and balance, along with takeoff speed and distance. They calculated a new takeoff roll of 9,400 feet.

The weather briefing was conducted by Lt George Miller from the 26th Weather Squadron. The weather locally was good: high scattered clouds, visibility at fifteen miles, temperature 71 degrees with light wind from the south. Weather along the route was good. No major problems would hamper the mission. Everything looked copacetic.

Grabbing their flight gear and lunches, the crew left Base Operations, reported to 2111 and began their preflight. The walkaround went like clockwork. No major leaks, just the usual expected smears and smudges. Engines were started and 2111 taxied out of her slot on the ramp twenty minutes before scheduled take off time. Copilot Wesner monitored the engine instruments while they taxied and everything was normal. This was scheduled to be a rolling takeoff, so the crew held short of Runway 17 and went through their last-minute checks.

Capt Holst called the tower at 2101 for takeoff clearance. They still had a few minutes before they were supposed to take off. There was some small talk about the nice weather and that Wesner was going on leave next week. A couple of last-minute checks and they were ready to roll.

Turning onto Runway 17, Capt Holst pushed the six throttles forward to a hundred per cent and lined up on the center stripe. Water alcohol injection came on with six red lights out. They were rolling on time at 2115 local time. 2111 began moving down the runway, speed building with each turn of the turbines.

Wesner scanned the panel. "Coming up on 70 knots." "70 knots-- NOW!," called Holst. In the nose, Marinich replied "Hack!" and started his stopwatch for the acceleration check. At the end of the check their speed was 125 knots, three knots higher than the computed airspeed. Engine instruments were normal. Wesner glanced out of the canopy, but in the dark he couldn't see much. More important, he didn't see anything indicating trouble, like fire coming from the engines.

Men in the control tower were watching 2111 on her takeoff roll like they were supposed to. About 1000-2,000 feet after the timing check the tower saw sparks coming from the #6 engine. The sparks turned to flames, shooting five to fifteen feet to the rear of the engine. The tower called 2111 to warn them. The warning fell on deaf headphones. The crew had changed to the departure control frequency before starting to roll.

About 9,000 feet down the runway Holst remarked, "We should be getting off soon." Airspeed was about 145 knots, not the planned 163 knots. Something was wrong! Ever so slowly the airspeed came up. As they approached the 12,000 foot mark of the takeoff roll, Wesner took his right hand off the throttles and wrapped his fingers around the yoke. As he did, he could feel Holst pull the yoke back slightly to the take off position. 2111 did not respond by leaving the runway like she should. Holst applied a little more back pressure on the yoke; 2111 struggled into the air, but as the nose came up, the aircraft began to buffet as speed fell off towards stalling. Holst pushed the yoke forward to get the nose down a little. The buffeting continued as 2111 approached stalling. The right wing started to drop. Holst yelled, "LET'S GET OUT!"

Wally Wesner reached down and grabbed the handles on his ejection seat and pulled them upward. The canopy blew off into space. In a millisecond Wesner glanced down at the airspeed indicator: 150 knots. The right wing was now at about a forty-five degree bank as Wesner's seat fired him out of 2111. His zero-delay lanyard worked to perfection; the seat fell away and his chute started to billow.

2111 continued to roll to the right until it hit the ground 2,950 feet from the end of Runway 17. For a moment, Wesner thought he was going to be caught in the billowing fireball of the crash. Whether it was luck or perhaps air movement by the concussion, Wesner swung once in his chute and landed near a country lane off the end of the runway.

By the time Capt Holst ejected the aircraft was beyond forty-five degrees right wing down attitude. There wasn't enough time for him to separate from the seat and the chute to open. The other crewmen had no chance to escape from the falling B-47.

Paul Koski lived at the Ring Trailer Park on West "O" Street. The trailer park was about a mile or two from the end of the runway. Paul remembered that sad night:

"My wife and I were in our trailer, which was about one or two miles from the end of the runway. We had all of our windows open, trying to get some fresh air. There were stock car races going on around five blocks away and you could hear the noise of the cars as they raced around the course. We also had aircraft taking off all evening.

"I heard this one aircraft, the engines sounded like they had changed pitch. I told my wife that aircraft was in trouble and ran to the door. I wanted to make sure we weren't in the path of the aircraft and we could get out of the way if it crashed. When I got to the door and looked west, the whole sky lit up as the aircraft went in. It was less than a mile from our house.

"The next thing I knew, the people from the stock car races were streaming by with their cars to see the accident. My wife asked. 'Why don't you go see if you can help?' I said, 'There's nothing that anyone could do!'"

Great White Father had promised to take SAC BRAT to the races at Capital Beach that Sunday night. It was quite a night for car racing. Louie Quotroccii and his crew from IGA Food King had managed to win their heat in #17 and were going to run against the dreaded purple 4x in the main event.

The racetrack at Capital Beach was about a mile and a half from the runway. There had been several B-47 take offs that night and young SAC BRAT watched them take off like he always did. The bleachers at the racetrack were a great place to watch B-47s take off and the stock car races. Kind of the best of both worlds.

Just before the main event another B-47 was taking off. "He doesn't sound right," remarked Great White Father. SAC BRAT focused on the runway to the northwest. He could see the B-47; there appeared to be fire coming from the right side of the plane and it was heading towards the ground. Then the plane went behind some trees and disappeared. A second later the sky turned to a brilliant orange for a moment, then returned to dusk. The youngster turned to his dad and asked if they should go and try to help. His dad's answer was direct and simple. "Sit still son. There's nothing we can do to help them. They're in God's hands now."

Fire units from the base and Lincoln converged on the crash site to fight the fire before it could spread any further. One of the trucks spotted someone waving at them from a ditch near the billowing flames; it was Capt Wesner, the copilot. He was taken to the base hospital for treatment of some cuts, bruises and further observation.

There was another accident that night. Col Walter Duch saw the accident and jumped into a car. He went pell-mell down the taxi way and onto the end of the runway. He went over the bank of Oak Creek and down into the creek bed. The car was demolished and Col Duch suffered a broken leg.

The next morning, the first phase of the investigation began with documenting the entire area with photos. Photographs were taken from almost every conceivable angle, including aerials. All of the records on 2111 were gathered for close examination. As soon as the doctors allowed, Capt Wesner was interviewed in great detail concerning the entire mission, from flight planning to the moment he landed after ejecting.

On Monday, the troops reported for duty at the usual 0745. There was a visible air of sadness within the ranks. They all knew the wing had lost an aircraft and crew. It was never good to lose a bird; it always left a knot in your gut. They had to move on to the work of the day. Every now and then, they couldn't help but take time for a momentary glance towards the south end of the runway where 2111 lay in pieces.

On Tuesday, June 20th, there was the usual weekly Reflex deployment, but this one was a little different. There were four B-47s heading to Spain. The fourth aircraft was part of the gradual force build up in response to the Soviet threats in Berlin.

The 307th flew the monthly Big Blast mission on Friday, June 21st. Six aircraft launched for the eight-hour mission at 1800 and headed north into Canada. Near Churchill, they turned and started for their ECM target near Detroit. They turned on their music and played the tunes until they were about two hundred miles south of the target. After logging all of the radar lock-ons they turned for home.

Shortly after the loss of 2111, an accident investigation board was formed to probe the accident and determine what had happened to cause the loss of the crew and the three million dollar B-47. Glen Hesler was one of the officers on the board. He recalled the board was chaired by a major general from 2nd Air Force headquarters. To Glen, it appeared the General was in a hurry to get the investigation over. Glen recalled feeling ill at ease with the chairman of the board. To the general, the cause of the accident was obvious, "PILOT ERROR". Glen disagreed and could never fully accept the general's manner of conducting the investigation. Another officer serving on the board was Robert Byrom:

"I had been assigned to help investigate the takeoff accident of Russ Holst and his crew as the Wing Operations member. The investigation went fast, too fast I thought, for the board to look carefully at all possible causes. We knew that one outboard engine had lost RPM and power, but there were other factors that could have caused loss of thrust and increased drag, like water alcohol injection malfunction, brake or tire problem, inadvertent deployment of one of the drag chutes on the airplane. I thought we should look harder at the performance charts because they showed the same degraded takeoff performance with loss of an outboard or inboard engine."

Another Reflex deployment left Lincoln on Tuesday, June 27th. This flight consisted of four aircraft, again reflecting the increased Alert build up and the situation brewing in Berlin. There were a few anxious moments during arrival at Morón. High winds blowing across the Spanish plain made landing interesting after a long flight when fatigue was creeping into the bodies of the crewmen.

Problems at the depots were causing a lot of extra work locally for the Clip In project. 53-1872 came out of the docks on June 27th. She had returned from Tulsa and was found to have 97 defects in the Clip In modification. Defects included oversized holes, bent bolts, improper trimming, and in general the same unreliable sheet metal work that had been found on other aircraft coming back from the depots.

On June 29th, 53-1829 arrived back at the patch from Marietta, Georgia. To say the least, she was a mess. There were 44 defects noted. There were structural repairs that had to be redone. Holes were drilled too close together. 25 bushings had to be made at Lincoln. Additional engineering assistance was required from Tinker AFB.

Tuesday, July 4th, was a routine day on the flight line. Launch crews got four birds off on Reflex deployment. That night, there was a gala fireworks display at Bowling Lake. The Nebraska sky lit up as star shells burst and cascaded to earth in beautiful multiple colors. Since the fireworks were fired from the island the resident sheep herd had been brought ashore for the night.

The Reflex flight was treated to a beautiful sight as they flew towards the East. From the air they could look down and see fireworks being fired from various cites along their route. It was an interesting and beautiful change from the usual night flight for the Spain-bound fliers.

The Kennedy Administration had taken a look at the policies regarding nuclear response to any Soviet threat around the world. Under President Eisenhower the policy had been fairly simple. If the United States were attacked, we would respond with everything we had. Kennedy believed this "Massive Retaliation" strategy was dangerous and lacked credibility. The administration came up with the idea of Flexible Response. They also made moves to enhance the military's ability to respond to a non-nuclear incident or limited war.

The concept of Flexible Response would be fine as long as the other side played by the same rules. However, the Soviet Bloc countries had a vast superiority in ground forces along the Iron Curtain. Who could say if they would use their conventional superiority or use tactical nukes if they made a move to throw the Allies out of Berlin? The old axiom of get there first with the most was being replaced by, "Let's wait and see what you got, then we'll let you know what we plan to do."

This policy under the Kennedy Administration would eventually allow the Soviet Union to build its nuclear capability until it was equal to the United States, thus spawning the concept of Mutual Assured Destruction (MAD) if either side pulled the trigger.

With this change in policy, the Soviets saw a possible weakness to exploit. They began turning the screws on the isolated city of Berlin. It was getting harder to cross the East-West border. There were also reports of military forces being increased along the checkpoints. A strong debate between the Allies and the Soviets began at the United Nations. As the debate heated up, it was fairly apparent the world was heading for another Berlin Crisis.

On Monday, July 10th, members of the 3980th Strategic Standardization Group arrived at the base. They arrived with no advanced notice in a KC-135 that pulled into the pattern and declared a low fuel situation. It had all the bad smells of an ORI. After all, the wing was vulnerable for one.

It wasn't an ORI, but for the next twelve days they would evaluate crews of the 307th. Crewmembers were given oral and written examinations on Alert procedures, EWO procedures, security, mission planning and other areas. Then, it was out to the planes to fly a mission under the watchful eye of the "stan-eval" member. This kind of flight was standard procedure using wing personnel and they were tough. The check flights under the watchful eye of the 3980th were murder. Four crewmen failed the oral and written exams. They were tested again on July 15th and passed. The failure on the first series cost the wing MCS points for the overall score.

During the flight evaluations the crews were under the microscope for the entire time, from mission planning to final debriefing. Absolutely everything was scored under the watchful eye of the umpire. Everything had to be done right, according to SACREGS and the checklist.

One crew failed the check ride evaluation. Along with the written test failure the wing scored a total of 92.9%. Passing for the 2nd Air Force was 83%, and passing for SAC was 87%. Overall, the 307th had scored well enough to place the wing in the top 2% of the wings scored in the last several months.

While the 307th was being evaluated, two crews from the 307th were competing in the 2nd Air Force Bombing Competition. The competition was held to determine who would represent the 2nd Air Force in the big event at Fairchild AFB, Washington, in September. The crews staged out of Lincoln and flew special routes that had been developed by 2nd Air Force for the competition.

The 307th Bomb Wing was represented in the 2nd Air Force competition by a crew commanded by Maj William Stringfellow. His copilot was Lt Yale Davis and Capt Donald Kellum flew as Navigator/Bombardier. Maj Dale Christians was aircraft commander of the other crew representing the wing. His crewmen were Capt Donivan Jordan, copilot, and Capt Charles Schisler, Nav/Bomb. Dale's usual navigator, Maj Noble Timmons, had to be replaced at the last minute due to a bout with the mumps.

The *Jet Scoop* headlines for July 21st proclaimed "307TH NAMED BEST IN 2ND AIR FORCE." Maj Stringfellow's crew took top honors with Best Overall Crew, Best Crew in Bombing and Best Crew in Navigation. Maj Christians' crew was second in navigation, making it a one-two sweep for the 307th in that category.

The two crews would be headed to Fairchild in September for the SAC-wide "World Series of Bombing". It would be Dale Christians' second trip to the big one. His crew helped bring home the Fairchild Trophy during the 1959 Bomb Comp. Since it was his second trip to the big one, he knew what it would be like and what was needed to bring home the bacon.

During the entire month of July the U.S. and Soviet delegates to the United Nations were locked in heated debate over the situation in Berlin. It was clear the Soviets wanted the Allies out of the city. It was also clear the Allies had no intention of letting that city be swallowed up behind the Iron Curtain. What was not clear was what the next move by the Soviets would be.

With the situation in Berlin warming up towards a boiling point on almost a daily basis, the Kennedy Administration called a halt to the phase out of the B-47 under the Fly Fast program on July 25th. They might just be needed in the near future.

There was also a change in the Reflex schedule in the works due to the growing crisis in Berlin. More aircraft and crews would be flying across the pond in the near future. The increase would be a slow buildup of Alert aircraft in Europe. It's a matter of SAC clenching the mailed fist tighter on the lightning bolts and olive branches. Let the Soviets decide which one was to be hurled.

The near future arrived on August 2nd with a new wrinkle to the Reflex operations. That Wednesday night a single B-47 launched towards Spain. Reflex deployments would now be twice a week, Monday and Wednesday. Redeployment would leave Morón on Wednesday and Friday. Deployments would either be a single ship or two-ship cells. With aircraft in the air on Wednesday using the Blue Route, it was theoretically possible for the 307th to meet itself coming and going.

In early August, the accident report was filed on the June 18th crash of 53-2111. Like everyone figured, the primary cause of the accident was ruled Pilot Error. There were several contributing factors listed. One was the loss of power on the #6 engine during the take off roll. A detailed tear down of the engine revealed no reason for the failure. The board could find no cause for the loss of power on the engine. It was also noted the #6 engine aft mounting bolt was fractured at some time during engine maintenance, but was not a contributing factor in the accident.

There were a lot of people who could not accept the Board's final verdict. One member of the Board refused to sign the final report in protest to the final findings of the investigation board. Since the loss of power happened after the aircraft had reached S1, Capt Holst had no choice but to try to take off and to stay in the air for an emergency landing. There wasn't enough runway left to attempt stopping the B-47 without going off the end and into Oak Creek. It was a "damned if you do, damned if you don't" situation.

The klaxon went off on August 5th, shattering an otherwise quiet Saturday afternoon. The crews scrambled to their birds and started engines. When they checked in as "**Ready to Taxi**", they were informed, "**This is a Green Dot Two, Practice, REPEAT, Practice Bravo Response.**"

There was another single ship Reflex launch on Wednesday, the 9th. The flight over was uneventful. Letdown and landing were also uneventful. The crew was happy to get out and stretch their legs after the long flight. They did a quick walkaround to see if the wings were still attached or if there was anything wrong to write up on the Form 781. Everything was still in the same place after almost thirteen hours in the air. The bomb bay doors had been opened and the ground crews were busy removing the "travel package" and any cargo that had been sent over.

The crew was tired and they were ready to go to debriefing and get some grits to pack the belly. Without warning, the area reverberated with a loud KA-BANG! Instinctively, people ducked as if trying to get out of the way of whatever was happening.

At first, nobody could figure out what happened. Then, someone noticed a slight list in how the aircraft sat on the ramp. The right rear main tire was flat and there were several large chunks of rubber lying nearby. They were lucky that no one was standing close by when the tire blew. Well, another write-up in the 781, "Change right rear tire."

August 13th began as a normal Sunday at Lincoln. Flight crews did the usual morning checks on the Alert birds, then some of them headed for services at the chapel. Across the Atlantic, things were beginning to approach the boiling point in Berlin.

East German authorities closed the borders between East and West Germany. Soldiers began building what would become the infamous Berlin Wall. At first, it was a hastily thrown up series of barbed wire and wooden barricades. East German military units appeared, poised to move out for possible attacks against NATO forces.

SAC was placed on increased readiness at bases worldwide. The 307th began a "standby alert" readiness posture. Off-duty personnel were subject to a telephone pyramid alert. The rest of the day was filled with higher tension for the Alert crews. Everyone figured that, if the klaxon went off, it would be the real deal.

Monday morning there was more than the usual activity on the flight line. Two B-47s were being generated for Reflex launch late that afternoon. This Reflex launch was different from a normal launch. After returning from the refueling pits the two aircraft were placed under heavy guard. They were uploaded with nuclear weapons instead of the usual cargo rack for the trip to Spain.

Reflex with weapons aboard was not a normal procedure under SAC protocol. B-47s would carry weapons on Reflex flights from time to time, but it was not an everyday occurrence. These aircraft were "packing" so that, when they arrived in Spain, they could be turned around and on alert quicker than under normal Reflex guidelines. The flight crews were also given a special briefing that afternoon. Just before going to the aircraft, the cell leader was given a special package to deliver to the Alert commander at Morón. Flying across the pond was always filled with a certain amount of tension. Doing it with a real weapon just twenty feet away from you increased the pucker factor by several levels.

Reflex continued with another flight of two on Wednesday, the 6th. Like Monday's flight, they were loaded with weapons and carried special dispatches for the Alert commander at Morón. These two aircraft had been through Clip In, so there was the capability for them to carry four weapons on the flight.

Two B-47s and their crews left Morón on the 16th for the flight back to the States. They also flew the northern route back. Coming home, they faced brutal headwinds all the way across the Atlantic. By the time they arrived in the refueling area they were at minimum fuel reserves. The two B-47s hit the tankers and got their fuel.

On the 17th, word came down from SAC that, even with the Berlin pot simmering, the policy of no-notice practice alerts would continue. So the Alert crews could look forward to the blare of the klaxon at any time. Like before, they wouldn't know if it was practice or a real EWO launch.

Thunderstorms raked the Eastern part of Nebraska overnight on August 20th. Two aircraft had to divert to McConnell AFB due to the weather. After crew rest and refueling the planes headed back to Lincoln on the 21st.

The weather system that had caused the thunderstorms was still close enough to cause more thunderheads to start building early on the 21st. The two B-47s that started back from Wichita reported from their perch at 35,000 feet that it looked like there was a nasty line of "builders" to the south and west of Lincoln. The weather wizards gazed into their weather crystal balls and confirmed there was a good possibility of strong storms arriving in the area around noon.

52-0353 was scheduled for launch on a round robin training mission that day. The flight crew arrived at base operations and had a look at the weather charts. If they were able to make their noon takeoff, they might beat the line of storms moving in from the west.

With the fire guard standing by, the crew spooled up #4 and continued through the other five. While they were going through the startup procedures, they kept one eye on the engine gauges and the other eye peeled on the southwestern sky. It was getting darker by the minute as the clouds raced across the plains towards the base. The distant rumble of thunder rolled across the countryside. Within a few minutes they got a call from the tower advising them the storm would be on them before they could get off the ground. The crew had no choice but to shut down, button up and wait out the bad weather.

Bad weather wasn't exactly the word for it. Severe weather would be more like what was bearing down on the flight line. The gentle morning breeze died without warning to dead calm. Lightning danced across the western hills and thunder cracked across the countryside. The dark clouds turned an ugly greenish-yellow. Within seconds, heavy rain lashed the flight line. Men scrambled for cover in vehicles, buildings and inside the aircraft on the flight line. High winds rolled across the flight line, causing the B-47s to rock and roll against the chocks.

After about twenty minutes of wind, rain, flashing lightning and crashing thunder, the line of storms passed on to the east and activity on the ramp moved back to normal. The flight crew went back to 0353 and started the engines at 1400, then taxied at 1415. While heading to the runway the Bomb/Nav System malfunctioned. So they had to taxi back, park and let the specialists troubleshoot the problem.

A special train left the Ogden, Utah, rail yards on August 21st. It was officially designated as RBS Express Train #3. The train was headed east for the Alabama Ordnance Works at Childersberg, Alabama. This was a specially built train capable of being used as a mobile bomb-scoring unit. The idea of the train was to keep moving it around the countryside to give the flight crews experience in attacking different targets. It was felt the crews were getting complacent bombing the same targets at the established RBS units. So, if you varied the targets frequently, it would give the crews more realistic training in target study and bombing.

RBS Express Train #2 left Ogden around 1900 on 22 August. They were headed for a remote rail crossing near Rhame, North Dakota. The train was supposed to be operational in time for the upcoming SAC-wide Bombing competition.

A morning launch was scheduled for 53-2330 on Friday the 25th. The crew arrived, went through preflight and started engines. At the end of the runway, they went through the checklist and got the go-ahead from the tower. At 1120 the aircraft commander pushed the throttles forward and hit the WAI after the power was stable. After rolling about 300 feet, the water alcohol cut out on the #6 engine. Without the thrust they had to abort and taxi back to the ramp. A defective airflow valve was found and a call went out for a new unit. Supply had problems finding the right kind of valve. It was finally delivered to the aircraft at 1600. By then it was too late and the profile was canceled. More MCS points down the drain.

The last Reflex deployment for August left Lincoln on Wednesday the 30th. That single ship left Lincoln at 1700 for the flight to Spain. That same day 2 B-47s left Morón to fly back to Lincoln. Somewhere over the Atlantic their paths crossed.

Project Clip In was officially completed on 31 August. The project was completed a month later than projected. The delay in completing the work was due to trouble getting parts and defects that had to be reworked after coming back from the depots. The project required 9,424 man-hours to complete. 1,804 of those hours were due to work that had to be done a second time in order to accomplish Tech Order Compliance.

August ended with the usual monthly report going to SAC and 2nd Air Force Headquarters. Again, there was the plea for more manpower to cover areas like the A&E Squadron and the engine shop. The wing flew 249 sorties and spent 1,701 hours in the air. The situation in Berlin caused the 307th to increase readiness through changes in the Reflex schedule and placing several more aircraft on ground Alert at Lincoln.

Back in March, the 307th had been advised they would participate in Operation Big Switch. This was to evaluate the use of mobile RBS sites mounted on specially built trains. The first two RBS Express trains were operational and were in place. The 307th was assigned to the train now at Childersberg, Alabama, on the Tree Trimmer OB route. The first mission scheduled to Tree Trimmer was set for 6 September.

The first Reflex deployment to Spain for the month left on Monday, 4 September. The Reflex schedule would see aircraft leaving on Monday and Wednesday as they had done in August.

The 6th also saw the first mission against the RBS Express train. The B-47 launched from Lincoln and flew a regular round robin mission. They made a Short Look bomb run after flying the low-level route. As may be expected, the first run at the new target wasn't the best. Approaching the target, the aircraft pulled up to about 4,000 feet and began the run. There was trouble identifying the aiming point. The score came back as unreliable. Not a very good beginning.

# 1961

More and more, Col Read's prophetic words, "You can't fly 'em, if you can't fix 'em" was becoming a common occurrence. There were more and more incidents of late takeoffs or aborts due to equipment failure. Very interesting in view of the record established by the wing only two years previously.

On the 6th, 53-2416 was scheduled for a 1650 take off for a 50-8 training flight. During taxi to the runway the navigator lost his Bomb/Nav System. You can't hit the target if your system is haybags. They came back to the ramp and shut down at 1625. An urgent call was sent out for a B/N specialist. None was available until 1900. Troubleshooting and replacement of several components were finished by 1920. The flight crew arrived back at the aircraft and stood by while last-minute adjustments were made. Finally, the crew started engines and taxied at about 1950. The takeoff was aborted when the copilot reported seeing fire in the area of the #4 and #5 engines. The flight was postponed for twenty-four hours. Maintenance crews could not find anything wrong with the engines.

Another mission to the RBS Express in Alabama was flown Friday the 8th. After refueling and a two-hour nav leg the crew entered the Tree Trimmer route. This time, the crew was able to find the target and sent a radar bomb to be scored by the Alabama choo-choo. The score came back as being within 500 feet of the target.

The Combat Competition crews headed for Fairchild on Wednesday, 13 September. There were six B-52 wings and six B-47s wings in the competition. There were twelve squadrons of KC-135s and KC-97s to provide refueling support and competition. This year a weapons loading competition was included. The score from this event would be used in the final determination for the Fairchild Trophy.

Opening ceremonies began at 1000 on 16 September. After the opening ceremonies the crews went to the competition briefing at 1300. At the briefing they were given the details of the rules and routes of the competition. They also drew their bomb targets and the order for standing "Alert" for their mission.

Competition guidelines had changed since 1959. Each crew would fly one mission. The flight would include a navigation leg, air refueling, ECM run and bomb runs on two different targets. One would be a low-level Short Look, while the other would be a high altitude bomb run. There were two different targets for the low-level run: one was at Hastings, Nebraska; the other was at the RBS Express train located at a railway crossing near Rhame, North Dakota. The low-level target to be used was determined by random drawing. Another new wrinkle in the competition was the launch of the aircraft. The crews were to execute a scramble type launch as they would under EWO conditions.

Right away the B-47 crews thought they might be competing against a stacked deck in favor of the B-52s. There were no sharp turns along the bomb run routes so the big lumbering B-52s could make long slow turns, giving their newer bombing system more time to compute the drop. Likewise, the nav leg was laid out in a big W pattern with wide turns again. Then, there was the fact the B-52s had two men to collaborate on the job that the one man in the nose of the B-47 had to accomplish.

Maj Stringfellow's crew was the first 307th crew at bat in the competition on 17 September. They did the preflight on 53-1872 at 1500 and reported to the Alert Facility. At 1800 the first crew was called to react to the scramble and fly their mission. Don Kellum remembered:

"We were all in one room, the horn would blow and they would shout out a crew number. Then we'd scramble for the takeoff. They gave us a certain amount of points for the scramble. We had fifteen minutes to get into the air."

Maj Stringfellow's crew scrambled to their awaiting aircraft and was airborne with a few minutes to spare. They climbed out and headed for the refueling area. Their refueling was right out of the textbook. Stringfellow slid into the refueling envelope, moved in and took on the offload without a disconnect. They flew the ECM run and played their music without a missed beat. Don Kellum's navigation was right down the middle of the route. The low-level bomb run was classified as excellent. They made the long climb back to altitude for the high altitude run on a target near Seattle, Washington. After the tone cut off on the last run they figured they had done very well.

When they landed, they had to wait for the scores to be forwarded from the bomb plots. There had been no problems during the mission. When the score was posted on the big board, the 307th was on top and on the way to a second Fairchild Trophy win.

On September 19th, the final round of the weapons loading competition was held. The competition included preparation of the weapon and loading it into the assigned aircraft using the checklist and proper procedures. The crews were graded on speed and efficiency.

The ground crews for the 307th used the time between flights to make sure that 1872 was in the best shape possible. They went over her with a fine-tooth comb to make sure that there weren't any discrepancies that might cause problems on the next flight. They got out the paint and tidied up a couple of rough looking spots on her aluminum hide.

When the second round of competition missions started on September 19th, Maj Dale Christians' crew was at bat for the 307th. Dale's regular Navigator, Noble Timmons, was over the mumps and ready to reclaim his cramped office in the nose. Dale's crew had been here before in the 1959 Bomb/Comp. They knew the pressure was on for another late-inning score.

Dale and his crew preflighted the aircraft at 1500, then went to the Alert Facility. All of the crews were isolated at the Alert pad by 1600. All they could do now was sit around like everyone else and wait for the horn to go off. The horn for the first crew to fly started at 1800.

A little-known event at the 1961 Bombing Competition proved the resourcefulness, competitiveness, dedication and good old Yankee ingenuity of the 307th participants. Gene Lee and Frank Fish, 307th electrical specialists both, decided it was high time to invent "Fast Start Technology". To do this, they wired the starter switch for #3 engine to the starter motors for engines 2 and 3, and did the same with the starter switch for #4 for engines 4 and 5. Thus, when the starter switch was activated, two engines would start rotating simultaneously for start. This enabled Bill Stringfellow, whose aircraft was the guinea pig, to fire up and roll two and a half minutes faster than any other competitors. Points accrued to the 307th!

Fish and Lee, firm believers in process improvement, thought, "Surely we can do better than that". So, the second night of the competition with Dale Christians and crew coming up on their turn in the barrel, the two innovators tied a string to the #4 starter switch and ran the string down the entrance ladder so Dale could pull it and begin the start sequence when his foot hit the first rung of the ladder. Alas, sometimes improvement processes need refining and this was one of those times. When the string was pulled it broke and the starter switch spring loaded to "Off" and aborted the start. The net result was that, for want of a string, 30 seconds of the fast start were lost. Maybe they would have been luckier if "Stringfellow" had been second, rather than first?

When the call came in for Dale's crew to scramble they hit the ladder, spooled up and launched within the competition guidelines, despite the broken string. Unfortunately, they quickly discovered a problem with the

## Cold War Cornhuskers: The 307th Bomb Wing Lincoln Air Force Base Nebraska 1955-1965

Bomb/Nav System. They weren't getting an airspeed reading through the system. So, right away it was a matter of "Continuous talking on the UHF and HF radio, trying to get the radar fixed," Dale remembered. They tried this, then that, but nothing they tried brought the radar equipment back.

Dale knew they had to press on with the mission or be scored as an abort, which of course would kill any chance of winning the competition. They rendezvoused with the tanker and took on the full fuel load in one gulp without a disconnect. Timmons was near perfect on the navigation legs. Now, head for North Dakota and see what happens on the bomb run. Even at this point they were still trying everything possible to get the radar to work.

Without the radar the crew was competing under a severe handicap. There was nothing they could do except turn to a heading that would take them to Rhame, North Dakota, and the target near the RBS Express train sitting on a siding just outside of town.

Again and again they tried to come up with some kind of fix that would get the radar back up and running before they committed to the bomb run. No matter what was suggested or tried, the radar would not work. Dale wrote, "We couldn't use the computer on either run and had to go to fixed angle for the bomb runs which was the last resort method and naturally our scores were a lot higher in distance from the target."

There wasn't a lot that could be done except head back to Fairchild and wait for the scores to be posted. But the tension for Dales' crew wasn't over. During letdown and approach there was a problem. "When we got back to Fairchild, there was a big delay in landing and I had to declare a low-fuel emergency and landed on fumes. I still have some gray hairs from that mission," Dale wrote.

When they got back, they started checking to see what had caused the problem with the Bomb/Nav System. They found, when things were being tidied up, someone had painted over the true airspeed port for the Bomb/Nav System. With the painted port on the outside of the airplane, they had their explanation as to why they couldn't fix it in the air.

In the final inning of the competition the B-52 crews put together some great missions. They were the favorites to win and the whole set-up seemed to be in their favor. After the second wave of flying by the B-52 wings, the scoreboard showed the B-52s were in the lead for the Fairchild Trophy.

When the final results were posted, the 4137th Strategic Wing from Robins AFB, Georgia, had won the Fairchild Trophy. The wing was flying the latest B-52G with upgraded radar and bombing systems. Maj Stringfellow's crew was the Best B-47 crew in the competition. The 307th placed 5th overall out of the twelve wings at the competition.

While the 307th wouldn't bring home the top honors, they showed they could perform very well under pressure with equipment problems. In view of competing against a stacked deck, the wing could be very proud of the crews who had represented the wing.

During the Combat Competition, the crews at Lincoln stayed busy flying 50-8 profile missions to fill in the squares on the training board. There were Reflex flights to Spain and redeployment flights back to the USA. The buildup of aircraft due to the Berlin situation continued. While we built up our Alert commitment overseas, the Soviets continued to build the wall around Berlin.

The increase in Reflex and Alert posed manpower problems for the already short-manned 307th. A review of manpower in the military revealed it wasn't just the 307th that was short of personnel. The problem extended throughout the entire United States military. To avoid an even more critical shortage, the Kennedy Administration froze the separation dates of military personnel who were eligible for discharge for the duration of the Berlin situation. To say the least, this move was not well accepted by "short timers" who were looking forward to getting out.

The 307th had problems adjusting to the RBS Express train site on the Tree Trimmer route at Childersberg, Alabama. On September 20th, a B-47 on a low level bomb run pulled up to release altitude and released their radar bomb on the site. The results were, shall we say, not good. The circular error was scored at over 23,000 feet from the target. They had missed the target by almost four country miles!

Leo Porter and his ground crew were getting 53-4236 ready for an 1155 launch on the 26th. Everything was fine during preflight. Engine start went like clockwork until they started #3 engine. Just before moving to start #2, Leo noticed excessive fuel coming from the spider drain on #3. The fuel flow increased with any increase in power. The engine was shut down and the cowling pulled.

The fuel pump had ruptured a diaphragm, allowing fuel to leak out. The pump was changed in record time, the engines restarted, and 4236 taxied to the end of the runway. The crew radioed the tower for takeoff clearance. There was no response from the tower, just static. 4236 started back to the ramp. Then on the way back, the radio crackled with the tower asking the reason for the return taxi. So it was turn around and head back towards the runway again. A crew towing a B-47 from the compass rose spotted fuel coming from the #3 engine again. So turn around again and drive back to the ramp. The sortie was canceled at 1445.

All during the year incidents of late takeoffs or canceled missions had been on the increase. Several factors played heavily together to cause this increase. First, the B-47 fleet was getting older with every mission flown. The birds of the 307th had had a lot of air across their wings. Since the B-47 was to be phased out, no additional funds were available for needed updates. Add to this the manpower situation; planes that cannot be maintained properly are going to have problems.

There were problems again on September 27th. 53-1843 was scheduled for a 0020 takeoff. They couldn't get any RPM on the #2 or #3 engine. A broken relay switch was causing the problem. Then there was a fuel leak in the forward tank. After repairing multiple problems, 1843 launched at 0135 that morning.

Col Berg's report for September was again filled with the same basic message of being low on men, low on parts, high on aircraft breakdowns, and high on flying hours brought on by the situation in Berlin. He brought out there were not enough hours in the day to complete maintenance with the manpower available. Col Berg pointed out the situation was serious and that, without proper staffing, the efficiency of the wing would suffer.

October started with a two-ship Reflex launch on Monday, the 2nd. It was another fairly routine Reflex flight filled with the usual pucker factor in the refueling area and the same factor for the duration of the flight across the Atlantic.

Wednesday, the 4th, started with the same routine. Alert crews arrived at their birds and went through the morning preflight, making sure the aircraft was cocked and ready. Ground crews took care of anything that may have surfaced overnight. No major discrepancies were found, so all of the birds were cocked.

The morning hours were filled with getting another Reflex flight ready for launch early that evening. About noon, the troops started heading for the chow halls for a bite to eat. At the alert pad the crews were lining up to have a look-see at what was on the menu. Some already had their trays and were sitting down to enjoy the meal.

A quiet meal was not to be. The klaxon interrupted lunch. The crews hit the doors and then out through the tubes to the Alert birds. Across the pad, the whine of J-47 engines spooling up replaced the usual flight line sounds. Those not on alert stole a glance towards the pad to see what was going to happen next.

The crews got the word. It was a Green Dot practice Coco Alert. Practice or not, everyone wanted to be first to taxi. The first B-47 started

176

to move six minutes after the klaxon went off. Out of the Alert ramp, and a short taxi to the end of Runway 17. Power up and roll, then pull the power off and finish the alert. The last bird in line was ready to taxi fourteen minutes after the klaxon.

Oh well, another lunch shot in the head. By the time the Alert was over and they got back their food was cold, so they looked to see what kinds of sandwiches were available. Meals weren't always interrupted by the klaxon, but the crews remembered those that were.

Paul Koski recalled an interesting Alert response during mealtime:

"We started our 48-hour shift that morning. During the morning briefing, we were told that a SAC inspection team would be in late that night or first thing in the morning to inspect our procedures and response time with the aircraft. They would also inspect our Alert facilities at the 'mole hole.' We knew the meals would be special since the dining facility wanted to make a good impression and pass their portion of the inspection. Not that we didn't get good food normally while were on Alert, but this would be above average.

"The inspection went fine. They interviewed some of the people, not only the flight crews but also anyone at the "mole hole". When five o'clock came, we went to the dining facility for dinner. The cooks had outdone themselves: we had steaks that looked like they were cooked to perfection, baked potatoes and corn on the cob, with ice cream or pie for dessert. We had gone through the line, picked up our food and found an empty table.

"I was just about to take a bite from my steak when a feeling came over me to look up. There, looking through the window of the doors that led to the dining area was a full colonel from the inspection team. I thought, 'No, they wouldn't blow the klaxon now.' You guessed it. The horn sounded and, within a second, I hit the door with about five other people. Well, the colonel didn't have a chance to get out of the way. The last I saw of him was when he was sliding down the wall across from the door. We couldn't stop to help him. We completed the exercise and got back to the mole hole. The dining area was all cleaned up; no steaks, but the cooks did have cold cuts and juice or milk."

53-2349 was scheduled for a 0215 launch on a round robin 50-8 mission. The flight crew found a fuel leak in the bomb bay. You can't go poking around looking for the source of the leak with all that JP-4 in the tanks, so 2349 was towed to the fuel pits and defueled. Specialists hunted for the leak and started their repairs at 0150. It took almost twelve hours of dirty, cramped work to get at the leak and get it fixed. At about 1358, 2349 was back at the pits for refueling. She finally launched at 1515 on the afternoon of the 6th.

Routine 50-8 missions continued on a daily basis. On the 9th, 53-1897 was serviced and ready for launch at 1121. The crew departed Lincoln and climbed out towards the south. Over Beatrice, the navigator gave a course correction and the B-47 turned towards the west. Near Cheyenne, Wyoming, the crew turned and flew a short navigation leg to Gillette, Wyoming, then on to Sheridan. Just north of Sheridan they turned back east to meet their tanker for refueling.

Rendezvous with the KC-135 went without a hitch, but at first they had a problem getting fuel when a valve stuck in the closed position. The tanker crew was able to get the fuel flowing and 1897 got their total SAC SNACK.

After refueling, the crew started coming down from refueling altitude for their low-level bomb run. Their target was the RBS Express train at Rhame, North Dakota. They approached from the west at low level, skirting the bluffs. Their target wasn't the easiest to find with all of the bluffs and buttes in the area, causing plenty of strange radar returns.

A couple of wind runs and the bomb system had the numbers. Tone cut off signaled bomb away. The results came back as within effective range. After the run on Rhame, 1897 and her crew flew another short nav leg, then headed for Lincoln.

Another mission up to the Dakotas was scheduled to leave Lincoln at 2156, 12 October. The crew arrived and did the preflight prior to engine start. As usual, the fireguard was standing by for the engine start and runup. Engines 4, 5, and 6 started with no problem. The ground crew moved to the left side and stood by on #1. That engine started with no problems.

They started turning #2; fuel flow normal, ignition and RPM came up, and so did the EGT. The temperature came up and then moved beyond 950 degrees. Watchful eyes saw it climb higher and stay there. The pilot pulled the power off and hit the cut off switch. They had had an infamous "hot start". According to procedures, they had to shut down the other engines and have the engine inspected. The mission was canceled when they determined the engine had to be changed.

Engine shop personnel arrived and moved the engine hoist into place and attached the J-shaped engine hook to the damaged engine about 2230. Fuel lines, electrical lines and connectors had to be disconnected and placed out of the way. The damaged engine was removed and the new one hung in place by 2323. Within another thirty minutes the engine was in the final checkout stage. The ground crew topped off the tanks and serviced the water-alcohol system. The crew arrived back at the aircraft and was airborne by 0037.

Two birds launched on Saturday, the 14th, for a training flight. The aircraft took off about thirty minutes apart and flew their individual routes. One went towards Joplin, Missouri; the other headed for a run on the Minneapolis bomb plot. They both recovered at O'Hare airport near Chicago as part of the monthly Clutch Pedal program.

During mid-afternoon on Tuesday, the 24th, the command post got a message from Jumbo for a Green Dot Bravo Alert. The klaxon wailed and the crews scrambled up the ladders. The first bird was ready to roll in four minutes. The rest checked in when their engines were running and ready to taxi. As soon as the alert was over ground crews moved in and serviced the Alert planes. The flight crews went through the checklist and recocked the aircraft.

An hour or so later the control tower got an urgent call from a KC-135 about seventy-five miles south of Lincoln. They reported they were having trouble with the fuel transfer system and couldn't pump fuel into their main flight tanks. They were afraid they couldn't make it back to their home base and were declaring a low fuel emergency and asking Lincoln for clearance to land.

Transient aircraft landing at Lincoln was an almost daily occurrence. A lone KC-135 arriving unannounced and declaring an emergency to get landing clearance almost shouted an ORI was about to be thrown at the base. The tower personnel called the 818th Air Division and told the command staff what was happening. The staff agreed that it sure smelled like an ORI.

The 135 landed and taxied in, parking near Base Operations. Within a few minutes several officers from the tanker left the flight line in staff cars that had been sent for them. Whoever they were, they were important enough to get a greeting and staff car ride off the ramp. So much for the break in the routine; it was time to get back to work.

Arriving at the command post, the battle staffs from the 98th and 307th were assembled in one of the briefing rooms. They were informed the unexpected visitors were members of the SAC Inspector General Staff and the 818th Air Division could expect a message from Omaha to execute Quick Kick Bravo. It *was* an ORI!

Within the hour the message arrived from Omaha. It was authenticated and word was sent out to the Alert pad. The Alert Commander reacted by

## Cold War Cornhuskers: The 307th Bomb Wing Lincoln Air Force Base Nebraska 1955-1965

hitting the klaxon. The crews scrambled for the aircraft for the second time that afternoon. As always there was a race to see who would be first to check in.

Like almost all ORIs, Quick Kick Bravo began with a Coco Alert. The B-47s were fast taxied through the alert procedures then back to the Alert pad. Under normal ORI procedures, these birds would be downloaded and serviced for the first wave of the mission. This time it was different. With the situation in Berlin, the Alert birds would be recocked and continue standing alert.

The Alert crews wouldn't fly this ORI, but they weren't finished with their part of the exercise. When the aircraft were recocked, they reported to the Alert briefing room and were tested by the IG Staff on EWO knowledge and procedures. The test covered everything from engine start procedures under EWO conditions to questions on how long to remain at the Positive Control Turnaround Point before returning to base. Failure on this test was not an option.

The Wing Plans staff pulled the Operations Plan for Quick Kick Bravo and started putting the plan into action. The mission requirements called for generation of all available aircraft under peacetime guidelines. The force would be required to fly a heavyweight take off, celestial navigation grid leg, electronic rendezvous and air refueling, ECM, controlled ETA at the H- Hour Control Point, low-level navigation, Short Look RBS, high altitude run on a Nike site and High Pass tactic on a Nike site.

With the increase in the SAC Alert posture and Reflex commitment since the original plan was drafted, there were several modifications made and approved by the IG Staff. The major change was the fact the alert aircraft would not fly. Another major change was the number of aircraft that would actually fly the mission. The follow-on force would be generated as usual. Thirteen aircraft would be selected to fly the actual ORI missions. There was also a change in the launch schedule. Two aircraft would fly every other day, alternating with the 98th Bomb Wing.

It didn't take long for the word to spread across the ramp. "It's an ORI. Generate the Force!" Now the flight line troops started scrambling to get the birds ready. The first ones ready were three B-47s that had been scheduled for a round robin mission that night. They would lead the wing into the air with the first cell on Thursday, the 26th.

For the next week, Lincoln Air Force Base would be under the ever-watchful eye of the SAC IG Staff. Everything on base would be observed, checked and scored. An inspector would be poking into everything from aircraft maintenance to temperatures in the cooler at the Commissary to the height of the grass in the housing area. Legend had it that they even checked the level of the water at Bowling Lake.

Thursday the 26th was filled with mission planning, briefings and aircraft servicing, all under the eye of the umpires. So far, the local weather had cooperated with mild temperatures and beautiful blue Nebraska skies. The normal pressure to get the birds ready for a mission was kicked up to a notch equal to an actual EWO mission.

The first two aircraft were to take off early that evening. The ground crew on old reliable 6244 had her serviced and went through their ground preflight. Everything appeared ready for the mission. The flight crew arrived and did their preflight. Scheduled take off was set for 1940. The crew climbed aboard and began starting engines at 1900. All of the engines were started and 6244 was ready to taxi at 1915. Just before moving out the aircraft commander reported his attitude gyro was inoperative.

An instrument specialist was called and arrived at 1935. The pressure was on, in spades. The specialist located the problem in a control box. A frantic call was made for a replacement unit, which arrived in record time. 6244 pulled out of her slot and headed for the end of the runway with the specialist still aboard working frantically to get the unit changed and checked out. A Metro truck followed 6244 down the taxiway.

At the end of the runway, the specialist gave thumbs up and scrambled down the ladder. The crew chief was out of the Metro like a shot and buttoned up the ladder and entry door. He gave the AC the signal everything was "go" and ran like hell back to the Metro.

The throttles were pushed up and 6244 started down the runway in a cloud of black water-alcohol smoke. At S1, the speed was good and 6244 lifted off the runway just after passing the 9,000 foot marker. A quick glance at their watches gave the launch crew a sinking feeling in their gut. Lift off was at 1947. Scheduled take off was 1940. Under ORI guidelines there was a five-minute window. 6244 was seven minutes past her takeoff time and two minutes over the ORI guideline limit. 6244 was scored as an abort. What a way to start an ORI!

The other scheduled aircraft was supposed to take off at 1941 that night. With the problems causing 6244 to be late, the other aircraft taxied and launched on time in front of 6244. At least they had one bird in the air and on time. It didn't take a major league scorekeeper to figure it out; one more abort and the wing would bust the ORI.

The next day was the same ORI grind. The ground crews spent the day getting the next cell ready for takeoff. Several problems surfaced during the servicing of one of the birds. They had trouble transferring fuel from one tank to another. The problem was located and fixed. It all took time, precious time, with the ORI umpires breathing down their necks. Extra time was something they just didn't have.

The IG Staff was poking into every nook and cranny of Lincoln Air Force Base and the 307th Bomb Wing. They were not there only to see how well the 307th could maintain and fly B-47s; they were there to see how well the 307th did *everything*. They inspected how well the records and paperwork were done. They looked at how the wing maintained security in areas where classified material was used and stored. No area or airman was immune from the scrutiny of the IG Staff during the ORI.

The second cell launched on time for the second night of flying. The launch was a bit of a nail-biter when one of the aircraft seemed to use too much runway to get airborne. Some on the ground swore she didn't clear the knoll off the end of Runway 17 by much.

The two B-47s climbed into the early evening sky. When they got to altitude, they began the two-hour celestial navigation leg of the mission. Both copilot and navigator spent a lot of time hanging from the sextant, checking and double-checking their fixes to make sure that they were where they were supposed to be.

After the navigation leg they headed for their individual refueling rendezvous points. Within minutes of arriving at the refueling area, they spotted the tanker on radar and made radio contact. Slowly, the B-47s closed the distance on the tankers. At night there was very little visual reference to fly into refueling position. It had to be done by radar and the indicator lights on the belly of the tanker. Skill that had been honed by practice mission after practice mission paid off.

Within moments the bombers were hanging on the boom and fuel surged through the nose receptacle while the copilot watched the gauges to make sure the fuel was going to the right tank. As the B-47 got heavier with fuel, the tanker got lighter. Only constant attention to what was going on kept the two planes together. Fuel offload completed, the B-47s dropped off the boom and slid away into the darkness until only blinking lights could be seen in the distance.

With the refueling complete, the bombers headed for the ECM portion of their mission. Approaching the ECM target area, the planes tuned up and started their music. They played it long and loud, trying to ward off the "enemy" ground radar trying to track them. When they did get a lock-on, they tied their best to play enough of the right music to break the lock.

The next phase of the mission was to make the H-Hour Control Line. If they didn't make the control line, they would be scored as late and could be given an air abort. An air abort at this point would cause the wing to fail the ORI since they already had one abort. Passing the control point, the planes descended to enter the low-level navigation Oil Burner run which would end with a Short Look bomb run. Flying on the deck on an Oil Burner route during the day was a real thrill, a bomber pilot's dream come true. At night, it could be a pilot's worst nightmare.

Imagine hurtling through the night sky at between 500 and 1,000 feet above the ground. Unlike driving a car at night, there are no headlights shining to show what lies ahead. You know the ground is out there ahead of you. The radar is the only thing that can point out obstacles. You hope there isn't a radio tower with a light out, or a hill that wasn't charted correctly, lurking out there in front of you.

At the end of the navigation leg they were ready for the Short Look bomb run. They contacted the bomb plot about seventy miles out from the target for positive identification. They started climbing to the release altitude and put the bombing offsets into the system. Fifteen seconds before release the tone came on; at release the tone cut off. On the ground, the pen lifted from the plotting paper.

After the low-level run they climbed back up to higher altitude for the high-level run on a Nike site. After hitting the Nike site, they did the High Pass ECM run on another Nike site. Mission completed, they turned for Lincoln.

By Tuesday, the 31st, the 307th had flown eight of the ten scheduled ORI missions. The bombing scores on most of the runs were good. So far, there had been two bombs scored as unreliable. If the wing had two more bad runs the ball game would be over. That night's mission had an unreliable bomb run. The 307th was now in deep trouble.

So far, it had been the worst showing the 307th had put in during an ORI. The wing had problems with the exercise from the very beginning. Equipment problems, aborts and bad bombing had put the wing in a precarious position. The wing was teetering on the brink of failing the ORI. Everyone knew what would happen if the wing failed. The men of the 307th dug deep for the final inning of the ORI.

The final results came in on the final night's flying. The 307th had struck out. The ORI was over and the wing had failed. Emotions ran from feeling as low as a snake's belly to a two-cent postage stamp with the glue licked off. Nothing to do but report to the Base Theater for the tongue lashing by the SAC IG.

During the post-exercise critique, the SAC IG went through page after page of recommendations. The IG Staff found problems in the Control Operations area. The building was not equipped with electrical alarm systems. The building was secured by chain link fence; however, there were several places where a person could crawl under. The windows and doors were not secured. It was also pointed out the EWO study rooms had unsatisfactory security.

Bomber maintenance was listed as unsatisfactory due to mechanical failures that caused last-minute emergency bomb runs on two sorties. The generation phase was scored marginal due to late starts on aircraft generation. Then there was the one late takeoff of 6244, which was scored as a mission abort.

Navigation and ECM were listed as outstanding. However, it doesn't count if you can't hit the target when you get there. The wing had four unreliable bomb runs. The failure to identify the correct aiming points was listed as the primary cause of the unreliable bomb runs. The four botched bomb runs were the ultimate cause for the wing to fail the ORI.

Along with the outstanding navigation and ECM, there were several other high points. The IG pointed out that the personnel records section was the best that he had seen in several months. It was also mentioned the response of the alert crews was excellent. They finally mentioned the cleanliness of the large south hangar, Big deal! All nice to mention, but failing an ORI was a bitter pill to swallow. As always with an ORI failure, changes would have to be made. Several who attended the critique recalled Col Berg endured the entire post-ORI briefing with his head hung low. There was only one real bright spot, if you could call it that. The 98th Bomb Wing had failed their ORI too. So they were in the same boat as the 307th.

The next several weeks would be recorded as the lowest morale period in the history of the 307th. It was well known what the results of busting an ORI in SAC would be. SAC couldn't have any of their bomb wings not measure up to SAC standards. Mike Gingrich recalled, "It was a bloody time in the 307th. We thought we were at the top of the heap and it was a great comedown. There were bloodletting and recriminations, some of which I personally witnessed."

Failing the ORI meant that the 307th would be under the watchful eye of both Omaha and Barksdale until they could pass another ORI, which, of course, they could expect within the next several months. In the meantime, life continued with Reflex deployments on November 1st, 2nd, and 3rd.

On 14 November the following message arrived at the 307th Bomb Wing Headquarters from Offutt.

FR: SAC OFFUTT AFB, NEBR
TO: 2ND AF BARKSDALE AFB, LA
Info: 818th AIRDV, Lincoln AFB, Near

Confidential DO 3682
(U) Unit Probation. This message in four parts.

Part I. The 307th Bomb Wing is placed on probation in Accordance with Chapter 1, Paragraph 58, SACM 51-1.
    Part II. Unit probation is due to failure of Operational Readiness Inspection.
Part III. Removal of 307th BW from unit probation will be accomplished in Accordance with Chapter 1, Paragraph 6, SACM 51-1
Part IV. The 307th BW will forfeit all MCS points available for the unit reliability for the Oct/Dec 61 training period.
    IAW Chapter 1, Para 5 note 1 SACM
    Dated 18 Sept. 61 SCP-4
    14 Nov.

The Berlin crisis caused a continued build up of Reflex aircraft at Morón. The 307th might have been on probation, but they were still required to contribute to the overseas Alert force. The 307th launched Reflex missions on a daily basis, November 13th through the 16th. The first return flights from Morón began on the 18th and continued every other day until the 30th. This build up was part of Operation Quick Change.

The weather at the patch on Wednesday, November 15th, was typical for November in Nebraska: low clouds, cool temperatures and the wind blowing out of the north. All day, the low clouds looked as if they could start spitting rain or snow at any moment. By 1800 the temperature had fallen to 38 degrees and the wind was gusting to 38 knots out of the north.

307th launch crews worked through the miserable afternoon to get their aircraft in the air for routine 50-8 training missions. By the time the last bird was airborne light rain was falling and the clouds had dropped even lower. The crews from the 307th were glad the birds were in the air. Now, they could clean up the area and get out of the weather.

# Cold War Cornhuskers: The 307th Bomb Wing Lincoln Air Force Base Nebraska 1955-1965

Most of the launch crews were still on the flight line when 52-0347 from the 98th Bomb Wing taxied towards the end of Runway 35 for departure on a 50-8 mission. Several paused to watch the takeoff. Within a few minutes 0347 rolled down the runway, lifted off, and was almost immediately swallowed by the low scud clouds.

About two minutes later there was a dim flash of light, followed by a muffled explosion to the north. At first no one seemed to know what happened. The wail of the fire trucks charging out of their barns was the first concrete indication the base had lost a bird.

Within a few minutes worst fears were confirmed: 0347 had gone in about three miles off the end of the runway. So far there was no word on the fate of the crew. Across the flight line the mood became very somber, knowing a bird was lost. Later that evening it was confirmed that the four crewmen had perished in the crash. There was no explanation as to what might have gone wrong. Everyone who saw the B-47 takeoff agreed that it looked like a normal takeoff.

The Reflex departure on the 16th was delayed for several hours due to the return of Old Man Winter. An early snowstorm moved out of the Rockies and started covering the flight line in a heavy blanket of first-of-the-season snow. The snow continued through the night and through most of the 17th.

On the 18th, 53-1872 was scheduled for a 1035 take off. At 0530 the launch crew started getting her ready. They removed the engine covers and got a big surprise. The engine intakes were full of snow and ice. They called for ground heaters to melt the snow. As usual, the ground heaters were not only late in arriving, but they also wouldn't start. After getting the heaters fixed they started at the #6 engine and worked towards #1. After getting the intake clear #4 engine was started and allowed to run for a few minutes. The other engines were started at about 0830, then shut down.

The crew continued to preflight the aircraft until they found bent inlet guides and damaged compressor blades on the #4 engine. Engine shop specialists arrived and started changing the engine. The new engine was mounted and checked out at 1730. It was believed that, after the intakes had been cleared, the water refroze and then broke loose during the engine runup, causing the damage.

In spite of the snow and cold, the launch crews were able to dig the aircraft out and launch a routine profile flight, which was to end up as a Clutch Pedal recovery at O'Hare. The regular part of the mission went according to the planned mission profile. The recovery at O'Hare was interesting due to the falling snow and limited visibility. The Clutch Pedal flight was able to return to Lincoln on Sunday, November 19th.

The 307th took a short break from operations to celebrate Thanksgiving on November 23rd. As always, the mess halls went all out to give the troops a wonderful home-style feast. Turkey and all the trimmings were provided at all of the dining areas. Alert crews were treated to two things that day: families were allowed to visit and have dinner with the Alert crews and they were also blessed with a silent klaxon.

At 0450, Friday, November 24th, the Alert crews were jolted from their slumber by the blare of the klaxon. Flight crews scrambled into their flight suits and boots and headed for their aircraft. The first B-47 ready to taxi called the tower in six minutes. They were informed this was a Blue Dot Delta Alert!

A Blue Dot Delta was a launch order of the Alert force under Positive Control! "**Good God! This is it! Somebody must have pulled the trigger!**" The heavily laden B-47s pulled out of their spots and headed south for takeoff on Runway 35. A plethora of emotions flashed through the minds of the crews as they taxied toward the launch end of the runway: "Could we get off the ground before Lincoln disappeared in a white flash of nuclear destruction? Who pulled the trigger? Why? What are our chances of getting through to the target? What about our families; they have no idea of what's going on?"

The lead B-47 was just about to make the rolling turn onto the runway when the Alert Control Room broadcast one word over the radio, "Crabapple". It was the recall signal. The next thing the crews heard was "Continue Green Dot Coco, Practice, Repeat, Practice Alert."

The force continued with the Coco Alert. Back at the pad, the flight crews stayed with their birds until they were serviced and recocked for alert. When they got back to the "mole hole", there was no explanation of what had happened. Something major surely had to have gone down to cause a launch order to be issued.

It would take several hours for the adrenaline to work its way out of their systems. No sense trying to go back to sleep; everybody was too "keyed up" even to try. Everybody agreed that it was the longest fifteen minutes they had experienced in SAC. Some mentioned the pucker factor was so tight an arrow wouldn't have penetrated. Others said, "Pucker factor? Hell, that scared the sh.. out of me!"

The Alert crews never got a straight answer on what had happened. Historically, it would be known as the "Black Forest Incident". At about 1045 Zulu, all communications between the BMEWS system at Thule and the SAC Command Post was lost. Everything—primary, backup and emergency communications systems—went out at the same time. SAC knew that a total knockout of these systems would most likely be the first indication of a Soviet attack. With an all-out attack on the United States apparently underway, SAC Headquarters pushed the button to flush the Alert birds from the nest.

During the next few minutes SAC was able to communicate with a B-52 bomber airborne near Thule. The crew reported no nuclear flash or mushroom in the area. The B-52 radioed Thule and found there was nothing out of the ordinary going on. No blips coming over the pole; everything was normal.

It was later found that all of the communication lines between NORAD, Thule and SAC ran through different routes; however, there was one common point where they all ran through a common relay station in Colorado. A motor had overheated and popped a relay, which in turn caused the entire system to fail.

Two things were learned from the Black Forest Incident. First, a weak link was found in the ability to communicate between NORAD and SAC. Changes would have to be made to ensure that the failure of a single relay would not cause the failure of the entire communications system. It also showed that a launch order could be given, executed and recalled under Positive Control. That morning, over 550 Alert Crews scrambled to their nuclear-laden bombers. They all got the recall message before leaving the runway.

Since the arrival of the probation message after the busted ORI, the wing had a constant stream of visitors from Omaha and Barksdale. Officially they were at Lincoln to help the wing locate, identify and eliminate the problems that caused the wing to fail.

If what the visitors provided was help, most of the witnesses knew what the Spanish Inquisition had been like. The wing would be subjected to reorganization of several squadrons. There were "changes" in several key personnel. It started at the top. On November 27th, Col Walter Berg was replaced by Col William Bertram.

Along with the reorganization, the 307th A&E Squadron was to undergo all kinds of changes. There was promise of additional personnel to help alleviate the workload. There would be changes in some of the section leaders and work schedules. Other areas were scheduled to feel the help of SAC.

It is interesting to note that from the very beginning of the 307th Bomb Wing at Lincoln, every wing commander had mentioned in numerous monthly reports the shortages of personnel in key areas like the A&E Squadron and the Engine Shop. They also forecast that these shortages would eventually have an adverse effect on the wing's efficiency and ability to perform its mission. Sadly, it took failing an ORI to open the eyes of SAC HQ and finally get something going in the personnel pipeline.

Every man in the 307th was down in the dumps over the ORI. Each man dug deep and did a lot of soul-searching to see if he had personally failed the wing at a critical moment. These were the same men who had put together the unbeatable string of takeoffs. The 307th Bomb Wing was engraved on the Fairchild Trophy as the Best of the Best in 1959. They were the Champs of the 2nd Air Force in 1961. They were the same people who pulled Alert and Reflex, or sweated blood over their birds on takeoff. Many felt that it really wasn't the men of the 307th who failed the ORI, but rather SAC's inflexible policy of "Don't tell me about your little problems. We are just interested in results."

The first December Reflex deployment was scheduled for the 6th. Billy Lyons was on one of the early December deployments and wrote:

"We deployed in early December 1961, which would result in our being in Spain during the Christmas holiday period. We didn't like it, but, when you're the new kid on the block, you don't have much choice. Going to Spain, we were scheduled to be number three in a three-ship formation going the southern route, coasting out near Jacksonville, Florida, refueling from tankers from an East Coast base in a refueling area near the Island of Bermuda and proceeding across the ocean to Spain.

"We had three tankers (KC-135s) and as number three we would refuel with the second tanker. Before coasting out, the lead aircraft discovered that the wing tanks wouldn't feed. They could not continue to Spain in this situation and left the formation to go to a missed-air refueling base on the East coast. The number two in our formation took over as lead and we proceeded to the air refueling area. Now we are down to two-on-two situation with the tankers. As we closed on the tankers during the rendezvous, the lead tanker announced they couldn't get the boom down. This meant they couldn't refuel the new lead aircraft in our cell and so the lead also headed for the missed-refueling alternate. That left us, the 'newbies', three 1st lieutenants, all by ourselves to complete the refueling and find our way across the Atlantic.

"After their departure, our tanker started working on an OK from his wing to refuel both of the B-47s and divert to Ramey AFB, Puerto Rico. He got the OK to refuel both our aircraft, land at Ramey, refuel, and then return to his home base. We got word to our second aircraft to turn around and re-rendezvous with us and get his fuel, which they did, and we proceeded to Morón."

Another Reflex flight was scheduled for the 11th. Changes in the deployment route were made due to weather and headwinds in the northern route. The prospects for the launch started looking dim. Weather reports indicated a major winter storm was brewing to the west and had Lincoln Airplane Patch in its sights.

The Reflex birds were towed back from the refueling pits and the launch crews started their ground preflight. While they were working, low gray clouds moved in from the west and the temperature started to plummet. About 1600 gentle light snow began falling. If it didn't get any worse, the Reflex flight would be able to get off without delay.

The light snow continued until the flight crews climbed the ladder and spooled the engines up. They taxied out, called the tower for clearance and pushed the throttles forward. The two B-47s rolled down the runway on time and lifted into the dark sky. The clouds swallowed them before their altimeters read 500 feet.

They got out of Lincoln in the nick of time. The winds picked up and the snow became heavy. Well, it seemed heavy. It was hard to tell if the snow was falling or rushing sideways in the wind. By 1900 that night all air operations were shut down.

The storm showed no signs of leaving the State of Nebraska in the near future. Heavy snow fell all night and into the afternoon of the next day. By the evening of the 12th, the snow was piled up in drifts four- to six-feet high in places. And those were the *small* drifts. It was hard to figure how much snow actually blanketed the base. Officially, Lincoln got just over twelve inches of the white stuff during the forty-eight hour storm.

As soon as the storm moved on the snowplows hit the runway and taxiways. It took another thirty-two hours of non-stop plowing to clear the snow from the flight line and runway so that air operations could get underway. A couple of days later the streets on base and housing area were plowed and the base was back to normal winter conditions.

The accident investigation report on the crash of 53-0347 from the 98th Bomb Wing was completed and forwarded to SAC Headquarters on December 12th. The findings of the board showed there had been no mechanical failures aboard the aircraft. The primary cause cited was, "The pilot had an incapacitating heart attack at a critical phase of flight." It went on to say the copilot was unable to gain control of the aircraft in time to prevent the accident.

The Reflex deployment for December 13th was delayed by the snowstorm. Since they couldn't get off the ground at Lincoln, the return flight was delayed in deploying back to the States. Both flights were able to finally get into the air on the 14th.

There was a Clutch Pedal flight on December 18th. The single B-47 launched at 0925 Saturday morning and flew a normal 50-8 training mission. They recovered at Billy Mitchell Field, Milwaukee, Wisconsin. The facilities at Milwaukee were about the same as O'Hare. The taxi strips were just wide enough to accommodate the B-47. They fired up the engines and returned to Lincoln the next morning.

The last Reflex flight before Christmas left Lincoln on December 20th. This deployment flew the southern route. They coasted out and refueled near Grand Bahamas Island. Then it was the long flight across the pond. It was over a thousand miles longer than the northern route. The two crews were glad to get on the ground, even if they would be in "Sunny Spain" for the holiday.

Gentle snow began to fall on Christmas Eve. There were special candlelight services that Sunday night at the Base Chapel. The light snow continued through the night. Christmas morning saw a new layer of snow on the ground. It was a beautiful morning to celebrate the season by opening presents and spending time with the family, if you could.

Like Thanksgiving, Alert crews were able to spend some time with their families at the Service Club. The sound of tearing paper and gleeful children rang through the club, drowning out the Christmas music being played. Papa SAC gave the crews a present that day; the klaxon was silent that night.

Across the Atlantic, the Reflex crews observed the Holiday in various ways. Billy Lyons wrote:

"I spent Christmas on R&R in Palma. Some American people who owned a restaurant there invited the R&R troops to Christmas dinner. Turkey, dressing and all the trimmings. Very nice of them, but nothing like home. We would have rather been home with family even if it meant fighting the cold and snow."

The year had been full of high and low points. The world situation had brought changes in flight operations. It had been announced the B-47

## Cold War Cornhuskers: The 307th Bomb Wing Lincoln Air Force Base Nebraska 1955-1965

would be retired on a very fast schedule, but then it was put on hold when President Kennedy realized he just might need the old gal. Of course, the lowest point for the wing was failing the ORI. The wing was resilient; they would be back, with hard work. They would show SAC that you couldn't keep a good wing down.

The year ended as it began. Alert crews huddled in the "mole hole" waiting for the klaxon. Silent sentinels standing their post outside with the Alert birds. As midnight approached one of the guards reached down and petted his faithful sentry dog. "Good boy, Hercules. I know it's cold, but we got a job to do." Just before the stroke of midnight light snow started falling; across the ramp the guards pulled their parka hoods up. It looked like another long night in the snow and cold. Sleep well tonight. SAC is on Alert.

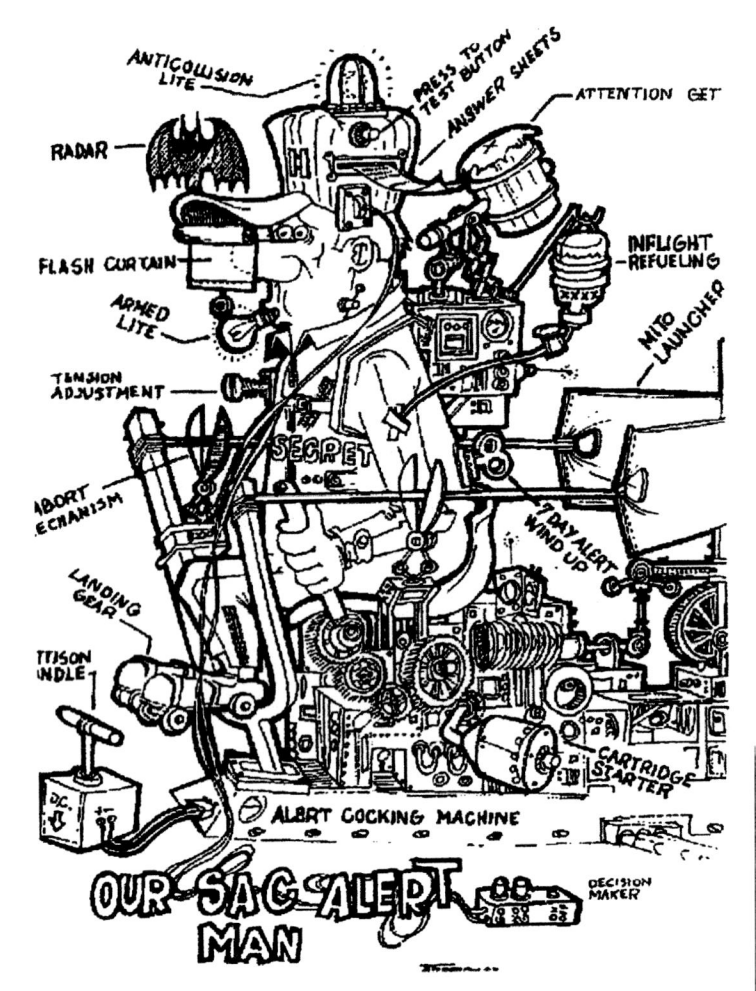

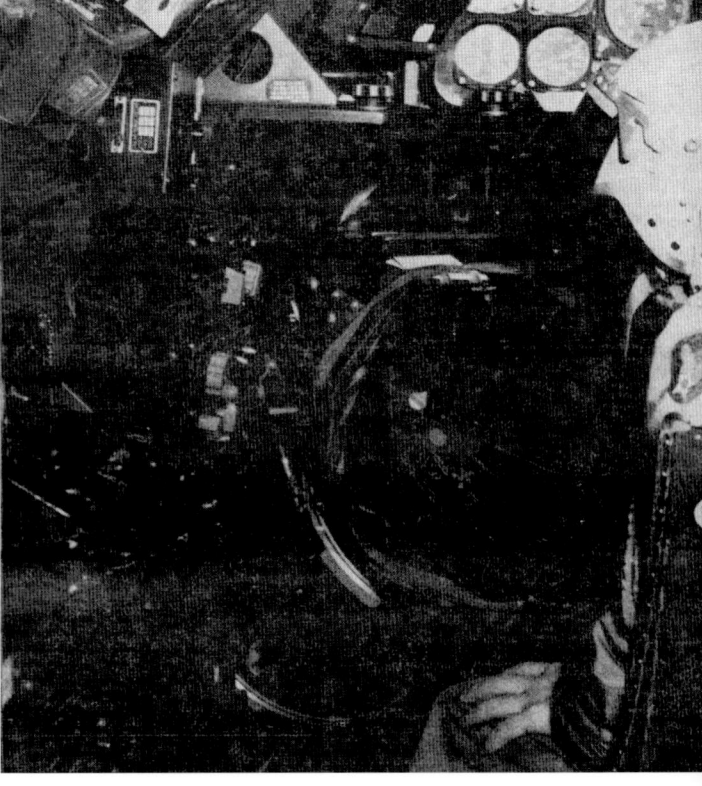

Capt. James Jacobs in his office. (JET SCOOP)

182

## 1961

L-R Col. Mark Burke, Norm Menke, Bud Timmons, Doug Valen, Col. Walter Berg. (USAF)

The Clip In would allow the B-47 to carry four Mark-28 nuclear weapons. (M Hill)

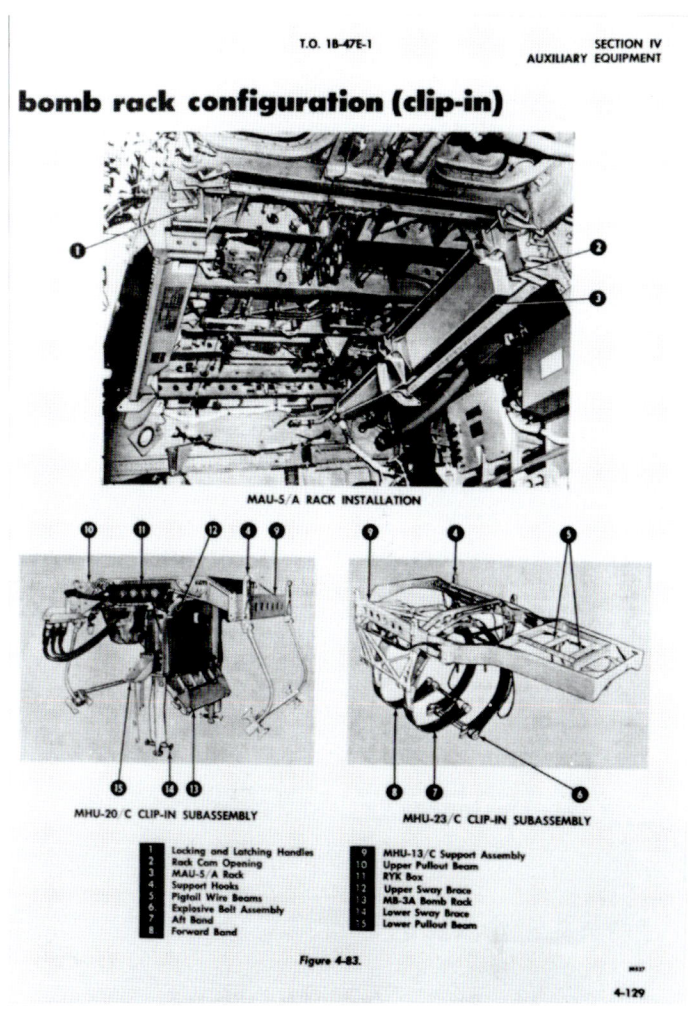

Bomb Rack Configuration (Clip In) from the B-47 Dash-1.

L-R Russell Holst, Tom Wessner, James Moon. Jim Moon was not on the crew when 2111 crashed on take off. Tom Wessner managed to eject. Russell Holst was killed in the accident. (USAAF)

2nd Air Force Bomb Competition winners. L-R. MGen. John D. Ryan, Col. Walter Berg, Maj. William Stringfellow, Lt. Yale Davis, SSgt. Donald Mowery, TSgt George Barnhart. (USAF via Mowery)

183

# Cold War Cornhuskers: The 307th Bomb Wing Lincoln Air Force Base Nebraska 1955-1965

Nebraska Governor's Secretary and Maj. William Stringfellow naming 53-1872 for the 1961 SAC Bombing Competition. (Mowery)

L-R, SSgt. Donald Mowery, Capt. Donald Kellum, Lt. Yale Davis, Maj. William Stringfellow. (Mowery)

Representatives of the 307th Bomb Wing at the 1961 Combat Competition. (Christians)

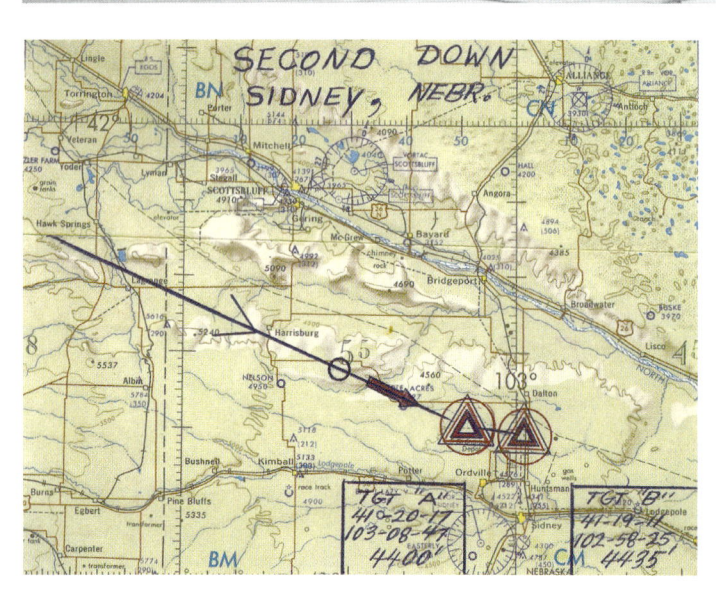

1961 Combat Competition Patch. (Mowery)

Target: SECOND DOWN, Hastings Nebraska. (Kellum)

184

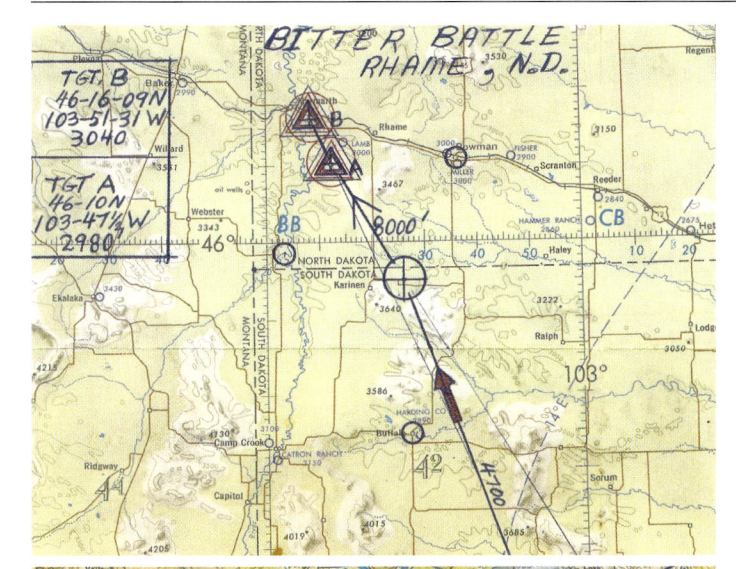

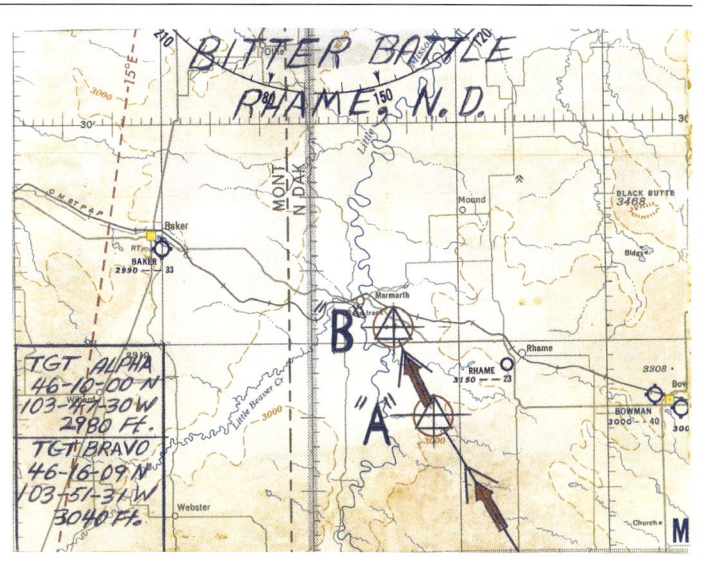

*1961*

Clockwise from above left: Target: BITTER BATTLE, Rhame, North Dakota, BITTER BATTLE, and Target: SPOKANE Spokane, Washington (Kellum)

Ground crew use the J-Shape crane to change an engine. (USAF)

Col. William Bertran assumed command of the 307th on November 27, 1961. (USAF)

185

# 1962

The blare of the klaxon ushered in the New Year at 0320. Alert crews shook off sleep and struggled into their flight suits and boots, then hit the tunnels on a dead run. Arriving at the aircraft, they grabbed their helmets and tuned in the radio to hear what was going on. Crew chiefs fired up ground power units and within six minutes the first bird was ready to taxi.

The Alert crews executed a Coco Alert. The wind was from the south, so it was a short taxi to Runway 17. As each aircraft lined up on the runway they went to full power for about 1000 feet, then backed off and finished with a fast taxi down Runway 17, returning to the Alert pad via the taxiway. Arriving back at the pad, the crew chiefs stood by to get the aircraft serviced and recocked.

When it was over the crews went back to the "mole hole" and tried to relax enough to climb back in the sack for a couple of hours. Those that couldn't relax got a cup of coffee and sat around in an impromptu bull session about Alert and sleep deprivation.

As part of the reorganization of SAC and phase out of the B-47, the 424th Bomb Squadron was officially deactivated effective January 1, 1962. Aircraft and personnel were distributed among the other three squadrons. While this provided more crew personnel for the other squadrons, it didn't help the problem in the maintenance units, which really needed more qualified specialists.

A Reflex deployment should have been launched on Monday the 1st, but was held off because of the holiday. The first Reflex flight was launched on Wednesday, January 3rd. The three-ship cell launched early in the evening and flew the southern route to Spain. To make up for the holiday, another Reflex flight was launched on Thursday the 4th.

Making up for the holiday was fine with the crews that spent the last several weeks in Spain. They were chomping at the bit to get in the air headed home. Billy Lyons recalled:

"Our tour was extended so some crews wouldn't have to deploy to Morón during the time right after Christmas. Thanks a lot! We got back early in January. It was a long flight home via the southern route (near Lajes in the Azores and on to Bermuda and coast-in near Jacksonville, Florida) due to high winds along the northern route.

"First refueling was with a KC-97 near Lajes. As we moved into pre-contact position, the crew notified us they had 50,000 pounds of contaminated aviation gas for us. No problem, except you don't get as much range from av gas as you do from jet fuel, but at that point we were willing to take whatever they had if it meant we could get back to Lincoln without having to ground stage somewhere.

"We spent thirty minutes on the boom, the longest contact I ever had with a KC-97. At one point, the copilot advised that we were losing ground, burning more fuel than we were taking on. The tanker had to pump the last part of the onload from the wing tanks and that was a slow process. We got a KC-135 for the second refueling near Bermuda and that 35,000-pound onload seemed a breeze. We flew thirteen and a half hours, enough in a B-47."

Problems during Reflex didn't always center on getting enough fuel onboard to get home. Pete Todd remembered an interesting problem:

"My crew was redeploying from a Reflex tour in Spain. Everything seemed normal on climb-out until a mild vibration became a loud banging that sounded like it was coming from the left side of the aircraft under the crew compartment. All systems and instruments registered normal so we surmised the entrance door must have been improperly secured by the ground crew before we departed and had become unlatched after takeoff.

"This probably wasn't an immediate safety-of-flight issue, but we realized that we couldn't fly the whole way back to Lincoln with the hatch banging against its housing without some damage to the aircraft, possibly even a hinge failure and loss of the hatch. Therefore, the choice was either to abort the mission and return to our departure base or figure out some way to get the hatch closed. The crew decided to attempt the latter.

"(For those readers who might not be familiar with the interior configuration of the B-47, access into and out of the aircraft was gained by means of a retractable ladder mounted on the inside wall of a four-foot vertical chute below the crew compartment. After the crew boarded the aircraft, the ground crew would normally close the inside pressure door, then stow the ladder and close and latch the entrance hatch. The process would be reversed after landing.)

"By majority vote of the other crewmembers, the copilot (me) was elected to try to secure the door. We leveled off at 10,000 feet since we were going to have to depressurize the aircraft to get to the flopping outer door (remember the inner pressure door?) and I was going to have to scramble around inside the entrance chute without the supplemental oxygen normally available inflight (not considered safe above 10,000 feet).

"I also realized I was going to have to scramble around inside said entrance chute **without** my parachute! The backpack would have been too bulky to permit the kind of contortions that were going to be required in that confined space. My ever-helpful aircraft commander (Gene Hickman) said, 'Don't worry, Pete. Even if you slip and land on the entrance hatch, the air pressure from the slipstream will support your weight and you won't fall out.' I accepted this reassurance with considerable skepticism and decided not to try a field test.

"We depressurized the jet and I climbed out of my seat to release the pressure door. As soon as I had done so, it was obvious that our hypothesis had been correct. The outer entrance hatch was oscillating rapidly and loudly and I could see daylight around the edges.

"There was little time to waste; we couldn't stay at 10,000 feet too long (much higher fuel consumption than at cruise altitude) without compromising our fuel reserves for the long flight across the Atlantic and half the country. It would have been easier if I could have just lain on the floor of the crew compartment and reached down to the open latch. Unfortunately, one would need the trunk and wingspan of a pro basketball player to do this, so it was going to have to be feet first. I took a deep breath, edged my feet into the entrance chute and prepared to lower myself into the (seemingly) gaping abyss.

"My target was the inside handle that was designed to lock or release the hatch. (The B-47's designers had cleverly configured both the entrance hatch and the ladder so that they could be operated from either inside or outside the aircraft.) I needed to lower myself to the point where I could grasp a crossbar on the hatch with one hand, then pull it closed and simultaneously rotate the locking handle with the other hand to secure the hatch. To do that, I needed a foothold.

"When I stopped hyperventilating, I realized that one foot could just barely reach the opening of the crawlway that extended from the bottom of the entrance chute aft to the forward wheel well. In less time than it takes to tell, I wedged my boot into the space, lowered myself to within range of the door (which suddenly looked **VERY** flimsy), grabbed the crossbar, closed and locked the hatch and vaulted back up into the crew compartment faster than a Whack-a-Mole. With pressure door closed, we repressurized the aircraft and climbed to cruising altitude, continuing homebound to our families without further incident. Just another day at the office for the SAC warriors."

January was the first month of the Centralized Scheduling Concept. Flight scheduling would be done through the Deputy Commander for Operations office. Under this concept, squadron planning staff would act as liaison between the crews and central scheduling personnel. Hopefully, this would make flight scheduling for the month easier for flight crews who needed to complete 50-8 training requirements.

The wing operations plan called for maximum use of the RBS Express trains for bomb scoring. The wing would also continue to use RBS sites at Hastings, Nebraska; Ironwood, Michigan; and Joplin, Missouri. To ensure maximum use of the sites, a racetrack pattern had been established to allow bomb runs to be scored every twelve minutes. Nike sites would be able to handle a bomb run every fifteen minutes.

The operations plan also outlined areas that had to be accomplished by all personnel during the upcoming year. Personnel had to qualify as "Marksman" on the firing range. They were also required to pass an open-book test on the Code of Conduct and a fifty-question open-book exam on Disaster Procedures. Personnel who were members of flight crews were required to attend a class on ejection seat procedures.

Along with reorganization, the 307th faced a tight flying schedule to prove to SAC Headquarters that the wing could bounce back from the October ORI debacle. The 307th would launch a minimum of ten sorties each day that weather permitted flying. In January, weather was the big question when it came to air operations.

January 11th found the wing launching six B-47s for training profile missions. Five of the missions went very well. The sixth mission encountered tremendous crosswind conditions during the grid navigation leg. At the end of the leg the B-47 was thirty miles off the planned route. The leg was scored as ineffective, the fourth ineffective navigation leg the wing had during the month.

On January 18th, the B-47 simulator reopened for business. The "sim" had been shut down since the first of the month for a complete update and overhaul. Wing scheduling sent a full schedule to the simulator so crews could get on the list to fulfill the requirement for sim time.

January 22nd dawned clear and cold. Flight crews scheduled to fly didn't like what they heard at the weather briefing. Another storm was headed towards Lincoln. It was due to arrive around noon and could dump six to twelve inches of the white stuff on the patch before moving on to the east.

Sure enough, low clouds and light snow arrived just after 1300. The snowfall continued to get heavier as the afternoon progressed. By 1700 visibility was down to a quarter of a mile with snow slithering across the flight line like large white snakes. The scheduled Reflex launch, along with all other sorties, was called off. Flights that had launched before the storm arrived were diverted to other bases.

Cold weather and snow not only interfered with the flying schedule; they also caused problems with Alert aircraft sitting on the pad waiting for the klaxon to go off. Paul Koski recalled a problem he experienced:

"We were in the Alert quarters playing poker with some of the flight crews when it was announced that the crew of 4212 should report to the aircraft. It was one of those nights when the temperature was around 20 degrees and blowing snow. We knew it had to be important since nobody in their right mind would want to be out in this type of weather.

"When we got to the aircraft, we were met by several people: the Alert duty officer, fire department and, of course, Security Police. It was the guard who had discovered the fuel leak and called it in; fuel was dripping from the bomb bay doors. We had a high level discussion of what we were going to have to do and what our options were. I told them until we found out where the fuel was coming from we couldn't make a rational decision. I told them we couldn't put power on the aircraft because of the leak. They wanted to know how we would open the bomb bay doors without power and how we would download the bomb and all the suppositions on what we should do.

"I said that I would open the bomb bay doors and went into the wheel well, climbed up to the hydraulic area and pulled the cable that releases the bomb bay door latches, whereupon about a gallon of fuel poured onto the ramp. Several officers were panic-stricken and one said, 'You know if you had pulled the wrong way you would have jettisoned the bomb on the ramp.' I told them of course I knew that, but I also knew the system and which way to pull the cable, and anyway I didn't drop the bomb.

"I started to go into the bomb bay to check for the leak, but was stopped and told I couldn't go in there because I didn't have top secret clearance. I said, 'Fine, you find the damn leak and tell me what options we have to fix it.' The flight crew said that fuel was coming from a drain valve and dripping around twenty drops a minute. We opened the discussion of what to do:

"1. We could plug the drain until we got off Alert. Estimated time: 1 hour.

"2. We could plug the line, put power on the aircraft and download the weapon, defuel the aircraft, change the valve and upload the bomb. Estimated time: 5 hours.

"3. I could get a new valve and install it by placing my finger on the hole. We would lose a little fuel, but it could be done. However, there was a risk that I could cross thread the valve and we would still have to defuel and remove the bomb.

"I told them that, whatever they decided, I would still have to verify which valve and, if we had to plug it, I would need to know what size Dow rod we would need. If they elected to change the valve, I would need to know which valve and the part number of the valve. This meant I would have to be able to get into the bomb bay. They finally waived the top-secret clearance and let me inspect the valve. Naturally, we observed the two-man concept. Security police weren't too happy.

"I told them I could change the valve, but it would take about thirty minutes to get it from supply and another thirty minutes to change the valve and wash the accumulated fuel from around the area. This included a leak check of the valve. In case you're wondering, I did cycle the valve several times because sometimes the 'O' ring takes a seat and you can reseal it. It didn't work; it still leaked.

"To expedite getting the aircraft back on Alert, they let me change the valve. It took less than an hour to fix the leak, but it took almost two hours to decide what to do. We had the aircraft back on Alert in about three hours, since they had to recock the bird."

January was a busy month for the 307th. Due to the weather it was a constant battle to get aircraft launched. The wing was scheduled to fly 186 sorties; 158 were flown as effective sorties. 18 of the ineffective sorties were due to weather cancellations. The wing chalked up over 2,065 hours in the air.

February started with a Reflex deployment back to the U.S. from Spain on February 2nd. They traveled the southern route, meeting tankers near the Azores and then another refueling near Bermuda. In spite of the snow and cold at Lincoln, the crews were glad to be back home with family and friends.

February 5th saw the first Reflex sorties for the month headed towards Spain. On the way over, they filled a 50-8 requirement by making an RBS run on a Nike site. After the run it was find the tankers, refuel and on to Spain. With the arrival of this deployment, the 307th had ten B-47s sitting on the Alert at Morón. Crews were hoping the simmering Berlin situation would cool down so there wouldn't be so many Reflex sorties coming and going at the same time.

Missions scheduled for February included low-level Short Look runs against the Big Talk Express site near Barksdale AFB, Louisiana. The first missions had problems due to the bad selection of aiming points. The 307th got a TWX from Barksdale saying that the use of Big Talk would end on February 9th.

Wing headquarters received a scathing message from 2nd Air Force on the 9th. The message was the result of the last quarter MCS review by 2nd Air Force. It pointed out that the wing failed to meet 50-8 requirements and the wing reliability was 0% due to the failed ORI. The 307th was listed as unsatisfactory and not up to 2nd Air Force standards. "It is indicative of poor management and control in all areas. Immediate action must be taken to review control, management and procedures in all areas to assure satisfactory performance and compliance with existing directives."

The wing staff was thunderstruck by the message. They knew the MCS points and wing efficiency would be rated at 0%. Also, the wing would be penalized in the 50-8 training area. But why bring all of this out again almost three months after the fact? The wing had been busting backside since October to bounce back from the ORI. They felt this harsh message was an unwarranted "kick in the gut while they are down, just to see if they could get back up" maneuver from 2nd Air Force.

Sunday afternoon, February 11th, was a cold, crisp sunny day on the Alert pad. At 1505 the klaxon went off, sending the crews towards their aircraft. The first bird was up and running within six minutes. They contacted control and were given a Blue Dot Delta Alert response message. It was the order to launch! The crew chiefs pulled the chocks and the lead aircraft started down the taxi strip towards Runway 35. By the time the first aircraft reached the end of the runway, the Alert was downgraded to a Coco response. The Alert lasted a total of thirty-six minutes.

Ever since the Black Forest Incident back in November, SAC had called one Delta Alert a month. The exact reason for taking the Alert crews to the brink of launching under Positive Control was never explained to the crews. Under SAC Alert Guidelines, a minimum of eight Bravo and two Coco practice Alerts were required during the month. 2nd Air Force and the 818th Air Division could call a practice Alert at any time, with no limit.

Two routine missions launched from Lincoln on the morning of February 16th. The two B-47s flew a standard profile with navigation legs and bomb runs on low-level targets, along with a high altitude run. After the mission they recovered at Billy Mitchell Field, Milwaukee, Wisconsin, as part of the Clutch Pedal program. Some of the crews that had to recover at the dispersal bases thought the exercise was a pain in the backside, but the experience gained would prove invaluable before the year was out.

Weather remained the number one enemy of the 307th in February. Cold weather brought out the primary winter problem of the B-47 fleet: fuel leaks. Great strides had been made in sealing the fuel tanks against the icy grip of old man winter. There were still some aircraft prone to leaks, but it was nowhere near what it had been in previous winters.

The Nebraska winter "Hawk" was the real problem. The snow from one storm would just be cleared away and the weather forecast would find another storm bearing down on the patch or messing things up in the scheduled oil burner routes.

On Monday, the 19th, the wing had a full launch schedule. Three Reflex deployments were supposed to leave around 1800. There were seventeen other sorties scheduled to launch to fill 50-8 requirements. The night before, KOLN-TV posted a forecast for heavy snow beginning around 0800.

Shortly after the troops reported for duty at 0745 the snow started falling. It went from light to heavy in a matter of just a few minutes. The "Hawk" had arrived. It was evident very early in the day that the entire flying schedule was in jeopardy. Before noon, the men in the Control Tower couldn't see the aircraft parked at Papa 1, which was the parking spot nearest them. All air operations were canceled for the day.

The storm moved out in the early morning hours of the 20th. Snowplows were unleashed as soon as the snow slowed enough for the plows to be effective. They worked through the night and on past dawn to clear the concrete. It was another long night for the snow crews in the cabs of their plows.

While the snow crews were busy trying to clear the snow, those who could huddled around the nearest TV. That morning, Col John H. Glenn was launched into orbit around the earth as part of Project Mercury. After several delays that morning, the Atlas rocket boosted Glenn into orbit, where he made three circuits of the earth before his splashdown in the Atlantic. The United States had finally put a man in space.

The delayed Reflex flight was finally able to launch for Spain on the 21st. That evening, there were six B-47s headed for Spain along the southern route. Refueling was a bit dicey since there were six bombers to refuel instead of the usual three. Arrangements had been made to have extra tankers for the mission. The flight actually qualified for a mass gas refueling over the Bahamas.

There were several other sorties launched that day. Two of the profiles included RBS runs on the Go Boy route near Corsicana, Texas.

188

## 1962

After takeoff, the two B-47s climbed out of Lincoln and headed to their refueling rendezvous over Missouri. The tankers were waiting on the refueling track and the B-47s adjusted speed and slowly moved in and hooked up. After they got their offload, the two bombers slid away from the tankers and headed on to their individual profiles.

Each bomber crew flew a navigation leg lasting about two hours, then a high altitude bomb run, followed by a low-level run on the Go Boy RBS site. These were the first missions against that particular RBS site. The 307th was scheduled to use this site until March 31st. After visiting Corsicana, the planes flew another short nav leg and then headed back for Lincoln.

February was a short month, so the wing had to cram as many sorties into the schedule as possible. Add weather problems and the 307th had trouble filling all the 50-8 squares desperately needed to get back in the good graces of 2nd Air Force and SAC Hq.

The wing finished the month with a Reflex deployment on Wednesday, the 28th. The flight of three B-47s left Lincoln at about 1800 and flew towards Florida, coasting out near Jacksonville. After refueling near Bermuda, they headed out over the Atlantic for the long flight to Spain.

The wing flew 174 sorties during February, 138 of which were scored as effective. The wing lost 20 sorties to either bad weather at launch or bad weather in the refueling area. During the month bombing scores improved over January's. The wing scored 31 effective Long Look Large Charge bomb runs out of 34 attempted. The Short Look Large Charge bomb runs were still giving the wing problems. The wing made 162 short look large charges, of which 142 were scored effective.

Three aircraft left Morón on March 2nd for redeployment to Lincoln. They traveled the southern route, refueling near the Azores and again over the Bahamas. Coming in towards Lincoln, they made a bomb run on the Rough Road bomb plot near Joplin, Missouri.

The first March Reflex flight from Lincoln departed on the 5th. For a while, it looked like it would be canceled due to low clouds and snow that afternoon. The system moved out just in time for the mission to be launched. One of the Reflex aircraft was unable to refuel when the tanker couldn't transfer fuel and had to divert to an East coast base and ground stage the next day.

Late evening on the 5th, another weather system moved in on the heels of the earlier storm. This one was typical for March: not much snow, just a lot of freezing drizzle to turn the ramp into a skating rink. About midnight, the drizzle ended and banks of thick fog began rolling in. Visibility was down to zero and stayed there through the night.

The sun came up, but the fog hid it from view until 1000, when it finally burned through and started shining on the ice-covered patch. 2nd Air Force called a Coco Alert at 1120. The first crew reported ready in nine minutes. The planes taxied very slowly through the entire Alert due to the conditions on the runway and taxi strip. It took over forty-five minutes to complete the exercise.

An event across the Atlantic in France would have a sad effect on a lot of the maintenance troops of the 307th. On Thursday, the 8th, a C-130 Hercules, 55-0020, from the 317th Troop Carrier Wing crashed near Alençon, France. The C-130 was returning to its base after a routine paradrop training flight. All fifteen aboard were lost.

One of the crewmen aboard was TSgt Robert Conway, former member of the 307th OMS. When news of Bob Conway's loss arrived, the troops on the flight line who knew and worked with him were devastated. He was well liked by everyone who had known and served with him.

Bob had served as a gunner during World War II. He flew on B-26 Marauders and was assigned to Russell Bowling's crew for most of his service. Mary (Bowling) Ashton wrote:

"Bob was a member of Russ's crew from April 1943 until his plane was shot up and they crash-landed back in England. Bob was on most of the 47 missions Russ flew in the European Theater. Another of that crew in England during WW II sent me many interesting tidbits about Bob and the rest of the crew. Shortly after their training began in the B-26 Marauder, known as the 'Widow Maker', with a reputation for 'One-a-day in Tampa Bay,' an emergency bailout procedure arrived from Wing Headquarters. The pilot was to ring the bailout bell and repeat the word 'jump' over the intercom three times. As they prepared for their next flight, Bob asked if Russ would use the procedure. Russ replied, 'I certainly will, but you better go out on the first 'jump' if you want to hear the other two!'"

Ernie Pence knew Bob and wrote:

"Many of our comrades-in-arms were veterans of WW II. I happened to have had the pleasure of working with many of those fine people. One was TSgt Robert Conway. He had so many medals, it was embarrassing to stand next to him in formation. His aircraft had been shot down three times. It flew round-robins for 24 hours on D-Day before the maintenance officer grounded it, saying, 'That thing will fall apart in the air if it goes up again; too much damage.' Sgt Conway was a tail gunner on a B-26.

"His recollections of those desperate days were spellbinding for those of us that had the opportunity to hear them. He told of hedgehopping in France on D-Day to avoid flak. In one incident, he recalled popping over a hedgerow and the navigator spotted a German crew unloading a 60-ton Tiger tank from a flatcar on a railroad siding. The navigator called, 'Power, power, power, climb!' He toggled a bomb that went off right under the tank. As tail gunner, he marveled at the sight of the big tank rising up in the air and tumbling with the crew around it doing the same thing.

"The Hill family knew Bob and his wife, Annabelle. They lived in a mobile home park on top of a hill near the West "O" Drive-In. Mom and dad would get together with the Conways and play cards. Mike Conway and I would spend some of the time flying balsa wood gliders and other SAC BRAT activities. I remember when dad told me of Sgt Conway's loss. I was saddened for Mike and the family over the loss of his dad. I could only imagine how I would feel if I had suddenly lost my dad.

"There was talk of sending a delegation from the 307th to the funeral. Somehow it never developed. Dad took up a collection from the troops who knew Bob Conway and managed to get it to the family. TSgt Robert Conway rests with his comrades-in-arms in Section 42, Site 305 of Arlington National Cemetery, Washington, D.C."

On Monday, March 19th, 2nd Air Force sent a message to SAC Headquarters requesting the 307th be taken off probation. The message pointed out action had been taken to clear all of the deficiencies found during the October ORI. This included key personnel changes, retraining and reorganization of the A&E Squadron. The message was a nice way of informing SAC Headquarters that the rehabilitation of the 307th Bomb Wing had been completed.

SAC sent a message on the 21st saying there would be no more "Delta" practice Alerts. That was fine with the Alert crews, who could never understand the reason to issue a launch order, then downgrade the entire Alert to a Coco Exercise.

The "Hawk" paid another visit to the patch on the 22nd. Snow and freezing rain pelted the base all morning and afternoon. Low clouds and high winds caused air operations to cease until the weather conditions improved. However, just because flight operations were called off didn't mean the wing took a holiday. Flight crews used the time to do more target study and mission planning. The troops on the flight line kept working on the aircraft in the cold and freezing rain.

While the "Hawk" was visiting the patch, a message arrived from Offutt dealing with some revisions in Alert procedures. During a Coco Alert, the Mobile Strike Force was to do a complete sweep of the taxiway used. They were then to go to the end of the runway and position themselves for perimeter protection of the Alert aircraft.

There were also revised procedures for Minimum Reaction Posture under DEFCON 1. The new procedure called for the Alert force to taxi to a point just short of the runway. The operational concept was that the force would either launch under Positive Control or return to the Alert ramp. In the event CINCSAC desired the aircraft be maintained at MRP, they would keep minimum engines running to provide starting power for all engines without the need for ground power units.

Official notification that the 307th was taken off probation was received by the wing staff on March 27th. However, everyone knew the 307th wouldn't be completely off the hook and back in the good graces of SAC until they passed the next ORI.

The first Reflex flight of April deployed from Lincoln on the 2nd. The flight of three B-47s flew the Southern route refueling near the Bahamas, then flew on to Spain. With the situation in Berlin at a stalemate, Reflex had been scaled back to almost pre-crisis level.

The 307th may have been taken off probation, but everyone was still "nervous in the service" about when the next ORI would put the wing in the hot seat to perform and show SAC Headquarters the 307th was again up to snuff. Every time a transient KC-97 or KC-135 landed, every eye on the flight line would follow the arrival and get "that old feeling" that maybe the arrivals were going to call an ORI.

On the morning of April 10th, a staff car arrived at the main gate. The Air Policeman on duty waved them through after checking for the appropriate vehicle sticker in the corner of the windshield. After all, staff cars came and went on a daily basis. This particular car headed down 9th Street towards Base Headquarters. On arrival, they headed for the 818th Commander's office and demanded an immediate meeting. The SAC IG had managed to sneak in the back door (actually the main gate).

Within moments of the IG's arrival the 307th battle staff was summoned. The klaxon blared, sending the Alert crews on a mad dash to their aircraft. The first aircraft was ready to taxi in four minutes. The short reaction time for the first aircraft was because the crew was preparing to move the aircraft a few feet to prevent the tires from getting flat spots sitting under the weight of the EWO load.

The birds taxied to the end of Runway 17 and executed the usual full power, then fast taxi down the runway and return to the Alert ramp. Arriving back at the Alert area they were met by the crew chiefs and munitions maintenance crews, who started downloading the nukes. By now, there was no question in the minds of the men of the 307th. It was a full-blown ORI!

While the Alert birds were being downloaded for the first ORI mission, the crews assembled in a briefing room to take an examination on EWO procedures. Everyone knew they had to pass the exam or the ORI would be busted before it really began. After the test, the crews were briefed on the mission they would fly for the ORI.

At the briefing, they learned the mission would begin with the six Alert aircraft launching in three-ship MITO cells with ten minutes between the two cells. After the heavyweight takeoff they would fly individual profiles consisting of a two-hour navigation leg, air refueling, ECM, H-Hour Control ETA, low-level nav leg, Short Look RBS and high altitude Large Charge RBS runs.

Out on the ramp, the ground crews had gotten the word to generate the follow-on force. The wing would be required to generate and fly a total of thirty sorties, including the Alert aircraft. Six aircraft would fly each day over the next five days. Each B-47 would be generated to EWO mission status except for nuclear weapons.

There were several aircraft that had been scheduled to fly training missions when the ORI began. They were the first to be generated for the follow-on force. There was a constant stream of B-47s being towed to the refueling pits for servicing, then towed back to their slot on the ramp. The 781 Forms were checked and double-checked to make sure there was nothing that hadn't been taken care of. Oxygen, engine oil, hydraulic fluid and water injection were topped off and double-checked.

Whether it was an ORI or routine flying, servicing the aircraft had to be done according to the checklist. Jim Villa recalled:

"When arriving on the fuel pit location, the airplane would be chocked and the five point grounding wire would be attached. The grounding wire would be attached to each of the four landing gear struts and one end of the grounding cable to a grounding point in the concrete slab. Care would have to be taken so the chocks were not too close to the wheels. If the chocks were too close to the wheels, the chocks would become jammed under the tires when the weight of the fuel was put on the airplane. The MD-3 power unit would be positioned and power put on the airplane. The standing procedure was to have the power unit upwind from the airplane so fuel vapors would not be traveling to the MD-3 power unit.

"During refueling and defueling, the man in the cockpit would move to the copilot's position and operate the copilot's fuel panel switches and monitor the individual fuel tank gauges. He would have a headset on and there was an individual (usually the NCOIC) on the ground headset watching the operation from outside the airplane. One man would be stationed at the MD-3 power unit and the other man would be stationed at the refueling pit. The connecting hose was a four-inch flexible with twist-on locking connections. The Coleman driver always stayed in or near the towing tractor during fueling operations."

The first launch would be a three-ship MITO at 1830. It would be followed at 1840 by the next three B-47s launching in MITO configuration. The first three aircraft spooled up and taxied to the end of Runway 17. They launched at fifteen second intervals. Everyone who could spare a moment turned and watched the launch. It was impressive to see three B-47s rolling down the runway at the same time.

Ten minutes later the next three B-47s were rolling down the runway, leaving massive clouds of black smoke hanging in the air. The last one seemed to use more runway than she should have before getting into the air at what seemed the last moment. The men on the ground watched as the three ships fanned out a little to avoid the jet wash and wake turbulence of the B-47 in front of them.

About eight hours later the birds returned to the nest. The crews were tired after the long mission. The first question posed to them was about how the mission had gone. Everyone got the required fuel load, navigation looked good, and there weren't any major problems on the bomb runs. So far, so good!

When the first wave landed they were towed to the refueling pits and refueled. Then they were serviced with everything needed for an immediate turnaround flight. Weapons carriers arrived and the aircraft reloaded for Alert. When they were serviced and loaded, they were taxied back to the Alert pad and recocked by the crews.

Every day it was the same pressure-cooker atmosphere. Get the aircraft serviced and ready to fly, each and every move under the watchful eye of the IG Staff. One major problem or false move on any aircraft could spell disaster for the wing. It was critical that everything went according to the ORI schedule and guidelines.

Other members of the IG Staff were busy checking other areas that had failed during the last ORI. They spent a lot of time in the Command Post, Operations, and target study areas. They also went through the Alert "mole hole" with a fine-tooth comb.

## 1962

There was a Reflex deployment scheduled for Monday, the 16th. Three aircraft were to depart for Sunny Spain. Although they were leaving families, the crews were almost glad to get away from the tension-filled environment of the ORI.

Just after the Reflex flight departed Lincoln, the last six crews were getting their final weather briefing for the last wave of the ORI. The local weather and weather over the targets looked good. It was the weather in the refueling area that gave the crews some concern. There was the possibility of thunderstorms along the refueling track.

Flight crews for the last wave reported to their aircraft and started the preflight walkaround. Because they were under the eyes of the umpires, the crews took a little extra time to be sure that everything was done by the checklist and as mechanically perfect as humanly possible.

The lead aircraft was 53-6244, whose abort during the last ORI had contributed to the wing failing. There was a certain amount of trepidation about flying 6244 in the ORI, but there really wasn't any choice. She was available, so she had to be used. The flight crew climbed aboard and began starting the engines. This time old 6244 was up to snuff and led the way to the runway, then into the air for the last wave of the ORI.

All six aircraft launched on time and headed into the wild blue ocean of air. The first nav leg went according to the flight plan. Aerial refueling was next. Approaching the refueling area, it was plain to see that the weather wizards were right. Thunderheads were popping up all over the place.

Turbulence caused problems in the refueling area for the last aircraft. By the time they arrived, the thunderstorms were boiling upwards beyond their altitude with angry black centers. The crew managed to find the tanker and moved into position. With all of the bouncing around there were several disconnects, but each time they moved back in and hooked up. It took awhile, but they managed to take on enough fuel to be scored as effective for the ORI.

When the birds arrived back at Lincoln there was the usual, "How'd it go?" They would have to wait with bated breath for the bomb scores to come in. The crews believed they had flown the profile according to the mission plan. There hadn't been any major problems during the last mission. One of the crews believed they might have scored a "shack" on the final bomb run.

It was an entirely different mood at the Base Theater for this ORI briefing. By now it had leaked out that the wing had passed. It was only a formality, but everyone wanted to find out just how well the wing had done. There were some recommendations brought out by the IG. None of them were major problems, just basic housekeeping recommendations. The wing scored "Excellent" in the generation of the force. Navigation was "Outstanding". Refueling was scored as "Excellent" in spite of the problems with the thunderstorms. ECM runs were "Satisfactory". The all-important bombing scores were "Excellent". The crew aboard 6244 had indeed scored a shack during their final high altitude bomb run. When all of the scores were tabulated the wing was rated as "Outstanding" for the ORI. There was some celebrating at the various clubs on and off base that night, even if it was Tuesday.

During April, several of the 307th B-47s were sent to the depot for Project Red Barn. This was for inspection of the wings at Wing Station 354. Modifications were done to eliminate any problems, such as cracks which may have been found during the inspection.

The last Reflex deployment for April launched at 1820 on the 31st. Reflex sorties had continued to be one of the major flying activities for the wing. With the commitment to maintain 50% of SAC bombers on ground Alert status, the 307th would continue to send aircraft and crews to Spain every Monday and Wednesday.

May would be recorded in the wing history as a routine training month. Home Alert and Reflex would make up the majority of the operational activities for the month. Since the wing had just passed an ORI, there shouldn't be any worry about another one so close after the one in April.

On the home front, there were a lot of officers and airmen furthering their education. 53 Airmen completed requirements for High School through either GED or Lincoln Adult High School. There were also 112 airmen taking Extension Course Institute (ECI) courses. Over 52% of non-college graduate officers were working towards their degree.

A message from SAC Headquarters arrived on May 14th. The directive stated that any major work on an engine would no longer be done while the engine was mounted on the aircraft. The directive would certainly result in more engine changes in the future. It would also mean a heavier workload for the short-staffed engine shop.

There was the usual Monday Reflex deployment scheduled for May 7th. The flight crews reported for the flight and received the latest weather briefing at Base Operations. They got their flight lunches and headed for their aircraft. The preflight was done by the checklist and everything looked good.

With the fire guards posted, the crews began starting the #4 engine on each of the Spain-bound birds. Engine start was completed and the three B-47s taxied out towards Runway 35. The first two aircraft launched with no problem. The last aircraft, 53-1812, moved onto the runway and was given takeoff clearance. The pilot pushed the six throttles forward and then hit the water injection switch. Clouds of black smoke billowed from the engines as the water alcohol mixture poured into the combustion chambers of the J-47 engines.

Just as the brakes were released, the flow of water alcohol in the number six engine failed. The crew pulled the power off and aborted the take off. After returning to the ramp, the ground crews tore into the innards of the bomber to find and correct the problem. Repairs would take at least two hours, so the flight was postponed.

Another Reflex flight was on tap for Wednesday, May 9th. By now, 53-1812 had been repaired and would join the other three aircraft for the long haul to Spain. Adjustments had been made for the extra aircraft in the refueling area. After getting airborne, the four B-47s completed the flight with no major problems.

Two B-47s launched for routine 50-8 training sorties on May 10th. The crews flew a standard profile with nav leg, air refueling and several bomb runs. Their missions went according to the planned profile. At the end of the mission they landed at Milwaukee as part of the Clutch Pedal program.

During the last several weeks, B-47s on routine training flights over southern Florida had been receiving some strange radar signals. A copilot from the 2nd Bomb Wing realized they were being painted by Soviet Fan Song radar. He made some notes as to the time and area the signals had been encountered. At mission debrief he reported the incident.

At first, it was believed the signals had come from Eglin AFB, Florida. It was later determined that Eglin had not been conducting any type of radar tests, much less using anything like a Soviet Fan Song. This brought up some interesting questions.

The copilot was given a rather long series of tests to determine if he could actually identify Fan Song signals on his AN-APS-54 unit. The tests showed he was able to identify the Fan Song signal every time it was sent. The big questions now became "Where had the signal originated? Who was equipped with the latest type of Soviet anti aircraft radar?"

There was only one place friendly enough with the Soviet Union and close enough to Florida to paint an aircraft with that type of radar. The radar signals had to be coming from the island of Cuba. That answered one question but posed others. Why did Cuba have the radar and what were they trying to protect?

There was a Coco Alert on the afternoon of the 15th. During engine start the #1 engine on 53-4218 would not start. The crew tried several times to get the engine started. The engine would rotate, but there was no ignition. For a moment the crew gave serious consideration to taxiing on five engines, but decided against it and 4218 aborted the Alert. Before the Alert aircraft were back on the pad, the ground crew was digging into the problem on 4218. The aircraft had to be downloaded and defueled before anything could be done about the engine. Another B-47 was brought up to the Alert pad and cocked to replace 4218.

The 307th had been assigned the Steelman Express Route for low-level bomb scoring. The crews had problems on the route from the very beginning. Several mentioned the charts did not match the actual lay of the land. The aiming points that had been selected were not in the right place, according to the charts.

On May 30th, the last Reflex deployment for the month left Lincoln for Spain. On that same day, three B-47s departed Morón for the long flight home to Nebraska. The aircraft headed home would try something that hadn't been done for quite some time. They attempted a fireout of the 20 mm tail guns. Over the mid-Atlantic, the copilots turned their seats and warmed up the gun radar. After going through the safety checks they depressed the fire button. Two of the B-47s got a 50% fire out, while the third achieved over 70% fire out.

During May, the 307th spent 1,909 hours in the air completing 239 sorties. Short Look bomb runs improved during the month. There were 58 attempts and 56 were scored reliable. Long Look bomb runs were one hundred per cent effective. The wing was 95% effective on their air refueling sorties.

The 307th and 98th Bomb Wing Alert forces were combined to form the 818th Strategic Aerospace Division Alert Force.

The Steelman Express route gave the wing all kinds of problems during May. The problems were primarily the result of the poor quality of the 200-Series Air Target Charts. The charts available to the wing were inadequate in terrain features and did not indicate bright cultural radar returns in the aiming point area. Moreover, the selected aiming points were less than 70% of the predicted radar intensity. These factors were blamed for the low (77% effective) score on that route.

May saw a lower than normal reenlistment rate for the wing. One of the reasons for the lower rate was the release of those who had been frozen during the Berlin Crisis buildup. Those who were "short" and extended during the crisis were now getting out. The 307th OMS was the only squadron that reported 100% reenlistment for those eligible.

There were, of course, those who were glad the Berlin situation had settled down enough to finally get out of "this man's Air Force". Promotions were slow, hours were long, pay was low, and there was not much hope of things getting better. Then there was pulling Alert, Reflex and TDY. For a lot of the troops, it wasn't at all the glamorous life painted by the recruiter when they signed up. They figured they had given enough of themselves to their country and could do a lot better on the outside.

Since SAC had sent the directive about major engine work not being done while the engine was mounted on the aircraft there had been a lot more complete engine changes. The directive meant longer hours for the engine shop personnel. During May there were fourteen complete engines changes.

With the start of another month, there were always housekeeping changes that had to be accomplished. Several of these changes dealt with security. The changes included changing the password on the Alert ramp and safe combinations. Changes like this could cause problems. Doug Valen wrote:

"One of our normal training mission requirements was for the copilot and navigator to copy a simulated 'go-code' message on the high frequency radio sometime during the mission. Then, using some special documentation from our 'Communication Kit', we would practice decoding the message and fill out a log to be turned in with our mission papers.

"These documents at that time were referred to as KAA-29 and KAC-72, if my memory serves me correctly. They were highly classified and controlled, and had to be accounted for at all times when they were out of the 'safe'. These kits were numbered and kept in small olive drab bags in the Squadron safe. The copilot would check them out of the safe in the squadron before every flight and then lock them back in the safe after the flight. The forms changed each month and were replaced by updated information on the 1st of the month.

"We didn't always have time to do the decoding during the mission, so we would occasionally write down the message and then wait till we returned to the squadron and do the practice decoding during our mission debriefing before turning in the 'Comm Kit'.

"Our crew had taken off on a mission one evening on the last day of the month and returned early in the morning of the 1st day of the next month. I had all the necessary forms to decode, but the squadron changed the lock combination on the safe and I didn't have the new combination.

"I did my decoding at debriefing and put the 'Comm Kit' back in my flight bag for later locking in the safe. Norm Menke apparently pulled the kit out of my bag to do his checking and neglected to put the kit back in my bag. At the end of debriefing, I went to the safe, thinking the 'Com Kit' was safely in my bag, but I could not get the safe open. Then I noticed a sign reminding us that the safe combination had been changed earlier in the evening. I had no place to put the 'Comm Kit' so I took it home, thinking it would be safe locked in my house.

"The next morning I received a call from the Squadron Ops Officer, Maj Frank Fish. He asked me where my 'Comm Kit' was, and I said right here in my bag. I explained the problem with the safe combination. He sternly told me to get it out of my bag. When I attempted to do so, I could not find it. At that point he told me he had found it lying on the table in the debriefing room. I then realized what had happened.

"There was a long silence and he asked me what the classification of the 'kit' was. He then said that what he probably **should** do was take me out behind the Squadron and shoot me! I guess as a brand new copilot, I was not real sure just what he would do. Needless to say, it was a good lesson in 'security' and I never made that mistake again."

Harold "Butch" Leppi recalled a password change that caused problems for him:

"My aircraft was going to be towed to the Alert area. When we were ready to go, servicing showed up to do the towing. The password had been changed to 'Lost Cause 28'. If a security airman challenged you with 'Lost 28', you were supposed to answer 'Cause 28'.

"After going up and down the Alert line looking for our parking spot, a security pickup with about six guards in the back stopped us, challenged us saying, 'Lost 28'. I had forgotten the new password, getting uploaded and ready to go on Alert. I looked at the towing crew, like, 'Can you help me here?' No one said anything. The guard again issued the challenge. 'Lost 28'. I said, 'You ain't shitten.' I hadn't heard anything but the word, 'Lost'. Needless to say, we were then told to spread-eagle on the flight line

# 1962

and stayed there until our squadron commander came and vouched for us. Not a good way to start Alert."

Flying for the month kicked off on Friday, June 1st. There were seven launches in the morning, followed by seven in the early evening. Getting the birds ready for a morning takeoff could be an all night job for the ground crews. Butch Leppi wrote:

"My aircraft was parked on Pit 20 with a bomb bay tank fuel leak. After the leak was fixed, we had to change a water-alcohol pump on the left side of the aircraft prior to a scheduled takeoff the next morning. Ernie Pence (one hell of a good mechanic) volunteered to stay and help Kenny and me change the pump. It was a good thing, as he was small enough to fit through the access hole in the wing up to his waist. We were towed to R-1 and cocked at an angle so we could run the engines to check it out after we changed the pump.

"Prior to being towed to R-1, we ordered an MD-3, floodlights, and a B-1 stand. So we went to ops to get some coffee until the equipment arrived. Ernie said he would change the pump only if he could run engines to check it out. We all agreed. After we got the equipment, Kenny and I were working on other discrepancies in the aircraft forms. Ernie, with a heater duct tied to his butt, disappeared up inside the wing to start pulling the bad pump.

"We worked all night and Ernie completed the pump change around 0430. We ordered water alcohol servicing, filled her up and Ernie went upstairs to start engines. Well, after checking out the pump (the noise at that time of the morning was horrendous with the engine running), we shut it down. Our maintenance truck pulled up and the night line chief said, 'Didn't you guys know that there were to be no engine run-ups from midnight to six in the morning?' We said, 'We were not aware of any SOP stating that.' The chief said it was by Col Corbin's order."

June's first Reflex deployments left Lincoln at 1800 on the 4th. The 307th would launch Reflex flights every Monday and Wednesday during June. The wing would continue to deploy to Morón, Spain, but notification had been received from SAC Headquarters that there would be a change in the Reflex commitment in August.

During the last several months there had been a lot of TWX traffic between Omaha, Barksdale and the 818th Headquarters regarding the status and control of Base Flight Operations at Lincoln Air Force Base. At first, it appeared that the 98th would be given control of Base Flight. After a long TWX debate on the pros and cons of each wing, it was decided the 307th would have the responsibility for maintaining Base Flight Operations.

SAC Headquarters sent a TWX to the 307th Wing Headquarters on the subject of Reflex. Under the Single Integrated Operations Plan (SIOP) for Fiscal Year 1963, the 307th Reflex commitment would change from Morón, Spain, to Greenham Common RAF Base, UK. The effective date for the change was set for August 1, 1962.

SAC had always been hypersensitive about communications with the bomber fleet in the air. To safeguard against the possibility of an accidental nuclear exchange, the system of Positive Control procedures had been formulated and drilled into the flight crews. SAC had also pioneered the airborne command post concept with Looking Glass. The primary problem at the moment was that there were not enough Looking Glass aircraft available to fulfill the mission. Also, there was the question of possible blind spots in the system between the Looking Glass aircraft and the bomber force.

SAC came up with the idea of modifying certain B-47s to act as radio relay aircraft. The specially modified B-47s would be the first aircraft to launch during an Alert and proceed to an area where they would be able to establish a radio link between Looking Glass and the airborne bomber strike force. Since the fall of 1961, SAC had been working on this concept under the Code name Pipe Cleaner.

The 307th was officially notified they would assume operational control of the 4362nd Airborne Communications Relay Squadron. The official activation would be effective July 1, 1962. The squadron would be one of the lead squadrons in proving the concept of radio relay communications. They would also be responsible for establishing Alert and launch criteria and tactics. The squadron was finally organized on 20 July as the 4362nd Post-Attack Command & Control Squadron (PACCS).

A routine mission left Lincoln on Friday, June 15th. That morning the crew preflighted 53-4217 and climbed the ladder for what was scheduled to be a 50-8 training flight. Everything went according to the mission plan until they were on the low-level navigation leg. Hurtling along the Rough Road oil burner route, the crew was about to contact Joplin bomb plot for entry into the bomb run corridor. The crew felt a faint thump somewhere on the left side of the aircraft. Moments later they felt vibration coming from the left wing and the EGT on #1 started to climb.

It was obvious something was wrong with the engine. The crew contacted Joplin to inform them of the problem and advised they were aborting the bomb run. The aircraft commander began a slow, cautious climb out of the oil burner route. They might need the altitude if they had to eject. Within a few moments the vibration had almost stopped, but the EGT continued to climb.

The aircraft commander shut down the #1 engine after they had climbed to about 7,000 feet. The vibration ceased and the EGT started falling. The crew contacted the Command Post and advised them of the situation. They aborted the mission and headed back towards Lincoln. While there shouldn't be a problem getting home on five engines, the crew would be sitting on ejection seats full of pins and needles until they were on the ground.

As they approached Lincoln, the crew refigured their landing weight and figured the best flare speed. Coming across the fence, the pilot adjusted the sink rate and flared the B-47 for landing. She only bounced twice according to eyewitnesses. The main chute blossomed and 4217 started slowing down. All they had to do was taxi in and shut down. They had snatched another one from the gods!

When the crew came down the ladder, they joined the ground crew, fire crews and wing officials around the #1 engine. You don't declare an emergency and not have half the base show up to see what happened. Looking into the intake, it was clear to see the inlet vanes were bent and it appeared several of the compressor blades were bent or missing. There was also a ragged hole in the bottom of the engine cowling. There appeared to be blood and what looked like feathers on the bent inlet guide vanes. Later investigation confirmed the aircraft had been struck by what was believed to be a large goose.

The wing continued to shuttle B-47s back and forth for Project Red Barn. This inspection and repair of the wings was a continuation of the original Milk Bottle project back in 1958. With the B-47 fleet spending more and more time at low altitude, it was important to make sure the wings could take all of the bumps and thermal potholes encountered at low-level. During June, the 307th would send nine aircraft for Red Barn.

June 27th saw three crews preparing for the last Reflex deployment of the month. The flight launched at 1800 that Wednesday and flew the southern route. Refueling went according to the profile, then the three ships headed on towards Spain. Over the mid-Atlantic, one of the aircraft ran into a problem when they discovered they couldn't transfer fuel from the right external wing tank. If they couldn't get the fuel out of the tank they wouldn't be able to make it all the way to Morón.

# Cold War Cornhuskers: The 307th Bomb Wing Lincoln Air Force Base Nebraska 1955-1965

They managed to rendezvous with their scheduled tanker near the Azores and take on fuel. After getting the fuel, they had to come up with a revised flight plan and options. First, they could turn around and head for Lajes AB, Azores, and land. After taking on the fuel they would have to spend a couple of hours trying to burn off fuel and get down to a safe landing weight. Making it all the way to Morón was not a problem now, even with unusable fuel in the wing tank. Since they didn't have to worry about running out of fuel, they could concentrate on the problem at hand.

A quick review of the Dash-1 showed several options available to the crew. They could keep both wing tanks full, now that they had refueled. That would mean landing with full tanks hanging off of both wings, necessitating a higher approach speed during landing. Another option was to use the emergency procedure to gravity feed from the right wing tank. This would mean shutting down the #5 engine. Shutting down a good engine over water is not the best option with a lot of ocean yet to cross. The final option was to use the fuel in the left external tank first, then jettison both tanks over the water. The primary problem with that option was the possibility of one of the tanks failing to jettison. After consulting with the Reflex Commander at Morón, it was decided they would use the fuel from the left tank, then drop them into the ocean when they reached a point where they were assured of reaching Morón with fuel reserves.

While the copilot double-checked the remaining fuel on board and the reserves, the navigator checked the area below with the radar. They had enough fuel to make Morón. The radar showed the area was clear below; no one would get an unexpected surprise from above. The pilot reached for the guarded switch and pushed the switch to R.H. TANK to jettison the fuel laden right wing tank first. As soon as the tank fell from the wing he pushed the toggle up to L.H. Tank. Both tanks fell from the wings and headed towards the water.

It was a happy flight crew when they got on the ground at Morón. The last few hours in the air had been some of the longest they had experienced. They didn't care at the moment that they would be going on Alert in the next 24 hours. They were just glad to have made it across the pond safe and sound.

On June 28th, the #1 engine on 53-2342 was being run up at 70% power to locate an oil leak in the accessory section. A previous check at idle had revealed no leaks. A ground observer was standing at the side of the engine, close to the accessory section. Without warning, the spring holding the foam rubber piece around his microphone and the clip on the microphone came loose and were sucked into the engine. The engine had a total of six hours on it at the time of this Foreign Object Damage (FOD) incident.

During June, there were several bomb runs scored as ineffective due to equipment failures. On June 29th two MADREC units arrived. (These were electronic diagnostic units used to trouble shoot Bomb/Nav malfunctions.) With the arrival of the two units, there would be a total of three of them in the Bomb/Nav Section. It was hoped the units would cut down on the time required to find and repair problems in the Bomb/Nav System.

Ever since the first sign of Soviet Fan Song radar had surfaced, there had been aerial recon flights to Cuba. A U-2 flight over Cuba on Friday, June 29th, brought back some interesting photos. Photo interpreters confirmed construction was under way to receive Soviet-built SA-2 Guideline Surface-to-Air missiles. There were also photos of at least two operational SA-2 sites. This information was sent from SAC Headquarters to Washington and presented to the CIA, National Photographic Interpretation Center for the Air Staff and other high level agencies in the Pentagon, including the Secretary of Defense. No action was taken at the time except to increase surveillance on what appeared to be a Soviet buildup on the island of Cuba.

July saw the official activation of the 4362nd Post-Attack Command & Control Squadron. The squadron would use specially modified B-47s, designated as EB-47L, which had been modified by Tempco Aircraft, Dallas, Texas. The aircraft were equipped with AN-ARC-89 relay system and AN-ART-42 transmitters. During a mission, the Pipe Cleaner aircraft would launch before the Alert force and fly to a predetermined track and stand by to relay messages from the SAC Command Post or Looking Glass.

The 307th also assumed control of Base Flight on July 1st. The 307th would now be responsible for maintaining all Base Flight aircraft, along with servicing and supporting all transient aircraft arriving at Lincoln Air Force Base. The increase in responsibility came without an increase in personnel to help cover the workload.

The first Reflex flight for the month of July departed for Spain on Monday, July 2nd. Three aircraft left Lincoln at 1815 and flew the southern route to Spain. The flight was routine, with no major problems along the way.

Bowling Lake was the scene of the gala base fireworks display on the evening of the 4th. People jammed the roads and nearby picnic areas to watch the show. Just after the last star cluster drifted to the ground, Mother Nature arrived with her own display of natural fireworks in the form of a thunderstorm. People were treated to a double-dose aerial display that night.

A Reflex redeployment on Wednesday, the 18th, was routine until the flight arrived in the refueling area. The tankers had been grounded due to bad weather at their base. The inbound B-47s could not make Lincoln with their present fuel load. They had to land at McCoy AFB, Florida, and ground stage to Lincoln the next day.

Bad weather at Lincoln caused the Reflex deployment headed for Morón to hold for twenty-four hours. One of the crews that were supposed to deploy was commanded by Gene Hickman. His navigator left on emergency leave. They had to find a replacement for him before they could leave. R.T. Boykin recalled, "Early in the morning, I was awaked by the phone. I was told to grab my bag because I was going Reflex with Gene Hickman and Pete Todd. Their navigator had gone on emergency leave and I was the only one available."

This last minute change would throw a small monkey wrench into the flight schedule. R.T.'s regular crew, S-97, was scheduled to fly a routine training mission on the 19th. At this point his aircraft commander had to find a navigator. Not that big of a problem since the flight had originally been scheduled as a four man flight with two navigators. With R.T. headed for Spain, the mission would be flown without the navigation upgrade. Walter Snyder would fly in the nose and navigate for Crew S-97 during the July 19th mission.

With the schedule shuffled, LtCol Art Stokes (AC), 1Lt Gerald Bachner (CP), and 1Lt Walt Snyder (Nav) got their final weather briefing before blasting off into the wild blue. According to the weather section, the wild blue could be exactly that, "wild"! The forecast called for the possibility of strong to severe thunderstorms in the Lincoln and surrounding area of the Midwest. Capt Bill Rogers had been one of the staff briefing officers that day. In view of the forecast he commented to the crew about having a toothbrush and razor in case they had to RON due to weather.

Crew S-97 arrived at 53-4218 at about 1400 and began their preflight. There was a slight change in the situation. SSgt Walter Fonderhide would be going along since the fourth man seat was vacant. He needed the flight time to qualify for his flight pay.

By 1530, Czar 14 was airborne headed for Mankato, Kansas, for a celestial navigation leg, taking them north to Cheyenne, Wyoming. The nav leg ended near Minneapolis, Minnesota. They flew a leg east to Grand Rapids, Michigan, then entered the Long Hike low level route for a low-level bomb run. They had to do some ECM work on a Nike site along with other 50-8 requirements. By 2030 they were back at about 36,000 feet near the Jamestown, North Dakota, VOR. So far it had been just another routine mission.

Back at Lincoln, a three-ship Reflex flight departed Lincoln on time, just in front of some massive storms brewing to the west and southwest of Lincoln. They climbed out and turned southeast towards coast out near Jacksonville, Florida. They got their tankers and took on enough fuel to make the trans-Atlantic flight. Like all Reflex flights, it would be a long night over the Atlantic.

At 2045, Art Stokes and crew had been advised by radio contact with Minot, North Dakota, of the weather brewing around Lincoln. The storms had mushroomed into supercells. There were multiple lines of these supercells blocking the route back to home base. The crew made radio contact with Minneapolis Center and modified their flight plan for a direct return to Lincoln. Near Huron, South Dakota, Walt Synder picked up the boiling thunderstorms on his radar scope. For a while, no matter which way they turned, they were blocked by clouds. Walt Snyder was getting a good workout in the nose of 4218 trying to navigate a clear path around the danger, which seemed to cover the entire horizon. The problem facing the crew was related by Gerald Bachner. "We used a lot of fuel trying to navigate around the bad weather." The Command Posts at Lincoln and Omaha were monitoring the situation. There were two 307th aircraft trying to get around the storms. Fuel was starting to become a concern for both crews. They either had to get around the storms and land or get a tanker.

The storms blocking the return of 4218 ran along a line from Kansas up through Nebraska and into the Dakotas and Minnesota. Czar 14 finally managed to get around the line of storms and headed south towards Des Moines, Iowa. 4218 wasn't the only B-47 in the area having problems with the weather. Czar 37 from the 307th was trapped behind the line of storms and had been working with the Command Post on getting a KC-97 for refueling.

The tanker had launched from its base in Missouri and was now in position to refuel the other aircraft just south of Des Moines. The 307th Command Post let Czar 14 know there was a tanker in the area and got the OK from SAC for Czar 14 to rendezvous and get enough fuel to return to Lincoln with a 12,000-pound fuel reserve. There was a problem with the communications between the aircraft involved in this incident. While Czar 37 was refueling with the KC-97, they disrupted the airways by communicating on the guard channel. This interfered with the ability of Czar 14 to receive further instructions from the Command Post. Gerald Bachner recalled:

"When we finally got through the bad weather, the tanker had gotten a hundred miles or so south of Des Moines while he was finishing the refueling he was doing. In order for us to get to him, we would have to fly away from Des Moines. If we missed the tanker or had problems getting fuel, we wouldn't have a legal reserve to get back to Des Moines. The area was pretty calm; it seemed like a logical decision to go and land there. Art Stokes was a good pilot and aircraft commander. We all discussed the situation and had a say in the decision to go to Des Moines."

Des Moines had been part of the 307th evacuation plan since it was first developed. At the time the airport was undergoing runway improvements. The north-south runway had just been lengthened to 8,000 feet and resurfaced. At the north end of the runway there was a two-foot drop off where the ground had not been contoured to match the runway surface. With two feet of concrete sticking up in the air, authorities had placed a barricade across the runway with low powered lights marking the end.

Art set up for the approach on the runway from the north. Since the runway was still under construction there were no approach lights. "It was a black hole until we got to the runway," Gerald related. As they approached the runway, there was no way to see the drop off at the end of the concrete. Everything went well until they reached the threshold. As Art began to flare for landing, the forward main gear hit the drop and sheared off. At 2211 Czar 14 slammed down onto the concrete nose first, bounced into the air, then hit the runway about a thousand feet from the first impact. It then slid for over 2,500 feet in a shower of sparks and shedding parts of the aircraft. Stokes pulled the throttles back and hit the cutoff switches, then hung on for a wild ride. Sharp edges of sheared metal punctured fuel tanks, allowing fuel to spill out and into the sparks. Fire erupted, but it wasn't the explosive conflagration it would have been if the fuel tanks had been full of JP-4.

"We were on fire as we slid down the runway," Gerald recalled. "And we really started to burn as we slowed down. When the airplane started to veer off the runway to the left, I reached down and blew the canopy off the airplane. We slid off into the grass and down a slight valley."

When Czar 14 finally slid to a stop, it was a mad scramble to get out of the burning aircraft. "We got up on the open canopy rail and moved forward, slid off the nose of the aircraft since it was close to the ground." Gerald continued, "We were lucky to have blown the canopy when we did. If the fuselage had buckled during our slide, it might have fouled the canopy railing enough so we wouldn't have been able to blow it after we came to a stop."

Everyone got out with minor scrapes and abrasions. They all agreed they had been pretty lucky. Walt Fonderhide wondered if it was worth the risk for the extra flight pay. Walt Snyder was heard to say, "I thought it was a pretty normal landing until the radar scope fell in my lap!" Well, like they say, any landing you can walk away from is a good one.

When the Reflex crew of Hickman, Todd and Boykin arrived in Spain there was a little excitement. R.T. Boykin recalled:

"The published schedule showed Crew S-91 as Stokes, Bachner and Boykin, so there was confusion as to who was on the Des Moines flight. We, (Hickman, Todd, Boykin) landed at Morón, Col Lally met us and verified I was aboard, then filled us in on the details of the crash landing at Des Moines."

Two B-47s arrived at the patch on July 23rd. They looked like any other B-47, except for a couple of strange looking air scoops protruding from the bomb bay doors. The B-47s, 52-0329 and 52-0292, were prototype EB-47L Pipe Cleaner aircraft. The first two aircraft assigned to the 4362nd PACCS had arrived at Lincoln airplane patch.

At Morón, the 307th was preparing for the change in Reflex commitment to England. There had been several loads of equipment and personnel flown to Greenham Common by transport aircraft. The skeleton crew would be in place when the actual changeover date arrived.

July 31st, three B-47s departed Morón, Spain, and flew towards the northwest, then turned towards England. They coasted in and flew on to Greenham Common, just west of London. They were the first 307th aircraft to arrive at the new Reflex base. To help with the move they carried a full load of weapons. Arriving in England, they would be turned around and cocked in almost record time.

There was a redeployment flight headed back to Lincoln the same day. This would be the last flight back from Morón. A last flight from anywhere almost demands a special farewell. Don Kellum recalled his farewell flight from Morón with William Stringfellow:

# Cold War Cornhuskers: The 307th Bomb Wing Lincoln Air Force Base Nebraska 1955-1965

"We cut about ten rolls of toilet paper in half and taped it in under the aft camera doors before departure from Morón to return home from Reflex. After takeoff we requested a flyby to look us over due to vibration. When abeam of base ops, we released the paper and it looked like a stream of chaff and really cluttered up the Moron ramp. We were leading a flight of three who waited on us at coast-out for the return to CONUS."

Deployment for Reflex would now be a flight to England via the northern route. There would also be a change in the schedule. Deployment would be on Mondays, with the returning flight departing England on Wednesday. The first deployment to Greenham Common from Lincoln was scheduled for Monday, August 6th.

At Lincoln, the klaxon blared for the first time in August on the afternoon of August 7th. Scrambling to the Alert aircraft, the crews donned their "brain buckets" and tuned in to hear what kind of response they were to accomplish. Before they had the word, engines were starting to whine as they spooled up through idle.

The crew assigned to 53-4226 was ready to start engines. A2C Matthew Boylan was standing by as fireguard near the #4 engine. The engine was turning, but there was no ignition. Without warning residual fuel ignited, causing a fire around the engine. The flames spread across the ramp from JP-4 spilling from the engine.

Boylan grabbed his fifty-pound carbon dioxide fire bottle and started fighting the fire in the engine. He was able to extinguish the flames in the engine, then turned his attention to the flames dancing on the ramp below the wing. The crew chief notified the crew of the fire and they abandoned the aircraft in near record time.

Within a few minutes the base fire units came screaming down the flight line. By the time they arrived, Boylan was standing by with an empty fire bottle and a pounding heart. His quick action had prevented a major fire in the Alert area. His only comment was, "I just did what I was supposed to do. That's why we have a fireguard standing by."

August 6th, the first Reflex flight to England was ready to launch. There were thunderstorms rumbling across the plains of Nebraska. It looked pretty dark to the southwest as the storms raced towards Lincoln. The Reflex launch was lucky; the storms held off just long enough for the crews to get into the air. Billy Lyons recalled his first Reflex to England:

"First Reflex trip to England in the fall of 1962. Not a bad trip over, shorter than the trip to Morón. We could refuel over Canada, coast out near Goose Bay, Labrador, fly near the southern tip of Greenland and then on to the British Isles. On that trip we were a single ship. We were assigned a single altitude coasting out and were in thick cirrus clouds at that altitude. We couldn't contact the controlling air traffic agency on the high frequency radio to get a higher altitude because of the static created by the clouds. Also, we couldn't shoot the sextant for celestial fixes because of the clouds. So, it was dead reckoning and a fix off the southern coast of Greenland. We made it to the British Isles like we knew what we were doing!

"Entirely different surroundings in England. The base had been used during WW II, but had significant modifications to fit the needs of a B-47 Reflex base. Air traffic was more congested than in Spain, but no big difficulty. On our first trip, as we were in the landing flare at Greenham Common, I hit one of the Queen's pheasants. I caught sight of something coming from the right side in the landing flare and heard a thump as the bird hit the aircraft just aft of the nav's compartment. Didn't find any dents in the aircraft during postflight, but I was sure there was one less pheasant in the UK."

Friday, the 17th, found the crews preflighting the two Pipe Cleaner aircraft for their first mission at Lincoln. After taking off they headed for the prescribed orbit areas. Arriving in the northeast orbit area, the two EB-47Ls established contact with Looking Glass and started receiving. The Looking Glass aircraft complained of a lot of noise in the system. There were also a lot of fadeouts in communication. The system worked, but there were a lot of bugs to work out.

The second Pipe Cleaner mission launched on Tuesday, the 21st. 52-0329 and 52-0292 departed Lincoln and flew to the Delta and Echo orbit areas. Both aircraft established contact with Looking Glass. There was noise reported in the system when Grayson, the 8th Air Force auxiliary command post, entered the area. The noise was traced to 0292 (Pincher 14).

Pincher 14 flew a local test flight on the 23rd to see if the noise in the system had been eliminated. The crew established a link with Looking Glass. After several link-ups between the two aircraft, the system was noise-free and there was clear transmission between the two aircraft.

While the Pipe Cleaners were trying to work out the bugs in their system, Base Flight was getting the first major workout since the 307th assumed control. Base Flight crews provided support for Swift Strike II, August 17th through the 24th. Lincoln was used as a stopover for troops and equipment being ferried from Pueblo, Colorado, to the war game site in South Carolina. The crews at Base Flight serviced 275 C-124 aircraft during the week.

The Pipe Cleaners were in the air again on the 24th. 52-0329, Pincher 15, attempted to establish a link with Stepmother, the 15th Air Force Command post. Pincher 15's equipment would work only intermittently. After several hours of problems the mission was aborted.

During July and August, the wing had been assigned to the Long Hike RBS Express route. Most of the flight crews had no idea this route in central Minnesota ran right through the middle of turkey farm country. In late August, word came in from Offutt changing two of the turn points on the route to avoid several turkey farms near Henning, Minnesota.

Turkeys have never been at the top of Mother Nature's list when it comes to intelligence. Place a couple thousand gobblers in a large coop and subject them to sudden, loud noise of a B-47 flashing overhead at low-level and you have the makings of instant gobbler mayhem. SAC learned that low-flying B-47s and turkeys don't mix. Apparently, the turkeys thought the B-47s were very large silver hawks. When the silver hawks passed over the turkeys would run to one side of the coop, pile up and suffocate by the hundreds. SAC paid for a lot of gobblers before the route was changed to avoid the farms.

In his monthly report, Col Bertram compiled the activity of the 307th for the month of August. The wing flew 268 sorties, spending 1,791 hours in the air. The wing had 51 aircraft assigned and 81 combat ready crews to man them. The wing posted one of the best months in bombing accuracy.

During the month the wing responded to seven Bravo Alerts. Reaction time was excellent. There were two Coco Alerts with one downgraded to a Bravo due to runway repairs. The reaction time for the Coco was considered good, with the first aircraft ready to roll six minutes after the klaxon went off. All in all it had been a routine, yet busy month for the 307th.

During August, the 307th received the Operations order for Sky Shield II. This was a Joint Chiefs of Staff-directed mission to test the capability of NORAD to detect and intercept an enemy bomber attack on the United States. The 307th would be required to launch eleven aircraft to simulate a Soviet attack.

# 1962

The 307th got the word to execute Sky Shield II on September 2nd. They generated eleven aircraft and were ready for the launch order by 1800 that evening. When the launch order arrived, all eleven aircraft launched on time and headed north into Canadian airspace. Near Churchill, Manitoba, they turned back towards the States and dropped to low-level for penetration of the defended area.

The eleven B-47s arrived at the control point on time and started playing their music. NORAD was on the ball and managed to detect six bombers before they crossed into U.S. airspace. These were listed as "destroyed" by Nike missiles. Two B-47s were scored as effective in sneaking in and dropping their weapons on target. The final score listed NORAD as having done very well. However, if it had been "real world", Minneapolis and Detroit would have vanished in a nuclear flash.

The wing got a message from Omaha outlining the participation of the Pipe Cleaner aircraft in the upcoming "Dominic" nuclear test shot in the Pacific. Under the original order, aircraft and support personnel were to deploy and arrive at Hickam AFB, Hawaii, on September 24th. Support personnel were to travel by KC-135s. Like most tests, the deployment date would be delayed several times.

The first Reflex deployment for September departed Lincoln on September 3rd. That afternoon, the ground crews prepared 53-1918, 53-1853 and 53-2143 for the flight to England. Going over along the northern route, the three B-47s would refuel near Goose Bay and head out over the North Atlantic. Total flight time would be about ten hours.

Preparing for Reflex could have profound effects on a crew. Dave Bowersock related:

"Our crew was scheduled for target study and flight planning prior to going Reflex to Greenham Common RAFB. When Gene (Van Meter) arrived, he asked Neal (Amtmann) and me where Kiev was. We checked it out on our maps and learned that Kiev was a city in the Ukraine, about 470 miles southwest of Moscow, with a population of over three million. It was a major industrial, transportation and military complex. Gene told us that he had dreamed that a war started and our target was Kiev. His dream ended with no conclusion to the mission, only that he remembered Kiev and going through our bomb run procedures. Our targets for this Reflex mission weren't near this area so we laughed about it and went on with our planning for England.

"Our first week of Alert at Greenham Common was routine. Prior to starting the second week, we were told that we would be changing our flight plan and target, to cover for a B-47 out of Dyess AFB, Texas, that was delayed getting to England. We were given the new "package" and, you guessed it, the target was Kiev. I felt like we were in a twilight zone with some inexplicable force writing the script. We had one exercise that week and I was fully convinced we were on our way to war. Well, of course, it didn't happen. We finished that otherwise uneventful week and never did see Kiev as a target again. I suppose it was just one of those weird things that sometimes happens during our lives."

On the sixth, the 307th Command Post began Operation High Heels II. This was an Air Force-wide exercise for Command Post personnel that would last for three weeks. Umpires would be on site to observe the activities of the Command Post daily activities and special operations received during the exercise period.

2nd Air Force officials arrived via KC-135 on September 6th. The Thursday arrival was a scheduled visit in conjunction with High Heels II. The Command Post knew they were coming due to the exercise and figured 2nd Air Force might just try and throw the wing a curve ball.

As long as the 2nd Air Force staff was at Lincoln to observe the Command Post in action, let's see how they would react in an ORI recheck to see if the deficient areas from April's ORI had been corrected. The blare of the klaxon signaled the start of the ORI recheck at 1300 that afternoon. The first aircraft reported ready to taxi four minutes after the Alert started. It took six minutes for the aircraft to be at the end of Runway 17 and report they were ready to roll.

This would not be a full ORI, so the Alert birds were brought back to the Alert ramp, serviced and recocked. Flight line troops got the word to generate six aircraft for the ORI. A quick check of the flying schedule showed 53-1887, 53-1910, 53-1932, 53-4227, 53-1829 and 53-1843 were supposed to fly that day. They would be serviced and generated for the ORI mission.

Crews flying the mission reported for the briefing and were given the details for the flight. The mission plan called for a heavyweight takeoff, navigation leg, air refueling, Short Look and a Long Look bomb run. There was also an ECM run scheduled during the Long Look bomb run.

All of the B-47s launched on time, flew the navigation leg, then headed for the refueling area. Five of the B-47s got their offload without difficulties. The other aircraft was delayed when the tanker reported trouble with a transfer pump. The tanker crew did some quick inflight maintenance and solved the problem in time to complete the refueling within ORI guidelines.

The rest of the mission was flown within the ORI guidelines. The bomb runs were scored "Satisfactory". Two bomb runs were ineffective when the Bomb/Nav system on 53-4227 malfunctioned. ECM runs were scored as "Satisfactory". Generation, navigation and bomb scores were scored as "Outstanding". One area that caused problems was in the EWO procedures examination given to several of the crews. Five specific questions gave the crews the most problem. The most frequently missed question was, " How many engines not taking WAI can be had and still take off?"

The wing passed with minimum recommendations from 2nd Air Force. One interesting item brought out was when the umpires wanted to observe the walnut shell dispensing unit for cleaning compressor and turbine blades. The answer was, "What walnut shell dispenser? Oh, you mean the one-striper on a safety harness." Several of the crew chiefs chuckled and thought the umpires were throwing a curve, like the age-old bucket of propwash, or left-handed monkey wrench. No, the umpires were serious about it. The crew chiefs were informed the equipment did exist, to which the older crew chiefs remarked, "What will they come up with next?"

A single FOD incident occurred on September 18th. A three-ship MITO launched and flew a routine mission. The recovery crew on 53-2392 discovered a torn turbine blade and several others nicked. 2392 was the third ship in the MITO, and it was believed that the damage was due to ingestion of an object during taxi or runup. This was the fourth such incident associated with MITOs during the month.

Pipe Cleaner aircraft launched at 0735 on September 19th for another system check. An FM link with Looking Glass was established, but right away there was a problem on 0329. She could be heard transmitting; however, there was no acknowledgment they were receiving anything. It was determined all three of the receiver units were not working.

The mission was aborted and 0329 headed back to Lincoln. On arrival, she was defueled due to a boost pump problem. Investigation revealed a ground crew had done some work on one of the fuel cells. They had disconnected the RF cables from the tuner to do their work. When they reconnected them they connected the input cable into the output jack, which explained the failure to receive any of the messages.

Three Reflex aircraft launched from Greenham Common on the 19th for the return trip to the USA. One of the aircraft had to return due to loss of the #3 engine just after coasting out. The B-47 managed a safe landing

*197*

at Greenham Common on five engines. Billy Lyons recalled an interesting flight back from England:

"Ever hear of bootlegging a tanker on a Reflex return? We did it on a return trip from Greenham Common. Lots of questions to be answered, but this is how it went. We were to launch with our normal three ships to return from Greenham to Lincoln, but we couldn't get an engine started. By the time we got it fixed, we were too late to catch the other two aircraft and would lose our tanker and have to ground stage through Goose Bay. At another UK base, a B-47 Reflex return three-ship formation was preparing to launch about an hour after our originally scheduled launch time to return to their stateside base. One of their aircraft could not launch with the formation and they pressed on as a two-ship.

"As we coasted out, I heard the crews from the other UK base. They were flying the same route and were about thirty minutes ahead of us. I recognized the voice of the lead AC and asked if we could join their formation, tack on to their altitude reservation flight plan and share their tankers. We were able to work it out and increased our speed to catch them. As they did a 360-degree turn near the refueling initial point to lose some time and rendezvous with the tankers at the scheduled time, we caught up and joined their formation as number three.

"We got our onload and stayed with them until near St. Louis. They were from Whiteman AFB near Kansas City. We left the formation and proceeded to Lincoln, thanking the Whiteman crews again for letting us join them on the return trip. I had some explaining to do after we landed. Seems some people in the wing had never heard of bootlegging a tanker on a Reflex return trip."

Air reconnaissance over Cuba from 15-20 September showed Medium Range Ballistic Missile sites were being placed at several locations on the island. The work at these sites had reached a fever pitch. On Friday, September 28th, recon photos showed there were IL-28 Beagle medium range bombers being readied for flight. There was also evidence that the Cuban Air Force had MiG-21 fighters.

The last Reflex flight for September was set to launch on the 24th. That afternoon 53-1897, 53-1902 and 53-2097 were serviced and preflighted for the flight to England. The flight over was a routine ten-hour mission. On the 26th crews launched in 53-1918, 53-1853 and 53-2143 for the return to Lincoln. The return flight ran into headwinds that depleted fuel reserves to danger levels. The flight was able to meet the tankers and take on the needed fuel load to get home to Lincoln.

High winds aloft caused problems anytime they were encountered. "The longest flight I was ever on was seventeen hours, coming from England to Lincoln," Paul Koski recalled:

"About half way across the pond, we hit 250 knot headwinds. We ended up with three air refuelings. The helmet felt like it was boring a hole in my head and I know my ears were permanently flattened. At least the Nav and I could move around, but I really felt sorry for the pilot and copilot. If I was miserable, they must have gone through hell; they had to sit there and feel all the agony of the chute cutting through their legs and the same helmet problems everyone had.

"The aircraft had cold-soaked for all that time at 60° below. The copilot had picked up a slab of Italian Marble that he was going to make into a coffee table. I had put three bottles of the good stuff in my duffel bag and wrapped it very carefully with my clothes. When we landed, it wasn't one of the "greased" landings that we normally had; we hit hard and bounced several times. We were just glad it was over with. When we unloaded the marble, it all ran out about the size of crushed rock. My duffel bag was dripping as I carried it across the ramp; all the bottles had broken.

"When we landed and climbed off the aircraft, none of us could stand up straight. We were all kind of bent over and you talk about being stiff, we could barely walk. They took us to debriefing and the base doctor handed us a foam cup with medicinal alcohol, about six ounces in a ten-ounce cup. It burned all the way down, but, you know, after about ten minutes I didn't feel so bad."

September had been a busy month for the 307th. Flight crews spent 1,644 hours in the air during 241 sorties. They made 230 effective air refuelings. Operation High Heels II presented an interesting time for the Command Post. During that exercise, the Command Post was tasked with not only the exercise operations, but also a real ORI recheck. It was believed there was too much radio and TWX traffic. There were also too many changes in procedures. Under EWO conditions there wouldn't be the changes coming in one after another.

The wing was still short of personnel. The number one area remained the Bomb/Nav section. This section was authorized 173 technicians and had 113 assigned by the end of the month. In spite of being short of technicians, an almost perfect reliability in Bomb/Nav equipment was turned in.

October began with preparations for a three-ship Reflex deployment early that evening. During the day there were several routine launches for training flights. The Reflex crews departed Lincoln on time. As the crews flew towards the East, they had no idea of the events that would soon transpire in Washington, D.C., or the effect those events would have in the next few weeks.

During the last several weeks, intense aerial photo recon over Cuba brought back disturbing information. Intelligence authorities presented briefings on the photo evidence to Defense Secretary McNamara, the President, and other high-level Administration officials. There was now evidence confirming the presence of Soviet built bombers, SA-2 Guideline antiaircraft missiles, and the presence of Medium Range Ballistic Missiles in Cuba.

After the mid-October meetings, McNamara directed the JCS to begin developing contingency plans for a naval blockade of Cuba. He also directed that military forces be mobilized for a possible invasion of Cuba, preceded by massive air strikes against the missile sites. With the recon photos pointing to a Soviet build-up in Cuba, the evidence forced the Kennedy Administration to address the situation brewing off our coast.

Word came in to the 307th that the Pipe Cleaner aircraft were to deploy to Hickam AFB, Hawaii, being in place by October 7th. The Pipe Cleaner aircraft departed Lincoln on the 5th. Support personnel departed for the Pacific that same day aboard KC-135s. If conditions were right, the atomic test would be conducted on the 8th. The test date was postponed at the last minute to October 12th.

With some time on their hands before they had to fly the real mission, the crews flew a test flight on October 9th. A crew boarded 52-039 and flew to Midway Island testing the radio link. Everything checked out according to the checklist. The crew felt everything was ready for the test.

A Reflex flight returned to the patch on Wednesday, October 10th. It was a long flight and the crews were bone-tired after crossing the Atlantic, then making the obligatory bomb run on one of the RBS sites. They may have been tired, but nothing beat being back home with their families. The rest of the Wednesday afternoon was spent getting aircraft that were scheduled to fly ready for their mission.

Thursday, the 11th, started like another normal day for the 307th. First shift reported for duty at 0745 and briefed on the day's workload. There were several launches scheduled for the morning, along with recovering two aircraft that had flown during the night. First shift was just about through with their day when a KC-135 landed and taxied to the transient area near Base Operations. The second shift reported at 1615 and took over for the evening at 1645. Base Flight crews were busy servicing the KC-135 that arrived earlier. It was supposed to leave later that evening, but so far the crew hadn't returned to the aircraft.

The SAC IG had arrived on the KC-135 that afternoon. Arriving at the Command Post, they informed the Battle Staff of the impending message from Omaha. They stated that no one was to leave the Command Post or make any phone calls until the message arrived. At 1820, the Command Post got a fast reaction message from Blackjack. Authentication confirmed that it was the execution order for Golden Jet Bravo.

Within moments of authenticating the message, the blare of the klaxon sent the Alert crews towards the entry hatch ladders. Ground crews pulled the engine and pitot covers while the crew chiefs put power on with the MD-3s. Following the message from the Command Post, Alert aircraft executed a Coco Alert and returned to the Alert pad for their briefing on the ORI.

Under the operations plan, the 307th was required to reconfigure and launch fourteen bomber Alert sorties in two waves of seven aircraft over a two-day launch window. While the flight crews were at the briefing, the ground crews had started downloading the aircraft for the upcoming ORI mission.

When the last ORI sortie landed on Saturday the 13th, everyone figured the wing had passed. During debriefing they found out the wing had, indeed, passed, but there were a few bumpy spots. The bomb runs had been scored "Outstanding" and generation was also given an "Outstanding" rating. Eleven of the fourteen aircraft were scored as effective. One was scored as an abort due to fluctuating EGT. The other abort was caused by one aircraft failing to take on the required fuel load by the end of the refueling point. There were several areas regarding personnel records that were not up to par. These were not considered bad enough to fail the wing.

Members of the 307th were happy the ORI was over. They could hardly believe the wing had been hit with three ORIs during the year so far. Maybe that was the price to pay for failing an ORI. They figured the pressure would be off after passing the next ORI. It just went to show you were never out from under the watchful eye of SAC.

Right on the heels of the ORI the wing was alerted for Operation Mute II. This would be a Sky Shield type mission. The 307th was required to launch six aircraft on Sunday, October 14th. One aircraft (53-2143) was scored as a ground abort. Another B-47 (53-1932) aborted in the air when the Bomb/Nav system failed. The other four B-47s flew north into the Canadian tundra, then turned for their bomb runs on Detroit, Michigan, and Chicago, Illinois.

While the 307th was busy flying Operation Mute II, Maj Richard Heyser was high over western Cuba in a U-2 taking more photos. After making several north to south camera runs he turned back to the north and landed at McCoy AFB, Florida. He was met by Gen Robert Smith, Director of SAC Intelligence. Gen Smith loaded the raw film aboard a KC-135 for the flight to Washington, D.C. Other film canisters were loaded onto another KC-135 and flown to Omaha.

Out in the Pacific, the Pipe Cleaners had been busy trying to get test flights in and waiting for the big blast to go off. The first shot, Blue Gill Double Prime, was aborted by Range Safety on October 15th. 52-0329 flew the communications test during the test. On the 19th, both aircraft flew during Dominic Checkmate. This test was completely successful. Both Pipe Cleaners also flew the Blue Gill Triple Prime shot on October 26th. The Pipe Cleaners were there to test the effects of nuclear blast on communication aircraft and if message relay could be accomplished after detonation of nuclear weapons.

Another Reflex flight left Lincoln on Monday, October 15th. The three crews flew across the Atlantic for what they believed would be a normal three-week Reflex tour. They had no idea their Reflex tour would turn into one of the longest, most tension-packed Reflex tours they would pull.

The photos taken on the 14th had been processed and gone over with a fine-toothed magnifying glass by photo interpretation experts. The photos showed there were indeed Soviet Medium Range Ballistic Missiles in Cuba. The most disturbing aspect was that the MRBM sites could be operational in less than two weeks.

In Washington, there were constant briefings and meetings among all high-level members of the Kennedy administration. The news media began sniffing around for a leak to break everything open and explain what was going on. Government officials tried to keep the lid on what was becoming a boiling pot. On Friday, the 19th, President Kennedy was on the campaign trail in support of Democratic candidates for the midterm election. He cut his trip short and headed back to Washington under the cover story of having caught a cold.

The Pentagon was still trying to keep the lid from flying off the pot. On the 19th, a high-level Defense Department spokesman replied to media questions that there was no indication of Soviet missiles in Cuba. There were also denials of any measures being taken by the United States to increase the readiness of the military.

During the weekend the President was given several more briefings. There was photo evidence showing 22 IL-28 Beagle bombers in various stages of assembly. Other aircraft included 39 MiG-21 fighters, along with MiG-17s. Photos identified 16 SS-4 MRBM and 24 SA-2 SAM sites on the island. Two of the MRBM sites near San Cristobal would be able to target Washington, D.C., St. Louis, Missouri, and Dallas, Texas. Other sites showed, with a range of over 2,000 miles, most of the United States would be on the target list.

Ever since he had been badly burned by the Bay of Pigs fiasco, President Kennedy had maintained a *laissez faire* attitude towards Cuba. This evidence, however, changed everything. In one sense, the force in Cuba was small change compared with the military might of the United States. However, small change or not, a missile launched from Cuba could reach the target in the U.S. with absolutely no warning time to react. President Kennedy could no longer ignore the danger posed by hostile missiles so close to our border.

Late Sunday evening, October 21st, the 307th Command Post got a strange call from Omaha. They requested specific aerial charts and combat mission material to be delivered to Omaha as quickly as possible. A member of the 307th Battle Staff made two trips to Offutt in a Base Flight C-47 to hand-carry the material to Offutt. He couldn't help but notice that Offutt was a beehive of activity that night. In view of his late night mission and the activity at Offutt, he knew something big was brewing.

First shift reported as usual at 0745, Monday morning, October 22nd. There was some small talk about several of the news reports that had been on TV last night. There was mention about unconfirmed reports of Soviet missiles being in place in Cuba. So far there was nothing official from the White House, although there were reports of high-level officials coming and going.

Several flight crews reported for duty and started mission planning for training flights the next day. They sat through the usual morning briefing on the world situation, weather, and other mission essential details. One of the crews that morning was E-42. Capt Paul Canney was the aircraft commander, Capt Dick West, copilot, and 2Lt Don Hickman, who had just been assigned to the crew as Navigator. The mission they were planning would be a practice flight so Don Hickman could become combat qualified.

Earlier that morning the Command Post received a "standby Alert message" from Omaha. This usually preceded some kind of communications check or notification of an operation called by Offutt. Even though they were routine, the Command Post still had to play the game for the MCS points.

When the message arrived at the Command Post, there was a momentary air of disbelief. The message was a "Triple Flash, Quick Reaction" message in eight parts. The first part of the message emphasized this was a "real world" message. The orders went on to say that the bombers would be generated to EWO status. It also emphasized these orders constituted a generation and execution order to disperse the entire bomber force under the pre-arranged guidelines of Clutch Pedal.

Aircraft would be dispersed to Duluth Airport in Minnesota and Gen Billy Mitchell Field Milwaukee, Wisconsin. Generation and dispersal would be done as outlined in Annex 1, SAC Emergency War Order (EWO) 50-63, to include issuance of authentication code envelopes to crews prior to dispersal. Also, all procedures outlined in SAC Manual 55-2A applied to the execution of the strike force once they were dispersed.

Other parts outlined the basic situation, which had prompted the action and why it was considered a real world message. It was noted that, for the time being, SAC would maintain a DEFCON 4 level of readiness, although that status could change as the situation demanded. The last part of the message stated all 50-8 training requirements were suspended until further notice. With that the Command Post knew something serious was brewing. There was only one reason for SAC to suspend all further training: SAC might be going to war!

The Command Post authenticated the message, and within a matter of moments became a beehive of activity. The Battle Staff began meeting to implement the various parts of the message outline. Special operations folders were pulled from the safe and reviewed before activating the alert.

One would expect the activation of a triple flash message would be a wild, mad dash to implement the reaction message from SAC. Nothing would be farther from the way it began. It was a quiet, methodical step-by-step movement. Wally Whitehurst remembered, "Our crew, L-80, was preflighting a B-47 for a mission when we got a 'real world' message to shut down and we did as we were told."

Jarvis "Flip" Latham wrote:

"Our crew had been scheduled for a six-hour daytime pilot proficiency mission. At about 1400 Z (0800 C) we had taxied into position for a copilot takeoff, when the tower called and told us (without explanation) to return to the parking area and report to the Command Post. We didn't have a clue about what was going on until our squadron commander told us we had thirty minutes to go home, get our survival bags and report back to Target Intelligence. We were told to tell our families nothing about where we were going, except to say that we were leaving on a mission and would be gone indefinitely.

"We went to the Target Intelligence Center and were given targets in the Asian communist world that we had never studied. These were what SAC called "follow-on" or non-first strike sorties. We studied the new targets all afternoon while our aircraft was being configured for an EWO mission. We watched television right after our target study session and saw President Kennedy brief the nation on some of what was going on. A short time later we were told that our crew was one of several (eight) assigned to fly a fully loaded (with ATO rack and weapon aboard) B-47 to Duluth Airport, Minnesota, where we were to stand Alert and wait for further orders. Incidentally, the Mark-28s were chained in, so they could not possibly be dropped between Lincoln and Duluth and the ATO was disarmed until we reached our new base. We took off for Minnesota sometime just before midnight Central Time."

Don Hickman's crew was busy planning for his check ride the next day and recalled:

"Suddenly, the door to the room we were in opened and a captain told us to report to the main briefing room." When they arrived in the briefing room, the crews were addressed by a full colonel. His exact words are lost to history, but it went something like this, as Don recalled.

"Gentlemen, we have a serious 'real world' situation developing. All training missions for tomorrow have been canceled. You may have been following the TV news the last few days and realize that the government is very concerned about developments in and around Cuba. President Kennedy will be speaking to the nation, probably today, and explaining what is going on. But before that speech, we have a job to do. We are dispersing the B-47 fleet to some civilian airfields to make sure they cannot be easily destroyed. As I am talking with you, the maintenance troops are generating every available bomber at Lincoln and loading them with nuclear weapons. Any aircraft capable of flying and not sent to a civilian airfield will be placed on Alert here at Lincoln. All deployments to Reflex bases in England have been stopped. Those aircraft and crews already deployed will remain until further notice.

"In a moment we will call out crew numbers and send you home to pack your bags. Be prepared to stay on Alert for a minimum of thirty days and possibly longer. When you return from home, you will be briefed separately on your destination and your individual war plan mission. Some crews will be placed on Alert here at Lincoln and these crews should also be prepared for a minimum thirty-day Alert. There is no time to answer questions. We need to get the crews moving. I and several of my staff will be available to answer individual questions after we call out the crew numbers. You should also be advised that increased security has been implemented at all gates of the base. We are now at DEFCON 4. Gentlemen, this is not an exercise. This is the real thing. Do not discuss anything with anyone, including your wives. Going home, please drive safely, do not speed, but get back here as soon as you possibly can and report to your squadron buildings. Godspeed! Major, the podium is yours."

On the flight line section chiefs, crew chiefs and all essential maintenance personnel had been pulled off the line for their briefing. The briefing was painfully simple: generate the force to EWO status and stand by for further instructions. Every B-47 in the 307th that was capable of flying would be generated. The only exceptions were aircraft that were down for major repair or inspection.

By noon, the flight line looked like an anthill that had been kicked by a size twelve boot. B-47s were moving back and forth to the refueling pits. Other liquids like water-alcohol, hydraulic and engine oil were serviced. ATO racks were towed into place, then wrestled into position on the aircraft. Armament specialists filled the ammo drums for the tail guns with live twenty "mike-mike". Finally, weapons transporters arrived with their lethal cargo to begin the uploading process. When the aircraft were loaded they were placed under guard until the flight crews arrived.

In late afternoon the first wave of aircraft was ready for dispersal. The crews that would fly to the dispersal bases were briefed on the route they would fly and what they were to do after arrival. They were briefed on how they were to set up a command post and monitor for further instructions.

The crews being dispersed were considered the follow-on force, or second strike team. If the nuclear trigger were pulled, the primary ground Alert aircraft would launch first and fly the first strike mission. The follow-on force would launch later to strike other targets. At every SAC base across the United States and around the world, the mailed fist was being prepared to unleash its awesome power if called upon by the President.

School ended that day and SAC BRAT headed for football practice. He walked to Lincoln High School from Everett Junior High for another practice session of freshman football. It was a regular gridiron practice, and when it was over he headed for the parking lot. Dad always picked him up from practice. That night, mom was sitting in the car waiting.

"Where's Great White Father?"

"I don't know. He came home about 10, grabbed his flight bag and said not to worry. He would be gone for a while. He said to watch TV; the President was going to speak to the nation."

Dad wasn't one to push the panic button, but if he said, "Don't worry", well, that was exactly the time to be worried. That was my introduction to the Cuban Missile Crisis. Things really started popping after 6 PM that evening. For a while there was a constant stream of B-47s taking off. Then there were the vague news reports on the evening news and the announcement that the President would speak to the nation that evening. Throw in the fact that dad wasn't at the supper table that evening, and it didn't take a military genius to put two and two together. SAC BRAT knew something very big was brewing.

President Kennedy addressed the nation on TV at 7 PM, October 22nd. His speech to the nation lasted about 17 minutes. He mentioned "unmistakable evidence" of Soviet MRBM and IRBM sites, along with nuclear bombers in Cuba. He went on to talk about the first steps being taken to ensure a quarantine of any further military buildup in Cuba. The most chilling part of the address was his statement about "any nuclear missile launched from Cuba against any nation in the Western Hemisphere would be regarded as an attack by the Soviet Union on the United States, requiring a full retaliatory response against the Soviet Union."

While most Americans watched the President on TV, there were those who were not near a tube. Pete Todd recalled, "I vividly remember listening to the President's speech that evening on the airplane's radio while orbiting over Milwaukee (with a nuclear weapon in the bomb bay) as we waited to land at our dispersal base. One of the more sobering broadcasts I've ever heard in my life."

During the President's speech to the nation, SAC Headquarters sent a message to all SAC Bases. The content of the message had been directed earlier during the day by the Joint Chiefs. Since there was no way of predicting the reaction of the Soviet Union to the President's address, all military forces would go to DEFCON 3 at 1900 on October 22nd.

Conditions at the dispersal bases could be described as rather spartan at first. Wally Whitehurst recalled Duluth:

"We slept anywhere we could in a large room, a briefing room for the fighter organization there. 'Skip' Heller commandeered a local motel for us, set up a secure command post and all the other things he had to do; did a helluva good job, too. We were there for several days, then were deployed to Billy Mitchell Field where other 307th crews were, then flew back to Lincoln."

Pete Todd recalled Milwaukee:

"We all slept in a medium sized, open-bay building. I don't remember whether it was a barracks or a Quonset hut. We'd go out and preflight our aircraft every day, then go back to our hut and think about war. I believe all of our meals were in civilian restaurants in town. We had either rental cars or military staff cars and the crews went to eat in shifts. I also remember that we were a little spooked about the possibility of assassination squads. Guys driving around town and going to Denny's in smelly flight suits would have been a pretty visible target. In the first few days, most of us traveled armed while in town. A visit by some senior Lincoln staff during the first week promptly put a stop to carrying weapons off base.

"Fatigue, cold, boredom and breathing each other's air took its toll. Most of us had colds by the end of the week. It was about that time that a senior officer from SAC HQ paid us a visit and was appalled at the living conditions. Within a day or two, we were moved to motels to sleep, though still using the previously mentioned building as the gathering place to watch and wait. A hot shower never felt so good!"

Then, there was the Legend of Lt Jim Stevens in one of the first aircraft to deploy. In the legend he arrived and began to set up a command post. Since his bird needed fuel, it was said he pulled out his Gulf Credit card so the locals would refuel the aircraft. One can only wonder what his credit limit was in order to refuel a B-47?

By midnight, October 22nd, SAC had responded to the building crisis. Nuclear-armed B-52s were flying airborne alert under the code name Chrome Dome. Across the United States and Reflex bases, cocked B-47s stood ready to respond. The dispersal of loaded B-47s to civilian airfields continued. Along with the aircraft, there were SAC missiles standing by in case the keys had to be turned.

Don Hickman hadn't flown his check flight to become combat qualified. His crew had been given a combat qualified navigator, and they were pulling Alert at Lincoln as part of the increased Alert posture. Don was assigned to check, then double-check routes for the strike aircraft on maps. "Boring, yet essential work. I felt left out of the real activity."

On the morning of October 23rd, 2nd Air Force sent a message requiring a field grade officer to be in command at the dispersal bases. LtCol James Pumford assumed command at Milwaukee, while Maj Russell Heller took command at Duluth. The same message outlined control of personnel at the dispersal bases. The onsite commander had to be aware of personnel locations at all times and be able to muster them within thirty minutes.

With the first wave of aircraft dispersed to Milwaukee and Duluth, the flight line crews continued to generate more aircraft to EWO configuration. It was a constant stream of aircraft being refueled, loaded and placed under guard. For these unsung heroes, there was no such thing as a first or second shift now. They kept working until the job was completed, then maybe they grabbed a little sack time wherever they could.

Within a couple of days of this pressure cooker beginning a problem began to surface. The problem was keeping the Combat Mission Folders (CMF) at the dispersal bases current. There was only one folder per aircraft, which had to be kept in the safe, leaving no target folder for the crew to study. The situation was taken care of by sending extra CMFs to the dispersal base by special courier.

Don Hickman made one of the night trips to Duluth and Milwaukee aboard a Base Flight C-47. He was armed with a sidearm and had a briefcase handcuffed to his wrist. On arrival at the dispersal bases he reported to the commander. They, in turn, would unlock the briefcase and take out the needed material. Then it was off to the next base to repeat the process. The flight took all night to accomplish. Don remarked he was glad to get home and get the handcuffed briefcase off his wrist.

The crisis continued with daily changes in the heat level. On Wednesday, the 24th, the quarantine was in place, ready to stop and search any ship heading for Cuba. There were meetings within the administration formulating contingency plans of action. Intelligence briefings on how the Soviets might react to the searches and other questions regarding our reaction if any of our recon aircraft were lost are gone over.

Under the direction of the Joint Chiefs of Staff, SAC was elevated to DEFCON 2 at 1400 Zulu on the 24th. This was the first time in history that the awesome power of the command had been placed just one step away

## Cold War Cornhuskers: The 307th Bomb Wing Lincoln Air Force Base Nebraska 1955-1965

from a condition of nuclear war. Gen Thomas Power took the DEFCON 2 status a step further by broadcasting the change of orders in the clear. He was sending the Soviet Union a message: his "mailed fist" was ready to carry out any strike order issued by the President. Along with his message, there was an increase in radio traffic from the airborne B-52s. They broadcast position reports to Omaha in the clear. It was another message to the Soviets that SAC was not only ready, but in the air, unable to be caught on the ground. At this point, the Russian Bear and the American Eagle stood claw to talon, waiting for one of them to blink.

On Thursday, October 25th, the crisis was highlighted by an event taking place on the floor of the United Nations General Assembly. It was there that UN Representative Adlai Stevenson confronted the Soviet Representative Zorin. Stevenson asked for a simple yes or no answer to the question about the presence of Soviet missiles in Cuba. Zorin replied that Stevenson would have his answer in the due course of time. Stevenson answered with his famous, "I am prepared to wait for my answer until Hell freezes over!"

On Friday, the 26th, the blockade intercepted the Soviet tanker Vinitsa. It was allowed to proceed without boarding. Ironically, it was the destroyer U.S.S. *Joseph Kennedy* that stopped and boarded the cargo ship *Marcula*. After a quick inspection the *Marcula* was allowed to continue.

On base, leaves had been canceled for the duration of the situation. Al Ottaviano wrote:

"I was on leave in California and received an urgent telegram to return to Lincoln immediately. Upon my arrival, I was crewed up with the first available pilot and copilot for dispersal to an International Airport. The aircraft commander was LeRoy McMath, a great guy and superb pilot and, incidentally, the only black aircraft commander at Lincoln AFB at the time. Few people knew of our missions during that emergency action. Our aircraft were fully loaded with the nukes and we were prepared to fly strike missions into Russia, if it was so decided in the White House. We were at DEFCON 2, which was one step below readiness for all-out war. We flew out of Lincoln to the dispersal station and lived in flight suits for 12 days until the Russians backed down. You want to talk about memorable flights, one out and finally back to Lincoln, without a call to action. We were prepared and ready, but it was another win in the Cold War."

Dave Bowersock wrote:

"At Lincoln AFB, all crews that were not on Alert status were called to the base. We were advised of the situation, told we were going to deploy (destination unknown) and that we had one hour to pack a bag and return to the base. (Gene had a feeling and had come with a bag already packed). I called Loretta, asked her to pack my bag and made a fast trip to get it. Later, when I opened it, I had both Bermuda shorts and long underwear. Good thinking!

"We were in a group of six aircraft, with nuclear bomb loads, that deployed to Billy Mitchell Field in Milwaukee, Wisconsin. The US was dispersing our forces for maximum survivability in the event of a sudden missile attack. Cots were set up in the National Guard Armory to accommodate the crewmembers. Our time was spent on flight planning, target study, preflighting the aircraft and updated briefings on the situation.

"A Command Post was set up in the armory with about five phones including a RED one, which was a direct line to the SAC Command Post, Offutt AFB, Nebraska. The aircraft commanders rotated the CP duty and manned the phones around the clock. One afternoon we had an "Official" briefing from SAC. The briefing officer impressed on us that this was not an exercise and if the RED phone rang, the duty officer should immediately turn on the lights and get the crews up even before answering it. We would be at war.

"I had the duty starting at midnight and there was just enough traffic on the phones to keep me busy and my mind off what might be happening. Around 0200 hours the phone rang and I picked up the one I thought it was. With the phone in my hand, I heard the ring again and I realized it was the RED phone. There is no way I can make you, the reader, fully aware of the feeling of my adrenaline rush: we were going to war!

"I flicked on the light switch, yelled at the crews, then answered the phone. From the background noise it sounded like Looking Glass, the airborne command post. A voice came on and we went thru code authenticating procedure. By this time the crews were gathering around me.

"The telephone voice asked the operator's name (meaning me). I said Bowersock and at his request repeated it twice. He asked me to spell it phonetically. I began, 'Baker, Oboe, ...ah, I mean, Bravo, Oscar…' (a few of the letters of the phonetic alphabet had recently been changed). I can normally do this in about five seconds, but my moment in the spotlight was making me sound like an idiot. The crewmembers, realizing what I was doing and began 'helping', which resulted in a noise much like a stirred-up hen house. When I finally got it out, the voice on the line was laughing and replied, 'Roger, I copied Bowersock. This is Looking Glass with a communication check. Thank you, out.' There were only a few that got back to sleep that night."

Saturday was usually the day for Mom and SAC BRAT to drive to the base for grocery shopping at the Commissary. It was just a short drive from Ring Trailer Park on West "O" Street. Unlike a normal trip to the base, there was a long line of cars backed up almost to the old south gate near the Boy Scout Hut. The SAC Decal in the lower left corner of the windshield wasn't getting the usual white glove wave in by the guards. They were checking ID Cards! I hadn't seen that at the patch in a long time.

Groceries in the station wagon; time for a short joy ride over to the BX Annex and check out the model airplane kits. Also a chance to scope out the flight line, one of SAC BRAT's favorite on-base activities. OK, no neat models, but look at the flight line! Never had it been so deserted, yet full of B-47s spread out in all directions. Almost all of them had ATO racks. It took a little bit of begging and pleading, but Mom gave in and took the long way home. Out the north gate and back along Cornhusker Highway so SAC BRAT could have a look at the base from the other side. What a sight to behold! B-47s parked all along the flight line with ATO bottles attached! It was a sobering thought, knowing each one of them was loaded with nuclear weapons and ready to scramble at a moment's notice.

On the Cuban front that day, things heated up almost to the boil over. A U-2 flying a routine air-sampling sortie accidentally crossed into Soviet airspace over the Chukotski Peninsula. The Soviets scrambled MiGs to intercept the intruding U-2. Alaskan Air Command launched several F-102s to protect the U-2. The wayward U-2 managed to exit Soviet airspace without any shots being fired by either side.

Maj Rudolph Anderson was over Cuba in his U-2 taking more photos of the areas that had been covered on previous flights. The purpose of the retake was to check the progress being made at those areas. As he passed overhead near the Cuban naval base at Banes an SA-2 was launched. The missile detonated close enough to the U-2 to inflict mortal damage to the aircraft and the loss of the pilot.

SAC lost an RB-47 from the 55th SRW deployed to Kindley AFB, Bermuda. The crash was caused by problems in the water-alcohol augmentation system. The crew was killed in the crash. The photo recon

RB-47s were in Bermuda photographing ship traffic headed for Cuba. Saturday would go into the history of the crisis as the darkest day for SAC.

Under the original crisis management plans, the Kennedy Administration would respond to the loss of an aircraft by launching air strikes against the offending SAM Site. In this instance, Kennedy did not order retaliation against the missile site. The Joint Chiefs were furious over the President's inaction, but history shows that Kennedy's restraint at that moment was the best possible course he could have taken.

Even in the middle of the most serious crisis in the history of the Cold War, one could not escape the ever-watchful eye of the SAC IG. The 307th Command Post got a TWX from Offutt informing the wing that one of the EWO cocked B-47s at Duluth was parked too close to a building.

Late on the afternoon of the 27th, the wing received instructions to place three more B-47s on ground Alert at Lincoln. With this, the wing had seventeen aircraft on home station primary Alert, ten on ground Alert at Greenham Common, ten on first cycle home station Alert, and twelve aircraft on second cycle ground Alert at the dispersal bases. This added up to forty-nine of the fifty aircraft assigned to the 307th now generated to EWO status. Never before in the history of the wing had there been that many B-47s on Alert for a possible EWO mission.

Every day, it was the same grim task for the Alert crews at Lincoln and at the dispersal bases. Check and preflight the aircraft twice a day, then go back to the "ready room" and listen to the radio for any word from SAC. There were deep thoughts about the fact that this just might be the real thing. If the decision was made, everyone was confident they would be able to complete the mission they had trained for.

Some SAC families had discussed what they would do if the situation boiled over. Some had their own evacuation plans to get the car packed and leave town if the balloon went up. Others never contemplated leaving the area. It was just assumed they would sit tight and wait for the nuclear flash at home.

Some of the dispersed crews tried to call home. This could lead to an interesting situation, as Jarvis Latham recalled:

"I inadvertently tipped off our folks in Lincoln of our whereabouts by making a collect call to my wife. I knew I had screwed up when I heard the long distance operator ask my wife if she would accept a collect call from Captain Latham in Duluth, Minnesota."

By the afternoon of October 27th, there was a glimmer of hope the crisis could be resolved without a nuclear exchange. All during the crisis there had been constant, behind-the-scenes diplomatic moves. After the Stevenson-Zorin debate at the United Nations, world opinion started to shift against the Soviet Union. The final straw was Stevenson's producing aerial photos showing the Soviet build-up and placing them on display at the United Nations. With the evidence on the table in front of the world, Khrushchev had been caught red-handed in his denial of having missiles in Cuba.

Khrushchev agreed to withdraw the missiles under UN supervision and not send any more weapons to Cuba if the United States promised not to invade Cuba. Of course the United States would agree to such a proposal. Both countries stepped back from the brink of war to contemplate the next step. For the moment the crisis was over, yet the tension continued.

Col Bertram issued instructions to the battle staff to formulate a written plan for the recovery of aircraft, equipment and personnel from the dispersal bases on October 30th. Although there had been no word from SAC regarding recovery of the force, it was never too soon to plan for that eventuality. Everyone knew that, when the word came down from Omaha, there would be a mad dash to get everyone back to Lincoln as quickly as possible.

R.T. Boykin was one of those caught in England when the crisis began. He recalled:

"I had completed the first week of Alert at Greenham Common and was on my first day of R&R. I was visiting my good friends that lived in Oxford, Gordon Excell and his wife Marian. (Marian was the sister of Pat McComb--Pat was married to Leo McComb, a navigator who was killed when a B-47 from Little Rock attempted a 'poorly executed roll' while climbing out from a low level route. The crash was near Crystal City, Texas.) I had been at Gordon and Marian's home maybe three hours when an English Bobby knocked on the door and told me to return immediately to Greenham. Gordon and Marian drove me back in their car.

"Several hours after I signed in at Greenham, we reported to the briefing room and heard President Kennedy's speech about Cuba. After the speech we were briefed and went back on Alert. The aircraft that were scheduled to return to Lincoln were retained at Greenham and placed on Alert. As I recall at that moment we had nine aircraft and twelve crews at Greenham. The three crews that were originally scheduled to return to Lincoln were bused to Brize Norton and flown back to Lincoln on a MAC bird.

"We remained on Alert at Greenham for the next four weeks and finally some relief crews were flown over by MAC and we were relieved, bused to Brize Norton and flown back to Lincoln. The KC-135 landed at McConnell and we were bused to Lincoln.

"After returning to Lincoln we were allowed to go home for one day, just long enough to get a change of underwear. The next day, we were back on base checking into the 'The Lincoln Hilton'-- ' The Lincoln Hilton' was any place a bunk could be placed for air crews, ground crews, air police, etc., to get a little sleep while waiting for the 'Big One' to be started over Cuba. We had planes deployed to forward bases and they rotated, which gave us sort of an airborne Alert capability in that we could be diverted to a target in case the 'Big One' started. So I experienced the Cuban Missile Alert abroad, at home and at stateside forward bases."

October 1962 would be recorded as one of the busiest months the 307th ever had. The wing passed an ORI, flew a Sky Shield-type mission, and deployed the Pipe Cleaners to the Pacific for Operation Dominic. The largest event, of course, was the Cuban Missile Crisis. The wing responded to the situation like the true SAC warriors they were. Each member of the wing gave more than a hundred per cent to get the wing ready and deployed to the dispersal bases. The fact that the 307th was one of the first wings in SAC to actually generate and launch aircraft in response to the national emergency showed the ability and dedication to duty of the men serving with the 307th.

On November 2nd, SAC stepped down from DEFCON 2 and went back to DEFCON 3. With the change in Alert posture, some of the crews were brought back from the dispersal bases. Pete Todd wrote:

"Our crew remained at Billy Mitchell Field for about two weeks. We were then relieved by other crews from Lincoln and returned to home base for a brief R&R. Tensions were still high and my crew deployed shortly afterwards to our Reflex base at Greenham Common in England to relieve a crew that had been on Alert since the crisis began. We were just glad to be home when it was all over, having pulled back from the brink of nuclear war."

By November 7th, the White House announced the missiles in Cuba were on the way back to the Soviet Union. Castro refused to allow any United Nations verification that the missiles were gone. Perhaps this was his way of protesting over the loss of his new toys and never being consulted during the crisis.

# Cold War Cornhuskers: The 307th Bomb Wing Lincoln Air Force Base Nebraska 1955-1965

The 307th now faced the task of recovering the dispersed B-47s back to Lincoln. The deployment from Duluth went without a hitch. Crews packed their bags and checked out of their motels. They arrived at the airport, preflighted their aircraft, and launched into the skies of Minnesota for the return trip to the patch.

At Billy Mitchell Field things were different. The crews had gotten the general word the crews from Duluth had gone back to Lincoln. So far they had not gotten a valid recall from SAC, so they were staying put. Thus began the short-lived mutiny of the 307th. Bud Flanik wrote:

"An item of note was the way the flight crews 'stood down' at the end of the crisis. SAC Headquarters refused to send a recall message ordering the planes to redeploy back to their home base. Someone at Offutt called our detachment and told our officer on duty to send the planes back home. The duty officer requested a properly authenticated recall message be sent and we would comply with the contents. As a navigator, I was out of the loop and the direct line of fire. This was one of the few times I was pleased that I didn't have the authority to make the decision to refuse a nonstandard order from Offutt.

"We all knew the other staging bases had closed down, but the overwhelming consensus (100%) of the flight crews at General Mitchell Field was that we would not redeploy without a valid recall message from SAC Headquarters. Things got butt-ugly for a while and Offutt finally flew a C-54 into Milwaukee two days later. A senior officer deplaned and gently chatted with our pilots. We then took off for Lincoln, never getting a valid recall message that we had so diligently trained for over the years."

SAC slowly returned to normal and, by November 20th, was back to the previous status of having fifty percent of the bombers on Alert. With that the military was also reduced back to DEFCON 4 status. Alert crews that had been caught overseas on Reflex came home as the Reflex schedule was reworked and adjusted so they could have a few days off and spend time with their families.

Don Hickman finally flew his mission to become combat ready. It was a normal mission until they made the bomb run on the Hastings bomb plot. He had everything lined up and ready. The TGI was moving towards zero when the radar scope went blank. He had lost the system due to two blown fuses. He grabbed two spares and jammed them into the proper spots, but they sparked and blew. He grabbed another set and replaced the blown fuses. They worked. At the last second the radar came back up and they were able to release on time. After the bomb run they did a nav leg and finally headed back to Lincoln.

Thanksgiving Day 1962 was celebrated with more meaning than ever that year. Everyone was THANKFUL the crisis was over and most of the crews were back home with families. We were THANKFUL for not having been vaporized in a nuclear exchange between the Soviet Union and the United States. The mailed fist of SAC had been clenched tighter than it had ever been, ready to release its grip of awesome power against the Russian Bear. We were THANKFUL this power didn't have to be used. Jim Villa recalled:

"The day before Thanksgiving, I began having pain in my lower jaw (both sides). What really set in was the anxiety that my enjoyment of the approaching Thanksgiving meal would be foiled. Sure enough, Thursday morning the pain was at full throttle setting. It didn't completely foil the enjoyment, but I do enjoy eating without any distraction.

"I didn't sleep much that night and the next morning when I looked at the guy in the mirror, both jaws were swollen. I decided I had better see our Alert maintenance officer and see if I could get to the dental clinic. He declined and I guess he had his reasons. His was that no one could be excused from duty due to the Alert status we were in.

"We went down to the airplanes at about nine o'clock to do the regular check of the uploaded birds. There would be a crew change this morning. Capt Paul Pudwill and his crew would be coming on duty with my assigned plane. I went over to the power unit and had it running when both crews arrived. I flipped the power onto the bird when they started doing their change out, went over and put the headset. I did the walk around under the airplane and was waiting by the entrance ladder when the crew came out of the cockpit.

"Capt Pudwill turned to me and was about to convey what I needed to know about the LOX gauges when he saw the swollen state of my face. He asked what was wrong and I explained. He told me to get to the dental clinic and I relayed the maintenance stance. He turned to his crew and told them to ride with the crew who were parked next to us. He then turned and got in his Alert vehicle and away he went. By the time my partner and I had topped of the LOX systems on both our airplanes, he was back.

"Capt Pudwill told me to get into the truck and we were going to the dental clinic. It appeared things had been sorted out up on the hill. The captain told me to go into the dental clinic and have them do what they needed to. He told me if the klaxon went off, get them to do what was necessary to get me on my feet, he would be waiting to get us to the airplane. (So, Nikita and Fidel, you would have to wait on us.)

"The dental people found that I had both of the bottom wisdom teeth coming in under the back teeth. They did a little cutting and told me to come back at a later date for them to take the suckers out. The captain and I returned to the Alert area and, in a few days, the all clear sounded for us to stand down."

There was a change in the command structure within the 307th. On December 2nd, LtCol Warren Franscioni replaced Col Walter Duch as the Deputy Commander of Maintenance. LtCol Franscioni had served as the 307th OMS commander for the last year.

Reflex got back to a normal schedule with the first deployment of three aircraft leaving Lincoln on Monday, the 3rd. Like before the Cuban interruption, Reflex would leave on Monday with the returning crews coming back on Wednesday.

Another Pipe Cleaner aircraft arrived on December 10th. 52-0031 would be assigned to the squadron to train the crew in radio relay procedures. This aircraft flew a training sortie on December 14th. A radio link was established with Grayson. The mission was successful and all training items were accomplished according to the mission profile.

Pipe Cleaner aircraft were in the air again on December 20th. That Thursday, 0031 and her crew teamed up with the other two crews assigned to the squadron for another test of equipment on 0031. Links were established with Looking Glass and were maintained during the entire mission. At the end of the mission, 0031 and her crew recovered at Lockbourne AFB, Ohio, to become part of the Pipe Cleaner squadron based there.

Any time a crew flew in a B-47 there was a certain element of risk. To return safely to the ground after a mission was always a welcome relief. Even a routine ferry flight to a depot could have an element of danger. Bill Rogers recalled a ferry flight on December 22nd to Wichita that ended up being more than routine:

"Both the aircraft commander and co pilot were staff officers, but I can't remember who they were. Sometimes it was difficult for staff officers to get flying time, so this relatively short daytime flight was just the ticket. There was also a crew chief flying in the fourth man seat to get flying time.

"The mission was a simple one. Take off from Lincoln, fly to Wichita, Kansas, deliver the bird to the Boeing factory, but before landing, fly a couple of hours of instrument work there. We were at 25,000 feet and had just arrived at the Wichita VOR. I had taken off my oxygen mask and was monitoring our position when I smelled smoke typical of an electrical fire.

"I immediately asked on the intercom if anyone else smelled or saw it. Pretty quickly, the copilot said he smelled it. At about the same time, I had shut down the radar, gone on 100% emergency on my oxygen, and was scanning the area like crazy. Suddenly, flames erupted behind my right shoulder, so I called for the crew chief to bring a fire extinguisher that was by his position.

"In the meantime, either the pilot of copilot called Air Traffic Control and advised them of a fire in the cockpit and they immediately cleared us to all altitudes within a 50 mile radius from the VOR. Following emergency procedures, we dumped the cabin pressure and descended to 10,000 feet.

"I turned around with the fire extinguisher (CB) and squirted it at the biggest bonfire I have ever seen, but the fluid hit a bulkhead and splashed back in my face and eyes. I started to unbuckle from the ejection seat, but realized that there might be a need to use it on short notice so didn't unbuckle. I lunged around and pulled the trigger again and the flames went out, but they immediately re-ignited. I lunged again, squeezed the trigger and the flames went out for good.

"Because CB is very toxic and had gone into my eyes, I asked the crew chief to bring me the water bottle, but the copilot said he hadn't gotten water--just coffee and lemonade. I said bring me the coffee, but he couldn't tell which was which, so I said it didn't matter, just bring me one of them. It turned out to be lemonade and that did smart when it was splashed into my eyes.

"During that time, the pilot asked for the weather at Wichita and it was below minimums, so they began searching for a B-47 base that had good weather, but there wasn't one anywhere close. Finally, the SAC Airborne Command Post boomed in with 'Go to Walker AFB, NM,' so we headed in that direction.

"After washing out my eyes and figuring a course to fly to Walker, I scanned the circuit breaker panel behind my head and found that the windshield anti-ice circuit breaker had popped out, indicating a short in that circuit. (It was later determined to be the windshield anti-ice transformer that had caught fire.)

"On the way to Walker, we flew near a SAC base (B-52) in Western Oklahoma and found they were above minimums for landing. We were too heavy to land at the time we got there, so had to go into a holding pattern to burn off fuel. Since we knew what the problem was, there was no threat to our staying in the air for a short time more.

"When we landed, an ambulance met the airplane and took me to the flight surgeons office to be checked. When I related to the doctor that I had used lemonade to wash out my eyes, he said that was a good thing to use because the acidity of the lemonade counteracted the base in the CB! But, his weren't the eyes that got the bath!

"The next day, the weather had lifted at Wichita and we were cleared to fly there without repairing the windshield anti-ice system. We landed at Wichita, picked up the bird we were sent for and returned to Lincoln.

"It turned out that when I twisted around to fight the fire, I hurt my back on the right side and wound up being grounded from flying, off and on, for several months. From time to time, I still have problems with that area of my back."

Three crews deployed to Greenham Common on Monday, December 24th. The Christmas Eve deployment flew the usual northern route. While refueling near Goose Bay they were advised to be aware of possible "special traffic" in the area coming down from the North Pole. The crews kept a sharp watch, but never caught a glimpse of a red sleigh and eight tiny reindeer.

Christmas Day was celebrated on Tuesday with services at the chapel observing the day with thanks to world leaders in view of the events of the last several months. Again, there was special meaning in the celebration of Peace on Earth, even if it was still quaking from being near the brink of war.

The monthly report showed the 307th had flown 1,421 hours during the month. The wing had 46 B-47s assigned to the wing along with 2 Pipe Cleaner aircraft. There was the promise of more EB-47Ls on the way, but so far it was just that, a promise. Bombing effectiveness was rated at 92%; Navigation was 100% effective. Again, there was the same shortage in personnel within the wing. There was no immediate relief in sight, as there was a shortage of personnel across the board in SAC.

During the year, the wing had continued to maintain its commitment to ground Alert and Reflex to both Spain and England. The wing proved its capabilities by passing three ORIs during the year. It helped pioneer the use of airborne command radio relay through the use of the Pipe Cleaner aircraft. The wing's safety record was marred by the loss of the B-47 at Des Moines. The single most important event of the year was the wing's response during the Cuban Missile Crisis. At the peak of the crisis the wing had generated forty-nine of the fifty B-47s assigned to the wing to EWO status. SAC Headquarters commended the wing on being one of the first wings to generate and disperse aircraft after receiving the directive. To the last man, wing personnel had performed their duties in the highest professional manner that could have been expected.

Looking up from the aisle way. Pilot seat at left. (M.Hill)

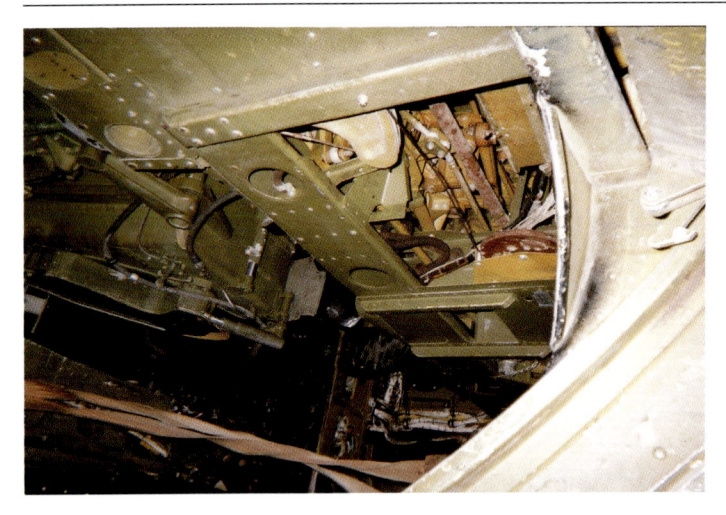

# Cold War Cornhuskers: The 307th Bomb Wing Lincoln Air Force Base Nebraska 1955-1965

Pete Todd's view from the cabin pressure door. (M. Hill)

52-6244 on the 307th flight line. (Villa)

After the May 14th directive, crews would have to remove the engine from the aircraft to work on it. (USAF)

Changing combustion chambers burner cans. (USAF)

A "LOOKING GLASS" aircraft taxis for another mission. (Campbell)

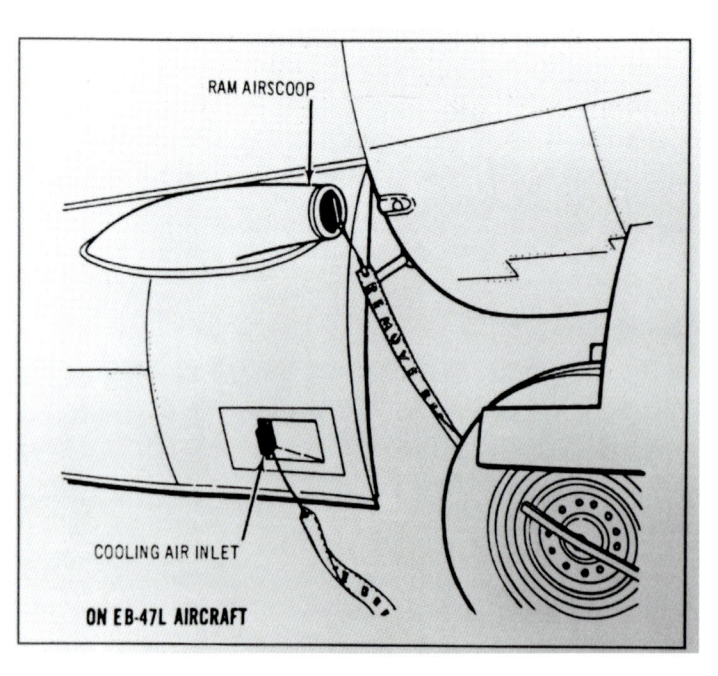

External air scoops on the EB-47L "PIPECLEANER". (Boeing)

*1962*

Aerial view of the 307th flight line. (JET SCOOP)

A view of the flightline from one of the barracks. (307th BWA)

A KC-135 refuels a B-47.

MiG 21 preserved at the Air Force Museum. (M Hill)

207

# Cold War Cornhuskers: The 307th Bomb Wing Lincoln Air Force Base Nebraska 1955-1965

MiG 17 preserved at the Air Force Museum. (M Hill)

Sac Command Post at Offutt Air Force Base, Omaha. (SAC)

Mark 28 nuclear weapons were carried by 307th B-47s during the Cuban Missile Crisis. (M Hill)

SAC dispersed the B-47 fleet to civilian airports around the country during the Cuban Missile Crisis. (SAC)

Nuclear armed B-52s maintained 24 hour airborne alert under the code name CHROME DOME. (Titus)

A SA-2 Ground to Air Missile like this one brought down a U-2 piloted by Maj. Rudolph Anderson on October 27th. This brought the crisis even closer to nuclear Armageddon. (M Hill)

*1962*

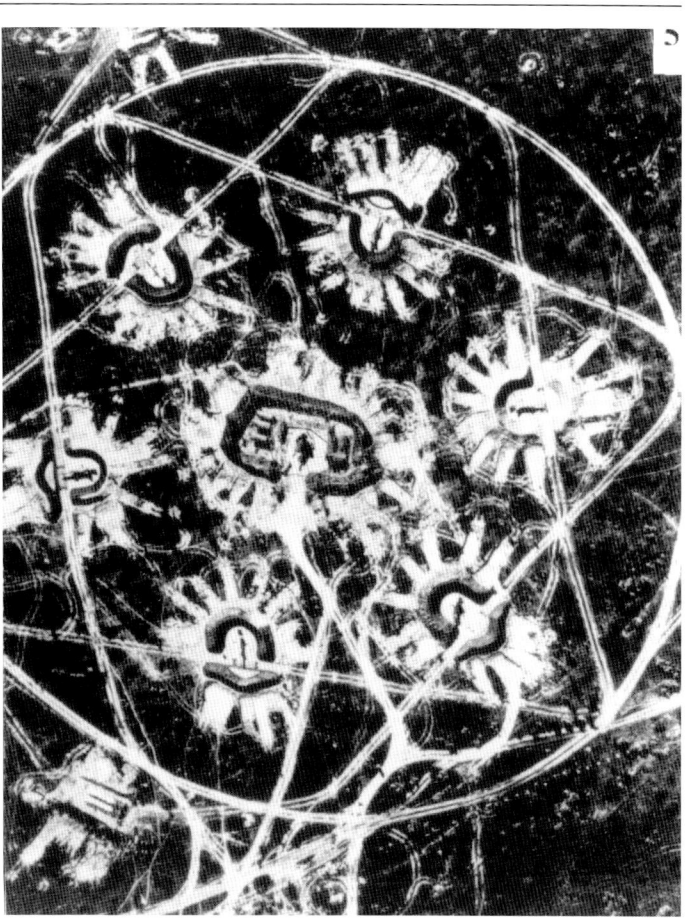

October 15th Recon photo: San Juan Airfield showing IL-28 bomber crates. (USDS)

SA-2 ground to air missile site. (USDS)

October 23rd Recon Photo: Medium Range Ballistic Missile (MRBM) Site, San Cristobol, Cuba. (USDS)

Medium Range Ballistic Missile site, Sagua La Grande, Cuba. (USDS)

# Cold War Cornhuskers: The 307th Bomb Wing Lincoln Air Force Base Nebraska 1955-1965

October 27th, United States Ambassador Adlai Stevenson (Seated Rt) produces photo evidence of Soviet missile in Cuba. (USDS)

October 29, 1962. San Cristobol site showing removal of MRBMs. (USDS)

November 6, 1962. Casilda Port, Cuba, photo shows loading of missile transporter and Soviet personnel on a ship for journey back to Soviet Union. (USDS)

Harold "Butch" Leppi (right) gets a three day pass from Col. Corbin for being one of the top Crew Chiefs with 70 on time take offs. (Leppi)

424th Bomb Squadron flight crews pose for a portrait.

# 1963

The New Year arrived in the usual Nebraska fashion, cold and snowy. The first few days of the year brought literally tons of snow to cover the flight line and the roads around the base. While some partied to celebrate the New Year, the snow removal crews worked overtime to clear the concrete.

Last October, before the Cuban Missile Crisis threw a monkey wrench into the SAC training program, the 307th had been alerted for a command-wide change in the way training flights would be conducted. According to the directive there would be two types of training missions.

Crews would continue to fly standard "profile" missions. These would be based on the regular 50-8 training requirements. The other type of mission would be classified as "Bar None". These were evaluation missions and would be used to evaluate the crews' performance. They would be planned by the wing planning staff and could also be used for ORI missions. The "Bar None" missions were designed to be tougher than the normal training flights. Timelines would be more critical. Aircraft would have to take off within a 0 to +5-minute window of the scheduled take off time. During the mission, CEG or a standboard staff member might be assigned to fly with the crew. The implementation of the program was postponed until January due to the disruption of the training schedule during the Cuban Missile Crisis.

The first Reflex flight of the year was a return flight to Lincoln on January 2nd. The crews were glad to leave England and return home. So far, the winter in England had been one for the record books. Snowfall had been higher than normal during November and December. Constant frontal systems made flying in and out of England hazardous.

Winter weather in England and the U.S. prompted the 307th staff to increase briefings on the "do's" and "don'ts" for working on the flight line in severe cold or blizzard conditions. Flight crews were reminded to brush up on the Cold Weather Operations section of the Dash-1. Special briefings on the effects of cold weather and the effect it had on water-alcohol augmentation were held. Included in the briefings was a warning that engines were more prone to compressor stalls at lower temperatures. Pilots were briefed on the correct use of the Emergency Stall Prevention (ESP) switch.

Flight crews and ground crews were glad to get out of the icebox in England and into the freezer at Lincoln. Paul Koski had just returned from England and related:

"We were at RAF Base Greenham Common, England, and it was just before Christmas. England had the worst snowfall in one hundred years, or so they said, with two to three feet of snow and drifts up to six feet. They said they were having trouble getting milk to London. Since England hadn't had much snow in many years, the Air Force in their wisdom sent all of the big snowplows to northern Spain. Their winters were by far harder than England's. We did have some six by six trucks with snow blades attached, but their priorities were the runways and taxiways. We had the task of shoveling out the aircraft, which took most of the day. I don't know if they changed our Alert status, but we sure couldn't launch any aircraft for awhile."

The first Reflex flight of the year from Lincoln to Greenham Common departed on January 7th. The flight of three flew the northern route arriving in England in bad weather. Snow and blowing snow caused problems with the arrival. Using GCA (Ground Controlled Approach), the three B-47s managed to land on the snow-swept runway.

Arriving in bad weather always caused the pucker factor to climb several notches. Doug Valen recalled an arrival his crew made:

"We flew into Greenham Common one day and the weather over most of England was socked in. We evaluated our options and chose to land at Greenham, in spite of no radio. This made GCA unavailable, but we seemed to have some kind of navigation that got us over the end of the runway, but too far to one side to make a safe landing. So Bud (Norm Menke) flew a 'box pattern' with timed legs and we got a little closer the second time. So, around we went again, timing the legs and got close enough to land on the third try. We were met by the Alert Force commander who was extremely upset we had landed in questionable weather. I remember him yelling at Bud, 'Why the hell did you land?' Bud calmly responded, 'Because I couldn't park it up there!'"

January 9th began as another cold day at the patch. Low gray clouds hung over the base. The weather boys said there was a good chance of snow arriving that night. There was a full flight schedule, with five launches during the day and another five scheduled to start launching at 1800. Ground crews spent the day getting the B-47s ready for the evening launch. At 1115, the five day-flight aircraft started launching and were immediately swallowed by the low-hanging clouds.

# Cold War Cornhuskers: The 307th Bomb Wing Lincoln Air Force Base Nebraska 1955-1965

Late that afternoon, Crew E-18 reported for their flight that evening. Capt Paul Pudwill (AC) along with Lt Frank Medrick (CP) and Capt Harry Jones (Nav) had planned a routine flight lasting just over eight hours. They spent time checking the weather and getting a preflight briefing before going out to their assigned aircraft. According to Base Weather, another frontal system was moving into the Midwest and would arrive at Lincoln sometime after midnight. At this point it looked like the front would cause light snow and gusty winds for the return to Lincoln early the next morning.

When the flight crew arrived at their aircraft, James Burns and his ground crew had 53-2097 ready for the walkaround preflight. The walkaround was normal, no fuel leaks, no leaks of any kind in any place. The crew climbed aboard 2097 and started engines. It all went like clockwork. At the scheduled time hack, Paul Pudwill pushed the six throttles to full power and started the takeoff roll. Speed built up and, at the computed speed, Jonas 37 lifted off the runway and into the night sky.

Their mission that night was a routine training flight. There were several nav legs and a couple of bomb runs on simulated targets. They were continuously communicating with the Command Post on the weather conditions at Lincoln. Everything on the mission profile was going according to the plan, except for the weather at home plate.

Shortly after midnight, snow began falling at Lincoln. At first, it was light, then it turned to a heavy snowfall. Within the hour, the wind picked up and visibility dropped to less than a half a mile. As the night continued, the snow and wind kept intensifying. By 0300, the forecast was revised for continued snow and increasing winds.

The 307th had five birds in the air that night. As weather at Lincoln continued to go to hell in a hand basket, it became obvious the five aircraft were not going to land at Lincoln. The Command Post was watching the situation. They had been communicating with other bases in the area to find out which one had the best weather. It looked like McConnell AFB, Kansas, was still open, so the Command Post advised all five aircraft to divert to McConnell.

Jonas 37 diverted to McConnell along with the other four 307th aircraft. Jonas 37 landed at McConnell at 0515 and taxied to the ramp. They were the last 307th aircraft to land. The crew went to Base Operations and debriefed. By the time they finished debriefing and were transported to an off-base motel, it was 0945 before the tired crew was able to climb into the sack for some much needed crew rest.

Around noon, one of the other aircraft commanders called the 307th Command Post to discuss how and when the diverted crews would return to Lincoln. The Command Post directed the five crews to return to Lincoln that evening. To make the best of the situation, they were to fly a training mission on the way back. After the discussion, the departure times from McConnell were established. Crew E-18 was scheduled to depart McConnell at 2016 for the return flight to Lincoln.

Paul and his crew were awakened by a loud knocking on the motel door about 1230. It was the aircraft commander who had called Lincoln. There was a discussion about what the Lincoln Command Post had said and just what the return flight was supposed to accomplish. Crew E-18 climbed into their flight suits and proceeded back to McConnell at about 1650. They were still tired since they had only been able to sleep for about three hours since arriving at Wichita.

At Base Operations, the crews planned for the return to Lincoln. The crew arrived at 53-2097 and began to preflight the aircraft. The aircraft was covered with a thin layer of ice from the weather that had moved into Wichita. It was obvious that the ice made flying 2097 unsafe, so they called for a deice truck. With the delay, it was obvious the departure time would have to be moved back.

The weather at McConnell was starting to go downhill rapidly. The ceiling was down to 1500 feet with fog, light snow and intermittent light freezing rain. While the aircraft were being deiced, the crews contacted the Command Post at Lincoln with an update. They expected Lincoln to tell them to stay put until the weather improved. The Command Post directed that, unless McConnell closed due to the weather, they were to launch for the return flight to Lincoln. The crews questioned the decision, but would comply with the order from the Command Post.

Paul and his crew went back to 2097 and started engines at 2124. They were number two in the Lincoln-bound launch of five B-47s. While they were waiting for clearance and their turn to take off, the crew would run up the engines to keep the ice clear of the nacelles. They also had the anti-ice system on to keep the surfaces clear. Since 2097 had been deiced, there should be an hour window for the takeoff.

While they were waiting in line for takeoff, the crew engaged in some small talk about the weather. "Just like Greenham Common. You can't see either end of the runway." "Yeah, I'll be glad to get airborne and get above of this crap!" The lead aircraft had a problem, so Jonas 27 moved towards the runway for takeoff.

At 2204, Paul Pudwill pushed the six throttles forward to a hundred percent and let the power stabilize. The water alcohol kicked in, brakes were released, and 2097 started rolling down the runway. Speed built up slowly at first as thrust overcame the 190,000-pound weight of the B-47. At S-1, acceleration was good; they were committed. When they reached S-2, Paul gave a gentle pull on the control wheel and 2097 left the runway and climbed into the snowy night sky.

As they climbed towards the bottom of the low scud clouds, Paul called for gear to be retracted. Copilot Frank Medrick pulled the gear lever up and waited for the gear to retract. When the gear cycled, there was an "intermediate" indication on the forward main gear. Medrick checked the circuit breaker and recycled the gear. Again, the forward main indicated "intermediate".

After the second intermediate indication, there was a quick discussion by the crew about the situation. Paul decided to continue to climb out and get on top of the soup, then figure out what to do about the landing gear situation. The flaps would be left down as recommended in the Dash-1. 2097 began a slow climbing turn to the right. The climb was slower than normal because of the extended flaps.

Breaking out of the clouds at about 6,000 feet, Paul rolled back out of the turn. As he did, the airspeed started to drop. Paul pushed the wheel forward to lower the nose of the aircraft. Airspeed came up a little. Frank Medrick noted they were climbing a little, but the airspeed started to fall again. Both Medrick and navigator Harry Jones confirmed the falling airspeed. Paul was working hard, fighting the wheel to maintain control of 2097. "I've lost the artificial feel. I can't control her!" Paul yelled. He pushed the nose forward again and 2097 started to buffet, airspeed kept falling, and 2097 was back in the clouds.

Breaking out of the bottom of the cloud layer at about 2,500 feet, Paul tried to get the nose to come up again. Airspeed fell off again when the nose started coming up. 2097 started shaking again like a dog shaking off water. Below, in the murky darkness, Paul could see the lights of houses; he fought the controls desperately to keep the bucking B-47 in the air long enough to clear the houses. They were coming down fast, in a last ditch effort, Paul pulled the controls back, 2097's descent slowed, the nose came up and she started shaking again. Paul's last-ditch effort had gotten them away from the houses; it was time to save themselves. Paul yelled into the intercom, "EJECT, EJECT, EJECT!!" Harry Jones wrote:

"When Paul said let's get out of here, I initiated the ejection procedure by rotating the arm braces forward. This started a series of events: the shoulder harness and lap belt retract and lock, holding you back in the seat, and the D-ring is released from the seat and flips up in front of you. After rotating the arm braces forward I reached for the D-ring, but it wasn't where it was supposed to be. I leaned forward and saw that it had unlocked from the stowed position, but had not flipped up to where I could grasp it. I bent further over and grabbed the D-ring and pulled up and I ejected.

"If the shoulder harness and lap belt had retracted and locked as they were designed to do, I don't think I would have had time to release everything and start the ejection sequence again. I was fortunate in having a double malfunction. It was determined later that a pin had been installed backwards and it prevented the D-ring from springing upright. Upon checking the B-47 fleet, six aircraft were found with this pin installed backwards.

"The gas initiators firing made me think that the seat had eaten a lot of beans, quite gassy and noisy. I blacked out, but the chute popping open woke me. I saw another chute in the air in front of me, but I had no idea who it was. Looking down I saw that I was going to land on a road. I reached for the shroud lines to guide myself away from the road, but I missed. Before I could try again, the chute swung for the first time, picking my legs up in front of me, and then I hit the ground rear end first. That resulted in two compression fractures in my lower vertebrae. At the time, I had the lowest successful downward ejection from a B-47. I was less than 800 feet above the ground when I ejected. It might have been the difference in G force, i.e., up or down ejection, but my winter gloves in my lower flight suit pocket ripped out and were gone. The copilot had a G.I. flashlight in his lower pocket and it stayed in the pocket."

Frank Medrick reached down and pulled the handles up which blew the canopy. He squeezed the handgrip with his gloved right hand. He and his seat were blown upward into the darkness. The zero-delay worked perfectly and he separated from his seat. His chute billowed, he swung in the shroud lines once and hit the ground.

With his crew out of the doomed B-47, Paul reached down and pulled the seat handles upward and squeezed the trigger. His seat fired and catapulted upward. He was low, too low for his chute to fully open and break his fall. He gave his last full measure to save his crew and the unsuspecting people on the ground.

2097 had almost recovered from the stall after the crew ejected. She hit the ground with one wing slightly low on the north side of Highway 54 at the Butler County line. The B-47 exploded on impact showering the highway with flaming debris in a 300 by 1100-foot path of destruction. Some of the wreckage blocked the highway.

Harry Jones landed on Highway 54, about a half a mile from the burning wreckage. Frank Medrick landed on the south side of the highway, just a couple of hundred yards from Jones. Both were shaken by their low level ejection. Now they faced another problem. They were wet and cold due to the combination of weather and shock to their bodies. Their entire flight had lasted about four and a half minutes.

Richard Clarkson was headed east on Highway 54. He had been in Wichita covering a basketball game for the Topeka *Capital Journal*. He saw the crash and filed the story for a Wichita paper. "I was leaving Wichita on US-54 east of the city. Light snow, flurried by a due north wind, had been falling for almost three hours. The cloud ceiling was low, so low that each clutter of business buildings on the route, Kellogg Street, reflected its own bright spot on the clouds. I was startled by the noise of a jet. I rolled down the window of my car to look up for it. At first, I didn't see it. And suddenly there it was two or three miles ahead--a mushroom fireball spreading across the highway. It was so fierce that it was clearly visible through the wind whipped snow. At first it was a huge fireball. Then it cascaded across the highway and into the fields on the other side.

"It was there only a couple of seconds. The orange glow that reflected off the clouds of the eastern sky quickly died to dim reflections of small fires. At the crash site there was no sign of life except for stopping motorists who couldn't continue through the four lane US-54 that was now strewn with burning wreckage."

Harry Jones was picked up by one of the fire trucks responding to the fire. The firefighters put him inside the truck to warm up. Frank Medrick was picked up by a local family who had started driving towards the accident. They found the firefighters and took both Jones and Medrick to McConnell AFB for treatment of any injuries they may have sustained in their low altitude ejection. Harry Jones sustained back injuries that would not show up until examined later when they got back to Lincoln.

Dave Bowersock was flying one of the other B-47s that had diverted to McConnell. He recalled:

"We landed at McConnell early enough for me to call an old friend, George Jabara, who insisted that I spend the night with him. The next morning, I called the base and was told our return to Lincoln was delayed because it was still weathered in. Not long after that, my crew called to tell me that I needed to return to base because all the B-47s diverted to McConnell were to fly another mission that night.

"I need to point out here that SAC was operating under a very competitive system of points given for every phase of the training program. This so-called, motivational game pitted crews, squadrons, wings and even divisions against each other. Promotions and careers were very much influenced by this competitive score keeping. Thus, Lincoln was still socked in, so we were ordered to fly the scheduled missions they couldn't fly from Lincoln.

"We planned and did our target study all that day with a takeoff time that night. As the takeoff time approached, a light freezing drizzle began. The deicing trucks sprayed all of our planes with their liquid deicing solution. During our preflight, we discovered some areas that perhaps the truck missed and were icing over again. As our start engines time was passing by, we were still waiting for the deicing truck, with fatigue and stress taking their toll. The weather conditions were deteriorating as we pulled out to taxi. We were scheduled for the first takeoff but Paul Pudwill had no delay in starting so they switched our take off time, making him first.

"As we watched Paul's plane take off and disappear into the night, we waited for the tower's instructions to take the runway. After a lengthy delay, the tower ordered all aircraft back to their parking spots on the ramp. We were eventually informed that the first aircraft had crashed.

"We parked the aircraft, sat in stunned dark silence and I think each of us cried. I took off my helmet. Angry and frustrated, I threw it down, intending for it to land on the walkway. Unfortunately it went thru the hatch and fell about twenty feet to the concrete ramp."

From the very beginning of Alert operations, SAC had concern about the capability to launch the fleet and remain in communications with the outbound strike force. They had implemented Positive Control Procedures along with Looking Glass, and the Pipe Cleaner aircraft. On January 11th, a new system became operational. Taped messages were placed in the nose cones of Blue Scout missiles. The idea was that, if the strike force was launched and all other communication was lost, the missiles would be launched to play the tape containing the "Go Code". These missiles were based at Tekamah, Wisner and West Point, Nebraska.

On the heels of the eight-inch snowfall hitting Lincoln on the 9th, more snow arrived on the 14th. The storm dumped another five inches of the white stuff on the base. Visibility was reduced to less than a half a mile. In view of the loss of 2097 in similar conditions, the Reflex launch scheduled for that evening was held off for twenty-four hours.

Cold weather and snow continued to plague the 307th during the entire month of January. Air operations suffered as flights were canceled or rescheduled. The crews who managed to fly the new Bar None missions agreed that they were like flying a mini-ORI.

January 30th was one of the few normal days during the month. It was clear and sunny, with no snow in the forecast. There was the normal briefing for crews scheduled to fly that day. There was another briefing and mission planning session for the crews that were going Reflex on February 4th.

On January 30th, the accident investigation board published the findings on the loss of 2097 at McConnell. Supervisory personnel at the Lincoln Command Post were listed as the primary contributing factor, for scheduling the return flight without allowing adequate crew rest. They were also cited for ordering the launch into known icing conditions. Pilot factor was mentioned because the crew took off into bad weather. It was also noted recovery could not be accomplished due to loss of artificial feel caused by Q-Spring icing.

Friday, February 1st, was another snowy, blustery day at LAFB. A Base Flight T-33 returned from a local pilot proficiency flight that afternoon. As they turned off the runway, they hit a patch of ice and started sliding. The T-33 went off the taxiway and into the snow. The forward momentum was just enough to cause the nosewheel to bury itself in the snow with the tail blocking the taxiway. It took about two hours to dig the nosewheel out and tow the T-Bird back to the ramp. Just another day at the frozen patch.

Bright and early Monday morning, February 4th, the flight line troops reported for duty and were briefed on the day's activity. If the weather held, there were four birds to launch for routine training profiles in the morning and five more for the afternoon. The launch crews were also busy preparing three aircraft for a Reflex launch that evening. One of the B-47s being serviced was 53-2134. She had been the 1959 Bomb/Comp aircraft and had brought the Fairchild Trophy home to Lincoln.

The flight of three, call sign "Willow", would be led by Crew S-97, commanded by Alfred Hunt. The copilot was Roger Beamer. Plotting the course from the nose would be R.T. Boykin, Jr. Flying the #2 position would be Crew S-57, William Schwob (AC), Jerry Lanning (CP) and Peter Kraska (Nav). Flying in the #3 slot would be Crew E-58. Paul Canney was aircraft commander, Richard West would fly in the back seat and Don Hickman would be in the nose as navigator.

This would be Don's first trip across the pond. He and Paul had talked about going to London on their R&R. Don looked forward to the trip with mixed emotions. Somewhat excited about his trip across the ocean and seeing exotic places in England, yet sad about being away from his family.

The crews reported at 1800 and were briefed for the Reflex flight. The weather briefing for takeoff looked good. There was a weather system to the east, but by the time the flight reached it they would be at cruising altitude above the weather. The flight across the Atlantic looked good. No major weather systems along the way. The weather at Greenham Common would be another story. It looked like Willow flight would arrive on the heels of another bad weather system in Europe.

The three crews climbed aboard their aircraft. Don Hickman recalled:

"I hauled my heavy nav bag and my flight lunch up the ladder, completed my interior inspection and pulled out all of the tools of my trade. Paul and Dick climbed aboard and I heard someone else coming up the ladder and down the aisle toward my seat. It was crew chief, SSgt Bobby Odom. He would be riding with us using the fourth man seat that was to the left and just below the copilot's seat. Not a very comfortable place to sit and there was no ejection capability. If a bailout became necessary, he would have to drop out through the entry hatch. We introduced ourselves, shook hands and he headed back toward his seat. I slipped on my helmet and strapped myself into my ejection seat."

One by one, the three England-bound B-47s started engines, taxied to the end of Runway 35 and held for the tower to clear them for takeoff. The lead aircraft, flown by Al Hunt started its takeoff roll at 2140, followed at one-minute intervals by the remaining aircraft. ATC had cleared Willow flight for a Dodge Departure. The three B-47s would climb out over Wahoo, Nebraska, then continue on a heading of 342 degrees until they reached Dodge, Nebraska. Passing over Dodge, they would turn towards Sioux City, Iowa, and then on to the east.

"I kept track of our position using radar returns from the ground until we hit the East Coast." Don recalled. "It was dark and I opened my optical sight to look at all the lights. It was gorgeous and I felt quite small and insignificant as I gazed at all the twinkling lights of the cities along the coast below. I couldn't help but wonder what all of those people below were doing tonight."

After coasting out, Willow lead began trying to make contact with Tonto 41, the lead KC-135 tanker. At first, there was nothing but static on the airway. Finally, contact was made and rendezvous with the tankers began. The tankers were spotted on radar and the three B-47s formated with the tankers for refueling. There were a few moments of concern when Tonto 41 reported they were having problems with their boom. After a few anxious moments, the tanker crew was able to resolve the problem and continued with the refueling.

The Reflex flight continued out over the Atlantic. The hours of flying in the cramped quarters of the B-47s were starting to take their toll on the crews. "As time ticked away, my buttocks started to get numb, so I loosened my lap belt and squirmed around a bit," Don recalled:

"That helped for a time, but then I decided I would get out of my seat, leave my parachute behind and try to stand up and stretch. Hunched over, I made my way back along the aisle to a position below and to the left of Paul. There wasn't enough room to stand straight up so I put my head next to Paul's left leg stretching out as much as possible. Paul just looked down at me, moved his leg a bit to give me more room and gave me the 'thumbs up' signal. I returned to my seat and strapped back in. I began to think that next time I might bring a small pillow with me."

In the lead aircraft, R.T. Boykin kept busy navigating for the flight. He recalled:

"Just prior to the point of no return, we conducted routine checks and received a European weather report. We proceeded on and about 500 miles out from England, Schwob reported hydraulic problems. We got an updated weather report on European bases and, based on the report, Al, my AC, ordered Schwob to divert to Spain."

Bill Schwob left the Reflex cell and headed for Spain. After some anxious time enroute they landed safely in Spain.

Willow flight continued on course for England. R.T. Boykin recalled:

"Our flight plan had us coasting in near Prestwick, Scotland, and proceeding southwards to Greenham. About 15 minutes before coast in, Roger (Beamer) reported that oil pressure was dropping in number 3 engine. A few seconds later, Al reported he was shutting down number 3. We were truly committed to landing in England and, while the weather (especially the crosswind) was marginal at Greenham, the weather there was the best available. Al declared an emergency and we proceeded to land at Greenham. The emergency equipment was in place for our landing."

GCA had gotten Willow lead down safely. With the crosswinds and snow blowing across the runway, it was, to say the least, an interesting landing approach. Willow 37 was now in contact with Midlands Approach Control and got the latest weather information at Greenham. At the moment, they were reporting scattered clouds at 2,500 feet with 8,000 feet broken. Visibility was seven miles, winds at 170 degrees at 16 knots with gusts to 23, temperature was 31 degrees.

Aboard Willow 37, Paul Canney and Dick West went through the checklist. **"ESP Switch...ON; Pitot Heat...ON; Engine Anti Icing... ON"** Midlands Control handed Willow 37 off to Greenham Common GCA for the final letdown and approach. The final transmission from GCA was when Willow 37 was about six miles out and had the runway in sight. **"One Four Zero, Winds variable at one seven zero degrees at fifteen gusting to twenty two knots. On course and on glide path."** Don Hickman wrote:

"It seemed very normal to me. I had heard these calls many times, on every approach we had flown with GCA. We began to experience some turbulence as we descended on final approach. The wind seemed to be kicking us around a little and the closer we got to the runway the worse it seemed to get. I took one last peek out my optical sight and could see the runway straight ahead of us. It looked like there was a lot of snow piled up along the edges of both sides of the runway. The wind was blowing snow from the tops of these piles across the runway in sheets like I had seen many times on roads in the Midwest. I closed the cover on the sight, remembering the cost to me if it got broken.

"As I heard the power reducing for the touchdown, I put the safety pins into my ejection seat and began putting my charts and other equipment in my bag. I was anxious to see England for myself. I sat back in my seat as I heard the engine noise reduce close to idle making me think we were about to touchdown. Then, I heard the noise increase as if Paul needed just a bit more power to touchdown where he wanted to or maybe the airspeed was a bit low for our altitude above the runway. He was always proud of his smooth touchdowns. Then, the power came up to the point I thought we were probably aborting the landing and making a go-around for another landing attempt. I tried to decide if I should pull my ejection seat pins back out again, and then it happened."

In the front seat, Paul Canney was trying desperately to keep 2134 lined up with the runway. Because of the crosswind, he was trying to hold his airspeed about ten knots above his best flare speed of 136 knots. He was also holding a slight right crab to help account for the crosswind. Looking out of the windshield, Paul could see the runway, then it disappeared in the blowing snow. In a heartbeat, it appeared again, then he lost it in another wave of blowing snow.

Paul lost depth perception and couldn't judge his landing anymore. Time to play it safe and go around for another try. Paul knew he would get a lot of good-natured razzing by his fellow pilots. This wasn't the time to care about ribbing and try to grandstand. Play it safe, go around and try it again. Paul pushed the throttles forward to go around.

Standing out in the cold, a young copilot from Dyess AFB had been filming B-47s taking off. He was trying out the new 8 mm movie camera he had purchased at the BX and he had some film left. The emergency equipment had come out to the edge of the runway. With an emergency in progress, he decided to stay and film it. The first B-47 had declared the emergency and they (Al Hunt) landed without incident. Oh well, there's another B-47 on approach, so why not use the rest of his film on that one. He squinted through the viewfinder and framed the approaching B-47 in the center. He pressed the shutter and followed the approaching B-47.

2134 floated just above the runway for about 2,500 feet while the engines started spooling up to full power for the go-around. Five engines came up to power, but number six went into compressor stall. The asymmetric thrust caused the right wing to drop suddenly while the nose started to come up. The right wing continued to fall towards the runway until it hit the snow and started dragging across the hard packed snow. Paul cranked full left aileron to get the dragging wingtip up and he pulled the power back on number six trying to get it out of the stall. To counteract the asymmetric thrust, he pulled power back on number one. The number six engine smashed into a snow bank alongside the runway causing the right wing to bounce.

For a brief moment, the wings came back almost level. The stalled engine started coming back to life. The increasing power on the right side now caused the under-powered left wing to drop towards the ground while the aircraft drifted to the right. Paul Canney was using every ounce of his skill as a pilot to regain control of the runaway B-47. The left wing continued to drop until the aircraft was almost at a 30 degree left bank and heading off the runway towards the taxiway.

Sitting in the fourth man seat Bob Odom couldn't see what was going on. His helmeted head was almost at the same level as the bottom of Dick West's ejection seat. He knew no matter what happened, he would have to ride it out since he didn't have an ejection seat. All he could do was hang on for dear life and rely on his pilot to pull them through.

With the left wing almost dragging the ground, Dick West reached down and tapped Odom on the shoulder and gestured by crossing his arms across his chest. Without warning, Dick West blew the canopy and ejected. Bob Odom recalled. "That scared the hell out of me when he ejected. His seat was right by my head!"

Dick West and his seat rocketed out of the aircraft into the air. What no one knew was there was a partial malfunction of the seat. Part of the railing and tube twisted and blew downward cutting some of the control cables. Paul Canney now had no way of controlling 2134. Number one engine smashed into the ground followed by the outrigger. The nose came down on the forward main gear, then the rear main gear.

Sitting on the taxi way was an AFEX "Snack Bar" vehicle. The driver sat frozen in his right hand seat as the huge runaway B-47 hurtled towards him. At the last second, 2134 bounced into the air. The number three engine smashed into the left front side of the truck, while the left front main gear door sliced through the rear corner of the vehicle.

Both landing gear slammed into the ground again slewing the aircraft almost ninety degrees. Sliding sideways in a cloud of snow, she finally swung back, coming to a grinding halt almost on the taxiway. Before 2134 had stopped sliding, the emergency equipment sitting on the taxiway was rolling towards the crash. The drivers knew somewhere within the billowing cloud of snow a crew was in trouble.

2134 came to a stop with the left wing down and the number one engine lying on the ground. The entire left inboard engine nacelle was missing. The rear engine mount on the number six engine had broken and the engine was hanging from the front mount running at almost full power. Paul frantically pulled the throttles back to cut off. When he did, 2134 rolled back to the right settling on the right wingtip and engine.

Bob Odom unbuckled his lap belt and climbed for the empty copilot position. Don Hickman unstrapped from his seat and pulled the release on his escape hatch. Looking out of the window, he figured it was too far to the ground. Paul Canney pulled the release on his straps and climbed towards the rear, followed by Hickman. They climbed out onto the fuselage and scrambled down the right wing.

The copilot from Dyess dropped the camera from his eye. He couldn't believe what he had just witnessed through the viewfinder. He looked at the film counter, sure enough it had moved from the last count. He had captured the entire crash-landing on film. He knew it had to be turned in for the investigation board. Perhaps his film would help in finding the cause of the accident.

Before the three shaken crewmen could hardly look around, they were inside an ambulance on their way to the hospital. They kept asking about Dick West, but no one seemed to have any idea of what had happened to him or if he was OK. The three were examined by the doctors and pronounced to be in good shape. They were shaken up a bit. The worse thing was, no one could, or would, tell them a thing about their copilot. After what seemed an eternity, a doctor came in and gave them the bad news; Dick West didn't survive his low level ejection. Don said, "Paul and I were speechless. Tears came to both our eyes."

That night in their hospital room, Paul was busy writing on a note pad. Don asked him what he was doing. "I am writing every single detail I can think of regarding the crash," he replied. "You know, I can't think of a single thing I would do differently. I wasn't proud. I decided to take it around for another try. I knew I'd get razzed by some of the guys about it, but I lost all my depth perception because of that stupid snow blowing across the runway. It was like a complete 'white-out'. Then that damn number six stalled and rolled back on me. When Dick punched out, I thought we were in the best shape we had been in. We'll never know why he did that. I'm writing all the things I can think of. The accident board will want to know everything."

After twenty-four hours of observation in the hospital, Paul and Don were released. A car arrived to take them to the BOQ. Don Hickman recalled the ride. "It was very cold outside but the car was warm. We had to cross the runway. The normal crossing spot near the center was blocked because of debris still there from our accident. The driver told us that the man who was driving the snack bar van we hit couldn't be found. He took off running immediately after the collision and hadn't been seen since. Everyone was still looking for him.

"As we approached the runway area, we could see our airplane sitting like a helpless, wounded bird. We used the parallel taxiway to get further south and crossed the runway to the other side. As we crossed the runway, I noticed that snow was piled at least six-feet high along either side of the runway. We headed back north and could see our bird sitting between the runway and the taxiway. Paul asked the driver to slow down so we could get a better look. As we came abeam the aircraft, Paul asked the driver to stop. It was an eerie feeling that engulfed my body and mind. Ground crew personnel had covered the cockpit area with a tarp and they had replaced the escape hatch in the nose that I had jettisoned. I was looking at an aircraft that I had been sitting in just yesterday morning and could have died in.

"It was sad to see the magnificent airplane now damaged, probably beyond repair. The canopy was missing and the aft main gear was severely bent. There were fuel and hydraulic lines dangling from the wing where the number two and three engines had been and the right external fuel tank was lying on the ground under the left wing. I took a deep breath as I began to realize how close to a horrible disaster we had been."

Within a week, the accident investigation board was assembled to find the cause of the accident. The three surviving crewmen were summoned to relive the accident from their perspective and to present testimony to the accident board. The board had one thing very few accident investigation boards had to work with. They had about thirty seconds of 8 mm movie film that captured the entire accident. The board reviewed the film over and over, frame by frame. The film was shot from the east side of the runway so the accident was viewed from the right side of 2134.

Like the investigation board, I have reviewed the film hundreds of times during my research for this history. I have watched it at normal speed, slow motion and stop frame. Each time, I have spotted something I hadn't observed before: Small things, like the #6 engine bouncing as it scraped along the runway. The collision of the engine and the snow piled on the side of the runway. The clouds of snow kicked up as the #1 engine and outrigger hit the runway. The final impact of 2134 as it disappeared in a cloud of churned up snow. But every time I review the footage, I cringe momentarily when I see Dick West eject and separate from the seat, then disappear in the cloud of snow, knowing the final outcome was fatal.

There was a sad ironic twist to the accident. Just days before leaving Lincoln, Dick West had talked to Paul Canney. He told his aircraft commander he didn't want to fly in the B-47s any more. He was ill at ease in the aircraft. Both of them talked to their squadron commander. It was too late to change the Reflex schedule, so Dick agreed to fly one last Reflex deployment before getting off the crew and getting into maintenance.

The effect of the accident in England had a profound ripple effect on the 307th. The wing had lost two aircraft in less than thirty days. Both of them occurred during cold, adverse winter weather. So, once again, there were more briefings on the effects cold weather could have on air operations. Everyone pulled out the old Dash-1 and reviewed the section on cold weather operations, emergency procedures for loss of artificial feel and how to deal with compressor stall in an engine.

Winter weather at Lincoln continued to border on record-breaking. Almost every other day it either snowed or the snow that was on the ground was rearranged by gusty winds. Then, the bottom would fall out of the thermometer. It was another winter battle with Mother Nature to keep the planes cocked for Alert, repaired for the next flight, then getting off the ground and safely back onto terra firma. Paul Koski remarked, "Remember, this was the 'Cold War' we were in, I think it was between Lincoln's winters and the USAF!"

The 307th launched three aircraft early on Wednesday, February 20th. They were followed by a three-ship cell from the 98th Bomb Wing. All six aircraft were scheduled to fly a Bar None training sortie. By 1630, that afternoon five of the B-47s had returned to the base. 52-563 from the 98th had not returned. They had not been heard from since their last transmission to Minneapolis Center when they left the Big Stick RBS at 1406.

Later that evening, word spread across the base. The 98th aircraft had crashed about three miles northwest of Comfrey, Minnesota. Two of the crew had apparently ejected and were listed as missing. The other two crewmen had perished in the crash. Local officials in Minnesota were searching the area near the crash site for the missing airmen.

First shift reported for duty as usual on the morning of the 21st. The mood was subdued during briefing due to the accident the previous day. The low clouds and misty skies added to the mood as the troops started their daily routine. By the time the troops returned from noon chow, word had arrived concerning the missing airmen. They had been located, but there was horrible news: neither of them had survived ejection from the doomed B-47. The crash of 563 was the third fatal accident for Lincoln Air Force Base in the first two months of the year. There was some small talk about maybe the base was snakebit.

# 1963

February 27th was another Wednesday of fighting the cold. The scheduled Reflex flight was delayed due to—you guessed it—bad weather in England, over the pond and almost all points in between. That afternoon the low-hanging clouds dropped even lower. Light snow began falling; by 1800 another inch of "partly cloudy" covered the streets and flight line. There was a small crowd that night at the base theater. Along with the popcorn, the movie fans enjoyed *The Guns of Navarone*. What a surprise they got when they walked out of the theater. While they were inside watching Gregory Peck put the big guns out of action, almost five inches of snow had piled up on their cars.

Over the next three days, Lincoln was almost brought to a halt with over twelve inches of snow, which was constantly rearranged by high gusty winds and snowplows. After the snow stopped, it took another couple of days to get the runway, taxiways and streets plowed so that normal operations could resume.

Native Nebraskans say that if you don't like the weather, just wait a few minutes and it will change. Well, they were right. On the heels of the snowstorm, the skies cleared and a strange bright yellow white orb appeared in the sky. The sun had been hiding for about a week, so when it appeared after the storm there were some jokes about the new object in the sky. The cold weather abated and the yellow orb in the sky beat down on the ramp with a new vengeance, filling the area with rays of unseasonable warmth. The piles of snow along the runway actually started to get smaller as the sun worked its magic.

The accident report on the crash of 52-563 from the 98th was forwarded to SAC Headquarters on March 2nd. The board concluded the primary cause of the accident was the failure of the #1 engine turbine wheel, which caused the engine and twelve feet of the left wing to depart the aircraft. This caused a rapid roll rate, which in turn caused the #6 engine and both wing fuel tanks to depart the aircraft.

On March 4th, the first Reflex deployment of the month departed for Greenham Common. There were a few problems with the weather, but not half as many as there had been during the last several months. The warm weather had made it to Lincoln, but it hadn't arrived in England. Snow was still piled high along the runway and taxiways.

Thursday, March 5th, was a scheduled Alert changeover day at home. Several of the aircraft that had been standing Alert were uncocked, downloaded and replaced by other B-47s. One of the B-47s that came off Alert was 53-4226. In accordance with current SAC policy, 53-4226 would fly the first sortie after Alert with no major maintenance being done unless there was a flying safety issue. This was to see how well the aircraft would have been able to accomplish an EWO mission if it had been launched.

Crew S-84 was on the flying schedule for Thursday. They spent Wednesday planning their mission. They would make an ATO takeoff to fill their annual 50-8 requirement. Aircraft commander, Capt N.V. "Old Soldier" Meeks, would make the take off. Another planned item was a 60-1 instrument check for the copilot, 1Lt Larry Talovich. Another copilot from Crew E-59, Capt Art Ingle, would go along for his 60-1 instrument check. Navigating on the mission would be Capt Clifford Cork.

Along with the ATO take off and instrument check ride, the crew planned several navigation legs, a Short Look and Short Look Large Charge bomb run. During the flight planning, Meeks did the preflight emergency procedures briefing. In all, it would be about eight hours in the air. Weather for takeoff looked good at the moment, but there was always the chance the Nebraska weather could change at the last second.

Bright and early, 0715 to be exact, Crew S-84 arrived at Base Operations on Thursday, March 7th. They checked the weather for the local and enroute conditions. For once, there were no major frontal systems to contend with. They checked their flight plan for the needed clearances and filed it with the operations section. Flight plan filed, weather looks good, time to get their flight lunches, personal equipment and head out to their bird.

When they arrived, the crew chief and his crew were standing by. There were a few comments about the cool weather and the light snow that had fallen during the night. The temperature that morning was about normal for Nebraska. The thermometer hovered in the high twenties. No serious problems with the weather, just enough to make for some good preflight chitchat.

The crew split up for the walkaround. Meeks started for the right side, while Larry Talovich and Art Ingle would check the left side of the aircraft. Every aircraft commander had a Pet Preflight Peeve. For "Old Soldier" Meeks it was the brake settings. Paul Koski remembered:

"It seems like every crew had some pet thing they wanted or did on preflight. Capt Meeks wanted his brake clearances set at thirteen thousandths and the first time I met him, I told him they were within book limits, five to fifteen thousandths and I had checked them. He said, 'I still want them set at thirteen', in a very demanding way. You know what, he even had his own feeler gauge to check them. So, from that day forward, if he was going to fly my plane, they were set at thirteen before he got to the plane. It also made for good relationship and preflight went a lot smoother."

As part of their preflight, Larry and Art checked the ATO rack. The rack was secure; all of the bottles were hanging tight in their mounts. The pull-out plugs were disconnected according to the checklist. When they met at the tail, they checked the guns and turret. Their final preflight ritual was to install the drag chute and make sure it was ready.

The crew climbed the ladder and went through the preflight checklist inside. They checked the ATO circuits according to the checklist; the ground crew then installed the pull out plugs. Everything on the preflight had gone like clockwork. They didn't find any leaks and everything was in the right place. The crew chief pushed the ladder up and closed the entry door. Time to go fly.

With the fire guard standing by, they started engines at 0935. Meeks contacted the tower when he was ready to taxi. While they taxied to the end of Runway 35, the #1 engine kicked up some snow and debris from the edge of the taxi strip. There was a lot of snow and ice on the run-up pad so they held a little short of the pad for the final takeoff checklist.

Final takeoff clearance was given and, at 1015, Meeks pushed the throttles to 85% and let the power stabilize. Brakes were released and 4226 crossed the run up pad and turned sharply onto Runway 35. Throttles were pushed to 100%, they got "Six Reds Out" when the water alcohol kicked in. "**4226 Rolling.**"

4226 rolled north on Runway 35 gaining speed every second. Approaching 70 knots they got ready for the timing check. "**70 knots… Now!**" The stopwatch started ticking away the seconds. "**Coming up on S1...Hack. Speed 109 knots, Looks Good, we're committed!**" Meeks reached down for the ATO. "**Arming ATO**". The green light came on. "**Firing ATO!**"

Jim Villa had reported for first shift that morning. About 0950 he and Harlan Tordoff had taken a break and headed for the Base Ops Snack Bar for a cup of swamp water. They were on their way back to work when they spotted a B-47 taking off. Like a lot of the flight line troops, he liked to watch the birds leave the nest, especially when it was an ATO takeoff. Jim continued:

"It wasn't but a few seconds and we could see flames trailing from the airplane from the right side of the fuselage. Horror struck very quickly;

the airplane was on fire! By the time the B-47 got directly across from the parking area, flames were trailing a great distance behind the airplane. For the first time in my life, I felt so helpless. It also hit home the B-47 was 53-4226. This was the same 4226 I had Alert-crewed while at Greenham Common, England, when the Cuban Missile Crisis started."

Young Airman James Archer was sitting in one of the flight line trailers that morning listening to a safety briefing. It was his very first day on the flight line. "I was watching this B-47, while at the same time trying to pay attention to the safety briefing from the sergeant. As the takeoff roll progressed and the airspeed increased, the aircraft commander fired the ATO bottles for additional thrust.

"After the plane moved a couple of hundred feet further, I interrupted the sergeant and asked if the bomber was supposed to be making all that fire. (He had his back to the flight line). He said, 'ATO takeoffs always make fire when ignited.' I had never seen an ATO takeoff before. I then said, 'Sergeant, the fire is engulfing the fuselage and parts are falling off the plane.' We both ran out of the trailer just in time to see the bomber lift off the runway into the air.

"Tordoff and I watched the plane climb rapidly and clear the north end of the base," Jim Villa recalled. "Other than the long flame coming from the right side of the fuselage, the airplane was flying perfectly."

Inside the cockpit, things were about to go from normal takeoff to a full-blown emergency. As 4226 lifted off the runway, the crew retracted the landing gear. The flaps were brought up quickly because of the increased speed provided by the ATO. Suddenly the crew got a frantic radio call from the tower. **"4226, you're on fire from the ATO unit to the tail!"**

The call from the tower was the first indication to the crew they were in trouble. Instinctively, Meeks and Talovich shot a quick look over their shoulder. Larry Talovich remembers, "I was the only guy in the crew that could see the fire. I remember looking over my shoulder and seeing the fire. At first, it didn't look too bad, but as time went on, I knew we were in big trouble."

4226 kept climbing into the Nebraska sky, leaving a trial of billowing fire and smoke. The ATO ran out and, as it did, one of the bottles fell from the rack hitting the ground about 1300 feet from the north end of the runway. Fire now licked back beyond the tail of the B-47. "People on the ground said we looked like a Roman Candle," Talovich recalled. Two more bottles fell from the rack along with other parts of the aircraft that had burned away.

"Meeks kept asking me what it looked like. I told him the fire was getting worse. He replied, "No way we're gonna get around for a landing. She could blow any second. **PREPARE TO BAIL OUT!"**

Meeks and his crew had taken off from Runway 35 many times. He had seen the small country schoolhouse several miles off the runway and knew there were school children in the path of the burning bomber. Meeks pulled the yoke back to "zoom" the burning B-47, trading his airspeed for altitude so his crew could bail out and the aircraft would crash beyond the school. He hit the alarm bell and gave the order to bail out. The nose of 4226 came up, responding to the pull on the yoke.

Clifford Cork reached down and pulled the handles on his seat up to rotate the leg braces. The hatch below his seat blew away. He grabbed the D-ring and pulled upward. He and his seat were blasted downward into the slipstream. Larry Talovich pulled his seat handles up, the control column disengaged and jerked forward and the canopy departed the aircraft. He squeezed the grip with his right hand to fire his seat out of the B-47. Art Ingle had moved from his fourth man seat after getting the "prepare to bail out" signal. When he pulled the pressure door handle, the inner pressure door retracted and the ladder and outer entry door released. For a moment, aerodynamic pressure held the entry door in place, but Art kicked at the ladder with his foot and the ladder and door fell away. Grabbing his parachute ripcord he jumped downward through the hatch and into the air, pulling the ripcord as soon as he felt the slipstream and was free of the burning B-47.

On the ground Jim Villa recalled, "I saw a parachute, then two more chutes. We breathed a sigh of relief!" Jim Archer watched. "The navigator ejected downward, but almost horizontally due to the aircraft's nose high attitude. Next, I saw the canopy blow off preceding the copilot's ejection. His and the navigator's chutes fully blossomed without much room to spare before they hit the ground."

Both of the men on the ground had made a logical assumption: Three good chutes, everyone is out of the burning aircraft. They had no way of knowing there were four men aboard 4226 that morning. "Old Soldier" Meeks was still aboard the B-47, fighting the controls to make sure the blazing B-47 would clear the school.

Robert Flader was outside doing morning chores on his farm near the school. Like so many times before, he glanced up when he heard the approaching B-47. He was horrified to see fire trailing from the aircraft as it came towards him. He saw the crew leaving the bomber, one of them floating in his parachute towards his farm.

His daughter, Kathy, was at the school that morning. The children heard the bomber coming. Aircraft taking off passed right over the school. The noise would momentarily interrupt their education. The noise was much louder than normal, prompting several of the children to leave their seats and go to the window, just in time to see the B-47 pass overhead.

Meeks had fought the B-47 long enough. He knew the burning bomber would crash beyond the school. He reached down and pulled the handles on his seat up and squeezed the right handle firing his seat out of the B-47. He had enough altitude to make it under normal conditions. However, his seat had a defective component in the separation mechanism. He couldn't separate from his seat and deploy his chute. N.V. "Old Soldier" Meeks gave his life for his crew and twenty-one school children.

"When the B-47 hit the ground, a huge orange fireball lit up the horizon and was followed by a large plume of black smoke that went high into the sky. This was indeed a sickening, helpless feeling that I experienced," Jim Archer recalled. "I was only 18 years old. Reality kicked in; this was my time to grow up, and I mean fast!"

4226 crashed into the Nebraska soil about four and a half miles north of the runway. The flight had lasted one minute and twenty-three seconds. For those who saw it and the crewmen aboard, it was a frantic frightening minute and twenty three seconds that would be indelibly etched into their memory.

Base fire units responded to the crash site and fought the billowing flames for over an hour to bring them under control. The crew was brought back to the Base Hospital for observation and treatment of any minor injuries they had sustained. By mid afternoon, the fire had been beaten down to a pile of smoldering wreckage.

Jim Villa said, "Forty-some years later, I can still see 4226 climbing into the sky with flames trailing. But, I remember Meeks another way. I was assisting another crew chief launch Capt Meeks on a regular training mission. This would be a night launch and the weather was very cold. When Meeks and his crew arrived at the airplane, he was wearing his G.I. pile cap with the earflaps down. I can still see him standing in the forward wheel well with his two crewmembers reviewing the airplanes 781. He was in a very jolly mood. This is what I remember best about him. It was an honor and privilege to have known him."

Copilot Larry Talovich recalls, "He was a good pilot. He was one of those guys who would hoot and holler on the ground, but was all business

## 1963

in the air. It was quite a feat of airmanship to control the airplane as long as he did. I wouldn't be here today if it wasn't for his skill as a pilot. I owe my life to him. People should remember people like N.V. Meeks for the contribution and sacrifice they made for their country."

A special memorial service was held at the base chapel on Saturday. The chapel was packed with those who had known "Old Soldier" Meeks. After the service, a lot of the attendees retired to the club to remember and toast the memory of their friend and comrade. Several of the club goers thought it would be a good idea to organize some kind of ongoing memorial to their fallen comrade. The accident was the fourth Class A accident in the first three months of the year.

On March 11th, another Reflex deployment departed Lincoln for England. The long flight across the pond was routine until they reached the English shore. Once again, the weather made letdown and landing "Bloody Awful".

Wednesday, March 13th, a KC-135 pulled into the pattern and landed. The troops on the flight line thought it may have signaled the start of an ORI when they saw staff cars arrive and whisk those aboard off the flight line. It wasn't an ORI at all. Aboard the KC-135 was LtGen John D. Ryan, Deputy Commander-in-Chief of SAC. He had arrived for a special ceremony that day. At 307th Wing Headquarters, he presented the Distinguished Flying Cross to Ruth Meeks, in honor of her husband's sacrifice. He also announced "Old Soldier" Meeks had been posthumously promoted to the rank of Major.

Sunday, the 17th, was a special Sunday at the base chapel. During the services, the 5th Annual SAC Memorial Sunday was observed. The special service was a tribute to all who were serving in SAC. There was a special memorial observance for all who had given their lives while serving. The service had a special meaning for the 307th in view of the loss of three crewmen in the first three months of the year.

The bible on the altar was opened to the book of Isaiah. "I heard the voice of the Lord, saying, 'Whom shall I send, and who will go for us?' Then said I, 'Here am I, send me.'" To the left side of the altar, three large candles were lit in memory of Capt Paul Pudwill, Capt Richard West, and Maj N. V. Meeks from the 307th Bomb Wing. On the right side of the altar four candles burned in memory of LtCol Lamar Ledbetter, 1Lt Thomas Hallgrath, Capt Donald Livingston and Lt Michael Rebmann from the 98th Bomb Wing.

Crews on Reflex looked forward to their period of R&R during their tour. Most crews would spend the time traveling around England to see the sights. Jarvis "Flip" Latham recalled, "In March 1963 during my last Reflex tour at RAF Greenham Common, a fellow copilot, Art Hood, and I decided we wanted to spend our days off Alert doing something more useful than partying in London. We talked to the RAF liaison officer on base to inquire about a visit to one of the Bomber Command bases. They were delighted to set us up with a trip to RAF Waddington in Lincolnshire, one of the AVRO Vulcan aerodromes. They even came to get us in a small twin-engine executive transport. Little did we realize that we were not only going to get a tour of the base, but would also each do a mission planning session and a five and a half hour flight with one of the combat-ready Vulcan crews.

"The Vulcan was an impressive flying machine--on the ground as well as in the air. Unlike our B-47, which had an optimum altitude of 28,500 feet just after takeoff with a full load, we took off on the morning of 19 March with a Vulcan full of fuel and climbed immediately to 50,000 feet to let RAF Lightning fighters try to make passes at us. They couldn't touch us at that altitude. Our AC, Flight Lieutenant Wally Wallbank, put me in the right seat for an hour just before landing. It was like driving a Mercedes. There was no comparison to the B-47 in terms of performance or ease of handling.

"When we got back to Greenham, our base commander met us and commented, 'I've been trying to get a ride in that thing for three years, and here you guys did it without even trying.'"

The "Hawk" returned to Lincoln airplane patch on the 20th. Low clouds arrived from the west about 1100. The wind shifted to the north and a fine freezing mist started falling about noon. The temperature fell below freezing and the flight line was shortly a skating rink. By 1500, the visibility was down to half a mile with drizzle and intermittent snow. All further air operations were called off. The Reflex redeployment had to be diverted to Pease AFB due to the weather at Lincoln.

The bad weather hung around until Sunday. It took another forty-eight hours to clear the runway and streets before air operations could get back to normal. The Reflex flight scheduled for the 25th was held for twenty-four hours. The diverted deployment was finally able to return from Pease on Wednesday the 26th.

At the Wing Staff meeting on Friday, March 28th, there was special discussion about establishing a special memorial to Maj Meeks. Several suggested a trophy should be established in his name for special accomplishment by crews. A committee was formed to work on the suggestion and come up with the type of award and the criteria for the award.

April started with the launch of a Pipe Cleaner mission on Monday, the 1st. The three EB-47Ls departed Lincoln and flew southwest to western Texas and Orbit Area 15. When they arrived, they began to fly a racetrack orbit near Odessa, Texas. They established a radio link with Looking Glass, sending and receiving radio messages. When the tests were over, the Pipe Cleaners spent the next five hours flying in the orbit waiting for further radio traffic to be relayed. After what could be described as a long, boring tour of Texas, they returned to Lincoln.

At 0951 on the 2nd, the blare of the klaxon sent the Alert crews scrambling for their birds. Within five minutes, the low whine of engines starting replaced the normal sounds on the flight line. As power came up, the aircraft reported when they were ready to taxi. They were informed it was a Bravo response. They shut down the engines and prepared to recock the Alert birds.

Later that morning, there was a formal change of command ceremony at 307th Headquarters. Col. William Riggs replaced Col. William Bertram as the Wing Commander. It was announced there were other changes in the wing command structure pending. It was part of the general realignment in the command structure of SAC.

Three Pipe Cleaners left Lincoln on the 5th to fly another relay training flight. They flew to Orbit 15 and began flying their orbit pattern while trying to set up a radio link with Looking Glass. After they completed their relays and the required time in the orbit area, they turned to the northeast and flew back to Lincoln.

Along with the regular flying schedule on the 8th, two Pipe Cleaners launched and flew another mission to Orbit 15. 52-0298 and 52-0071 established the radio link and practiced relaying messages between Looking Glass and another B-47 that was on a training flight. The mission was scored as 100 % effective.

53-1941 was on the flying schedule to fly a Profile Mission on Thursday, the 9th. It would be a routine flight with 50-8 training requirements being checked off the list. The preflight was accomplished and the engines were started on time. The weather wasn't the best that morning. Low clouds hung in the Nebraska sky and it appeared the "Hawk" was about to pay another visit to the patch. When 1941 left the concrete, she was quickly swallowed by the low hanging scud clouds.

Just before they broke out VFR On Top, they started having problems with the Bomb/Nav System. The navigator went through several checks, but his efforts were fruitless. The entire Bomb/Nav System went out.

# Cold War Cornhuskers: The 307th Bomb Wing Lincoln Air Force Base Nebraska 1955-1965

Without it, they couldn't navigate very well, let alone bomb a target. The mission was aborted. Now all they had to do was get back down through the soup and get 1941 on the ground.

It took the usual good work by GCA to get 1941 down through the soup and lined up after they burned enough fuel to make a safe landing. GCA literally talked 1941 down to the end of the runway. About the time they crossed over "O" Street, the pilot could finally make out the high-intensity approach lights off the end of Runway 35. A little left rudder and they were lined up. Power back a little, as they floated over the threshold. A little more rudder, then flare and finally the tires kissed the pavement. Brake chute kicked out, and the B-47 started to slow as she rolled down the runway. The crew may not have filled many 50-8 squares, but the pilot certainly had completed an instrument approach and landing requirement under real conditions.

The weekly issue of the *Jet Scoop* came out on April 12th. As always, it was full of the latest news from around the patch. There was a timely article about several 307th crew chiefs. During the week, LtCol John Crook had presented the coveted Master Crew Chief patch to six crew chiefs. Receiving the award were SSgts Virgil Cheney, George Sherwin, Graydon Garlough, Joe Fuqua, Paul Koski and Joe Pen.

To achieve the award, they had to be a crew chief for at least one year. Their aircraft had to meet all flying and Alert assignments for a six-month period. They had to maintain their aircraft at above average standards during Periodic Inspection and aircraft record inspection. The six Crew Chiefs could now sew the Master Crew Chief patch on their fatigues, showing they were some of the best crew chiefs in SAC.

There was a lot of commotion going on up in the 98th area on Monday morning, April 15th. There was a special departure ceremony after the crew preflighted KC-97 #52-2723. After the ceremony, the crew climbed aboard and fired up the four big radial engines and taxied to the end of the runway. The takeoff marked the end of KC-97 tanker support at Lincoln Air Force Base. For the first time in nine years, there would be no tankers sitting on the flight line.

Later that evening, another Reflex deployment left Lincoln for England. Like so many times before, they flew the north route across the Atlantic, refueling off the coast of Maine. The weather in England had improved, so this time, there were no weather-related problems getting into Greenham Common.

Tuesday, April 16th, saw a full training schedule for the crews scheduled to fly that day. There were four Bar None flights scheduled for the day launch. Five Profile missions were on tap for later that afternoon. The Bar None missions launched within the guidelines.

About two hours into the mission, 53-1918 started having problems that would jeopardize the mission. The left wing tank stopped feeding fuel. That problem was shortly compounded by fluctuating oil pressure and vibration in the #3 engine. After watching the oil pressure fall below operational limits, the crew shut the engine down and aborted the mission. They limped home to Lincoln on five engines and a heavy wing.

The evening launch of the Profile missions went without a hitch. With the aircraft gone, the ground crews could work at recovering and servicing the planes that had returned. Down on the ramp, the cowling had been pulled of the #3 engine on 1918 to see what had caused the problem. Since the oil pressure had fallen below safe limits, they called the engine shop to get the ball rolling on an engine change.

Up in the Alert area, the crews were spending a quiet evening buried in the mole hole. As usual, there was a crowd around the boob tube, watching TV and going through endless channel checks. Others were embroiled in a marathon game of poker. A couple of guys headed for the dining room to see what was available for a late evening snack.

At 2100, the blare of the klaxon ended the quiet evening and sent the crews on a mad dash for their aircraft. After crawling up the ladder, strapping in and hitting the engine start switch, they called the command post when they were ready to taxi. They copied and authenticated a Green Dot Practice Bravo Alert message. They shut down, then recocked the aircraft. Back in to mole hole there were the usual post-Alert comments about who was the first to report along with the grumbling about calling so many practice Alerts.

April 17th was another routine day at the patch. The daily duty was full of routine mission launches. There were a couple of Bar None flights along with Profile missions on the board. The routine day was interrupted by the klaxon going off at 1300. Once again, the crews scrambled to the Alert planes, started engines and called the command post. This was a Green Dot Practice Coco Alert. The planes taxied from the Alert area to the south end of the runway. Troops on the flight line paused their daily duty to watch the parade of B-47s taxi by. Hitting the end of the runway, the throttles went to full power for the takeoff roll, the decibel level rose, then fell as the throttles were retarded for the taxi back to the Alert pad. What a show for the troops and travelers along Cornhusker Highway. A lot of JP-4 had been turned into black smoke and pungent fumes. When the planes parked back at the Alert ramp, they had to be serviced and then recocked. Not really a fun way to finish the afternoon, but then, that was SAC.

On April 26th, another Pipe Cleaner flight was scheduled to depart Lincoln. Three EB-47Ls launched and flew three different routes to their respective orbit areas. All three established a radio link with Looking Glass. Two were scored as 100% effective and returned to Lincoln. 52-0061 had been the last to launch. They were on their fourth orbit when they got some disturbing news from home plate in the form of a weather update. There was a line of thunderstorms building between them and Lincoln. They had made their radio link up with Looking Glass, transmitted and received several messages as practice. Another orbit wouldn't accomplish anything. If they headed for home, they might be able to beat the weather.

061 broke out of their orbit and pushed the throttles forward a little for the dash back to Lincoln. Back up across Oklahoma and into Kansas, they had to constantly thread their way through billowing clouds and nasty looking thunderheads. Crossing into Cornhusker airspace, they could see a line of really bad looking cumulonimbus clouds building about a hundred miles southwest of the patch. 061 high-tailed it home and got down before the storm clouds cut them off.

Col. Riggs prepared his first monthly report as the 307th Wing Commander. Like all of his predecessors, he noted the shortage of qualified specialists in the maintenance areas. The wing had flown 31 of 36 scheduled Bar None missions of which 27 were scored as effective. Along with that, the wing flew 188 Profile missions scoring 176 as effective. After reviewing the bombing statistics, aiming point identification was found to be the primary problem.

There were 54 B-47s assigned to the wing, 43 listed as available. Along with that there were 7 Pipe Cleaner B-47s with another due to arrive in May. It was noted that May would be the first month with a Pipe Cleaner standing Alert. In case of launch, the EB-47L would launch first and be ready to relay the "go code" if needed.

May started on Wednesday with the usual report for duty, then get ready for another day in SAC. People were busy moving files and equipment out of one of the last remaining wooden hangars from World War II. The large hangar was scheduled to be torn down in July, so everything had to be taken out. About 1000, those inside were about to knock off and get a cup of coffee. Without warning, they heard a weak moan, followed by a sound described as "the crack of a rifle". Looking around, they spotted dust and debris falling from one of the main ceiling rafters. Then it slowly started to sag and buckle. Below, everyone scattered for the nearest door. It took over an hour for the old hangar to completely cave in and give up the ghost.

## 1963

The previous month, there had been a change of Wing Commander and there were other changes in the wind. LtCol. Jack Crook officially assumed command of the 307th Field Maintenance Squadron. He took command of the squadron when it was at 82% of authorized manpower. Being short of manpower was something the squadron troops had learned to live with over the years.

Three B-47s returned from Reflex on May 1st. For the crews, it was good to get home. Before they could relax at home, they had to download their bags and any "goodies" they brought back. They also had to debrief and make sure the forms were all filled out. Coming back, they had tried a fireout over the Atlantic. None of them had achieved better than 75% fire out. 53-2353 had fired out only 40%. There had to be a reason, so all three wrote up the problem to be checked out by specialists. The A&E boys weren't going to be able to check it out that day. So, the three aircraft were parked and other writeups were taken care of.

Bright and early the next day, the A&E troops showed up to troubleshoot the problem on the guns. After they opened the panels to get to the ammo and feed chutes, it was obvious what had caused the problem. The ammo belts were so badly rusted, the belted ammo was not flexible and wouldn't feed right.

May 7th, saw more Reflex returns to Lincoln. Like the last flight, they had scored badly during the fireout. 53-2392 had scored a 70% fire out. Like before, the ammo links were badly rusted to the point they were not flexible. It was also found that some of the rounds were in very bad condition. The other two aircraft had rusted feed links and corroded ammo.

The flying schedule was full of missions to be flown on the 8th. The wing was suffering from a rash of poor bombing scores on the bomb runs. Last month's problem of aiming point identification continued into May. 53-1918 was flying a Profile flight that day. Approaching the Clearview bomb plot, the aiming point was misidentified big time. The crew bombed Grand Island, Nebraska, instead of the plot at Hastings. They had missed the target by almost twenty miles. Talk about "gross error". The crew would have a lot of explaining to do when they got back to home plate.

Rotten bombing struck again the next day. This time it was a double whammy. 53-6244 was preflighted and ready to take to the skies. During engine start, the #2 engine refused to start and come up to power. The trouble was repaired and 6244 took off two hours and forty-five minutes late. Not a good start! Then, during the bomb run the aim points were mistaken, causing an error of over six thousand feet. That was two missions that could be classified as FUBAR in a two-day period. No bad weather, no mechanical failures in the bombing system, just bad procedures.

The weekly issue of the *Jet Scoop* for May 17th announced the creation of the N.V. Meeks Memorial Trophy, in memory of Maj Meeks. The award would be presented in recognition of the timeliest completion of quarterly 50-8 requirements. It would be based on flying time used to complete the requirements along with the best crew score in navigation, bombing, air refueling and ground training. The trophy would be presented twice a year.

Saturday May 18th, Lincoln Air Force Base opened the gates to the public at 1000 for Armed Forces Day. The flight line between the two big hangars was filled with all kinds of aircraft on display. A lot of the aircraft were open so that people could go inside and get up close and personal with their tax dollars. Among the 25,000 people on the ramp that day was none other than SAC BRAT. Since he was plane crazy, he never missed a chance like this; what made it even better, it was a father and son outing.

The two arrived at 0900 that morning before all of the local tourist traffic. It would be not only a day to see airplanes, but also to work at the open house. Boy Scout Troop 98 had set up a booth and had the grills going to sell hamburgers and hot dogs to the crowd as a money-making project. Although there was a lot of grillin' and chillin' to be done, there was also time to see all of the planes.

Now, as luck would have it, one of the aircraft on display was a B-47 from the 307th. 53-2392 had been towed to the display area Friday afternoon. As luck would also have it, her crew chief, Jim Yandle, was a good buddy of my father. It didn't take long for Jim and dad to link up under the wing of the bird. There was some muffled conversation going on between the two while the young one wondered around marveling at how close he was to a real B-47. Jim went over to the entry door with a small crew stand. He climbed up and opened the door and dropped the ladder. "Hey, Scout, you want to go up inside?"

Well now, Mrs. Hill didn't raise her b-boy to shy away from a gift horse staring him in the face. I was up the ladder as if the klaxon had just gone off. Jim was right behind me to make sure I didn't do anything foolish. He showed me everything inside. The cockpit, the ejection seats, along with a few stolen moments in each of them. Then, it was up to the nose and sit in the navigator's seat and look at all the equipment. I just sat there drinking everything in I could. Even though I was just a teenager, I couldn't get over just how small and cramped the inside of the plane was.

All too soon, Jim had to button her up before the crowd arrived so we had to climb back down the ladder. I couldn't thank Jim and dad enough for the secret arrangement they had made under the wing of 2392. It was a kid's dream come true. That whole day, while flipping burgers, I would steal a glance at 2392 and kinda smile to myself. I'd been in a real B-47 that morning. Not many tourists in the crowd could say the same.

Monday, the 20th, would prove to be a high and low point in the monthly bombing scores for the 307th. That day, 53-4219 launched for a Profile mission. The crew flew the usual 50-8 requirements. During one of the bomb runs everything went well until release. The tone failed to cut off, for several seconds there was no effort to manually cut it off. Another gross error for the wing.

53-0583 departed the patch for a Bar None. Crew E-05, William Barnicoat, Neal Cosentino and James McElvain flew a good mission. Take off was on time, the nav legs were right down the middle of the map line. Air refueling with the KC-135 was just like it had been planned. The bomb runs were good. On the last run, McElvain put the offsets in and made a final wind run. Tone came on fifteen seconds before release. At release, the tone cut off. From the nose of 0583 it looked like it had been another good run. The score came back; it wasn't just another good run, it was a shack!

Fire out during Reflex return had caused a lot of problems during the month. Another flight returned on Wednesday, the 22nd, with the same rusty links and badly corroded ammo rounds which had been coming back from England all month. This was supposed to be the same ammo being loaded into the Alert aircraft at Greenham Common. There was a lot of concern about the problem; something had to be done about it. The 307th sent a strongly worded message to Greenham about the situation and asked them to look into it.

Aircraft returning to Lincoln late in the afternoon of the 22nd had to thread their way through a lot of thunderheads to the southwest of the base. Lincoln was reporting clear skies and light winds, so if they got ahead of the front, they could make a normal approach. On the ramp, old timers felt the hot sticky air and looked up at the billowing cumulus clouds. They knew from experience the weather was about to change.

Arrival of the storm was heralded by the rumble of thunder in the distance. What little wind there was suddenly went dead calm as the thunder came closer and more audible. The approaching clouds went from dark blue-gray to an ugly yellow-green in just a few seconds. Native Cornhuskers knew the signs; they could almost smell a twister brewing somewhere in the boiling greenish mass overhead. In a heartbeat, the wind went from calm to intense, as the gust front arrived signaling the front edge of the supercell.

Rain arrived as a wall of water, driven by the gusty wind till it was hitting the ground in almost horizontal sheets. Visibility dropped with the rain and wind. Lightning danced across the sky and jabbed towards the ground. Thunder bellowed after each flash, till there was a concert of sharp cracks and distant rumbles.

The flight line troops knew the wide-open space of the concrete ramp was no place to be during one of these chock washers. Before the gust front arrived, most of the troops headed for the higher ground safety of Base Operations. There were thrill some seekers who decided to ride out the storm in a vehicle or inside one of the B-47s.

Rain let up momentarily. Then, there was the tell-tale sound of small hail smashing into the concrete at over a hundred miles an hour. The size of the hail got bigger until it was the size of marbles, then some of it was the size of golf balls. Inside a Metro, the sound of the hail banging on the roof was almost unbearable, but it beat getting beaned in the noggin by the falling ice. Within a matter of moments, the ramp was awash in water and floating balls of ice.

Just to the north of the base a low hanging wall cloud appeared on the back edge of the storm. Then, a spiraling finger dropped from the base of the cloud and spun towards the ground. The funnel dropped closer to the ground followed by a momentary cloud of debris as the funnel touched down. As quickly as it formed, the funnel broke ground and slowly retreated upward into the cloud base.

Within the hour, the storm moved on to the east, pelting the rest of the state with rain, hail and several more tornadoes. At the patch, people came out of their cover to survey the damage left by the storm. Several windshields in cars had been broken by the hail; trash cans were strewn all over the place. The worst damage was to two Base Flight C-47s parked near Base Operations. The fabric control surfaces hung in tattered shreds due to the beating by the hailstones.

The monthly report for May was a little better, but still wasn't within 2nd Air Force guidelines. Out of 21 Bar None missions scheduled, 12 were effective. The wing had 108 effective Profile missions out of 133 flown. There were 54 B-47s assigned to the wing with 7 EB-47L Pipe Cleaner aircraft. The wing had 90 combat ready crews to man the Alert, Reflex and training schedule.

On Memorial Day the wing paused to remember those who had given their lives while serving their country. There was a special service at the base chapel to remember the self-sacrifice of heroes who had served during the major wars and those who had given their lives during the Cold War.

At the Wyuka Cemetery in Lincoln, 818th Air Division Commander, BGen Lewis Lyle, presided over a special Memorial Day ceremony. During the ceremony, he presented the Distinguished Flying Cross to Shirley Pudwill in honor of her husband Paul's sacrifice in January. The ceremony was a quiet, fitting tribute to an airman who gave his life so others may live.

We now do a historical fast forward to military action during Operation Desert Storm. Paul's son Dominic Pudwill Gorie had grown up and was serving as a pilot and Commander in the United States Navy. For his action during Desert Storm, he was awarded the Distinguished Flying Cross. At the formal presentation ceremony in Florida, there was a major fly in the ointment. The medal for the ceremony had not arrived. Quick action on Shirley Pudwill's part saved the day. The DFC presented to Dom's father, Paul, in 1963, stood in for the missing decoration. Shirley recalled, "I think Paul must have been looking down and grinning from ear to ear."

Dominic went on to further fame in the astronaut program. On June 2, 1998, Space Shuttle mission STS-9 lifted off from Cape Kennedy. Dominic was one of the crew on the mission. Tucked away in his personal mementos was the DFC that had been presented to his father and had stood in for his own DFC presentation ceremony. Dominic's career as an astronaut was not limited to the one flight. On May 9, 2008 he was the mission commander for STS-123. It was the longest shuttle flight to date, spending over sixteen days in space. It was his fourth trip in the space shuttle program.

In May, rumors started floating around that the Reflex commitment was going to change. Now, we all know how rumors are: just that, rumors. This time the rumors were confirmed as being correct. On Monday, June 3rd, a message came down from Omaha stating that, effective July 1st, the 307th Reflex commitment would change to Zaragoza, Spain. That meant flying the southern route and spending fifteen to sixteen hours in the air.

Three aircraft and crews left Lincoln for England on June 3rd. They flew the north route and had a favorable tailwind all the way across the pond. During the flight, they had a fireout, each of the three scoring 90% fireout. Amazing what could be accomplished with good links and rounds.

Three B-47s left England on the 5th for the weekly return flight. Out over the Atlantic, they cleared the area for a fireout. One got a 50 % fire out, then the chatter of the guns stopped. The next one managed a 70% fire out before the guns stopped. The third fireout saw the rounds counter stop after ten rounds. When they arrived at Lincoln more rusty links and bad looking rounds were discovered. The proverbial you-know-what was about to contact the rotating blades.

Photos were taken of the rusty links and corroded ammo from almost every angle. Several 8x10 glossy prints were made and the report was sent to SAC Headquarters. An extra copy of the report was also placed in a courier bag to go to England aboard the next Reflex flight on Monday, June 10th. Along with the report, there was a letter to the base commander at Greenham Common letting him know that the original report had been sent to SAC Headquarters.

There was another change in the command structure on June 6th. Col Patrick Ness took over the duties as Deputy Commander for Operations. Again, this was part of command realignment due to transfers and retirements.

At 1900 that day, the relative calm was broken by the klaxon going off. Like always, the Alert crews went from zero to nine point five on the pucker scale as they raced for the aircraft. It turned out to be a Green Dot Bravo. All they had to do was start engines and report when they were ready to taxi. Then, the work began to get the aircraft serviced and recocked.

June 13th would be a busy day for the 307th. There were several launches on tap for the morning, several more for late afternoon. There was also the recovery of flights that had been flying during the night, and then recover the morning flights late that afternoon. Along with the routine missions, two B-47s were scheduled to go to the depot for ECM updates. 53-6244 was scheduled for an 1125 takeoff that day. The crew went through a routine preflight and engine start. Everything was ready as they stated to taxi towards the south end of Runway 35. They were on the taxiway when the klaxon went off at 1115. This situation could get interesting.

Up at the mole hole, the crews responded to the horn with the usual mad dash for the Alert aircraft. Within minutes, engines were coming up to power and they were reporting ready to taxi. They got a Green Dot message to execute a Coco Alert. The first aircraft ready pulled out of its slot and headed for the south end of the runway. Shortly, the 307th had eight of the ten Alert birds doing a fast taxi parade.

## 1963

Now for the fun part. The crew aboard 6244 was between the oncoming Alert aircraft and the end of the runway, kind of like being between a rock and a hard place. Looking over his shoulder, the copilot could see the entire Alert force behind them and gaining. The Alert had priority; 6244 couldn't make the runway and launch before the parade overtook them.

Aboard 6244, the pilot edged the throttles forward to gain a little speed. The Alert force was still gaining on them. To one of the troops on the flight line, it looked like a band of Indians chasing a wagon in a John Wayne movie. When 6244 hit the edge of the runup pad they pulled off and headed for the compass rose. It may have looked exciting, but 6244 was almost turned around on the compass rose when the first Alert bird hit the runway for power up.

Back on the Alert ramp, two aircraft hadn't made the Alert. One had developed a problem with the liquid oxygen converter. The other had an oil leak in the #3 engine. They were uncocked for over two hours while the problem was found and repaired. Then, the crews recocked the aircraft and went back to the mole hole. The rest of the day was normal: the usual hubbub of recovering aircraft, getting the birds ready for Reflex and the evening launch.

Reflex-bound crews arrived at Base Ops for the usual ritual of briefing, weather updates and getting the aircraft ready for the long trip to England. Helmet bags and lunches in hand, they headed for their aircraft and preflight. Everything was ready, so they climbed aboard and started engines. They left the parking slot and headed for the runway at 1640.

At 1645, the blare of the klaxon sent the Alert crews rushing for the Alert aircraft for the second time in less than six hours. The Alert crews climbed the ladders, strapped in and started engines. The Reflex bound B-47s were about half way down the taxi strip when the klaxon blew. It looked like it might be a repeat performance of the morning Alert.

The three Reflex aircraft were advised there was an Alert in progress and to expedite their taxi. One could head for the compass rose, while the other two would have to go dangerously close to the edge of the runup pad and hold for the Alert. The Alert turned out to be a Green Dot Bravo response. There would be no race for the compass rose or runup pad for the Reflex crews. The three England-bound B-47s arrived at the end of the runway and launched on time in spite of the klaxon.

Back at the mole hole, the conversation at the chow table centered on the two Alerts. Two in one day, while not a common occurrence, did happen from time to time. Didn't SAC communicate with 2nd Air Force and vice versa? Of course they did. The cynics speculated whether it was really needed practice or just fun for the higher commands to call an Alert and harass the crews to see just how much pressure they could take.

Another topic of conversation was how much money had gone up in smoke with all of the JP-4 they used. For a few minutes they calculated, so much for the taxi to the south, X amount for the runup, then Y for the fast taxi back to the mole hole and shut down. They all agreed they could run their cars a couple of years with the fuel they had turned into a lot of noise and pollution that day.

At 307th Headquarters, Monday morning, June 24th, there was a special recognition ceremony. A2C Matthew Boylan was awarded the Airman's Medal. He was cited for his actions on August 7, 1962, when he was standing fire guard and fought a fire during engine start while an Alert exercise was in progress. His comment after the presentation was the same as his comment in August. "I only did what I was supposed to do. That's why we stand by as fire guard."

The last Reflex return flight of the month came back on June 24th. In view of the recent problems with fireouts, the three crews were instructed not to use the guns during the trip home. It was kind of a hush-hush 307th secret. The idea was to see what kind of ammo and links had been loaded. When the ammo drums and feed chutes were inspected, they were filled with what appeared to be brand new ammo and feed links. Complaining to SAC Headquarters seemed to have gotten the problem solved. It really didn't matter, since the 307th would be changing Reflex base location within a week.

The June report to SAC and 2nd Air Force was jammed with MCS statistics reflecting the ever-growing use of figures and graphs to show how well the wing was doing. The maintenance section of the report was all graphs and stats, just what the MCS wizards wanted.

The wing spent 1,808 hours in the air and completed 100 % of the 50-8 requirements. There were 54 B-47s assigned to the wing with 41 available for missions. The wing flew 15 Bar None missions with 14 scored as effective. Bombing was scored at 93% effective. The wing did better against Express Train sites than in previous months. There were 95 runs on Express sites with 92 scored reliable. The 307th scored a major victory in the battle of rusty links and bad ammo with the direct report to SAC Headquarters to prove a point.

SAC underwent a major realignment of the three major Air Forces under its control. The 8th Air Force, headquartered at Westover AFB, would oversee wings along the eastern portion of the country. 2nd Air Force at Barksdale AFB would control the middle half of the country. The 15th at March AFB would take over SAC bases in the western part of the nation. Effective July 1st, the 2nd Air Force gained control of two northern tier bases that had been under the 15th. Grand Forks and Minot, North Dakota, would now be part of the 2nd Air Force.

The first Reflex deployment of the month left Lincoln on Monday the 1st. It would also be the inaugural flight to Zaragoza, Spain. Leaving home plate, the three B-47s headed southeast, coasting out along the South Carolina coast. They met up with their KC-135 near Bermuda and took on their SAC Gulp of JP-4, then headed on across the Atlantic. Fifteen and a half hours later, they landed at Zaragoza.

307th aircraft in England were ferried to Zaragoza. The aircraft had to coast out and fly over the Atlantic. The French Government would not allow aircraft loaded with nuclear weapons to fly in their airspace. That added a lot of miles to the flight, just as when the wing ferried the Alert birds from Morón to Greenham Common the previous year. Jim Villa recalled the move:

"The 307th would move back to Spain on July 1st. I believe Little Rock AFB B-47s replaced us at Greenham Common. By this time, many of our guys had gotten into liking some of England's offerings. A few of them were very sad to depart.

"We would be taking a nuclear weapon with us to Zaragoza. This meant we wouldn't have a cargo platform hung in the bomb bay. I have been known to be a bit of a pack rat and wouldn't be able to take some of my 'accumulated valuables' that I had stowed away. We barely had enough room to tie our baggage on the walls of the bomb bay. I had a number of rolls of discarded brake chute straps, which I had planned to make into vehicle tow straps. Since this would be my first ride in a B-47, I was very excited to say the least.

"Our good friends, the French, would not allow nuclear weapons to be transported over their country. We would have to go out over the Atlantic and go in over Portugal. When we took off, the weather at Greenham was, as usual, raining. When we landed at Zaragoza, it was just the opposite, hot and dry. I don't think the flight lasted more than three hours."

Thursday, the 4th of July, proved to be a normal day of flying and fixing at the patch. There were a lot of ball games played on the base diamonds along with picnics and other special events. That night, crowds of people lined the roads around Bowling Lake for the annual fireworks

223

show. As always, it was a show not to be missed. A magnificent display of aerial pyrotechnics. Star clusters and whistling shells blanketed the night sky and reflected from the shimmering water of Bowling Lake. What a way to finish off a day of ball games and picnics.

Monday evening, the 8th, saw the launch of three B-47s for Reflex to Spain. There were a lot of new things to get used to at the new base. Billy Lyons wrote:

"Zaragoza was much better for pulling Alert (my opinion) than Morón; we had some memorable moments during our three tours there. I remember the long parallel taxiway and some guys (not 307th) attempted to land on this taxiway. We were specifically cautioned not to land on the taxiway when we were preparing for our first trip to Zaragoza. There was a golf course on base and, as I recall, you could play golf on Alert. There were klaxons strategically placed on the course so you wouldn't miss an Alert."

On Friday, July 12th, three B-47s from the 307th were being prepared to launch and deploy from Zaragoza to Lincoln. The three crews were anxious to get in the air and head for home. They had been delayed twenty-four hours due to weather along the route across the Atlantic.

The three 307th B-47s would launch about an hour behind three aircraft from the 98th Bomb Wing. The three birds from the 98th had gotten off the ground at 1010 that morning. Preflight for the 307th birds was proceeding according to the checklist. Bags were packed and their "special" personal cargo was secured in the bomb bay.

The crews climbed the ladders and began the engine start checklist. Several noticed a lone B-47 pull into the pattern and rock its wings to signal their radio was out. The B-47 flew down the runway, then made a slow turn for a go around. Within a few seconds, the tower informed the waiting crews to standby, there was an emergency landing in progress.

Those on the ground watched as the 98th Bomb Wing B-47 lined up on the runway. From the ground, it appeared they were coming in pretty hot. There was no approach chute and it didn't look like they had the flaps set for landing.

The B-47 touched down, the brake chute popped out, billowed, then broke away. The bomber was a runaway, charging down the runway in a cloud of smoke as the brakes were applied then appeared to lock up. About two thousand feet down the runway, the left forward tire blew sending rubber shrapnel flying in all directions.

Hurtling down the runway, 53-2160 showed no signs of slowing to a safe stop. The aircraft went off the overrun and struck a hump in the ground and bounced into the air striking the ground 325 feet off the end of the overrun.

Fire erupted as the B-47 continued to slide another 500 feet. Crash and rescue equipment had chased the runaway plane down the concrete and were on the scene as 2160 ground to a stop in a cloud of smoke and dust.

Rescue crews fought their way through the smoke and flames and were able to rescue the pilot, copilot and crew chief, all of whom suffered second and third degree burns. The navigator was fatally injured in the crash.

With all kinds of debris on the runway, the 307th crews were delayed for another twenty-four hours before they could get airborne and head for home. It was the first major accident at Zaragoza since the Reflex program had begun.

The investigation board determined that, shortly after takeoff, 53-2160 experienced major problems with the electrical system. The crew turned back for Zaragoza with no radio and very little power left in the batteries to power critical systems they would need for landing. By the time they arrived over Zaragoza, the electrical system had failed completely. Battery power ran out before they could land. The brake chute failed due to their higher than normal touchdown speed. Without electrical power, the anti skid system for the brakes was inoperative causing the brakes to lock up and blow the tire.

The flying schedule for Thursday, the 18th, was full of Bar None and Profile missions. 52-0549 was at bat for a Bar None. This would be the second mission after returning from Reflex deployment from England for the aircraft. She was scheduled to launch at 1300 that day for an eight-hour mission. Preflight, engine start and takeoff were all within the Bar None guidelines. They had been cleared for a Geneva Departure, so they maintained a 230 degree radial course from the Raymond VOR as they climbed to 35,000 feet. Over Geneva, Nebraska, they turned towards Wichita to rendezvous with the tanker for refueling.

Approaching Wichita, the crew felt a vibration on the right side of the aircraft. They did a quick scan of the engine instruments, seeing nothing out of place. Within moments, the vibration became more pronounced. Another scan of the instruments; this time, the EGT on #4 was going up, while the oil pressure was falling. They pulled the power off and shut down the sick engine.

They contacted the command post, advised them of the situation and said they were going to RTB (Return To Base) via the shortest route. They banked back towards Lincoln for a five-engine landing. On the way back the oil pressure on #5 started to fluctuate up and down. It never approached the danger level so they kept it running for the time being. It was a routine landing, if you consider landing on five engines with fire trucks lining the runway as normal.

Climbing down from the aircraft, they walked around to the right side of the aircraft. They could see that the entire inner nacelle was bathed in oil. Later, it was found a coupling on a feed line had broken, causing the massive leak. At the end of the day, it was another Bar None down the tube and another unscheduled engine change for the engine shop.

Staff members from the 818th Air Division showed up at the 307th's doorstep at 0900 on Wednesday the 25th. The purpose of their visit was to inspect the 307th. Call it a local mini ORI, only without flying. For the next couple of days, they'd be looking into every aspect of wing operations, right down to personnel medical records.

At 0955, one of the Air Division inspectors had the klaxon go off. At the mole hole, the crews raced for the aircraft and started engines. When they reported in, they were told it was a Bravo response. Just part of the inspection, it meant extra work to get the planes recocked while under the watchful eyes of the umpires. The rest of the day was spent checking actual launch times against the planned times. Other umpires were digging into the aircraft records to check for dotted i's and crossed t's.

The next morning, the Air Division staff was back at the 307th. They had arranged a morning of special activities. Out on the flight line, a B-47 was being prepared for Alert uploading. At 0900, the klaxon went off sending the Alert crews to the aircraft again for yet another Bravo Alert.

Before the whine of the last engine faded into silence, the umpires started another game for the 307th. One of the inspectors placed a thermos bottle near the bomb bay of the B-47 being uploaded for Alert. The thermos was marked Mark-28. He informed the ground crew the weapon had accidentally dropped during the upload and they now had a "Broken Arrow".

For the next several hours, the flight line was a beehive of activity as planes were towed or taxied clear of the danger area. Specialists arrived to inspect and make sure the weapon hadn't been damaged when it fell to the concrete. Any casualties were taken to the aid stations or hospital. In all, the response by the 307th was rated as "Outstanding".

## 1963

The finale for the exercise brought a couple of comments and chuckles from those near enough to see what happened. In a final gesture, the umpire walked over and picked up the "Mark-28" thermos, unscrewed the lid and poured himself a cup of "hot" coffee.

The inspection rehash was held on Friday. Air Division couldn't find any major problems, only a couple of small housekeeping items. In all, the 307th was rated as "Excellent" for the annual inspection by the host 818th Air Division.

August 1st fell on Thursday. Wing personnel reported for duty and prepared for another day of serving their country in the United States Air Force. Across the flight line there was a lot to accomplish. Aircraft had to be serviced for the morning launch and recovery teams were busy taking care of the planes that had flown during the night. Routine repairs on aircraft, a PCU change, check the alternator on a sick #3 engine, tow a bird to the compass rose and swing the compass, check the gear doors for small cracks and stop-drill the small ones. Little things and major repairs, all needed to keep the wing ready to respond at a moment's notice.

The first Reflex flight of August left Lincoln on Monday, the 5th, at about 1800 for the fifteen-hour flight to Zaragoza. Meeting the tankers near Bermuda, they took on fuel and flew across the Atlantic. Roman lead contacted Zaragoza and the three planes started down for approach and landing. Roman lead was about fifteen miles from the threshold when they received a call from the tower informing them a Coco Alert had just been called and instructing them to prepare to hold for at least thirty minutes. A quick check of their fuel reserves showed they had a forty-minute reserve if everything went according to plan. So, they turned away and toured the Spanish countryside while the Alert crews completed the Coco exercise.

The last Alert aircraft wasn't off the runway before Roman lead was back in the pattern and final approach. The other two Romans slid in behind and started for the runway. They still had enough fuel for one missed approach, but that would be it. There wouldn't be a second go around. One by one, with approach chutes billowed, the three B-47s crossed the threshold and landed.

Concert lovers started heading for Pioneers Park early on the evening of August 7th. That night the SAC Band was appearing at Pinewood Bowl. Pinewood Bowl was a popular outdoor amphitheater at the park on the southwest edge of Lincoln. At 8 p.m., the crowd had filled the seats and the lights went down. The sound of music filtered through the pine trees and echoed across the countryside. Part way through the concert, several B-47s launched using Runway 17. By the time they flew over Pioneers Park they were about two thousand feet off the deck and climbing at full power. The noise of the jet engines was enough to drown out the music for a few moments.

On Thursday, the 15th, the "O Club" was full of activity as it was prepared for the evening activity. Those who would attend dug out their formal mess dress uniforms and made sure all their ribbons were in the right place and their wings were bright and shiny. The 307th hadn't had a formal Dining In for several years, so they all wanted to look sharp for the evening.

The Wing Commander, Col. William Riggs, presided as the Master of Ceremonies for the evening. There was a nice social hour for the crews to move about, mingle and engage in the normal informal chitchat. The meal was great, as usual for a formal affair. Sitting at the head table was a very familiar face to a lot of the officers of the 307th Bomb Wing.

The guest speaker for the evening was none other than Col. Elkins Read, Jr., former commander of the 307th. He came down from Omaha to spend the evening with his old wing. His sense of humor and rapier wit hadn't been dulled by his close proximity to the SAC Big Wigs at Offutt. That night he regaled his "fellow sheep herders" with memories and tales of his days with the 307th.

After the meal, speeches and entertainment came awards. Col. Read presented 1,000 hour pins to those who had racked up the time in the B-47. Crew of the month awards along with recognition for the best bombing scores were also presented. The highlight of the evening was the first presentation of the N.V. Meeks Memorial Trophy. Along with Col. Read, Mrs. Ruth Meeks was on hand to present the trophy honoring her husband.

The first presentation of the trophy went to Crew S-97, of the 371st Bomb Squadron. Maj Alfred Hunt, Capt Roger Beamer and Capt R. T. Boykin stepped forward for the honor. R. T. Boykin recalled:

"The bomber crew with the best performance during a training period was awarded the trophy. Everything a crew did in the air and on the ground was measured: bomb scores, ground training, mission planning, Stan Eval check rides, mission briefings, knowledge of war plan, Alert and Reflex missions. The competition was keen, the crew scores were just fractions apart. In my opinion, winning the N.V. Meeks Trophy would be similar to winning the NFL's MVP for the season."

In the sky above Lincoln on August 14th, there was a B-47 in trouble. 52-0549 had returned from Spain. The crew made a normal jet penetration and let down according to the checklist. Everything went well until they lowered the landing gear. They got three greens, but the forward main gear did not indicate down and locked. The copilot checked the circuit breaker, then recycled the gear. The front main was still showing a red light. The command post was advised of the situation and advised they had about forty minutes of fuel left.

They requested a tower fly by to check the landing gear. The tower reported the forward gear was down all the way and looked like it was in the locked position. At least the news from the ground was positive. As they passed the north end of the runway, they were talking with the command post. Again, they checked the Emergency Procedures checklist. After some discussion between the crew and the command post, they decided the best option was the ELGE. They checked that the gear lever was in the off position, then the copilot pumped the ELGE handle for the forward main gear. It was hard to move the handle back and forth from the start. After about ten very hard strokes the green light at the base of the pedestal came on, indicating down and locked. Another pass by the tower again confirmed the gear was down.

While the crew tried to figure out the problem, the other two B-47s had pulled into the pattern and landed. With two birds back in the nest, the troubled B-47 went around and set up for landing. Fire and rescue trucks had been positioned along the runway.

The navigator moved from his front seat and strapped into the fourth man seat. If the gear failed, his seat in the nose would not be the safest place to be. He wouldn't have an ejection seat, but it didn't matter; they were too low to use it anyway.

They lined up on Runway 35 and made their final approach. Over the threshold power was adjusted and they flared out. The rear main touched down followed by the front gear. The tires squealed in protest as they spun up from zero to landing speed in a matter of seconds.

The gear held in place, no collapse; just a nice sweet landing. They popped the drag chute and rolled down the runway, just like a normal landing, except for the pucker factor. At the turnoff, they left the runway and taxied back to the ramp. After shutting down, they climbed down the ladder and walked back to the main gear well. A quick look in the well showed the switch actuator and striker were in the correct position for down and locked. Further inspection showed everything was normal. At the moment there was no quick answer to the problem. Needless to say, the crew made the appropriate notation on the Form 781.

## Cold War Cornhuskers: The 307th Bomb Wing Lincoln Air Force Base Nebraska 1955-1965

The crew chief and maintenance crews started trouble-shooting the problem. Everything seemed to check out; maybe it was one of those gremlin creatures the old WW II Sarges talked about. After checking everything again, they found a loose wire on the indicator light. After fixing that, they also found the bulb had burned out. A retraction test proved the gear worked and the light was fixed.

August continued to be a routine month. Reflex flights to and from Spain continued on a weekly basis. Regular 50-8, Profile and Bar None missions dominated the flying schedule. With each return came the recovery, servicing and taking care of writeups on the Form 781.

September got off to a start with a Reflex launch on Monday, the 2nd. The three aircraft launched on time and headed southeast to coast out and fly the southern route to Spain. It was a routine flight all the way across the Atlantic. Just after coast-in, one of the aircraft reported a problem with the hydraulic system. It turned out to be minor, the flight continued to Zaragoza and landed without incident.

Three crews boarded their aircraft and launched for their return flight to Lincoln on September 4th. The return flight was uneventful until they arrived in the refueling area. The tanker had aborted with mechanical problems. Another KC-135 on strip Alert was scrambled. They rendezvoused with the thirsty B-47s and offloaded fuel for the rest of the flight.

Just after the Reflex aircraft landed at Lincoln, the klaxon went off, signaling another practice Alert. It was a Bravo response. After checking in when they were ready to taxi, the crews shut down and recocked the Alert aircraft. The Alert crews headed back to the mole hole and went on with the daily routine of being on Alert.

During the first two weeks of September, the wing flew as much as possible since the runway was scheduled to be closed down for several days for repair. There would be several more days that the runway would be available for limited use. The start day for the repairs was September 16th. By the 25th, the entire runway would be closed to operations for at least three days.

With the runway closed, there were plans to disperse the Alert aircraft if needed. The wing would also disperse aircraft for the Reflex launch. The aircraft were to fly to Forbes AFB, Kansas, and launch for Spain from there. A Pipe Cleaner mission scheduled for the 23rd was to stage out of Offutt.

A Pipe Cleaner mission launched on September 12th during a Bravo Alert. It was a routine mission with a nav leg and flight to Orbit Area Alpha near Lake McConaughy in western Nebraska. Like most relay missions, it was long and somewhat boring. When they arrived on station, the copilot turned his seat around to the old gunnery position, only now it was a special radio operator's position. They established a link with Looking Glass and practiced sending and receiving "Noah's Ark" messages. With the mission finished, they returned to Lincoln. During the postflight equipment checks they found all of the ARC-89 equipment was wet. They couldn't find any leaks and they hadn't flown through any weather on the way back.

The weekly Reflex launch was on tap for Monday, the 16th. Ground crews spent most of the morning getting the three aircraft serviced for the flight. The klaxon blared at 1300, sending the Alert crews to their aircraft. They received a Coco Alert response, which was downgraded to a Bravo because of the runway repair. Later that evening the Reflex birds left the nest after the equipment had stopped working on the runway.

Another EB-47L launched on the 16th for a day filled with taking and relaying practice messages. They flew to Orbit Charlie and orbited between Kimball, Nebraska, and Cheyenne, Wyoming. When they returned, they noticed water dripping from the intake scoops in the bomb bay. The equipment was wet. Again, they hadn't flown through any bad weather. The wet radio equipment had to be removed and completely dried out. Then, it had to be checked to make sure it worked and replaced in the aircraft. The problem was traced to the unheated and unpressurized bomb bay causing condensation to build up on the equipment.

Three B-47s departed the patch on Monday, the 22nd. They had a short flight to the Land of Oz at Forbes AFB, Kansas. Since the runway would be under repair, they would stage from Forbes for the Reflex flight. That same day a Pipe Cleaner left for Omaha, to stage from there the next day. It was agreed by all that the runway repair was a pain in the backside.

Well, if the runway is closed and you can't fly, no better time than now to have a ground exercise. After getting off to a false start by calling it an Alert, the annual Great Effort exercise began at 0800. For the next twelve hours, all base and housing area personnel would participate in the war game. The purpose was to simulate a nuclear attack and see how the base would respond. The base was closed to all non-duty personnel. The BX and Commissary would be closed for the entire duration of the war game. Overall, the 307th did very well. Umpires did note that the command post was not in a sheltered building.

The runway work was finished and reopened on the 29th. The wing launched a full flying schedule that morning with another string of missions that night. Four of the launches were Bar None missions. They launched on time. All of the Bar None missions were scored as effective.

September 30th, found a message arriving from Omaha regarding Pipe Cleaner mission launches. To add realism to the mission, the Alert Pipe Cleaner could be launched by a special Green Dot message after the klaxon goes off. If the Pipe Cleaner crew decodes a special launch message, they would launch regardless of what type of Alert is called.

Later that afternoon, the klaxon went off, initiating a Bravo Alert. After the Alert, three crews preflighted their aircraft and launched for the last Reflex deployment of the month. By the time they arrived in Spain, they were suffering from an acute case of TB (Tired Butt) and aching muscles from being cramped in the close quarters of the B-47 for fifteen hours.

That evening the final Bar None mission of the month departed the runway at 2100 for an eight-hour flight. When they returned at 0500 the next morning, the tired crew was happy; they gave the wing a 94.5 % effective rating on Bar None missions for the month.

Three Bar None flights launched on October 1st. 53-1901 was one of the aircraft flying the mission. They climbed out and headed for their refueling area in eastern South Dakota. Refueling time was within the guidelines and they took on the required fuel load. The nav leg to Rapid City and into Montana went according to the mission profile. Then, they headed for their bomb run at Scenic Badlands RBS site near Rapid City. During the checklist, they found a problem with the radar. After checking the system, the crew could not get a good radar return. They made a last resort bomb run and hoped for the best. The best wasn't to be that day. Before they could turn for the second target, the Bomb/Nav System went out completely. They had to abort, scoring an ineffective Bar None.

2nd Air Force published the wing standings on Sunday the 6th. The 307th was in 5th place in overall mission effectiveness. The wing had moved up to third place in bombing effectiveness and accuracy. The report also showed the 307th was at the top of the heap in maintenance and on-time launches.

Monday, the 7th, the 307th posted a full flying schedule. There were the usual morning takeoffs for training missions along with more launches in the afternoon. Three Reflex launches were on tap for that evening. There were two Bar None launches that day. 53-1941 and 53-1834 were launched in the morning. Each of the aircraft was scored ineffective due to misidentification of the aiming point on the bomb run.

## 1963

Members of the 4362nd Airborne Communications Relay Squadron were informed by SAC of a command wide operation for the Pipe Cleaner aircraft to be flown on October 10th. Ground crews worked overtime to get the EB-47Ls serviced and ready for the mission. That afternoon, the crews assembled for the briefing and got their individual aircraft and mission assignments.

Operation Top Rung began at 0800 on Thursday with the execution message arriving at the command post for the aircraft to launch at 1000 that morning. Crews that were going to fly reported to Base Ops for final briefing and weather updates along with the routes they would fly.

The mission outline was simple. The first Pipe Cleaner would launch at 1000 and fly a nav leg and air refueling before heading for the relay orbit point. Arriving at the orbit point, they would establish a radio link with Looking Glass and relay "Noah's Ark" messages. The other three aircraft would launch at two-hour intervals, fly the nav leg and refuel, then head for their respective orbit areas and relieve the Pipe Cleaner on station.

The first aircraft launched on time, flew the nav leg and rendezvoused with the tanker. After refueling, they headed to Orbit Area Alpha near Lake McConaughy, Nebraska, and contacted Looking Glass

The second aircraft launched at 1200 and repeated the flight. Their orbit area was the Delta area, orbiting from near Kimball, Nebraska, to Cheyenne, Wyoming. The third arrived in Orbit Charlie near Akron, Colorado, and flew their orbit to Denver and back. The final Pipe Cleaner launched at 1600. They arrived at area Bravo, just west of McCook, Nebraska, and relieved the aircraft on station after establishing a radio link with Looking Glass. When the final results for Operation Top Rung arrived at the command post, they showed that the 4362nd had scored very well. For their twenty-four hours in the air, they scored 94% effective overall. It was the highest score posted of any of the Pipe Cleaners participating. SAC Headquarters commended the unit on their fine effort.

Alert crews were starting to get a little antsy. There hadn't been an Alert of any kind so far during the month. It was unusual not to have an Alert of some kind during the week. It just wasn't natural to go that long without having to react to the sound of the klaxon. The Alert drought was broken at 0845 on October 21st. The klaxon went off and the crews responded to the Green Dot Bravo. The first aircraft was ready to taxi six minutes after the klaxon wailed.

Later that morning, 53-2337 launched on a routine 50-8 Profile mission. Air refueling over central Missouri went without a hitch. They turned towards Iowa for a two-hour nav leg. About halfway through the leg, they started having problems with the #1 engine. It had to be shut down when the EGT went above normal operating temperature. They lost #6 alternator shortly after they shut the sick engine down. 2337 was scored as an air abort.

Late that afternoon, three B-47s launched for Reflex in Spain. The tanker was waiting near Bermuda and the three birds took on their required fuel load for the rest of the trip across the pond. As usual, the trip was long and the crews were glad the flight was over. They were more than ready to get some sack time before going on Alert the next day.

Alert crews scrambled to their aircraft at 0831 on the morning of October 28th. After decoding a Bravo response, the crews began shutting down the engines. One of the aircraft pulled out of their slot and headed for Runway 17. The Pipe Cleaner crew had authenticated a launch code for a practice launch and relay mission.

The crew climbed out over Beatrice, then turned and flew towards western Nebraska. Near McCook, the copilot turned his seat to the rear and warmed up his radio equipment. They got a good link with Looking Glass and started relaying "Foxtrot" messages to other aircraft in the area that were flying training missions. After spending two hours flying orbits from McCook to Akron, Colorado, the Pipe Cleaner broke out of orbit, flew a nav leg for practice and returned to Lincoln late that afternoon.

During October, the 307th flew a total of 280 sorties, spending 2,097 hours in the air. Pipe Cleaners flew 53 sorties for 350 hours. There were 60 B-47s assigned to the wing, with 47 available. Wing bombing scores were better during the month, posting a 95.8 effective rating for October.

LtCol James Pumford, Commander of the 4362nd Airborne Communications Relay Squadron retired from the Air Force at the end of the month. LtCol Russell Heller Jr. assumed command of the squadron effective on November 1st.

Thursday evening, the 31st, base housing came alive with ghosties and hobgoblins as Trick or Treaters made their way through the streets in search of their favorite Halloween goodies. Some thought they heard the wail of a Banshee. Actually it was the wail of the klaxon sounding, followed by the rush for the aircraft. It was a Bravo Alert, so the crews were back in the mole hole within an hour.

Before the Cuban Missile Crisis, SAC had been retiring the B-47 from active service. The B-47 got a short reprieve because of the situation in Cuba. With the world situation back to normal Cold War tension and more ICBMs reaching Alert status, the program to retire the B-47 was again in full swing. With that, everyone at Lincoln Air Force Base knew it was just a matter of time before word would arrive from Omaha for the B-47s to start heading for retirement at the "boneyard". On November 1st, the 307th got word to start sending the "high time" aircraft to the boneyard. The announcement on Friday was received with mixed emotions. Crew chiefs didn't want their bird to go to the boneyard; after all "she" was still a good airplane and had a lot of flight time left. Others thought if the wing started sending aircraft to retirement, that might mean a transition to a new aircraft, like maybe the B-52H.

Monday, the 4th, saw the first Reflex flight of the month. Three B-47s departed on time and flew to Spain on the usual southern route. Out over the Atlantic, one of the aircraft was drinking fuel faster than normal. There were no headwinds to cause the high fuel consumption, the bird was just burning fuel at a higher than normal rate. They were able to get a tanker launched from the Azores and take on enough fuel to make it to Zaragoza.

Tuesday, the 5th, 52-0583 launched for a routine training flight. She had been on the Alert pad and this was the first mission after being downloaded from Alert status. There had been no major maintenance after Alert in accordance with SAC policy to see how well the aircraft would perform. About an hour into the mission, the Bomb/Nav system started having problems. Next, they got a high EGT indication on the #3 engine. Other small problems cropped up. It all totaled up to an ineffective mission for 0583.

Wednesday, the 6th, started like any other day at the patch. Training missions were on the flying schedule, along with the usual "keep em flying" work on the flight line. There was a Reflex flight on the way back from Spain that would arrive at home plate at about 2100 that evening.

At Zaragoza, the Reflex return flight had prepared for launch. During engine start, the fuel pump on #5 engine on 53-2342 was leaking. The crew had no choice but to stand by and wait for the fuel pump to be changed. The other two aircraft launched on time to begin the long flight back to the states. After changing the pump and checking it out, the other aircraft had to revise clearances and tanker support. They would launch as a single ship the following day.

At 0730 that morning, the 307th Command Post got a TWX from Omaha to stand by for an execution message. Since the wing was vulnerable for an ORI, those in the command post could almost smell what was coming down the pipe from Omaha. Under the rules of the game, the command post could not warn anyone about their suspicion.

# Cold War Cornhuskers: The 307th Bomb Wing Lincoln Air Force Base Nebraska 1955-1965

A KC-135 touched down at 0800 and taxied to Base Operations. Several staff cars arrived and whisked several officers off the flight line. Old timers who saw the 135 got that "old feeling" about what was going on. They figured they could expect the blare of the klaxon within the hour signaling the start of an ORI.

The Battle Staff assembled in the 98th BW Conference Room for the briefing on the conditions and ground rules for the ORI. Both wings would be under the watchful eye of the 2nd Air Force IG for the next several days until the entire force had completed the mission.

Alert crews scrambled to the birds when the klaxon went off at 0915. They spooled up, lit the burner cans and decoded a Green Dot message for a Coco Alert. One by one, they made the short taxi to Runway 17 and pushed the throttles forward for the simulated launch. Black smoke and pungent fumes covered the north end of the field as the entire Alert force got the ORI started. When the crews returned to the Alert pad, they shut down and reported to the mole hole to take a test on EWO knowledge. While the crews were taking their test, the aircraft were being downloaded for the mission.

Crew chiefs and line chiefs were summoned from the flight line for the ORI briefing. Aircraft scheduled to fly a mission during the day would be the first to be generated for the ORI mission. After the briefing, the crew chiefs hit the flight line and started getting their bird ready for the ORI. They had been told in the briefing the aircraft would be making an ECM run. During the low level run, the aircraft would be using chaff to confuse the radar. Each aircraft would be loaded with 192 bundles of chaff on each side of the dispenser, which added up to about 370 pounds of chaff to be loaded by hand.

Flight crews reported for the ORI briefing. The route was studied along with the air refueling area and time line. The mission would be flown in two ship cells using MITO for takeoff. There would be thirty minutes between cells. For the next three hours, the 307th would be filling the sky with fourteen aircraft for the first wave.

The first wave of fourteen aircraft was scheduled to begin launching at 1330 that afternoon. Last-minute weather looked good except for the north end of the mission. There was a low-pressure area moving into Minnesota. Depending on which way it tracked and the speed of the system, it could cause some problems on the Big Stick oil burner route.

Two leadoff crews preflighted their aircraft, started engines and taxied towards the end of Runway 35. They held short until the launch time arrived. At 1330, the first B-47 turned onto the runway, went to take off power and started rolling down the runway. Fifteen seconds later, the second B-47 was rolling on the concrete ribbon. Operation Golden Jet Bravo was underway.

Climbing out from Lincoln, the two aircraft turned to a heading of 325 degrees and headed for a Stanton departure. Over the small town of Stanton, they turned for the Sioux City VOR. From Sioux City, Iowa, they flew to a point just southeast of Spencer, Iowa, and turned towards the checkpoint at Des Moines. Passing to the north of Des Moines, they made a required radio checkpoint and continued on course towards the turn point near Moline, Illinois.

Mission aircraft turned to 254 degrees and began the refueling checklist as they flew towards the Cave Inn refueling area. KC-135s from the 914th AREFS out of Blytheville AFB, Arkansas, were on the Cave Inn racetrack waiting at 25,000 feet for the oncoming B-47s. Rendezvous was made near the Lamoni VOR. Red Cell slid into position and slowly moved into the observation position below the hanging booms. Slipway doors opened, signaling **"READY FOR CONTACT"**. Skillful hands of the boomer in the tanker flew the boom into the receptacle. **"CONTACT"**. Both aircraft took on the required 35,000 pounds of fuel by the time they reached the end refueling point over Hill City, Kansas.

Just beyond Hill City, they did a timed turn to the right until they were on a heading of 130 degrees. The navigation leg began as they passed over Great Bend, Kansas, with the required radio check. The first nav leg would take them to the turn point over Russellville, Arkansas. Before turning for the next leg they checked in with Ft. Smith radio.

Red Cell made another slow timed turn to the left, rolling out on a heading of 351 degrees for the longest navigation leg of the mission. Flying north, the navigator was busy plotting position points and calling for corrections to stay on course. There was a mandatory checkpoint as they passed Des Moines and continued towards Minnesota. Two hours and thirty minutes after starting the nav leg, the lead aircraft made the final radio checkpoint just east of Minneapolis. Staying on course, they started descending from 35,000 feet to low level for the oil burner route. By now, the fourteen aircraft of the first wave were airborne and strung out along the mission route. So far, everything was going according to the operations plan.

Just north of Duluth, Minnesota, the aircraft crossed the H-Hour Control Line on time. They made a correction to the left towards International Falls. Twenty miles from International Falls they turned for the oil burner route checkpoint at Bemidji. Starting at this point, the B-47s were using maximum ECM and kicking out chaff.

By the time they made their checkpoint at Bemidji, it had been dark for several hours. Flying an oil burner route during the day was hard enough. Flying in the dark with few visual references could turn into a real nightmare. The crew had to rely on radar and instruments to make sure they didn't end up in the tall pine trees or the side of a hill.

At Grand Rapids, Minnesota, they turned towards the southwest for their short look run on Brainerd. Offset points and coordinates were programmed into the Bomb/Nav system. They went through the checklist and contacted the RBS Express for the Big Spike express route. The navigator called for "Second Station". A last second wind run, then a slight correction to the right and at fifteen seconds to go, the tone came on. The TGI (time-to-go indicator) counted downward as the B-47 hurtled towards the target. At zero, it was "BOMB AWAY". From inside the bomber it looked like a good run.

At tone cut off, the pilot made a right turn and started climbing on a heading of 190 degrees towards Ft. Dodge, Iowa. At the Ft. Dodge checkpoint, they made a slight correction to a heading of 189 degrees, for the IP and their last bomb run. Omaha was the turn point for the IP and they changed course to a heading of 232 degrees. Contact was made with the Hastings RBS. They made a positive identification for scoring the bomb run. Again, the man in the nose called for second station; it was his airplane for the duration of the bomb run.

When the tone cut off at Hastings, the aircraft commander took control and racked the B-47 into a hard right breakaway turn. Completing an almost 180 degree turn, the B-47 headed back towards Lincoln for letdown and landing. They had been flying for just over eight hours and saw a lot of country. More important, they had flown an excellent ORI mission.

Meanwhile, up in Minnesota, things were falling apart for the last four aircraft in the wave. They made the control point, then started down for the oil burner route and the Short Look bomb run. All four aircraft had been monitoring the command post and heard the last aircraft report low clouds and snow along the route. They also reported the wind was picking up.

Gray Cell lead was about to enter the oil burner route. They were down to about two thousand feet and couldn't see a thing because of the blowing snow. Wind was almost ninety degrees off the right wingtip. They edged down to fifteen hundred feet and still had no idea of where the ground was. They were now in a ticklish situation. Keep going to finish

228

## 1963

the oil burner route and they could end up plowing a flaming trail through the tall pine trees. After conferring with the command post, Gray Cell lead aborted the oil burner route and started back up through the soupy clouds. Gray Cell 2 heard the call to abort and pulled up, straining for altitude in the icy conditions. Both aircraft in Pink Cell heard the call and aborted.

Although aborting the low level run, the last four B-47s completed the rest of the mission with excellent results on the bomb run at Hastings. All they could do was wait and see how the umpire would score the low-level oil burner abort. By 0100, the first wave aircraft were back on the ground. The engines had hardly started to cool down before the recovery crews were busy getting them serviced for Alert uploading.

Wave two was scheduled to start launching at 0730 the next morning. White Cell Lead launched on time to start the morning off. Again, there would be two-ship cells using MITO every thirty minutes until there were another fourteen aircraft in the air flying Golden Jet Bravo.

By the time the lead crew reached the Big Spike oil burner route the bad weather had moved out and it was now CAVU (Ceiling and Visibility Unlimited). Flying down the oil burner route, the pilot and copilot had a beautiful vista of fresh snow in the pine trees as they flashed by at about 400 knots indicated air speed. There wasn't time to do any sightseeing. They couldn't even sneak a quick wave to Paul Bunyan and Babe The Blue Ox as they passed near Bemidji.

Even if they couldn't see the sights, they could help with redecorating the countryside. Hurtling down the oil burner route the B-47s were kicking out chaff. Each aircraft carried about 370 pounds of chaff. That's a lot of foil fluttering down into the tall pines below. By the time the last aircraft in the second wave pulled out of the oil burner route, the 307th had decorated the landscape with over 5,000 pounds of tinsel.

The last aircraft of the second wave came back to the patch. After shutting down they went to debriefing and rehashed the mission in detail. The 98th was still in the air flying their second wave mission. Their last ship wouldn't recover until early in the morning. The results of Golden Jet Bravo would have to wait until 0900, when the ORI critique would be held in the base theater.

Things were tense when the men of the 307th filed into the theater for the ORI rehash. Four aircraft had aborted the short look bomb run on the Big Stick RBS Express. Four aborts during an ORI was bad news. With the bad weather along the route, the crews felt justified in aborting due to unsafe peacetime conditions. It all boiled down to how 2nd Air Force scored the mission.

The 307th scored "Outstanding" for the initial Alert response and generation of the ORI force. Navigation was another "Outstanding" score for the wing. Then came the bombing and the room was so quiet you could hear a pin hit the carpet. The IG mentioned the four aborts and, as such, no score could be rated. He stated the weather conditions were such that, under peacetime exercise guidelines, the 307th had made the right call. He announced that the entire first wave of the 98th had aborted the low level run due to weather. It would not be fair to fail the wing under circumstances that were not only unsafe, but beyond the control of mortal man. The bottom line: the wing passed with an overall rating of "Excellent".

Routine training missions filled the schedule for the week after the ORI. On Monday, November 11th, three B-47s deployed for Reflex in Spain. There was a return flight back to the states on Wednesday. The best way to return home was by B-47. Sometimes, there was a change in the rotation of aircraft and crews, which meant riding back to Lincoln in a KC-135. Billy Lyons recalled:

"On one return trip from Zaragoza to Lincoln, we were flying as passengers in a KC-135. On this particular return trip there were 30 to 40 Reflex troops plus, fortunately, an Air Force Flight Surgeon. After level-off at 28,000 feet, the crew inadvertently dumped the cabin pressure while attempting to adjust the temperature. Explosive decompression! Just like being in the altitude chamber. Cargo compartment fills up with vapor. Dust flies and guys grab for their oxygen masks and emergency oxygen bottle.

"The aircraft crew chief collapsed in the aisle while attempting to get all the people on oxygen. We each had an oxygen mask with an emergency bailout bottle like the ones we used in our parachutes. Some guys activated the emergency bottles (pulled the green apple) while others didn't even get that far and had to have some help. The guy I was sitting next to passed out almost immediately and I had to activate his emergency bottle and put the mask up to his face. I did not have to activate my emergency oxygen fortunately.

"The crew declared an emergency and descended to 10,000 feet. One guy had ruptured his eardrums from the rapid decompression and the flight surgeon was able to help him some, but it was still a painful situation for him. Although there was technically nothing wrong with the aircraft, we didn't have enough fuel to make it to our East coast base in the United States with required reserves. Also, half the passengers had activated their emergency oxygen bottles, which would have to be replaced before we headed across the pond. So we returned to Zaragoza, refueled, robbed the life support shop of some replacement emergency oxygen bottles and tried again.

"Most of us made it on the second try. The guy with the ruptured eardrums and a couple of others couldn't make it and had to remain there for further evaluation. Made us late getting back to Lincoln because we had to make a couple of stateside stops to let people off before we got home. Families not too happy. Had to drag the kids out or get a sitter at a late hour, but that's the business."

Friday, November 22nd, dawned like any other November morning. The air was crisp with a hint of approaching winter. At the patch there were the usual morning launches for 50-8 training flights. The flight line was buzzing with the usual fix and repair daily routine. SAC BRAT rode the bus to Lincoln High School and started another day of education. Few of us knew President Kennedy was going to be in Dallas, Texas, that afternoon. It was just another day.

One of the B-47s in the air that day was commanded by Capt Harold "Red" Duffer. His copilot was Miller Peeler. Sitting in the navigator's seat was Don Hickman, who recalled:

"We started to hear some rather unusual transmissions on the radio and couldn't figure out what was going on. 'Red' made a call to the Lincoln AFB Command Post and asked if anything was happening that we needed to know about. They gave us instructions to just continue with our mission with no explanation as to why there was such an increase in radio traffic."

At Lincoln High School, SAC BRAT was in the swimming pool during the noon hour. The swimming team was getting in a special practice before an upcoming swim meet. Coach Gene Cotter was talking with the team just before we hit the shower. A girl burst through the door to the hallway yelling, "The President has been shot! The President has been shot!" Her frantic voice reverberated off the water and the high walls of the pool.

Going to Mr. Franklin Burden's geometry class, the hallowed halls of Lincoln High School were buzzing with more than the usual between-class commotion. Inside Room 103, there was a lot of chatter about rumors of the President being shot in Dallas. When the final class bell rang, Mr. Burden came into the room and he didn't seem his usual jovial self. He

## Cold War Cornhuskers: The 307th Bomb Wing Lincoln Air Force Base Nebraska 1955-1965

looked shaken and serious. He announced there were unconfirmed reports that President Kennedy had been shot during a motorcade in Dallas, Texas.

Within a few minutes of the last class bell, the Principal came over the intercom. He confirmed the rumors circulating that the President had been shot in Dallas, Texas. Within moments of the announcement girls started sobbing, guys sat in shocked silence. Mr. Burden made several comments about the significance of the event and how it could affect our nation. Then he offered a moment of silence and prayer for our fallen President and the nation. Don Hickman recalled:

"When we finally landed, we were told President Kennedy had been shot and killed in Dallas, Texas. It was November 22. We quickly debriefed the mission and were told that we should stand by our phones in case they needed to recall us to the base. Security had been increased and checks were again being made at the gates."

In the immediate aftermath of the assassination, there was an air of confusion as to exactly what was going on. In Washington, there was a strong belief that killing of the President might be the initial phase of a Soviet attack. With that possibility looming over the country, Defense Secretary McNamara ordered the military to increase their Alert posture, just in case.

On base, security was tightened. Cars coming on base were subject to search and the guards were checking ID cards. Five more B-47s were generated to EWO status and placed on Alert. Crews on Alert were briefed about the situation. For the moment, practice Alerts were curtailed. If the klaxon went off it would be a launch response under EWO conditions. Across the country, we as a nation mourned the loss of our President. Like him or not, he was our leader. With his loss came an end to his Presidency and the era of Camelot.

Out of respect for the fallen President, most of the college football games were postponed or canceled. There was some controversy when the University of Nebraska announced the Cornhuskers would play at Memorial Stadium on Saturday as scheduled. Boy Scouts from Cornhusker Council served as ushers at the home games. SAC BRAT reported at noon and took his position on the top deck of the stadium. The crowd that afternoon was quiet and subdued as they filed in and took their seats. Even when Big Red scored, there wasn't the usual Husker Havoc.

Like a lot of families, we went to Sunday services at the base. Chapel services were filled with prayers for our nation and our leaders during the terrible time of national shock and mourning. It was one of those times when the actual service would be remembered for a long time because of the significance of the events in our nation's history.

Arriving home, we turned on the tube to check on the latest news. We were just in time to watch in horror as Jack Ruby emerged from the crowd and fired his pistol at Lee Harvey Oswald in the basement of the Dallas Police Department. Was it Jack Ruby's rage, a conspiracy, or was it another step towards a Soviet attack?

The nation paused to witness the State Funeral for our slain President. We watched as thousands passed by in silent respect as he lay in state below the rotunda of the Capitol. We too were silent. We watched a small boy salute his fallen father. We were touched. We listened to the beat of muffled drums and the clatter of shod hooves on the pavement. We watched the riderless horse, boots turned to the rear and the caisson carrying our fallen President as he was taken across the Potomac River to Arlington. We were saddened. We watched his wife as she lit an Eternal Flame. We held her in silent respect. We heard the bugler play the haunting notes of Taps and its echo among the silent white crosses of Arlington National Cemetery. We wiped away a tear.

Thanksgiving Day that year was filled with subdued celebration. Families and friends gathered for the traditional feast of the day. Special prayers were said for our nation and our leaders in Washington. We were thankful the horrible events a week ago didn't signal the beginning of Armageddon.

A Bravo Alert at 0900 kicked off the month of December on the 2nd. Later that evening, three aircraft launched for Reflex in Spain. It was a routine flight, although there were a few tense moments when the tankers were late arriving in the refueling area.

On the 4th, the Winter "Hawk" arrived with the first real snowfall of the season. It was only three inches, but it was enough to slow traffic, especially newcomers to the base who hadn't had the pleasure and thrill of driving in snow. For old hands, a mere three inches was just a drop in the bucket. The snowfall delayed the Reflex flight returning home from Spain by twenty-four hours.

Pipe Cleaner aircraft of the 4362nd Airborne Communications Relay Squadron participated in Top Rung II on December 6th. Nine aircraft launched at three-hour intervals, flew a nav leg, air refueling and arrived at their designated orbit areas. They practiced relaying "Noah's Ark" messages until they were relieved by the next aircraft on station. Eight of the nine missions were scored as effective.

On the morning of the 9th, the Alert crews were heading out of the mole hole for the morning preflight when the klaxon went off. Since they were already near their aircraft, it was a near-record Bravo response. One of the aircraft aborted when the #1 engine would not start. The Alert was supposed to signal the launch of Spurt 42, the Alert Pipe Cleaner for a relay mission. There was one major problem with Spurt 42. Somehow, someone had not placed the current KAC-29 Codebook aboard the aircraft. There was a mad dash to get the current codebook, then a mad scramble to get Spurt 42 in the air. Needless to say, the crew had a date with Col Heller to explain the foul up.

Wednesday, December 11th, saw the return Reflex aircraft getting back to Lincoln by the skin of their teeth. Low clouds moved into the area and started a combination of sleet and snow. Oxide flight managed to feel their way down to the runway with the help of GCA and land before the runway became an icy slab of concrete. By the next morning, the roads to the base were covered with snow and a nice layer of ice, which made driving to the base very hazardous.

Ice covering the ramp and runway caused all kinds of problems during the Bravo Alert that started at 0932 on the 12th. Alert crews had trouble getting to their aircraft. One of the Alert crews nearly ran into an MD-3 power cart trying to stop on the ice. Several ground troops took a nosedive, others did a triple back flip landing on their kiester. All aircraft reported in when they were ready to taxi. After the Alert, the engines were shut down and the aircraft recocked, which, of course, was made even harder by the cold and snow. Just another morning Alert on the ice-covered pad to show that the 307th was always ready.

Monday, the 16th, more snow fell on the patch giving an even more festive look for the Christmas Season. At 0915, the Alert crews responded to another Bravo Alert. The Pipe Cleaner aborted launch when an alternator shaft sheared. Spurt 83 was taken off Alert and replaced with another aircraft.

Later that afternoon, three aircraft departed Lincoln for Sunny Spain. The crews would fly the southern route as usual. Air refueling went according to the flight plan. Several of the crews at Zaragoza were happy to see the arrival of three B-47s with a green stripe on the tail. That meant their relief had arrived and they would be homeward bound in time for Christmas.

53-2366 launched for a Bar None mission on Wednesday morning, the 18th. Takeoff was on time, but a little shaky since there were still patches

230

of ice on the runway. The mission went well. The Bomb/Nav system had been repaired since aborting the mission on the 5th. The bomb runs were excellent, with no problem centering the PDI. Weather at Lincoln caused 2366 to divert to Forbes AFB in Kansas. A Reflex return flight also had to divert to the Land of OZ.

A blaring klaxon sent the crews scrambling to the Alert birds at 0915 on the 19th. The Bravo Alert response was scored "Excellent" for the 307th. The first aircraft reported ready to taxi five and a half minutes after the klaxon. The time was remarkable considering the icy conditions on the ramp.

There was an interesting sidelight to this particular Alert. An aircraft from the 98th aborted due to a "7-High" investigation. There was no indication whether this was practice or a real sabotage investigation in the official microfilm history of the 307th.

The klaxon blared again at 1400 that afternoon. This time it was a Coco response. A total of five aircraft on the Alert ramp aborted with mechanical problems. The Alert force had to taxi very slowly due to the icy conditions on the taxiway and runway. With safety a big concern, the power up and fast taxi down the runway was called off. If it had been a real EWO launch, it is doubtful the entire force would have been able to get off the ground. Score another point for Nebraska weather versus SAC.

The weather system that dumped the freezing rain and snow moved out overnight and brilliant sunshine greeted those who managed to slip and slide to the base on the 20th. The sun may have been shining, but it was frigid on the flight line. How cold was it? Officially, the temperature was -11 degrees reported at 0900. From there the mercury kept slipping until it reached a low of -18. That set a record for that date in the weather book. They didn't call Lincoln Air Force Base the "Icebox" for nothing!!

All training flights were to be completed by December 20th due to the approaching Holiday. There was a Reflex deployment launch on the 23rd. The unlucky flight crews who drew the short straw on the schedule were, to say the least, not thrilled by the idea.

Christmas Eve, the weather was still cold with that four-letter word "snow" in the forecast. At least the patch could look forward to a White Christmas. No flying was scheduled due to the Holiday. Except for a skeleton crew, the flight line was almost vacant of the usual activity.

Alert crews reported to their aircraft for the morning preflight at 0930, Christmas Eve. They had just started the preflight when the klaxon went off. The crews dropped the checklist and climbed the ladders. MD-3 power units coughed to life, electrical power surged through the cables and into the cold-soaked aircraft. Engines went from silent to a throaty whine as they spooled up. Checking in, they were informed it was a Bravo Alert. The noise of jets engines died as the crews shut down and prepared to recock the aircraft. There was some grumbling about the Alert, especially on Christmas Eve. The comments reached +10 on the grumble scale when they found out the Alert was not scheduled by either SAC or 2nd Air Force. It had been called by the 818th AD.

Christmas morning fell on Wednesday. In most of the base housing units, the sound of tearing paper echoed as SAC BRATS and family members opened gifts that sat below the traditional tree. New sleds got a test flight down the hill, while others struggled with tracks for their new electric train.

Three families got a special Christmas present later during the day when three crews returned from Reflex. It may have been cold on the flight line, but the homecoming reception helped warm things up. It was always nice to get home after Reflex. Arriving home on one of the most special days of the year made the holiday a little more meaningful for these three families who also served and suffered in SAC.

Monday, December 30th, was the last of the flying days for the year. There were eight scheduled training launches and three Reflex deployments for the day. The "Hawk" had other ideas about the schedule. Early that morning, the temperature was a balmy 22 degrees. The forecast called for partly cloudy with a slight chance of snow. Well, the forecast was off just a little. The flakes started falling about 0900. The wind shifted to the northwest signaling the arrival of the "Hawk".

Snowfall went from light to heavy, the winds picked up and the visibility dropped. By noon, there were three inches of "partly cloudy" on the streets and flight line. Visibility was less than a quarter of a mile with huge snow snakes slithering across the ramp. All flying was canceled due to the weather.

The 307th spent News Year's Eve digging out from the eight-inch snowfall the "Hawk" had deposited on the patch. Snowplows hit the runway to clear it of the heavy white stuff. While the plows were working, ground crews grabbed shovels and attacked the drifts surrounding the aircraft on the flight line. By late evening the three crews who were supposed to have launched on Monday for Reflex were able to get off the ground. They spent News Year's Eve flying across the Atlantic to Zaragoza. They were late getting to Spain, but at least they had arrived. The Alert crews they relieved were glad to see them, even if they were late. They knew even the Almighty Mailed Fist of SAC could not control the weather.

"I think I can speak for many of the 818th CDS APs when I say we really appreciated the consideration and kindness shown by the aircrew and ground crew members," Dan Brant wrote. "During one of the colder nights on the ramp an Alert bomber crew member asked if we were getting breaks and coffee. I told him I had not seen a CDS truck or coffee since I had been posted several hours before. They finished their business with the aircraft and left the Alert area, only to return about a half an hour later with two large thermoses of hot coffee and a sleeve of cups. I shared it with the other plane guards and the perimeter guards. They were back in the early morning hours and picked up the thermoses. I can remember many occasions when ground crew members would be running up the engines on the non-Alert birds just outside the south Alert ramp. We'd 'stretch' our post limits a little and stand with our backs to the jet wash. Man, was that nice. Bathed in the warmth and heavy kerosene fumes from the exhaust. I can remember several of those occasions when the man in the cockpit surged the engine and 'bounced' me as I was leaning back into the wash."

The 307th had another year under their belt. It had been a year filled with flying to fill in 50-8 squares, Bar None and Profile Missions. There was more emphasis on low-level flying. The wing was saddened by the loss of fellow airmen and shocked by the assassination of the President. The wing knew it was a matter of time until the B-47 would head for the boneyard. Then maybe, just maybe, the wing would get their hands on the B-52, or something even better

# Cold War Cornhuskers: The 307th Bomb Wing Lincoln Air Force Base Nebraska 1955-1965

53-4222 taxis at a winter locked Greenham Common, England. (Erickson)

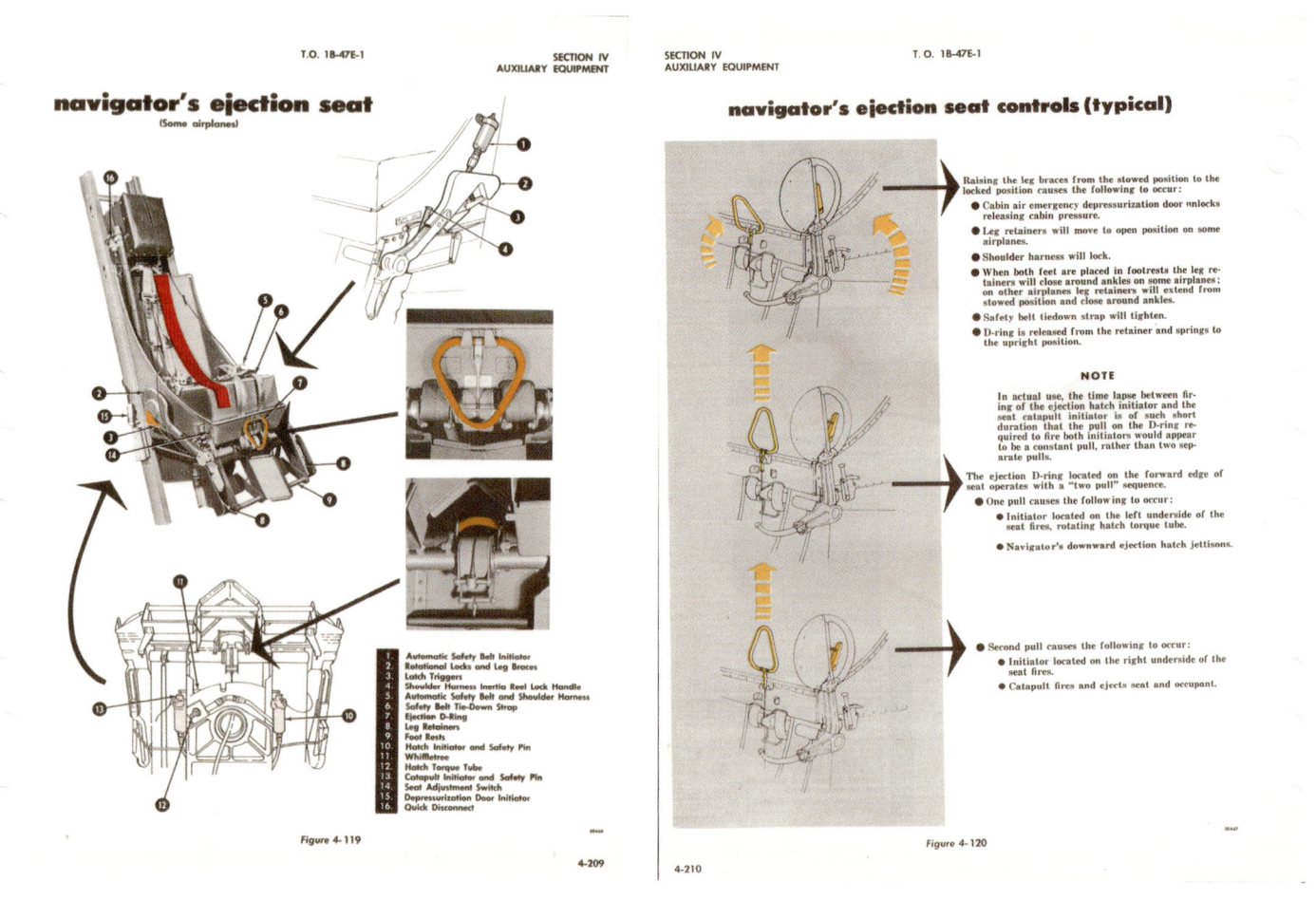

Navigator Ejection Seat diagram from the B-47 Dash-1.

Navigator's ejection seat controls diagram from the B-47 Dash-1

232

# 1963

Wreckage covers Highway 54 at the Butler County Line. (Alexander)

Harry Jones warming up in a fire truck after his low altitude ejection. (Alexander)

Capt. Paul Pudwill (S.Pudwill)

4th man station on the B-47. Note the hinged backrest at the top of the step. (M.Hill)

233

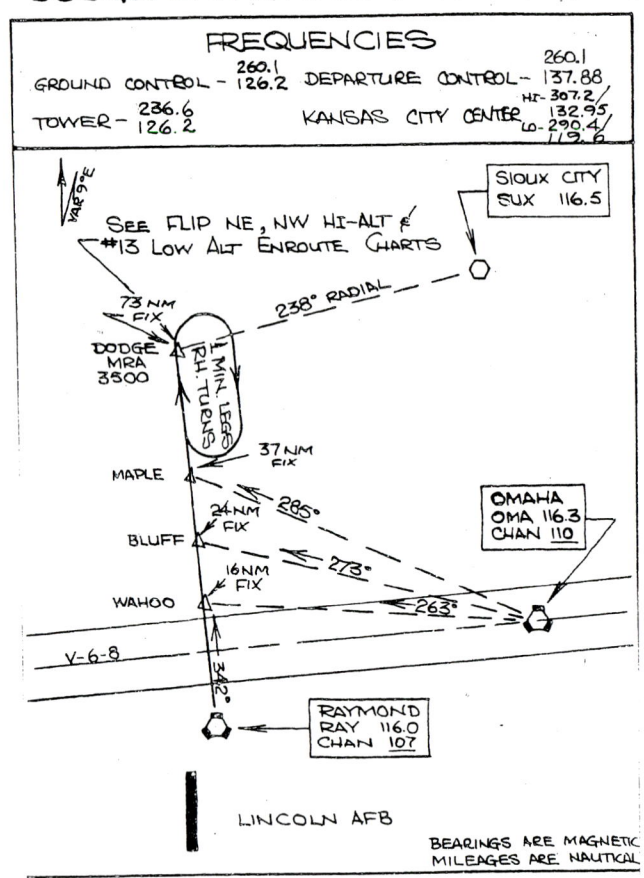

# Cold War Cornhuskers: The 307th Bomb Wing Lincoln Air Force Base Nebraska 1955-1965

DODGE DEPARTURE (Parks)

Periscopic Bombsight used on the B-47. (M Hill)

Navigator's escape hatch. (M. Hill)

53-2134 after the crash landing at Greenham Common, England. (Hickman)

## 1963

2134 sits like a huge wounded bird. Note the fuel tank under bomb bay, missing inboard engine pod and damage to the left fuel tank. (Hickman)

ATO take offs were always spectacular and dangerous as this early Air Force photo shows. (USAF)

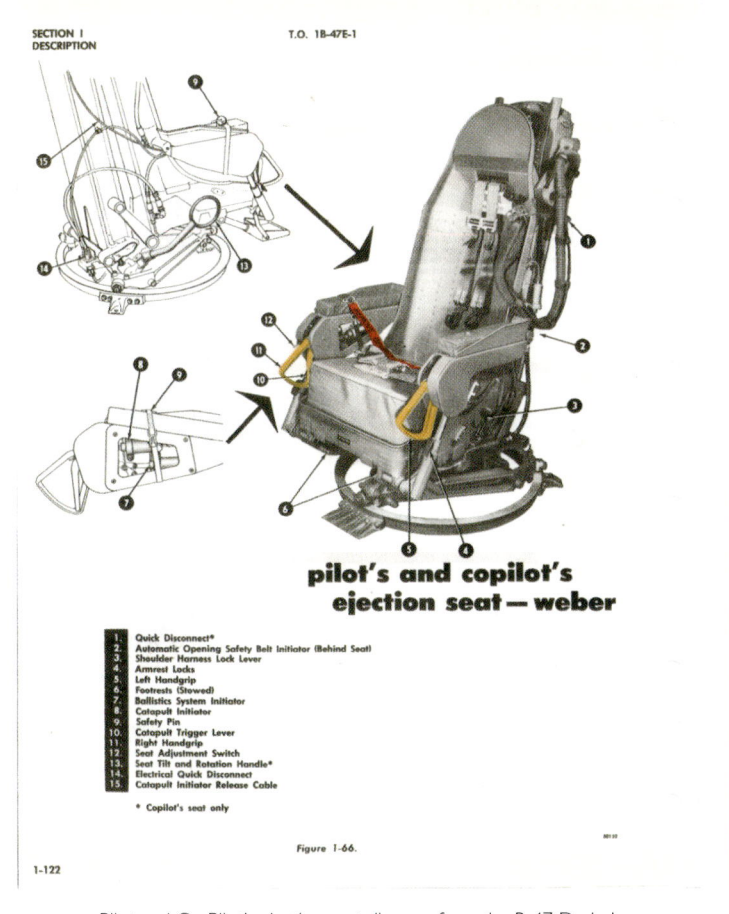

Pilot and Co Pilot's ejection seat diagram from the B-47 Dash-1.

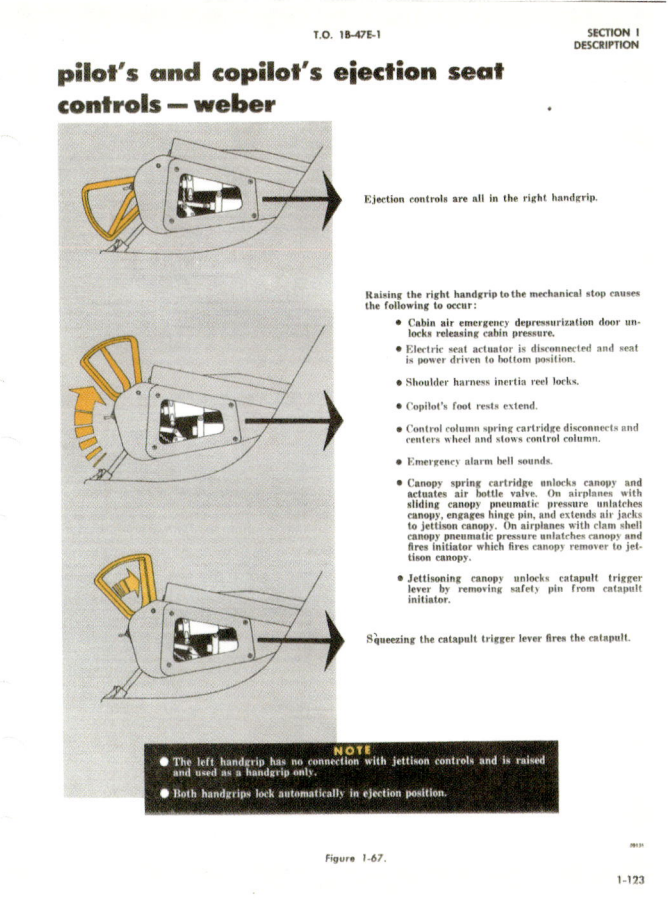

Ejection seat controls from the B-47 Dash-1.

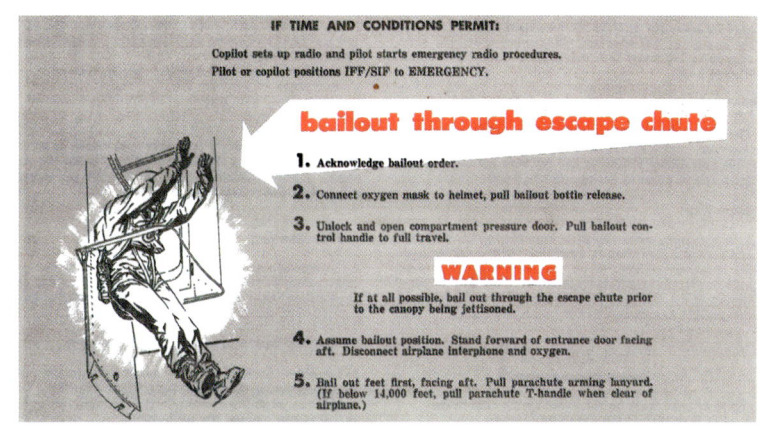

Alternate bail out procedure used by Art Ingle to escape the burning B-47.

# Cold War Cornhuskers: The 307th Bomb Wing Lincoln Air Force Base Nebraska 1955-1965

Maj. N.V. "Soldier" Meeks. (USAF)

Col. Walter Berg assumed command of the 307th on April 5, 1963. (307th BWA)

Ruth Meeks receives the Distinguished Flying Cross from LtGen. John D. Ryan, Commander of the 2nd Air Force. (JET SCOOP)

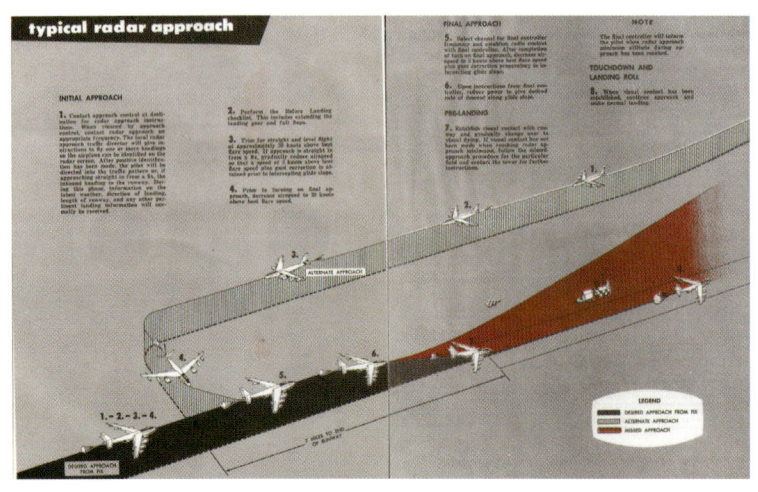

Typical Radar Approach diagram from the B-47 Dash-1.

*1963*

Master Crew Chief Patch (Avery)

2nd Air Force Master Crew Chief Patch. (Avery)

393 "cocked" on the alert ramp at Greenham Common, England. (Avery)

The N.V. Meeks Memorial Trophy. (USAF)

Shirley Pudwill receives the Distinguished Flying Cross on behalf of her husband's sacrifice. The medal was presented by BGen Lewis Lyle, 818th Strategic Aerospace Division Commander. (JET SCOOP)

# Cold War Cornhuskers: The 307th Bomb Wing Lincoln Air Force Base Nebraska 1955-1965

53-1867 Reflex bound to Greenham Common, England. (307th BWA)

53-2342 taxis in at Greenham Common during Reflex deployment. (Avery)

A2C Matthew Boylan receives THE AIRMAN'S MEDAL on June 24th for his actions on August 7, 1962. (JET SCOOP)

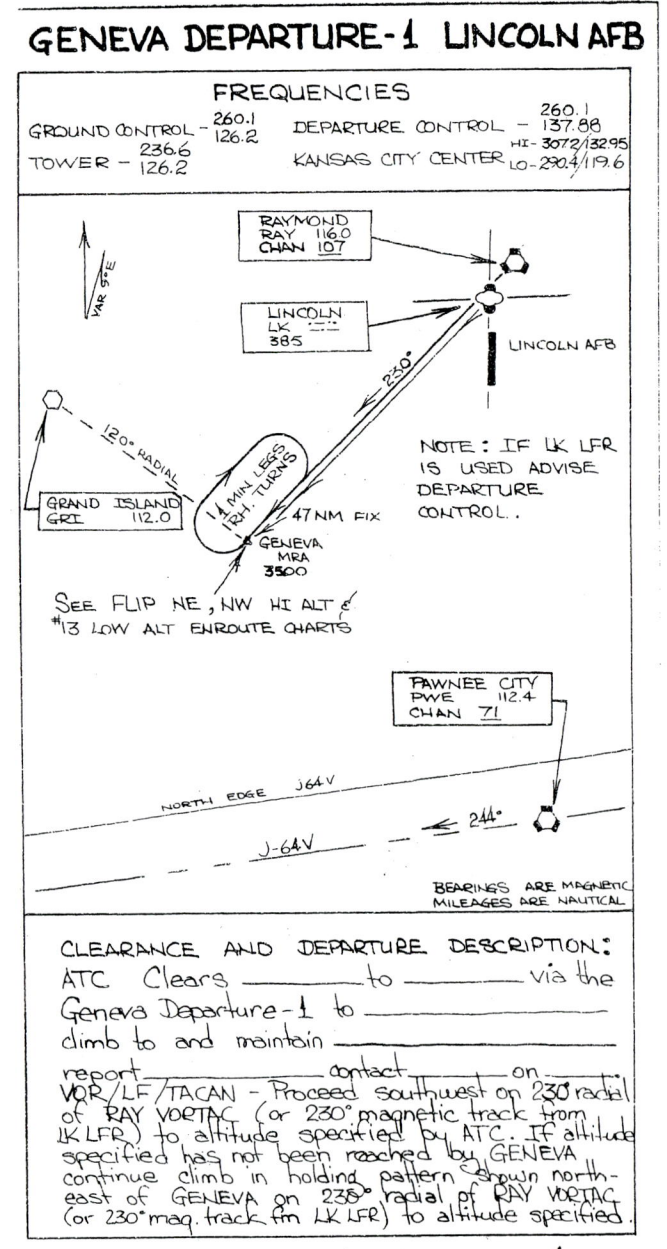

GENEVA DEPARTURE diagram. (Parks)

## 1963

Col. Elkins Reed was the special guest at the Dining Inn, August 15th. (JET SCOOP)

Crew S-97 were the first recipients of the N.V. Meeks Memorial Trophy. (JET SCOOP)

The Emergency Landing Gear Extension controls. (M.Hill)

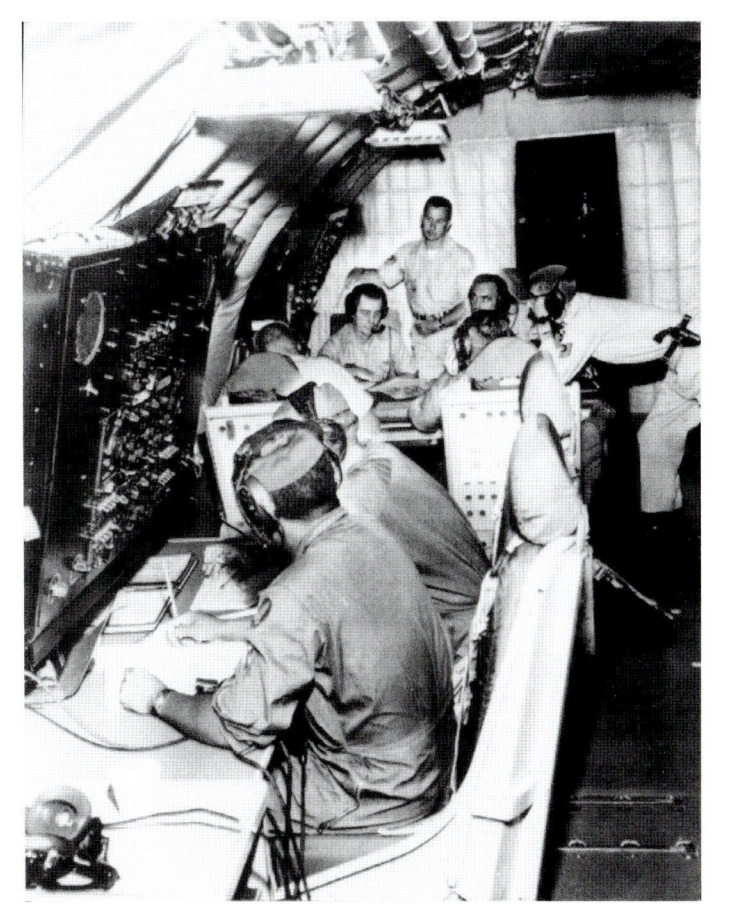

A LOOKING GLASS crew performs communication tests with other SKY KING aircraft. (USAF)

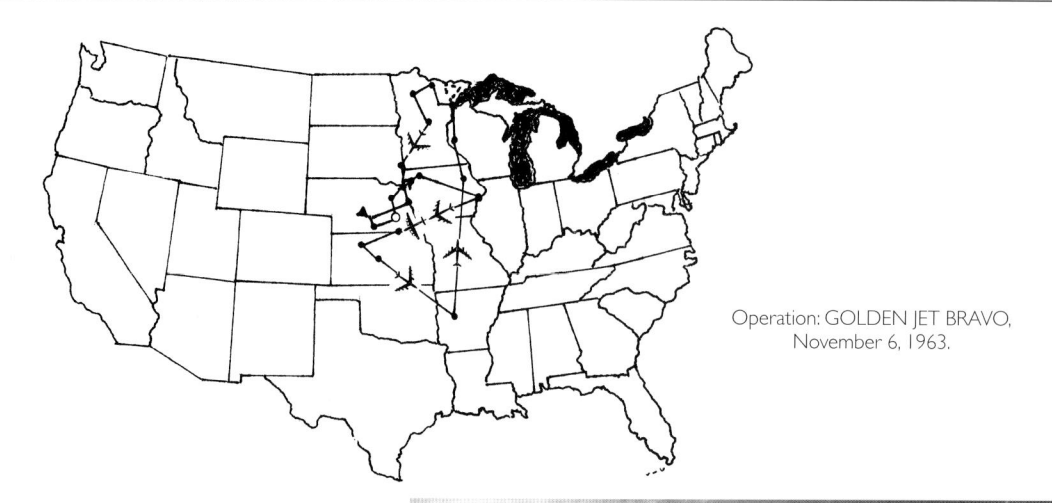

## Cold War Cornhuskers: The 307th Bomb Wing Lincoln Air Force Base Nebraska 1955-1965

Operation: GOLDEN JET BRAVO, November 6, 1963.

STANTON DEPARTURE. (Parks)

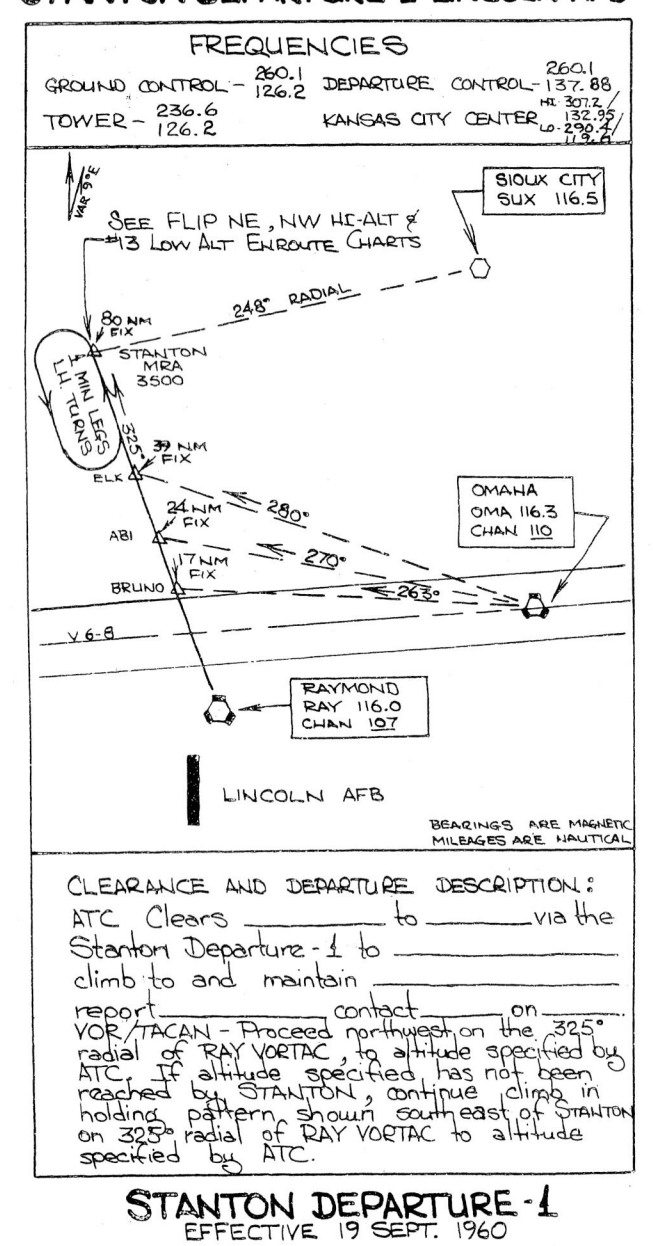

Copilot view of a air refueling. (USAF)

# 1964

New Year's Day fell on Wednesday, a normal workday at the base. There was still clean-up underway out on the flight line from the latest snowfall. There were four scheduled launches for training flights and three B-47s enroute back to Lincoln from Spain.

Word came down from SAC there was an administrative change. Effective on the first, the 4362nd Airborne Communications Relay Squadron would be known as the 4362nd Post-Attack Command and Control Squadron or PACCS. It was just a change in name, as there would be no change in personnel or mission.

There was also a message from SAC related to EWO launch criteria and Coco Alerts. Reaction time must remain as quickly as possible and no later than the BMEWS warning reaction time for either runway. That would give about fifteen minutes to launch the force. The wing was directed to develop procedures to launch all bombers downwind and to preposition aircraft at the non-optimum end of the runway to enable the force to meet the new timing criteria. The new criteria would be used during future ORIs.

The first mission under the new designation for the 4362nd PACCS was flown on January 2nd. The mission went off without a hitch. The crew spent eight hours in the air with nav legs, air refueling and relay of practice "Noah's Ark" messages.

Problems with the Bomb/Nav system cropped up again on January 6th. 53-2330 was flying a profile mission to fill in 50-8 squares. During the bomb run on the Rough Road bomb plot near Joplin, Missouri, the Bomb/Nav system started having problems. The crosshairs would not respond when the navigator tried to make last second adjustments with the tracking handle. A last resort bomb run was tried; however, like most last resort efforts, it was ineffective.

Bomb/Nav problems caused another ineffective score on the 10th. 53-1932 had two tubes go bad in an antenna server. "Tubes?", you say. That's right. This was before the advent of "solid state" and other technological advances. The bombing system on a B-47 was full of vacuum tubes, which would burn out and cause failures in the system at the most inopportune times.

At 1345 on the 12th, the klaxon sent the Alert crews dashing towards the Alert aircraft. Checking in, the crews were informed it was a Coco response. The first aircraft reported ready to taxi, moved out of their Alert slot and headed for Runway 17. Using MITO procedures, they hit the threshold and pushed the power to 80% for 1,000 feet, then pulled the power back. Under the new guidelines, water augmentation was simulated. As the aircraft returned to the Alert ramp, they were serviced and recocked. Since the water augmentation was simulated, there was one less item to service.

Late that evening, low clouds moved into the area and it looked like the "Hawk" was about to pay another visit to the patch. By 0200, light snow drifted to the ground. Aircraft returning from training flights were able to get back on the ground with the help of GCA. The snow kept falling for the rest of the night. By morning there were about four inches of new snow on the ground.

The 307th was hit with another Bar None ORI on the 13th. Alert aircraft responded to a Coco Alert, then downloaded the weapons and prepared for the ORI mission. While the aircraft were being serviced, the flight crews assembled to prove their knowledge of EWO procedures. The new-fallen snow caused a slowdown in the downloading procedure to ensure all safety measures were taken.

On the flight line, the ground crews started generating the mission aircraft for the follow- on force. Several had to be dug out of the snow and they all had to be swept clean of snow and inspected for possible ice. Bone-chilling cold made life on the ramp miserable for the ground crews. The download and generation were going well when the first flakes of snow started falling from the clouds. It wasn't heavy snow, just enough to slow things down even more.

The Alert crews would fly first. They were given the mission briefing and had a chance to study the route and targets. Takeoff order had been determined by the Coco Alert. The first crew that taxied would be the lead-off crew for the ORI. All they had to do was wait for the aircraft to be declared ready to fly.

The first wave would launch a total of fourteen aircraft in two-ship cells, with ten minutes between cells. Takeoff would use MITO procedures with fifteen seconds between aircraft. The 4362nd PACCS would launch three aircraft at one-hour intervals. Each of them would fly to a different orbit area and establish radio link with Looking Glass.

Low clouds and light snow continued to slow the ORI. The first two aircraft taxied out, crossed the runway threshold then started the takeoff run. Within moments of lifting off Runway 17, the low clouds swallowed the B-47s from view. Climbout was on the runway heading until they broke through the murky clouds. Once out of the clouds, the aircraft turned and headed for the refueling area near Rapid City, South Dakota.

Rendezvous and refueling went according to the mission profile. When the last drop of fuel was in the tanks, the bombers dropped off the boom and climbed back to their mission altitude. The navigation leg entry point was near Fargo, North Dakota. There, they changed heading for the radio checkpoint at Bemidji, Minnesota, then on to Brainerd, Minneapolis and another checkpoint. From Minneapolis, they turned for a checkpoint near Green Bay, Wisconsin. The final navigation checkpoint was over Davenport, Iowa.

Passing over Davenport, the aircraft started descending from 35,000 feet for the first bomb run on the Rough Road corridor near Joplin, Missouri. The winter weather that caused problems at takeoff was to the north of Joplin. The B-47s had no problem getting down to low level to make a Short Look Large Charge run without bad weather causing problems.

After the run on Joplin, they turned towards Wichita, Kansas, to set up for the next bomb run on Hastings, Nebraska. The run on Hastings was flown at high altitude; the low clouds and snow couldn't hide the target from the pulsing radar. After the attack on the Clearview RBS, the bombers did a tactical breakaway and headed back to home plate at Lincoln.

Arriving back at Lincoln, the crews contacted Approach Control and GCA for help in getting down through the overcast. Getting down was one thing; landing and slowing down on a snow-covered strip of concrete could be a whole new ballgame. Touchdown and rollout were a bit dicey, but they managed it with the professional skill that came from hours of training.

When the 28th and final sortie popped the drag chute, the 307th figured they had completed a good ORI. When the results were posted, the 307th had indeed flown a good ORI. Generation of the force was rated as "Outstanding" in spite of the snow and cold. Navigation and refueling were "Excellent". Bombing scores were rated 97.8% effective for a score of "Outstanding". Overall, the wing was rated as "Outstanding" for the ORI.

Col William Riggs and several members of the wing staff flew to Barksdale on Monday, January 20th, for the 2nd Air Force Commanders' Conference. After the official meetings, there was a special evening social and dinner. After dinner, there was a presentation of awards. The 307th was awarded the Revere Bowl Trophy for having the best Bar None results in the 2nd Air Force for the period of July 1 to December 31st.

53-2307 launched for a Profile Mission on Wednesday morning, the 22nd. After flying to the refueling rendezvous point, they started closing with the tanker. The crew went through the checklist before easing into the observation position. They slowly moved forward into the slot, trying to match their speed with the hovering tanker.

The copilot reached down and flipped the slipway door switch. The amber "READY FOR CONTACT" light remained dark. The navigator reported he heard a noise coming from the area of the slipway door. The pilot also heard the noise. The copilot tried the switch again with no change in the amber light. In the tanker, the boom operator confirmed the slipway door was not open. After trying everything they could think of, they had to abort the refueling and return to Lincoln.

After landing, the maintenance crew found an eyebolt connecting the hydraulic actuator to the door opening mechanism had failed. Further investigation revealed that, on a previous mission, the door had been struck by the boom while open, causing damage to the door and stressing the bolt to the failure point.

There was a Reflex launch on the 27th. The flight to Spain was a normal fifteen-hour flight. The crews who were relieved departed Zaragoza and returned to Lincoln on Wednesday, the 29th. The return flight was flown with no major problems.

At Zaragoza, there was a Bravo Alert on January 30th. The Alert crews scrambled to the aircraft and started engines. On one of the B-47s, the EGT climbed beyond normal limits during start-up on #4. The pilot pulled the throttle back, but the EGT stayed above the limit. They had no choice except to shut it down and were scored ineffective due to the "hot start".

January 1964 went into the books as a good month for the 307th. The wing had 60 aircraft assigned to the wing while authorized a total of 45. Flight crews spent 2,011 hours in the air during 284 sorties. Bombing scores were better than past months'. There were 303 high altitude runs with 297 scored effective. There were 346 low-level runs, all of which were scored effective. Air refueling was 99.5 % effective.

February would be a short month, so the 307th would try and cram as much flying as possible into the month. They started bright and early on Monday, the 3rd, with four launches for Bar None missions. All four flew the mission and were scored as effective. The ground crews kept busy servicing three B-47s for Reflex departure early that evening.

Three aircraft launched on time that evening for the flight to Spain. They coasted out near Charleston, South Carolina, and headed for the refueling area. There was concern when the tankers were late for rendezvous. The flight made a head on rendezvous, refueled and continued across the Atlantic to Sunny Spain.

Gray skies and low clouds greeted the men of the 307th reporting for duty on Friday morning, February 7th. It looked like it could start snowing at any minute. There was a full launch schedule on tap for the morning and afternoon. By 0900, light flakes of snow were drifting down from the clouds.

Anyone who worked on the flight line knew there were only two seasons on the ramp: hotter than hell, or colder than a brass monkey. No matter which season it was, the daily work of fixing and flying had to be accomplished.

At 1020, the wail of the klaxon sent the Alert crews scrambling to their aircraft for a Bravo Alert. One aircraft was ineffective when the MD-3 unit failed to start. Try as they could, the MD-3 just refused to fire up and supply power for the engine start. Starting up the power cart in cold weather was always a challenge. Paul Koski recalled an incident with a MD-3 and cold weather:

"We were on Alert and the temperature was about twenty below zero. We had to go out to the aircraft every hour or so and start the MD-3s and run them for about ten minutes. The flight crews said they were sure glad they didn't have to go out in the cold. Around three o'clock, I tried to start my MD-3 and it would barely turn over. The Alert truck was towing an MD-3 that had been running all night to help get other units started that wouldn't start. The procedure was to take the power cable from the one that was running and plug it into the back side of the one that wouldn't start. Then, turn the generator switch on; that supplied power to your unit, just like jumping a car. The problem was, when the switch was thrown, the power not only went to the MD-3, but also the aircraft.

"It lit up like a Christmas tree, all the lights on, even the rotating beacon. They had to call for the flight crew to go to the aircraft and recock it. You don't think they were mad? They even accused me of doing it on purpose just to get them out there. I assured them it wouldn't happen again and it was an accident."

Don Brandt served with the 818th Combat Defense Squadron and recalled a unique use of the MD-3:

"I remember one exceptionally cold night when I got so desperate to get out of the piercing cold wind that I climbed into an MD-3 unit. I had seen the inside of the unit when ground crews had opened the double doors and thought there might be enough space in front of the engine for a skinny person like me to fit. Probably could have died from carbon monoxide poisoning if the wind hadn't been blowing so hard. I was watching my post through the vent louvers on the side so my face was close to openings. Even so, the fumes were so strong that I only spent a few minutes in there and never did that again."

By the time the troops broke for chow, the snow was starting to come down a little heavier. It looked like about an inch had fallen since it began. Nothing serious, just enough to make life miserable on the ramp. Unless the snow got worse, air operations would continue.

Snow stopped falling by late afternoon. There was hardly enough to call out the plows, but as soon as the last flake had settled on the concrete, the plows were charging up and down the runway and taxi strips to clear the white stuff.

Monday, the 10th, started out with the normal report for duty, briefing, then hit the flight line. Recovery teams were working on aircraft that had returned from night missions. Launch crews started getting aircraft ready for the flight crews. About 1045, the blue sky turned gray and low clouds moved in from the west. It looked like another bout of Nebraska winter was about to arrive at the patch.

About noon, the snow started falling and the wind increased. The ever-present winter snow snakes started slithering across the ramp. Within the hour, snow was falling heavier than the last several storms. Visibility dropped to about half a mile due to the blowing snow.

The klaxon went off at 1345. Alert crews piled out of the mole hole like ants racing out of an anthill. Crew chiefs pulled the intake and exhaust covers, then grabbed the red "Remove Before Flight" flags. Inside the aircraft, the crews copied the Alert message. It was a Green Dot Coco Alert message.

They made the short taxi to the end of Runway 17 and turned onto the snow swept runway. Throttles were pushed to 80% and, one by one, they simulated the launch. With the low visibility, each crew kept an ear tuned to the tower frequency to hear if there were any problems with the aircraft on the runway ahead. The pucker factor was a lot higher than normal as the crews watched the aircraft in front of them power up, move forward, then disappear in clouds of blowing snow and billowing exhaust.

The long taxi back was also filled with tension. There were times when only a faint flashing red light from the tail of the aircraft in front could be seen in the murky distance. Arriving back at the Alert ramp, the aircraft were shut down and the crews went through the process of recocking in the cold blowing snow.

Back at the mole hole, the crews spent some time discussing the Alert. Most agreed it seemed foolish to have an Alert in the middle of a snowstorm. Maybe SAC wanted to see if the force could get off the ground in the blowing snow, or was it just a move to see if the crews still had the right stuff to be in SAC? They all agreed it had been one of the hairiest Alerts they had pulled.

By 1500, the patch was below minimums for safe air operations. The Reflex launch was postponed along with the remainder of the flying schedule for the day. Everything would have to wait until the winter "Hawk" stopped flapping his wings and the weather improved enough to clear the planes of the snow.

When the "Hawk" moved on, the plows hit the runway with the conga line to clear the drifts from the concrete. Ground crews manned the Mark-1 shovel and dug the aircraft out of the snow. Within hours, the flight line was almost back to normal winter operations. That meant back to work getting the planes ready for the next mission.

The "Hawk" may have moved on, but, on the heels of his visit, the thermometer dropped to five below zero. The flight line troops donned their special winter gear and went about the daily business regardless of the temperature. It was a fact of life: any problem that cropped up in cold weather was always in the worst possible place to get to for repairs. It always required taking off gloves or heavy clothes just to get to the problem. Without gloves to protect the exposed flesh, fingers and hands became cold and stiff in a matter of seconds. A simple job turned into a major, time consuming task. Cold or not, the work on the planes had to be completed. The lives of the crew would depend on how well the men on the ground did their job; cold fingers or frostbite was not an excuse. Copilot Larry Talovich remarked:

"The crew chiefs had a lot of pride in their aircraft. I remember one time we were having trouble with our oxygen system. This young troop worked his tail off trying to get it fixed. His fingers would stick to the piping. I told him to forget it, we could get along OK. But he stayed with it until it was fixed."

The Reflex flight to Spain left Lincoln on Wednesday, the 12th. When they finally arrived at Zaragoza, they were greeted with some good-natured razzing. "Where the hell have you been? It doesn't take 48 hours to fly from Lincoln to Zaragoza!" The crews who were returning to Lincoln were anxious to get back. They knew the real reason the relief crews were late. They hoped they could get going and return to Lincoln before the next bout of bad weather arrived.

Friday, the 21st, dawned cold and crisp at the patch. The temperature hovered around five below, typical Nebraska winter morning. That morning, 53-1919 was scheduled to fly a Bar None. The flight crew reported to the aircraft and went through preflight, engine start and taxi. At the end of the runway, they held short until the scheduled takeoff time. The takeoff and climb out went according to the mission plan.

Over Beatrice, Nebraska, 1919 turned and climbed towards Grand Island, then turned towards Sioux Falls, South Dakota, to meet their tanker. Rendezvous and refueling went according to the mission plan taking on the required fuel load within the Bar None time guidelines. The crew flew a nav leg through central Minnesota and down through Iowa. They then started to set up for a Short Look bomb run at the Joplin RBS.

So far, the mission had been textbook. Checkpoints were within the guidelines. Refueling had been accomplished with one gulp. Navigation had been right down the centerline. The crew set up for their run and crossed the Pre-Initial Point. At the IP, they checked in with the Joplin bomb plot and started their run. When the TTGI hit zero, the tone cut off. At the RBS scoring room, the tracking pen lifted from the paper. When the score was plotted, it was a shack.

Arriving back at Lincoln, 1919 and her crew approached from the north and landed on Runway 17. After shutting down and going through the post-flight checklist, the tired crew climbed down the ladder and headed for mission debriefing. 53-1919 and her crew had flown a near perfect Bar None. Their score would help the wing standings in the 2nd Air Force.

The 307th finished February with a Reflex flight to Spain on Monday, the 24th, with the relieved crews returning to the US on the 26th. The return flight had to divert to Whiteman AFB, Missouri, when the base was under another winter siege. The return flight was able to get in the air for the short flight home on the 28th.

Jim Villa recalled the bad weather and an interesting event:

"The Clay-Liston fight was to be held on February 25. I'm not a boxing fan, but I wanted to see 'Sonny' punch Clay clear back into the dressing room. What took place that night, I'm sure didn't happen on many occasions. It had snowed a lot and base maintenance was scheduled to clean off the accumulated snow on the 'hill' Alert area, so we moved all the Alert birds from up on the hill down to the area adjacent to Base

Operations. After getting all of the airplanes started and closed up, they loaded all of us crew chiefs in the Metros and we took off down the flight line taxiway so we would be on location.

"Since some of us wanted to listen to the fight, someone had brought a portable radio along and we were listening to the before-fight stuff as we went down the taxiway. It just so happened that the bird I was on was the first to arrive at the Base Ops area. I stepped out of the Metro before the fight started.

"It was a cold night. I can still see those 'big beauties' coming down the taxiway, one after another. There they were with their landing lights shining so brightly in the night. I still feel a little thrilled thinking about what I saw. I guided the AC into the parking slot, hooked into the bird with headsets and ground cord. Ground power had delivered the MD-3, so my partner and I wrestled the fifty-foot cables into place and plugged them in.

"After we got both airplanes shut down and recocked, I stepped into the Metro van and asked, 'What round is the fight in'? Someone said it didn't last long and Sonny threw in the towel. Best I recall, I was speechless.

"Yes, that was a special night. Seeing those B-47s in their fineness was something that was rarely seen. But, there was something else to remember. When we pulled up to park the vans at the Alert building, we could see the ground power and other equipment still sitting on the parking slots where the airplanes had just been sitting a couple hours ago. It gave me an idea what might happen if we had a full scale launch."

February went into the wing history as a month plagued with bad weather at the base, hampering flight operations. Over two hundred sorties were canceled because of the weather. Even with the canceled flights and short flying schedule, the wing managed to score 96.4% on bombing reliability. Refueling was scored at 94% while navigation was rated at 98%.

The wing started March with another bout of weather on Monday, the 2nd. The snowfall wasn't enough to postpone flying; it just made getting off the ground and back down a lot more difficult. The scheduled Reflex launch left on time. It appeared Old Man Winter would be around for a while.

Lt Gen David Wade, 2nd Air Force Commander, had arrived at the base on Sunday, March 1st. He spent the following three days looking over the base and conferring with the command staff of the base. He commended the 307th for their last quarter Bar None ratings.

A flight crew reported to Base Operations on the morning of March 3rd. They checked the weather and filed their flight plan. They arrived at their assigned aircraft and began the preflight like they had done so many times before. After preflight, they climbed aboard 53-0618 and went through the usual checklist procedures for engine start, taxi and takeoff.

When 0618 left the ground and cleaned up the landing gear, a lot of flight line troops who watched figured she'd be back on the ramp in about eight hours. They were wrong; 0618 would never return to the ramp at Lincoln. This was not another routine 50-8 mission. After completing a refueling, nav leg and bomb run, the crew would head for recovery at the aircraft storage facility in Arizona. 0618 was a high-time B-47 and was being retired from service to the boneyard. Retirement of 0618 was part of the Fly Fast project to retire the B-47. From now on, the 307th would continue to send high-time aircraft to the boneyard.[2]

The weekly Reflex launch left Lincoln on Monday, the 10th, and, except for some bad weather along the East coast causing the tankers to be late, it was a normal Reflex deployment. When the crews arrived, the aircraft were serviced and uploaded for Alert.

Tuesday, the 11th, the klaxon went off at 0945. The crews hit the Alert pad and started engines, and executed a Bravo Alert. The Pipe Cleaner crew decoded a launch order for a practice flight. They taxied to the end of the runway and launched. They would fly a nav leg and air refueling before taking up their station. Pipe Cleaner missions were usually long and boring. Every once in awhile, though, they could go from routine to downright scary in a matter of seconds. Bud Martin recalled such a mission:

"The mission of the 4362nd PACCS was to fly around in circles using the AN/ARC-89(V) UHF transponders. Similar sorties were launched from other bases, so the country could be served by reliable communications between SAC and the major AF headquarters. When a Green Dot message launched the single Alert Pipe Cleaner from Lincoln to circle around Lake McConaughy, it was six hours of boredom. At least one LtCol I flew with was known to nap for most of the mission.

"Not all flights were uneventful. On one occasion, with the usual dull conversation dwindling and nothing heard on the HF radio 'Ham' band, I noticed smoke in the cockpit, at least in the nose. I asked the copilot if he was smoking (he promised to give it up), thereby alerting the rest of the crew to the condition. There was a flurry of activity behind me as I looked over my shoulder. The AC stowed the smoking autopilot (that got more than normal use), but the smoke was still coming out of the inspection holes under his seat. 'OK, Nav; you're the primary firefighter. Come back here and see what you can do.'

"I thought, 'Those guys are sitting on ejection seats and I have to get out of my parachute.' Because of the location of the smoke (Where there's smoke there's fire, right?), no access to the source could be reached with an extinguisher. So, with a gloved hand inserted through the inspection port, I squeezed the bundle of hot wires serving the autopilot until the smoke dissipated. Mighty Mouse saved the day!

"Well, so much for that. We didn't even abort the mission. However, later, ready for landing, the forward gear indication was intermediate, and guess who had to get out of his parachute again and open the inspection plate to visually check the position. It looked OK to me, but my maintenance experience was with electronics. As we circled the base with the approach chute out, the AC talked with the ground about options. I was offered the choice of parachuting, or sitting on the step for landing, as a nose gear collapse would be more dangerous at the navigator's position. The idea of jumping out of a functioning machine at 0330 dark was not attractive, so I sat next to the copilot's leg while we made a normal landing. 'Those were the days my friends. We thought they'd never end.' But, they did."

The 307th had been alerted for participation in Operation Top Rung III, to be flown on Friday March 13th. During the first two Top Rung operations, the 4362nd had flown message relay missions. During Top Rung III, the Pipe Cleaner aircraft would be joined in the air with other B-47s from the 307th.

During the exercise, SAC B-52s and B-47s would fly low level attacks on selected targets in Nevada and Utah along with attacks on cities along the west coast. The 307th would launch eight B-47s and eight Pipe Cleaners during the two-day operation. Four B-47s and four Pipe Cleaners would launch each day. The B-47s would fly north into Canadian airspace, then turn and fly back towards the border. The Pipe Cleaners would launch and fly a short nav leg, then take up station at the designated orbit area. The relay aircraft would broadcast "Noah's Ark" messages to the mission aircraft to help test the system. The mission aircraft would decode the messages and continue to their target if it contained a valid go code for the exercise.

# 1964

The lead off Pipe Cleaner launched at 0820, and headed for the orbit point. The crew would complete a nav leg and air refueling before taking up station for their relay mission. The lead aircraft would be followed by another Pipe Cleaner at four-hour intervals.

The first two aircraft of the initial wave taxied to the runup area and held for the takeoff time hack. At 0850, the first aircraft advanced power, turned onto the runway and began the takeoff roll. Fifteen seconds later the second aircraft was on the runway, rolling at full power. As they lifted off, the water-alcohol augmentation system on the #6 engine quit. The asymmetric loss of thrust caused the aircraft to yaw to the right, but the pilot was able to stay on heading until the water-alcohol was exhausted on the other engines.

After takeoff the B-47s turned for the Geneva departure. Over Geneva, they turned and flew to Grand Island for the climb to refueling altitude. By the time the bombers reached Sioux Falls, they had made contact with the tankers and started easing into position behind the KC-135s from the 905th AREFS out of Grand Forks AFB, North Dakota.

The first B-47 took on fuel with a single hook-up. The second B-47 slid into position and moved in for hook-up. The hook-up went well, but the tanker was unable to transfer fuel. The tanker crew went through the checklist trying to isolate and correct the problem. The bomber disconnected and moved back into the observation position in case the problem was solved. Several of the crew may have made a remark about flying on Friday the 13th.

There was another tanker in the area. A quick conference with the command post and the second tanker was dispatched to rendezvous with the #2 B-47. This time, the hook-up and transfer went without any further problems. After refueling, the B-47 dropped off the boom and headed for the beginning of the nav leg at the Minot VOR. The second ship was now about forty minutes behind the first B-47. At least they wouldn't have to fly the timing triangle in Canada before turning towards the target.

Arriving over Estevan, Saskatchewan, the lead B-47 made the radio checkpoint and reported in. From Estevan they made a slight correction and headed for the next checkpoint over Regina. By now, the second aircraft was beginning their nav leg. Back along the route, the other two B-47s had launched and were headed for the air refueling control point.

Pipe Cleaner Spurt 42 had flown their nav leg and had taken on a full load of fuel. They had arrived on station near Kimball, Nebraska. The copilot rotated his seat and warmed the radio equipment up. He made the call and got an uplink with Looking Glass. Unlike most missions, once they were on station, the copilot stayed busy monitoring the radio and relaying messages that came in.

Near the H-Hour Control Point at Calgary, Alberta, the lead aircraft had finished the nav leg and was monitoring the radio for the authority to turn and head for the target. So far, they had suffered no problems like their sister ship. Just after reaching Calgary, the crew's earphones crackled with **"Sky King, Sky King....This is Noah's Ark. All Sky King aircraft stand by to copy a Foxtrot message."** The bomber crew opened the codebook and decoded the message. After cracking their plastic "cookies", they verified the message. Looking at the combat mission folder, they turned south toward their target near Salt Lake City.

Hugging the eastern slopes of the Rocky Mountains, the lead aircraft flew south, crossing into United States airspace near Cut Bank, Montana. They pulled up to gain enough altitude to clear the oncoming mountains. They would skim the peaks and fly through valleys when possible. The route took them down the west side of the Grand Tetons, then south to the Wasatch Range in Utah. Over Willard Bay, they changed course for the target range west of the Great Salt Lake. They made a Short Look bomb run on a radar target and turned towards Denver and a checkpoint.

From Denver the lead ship flew east and set up for a Long Look bomb run on the Hastings bomb plot. After Hastings, it was a short flight back to the patch. The lead bomber had completed the mission with very few problems. Back along the route, the remaining aircraft were still trying to fly the profile.

The crew of the second aircraft in the lead cell seemed to have more than their share of problems. During the nav leg, they had problems with the radar. Approaching the H-Hour control point, their radio started acting up. They almost missed the "Noah's Ark" message. It was garbled, but the repeat transmission came through. They turned south and picked their way through the mountains for the run on the first target.

Their Friday the 13th wasn't over yet. After the Long Look run on Hastings, they flew a flawless approach and flared for landing. On touchdown, the drag chute billowed and then collapsed as it sheared away from the rolling B-47. It took a lot more concrete than normal to slow the big bird down, but they made the turnoff and taxied back to the flight line.

On Saturday, the 14th, the 307th and the 4362nd repeated the mission with another Pipe Cleaner relay wave and more B-47s heading north to Canada. Saturday's mission had no mechanical problems. The entire mission was considered textbook. One aircraft scored a shack on the target in Utah and another on the Hastings bomb plot. The 307th received an "Outstanding" rating for their flying during Top Rung III.

On Sunday, the 15th, there were special services at the base chapel. The services were in observance of the 6th Annual SAC Memorial Sunday. Special moments of silence were observed for those who had given their lives while serving in SAC.

Julius Caesar was told, "Beware of the Ides of March". That was a fateful day in Rome centuries ago. March 16th was a fateful day for the 307th. Word came down from Omaha that the 307th Bomb Wing would not transition to a new mission aircraft. The wing would be deactivated, with an effective date of late March 1965. The news of deactivation was received with mixed emotions throughout the wing.

During a Wing Staff Conference held in Omaha on March 18th, the 307th Wing met with SAC officials to plead their case against deactivation. The bottom line was if another mission for the 307th could be found, then the wing would survive. At the moment, it didn't look good for the 307th's survival beyond next March.

Winter weather returned to the base on March 18th. A fine freezing drizzle started about 1000. By noon, the flight line troops were joking about getting their ice skates out and skating over to Base Ops for a quick burger before skating around the flight line for the rest of the afternoon. Heavy snow replaced the drizzle about 1400. Now, there was snow on top of the ice, making movement even more difficult.

Alert crews boiled out of the mole hole tunnels at 1400 and hit the six-pack trucks for the short slide to the Alert birds. Crew chiefs already had dropped the ladders on most of the birds. While the flight crews climbed aboard and strapped in, the ground crews pulled red ribbons from the pitot tubes and cranked up the MD-3s.

Within four minutes of the klaxon's wail, the first B-47 reported they were ready to roll. From inside the canopy, the pilots gave the signal to pull the chocks. Chocks, ground cords and the power carts were removed from the area around the front of the aircraft. Power was pushed up to get the old gal moving. The first plane to taxi was a bird from the 98th Bomb Wing.

Once the EWO-laden B-47 was moving, it had to turn sharply to get onto the runway. When the pilot tried to make the turn, the B-47 had other ideas and continued straight ahead, sliding on the ice until the forward main gear slid off the concrete and buried itself in the snow. The big B-47 wasn't going anywhere and neither were the rest of the Alert aircraft. The taxiway was blocked.

Most of the Alert aircraft hadn't moved from their slots. They sat for a few moments with engines idling waiting for the word on what to do next. There were other ways to get around the blocked taxiway, but they had the potential of causing even more problems. Finally, they were told to shut down, since the Alert had been downgraded to a Bravo Alert in view of the conditions and one bird stuck in the snow.

It took over three hours to defuel, dig, and then pull the stuck B-47 out of the snow and clear the taxiway. The crew was summoned to meet with their wing commander to explain what happened to cause the aircraft to slide off the taxiway. The final verdict was too much power applied, which caused too much speed to make the turn under the icy conditions.

Three Reflex redeployment aircraft ran into problems trying to get back to Lincoln that day. Weather between the east coast and Nebraska wasn't the best. In fact it was downright rotten. The crews were forced to divert to McCoy AFB, Florida, where they were marooned in the balmy sunshine for forty-eight hours.

By March 23rd, the runway was clear of ice. Air operations were back to a normal fever pitch to try and make up for lost time in the air. Four aircraft launched in the morning for routine training flights. There were four more launches that afternoon. That evening, three B-47s launched for Reflex, landing at Zaragoza about fifteen hours later.

During the morning preflight on the Alert pad, a problem was discovered with one of the aircraft. There appeared to be a major leak in the water-alcohol system. After checking things out, a leak was found in one of the pumps. The aircraft was scheduled to come off Alert that day so repairs were postponed until the weapon was downloaded. Jim Villa recalled a similar problem and how it was fixed:

"Mike Fox and I went up to Alert with 4227. Mike was one of the best guys for anyone to have as a partner on Alert. Anyway, when Mike went out to 4227, they did the external check and the water-alcohol pumps in the right wing were leaking--BAD! So, it fell to Mike to fix the problem; this type of repair was done by the maintenance section. The bird had to be uncocked and taken off Alert status.

"The pumps were located inboard of the #4 and #5 engines and had access through a 'hell hole' in the bottom of the plane's wing. We called these accesses hell holes since we had to work in such tight places. In this case, a maintenance stand had to be placed under the wing at the height where a man could squat, then put his arms above his head and ease up through the hole. There was only enough room for the man's body above his armpits. Also, he would have to thread his arms and hands into a lot of tight places and positions. This meant he would have to slip in and out of the 'hell hole' many times so as to get at what he needed to do. It would be best that the man would take off clothes above the waist, but this event took place in cold winter weather. There were portable heaters, but a person couldn't have the heater ducts blowing into the tight compartment; there was no room. Also there would be fumes coming from the heater. So, that meant a man's bottom part could be warm and the top frozen.

"Mike and his partner worked all day and through the night. The Alert maintenance supervisor called me in to replace Mike so he could go to the barracks and get some well-deserved rest. When I got there, Mike had discovered a very disheartening problem after he thought completion was near. 'Murphy's Law' had stepped in; the clamp that held the pumps to the water manifold could not be tightened. A person couldn't get to the clamp because of the pumps and hardware.

"No matter what we tried, that !$**&^# clamp could not be reached and tightened. We decided everything would have to come out again and the clamp would have to be tightened before any of the other parts were put in place. It took my partner and me the same amount of time Mike and his partner endured to do the work. At my age now, I wouldn't be able to twist my arms and hands to do what was needed. Also, I wouldn't be able to put my body in that hole.

"Mike came back about the time we completed the work. He would have a seven-level skilled person inspect our work. The airplane was serviced with water alcohol and recocked."

During the last week of March, it appeared old man winter was about to release his grip on the Plains of Nebraska. The mercury started moving higher and higher in the thermometer. As the temperature rose, the piles of snow started to diminish in size.

March would go into the wing history as the beginning of the end for the 307th at Lincoln Air Force Base. With SAC calling for the deactivation of the wing, it would take a miracle for the 307th to survive beyond March 1965. At the moment, there didn't appear to be any hope of a miracle for the 307th.

Mother Nature played an April Fools prank on the base on the 1st. Late that morning clouds moved in and a thunderstorm dumped rain on the base. It was almost a pleasant surprise in view of the miserable winter weather that had plagued the base for the first three months of the year. The storm washed a lot of the accumulated winter grunge into the gutters. After the storm there was a smell of spring on base.

Earlier that morning, a flight crew preflighted for a routine flight in 52-0323. The old gal arrived last August and over her career, she had a lot of air flow across her wings. The crew started engines and launched for a routine 50-8 mission. The final leg of the mission was to deliver 0323 to the boneyard in Arizona.

At Wing Headquarters, the staff reviewed aircraft records to determine which were the high-time birds in the wing. These would be the first aircraft to be sent to the boneyard and retirement. The high-time aircraft would be culled from the wing to make room for lower-time aircraft being transferred to the 307th from other wings being deactivated.

Along with the beginning of sending aircraft to retirement, the 307th home Alert commitment was changed from fourteen aircraft to nine B-47s at Lincoln. There would also be four Pipe Cleaner aircraft on Alert. With B-47 wings being deactivated, the 307th Reflex commitment was also changed. The 307th would now maintain twelve B-47s at Zaragoza instead of nine.

Reflex launches would change to two launches per week, on Monday and Wednesday. Return deployment would be on Wednesday and again on Friday. There was also a change of the Reflex station in the mill. The 307th was alerted to change from Zaragoza back to Morón effective June 1, 1964.

The 4362nd PACCS received a message to prepare three aircraft for Operation Garlic. The operations plan called for three aircraft to deploy to Eielson AFB, near Fairbanks, Alaska. They were to fly message relay missions for the B-52s flying polar airborne Chrome Dome Alert. The first three aircraft departed Lincoln on April 9th.

Arriving in Alaska, they flew the first Garlic mission on Monday April 9th. They flew north across the Arctic Circle and established an orbit over the frozen tundra. Establishing a radio link with a Looking Glass, they relayed radio traffic to the Chrome Dome B-52s.

The 13th saw the launch of four B-47s from Lincoln for Reflex duty in Spain. The fourth aircraft in the flight reflected the change in the Reflex commitment for the 307th at Zaragoza. Another four aircraft Reflexed to Spain on the following Wednesday.

A blaring klaxon sent the crews running for their Alert vehicles early on the morning of April 16th. Scrambling up the crew ladder, the crews clambered into their seats, donned their helmets and started engines. When they checked in, they received a Green Dot Bravo response message. No further action was required, so they shut down the engines and began the process of recocking their aircraft.

About 1015, a C-130 landed and taxied to Base Operations. The cargo ramp dropped and pallets of equipment started rolling down the ramp. Several members of the crew went into Base Ops. The troops on the flight line hardly noticed the arrival; after all, they had work to do. None of the troops had any idea that a 2nd Air Force inspection team had arrived aboard the C-130.

The klaxon blared again at 1145 sending the crews back to the Alert birds. Checking in, they received a Green Dot Coco Alert message and were informed this was the beginning of a no notice ORI. Ground crews buttoned up the aircraft and pulled the chocks. The first bird called in six minutes after the Alert began. They made a fast taxi to the south end of the field and hit the runway for the simulated launch.

Arriving back at the Alert ramp, the crews shut down the engines and climbed down the ladders. They reported to the briefing room and waited for the arrival of the ORI inspection team. One aircraft from the 98th aborted the Alert due to a hot start and small fire on the #3 engine. All of the 307th aircraft were scored effective for the Alert.

While the flight crews were getting their briefing and confirming their EWO knowledge, the Alert area was a beehive of activity. Munitions crews had arrived and were downloading the Alert force for the ORI. After the aircraft were downloaded, they were serviced with fuel and were preflighted for the upcoming mission.

307th Wing Staff pulled a Bar None mission folder from the safe to establish the mission that would be flown. The route was filed with ATC, who issued clearances for the mission. Air refueling support was also established. Seven of the nine Alert crews would fly the first wave. The second wave would be generated and follow up with a mission on Friday.

The 307th would launch seven aircraft on the first wave. There would be two cells, one cell of three, the other of four. The cells would launch one hour apart, each cell using MITO procedures for the launch. Runway 17 would be the active runway for the first wave. Climbout would be according to the Dodge Departure procedure.

After reaching a mission altitude of 35,000 feet, the B-47s would turn and fly over Sioux City, Iowa, then head to the turn point at Storm Lake, Iowa. From there, the route took them southeast to Des Moines and their first radio checkpoint. Quincy, Illinois, was the turn point for the air refueling control point at St. Joseph, Missouri.

Air refueling would be in Area 22 "Cave Inn", between St. Joseph and Hill City, Kansas. The air refueling requirement was to take on 35,000 pounds of JP-4 before the end of the refueling track. To score as effective, the crews had to take on at least 25,000 pounds of fuel.

At the end of the refueling track, there was a spacing triangle built in to provide a fifteen-minute gap between the bombers for the rest of the mission. Leaving the refueling area, the aircraft would turn north towards North Platte, Nebraska, and the first nav leg checkpoint.

Checking in over North Platte, the B-47s turned to a heading that would take them to Scottsbluff, then turn towards Rapid City, South Dakota. At Rapid City, they would turn for the next checkpoint over Mobridge, South Dakota, then on to Fargo, North Dakota, ending the nav leg.

Over Fargo, they would start descending from 35,000 feet for the first low-level bomb run. There was a short dogleg to the north, then a turn towards Bemidji, Minnesota, to enter the "Big Spike" oil burner route. They would set up for a Short Look bomb run on the RBS Express unit at Brainerd, then begin climbing back to high altitude for a bomb run on Madison, Wisconsin. After leaving the land of milk and cheese, the mission aircraft would turn and fly back to Lincoln.

The initial launch of the first wave went off within the time window established for the ORI. The refueling and navigation leg were textbook. Bombing scores for the first wave were scored at 98% effective. After the first wave, the wing was off to a very good start.

The second wave began launching at 0940 on Friday morning to fly the second wave of the ORI. Takeoff went according to the mission plan until the last aircraft turned onto the runway and started rolling. Just before they reached S1, the water-alcohol system failed. With the loss of the extra thrust, the crew had to abort the take off. The AC pulled the power back and called for the drag chute. The B-47 slowed to safe taxi speed, turned off the runway and taxied back to the flight line.

The rest of the ORI mission was flown with minor problems in the refueling area when one of the tankers was late for rendezvous. There was a major setback during one of the bomb runs at Madison. A B-47 started having problems with the stabilizer unit in the Bomb/Nav system. Then, just after crossing the IP, the system had multiple failures. Without the capability to bomb accurately, the aircraft was scored as ineffective.

During the ORI critique, the 307th was praised for the conduct of the ORI. Navigation was rated "Outstanding" along with the generation of the follow-on force. Air refueling was rated "Outstanding". Bombing was rated "Satisfactory". The two aborts gave the wing an overall rating of "Excellent" for the ORI.

Monday, the 20th, saw the launch of a Reflex flight to Zaragoza. The flight was normal until the three B-47s landed at Zaragoza. During landing rollout, the left outrigger tire on 53-1829 blew, sending rubber shrapnel flying in all directions. Before they could slow down, the blown tire was worn to the rim, which was getting hotter by the second. When the crew finally brought the beast to a halt, there wasn't much left of the tire or wheel. The ground crews grabbed their trusty toolboxes and started working on the outrigger to get it changed and checked out.

Word came down from Omaha for the 307th to begin planning for a change in the Reflex station. Effective June 1st, the wing would change from Zaragoza back to Morón, Spain. The wing would have to begin the change in mid-May, so men and equipment could be in place at Morón by the end of the month. Aircraft would transfer to Morón during the last week of May and placed on Alert as quickly as possible.

At Zaragoza, the Alert crews were getting a bit "antsy". They hadn't been subjected to an Alert in almost a week. Ask any SAC crew dog, they will tell you, when you are pulling Alert, you are supposed to have the klaxon go off at least once during your tour; it's a SAC fact of life! No klaxon to get the adrenaline pumping and you get antsy. Some would even say that the blare of the horn would actually relieve the tension of being on Alert for a little while.

Sweet dreams of home and family for the Alert crews at Zaragoza were shattered by the blaring klaxon at 0215 on the 23rd. There was a mad scramble to don flight suits, stuff their feet into boots and pull the zippers closed. Then, there was a dash to the vehicles and a fast drive to the cocked birds.

The crews copied a Green Dot Bravo response message. Two aircraft were ineffective. One couldn't start the #6 engine. The other had an alternator shaft shear. The flight crews could return to the mole hole and try to get back to dreamland. Broken birds meant hauling out crew stands and lights to get the birds repaired and back on Alert in the shortest time possible. Repairing the Alert birds meant more lost sack time for the crew chiefs.

There was a Reflex return flight launched on Thursday the 30th. Like most return flights it was long and, for the most part, uneventful. There was a twist to this return flight. From time to time, the profile would call for jettisoning the wing fuel tanks to verify the system. This would usually be done off the coast of the US after the fuel had been used. Approaching the drop area, the navigator would sweep the area below to make sure

## Cold War Cornhuskers: The 307th Bomb Wing Lincoln Air Force Base Nebraska 1955-1965

there was no ship traffic in the area. There being no ships in the area, he cleared the pilot for the drop. The pilot reached down and lifted a guarded switch, then lifted the toggle for the left tank. A small drag chute deployed from the rear of the tank, then it fell away from the left wing. The pilot dropped the switch to the right tank position. With a slight rock of the wing, the tank fell away towards the ocean below.

During most of the time in the air, there wasn't a lot for the copilot to do. There was managing the fuel panel during air refueling and helping the navigator with sextant shots. He helped run the checklists and sometimes actually flew the airplane. But there was a lot of time to look around and see the sights. That is, whatever could be seen from high altitude. Several copilots carried movie cameras with them and would film images from the backseat.

Neil Cosentino managed to capture dropping wing tanks on film. The film shows the left, then the right tank leave the aircraft. Then the aircraft banks in an attempt to follow the falling drop tanks. Neil's camera also caught a fireout during a Reflex return. With guns pointed towards the sky, you can almost hear the sound of the 20 mm guns barking away as the turret swings from side to side, spraying the sky with rounds of 20 "mike-mike".

May Day fell on Friday. There were three Bar None launches scheduled for the morning and four profile missions on tap for the afternoon. The three Bar None missions launched on time and flew the mission according to the flight plan. All were rated as effective.

The *Jet Scoop* hit the newsstands on base that Friday with the latest news from around the patch. There were several articles about the upcoming softball season and whom to contact if you wanted to play. The movie feature for that night and the weekend was the World War II epic, *The Longest Day*. That night, the popcorn machine worked overtime as the D-Day docudrama played to a packed house.

Ground crews worked most of the morning of the 4th to get three B-47s ready for the evening Reflex launch. About an hour before the launch, the klaxon went off sending crews to the aircraft for a Bravo response. The launch and flight across to Zaragoza were routine. The flight may have been routine, but shortly after landing, the klaxon went off sending the Alert crews to the birds. What a way to start Reflex: an Alert at Lincoln before they left and now they were greeted by another Alert in Spain. During the Alert, Crate 14 was scored ineffective when there was a hot start on the #4 engine.

On Tuesday, the 19th, the weather was unseasonably hot. High humidity made it not only hot, but also muggy. Working inside a B-47 was almost unbearable as the temperature inside passed the century mark. In the hot muggy air, clothes stuck like glue as the sweat poured off.

That morning, 53-2327 launched for her final flight from the patch. After flying a 50-8 mission, the crew turned and headed towards the boneyard in Arizona. Their route took them through western Kansas, where they reported thunderstorms building across the horizon. The storms looked like they were headed northeast, towards Huskerland.

As the sun climbed higher in the sky, so did the heat and humidity. With little wind, conditions on the sun-baked concrete were hard to bear. Shimmering waves of heat danced off the flight line. Three aircraft launched at 1430 for a 50-8 profile mission. In the hot humid air, they used most of the runway to struggle into moisture-laden air.

Late afternoon, the first clouds appeared on the western horizon. They boiled and billowed, sucking in the hot moist air from the prairie as they rumbled northeast. As they got closer, the western sky started to darken. Soon, the distant rumble of thunder echoed across the countryside.

By the time the gust front arrived, most of the people on the flight line had taken cover. Looking to the southwest, the hills disappeared as the wall of rain approached. Within moments, the flight line was peppered with huge drops of rain. Gusty winds picked up, blowing sheets of water across the ramp. Lightning flashed, followed by the crack of thunder as the full force of the storm lashed at the base.

Wind gusts increased to 45, then 50 miles per hour. Anything that wasn't secured became airborne. Then a peak gust of 58 miles per hour was recorded as it rocked Base Operations. A few moments later, the rain let up for a moment, then returned with even more fury.

For over forty-five minutes, the base was hammered by high winds, rain and hail. Slowly, the storm moved on to the northeast. Behind the storm, the western sky was filled with another line of approaching dark clouds. These looked just as dark and threatening as the clouds that had just dumped over two inches of rain.

The next line of thunderbumpers arrived with the same fury as the first. High wind and more rain pummeled the patch. Just southwest of the base, a funnel cloud dropped from the low-hanging clouds. It passed over the south end of the runway, then retreated skyward disappearing into the base of the wall cloud.

When the storm was over, people emerged to see if there was any damage. The base was littered with overturned trashcans and other debris. Near Base Supply, the wind had toppled several crates of wing tanks that formed the wall around the supply compound. An unknown object had smashed into the tail of a B-47 denting the aluminum. Luckily, there was no major damage.

The storms may have moved out, but the gusty winds remained on the backside of the storm. It seemed the wind was coming from every point of the compass as it changed from moment to moment. There was a B-47 on final approach for Runway 17, trying to sneak in behind the storm front. At the last second, the wind shifted. The crew noticed they were dropping out of the sky like a rock. The pilot pushed the throttles to full power, the aircraft continued to sink towards the runway. He pulled back on the yoke as the power started coming up. The bomber touched down on the front main gear and bounced back into the air. There was a lot of yoke yanking and rudder tramping as the pilot fought to correct the dreaded porpoise action of the B-47. He was able to correct just enough to get the B-47 down on the runway with the help of pulling the drag chute while still in the air. At this time, there was very little known about the phenomenon of wind shear.

Pipe Cleaners from the 4362nd were back in the air for Top Rung IV on Thursday and Friday, the 21st and 22nd. During the exercise, ten aircraft were launched, each flying to its designated orbit area. Eight of the sorties were scored effective. Two aircraft had transmitter problems, which caused them to be scored ineffective.

Friday, the 22nd, saw all kinds of military aircraft landing at the base. Unlike usual procedures, they taxied to the east side of the base and parked on the civilian airport ramp. The arrivals were part of the huge Aviation Day in conjunction with the dedication of the new facilities at the Lincoln Municipal Airport.

At 0900 on Saturday morning, SAC BRAT and fellow Explorer Scouts from Air Explorer Squadron 99 arrived at the new airport area. They were there to help park cars and man the first-aid station. They would also sell burgers and hot dogs to help make some money for the squadron coffer.

Before the crowd arrived, there was some time to look the aircraft over. SAC BRAT was drawn to the B-58 Hustler like a bee to honey. It was his first time to get close and personal with the sleek delta-wing bomber. Just sitting there on the ramp on its stork-like landing gear, it appeared to be going Mach 2. What a beautiful aircraft!

After the dedication ceremonies for the new terminal and airport facilities, the crowd was able to move out on the ramp and see such aircraft as the B-52, B-58, B-47, and KC-135 along with a host of other aircraft.

# 1964

The Nebraska Air National Guard showed off their new RF-84 along with the old F-86L in a farewell flight for the old Saber Jet. There was a mock refueling with a B-47 and KC-135. Then the Navy Shooting Stars parachute team thrilled the crowd with their aerial antics under a silk canopy.

Bob Hoover climbed into his bright yellow P-51 Mustang wearing his trademark business suit. He fired up the big Merlin engine and taxied to the runway. For the next fifteen minutes, he thrilled the crowd with loops, figure eights, snap rolls and high speed passes. He finished his flight with his signature landing. Touching down on one tire, then lifting and touching down on the other, repeating the process several times before settling on the landing gear and taxing back to the crowd line for a rousing round of applause.

There were other demonstrations at the show. Don Hickman recalled:

"Most of the aircraft made fly-bys and one in particular caught my eye. It was the brand new trainer being phased into pilot training called the T-38 Talon. It was painted a very bright white and had the shortest wings I had ever seen on an aircraft. It looked like it was traveling at 1000 miles per hour just sitting on the ramp. And when the two pilots climbed in and became airborne, I was thoroughly impressed by the takeoff. They flew this sleek new bird around the pattern and then approached the runway from the north at a very, very high rate of speed. In front of the crowd, the nose came up and this marvel of flight pointed up into a vertical climb. It kept climbing and climbing until it went completely out of sight in the crystal-clear dark blue sky. I kept looking and finally saw a very small white dot in the dark blue sky as they came back to level flight. I was so impressed with the T-38 that I told Bonnie that someday I would fly that bird."[3]

On Sunday, the air show crowd was given a special demonstration that wasn't on the program. The wail of the klaxon interrupted the air show at 1405. The Alert crews dashed to the aircraft and responded to a Coco Alert. To say the least, the Alert interrupted the show. Bob Hoover was in the air and was told to orbit south of the base. He pulled up and away and started his orbit near Pioneer's Park.

Within six minutes of the klaxon, the first bomber was rolling towards the south end of the ramp. When they arrived at the end of Runway 35, they poured on the power and moved down the runway for about a thousand feet, then pulled the power back. It was impressive to see the B-47s hit the runway at fifteen-second intervals. On the east side of the field, pungent clouds of black exhaust wafted towards the crowd.

One of the B-47s had a problem with its brake system and the crew deployed the drag chute, another unexpected thrill for the crowd. A lot of the air show crowd believed the Alert was staged as part of the show. Not really; it was just another routine Alert to keep the crews on their toes, air show or no air show. Regardless, the crowd loved it.

As soon as the runway was clear, Bob Hoover was cleared to continue his routine. His reentry was a low-level run with the Merlin engine screaming at full power, then pulling up in a spiraling aileron roll towards the heavens, completed by a roll over and Spilt-S back in the direction he had just come from. I have seen Bob Hoover fly his routine many times, but I will always remember that first time there at Lincoln.

It was back to air operations on Monday the 25th. Five aircraft launched for 50-8 training missions. Five more were scheduled to launch that afternoon for more training missions. Three crews would head for Spain for Reflex. Just another day at the patch.

May went into the books as a good month for the wing. There were 302 sorties flown. Bombing scores for the month were some of the best of the year with 98.8% effective. Air refueling rated a 97% effective and navigation was scored at 98.2 % effective. As the month ended, the wing had 1,219 officers and airmen assigned to the 307th. So far, there was no reprieve insight regarding the deactivation of the 307th.

Monday, June 1st, found the 307th launching the scheduled Reflex deployment to Spain. The changeover to Morón had been completed during the last week of May. The three Reflex bound B-47s landed at Morón and began the process of uploading for Alert.

Capt LeRoy McMath and Crew E-06 spent most of Monday planning for a routine training mission. Flying in the back seat would be Capt Stanley Toney. Capt Thomas Package would fill in for the regular navigator. They would be the third aircraft in a MITO launch scheduled for 0240 on June 3rd. The planned profile called for an air refueling, nav leg and a couple of bomb runs to hone the crew's SAC skills.

The crew arrived at Base Operations at 2330 on June 2nd. They went through another briefing and weather update. Engine start time, taxi and MITO procedures were coordinated among the three crews. Everything was ready, so they headed out to their assigned aircraft.

Arriving at 53-2363, Crew E-06 began the preflight walk around at 0040. Several minor discrepancies were found, none serious enough to cause a safety concern. The three captains climbed the ladder and squeezed into their seats to begin the pre-start checklist. At 0200, Capt McMath turned the engine start selector to #4 and began starting the engines.

The three aircraft moved out of their slots on the ramp and headed for the south end of the runway. Halting at the runup area, the three crews went through the before-takeoff checks. Radio checks, along with the "Guard" channel were made. At 0239 the lead aircraft called the cell to go to 80% power and stand by for brake release. At 0240, the lead aircraft released brakes and began the takeoff roll followed by the second B-47 fifteen seconds later.

Capt McMath released brakes and rolled onto Runway 35. He pushed the throttles forward to 100 %, waited for the power to stabilize, then hit the water alcohol switch. 2363 began rolling down the runway gaining speed with every turn of the tires.

Copilot Toney called, "60 knots.....NOW!" Moments later McMath called, "70 knots.....NOW!" In the nose, Tom Package started the timing check as 2363 continued to gain speed. Toney glanced at the engine instruments; everything was normal. McMath stole a glance at the instruments; again, everything was normal. So far it was a normal takeoff run.

About 3,200 feet down the runway, a compressor blade in the #3 engine fractured, pieces flew into other whirling blades, causing shrapnel like shards of metal to puncture the engine cowling. Within seconds the engine caught fire, fed by spraying JP-4 from punctured fuel lines.

Tower personnel saw the fire erupt and called. "Crate 21, you're on fire! ABORT, ABORT. ABORT!" Almost at the same instant, the crew saw the fire. McMath hit the intercom. "We have fire in #3. ABORT, ABORT, ABORT!" By this time, 2363 was hurtling down the runway at about 120 knots.

McMath pulled the throttles back to idle, shut down #2 and 3 and pulled their fire cutoff switches. He then pulled the drag chute lever. In the back seat, Toney deployed the approach chute. Standing on the brake pedals, McMath and Toney could feel the aircraft starting to slow down.

About 7,500 feet down the runway, 2363 ground to a halt with the brakes squealing. Inside, there was a mad scramble to get out of their seats and vacate the burning B-47 before she erased herself in a blinding explosion. There was a moment of near panic when the crew had difficulty getting the entry door open and the ladder down. The ladder and door hadn't been designed for easy deployment from inside the aircraft. Finally, the crew was able to get the door open and scrambled down the ladder.

Hitting the ground on a dead run, they raced away from the growing inferno. LeRoy McMath recalled:

"I heard an explosion and saw a flash. Almost immediately, the tower told us to abort the take off. We applied both brake and drag chutes and applied wheel brakes to stop the plane as soon as possible. We were able to go through our emergency procedures and, by the time we got out of the airplane, the fire trucks had already arrived. My track coach would have been proud of me. I set a new speed record running away from the burning aircraft."

Jim Rusher was working the night shift and recalled:

"53-2363 began its takeoff roll and after a few hundred feet of rolling, the #2 and #3 engine nacelle burst into flames which immediately engulfed the top and bottom of these engines and over and under the left wing. The aircraft commander chopped the throttles and started applying the brakes. The brakes emitted a sound that resembled the sound elephants would make.

"As the fire was still growing larger by the second and also illuminating the dark sky, the aircraft commander deployed the chutes in an attempt to slow the stricken bird to a stop. By this time the fire was really going. The fire was working up the wing and fuselage.

"All of us piled into a Metro maintenance van and drove up the ramp towards the burning B-47 in hope of possibly helping those on board get out. By the time we got closer, we saw the pilot and copilot on the ground running away from the plane. Someone found the navigator some time later.

"All that could be done now was to helplessly watch the plane burn. It was no doubt the biggest fire I had ever seen. This might sound crazy, but after the excitement was over, a thought came into my mind. At the time, a local radio station KLMS was offering $40 to anyone who called in the top news story of the day. I seriously thought about making the call. I never made the call to KLMS for fear I might very well suffer some serious disciplinary action from the Air Force for doing it. I always wondered who did collect the $40."

Base fire equipment arrived almost before the B-47 came to a stop. They began spraying the inferno with foam to suppress the fire. With a takeoff load of JP-4 aboard, they were fighting a losing battle. All they could do was try and contain the conflagration to the immediate area.

Everyone, especially the crew, knew Lady Luck had been riding in the fourth man seat that night. If the engine had failed just ten to fifteen seconds later, the aircraft would have been beyond refusal speed for a safe abort. If they had been making an ATO take off, they would have been committed to take 2352 into the air. Either way, the results most likely would have been fatal.

By daylight, 2363 was just a smoking pile of burnt aluminum junk. Since the main runway was blocked, airlines had to use the shorter diagonal runway on the north side of the base. Later that day, the investigation began to pursue the cause of the accident. The first step was debriefing the crew and tower personnel.

The accident on June 3rd was the first major accident for the 307th since March 7, 1963. The wing had flown over four thousand sorties and over 28,260 accident free hours. By late Friday afternoon, the site had been cleared and the main runway was back in service. The Reflex deployment on Wednesday and the return flight from Spain had to be delayed due to the accident; these flights were able to launch late Friday night.

On Monday, the 8th, two crews arrived on the flight line for routine training flights. The two crews went through preflight on 52-0331 and 53-2098. It was a regular mission except for the recovery of the aircraft. Instead of landing at Lincoln, they landed at the boneyard in Arizona. Later that day, three B-47s launched for Spain. They flew the Southern route and recovered at Morón about fifteen hours later.

Wednesday, the 10th, saw the launch of 53-2090, 53-1853 and 52-0335. The launch of these three aircraft was the first triple launch of aircraft headed for retirement. With five aircraft retired in the last two days, it was evident that the 307th was beginning to downsize as a result of the deactivation order.

The klaxon sent the Alert crews dashing to their planes at 1240 on June 17th. They climbed the ladder and prepared for engine start. Within six minutes, the first aircraft was ready to roll. They moved out and began taxiing towards Runway 17. After the Coco Alert, the planes made the long taxi back to the Alert pad, shut down and began the process of recocking the aircraft.

Thursday, the 25th, began like any other day at the Lincoln airplane patch. There was the normal report for duty and get cracking on the daily routine of getting the birds ready to fly. There was a Reflex return flight scheduled to arrive that evening. Along with the Reflex launch, there were several launches during the afternoon.

By noon, the sun was at its apex, beating down on the flight line with typical June vengeance. Along with the heat, the humidity was high, making for miserable, muggy conditions on the ramp. Base weather had forecast thunderstorms in the area for late afternoon and evening. With the hot and humid weather, both of the base swimming pools were packed with bathers trying to beat the heat.

Late that afternoon, large billowing clouds appeared from the southwest. With hot, humid air, residents of the patch knew a good old Nebraska thunderstorm was taking aim at Lincoln. Within minutes, the low rumble of distant thunder signaled the approaching thunderstorm. The sound of thunder was usually the first signal to the flight line troops to button up and head for higher ground, or at least shelter of some kind.

The storm arrived in typical fashion. Jagged bolts of lightning flashed across the heavens, followed by ear-splitting cracks of thunder. The first large drops of rain hit the ramp with a loud splat. Within minutes, the flight line was awash with water from the sky. High winds blew the rain in sheets across the base. Anything not secured went tumbling off, to who-knew-where.

For about twenty minutes, the storm pelted the area with heavy rain, high winds and marble size hail. On the backside of the huge supercell, a low hanging wall cloud produced a tornado that briefly touched down near Raymond. There were several farms damaged, but no one was injured.

For the rest of the night, line after line of thunderstorms moved across Lincoln and dumped heavy rain on the area. None of the storms was as strong as the first cell. They were just small storms adding more rain to the growing total. By midnight, almost four inches of rain had fallen in the Lincoln area. With all of the rain, Oak Creek was running bank full.

Regardless of the weather, the Alert birds were under constant guard by Combat Defense personnel. Don Brant wrote, "I smoked back then and we were allowed to smoke in the Alert areas, but had to move off-post to the center of the taxiways. That's where we did most of our talking. The worst part was when the MMS (Munitions Maintenance Squadron) guys would run out of daylight on the Christmas tree area and park a line of bomb cradles with nukes at the side of the access taxiway away from the Alert birds. It was inside the secure fenced area so only one guard would be posted with the bombs. It didn't happen often, but for us it was too often. You were posted alone in relative darkness and seldom, if ever, saw a supervisor in a CDS truck with coffee. Eight to twelve hours is a long time to listen to crickets and slap mosquitoes. It was even worse when rumors of an imminent ORI were circulating.

# 1964

One of my worst nights was on that post in a night-long rain. I never saw a supervisor and spent the entire night babysitting those eggs alone, wet, hungry and cold. I was so angry and miserable, I wet down a tire on one of the bomb cradles. Didn't do much; rain washed it off. But I felt somehow better after my 'reckless, rebellious and totally unobserved protestation.'"

Except for the accident on June 3rd, the 307th had posted a good month. At the end of the month there were 1,219 officers and airmen assigned to the wing. The wing had flown over 1,900 hours during June. The 307th made the changeover to the new Reflex base without major difficulties. Fourteen high-time B-47s had been retired to the boneyard during the month. This reflected the continued phasing out of the B-47 as a deterrent force in SAC.

Wednesday, July 1st, was another day at the base. There were the usual training flights launching during the day, along with a Reflex return flight from Spain that was to arrive home later that day. There was a Bravo Alert late that afternoon, sending the Alert crews scrambling to the birds for yet another practice Alert to keep the crews honed to a razor edge.

The accident investigation board finished their report on the June 3rd accident. Their report and conclusion centered on the failure of compressor blades in the #3 engine. The failure apparently occurred during a momentary compressor stall during water augmentation. The blade failure caused a fire that spread from the engine nacelle and caused the destruction of the aircraft.

The board was critical of the use of night MITO procedures during training flights:

"It is the opinion of the board that night MITO training is not valid as a <u>reoccurring</u> training requirement in view of the catastrophic accident potential created. While the board is of opinion that MITO abort procedures under optimum execution are adequate for the safety of the aircraft and crew involved, the realization that this requirement exists primarily as a one-time EWO launch procedure gives rise to the question of its value as a <u>reoccurring</u> training item. In this connection, it should not be overlooked that, had this been an ATO takeoff, the ATO would already have been fired and the pilot committed to takeoff when the engine exploded."

At 1520 on Friday, the 3rd, the klaxon went off for the first time in July. It was a Green Dot Coco response. All of the 307th aircraft except one were scored effective. PASTE 47 missed the Alert because the #2 engine scavenger pump was leaking. The aircraft was repaired and recocked for Alert.

Over in Spain, Billy Lyons was looking forward to returning to Lincoln after pulling a Reflex deployment. He recalled:

"We were preparing for return to Lincoln from our tour on July 3rd, leading a two-ship cell. After completing preflight, the other AC and I were standing out in front of our aircraft stretching our legs before getting back in for engine start. We were watching, as a Northrop test pilot was demonstrating a NF-5 (fighter version of the T-38) to the Spanish Air Force 'heavies' with a Spanish AF general in the back seat. His finale was a loop right over the runway. He apparently entered the loop too low (the field elevation is about 2,000 feet) and did not have enough altitude to complete the loop without hitting the ground. They hit alongside the runway doing about 350 knots pulling 8 G's and scattered debris along and on the runway. Unfortunately, both pilots were casualties.

"We were about thirty minutes from our scheduled takeoff time and, if we were not airborne within 30 minutes after our scheduled takeoff time, we would lose our clearance and probably our tankers for a nonstop flight to Lincoln. We really didn't have a lot of hope getting off within these limits and started to mentally map out a backup plan. All our maintenance troops who were going to launch us were picked up to help clear the debris off the runway.

"Another factor was that a KC-135 tanker had launched earlier from Torrejon and was due to land in a few minutes after giving a maximum offload to an Airborne Alert B-52 in an air refueling area near the base. The tanker was at minimum fuel and would have to land soon.

"The runway was quickly cleared and we were instructed to start engines and prepare to take off as soon as our maintenance troops returned from clearing the runway. We expedited engine start and taxi and made it to the number one position for takeoff with about one minute left for both of us to start takeoff or we would lose our overwater clearance.

"I told number two to 'tuck it in,' which he did. Normally, he would have been about a minute behind us but, not wanting to be left behind, he was somewhat less than a minute in trail, probably somewhat like a MITO we had practiced back home.

"It was a warm July day and we had a long takeoff roll from being somewhat heavier than planned and the high field pressure altitude. The water-alcohol augmentation we used to get extra thrust from the engines for takeoff was expended just after we broke ground and had the gear coming up. We didn't have much climb capability. I could see the prongs on the TV antennas on the apartment buildings in Madrid as we flew over them. Have a Nice Siesta! We got our tankers and made it home without further delay."

The 4th fell on Saturday. Across the base, the day was filled with jammed picnic areas and a lot of boats on Bowling Lake. Every ball diamond on the base was busy with marathon softball games. That evening, folks lined up early around Bowling Lake for the gala fireworks show. When darkness finally fell, the sky above the lake erupted in a magnificent patriotic show of blazing star shells and cascading colors.

After a fun filled weekend of celebration, it was back to the job at hand of keeping the force ready. That Monday, there was the usual Reflex launch and scheduled morning and afternoon training flights. All of the launches went off on schedule that day.

The July 10th edition of the *Jet Scoop* featured a special section on the 307th Recovery Section. The full page showed photos of the team going about the daily business of getting the B-47s ready for the next flight. The front page had a rather interesting photo of the number six engine on a B-47. It showed TSgt Billy Hill in the intake and an unknown pair of legs protruding from the back of the tail cone. It was captioned, "Quite A Stretch".

Launch crews were preparing 53-4223 for a Bar None mission on Tuesday, July 14th. She had been towed to the refueling pits and was taking on a full fuel load. A valve stuck open and within seconds, hundreds of gallons of JP-4 covered the concrete around the aircraft. One stray spark, it would be bye-bye bird, along with others in the nearby flock. Fire equipment responded and hosed the fuel spill down with foam to prevent a fire. Other aircraft were towed out of harm's way. It took over four hours to clean up the smelly mess. With all of the fumes from the foam and fuel floating along the flight line, a lot of the troops lost their lunch and came away with unbelievable headaches.

Three B-47s left Morón on Tuesday, July 21st for the return trip to Lincoln. The flight was routine all the way across the pond until the B-47s were just off the coast of South Carolina. The three crews reported they were being painted by some type of radar and the radio frequencies were being interfered with. This type of incident happened from time to time when Soviet "fishing" vessels were in the area off the US coast. Everyone knew they were there and they were doing more than just fishing. It all added up to another game of Cold War cat and mouse.

## Cold War Cornhuskers: The 307th Bomb Wing Lincoln Air Force Base Nebraska 1955-1965

Capt Thomas Sutton and Crew E-69 spent July 23rd planning for a mission scheduled for an early launch on July 24. The mission included a navigation evaluation by Maj John Sakry of the 307th Standardization Division. The mission was canceled due to a lack of time for adequate crew rest following the mission planning and briefing. The mission was rescheduled for Monday, the 27th. Maj Sakry was scheduled to fly with a different crew that day, so the evaluation portion of Crew E-69's mission was canceled. In view of the cancellation, Crew E-69 spent the weekend relaxing and spending time with their families.

Crew E-69 reported to Base Operations at 0455 on Monday, July 27th. They were briefed on last-minute changes in the mission along with the latest weather along their planned route. The weather looked good, so there should be no major problems along the way. There was a slight chance of thunderstorms moving into the Lincoln area late that afternoon.

SSgt Bill Baker had originally been scheduled to fly on the 24th as the fourth man so he could get his flight time in for the month and get his flight pay. With the change in the mission plan, he had been bumped from the flight. Then, there was the cancellation and rescheduled flight, so Baker was cleared again to fly. He was waiting for the crew when they arrived at the aircraft at 0545 that morning.

Preflight walk around was completed with no major problems found. The crew climbed aboard and went through the pre-start checklist. Engines were started on time and the aircraft was ready to taxi. At that time, the routine flight became a little confused.

A last-second cancellation of another flight made Maj Sakry available for the navigation evaluation again. The command post did some shuffling and quick-change paperwork and the evaluation flight was on again. Jim Rusher recalled:

"Baker and I told the aircraft commander that after all engines were running and after everything was ready, he (Baker) would board the aircraft with his parachute and helmet and take his position in the fourth man seat. I would push the ladder up and close the latch on the entrance hatch and pull the chocks. The aircraft commander checked Baker's orders and signed them so Baker could get his flight pay.

"Once all the engines were running, the first B-47 began to taxi out. I had helped Baker on board and secured the aircraft. I disconnected my intercom headset from the J-box and pulled the wheel chocks. Then I ran over to the nose of my aircraft and gave the aircraft commander on 2366 the signal to roll. 2366 began to roll and after just a few feet came to a full stop. The aircraft commander looked directly at me and gave me the signal to install the chocks and plug my headset back into the J-box. I wondered what was going on!

"After I plugged into the intercom, the aircraft commander told me to open the entry hatch and lower the ladder. I asked him what was going on. He responded by saying that he just received a radio call that Baker had been bumped from the flight. About that time, a vehicle drove up and stopped right in front of the airplane. A major got out of the car and grabbed his equipment out of the back of the vehicle.

"Baker had walked over to my idling B-47 along with his flight gear and was fuming over getting 'bumped'. I finished buttoning up 2366 and gave the aircraft commander the signal to taxi. Baker was very angry he had been bumped from the flight at the last possible moment. Baker, another crew chief and I began picking up and loading our tools and equipment into our vehicles while waiting for the birds to fly. As crew chiefs, we couldn't leave the flight line until our airplanes were in the air."

After the change, Swan 12 taxied to the end of Runway 17, with the other aircraft in the lead. They waited at the runup pad for the first B-47 to depart. When the lead aircraft was breaking ground, Sutton called the tower for final take off instructions and clearance for a southbound takeoff. Sutton pushed the six throttles forward with his right hand and waited for the power to stabilize at 100% power. Clouds of black exhaust billowed back as the engines burned the combination of JP-4 and water-alcohol. Brakes were released and Swan 12 started rolling down the runway.

Like always, a lot of the troops on the flight line paused for a moment to watch the takeoff. At the 70-knot check everything was normal. When SWAN 12 reached the liftoff position, Sutton put gentle back pressure on the yoke to ease the B-47 into the air. Swan 12 stayed on the runway, eating up distance for several hundred feet more. Then, she slowly lifted into the air, but stayed dangerously close to the runway. Those watching the takeoff knew Swan 12 was in trouble.

At what seemed to be the last second, the B-47 climbed for a moment. Then it started to veer towards the right and settled towards the ground. Swan 12 was barely in the air when it crossed the end of the runway and cleared Oak Creek. Then, the #6 engine hit the ground near a country road just off the end of the runway. On the other side of the road the B-47 impacted the ground and was engulfed in a sliding fireball. Jim Archer wrote:

"Shortly after liftoff and passing over the end of the runway, I noticed something very different about this take off. Black smoke that is characteristic of the J-47 engine ceased coming from the number six engine. Number six is attached to the wing near the tip of the right wing. The obvious loss of power on this engine on takeoff while the other five were at full power caused the crippled aircraft to yaw to the right and then begin its descent toward the ground.

"The best way I can describe it is to say that 2363 kind of pancaked into the ground in a right yaw. There was never enough altitude for anyone to eject. The airplane struck the ground and was followed by a huge orange fireball and plume of black smoke.

"Baker and I just looked at each other in disbelief. He said to me, 'That was supposed to have been me!' I can tell you he was white as a sheet, as he had just cheated death. I don't remember any enlisted crew chief ever complaining again about being 'bumped.'"

Within moments of the crash, fire equipment arrived on the scene and started fighting the inferno. The crash site was just a couple of hundred yards from Interstate 80 and the fire appeared to be spreading towards the highway. It took several hours to beat the fuel fed inferno into submission. Base security forces secured the crash site so onlookers couldn't interfere with the efforts to control the fire.

SAC BRAT happened to be up that morning and heard the sirens from the Lincoln Fire Department as they went whizzing by on West "O" with sirens wailing. Looking to the west, there was a black cloud of smoke that could be seen through the trees. He jumped on his trusty bike and headed in the direction of the commotion. SAC BRAT managed to get to an overpass for I-80 near Garfield Elementary School. From there he could see the crash site and the flaming wreckage of a once-proud B-47. It was a terrible scene of destruction that was firmly etched into the mind of the young teenager.

Later that morning, operations resumed with the launches flying over the charred remains of Swan 12. It was a grim reminder that flying could go from routine to tragic in a matter of seconds. Before the wreckage was cool, the investigation began with the gathering of flight records and taking photos of the crash site from every angle possible.

In mid-July, the 818th Strategic Aerospace Division held a local competition between the 98th and 307th to pick a crew to represent the Division at the Emergency War Order Competition. The local competition was a "knock down, drag out" affair. When the competitive dust settled, Crew E-65 from the 307th was on top of the heap. Capt Eugene Hickman (AC), Capt Harold "Pete" Todd (CP) and Capt Laurie Bunten (Nav) were off to Barksdale to represent Lincoln at the 2nd Air Force EWO Knowledge Competition on July 30th. Pete Todd recalled the competition:

"I don't know what started the competition, but it had been underway for most of the year, at least in 2nd Air Force units. It didn't become an annual event, probably because it was found to be too expensive and cumbersome to administer. Throughout the competition, each time a crew went on Alert, there was a head-to-head competition among the crews on Alert in what I recall as a single elimination format. I believe the questions for the quiz format were developed by the Wing EWO plans staff and covered any and all aspects of EWO operations.

"Eventually, our crew made it to the wing championships and won. I would have thought that both the 307th and 98th BWs would send their top crews to the SAC finals, but for some reason (cost?), only one crew was to represent LAFB, so our crew met the 98th top crew at the Alert facility briefing room for the 818th Air Division 'playoffs'. The two wing staffs collaborated on the questions to be posed. A moderator would ask the question and the crew, using only materials they would have available in their Combat Mission Folders (CMFs) on an actual combat mission, raced to come up with a collective response. Whoever was to answer would press a large knob on a tabletop box that would activate a buzzer and simultaneously inactivate the opponents' buzzer (to avoid 'photo finishes').

"The 98th-307th competition was hard fought. The 98th Wing Commander was in the room as well as all the Alert crews from both wings. (The 307th Wing Commander was absent). I don't remember the actual number of questions, but the first crew to get three out of five or four out of seven or whatever answers, would win. On one particularly complex question, I hit the buzzer and delivered the answer. The 98th Wing Commander (who was supposed to be there as an observer) declared my response wrong/incomplete and nobody tried to overrule him. That made the competition personal for me. I wanted not only to beat the other crew, but also this colonel who had blatantly subverted the competition.

"At the finish, each crew had the same number of 'correct' answers with one question to go. The final question asked for the IFF (radar transponder) settings for a particular in-flight situation. I was exultant because I knew the answer cold from previous study. While the other crew was scrambling to locate the information in their reference materials, I locked eyes with the 98th Wing Commander, reached over, tapped the buzzer and said firmly, "Mode 1, code 73; Mode 3, code 77." My crew had won the competition and the wing commander stalked out of the room with hardly a perfunctory 'congratulations'. The crew we had beaten was considerably more gracious.

"An interesting historical sidelight: The aircraft commander of the crew we beat that day, C. Truman Spangrud, and I, crossed paths often in our respective Air Force careers. In 1986, he became a three-star General and, as Commander of Air University (AU) at Maxwell AFB, Alabama, he was my boss in my roles as Vice Commander of the AU and Commandant of the Air War College. He was never anything but complimentary and respectful about our clash so many years before.

"The 2nd Air Force-level competition was held at Barksdale AFB, LA. We were to fly there on a C-47, but takeoff was delayed due to Tom Sutton's crash that morning, a somber beginning for what should have been a fun trip."

The competition format at Barksdale was different from the wing-level, head-to-head crew competitions used previously. Each crew was in a separate room with a moderator posing the questions and a SAC officer observing the process. As before, the only reference materials that could be consulted were those that would be available to a crew in-flight on an EWO mission. Not all the questions were drawn from those materials; some came out of tactical doctrine manuals and other documents that were studied at home, but not carried on an EWO mission.

Each crew, by aircraft type, answered a set of questions that were identical and specific to that aircraft's mission. Results were tallied later and a winning crew determined in each aircraft category. Crew E-65 from the 307th won the B-47 division in the 2nd Air Force. They were presented with the awards and honors at the presentation ceremonies by Lt Gen David Wade, Commander of the 2nd Air Force. Even though the B-47 was being phased out, it was quite an honor for Crew E-65 and the 307th.

The 307th started air operations for August on Monday the 3rd. It was another day of routine launches for training flights across the country. There was a Reflex deployment to Morón as part of the usual Monday activities. One of the aircraft flying to Spain had a minor problem with the hydraulic system. After consulting with the command post, the problem was resolved and the mission was completed without further problems.

On the 5th, the 307th was given a special operation to accomplish. They were going to do something the wing hadn't done in a while. The mission called for a mass gas air refueling. The 307th would provide a total of twelve aircraft for the mission. Six would fly on the 5th and the other six would launch on the 6th.

Planning for the operation had started with a directive from SAC on July 31st. The directive outlined the mission and what part the 307th would play. The first six aircraft would be generated and ready for the execution order by 0900 on August 5th. When the execution message arrived, the first three aircraft would launch using MITO procedures. The second wave would launch an hour later using MITO to get airborne.

"Jumbo" sent the execution message for the mission at 0920 for a launch window beginning at 1140 on the 5th. The crews scheduled to fly were ready and waiting for the word to come down from SAC. They headed for their aircraft and preflighted the planes. Engine start was on time and the first three B-47s taxied to the end of Runway 17.

The lead ship held short for final clearance with the two sister ships holding in place for the MITO. The tower cleared the cell for takeoff. Throttles were pushed to takeoff power and the first B-47 began rolling down the runway, followed by the others at fifteen-second intervals. The lead climbed straight ahead, while the other two pulled a little left or right to avoid the jet wash and wake turbulence of the bomber ahead.

Climbout was according to a Geneva Departure. Over Geneva, Nebraska, the cell turned and flew north to Rapid City, South Dakota. Near Rapid City, they made contact with their three KC-135s from the 906th AREFS out of Minot Air Force Base. Rendezvous was accomplished with no problems. The bombers slowly moved into position, hooked up and started taking on fuel. The three B-47s took on their fuel as the profile called for, then the cell broke up with each aircraft flying its individual mission profile.

The second wave departed Lincoln and flew the same route to the tankers. The first two bombers refueled with no problems. By the time the third B-47 started moving into position, they were getting close to a line of billowing thunderheads over the eastern part of North Dakota. Moving into the weather, there were several disconnects and a bumpy ride as they broke in and out of the clouds. After about forty minutes of white-knuckle, roller coaster flying, the fuel transfer was completed and the final B-47 disconnected and continued its profile flight.

The wing repeated the mission the next day. The first wave flew the mission with no problems for a textbook mission. The second wave found the same problem with weather as the day before. This time the clouds

# Cold War Cornhuskers: The 307th Bomb Wing Lincoln Air Force Base Nebraska 1955-1965

were big and angry looking supercells. Only one aircraft was able to refuel. The turbulence was beyond safety limits for the other two aircraft to attempt hook- up.

The two-day operation had garnered the 307th ten effective refuelings and two scored as aborts due to weather. The bombing scores for the operation were "Outstanding". One crew scored two shacks on their Short Look Large Charge bomb run. SAC HQ sent an "attaboy" message to the wing for the way the 307th had conducted the mission.

The August flying schedule was plagued by bad weather at Lincoln and all across the Midwest. Thunderstorms ravaged the patch during mid-month, causing cancellations, postponements and diversions to other bases. Reflex deployments and return flights were delayed due to weather. Mid-August would go into the record as one of the stormiest on record.

On Friday, August 21st, there was a formal Dining-In at the Officers' Club. The guest speaker for the evening's affair was Maj Gen William Martin from the Pentagon. After dinner and speeches, he presented several awards to the crews of the 307th. The trophy for the best bombing score on the Cozy Couch route went to Maj Glen "Pappy" Hesler and crew. The N.V. Meeks Memorial Trophy was awarded to the 371st Bomb Squadron.

The weekly Reflex flight launched for Spain on Monday, the 24th. The flight was routine until just after coasting out. One of the aircraft started getting an abnormal EGT reading on the #5 engine. They pulled the power back a little, but the temperature stayed in the abnormal range. The crew had no choice but to shut the engine down and turn back towards the coast. They landed at Hunter AFB, Georgia, on five engines and spent several days waiting for the engine to be fixed.

The last Reflex return flight of the month left Morón on the 27th. Out over the Atlantic, the homeward bound B-47s performed a fireout of the tail guns. Each of the aircraft scored 80% fireout. The rest of the flight was just another routine crossing of the pond.

A blaring klaxon kicked off September at 0640 on the morning of the 1st. Alert crews stumbled out of their sacks and climbed into their flight suits, grabbed their boots and headed for the door. Scrambling up the ladders, they climbed into their ejection seats, stuffed their heads into helmets and began turning #4. The earphones crackled with a Green Dot message to execute a Coco Alert.

The first 307th aircraft was rolling six minutes after the klaxon went off. The active runway was Runway 17, so it was a short taxi, then a rolling start at full power. Water-alcohol was simulated, then the power was pulled back as the one thousand foot marker flashed by. After turning off the runway, there was the two-and-a-half-mile taxi back to the Alert ramp.

The last B-47 to hit the runway was a 98th bird. They started their roll seventeen minutes after the klaxon went off. That was two minutes over the warning criterion from BMEWS. Shortly after arriving back at the mole hole, the crew was summoned to a briefing room. They had to explain why it had taken seventeen minutes to respond to the Alert. When they emerged from the briefing room, they had the unmistakable look of having experienced a high-level butt chewing.

307th Headquarters received an operational message from Omaha regarding the flying schedule. The TWX came in on Wednesday the 2nd. Starting on the 15th, training missions would include fighter intercepts as part of the profile. The program was designed to give pilots from Air Defense Command, training in ground-controlled intercepts and making passes at bombers along the northern tier of the country.

Friday, the 11th, was another busy day on the flight line. Aircraft were serviced for launch on the regular flying schedule. There was a Reflex launch early that evening. Along with the flying that day, there was a Bravo Alert sending the crews dashing to the Alert birds. All aircraft from the 307th were scored effective with an average response time of five and a half minutes.

The big news of the day came that evening during the nightly news programs. Earlier that day, the Pentagon announced a list of military bases that would be closed as part of budget cutbacks in the military, along with the never-ending changes in strategic thinking by McNamara and his Whiz Kids. The city of Lincoln was shocked with the news: Lincoln Air Force Base would be closed, with a target date of December 1965. This appeared to be the final nail in the 307th's coffin. Not only would the 307th be deactivated, the 98th and all military units at the base would be deactivated.

Monday, the 14th, saw another routine day at the patch. There were the usual launches for training flights and another Reflex deployment. Crews scheduled to fly on Tuesday spent the better part of the day planning their missions. Every detail of the flight was planned down to the second. Gross takeoff weight, S1 and S2 speed, headings for the legs to be flown, refueling time and how much fuel would be taken on. Targets were studied for offset points and radar photos were reviewed. By the time they briefed back the mission, the crews could almost fly the mission blindfolded.

One special aspect of the mission plan was the addition of fighter attacks. During the latter part of the nav leg, the crews were to participate in the fighter intercepts. According to the Omaha directive, fighters would intercept the B-47s along the northern tier. The B-47s would fly straight and level like a sitting duck. The bomber crew would defend themselves only during the final fighter pass only. After a full day of planning, the flight crews went home for crew rest.

On the 15th, 53-2139 was on the flying schedule. Her crew reported to Base Operations for final mission briefing and weather update. The crew arrived at the aircraft and went through preflight. Climbing the ladder, they moved to their positions and strapped into their seats. They went through the checklist and started engines. At the end of Runway 17, they powered up and started takeoff. At the correct S2 speed, they lifted off and started climbing into the clear Nebraska sky.

2139 continued climbing and, over Beatrice, they began a turn that would take them towards Grand Island and another turn for Sioux City. From there it would be a gentle turn towards Des Moines and the air refueling control point. They rendezvoused with the tanker and took on the required fuel load.

Dropping off the boom, 2139 started climbing back to 35,000 feet near Moline, Illinois, then a heading correction for a radio checkpoint at Milwaukee. Over the famous beer city, they made a turn and flew northwest to the gunnery range over Lake Michigan. They were not going to fire the guns; the range was another checkpoint to start descending for the low-level oil burner route.

Crossing of the Mackinac Straits, they could see the beautiful bridge across the straits. There may have been a momentary urge to line up and fly under the bridge. The urge evaporated knowing what happened to the pilot that flew his B-47 under the bridge back in 1959. It wasn't worth getting grounded for a thrill-seeking moment.[4]

Turning north, they flew over Sault St. Marie, Michigan, and out over Lake Superior for a fifty-mile leg before turning back. By now, they were flying about five hundred feet above the blue water of the big lake. The crew of the big iron ore boat most likely never saw the B-47 boring down on them until it flashed by in a roar of six jet engines. It would take several days for the ore boat to reach Duluth; 2139 would be there in less than an hour.

2139 entered the Iron Man oil burner route and flew west for the Short Look bomb run, then climbed out of the oil burner route near Hurley, Wisconsin. Climbing out, they made a radio check at Duluth, then turned towards Fargo, North Dakota, and another checkpoint.

254

# 1964

Just west of Fargo, 2139 was intercepted by an F-106 from the 5th Fighter Interceptor Squadron out of Minot. For about the next twenty minutes the crew played target, as the graceful delta winged "Six-pack" made pass after pass from the rear. On the last pass, the copilot turned his seat to the rear and tracked the incoming fighter on radar. The 106 pulled alongside the left wing for a moment, the pilot gave a thumbs-up, then gracefully banked and slid away, disappearing in the distant clouds.

After the fighter attacks, the crew pointed 2139 towards the south for a leg to Hastings, Nebraska, for a Short Look bomb run. Leaving Hastings bomb plot, they flew into the Nebraska Sandhills, then turned for home plate. Letdown was from the north for landing on Runway 17. Gear down and four green, approach chute out, best flare speed plus five, flaps set. Across Highway 34, let her float a little. Over the numbers, the B-47 settled towards the concrete. With a squeal and puff of smoke the rear tires touched down, then the drag chute billowed, slowing the B-47 to manageable speed. Mission Accomplished.

For the rest of the month, crews from the 307th would repeat the role of acting as targets. They would provide training for the Montana, Minnesota and North Dakota Air National Guard as well as regular Air Force fighter units along the northern tier of the United States. The Air Defense Command, Operation "Turkey Shoot" had been aptly named in view of the B-47s' being unable to defend themselves.

The *Jet Scoop* edition for September 20th was full of the latest news from around the patch. On page twelve, there was an article of personal interest titled "Base Sharpshooters Earn Trophies". The article centered on the base rifle team's performance at the Nebraska State Championship Smallbore Match held at Omaha the previous weekend.

The team came away from the match with fifteen trophies. Team members were MSgt Ralph Peak, 98th A&E, TSgt Sedgefield Hill, 307th Headquarters Squadron, A3C James McCabe, 818th CE, and A3C Marion Brown, 818th Supply. Sedge "Red" Hill took top honors, winning first place in the Grand Aggregate Sharpshooters Class in a total of 13 matches. The win gave "Deadeye Red" the honor of being the best smallbore rifleman in the State of Nebraska for 1964. Several more medals and trophies were added to the growing collection at the Hill House.

Almost everyone on base knew what was coming on Monday, the 28th. That was the day Operation Great Effort was scheduled. It was the base wide yearly exercise to see how the base would react and function during a nuclear attack. The Base Exchange, Commissary and Service Station would be closed for the entire day. The base would be closed to all except essential duty personnel.

For once, the Alert crews knew the klaxon was going to go off. It would be the signal to start the exercise. They had done the regular morning preflight early so they would be inside the mole hole and waiting for the war games to begin. Right on time, the klaxon went off at 0915, sending the crews to the Alert aircraft. They would execute a Coco Alert to see how many birds could be flushed before the incoming nuclear weapon detonated.

Within four minutes, the first B-47 was ready to roll. They made a quick taxi to Runway 17 and poured on the JP-4 for the rolling start. All of the aircraft were scored effective. Arriving back at the Alert ramp, the birds were serviced and recocked. The Alert crews and other personnel were exempted from the war games since they had to be ready, just in case Great Effort turned out to be Armageddon.

Shortly after the klaxon went off, the sirens on base went off signaling all base personnel to take cover and begin the activities of the day. Personnel went to their respective shelters and, for the next eight hours, reacted according to the emergency plan that would be used in case of a real nuclear attack.

The reaction plan was full of well-planned ways for the base to function. There were the designated shelters and casualties were taken to aid stations for triage and treatment. Fire crews stood by to fight fires. The command post would be in contact with Omaha via special links for further instructions.

October began by launching a Reflex deployment on the 1st. It was a normal fifteen-hour flight in the confined cramped quarters of the B-47. We have to remember, there were no rest areas to pull off the road and stretch their legs.

During a trip to Nebraska, I was granted the privilege of getting up close and personal with the B-47 preserved at the Strategic Air and Space Museum near Ashland, Nebraska. As I climbed the ladder into the belly of the B-47, my mind wandered back to the last time I had been in a B-47 over forty years ago. I was a lot younger back then and a great deal smaller around the middle.

For over forty minutes, I moved around inside the old bird taking pictures. I squeezed into the nose and fought my way into the navigator's seat. Then, I moved down the very narrow aisle, stopping to climb up into the front seat, then back seat. I tried to make mental notes to compare with the Dash-1 when I got home. After shooting a couple of rolls of film, I struggled back down the ladder.

Even though the B-47 was inside an air-conditioned building, it was still very hot inside. By the time I got back down the ladder, I was wringing wet. I came away from my adventure with a renewed, healthy respect for those who had to work inside the cramped confines of the cockpit and flight crews who spent hour after hour strapped to those wonderfully "comfortable" ejection seats, or the slab of aluminum known as the fourth man seat.

Even though the 307th was scheduled to be deactivated within six months, there was no word as to when the wing would stop Reflex deployments or stand down from Alert. Until the word comes in from Omaha, it would be business as usual for the 307th at Lincoln airplane patch.

So, it was a full flying schedule for Monday, October 5th. Five Bar None flights were launched during the morning, followed by six 50-8 training flights that afternoon. Along with that, there were three aircraft departing for Reflex. It all added up to a lot of work for the launch and recovery crews.

On Wednesday, the 7th, a crew preflighted 53-4219 for a mission to fill some 50-8 squares. After preflight, the crew climbed aboard and began going through the fifty-two item pre-engine start checklist. With the fireguard standing by, they began turning #4 engine. At the preplanned time, they taxied to the end of the runway and held for tower clearance and time hack for takeoff.

Another B-47 taxied out behind 4219 and was holding short of the runway waiting for 4219 to roll. They could see the power come up to a hundred percent, then the unmistakable sign of the water-alcohol kicking—plumes of dense, black exhaust boiling from the engines, as 4219 started rolling down the runway.

Airspeed started building as raw thrust overcame the inertia of the aircraft. "Coming up on 70 knots...Now!' In the nose, the navigator pressed his stopwatch for the timing check. Everything was going according to the profile. "S1...Now! Airspeed looks good. We're committed!"

Without warning, the water alcohol cut off, producing a noticeable loss of thrust. They had plenty of runway ahead and, at the moment, it looked like it would be needed. The seven thousand foot marker flashed by, then the eight thousand foot marker. Speed was 140 knots, then it climbed to 145, the computed take off speed. Gentle back pressure on the yoke and 4219 lifted off the concrete. As she started a slow climb, the gear came up and settled into the wells. They hurdled the low hill at the end of the runway and crossed "O" Street a little lower than normal, but they were in the air to stay.

The rest of the mission was completely routine. At the mission debriefing, the crew filled out the paperwork including a write up on the 781 about the water-alcohol system. Just another mission in the day-to-day operations of the 307th. Routine, yes, but good planning and crew coordination overcame a potentially dangerous situation. They all agreed it got a bit hairy for a few moments. Training and following procedures had snatched another one from the Grim Reaper.

The 307th was hit with a no notice ORI on Tuesday, the 13th. It all began with the irritating wail of the klaxon at 1020 that morning. Like always, the Alert crews piled out of the mole hole like NFL running backs and scrambled to the aircraft. The first aircraft reported ready in five and a half minutes. They were informed to execute a Coco Alert and it was the beginning of an ORI.

While the Alert crews were executing the Alert, the 307th wing staff was busy pulling mission folders to use on the ORI. Other members of the battle staff were spreading the word that the wing was under the watchful eye of the ORI umpires. Word spread across the flight line like wildfire.

Alert crews reported back to the mole hole for the test on their knowledge of EWO procedures. Out on the ramp, munitions crews pulled out the download checklist and started removing the weapons from the Alert aircraft. The aircraft on Alert would fly the first wave so they could be recocked and placed back on ground Alert as quickly as possible.

The ORI mission would be based on a Bar None evaluation sortie. The nine Alert aircraft would lead off, followed by nine other aircraft, which were presently being generated. Launch would consist of three cells of three aircraft using MITO to get off the ground. There would be one hour between cell launches. The follow-on force would fly the same mission profile the following day.

Later that afternoon, the aircraft had been downloaded and prepared for the first wave. Flight crews had a chance to study the mission profile and study the target. The crews reported to their aircraft and went through the preflight walkaround. Everything checked out; no major problems. It was time to climb aboard, start engines and fly the mission.

The first three aircraft taxied to the end of Runway 17 and held short for final clearance from the tower. The tower cleared them for takeoff after giving a final report on wind and local conditions. The lead aircraft went to 80% power, released brakes and turned onto the runway. As soon as they were lined up on the center strip, they pushed the throttles to full power, let it stabilize, then hit the water-alcohol switch. Clouds of black smoke billowed as the first B-47 started rolling down the runway. Fifteen seconds later the second B-47 was rolling.

By the time the third aircraft powered, up the runway was covered with thick clouds of black exhaust from the other two aircraft. Forward visibility was next to nothing. So far, they hadn't heard anything on the radio from the tower that would signal an abort. At 100% power, they started rolling down the runway. As they lifted off, the B-47 shuttered and rocked in the turbulent jet wash of the preceding two aircraft. As soon as they were in the air they banked a little to the right and smoother air.

The profile called for a Fairbury Departure. The cell flew a 200-degree heading for the forty-two nautical mile climb out. Over Fairbury, they turned to a heading of 294 degrees and flew to Grand Island. Arriving over the city, they turned south towards Hill City, Kansas, the Air Refueling Control Point.

At the ARCP, the cell began rendezvous with the KC-135s. The cell leader moved into the position, made contact and began the fuel transfer. When the transfer was complete, the lead aircraft dropped away from the boom and continued to the next leg of the mission. The refueling served as a built-in cell separation device for the mission. It would allow at least thirty minutes between aircraft for the bomb runs later in the mission.

After refueling, the lead aircraft turned over Brookfield, Missouri, and headed for St. Louis, the entry point for the navigation leg. Checking in over St. Louis, they turned and flew to Decatur, Illinois, their first mandatory checkpoint. From Decatur it was on to Chicago, Madison, and Minneapolis, finishing that leg just south of Aberdeen, South Dakota. At Aberdeen, there was a heading change towards Grand Forks AFB, the end checkpoint for the navigation leg.

At Grand Forks, they turned towards Bemidji, Minnesota, and began descending for the oil burner route and bomb run. The bomb runs would be made at the RBS Express located at Brainerd, Minnesota. After completing the Short Look Large Charge run, the profile called for a climb to 28,000 feet and employing ECM procedures between St. Cloud, Minnesota, and Des Moines, Iowa. When they arrived at Des Moines, they would turn to a heading that would take them back to Lincoln and home plate.

The scores for the first wave were outstanding. No aborts, navigation was right down the centerline. Bomb scores were some of the best ever posted during an ORI. The 307th was off to a good start. All they had to do was repeat the performance during the follow up mission.

Weather on the 14th, caused problems with the ORI. Low clouds and light rain had moved into the Lincoln area. The lead aircraft began rolling, followed by the rest of the cell at fifteen-seconds intervals. The last aircraft had to contend with thick clouds of exhaust smoke, jet wash and light rain before being swallowed by the low hanging clouds just after lifting off the runway.

Launching in the low clouds and rain was the biggest problem for the mission. After getting on top of the muck, the rest of the mission was flown according to the profile with excellent results. One crew scored a double shack on their bomb run. The 307th passed the ORI with an "Outstanding" rating.

There was one aspect of the ORI that wasn't exactly according to the planned ORI profile. The *Jet Scoop* edition for Friday, the 16th, featured an article covering the ORI. The non-routine part of the ORI was that the wives of the flight crews had cooked a special "glad you're home from the ORI" meal at the O Club while the mission was being flown. So, after debriefing, the tired SAC warriors were able to sit down and have a good old fashioned, home cooked meal. It was a nice special touch and greatly appreciated by the crews.

The October 23rd, *Jet Scoop* came out on Friday as usual. Inside, it was noted that the 307th was the first unit on base to achieve 100% participation in the United Appeal Campaign. The wing raised a total of $8,249.31 for the drive.

Also noted was Brig Gen Lewis Lyle's trophy presentation for the best bombing score on the "Rusty Spur" RBS Express target. The trophy went to Capt John Blewitt (AC), 1Lt Charles Adams (CP), and Capt Benjamin Overstreet (Nav) from the 372nd Bomb Squadron.

Reports were written and sent to Col Riggs for his signature, then forwarded to Barksdale and Omaha. After all, no month is complete until the paperwork was done. There are a lot of forgotten, unsung airmen who manned the typewriters at Wing headquarters who typed, filed and, in some cases, retyped thousands of pages of reports, orders, flight plans and other daily humdrum items. They accomplished their equally important part of the wing mission without fanfare, yet with the same professional dedication that was the hallmark of the 307th.

The wing started November with Reflexing three aircraft to Spain on Monday, the 2nd. The launch got off to a shaky start due to weather at Lincoln. Low clouds hung from the skies and there was a light rain or snow in the forecast. By launch time, light rain was falling with about two miles visibility. The three aircraft launched and climbed through the

## 1964

soup. After getting on top of the clouds they had clear flying all the way to Spain.

A blaring klaxon sent the Alert crews to their aircraft at 1420 on the 5th. The crews decoded a Green Dot message for a Bravo Alert. After spooling up the engines, the first aircraft reported ready to roll in five and a half minutes. The last crew reported ready at nine minutes after the horn.

During the Alert, the Pipe Cleaner Alert bird moved out of her spot on the Alert ramp and headed for Runway 17. The crew had decoded a launch message for a communication validation mission. Hitting the end of the runway, they poured on the JP-4 and rolled down the runway. After climbing out, they turned west and headed for the orbit area near Kimball, Nebraska. For the next five hours they flew the orbit between Kimball and a point just east of Denver. They had established an uplink with Looking Glass and practiced communication procedures along with relay of practice Foxtrot messages for all Sky King aircraft.

Launch crews prepared 53-0523 for a final launch on November 9th. After a four-month hold on sending aircraft into retirement, the 307th started sending the highest-time aircraft into retirement in the Arizona desert. Later that Monday, Reflex bound crews launched for the fifteen-hour flight to Morón, Spain.

The 307th was less than six months away from deactivation. Across the wing, people were trying to figure out which base they should forecast for their Permanent Change of Station (PCS). Everyone knew it was just a matter of time before their orders would arrive. Others had to make life-changing choices: should they stay in the Air Force or get out? Lives that had been secure at Lincoln were now in turmoil, uncertain about when they would be on the road to who-knew-where.

Going along with the deactivation, the grapevine was grinding out all kinds of "straight dope" rumors about the upcoming months. There were rumors about when the wing would end Alert and Reflex, when the last B-47 would leave and which aircraft it would be. Further speculation started floating around in mid November about when Old Man Winter was going to arrive and spread his icy grip on the plains of Nebraska. So far, it had been a very mild fall. There was only the morning chill, which left by noon and turned into beautiful afternoons.

Questions about the weather were answered on Thursday the 19th. Those reporting for duty drove to the base under a curtain of low clouds. There was also the unmistakable feeling it could snow at any moment, which turned out to be about 1000 that morning. Light mist formed, then snow began falling, signaling the arrival of Old Man Winter.

The weather wasn't bad enough to curtail air operations. It just made taking off and landing more interesting. Aircraft returning from missions had to be talked down by GCA. The old pucker factor could hit nine plus when you went over "O" Street and could barely see the high intensity approach lights off the end of the runway.

By that evening, the base was shrouded in fog and snow. Flights trying to return were diverted to other bases as the patch had gone below safe minimums. The Reflex return flight was diverted to Florida for a two-day hold due to weather.

On Monday, the 23rd, two Alert crews from the 4362nd PACCS stood down from Alert. The two Pipe Cleaner birds were towed back to the south end of the ramp and parked near Base Operations. With the stand down, the 4362nd ended its almost two-year Alert commitment at Lincoln Air Force Base.

Thanksgiving was celebrated on Thursday the 26th. Most of the 307th personnel realized it would be their last one with the friends they had made at Lincoln. Thanks were given for another year of relative world peace. Most families sat down to the traditional meal of the day and, as usual, managed to have one helping of turkey, dressing, sweet spuds and hint of cranberries more than they should.

SAC Headquarters at Omaha was filled with pomp and circumstance on Monday the 30th, for the formal change of command. Gen John D. Ryan assumed command of SAC with the retirement of Gen Thomas Power from the Air Force.

Gen Power had been Commander-in-Chief, Strategic Air Command, since he took over from Gen LeMay on July 1, 1957. His command legacy included operations during what has been described as the hottest portion of the Cold War. New aircraft came into service and the ballistic missile weapons systems came online. He helped SAC grow to its zenith as the premier deterrent force in the United States military. He commanded with a no-nonsense, no-excuse, tight fist. There were those who joked that it was his hand inside the mailed fist of the SAC emblem. Gen LeMay was "the Father SAC" and Gen Power built on his foundation.

During November, the 307th spent 1,831 hours in the air during 268 sorties. The wing continued the Reflex commitment in Spain regardless of the upcoming deactivation. The wing posted some of the best bombing scores of the year during November. The wing scored a 98% effective rate in bombing for the month. Not too shabby for a wing flying older aircraft and about to be deactivated.

Thursday, December 1st, launch crews prepared 52-0067 and two Pipe Cleaners, 52-0068 and 52-0078, for launch. It would be their final flight from Lincoln. The three crews preflighted and launched for a direct flight to Arizona and retirement. Friday, the 2nd, saw 53-2368 and 53-1964 take to skies and head for the boneyard. The launch of five aircraft in two days for the boneyard drilled home the fact that the 307th was starting the final downsizing towards deactivation.

It now became a scheduling nightmare to have enough aircraft to meet the regular flying schedule, not to mention Reflex and Alert. Although the wing still had fifty aircraft officially assigned, there were actually forty-seven available for the 307th to use. With nine on Alert and fourteen B-47s in Spain, that left twenty-three on the ramp for training flights.

With the wing in the process of shutting down, there was a constant arrival and departure of aircraft with high-ranking staff from Barksdale and Omaha. A shiny KC-135 arrived at the patch on Sunday, December 6th; there weren't many troops on the flight line to even notice the arrival. After all, it was Sunday and only those who had drawn weekend duty were manning the flight line.

To say the least, the command post staff was surprised when the 2nd Air Force inspection team showed up at the door and announced they were there to conduct a Bar None no-notice ORI. For a brief moment, the staff may have thought it was someone's idea of a joke. After all, the wing was going to be deactivated in four months and had just gone through an ORI in October.

It wasn't a joke, though; these guys were serious! They informed the staff an execution order would arrive from Barksdale within the hour. At that time, they would notify the wing staff of the situation in the command post and execute the beginning phase of the ORI.

A Green Dot execution message arrived from "Iron Horse" setting the ORI in motion. The command post contacted the wing battle staff and told them to report for duty. Other wing, and squadron personnel were called in. The telephone pyramid was implemented to bring in essential personnel for the ORI.

Alert crews were headed for the tunnels leading out of the mole hole before the klaxon stopped its infernal wail. At the base chapel, the red lights came on and started rotating. Alert crews forgot the sermon and headed for the door, then to the Alert area as fast as their trusty "six-packs" could go.

A casual observer might think an Alert was like a Chinese Fire drill. But watching crews respond to the klaxon was actually like watching a well-choreographed Broadway play. It was a true symphony of hectic,

# Cold War Cornhuskers: The 307th Bomb Wing Lincoln Air Force Base Nebraska 1955-1965

chaotic motion, with everything happening at once. The crew chief fired up the MD-3 ground power unit while his assistant started pulling intake and exhaust plugs from the engines. When the flight crew arrived, the pilot and copilot scrambled up the ladder while the navigator took over for the Crew Chief at the MD-3. The crew chief ran to help pull plugs and red REMOVE BEFORE FLIGHT streamers from the aircraft. Inside the aircraft, the two crewmen grabbed their brain buckets and strapped in.

The crew chief was now on the right side of the aircraft with his headset on, plugged into the J-Box. "AC, Ground. Clear to start #4, Fireguard Standing By!" "Roger, Ground, Turning #4". The engine comes to life with a low whine, increasing pitch as the engine spools up. A small flame licks from the exhaust as the combustion chambers ignite. In less than a minute the engines on the right side of the aircraft are started. The ground crew races to the left side of the B-47 and stands by. As the #1 engine comes up and the starter cuts out, the navigator leaves the MD-3 and clambers up the ladder.

The ground crew scrambles to disconnect the MD-3 and push it clear of the aircraft. Then they button up the aircraft, pull the chocks and disconnect their headsets from outlet box. A quick look around to make sure everything is clear of the aircraft, then give a thumbs up signal to the pilot.

Inside, the crew has decoded a Green Dot message for a Coco Alert and the word that this is an ORI. "Skate 13, Ready to taxi!" A gentle nudge on the blue tipped throttles and Skate 13 moves forward towards the runway. It has been six minutes since the klaxon went off.

One by one, the B-47s respond and move toward the runway. Full power for about a thousand feet, then back on power and fast taxi down the rest of the runway and back to the mole hole. Arriving back at the Alert ramp, they went through engine shut down and headed back to the mole hole for debriefing.

Preparation for the ORI mission began the moment the klaxon went off. Munitions crews were arriving on the Alert pad to begin downloading the weapons from the Alert birds. Like always, it was done by the checklist. This time it was under the probing eye of the ORI team. The battle staff was busy pulling mission folders and getting set up for the mission briefing. It would be a typical Bar None mission. The mission would include launch, air refueling, navigation leg, bomb runs and return to Lincoln. It would be about seven and a half hours in the air for the flight crews, every minute of it under ORI pressure.

The telephone pyramid Alert worked exactly as planned. Within an hour of implementing phone calls, personnel were arriving to generate the follow-on force for the second wave. It may have been a follow-on force, yet there was typical urgency to get the birds ready within the ORI guidelines.

Flight crews were assembled for the mission briefing. Everything was gone over with a fine-tooth comb: takeoff time, routes, refueling offload and bombing offset points were reviewed. After briefing, the crews were given a little time for last minute target study and mission planning. Takeoff order had been determined by the order they reported ready for the Coco Alert.

Alert aircraft had been downloaded, serviced and preflighted by the ground crews. The planes were as ready as humanly possible for the mission. Weather briefing was full of good conditions for the entire route. Flight crews were given their final briefing and their targets were given one last look. The first wave was ready, ready for the third ORI in less than six months. With all of the practice, the wing should have a good exercise.

This ORI would be conducted a little differently than the last one. The first wave would be flown by the nine crews that had been on Alert. They would launch as single ships with thirty minutes between aircraft. Each crew would fly the route as a single attack aircraft. On return to Lincoln, the first-wave aircraft would be refueled and recocked for Alert immediately.

At the scheduled time, the lead-off crew started the takeoff roll down Runway 17, climbing out for a Fairbury departure. They flew to the air refueling area and rendezvoused with the tanker. Hook up and transfer of fuel were completed according to the profile. After leaving the refueling track, the crew turned and headed for the first navigation checkpoint.

For the next two hours the crew was busy checking their position along the nav leg, using radar, sextant shots and maybe a little dead reckoning thrown in for good measure; the crew plotted the route and made the radio checks over the required checkpoints.

After the navigation leg, the crew headed for the RBS Express target near Kirksville, Missouri. They were required to make a Short Look Large Charge attack on the targets. As they approached at low level, they made contact with the scoring site and transmitted their identification information for scoring the run.

The tone came on with fifteen seconds to go on the counter, then it was bomb away and a turn to the second target. The results for both looked good from inside the B-47. All they had to do now was fly home to Lincoln and wait for the scores to arrive. Over two days of ORI flying, there had been no aborts on any part of the mission. It appeared the wing had flown a near perfect ORI. All they had to do was wait for the final results and the ORI debriefing at the base theater.

There were a lot of smiles at the critique for the ORI. The 2nd Air Force inspection team praised the 307th for the "outstanding professional manner" in which the wing conducted the exercise. They pointed out the results were exceptional, especially in view of the impending deactivation of the wing.

The wing had gotten off to a good start during the "kick off" Coco Alert. All of the aircraft were scored effective. Generation of the force was "Outstanding". Navigation and refueling were also rated "Outstanding". Then there were the comments about the bomb scores. In a nutshell, the results of the wing on the Kirksville target were, you guessed it, "Outstanding". Every aircraft was scored effective.

Each crew attacked two targets for a total of thirty-six bomb runs. There were fifteen bombs with a circular error of a thousand feet or less from the target. There were five shacks, including a double shack for one of the crews in the second wave; they had 'pasted the target'. It added up to some of the best results ever posted for an ORI.

Three crews were singled out for their "outstanding" Bar None missions during the ORI. Capt Leroy McMath's crew was singled out as having the best score for bombing during the second wave with their double shack. Capt Stanley Toney flew as copilot and Capt Pete Revello was at the bombsight as navigator. "Outstanding" navigation went to the crew of Maj Frank Kisner, Capt Richard Storr and Capt William Rogers, Jr. Best overall bombing went to the crew under the command of Capt James Hughes. His copilot was 1Lt Clifford Thomas. Capt Donald "Brent" Horn flew as the navigator.

When the 307th bombing scores reached SAC Headquarters, the results turned a few heads at the "head shed". The SAC Director of Operations sent a message to B-52 units in SAC pointing out that 307th crews flying older aircraft with less sophisticated bombing capability had scored better than B-52s at the Kirksville target.

There was a special "attaboy" message from the SAC DO to Col Riggs at 307th Headquarters. It commended the 307th's professional conduct of the mission and the outstanding results in view of the wing's deactivation. Deactivation or not, the 307th had proven again that they were still near the top of the SAC heap.

# 1964

December 7th, found the wing preparing three aircraft for Reflex launch. The three crews would spend the holiday season in Spain standing Alert so there would be no repeat of an attack like the one twenty three years ago at Pearl Harbor.

During the next two weeks, the 4362nd PACCS sent their high-time birds to Davis-Monthan AFB for retirement in the desert. The low-time aircraft would be transferred to Lockbourne AFB, Ohio. The 4362nd was deactivated with a ceremony on Thursday, December 24th.

Late afternoon on the 24th, three B-47s began letting down for landing at the patch. They were returning from Reflex in Spain. The return of the crews was a special Christmas Eve present for the families. It was special to be back home with the wife and kids for a most special time of the year.

Those three crews were happy to be home, but there were three crews who were not going to spend Christmas with their families. They would be headed for Spain and Reflex. What a crummy time to be going Reflex. There was only one bright side to the deployment. It would be the last time they would be traveling across the pond for Reflex.

That afternoon found the launch crews preparing three B-47s for Reflex deployment, just like they had done hundreds of times since Reflex began in 1957. This Reflex would be different, though. It would be the last time these three crews from the 307th would point their B-47s towards the east and fly across the pond to Sunny Spain. That morning, 53-6236, 53-2140 and 53-1956 were towed to the refueling pits and serviced with a full load of JP-4.

Late that afternoon, the ground crews went through their preflight checklist, making sure the aircraft were ready for the long flight ahead. Write-ups on the Form 781 were checked, then double-checked to make sure they had been taken care of. Fuel tanks had been checked with the dipstick and double-checked against the refueling forms. The three aircraft were ready for the flight crews and their preflight walkaround.

Flight crews arrived at Base Operations for their final briefing on ATC clearance and enroute weather. There was a healthy weather system between Lincoln and the East coast. The Spain bound B-47s would be high enough so the weather wouldn't cause problems. Refueling would be just north of Bermuda by two KC-135s.

Preflight walkaround went according to the checklist. No major problems were found. The crews boarded the aircraft, started engines and taxied to the end of Runway 17. One by one, they poured on the power and took off into the night for their last Reflex.

Two tankers were waiting for the thirsty B-47s right where they were supposed to be. The three B-47s found them on radar and slowly moved into the slot below and behind the tankers. Transfer was completed with no major problems. After taking on enough JP-4 to make it across the Atlantic, the three bombers pulled away from the tankers and began the long, lonely flight to Spain.

The flight was routine. Hours of listening to the sound of the engines hammering the eardrums through the helmets and occasional radio traffic. Sextant shots to check their position along the invisible aerial highway. In-flight meal was steak cubes wrapped in tinfoil, which they heated on the amplifier racks and washed down with coffee or water.

Flying east, the black sky began changing to ultramarine blue. Then the first bands of orange and yellow appeared on the horizon. Flying at jet speed, the sun seemed almost to leap over the horizon, flooding the cockpit with blinding rays of light.

When the coastline appeared on the radar, it was a welcome sight. It was still a long way to coast-in, but at least they could see it on the radar. Within a few minutes, the faint outline of the coast appeared on the horizon. The long flight over the water was just about over.

One by one, the three B-47s let down from altitude and made their approach. After landing, they taxied to the ramp and went through the engine shutdown checklist. The crews were glad to get out of their seats and climb down the ladder and plant their stiff legs on terra firma for the first time in over fifteen hours. It felt good to walk around for a minute and get the feeling back in their stiff backside and the kinks out of their legs. They were met by the crews they were going to relieve. "Merry Christmas! About time you got here!"

Everyone knew this would be the last Christmas at Lincoln. For many, it would be spent with friends and family, like Christmas should be celebrated. There were those who went, well should we say, a little beyond the usual call of duty to make this Christmas a little more special. Neil Cosentino recalls:

"It was a week before Christmas 1964, and we had some time left to fly around a bit after RTB to Lincoln. I talked Barney (Capt William Barnicoat, Jr.) into flying about 1,000 feet to look for Christmas trees. I was the copilot on this B-47E and I was looking for the right size tree away from farmhouses out in the open range.

"The mission was to find one, go there after landing, cut it down and take it home for Christmas. Mac (James McElvain, Capt) our navigator was looking through the zoom of the optical bombsight and we both gave directions to Barney about where to fly. We spent about a half hour looking around until I spotted what looked like a good tree near a snow covered county road with good access and no farmhouses around! Now to land, then go out and cut the tree and haul it home on the top of my car.

"All went well after landing-we (Mac and I) drove out to the area and finally found the location, which was no easy task. When we reached the open field there was light snow falling on us. Everything looked much different from the air. The size of that lone Christmas tree looked about right, but its location in that field was a different matter. The walk in deep snow out to it, across that windswept snowfield, seemed to us as if we were E&Eing across the steppes of Russia! But, we had gotten that far and were now determined to keep going all the way.

"With ax in hand we headed out. The snow began falling heavier, but we kept on course in the 'whiteout,' finally getting to the tree. It turned out to be a **cedar** tree! It sure looked good at 1,000 feet and 250 knots, and from the road a half-mile away, but up close it was one that would cost less than $5 even today, the kind that would be the last to sell on Christmas Eve. It was a tough, shaggy tree that had survived years in the winter winds out there in the middle of nowhere, a tough survivor on the Western Prairie, and very special to us.

"When we reached it, the snow started to fall harder than ever, coming down so suddenly that it was like being hit by a small avalanche, pressing down, a strange sensation, it was sucking our breaths away! We cut the tree down and started back across the field, still in a whiteout. The snow continued to fall and then started to blow like a blizzard in strong horizontal bands. It was like walking across the front of a giant Langley wind tunnel with horizontal streams of snow that looked like the smoke trails in a wind tunnel.

"This has a wonderful happy ending: A very Merry Christmas season, which we celebrated in the great German tradition of drinking the best red wine in a heated silver lined bowl with the best brandy and with orange rings floating on top of the wine. The wine we had brought back from Spain while SAC Reflexing there! We toasted our tree many times. We had the poorest tree, but with Maria decorating, it looked wonderful! It was the most memorable tree I can remember! A Christmas at home for a change, never to be forgotten, with a tree that no one but Barney, Mac and I, and our wives, knew where it came from and how we used a SAC bomber to find it!"

## Cold War Cornhuskers: The 307th Bomb Wing Lincoln Air Force Base Nebraska 1955-1965

At the end of December, the wing still had 90% of their authorized manpower assigned. During the month, the wing flew 187 sorties, spending 1,331 hours in the air. During the month, more aircraft were retired from service until the wing finished the year with fifty-one assigned aircraft.

1964 had been a year of highs and lows for the 307th. The wing had been subjected to three ORIs since April, all of which had been sprung on the wing after deactivation of the wing had been announced. The wing showed SAC Headquarters even though the 307th's days were numbered, the wing maintained the same level of professionalism that had always been the hallmark of the 307th.

The wing suffered two Class A accidents during the year. The wing was saddened by the loss of one crew in the July accident. Everyone in the wing agreed it was a near miracle the accident on June 3rd was confined to the loss of the aircraft and not the crew. Lady Luck had been on their side that night.

Everyone in the wing knew that, with the arrival of the New Year, orders would be coming down the pipe for transfers to new duty stations. As always, there were parties around the base. They had special meaning since they would be the last ones at Lincoln as part of the 307th Bomb Wing.

A note concerning the organizational designation of the squadron flying the Pipe Cleaners:

Astute readers may have noted seeming discrepancies in the years 1962, 1963 and 1964 regarding the identification of the 307th Bomb Wing organization responsible for operating the B-47L Pipe Cleaner aircraft. In this document, the organization in 1962 is identified both as the 4362nd Airborne Communication Relay Squadron (ACRS) and as the 4362nd Post Attack Communication Squadron (PACS). In 1963 it is identified as the 4362nd ACRS, and in 1964 it is noted that SAC changed the name from 4362nd ACRS to the 4362nd Post Attack Command Control Squadron (PACCS). At the time, those of us on the scene, but not directly involved, were quite content with referring to it as the "Pipe Cleaner Squadron"

As researchers putting this history together, we wanted to resolve these discrepancies. Despite consulting different resources, we were unsuccessful!

The source for the nomenclature evolution shown above is the 307th BW historical microfilm obtained from the Air Force Historical Research Agency (AFHRA) at Maxwell AFB. Back in the 1990s, Ernie Pence obtained 307th microfilms from the same agency and used them to produce a wing history outline that was published in limited numbers in 2000. Pence's document refers to the Pipe Cleaner squadron throughout as the 4362nd PACCS. Lt Col Russ Heller, assumed command of the squadron on 1 November 1963 from retiring Lt Col James Pumford, who was the initial commander. Heller remained as commander until the squadron's deactivation. He states that "4362nd PACCS" was the only name ever assigned to the squadron.

In December 1991, a report published by the SAC Historian entitled *Alert Operations and the Strategic Air Command 1957-1991*, states, "1961- Strategic Air Command also expanded its airborne command post operations. In April 1962, the Post Attack Command Control System or PACCS was augmented with three auxiliary airborne command posts. The new aircraft were established at Barksdale AFB, Louisiana; Westover AFB, Massachusetts; and March AFB, California. SAC then organized four support squadrons on 20 July at Mountain Home AFB, Idaho; Lincoln AFB, Nebraska; Lockbourne AFB, Ohio; and Plattsburgh AFB, New York. The command equipped the squadrons with EB-47L aircraft (B-47s modified with communications equipment) and redesignated them Post Attack Command Control Squadrons.

The nomenclature "support squadron" pops up above and in an AFHRA fact sheet without elaboration. It can be inferred that perhaps these units were referred to in this manner until they were organized and had rubber on the ramp.

No sources to support the nomenclature ACRS or PACS could be found other than the cited microfilm. The SAC Historian's report and surviving, but fallible, corporate memory lead one to favor 4362nd PACCS as the operative historical designation.

Mission Briefing for BAR NONE ORI. (JET SCOOP)

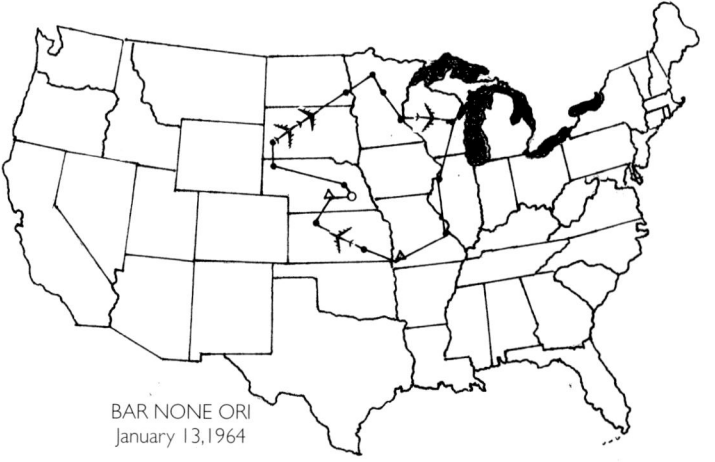

BAR NONE ORI
January 13, 1964

## 1964

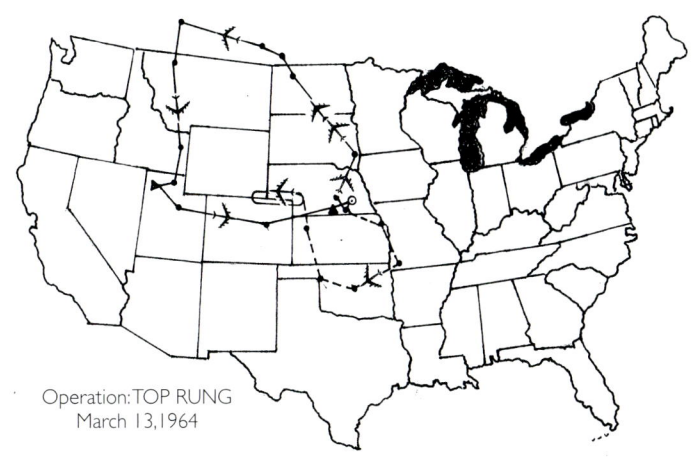

MD-3 Generator. (M Hill)

Operation: TOP RUNG
March 13, 1964

KC-135 from the observation position. Within moments the receiver will ease into position for "Contact". (USAF)

If a B-47 required extensive work or periodic inspection, they were towed to the nose docks near the large north hanger. (M.Hill)

Adorning the walls of the nose docks were these cartoon adventures of T.O. Joe, the wise old "Sarge" (Godemann)

261

# Cold War Cornhuskers: The 307th Bomb Wing Lincoln Air Force Base Nebraska 1955-1965

These figures are over twenty feet in length. (Godemann)

The cartoon figures were rediscovered in the summer of 2009 by Darwin Godemann while working for Duncan Aviation. (Godemann).

The figures admonish the crews to check the technical orders. (Godemann)

Follow the proper procedure or face the consequences. (Godemann)

"But Sarge, The Ball Game is on" (Godemann)

# 1964

We THANK Darwin for finding and sharing a lost part of the 307th BW history. (Godemann)

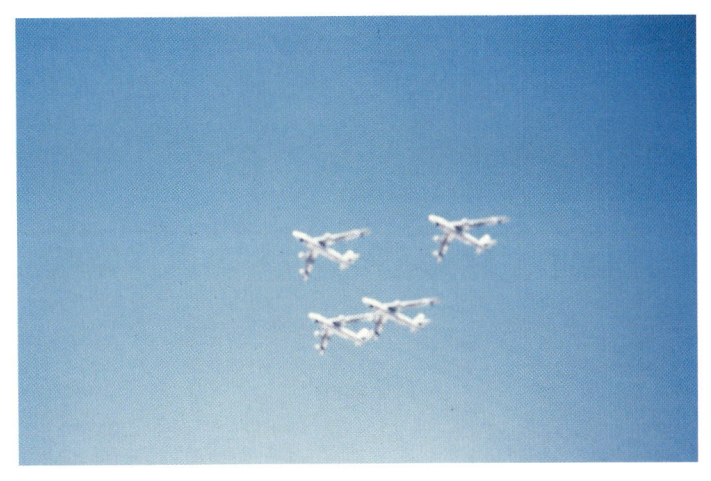

A 307th imitation of the Thunderbird Diamond formation during a Reflex arrival in Spain. (S.D. Hill)

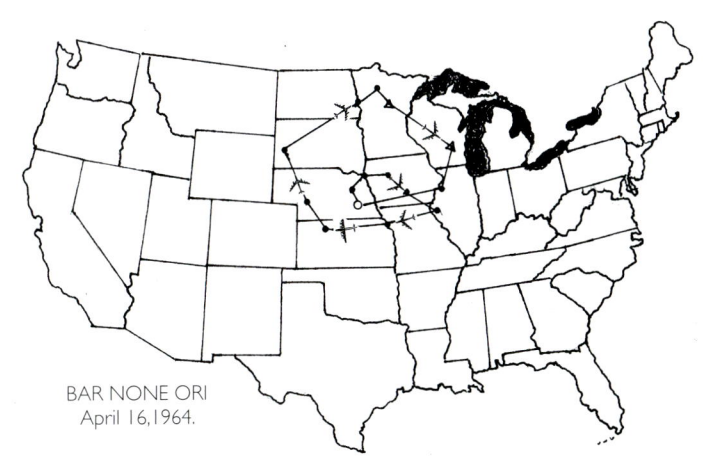

BAR NONE ORI
April 16, 1964.

Alert B-47s at Zaragosa, Spain. The seventh B-47 is 53-1956 from the 307th. Beside her is 53-2363 and 53-2341 from the 307th. (USAF)

A 307th crewman passes time on alert in Spain by building a model airplane. (USAF)

Arriving in Spain a B-47 flies low over a historic Spanish castle. (USAF)

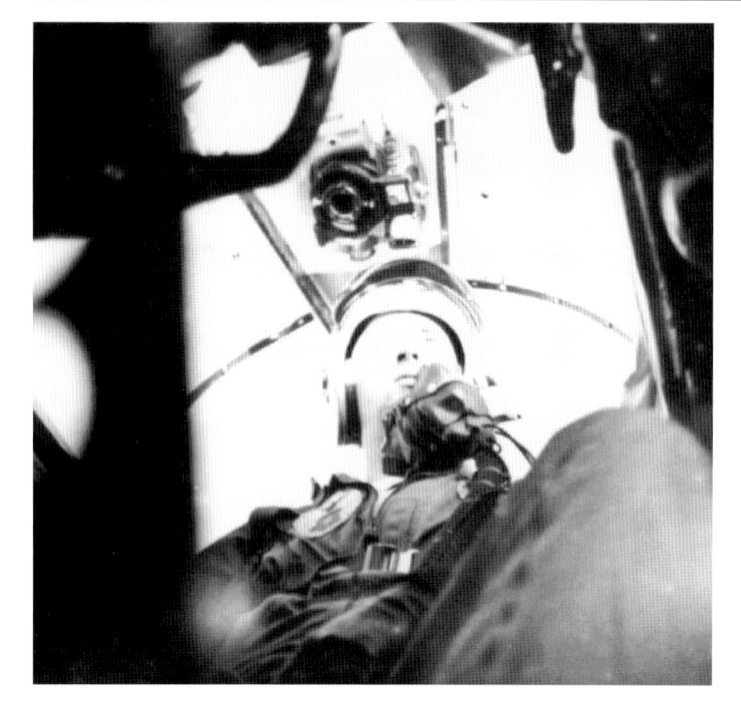

# Cold War Cornhuskers: The 307th Bomb Wing Lincoln Air Force Base Nebraska 1955-1965

B-58 Hustler on display for the air show on May 23, 1964. (M.Hill)

Mike Gingrich performing routine co pilot duties during a long mission. (Gingrich)

Fire crews battle the flames that consumed 53-2363 in the early morning hours of June 3rd. (USAF)

Aerial view of Lincoln Air Force Base and the new airport on the East side of the base. (USAF)

The July 10th JET SCOOP featured the 307th Recovery Section. (JET SCOOP)

Engine run up. (JET SCOOP)

## 1964

Hooking up to tow a B-47. (JET SCOOP)

Air Force officials survey the crash site of 53-2366.

An engine laid near the main crash site. (LINCOLN JOURNAL-STAR)

The fire damaged these small trees near the main crash site. (LINCOLN JOURNAL-STAR)

The crash area as it appears today. The main crash area was near the clump of three trees in the center-left. (M.Hill)

A F-106 from the 5th FIS. They flew fighter intercepts using 307th B-47s as target. (USAF)

265

# Cold War Cornhuskers: The 307th Bomb Wing Lincoln Air Force Base Nebraska 1955-1965

FAIRBURY DEPARTURE. (Parks)

A "special" post ORI meal was prepared by the wives of the flight crews. (JET SCOOP)

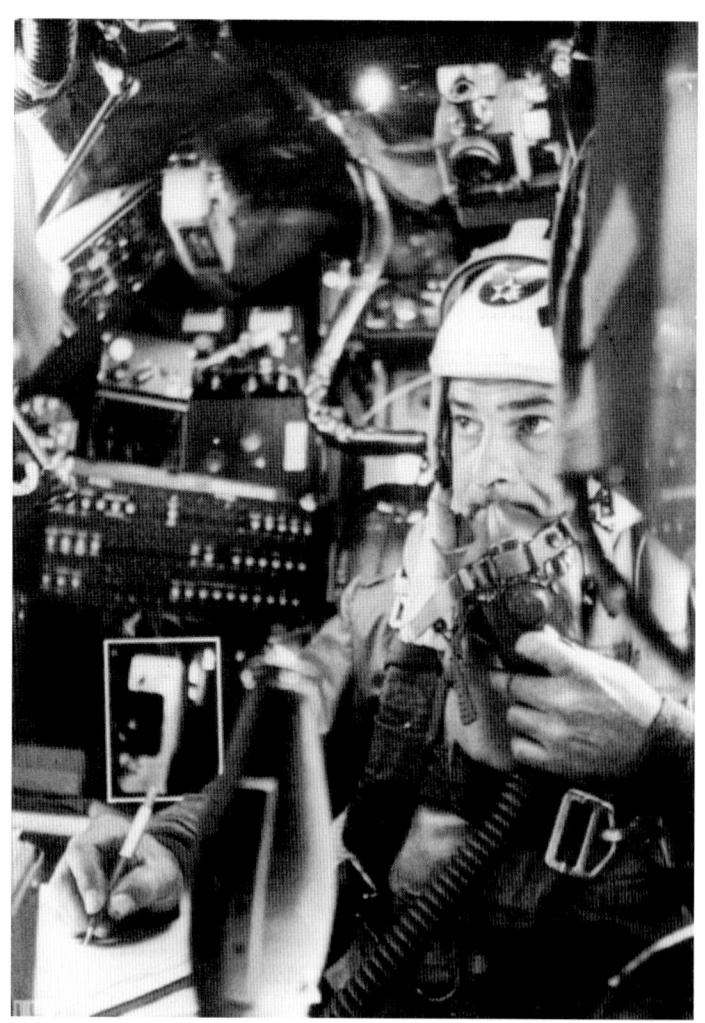

An unusual view of the navigator station on a B-47. (LIFE)

The 4362nd PACCS stood down from alert on November 23rd. (JET SCOOP)

# 1964

LeRoy McMath and Crew. (JET SCOOP)

Frank Kisner and Crew. (JET SCOOP)

James Hughes and Crew (JET SCOOP)

The Christmas Tree Crew. L-R: James McElvain, W.J. Barnicort, Neil Consentino. (Consentino)

# 1965

Operations within the 307th showed no sign of slowing down as the New Year began. Operation Swan Song outlining the deactivation of the 307th and 818th Air Division called for the deactivation to be complete by March 25th. There had been no word from SAC Headquarters as to exactly when the wing Alert and Reflex commitments would end.

Under the original Swan Song operations orders, the 307th was to stand down from Alert and Reflex on January 15th. SAC Headquarters amended the OPSORD to have the wing continue operations until a stand down notification order from Omaha was received. The reason was never officially defined, but apparently was so the US would be able to maintain adequate deterrent capability in view of the developing situation in Southeast Asia.

Ground crews prepared three aircraft for a Reflex launch on Monday, the 4th of January. Originally, 53-6244 had been on the schedule to Reflex to Spain. The schedule had to be changed in December when 6244 was scheduled to be retired to the Air Force Museum at Dayton, Ohio. Another aircraft was selected to stand in for 6244 on the Reflex flight. The Reflex aircraft launched on time that day for the long flight to Spain.

Alert crews responded to a Bravo Alert on Tuesday, the 5th. After starting engines and reporting ready, the ground crews removed the chocks and the aircraft surged forward about two feet, then stopped. The two-foot taxi was to rotate the tires, preventing flat spots due to the weight of the aircraft. They recocked the aircraft so they were ready for the next Alert or EWO launch.

By 1965, SAC was no longer the dominant part of the U.S. military structure. Now, SAC had to compete with not only the rest of the Air Force, but also the other services for budget dollars to continue operations. SAC was forced to cut back in certain areas. One area that could be cut back was the number of Coco Alerts that were called.

During a Coco Alert, nine B-47s from the 307th would be started, taxied to the runway and throttled up to full power, then taxied to the end of the runway and all the way back to the Alert pad. That's a lot of JP-4 burned for just the 307th. Multiply that across the entire Alert force and it adds up to a lot of black smoke and burnt JP-4 just for a ground exercise. At least for the time being, SAC would curtail Coco Alerts.

The 1st Combat Evaluation Group had arrived on the 5th. They were on base to evaluate the standardization evaluation program for both wings. At first glance, the visit seemed ridiculous in view of the deactivation. They would spend the next two weeks at the patch. They would be checking records for the 307th personnel for past stan eval flights to make sure the records were up to snuff and ready for their next duty station.

As long as they were at the base, they would also fly a couple of missions with crews just to make sure the program and the crews were proficient. The missions would be Bar None profiles and the crews would be selected from crews who were due to be evaluated.

Back in December, arrangements had been made to send 53-6244 to the Air Force Museum at Dayton, Ohio. Since she was going to the museum, the 307th wanted her to look good. She had been towed to the big south hangar and would spend her remaining days with the 307th inside the hangar. First, she was scrubbed down from wingtip to wingtip. Then, ground crews spent hours cleaning the cockpit and touching up the paint. Other ground crews spent hours polishing her aluminum skin. Jim Villa recalled, "A1C James Sine and I volunteered to work at night on 6244 because everything was quiet then. It took a night each to polish the two wing tanks."

Crews spent over four hundred hours polishing and about five hundred pounds of compound on the "Old Warrior". By the time they were finished, she looked better than the day she came off the production line at Wichita. 6244 was the 1,390th B-47 to roll out of Wichita. More important, she was the end of the line at that plant. She had a reputation for being a good reliable aircraft. Perhaps the production crew at Wichita had given her special attention since she was the last one to roll out.[5]

There was a Reflex deployment to Spain scheduled for Monday, the 11th. Everyone wondered when SAC would send word to stand down from Reflex. Until the word came in, it would be Reflex as usual on Monday, with the return crews coming back to Lincoln on Wednesday.

At 307th Headquarters, there was a change of command ceremony on Monday, the 18th. Col William Riggs was being transferred to his new duty station. At the ceremony he handed the reins of the 307th over to Col Arthur Holderness, Jr., who had served as Deputy Wing Commander. Col Holderness would close the wing out as commander.

Tuesday, the 19th, saw 53-0608 and 53-0529 launch for their final flight from the patch. Leaving Lincoln, the crews flew to Arizona where the two birds joined hundreds of B-47s in retirement at Davis-Monthan AFB, better known as the boneyard.

A TWX arrived at wing headquarters on Wednesday, the 20th. The message contained what the wing had been waiting for. The 307th would deploy the last Reflex mission on Monday, February 1st. The aircraft and crews would redeploy to the US on February 22nd after their Reflex tour. The wing was instructed to stand down from ground Alert at Lincoln effective 1200 hours on Sunday, February 28th. Crews that had been on the schedule after those dates were overjoyed at the prospect of not having to continue Alert or Reflex.

Just because the wing was deactivating was no excuse to have those 50-8 squares blank. It would be "fly as usual" until the last minute. On Thursday, the 21st, 53-1882 was scheduled for a mission. During the mission, the crew had problems transferring fuel to keep the aircraft balanced correctly. The crew aborted the mission and returned to Lincoln. They landed heavier than normal and used a lot more runway to get 1882 slowed down.

Early on the morning of Friday, January 22nd, the south hangar doors opened and 53-6244 was towed to the refueling pits. After taking on fuel, she was towed to a slot near Base Operations to await her crew. Jim Villa recalled that morning:

"During the entire preparation time of 6244, she was kept in the southeast quarter of the south hangar. The airplane was taken out only to be defueled and for running the engines. Then she was towed back to the hangar. A2C Bruce Stufflebeam and I would do some of the maintenance ground preflight in the hangar on the morning of the Museum launch. Before daylight, she was towed and parked in front of Base Operations. We continued our ground preflight with power connected."

The honor of flying "Old Warrior", as she was known, went to Capt Gene Hickman's Crew E-65. They had taken top honors at 2nd Air Force EWO Knowledge Competition in July 1964. Capt "Pete" Todd would fly copilot. Capt Al Ottaviano would guide the way to Dayton as navigator. A1C Jim Sine flew in the fourth man seat as crew chief.

The flight was scheduled to be a media event. Local television and papers were invited to be on base for the departure of the historic aircraft. The low-hanging clouds and cool temperature may have been too much for the media; very few turned out for the event.

When the sun was supposed to rise, it was hidden by low clouds, fog and intermittent light drizzle. For a while it looked like the flight wouldn't get off the ground. Pete Todd recalled the morning. "Ever been in Nebraska in January? Well, on this particular day, the fog would have made Londoners green with envy. The bright, sleek machine was dulled by the weather into a barely discernible hulk looming in the murk. The media people were disappointed; the wing commander was apoplectic; the flight crew was just happy the weather lifted enough to get us off the ground with our treasure."

As the time for engine start approached, the fog began to lift a little. Gene Hickman and crew arrived at 6244 for preflight, after which there was a photo session with Col Holderness, the wing commander, and other base officials. The crew climbed aboard, started engines and taxied to the fog-shrouded runway. Jim Villa recalled the launch of 6244:

"A1C Bruce Stufflebeam and I did the ground preflight. The aircrew climbed aboard and commenced engine start. Bruce and I closed up 6244 for the last time. As Capt Hickman took off in 6244, LtCol John Crook, Bruce and I sat in the colonel's car to watch 6244 take off for her last time and disappear in the low overcast."

The flight to Dayton lasted less than two hours. Pete Todd wrote:

"The flight itself was unremarkable, except that the bird was so slick and shiny we actually got about ten knots of extra airspeed out of her at cruise power setting. Arrival at Wright-Patterson was more festive. The airplane was met with all appropriate pomp. Gene signed over the aircraft and we hauled our gear, including parachutes, to a local motel for the night. We flew back to Lincoln via commercial air the next day and got some curious looks and witty comments when we delivered our parachutes as checked baggage. ('You guys know something about this flight that we don't?')"

Al Ottaviano recalled:

"The actual flight to Dayton was quite short; Lincoln to Dayton, maybe 500 miles or so. Not much of a flight plan. One hour, fifteen minutes takeoff to landing. I used radar to check where we were going. Pete had us on VORTAC radials all the way in. They treated us very nicely at Wright-Patterson AFB."

After her departure from Lincoln, some of the ground crews gathered for morning coffee and remembered old 6244. "Hey, remember that time on Reflex when they launched to come back and couldn't get the forward gear to retract. Steve Vensky had to climb down in the crawlway and check the gear while they were in the air." "Yeah, then there was that flight when the crew lost an engine on final." "How about the time during the ORI when she was scored as an abort because she missed take off by about two minutes." "Yup, she was a pretty good old bird; at least she will be kept at the museum."

After 6244 disappeared in the clouds, it was back to business as usual on the flight line. Two aircraft launched for training flights that afternoon. The low clouds swallowed them before they reached the end of the runway. After breaking out of the clouds, the mission was routine until they returned. The low murk and scud still covered the patch so they had to use GCA to get back on the ground.

One of the aircraft that launched for a 50-8 mission was 53-2416. The crew had gone through a normal preflight, started engines and took off. When they started retracting the landing gear the forward main indicated an intermediate condition. The crew went through the checklist. Circuit breakers checked, everything appeared normal. After recycling the gear, the forward main indicated down and locked.

After conferring with the command post, they made a tower flyby. In the murk and scud they could barely be seen from the tower as they flew down the runway. Sure enough the forward gear was down. The crew tried to recycle the gear once more, no luck. They had little choice but the abort the mission. Now, all they had to do was fly around and burn off enough fuel to make a safe landing. The primary problem was, with the field under the shroud of fog, a normal landing would be a bit dicey. In this case, it would be on the dangerous side. The crew was instructed to head for their weather alternate at McConnell AFB near Wichita, Kansas. With the gear down, they burned off fuel at a higher rate. Arriving at Wichita, they stayed in the pattern until they had burned off enough fuel then made a relatively normal landing. A faulty switch was later found to be the culprit for the gear failure.

The day ended with a Bravo Alert when the klaxon went off at 2115 hrs. Alert crews hit the tunnels and headed for the six-packs for the short drive to the aircraft. By this hour the fog had rolled in even thicker than it had been during the day. When you're in a hurry, trying to find a B-47 parked somewhere out there in the foggy glare of headlights is almost impossible. You know it's out there, but where? After groping around in the fog, the phantom shape of a B-47 emerged from the murky darkness. After finding their birds, it was a rather simple matter to climb aboard, spool up engines and report when they were ready to taxi. Taxi? Where the hell is the taxiway?

## Cold War Cornhuskers: The 307th Bomb Wing Lincoln Air Force Base Nebraska 1955-1965

After checking in, they shut down the engines and started the checklist to recock the aircraft:

1. Parking Brakes- SET
2. Engines- CUTOFF
3. Flight Controls- LOCKED & ENGAGED
4. Aileron Power Control Switches- OFF
5. Fuel Selector Switches- TE
6. Fire Cutoff Switches- PULLED
7. Oxygen Regulators- 100 % OXYGEN LEVER OFF
8. Battery Switch- OFF
9. Ejection Seat & Canopy Pins- INSTALLED
10. Chocks- SET

With the birds recocked and ready in case they had to be flushed from the nest, the crews climbed aboard their six-packs and headed for the mole hole. All they had to do was find it out there, somewhere in the fog. Getting back would be just about as easy as finding the aircraft in the thick soup. They all agreed it would have been next to impossible to have launched if it had been a Red Dot Delta message.

53-1909 was preflighted and ready for her mission on Wednesday, the 27th. The crew had gone through the preflight and nothing that would cause a safety problem was found. 1909 taxied on time and got final clearance from the tower. Everything about the take off was normal, that is, until the pilot called "gear up". The forward main would not come up into the well. The aircraft commander flew the aircraft while the copilot checked the circuit breakers and recycled the gear. Still no retraction. Check the breakers and try again. No luck, the gear was still down. Here we go again!

Conferring with the command post brought no inflight solution. There was only one thing to do. Stay in the air and burn off enough fuel for a safe landing. After several hours of flying around the area between Lincoln and Omaha, the B-47 had burned enough to get down to a safe landing weight. They pulled into the pattern and made a long approach to Runway 35. Crossing the threshold with the approach chute bobbing in the slipstream, 1908 made a fairly normal landing. This was the second gear problem in less than a week. Was it a matter of the old birds getting too old to fly or something else? Again, a faulty switch was found to be the culprit.

Not all retraction problems were caused by mechanical failure. Sometimes there was another reason. Paul Koski recalled an incident that happened early in wing history at Lincoln:

"I had just launched my airplane when my flight chief asked me and my assistant to help another crew chief launch his aircraft. They were running late and it was going to be tight making takeoff on time. The flight crew was making their walkaround, checking all open panels and we secured them after they were inspected.

"We had pulled the nose gear, right outrigger and bomb bay locks. We headed for the rear wheel well, when the brake chute and approach chutes arrived. To expedite the time, we went and installed the chutes and closed the doors. We continued our walkaround on the left wing and pulled the left outrigger down lock. The flight crew climbed aboard and we passed the down locks up to them. Engines started and the aircraft was going to make its takeoff time. We felt proud of ourselves since we had busted our tails to make it on time.

"We saw the aircraft off and my assistant and I went to the maintenance trailer to finish the paperwork on my aircraft. Our flight chief came in about 30 minutes later and said he had just gotten word the aircraft we had just launched couldn't get its aft main gear up. He asked if all the gear locks had been removed. Although we didn't remember seeing the aft lock removed, we assumed someone had removed it. We elected not to tell anyone there was a possibility that the lock still might be there; no sense borrowing trouble until we knew for sure. Besides, the flight crew could check the locks they had aboard.

"We told control that we would meet the aircraft at the end of the runway to install the locks since we didn't want any landing accident. The aircraft flew for about four hours to burn off enough fuel to land. We didn't have a fuel dump system like other aircraft so all you could do was burn it off.

"We met the aircraft at the end of the runway and installed the down locks. However, the aft lock was already installed, but there wasn't a REMOVE BEFORE FLIGHT streamer on it. It could have blown off, but I doubt it. Intake covers and exhaust covers, as well as most of the streamers, were either missing or torn on these older birds. That's no excuse for what happened, but it could have been a contributing factor.

"We didn't tell control that the lock was left in and the flight crew went along with our decision since they were as much at fault as we were. We did have to make a retraction test and answered the form write up with 'could not duplicate the problem.' A report would have to be sent to SAC if anything had been said about the lock not being removed. We put new streamers on all the aircraft as soon as supply received enough of them. The flight crews now had a procedure to count the locks before passing them to the cockpit."

During the last week in January, the 307th had the usual nine aircraft cocked on the Alert pad. What made it unusual were the tail numbers. Sitting on the ramp were 53-4222, 53-4223 and 53-4224, three aircraft with consecutive tail numbers. It was rare that three consecutive tail numbers would be on Alert at the same time. What happened on Thursday the 28th was a mathematical improbability. "Can't happen, but did."

The klaxon wailed, sending the crews scrambling to their birds. Within a few minutes, the low whine of engines spooling up to power could be heard coming from the Alert ramp. It was a now-routine Bravo Alert, so the crews had to spin em up, juice em, spark em, then report when they were ready to roll. Much easier and less time-consuming than those darn old Coco Alerts. No problem; the crews would be snug as a bug in a rug at the mole hole pretty soon.

One by one, the aircraft checked in when they were ready to taxi, That is, everyone except—that's right—4222, 4223 and 4224! On 4222 there was no ignition on #2 engine. 4223 had radio problems; it took over six minutes for the radio to warm up so they could report in. 4224 couldn't get ignition on #3 engine. The three were scored ineffective for the Alert. The mathematical probability of those three aircraft being on Alert at the same time was one thing. For them all have problems at the same time during an Alert was beyond comprehension.

January went into the wing history as a good month. It was one of the few times the wing was able to report fewer than fifteen flights canceled due to weather. The wing flew 247 sorties for a little over 1,500 hours in the air. Total manpower was listed as 86% of the authorized level. Personal were beginning to transfer or muster out at an ever-growing rate. Overall, it was a good month operationally in view of the March target date for completion of deactivation.

The wing started February with a Bravo Alert at 1140 on the 3rd. Alert crews tumbled out of the mole hole and headed for the Alert aircraft. Climbing aboard, they went through engine start up and checked in when they were ready to taxi. The average response time for the Alert was six minutes. All 307th Alert birds were scored effective.

The *Jet Scoop* edition for Friday, the 5th, carried an article about a very special ceremony that took place during the week. Col Arthur

## 1965

Holderness, wing commander, presided at the ceremony at wing headquarters to present the N.V. Meeks Memorial Trophy to Ruth Meeks for her permanent possession in view of the upcoming deactivation of the 307th. The trophy had been created in honor of her husband, Maj N.V. Meeks, who lost his life in the line of duty. The trophy had been presented to crews who accomplished 50-8 training requirements in the timeliest fashion since March 1963.

So far, Old Man Winter had not sent the "Hawk" to visit the patch. It had been a mild winter thus far. Cold temperatures, yes, but very little snow had fallen. As a matter of fact, the ground was almost bare. Air operations hadn't suffered the historical problem of dealing with piles of snow covering the flight line. Maybe Old Man Winter had taken pity on the 307th since the wing would be leaving his domain.

Sunday, the 7th, dawned with crisp air and low clouds covering the patch. There was that certain itchy feeling the low clouds could start dropping snow at any minute. That afternoon, the wind shifted to the northwest. In a short time, the wind picked up signaling the approach of a storm. Wind-driven snow arrived, reducing visibility to less than a half a mile. By late afternoon drifts were forming across the flight line. The "Hawk" had arrived at the patch, once again!

By Monday morning, the 8th, almost ten inches of snow had fallen. Wind had piled drifts across the streets on base and in the housing area, making travel next to impossible. Snow was still falling at noon and showed no signs of abating. Visibility was next to nothing. Air operations were halted and only duty essential personnel reported for work.

Late that afternoon the snow slowed, then stopped, and the task of digging out began. The first priority was getting the Alert ramp, taxiways and runway clear of snow. With all of the wind, the runway had stayed fairly clear of drifts. A couple of passes with the plows and it was ready.

A B-47 sitting on the ramp covers a lot of concrete. Enough to break the wind and cause drifts to form around the large aluminum hulk. Most of the Alert birds were up to their engines in white stuff. As soon as the wind let up enough, ground crews manned the shovels and started digging the birds out of the drifts. It was no easy chore since most of them were buried up to the engines and wing tips in solid, wind-driven snowdrifts.

Most people who served in SAC were convinced that the "stars" at the head shed were always dreaming up special ways to test or harass the troops. So, here's the situation: Nine 307th B-47s cocked and ready for immediate response launch. The problem is, at the moment, they are up to their ATO bottles in snowdrifts. Crew chiefs are working feverishly to dig them out with the trusty Mark-1 snow shovel. Now would be a great time to catch part of the SAC flock in the nest.

The klaxon went off, sending the crews on a mad scramble to get to their cold-soaked birds. Crew chiefs dropped the shovels, responding to the klaxon. They opened the entry door and dropped the ladder for the crew. Now, get the MD-3 fired up and put power on the aircraft. Alert vehicles arrived, some plowing snow with their bumpers as they slid to a stop. Then a mad dash for the crew ladders. Across the ramp, the sound of MD-3s was slowly drowned out by the low whine of J-47 jet engines starting and coming up to power. That is, except for 53-2140.

Her crew chief couldn't get the MD-3 started. The cold soaked battery didn't have enough power to get the engine started. He signaled for the backup MD-3 to try and jump-start the generator. Even with the warm MD-3 running they couldn't get the frozen generator to fire up. Since they couldn't start any of the engines, 2140 was scored ineffective.

Up in the frigid cockpit, Capt Hank Grogan could only throw his hands up in the air and say a few choice words in despair, unbuckle and climb down the ladder. "More than a few times while on Alert, we had a mini-blizzard", Hank wrote. "Like a foot of snow on the ground and drifts five and six feet deep around the outboard engine pods on the 47s. Snow was above the lips of the engine nacelle, level with the 'dog pecker'. No way could we start engines and taxi. Made no difference to SAC; there would never be a downgrading of the Alert force. As in, 'Damn the torpedoes, full speed ahead.'"

The Alert had been a Bravo Alert. Eight of the nine aircraft were effective, with an average response time of seven minutes and twenty seconds. Not too bad considering the weather and conditions on the Alert pad. Most agreed it would have been difficult to taxi and launch if it had been for real. Rest assured, if it had been an EWO launch the crews would have made a superhuman effort to get off the ground, or die trying.

Snow removal crews continued to dig the base out after the snow stopped that evening. They were making good progress until the "Hawk" returned for round two about midnight. Snow started falling and the winds picked up again, blowing snow back into drifts that had just been cleared. With the wind blowing and snow piling up again, the snow crews were fighting a losing battle against nature. Shortly after 0200, they were pulled until the snow slowed down.

By morning, the storm showed no sign of moving on. Duty essential personnel fought their way to work. There wasn't much that could be done out on the flight line. A lot of people who made it to work spent the day cleaning up paperwork and waiting for the snow to slow enough to get back outside.

Late afternoon on Tuesday, the 9th, the snow started to let up. By 1800, it had almost stopped completely. Snowplows fired up and charged down the runway in a three abreast conga line. The runway and taxi strips were cleared first, then they hit the Alert pad. Ground crews grabbed their trusty shovels and started digging the aircraft out of the drifts by hand again. By midnight, enough snow had been hauled away so the Alert aircraft could be launched if needed.

Three crews preflighted their aircraft for the return flight from Spain on the 10th. Since the 307th would be ending Reflex, they would return to Lincoln with a belly full of weapons. It was the easiest and safest way to get the Mark-28s back to the US. The weapons would be safetied and chained into the aircraft to prevent accidental release.

The three loaded birds launched and headed out over the Atlantic for the long flight back to the States. If everything went according to the flight plan, the aircraft should arrive at Lincoln about 1300 on the 11th. Like all returning Reflex crews, they were happy to get the show on the road and head towards home and family. That left just three aircraft and crews on Alert in Spain.

The weather wizards had been watching an intense low-pressure area emerge and boil out of the Rockies. Everything indicated the system was heading out onto the plains and gaining strength as it moved. At the moment, it looked like the intense weather was headed for Nebraska and setting its sights on Lincoln.

While the Hawk was approaching, members of the 307th who had received orders were trying to "get out of Dodge" before the storm hit. Wally Whitehurst recalled:

"I left LAFB in February as the wing was breaking up. Interestingly enough, I was assigned to the 370th Bomb Squadron for the last two days and the only person I saw in the squadron was Hale Dodge, who was then the squadron commander. I was leaving the next day and Hale gave me a Certificate of Performance in the 370th Bomb Squadron for the period of 9 Feb to 10 Feb, 1965, which I still proudly display. We talked about our years together in the 307th BW for an hour or so, and Hale said he'd sign me out the next day and give me a head start out of Lincoln and on to our next assignment. Then it snowed over 25 inches in Lincoln on the day we were to leave and we had to stay over for another day. It took us over four hours to drive from Lincoln to Beatrice, about forty miles."

# Cold War Cornhuskers: The 307th Bomb Wing Lincoln Air Force Base Nebraska 1955-1965

The storm arrived just after midnight on the 11th. It started with light snow, which increased to heavy snowfall in a matter of minutes. Within an hour of its arrival, the wind picked up, sending slithering snow snakes blowing across the freshly plowed flight line. By morning, the "Hawk" was almost at its full fury.

Snow and high winds pummeled the patch all day. Sustained winds at fifteen to twenty knots piled drifts of snow higher and higher across the base. Snowplows were called in after fighting a losing battle with the "Hawk". All air operations were called off until weather conditions improved.

The homeward-bound Reflex crews were in contact with the command post and knew that Lincoln was closed. They were diverted to a weather alternate until Lincoln reopened. Since the aircraft were "packing" a full load, they were placed under guard for security.

Back at the patch, the full fury of the winter storm had arrived. Wind was gusting from 33 to 38 knots with blowing snow. Visibility? Well there wasn't any; maybe a city block. Drifts continued to grow like corn during the Nebraska summer. In some places, they were over six feet and growing with each gust of wind.

By the time the "Hawk" moved on, drifts were piled up nine to twelve feet in places. Streets on base and in the housing area were clogged with impassable drifts. Snowplows hit the ramp and carved a path to the runway. Other plows worked to get the taxiways and streets clear enough to drive on. The storm set a new record for a twenty-four hour period, dumping over nineteen inches of snow on Lincoln. That closed schools down and personnel were told not to report for duty. A decree like that was a rarity in SAC life.

It took most of the weekend to clear away tons of snow from the flight line, runway and streets. Mountains of snow where piled up on the golf driving range on the south end of the base. At least the streets were passable and people could get to the commissary for needed groceries.

At Ring Trailer Park on West "O" Street, we didn't have the benefit of snowplows coming to the rescue. It started with people trying to dig their cars out of the snow so they could get to the base or town. One problem: the street was full of snow so even if you could get out, you weren't going very far. Almost the whole trailer park turned out with shovels in hand and dug out the streets within the park. It took all day, but who cared? We didn't have to go to school and military personnel didn't have to report for duty. Besides, we weren't going anywhere until we shoveled a path so the cars could move.

The three Reflex birds trying to get back to Lincoln were finally able to return on Sunday afternoon. The crews were glad to get home from their last Reflex flight. Before the engines were cool, munitions crews were busy downloading the weapons from the racks and transporting them to the storage area northwest of the base. When the weapons were gone, the three aircraft were towed back to an open spot on the snow-covered ramp.

Operations opened again on Monday, the 15th. That morning, three B-47s were preflighted for their one-way trip to Arizona and retirement. Over the last month, more and more birds were retired. By now, the 307th's portion of the flight line was almost bare of aircraft. Another three aircraft left the patch for the boneyard on the 18th.

Sunday afternoon, the 21st, preparations were underway at the O Club for a gala evening. That evening, there was an Open Mess farewell party for the officers and wives of the 307th. It was the last time for a formal get-together. The evening was filled with farewell speeches, dinner and dancing. There was a lot of small talk, memories of Lincoln, war stories and comparing notes about where everyone was headed.

On Monday, the 22nd, the last remaining 307th Reflex crews in Spain preflighted their aircraft and started engines. They bid a not-so-fond farewell to Spain and headed their birds out across the Atlantic for the long flight home. Like always, it was a flight filled with the usual operational business at hand. This time there was a little different feeling as they approached the United States coastline. They knew it was the last time they would pull Reflex in the 307th.

Arriving at Lincoln, the three aircraft taxied to the almost vacant south end of the ramp. After shutting down the engines, the tired crews were met by munitions specialists who began the process of downloading the weapons from the bomb bay. As soon as the nuclear cargo was on the transporters and signed for, the crews departed the area for debriefing, then home. The Reflex commitment for the 307th had come to an end.

During the month, more and more transfer orders had come in. 307th personnel were leaving for all points of the compass. Some would stay in B-47s either at Pease, Plattsburgh or Mountain Home AFBs. 80 officers and airmen were transferred to the 98th and would stay at Lincoln for the time being. Others would go to B-52 or B-58 units. In the housing area, there was a constant stream of moving vans backing into driveways and loading up for the move to the next duty station.

Sunday, the 28th, dawned bright and sunny. Alert crews had breakfast at the mole hole just like they had countless times before. This time it was different: it would be their last breakfast in the mole hole at Lincoln Air Force Base. Even though the wing would stand down from Alert at 1200, they still had to do the required preflight. The wing may stand down at noon, but until that golden moment, they were still on Alert and ready to launch if the balloon went up.

After morning preflight, the crews headed back to the mole hole for the last several hours on Alert. The crews had just settled in when the klaxon sent them charging for the tunnels and to the cocked aircraft. Scrambling up the ladders, they grabbed their helmets and started spooling up the #4 engine. The radio crackled with a Green Dot Bravo message. One by one, they reported when they were ready to taxi. At the end of the Alert, they climbed back down the ladder. All nine aircraft were scored effective. When they finished the Bravo Alert, they recocked the aircraft, went back to the mole hole and waited for the stroke of noon.

At noon, on the 28th, the 307th Command Post sent a message to Barksdale and Omaha. The message informed the head sheds that the 307th Bomb Wing was standing down from ground Alert in compliance with the wing deactivation procedure as outlined in Operation Swan Song.

Flight crews arrived at their aircraft and climbed the ladders. One by one they went through engine start on the nine B-47s. When everyone was up and running, the first aircraft commander pushed the throttles forward a little to get the bird rolling. Each Alert bird moved forward from its Alert slot and started a slow taxi to the south end of the flight line. They were escorted by security trucks with the red light flashing as they formed a ground formation for the historic event.

It was an impressive, yet sad parade. Nine B-47s in a row doing a final slow taxi to the ramp near Base Operations. Arriving at the end of the ramp, they turned and moved towards a parking spot on the almost-vacant flight line. The engines wound down from a high-pitched whine to silence. When the chocks were in place, the bomb bay doors opened. Security forces were posted at each aircraft ready to repel any intruder.

The crews climbed down the ladder burdened with their flight gear and black boxes filled with EWO strike folders. They piled their gear into waiting trucks and signed the Combat Mission Folders over to the appropriate officials. Munitions crews pulled out the download checklist and began the task of removing the weapons from the racks. When the "nukes" were secured to the dollies, they began the long slow trip to the storage area under heavy security guard.

As soon as their aircraft was unloaded, the crews went to debriefing and again signed a lot of paperwork. When they were finished, they left the flight line and went home to their families. The final Alert tour for the 307th was finished. Crews could relax a little. If the klaxon went off, there wouldn't be a mad dash for the Alert birds; the 98th would have to take care of that.

At the end of the month, the 307th had thirteen B-47s sitting on the ramp, including the nine that had just come off Alert. Almost 57% of the personnel had been transferred out to their new duty stations. Those left would continue the task of closing out the wing at Lincoln.

March 1st dawned clear and bright. The sun came over the eastern hills like it had since the 307th began operations almost nine years ago. But, that Monday morning it was different. It was the first day of the last month the 307th would be at Lincoln airplane patch.

During the last few weeks of February, the weather had been unusually mild. As a matter of fact, the unseasonably mild weather had broken several records for high temperatures. Most of the snow had melted and the ground in many places was devoid of any of the white stuff. Who would have believed the mounds of snow would melt so quickly? The mild weather made it easier on the moving vans to take on the valuable loads of household goods up in the housing area.

Ground crews serviced and went through ground preflight on 53-1902 and 53-1867 on Tuesday morning, the 2nd. Later that morning, the flight crews arrived and went through their preflight, startup and taxi. They lined up on the runway, went to full power and took off. They were headed for Arizona and the boneyard. They were the first of the last wave of B-47s from the 307th headed for retirement. During the rest of the day, 307th personnel continued to pack equipment for transport or transfer to the 98th.

The next day, three more B-47s departed the patch for Arizona. The flights were routine, lasting about three hours. Arriving in Arizona, the crews would sign the aircraft over to the boneyard, collect their flight gear and spend the night either at the base or at a motel before heading back to Lincoln. During the next few days, the number of B-47s on the south end of the ramp continued to dwindle as they left the patch for Arizona.

By Tuesday, the 9th, there were three birds with the 307th insignia sitting on the barren end of the flight line. Launch crews prepared 53-2140 and 53-1911 for a morning launch. There was some small talk as the crews went through preflight. The crew chiefs had done their usual professional job of getting the aircraft ready for the final flight. When the flight crews taxied out and took off, there was one B-47 sitting all alone on the ramp.

Alone on the flight line was 53-4223. She had been assigned to the wing since April 1956, a replacement aircraft for one of the original aircraft assigned to the wing. When the wing went TDY to England, 4223 flew in the second wave. She went through Project "Milk Bottle" and returned to the 307th. The old gal pulled her share of Alert and went Reflex to England and Spain. During the Cuban Missile Crisis, she stood Alert, ready to respond if the balloon went up.

The flight crew arrived for the final preflight. Flying in the front seat as aircraft commander was LtCol H.T. Moore. LtCol John Allison would fly copilot and LtCol Alan Simpkins would be in the nose as navigator. Her crew chief for the mission was SSgt James Weatherby. The preflight walk around was completed without major problems. After a photo session to record the historic event, the crew climbed the ladder and started engines.

While the aircraft taxied to the end of Runway 17, Col Arthur Holderness drove to the turnoff point about halfway down the runway. At the far end of the runway, 4223 held short for final clearance from the tower. When the tower cleared them for take off, LtCol Moore pushed the throttles to full power, waited for it to stabilize, then hit the water-alcohol augmentation. 4223 started down Runway 17 for the last time. Gaining airspeed as each marker flashed by, the crew went through the acceleration timing check. At the calculated take off speed, the old bird lifted off the concrete and started climbing into the air.

Col Holderness had left his staff car and was standing beside the runway as 4223 approached. As 4223 flew past, Col Holderness gave her and her crew a snappy farewell salute. He watched as the last 307th B-47 disappeared in the distance, leaving only a trail of black smoke to mark her passing into history.

With the departure of 4233, air operations of the 307th came to an end. No more Reflex; no more 50-8 squares to fill in; no more Alert. Since the 307th didn't have any aircraft, it was almost safe to say no more ORIs. Now, those who remained would concentrate on the business of packing up and closing the wing down.

The *Jet Scoop* issue for Friday, March 12th was a farewell to the 307th. Practically the whole issue was devoted to the wing. There was a brief history of the wing from World War II to the present. There were articles devoted to the accomplishments of the wing during service at Lincoln. Other articles covered the saga of 6244 going to the Air Force Museum at Dayton, Ohio, along with the departure of the last B-47. In all, it was a fitting farewell to the wing.

*"To all members, past and present, of the 307th Bomb Wing:*

*Farewell. I am immensely proud of the outstanding record the 307th Bombardment Wing has compiled during the past years. Your inspiring display of cooperation, loyalty and high resolve have carried the 307th Bomb Wing to the epitome of professional competence. Throughout the years, our military environment has demanded great patience, restraint and dedication. All of you have met and exceeded these demands. I am certain that each of you throughout the remainder of your military career will continue to exercise that same high degree of vision, integrity and devotion to duty which has earned the 307th Bomb Wing the highest of professional standings. Accept my thanks and sincere appreciation for a job superbly accomplished. My best wishes go with each and every one of you.*

*Col Arthur W Holderness*
*Commander, 307th Bomb Wing"*

Deactivation of the wing hit high gear. Every day, literally tons of equipment were inventoried, packed, the inventoried again. Tons of paperwork were filed, packed and loaded for transport to storage for later consideration and disposal. Equipment that could be used by other wings was crated and shipped to a new location.

Remaining personnel went through the process of transferring out. The process could take hours or just a few minutes depending on how up-to-date the paperwork was. There was the 201 file which had to be up to date, medical records, pay records and, oh yeah, orders, in triplicate of course. With this in hand, it was then the simple matter of signing out of the squadron and clearing the base. Don Hickman recalled:

"It was announced the 307th Bomb Wing was being deactivated and the assignments started pouring in. 'Red' Duffer was headed for B-52s. Miller Peeler had upgraded to aircraft commander and he and I agreed to go together as a crew to either Mountain Home AFB, Idaho, or Plattsburgh AFB, New York. Together, we decided Plattsburgh would suit us better and applied for it as our first choice. Finally, believing that wonders never cease, we actually got what we asked for. In March of 1965, the movers came to the house, packed us up and we headed for upstate New York."

Most of the equipment had been crated up and either sent out or hauled over to base supply. With most of the equipment gone, there wasn't

# Cold War Cornhuskers: The 307th Bomb Wing Lincoln Air Force Base Nebraska 1955-1965

a lot left to do for those who still manned the fort, wing, that is. There was a somewhat comical sign posted on the door of wing headquarters that read, "The last one to leave, PLEASE shut off the lights and lock the door."

The wing commander, Col Arthur Holderness, presided over a formal deactivation ceremony for the 307th on March 25th. After several speeches by SAC officials, Col Holderness stood by as the colors for the wing were retired and encased for the last time at Lincoln Air Force Base, Nebraska.

After the official deactivation was completed, there was only one thing to do. Sign out of the wing and leave the base. The last members of the 307th Bomb Wing to sign out were Maj Leroy Kutscher, 307th A&E Squadron; Lt Richard Dinwiddie, 307th OMS; LtCol Hale Dodge, 370th BS Commander; Maj Fred Varn, 372nd BS Commander; A1C Timothy Joiner, 307th OMS; and Col Arthur Holderness, 307th BW Commander. With the final sign-out completed, the 307th BW was officially no longer active. Thus ended almost nineteen years of service in the Strategic Air Command.

**Author's Postscript**
Towards the end of February, the Hill family got their marching orders to move on to the next base. The hope had been to go to Omaha and finish Air Force life in Nebraska. SAC BRAT wanted to attend the University of Nebraska. The United States Air Force had decided that TSgt Hill's expertise was needed at Minot Air Force Base, North Dakota, wherever that was.

When SAC BRAT's neighborhood buddies found out he was headed for the American version of Siberia, they didn't have a going away party, they held a "wake". Young SAC BRAT assured his buddies that as soon as he was out of high school he'd be back in Huskerland to go to college.

Monday, the 15th, found the Hill family ready to "head 'em up; move 'em out" for Minot. Dad had spent the last several days getting our mobile home ready for the trip. It was hitched to the truck and ready to roll. That morning he pulled it out of Lot 10 and parked it on the street for the final preflight check. Mom and SAC BRAT would follow, pulling a 1955 Ford sedan that SAC BRAT had just acquired.

After a day-long drive up Highway 81 the clan arrived at Ellendale, North Dakota, the port of entry for North Dakota. First SNAFU: the permit to tow the "long wide load" hadn't arrived from Bismarck; "they should be here tomorrow". So, it was across the highway to a motel for the night. Supper that night was at the Ellendale Hotel in beautiful downtown Ellendale. The hotel looked like it was right out of "Gunsmoke". About all that was missing was Marshall Dillon, Miss Kitty, Doc and Chester.

Next morning, checking with the port of entry weight station across the highway, we found the permits had arrived. So, it's on the road towards Minot, right? SNAFU #2: along with the arrival of the permit, a good old fashion NODAK blizzard had arrived from the north. This one made the Nebraska "Hawk" look like a sparrow. Wind at 40-45 knots, and that's during the calmer moments. Snow coming down like crazy. Visibility wasn't much beyond the hood of the car. Along with the wind and snow there was the temperature, or lack of it. It was colder than a brass monkey's backside. SAC BRAT thought that if this was what North Dakota was like, he wanted no part of it!

Since the Highway Patrol had pulled their "Smokeys" off the road, it was obvious the Hill family would have to wait out the blizzard at the motel. Later, there was the thrilling, less-than-a-mile drive to the Gunsmoke Hotel for lunch and supper. Why was it thrilling, you ask? The wind was howling like a banshee, bumper deep snow, not much to see beyond the hood ornament and that's in town. You almost needed a GCA to find the hotel and we were on the ground!

The NODAK whiteout showed no signs of abating the next day. So, it was a couple of more trips back to Gunsmoke and watch the one station available on the television. At times the reception was about as snowy as it was outside.

By late morning on the 18th the snow had slowed; the wind calmed down enough so you could see about a half a mile. Dad said, "Saddle up, we got to get movin'. We're burnin' daylight!" Daylight, what daylight? Oh, you mean the gray soupy mess outside. Out on the road, dad took the lead with the mobile home in tow while mom and SAC BRAT followed close enough so we wouldn't get swallowed in the blowing snow.

Somewhere south of Jamestown, the wind ripped the plywood covering the expandable section of the living room off. It was last seen heading east across Farmer Brown's fields. This opened the living room to the fury of the elements. Can't stop and try to find the plywood. Only choice was to limp into Jamestown. SNAFU #3: arriving in Jamestown, we found a lumber yard, got another sheet of plywood, then spent over an hour securing it to the proper place. Ever try securing plywood using sheet metal screws at minus eighteen degrees? NOT FUN AT ALL, ME BOYO! We could get two or three screws fastened before fingers started feeling like ice cubes.

By the time the plywood was secured the snow had almost stopped. The wind was still blowing, but at least the weather was improving. Considering the conditions that we left behind, the final one hundred and seventy-five miles to Minot were a breeze. So, the Hill family arrived at their new station. New friends would be made, time would march on, but there would always be a special feeling for the years spent at Lincoln.

53-6244 in the south hangar. Hours of work will make her look "factory fresh" for her trip to the Air Force Museum. (Villa)

*1965*

Bruce Stufflebeam and 6244 at the refueling pits prior to departure for Dayton. (Villa)

Museum Aircraft. (JETSCOOP)

Without a reliable MD-3 unit, it was almost impossible to get the engines started. (M Hill)

307th OMS members pose with 53-4223 March 1965. L-R: William Sullivan, unknown, Sgt. Herr, unknown, Melvin Taylor, John Laws, Shields, Gary Leslie, Ron Short, Robert Holly. Front L-R: Ken Harraburda, Melvin Cihal, David Peltz, Robert Loffredo, Sheldon Thomas. (Loffredo)

# Cold War Cornhuskers: The 307th Bomb Wing Lincoln Air Force Base Nebraska 1955-1965

The last 307th crew. (JET SCOOP)

Col. Holderness gives a farewell salute as 4223 takes off for Davis Monthan. (JET SCOOP)

Col. Arthur Holderness, last commander of the 307th BW. (JET SCOOP)

# Memorials

*IN HONORED MEMORY:*
*Isaiah 6:8 "Whom shall I send and who will go for us?....*
*Here am I! Send me!"*

July 1, 1955 LAFB: KC-97 Ground Accident A1C Willie L. Ezell Jr.

April 6, 1956 Ceresco, Nebraska: B-47 53-4209 Capt James W. Sullivan, AC
Lt Anthony C. Marcanti, CP, Lt Lawrence A. Schmidt, Nav, A1C James J. Berry, Crew Chief

July 28, 1956 RAFB Lakenheath England: B-47 53-4230 Capt Russell R. Bowling, AC, Lt Carroll W. Kalberg, CP, Lt Michael J. Selmo, Nav, TSgt John Ulrich, A/E Tech

October 10, 1956 Lost between Lakenheath and Lakenheath: R6D-1 (C-118) #131588 *Navy Crewmen:* Lt Cmdr Fred Lowe, Lt Cmdr William Willis, Lt (jg) Dominic Cirbus, Aviation Electrical Technician Roger Jokela, Chief Aviation Technician Robert Miney, Airman James Ringler, Aviation Machinist Mate 1C Herman Stone, Aviation Machinist Mate 2C Frank Smith

*307th Bomb Wing Passengers:* Capt Kenneth E. Goodroe, Capt Robert W. Ryan, MSgt William A. Caisse, SSgt Thomas I. DeCota, A1C Alton J. Gaines, A1C Orest D. Giancola, A1C Billy B. Grogan, A1C Eugene D. Gruenberg, A1C Richard K. Hunter, A1C Ronald L. King, A1C Robert Lada, A1C Joseph D. Loontiens, A1C Michael C. Macedonia, A1C Ronald F. Mountain, A1C Stanley L. Osgar, A1C Keith A. Peterson, A1C James L. Schorr, A1C Robert C. Urban, A1C Earl F. Vasey, A1C Herbert A. Banks, A2C Albert L. Beard, A2C Dale R. Brockman, A2C Conrad J. Buehler, Jr., A2C Edmond R. DeWolf, A2C John F. Disanto, A2C Raymond E. Drake, A2C Lyle C. Giberson, A2C Gene O. Godfrey, A2C Cloyse A. Hepler, A2C Gerard A. Hummel, A2C Robert H. Lipina, A2C George F. Luce, A2C William R. Ray, A2C Leonard J. Roman, A2C Henry J. Schuver, A2C Robert D. Spurling, A2C James B. Whitlock, A2C Frank C. Williamson, A3C Roscoe F. Deel, A3C Willie B. Ferguson, A3C Ronald L. Gardner, A3C Charles W. Hannah, A3C Lloyd D. Harding, A3C Lee R. Kane, A3C Sherman W. Lock, A3C Donald L.

Reynolds, A3C Abelardo Siller, Jr., A3C Bruce B. Stewart, A3C Earl E. Tanner, November 17, 1956 LAFB: Nebraska ANG F-80 crashed into fuel pits destroying 2 B-47s. A1C John L. Delancy, A2C Donald R. Price.

October 8, 1959 LAFB: B-47 51-5248 Maj. Paul R Ecelbarger, IP, 1Lt Joseph R Morrissey, Jr., FBAC, Capt Lucian W Nowlin, Nav, Capt Theodore Tallmadge, NAV

June 18, 1961 LAFB: B-47 53-2111 Capt Russell Holst, AC, Capt Allan Matson, CP, Capt Albert Marinich, NAV

January 11, 1963 McConnell AFB, Kansas: B-47 53-2097 Capt Paul Pudwill, AC

February 3, 1963 RAFB Greenham Common England: B-47 53-2134 Capt Richard C West, CP

March 7, 1963 LAFB: B-47 53-4226 Maj N. V. Meeks, AC

July 27, 1964 LAFB: B-47 53-2366 Capt Thomas E. Sutton, AC, 1Lt David C. Williams, CP 1Lt Terrance P. Murphy, NAV Maj. John F. Sakry, IN

**Killed In Action: Southeast Asia Conflict**
Earl M. Freeman,
Ivel D. Freeman
Otis Gordon, Jr.
Andrew Matyas
Maj James R. McElvain December 18, 1972
Robert D. Morrissey.
Lt George K. Sisler, US Army Special Forces (Awarded the Medal of Honor)
Leon G. Smith, Walter H. Trisko
Courtney E. Weismueller

**Lost In Other Military Aviation Accidents**
Selfridge AFB, Michigan, February 28, 1961: KC-97 53-0331, Capt Lindell Hagood, 1Lt John Dibble, 1Lt Robert Lewis, TSgt Robert Derby
Curtiss E. Robertson
TSgt Robert L. Conway
1Lt Michael Eyre, killed in a Civil Air Patrol Accident at LAFB September 1964
Clifford E. Hanna, USCG

# 307th Bomb Wing Aircraft Assignments

**B-47 Aircraft Assigned to the 307th Bomb Wing**

51-15808
Assigned to the 307th Bomb Wing (BW), 370th Bomb Squadron (BS), Lincoln AFB, NE, July 1958. Crew Chief T.R. Taylor. Transferred January 1961 to the 68th BW, Chennault AFB, LA. Sent to the Military Aircraft Storage and Disposition Center (MASDC), Davis-Monthan AFB, AZ, February 1, 1963. Scrapped October 17, 1967.

51-17380
Assigned to the 307th BW, 372nd BS, 1958. Transferred to 98th BW, Lincoln AFB, NE. Sent to MASDC June 1, 1961. Scrapped March 10, 1964.

51-2087
Assigned to the 307th BW, 372nd BS, from McConnell AFB, KS, on May 15, 1957. As a TB-47, it was used as a pilot proficiency aircraft. Sent to MASDC October 28, 1958. Scrapped April 15, 1959.

51-2207
Research indicates this was the first B-47 to be assigned to the 98th BW at Lincoln AFB, arriving December 1955. Transferred to the 307th BW, 370th BS, in January 1958. Crew Chief Sedgefield Hill. Assigned to the 340th BW, Whiteman AFB, MO, September 1958. The aircraft was later transferred back to Lincoln AFB, NE. It was demilitarized and placed on display near the BX Annex. After the base closed, it was towed across the runway and used as a fire practice aircraft.

51-2364
Last assigned to the 307th BW, 370th BS. Sent to MASDC on February 15, 1961. Scrapped May 11, 1963.

51-5234
Last assigned to the 307th BW, Lincoln AFB, NE. Sent to MASDC and scrapped on January 16, 1964.

51-5235
Assigned to the 307th BW, 371st BS. Crew Chief Donald Watts. Sent to MASDC on June 14, 1961, and scrapped on February 5, 1964.

51-5237
Assigned to the 307th BW, 370th BS, October 1959. Sent to MASDC on June 14, 1961, and scrapped on December 31, 1965

51-5248
Assigned to the 68th BW, Lake Charles AFB, LA (1953). Transferred to the 307th BW, 372nd BS, June 1959. Crashed on takeoff during a northbound ATO takeoff on October 8, 1959. Maj Paul Ecelbarger (IP/CP), Lt Joseph Morrissey, Jr. (Student AC), Capt Lucian Nowlin (Instructor Nav) and Capt Theodore Tallmadge (Nav) were killed in the accident.

51-7065
Assigned to the 307th BW, 371st BS, August 1958. Sent to MASDC April 28, 1961. Scrapped February 4, 1964.

52-040
Assigned to the 307th BW June 1958. Transferred to 98th BW July 1959. Last Assigned to the 4347th CCTW, McConnell AFB, KS. Sent to MASDC June 13, 1963. Scrapped October 17, 1969.

52-054
One of the original B-47s assigned to the 307th BW, 370th BS, March 15, 1955. Overshot runway on May 27, 1955. Damaged beyond repair, dropped from the inventory in October 1955. Salvaged for usable parts. The fuselage was placed near the auto hobby shop at Lincoln AFB.

52-058
One of the original aircraft assigned to the 307th BW, 370th BS, March 15, 1955. Transferred May 2, 1956, to the 306th BW, MacDill AFB, FL. Sent to MASDC February 8, 1963. Scrapped October 18, 1967.

52-060
Assigned to the 307th BW, 371st BS. Crew Chief Ansel B. Chase. Transferred to 98th BW October 1959. Last assigned to the 9th BW, Mountain Home AFB, ID. Sent to MASDC May 13, 1964. Scrapped July 9, 1968.

# Cold War Cornhuskers: The 307th Bomb Wing Lincoln Air Force Base Nebraska 1955-1965

52-061
One of the original aircraft assigned to the 307th BW, 371st BS, March 14, 1955. Transferred May 3, 1956. Modified to EB-47L Pipe Cleaner (1962). Returned to the 307th BW, 4362nd PACCS, summer 1962. Sent to MASDC December 1, 1964. Scrapped October 2, 1968.

52-064
One of the original B-47s assigned to the 307th BW, 370th BS, March 14, 1955. Crew Chief Edward Seagraves. Transferred May 7, 1956, to the 40th BW Smoky Hill AFB, KS. Sent to MASDC June 13, 1961. Scrapped March 31, 1964.

52-066
Arrived March 14, 1955, as one of the original B-47s assigned to the 307th BW, 371st BS. Departed May 8, 1956. Modified to EB-47L Pipe Cleaner (1962). Returned to the 307th BW, 4362nd PACCS. Transferred to the 380th BW, Plattsburgh AFB, NY. Sent to MASDC August 22, 1964. Scrapped October 2, 1968.

52-067
Assigned to 307th BW, 370th BS (1958). Transferred to 98th BW October 1959. Modified to EB-47L Pipe Cleaner (1962). Last assigned to the 9th BW, Mountain Home AFB, ID. Sent to MASDC February 24, 1965. Scrapped December 13, 1968.

52-069
Modified to EB-47L Pipe Cleaner (1962). Assigned to the 307th BW, 4362nd PACCS. Sent to MASDC December 1, 1964. Scrapped October 2, 1968.

52-071
One of the original wing aircraft, arrived March 14, 1955. Transferred May 9, 1956. Modified to EB-47L Pipe Cleaner (1962). Last assigned to the 376th BW Lockbourne AFB, OH. Sent to MASDC February 26, 1965. Scrapped December 13, 1968.

52-075
Assigned to the 307th BW summer 1958. Transferred November 1958 to the 4347th CCTW, McConnell AFB, KS. Sent to MASDC April 26, 1963. Scrapped October 18, 1967.

52-077
Assigned to the 307th BW, 372nd BS, March 14, 1955, as an original aircraft. Departed 307th on May 9, 1956. Assigned to the 307th BW May 1959. Transferred to 98th BW August 1959. Last assigned to the 4347th CCTW, McConnell AFB, KS. Sent to MASDC June 5, 1963. Scrapped October 18, 1967.

52-078
Modified to EB-47L Pipe Cleaner (1962). Assigned to the 307th BW, 4362nd PACCS, September 1962. Sent to MASDC December 1, 1964. Scrapped January 14, 1969.

52-082
Assigned to the 341st BW, Dyess AFB, TX. Modified to EB-47L Pipe Cleaner (1962). Transferred to the 307th BW, 4362nd PACCS, December 10, 1964. Last assigned to the 380th BW, Plattsburgh AFB, NY. Sent to MASDC November 23, 1964. Scrapped October 2, 1968.

52-120
Assigned to the 307th BW March 14, 1955, as one of the original B-47s. Transferred March 12, 1956, to the 305th BW, Bunker Hill AFB, IN. Sent to MASDC May 18, 1960. Scrapped July 1, 1960.

52-154
Assigned to the 301st BW, Lockbourne AFB, OH. Transferred to the 307th BW, 372nd BS, July 1958. Transferred out August 1959. Modified to EB-47L Pipe Cleaner (1962). Assigned to the 307th BW, 4362nd PACCS, August 1963. Last assigned to the 380th BW, Plattsburgh AFB. NY. Sent to MASDC November 19, 1964. Scrapped October 2, 1968.

52-214
Assigned to the 307th Bomb Wing, 372nd BS July 1958. Transferred to 98th BW August 1959. Modified to EB-47L Pipe Cleaner (1962). Last assigned to the 9th BW, Mountain Home AFB, ID. Sent to MASDC May 27, 1963. Scrapped January 14, 1969.

52-217
Assigned to the 307th BW, 372nd BS, 1958. Transferred to 98th BW September 1959. Modified to EB-47L Pipe Cleaner (1962). Last assigned to the 376th BW, Lockbourne AFB, OH. Sent to MASDC December 18, 1964. Scrapped January 14, 1969.

52-224
Assigned to 307th BW, 4362nd PACCS. Modified to EB-47L Pipe Cleaner (1962). Transferred July 12, 1964, to the 380th BW, Plattsburgh AFB. NY. Sent to MASDC November 19, 1964. Scrapped October 2, 1968.

52-228
Assigned to the 307th BW, 371st BS, 1955. Transferred out April 11, 1956, to the 306th BW, MacDill AFB, FL. Sent to MASDC January 23, 1963. Scrapped October 11, 1967.

52-231
Assigned to the 93rd BW, Castle AFB, CA (1954). Transferred to the 307th BW, 370th BS, 1955. Assigned April 2, 1956, to the 40th BW, Forbes AFB, KS. Sent to MASDC January 21, 1962. Scrapped October 19, 1967.

52-233
Assigned to the 307th BW, 371st BS, 1955. Assigned April 4, 1956, to the 9th BW, Mountain Home AFB, ID. Sent to MASDC January 27, 1965. Scrapped October 6, 1968.

52-234
Assigned to the 307th BW, 370th BS, 1955. Crew Chief William Gallagher. Assigned April 6, 1956, to the 509th BW, Pease AFB, NH. Sent to MASDC October 27, 1965. Scrapped October 23, 1968.

52-235
Assigned to the 307th BW, 372nd BS 1955. Transferred April 9. 1956, to the 306th BW, MacDill AFB, FL. Crashed on April 15, 1958, about five minutes after taking off. There were thunderstorms in the area at the time. Investigation revealed that there was a fatigue crack in the wing. It is believed that the extra stress imposed by wind gusts from the thunderstorm caused the wing to fail.

# 307th Bomb Wing Aircraft Assignments

52-236
Assigned to 307th BW, 370th BS, 1955. Transferred April 11.1956, to the 4347th CCTW, McConnell AFB, KS. Sent to MASDC June 11, 1963. Scrapped October 19, 1967.

52-238
Assigned to the 307th BW, 372nd BS 1955. Assigned April 13, 1956, to the 4347th CCTW, McConnell AFB, KS. Sent to MASDC March 26, 1968. Scrapped October 19, 1967.

2-241
Assigned to the 307th BW, 372nd BS, 1955. Assigned April 17, 1956, to the 306th BW, MacDill AFB, FL. On December 4, 1957, this B-47 crashed at the Eglin AFB, FL, bombing range.

52-242
Assigned 307th BW, 370th BS 1955. Assigned April 18, 1956, to the 306th BW, MacDill AFB, FL. On January 31, 1958, the aircraft was destroyed on the runway at Sidi Slimane, Morocco. Responding to a "COCO ALERT" the aircraft blew a tire, which sent fragments in all directions. The aircraft caught fire and burned for over seven hours. The fire burned a 100-foot gap into the runway. The aircraft was loaded with a nuclear weapon. In response to the danger the base was evacuated. No explosion of the weapon occurred.

52-243
Assigned to the 307th BW, 371st BS 1955. Assigned April 20, 1956, to the 4347th CCTW, McConnell AFB, KS. Sent to MASDC May 24, 1963. Scrapped October 19, 1967.

52-244
Assigned to 307th BW, 371st BS 1955. Assigned April 24, 1956, to the 306th BW, MacDill AFB, FL. On March 21, 1958, the aircraft had completed a series of low-level bomb runs at the Avon Park, FL, range. Returning to the base the aircraft made low pass by the control tower and pulled up into a climbing turn to the left. The left wing snapped and the aircraft burst into flames and crashed. The crew was killed.

52-245
Assigned to 307th BW, 371st BS, 1955. Assigned February 26, 1956, to the 4347th CCTW, McConnell AFB, KS. Sent to MASDC June 11, 1963. Scrapped October 19, 1967.

52-246
Assigned to the 307th BW, 371st BS, 1955. Assigned May 1, 1956, to the 9th BW, Mountain Home AFB, ID. Sent to MASDC August 31, 1964. Scrapped July 9, 1968.

52-247
Assigned to the 307th BW, 370th BS, 1955. Transferred May 2, 1956, to the 306th BW MacDill AFB, FL. On December 16, 1958, the pilot reported a fire in the right aileron pack about four minutes after takeoff. The aircraft crashed into Tampa Bay killing the crew. Investigation showed that the right aileron PCU return line had pulled loose allowing fluid to pool in the canoe fairing above the #6 engine. This caused a fire burning the aileron pulley and causing the cable to slip, which caused loss of aileron control during the final turn.

52-248
Assigned to the 307th BW, 371st BS, 1955. Transferred May 3, 1956, to the 4347th CCTW, McConnell AFB, KS. Sent to MASDC May 17, 1963. Scrapped October 19, 1967.

52-250
Assigned to the 307th BW, 371st BS, 1955. Assigned May 7, 1956, to the 3918th Combat Support Group, RAF Upper Heyford, UK. Scrapped there in February 1962.

52-251
Assigned to the 307th BW, 371st BS, 1955. Transferred April 11, 1956, to the 305th BW, Bunker Hill AFB, IN. Status change to "W" for school use. Ultimate disposition unknown.

52-252
Assigned to the 307th BW, 371st BS, 1955. Transferred May 10, 1956, to the 305th BW, Bunker Hill AFB, IN. Status changed to "W" for use in schools. Ultimate disposition unknown.

52-255
Assigned to the 307th BW, 370th BS, 1955. Transferred May 14, 1956, to the 305th BW, Bunker Hill AFB, IN. Last assigned to the 3919th Combat Support Group, RAF Fairford, UK, and scrapped there on May 19, 1959.

52-256
Assigned to the 307th BW, 370th BS, 1955. Transferred May 16, 1956 to the 305th BW, Bunker Hill AFB, IN. Status changed to "W" for school use. Ultimate disposition unknown.

52-257
Assigned to the 307th BW, 370th BS, 1955. Transferred May 18, 1956, to the 305th BW, Bunker Hill AFB, IN. Sent to MASDC June 7, 1960. Scrapped February 13, 1961.

52-258
Assigned to the 307th BW, 372nd BS, 1955. Assigned May 21, 1956 to the 305th BW, Bunker Hill AFB, IN. Transferred to the 3909th Combat Support Group, RAF Greenham Common, on May 18, 1959. Dropped from inventory in May 1959. Used for special weapons loading training and scrapped in May 1963.

52-260
Assigned to the 307th BW, 370th BS, 1955. Transferred April 10, 1956, to the 305th BW, Bunker Hill AFB, IN. Sent to MASDC June 2, 1960. Scrapped February 13, 1961.

52-262
Assigned to the 307th BW, 370th BS, 1955. Transferred June 1, 1956, to the 305th BW, Bunker Hill AFB, IN. Sent to MASDC May 4, 1960. Scrapped July 1, 1960.

52-263
Assigned to the 307th BW, 371st BS, 1955. Transferred June 4, 1956, to the 4347th CCTW, McConnell AFB, KS. Sent to MASDC June 20, 1960. Scrapped February 14, 1961.

52-264
Assigned to the 307th BW, 372nd BS, 1955. Transferred June 6, 1956, to the 305th BW, Bunker Hill AFB, IN. Sent to MASDC May 17, 1960. Scrapped July 1, 1960.

# Cold War Cornhuskers: The 307th Bomb Wing Lincoln Air Force Base Nebraska 1955-1965

52-267
Assigned to the 307th BW, 370th BS, 1955. Transferred June 8, 1956, to the 305th BW, Bunker Hill AFB, IN. Sent to MASDC May 10, 1960. Scrapped July 14, 1960.

52-270
Assigned to the 307th BW, 372nd BS, 1955. Transferred June 13, 1956, to the 305th BW, Bunker Hill AFB, IN. Sent to MASDC June 9, 1960. Scrapped February 14, 1961.

52-288
Assigned to the 307th BW, 371st BS, 1955. Transferred June 13, 1956, to the 305th BW, Bunker Hill AFB, IN. Sent to MASDC May 12, 1960. Scrapped January 26, 1961.

52-292
Assigned to 307th BW 1958. Transferred to 98th BW September 1959. Modified to EB-47L Pipe Cleaner (1962). Last assigned to the 9th BW, Mountain Home AFB, ID. Sent to MASDC March 24, 1965. Scrapped January 14, 1969.

52-298
Modified to EB-47L Pipe Cleaner (1962). Assigned to the 307th BW, 4362nd PACCS. Transferred November 15, 1964, to the 9th BW, Mountain Home AFB, ID. Sent to MASDC March 26, 1965. Scrapped January 14, 1969.

52-323
Last assigned to the 307th BW, Lincoln AFB, NE, August 1963. Sent to MASDC April 1, 1964. Scrapped September 11, 1968.

52-331
Last assigned to "A" Section, 307th BW August 1963. Sent to MASDC June 8, 1964. Scrapped September 10, 1968.

52-353
Last assigned to the 307th BW in September 1960. Sent to MASDC June 10, 1964. Scrapped July 9, 1968.

52-358
Assigned to the 307th BW, 372nd BS, 1955. Transferred April 13, 1956, to the 40th BW, Smoky Hill AFB, KS. Sent to MASDC June 24, 1964. Scrapped July 9, 1968.

52-362
Assigned to the 307th BW, 372nd BS, 1955. Transferred April 16, 1956, to the 384th BW, Little Rock AFB, AR. Sent to MASDC July 17, 1964. Scrapped September 11, 1968.

52-390
Assigned to the 307th BW, 372nd BS, 1955. Transferred April 16, 1956, to the 96th BW, Dyess AFB, TX. On July 23, 1962, the aircraft crashed into Emigrant Mountain, MT, at the 8,000-foot level. The crew of four were killed.

52-398
Assigned to the 307th Bomb Wing 1955. Transferred April 1956. Modified to EB-47E Blue Cradle. Assigned to the 376th BW, Lockbourne AFB, OH. Sent to MASDC January 21, 1965. Scrapped January 31, 1969.

52-402
Assigned to 307th BW, 372nd BS, 1955. Transferred April 1956. Modified to EB-47E Blue Cradle. Assigned to the 376th BW, Lockbourne AFB, OH. Crashed on takeoff on October 23, 1958. During takeoff, the aircraft gained about 300 feet altitude, dropped off on the right wing and crashed and burned on the runway. Investigation showed that the accident was caused by improper CG of 39.9 %. The forward main fuel tank had 8,000 lbs less fuel than indicated. Capt George Berliner, Lt Carl Atherton and Capt Thomas Henry were killed.

52-406
Assigned to 307th BW, 372nd BS, 1955. Modified to EB-47E Blue Cradle. Assigned to the 376th BW, Lockbourne AFB, OH. Sent to MASDC October 11, 1964. Scrapped January 13, 1969.

52-408
Assigned 307th BW, 372nd BS, 1955. Modified to EB-47E Blue Cradle. Assigned to the 376th BW, Lockbourne AFB, OH. Sent to MASDC December 3, 1964. Scrapped January 13, 1969.

52-432
Assigned to the 307th BW July 1963. Sent to MASDC June 10, 1964. Scrapped September 10, 1968.

52-536
Assigned to the 307th BW 1963. On September 9, 1964, it was transferred to the Navy and sent to China Lake, CA.

52-548
Assigned to the 307th BW. Sent to MASDC November 16, 1964. Scrapped September 11, 1968.

52-549
Assigned to the 307th BW August 1963. Sent to MASDC June 15, 1964. Scrapped September 11, 1968.

52-550
Assigned to the 307th BW. Sent to MASDC December 14, 1964. Scrapped September 11, 1968.

52-583
Assigned to the 307th BW July 1963. Sent to MASDC June 19, 1964. Scrapped September 30, 1968.

52-522
Assigned to the 307th BW. Sent to MASDC February 13, 1963. Scrapped October 20, 1967.

52-523
Assigned to the 307th BW. Sent to MASDC November 9, 1964. Scrapped September 11, 1968.

52-529
Assigned to the 307th BW. Sent to MASDC January 19, 1965. Scrapped October 17, 1968.

52-548
Assigned the 307th BW. Sent to MASDC November 16, 1964. Scrapped September 11, 1968.

# 307th Bomb Wing Aircraft Assignments

**52-549**
Assigned to the 307th BW. Sent to MASDC June 15, 1964. Scrapped September 11, 1968.

**52-550**
Assigned to the 307th BW. Sent to MASDC December 14, 1964. Scrapped September 11, 1968.

**52-557**
Assigned to the 307th BW. Sent to MASDC January 26, 1965. Scrapped October 17, 1968.

**52-602**
Assigned to the 307th BW. Sent to MASDC February 10, 1964. Scrapped October 16, 1968.

**52-604**
Assigned to the 307th BW. Sent to MASDC February 10, 1965. Scrapped October 16, 1968.

**52-605**
Assigned to the 307th BW. Sent to MASDC February 15, 1965. Scrapped October 16, 1968.

**52-607**
Assigned to the 307th BW. Sent to MASDC February 15, 1965. Scrapped October 16, 1968.

**52-608**
Assigned to the 307th BW. Sent to MASDC January 19, 1965. Scrapped October 16, 1968.

**52-611**
Assigned to the 307th BW. Sent to MASDC March 18, 1965. Scrapped October 20, 1967.

**52-616**
Assigned to the 307th BW. Sent to MASDC February 4, 1965. Scrapped October 16, 1968.

**52-618**
Assigned to the 307th BW. Sent to MASDC March 3, 1965. Scrapped October 16, 1968.

**53-1829**
Assigned to the 307th BW June 29, 1961. Sent to MASDC June 4, 1964. Scrapped September 11, 1968.

**53-1834**
Assigned to the 307th BW June 1963. Sent to MASDC June 4, 1964. Scrapped September 11, 1968.

**53-1843**
Assigned to the 307th BW May 1958. Crew Chief Robert Hart. Sent to MASDC June 12, 1963. Scrapped October 1, 1968.

**53-1844**
Assigned to the 307th BW April 1958. Assigned to the 96th BW, Dyess AFB, TX. Sent to MASDC February 1, 1963. Scrapped July 31, 1967.

**53-1853**
Assigned to the 307th BW summer 1958. Sent to MASDC June 10, 1964. Scrapped September 11, 1965.

**53-1866**
Assigned to the 307th BW. Sent to MASDC February 4, 1965. Scrapped October 16, 1968.

**53-1867**
Assigned to the 307th BW. Sent to MASDC March 3, 1965. Scrapped October 16, 1968.

**53-1870**
Assigned to the 307th BW, 372nd BS, summer 1959. Assigned to the 380th BW, Plattsburgh AFB, NY. Sent to MASDC December 9, 1965. Scrapped January 28, 1969.

**53-1872 CORNHUSKER SPECIAL**
Assigned to the 307th BW 1959. Represented the 307th at the 1961 SAC BOMB/COMP. Crew Chief Donald Mowry. Sent to MASDC January 26, 1965. Scrapped October 16, 1968.

**53-1882**
Assigned to the 307th. Sent to MASDC February 2, 1965. Scrapped October 16, 1968.

**53-1885**
Served with the 380th BW, Plattsburgh AFB, NY. Last assigned to the 307th BW. Sent to MASDC March 3, 1965. Scrapped October 16, 1968.

**53-1897**
Assigned to the 307th BW, 372nd BS, November 1960. Sent to MASDC March 19, 1965. Scrapped October 16, 1968.

**53-1900**
Assigned to the 307th BW, 372nd BS, March 1956. Modified to EB-47E (Phase V) and last assigned to the 376th BW, Lockbourne AFB, OH. Sent to MASDC January 18, 1965. Scrapped January 13, 1969.

**53-1901**
Assigned to the 307th BW summer 1956. Sent to MASDC January 21, 1965. Scrapped October 16, 1968.

**53-1902**
Assigned to the 307th BW, 371st BS, April 1956. Sent to MASDC March 2, 1965.

**53-1906**
Assigned to the 307th BW, 372nd BS, May 1956. Crew Chiefs Robert Bergene, Theodore Heglee, Paul Koski. Sent to MASDC February 18, 1965. Scrapped October 16, 1965.

**53-1909**
Assigned to the 307th BW 1956. Crew Chiefs William Filpula, Paul Koski. Sent to MASDC March 3, 1965. Scrapped October 24, 1968.

**53-1910**
Assigned to the 307th Bomb Wing, 372nd BS, May 1956. Last assigned to the 3960th SW, Andersen AFB, Guam. Sent to MASDC October 29, 1965. Scrapped October 24, 1968.

## Cold War Cornhuskers: The 307th Bomb Wing Lincoln Air Force Base Nebraska 1955-1965

53-1911
Assigned to the 307th BW, 371st BS. Crew Chiefs James Dewett, Jerome Hoffman. Sent to MASDC March 9, 1965. Scrapped October 24, 1968.

53-1912
Assigned to the 307th BW, 371st BS, 1956. Crew Chief William Nelson. Sent to MASDC March 30, 1965. Scrapped October 24, 1968.

53-1915
Assigned to 307th BW 1956. Modified to EB-47E (Phase V) and transferred to the 301st BW, Lockbourne AFB, OH, May 29, 1958. Last assigned to the 376th BW, Lockbourne AFB, OH. Sent to MASDC February 23, 1966. Scrapped December 13, 1968

53-1916
Assigned to the 307th BW 1956. Crew Chiefs Richard St. Louis, Robert Tysinger. Last assigned to the 100th BW, Pease AFB, NH. Sent to MASDC November 4, 1965. Scrapped October 24, 1968.

53-1917
Assigned to the 307th BW, 372nd BS, 1956. Crew Chief Robert Rosario. Sent to MASDC February 18, 1965. Scrapped October 21, 1968.

53-1918
Assigned to the 307th BW. Last Assigned to the 3960th SW, Andersen AFB, Guam. Sent to MASDC March 13, 1966. Scrapped May 27, 1966.

53-1919
Assigned to the 307th BW. Sent to MASDC February 15, 1965. Scrapped October 21, 1968.

53-1932
Assigned to the 307th BW, 370th BS, 1959. Crew Chiefs Harold Ross, Billy Williams. Sent to MASDC March 4, 1965. Scrapped October 22, 1968.

53-1935
Assigned to the 307th BW. Sent to MASDC March 8, 1965. Scrapped October 22, 1968.

53-1938
Assigned to the 307th BW. Transferred to the 9th BW, Andersen AFB, Guam. Sent to MASDC January 6, 1966, Scrapped January 28, 1969.

53-1939
Assigned to the 307th BW. Sent to MASDC January 26, 1965. Scrapped October 22, 1968.

53-1941
Assigned to the 307th BW, 370th BS, 1959. Crew Chief George Nigh. Sent to MASDC March 4, 1965. Scrapped October 22, 1968.

53-1956
Assigned to the 307th BW, 371st BS, July 1959. Sent to MASDC March 25, 1965. Scrapped October 22, 1968.

53-1958
Assigned to the 307th BW, 372nd BS, August 1959. Sent to MASDC March 3, 1965. Scrapped October 22, 1968.

53-1964
Assigned to the 307th BW. Sent to MASDC December 2, 1964. Scrapped July 12, 1968.

53-2090
Assigned to the 307th BW June 1962. Sent to MASDC June 10, 1964. Scrapped September 11, 1968.

53-2097
Assigned to the 307th BW July 12, 1961. Crashed January 11, 1963, after takeoff from McConnell AFB, KS. Crashed on Highway 54 during a snowstorm when the aircraft experienced control failure due to icing and weather complications. Capt Paul Pudwill was killed in the crash when he stayed with the aircraft to fly it away from a populated area. Capt Fred Medrick (CP) and Capt Harry Jones (NAV) were able to eject from the aircraft.

53-2098
Assigned to the 307th BW, July 12, 1961. Sent to MASDC June 8, 1964. Scrapped September 11, 1967.

53-2101
Assigned to the 307th BW June 1963. Sent to MASDC April 16, 1964. Scrapped September 12, 1968.

53-2111
Assigned to the 307th BW, 370th BS, 1958. On June 11, 1961, while making a southbound takeoff, the aircraft was unable to gain flying speed. The B-47 crashed just off the end of the runway. Capt Russell Holst, Capt Albert Marinich and Capt Allan Matson were killed. Lt Thomas Wesner was able to eject safely.

53-2112
Assigned to the 307th BW. Sent to MASDC February 26, 1965. Scrapped October 21, 1968.

53-2125
Assigned to the 307th BW. Sent to MASDC February 2, 1965. Scrapped October 21, 1968.

53-2128
Assigned to the 307th BW, 372nd BS, March 1956. Later modified to EB-47E (Phase V) and assigned to the 376th BW, Lockbourne AFB, OH. Sent to MASDC December 10, 1964. Scrapped June 21, 1966.

53-2134 CITY OF LINCOLN
This B-47 was the Winner of the Fairchild Trophy in the 1959 SAC Bomb/Comp (307th BW). Crew Chief Jerome Hoffman. Assigned to the 307th Bomb Wing. On February 3, 1963, this aircraft was declared Class 26 after an accident at RAF Greenham-Common, UK. During a snowstorm, strong crosswinds caused the landing aircraft to drift off the runway. The crew attempted to go around, but the number six engine failed to accelerate causing asymmetric thrust. The wing began to drag. Capt Richard West (CP) elected to eject. His seat malfunctioned and he was killed. Capt Paul Canney (AC), Lt Don Hickman (NAV) and SSgt Bobby Odom survived.

53-2135
Delivered to the 44th BW, Lake Charles AFB/Chennault AFB, LA. Also assigned to the 68th BW, Chennault AFB, LA. Assigned to the 307th BW, 371st BS, November 1956. Transferred June 1958 for Project "Milk

Bottle". Modified to EB-47E (Phase V). Served with the 301st and 376th Bomb Wings at Lockbourne AFB, OH. Sent to MASDC December 3, 1964. Transferred to the Pima Air Museum, AZ, January 13, 1969.

53-2138
Assigned to the 307th BW, 371st BS, March 1956. Crew Chief Henry Paulin. Transferred June 1, 1958, to the 100th BW, Pease AFB, NH. Modified to EB-47E (Phase V). Last assigned to the 376th BW, Lockbourne AFB, OH. Sent to MASDC February 23, 1965. Scrapped December 13, 1968.

53-2139
Assigned to 307th BW, 370th BS, 1956. In September 1960, during a "Coco" Alert while taxing to the active runway, an outrigger tire blew, which wore down to the rim causing a fire. The aircraft was repaired. Crew Chief Richard Lauk. Sent to MASDC March 5, 1965. Scrapped October 11, 1968.

53-2140
Assigned to the 307th BW, 370th BS, 1956. Crew Chief George Nigh. Sent to MASDC March 9, 1965. Scrapped October 11.1968.

53-2141
Assigned to the 307th BW, 372nd BS, 1956. Crew Chief Homer Mosser. Transferred to the 98th BW, Lincoln AFB, NE. Sent to MASDC November 3, 1965. Scrapped October 24, 1968.

53-2142
Assigned to the 307th BW, 372nd BS, 1956. Transferred to the 98th BW, Lincoln AFB, NE. Sent to MASDC November 11, 1965. Scrapped October 24, 1968.

53-2143
Assigned to the 307th BW, 372nd BS, November 1959. Crew Chiefs Elmer Sensening, Kenneth McGee. Transferred to the 9th BW, Mountain Home AFB, ID. Sent to MASDC January 18, 1966. Scrapped January 30, 1969.

53-2144
Assigned to the 307th BW, 372nd BS. Crew Chief Donald Mowry. Transferred to the 9th BW, Andersen AFB, Guam. Sent to MASDC January 22, 1966. Scrapped January 30, 1969.

53-2266
Assigned to the 307th BW, 371st BS, May 13, 1958. Last assigned to the 68th BW, Chennault AFB, LA. Sent to MASDC February 15, 1963. Scrapped October 31, 1967.

53-2278
Assigned to the 307th BW, 371st BS. Crew Chief Ansel Chase. Sent to MASDC June 26, 1964. Scrapped September 30, 1968.

53-2289
Assigned to the 307th BW August 1963. Sent to MASDC May 5, 1964. Scrapped September 10, 1968.

53-2292
Assigned to the 307th BW, 372nd BS, 1958. Transferred to the 98th BW, Lincoln AFB, NE. Sent to MASDC July 8, 1964. Scrapped September 30, 1968.

53-2297
Assigned to the 307th BW 1958. Crew Chief Donald Avery. Transferred to the 98th BW, Lincoln AFB, NE, May 14, 1960. Sent to MASDC July 9, 1964. Scrapped September 30, 1968

53-2307
Assigned to the 307th BW June 1963. Sent to MASDC April 23, 1964. Scrapped September 10, 1968.

53-2322
Assigned to the 307th BW August 1963. Sent to MASDC June 2, 1964. Scrapped September 11, 1968.

53-2324
Assigned to the 307th BW August 1963. Sent to MASDC June 15, 1964. Scrapped September 11, 1968.

53-2327
Assigned to the 307th BW August 1963. Sent to MASDC May 19, 1964. Scrapped September 10, 1968.

53-2329
Modified to EB-47L Pipe Cleaner (1962). Assigned to the 307th BW, 4362nd PACCS, July 1962. Last assigned to the 9th BW, Mountain Home AFB, ID. Sent to MASDC March 25, 1965. Scrapped January 14, 1969.

53-2330
Assigned to the 307th Bomb Wing June 29, 1961. Sent to MASDC July 31, 1964. Scrapped September 30, 1968.

53-2337
Assigned to the 307th BW. Sent to MASDC June 8, 1964. Scrapped September 11, 1968.

53-2341
Assigned to the 307th BW July 1961. Sent to MASDC June 2, 1964. Scrapped September 11, 1968.

53-2342
Assigned to the 307th BW April 14, 1961. Sent to MASDC July 15, 1964. Scrapped September 30, 1968.

53-2348
Assigned to the 307th BW April 27, 1961. Sent to MASDC June 22, 1964. Scrapped September 30, 1968.

53-2349
Assigned to the 307th BW 1962. Sent to MASDC May 11, 1964. Scrapped September 11, 1968.

53-2351
Assigned to the 380th BW, Plattsburgh AFB, NY. Assigned to 307th BW, May 13, 1958. Transferred late 1961 to the 310th BW, Schilling AFB, KS. Sent to MASDC February 16, 1965. Scrapped October 21, 1968.

53-2353
Assigned to the 307th BW, 371st BS, May 1958. Sent to MASDC March 19, 1964. Scrapped September 11, 1968.

# Cold War Cornhuskers: The 307th Bomb Wing Lincoln Air Force Base Nebraska 1955-1965

53-2362
Assigned to the 307th BW. Crew Chief Charles Baker. Transferred to the 98th BW, Lincoln AFB, NE. Sent to MASDC November 11, 29, 1965. Scrapped October 23, 1968.

53-2363
Destroyed by fire June 3, 1964. During a three ship MITO at 2:42 a.m., the number three engine caught fire. The crew aborted the takeoff and made an emergency egress from the aircraft. The aircraft burned on the runway. Capt Leroy McMath (AC), Capt Stanley Toney (CP) and Capt Thomas Package (Nav) survived.

53-2364
Assigned to the 307th BW, 370th BS, August 1963. Sent to MASDC March 3, 1965. Scrapped October 21, 1968.

53-2366
Assigned to the 307th BW. Crashed on takeoff, July 27, 1964. During a southbound takeoff at about 8:12 a.m., the aircraft failed to accelerate to flying speed. The aircraft crashed in a field off the south end of the runway about a quarter of a mile from Interstate 80. The aircraft veered to the right of the runway and appeared to have hit near a country road, then careened into a cornfield on the other side. Killed in the crash were Capt Tom Sutton (AC), Lt David Williams (CP), Lt Terrance Murphy (Nav), and Maj John Sakry instructor navigator. SSgt Billy Baker had been scheduled to fly that day. A schedule change placed Maj Sakry on the plane instead of Sgt Baker.

53-2368
Assigned to the 307th BW. Sent to MASDC December 2, 1964. Scrapped September 11, 1968.

53-2387
Assigned to the 307th BW, 372nd BS, in late 1958. Crew Chief Jim Lancaster. Sent to MASDC March 4, 1965. Scrapped October 21, 1968.

53-2392
Assigned to the 307th BW, 371st BS, 1958. Crew Chief James Yandle. Sent to MASDC February 18, 1965. Scrapped October 21, 1968.

53-2393
Assigned to the 307th BW, April 1963. Last assigned to the 98th BW, Lincoln AFB, NE. Sent to MASDC November 18, 1965. Scrapped January 30, 1968.

53-2413
Assigned to 307th BW, March 1956. Modified to EB-47E (Phase V). Transferred June 1958 to the 301st BW, Lockbourne AFB, OH. Sent to MASDC May 25, 1964. Scrapped October 3, 1968.

53-2416
Assigned to the 307th BW, 372nd BS, March 1956. Sent to MASDC February 26, 1965. Scrapped October 21, 1968.

53-2417
Assigned to the 307th BW, 372nd BS, April 1956. Sent to MASDC March 3, 1965. Scrapped October 21, 1968.

53-4208
Assigned to the 307th BW, 370th BS, March 1956. Departed for factory updates November 1958. Crew Chief James Sutton. Crashed February 17, 1959, at Lockheed, Marietta, GA, during a test flight. Two Air Force crewmen and one civilian were killed.

53-4209
Crashed on April 6, 1956. This aircraft went down about fifteen minutes after takeoff from LAFB, near Ceresco, NE. The aircraft broke into three sections. Killed were Capt James Sullivan (AC), 2/Lt Lawrence Schmidt (CP), Lt Anthony Mercanti (Nav) and A1C James Berry, crew chief.

53-4210
Assigned to the 307th BW, 370th BS, March 1956. Modified to EB-47E (Phase V). Assigned to the 301st Bomb Wing, Lockbourne AFB, OH. Sent to MASDC April 30, 1964. Scrapped May 12, 1966.

53-4214
Assigned to the 307th BW, 370th BS, April 1956. Crew Chief Paul Koski. Modified to EB-47E (Phase V). Assigned to the 301st BW, Lockbourne AFB, OH. Sent to MASDC May 7, 1964. Scrapped October 3, 1969.

53-4216
Assigned to the 307th BW. Crew Chiefs George Davis, Rudolph Nieman. Transferred to the 98th BW, Lincoln AFB, NE. Sent to MASDC October 23, 1965. Scrapped October 25, 1969.

53-4217
Assigned to the 307th BW, 371st BS, April 1956. Crew Chiefs James Boothe, Lawrence Hall, Bill Martin, George Davis. Sent to MASDC March 3, 1965. Scrapped October 21, 1969.

53-4218
Assigned to the 307th BW. On July 19, 1962, the aircraft was unable to return to Lincoln due to thunderstorms in the area. Maj Art Stokes elected to land at Des Moines, Iowa, airport. The primary runway was under construction at the time. The overrun had been excavated and there was a 24-inch lip at the end of the paved runway. The aft landing gear caught the lip and was torn off. The B-47 slid about 3,000 feet down the runway before coming to a stop and catching fire. The crew escaped. The aircraft was salvaged and trucked to Lincoln AFB.

53-4219
Assigned to the 307th BW, 371st BS, April 1956. Sent to MASDC February 26, 1965. Scrapped October 21, 1968.

53-4220
Assigned to 307th BW, 370th BS, April 1956. Modified to EB-47E (Phase V). Assigned to the 301st BW, Lockbourne AFB, OH. Sent to MASDC April 15, 1964. Scrapped May 12, 1966.

53-4222
Assigned to the 307th BW, 370th BS, March 1956. Crew Chiefs Vernon Dixon, Paul Koski, Fred Lally, Jim Lancaster, Jim Lentz. Sent to MASDC March 5, 1965. Scrapped October 31, 1969.

## 307th Bomb Wing Aircraft Assignments

53-4223
Assigned to the 307th BW, 372nd BS, April 1956. Crew Chiefs T.R. Taylor, Vonzell Carter. Sent to MASDC March 9, 1965. Scrapped October 23, 1969. This was the last B-47 officially assigned to the 307th BW to depart Lincoln AFB.

53-4224
Assigned to the 307th BW, 370th BS, March 1956. Crew Chief Willard Owensby. Sent to MASDC March 8, 1965. Scrapped October 21, 1969.

53-4225
Assigned to the 307th BW, 372nd BS, March 1956. Transferred June 1958 to the 380th BW, Plattsburgh AFB, NY. Sent to MASDC December 13, 1965. Scrapped January 30, 1969.

53-4226
Assigned to the 307th BW, 371st BS, March 1956. Crashed on takeoff from LAFB on March 7, 1963. The aircraft caught fire during an ATO takeoff. Maj N.V. Meeks held the B-47 under control so the crew could bail out. Navigator Clifford Cork, and copilot Larry Talovich ejected. The fourth man, Arthur Ingle (2nd copilot), was able to bail out via entrance hatch. Maj Meeks ejected but his lap belt malfunctioned and he was unable to separate from the seat before impact. The 307th BW established the N.V. Meeks memorial trophy in memory of Maj Meeks. Crew Chiefs Vonzell Carter, David Bench, Joseph Charbonneau.

53-4227
Assigned to the 307th BW, 371st, and 372nd BS, April 1956. Sent to MASDC December 17, 1964. Scrapped September 12, 1969.

53-4228
Assigned to the 307th BW, 371st BS, April 1956. Transferred July 1958 to the 380th BW, Plattsburgh AFB, NY. Sent to MASDC October 20, 1965. Scrapped October 25, 1969.

53-4230
Assigned to the 307th BW, 371st BS, April 1956. Crashed at RAF Lakenheath, UK, on July 28, 1956. The aircraft was shooting touch-and-go landings. On the fourth approach, the aircraft porpoised, a go around was attempted, but the right wing tip dragged causing the aircraft to crash. Killed in the crash were Capt Russell Bowling (AC), 2/Lt Carroll Kalberg (CP), Lt Michael Selmo (Nav) and TSgt John Ulrich, A&E Technician. Bowling Lake at LAFB was named in honor of Capt Bowling.

53-4232
Assigned to the 307th BW, 370th BS, April 1956. Transferred April 1958 to the 9th BW, Mountain Home AFB, ID. Sent to MASDC January 6, 1966. Scrapped January 30, 1969.

53-4233
Assigned to the 307th BW. Crew Chiefs Vonzell Carter, James Pepper, Bob Fontaine. Last assigned to the 9th BW, Mountain Home AFB, ID. Sent to MASDC October 25, 1965. Scrapped October 25, 1969.

53-4234
Assigned to 307th BW, 371st BS, March 1956. Transferred June 1958 to the 9th BW, Mountain Home AFB, ID. Sent to MASDC October 25, 1965. Scrapped October 25, 1969.

53-4235
Assigned to the 307th BW, 372nd BS, March 1956. Destroyed on the ground by crash of a Nebraska Air National Guard F-80 on November 17, 1956. The F-80 landed on the taxiway by mistake and crashed into the B-47. Crew Chief A1C John Delancy and A2C Donald Russell were in the bomb bay working and were killed in the accident.

53-4236
Assigned to the 307th BW, 370th BS, April 1956. Crew Chiefs Warren Lechot, Merrill Sinclair. Sent to MASDC March 2, 1965. Scrapped October 21, 1969.

53-4237
Assigned to the 307th BW, 370th BS, August 1958. Last assigned to the 9th BW, Mountain Home, AFB, ID. Sent to MASDC January 14, 1966. Scrapped January 30, 1969.

53-4240
Assigned to the 307th BW, 371st BS, May 1956. Transferred May 19, 1958 to the 9th BW, Mountain Home AFB, ID. Sent to MASDC October 25, 1965. Scrapped October 25, 1969.

53-4241
Assigned to the 307th BW, 370th BS, March 1956. Transferred for Project "Milk Bottle" May 1, 1958. Last assigned to the 9th BW, Mountain Home AFB, ID. Sent to MASDC January 26, 1966. Scrapped January 30, 1969.

53-4242
Assigned to the 307th BW, 370th BS, January 1957. Transferred April 1958 for "Milk Bottle" update. Modified to EB-47E (Phase V). Assigned with the 376th BW, Lockbourne AFB, OH. Sent to MASDC December 17, 1964. Scrapped January 13, 1969.

53-4243
Assigned to the 307th BW, 371st BS, January 1957. Transferred for "Milk Bottle" update May 16, 1958. Last assigned to the 9th BW, Mountain Home AFB, ID. Sent to MASDC May 1, 1966. Scrapped January 30, 1969.

53-6236
Assigned to the 307th BW, 372nd BS, August 1959. Sent to MASDC March 8, 1965. Scrapped October 21, 1968.

53-6243
Assigned to the 307th BW. Last assigned to the 9th BW, Mountain Home AFB, ID. Sent to MASDC October 29, 1965. Scrapped October 24, 1968.

53-6244
Delivered to the 40th Bomb Wing at Smoky Hill AFB, KS, on October 23, 1956. Transferred to the 307th BW January 1957. Crew Chiefs Steven Vensky, Don Kimmel. Logged over 1,947 hours while assigned to the 307th. On January 22, 1965, she was flown to the Air Force Museum, Dayton, OH, by Capt Gene Hickman (AC), Capt Pete Todd (CP) and Capt Al Ottaviano (Nav). At the time of her retirement, she had logged over 2,991 airframe hours. She was placed on display at the museum until the move to the present facility. It was deemed unfeasible to move 6244. She served as a gate guard until turned over to the base fire department for training.

*Cold War Cornhuskers: The 307th Bomb Wing Lincoln Air Force Base Nebraska 1955-1965*

**KC-97 Aircraft Assigned to 307th Air Refueling Squadron**
**KC-97F**
51-375
Assigned to the squadron Fall 1954
Crew Chiefs: Russ Geisler, Bobby Moorehead, Jack Orewyler
Sent to MASDC 1965

51-376
Assigned to the squadron Fall 1955
Crew Chiefs: Robert Games, Claude Harris
Asst. Crew Chief: Francis Vickers

51-377
Assigned to the squadron Fall 1955
Crew Chiefs: Jack Wilkins, Lee Cullimore, Connelly
Asst. Crew Chiefs: Maurice Chapman, Ken Tarwater

51-378
Assigned to the squadron Fall 1955
Crew Chiefs: Robert Stanley, Robert Newman
Asst. Crew Chief: Bernard Jump
Later sold to the Israeli Air Force and modified to an ELINT aircraft

51-379
Assigned to the squadron Fall 1955
Crew Chief: Perry Meixsel
Asst. Crew Chief: Ray Jones

51-380
Assigned to the squadron 1955
Crew Chiefs: Robert Greenwald, James Blain

51-381
Assigned to the squadron Fall 1955
Crew Chief: Gordon Hazzard
Asst. Crew Chief: Gerald Barker
Sent to MASDC 1965

51-382
Assigned to the squadron Fall 1955
Crew Chief: Glen Pinnick, Melvin Patterson
Asst Crew Chief Stephen Luster

51-383
Assigned to the squadron Fall 1955
Crew Chiefs: Donald Darling, Lillard Chadwell
Asst. Crew Chief: William Apger

51-384
Assigned to the squadron Fall 1955
Crew Chiefs: Donald Tubbs, Arnold Fall, John Gafford

**KC-97G**
52-0919
Transferred to squadron March 1960
Crew Chief: Robert Chapin
Asst. Crew Chief: Melvin Furgeson
Destroyed April 15, 1960 in takeoff accident at Lincoln AFB.
Everyone aboard managed to escape.

52-2667
Assigned to squadron Fall 1955
Crew Chief: Donald "Shorty" Grove
Asst. Crew Chief: Gaylord Back
Converted to a C-97G, later sent to MASDC

52-2790
Assigned to squadron Fall 1955
Crew Chief: Glenwood Johnson
Asst. Crew Chief: Jerry Moulton
Converted to a C-97K. Sent to MASDC February 3, 1971

52-2791
Assigned to the squadron Fall 1955
Crew Chief: Marvin Rogers, Thomas Propes
Asst. Crew Chief: Bill Tuley
Converted to HC-97. Sent to MASDC June 21, 1972

52-2792
Assigned to squadron Fall 1955
Crew Chief: Paul Sweetman
Asst. Crew Chief: John Lysher
Sent to MASDC October 1, 1964

52-2793
Assigned to Squadron Fall 1955
Crew Chiefs: Marty Jetton, Carl Dobish
Asst. Crew Chief: James Falkner
Sent to MASDC

52-2794
Assigned to squadron Fall 1955
Crew Chief: Cicle (Ollie) Oliver
Asst. Crew Chief: Robert Jatczak

52-2795
Assigned to squadron Fall 1955
Crew Chiefs: June Thomas, Oscar White
Asst. Crew Chief: Julius Gator

52-2796
Assigned to squadron Fall 1955
Crew Chiefs: John Zlomac, Ron Ralston
Asst. Crew Chief: Chuck Sweeney
Sent to MASDC October 1, 1964

52-2797
Assigned to squadron Fall 1955
Crew Chiefs: Menno Weims, Richard Miller, Thomas Haas
Asst. Crew Chief: Connie Manners
Converted to HC-97G. Sent to MASDC June 21, 1972

52-2798
Assigned to squadron Fall 1955
Crew Chief: Walt Hege
Asst. Crew Chief: James Samson

## 307th Bomb Wing Aircraft Assignments

52-2799
Assigned to squadron Fall 1955
Crew Chiefs: Cliff Gustason, Delbert Greve
Asst. Crew Chief: George Lewis
Converted to C-97K. Sent to MASDC March 27, 1970. Later sold to Israel and served as a military transport with the Israeli Air Force.

52-2800
Assigned to squadron Fall 1955
Crew Chiefs: Everett Sutherland, Marvin Rogers
Asst. Crew Chiefs: Stephen Luster, John Tomaselli
Sent to MASDC September 25, 1964

52-2801
Assigned to the squadron Fall 1955
Crew Chief: Leo Halpin
Sent to MASDC November 2, 1965

52-2802
Assigned to the squadron Fall 1955
Crew Chiefs: Dennis Back, ? Thamason
Asst. Crew Chief: George Lewis
Sent to MASDC November 2, 1965

52-2804
Transferred to 307th from 98th AREFS June 11, 1957
Crew Chiefs: Richard Miller, Sam Sloan
Asst. Crew Chief: Ken Tarwater
Represented the 307th at the 1959 SAC Bomb/Comp

52-2833
Crew Chief: Don Goble
Asst. Crew Chief: Eugene Shelton

53-0331
Arrived May 1960 to replace 52-0919. Crashed on takeoff February 28, 1961 at Selfridge AFB, MI, during an ORI mission. All five-crew members were fatally injured.

# Flight Crews

Bill Howell, Fisher, Merrill Powell

Frank Kisner, Don Daly, Earl Buys

Bill Heald, Bob Byrom, Dick Storr

Bob Hanson, Roger Beamer, Ivan "Buck" Buchanan

Al Masserini, Vince Kovacich, Merrill Powell

## Flight Crews

Jack Jones, Gene Hickman, Bill Howard.

Tom Powell, Clarence Purcell, Bill Rogers.

Howard Solomon, Mike Gingrich, Joe Miller

Joe Rogers, Dan Stallard, Bill Carrier.

LeRoy McMath, Pete Todd, Al Ottaviano

Jim Shelton, John Puckropp, Simcox.

# Cold War Cornhuskers: The 307th Bomb Wing Lincoln Air Force Base Nebraska 1955-1965

Lewis Wilson, Thomas Wesner, Jim Moon

Bill Oretel, Everett Vaughn, Charles Takacs

N.V. Meeks, Bill Sund, Don Simmons

## Flight Crews

Art Stokes, Roger Beamer, Ivans Buchanan

Otis "Flash" Gordon, Bob Boulware, Bob Ace.

Charles Watt, Orin Shellhamer, Robert Bauer.

Curtis Robertson, Bob Kelly, James "Wally" Whitehurst

293

# B-47 and KC-97 Walkaround

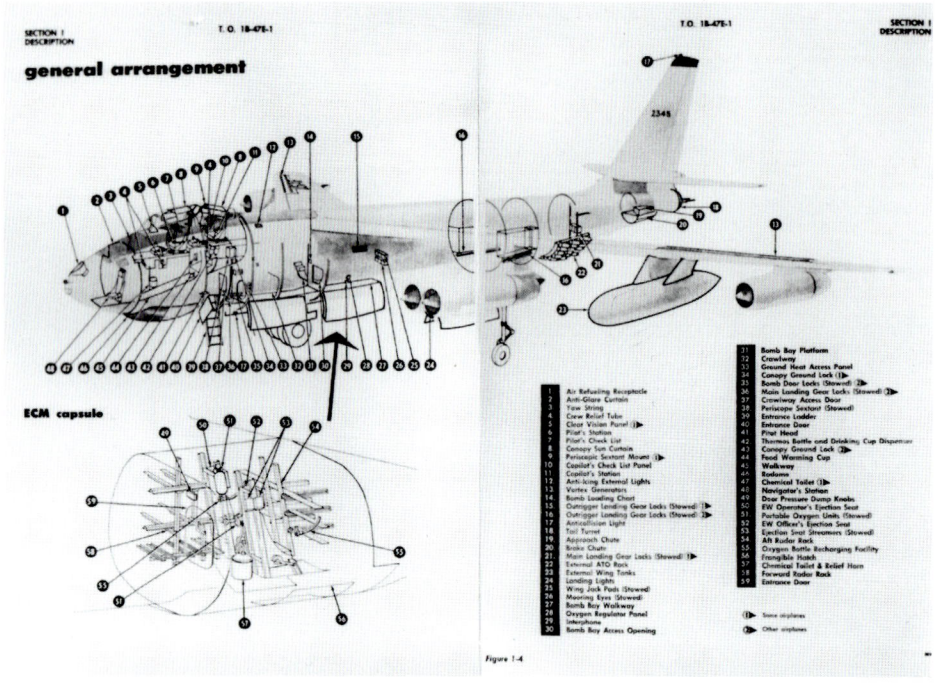

B-47 General Arrangement

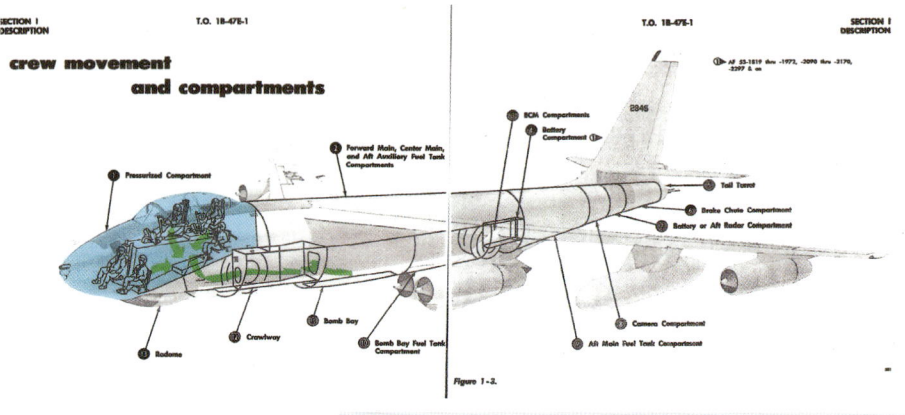

Crew Movement and Compartments

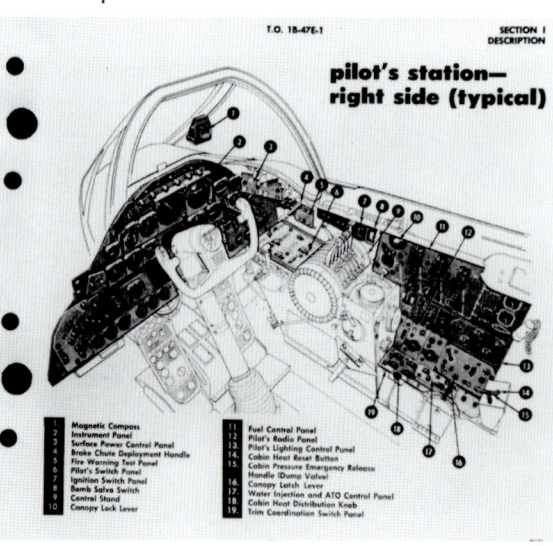

Pilot's Station Right Side

## Pilot's Station Left Side

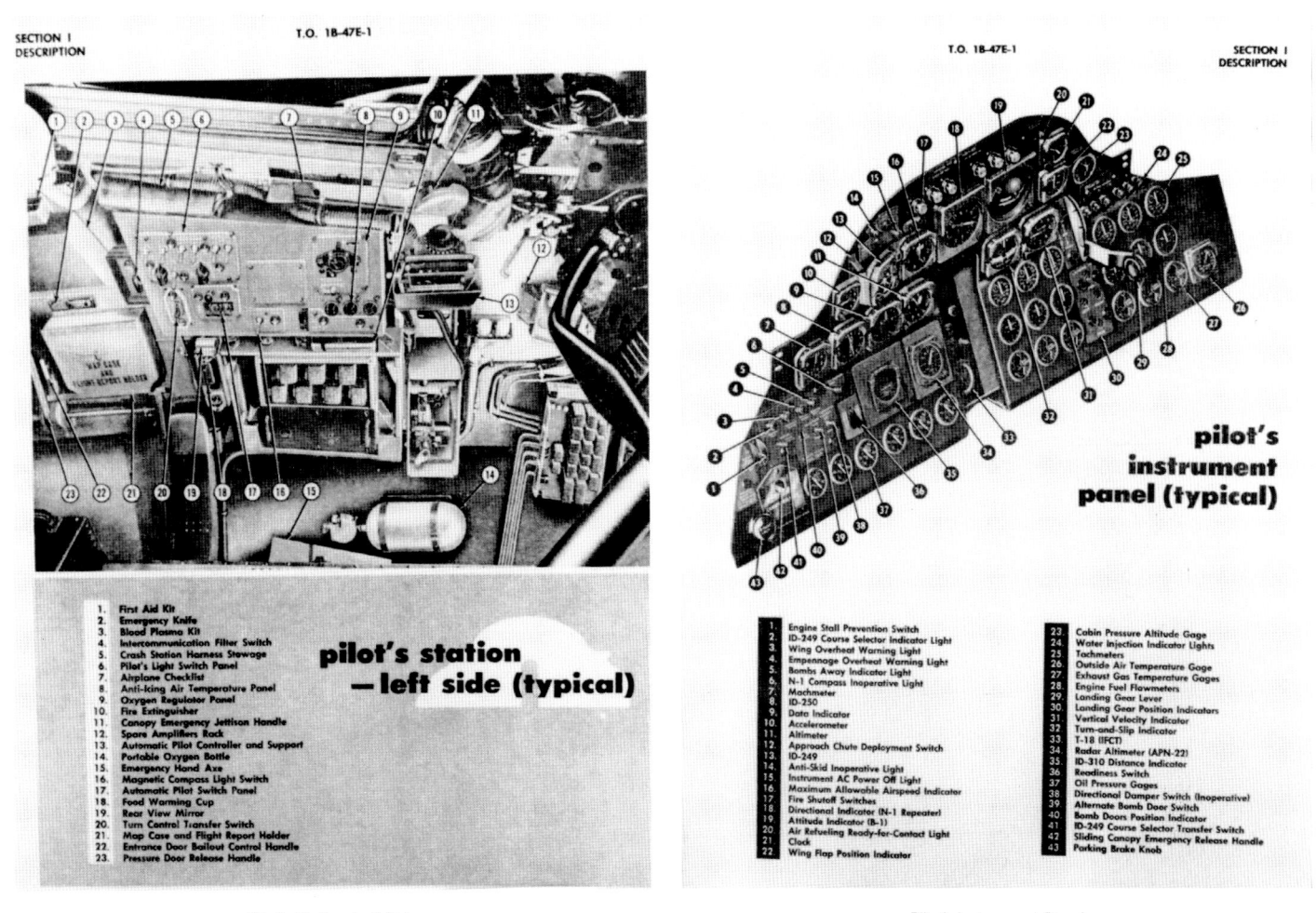

1. First Aid Kit
2. Emergency Knife
3. Blood Plasma Kit
4. Intercommunication Filter Switch
5. Crash Station Harness Stowage
6. Pilot's Light Switch Panel
7. Airplane Checklist
8. Anti-Icing Air Temperature Panel
9. Oxygen Regulator Panel
10. Fire Extinguisher
11. Canopy Emergency Jettison Handle
12. Spare Amplifiers Rack
13. Automatic Pilot Controller and Support
14. Portable Oxygen Bottle
15. Emergency Hand Axe
16. Magnetic Compass Light Switch
17. Automatic Pilot Switch Panel
18. Food Warming Cup
19. Rear View Mirror
20. Turn Control Transfer Switch
21. Map Case and Flight Report Holder
22. Entrance Door Bailout Control Handle
23. Pressure Door Release Handle

## Pilot's Instrument Panel

1. Engine Stall Prevention Switch
2. ID-249 Course Selector Indicator Light
3. Wing Overheat Warning Light
4. Empennage Overheat Warning Light
5. Bombs Away Indicator Light
6. N-1 Compass Inoperative Light
7. ID-250
8. Machmeter
9. Data Indicator
10. Accelerometer
11. Altimeter
12. Approach Chute Deployment Switch
13. ID-249
14. Anti-Skid Inoperative Light
15. Instrument AC Power Off Light
16. Maximum Allowable Airspeed Indicator
17. Fire Shutoff Switches
18. Directional Indicator (N-1 Repeater)
19. Attitude Indicator (B-1)
20. Air Refueling Ready-for-Contact Light
21. Clock
22. Wing Flap Position Indicator
23. Cabin Pressure Altitude Gage
24. Water Injection Indicator Lights
25. Tachometers
26. Outside Air Temperature Gage
27. Exhaust Gas Temperature Gages
28. Engine Fuel Flowmeters
29. Landing Gear Lever
30. Landing Gear Position Indicators
31. Vertical Velocity Indicator
32. Turn-and-Slip Indicator
33. T-18 (IFCT)
34. Radar Altimeter (APN-22)
35. ID-310 Distance Indicator
36. Readiness Switch
37. Oil Pressure Gages
38. Directional Damper Switch (Inoperative)
39. Alternate Bomb Door Switch
40. Bomb Doors Position Indicator
41. ID-249 Course Selector Transfer Switch
42. Sliding Canopy Emergency Release Handle
43. Parking Brake Knob

## Co-Pilot's Station Right Side

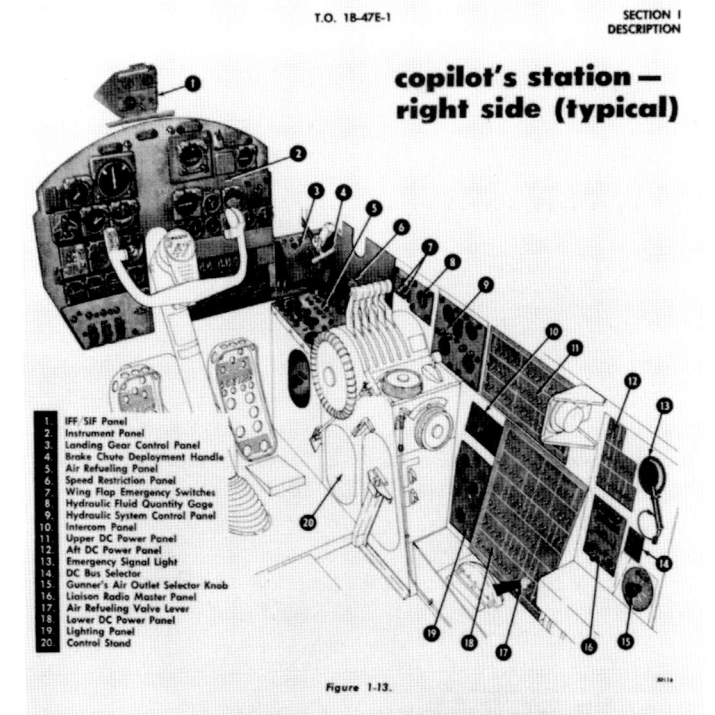

1. IFF/SIF Panel
2. Instrument Panel
3. Landing Gear Control Panel
4. Brake Chute Deployment Handle
5. Air Refueling Panel
6. Speed Restriction Panel
7. Wing Flap Emergency Switches
8. Hydraulic Fluid Quantity Gage
9. Hydraulic System Control Panel
10. Intercom Panel
11. Upper DC Power Panel
12. Aft DC Power Panel
13. Emergency Signal Light
14. DC Bus Selector
15. Gunner's Air Outlet Selector Knob
16. Liaison Radio Master Panel
17. Air Refueling Valve Lever
18. Lower DC Power Panel
19. Lighting Panel
20. Control Stand

Figure 1-13.

gine 4," "Engine 5," and "Engine 6" on the "Throttle & Engine Control" portion of the lower DC power panel.

**Starter Emergency Override Switch**

A two-position START—OFF starter emergency override switch (11, figure 1-10), spring-loaded to the OFF position, is located on the pilot's switch panel. In the START position, the starter bus is connected to the airplane DC system bus. Actuating the starter switch simultaneously with the override switch permits engine starting from the airplane batteries through the normal airplane bus or from an external power source connected to the normal airplane bus. In OFF position, the starter-generators may be motorized by actuating the starter switch with an external power source connected to the start and NORMAL portion of the external DC power receptacle. DC power is supplied to the starter emergency override switch through the "Start Control" circuit breaker on the lower DC power panel.

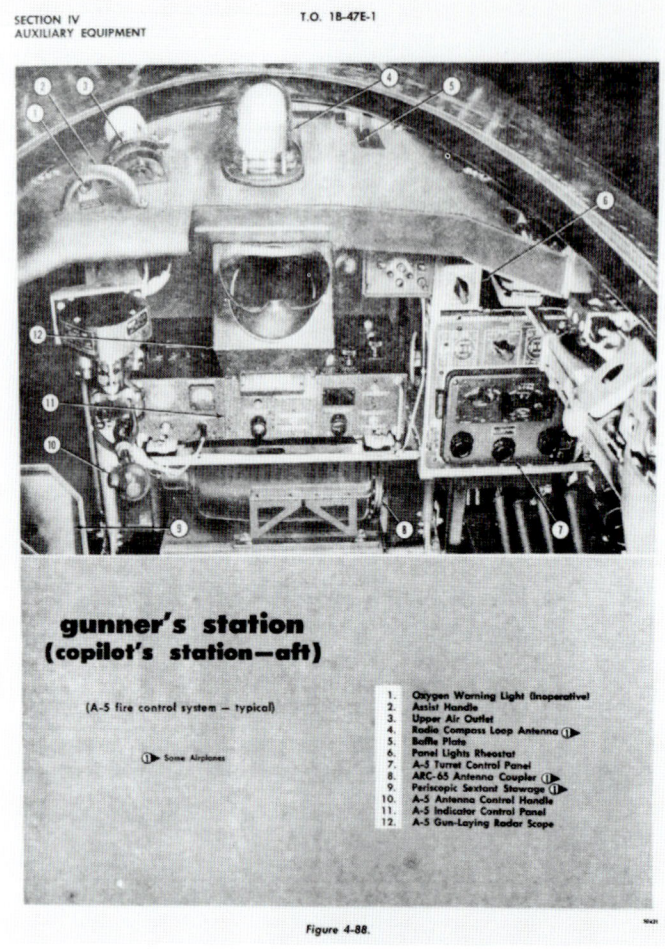

# Cold War Cornhuskers: The 307th Bomb Wing Lincoln Air Force Base Nebraska 1955-1965

Co-Pilot's Station Left Side

Gunner's Station-Co-Pilots Station Aft

Co-Pilot's gunnery station (M.Hill)

Copilot's gunnery station observed from copilot's seat. (M Hill)

# B-47 and KC-97 Walkaround

Looking forward towards Navigator's Station. (M.Hill)

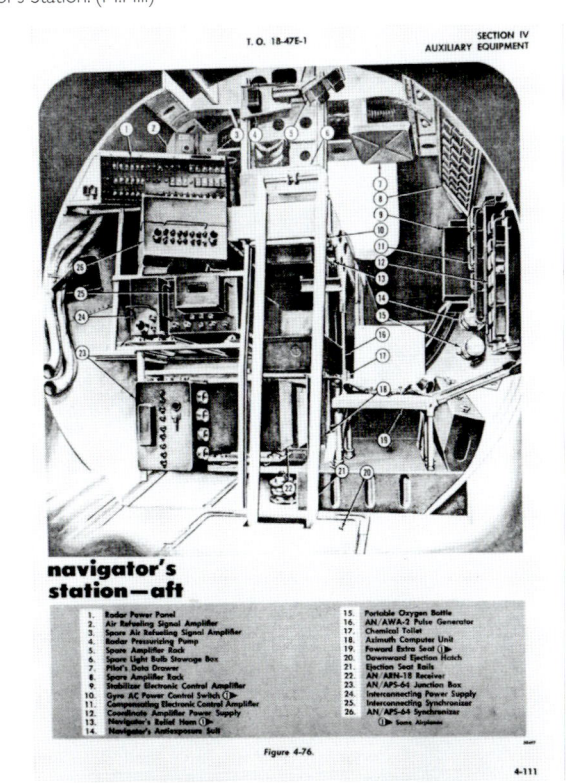

Navigator Station- forward.

Navigator Station -aft.

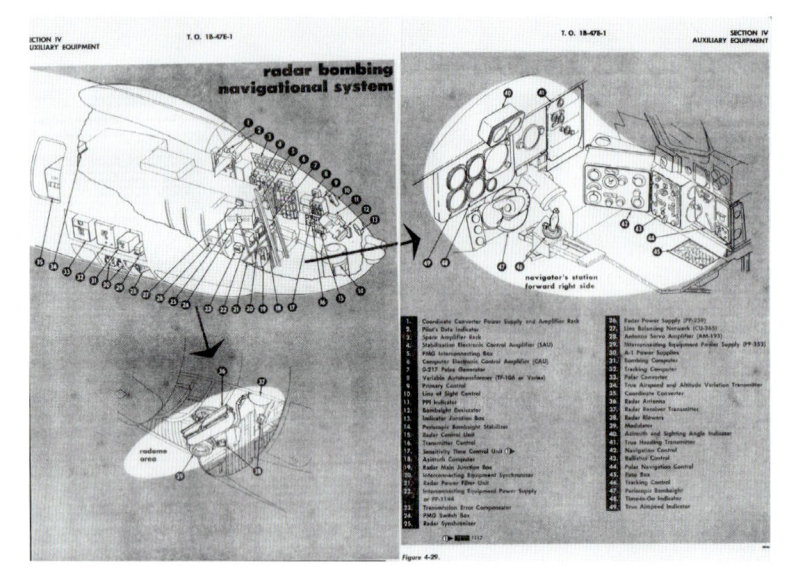

# Cold War Cornhuskers: The 307th Bomb Wing Lincoln Air Force Base Nebraska 1955-1965

B-47 Radar Bombing System

Navigator Station on EB-47E. (M.Hill)

Navigator Station. EB-47E at STRATEGIC AEROSPACE MUSEUM, Ashland, Nebraska. (M.Hill)

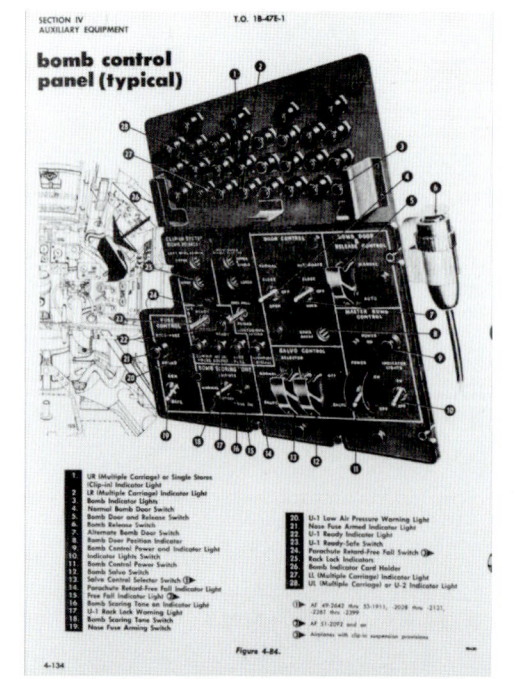

Bomb Control Panel

# B-47 and KC-97 Walkaround

B-47 Bombay looking aft. (M Hill)

Bombay looking forward. (M Hill)

Forward Bombay showing crawlway to forward area. (M Hill)

Cutaway of a J-47 jet engine. (M Hill)

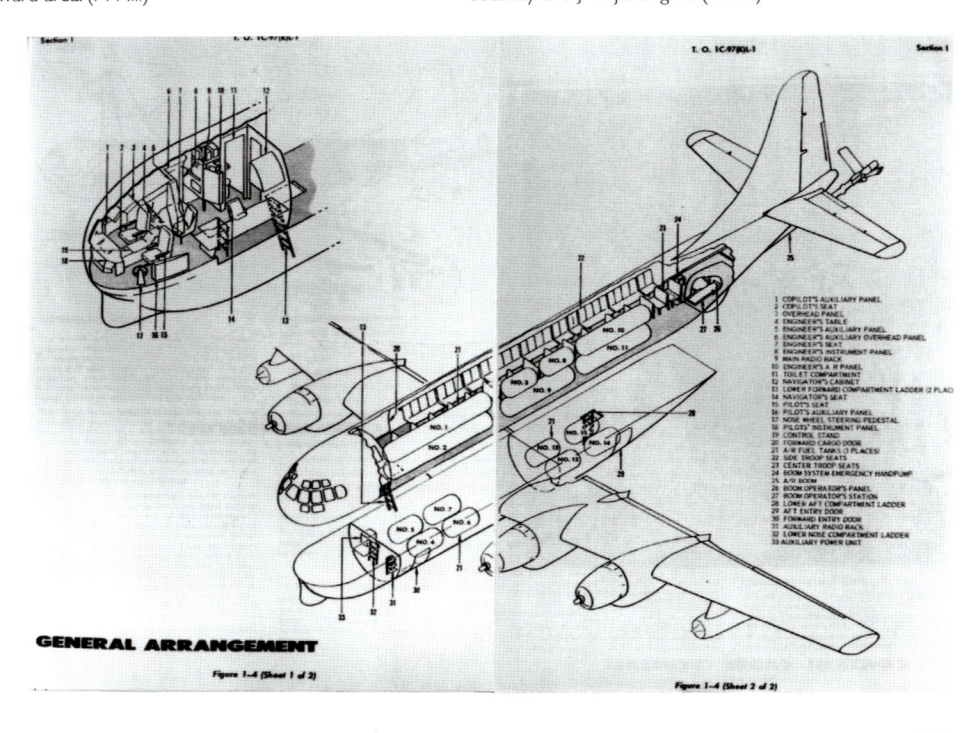

General Arrangement KC-97

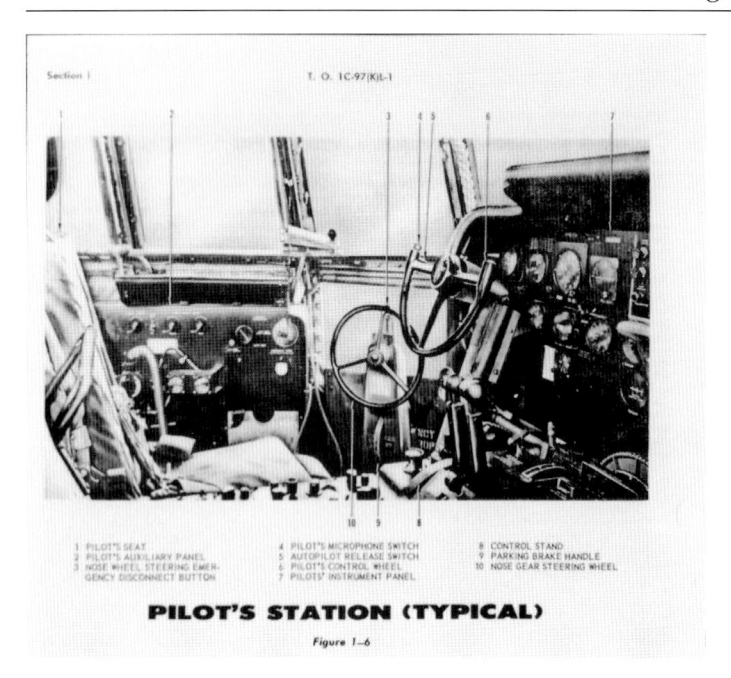

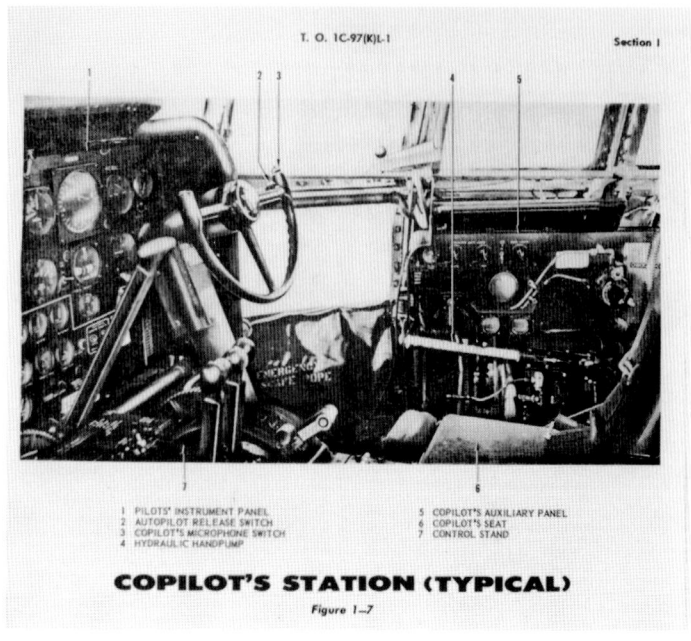

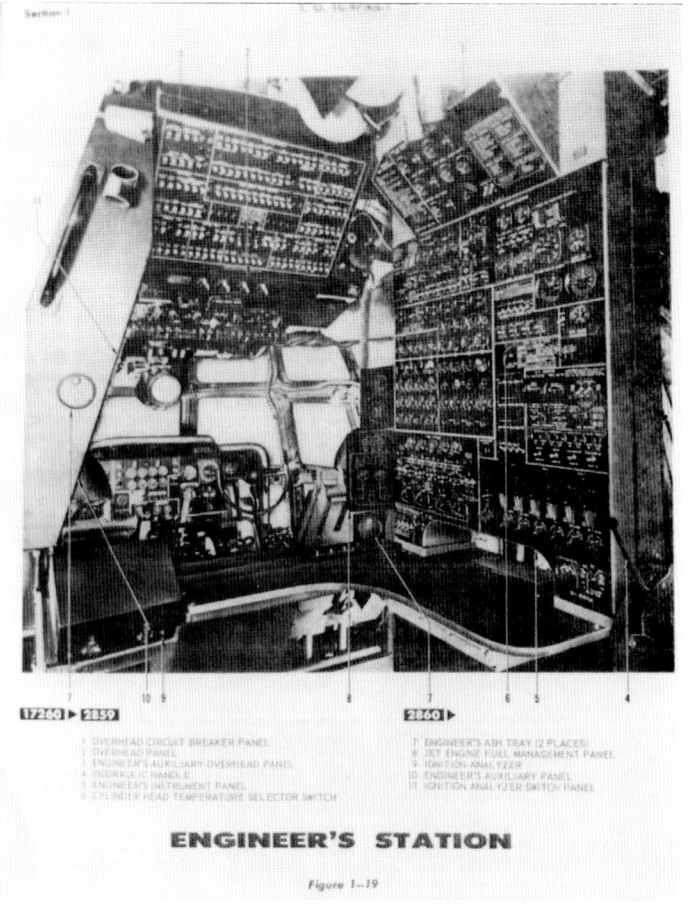

# Cold War Cornhuskers: The 307th Bomb Wing Lincoln Air Force Base Nebraska 1955-1965

**PILOT'S STATION (TYPICAL)**
Figure 1-6

**COPILOT'S STATION (TYPICAL)**
Figure 1-7

**CONTROL CABIN (TYPICAL)**
Figure 1-5

**ENGINEER'S STATION**
Figure 1-19

## B-47 and KC-97 Walkaround

Flight Deck KC-97G 52-2795. (Boeing)

A Flight Engineer at work (303rd ARS)

Radio Operator's Compartment (303rd ARS)

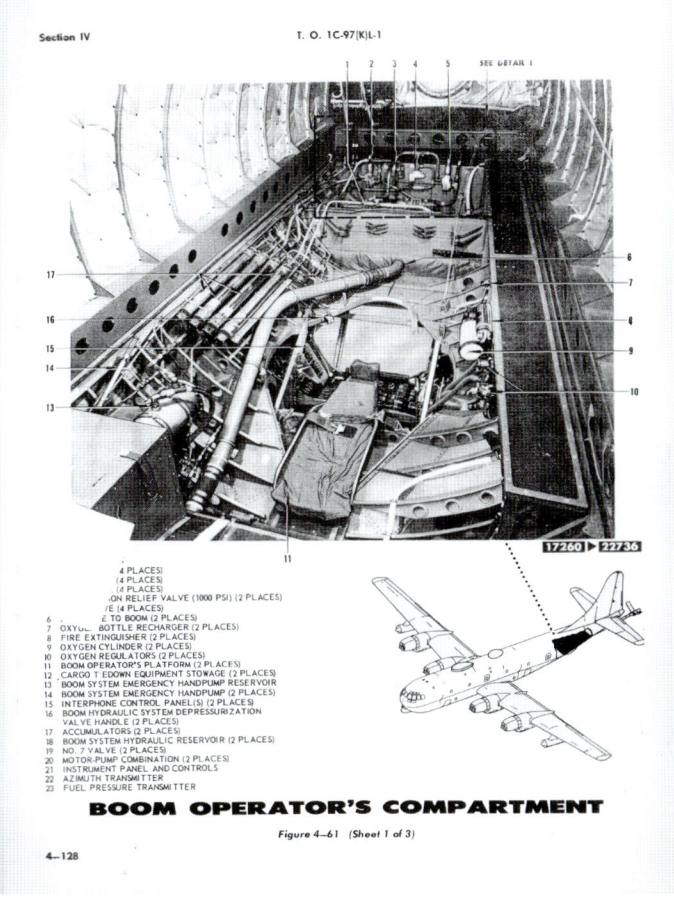

Boom Operator's Compartment

Navigator at work. (303rd ARS)

301

# Cold War Cornhuskers: The 307th Bomb Wing Lincoln Air Force Base Nebraska 1955-1965

Boom Operator about to go to work. (303rd ARS)

Business End of the Boom. (M.Hill)

Cutaway of a R-4360 engine. (M.Hill)

The #2 engine with the big 13 foot diameter propeller. (M Hill)

# Lincoln Air Force Base Then and Now

Main Gate Lincoln Air Force Base. (USAF)

Base Chapel

Base Chapel 2008 (M Hill)

Base Exchange

Base Exchange 2008 (M Hill)

Service Club 2008 (M Hill)

*303*

# Cold War Cornhuskers: The 307th Bomb Wing Lincoln Air Force Base Nebraska 1955-1965

Gymnasium 2008 (M Hill)

South Main Hangar 2008 (M Hill)

North Main Hangar and Nose Docks 2008 (M Hill)

Enlisted Men's Swimming Pool

Enlisted Men's Pool 2008 (M Hill)

818th Air Division Headquarters

## *Lincoln Air Force Base Then and Now*

Officer's Club and Swimming Pool

Base Operations

View of Barracks looking towards the Northwest. (Loffredo)

307th A & E Barracks (Loffredo)

Bowling Lake Park (M Hill)

Bowling Lake 1958 (JET SCOOP)

# Cold War Cornhuskers: The 307th Bomb Wing Lincoln Air Force Base Nebraska 1955-1965

Sportsman's Lodge

Sportsman's Lodge under construction (Mary Aston Bowling)

Entrance to Marina 2008. (M Hill)

Marina and Boat ramp 2008 (M Hill)

Looking north towards the boat ramp 2005 (M Hill)

Looking Northwest towards the Sportsman's Lodge 2005. Lodge was just above the concrete tramp at center. (M Hill)

# Lincoln Air Force Base Then and Now

Looking south from Sportsman's Lodge site 2005. (M Hill)

Aerial view of Base Housing looking North

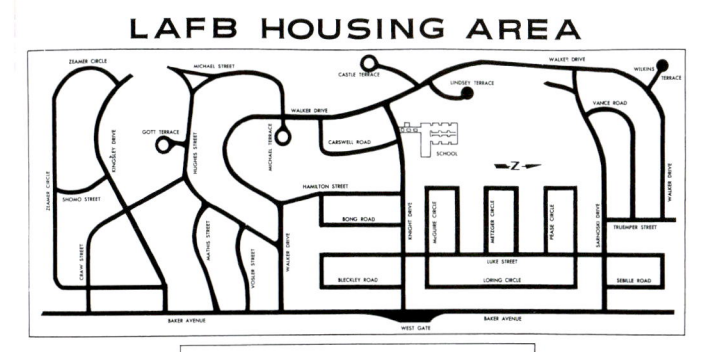

LAFB Base Housing Area Map.

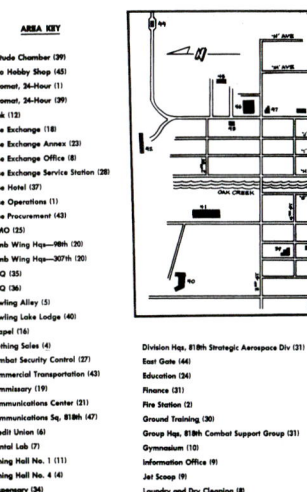

Lincoln Air Force Base Map.

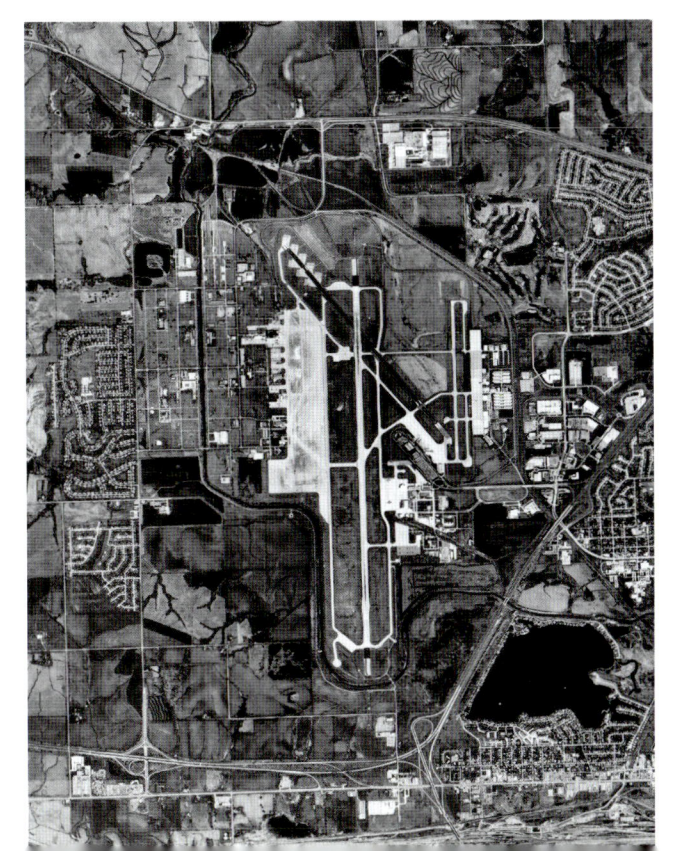

Aerial View of what was Lincoln Air Force Base 1990

307

# Glossary

| | |
|---|---|
| 731 Mod | A modification program to bring all aircraft up to the 731 airframe standard. (The 731st B-47 was 52-508.) All aircraft manufactured prior to that were brought up to that aircraft's equipment configuration (e.g., bomb/nav system, fuel tanks, etc.). |
| 781 | Form 781. A loose-leaf binder assigned to each aircraft, used by ground and aircrews to record discrepancies, maintenance actions, and aircraft loading (fuel, weapons, etc.). |
| 20 mike-mike | Slang for twenty millimeter ammunition used in B-47 tail guns. |
| ALFA | First letter of the international phonetic alphabet, representing the letter "A". An Alfa Alert required only that the Alert Force aircrew report "Ready to Taxi" by radio to the Command Post after engine start. |
| AOCP | Aircraft Out of Commission-Parts |
| APS-54 | An audio system that provided the copilot the ability to listen to ground and airborne radars. Each different radar type and its modes of operation would have different distinctive audio signatures. |
| APU | Auxiliary Power Unit |
| ARCP | Air Refueling Control Point |
| ARIP | Air Refueling Initial Point |
| ATC | Air Traffic Control |
| BMEWS | Ballistic Missile Early Warning System, a system of radars deployed across the northern arc from the UK to Alaska to provide advance warning of ICBM attack from the Soviet landmass. |
| BRAVO | Second letter of the international phonetic alphabet, representing the letter "B". A Bravo Alert summoned Alert crews to their aircraft for engine start and check-in, but did not require taxi. |
| Broken Arrow | Code word denoting a nuclear accident |
| CAVU | Ceiling and Visibility Unlimited |
| Chicks | Aircrew-speak for friendly fighter-interceptor aircraft sought to make tail aspect attacks for training so copilots could get live practice with the tail gun radar. To arrange this, the copilot would make a radio call to a GCI site and ask "Do you have any chicks for me?" |
| Christmas Tree (Alert area) | So called because the placement of the parking spots for the Alert aircraft resembled a Christmas tree when seen from above. |
| Class A Accident | The most serious level of aircraft accident, having resulted either in death or damage above a certain dollar level (variable over time). |
| CMF | Combat Mission Folder |
| COCO | Third letter of the international phonetic alphabet, representing the letter "C". A Coco Alert summoned Alert Crews to their aircraft and required them to taxi to and down the runway, briefly simulating initial takeoff actions. |
| CONUS | Continental United States (all states except Alaska and Hawaii) |
| Coleman | The tug vehicle used to move the B-47 and KC-97 |
| Crawlway | The aluminum tunnel between the entrance way and the bomb bay. About two feet square in cross section, it featured many sharp, protruding metallic edges, guaranteed to shred the clothing of anyone passing through. Virtually all copilots have horror stories about having to make an in-flight trip to the bomb bay to inspect something. |
| Dash-1 | The aircraft technical orders (T.O.s) were a series of operating and maintenance manuals divided numerically. The flight manual for aircrews was the first of the series (e.g., T.O. 1-1B-47/E-1). |
| Dead Reckoning | A somewhat macabre contraction of the phrase "deduced reckoning", an early, basic form of navigation performed without modern sophisticated navigation aids such as radar, inertial and GPS. Essentially, the pilot, navigator or mariner "deduced" his position from heading, estimated speed and forecast winds. |
| ECM | Electronic Countermeasures. Radio and other jamming techniques used to confuse and mislead enemy radar and communications. |
| EGT | Exhaust Gas Temperature, the temperature of the burned fuel-air mixture that is ejected from the tailpipe of a jet engine. |
| ELGE | Emergency Landing Gear Extension. A system for manually unlocking any or all retracted landing gear and extending them to the down-and-locked position with individual mechanical cranks, operated by hand-operated levers. |
| ELINT | Electronic Intelligence |
| EWO | Emergency War Order |
| FOD | Foreign Object Damage. FOD is a particular problem for jet aircraft because small items of debris on the ground can be sucked into the engine, causing possibly catastrophic damage. |
| GCA | Ground Controlled Approach, a system whereby a ground controller guides an aircraft for landing in cases of low ceiling or visibility. The controller "paints" the landing aircraft with a precision radar and issues course and glide slope guidance over the radio. |

# Glossary

| | |
|---|---|
| HHCL | H-Hour Control Line, an imaginary line surrounding enemy territory across which all attacking aircraft attempt to penetrate simultaneously to complicate the enemy's defensive efforts. |
| High Pass | A practice ECM run against ground-based missile control centers. |
| IP (2) | Instructor Pilot. |
| Initial Point | a geographic point over which a bomber turns and begins its bomb run on a target. |
| IRAN | Inspect and Repair As Necessary |
| KAC-72/KAA-29 | Documents carried by flight crews on training missions to authenticate and decode encrypted messages. |
| K-System | The B-47E bombing/navigation system |
| Large Charge | An attack on two or more targets in close proximity on a single bomb run. |
| Mail | Chaff dispensed from a bomber to confuse enemy radar. |
| MASDC | Military Aircraft Storage and Disposition Center, located at Davis-Monthan AFB, AZ. |
| MITO | Minimum Interval Takeoff. A standard EWO takeoff procedure (instituted in the early 1960s) to permit the Alert Force to take off quickly and gain separation from its base to counter reaction time compression brought about by the ICBM missile threat. Each aircraft in the takeoff stream would cross the runway threshold fifteen seconds after the preceding aircraft. |
| Mole Hole | Crew nickname for the Alert Facility |
| Music | Electronic jamming to confuse enemy radar and communication. |
| Noah's Ark Messages | A family of peacetime radio messages periodically broadcast from various command echelons in the Strategic Air Command to airborne crews. |
| NORAD | North American Aerospace Defense Command, a bi-national (US and Canada) command charged with surveillance and defense of the airspace over North America. |
| OAP | Offset Aiming Point, a radar-visible structure or terrain feature, offset from an actual, less radar-visible target by a known distance and used for aiming. The bomb/nav system computer compensates for the offset distance to deliver the bomb on the actual target. |
| OCAMA | Oklahoma City Air Materiel Area |
| Oil Burner Routes | A nationwide system of low-level navigation routes and targets used for peacetime training in all weather. |
| PCTAP | Positive Control Turnaround Point, a point beyond which an EWO bomber was prohibited from proceeding without a properly authenticated "go code." Usually referred to as the "Positive Control Point". |
| PDI | Pilot's Direction Indicator |
| Phase V Mod | A major aircraft modification in which certain B-47s were reconfigured from a bombing mission to an ECM mission and redesignated EB-47s. A large pod was built into the bomb bay, which would be occupied by two "Ravens" (ECM specialists) after takeoff. Their wartime mission was to penetrate enemy airspace along with the strike force and disrupt enemy air defense radars and communications. |
| Pre IP | Geographic point before the Initial Point where the flight crew begins to configure the aircraft and weapon for the start of the bomb run. |
| RBS | Radar Bomb Scoring. Ground based radars used to score practice "drops" made by the navigator. The drop point was signified by the cessation of a radio tone broadcast by the bomber. The bomber's position, speed, and heading at tone cutoff would be used by the RBS site to determine where the bomb would have hit. RBS radars were sometimes located on railroad trains to facilitate relocation to different targets. |
| Reflex | The nickname for a repetitive operation that sent aircraft, aircrews, and support personnel on a rotational basis to overseas bases (Canada, Europe, North Africa, and the Pacific) for purposes of standing Alert. A Reflex tour for an aircrew was typically 3 weeks or a month in duration. |
| S1-S2 Speeds | S-1: a minimum speed that must be reached during takeoff roll after a precomputed acceleration check time. Any lesser speed indicates that the aircraft is not accelerating properly and cannot safely continue the takeoff. |
| | S-2: The precomputed liftoff indicated airspeed based on aircraft gross weight, airfield temperature and pressure altitude |
| SACR 50-8 | The SAC regulation that prescribed quarterly and annual aircrew flying and ground training requirements. The expression "filling the squares" most often meant satisfying these requirements. |
| SACR 51-19 | The SAC regulation that specified the training requirements for each flight crewmember to achieve basic proficiency in his position. SACR 51-4 governed the training requirements to attain combat-ready status. |
| SAGE System | Semi-Automatic Ground Environment System. The air defense system in the US by which ground controllers could guide interceptor aircraft to a penetrator through automated electronic commands. |
| Seven High | Code Word for a suspected sabotage event. |
| Shack | A direct hit on a target |
| Six-Packs | Nickname for the six-passenger trucks used for Alert crews to respond to their aircraft when the klaxon blew. |
| T1A | A ground simulator mockup to provide copilots with training for the B-47 tail guns. It was dynamic, and the copilot was able to use the radar screen and control handle to lock on approaching threats. |

| | | | |
|---|---|---|---|
| T2A | A dynamic simulator to provide navigators training and practice with the bomb/nav system. Using photo and other sources of intelligence, specialists could construct ground features which, when viewed by the simulator's "radar", would look like actual targets. | TWX | An official electronic message between headquarters. Military "speak" for telegram. |
| | | USCM | Unit Simulated Combat Mission |
| | | VORTAC | A cockpit navigation instrument combining the features of the earlier Visual Omni-Range (VOR) which provided directional information to and from a station, and Tactical Air Navigation (TACAN) which provided distance from the station. |
| TDY | Temporary Duty, usually a temporary assignment to a location other than a member's primary base. | | |
| TTGI | Time-to-go Indicator, a reading on the pilot's PDI (see above) that indicates seconds to bomb release | | |
| | | WAI | Water-Alcohol Injection, a system on the B-47 that injected a mixture of water and alcohol into the engine exhaust during the takeoff roll to increase the mass flow, and therefore the thrust. |

# References

**Books**

Alexander, Sigmund; Colonel USAF (Ret). THE B-47 STRATOJET: CENTURION OF THE COLD WAR. C.C.C.P Publishing, San Antonio, TX.

Alexander, Sigmund; Colonel USAF (Ret). HISTORY OF THE 100TH BOMB WING. C.C.C.P. Publishing, San Antonio, TX.

Alexander, Sigmund; Colonel USAF (Ret). HEADQUARTERS SAC ANALYSIS OF B-47 ACCIDENTS. C.C.C.P Publishing, San Antonio, TX.

Alexander, Sigmund; Colonel USAF (Ret). B-47 AIRCRAFT LOSSES. C.C.C.P Publishing, San Antonio, TX.

Hesler, Glen. THE HEART OF THE TIGER. Privately published

Hill, Mike, John and Donna Campbell. PEACE WAS THEIR PROFESSION-STRATEGIC AIR COMMAND: A TRIBUTE. Schiffer Publishing Ltd., Atglen, PA. 1995

Hunter, Mel. STRATEGIC AIR COMMAND. Doubleday & Co., Garden City, NY. 1961

Lloyd, Alwyn T. A COLD WAR LEGACY-A TRIBUTE TO STRATEGIC AIR COMMAND 1946-1992. Pictorial Histories Publishing Co., Missoula, MT. 1999

Lloyd, Alwyn T. BOEING B-47 STRATOJET. Specialty Press, North Bank, MN. 2005

Natola, Mark. BOEING B-47, TRUE STORIES OF THE COLD WAR IN THE AIR. Schiffer Publishing Ltd., Atglen, PA. 2002

**Technical Orders**
T.O.1B-47E-1: Flight Manual-B-47B, B-47E, TB-47B & E-47B
U.S. Air Force, Jan 20, 1962

T.O. 1KC-97G-1

T.O. 1C-97(K)L-1 Flight Manual
U.S. Air Force, June 1,1966

**Additional References**
Microfilm History: 307th BW. Rolls 1-13
Alfred Simpson Research Center, Maxwell AFB, AL

Individual Aircraft Accident Reports
Kirtland AFB, NM

# Notes

1. The Organizational Readiness Inspection, or ORI, in later years became known as the Operational Readiness Inspection.

2. The well known boneyard is actually the Aerospace Maintenance and Regeneration Center, (AMARC) located at Davis-Monthan AFB in Tucson, Arizona.

3. Don's wish was to come true. He went to pilot training from Lincoln AFB and wound up being a T-38 instructor pilot. He was then sent to cross-train into helicopters and was subsequently assigned to a Special Forces unit in Viet Nam. On 3 February 1972, nine years to the day after being in the B-47 crash at Greenham Common, he was shot down near the DMZ, but fortunately was quickly rescued. His memoir February Third – The Story of a Green Hornet can be read or downloaded on the 307th website (**www.307bwassoc.org**). He was busy preparing his memoir for commercial publication when he unexpectedly passed away on October 21, 2006.

4. On 24 April 1959, Capt John Lappo, a pilot with an illustrious combat record, flying an RB-47E of the 352nd BS, 301st BW, Lockbourne AFB, Ohio, succumbed to the temptation of crossing under the bridge. After a General Court Martial, he received a mild fine and pay suspension, but couldn't win a reinstatement from the Flying Evaluation Board. He never flew again for the Air Force.

5. 6244 also earned a place in the tech order "Hall of Fame" when she became the photo frontispiece in 1-TO-B-47E-1, the so-called "Dash One," which was the aircrew's Bible for the airplane. 6244 is also memorialized in granite at the National Museum of the United States Air Force as the B-47 monument erected by the B-47 Stratojet Association bears the tail number 53-6244.